D0636482

COLLINS
POCKET
ENGLISH
DICTIONARY

HarperCollins*Publishers*

First Published 1984
New Edition 1992
© HarperCollins Publishers 1992
ISBN 0 00 470043-0 Hardback
ISBN 0 00 433632-1 Vinyl Cover

All rights reserved.

A catalogue record for this book is
available from the British Library.

Entered words that we have reason to believe
constitute trademarks have been designated as such.
However, neither the presence nor absence of
such designation should be regarded as
affecting the legal status of any trademark.

Computer typeset by Barbers Ltd
Wrotham, England

Printed and bound in Great Britain by
HarperCollins *Manufacturing*
PO Box, Glasgow G4 0NB

EDITORIAL STAFF

Managing Editor
Marian Makins

Senior Editor
Diana Adams

Editors
Alice Grandison
Danielle McGinley, Thomas Shearer
Elspeth Summers, Andrew Holmes

Pronunciation Editor
Judith Scott

Usage Editor
Ronald G Hardie

Computing Staff
Colette Clenaghan, Ray Carrick

USING THE DICTIONARY

Main Entry Words

printed in large red type, e.g.
> **abbey**

All main entry words, including abbreviations, foreign words, and combining forms, in one alphabetical sequence, e.g.
> **ensue**
> **en suite**
> **ensure**
> **ENT**

Variant Spellings

shown in full, e.g.
> **adrenalin, adrenaline**
> **guerrilla, guerilla**

Note: -ize, -ization spellings are used but -ise, -isation are equally acceptable.

Pronunciations

given for words that are difficult or confusing by respelling, with the stressed syllable in bold type, e.g.
> **acerbic** [ass-**sir**-bik]
> **aisle** [rhymes with **mile**]

Parts of Speech

usually shown as an abbreviation, e.g.
> **ablaze** *adj.*

When a word can be used as more than one part of speech, the change of part of speech is shown after a dash, e.g.
> **absent** *adj.* **1.** not present. ... –*v.* **4.** keep (oneself) away.

Parts of speech combined for some words, e.g.
> **alone** *adj., adv.* without anyone or anything else.

Cross References

shown in small capital letters, e.g.
> **aether** *n.* same as ETHER.

aseptic [eh-**sep**-tik] *adj.* germ-free. **asepsis** [eh-**sep**-siss] *n.* aseptic condition.

asexual [eh-**sex**-yew-al] *adj.* without sex. **asexually** *adv.*

ash[1] *n.* **1.** powdery substance left when something is burnt. —*pl.* **2.** remains after burning, esp. of a human body after cremation. **the Ashes** cricket trophy competed for in test matches by England and Australia. **ashen** *adj.* pale with shock. **ashtray** *n.* receptacle for tobacco ash and cigarette butts. **Ash Wednesday** first day of Lent.

ash[2] *n.* tree with grey bark.

ashamed *adj.* feeling shame.

ashlar *n.* square block of hewn stone used in building.

ashore *adv.* towards or on land.

ashram *n.* religious retreat where a Hindu holy man lives.

Asian *adj.* **1.** (also **Asiatic**) of the continent of Asia or any of its peoples or languages. **2.** of the Indian subcontinent. —*n.* **3.** person from Asia or a descendant of one. **4.** person from the Indian subcontinent or a descendant of one. **Asian pear** apple-shaped pear with crisp juicy flesh.
▷ Use *Asian* for 'someone who comes from Asia'. *Asiatic* in this context can be offensive.

aside *adv.* **1.** to one side. **2.** out of other people's hearing, e.g. *he took me aside to tell me his plans.* —*n.* **3.** remark not meant to be heard by everyone present.

asinine [**ass**-in-nine] *adj.* stupid, idiotic.

ask *v.* **1.** say or write (something) in a form that requires an answer. **2.** make a request or demand. **3.** invite.

askance [ass-**kanss**] *adv.* **look askance at 1.** look at with an oblique glance. **2.** regard with suspicion.

askew *adv., adj.* to one side, crooked.

aslant *adv., prep.* at a slant (to), slanting (across).

asleep *adj.* **1.** sleeping. **2.** (of limbs) numb.

asp *n.* small venomous snake.

asparagus *n.* plant whose shoots are cooked as a vegetable.

aspect *n.* **1.** feature or element. **2.** appearance or look. **3.** position facing a particular direction.

aspen *n.* kind of poplar tree.

asperity [ass-**per**-rit-ee] *n.* roughness of temper.

aspersion *n.* **cast aspersions on** make derogatory remarks about.

asphalt *n.* **1.** black hard tarlike substance used for road surfaces etc. —*v.* **2.** cover with asphalt.

asphodel *n.* plant with clusters of yellow or white flowers.

asphyxia [ass-**fix**-ee-a] *n.* suffocation. **asphyxiate** *v.* suffocate. **asphyxiation** *n.*

aspic *n.* savoury jelly used to coat meat, eggs, fish, etc.

aspidistra *n.* plant with long tapered leaves.

aspirate *Phonetics* —*v.* **1.** pronounce with an *h* sound. —*n.* **2.** *h* sound.

aspire *v.* (foll. by *to*) yearn (for), hope (to do or be). **aspirant** *n.* person who aspires. **aspiration** *n.* strong desire or aim. **aspiring** *adj.*

aspirin *n.* **1.** drug used to relieve pain and fever. **2.** tablet of this.

ass *n.* **1.** donkey. **2.** stupid person.

assagai *n.* same as ASSEGAI.

assail *v.* attack violently. **assailant** *n.*

assassin *n.* person who murders a prominent person. **assassinate** *v.* murder (a prominent person). **assassination** *n.*

assault *n.* **1.** violent attack. —*v.* **2.** attack violently. **assault course** series of obstacles used in military training.

assay *n.* **1.** analysis of a substance, esp. a metal, to ascertain its purity. —*v.* **2.** make such an analysis.

assegai *n.* slender spear used in S Africa.

assemble *v.* **1.** collect or congregate. **2.** put together the parts of (a machine). **assemblage** *n.* **1.** collection or group. **2.** assembling. **assembly** *n.* **1.** assembling. **2.** *pl.* **-blies.** assembled group. **assembly line** sequence of machines and workers in a factory assembling a product.

assent *n.* **1.** agreement or consent. —*v.* **2.** agree or consent.

assert *v.* **1.** declare forcefully. **2.** insist upon (one's rights etc.). **assert oneself** put oneself forward forcefully. **assertion** *n.* **1.** positive statement, usu. made without evidence. **2.** act of asserting. **assertive** *adj.* **assertively** *adv.* **assertiveness** *n.*

assess *v.* **1.** judge the worth or importance

of. **2.** estimate the value of (income or property) for taxation purposes. **assessment** n. **assessor** n.

asset n. **1.** valuable or useful person or thing. —pl. **2.** property that a person or firm can sell, esp. to pay debts.

asseverate v. declare solemnly. **asseveration** n.

assiduous adj. diligent and persevering. **assiduously** adv. **assiduity** n.

assign v. **1.** appoint (someone) to a job or task. **2.** allot (a task). **3.** attribute. **assignation** [ass-sig-**nay**-shun] n. **1.** assigning. **2.** secret arrangement to meet. **assignment** n. **1.** assigning. **2.** task assigned.

assimilate v. **1.** learn and understand (information). **2.** absorb or be absorbed or incorporated. **assimilable** adj. **assimilation** n.

assist v. give help or support. **assistance** n. **assistant** n. **1.** helper. —adj. **2.** junior or deputy.

assizes pl. n. court sessions formerly held in each county of England and Wales.

assoc. association.

associate v. **1.** connect in the mind. **2.** mix socially. —n. **3.** partner in business. **4.** friend or companion. —adj. **5.** having partial rights or subordinate status, e.g. associate member. **association** n. **1.** associating. **2.** society or club.

assonance n. rhyming of vowel sounds but not consonants, as in time and light. **assonant** adj.

assorted adj. consisting of various types mixed together. **assortment** n. assorted mixture.

asst assistant.

assuage [ass-**wage**] v. relieve (pain, grief, thirst, etc.).

assume v. **1.** take to be true without proof. **2.** pretend, e.g. I assumed indifference. **3.** take upon oneself, e.g. he assumed command. **assumption** n. **1.** assuming. **2.** thing assumed.

assure v. **1.** promise or guarantee. **2.** convince. **3.** make (something) certain. **4.** insure against loss of life. **assured** adj. **1.** confident. **2.** certain to happen. **assuredly** [a-**sure**-id-lee] adv. definitely. **assurance** n. assuring or being assured.

▷ When used in the context of business,

assurance and insurance have the same meaning.

astatine n. radioactive nonmetallic element, occurring very rarely in nature, and produced artificially by bombarding bismuth with alpha particles.

aster n. plant with daisy-like flowers.

asterisk n. **1.** star-shaped symbol (*) used in printing to indicate a footnote etc. —v. **2.** mark with an asterisk.

astern adv. **1.** at or towards the stern of a ship. **2.** backwards.

asteroid n. any of the small planets that orbit the sun between Mars and Jupiter.

asthma [ass-ma] n. illness causing difficulty in breathing. **asthmatic** adj., n.

astigmatism [eh-**stig**-mat-tiz-zum] n. inability of a lens, esp. of the eye, to focus properly. **astigmatic** adj.

astir adj. **1.** out of bed. **2.** in motion.

astonish v. surprise greatly. **astonishment** n. **astonishing** adj. **astonishingly** adv.

astound v. overwhelm with amazement. **astounding** adj. **astoundingly** adv.

astrakhan n. **1.** dark curly fleece of lambs from Astrakhan in the USSR. **2.** fabric resembling this.

astral adj. **1.** of stars. **2.** of the spirit world.

astray adv. off the right path.

astride adv., prep. with a leg on either side (of).

astringent adj. **1.** severe or harsh. **2.** causing contraction of body tissue. **3.** checking the flow of blood from a cut. —n. **4.** astringent substance. **astringency** n.

astro- combining form star.

astrolabe n. instrument formerly used to measure the altitude of stars and planets.

astrology n. study of the alleged influence of the stars, planets, and moon on human affairs. **astrologer** n. **astrological** adj.

astronaut n. person trained for travelling in space.

astronautics n. science and technology of space flight. **astronautical** adj.

astronomy n. scientific study of heavenly bodies. **astronomer** n. **astronomical** adj. **1.** of astronomy. **2.** very large. **astronomically** adv.

astrophysics n. science of the physical and

chemical properties of stars, planets, etc. **astrophysical** adj. **astrophysicist** n.

astute adj. perceptive or shrewd. **astutely** adv. **astuteness** n.

asunder adv. into parts or pieces.

asylum n. **1.** refuge or sanctuary. **2.** old name for a mental hospital.

asymmetry n. lack of symmetry. **asymmetrical**, **asymmetric** adj.

asymptote [ass-im-tote] n. straight line closely approached by but never met by a curve.

at prep. **1.** indicating position in space or time. **2.** towards. **3.** engaged in. **4.** in exchange for, e.g. *it's selling at two pounds.* **5.** indicating the cause of an emotion, e.g. *shocked at his rudeness.*

At Chem. astatine.

atavism [at-a-viz-zum] n. recurrence of a trait present in distant ancestors. **atavistic** adj.

ate v. past tense of EAT.

atelier [at-tell-yay] n. workshop, artist's studio.

atheism [aith-ee-iz-zum] n. belief that there is no God. **atheist** n. **atheistic** adj.

atherosclerosis n., pl. **-ses.** disease in which deposits of fat cause the walls of the arteries to thicken.

athlete n. person trained in or good at athletics. **athletic** adj. **1.** physically fit or strong. **2.** of an athlete or athletics. **athletics** pl. n. track-and-field sports such as running, jumping, throwing, etc. **athletically** adv. **athleticism** n.

at-home n. social gathering in a person's home.

athwart prep. **1.** across. —adv. **2.** transversely.

atlas n. book of maps.

atmosphere n. **1.** mass of gases surrounding a heavenly body, esp. the earth. **2.** prevailing tone or mood (of a place etc.). **3.** unit of pressure. **atmospheric** adj. **atmospherics** pl. n. radio interference due to electrical disturbance in the atmosphere.

atoll n. ring-shaped coral island enclosing a lagoon.

atom n. **1.** smallest unit of matter which can take part in a chemical reaction. **2.** very small amount. **atom bomb** same as ATOMIC BOMB.

atomic adj. **1.** of atoms. **2.** of or using atomic bombs or atomic energy. **atomic bomb** bomb in which the energy is provided by nuclear fission. **atomic energy** nuclear energy. **atomic number** number of protons in the nucleus of an atom. **atomic weight** ratio of the mass per atom of an element to one twelfth of the mass of a carbon atom.

atomize v. reduce to atoms or small particles. **atomizer** n. device for discharging a liquid in a fine spray.

atonal [eh-tone-al] adj. (of music) not written in an established key. **atonality** n.

atone v. make amends (for sin or wrongdoing). **atonement** n.

atop prep. on top of.

atrium n., pl. **atria. 1.** upper chamber of either half of the heart. **2.** central hall extending through several storeys of a modern building. **3.** main courtyard of an ancient Roman house.

atrocious adj. **1.** extremely cruel or wicked. **2.** horrifying or shocking. **3.** Informal very bad. **atrociously** adv. **atrocity** n. **1.** wickedness. **2.** pl. **-ties.** act of cruelty.

atrophy [at-trof-fee] n., pl. **-phies. 1.** wasting away of an organ or part. —v. **-phying, -phied. 2.** (cause to) waste away.

atropine n. poisonous alkaloid obtained from deadly nightshade.

attach v. **1.** join, fasten, or connect. **2.** attribute or ascribe, e.g. *he attaches great importance to his looks.* **attached** adj. (foll. by to) fond of. **attachment** n.

attaché [at-tash-shay] n. specialist attached to a diplomatic mission. **attaché case** flat rectangular briefcase for papers.

attack v. **1.** launch a physical assault (against). **2.** criticize. **3.** set about (a job or problem) with vigour. **4.** affect adversely. —n. **5.** act of attacking. **6.** sudden bout of illness. **attacker** n.

attain v. **1.** achieve or accomplish (a task or aim). **2.** reach. **attainment** n. accomplishment. **attainable** adj.

attar n. fragrant oil made from roses.

attempt v. **1.** try, make an effort. —n. **2.** effort or endeavour.

attend v. **1.** be present at. **2.** look after. **3.** pay attention. **4.** accompany. **5.** apply oneself (to). **attendance** n. **1.** attending. **2.** number attending. **attendant** n. **1.** person who assists, guides, or provides a service.

—*adj.* **2.** accompanying. **attention** *n.* **1.** concentrated direction of the mind. **2.** consideration. **3.** care. **4.** alert position in military drill. **attentive** *adj.* **1.** giving attention. **2.** considerably helpful. **attentively** *adv.* **attentiveness** *n.*

attenuate *v.* **1.** weaken. **2.** make or become thin. **attenuation** *n.*

attest *v.* affirm the truth of, be proof of. **attestation** *n.*

attic *n.* space or room within the roof of a house.

attire *n.* **1.** fine or formal clothes. —*v.* **2.** clothe.

attitude *n.* **1.** way of thinking and behaving. **2.** posture of the body.

attorney *n.* **1.** person legally appointed to act for another. **2.** *US* lawyer.

attract *v.* **1.** arouse the interest or admiration of. **2.** draw (something) closer by exerting a force on it. **attraction** *n.* **1.** power to attract. **2.** something that attracts. **attractive** *adj.* **attractively** *adv.* **attractiveness** *n.*

attribute *v.* **1.** (usu. foll. by *to*) regard as belonging to or produced by. —*n.* **2.** quality or feature representative of a person or thing. **attributable** *adj.* **attribution** *n.* **attributive** *adj.* *Grammar* (of an adjective) preceding the noun modified.

attrition *n.* constant wearing down to weaken or destroy, often *war of attrition*.

attune *v.* adjust or accustom (a person or thing).

atypical [eh-**tip**-ik-al] *adj.* not typical.

Au *Chem.* gold.

aubergine [**oh**-bur-zheen] *n.* dark purple tropical vegetable.

aubrietia [aw-**bree**-sha] *n.* trailing plant with purple flowers.

auburn *adj.* (of hair) reddish-brown.

auction *n.* **1.** public sale in which articles are sold to the highest bidder. —*v.* **2.** sell by auction. **auctioneer** *n.* person who conducts an auction.

audacious *adj.* **1.** recklessly bold or daring. **2.** impudent. **audaciously** *adv.* **audacity** *n.*

audible *adj.* loud enough to hear. **audibly** *adv.* **audibility** *n.*

audience *n.* **1.** group of spectators or listeners. **2.** formal interview.

audio *adj.* **1.** of sound or hearing. **2.** of or for the transmission or reproduction of sound.

audiotypist *n.* typist trained to type from a dictating machine. **audiovisual** *adj.* (esp. of teaching aids) involving both sight and hearing.

audit *n.* **1.** official examination of business accounts. —*v.* **auditing, audited. 2.** examine (business accounts) officially. **auditor** *n.*

audition *n.* **1.** test of a performer's ability for a particular role or job. —*v.* **2.** test or be tested in an audition.

auditorium *n., pl.* **-toriums, -toria.** area of a concert hall or theatre where the audience sits.

auditory *adj.* of or relating to hearing.

au fait [oh **fay**] *adj. French* **1.** fully informed. **2.** expert.

auf Wiedersehen [owf **vee**-der-zay-en] *interj. German* goodbye.

Aug. August.

auger *n.* carpenter's tool for boring holes.

aught *pron. Old-fashioned* anything.

augment *v.* increase or enlarge. **augmentation** *n.*

au gratin [oh **grat**-tan] *adj.* covered and cooked with breadcrumbs and sometimes cheese.

augur *v.* be a sign of (future events). **augury** *n.* **1.** foretelling of the future. **2.** *pl.* **-ries.** omen.

august *adj.* dignified and imposing.

August *n.* eighth month of the year.

auk *n.* northern sea bird with short wings and black-and-white plumage.

auld lang syne *n.* times past.

aunt *n.* **1.** father's or mother's sister. **2.** uncle's wife. **auntie, aunty** *n., pl.* **aunties.** *Informal* aunt. **Aunt Sally 1.** figure used in fairgrounds as a target. **2.** target of abuse or criticism.

au pair *n.* young foreign woman who does housework in return for board and lodging.

aura *n.* distinctive air or quality of a person or thing.

aural *adj.* of or using the ears or hearing.

aureate *adj.* **1.** covered with gold, gilded. **2.** (of style of writing or speaking) excessively elaborate.

aureole, aureola *n.* halo.

au revoir [oh riv-**vwahr**] *interj. French* goodbye.

auricle n. 1. upper chamber of the heart. 2. outer part of the ear. **auricular** adj.

auriferous adj. containing gold.

aurochs n., pl. **aurochs**. recently extinct European wild ox.

aurora n., pl. **-ras, -rae**. bands of light sometimes seen in the sky in polar regions. **aurora australis** aurora seen near the South Pole. **aurora borealis** aurora seen near the North Pole.

auscultation n. listening to the internal sounds of the body, usu. with a stethoscope, to help with diagnosis.

auspices [aw-spiss-siz] pl. n. **under the auspices of** with the support and approval of.

auspicious adj. showing signs of future success, favourable. **auspiciously** adv.

austere adj. 1. stern or severe. 2. ascetic. 3. severely simple or plain. **austerely** adv. **austerity** n.

austral adj. southern.

Australasian n., adj. (person) from Australia, New Zealand, and neighbouring islands.

Australian n., adj. (person) from Australia.

Austrian n., adj. (person) from Austria.

autarchy [aw-tar-kee] n. absolute power or autocracy.

autarky [aw-tar-kee] n. policy of economic self-sufficiency.

authentic adj. known to be real, genuine. **authentically** adv. **authenticity** n. **authenticate** v. establish as genuine. **authentication** n.

author n. 1. writer of a book etc. 2. originator or creator. **authorship** n.
▷ The word author should be used for both male and female writers. The form author-ess suggests a minor or amateur writer.

authority n., pl. **-ties**. 1. power to command or control others. 2. (often pl.) person or group having this power. 3. expert in a particular field. **authoritarian** n., adj. (person) insisting on strict obedience to authority. **authoritative** adj. 1. recognized as being reliable, e.g. the authoritative book on Shakespeare. 2. possessing authority. **authoritatively** adv. **authorize** v. 1. give authority to. 2. give permission for. **authorization** n.

autism n. Psychiatry disorder, usu. of children, characterized by lack of response to

people and limited ability to communicate. **autistic** adj.

auto- combining form self-, e.g. autobiography.

autobahn n. German motorway.

autobiography n., pl. **-phies**. account of a person's life written by that person. **autobiographical** adj. **autobiographically** adv.

autocrat n. 1. absolute ruler. 2. dictatorial person. **autocratic** adj. **autocratically** adv. **autocracy** n. government by an autocrat.

autocross n. motor-racing over a rough course.

Autocue n. ® electronic television prompting device displaying a speaker's script, unseen by the audience.

autogiro, autogyro n., pl. **-ros**. self-propelled aircraft resembling a helicopter but with an unpowered rotor.

autograph n. 1. handwritten signature of a (famous) person. —v. 2. write one's signature on or in.

automat n. US vending machine.

automate v. make (a manufacturing process) automatic. **automation** n.

automatic adj. 1. (of a device) operating mechanically by itself. 2. (of a process) performed by automatic equipment. 3. done without conscious thought. 4. (of a firearm) self-loading. —n. 5. vehicle with automatic transmission. 6. self-loading firearm. **automatically** adv. **automatic transmission** transmission system in a motor vehicle in which the gears change automatically.

automaton n. 1. robot. 2. person who acts mechanically.

automobile n. US motor car.

automotive adj. relating to motor vehicles.

autonomy n. self-government. **autonomous** adj.

autopsy n., pl. **-sies**. examination of a corpse to determine the cause of death.

autoroute n. French motorway.

autostrada n. Italian motorway.

autosuggestion n. process in which a person unconsciously influences his or her own behaviour or beliefs.

autumn n. season between summer and winter. **autumnal** adj.

auxiliary adj. 1. secondary or supplementary. 2. supporting. —n., pl. **-ries**. 3. person or thing that supplements or supports. **auxilia-**

ry verb verb used to form the tense, voice, or mood of another, such as *will* in *I will go.*

avail *v.* **1.** be of use or advantage (to). —*n.* **2.** use or advantage, esp. in *to no avail.* **avail oneself of** make use of.

available *adj.* obtainable or accessible. **availability** *n.*

avalanche *n.* **1.** mass of snow or ice falling down a mountain. **2.** sudden overwhelming quantity of anything.

avant-garde [av-ong-**gard**] *n.* **1.** group of innovators, esp. in the arts. —*adj.* **2.** innovative and progressive.

avarice [**av**-a-riss] *n.* greed for wealth. **avaricious** *adj.*

avast *interj. Naut.* stop.

avatar *n. Hinduism* appearance of a god in animal or human form.

Ave. Avenue.

Ave Maria [**ah**-vay ma-**ree**-a] *n.* same as HAIL MARY.

avenge *v.* take revenge in retaliation for (harm done) or on behalf of (a person harmed). **avenger** *n.*

avenue *n.* **1.** wide street. **2.** road between two rows of trees. **3.** way of approach.

aver [av-**vur**] *v.* **averring, averred.** state to be true.

average *n.* **1.** typical or normal amount or quality. **2.** result obtained by adding quantities together and dividing the total by the number of quantities. —*adj.* **3.** usual or typical. **4.** calculated as an average. —*v.* **5.** calculate the average of. **6.** amount to as an average.

averse *adj.* (usu. foll. by *to*) disinclined or unwilling. **aversion** *n.* **1.** strong dislike. **2.** person or thing disliked.

avert *v.* **1.** turn away. **2.** ward off.

aviary *n., pl.* **aviaries.** large cage or enclosure for birds.

aviation *n.* art of flying aircraft. **aviator** *n.*

avid *adj.* **1.** keen or enthusiastic. **2.** greedy (for). **avidly** *adv.* **avidity** *n.*

avocado *n., pl.* **-dos.** pear-shaped tropical fruit with a leathery green skin and yellowish-green flesh.

avocation *n.* **1.** *Old-fashioned* occupation. **2.** hobby.

avocet *n.* long-legged wading bird with a long slender upward-curving bill.

avoid *v.* **1.** keep away from. **2.** refrain from. **3.** prevent from happening. **avoidable** *adj.* **avoidance** *n.*

avoirdupois [av-er-de-**poise**] *n.* system of weights based on pounds and ounces.

avow *v.* **1.** state or affirm. **2.** admit openly. **avowal** *n.* **avowed** *adj.* **avowedly** [a-**vow**-id-lee] *adv.*

avuncular *adj.* (of a man) friendly, helpful, and caring towards someone younger.

await *v.* **1.** wait for. **2.** be in store for.

awake *v.* **awaking, awoke, awoken.** **1.** emerge or rouse from sleep. **2.** (cause to) become alert. —*adj.* **3.** not sleeping. **4.** alert.

awaken *v.* awake.

award *v.* **1.** give (something, such as a prize) formally. —*n.* **2.** something awarded, such as a prize.

aware *adj.* having knowledge, informed. **awareness** *n.*

awash *adv.* washed over by water.

away *adv.* **1.** from a place, e.g. *go away.* **2.** to another place, e.g. *put that gun away.* **3.** out of existence, e.g. *fade away.* **4.** continuously, e.g. *laughing away.* —*adj.* **5.** not present. **6.** distant, e.g. *two miles away.* **7.** *Sport* played on an opponent's ground.

awe *n.* **1.** wonder and respect mixed with dread. —*v.* **2.** fill with awe. **awesome** *adj.* inspiring awe. **awestruck** *adj.* filled with awe.

aweigh *adj. Naut.* (of an anchor) no longer hooked into the bottom.

awful *adj.* **1.** very bad or unpleasant. **2.** *Obs.* inspiring awe. **3.** *Informal* very great. **awfully** *adv.* **1.** in an unpleasant way. **2.** *Informal* very. **awfulness** *n.*

awhile *adv.* for a time.

awkward *adj.* **1.** clumsy or ungainly. **2.** difficult to use or handle. **3.** inconvenient. **4.** embarrassed. **awkwardly** *adv.* **awkwardness** *n.*

awl *n.* pointed tool for piercing wood, leather, etc.

awning *n.* canvas roof supported by a frame to give protection against the weather.

awoke *v.* past tense of AWAKE. **awoken** *v.* past participle of AWAKE.

AWOL [**eh**-woll] *adj. Mil.* absent without leave.

awry [a-**rye**] *adv., adj.* **1.** with a twist to one side, askew. **2.** amiss.

axe *n.* **1.** tool with a sharp blade for felling trees or chopping wood. **2.** *Informal* dismissal from employment etc. —*v.* **3.** *Informal* dismiss (employees), restrict (expenditure), or terminate (a project).

axil *n.* angle where the stalk of a leaf joins a stem.

axiom *n.* **1.** generally accepted principle. **2.** self-evident statement. **axiomatic** *adj.* **1.** containing axioms. **2.** self-evident.

axis *n., pl.* **axes.** **1.** (imaginary) line round which a body can rotate or about which an object or geometrical figure is symmetrical. **2.** one of two fixed lines on a graph, against which quantities or positions are measured. **axial** *adj.*

axle *n.* shaft on which a wheel or pair of wheels turns.

axolotl *n.* aquatic salamander of central America.

ayah *n.* in parts of the former British Empire, native maidservant or nursemaid.

ayatollah *n.* Islamic religious leader in Iran.

aye, ay *interj.* **1.** yes. —*n.* **2.** affirmative vote or voter.

AZ Arizona.

azalea [az-**zale**-ya] *n.* garden shrub grown for its showy flowers.

azimuth *n.* **1.** arc of the sky between the zenith and the horizon. **2.** horizontal angle of a bearing measured clockwise from the north.

Aztec *n., adj.* (person) of the Indian race ruling Mexico before the Spanish conquest in the 16th century.

azure *adj., n.* (of) the colour of a clear blue sky.

B

B 1. *Chem.* boron. **2.** magnetic flux density.

Ba *Chem.* barium.

BA Bachelor of Arts.

baa *v.* **baaing, baaed. 1.** make the cry of a sheep. —*n.* **2.** cry made by a sheep.

baas *n.* *S Afr.* boss.

baba *n.* small cake, usu. soaked in rum.

babble *v.* **1.** talk excitedly or foolishly. **2.** (of streams) make a low murmuring sound. —*n.* **3.** incoherent or foolish talk.

babe *n.* **1.** baby. **2.** *Informal* gullible person.

babel [**babe**-el] *n.* confused mixture of noises or voices.

baboon *n.* large monkey with a pointed face and a long tail.

baby *n., pl.* **-bies. 1.** very young child or animal. **2.** *Slang* sweetheart. —*adj.* **3.** comparatively small of its type. **babyish** *adj.* **baby grand** small grand piano. **baby-sit** *v.* take care of a child while the parents are out. **baby-sitter** *n.*

baccarat [**back**-a-rah] *n.* card game involving gambling.

bacchanalia *n.* drunken revelry or orgy. **bacchanalian** *n., adj.*

bachelor *n.* **1.** unmarried man. **2.** person who holds the lowest university degree. **bachelor girl** young unmarried independent woman.

bacillus [bass-**ill**-luss] *n., pl.* **-li** [-lie] rod-shaped bacterium. **bacillary** *adj.*

back *n.* **1.** rear part of the human body, from the neck to the pelvis. **2.** part or side of an object opposite the front. **3.** part of anything less often seen or used. **4.** *Ball games* defensive player or position. —*v.* **5.** (cause to) move backwards. **6.** provide money for (a person or enterprise). **7.** bet on the success of. **8.** (foll. by *onto*) have the back facing towards. —*adj.* **9.** situated behind. **10.** owing from an earlier date, e.g. *back pay.* —*adv.* **11.** at, to, or towards the rear. **12.** to or towards the original starting point or condition. **backer** *n.* person who gives financial support. **backing** *n.* **1.** support. **2.** musical accompaniment for a pop singer. **backward** *adj.* **1.** directed towards the rear.

2. retarded in physical, material, or intellectual development. **backwardness** *n.* **backwards** *adv.* **1.** towards the rear. **2.** with the back foremost. **3.** in the reverse of the usual direction. **back door** secret or underhand means of entry to a job etc. **back number** old issue of a newspaper or magazine. **back out** *v.* withdraw (from an agreement). **back room** place where secret research or planning is done. **back up** *v.* support. **backup** *n.* **1.** support or reinforcement. **2.** reserve or substitute.

backbencher *n.* Member of Parliament who does not hold office in the government or opposition.

backbiting *n.* spiteful talk about an absent person.

backbone *n.* **1.** spinal column. **2.** strength of character.

backbreaking *adj.* exhausting.

backchat *n.* *Informal* answering back, esp. impudently.

backcloth, backdrop *n.* painted curtain at the back of a stage set.

backdate *v.* make (a document) effective from an earlier date.

backfire *v.* **1.** (of a plan) fail to have the desired effect. **2.** (of an engine) make a loud noise like an explosion.

backgammon *n.* game played with counters and dice.

background *n.* **1.** person's social class, education, or experience. **2.** events or circumstances that help to explain something. **3.** space behind the chief figures in a picture.

backhand *adj.* *Tennis etc.* stroke played with the back of the hand facing the direction of the stroke. **backhanded** *adj.* sarcastic, e.g. *a backhanded compliment.* **backhander** *n.* *Slang* bribe.

backlash *n.* sudden and adverse reaction.

backlog *n.* accumulation of things to be dealt with.

backpack *n.* rucksack.

back-pedal *v.* retract or modify a previous opinion.

back-seat driver n. Informal a person who offers unwanted advice.

backside n. Informal buttocks.

backslide v. relapse into former bad habits. **backslider** n.

backstage adv., adj. behind the stage in a theatre.

backstairs adj. underhand.

backstroke n. swimming stroke performed on the back.

backtrack v. 1. return by the same route by which one has come. 2. retract or reverse one's opinion or policy.

backwash n. 1. water washed backwards by the motion of a boat. 2. repercussion.

backwater n. isolated or backward place or condition.

backwoods pl. n. remote sparsely populated area.

backword n. Brit. dialect failure to keep a promise.

bacon n. salted or smoked pig meat.

bacteria pl. n., sing. **-rium**. large group of microorganisms, many of which cause disease. **bacterial** adj. **bacteriology** n. study of bacteria. **bacteriologist** n.
▷ Note that the word *bacteria* is already plural and does not need an '-s'.

bad adj. **worse, worst. 1.** of poor quality. **2.** lacking skill or talent. **3.** harmful. **4.** immoral or evil. **5.** naughty or mischievous. **6.** rotten or decayed. **7.** severe or unpleasant. **8.** Slang good or excellent. **badly** adv. **badness** n. **bad blood** feeling of intense hatred.

bade v. a past tense of BID.

badge n. emblem worn to show membership, rank, etc.

badger n. **1.** nocturnal burrowing mammal with a black and white head. —v. **2.** pester or harass.

badinage [bad-in-nahzh] n. playful and witty conversation.

badminton n. game played with a racket and shuttlecock, which is hit over a high net.

baffle v. **1.** perplex or puzzle. —n. **2.** device to limit or regulate the flow of fluid, light, or sound. **bafflement** n.

bag n. **1.** flexible container with an opening at one end. **2.** handbag. **3.** amount of game killed by a hunter. **4.** Offens. ugly or bad-tempered woman. —pl. **5.** (foll. by of) Informal lots (of). —v. **bagging, bagged. 6.** put into a bag. **7.** (cause to) bulge. **8.** capture or kill. **baggy** adj. **-gier, -giest.** (of clothes) hanging loosely.

bagatelle n. **1.** something of little value. **2.** board game in which balls are struck into holes.

baggage n. **1.** suitcases packed for a journey. **2.** portable equipment of an army.

bagpipes pl. n. musical wind instrument with reed pipes and an inflatable bag.

bah interj. expression of contempt or disgust.

bail[1] n. **1.** Law money deposited with a court as security for a person's reappearance in court. **2.** person giving such security. —v. **3.** pay bail for (a person).

bail[2], **bale** v. (foll. by out) remove (water) from (a boat). **bail out, bale out** v. **1.** Informal help (a person or organization) out of a predicament. **2.** make an emergency parachute jump from an aircraft.

bail[3] n. Cricket either of two wooden bars across the tops of the stumps.

bailey n. outermost wall or court of a castle.

bailie n. Scot. municipal magistrate.

bailiff n. **1.** sheriff's officer who serves writs and summonses. **2.** landlord's agent.

bailiwick n. bailiff's area of jurisdiction.

bairn n. Scot. child.

bait n. **1.** piece of food on a hook or in a trap to attract fish or animals. **2.** enticement or temptation. —v. **3.** put a piece of food on or in (a hook or trap). **4.** persecute or tease.

baize n. woollen fabric used to cover billiard and card tables.

bake v. **1.** cook by dry heat as in an oven. **2.** make or become hardened by heat. **3.** Informal be extremely hot. **baker** n. person whose business is to make or sell bread, cakes, etc. **baker's dozen** thirteen. **bakery** n., pl. **-eries.** place where bread, cakes, etc. are baked or sold. **baking powder** powdered mixture containing sodium bicarbonate, used as a raising agent in baking.

baksheesh n. in some Eastern countries, money given as a tip.

Balaclava, Balaclava helmet n. close-fitting woollen hood that covers the ears and neck.

balalaika n. guitar-like musical instrument with a triangular body.

balance n. **1.** state in which a weight or

amount is evenly distributed. **2.** pair of scales. **3.** stability of mind or body. **4.** difference between the credits and debits of an account. **5.** amount that remains. —*v.* **6.** remain steady. **7.** weigh on a balance. **8.** consider or compare. **9.** equalize in weight, amount, etc. **balance of payments** difference between the payments for the imports and exports of a country. **balance of power** equal distribution of military and economic power among countries. **balance of trade** difference in value between a country's imports and exports. **balance sheet** statement showing the financial position of a business.

balcony *n., pl.* **-nies. 1.** platform on the outside of a building with a rail along the outer edge. **2.** upper tier of seats in a theatre or cinema.

bald *adj.* **1.** having little or no hair on the scalp. **2.** (of a tyre) having a worn tread. **3.** plain or blunt, e.g. *a bald statement.* **balding** *adj.* becoming bald. **baldly** *adv.* **baldness** *n.*

balderdash *n.* stupid talk.

bale[1] *n.* **1.** large bundle of hay or goods tightly bound together. —*v.* **2.** make or put into bales.

bale[2] *v.* same as BAIL[2].

baleen *n.* whalebone.

baleful *adj.* vindictive or menacing. **balefully** *adv.*

balk, baulk *v.* **1.** be reluctant to (do something). **2.** thwart or hinder. —*n.* **3.** obstacle or hindrance.

Balkan *adj.* of any of the countries of the Balkan Peninsula: Yugoslavia, Romania, Bulgaria, Albania, Greece, and the European part of Turkey.

ball[1] *n.* **1.** round or nearly round object, esp. one used in games. **2.** single delivery of the ball in a game. **3.** bullet. **4.** more or less rounded part of the body, e.g. *the ball of the foot.* —*pl.* **5.** *Taboo slang* testicles. **6.** nonsense. —*v.* **7.** form into a ball. **ball bearings** steel balls between moving parts of a machine to reduce friction. **ball cock** device with a floating ball and a valve for regulating the flow of water. **ballpoint, ballpoint pen** *n.* pen with a tiny ball bearing as a writing point.

ball[2] *n.* formal social function for dancing. **ballroom** *n.*

ballad *n.* **1.** narrative poem or song. **2.** slow sentimental song.

ballast *n.* **1.** substance, such as sand, used to stabilize a ship when it is not carrying cargo. **2.** crushed rock used for road or railway foundation. —*v.* **3.** give stability or weight to.

ballet *n.* **1.** classical style of expressive dancing based on conventional steps. **2.** theatrical performance of this. **ballerina** *n.* female ballet dancer.

ballistics *n.* study of the flight of projectiles, such as bullets. **ballistic** *adj.* **ballistic missile** missile guided automatically in flight but which falls freely at its target.

balloon *n.* **1.** inflatable rubber bag used as a plaything. **2.** large bag inflated with air or gas, designed to carry passengers in a basket underneath. —*v.* **3.** inflate or be inflated. **balloonist** *n.*

ballot *n.* **1.** method of voting secretly. **2.** actual vote or paper indicating a person's choice. —*v.* **-loting, -loted. 3.** vote or ask for a vote from. **ballot box**

ballyhoo *n.* exaggerated fuss.

balm *n.* **1.** aromatic substance used for healing and soothing. **2.** anything that comforts or soothes.

balmy *adj.* **balmier, balmiest. 1.** (of weather) mild and pleasant. **2.** same as BARMY.

baloney *n. Informal* nonsense.

balsa [bawl-sa] *n.* tropical American tree that yields light wood.

balsam *n.* **1.** aromatic resin obtained from various trees and shrubs. **2.** soothing ointment. **3.** flowering plant.

baluster *n.* set of posts supporting a rail. **balustrade** *n.* ornamental rail supported by balusters.

bamboo *n.* tall treelike tropical grass with hollow stems.

bamboozle *v.* **1.** *Informal* cheat or mislead. **2.** confuse, puzzle.

ban *v.* **banning, banned. 1.** prohibit or forbid officially. —*n.* **2.** official prohibition.

banal [ban-nahl] *adj.* ordinary and unoriginal. **banality** *n.*

banana *n.* yellow crescent-shaped fruit.

band[1] *n.* **1.** group of musicians playing together. **2.** group of people having a common purpose. **bandmaster** *n.* conductor of a band. **bandsman** *n.* **bandstand** *n.* roofed outdoor platform for a band. **band together** *v.* unite.

band² n. **1.** strip of material, used to hold objects together. **2.** *Physics* range of frequencies or wavelengths between two limits.

bandage n. **1.** piece of material used to cover a wound. —v. **2.** cover with a bandage.

bandanna, bandana n. large brightly coloured handkerchief.

b. and b., B and B bed and breakfast.

bandeau n., pl. **-deaux.** narrow ribbon worn round the head.

bandicoot n. ratlike Aust. marsupial.

bandit n. robber, esp. a member of an armed gang. **banditry** n.

bandoleer, bandolier n. shoulder belt for holding cartridges.

bandwagon n. **climb, jump on the bandwagon** join a party or movement that seems assured of success.

bandy adj. **-dier, -diest.** (also **bandy-legged**) **1.** having legs curved outwards at the knees. —v. **-dying, -died. 2.** exchange (words) in a heated manner. **3.** circulate (a name, rumour, etc.).

bane n. person or thing that causes misery or distress. **baneful** adj.

bang n. **1.** short loud explosive noise. **2.** hard blow or loud knock. —v. **3.** hit or knock, esp. with a loud noise. **4.** close (a door) noisily. —adv. **5.** with a sudden impact. **6.** precisely, e.g. *bang in the middle.*

banger n. **1.** *Slang* sausage. **2.** *Informal* old decrepit car. **3.** firework that explodes loudly.

bangle n. bracelet worn round the arm or the ankle.

banian n. same as BANYAN.

banish v. **1.** send (someone) into exile. **2.** dismiss from one's thoughts. **banishment** n.

banisters pl. n. railing supported by posts on a staircase.

banjo n., pl. **-jos, -joes.** guitar-like musical instrument with a circular body.

bank¹ n. **1.** institution offering services, such as the safekeeping and lending of money. **2.** any supply, store, or reserve. —v. **3.** deposit (cash or cheques) in a bank. **4.** transact business with a bank. **banking** n. **bank holiday** public holiday when banks are closed by law. **banknote** n. piece of paper money. **bank on** v. rely on.

bank² n. **1.** raised mass, esp. of earth. **2.** slope, as of a hill. **3.** sloping ground at the side of a river. —v. **4.** form into a bank. **5.** cover (a fire) with ashes and fuel so that it will burn slowly. **6.** cause (an aircraft) or (of an aircraft) to tip to one side on turning.

bank³ n. arrangement of switches, keys, oars, etc. in a row or in tiers.

banker n. **1.** manager or owner of a bank. **2.** keeper of the bank in gambling games.

bankrupt n. **1.** person declared by a court to be unable to pay his or her debts. —adj. **2.** financially ruined. —v. **3.** make bankrupt. **bankruptcy** n.

banner n. **1.** long strip of cloth displaying a slogan, advertisement, etc. **2.** placard carried in a demonstration or procession.

bannisters pl. n. same as BANISTERS.

bannock n. round flat cake made from oatmeal or barley.

banns pl. n. public declaration, esp. in a church, of an intended marriage.

banquet n. **1.** elaborate formal dinner. —v. **-queting, -queted. 2.** hold or take part in a banquet.

banshee n. in Irish folklore, female spirit whose wailing warns of impending death.

bantam n. **1.** small chicken. **2.** small but aggressive person. **bantamweight** n. boxer weighing up to 118lb (professional) or 54 kg (amateur).

banter v. **1.** tease jokingly. —n. **2.** teasing or joking conversation.

Bantu n. **1.** group of languages of Africa. **2.** *Offens.* Black speaker of a Bantu language.

banyan, banian n. Indian tree whose branches grow down into the soil forming additional trunks.

baobab [bay-oh-bab] n. African tree with a thick trunk and angular branches.

bap n. *Brit.* large soft bread roll.

baptism n. Christian religious ceremony in which a person is immersed in or sprinkled with water as a sign of purification and acceptance into the Church. **baptismal** adj. **baptize** v. **1.** perform baptism on. **2.** give a name to.

Baptist n. member of a Protestant denomination that believes in adult baptism by immersion.

bar¹ n. **1.** rigid length of metal, wood, etc. **2.** solid, usu. rectangular block, of any material. **3.** anything that obstructs or prevents. **4.** counter or room where drinks are served. **5.** heating element in an electric fire. **6.** place in court where the accused stands during trial. **7.** *Music* group of beats repeated throughout a piece of music. —*v.* **barring, barred. 8.** secure with a bar. **9.** ban or forbid. **10.** obstruct. —*prep.* **11.** (also **barring**) except for. **the Bar** barristers collectively. **barman, barmaid, bartender** *n.*

bar² *n.* unit of atmospheric pressure.

barb *n.* **1.** point facing in the opposite direction to the main point of a fish-hook etc. **2.** cutting remark. —*v.* **3.** provide with a barb or barbs. **barbed** *adj.* **barbed wire** strong wire with protruding sharp points.

barbarian *n.* member of a primitive or uncivilized people. **barbaric** *adj.* cruel or brutal. **barbarism** *n.* condition of being backward or ignorant. **barbarity** *n.* **1.** state of being barbaric or barbarous. **2.** *pl.* **-ties.** vicious act. **barbarous** *adj.* **1.** uncivilized. **2.** brutal or cruel.

barbecue *n.* **1.** grill on which food is cooked over hot charcoal, usu. outdoors. **2.** outdoor party at which barbecued food is served. —*v.* **3.** cook (food) on a barbecue.

barber *n.* person who cuts men's hair and shaves beards.

barberry *n.* shrub with orange or red berries.

barbican *n.* walled defence to protect a fortification's gate or drawbridge.

barbiturate *n.* drug used as a sedative. **barbituric acid** crystalline solid used in the preparation of barbiturates.

barcarole, barcarolle *n.* Venetian boat song.

bard *n.* *Lit.* poet. **the Bard** William Shakespeare.

bare *adj.* **1.** unclothed. **2.** without the natural or usual covering. **3.** unembellished, simple. **4.** just sufficient. —*v.* **5.** uncover. **barely** *adv.* only just. **bareness** *n.*
▷ As *barely* already has a negative meaning, it should never be used with *not* or other negatives.

bareback *adj., adv.* (of horse-riding) without a saddle.

barefaced *adj.* shameless or impudent.

barefoot, barefooted *adj., adv.* with the feet uncovered.

bareheaded *adj., adv.* with the head uncovered.

bargain *n.* **1.** agreement establishing what each party will give, receive, or perform in a transaction. **2.** something bought or offered at a low price. —*v.* **3.** negotiate the terms of an agreement. **bargain for** *v.* anticipate or take into account.

barge *n.* **1.** flat-bottomed boat used to transport freight. —*v.* **2.** *Informal* push violently. **bargee** *n.* person in charge of a barge. **barge in, into** *v.* interrupt rudely.

baritone *n.* (singer with) the second lowest adult male voice.

barium [**bare**-ee-um] *n.* soft white metallic element. **barium meal** preparation of barium sulphate swallowed by a patient before an x-ray of the alimentary canal.

bark¹ *n.* **1.** loud harsh cry of a dog. —*v.* **2.** (of a dog) make its typical cry. **3.** shout in an angry tone. **barker** *n.* person at a fairground who calls loudly to passers-by in order to attract customers.

bark² *n.* **1.** tough outer layer of a tree. —*v.* **2.** scrape or rub off skin. **3.** strip the bark from.

bark³ *n.* same as BARQUE.

barking *adj.* *Slang* mad.

barley *n.* **1.** tall grasslike plant cultivated for grain. **2.** grain of this plant used for food and in making malt. **barley sugar** brittle clear amber-coloured sweet. **barley water** drink made from an infusion of barley.

barm *n.* yeasty froth on fermenting malt liquors.

bar mitzvah *n.* *Judaism* ceremony marking the 13th birthday of a boy, who then assumes full religious obligations.

barmy *adj.* **-mier, -miest.** *Slang* insane.

barn *n.* large building on a farm used for storing grain. **barn dance** informal party with country dancing. **barn owl** owl with pale brown and white plumage. **barnstorm** *v.* *US* tour rural districts putting on shows or making speeches in a political campaign.

barnacle *n.* shellfish that lives attached to objects under water. **barnacle goose** goose with a black-and-white head and body.

barney *n.* *Informal* noisy fight or argument.

barometer *n.* instrument for measuring atmospheric pressure. **barometric** *adj.*

baron *n.* **1.** member of the lowest rank of

baronet *n.* commoner who holds the lowest hereditary British title.

nobility. **2.** powerful businessman. **baroness** *n.* baronial *adj.*

baroque [bar-**rock**] *n.* **1.** highly ornate style of art and architecture from the late 16th to the early 18th century. —*adj.* **2.** ornate in style.

barque, bark [bark] *n.* sailing ship, esp. one with three masts.

barrack *v.* criticize loudly or shout against (a team or speaker).

barracks *pl. n.* building used to accommodate military personnel.

barracuda [bar-rack-**kew**-da] *n.* predatory tropical sea fish.

barrage [bar-**rahzh**] *n.* **1.** continuous delivery of questions, complaints, etc. **2.** continuous artillery fire. **3.** artificial barrier across a river.

barrel *n.* **1.** cylindrical container with rounded sides and flat ends. **2.** amount that a barrel can hold. **3.** tube in a firearm through which the bullet is fired. **barrel organ** musical instrument played by turning a handle.

barren *adj.* **1.** (of land) unable to support the growth of crops, fruit, etc. **2.** (of a woman or female animal) incapable of producing offspring. **3.** unprofitable, e.g. *a barren period*. **barrenness** *n.*

barricade *n.* **1.** barrier, esp. one erected hastily for defence. —*v.* **2.** erect a barricade across (an entrance).

barrier *n.* anything that prevents access, progress, or union. **barrier cream** cream that protects the skin. **barrier reef** long narrow coral reef lying close to the shore.

barrister *n.* lawyer qualified to plead in a higher court.

barrow[1] *n.* **1.** wheelbarrow. **2.** movable stall, used esp. by street vendors.

barrow[2] *n.* mound of earth placed over a prehistoric tomb.

barter *v.* **1.** trade (goods) in exchange for other goods. —*n.* **2.** trade by the exchange of goods.

basal *adj.* **1.** of, at, or constituting a base. **2.** fundamental.

basalt [**bass**-awlt] *n.* dark volcanic rock. **basaltic** *adj.*

bascule *n.* drawbridge that operates by a counterbalanced weight.

base[1] *n.* **1.** bottom or supporting part of anything. **2.** fundamental part. **3.** centre of operations, organization, or supply. **4.** starting point. **5.** chemical compound that combines with an acid to form a salt. **6.** *Maths* system of counting and expressing numbers. —*v.* **7.** (foll. by *on* or *upon*) use as a basis (for). **baseless** *adj.*

base[2] *adj.* **1.** dishonourable or immoral. **2.** of inferior quality. **3.** debased or counterfeit. **basely** *adv.* **baseness** *n.*

baseball *n.* **1.** American team game played with a bat and ball. **2.** ball used for this.

basement *n.* partly or wholly underground storey of a building.

bases *n.* plural of BASIS.

bash *Informal* —*v.* **1.** hit violently or forcefully. —*n.* **2.** heavy blow. **have a bash** *Informal* make an attempt.

bashful *adj.* shy or modest. **bashfully** *adv.* **bashfulness** *n.*

basic *adj.* **1.** of or forming a base or basis. **2.** elementary or simple. **basics** *pl. n.* **1.** fundamental principles, facts, etc. **2.** *Chem.* of or containing a base. **basically** *adv.*

BASIC *n.* computer programming language that uses common English words.

basil *n.* aromatic herb used in cooking.

basilica *n.* rectangular church with a rounded end and two aisles.

basilisk *n.* legendary serpent said to kill by its breath or glance.

basin *n.* **1.** round open container. **2.** sink for washing the hands and face. **3.** sheltered area of water where boats may be moored. **4.** catchment area of a particular river.

basis *n., pl.* -**ses.** fundamental principles etc. from which something is started or developed.

bask *v.* lie in or be exposed to something, esp. pleasant warmth.

basket *n.* container made of interwoven strips of wood or cane. **basketwork** *n.*

basketball *n.* **1.** team game in which points are scored by throwing the ball through a high horizontal hoop. **2.** ball used for this.

basque *n.* tight-fitting bodice for women.

Basque *n., adj.* (member or language) of a people living in the W Pyrenees in France and Spain.

bas-relief n. sculpture in which the figures stand out slightly from the background.

bass[1] [**base**] n. **1.** (singer with) the lowest adult male voice. —adj. **2.** of the lowest range of musical notes.

bass[2] n. edible sea fish.

basset hound n. smooth-haired dog with short legs and long ears.

bassinet n. wickerwork or wooden cradle or pram, usu. hooded.

bassoon n. large woodwind instrument.

bast n. fibrous material obtained from jute and flax, used for making rope etc.

bastard n. **1.** person born of parents not married to each other. **2.** Offens. obnoxious or despicable person. **bastardize** v. debase or corrupt. **bastardy** n.

baste[1] v. moisten (meat) during cooking with hot fat.

baste[2] v. sew with loose temporary stitches.

bastinado n., pl. -**does**. **1.** beating on the soles of the feet with a stick. —v. -**doing**, -**doed**. **2.** beat (a person) thus.

bastion n. **1.** projecting part of a fortification. **2.** thing or person regarded as defending a principle.

bat[1] n. **1.** any of various types of club used to hit the ball in certain sports. **2.** Cricket batsman. —v. **batting, batted**. **3.** strike with or as if with a bat. **batsman** n. Cricket person who bats or specializes in batting.

bat[2] n. nocturnal mouselike flying animal.

bat[3] v. **not bat an eyelid** Informal show no surprise.

batch n. group of people or things dealt with at the same time.

bated adj. **with bated breath** in suspense or fear.

bath n. **1.** large container in which to wash the body. **2.** act of washing in such a container. —pl. **3.** public swimming pool. —v. **4.** wash in a bath. **bathroom** n. room with a bath, sink, and usu. a toilet.

Bath chair n. wheelchair for an invalid.

bathe v. **1.** swim in open water. **2.** apply liquid to (the skin or a wound) in order to cleanse or soothe. **3.** (foll. by in) fill (with), e.g. bathed in sunlight. —n. **4.** Brit. instance of bathing. **bather** n.

bathos [**bay**-thoss] n. sudden change in speech or writing from a serious subject to a trivial one.

bathyscaph, bathyscaphe, bathysphere n. deep-sea diving vessel for observation.

batik [bat-**teek**] n. **1.** process of printing fabric using wax to cover areas not to be dyed. **2.** fabric printed in this way.

batman n. officer's servant in the armed forces.

baton n. **1.** thin stick used by the conductor of an orchestra. **2.** short bar transferred in a relay race. **3.** policeman's truncheon.

batrachian [bat-**tray**-kee-an] n. **1.** amphibian, esp. a frog or toad. —adj. **2.** of or relating to frogs and toads.

battalion n. army unit consisting of three or more companies.

batten[1] n. strip of wood fixed to something, esp. to hold it in place. **batten down** v. secure with battens.

batten[2] v. **batten on** thrive at the expense of (someone else).

batter[1] v. hit repeatedly. **battering ram** large beam used to break down fortifications.

batter[2] n. mixture of flour, eggs, and milk, used in cooking.

battery n., pl. -**teries**. **1.** device that produces electricity in a torch, radio, etc. **2.** number of similar things occurring together. **3.** Law assault by beating. **4.** group of heavy guns operating as a single unit. **5.** series of cages for intensive rearing of poultry.

battle n. **1.** fight between large armed forces. **2.** conflict or struggle. —v. **3.** struggle.

battle-axe n. **1.** Informal domineering woman. **2.** large heavy axe.

battledress n. ordinary uniform of a soldier.

battlefield, battleground n. place where a battle is fought.

battlement n. wall with gaps for shooting through.

battleship n. heavily armoured warship.

batty adj. -**tier**, -**tiest**. Slang **1.** crazy. **2.** eccentric.

bauble n. trinket of little value.

baulk v., n. same as BALK.

bauxite n. claylike substance from which aluminium is obtained.

bawdy adj. **bawdier, bawdiest**. (of writing

etc.) containing humorous references to sex. **bawdiness** n.

bawl v. **1.** shout or weep noisily. —n. **2.** loud shout or cry.

bay[1] n. wide curving coastline.

bay[2] n. **1.** recess in a wall. **2.** area in which vehicles may park or unload. **3.** compartment in an aircraft. **bay window** window projecting from a wall.

bay[3] v. **1.** (of a hound or wolf) howl in deep prolonged tones. —n. **2.** deep howl of a hound. **at bay 1.** cornered. **2.** at a distance.

bay[4] n. Mediterranean laurel tree. **bay leaf** dried leaf of a laurel, used in cooking.

bay[5] adj., n. reddish-brown (horse).

bayonet n. **1.** sharp blade that can be fixed to the end of a rifle. —v. **-neting, -neted. 2.** stab with a bayonet.

bazaar n. **1.** sale in aid of charity. **2.** market area, esp. in Eastern countries.

bazooka n. rocket launcher that fires a projectile capable of piercing armour.

BB Boys' Brigade.

BBC British Broadcasting Corporation.

BC 1. before Christ. **2.** British Columbia.

BCG antituberculosis vaccine.

BD Bachelor of Divinity.

BDS Bachelor of Dental Surgery.

be v. present sing. 1st person **am**; 2nd person **are**; 3rd person **is**. present pl. **are**. past sing. 1st person **was**; 2nd person **were**; 3rd person **was**. past pl. **were**. present participle **being**. past participle **been. 1.** exist or live. **2.** used as a linking between the subject of a sentence and its complement, e.g. John is a musician. **3.** forms the progressive present tense, e.g. the man is running. **4.** forms the passive voice of all transitive verbs, e.g. a good film is being shown on television tonight.

Be Chem. beryllium.

BE Bachelor of Engineering.

be- prefix **1.** surround or cover, e.g. befog. **2.** affect completely, e.g. bedazzle. **3.** consider as or cause to be, e.g. befriend. **4.** at, for, against, on, or over, e.g. bewail, berate.

beach n. **1.** area of sand or pebbles on a shore. —v. **2.** run or haul (a boat) onto a beach. **beachcomber** n. person who searches shore debris for anything of worth. **beachhead** n. beach captured by an attacking army on which troops can be landed.

beacon n. **1.** fire or light on a hill or tower, used as a warning. **2.** lighthouse. **3.** radio or other signal used in air navigation.

bead n. **1.** small ball of plastic etc., pierced for threading on a string to form a necklace etc. **2.** small drop of moisture. **3.** small metal knob acting as the sight of a firearm. **beaded** adj. **beading** n. strip of moulding used for edging furniture. **beady** adj. **beadier, beadiest.** small, round, and glittering, e.g. beady eyes.

beadle n. **1.** Brit. formerly, minor parish official. **2.** Scot. church official who attends the minister.

beagle n. small hunting dog with short legs and drooping ears.

beak[1] n. **1.** projecting horny jaws of a bird. **2.** Slang nose. **beaky** adj. **beakier, beakiest.**

beak[2] n. Slang judge, magistrate, or headmaster.

beaker n. **1.** large drinking cup. **2.** lipped glass container used in laboratories.

beam n. **1.** long thick piece of wood, metal, etc., used in building. **2.** breadth of a ship at its widest part. **3.** ray of light. **4.** broad smile. **5.** narrow flow of electromagnetic radiation or particles. **6.** crossbar of a balance. —v. **7.** smile broadly. **8.** divert or aim (a radio signal, light, etc.) in a certain direction.

bean n. seed or pod of various plants, eaten as a vegetable or used to make coffee etc.

beano n., pl. **beanos.** Brit. slang celebration or party.

bear[1] v. **bearing, bore, borne. 1.** support or hold up. **2.** born in passive use. give birth to. **3.** produce as by natural growth. **4.** tolerate or endure. **5.** hold in the mind. **6.** show or be marked with. **7.** move in a specified direction. **bearable** adj. **bear out** v. show to be truthful.

bear[2] n. large heavy mammal with a long shaggy coat. **bear hug** rough tight embrace. **bearskin** n. tall fur helmet worn by some British soldiers.

beard n. **1.** hair growing on the lower parts of a man's face. —v. **2.** oppose boldly. **bearded** adj.

bearer n. person who carries, presents, or upholds something.

bearing n. **1.** relevance (to). **2.** person's general social conduct. **3.** part of a machine that supports another part, esp. one that reduces friction. —*pl.* **4.** sense of one's own relative position.

beast *n.* **1.** large wild animal. **2.** brutal or uncivilized person. **beastly** *adj.* unpleasant or disagreeable.

beat *v.* **beating, beat, beaten** or **beat.** **1.** hit hard and repeatedly. **2.** move (wings) up and down. **3.** throb rhythmically. **4.** *Music* indicate (time) by one's hand or a baton. **5.** stir or mix vigorously. **6.** overcome or defeat. **7.** *Slang* puzzle or baffle. —*n.* **8.** (sound made by) a stroke or blow. **9.** regular throb. **10.** assigned route, as of a policeman. **11.** basic rhythmic unit in a piece of music.

beater *n.* **1.** device for beating. **2.** person who rouses wild game.

beatify [bee-**at**-if-fie] *v.* -**fying,** -**fied. 1.** *RC Church* declare (a dead person) to be among the blessed in heaven. **2.** make happy. **beatific** *adj.* displaying great happiness. **beatification** *n.* **beatitude** *n.* supreme blessedness.

beatnik *n.* young person in the late 1950s who rebelled against conventional attitudes etc.

beau [boh] *n., pl.* **beaus, beaux. 1.** boyfriend or admirer. **2.** dandy.

Beaufort scale *n.* scale for measuring the speed of wind.

Beaujolais *n.* red or white wine from southern Burgundy in France.

beauteous *adj. Lit.* beautiful.

beautician *n.* person whose profession is to give beauty treatments.

beautiful *adj.* **1.** possessing beauty. **2.** very pleasant. **beautifully** *adv.*

beautify *v.* -**fying,** -**fied.** make or become beautiful. **beautification** *n.*

beauty *n., pl.* -**ties. 1.** combination of all the qualities of a person or thing that delight the senses and mind. **2.** very attractive woman. **3.** *Informal* something outstanding of its kind. **beauty queen** woman who has been judged the most beautiful in a contest. **beauty spot 1.** place of outstanding beauty. **2.** small black spot formerly worn on a woman's face. **3.** facial mole.

beaver *n.* **1.** amphibious rodent with a big flat tail. **2.** (hat made of) its fur. **beaver away** *v.* work industriously.

becalmed *adj.* (of a sailing ship) motionless through lack of wind.

became *v.* past tense of BECOME.

because *conj.* on account of the fact that. **because of** on account of.
▷ It is unnecessary to follow *because* with *the reason is/was: He was cold because the window was open* or *The reason he was cold was that the window was open.*

beck[1] *n.* **at someone's beck and call** subject to someone's slightest whim.

beck[2] *n. N English* stream.

beckon *v.* summon with a gesture.

become *v.* -**coming,** -**came,** -**come. 1.** come to be. **2.** (foll. by *of*) happen to. **3.** suit. **becoming** *adj.* **1.** attractive or pleasing. **2.** appropriate or proper.

bed *n.* **1.** piece of furniture on which to sleep. **2.** garden plot. **3.** bottom of a river, lake, or sea. **4.** layer of rock. —*v.* **bedding, bedded. 5.** plant in a bed. **6.** have sexual intercourse with. **bed and breakfast** overnight accommodation plus breakfast. **bedclothes** *pl. n.* coverings for a bed. **bed down** *v.* go to or put into a place to sleep or rest. **bedpan** *n.* shallow bowl used as a toilet by bedridden people. **bedridden** *adj.* confined to bed because of illness or old age. **bedrock** *n.* **1.** solid rock beneath the surface soil. **2.** basic facts or principles. **bedroom** *n.* **bedsitter, bedsit** *n.* furnished sitting room with a bed. **bedspread** *n.* top cover on a bed. **bedstead** *n.* framework of a bed.

BEd Bachelor of Education.

bedaub *v.* smear with something sticky or dirty.

bedding *n.* **1.** sheets and covers that are used on a bed. **2.** litter, such as straw, for animals.

bedeck *v.* cover with decorations.

bedevil [bid-**dev**-ill] *v.* -**illing,** -**illed.** harass, confuse, or torment. **bedevilment** *n.*

bedlam *n.* noisy confused situation.

Bedouin *n., pl.* -**in,** -**ins.** member of a nomadic Arab race.

bedraggled *adj.* untidy, wet, or dirty.

bee[1] *n.* insect that makes wax and honey. **beehive** *n.* structure in which bees live. **beeswax** *n.* wax secreted by bees, used in polishes etc.

bee[2] *n. US* social gathering to carry out a communal task, e.g. *quilting bee.*

Beeb *n. Informal* the BBC.

beech n. European tree with a smooth greyish bark.

beef n. **1.** flesh of a cow, bull, or ox. **2.** *Informal* complaint. —v. **3.** *Informal* complain. **beefy** adj. **beefier, beefiest. 1.** like beef. **2.** *Informal* strong and muscular. **3.** *Informal* fleshy, obese. **beefburger** n. flat grilled or fried cake of minced beef. **beefeater** n. yeoman warder at the Tower of London. **beef tea** drink made by boiling pieces of beef. **beef tomato, beefsteak tomato** large fleshy tomato.

been v. past participle of BE.

beep n. **1.** high-pitched sound, like that of a car horn. —v. **2.** (cause to) make this noise.

beer n. alcoholic drink brewed from malt and hops. **beery** adj.

beet n. plant with an edible root and leaves. **beetroot** n. type of beet plant with a dark red root.

beetle n. **1.** insect with a hard wing cover on its back. —v. **2.** *Informal* scuttle or scurry.

beetling adj. overhanging or jutting. **beetle-browed** adj. having bushy or overhanging eyebrows.

befall v. *Old-fashioned* happen to (someone).

befit v. be appropriate or suitable for. **befitting** adj.

before conj. **1.** earlier than the time when. **2.** rather than. —prep. **3.** preceding in space or time. **4.** in the presence of. **5.** in preference to. —adv. **6.** at an earlier time, previously. **7.** in front. **beforehand** adv. in advance.

befriend v. become friends with.

befuddle v. stupefy or confuse, as with alcoholic drink.

beg v. **begging, begged. 1.** solicit (for money or food), esp. in the street. **2.** ask formally or humbly. **beg the question** assume the thing under examination as proved. **go begging** be unwanted or unused.

began v. past tense of BEGIN.

beget v. **-getting; -got** or **-gat; -gotten** or **-got. 1.** cause or create. **2.** father.

beggar n. **1.** person who lives by begging. **2.** *Brit.* fellow. —v. **3.** **beggar description** be impossible to describe. **beggarly** adj.

begin v. **-ginning, -gan, -gun. 1.** start. **2.** bring or come into being. **beginner** n. person who has just started learning to do something. **beginning** n.

begone interj. go away!

begonia n. tropical plant with waxy flowers.

begot v. a past of BEGET. **begotten** v. a past participle of BEGET.

begrudge v. grudge.

beguile [big-**gile**] v. **1.** cheat or mislead. **2.** charm or amuse. **beguiling** adj.

beguine [big-**geen**] n. **1.** S American dance. **2.** music for this.

begum [**bay**-gum] n. Muslim woman of high rank.

begun v. past participle of BEGIN.

behalf n. **on behalf of** in the interest of or for the benefit of.

behave v. **1.** act or function in a particular way. **2.** conduct (oneself) properly.

behaviour n. manner of behaving. **behaviourism** n. school of psychology that regards the observation of the behaviour of organisms as the only valid subject for study. **behaviourist** adj., n.

behead v. remove the head from.

beheld v. past of BEHOLD.

behest n. order or earnest request.

behind prep. **1.** at the back of. **2.** responsible for or causing. **3.** supporting. —adv. **4.** in or to a position further back. **5.** remaining after someone's departure. **6.** in arrears. —n. **7.** *Informal* buttocks. **behindhand** adj., adv. **1.** in arrears. **2.** late.

behold v. *Old-fashioned* look (at). **beholder** n.

beholden adj. indebted or obliged.

behove v. *Old-fashioned* be necessary or fitting for.

beige adj. pale brown.

being v. **1.** present participle of BE. —n. **2.** existence. **3.** something that exists or is thought to exist. **4.** human being, person.

belabour v. attack verbally or physically.

belated adj. late or too late. **belatedly** adv.

belch v. **1.** expel wind from the stomach noisily through the mouth. **2.** expel or be expelled forcefully, e.g. *smoke belched from the factory.* —n. **3.** act of belching.

beleaguered adj. **1.** besieged. **2.** surrounded or beset.

belfry n., pl. **-fries.** part of a tower where bells are hung.

belie v. 1. show to be untrue. 2. misrepresent.

belief n. 1. principle etc. accepted as true. 2. opinion. 3. religious faith. **believe** v. 1. accept as true or real. 2. (foll. by *in*) be convinced of the truth or existence of. 3. think, assume, or suppose. **believable** adj. **believer** n.

Belisha beacon [bill-**lee**-sha] n. flashing orange globe mounted on a post, marking a pedestrian crossing.

belittle v. treat as having little value or importance.

bell n. 1. hollow, usu. metal, cup-shaped instrument that emits a ringing sound when struck. 2. device that rings or buzzes as a signal. **bell-bottoms** pl. n. trousers that flare from the knee.

belladonna n. (drug obtained from) deadly nightshade.

belle n. beautiful woman, esp. the most attractive woman at a function.

belles-lettres [bell-**let**-tra] n. literary works, esp. essays and poetry.

bellicose adj. warlike and aggressive.

belligerent adj. 1. hostile and aggressive. 2. engaged in war. —n. 3. person or country engaged in war. **belligerence** n.

bellow v. 1. make a low deep cry like that of a bull. 2. shout in a loud deep voice. —n. 3. loud deep roar.

bellows pl. n. instrument for pumping a stream of air into something.

belly n., pl. **-lies**. 1. part of the body of a vertebrate which contains the intestines. 2. stomach. 3. front, lower, or inner part of something. —v. **-lying**, **-lied**. 4. (cause to) swell out. **bellyful** n. Slang more than one can tolerate.

belong v. 1. (foll. by *to*) be the property of. 2. (foll. by *to*) be a part of. 3. have a proper or usual place. **belongings** pl. n. personal possessions.

beloved adj. 1. dearly loved. —n. 2. person dearly loved.

below prep., adv. at or to a position lower than, under.

belt n. 1. band of cloth, leather, etc., worn usu. around the waist. 2. circular strip of rubber that drives moving parts in a machine. 3. area where a specific thing is found. —v. 4. fasten with a belt. 5. Slang hit very hard. 6. Slang move very fast.

bemoan v. express sorrow or dissatisfaction about.

bemused adj. puzzled or confused.

ben n. Scot. & Irish mountain peak.

bench n. 1. long seat. 2. long narrow work table. 3. judge or magistrate sitting in court. **bench mark** 1. mark on a fixed object, used as a reference point in surveying. 2. criterion by which to measure something.

bend v. **bending**, **bent**. 1. (cause to) form a curve. 2. (often foll. by *down* etc.) incline the body. 3. (cause to) submit. —n. 4. curved part. —pl. 5. Informal decompression sickness. **bendy** adj. **bendier**, **bendiest**.

beneath adv., prep. 1. below. 2. not worthy of.

Benedictine n. 1. monk or nun of the order of Saint Benedict. 2. liqueur first made by Benedictine monks. —adj. 3. of the order of Saint Benedict.

benediction n. prayer for divine blessing. **benedictory** adj.

benefaction n. 1. act of doing good. 2. gift to charity. **benefactor**, **benefactress** n. someone who supports a person or institution by giving money.

benefice n. Christianity church office providing a living.

beneficent [bin-**eff**-iss-ent] adj. charitable or generous. **beneficence** n.

beneficial adj. advantageous.

beneficiary n. person who gains or benefits.

benefit n. 1. something helpful, beneficial, or advantageous. 2. payment made by a government to a poor, ill, or unemployed person. 3. theatrical performance or sports event to raise money for a person or a charity. —v. **-fiting**, **-fited**. 4. do or receive good.

benevolent adj. 1. kind and helpful. 2. generous or charitable. **benevolently** adv. **benevolence** n.

Bengali n., adj. (member or language) of a people living chiefly in Bangladesh and W Bengal.

benighted adj. ignorant or uncultured.

benign [bin-**nine**] adj. 1. showing kindliness. 2. favourable or propitious. 3. (of a tumour) not malignant. **benignly** adv. **benignity** [be-**nig**-nit-tee] n.

benignant *adj.* gracious and kind. **benignancy** *n.*

bent *v.* **1.** past of BEND. —*adj.* **2.** curved. **3.** *Slang* dishonest. **4.** *Slang* homosexual. —*n.* **5.** personal inclination or aptitude. **bent on** determined to pursue (a course of action).

benumb *v.* **1.** make numb or powerless. **2.** stupefy (the mind etc.).

benzene *n.* flammable poisonous liquid used as a solvent, fuel, etc.

benzine *n.* volatile liquid used as a solvent.

bequeath *v.* **1.** dispose of (property) as in a will. **2.** hand down. **bequest** *n.* legal gift of money or property by someone who has died.

berate *v.* scold harshly.

berberis *n.* shrub with red berries.

bereaved *adj.* having recently lost someone close through death. **bereavement** *n.*

bereft *adj.* (foll. by *of*) deprived.

beret [ber-ray] *n.* round flat close-fitting brimless cap.

berg *n.* iceberg.

bergamot *n.* small Asian tree with sour pear-shaped fruit.

beriberi *n.* tropical disease caused by vitamin B deficiency.

berk *n. Brit. slang* stupid person.

berkelium *n.* radioactive element.

Bermuda shorts *pl. n.* close-fitting shorts that come down to the knees.

berry *n., pl.* **-ries.** small soft stoneless fruit.

berserk *adj.* **go berserk** become violent or destructive.

berth *n.* **1.** bunk in a ship or train. **2.** place assigned to a ship at a mooring. —*v.* **3.** dock (a vessel).

beryl *n.* hard transparent mineral.

beryllium *n.* toxic silvery-white metallic element.

beseech *v.* **-seeching, -sought** *or* **-seeched.** ask (someone) earnestly.

beset *v.* **1.** trouble or harass constantly. **2.** attack from all sides.

beside *prep.* **1.** at, by, or to the side of. **2.** as compared with. **beside oneself** overwhelmed or overwrought. **besides** *adv., prep.* in addition.

besiege *v.* **1.** surround with military forces. **2.** hem in. **3.** overwhelm, as with requests.

besmirch *v.* **1.** dirty. **2.** dishonour.

besom *n.* broom made of twigs.

besotted *adj.* infatuated.

besought *v.* past of BESEECH.

bespatter *v.* **1.** splash, e.g. with dirty water. **2.** dishonour.

bespeak *v.* indicate or suggest. **bespoke** *adj.* **1.** (of clothes) made to the customer's specifications. **2.** making or selling such suits.

best *adj.* **1.** most excellent of a particular group etc. —*adv.* **2.** in a manner surpassing all others. —*n.* **3.** most outstanding or excellent person, thing, or group in a category. —*v.* **4.** defeat. **best man** groom's attendant at a wedding. **best seller** book or other product that has sold in great numbers. **best-selling** *adj.*

bestial *adj.* **1.** brutal or savage. **2.** of or like a beast. **bestiality** *n.*

bestiary *n.* medieval collection of descriptions of animals.

bestir *v.* cause (oneself) to become active.

bestow *v.* present (a gift) or confer (an honour). **bestowal** *n.*

bestrew *v.* scatter or lie scattered over (a surface).

bestride *v.* have or put a leg on either side of.

bet *n.* **1.** agreement that money will be paid to someone who correctly predicts the outcome of an event. **2.** stake risked. —*v.* **betting, bet** *or* **betted. 3.** make or place (a bet). **4.** *Informal* predict.

beta *n.* second letter in the Greek alphabet. **beta-blocker** *n.* drug used to treat high blood pressure and angina. **beta particle** electron or positron emitted by a nucleus during radioactive decay or nuclear fission. **betatron** *n.* particle accelerator for producing high-energy beams of electrons.

betake *v.* **betake oneself** go or move.

betel [bee-tl] *n.* Asian climbing plant, the leaves and nuts of which can be chewed.

bête noire [bet nwahr] *n., pl.* **bêtes noires.** person or thing that one particularly dislikes.

bethink *Obs. v.* **1.** cause (oneself) to consider or meditate. **2.** (often foll. by *of*) remind (oneself).

betide *v.* happen (to).

betimes *adv. Old-fashioned* early.

betoken v. indicate or signify.

betray v. 1. hand over or expose (one's nation etc.) treacherously to an enemy. 2. disclose (a secret or confidence) treacherously. 3. reveal unintentionally. **betrayal** n. **betrayer** n.

betroth v. Old-fashioned promise to marry or give in marriage. **betrothal** n. **betrothed** adj., n.

better adj. 1. more excellent than others. 2. improved or fully recovered in health. —adv. 3. in a more excellent manner. 4. in or to a greater degree. —pl. n. 5. one's superiors. —v. 6. improve upon. **get the better of** defeat or outwit. **betterment** n. improvement.

between prep. 1. at a point intermediate to two other points in space, time, etc. 2. indicating a linked relation or comparison. 3. indicating alternatives. —adv. 4. between one specified thing and another.
▷ Between is used when two people or things are mentioned: the war between Iraq and Iran. Otherwise use among.

betwixt prep., adv. Old-fashioned between.

bevel n. 1. slanting edge. —v. -elling, -elled. 2. slope. 3. cut a bevel on (a piece of timber etc.).

beverage n. drink.

bevy n., pl. **bevies.** flock or group.

bewail v. express great sorrow over.

beware v. be on one's guard (against).

bewilder v. confuse utterly. **bewildering** adj. **bewilderingly** adv. **bewilderment** n.

bewitch v. 1. attract and fascinate. 2. cast a spell over. **bewitching** adj.

bey n. in the Ottoman Empire, title given to provincial governors.

beyond prep. 1. at or to a point on the other side of. 2. outside the limits or scope of. —adv. 3. at or to the far side of something. —n. 4. the unknown, esp. life after death.

bezel n. 1. sloping edge of a cutting tool. 2. slanting face of a cut gem. 3. groove holding a gem, watch crystal, etc.

bezique n. card game for two or more players.

BFPO British Forces Post Office.

Bi Chem. bismuth.

bi- combining form twice or two, e.g. bifocal.

biannual adj. occurring twice a year. **biannually** adv.

bias n. 1. mental tendency, esp. prejudice. 2. diagonal cut across the weave of a fabric. 3. Bowls weight on one side of a bowl that causes it to run in a curve. —v. -asing, -ased or -assing, -assed. 4. cause to have a bias. **biased, biassed** adj. **bias binding** strip of material used for binding hems.

bib n. 1. piece of cloth or plastic worn under a child's chin to protect his or her clothes when eating. 2. upper front part of dungarees etc.

bibelot [**bib**-loh] n. attractive or curious trinket.

Bible n. 1. sacred writings of the Christian and Jewish religions. 2. (b-) book regarded as authoritative. **biblical** adj.

bibliography n., pl. -phies. 1. list of books on a subject. 2. list of sources used in a book etc. **bibliographer** n.

bibliophile n. person who collects or is fond of books.

bibulous adj. addicted to alcohol.

bicameral adj. (of a legislature) consisting of two chambers.

bicarbonate n. salt of carbonic acid. **bicarbonate of soda** powder used in baking or as medicine.

bicentenary, U.S. **bicentennial** adj. 1. marking a 200th anniversary. —n., pl. -naries. 2. 200th anniversary.

biceps n. muscle with two origins, esp. the muscle that flexes the forearm.

bicker v. argue over petty matters.

bicuspid adj. 1. having two points. —n. 2. bicuspid tooth.

bicycle n. 1. vehicle with two wheels, one behind the other, pedalled by the rider. —v. 2. ride a bicycle.

bid v. **bidding, bade, bidden.** 1. past **bid.** offer (a sum of money) in an attempt to buy something. 2. say (a greeting etc.). 3. command. —n. 4. offer of a sum of money. 5. attempt. **bidder** n. **biddable** adj. obedient. **bidding** n. 1. command. 2. invitation.

bide v. **bide one's time** wait patiently for an opportunity.

bidet [**bee**-day] n. low basin for washing the genital area.

biennial adj. 1. occurring every two years. —n. 2. plant that completes its life cycle in two years.

bier *n.* stand on which a coffin rests before burial.

biff *Slang* —*n.* **1.** blow with the fist. —*v.* **2.** give (someone) such a blow.

bifid *adj.* divided into two by a cleft in the middle.

bifocal *adj.* **1.** having two different focuses, esp. (of a lens) permitting near and distant vision. —*pl. n.* **2.** spectacles with bifocal lenses.

bifurcate *v.* fork into two branches.

big *adj.* **bigger, biggest. 1.** of considerable size, height, number, or capacity. **2.** important through having wealth etc. **3.** elder. **4.** generous, magnanimous. —*adv.* **5.** on a grand scale. **bighead** *n. Informal* conceited person. **big-headed** *adj.* **big shot, bigwig** *n. Informal* important person. **big top** *Informal* main tent of a circus.

bigamy *n.* crime of marrying a person while still legally married to someone else. **bigamist** *n.* **bigamous** *adj.*

bight *n.* **1.** long curved shoreline. **2.** curve or loop in a rope.

bigot *n.* person who is intolerant, esp. regarding religion or race. **bigoted** *adj.* **bigotry** *n.*

bijou [bee-zhoo] *adj.* (of a house) small but elegant.

bike *n. Informal* bicycle or motorcycle.

bikini *n.* woman's brief two-piece swimming costume.

bilateral *adj.* affecting or undertaken by two parties.

bilberry *n.* bluish-black edible berry.

bile *n.* **1.** bitter yellow fluid secreted by the liver. **2.** irritability or peevishness. **biliary** *adj.*

bilge *n.* **1.** ship's bottom. **2.** dirty water that collects in a ship's bilge. **3.** *Informal* nonsense.

bilingual *adj.* involving or using two languages.

bilious *adj.* **1.** sick, nauseous. **2.** *Informal* bad-tempered or irritable.

bilk *v.* cheat, avoid making payment to.

bill[1] *n.* **1.** statement of money owed for goods or services supplied. **2.** draft of a proposed new law. **3.** poster. **4.** *US* piece of paper money. **5.** list of events, such as a theatre programme. —*v.* **6.** send or present a bill to. **7.** advertise by posters. **bill of exchange**

document instructing a third party to pay a stated sum at a designated date or on demand. **bill of fare** menu. **bill of health** certificate that confirms the health of a ship's company.

bill[2] *n.* **1.** bird's beak. **bill and coo** (of lovers) kiss and whisper amorously.

bill[3] *n.* weapon with a narrow hooked blade.

billabong *n. Aust.* stagnant pool in an intermittent stream.

billboard *n.* hoarding.

billet[1] *n.* **1.** civilian accommodation for a soldier. **2.** *Informal* job. —*v.* **-leting, -leted. 3.** assign a lodging to (a soldier).

billet[2] *n.* **1.** chunk of wood, esp. for fuel. **2.** small bar of iron or steel.

billet-doux [bill-ee-doo] *n., pl.* **billets-doux.** love letter.

billhook *n.* tool with a hooked blade, used for chopping etc.

billiards *n.* game played on a table with balls and a cue.

billion *n.* **1.** one thousand million. **2.** formerly, one million million. **billionth** *adj.*
▷ Note that the use of the word *billion* has changed and may stand for different amounts according to the date of a book or article.

billow *n.* **1.** large sea wave. —*v.* **2.** rise up or swell out. **billowy** *adj.*

billy, billycan *n., pl.* **-lies, -lycans.** metal can or pot for cooking on a camp fire.

billy goat *n.* male goat.

bimbo *n. Slang* attractive but empty-headed young person, esp. a woman.

bimonthly *adv., adj.* **1.** every two months. **2.** twice a month.

bin *n.* container for rubbish or for storing grain, coal, etc.

binary [bine-a-ree] *adj.* **1.** composed of two parts. **2.** *Maths, computers* of or expressed in a counting system with only two digits, 0 and 1.

bind *v.* **binding, bound. 1.** make or become secure with or as if with a rope. **2.** place (someone) under obligation. **3.** restrain or confine. **4.** enclose and fasten (the pages of a book) between covers. **5.** provide with a edging. —*n.* **6.** *Informal* annoying situation. **binder** *n.* **1.** firm cover for holding loose sheets of paper together. **2.** person who binds books. **3.** *Obs.* machine for cutting and binding sheaves. **binding** n. **1.** book cover. **2.** strip of cloth used as edging.

bindweed n. plant that twines around a support.

binge n. Informal bout of excessive eating or drinking.

bingo n. gambling game in which numbers are called out and covered by the players on their individual cards.

binnacle n. box holding a ship's compass.

binocular adj. **1.** involving both eyes. —pl. n. **2.** telescope made for both eyes.

binomial n., adj. (mathematical expression) consisting of two terms.

bio- combining form life or living organisms, e.g. biology.

biochemistry n. study of the chemistry of living things. **biochemist** n.

biodegradable adj. capable of being decomposed by natural means.

biogenesis n. principle that a living organism must originate from a similar parent organism.

biography n., pl. -phies. account of a person's life by another. **biographical** adj. **biographer** n.

biological adj. of or relating to biology. **biological warfare** use of living organisms or their toxic products to kill or disable people or destroy crops in war.

biology n. study of living organisms. **biologist** n.

bionic adj. having a part of the body that is operated electronically. **bionics** n. study of the relation of biological and electronic processes.

biopsy n., pl. -sies. examination of tissue from a living body.

biosphere n. part of the earth's surface and atmosphere inhabited by living things.

bipartite adj. **1.** consisting of two parts. **2.** affecting or made by two parties.

biped [bye-ped] n. animal with two feet.

biplane n. aeroplane with two sets of wings, one above the other.

bipolar adj. **1.** having two poles. **2.** having two extremes. **bipolarity** n.

birch n. **1.** tree with thin peeling bark. **2.** birch rod or twigs used, esp. formerly, for flogging offenders. —v. **3.** flog with a birch.

bird n. **1.** creature with feathers and wings,

the female of which lays eggs. **2.** Slang young woman. **bird's-eye view 1.** view seen from above. **2.** general or overall impression.

birdie n. Golf score of one stroke under par for a hole.

biretta n. stiff square cap worn by the Catholic clergy.

Biro n. ® ballpoint pen.

birth n. **1.** childbirth. **2.** act of being born. **3.** origin or beginning. **4.** ancestry. **give birth to** bear (offspring). **birth control** any method of contraception. **birthday** n. anniversary of the day of one's birth. **birthmark** n. blemish on the skin formed before birth. **birth rate** ratio of live births to population. **birthright** n. privileges or possessions that someone is entitled to as soon as he or she is born.

biscuit n. **1.** small flat sweet or plain cake. **2.** porcelain that has been fired but not glazed. —adj. **3.** pale brown.

bisect v. divide into two equal parts.

bisexual adj. **1.** sexually attracted to both men and women. **2.** showing characteristics of both sexes. **bisexuality** n.

bishop n. **1.** clergyman who governs a diocese. **2.** piece at chess. **bishopric** n. diocese or office of a bishop.

bismuth n. pinkish-white metallic element.

bison n., pl. -son. large hairy animal of the cattle family.

bisque[1] n. thick rich soup made from shellfish.

bisque[2] adj. pink-to-yellowish-tan.

bistro n., pl. -tros. small restaurant.

bit[1] n. **1.** small piece, portion, or quantity. **2.** short time or distance. **a bit rather**, somewhat. **bit by bit** gradually.

bit[2] n. **1.** metal mouthpiece on a bridle. **2.** cutting or drilling part of a tool.

bit[3] v. past tense of BITE.

bit[4] n. smallest unit of information held in a computer's memory, either 0 or 1.

bitch n. **1.** female dog, fox, or wolf. **2.** Offens. spiteful woman. —v. **3.** Informal complain or grumble. **bitchy** adj. **bitchier**, **bitchiest**. **bitchiness** n.

bite v. biting, bit, bitten. **1.** cut off, puncture, or tear as with the teeth or fangs. **2.** take firm hold of or act effectively upon. **3.** (of corrosive material) eat away or into. —n.

4. act of biting. **5.** wound or sting inflicted by biting. **6.** snack. **biter** n. **biting** adj. **1.** piercing or keen. **2.** sarcastic.

bitter adj. **1.** having a sharp unpleasant taste. **2.** showing or caused by hostility or resentment. **3.** extremely cold. —n. **4.** beer with a slightly bitter taste. —pl. **5.** bitter-tasting alcoholic drink. **bitterly** adv. **bitterness** n. **bittersweet** adj. **1.** tasting of bitterness and sweetness. **2.** pleasant but tinged with sadness.

bittern n. wading bird like a heron.

bitty adj. **-tier, -tiest. 1.** containing bits. **2.** lacking unity. **bittiness** n.

bitumen n. black sticky substance obtained from tar or petrol.

bivalve n., adj. (marine mollusc) with a double shell.

bivouac n. **1.** temporary camp in the open air. —v. **-acking, -acked. 2.** camp in a bivouac.

bizarre adj. odd or unusual.

Bk Chem. berkelium.

blab v. **blabbing, blabbed. 1.** reveal (secrets) indiscreetly. **2.** chatter thoughtlessly.

black adj. **1.** of the darkest colour, like jet or coal. **2.** (B-) dark-skinned. **3.** without hope. **4.** angry or resentful, e.g. black looks. **5.** unpleasant in a macabre manner, e.g. black comedy. —n. **6.** darkest colour. **7.** (B-) member of a dark-skinned race, esp. a Negro. **8.** complete darkness. —v. **9.** make black. **10.** (of trade unionists) boycott (goods or people). **blackness** n. **blacken** v. **1.** make or become black. **2.** defame or slander. **blacking** n. preparation for giving a black finish to shoes, metals, etc. **black-and-blue** adj. bruised, as from a beating. **black-and-white** adj. **1.** not in colour. **2.** consisting of extremes. **black box** Informal flight recorder. **black eye** bruising round the eye. **black hole** Astronomy hypothetical region of space from which neither matter nor radiation can escape. **black ice** thin transparent layer of new ice on a road. **black magic** magic used for evil purposes. **Black Maria** police van for transporting prisoners. **black market** illegal trade in goods or currencies. **black pudding** black sausage made from blood, suet, etc. **black sheep** person who is regarded as a disgrace by his or her family. **black spot** place on a road where accidents frequently occur. **black widow** American spider, the female

of which eats its mate.

▷ When black is used as a political or racial term it has a capital letter.

blackball v. exclude from a group.

blackberry n. small blackish edible fruit.

blackbird n. common European thrush.

blackboard n. hard black surface used for writing on with chalk.

blackcurrant n. small blackish edible fruit that grows in bunches.

blackguard [**blag**-gard] n. unprincipled person.

blackhead n. small black spot on the skin.

blackleg n. person who continues to work during a strike.

blacklist n. **1.** list of people or organizations considered untrustworthy etc. —v. **2.** put on a blacklist.

blackmail n. **1.** act of attempting to extort money by threats. —v. **2.** (attempt to) obtain money by blackmail.

blackout n. **1.** extinguishing of all light as a precaution against an air attack. **2.** momentary loss of consciousness or memory. **black out** v. **1.** extinguish (lights). **2.** lose consciousness or memory temporarily.

blacksmith n. person who works iron with a furnace, anvil, etc.

blackthorn n. thorny shrub with white flowers and small sour plumlike fruits.

black-tie adj. denoting an occasion when a dinner jacket should be worn.

bladder n. **1.** sac in the body where urine is held. **2.** hollow bag which may be filled with air or liquid.

blade n. **1.** cutting edge of a weapon or tool. **2.** thin flattish part of a propeller, oar, etc. **3.** leaf of grass.

blain n. inflamed sore on the skin.

blame n. **1.** responsibility for something that is wrong. **2.** expression of condemnation. —v. **3.** consider (someone) responsible for. **4.** find fault with. **blameless** adj. **blameworthy** adj. deserving blame.

blanch v. **1.** become pale. **2.** prepare (vegetables etc.) by plunging them in boiling water. **3.** cause (vegetables) to grow white.

blancmange [blam-**monzh**] n. jelly-like dessert made with milk.

bland adj. **1.** dull and uninteresting. **2.** smooth in manner. **blandly** adv.

blandishments pl. n. persuasive flattery.

blank adj. **1.** not written on. **2.** not filled in. **3.** showing no interest, feeling, or understanding. —n. **4.** empty space. **5.** cartridge containing no bullet. **blankly** adv. **blank cheque 1.** signed cheque without the amount payable specified. **2.** complete freedom of action. **blank verse** unrhymed verse.

blanket n. **1.** thick covering for a bed. **2.** concealing cover, as of snow. —adj. **3.** applying to a wide group of people, situations, conditions, etc. —v. **4.** cover as with a blanket.

blare v. **1.** sound loudly and harshly. —n. **2.** loud harsh noise.

blarney n. flattering talk.

blasé [blah-zay] adj. indifferent or bored through familiarity.

blaspheme v. **1.** speak disrespectfully of (God or sacred things). **2.** utter curses. **blasphemy** n. **blasphemous** adj. **blasphemer** n.

blast n. **1.** explosion. **2.** sudden strong gust of air or wind. **3.** sudden loud sound, as of a trumpet. —v. **4.** blow up (a rock etc.) with explosives. **5.** make a loud harsh noise. —interj. **6.** Slang expression of annoyance. **blasted** adj., adv. Slang extreme or extremely. **blast furnace** furnace for smelting, using a preheated blast of air. **blastoff** n. launching of a rocket.

blatant [blay-tant] adj. glaringly obvious. **blatantly** adv.

blather v., n. same as BLETHER.

blaze[1] n. **1.** strong fire or flame. **2.** very bright light. **3.** outburst of passion. —v. **4.** burn or shine brightly. **5.** become stirred with anger or excitement.

blaze[2] n. **1.** mark made on a tree to indicate a route. **2.** light-coloured marking on the face of an animal. —v. **3.** mark (a tree etc.) with a blaze.

blaze[3] v. proclaim or publish widely.

blazer n. lightweight jacket, esp. in the colours of a school etc.

blazon v. proclaim publicly.

bleach v. **1.** make or become white or colourless. —n. **2.** bleaching agent.

bleak adj. **1.** exposed and barren. **2.** offering little hope.

bleary adj. **-rier, -riest.** with eyes dimmed, as by tears or tiredness. **blearily** adv.

bleat v. **1.** (of a sheep, goat, or calf) utter its plaintive cry. **2.** whine. —n. **3.** cry of sheep, goats, and calves.

bleed v. **bleeding, bled. 1.** lose blood. **2.** draw blood from (a person or animal). **3.** draw off or emit liquid or gas. **4.** Informal obtain money by extortion.

bleep n. **1.** short high-pitched sound made by an electrical device. —v. **2.** make a bleeping sound. **bleeper** n.

blemish n. **1.** defect or stain. —v. **2.** spoil or tarnish.

blench v. shy away, as in fear.

blend v. **1.** mix or mingle (components). **2.** look good together. —n. **3.** mixture. **blender** n. kitchen appliance for mixing food or liquid at high speed.

blende n. mineral consisting mainly of zinc sulphide.

blenny n., pl. **-nies.** small fish with a tapering scaleless body.

bless v. **1.** make holy by means of a religious rite. **2.** call upon God to protect. **3.** give thanks to. **4.** endow with health, talent, etc. **blessed** adj. **1.** holy. **2.** RC Church beatified by the Pope. **3.** Euphemistic damned. **blessing** n. **1.** prayer for God's favour. **2.** approval. **3.** happy event.

blether Scot. —v. **1.** speak at length, esp. foolishly. —n. **2.** foolish or babbling talk.

blew v. past tense of BLOW[1].

blight n. **1.** withering plant disease. **2.** person or thing that spoils or prevents growth. —v. **3.** cause to suffer a blight. **4.** frustrate or disappoint.

blighter n. Informal irritating person.

blimey interj. Slang exclamation of surprise or annoyance.

blimp n. small airship.

blind adj. **1.** unable to see. **2.** unable or unwilling to understand. **3.** not determined by reason, e.g. blind hatred. —v. **4.** deprive of sight. **5.** deprive of good sense, reason, or judgment. —n. **6.** covering for a window. **7.** something that serves to conceal the truth. **blindly** adv. **blindness** n. **blind alley** alley open at one end only. **blind date** date arranged between two people who have not met. **blind man's buff** game in which a blindfolded person tries to catch and identify other players. **blind spot 1.** area of the retina where vision is not experienced. **2.** place where vision is obscured. **3.** subject about which a person is ignorant.

blindfold v. **1.** prevent (a person) from seeing by covering the eyes. —n. **2.** piece of cloth used to cover the eyes. —adj., adv. **3.** with the eyes covered by a blindfold.

blink v. **1.** close and immediately reopen (the eyes). **2.** shine intermittently. —n. **3.** act of blinking. **4.** glance. **on the blink** Slang not working properly. **blinkers** pl. n. leather flaps on a horse's bridle to prevent sideways vision.

blip n. small light which flashes on and off regularly on equipment such as a radar screen.

bliss n. perfect happiness. **blissful** adj. **blissfully** adv.

blister n. **1.** small bubble on the skin. **2.** swelling, as on a painted surface. —v. **3.** (cause to) have blisters. **blistering** adj. **1.** (of weather) very hot. **2.** (of criticism) extemely harsh.

blithe adj. **1.** casual and indifferent. **2.** very happy. **blithely** adv.

blithering adj. Informal stupid.

blitz n. **1.** violent and sustained attack by aircraft. **2.** intensive attack or concerted effort. —v. **3.** attack suddenly and intensively.

blizzard n. blinding storm of wind and snow.

bloated adj. swollen up with liquid or gas.

bloater n. salted smoked herring.

blob n. **1.** soft mass or drop. **2.** indistinct or shapeless form.

bloc n. people or countries combined by a common interest.

block n. **1.** large solid piece of wood, stone, etc. **2.** large building of offices, flats, etc. **3.** group of buildings enclosed by intersecting streets. **4.** piece of wood or metal engraved for printing. **5.** obstruction or hindrance. **6.** Slang person's head. —v. **7.** obstruct or impede by introducing an obstacle. **blockage** n. **blockhead** n. stupid person. **block letter** plain capital letter.

blockade n. **1.** action that prevents goods from reaching a place. —v. **2.** impose a blockade on.

bloke n. Informal man.

blonde, (masc.) **blond** adj., n. fair-haired (person).

blood n. **1.** red fluid that flows around the body. **2.** race or ancestry. **3.** bloodshed. —v. **4.** initiate (a person) to war or hunting. **in cold blood** done deliberately. **bloodless** adj. **1.** without blood or bloodshed. **2.** pale. **3.** lacking vitality. **blood bath** massacre. **bloodcurdling** adj. terrifying. **bloodhound** n. large dog used for tracking. **blood poisoning** disease in which the blood contains poisonous matter. **blood pressure** pressure exerted by the blood on the inner walls of the blood vessels. **bloodshed** n. slaughter or killing. **bloodshot** adj. (of eyes) inflamed. **blood sport** sport involving the killing of animals. **bloodstream** n. flow of blood round the body. **bloodsucker** n. **1.** animal that sucks blood. **2.** Informal person who extorts money from other people. **bloodthirsty** adj. taking pleasure in violence. **blood vessel** tube that carries the blood in the body.

bloody adj. **1.** covered with blood. **2.** marked by much killing. —adj., adv. **3.** Slang extreme or extremely. —v. **4.** stain with blood. **bloody-minded** adj. deliberately unhelpful.

bloom n. **1.** blossom on a flowering plant. **2.** period when flowers open. **3.** flourishing condition. **4.** youthful or healthy glow. **5.** whitish coating on fruit, leaves, etc. —v. **6.** bear flowers. **7.** be in a healthy glowing condition.

bloomer n. Informal stupid mistake.

bloomers pl. n. woman's baggy knickers.

blossom n. **1.** flowers of a plant. —v. **2.** (of plants) flower. **3.** come to a promising stage.

blot n. **1.** spot or stain. **2.** something that spoils or stains. —v. **blotting, blotted. 3.** cause a blemish in or on. **4.** soak up (ink) by using blotting paper. **blotter** n. **blot out** v. darken or hide completely. **blotting paper** soft absorbent paper for soaking up ink.

blotch n. discoloured area or stain. **blotchy** adj. **blotchier, blotchiest.**

blotto adj. Slang extremely drunk.

blouse n. woman's shirtlike garment.

blow[1] v. **blowing, blew, blown. 1.** (of air, the wind, etc.) move. **2.** move or be carried as if by the wind. **3.** expel (air etc.) through the mouth or nose. **4.** cause (a musical instrument) to sound by forcing air into it. **5.** burn out (a fuse etc.). **6.** Slang spend (money) freely. **blower** n. **blowy** adj. windy. **blow-dry** v. style (the hair) with a hand-held dryer. **blowfly** *n.* fly that lays its eggs in meat. **blowlamp** *n.* small burner producing a very hot flame. **blowout** *n.* **1.** sudden loss of air in a tyre. **2.** escape of oil or gas from a well. **3.** *Slang* filling meal. **blowpipe** *n.* long tube from which darts etc. are shot by blowing. **blow up** *v.* **1.** explode. **2.** fill with air. **3.** *Informal* enlarge (a photograph). **4.** *Informal* lose one's temper.

blow² *n.* **1.** hard hit. **2.** sudden setback. **3.** attacking action.

blown *v.* past participle of BLOW¹.

blowzy, blowsy *adj.* fat, untidy, and red-faced.

blubber *v.* **1.** sob without restraint. —*n.* **2.** fat of whales, seals, etc.

bludgeon *n.* **1.** short thick club. —*v.* **2.** hit with a bludgeon. **3.** force or bully.

blue *n.* **1.** colour of a clear unclouded sky. **2.** sportsman representing Oxford or Cambridge University. —*pl.* **3.** feeling of depression. **4.** sad slow music like jazz. —*adj.* **bluer, bluest.** **5.** of the colour blue. **6.** depressed. **7.** pornographic. **out of the blue** unexpectedly. **bluish** *adj.* **bluebell** *n.* flower with blue bell-shaped flowers. **bluebook** *n.* government manual publication. **bluebottle** *n.* large fly with a dark-blue body. **blue-collar** *adj.* denoting manual industrial workers. **blue peter** blue-and-white flag displayed before sailing. **blueprint** *n.* **1.** photographic print of a plan. **2.** description of how a plan is expected to work. **blue ribbon** first prize in a competition. **bluestocking** *n.* intellectual woman.

bluff¹ *v.* **1.** pretend to be confident in order to influence (someone). —*n.* **2.** act of bluffing.

bluff² *n.* **1.** steep cliff or bank. —*adj.* **2.** good-naturedly frank and hearty.

blunder *n.* **1.** clumsy mistake. —*v.* **2.** make a blunder. **3.** act clumsily.

blunderbuss *n.* obsolete gun with a wide muzzle.

blunt *adj.* **1.** lacking sharpness. **2.** (of people, speech, etc.) straightforward or uncomplicated. —*v.* **3.** make less sharp. **bluntly** *adv.*

blur *v.* **blurring, blurred. 1.** make or become vague or less distinct. **2.** smear or smudge. —*n.* **3.** something vague, hazy, or indistinct. **blurry** *adj.* **-rier, -riest.**

blurb *n.* promotional description, as on the jacket of a book.

blurt *v.* (foll. by *out*) utter suddenly and involuntarily.

blush *v.* **1.** become red in the face, esp. from embarrassment or shame. —*n.* **2.** reddening of the face. **blusher** *n.* cosmetic for giving the cheeks a rosy glow.

bluster *v.* **1.** speak loudly or in a bullying way. —*n.* **2.** empty threats or protests. **blustery** *adj.* (of weather) rough and windy.

BMA British Medical Association.

BO *Informal* body odour.

boa *n.* **1.** large nonvenomous snake. **2.** long scarf of fur or feathers. **boa constrictor** large snake that kills its prey by crushing.

boar *n.* **1.** uncastrated male pig. **2.** wild pig.

board *n.* **1.** long flat piece of wood. **2.** smaller flat piece of rigid material for a specific purpose, e.g. *ironing board*. **3.** group of people who administer a company, trust, etc. **4.** meals provided for money. —*pl.* **5.** the stage. —*v.* **6.** go aboard (a train, aeroplane, etc.). **7.** cover with boards. **8.** receive meals and lodgings in return for money. **on board** on or in a ship, aeroplane, etc. **boarder** *n.* pupil who lives at school during the school term. **boarding house** private house that provides meals and accommodation for paying guests. **boarding school** school providing living accommodation for pupils. **boardroom** *n.* room where the board of a company meets.

boast *v.* **1.** speak too proudly about one's talents, etc. **2.** possess (something to be proud of). —*n.* **3.** boasting statement. **4.** something that is bragged about. **boastful** *adj.*

boat *n.* **1.** small vehicle for travelling across water. **2.** *Informal* ship. **3.** boat-shaped dish. —*v.* **4.** travel in a boat. **boater** *n.* flat straw hat. **boating** *n.* **boat train** train scheduled to take passengers to or from a ship.

boatswain, bo's'n, bosun [boh-sn] *n.* ship's officer in charge of the equipment.

bob¹ *v.* **bobbing, bobbed. 1.** move up and down repeatedly. —*n.* **2.** short abrupt movement.

bob² *n.* **1.** hair style in which the hair is cut level with the chin. **2.** weight on a pendulum or plumb line. —*v.* **bobbing, bobbed. 3.** cut (the hair) in a bob.

bob³ *n.*, *pl.* **bob.** *Brit. informal* shilling.

bobbin *n.* reel on which thread is wound.

bobble n. small ball of material, usu. for decoration.

bobby n., pl. **-bies**. Informal policeman.

bobsleigh n. **1.** sledge used for racing. —v. **2.** ride on a bobsleigh.

bod n. Informal **1.** person. **2.** body.

bode v. be an omen of (good or ill).

bodega n. shop in a Spanish-speaking country that sells wine.

bodge v. Informal make a mess of.

bodice n. upper part of a dress.

bodkin n. blunt large-eyed needle.

body n., pl. **bodies**. **1.** entire physical structure of an animal or human. **2.** trunk or torso. **3.** corpse. **4.** main part of anything. **5.** group regarded as a single entity. **6.** person. **7.** woman's one-piece undergarment. **bodily** adj. **1.** relating to the body. —adv. **2.** by taking hold of the body. **bodyguard** n. person or group of people employed to protect someone. **body stocking** woman's one-piece undergarment, covering the torso. **bodywork** n. outer shell of a motor vehicle.

Boer n. descendant of the Dutch settlers in S Africa.

boffin n. Informal scientist.

bog n. **1.** wet spongy ground. **2.** Slang toilet. **boggy** adj. **-gier, -giest**. **bog down** v. **bogging, bogged**. impede physically or mentally.

bogey, bogy n. **1.** evil or mischievous spirit. **2.** something that worries or annoys. **3.** Golf standard score for a hole or course.

boggle v. **1.** be surprised, confused, or alarmed. **2.** hesitate when confronted with a problem.

bogie, bogy n. pivoted undercarriage, as on railway rolling stock.

bogus [boh-guss] adj. not genuine.

bogy n., pl. **-gies**. same as BOGEY or BOGIE.

bohemian n., adj. (person) leading an unconventional life.

boil¹ v. **1.** (cause to) change from a liquid to a vapour so quickly that bubbles are formed. **2.** cook by the process of boiling. **3.** bubble like something boiling. **4.** be extremely angry. —n. **5.** state or action of boiling. **boiler** n. piece of equipment which provides hot water. **boiling point** temperature at which a liquid boils.

boil² n. red pus-filled swelling on the skin.

boisterous adj. **1.** noisy and lively. **2.** turbulent or stormy. **boisterously** adv.

bold adj. **1.** confident and fearless. **2.** immodest or impudent. **3.** standing out distinctly. **boldly** adv. **boldness** n.

bole n. tree trunk.

bolero n., pl. **-ros**. **1.** short open jacket. **2.** traditional Spanish dance.

boll n. rounded seed capsule of cotton, flax, etc.

bollard n. **1.** short thick post used to prevent the passage of motor vehicles. **2.** post on a quay etc. for securing mooring lines.

boloney n. same as BALONEY.

Bolshevik n. **1.** Russian Communist. **2.** Offens. political radical. **bolshie, bolshy** adj. Informal difficult or rebellious.

bolster v. **1.** support or strengthen. —n. **2.** long narrow pillow.

bolt¹ n. **1.** metal pin which screws into a nut. **2.** sliding metal bar for fastening a door etc. **3.** flash (of lightning). **4.** arrow for a crossbow. —v. **5.** fasten with a bolt. **6.** eat hurriedly. **7.** run away suddenly. **bolt upright** stiff and rigid. **bolt hole** place of escape.

bolt², **boult** v. pass (flour etc.) through a sieve.

bomb n. **1.** container fitted with explosive material. **2.** Slang large amount of money. —v. **3.** attack with bombs. **4.** move very quickly. **the bomb** nuclear bomb. **bomber** n. **1.** aircraft that drops bombs. **2.** person who throws or puts a bomb in a particular place. **bombshell** n. shocking or unwelcome surprise.

bombard v. **1.** attack with heavy gunfire or bombs. **2.** attack verbally, esp. with questions. **bombardier** n. noncommissioned rank in the Royal Artillery. **bombardment** n.

bombast n. pompous language. **bombastic** adj.

Bombay duck n. fish eaten dried with curry dishes as a savoury.

bombazine n. twilled fabric, esp. one of silk and worsted.

bona fide [bone-a **fide**-ee] adj. real or genuine.

bonanza n. sudden good luck or wealth.

bonbon n. sweet.

bond n. **1.** something that binds or fastens.

2. feeling, of friendship etc., that unites two people or a group of people. 3. written or spoken agreement. 4. *Finance* certificate of debt issued to raise funds. —*pl.* 5. something that restrains or imprisons. —*v.* 6. bind. **bonded** *adj.*

bondage *n.* 1. slavery. 2. subjection to some influence or duty.

bone *n.* 1. any of the hard parts in the body that form the skeleton. —*pl.* 2. human skeleton. —*v.* 3. remove the bones from (meat for cooking etc.). **boneless** *adj.* **bony** *adj.* **bonier, boniest.** 1. having many bones. 2. thin or emaciated. **bone china** porcelain containing powdered bone. **bone-dry** *adj.* completely dry. **bone-idle** *adj.* extremely lazy. **bone meal** ground bones used as a fertilizer.

bonfire *n.* large outdoor fire.

bongo *n., pl.* **-gos, -goes.** small drum played with the fingers.

bonhomie [**bon**-om-ee] *n.* happy friendliness.

bonk *v. Informal* 1. have sex with. 2. hit. **bonking** *n.*

bonkers *adj. Slang, chiefly Brit.* crazy.

bon mot [bon **moh**] *n., pl.* **bons mots.** clever and fitting remark.

bonnet *n.* 1. metal cover over a vehicle's engine. 2. hat which ties under the chin. 3. *Scot.* soft cloth cap.

bonny *adj.* **-nier, -niest.** *Scot.* beautiful.

bonsai *n., pl.* **-sai.** ornamental miniature tree or shrub.

bonus *n.* something given, paid, or received above what is due or expected.

bon voyage *interj.* phrase used to wish a traveller a pleasant journey.

boo *interj.* 1. shout of disapproval. —*v.* **booing, booed.** 2. shout 'boo' to show disapproval.

boob *Slang* —*n.* 1. foolish mistake. 2. female breast. —*v.* 3. make a foolish mistake.

booby *n., pl.* **-bies.** foolish person. **booby prize** prize given for the lowest score in a competition. **booby trap** 1. hidden bomb primed to be set off by an unsuspecting victim. 2. trap for an unsuspecting person, intended as a joke.

boogie *v. Informal* dance quickly to pop music.

book *n.* 1. number of printed pages bound together between covers. 2. written work. 3. number of tickets, stamps, etc. fastened together. 4. libretto of a musical etc. 5. record of betting transactions. —*pl.* 6. record of transactions of a business or society. —*v.* 7. reserve (a place, passage, etc.) in advance. 8. record the name of (a person) in a book or on a list. **bookish** *adj.* 1. fond of reading. 2. forming opinions through reading rather than experience. **booklet** *n.* thin book with paper covers.

bookie *n. Informal* short for BOOKMAKER.

book-keeping *n.* systematic recording of business transactions. **book-keeper** *n.*

bookmaker *n.* person whose occupation is taking bets.

bookworm *n.* 1. person devoted to reading. 2. small insects that feeds on books.

boom¹ *v.* 1. make a loud deep echoing sound. 2. prosper vigorously and rapidly. —*n.* 3. loud deep echoing sound. 4. rapid increase.

boom² *n.* 1. pole to which the foot of a sail is attached. 2. pole carrying an overhead microphone. 3. barrier across a waterway.

boomerang *n.* 1. curved wooden missile which returns to the thrower. —*v.* 2. (of a plan) recoil unexpectedly.

boon¹ *n.* something helpful or beneficial.

boon² *adj.* close or intimate.

boor *n.* rude or insensitive person. **boorish** *adj.*

boost *n.* 1. encouragement or help. 2. upward thrust or push. 3. increase. —*v.* 4. improve. 5. increase. **booster** *n.* 1. small additional injection of a vaccine. 2. radio-frequency amplifier to strengthen signals. 3. first stage of a multistage rocket.

boot¹ *n.* 1. shoe that covers the whole foot and the lower part of the leg. 2. space in a car for luggage. 3. *Informal* kick. 4. *Slang* dismissal from employment. —*v.* 5. *Informal* kick. **bootee** *n.* baby's soft shoe.

boot² *n.* to boot in addition.

booth *n.* 1. small partly enclosed cubicle. 2. stall where goods are sold.

bootleg *v.* **-legging, -legged.** 1. make, carry, or sell (illicit goods). —*adj.* 2. produced, distributed, or sold illicitly. **bootlegger** *n.*

bootless *adj.* vain or fruitless.

booty *n., pl.* **-ties.** valuable articles obtained as plunder.

booze v., n. Informal (consume) alcoholic drink. **boozy** adj. **boozer** n. **1.** Informal person who is fond of drinking. **2.** Informal pub. **booze-up** n. Informal drinking spree.

bop v. **bopping, bopped.** Informal dance to pop music.

borage n. Mediterranean plant with star-shaped blue flowers.

borax n. white mineral used in making glass. **boracic** adj.

Bordeaux n. red or white wine from SW France.

border n. **1.** dividing line between regions. **2.** band around or along the edge of something. —v. **3.** provide with a border. **4.** be adjacent to. **5.** be nearly the same as, e.g. his stupidity borders on madness.

bore[1] v. **1.** make (a hole) with a drill etc. —n. **2.** hole or tunnel drilled in search of minerals etc. **3.** (diameter of) the hollow of a gun barrel.

bore[2] v. **1.** make weary by being dull or repetitious. —n. **2.** dull or repetitious person or thing. **boredom** n.
▷ Bored is followed by with or by: ...bored by his conversation; ...bored with ...reading. The usage bored of is not fully accepted.

bore[3] n. tidal wave in a narrow estuary.

bore[4] v. past tense of BEAR[1].

boric adj. of or containing boron. **boric acid** white soluble solid used as a mild antiseptic.

born v. **1.** a past participle of BEAR[1]. —adj. **2.** possessing certain qualities from birth, e.g. a born musician.

borne v. a past participle of BEAR[1].

boron n. chemical element used in hardening steel.

borough n. town or district with its own council.

borrow v. **1.** obtain (something) temporarily. **2.** adopt (ideas etc.) from another source. **borrower** n.
▷ Borrow is followed by from: Borrow a pound from Frank. The use of borrow followed by off is nonstandard. Avoid confusing the meanings of borrow and lend.

borsch, borscht n. Russian soup based on beetroot.

borstal n. prison for young criminals.

borzoi n. tall dog with a long silky coat.

bosh n. Informal empty talk, nonsense.

bo's'n n. same as BOATSWAIN.

bosom n. **1.** chest of a person, esp. the female breasts. —adj. **2.** very dear, e.g. a bosom friend.

boss[1] n. **1.** person in charge of or employing others. —v. **2.** boss around, about be domineering towards. **bossy** adj. **bossier, bossiest.**

boss[2] n. raised knob or stud.

bosun n. same as BOATSWAIN.

bot. **1.** botanical. **2.** botany.

botany n. study of plants. **botanical, botanic** adj. **botanist** n.

botch v. **1.** spoil through clumsiness. **2.** repair badly. —n. (also **botch-up**) **3.** badly done piece of work or repair.

both adj., pron. two considered together.
▷ After both the use of of is optional: both of the boys or both (the) boys.

bother v. **1.** give annoyance or trouble to. **2.** pester. **3.** take the time or trouble. —n. **4.** trouble, fuss, or difficulty. —interj. **5.** Chiefly Brit. exclamation of slight annoyance. **bothersome** adj.

bothy n., pl. **-ies.** Chiefly Scot. hut used for temporary shelter.

bottle n. **1.** container for holding liquids. **2.** Slang courage. —v. **3.** put in a bottle. **bottle-green** adj. dark green. **bottleneck** n. narrow stretch of road where traffic is held up. **bottle up** v. restrain (powerful emotion).

bottom n. **1.** lowest, deepest, or farthest removed part of a thing. **2.** ground underneath a sea, lake, or river. **3.** buttocks. —adj. **4.** lowest or last. **bottomless** adj. **bottom out** v. reach the lowest point and level out.

botulism n. severe food poisoning.

bouclé n. looped yarn giving a knobbly effect.

boudoir [boo-dwahr] n. woman's bedroom or private sitting room.

bouffant [boof-fong] adj. (of a hairstyle) having extra height through backcombing.

bougainvillea n. climbing plant with red or purple flowers.

bough n. large branch of a tree.

bought v. past of BUY.
▷ Be careful not to confuse the past forms bought (from buy) with brought (from bring).

bouillon [boo-yon] n. thin clear broth or stock.

boulder n. large rounded rock.

boulevard n. wide road.

boult v. same as BOLT².

bounce v. 1. (of a ball etc.) rebound from an impact. 2. Slang (of a cheque) be returned uncashed owing to a lack of funds in the account. —n. 3. act of rebounding. 4. springiness. 5. Informal vitality or vigour. **bouncer** n. person employed at a disco etc. to remove unwanted people. **bouncing** adj. vigorous and robust. **bouncy** adj. **bouncier**, **bounciest**.

bound¹ v. 1. past of BIND. —adj. 2. destined or certain. 3. compelled or obliged.

bound² v. 1. move forwards by jumps. —n. 2. jump upwards or forwards.

bound³ v. 1. form a boundary of. —pl. n. 2. limit, e.g. his ignorance knows no bounds. **boundary** n., pl. -aries. dividing line that indicates the farthest limit.

bound⁴ adj. going or intending to go towards, e.g. homeward bound.

bounder n. Old-fashioned Brit. slang morally reprehensible person.

bounty n., pl. -ties. 1. generosity. 2. generous gift or reward. **bountiful**, **bounteous** adj.

bouquet n. 1. bunch of flowers. 2. aroma of wine. **bouquet garni** bunch of herbs tied together and used for flavouring soups etc.

bourbon [bur-bn] n. US whiskey made from maize.

bourgeois [boor-zhwah] adj., n. Offens. middle-class (person). **bourgoisie** n. middle classes.

bourn n. in S Britain, stream.

Bourse [boorss] n. stock exchange, esp. of Paris.

bout n. 1. period of activity or illness. 2. boxing or wrestling match.

boutique n. small clothes shop.

bouzouki n. Greek stringed musical instrument.

bovine adj. 1. relating to cattle. 2. rather slow and stupid.

bow¹ v. 1. lower (one's head) or bend (one's knee or body) as a sign of respect or shame. 2. comply or accept. —n. 3. movement made when bowing.

bow² n. 1. knot with two loops and loose ends. 2. weapon for shooting arrows. 3. long stick stretched with horsehair for playing stringed instruments. 4. something curved, bent, or arched. **bow-legged** adj. bandy. **bow window** curved bay window.

bow³ n. 1. front end of a ship. 2. oarsman at the bow.

bowdlerize v. remove words regarded as indecent from (a play etc.). **bowdlerization** n.

bowel n. 1. intestine, esp. the large intestine. —pl. 2. innermost part.

bower n. shady leafy shelter. **bowerbird** n. brightly-coloured songbird of Australia.

bowie knife n. stout hunting knife.

bowl¹ n. 1. round container with an open top. 2. hollow part of an object.

bowl² n. 1. large heavy ball. —pl. 2. game played on smooth grass with wooden bowls. —v. 3. play bowls. 4. roll smoothly along the ground. 5. Cricket send (a ball) towards the batsman. 6. dismiss (a batsman) by delivering a ball that breaks his wicket. **bowler** n. **bowling** n. game in which bowls are rolled at a group of pins.

bowler n. stiff felt hat with a rounded crown.

box¹ n. 1. container with a flat base and sides. 2. separate compartment in a theatre, stable, etc. 3. Informal television. —v. 4. put into a box. **boxy** adj. **boxier**, **boxiest**. squarish or chunky. **box junction** road junction marked with yellow lines which may only be entered if the exit is clear. **box lacrosse** Canad. lacrosse played indoors. **box number** number to which replies to a newspaper advertisement may be sent. **box office** place where theatre or cinema tickets are sold. **box pleat** flat double pleat.

box² v. 1. fight (an opponent) in a boxing match. 2. hit (a person) with the fist. **boxer** n. 1. man who participates in the sport of boxing. 2. medium-sized dog similar to a bulldog. **boxing** n. sport of fighting with the fists.

box³ n. evergreen tree with shiny leaves.

boxer shorts, boxers pl. n. men's underpants shaped like shorts but with a front opening.

Boxing Day n. first weekday after Christmas.

boy n. male child. **boyish** adj. **boyhood** n. **boyfriend** n. woman's male companion.

boycott v. 1. refuse to deal with or engage in. —n. 2. instance of boycotting.

BP blood pressure.

Br *Chem.* bromine.

bra *n.* woman's undergarment for supporting the breasts.

brace *n.* **1.** object fastened to something to straighten or support it. **2.** pair, esp. of game birds. *—pl.* **3.** straps worn over the shoulders to hold up trousers. *—v.* **4.** steady or prepare (oneself) for something unpleasant. **5.** strengthen or fit with a brace. **bracing** *adj.* refreshing and invigorating.

bracelet *n.* ornamental chain for the wrist.

bracken *n.* large fern.

bracket *n.* **1.** pair of characters used to enclose a section of writing. **2.** group falling within certain defined limits. **3.** support fixed to a wall. *—v.* **-eting, -eted. 4.** put in brackets. **5.** class together.

brackish *adj.* (of water) slightly salty.

bract *n.* leaf at the base of a flower.

brad *n.* small tapered nail. **bradawl** *n.* small boring tool.

brae *n. Scot.* hill or hillside.

brag *v.* **bragging, bragged. 1.** speak arrogantly and boastfully. *—n.* **2.** boastful talk or behaviour. **3.** card game similar to poker. **braggart** *n.* person who boasts loudly.

Brahma *n.* Hindu god, the Creator. **Brahman, Brahmin** *n.* member of the highest Hindu caste.

braid *v.* **1.** interweave (hair, thread, etc.). *—n.* **2.** length of hair, etc. that has been braided. **3.** narrow ornamental tape of woven silk etc.

Braille *n.* system of writing for the blind, consisting of raised dots interpreted by touch.

brain *n.* **1.** soft mass of nervous tissue in the head. **2.** intellectual ability. *—v.* **3.** hit (someone) hard on the head. **brainless** *adj.* stupid. **brainy** *adj.* **brainier, brainiest.** *Informal* clever. **brainchild** *n.* idea produced by creative thought. **braindead** *adj.* **1.** having suffered complete stoppage of breathing. **2.** *Informal* not using or showing intelligence. **brainstorm** *n.* sudden mental aberration. **brainwash** *v.* force (a person) to change his or her beliefs, esp. by methods based on isolation, pain, sleeplessness, etc. **brainwave** *n.* sudden idea.

braise *v.* stew slowly in a covered pan.

brake[1] *n.* **1.** device for slowing or stopping a vehicle. *—v.* **2.** slow down or stop by using a brake.

brake[2] *n.* area of dense undergrowth.

bramble *n.* **1.** prickly shrub that produces blackberries. **2.** *Scot.* blackberry.

bran *n.* husks of cereal grain.

branch *n.* **1.** secondary stem of a tree. **2.** offshoot or subsidiary part of something larger or more complex. *—v.* **3.** (of stems, roots, etc.) grow and diverge (from another part). **branch out** *v.* expand one's interests.

brand *n.* **1.** particular product. **2.** particular kind or variety. **3.** identifying mark burnt onto the skin of an animal. **4.** burning piece of wood. *—v.* **5.** mark with a brand. **6.** denounce or stigmatize. **brand-new** *adj.* absolutely new.

brandish *v.* wave (a weapon etc.) in a threatening way.

brandy *n., pl.* **-dies.** alcoholic spirit distilled from wine. **brandy snap** tube-shaped crisp sweet biscuit.

brash *adj.* self-confident and aggressive. **brashness** *n.*

brass *n.* **1.** alloy of copper and zinc. **2.** group of wind instruments made of brass. **3.** engraved brass memorial tablet in a church. **4.** *Informal* money. **5.** *Informal* bold self-confidence. **brassy** *adj.* **brassier, brassiest. 1.** like brass, esp. in colour. **2.** insolent or brazen. **brass hat** *Informal* top-ranking military officer.

brasserie *n.* restaurant specializing in food and beer.

brassica *n.* plant of the cabbage and turnip family.

brassiere *n.* bra.

brat *n.* unruly child.

bravado *n.* showy display of self-confidence.

brave *adj.* **1.** having or showing courage, resolution, and daring. **2.** splendid. *—n.* **3.** North American Indian warrior. *—v.* **4.** confront with resolution or courage. **bravery** *n.*

bravo *interj.* well done!

bravura *n.* **1.** display of boldness or daring. **2.** *Music* brilliance of execution.

brawl *n.* **1.** rough fight. *—v.* **2.** fight noisily.

brawn *n.* **1.** physical strength. **2.** pressed meat from the head of a pig or calf. **brawny** *adj.*

bray v. **1.** (of a donkey) utter its loud harsh sound. —n. **2.** donkey's loud harsh sound.

braze v. join (two metal surfaces) with brass.

brazen adj. **1.** shameless and bold. —v. **2.** brazen it out overcome a difficult situation boldly or shamelessly. **brazenly** adv.

brazier [bray-zee-er] n. container for burning charcoal or coal.

brazil nut n. large three-sided nut of a tropical American tree.

breach n. **1.** breaking or violation of a promise etc. **2.** serious quarrel or separation. **3.** gap or break. —v. **4.** break (a promise etc.). **5.** make a gap in.

bread n. **1.** food made of baked flour and water. **2.** Slang money. **breadwinner** n. person whose earnings support a family.

breadline n. **on the breadline** living at subsistence level.

breadth n. **1.** extent of something from side to side. **2.** lack of restriction, esp. of viewpoint or interest.

break v. **breaking, broke, broken. 1.** separate or become separated into two or more pieces. **2.** damage or become damaged so as to be inoperative. **3.** fail to observe (an agreement etc.). **4.** disclose or be disclosed, e.g. he broke the news. **5.** bring or come to an end, e.g. the good weather broke at last. **6.** weaken or be weakened, as in spirit. **7.** cut through or penetrate. **8.** improve on or surpass, e.g. break a record. **9.** accustom (a horse) to being ridden. **10.** (of the male voice) become permanently deeper at puberty. —n. **11.** act or result of breaking. **12.** gap or interruption in continuity. **13.** sudden rush, esp. to escape. **14.** Informal fortunate opportunity. **15.** Billiards, snooker series of successful shots during one turn. **break even** make neither a profit nor a loss. **breakable** adj. **breakage** n. **breaker** n. large wave. **break dance** acrobatic dance style of the 1980s. **break-dance** v. **break down** v. **1.** cease to function. **2.** yield to strong emotion. **3.** analyse. **4.** decompose or separate into component parts. **breakdown** n. **1.** act or instance of breaking down. **2.** nervous breakdown. **3.** analysis. **4.** decomposition. **break-in** n. illegal entering of a building, esp. by thieves. **breakneck** adj. fast and dangerous. **break off** v. **1.** sever or detach. **2.** end (a relationship etc.). **break out** v. begin or arise suddenly. **break-**

through n. important development or discovery. **break up** v. **1.** (cause to) separate. **2.** (of a relationship) come to an end. **3.** (of a school) close for the holidays. **breakwater** n. wall that extends into the sea to protect a harbour or beach from the force of waves.

breakfast v., n. (eat) the first meal of the day.

bream n. freshwater silvery fish.

breast n. **1.** either of the two soft fleshy milk-secreting glands on a woman's chest. **2.** chest. **3.** source of human emotions. —v. **4.** confront boldly. **5.** reach the summit of. **6.** meet at breast level, e.g. she breasted the finishing line. **breast-feed** v. feed (a baby) with milk from the breast. **breaststroke** n. swimming stroke performed on the front.

breath n. **1.** taking in and letting out of air during breathing. **2.** air taken in and let out during breathing. **3.** slight gust of air. **breathless** adj. **breathtaking** adj. causing awe or excitement. **breathe** v. **1.** take in oxygen and give out carbon dioxide. **2.** be alive. **3.** whisper. **breather** n. Informal short rest. **breathing** n.

Breathalyzer n. ® device for estimating the amount of alcohol in the breath. **breathalyze** v.

bred v. past of BREED.

breech n. **1.** buttocks. **2.** part of a firearm behind the barrel. **breech delivery** birth of a baby with the feet or buttocks appearing first.

breeches pl. n. trousers extending to just below the knee.

breed v. **breeding, bred. 1.** produce new or improved strains of (domestic animals or plants). **2.** bring up. **3.** bear (offspring). **4.** produce or be produced, e.g. breed trouble. —n. **5.** group of animals etc. within a species. **6.** kind or sort. **breeder** n. **breeder reactor** nuclear reactor that produces more fissionable material than it uses. **breeding** n. result of good upbringing or training.

breeze n. **1.** gentle wind. —v. **2.** move quickly or casually. **breezy** adj. **breezier, breeziest. 1.** windy. **2.** casual or carefree.

breeze block n. light building brick made of ashes bonded with cement.

Bren gun n. gas-operated light machine gun.

brent n. small goose with a dark grey plumage.

brethren *pl. n. Old-fashioned* used in religious contexts, brothers.

Breton *adj.* **1.** of Brittany. —*n.* **2.** person from Brittany. **3.** language of Brittany.

breve *n.* long musical note.

breviary *n., pl.* **-aries.** book of prayers to be recited daily by a Roman Catholic priest.

brevity *n.* shortness.

brew *v.* **1.** make (beer, ale, etc.) by steeping, boiling, and fermentation. **2.** prepare (a drink) by infusing. **3.** be impending or forming. —*n.* **4.** beverage produced by brewing. **5.** instance of brewing. **brewer** *n.* **brewery** *n., pl.* **-eries. 1.** company that brews beer etc. **2.** place where beer etc. is brewed.

briar[1], **brier** *n.* **1.** European shrub with a hard woody root. **2.** tobacco pipe made from this root.

briar[2] *n.* same as BRIER[1].

bribe *n.* **1.** anything offered or given to someone to gain favour, influence, etc. —*v.* **2.** give (someone) a bribe. **bribery** *n.*

bric-a-brac *n.* miscellaneous small ornamental objects.

brick *n.* **1.** (rectangular block of) baked clay used in building. **2.** *Informal* reliable or trustworthy person. —*v.* **3.** build, enclose, or fill with bricks. **brickbat** *n.* **1.** blunt criticism. **2.** piece of brick used as a weapon. **bricklayer** *n.* person who builds with bricks.

bride *n.* woman who has just been or is about to be married. **bridal** *adj.* **bridegroom** *n.* man who has just been or is about to be married. **bridesmaid** *n.* girl who attends a bride at her wedding.

bridge[1] *n.* **1.** structure for crossing a river etc. **2.** platform from which a ship is steered or controlled. **3.** upper part of the nose. **4.** dental plate with artificial teeth that is secured to natural teeth. **5.** piece of wood supporting the strings of a violin etc. —*v.* **6.** build a bridge over (something). **bridgehead** *n.* fortified position at the end of a bridge nearest the enemy. **bridging loan** loan made to cover the period between two transactions.

bridge[2] *n.* card game based on whist, played between two pairs.

bridle *n.* **1.** headgear for controlling a horse. **2.** something that curbs or restrains. —*v.* **3.** put a bridle on (a horse). **4.** restrain. **bridle path** suitable for riding horses.

Brie [bree] *n.* soft creamy white cheese.

brief *adj.* **1.** short in duration. **2.** concise. —*n.* **3.** condensed statement or written synopsis. **4.** set of instructions. —*pl.* **5.** men's or women's underpants. —*v.* **6.** give information and instructions to (a person). **briefly** *adv.* **briefcase** *n.* small flat case for carrying papers, books, etc.

brier[1], **briar** *n.* wild rose with long thorny stems.

brier[2] *n.* same as BRIAR[1].

brig *n.* two-masted square-rigged ship.

Brig. Brigadier.

brigade *n.* **1.** army unit smaller than a division. **2.** group of people organized for a certain task. **brigadier** *n.* high-ranking army officer.

brigand *n.* bandit.

brigantine *n.* two-masted sailing ship.

bright *adj.* **1.** emitting or reflecting much light. **2.** (of colours) intense. **3.** full of promise. **4.** clever. **brightly** *adv.* **brightness** *n.* **brighten** *v.*

brill *n.* European food fish.

brilliant *adj.* **1.** shining with light. **2.** splendid. **3.** extremely clever. —*n.* **4.** sparkling diamond. **brilliance, brilliancy** *n.*

brilliantine *n.* perfumed hair oil.

brim *n.* **1.** projecting edge of a hat. **2.** upper rim of a cup etc. —*v.* **3.** **brimming, brimmed. 3.** be full to the brim.

brimstone *n. Obs.* sulphur.

brindled *adj.* brown streaked with another colour.

brine *n.* salt water. **briny** *adj.* very salty. **the briny** *Informal* the sea.

bring *v.* **bringing, brought. 1.** carry, convey, or take to a designated place or person. **2.** cause to happen. **3.** *Law* put forward (charges) officially. **bring about** *v.* cause to happen. **bring off** *v.* succeed in achieving. **bring out** *v.* **1.** publish or have (a book) published. **2.** reveal or cause to be seen. **bring up** *v.* **1.** rear (a child). **2.** mention. **3.** vomit (food).

brink *n.* edge of a steep place. **on the brink** of very near.

briquette *n.* block of compressed coal dust.

brisk *adj.* lively and quick. **briskly** *adv.*

brisket *n.* beef from the breast of a cow.

brisling *n.* same as SPRAT.

bristle *n.* **1.** short stiff hair. —*v.* **2.** (cause to) stand up like bristles. **3.** show anger. **bristly** *adj.* **bristlier, bristliest.**

Brit *n. Informal* British person.
▷ *Brit* used to be regarded as suggesting hostility, but it is now often used neutrally.

Brit. 1. Britain. **2.** British.

Britannia *n.* female warrior personifying Great Britain.

Britannic *adj.* of Britain, esp. in *Her Britannic Majesty.*

British *adj.* **1.** of Great Britain or the British Commonwealth. —*n.* **2.** people of Great Britain.

Briton *n.* native or inhabitant of Britain.

brittle *adj.* hard but easily broken. **brittleness** *n.*

broach *v.* **1.** introduce (a topic) for discussion. **2.** open (a bottle or barrel).

broad *adj.* **1.** having great breadth or width. **2.** not detailed. **3.** extensive, e.g. *broad support.* **4.** vulgar or coarse. **5.** strongly marked, e.g. *a broad Yorkshire accent.* —*n.* **6.** *Slang, chiefly US* woman. **broadly** *adv.* **broaden** *v.* **broad bean** thick flat edible bean. **broadcloth** *n.* closely woven fabric of cotton or wool. **broad-leaved** *adj.* (of trees) having broad rather than needle-shaped leaves. **broad-minded** *adj.* tolerant. **broadside** *n.* **1.** strong verbal or written attack. **2.** *Naval* firing of all the guns on one side of a ship at once. **broadsheet** *n.* newspaper with a large format.

B-road *n.* secondary road in Britain.

broadcast *v.* **1.** transmit (a programme or announcement) on radio or television. **2.** make widely known. **3.** scatter (seed etc.). —*n.* **4.** programme or announcement on radio or television. **broadcaster** *n.* **broadcasting** *n.*

brocade *n.* rich woven fabric with a raised design.

broccoli *n.* type of cabbage with greenish flower heads.

brochure *n.* booklet that contains information about a product or service.

broderie anglaise *n.* open embroidery on white cotton etc.

brogue[1] *n.* sturdy walking shoe.

brogue[2] *n.* strong accent, esp. Irish.

broil *v.* grill. **broiler** *n.* young tender chicken for roasting.

broke *v.* **1.** past tense of BREAK. —*adj.* **2.** *Informal* having no money.

broken *v.* **1.** past participle of BREAK. —*adj.* **2.** fractured or smashed. **3.** (of the speech of a foreigner) imperfectly spoken, e.g. *broken English.* **brokenhearted** *adj.* overwhelmed by grief. **broken home** family where the parents are separated or divorced.

broker *n.* agent who buys or sells shares, securities, etc. **brokerage** *n.* commission charged by a broker.

brolly *n., pl.* **-lies.** *Informal* umbrella.

bromide *n.* **1.** chemical compound used in medicine and photography. **2.** boring or meaningless remark.

bromine *n.* toxic liquid element.

bronchus [bronk-uss] *n., pl.* **bronchi** [bronk-eye] either of the two branches of the windpipe. **bronchial** *adj.* **bronchitis** *n.* inflammation of the bronchi.

bronco *n., pl.* **-cos.** in the US, wild or partially tamed pony.

brontosaurus *n.* very large plant-eating four-footed dinosaur.

bronze *n.* **1.** alloy of copper and tin. **2.** statue, medal, etc. made of bronze. —*adj.* **3.** made of, or coloured like, bronze. —*v.* **4.** (esp. of the skin) make or become brown. **bronze medal** medal awarded as third prize.

brooch *n.* ornament with a pin for attaching to clothes.

brood *n.* **1.** number of birds produced at one hatching. **2.** all the children of a family. —*v.* **3.** (of a bird) sit on or hatch eggs. **4.** think long and morbidly. **broody** *adj.* **1.** moody and sullen. **2.** (of a hen) wishing to hatch eggs.

brook[1] *n.* small stream.

brook[2] *v.* bear or tolerate.

broom *n.* **1.** long-handled sweeping brush. **2.** yellow-flowered shrub. **broomstick** *n.* handle of a broom.

bros., Bros. brothers.

broth *n.* soup, usu. containing vegetables.

brothel *n.* house where men pay to have sex with prostitutes.

brother *n.* **1.** boy or man with the same parents as another person. **2.** close friend or comrade. **3.** member of a male religious order. **brotherly** *adj.* **brotherhood** *n.* **1.** fellowship. **2.** association, such as a trade union. **brother-in-law** *n., pl.* **brothers-in-**

law. **1**. brother of one's husband or wife. **2**. husband of one's sister.

brought v. past of BRING.

brouhaha n. loud confused noise.

brow n. **1**. forehead. **2**. eyebrow. **3**. top of a hill.

browbeat v. frighten (someone) with threats.

brown n. **1**. colour of earth or wood. —adj. **2**. of the colour brown. —v. **3**. make or become brown. **brownish** adj. **browned-off** adj. Informal bored and depressed.

brownie n. **1**. elf said to do household chores at night. **2**. small square nutty chocolate cake.

Brownie Guide, Brownie n. junior Guide.

browse v. **1**. look through (a book or articles for sale) in a casual manner. **2**. nibble on young shoots or leaves. —n. **3**. instance of browsing.

brucellosis n. infectious disease of animals which can be transmitted to humans.

bruise n. **1**. discoloured area on the skin caused by an injury. —v. **2**. cause a bruise on. **bruiser** n. strong tough person.

brunch n. Informal breakfast and lunch combined.

brunette n. girl or woman with brown hair.

brunt n. main force or shock of a blow, attack, etc.

brush[1] n. **1**. device made of bristles, wires, etc. used for cleaning, painting, etc. **2**. brief unpleasant encounter. **3**. fox's tail. —v. **4**. apply, remove, clean, etc. with a brush. **5**. touch lightly and briefly. **brush off** v. Slang dismiss or ignore (someone). **brush up** v. refresh one's knowledge of (a subject).

brush[2] n. thick growth of shrubs. **brushwood** n. cut or broken-off tree branches and twigs.

brusque adj. blunt or curt in manner or speech. **brusquely** adv. **brusqueness** n.

Brussels sprout n. vegetable like a tiny cabbage.

brute n. **1**. brutal person. **2**. animal other than man. —adj. **3**. wholly instinctive or physical, like an animal. **4**. without reason. **brutish** adj. of or like an animal. **brutal** adj. **1**. cruel and vicious. **2**. extremely honest in speech or manner. **brutally** adv. **brutality** n. **brutalize** v.

bryony n. wild climbing hedge plant.

BS British Standard.

BSc Bachelor of Science.

BSE bovine spongiform encephalopathy: fatal virus disease of cattle.

BSI British Standards Institution.

BST British Summer Time.

Bt Baronet.

bubble n. **1**. ball of air in a liquid. **2**. unreliable scheme or enterprise. —v. **3**. form bubbles. **4**. move or flow with a gurgling sound. **bubbly** adj. **-blier, -bliest**. **1**. excited and lively. **2**. full of bubbles. —n. **3**. Informal champagne. **bubble over** v. express an emotion freely.

bubonic plague [bew-bonn-ik] n. acute infectious disease characterized by swellings.

buccaneer n. pirate.

buck[1] n. **1**. male of certain animals, such as the deer and hare. —v. **2**. (of a horse etc.) jump with legs stiff and back arched. **buck up** v. make or become more cheerful.

buck[2] n. US, & Aust. slang dollar.

buck[3] n. **pass the buck** Informal shift blame or responsibility onto someone else.

bucket n. open-topped round container with a handle. **kick the bucket** Slang die. **bucketful** n. **bucket down** v. **-eting, -eted**. rain heavily.

buckle n. **1**. metal clasp for fastening a belt or strap. —v. **2**. fasten or be fastened with a buckle. **3**. (cause to) bend out of shape through pressure or heat. **buckle down** v. apply oneself with determination.

buckler n. small round shield.

buckram n. coarse stiffened cloth.

buckshee adj. Slang free.

buckteeth pl. n. projecting upper front teeth. **buck-toothed** adj.

buckwheat n. small black grain used for making flour.

bucolic [bew-koll-ik] adj. rustic.

bud n. **1**. swelling on a tree or plant that develops into a leaf or flower. **2**. partially opened flower. —v. **3**. budding, budded. **3**. produce buds. **4**. develop or grow, e.g. a budding actor.

Buddhism n. eastern religion founded by Buddha. **Buddhist** n., adj.

buddleia n. shrub with purple flowers that attracts butterflies.

buddy n., pl. **-dies**. Informal, esp. US friend.

budge v. move slightly.

budgerigar n. small brightly coloured Aust. bird.

budget n. 1. financial plan for a period of time. 2. money allocated for a specific purpose. —v. **-eting, -eted**. 3. plan the expenditure of (money or time). —adj. 4. cheap. **budgetary** adj.

budgie n. Informal short for BUDGERIGAR.

buff[1] n. 1. soft flexible undyed leather. —adj. 2. dull yellowish-brown. —v. 3. rub with soft material. **in the buff** Informal naked.

buff[2] n. Informal expert on a given subject.

buffalo n. 1. type of cattle. 2. US bison.

buffer[1] n. something that lessens shock or protects from damaging impact, circumstances, etc. **buffer state** small state between two rival powers.

buffer[2] n. Brit. informal stupid or bumbling man.

buffet[1] [boof-ay] n. 1. refreshment bar. 2. meal at which guests serve themselves.

buffet[2] [buff-it] v. **-feting, -feted**. 1. knock against or about. 2. hit, esp. with the fist. —n. 3. blow, esp. with the hand.

buffoon n. clown or fool. **buffoonery** n.

bug n. 1. small insect. 2. Informal minor illness. 3. small mistake in a computer programme. 4. concealed microphone. —v. **bugging, bugged**. 5. Informal irritate (someone). 6. conceal a microphone in (a room or phone).

bugbear n. thing that causes obsessive anxiety.

bugger n. 1. Taboo slang unpleasant or difficult person or thing. 2. person who practises buggery. —v. 3. Slang tire. 4. practise buggery with. **buggery** n. anal intercourse.

buggy n., pl. **-gies**. 1. light horse-drawn carriage having two or four wheels. 2. lightweight folding pram.

bugle n. instrument like a small trumpet. **bugler** n.

build v. **building, built**. 1. make, construct, or form by joining parts or materials. 2. establish and develop. —n. 3. shape of the body. **builder** n. **building** n. structure with walls and a roof. **building society** organiza-

tion where money can be borrowed or invested. **build-up** n. gradual increase. **build up** construct or establish gradually.

built v. past of BUILD. **built-in** adj. incorporated as an integral part. **built-up** adj. having many buildings.

bulb n. 1. glass part of an electric lamp. 2. onion-shaped root which grows into a flower or plant. **bulbous** adj. round and fat.

bulge n. 1. swelling on a normally flat surface. 2. sudden increase in number. —v. 3. swell outwards. **bulging** adj.

bulimia n. disorder characterized by compulsive overeating followed by vomiting.

bulk n. 1. great size or volume. 2. main part. —v. 3. **bulk large** be or seem important. **in bulk** in large quantities. **bulky** adj.

bulkhead n. partition in a ship or aeroplane.

bull[1] n. male of some animals, such as cattle, elephants, and whales. **bullock** n. castrated bull. **bulldog** n. sturdy thickset dog with a broad head and a muscular body. **bulldozer** n. powerful tractor for moving earth. **bulldoze** v. **bullfight** n. public show in which a matador kills a bull. **bullfinch** n. common European songbird. **bullfrog** n. large American frog with a deep croak. **bull's-eye** n. central disc of a target. **bull terrier** terrier with a short smooth coat.

bull[2] n. papal decree.

bull[3] n. Informal complete nonsense.

bullet n. small piece of metal fired from a gun.

bulletin n. short official report or announcement.

bullion n. gold or silver in the form of bars.

bully n., pl. **-lies**. 1. person who hurts, persecutes, or intimidates a weaker person. —v. **-lying, -lied**. 2. hurt, intimidate, or persecute (a weaker person).

bully beef n. canned corned beef.

bully-off n. Hockey method of starting play in which opposing players strike their sticks together before trying to hit the ball. **bully off** v. Hockey start play with a bully-off.

bulrush n. tall stiff reed.

bulwark n. 1. wall used as a fortification. 2. person or thing acting as a defence.

bum[1] n. Slang buttocks or anus.

bum[2] Informal, esp. US —n. 1. person who

avoids work, idler. —v. **bumming, bummed. 2.** cadge. —adj. **3.** of poor quality.

bumbag n. small bag attached to a belt and worn round the waist.

bumble v. speak, do, or move in a clumsy way. **bumbling** adj., n.

bumblebee n. large hairy bee.

bump v. **1.** knock or strike with a jolt. **2.** travel in jerks and jolts. —n. **3.** (dull thud from) an impact or collision. **4.** lump on the body caused by a blow. **5.** raised uneven part. **bumpy** adj. **bumpier, bumpiest. bump off** v. Informal murder.

bumper[1] n. bar on the front and back of a vehicle to protect against damage.

bumper[2] n. **1.** glass filled to the brim. —adj. **2.** unusually large or abundant.

bumph, bumf n. Informal official documents or forms.

bumpkin n. awkward simple country person.

bumptious adj. offensively self-assertive.

bun n. **1.** small round cake. **2.** hair gathered into a bun shape.

bunch n. **1.** number of things growing, fastened, or grouped together. **2.** group, e.g. a bunch of boys. —v. **3.** group or be grouped together in a bunch.

bundle n. **1.** number of things gathered loosely together. —v. **2.** cause to go roughly or unceremoniously. **bundle up** v. make into a bundle.

bung n. **1.** stopper for a cask etc. —v. **2.** (foll. by up) Informal close with a bung. **3.** Slang throw (something) somewhere in a careless manner.

bungalow n. one-storey house.

bungle v. **1.** spoil through incompetence. —n. **2.** blunder or muddle. **bungler** n. **bungling** adj., n.

bunion n. inflamed swelling on the big toe.

bunk[1] n. narrow shelflike bed. **bunk bed** one of a pair of beds constructed one above the other.

bunk[2] n. same as BUNKUM.

bunk[3] n. **do a bunk** Slang leave a place without telling anyone.

bunker n. **1.** large storage container for coal etc. **2.** sandy hollow on a golf course. **3.** underground shelter.

bunkum n. nonsense.

bunny n., pl. **-nies.** child's word for a rabbit.

Bunsen burner n. gas burner used in laboratories.

bunting[1] n. decorative flags.

bunting[2] n. songbird with a short stout bill.

buoy n. **1.** floating marker anchored in the sea. —v. **2.** prevent from sinking. **3.** encourage or hearten. **buoyant** adj. **1.** able to float. **2.** cheerful or resilient. **buoyancy** n.

bur n. same as BURR[1].

burble v. **1.** make a bubbling sound. **2.** talk quickly and excitedly.

burden[1] n. **1.** heavy load. **2.** something difficult to cope with. —v. **3.** put a burden on. **4.** oppress. **burdensome** adj.

burden[2] n. **1.** theme of a speech etc. **2.** chorus of a song.

burdock n. weed with prickly burrs.

bureau n., pl. **-reaus, -reaux. 1.** writing desk with shelves and drawers. **2.** office that provides a service.

bureaucracy n., pl. **-cies. 1.** an administrative system based on complex rules and procedures. **2.** excessive adherence to complex procedures. **bureaucrat** n. **bureaucratic** adj.

burette n. glass tube for dispensing known volumes of fluids.

burgeon v. develop or grow rapidly.

burger n. Informal hamburger.

burgess n. citizen or freeman of a borough.

burgh n. Scottish borough. **burgher** n. citizen.

burglar n. person who enters a building to commit a crime, esp. theft. **burglary** n., pl. **-ries. burgle** v.

burgundy n. type of French wine.

burial n. burying of a dead body.

burlesque n. artistic work which satirizes a subject by caricature.

burly adj. **-lier, -liest.** (of a person) broad and strong.

burn[1] v. **burning, burnt** or **burned. 1.** be or set on fire. **2.** destroy or be destroyed by fire. **3.** damage, injure, or mark by heat. **4.** feel strong emotion. —n. **5.** injury or mark caused by fire or exposure to heat. **burner** n. part of a stove or lamp that produces the flame. **burning** adj. **1.** intense. **2.** urgent or crucial.

▷ Either *burnt* or *burned* may be used as a past form.

burn² *n. Scot.* small stream.

burnish *v.* make smooth and shiny by rubbing.

burnous *n.* long circular cloak with a hood, worn esp. by Arabs.

burnt *v.* a past of BURN¹.

burp *v., n. Informal* belch.

burr¹ *n.* head of a plant with prickles or hooks.

burr² *n.* **1.** soft trilling sound given to the letter (r) in some English dialects. **2.** whirring sound. **3.** rough edge left after cutting.

burrow *n.* **1.** hole dug in the ground by a rabbit etc. —*v.* **2.** dig holes in the ground. **3.** live in a burrow.

bursar *n.* treasurer of a school, college, or university. **bursary** *n., pl.* **-ries.** scholarship.

burst *v.* **bursting, burst. 1.** (cause to) break open or apart noisily and suddenly. **2.** come or go suddenly and forcibly. **3.** be full to the point of breaking open. —*n.* **4.** instance of breaking open suddenly. **5.** sudden and violent outbreak or occurrence. **burst into** *v.* give vent to (an emotion) suddenly.

bury *v.* **burying, buried. 1.** place in a grave. **2.** place in the earth and cover with soil. **3.** conceal or hide. **4.** occupy (oneself) with deep concentration.

bus *n.* **1.** large motor vehicle for carrying passengers. —*v.* **bussing, bussed. 2.** travel or transport by bus.

busby *n., pl.* **-bies.** tall fur hat worn by certain soldiers.

bush *n.* **1.** dense woody plant, smaller than a tree. **2.** wild uncultivated part of a country. **bushy** *adj.* **bushier, bushiest.** (of hair) thick and shaggy. **bushbaby** *n.* small African tree-living mammal with large eyes. **Bushman** *n.* member of a hunting and gathering people of Southern Africa. **bush telegraph** means of spreading gossip.

bushel *n.* unit of measure equal to eight gallons.

business *n.* **1.** trade or profession. **2.** purchase and sale of goods and services. **3.** commercial establishment. **4.** proper concern or responsibility. **5.** affair, e.g. *it's a dreadful business.* **businesslike** *adj.* **businessman, businesswoman** *n.*

busker *n.* street entertainer. **busk** *v.* act as a busker.

bust¹ *n.* **1.** woman's bosom. **2.** sculpture of the head and shoulders.

bust² *Informal* —*v.* **busting, bust** or **busted. 1.** break. **2.** (of the police) raid (a place) or arrest (someone). —*adj.* **3.** broken. **go bust** become bankrupt. **bust-up** *n. Informal* **1.** quarrel. **2.** brawl.

bustle¹ *v.* **1.** hurry with a show of activity or energy. —*n.* **2.** energetic and noisy activity. **bustling** *adj.*

bustle² *n.* cushion formerly worn under the back of a woman's skirt to hold it out.

busy *adj.* **busier, busiest. 1.** actively employed. **2.** full of activity. —*v.* **busying, busied. 3.** keep (someone) busy. **busily** *adv.* **busybody** *n.* meddlesome or nosy person.

but *conj.* **1.** contrary to expectation. **2.** in contrast. **3.** other than. **4.** without it happening. —*prep.* **5.** except. —*adv.* **6.** only. **but for** were it not for.

butane [bew-tane] *n.* gas used for fuel.

butch *adj. Slang* markedly or aggressively masculine.

butcher *n.* **1.** person who slaughters animals or sells their meat. **2.** brutal murderer. —*v.* **3.** slaughter (animals) for meat. **4.** kill (people) brutally or indiscriminately. **5.** make a mess of. **butchery** *n.*

butler *n.* chief male servant.

butt¹ *n.* **1.** thick end of something. **2.** unused end of a cigar or cigarette.

butt² *n.* **1.** person or thing that is the target of ridicule. **2.** mound of earth behind a target. —*pl.* **3.** target range.

butt³ *v.* **1.** strike with the head or horns. —*n.* **2.** blow with the head or horns. **butt in** *v.* interrupt a conversation.

butt⁴ *n.* large cask.

butter *n.* **1.** edible fatty solid made from cream by churning. —*v.* **2.** put butter on. **buttery** *adj.* **butter up** *v.* flatter.

buttercup *n.* small yellow flower.

butterfingers *n. Informal* person who drops things by mistake.

butterfly *n.* **1.** insect with brightly coloured wings. **2.** swimming stroke in which both arms move together in a forward circular action.

buttermilk *n.* sourish milk that remains after the butter has been separated from milk.

butterscotch *n.* kind of hard brittle toffee.

buttery *n., pl.* **-teries.** in some universities, room where food and drink are sold.

buttock *n.* either of the two fleshy masses that form the human rump.

button *n.* **1.** small hard object sewn to clothing to fasten it. **2.** knob that operates a piece of equipment when pressed. —*v.* **3.** fasten with buttons. **buttonhole** *n.* **1.** slit in a garment through which a button is passed. **2.** flower worn on a lapel. —*v.* **3.** detain (someone) in conversation.

buttress *n.* **1.** structure to support a wall. —*v.* **2.** support with a buttress.

buxom *adj.* (of a woman) healthily plump and full-bosomed.

buy *v.* **buying, bought. 1.** acquire by paying money for. **2.** bribe. **3.** *Slang* accept as true. —*n.* **4.** thing acquired through payment. **buyer** *n.* **1.** customer. **2.** person employed to buy merchandise.
▷ Be careful not to confuse the past forms *bought* (from *buy*) with *brought* (from *bring*).

buzz *n.* **1.** rapidly vibrating humming sound. **2.** *Informal* sense of excitement. —*v.* **3.** make a humming sound. **4.** be filled with an air of excitement. **5.** *Informal* fly an aircraft very low over. **buzzer** *n.* **buzz around** *v.* move around quickly and busily. **buzz word** jargon word which becomes fashionably popular.

buzzard *n.* bird of prey of the hawk family.

by *adv.* **1.** near. **2.** past. —*prep.* **3.** used to indicate the person responsible for a creative work, e.g. *an opera by Verdi.* **4.** used to indicate a means used, e.g. *I go home by bus.* **5.** past. **6.** not later than. **7.** during. **8.** near.

9. placed between measurements, e.g. *a plank fourteen inches by seven.* **by and by** presently. **by and large** in general.

bye[1] *n.* **1.** *Sport* situation where a player or team wins a round by having no opponent. **2.** *Cricket* run scored off a ball not touched by the batsman.

bye[2], **bye-bye** *interj. Informal* goodbye.

by-election *n.* election held during parliament to fill a vacant seat.

bygone *adj.* **1.** past or former. —*pl. n.* **2. let bygones be bygones** agree to forget past quarrels.

bylaw, bye-law *n.* rule made by a local authority.

by-line *n.* line under the title of a newspaper or magazine article giving the author's name.

bypass *n.* **1.** main road built to avoid a city. —*v.* **2.** go round or avoid.

by-play *n.* action apart from the main action in a play.

by-product *n.* secondary or incidental product of a process.

byre *n.* shelter for cows.

bystander *n.* person present but not involved.

byte *n. Computers* group of bits processed as one unit of data.

byway *n.* side road.

byword *n.* **1.** person or thing regarded as a perfect example of something. **2.** proverb.

Byzantine *adj.* **1.** of Byzantium or the Byzantine Empire. **2.** of the style of architecture developed in the Byzantine Empire. **3.** complicated.

C

C 1. *Chem.* carbon. 2. Celsius. 3. centigrade. 4. the Roman numeral for 100.

c. 1. cent. 2. century. 3. circa. 4. copyright.

Ca *Chem.* calcium.

CA 1. California. 2. Chartered Accountant.

ca. circa.

cab *n.* 1. taxi. 2. enclosed driver's compartment on a train, lorry, etc. **cabbie, cabby** *n., pl.* -**bies.** *Informal* taxi driver.

cabal [kab-**bal**] *n.* 1. small group of political plotters. 2. secret plot.

cabaret [kab-a-ray] *n.* 1. dancing and singing show in a nightclub. 2. place providing a cabaret.

cabbage *n.* 1. vegetable with a large head of green leaves. 2. *Informal* person with no mental faculties.

caber *n.* tree trunk tossed in competition at Highland games.

cabin *n.* 1. compartment in a ship or aircraft. 2. small hut. **cabin boy** boy who waits on the officers and passengers of a ship. **cabin cruiser** motorboat with a cabin.

cabinet *n.* 1. piece of furniture with drawers or shelves. 2. (C-) committee of senior government ministers. **cabinet-maker** *n.* person who makes fine furniture.

cable *n.* 1. strong thick rope. 2. ship's anchor chain. 3. bundle of wires that carries electricity or telegraph messages. 4. telegram sent abroad. — *v.* 5. send (a message) to (someone) by cable. **cable car** vehicle pulled up a steep slope by a moving cable. **cable television** television service conveyed by cable to subscribers.

caboodle *n.* **the whole caboodle** *Informal* the whole lot.

caboose *n. US* guard's van on a train.

cabriolet [kab-ree-oh-**lay**] *n.* small horse-drawn carriage with a folding hood.

cacao [kak-**kah**-oh] *n.* tropical tree with seed pods from which chocolate and cocoa are made.

cachalot *n.* sperm whale.

cache [kash] *n.* 1. hiding place. 2. hidden store of weapons or treasure.

cachet [kash-shay] *n.* 1. prestige, distinction. 2. distinctive mark.

cachou *n.* lozenge eaten to sweeten the breath.

cack-handed *adj. Informal* 1. clumsy. 2. left-handed.

cackle *v.* 1. laugh or chatter shrilly. 2. (of a hen) squawk with shrill broken notes. —*n.* 3. cackling noise.

cacophony [kak-**koff**-on-ee] *n.* harsh discordant sound. **cacophonous** *adj.*

cactus *n., pl.* -**tuses, -ti.** fleshy desert plant with spines but no leaves.

cad *n. Old-fashioned* dishonourable man. **caddish** *adj.*

cadaver [kad-**dav**-ver] *n.* corpse. **cadaverous** *adj.* 1. deathly pale. 2. gaunt.

caddie, caddy *n., pl.* -**dies.** 1. person who carries a golfer's clubs. — *v.* -**dying, -died.** 2. act as a caddie.

caddis fly *n.* insect whose larva (**caddis worm**) lives underwater in a protective case of sand and stones.

caddy *n., pl.* -**dies.** small box for tea.

cadence [kade-enss] *n.* 1. rise and fall in the pitch of a voice. 2. close of a musical phrase.

cadenza *n.* complex passage for a soloist in a piece of music.

cadet *n.* young person training for the armed forces or police.

cadge *v.* get (food, money, etc.) by sponging or begging. **cadger** *n.*

cadi *n., pl.* -**dis.** judge in a Muslim community.

cadmium *n.* bluish-white metallic element used in alloys.

cadre [**kah**-der] *n.* (member of) a group of selected trained people forming the core of a military unit, Communist Party, etc.

caecum [**seek**-um] *n., pl.* -**ca** [-ka] pouch at the beginning of the large intestine.

Caerphilly *n.* creamy white mild-flavoured cheese.

Caesarean section [see-**zair**-ee-an] *n.* surgical incision into the womb to deliver a baby.

caesium n. silvery-white metallic element used in photocells.

caesura [siz-**your**-ra] n., pl. **-s, -rae** [-ree] pause in a line of verse.

café n. small or inexpensive restaurant serving light refreshments. **cafeteria** n. self-service restaurant.

caffeine n. stimulant found in tea and coffee.

caftan n. same as KAFTAN.

cage n. **1.** enclosure of bars or wires, for keeping animals or birds. **2.** enclosed platform of a lift, esp. in a mine. —v. **3.** confine in a cage.

cagey adj. **cagier, cagiest. 1.** not frank. **2.** wary. **caginess** n.

cagoule [kag-**gool**] n. lightweight hooded waterproof jacket.

cahoots pl. n. **in cahoots** Informal conspiring together.

caiman n. same as CAYMAN.

cairn n. mound of stones erected as a monument or landmark. **cairn terrier** small rough-haired terrier.

cairngorm n. yellow or brownish quartz gemstone.

caisson [**kay**-son] n. watertight chamber used to carry out construction work under water.

cajole v. persuade by flattery. **cajolery** n.

cake n. **1.** sweet food baked from a mixture of flour, eggs, etc. **2.** flat compact mass. —v. **3.** form into a hardened mass or crust.

calabash n. **1.** type of large gourd. **2.** pipe or bowl made from this.

calamine n. pink powder consisting chiefly of zinc oxide, used in skin lotions and ointments.

calamity n., pl. **-ties.** disaster. **calamitous** adj.

calces n. a plural of CALX.

calciferol n. substance found in fish oils and used to treat rickets.

calcify v. **-fying, -fied.** harden by the depositing of calcium salts. **calcification** n.

calcium n. silvery-white metallic element found in bones, teeth, limestone, and chalk.

calculate v. **1.** solve (a problem) mathematically. **2.** estimate. **3.** plan deliberately.

4. US suppose. **calculable** adj. **calculated** adj. premeditated or deliberate. **calculating** adj. selfishly scheming. **calculation** n. **calculator** n. small electronic device for making calculations.

calculus n., pl. **-luses. 1.** branch of mathematics dealing with infinitesimal changes to a variable number or quantity. **2.** Pathology stone.

caldron n. same as CAULDRON.

Caledonian adj. of Scotland.

calendar n. **1.** system for determining the beginning, length, and division of years. **2.** table showing such an arrangement. **3.** schedule of events or appointments.

calender n. machine in which paper or cloth is smoothed by passing it between rollers.

calends pl. n. first day of each month in the ancient Roman calendar.

calendula n. marigold.

calf[1] n., pl. **calves. 1.** young cow, bull, elephant, whale, or seal. **2.** leather made from calf skin. **calve** v. give birth to a calf. **calf love** adolescent infatuation.

calf[2] n., pl. **calves.** back of the leg between the ankle and knee.

calibre [**kal**-lib-ber] n. **1.** ability, personal worth. **2.** diameter of the bore of a gun or of a shell or bullet. **calibrate** v. **1.** mark the scale or check the accuracy of (a measuring instrument). **2.** measure the calibre of. **calibration** n.

calico n., pl. **-coes, -co.** plain white cotton cloth.

californium n. artificial radioactive element.

caliph n. Hist. Muslim ruler.

calk v. same as CAULK.

call v. **1.** name. **2.** shout to attract attention. **3.** ask to come. **4.** (often foll. by on) visit. **5.** telephone. **6.** (of an animal or bird) utter its characteristic cry. **7.** read (a list) aloud for checking. **8.** awaken. **9.** arrange (a meeting, strike, etc.). —n. **10.** telephone communication. **11.** shout. **12.** animal's or bird's cry. **13.** summons or invitation. **14.** visit. **15.** need, demand. **caller** n. **calling** n. vocation or profession. **call box** kiosk for a public telephone. **call for** v. need, demand. **call girl** prostitute with whom appointments are made by telephone. **call off** v. cancel. **call**

up v. **1.** summon to serve in the armed forces. **2.** evoke.

calligraphy n. (art of) beautiful handwriting. **calligrapher** n.

calliper n. **1.** (usu. pl.) metal splint for the leg. **2.** instrument for measuring diameters.

callisthenics pl. n. light keep-fit exercises. **callisthenic** adj.

callosity n., pl. **-ties.** callus.

callous adj. insensitive or heartless. **calloused** adj. (of skin) thickened and hardened. **callously** adv. **callousness** n.

callow adj. immature and inexperienced.

callus n., pl. **-luses.** area of thick hardened skin.

calm adj. **1.** serene, composed. **2.** still, peaceful. **3.** windless. —n. **4.** serenity, composure. **5.** stillness, peacefulness. **6.** absence of wind. —v. **7.** make or become calm. **calmly** adv. **calmness** n.

calomel n. colourless tasteless powder used as a cathartic.

Calor Gas n. ® butane gas liquefied under pressure in containers for domestic use.

calorie n. **1.** unit of measurement for the energy value of food. **2.** unit of heat. **calorific** adj. heat-producing.

calumny n., pl. **-nies.** slander. **calumniate** v. slander.

Calvary n. place outside the walls of Jerusalem where Jesus was crucified.

calves n. plural of CALF.

Calvinism n. theological system of Calvin, stressing predestination and salvation solely by God's grace. **Calvinist** n., adj. **Calvinistic** adj.

calx n., pl. **calxes, calces.** powdery metallic oxide left when an ore or mineral is roasted.

calypso n., pl. **-sos.** West Indian song with improvised topical lyrics.

calyx n., pl. **calyxes, calyces.** ring of sepals protecting a flower bud.

cam n. device which converts rotary motion to to-and-fro motion. **camshaft** n. part of an engine consisting of a rod to which cams are fixed.

camaraderie n. comradeship.

camber n. slight upward curve to the centre of a surface.

cambric n. fine white linen fabric.

camcorder n. combined portable video camera and recorder.

came v. past tense of COME.

camel n. **1.** humped mammal of Asia and Africa. —adj. **2.** fawn.

camellia [kam-**meal**-ya] n. evergreen ornamental shrub with roselike white, pink, or red flowers.

Camembert [**kam**-mem-bare] n. soft creamy French cheese.

cameo n., pl. **cameos. 1.** brooch or ring with a profile head carved in relief. **2.** small part in a film or play performed by a well-known actor or actress.

camera n. apparatus used for taking photographs or pictures for television or film. **in camera** in private. **cameraman** n. photographer, esp. for television or cinema.

camiknickers pl. n. woman's undergarment consisting of knickers attached to a camisole.

camisole n. woman's bodice-like garment.

camomile n. aromatic plant, used to make herbal tea.

camouflage [**kam**-moo-flahzh] n. **1.** use of natural surroundings or artificial aids to conceal or disguise something. —v. **2.** conceal or disguise by camouflage.

camp[1] n. **1.** (place for) temporary lodgings consisting of tents, huts, or cabins. **2.** group supporting a particular doctrine. —adj. **3.** suitable for use in temporary lodgings. —v. **4.** stay in a camp. **camper** n. **camp follower** civilian who provides services to military personnel.

camp[2] Informal adj. **1.** homosexual. **2.** consciously artificial or affected. **camp it up** Informal behave in a camp way.

campaign n. **1.** series of coordinated activities designed to achieve a goal. **2.** number of military operations for achieving an objective. —v. **3.** conduct or take part in a campaign.

campanile [camp-an-**neel**-lee] n. bell tower, not usually attached to another building.

campanology n. art of ringing bells. **campanologist** n.

campanula n. plant with blue or white bell-shaped flowers.

camphor n. aromatic crystalline substance used medicinally and in mothballs. **camphorated** adj.

campion n. white or pink wild flower.

campus n., pl. **-puses.** grounds of a college or university.

can[1] v., past. **could.** 1. be able. 2. be allowed.

can[2] n. 1. metal container for liquid or foods. —v. **canning, canned.** 2. put (something) in a can. **canned** adj. 1. preserved in a can. 2. (of music etc.) prerecorded. **cannery** n., pl. **-neries.** factory where food is canned.

Canadian n., adj. (person) from Canada.

canal n. 1. artificial watercourse. 2. duct in the body. **canalize** v. 1. convert into a canal. 2. give direction to.

canapé [kan-nap-pay] n. small piece of bread or toast with a savoury topping.

canard n. false report.

canary n., pl. **-ries.** small yellow songbird often kept as a pet.

canasta n. card game like rummy, played with two packs.

cancan n. lively high-kicking dance performed by a female group.

cancel v. **-celling, -celled.** 1. postpone indefinitely. 2. revoke or annul. 3. cross out. 4. mark (a cheque or stamp) to prevent reuse. **cancellation** n. **cancel out** v. counterbalance or neutralize.

cancer n. 1. malignant growth or tumour. 2. disease resulting from this. 3. evil influence that spreads dangerously. **cancerous** adj.

Cancer n. (the crab) fourth sign of the zodiac. **tropic of Cancer** see TROPIC.

candela [kan-dee-la] n. unit of luminous intensity.

candelabrum n., pl. **-bra.** large branched candle holder.

candid adj. frank and outspoken. **candidly** adv.

candidate n. 1. person seeking a job or position. 2. person taking an examination. **candidacy, candidature** n.

candle n. stick of wax enclosing a wick, which is burned to produce light. **candlestick** n. holder for a candle. **candlewick** n. cotton fabric with a tufted surface.

Candlemas n. Christianity Feb. 2, Feast of the Purification of the Virgin Mary.

candour n. frankness.

candy n., pl. **-dies.** 1. US a sweet, or sweets in general. —v. **-dying, -died.** 2. preserve with sugar. **candyfloss** n. light fluffy mass of spun sugar on a stick. **candy-striped** adj. having coloured stripes on a white background.

candytuft n. garden plant with clusters of white, pink, or purple flowers.

cane n. 1. stem of the bamboo or similar plant. 2. slender walking stick. 3. flexible rod used to beat someone. —v. 4. beat with a cane.

canine [kay-nine] adj. of or like a dog. **canine tooth** sharp pointed tooth between the incisors and the molars.

canister n. metal container.

canker n. 1. ulceration or ulcerous disease. 2. something that spreads and corrupts. —v. 3. infect or become infected with canker. **cankerous** adj.

cannabis n. drug obtained from the hemp plant.

cannelloni pl. n. tubular pieces of pasta filled with meat etc.

cannibal n. 1. person who eats human flesh. 2. animal that eats others of its own kind. **cannibalism** n. **cannibalize** v. use parts from (one machine) to repair another.

cannon[1] n. large gun on wheels. **cannonade** n. continuous heavy gunfire. **cannonball** n. heavy metal ball fired from a cannon.

cannon[2] n. 1. billiard stroke in which the cue ball hits two balls successively. —v. 2. make this stroke. 3. rebound, collide.

cannot can not.

canny adj. **-nier, -niest.** shrewd and cautious. **cannily** adv.

canoe n. 1. light narrow boat propelled by a paddle or paddles. —v. **-noeing, -noed.** 2. go in a canoe. **canoeist** n.

canon[1] n. 1. Church law or decree. 2. general rule or principle. 3. set of writings accepted as genuine. 4. piece of music on which the same melody is taken up in different parts. **canonical** adj. **canonize** v. declare (a person) officially to be a saint. **canonization** n.

canon[2] n. priest serving in a cathedral.

canoodle v. Slang kiss and cuddle.

canopy n., pl. **-pies.** 1. covering above a throne, bed, etc. 2. any large or wide covering. —v. **-pying, -pied.** 3. cover with a canopy.

cant[1] n. 1. insincere talk. 2. specialized

vocabulary of a particular group. —*v.* **3.** use cant.

cant[2] *n.* **1.** tilt or slope. **2.** sudden movement that tilts or overturns something. —*v.* **3.** tilt or overturn.

can't can not.

cantaloupe, cantaloup *n.* kind of melon with sweet orange flesh.

cantankerous *adj.* bad-tempered, quarrelsome.

cantata [kan-**tah**-ta] *n.* musical work consisting of arias, duets, and choruses.

canteen *n.* **1.** restaurant attached to a workplace or school. **2.** case of cutlery. **3.** flask for carrying water.

canter *n.* **1.** horse's gait between a trot and a gallop. —*v.* **2.** (cause to) move at a canter.

canticle *n.* short hymn with words from the Bible.

cantilever *n.* beam or girder fixed at one end only. **cantilever bridge** bridge made of two cantilevers which meet in the middle.

canto [kan-toe] *n., pl.* -**tos.** main division of a long poem.

canton *n.* political division of a country, esp. Switzerland.

cantonment [kan-**toon**-ment] *n.* military camp.

cantor *n.* man employed to lead services in a synagogue.

canvas *n.* **1.** heavy coarse cloth used for sails and tents, and for painting on. **2.** painting on canvas. **under canvas** in tents.

canvass *v.* **1.** try to get votes or support (from). **2.** determine the opinions of (people) by conducting a survey. —*n.* **3.** canvassing.

canyon *n.* deep gorge.

caoutchouc [cow-chook] *n.* raw rubber.

cap *n.* **1.** soft close-fitting covering for the head. **2.** small lid. **3.** small explosive device used in a toy gun. **4.** player selected for a national team. **5.** contraceptive device. —*v.* **capping, capped. 6.** cover with or as if with a cap. **7.** outdo. **8.** select (a player) for a national team. **9.** impose an upper limit on (a tax).

CAP in the EC, Common Agricultural Policy.

cap. 1. capacity. **2.** capital. **3.** capital letter.

capable *adj.* **1.** able, competent. **2.** (foll. by

of) having the capacity (for). **capably** *adv.* **capability** *n., pl.* -**ties.**

capacity *n., pl.* -**ties. 1.** ability to contain, hold, or absorb. **2.** maximum amount that can be contained or produced. **3.** physical or mental ability. **4.** position or function. **capacious** *adj.* roomy. **capacitance** *n.* (measure of) the ability of a system to store electric charge. **capacitor** *n.* device for storing electric charge.

caparisoned [kap-**par**-riss-sond] *adj.* dressed in rich clothing.

cape[1] *n.* short cloak.

cape[2] *n.* headland or promontory.

caper[1] *n.* **1.** high-spirited prank. —*v.* **2.** skip or dance about.

caper[2] *n.* pickled flower bud of a Mediterranean shrub used in sauces.

capercaillie, capercailzie [kap-per-**kale**-yee] *n.* large black European grouse.

capillary [kap-**pill**-a-ree] *adj.* **1.** (of tubes) having a fine bore. —*n., pl.* -**laries. 2.** very fine blood vessel.

capital *n.* **1.** chief town of a country. **2.** accumulated wealth. **3.** wealth used to produce more wealth. **4.** large letter, as used at the beginning of a name or sentence. **5.** top part of a pillar. —*adj.* **6.** involving or punishable by death. **7.** chief or principal. **8.** *Old-fashioned* excellent. **capitalize** *v.* **1.** convert into or provide with capital. **2.** write or print (text) in capital letters. **capitalize on** *v.* take advantage of (a situation). **capital gain** profit from the sale of an asset.

capitalism *n.* economic system based on the private ownership of industry. **capitalist 1.** supporter of capitalism. **2.** person who owns capital. —*adj.* **3.** of capitalists or capitalism.

capitation *n.* charge or grant of a fixed amount per person.

capitulate *v.* surrender on agreed terms. **capitulation** *n.*

capon [**kay**-pon] *n.* castrated cock fowl fattened for eating.

cappuccino [kap-poo-**cheen**-oh] *n., pl.* -**nos.** coffee with steamed milk.

caprice [kap-**reess**] *n.* whim. **capricious** *adj.* changeable. **capriciously** *adv.*

Capricorn *n.* (the sea goat) tenth sign of the zodiac. **tropic of Capricorn** see TROPIC.

capsicum *n.* kind of pepper used as a vegetable or as a spice.

capsize v. overturn accidentally.

capstan n. rotating cylinder on which a rope etc. is wound.

capsule n. **1.** soluble case containing a dose of medicine. **2.** seed vessel of a plant. **3.** detachable crew compartment of a spacecraft. **4.** membrane surrounding an organ.

Capt. Captain.

captain n. **1.** leader of a team or group. **2.** commander of a ship or civil aircraft. **3.** middle-ranking naval officer. **4.** junior officer in the armed forces. —v. **5.** be captain of. **captaincy** n.

caption n. **1.** title or explanation accompanying an illustration. **2.** title of a chapter or article. —v. **3.** provide with a caption.

captious adj. tending to make trivial criticisms. **captiously** adv. **captiousness** n.

captivate v. fascinate or enchant. **captivating** adj. **captivation** n.

captive n. **1.** confined or restrained person or animal. —adj. **2.** held prisoner. **3.** obliged to stay. **captivity** n.

captor n. person who holds someone captive.

capture v. **1.** take prisoner. **2.** gain control over. —n. **3.** capturing.

capybara n. very large S American rodent.

capuchin [**kap**-yoo-chin] n. S American monkey with thick hair on the top of its head.

car n. **1.** motor vehicle designed to carry a small number of people. **2.** passenger compartment of a cable car, lift, etc. **3.** US railway carriage. **car park** area or building reserved for parking cars.

carafe [kar-**raff**] n. glass bottle for serving water or wine.

caramel n. **1.** chewy sweet made from sugar and milk. **2.** burnt sugar used for colouring and flavouring food. **caramelize** v. turn into caramel.

carapace n. hard upper shell of tortoises and crustaceans.

carat n. **1.** unit of weight of precious stones. **2.** measure of the purity of gold in an alloy.

caravan n. **1.** large enclosed vehicle for living in, able to be towed by a car or horse. **2.** group travelling together for safety in the East. **caravanserai** n. large inn enclosing a courtyard, providing accommodation for caravans in Eastern countries.

caraway n. plant whose seeds are used as a spice.

carbide n. compound of carbon with a metal.

carbine n. light automatic rifle.

carbohydrate n. any of a large group of energy-producing compounds in food, such as sugars and starches.

carbolic, carbolic acid n. disinfectant derived from coal tar.

carbon n. nonmetallic element occurring as charcoal, graphite, and diamond, found in all organic matter. **carbonate** n. **1.** salt or ester of carbonic acid. —v. **2.** impregnate with carbon dioxide. **carboniferous** adj. producing coal or carbon. **carbonize** v. **1.** turn into carbon as a result of heating. **2.** coat with carbon. **carbon copy 1.** copy made with carbon paper. **2.** very similar person or thing. **carbon dioxide** colourless gas exhaled by people and animals. **carbon paper** paper covered with a dark waxy pigment, used to make a duplicate of something as it is typed or written. **carbonic acid** weak acid formed from carbon dioxide and water.

Carborundum n. ® compound of silicon and carbon, used for grinding and polishing.

carboy n. large bottle with a protective casing.

carbuncle n. **1.** inflamed boil. **2.** rounded garnet cut without facets.

carburettor n. device which mixes petrol and air in an internal-combustion engine.

carcass, carcase n. **1.** dead body or skeleton of an animal. **2.** Informal person's body.

carcinogen n. substance producing cancer. **carcinogenic** adj. **carcinoma** n. malignant tumour, cancer.

card[1] n. **1.** piece of thick stiff paper or cardboard used for identification, reference, or sending greetings or messages. **2.** one of a set of cards with a printed pattern, used for playing games. **3.** small rectangle of stiff plastic for use as a credit card or cheque card. **4.** Old-fashioned witty or eccentric person. —pl. **5.** any card game, or card games in general. **6.** employee's documents held by his or her employer. **cardboard** n. thin stiff board made from paper pulp. **cardsharp, cardsharper** n. professional card player who cheats.

card² n. **1.** machine or tool for combing wool before spinning. —v. **2.** process with a card or cards. **carder** n.

cardamom, cardamon n. seeds of a tropical plant, used as a spice.

cardiac adj. of the heart. **cardiogram** n. record of heart movements. **cardiograph** n. instrument which records heart movements. **cardiology** n. study of the heart and its diseases. **cardiologist** n. **cardiovascular** adj. of the heart and the blood vessels.

cardigan n. knitted jacket.

cardinal n. **1.** one of the high-ranking clergymen of the RC Church who elect the Pope and act as his counsellors. —adj. **2.** chief, principal. **3.** deep red. **cardinal number** number indicating quantity but not order in a group, for example four as distinct from fourth. **cardinal point** one of the four main points of the compass.

care v. **1.** be concerned. **2.** have regard or liking for. **3.** have a desire for. **4.** look after. —n. **5.** serious attention. **6.** protection or supervision. **7.** worry, anxiety. **8.** caution. **in, into care** made the legal responsibility of a local authority. **careful** adj. **carefully** adv. **carefulness** n. **careless** adj. **carelessly** adv. **carelessness** n.

careen v. tilt over to one side.
▷ Be careful not to confuse _careen_, 'tilt', with _career_, 'rush headlong'.

career n. **1.** profession or occupation. **2.** course through life. —v. **3.** rush in an uncontrolled way. **careerist** n. person who seeks advancement by any possible means.
▷ Do not confuse _career_ 'rush' with _careen_ 'tilt'.

carefree adj. without worry or responsibility.

caress n. **1.** gentle affectionate touch or embrace. —v. **2.** touch gently and affectionately.

caret [kar-rett] n. symbol (⁁) showing the place in written or printed matter where something is to be inserted.

caretaker n. person employed to look after a place.

careworn adj. showing signs of worry.

cargo n., pl. **-goes.** goods carried by a ship, aircraft, etc.

caribou n. N American reindeer.

caricature n. **1.** likeness of a person which exaggerates features for comic effect. —v. **2.** portray by a caricature. **caricaturist** n.

caries [care-reez] n. tooth or bone decay.

carillon [kar-rill-yon] n. **1.** set of bells played by keyboard or mechanically. **2.** tune played on this.

Carmelite n., adj. (friar or nun) of the Order of Our Lady of Carmel.

carminative n., adj. (medicine) able to remedy flatulence.

carmine adj. vivid red.

carnage n. slaughter.

carnal adj. relating to the appetites and passions of the body. **carnal knowledge** sexual intercourse.

carnation n. **1.** cultivated plant with fragrant white, pink, or red flowers. —adj. **2.** rosy pink.

carnelian n. reddish-yellow gemstone.

carnival n. **1.** festive period with processions and entertainment. **2.** travelling funfair.

carnivore n. flesh-eating animal or plant. **carnivorous** adj.

carob n. Mediterranean tree with edible pods used as a chocolate substitute.

carol n. **1.** joyful Christmas hymn. —v. **-olling, -olled. 2.** sing carols. **3.** sing joyfully.

carotid [kar-rot-id] adj., n. (of) one of the two arteries supplying blood to the head.

carouse v. have a merry drinking party. **carousal** n. merry drinking party.

carousel [kar-roo-sell] n. **1.** revolving conveyor. **2.** US merry-go-round.

carp¹ n. freshwater fish.

carp² v. complain or find fault.

carpal n. any bone of the wrist.

carpel n. female reproductive organ of a flowering plant.

carpenter n. person who makes or repairs wooden structures. **carpentry** n.

carpet n. **1.** heavy fabric for covering a floor. **2.** carpet-like covering. —v. **carpeting, carpeted. 3.** cover with a carpet. **on the carpet** _Informal_ being reprimanded. **carpetbagger** n. politician seeking office in a place where he or she has no connections.

carpus n., pl. **-pi.** set of eight small bones forming the wrist.

carriage n. **1.** one of the sections of a train

for passengers. **2.** four-wheeled horse-drawn vehicle. **3.** person's bearing. **4.** moving part of a machine that supports and shifts another part. **5.** act or cost of conveying goods. **carriageway** n. part of a road along which traffic passes in one direction.

carrier n. **1.** person or thing that carries something. **2.** person or animal that does not show symptoms of a disease but can transmit it to others. **carrier bag** large paper or plastic bag for shopping. **carrier pigeon** homing pigeon used for carrying messages.

carrion n. **1.** dead and rotting flesh. **2.** something filthy or vile. **carrion crow** scavenging European crow.

carrot n. **1.** long tapering orange root vegetable. **2.** incentive. **carroty** adj. reddish.

carry v. **-rying, -ried. 1.** take (something) from one place to another, transport. **2.** have on one's person. **3.** transmit. **4.** have as a penalty or result. **5.** bear (the head, body, etc.) in a specified manner. **6.** win acceptance for (a bill or motion). **7.** (of sound) travel over a distance. **carrycot** n. light portable cot for a baby. **carry on** v. **1.** continue or persevere. **2.** Informal fuss unnecessarily. **carry out** v. perform or complete. **carry through** v. accomplish.

cart n. **1.** open two-wheeled horse-drawn vehicle for carrying goods or passengers. **2.** small vehicle pushed or drawn by hand. —v. **3.** carry in a cart. **4.** carry with effort. **carthorse** n. large heavily built horse. **cartwheel** n. **1.** sideways somersault supported by the arms with the legs outstretched. **2.** large spoked wheel of a cart.

carte blanche n. French complete authority.

cartel n. association of competing firms formed to fix prices.

Carthusian n., adj. (member) of a strict monastic order founded by Saint Bruno.

cartilage [kar-till-ij] n. firm elastic tissue forming part of the skeleton. **cartilaginous** adj.

cartography n. map making. **cartographer** n. **cartographic** adj.

carton n. container made of cardboard or waxed paper.

cartoon n. **1.** humorous or satirical drawing. **2.** sequence of these telling a story. **3.** film made by photographing a series of drawings which give the illusion of movement when projected. **4.** preliminary sketch for a painting. **cartoonist** n.

cartouche, cartouch n. **1.** ornamental tablet or panel in the form of a scroll. **2.** oval figure containing royal or divine Egyptian names.

cartridge n. **1.** casing containing an explosive charge for a firearm. **2.** sealed container of film, tape, etc. **3.** unit in the pick-up of a record player holding the stylus. **cartridge paper** strong thick paper.

carve v. **1.** cut. **2.** form (an object or design) by cutting, esp. in stone or wood. **3.** slice (meat) into pieces. **carving** n. **carve out** v. Informal make or create (a career).

caryatid [kar-ree-at-id] n. supporting column in the shape of a female figure.

Casanova n. promiscuous man.

casbah n. same as KASBAH.

cascade n. **1.** waterfall. **2.** something that flows or falls like a waterfall. —v. **3.** fall in cascades.

cascara n. bark of a N American shrub, used as a laxative.

case[1] n. **1.** instance or example. **2.** matter for discussion. **3.** condition or state of affairs. **4.** set of arguments for an action or cause. **5.** person attended to by a doctor, solicitor, or social worker. **6.** lawsuit. **7.** grounds for a lawsuit. **8.** Grammar form of a noun, pronoun, or adjective showing its relation to other words in the sentence. **in case** so as to allow for eventualities.

case[2] n. **1.** container or protective covering. **2.** container and its contents. —v. **3.** Slang inspect (a building) with the intention of burgling it. **case-harden** v. **1.** harden (an iron alloy) by carbonizing the surface. **2.** make callous.

casein n. protein found in milk and its products.

casement n. window that is hinged on one side.

cash n. **1.** banknotes and coins. **2.** immediate payment for goods or services. —v. **3.** obtain or pay cash for. **cash-and-carry** adj. sold on the basis of cash payment for goods that are taken away by the buyer. **cash in on** v. Informal gain profit or advantage (from). **cash register** till that displays and adds the prices of the goods sold.

cashew n. edible tropical American nut.

cashier[1] n. person responsible for handling cash in a bank or shop.

cashier[2] v. dismiss with dishonour from the armed forces.

cashmere n. 1. fine soft wool. 2. fabric made from this.

casing n. protective case or covering.

casino n., pl. **-nos**. building or room for gambling in.

cask n. barrel, usu. for holding alcoholic drink.

casket n. 1. small box for valuables. 2. US coffin.

Cassandra n. anyone whose prophecies of doom are unheeded.

cassava n. flour obtained from the roots of a tropical American plant, used to make tapioca.

casserole n. 1. covered dish in which food is cooked and served. 2. food so cooked. —v. 3. cook (food) in a casserole.

cassette n. plastic case containing a reel of film or magnetic tape.

cassia n. tropical plant whose pods yield a mild laxative. **cassia bark** cinnamon-like bark used as a spice.

cassock n. long tunic worn by a clergyman.

cassowary n., pl. **-waries**. large flightless bird of Australia and New Guinea.

cast v. **casting**, **cast**. 1. select (actors) to play parts in a play or film. 2. direct (a glance). 3. let fall, shed. 4. throw with force. 5. give (a vote). 6. shape (molten material) in a mould. —n. 7. actors in a play or film collectively. 8. something shaped by a mould while molten. 9. mould used to shape something. 10. quality or nature. 11. slight squint in the eye. 12. rigid casing for immobilizing broken bones while they heal. 13. throw. 14. coil of earth left by an earthworm. **castaway** n. shipwrecked person. **casting vote** deciding vote used by the chairman when the votes on each side are equal. **cast-iron** adj. 1. made of a hard but brittle type of iron. 2. rigid or unchallengeable. **cast-off** adj., n. discarded (garment). **cast off** v. 1. abandon. 2. untie (a ship) from a dock. 3. remove (stitches) from the needle in knitting. **cast on** v. make (stitches) on the needle in knitting.

castanets pl. n. two small curved pieces of hollow wood clicked together in the hand, used esp. by Spanish dancers.

caste n. 1. one of the hereditary classes into which Hindu society is divided. 2. social rank.

castellated adj. having battlements.

caster n. 1. small swivelled wheel on a chair leg etc. 2. bottle with a perforated top for sprinkling sugar or flour. **caster sugar** finely ground white sugar.

castigate v. criticize or scold severely. **castigation** n.

castle n. 1. large fortified building. 2. rook in chess. **castle in the air** daydream.

castor n. same as CASTER.

castor oil n. oil obtained from an Indian plant, used as a lubricant and purgative.

castrate v. 1. remove the testicles of. 2. deprive of vigour or masculinity. **castration** n.

casual adj. 1. happening by chance. 2. careless or offhand. 3. appearing unconcerned. 4. for informal wear. 5. (of work or workers) occasional. —n. 6. occasional worker. **casually** adv.

casualty n., pl. **-ties**. 1. person killed or injured in an accident or war. 2. hospital department treating victims of accidents. 3. anything lost or destroyed.

casuistry n. clever but false reasoning. **casuist** n.

cat n. 1. small domesticated furry mammal. 2. related wild mammal, such as the lion or tiger. 3. Informal spiteful woman. **catty** adj. **-tier**, **-tiest**. Informal spiteful. **catkin** n. drooping flower spike of certain trees. **cat-call** n. derisive whistle or cry. **catgut** n. strong cord used to string musical instruments. **catnap** v., n. doze. **cat-o'-nine-tails** n. whip with nine knotted thongs. **Catseye** n. ® glass reflector set in the road to indicate traffic lanes. **cat's paw** person used as a tool by another. **catwalk** n. narrow pathway or platform.

catabolism n. breaking down of complex molecules into simple ones.

cataclysm [kat-a-kliz-zum] n. 1. disaster, such as an earthquake. 2. violent upheaval. **cataclysmic** adj.

catacomb [kat-a-koom] n. underground burial place consisting of tunnels with recesses for tombs.

catafalque [kat-a-falk] n. raised platform on which a body lies in state before or during a funeral.

catalepsy n. trancelike state in which the body is rigid. **cataleptic** adj.

catalogue n. **1.** systematic list of items. **2.** book of items for sale in a shop or by mail order. —v. **3.** make such a list. **4.** enter (an item) in a catalogue.

catalyst n. **1.** substance that speeds up a chemical reaction without itself changing. **2.** person or thing causing a change. **catalyse** v. speed up (a chemical reaction) by a catalyst. **catalysis** n. **catalytic** adj.

catamaran n. **1.** boat with twin parallel hulls. **2.** primitive log raft.

catapult n. **1.** Y-shaped device with a loop of elastic used for firing stones. **2.** Hist. weapon used for hurling large rocks. —v. **3.** shoot from or as if from a catapult.

cataract n. **1.** waterfall. **2.** eye disease in which the lens becomes opaque. **3.** opaque area of an eye.

catarrh [kat-**tar**] n. inflammation of a mucous membrane causing a flow of mucus. **catarrhal** adj.

catastrophe [kat-**ass**-trof-fee] n. great and sudden disaster. **catastrophic** adj.

catatonia n. form of schizophrenia characterized by stupor, with outbreaks of excitement. **catatonic** adj., n.

catch v. **catching, caught. 1.** seize or capture. **2.** surprise, e.g. catch someone red-handed. **3.** hit unexpectedly. **4.** be in time for. **5.** see or hear by chance or with difficulty. **6.** contract (a disease). **7.** understand. **8.** entangle or become entangled. **9.** check (one's breath) suddenly. **10.** begin to burn. —n. **11.** catching. **12.** thing caught. **13.** device that fastens. **14.** Informal concealed or unforeseen difficulty. **15.** Informal person worth having as a marriage partner. **16.** Music round with a humorous text. **catch it** Informal be punished. **catching** adj. infectious. **catchy** adj. **catchier, catchiest.** (of a tune) pleasant and easily remembered. **catchment area** area served by a particular school or hospital. **catch on** v. **1.** Informal become popular. **2.** understand. **catch out** v. Informal trap (someone) in an error or lie. **catchpenny** adj. designed merely to sell quickly. **catch phrase, catchword** n. well-known and frequently used phrase or slogan. **catch 22** inescapable dilemma. **catch up** v. reach or pass.

catechism [kat-ti-kiz-zum] n. doctrine of a Christian Church in a series of questions and answers. **catechize** v. **1.** instruct by using a catechism. **2.** question (someone) thoroughly. **catechist** n.

category n., pl. **-ries.** class or group. **categorical** adj. absolute or unconditional. **categorically** adv. **categorize** v. put in a category. **categorization** n.

cater v. provide what is needed or wanted, esp. food or services. **caterer** n.

caterpillar n. **1.** wormlike larva of a moth or butterfly. **2.** ® endless track, driven by cogged wheels, used to propel a heavy vehicle.

caterwaul n., v. wail, yowl.

catharsis [kath-**thar**-siss] n., pl. **-ses. 1.** relief of strong suppressed emotions. **2.** purgation of the bowels. **cathartic** adj. **1.** purgative. **2.** causng catharsis. —n. **3.** purgative drug.

cathedral n. principal church of a diocese.

Catherine wheel n. rotating firework.

catheter [**kath**-it-er] n. tube inserted into a body cavity to drain fluid.

cathode n. negative electrode, by which electrons leave a circuit. **cathode rays** stream of electrons from a cathode in a vacuum tube. **cathode-ray tube** vacuum tube in which a beam of electrons produces a visible image, as in a television set.

catholic adj. **1.** broad-minded. **2.** universal. —n., adj. **3.** (C-) (member) of the Roman Catholic Church. **Catholicism** n. ▷ Note that the meaning of catholic can change depending on whether it begins with a capital letter or not.

cation [**kat**-eye-on] n. positively charged ion.

cattle pl. n. domesticated cows, bulls, or oxen. **cattle-grid** n. grid over a ditch in the road to prevent livestock crossing.

Caucasoid adj. of the light-skinned racial group of mankind.

caucus n., pl. **-cuses. 1.** local committee or faction of a political party. **2.** political meeting to decide future plans.

caudal adj. like or in the position of a tail.

caught v. past of CATCH.

caul n. Anat. membrane sometimes covering a child's head at birth.

cauldron, caldron n. large pot used for boiling.

cauliflower n. type of cabbage with an edible white flower head.

caulk v. stop up (cracks, esp. in a ship) with filler.

causal adj. 1. of or being a cause. 2. of cause and effect. **causally** adv. **causality, causation** n. relationship of cause and effect.

cause n. 1. aim or principle supported by a person or group. 2. something that produces an effect. 3. reason or motive. 4. (matter giving rise to) a lawsuit. —v. 5. be the cause of.

cause célèbre [kawz sill-leb-ra] n., pl. **causes célèbres** [kawz sill-leb-ra] controversial legal case or issue.

causerie n. informal talk or piece of writing.

causeway n. raised road or path across water or marshland.

caustic adj. 1. capable of burning by chemical action. 2. sarcastic or cutting. —n. 3. caustic substance. **caustically** adv. **caustic soda** same as SODIUM HYDROXIDE.

cauterize v. burn (body tissue) with heat or a chemical to treat a wound. **cauterization** n.

caution n. 1. care, attention to safety. 2. warning. —v. 3. warn or advise. **cautionary** adj. warning. **cautious** adj. showing caution. **cautiously** adv.

cavalcade n. procession of people on horseback or in cars.

cavalier adj. 1. arrogant, offhand. —n. 2. courtly gentleman. 3. (C-) supporter of Charles I in the English Civil War.

cavalry n., pl. **-ries**. part of the army orig. on horseback, but now often using fast armoured vehicles.

cave n. large hole in a hill or cliff. **caving** n. sport of exploring caves. **cave in** v. 1. collapse inwards. 2. give in. **caveman** n. 1. prehistoric cave dweller. 2. Informal man who is primitive and brutal in his behaviour.

caveat [kav-vee-at] n. warning.

cavern n. large cave. **cavernous** adj.

caviar, caviare n. salted sturgeon roe.

cavil v. **-illing, -illed**. 1. make petty objections. —n. 2. petty objection.

cavity n., pl. **-ties**. 1. hole. 2. decayed area in a tooth.

cavort v. prance, caper.

caw n. 1. cry of a crow, rook, or raven. —v. 2. make this cry.

cay n. low island or bank composed of sand and coral fragments.

cayenne pepper, cayenne n. hot red spice made from capsicum seeds.

cayman n., pl. **-mans**. S American reptile similar to an alligator.

CB Citizens' Band.

CBE Commander of the Order of the British Empire.

CBI Confederation of British Industry.

cc cubic centimetre(s).

Cd Chem. cadmium.

CD compact disc.

Ce Chem. cerium.

cease v. bring or come to an end. **ceaseless** adj. **ceaselessly** adv. **cease-fire** n. 1. order to stop firing. 2. temporary truce.

cedar n. 1. large evergreen tree. 2. its wood.

cede v. surrender (territory or legal rights).

cedilla n. hooklike symbol placed under a letter c to show that it is pronounced s, not k.

Ceefax n. ® BBC teletext service.

ceilidh [kay-lee] n. informal social gathering for singing and dancing, esp. in Scotland.

ceiling n. 1. inner upper surface of a room. 2. upper limit set on something. 3. upper altitude to which an aircraft can climb.

celandine n. wild plant with yellow flowers.

celebrate v. 1. hold festivities to mark (a happy event, anniversary, etc.). 2. perform (a religious ceremony). 3. praise publicly. **celebrated** adj. famous. **celebration** n. **celebrant** n. person who performs a religious ceremony. **celebrity** n., pl. **-rities**. 1. famous person. 2. fame.

celeriac [sill-ler-ee-ak] n. kind of celery with a large turnip-like root.

celerity [sill-ler-rit-tee] n. swiftness.

celery n. vegetable with crisp juicy edible stalks.

celestial adj. 1. heavenly, divine. 2. of the sky.

celibate adj. 1. unmarried or abstaining from sex, esp. because of a religious vow of chastity. —n. 2. celibate person. **celibacy** n.

cell n. 1. smallest unit of an organism that is able to function independently. 2. small room for a prisoner, monk, or nun. 3. small compartment. 4. small group operating as the core of a larger organization. **5.** device which generates electrical energy from a chemical reaction. **cellular** adj. **1.** of or consisting of cells. **2.** woven with an open texture.

cellar n. **1.** underground room for storage. **2.** stock of wine.

cello [chell-oh] n., pl. -los. low-pitched instrument of the violin family. **cellist** n.
▷ It is not necessary to use an apostrophe before the word cello.

Cellophane n. ® thin transparent cellulose sheeting used as wrapping.

cellulite n. fat deposits under the skin alleged to resist dieting.

celluloid n. plastic formerly used to make photographic film.

cellulose n. main constituent of plant cell walls, used in making plastics, paper, etc.

Celsius adj. of the temperature scale in which water freezes at $0°$ and boils at $100°$.

Celt [kelt] n. person who speaks a Celtic language. **Celtic** [kel-tik, sel-tik] n. **1.** group of languages including Gaelic and Welsh. —adj. **2.** of the Celts or the Celtic languages.

cement n. **1.** fine grey powder mixed with water and sand to make mortar or concrete. **2.** adhesive. **3.** material used to fill teeth. —v. **4.** join with or as if with cement. **5.** cover with cement.

cemetery n., pl. -teries. burial ground not attached to a church.

cenotaph n. monument to people buried elsewhere.

censer n. container for burning incense.

censor v. **1.** ban or cut parts of (a film, book, etc.) considered obscene or otherwise unacceptable. —n. **2.** official employed to examine and censor films, books, etc. **censorship** n. **censorial** adj. **censorious** adj. harshly critical.

censure n. **1.** severe disapproval. —v. **2.** criticize severely.

census n., pl. -suses. official count, esp. of population.

cent n. hundredth part of a monetary unit such as the dollar.

centaur n. mythical creature resembling a horse with the head, arms, and torso of a man.

centenary [sen-teen-a-ree] adj. **1.** marking a 100th anniversary. —n., pl. -naries. **2.**

100th anniversary or its celebration. **centenarian** n. person at least 100 years old. **centennial** n. US centenary.

centi- prefix **1.** one hundredth, e.g. centimetre. **2.** a hundred, e.g. centipede.

centigrade adj. same as CELSIUS.
▷ Scientists now use Celsius in preference to centigrade.

centigram, centigramme n. hundredth part of a gram.

centilitre n. hundredth part of a litre.

centime [son-teem] n. hundredth part of a franc.

centimetre n. hundredth part of a metre.

centipede n. small wormlike creature with many legs.

central adj. **1.** of, at, or forming the centre. **2.** main or principal. **centrally** adv. **centrality** n. **centralism** n. principle of central control of a country or organization. **centralize** v. **1.** bring under central control. **2.** bring towards a centre. **centralization** n. **central heating** system for heating a building from one central source of heat. **central processing unit** part of a computer that performs logical and arithmetical operations on the data.

centre n. **1.** middle point or part. **2.** place for a specified activity. **3.** person or thing that is the focus of interest. **4.** political party or group favouring moderation. **5.** Sport player who plays in the middle of the field. —v. **6.** move towards, put, or be at the centre. **centrist** n., adj. (person) favouring political moderation. **centre on** v. have as a centre or main theme.

centrifugal adj. moving away from the centre. **centrifuge** n. machine which separates substances by centrifugal force.

centripetal adj. moving towards the centre.

centurion n. Roman officer commanding 100 men.

century n., pl. -ries. **1.** period of 100 years. **2.** cricket score of 100.

cephalic adj. of or at the head.

cephalopod [seff-a-loh-pod] n. sea mollusc with a head and tentacles, such as the octopus.

ceramic n. **1.** hard brittle material made by firing clay. **2.** object made of this. —pl. **3.** art of producing ceramic objects. —adj. **4.** made of ceramic. **5.** of ceramics.

cereal n. **1.** grass plant with edible grain,

such as wheat or rice. **2.** this grain. **3.** breakfast food made from this grain.

cerebellum [serr-rib-**bell**-lum] *n., pl.* -s, -la [-la] rear part of the brain.

cerebral [**ser**-rib-ral] *adj.* **1.** of the brain. **2.** intellectual.

cerebrum [**serr**-rib-rum] *n., pl.* -brums, -bra [-bra] main part of the brain. **cerebrospinal** *adj.* of the brain and the spinal cord.

ceremony *n., pl.* -nies. **1.** formal act or ritual. **2.** formally polite behaviour. **ceremonial** *adj., n.* **ceremonially** *adv.* **ceremonious** *adj.* **ceremoniously** *adv.*

cerise [ser-**reess**] *adj.* cherry-red.

cerium *n.* steel-grey metallic element.

cert *n. Informal* certainty, e.g. *a dead cert.*

certain *adj.* **1.** sure, without doubt. **2.** reliable or unerring. **3.** some but not much. **4.** named but not known, e.g. *he had written to a certain Mrs Smith.* **certainly** *adv.* **certainty** *n.* **1.** state of being sure. **2.** *pl.* -ties. thing sure to happen.

certificate *n.* **1.** official document stating the details of a birth, death, etc. — *v.* **2.** authorize by or present with a certificate.

certify *v.* -**fying,** -**fied.** **1.** declare formally or officially. **2.** guarantee. **3.** declare (someone) legally insane. **certifiable** *adj.* **certification** *n.*

certitude *n.* confidence, certainty.

cerulean [ser-**rule**-ee-an] *adj.* of a deep blue colour.

cervix *n., pl.* **cervixes, cervices.** **1.** narrow entrance of the womb. **2.** neck. **cervical** *adj.*

cessation *n.* ceasing.

cession *n.* ceding.

cesspool, cesspit *n.* covered tank or pit for sewage.

cetacean [sit-**tay**-shun] *n., adj.* (member) of the whale family.

cetane [**see**-tane] *n.* colourless liquid hydrocarbon in diesel fuel.

Cf *Chem.* californium.

cf. compare.

CFC chlorofluorocarbon.

cg centigram.

ch. **1.** chapter. **2.** church.

cha-cha-cha, cha-cha *n.* (music for) a modern ballroom dance from Latin America.

chafe *v.* **1.** make or become sore or worn by rubbing. **2.** warm by rubbing. **3.** make or be impatient or annoyed.

chafer *n.* large beetle.

chaff *n.* **1.** grain husks. **2.** chopped hay and straw used to feed cattle. **3.** worthless matter. **4.** light-hearted teasing. — *v.* **5.** tease good-naturedly.

chaffer *v.* haggle, bargain.

chaffinch *n.* small European songbird.

chagrin [**shag**-grin] *n.* **1.** annoyance and embarrassment. — *v.* **2.** annoy and embarrass.

chain *n.* **1.** flexible length of connected metal links. **2.** (usu. *pl.*) anything that confines or restrains. **3.** connected series of things or events. **4.** group of shops, hotels, etc. owned by one firm. **5.** unit of length equal to 22 yards. — *v.* **6.** confine or fasten with or as if with a chain. **chain gang** *US* group of prisoners chained together. **chain mail** flexible armour made of metal rings. **chain reaction** series of events, each of which causes the next. **chain-smoke** *v.* smoke (cigarettes) continuously. **chain-smoker** *n.*

chair *n.* **1.** seat with a back, for one person. **2.** official position of authority. **3.** person holding this. **4.** professorship. — *v.* **5.** preside over (a meeting). **6.** *Brit.* carry (a person) aloft in a sitting position after a triumph. **chairlift** *n.* series of chairs on a cable for carrying people, esp. skiers, up a slope. **chairman, chairperson, chairwoman** *n.* person who presides over a meeting.
▷ The use of *chairman* is sometimes felt to be sexist and the use of *chairperson* has been advocated. If this too is unacceptable, it may be better to use a different word, e.g. *President.*

chaise [**shaze**] *n.* light horse-drawn carriage.

chaise longue [**long**] *n.* sofa with a back and single armrest.

chalcedony [kal-**sed**-don-ee] *n., pl.* -nies. variety of quartz.

chalet *n.* **1.** kind of Swiss wooden house. **2.** house like this, used as a holiday home.

chalice [**chal**-liss] *n.* **1.** large goblet. **2.** goblet containing the wine at Communion.

chalk *n.* **1.** soft white rock consisting of calcium carbonate. **2.** piece of this, often coloured, used for drawing and writing on blackboards. — *v.* **3.** draw or mark with chalk. **chalky** *adj.* **chalkier, chalkiest.**

challenge v. **1.** invite (someone) to take part in a contest or fight. **2.** call (something) into question. **3.** be difficult but stimulating to. **4.** order (someone) to stop and be identified. —n. **5.** act of challenging. **6.** demanding or stimulating situation. **challenger** n.

chamber n. **1.** hall used for formal meetings. **2.** legislative or judicial assembly. **3.** compartment or cavity. **4.** compartment for a cartridge in a gun. **5.** Obs. bedroom. —pl. **6.** set of rooms used as offices by a barrister. **chambermaid** n. woman employed to clean bedrooms in a hotel. **chamber music** music for a small group of players. **chamber pot** bowl for urine, formerly used in bedrooms.

chamberlain n. official who manages the household of a king or nobleman.

chameleon [kam-**meal**-yon] n. small lizard that changes colour according to its surroundings.

chamfer [**cham**-fer] v. bevel the edge of.

chamois [**sham**-wah] n., pl. **-ois**. **1.** small mountain antelope. **2.** [**sham**-ee] soft leather. **3.** cloth of this.

chamomile [**kam**-mo-mile] n. same as CAMOMILE.

champ[1] v. **1.** chew noisily. **2.** be impatient.

champ[2] n. short for CHAMPION.

champagne n. sparkling white French wine.

champion n. **1.** overall winner of a competition. **2.** someone who defends a person or cause. —adj. **3.** Dialect excellent. —v. **4.** support. **championship** n.

chance n. **1.** likelihood, probability. **2.** opportunity. **3.** risk, gamble. **4.** unpredictable element that causes things to happen one way rather than another. **5.** fortune, luck. —v. **6.** risk. **7.** happen by chance. —adj. **8.** accidental. **chancy** adj. **chancier, chanciest.** risky.

chancel n. part of a church containing the altar and choir.

chancellery n., pl. **-leries**. **1.** residence or office of a chancellor. **2.** office in an embassy or consulate.

chancellor n. **1.** state or legal officer of high rank. **2.** head of a university. **chancellorship** n. **Chancellor of the Exchequer** cabinet minister responsible for finance.

Chancery n. division of the British High Court of Justice.

chancre [**shang**-ker] n. small hard growth which is the first sign of syphilis.

chandelier [shan-dill-**eer**] n. hanging branched holder for lights.

chandler n. **1.** dealer, esp. in ships' supplies. **2.** maker or seller of candles.

change v. **1.** make or become different. **2.** interchange or exchange. **3.** put different clothes or coverings on. **4.** exchange (money) for its equivalent in a smaller denomination or different currency. **5.** leave one vehicle and board another. —n. **6.** changing. **7.** variation or alteration. **8.** variety or novelty. **9.** coins of low value. **10.** balance received when the amount paid is more than the cost of a purchase. **changeable** adj. changing often. **changeling** n. child believed to have been exchanged by fairies for another.

channel n. **1.** band of broadcasting frequencies. **2.** means of access or communication. **3.** course along which a river, shipping, etc. moves. **4.** groove. **5.** broad strait connecting two areas of sea. —v. **-nelling, -nelled**. **6.** direct or convey through a channel.

chant n. **1.** short simple melody. **2.** psalm with such a melody. **3.** rhythmic or repetitious slogan. —v. **4.** sing or utter (a psalm or slogan).

chanter n. (on bagpipes), pipe on which the melody is played.

chanty n., pl. **-ties**. same as SHANTY[2].

chaos n. **1.** complete disorder or confusion. **2.** (often C-) disordered formless matter supposed to have existed before the ordered universe. **chaotic** adj. **chaotically** adv.

chap[1] n. Informal fellow, man.

chap[2] v. chapping, chapped. **1.** (of the skin) make or become raw and cracked, by exposure to cold. —n. **2.** cracked patch on the skin.

chapatti, chapati n. in Indian cookery, flat thin unleavened bread.

chapel n. **1.** place of worship with its own altar, within a church. **2.** similar place of worship in a large house or institution. **3.** Nonconformist place of worship. **4.** section of a trade union in the print industry.

chaperon, chaperone [**shap**-per-rone] n. **1.** older person who accompanies and supervises a young person. —v. **2.** act as a chaperone to.

chaplain n. clergyman attached to a chapel,

military body, or institution. **chaplaincy** *n.*, *pl.* **-cies.**

chaplet *n.* garland for the head.

chaps *pl. n.* cowboy's leggings of thick leather.

chapter *n.* **1.** division of a book. **2.** period in a life or history. **3.** branch of a society or club. **4.** group of canons of a cathedral.

char[1] *Informal* —*n.* **1.** charwoman. —*v.* **charring, charred. 2.** work as a charwoman.

char[2] *v.* **charring, charred.** blacken by partial burning.

char[3] *n. Slang* tea.

char[4]**, charr** *n.* small troutlike fish.

charabanc [shar-rab-bang] *n.* bus used for outings.

character *n.* **1.** combination of qualities distinguishing an individual. **2.** moral strength. **3.** reputation, esp. good reputation. **4.** person represented in a play, film, or story. **5.** notable or eccentric person. **6.** letter, numeral, or symbol used in writing or printing. **characteristic** *n.* **1.** distinguishing feature or quality. —*adj.* **2.** distinguishing. **characteristically** *adv.* **characterize** *v.* **1.** be a characteristic of. **2.** describe the character of. **characterization** *n.*

charade [shar-rahd] *n.* **1.** absurd pretence. —*pl.* **2.** game in which one team acts out a word, which the other team has to guess.

charcoal *n.* black substance formed by partially burning wood.

charge *v.* **1.** ask as a price. **2.** enter a debit against (a person or an account). **3.** accuse formally. **4.** assign a task to. **5.** make a rush or sudden attack (upon). **6.** fill (a battery) with electricity. **7.** fill or load. —*n.* **8.** price charged. **9.** formal accusation. **10.** attack or rush. **11.** command or exhortation. **12.** cartridge or shell. **13.** custody. **14.** person or thing entrusted to someone's care. **15.** amount of electricity stored in a battery. **in charge** in command. **chargeable** *adj.* **charger** *n.* **1.** device for charging an accumulator. **2.** horse used in battle.

chargé d'affaires [shar-zhay daf-fair] *n.*, *pl.* **chargés d'affaires.** head of a diplomatic mission in the absence of an ambassador or in a small mission.

chariot *n.* two-wheeled horse-drawn vehicle used in ancient times in wars and races. **charioteer** *n.* chariot driver.

charisma [kar-rizz-ma] *n.* **1.** person's power

to attract or influence people. **2.** *Christianity* divinely bestowed gift. **charismatic** [kar-rizz-mat-ik] *adj.*

charity *n.*, *pl.* **-ties. 1.** giving of help, such as money or food, to those in need. **2.** organization that does this. **3.** help given. **4.** disposition to think kindly of others. **5.** love of fellow human beings. **charitable** *adj.* **charitably** *adv.*

charlady *n.* same as CHARWOMAN.

charlatan [shar-lat-tan] *n.* person who claims expertise that he or she does not have.

charleston *n.* lively dance of the 1920s.

charlock *n.* weed with hairy leaves and yellow flowers.

charlotte *n.* dessert made with fruit and bread or cake crumbs.

charm *n.* **1.** attractiveness. **2.** trinket worn on a bracelet. **3.** small object with supposed magical powers. **4.** magic spell. —*v.* **5.** attract or delight. **6.** protect or influence as if by magic. **7.** influence by personal charm. **charmer** *n.* **charming** *adj.* attractive. **charmingly** *adv.*

charnel house *n.* building or vault for the bones of the dead.

chart *n.* **1.** information shown in the form of a diagram, graph, or table. **2.** map to aid navigation. —*v.* **3.** make a chart of. **4.** plot the course of. **the charts** *Informal* weekly list of best-selling pop records.

charter *n.* **1.** document granting or demanding certain rights. **2.** constitution of an organization. **3.** hire of transport for private use. —*v.* **4.** hire by charter. **5.** grant a charter to. **chartered** *adj.* officially qualified to practise a profession, e.g. *chartered accountant.*

chartreuse [shar-trerz] *n.* sweet-smelling green or yellow liqueur.

charwoman *n.* woman employed as a cleaner.

chary [chair-ee] *adj.* **-rier, -riest. 1.** cautious. **2.** sparing or mean. **charily** *adv.*

chase[1] *v.* **1.** run after quickly in order to catch or drive away. **2.** *Informal* hurry. **3.** *Informal* try energetically to obtain. —*n.* **4.** chasing or pursuit. **5.** unenclosed area of land used orig. for hunting. **chaser** *n.* drink drunk after another of a different kind.

chase[2] *v.* engrave or emboss (metal).

chasm [kaz-zum] *n.* **1.** deep crack or ravine in the earth. **2.** wide difference.

chassis [shass-ee] *n., pl.* **-sis.** frame, wheels, and mechanical parts of a motor vehicle.

chaste *adj.* **1.** refraining from sex outside marriage or altogether. **2.** (of style) simple. **chastely** *adv.* **chastity** *n.*

chasten [chase-en] *v.* **1.** correct by punishment. **2.** subdue.

chastise *v.* **1.** scold severely. **2.** punish severely, esp. by beating. **chastisement** *n.*

chasuble [chazz-yew-bl] *n.* long sleeveless outer vestment worn by a priest while celebrating Mass.

chat *v.* **chatting, chatted. 1.** talk in an easy familiar way. —*n.* **2.** easy familiar talk. **chatty** *adj.* **-tier, -tiest. chattily** *adv.*

chateau [shat-toe] *n., pl.* **-teaux, -teaus.** French castle or country house.

chatelaine [shat-tell-lane] *n.* (esp. formerly) mistress of a large house or castle.

chattels *pl. n.* movable possessions.

chatter *v.* **1.** talk about trivial matters rapidly and continuously. **2.** (of birds and monkeys) make rapid repetitive high-pitched noises. **3.** (of the teeth) rattle with cold or fear. —*n.* **4.** idle talk. **chatterbox** *n.* person who chatters incessantly.

chauffeur *n.* person employed to drive a car. **chauffeuse** *n. fem.*

chauvinism [show-vin-iz-zum] *n.* **1.** irrational belief that one's own race, group, or sex is superior. **2.** fanatical patriotism. **chauvinist** *n., adj.* **chauvinistic** *adj.*

cheap *adj.* **1.** low in price. **2.** of poor quality. **3.** of little value. **4.** mean, despicable. **cheaply** *adv.* **cheapen** *v.* make cheap or cheaper. **2.** degrade. **cheap-jack** *n. Informal* seller of cheap and shoddy goods. **cheapskate** *n. Informal* miserly person.

cheat *v.* **1.** act dishonestly to gain profit or advantage. **2.** deprive (someone) unfairly. —*n.* **3.** person who cheats. **4.** fraud or deception.

check *v.* **1.** examine or investigate. **2.** stop or hinder. **3.** *US* correspond. —*n.* **4.** examination or investigation. **5.** stoppage or restraint. **6.** *US* cheque. **7.** pattern of squares or crossing lines. **8.** *Chess* position of a king under attack. **checked** *adj.* having a pattern of small squares. **check in** *v.* register one's arrival. **checkmate** *n.* **1.** *Chess* winning position in which an opponent's king is under attack and unable to escape. **2.** utter defeat. —*v.* **3.** *Chess* place (an opponent's king) in checkmate. **4.** defeat. **check out** *v.* **1.** pay the bill and leave a hotel. **2.** examine or investigate. **3.** *Informal* have a look at. **checkout** *n.* counter in a supermarket, where customers pay. **checkup** *n.* general (medical) examination.

checkers *n. US* same as CHEQUERS.

Cheddar *n.* smooth firm cheese.

cheek *n.* **1.** side of the face below the eye. **2.** *Informal* impudence. —*v.* **3.** *Informal* speak impudently to. **cheeky** *adj.* **cheekier, cheekiest.** impudent. **cheekily** *adv.* **cheekiness** *n.*

cheep *n.* **1.** young bird's high-pitched cry. —*v.* **2.** utter a cheep.

cheer *v.* **1.** applaud or encourage with shouts. **2.** (often foll. by *up*) comfort or gladden. —*n.* **3.** shout of applause or encouragement. **4.** *Old-fashioned* state of mind. **cheerful** *adj.* **cheerfully** *adv.* **cheerfulness** *n.* **cheerless** *adj.* gloomy. **cheery** *adj.* **cheerier, cheeriest. cheerily** *adv.*

cheerio *interj. Informal* goodbye.

cheese *n.* **1.** food made from coagulated milk curd. **2.** shaped block of this. **cheesy** *adj.* **cheesier, cheesiest. cheeseburger** *n.* hamburger with cheese on it. **cheesecake** *n.* **1.** sweet tart with a cream cheese filling. **2.** *Slang* photographs of scantily clad women. **cheesecloth** *n.* loosely woven cotton cloth. **cheesed off** bored or annoyed. **cheeseparing** *adj.* mean.

cheetah *n.* swift spotted African animal of the cat family.

chef *n.* cook in a restaurant.

chef-d'oeuvre [shay-durv] *n., pl.* **chefs-d'oeuvre.** masterpiece.

chemical *n.* **1.** substance used in or resulting from a reaction involving changes to atoms or molecules. —*adj.* **2.** of chemistry or chemicals. **chemically** *adv.*

chemise [shem-meez] *n.* woman's loose-fitting slip or dress.

chemistry *n.* science of the composition, properties, and reactions of substances. **chemist** *n.* **1.** qualified dispenser of prescribed medicines. **2.** shop that sells medicines. **3.** specialist in chemistry.

chemotherapy *n.* treatment of disease by chemical means.

chenille [shen-**neel**] n. (fabric of) thick tufty yarn.

cheque n. written order to one's bank to pay money from one's account. **cheque book** book of detachable blank cheques issued by a bank. **cheque card** card issued by a bank guaranteeing payment of a customer's cheques.

chequer n. **1.** piece used in Chinese chequers. —pl. **2.** game of draughts. **chequered** adj. **1.** marked in squares. **2.** marked by varied fortunes, e.g. a chequered career.

cherish v. **1.** care for. **2.** hold dear. **3.** cling to (an idea or feeling).

cheroot [sher-**root**] n. cigar with both ends cut flat.

cherry n., pl. -ries. **1.** small red or black fruit with a stone. **2.** tree bearing this. —adj. **3.** deep red.

cherub n. **1.** angel, often represented as a winged child. **2.** sweet child. **cherubic** [cher-**rew**-bik] adj.

chervil n. herb with an aniseed flavour.

chess n. game of skill for two players with 16 pieces each on a chequered board (**chessboard**) of 64 squares. **chessman** n. piece used in chess.

chest n. **1.** front of the body, from the neck to the belly. **2.** large strong box. **chest of drawers** piece of furniture consisting of drawers in a frame.

chesterfield n. sofa with high padded sides and back.

chestnut n. **1.** reddish-brown edible nut. **2.** tree bearing this. **3.** horse of a reddish-brown colour. **4.** Informal old joke. —adj. **5.** reddish-brown.

chesty adj. **chestier, chestiest.** Informal suffering from a chest disease.

cheval glass [shev-**val**] n. full-length mirror mounted to swivel within a frame.

Cheviot n. **1.** large British sheep reared for its wool. **2.** (often c-) rough woollen fabric.

chevron [**shev**-ron] n. V-shaped pattern, esp. denoting rank.

chew v. grind (food etc.) between the teeth. **chewy** adj. **chewier, chewiest.** requiring chewing. **chewing gum** flavoured gum used for chewing. **chew over** v. consider carefully.

chi [kie] n. 22nd letter in the Greek alphabet.

chianti [kee-**ant**-ee] n. dry red Italian wine.

chiaroscuro [kee-ah-roh-**skew**-roh] n., pl. -ros. distribution of light and shade in a picture.

chic [sheek] adj. **1.** stylish or elegant. —n. **2.** stylishness.

chicane [shik-**kane**] n. obstacle in a motor-racing circuit.

chicanery n. **1.** clever but deceptive talk. **2.** trickery.

chick n. **1.** young bird. **2.** Slang young woman. **chickpea** n. edible pealike seed of an Asian plant. **chickweed** n. weed with small white flowers.

chicken n. **1.** domestic fowl. **2.** flesh of this used as food. **3.** Slang coward. —adj. **4.** cowardly. **chicken feed** Slang trifling amount of money. **chicken out** v. Informal fail to do something through cowardice. **chickenpox** n. infectious disease with an itchy rash.

chicle n. gumlike substance used to make chewing gum.

chicory n., pl. -ries. **1.** plant whose leaves are used in salads. **2.** root of this plant, used as a coffee substitute.

chide v. **chiding, chided** or **chid, chid** or **chidden.** rebuke.

chief n. **1.** head of a group of people. —adj. **2.** principal, foremost. **chiefly** adv. **1.** mainly. **2.** especially. **chieftain** n. leader of a tribe.

chiffchaff n. common European warbler.

chiffon [**shif**-fon] n. thin gauzy fabric.

chignon [**sheen**-yon] n. knot of hair worn at the back of the head.

chigoe [**chig**-go] n. tropical flea which burrows into the skin.

chihuahua [chee-**wah**-wah] n. tiny short-haired dog.

chilblain n. inflammation on the fingers or toes, caused by exposure to cold.

child n., pl. **children. 1.** young human being. **2.** son or daughter. **3.** product of an influence or environment, e.g. a child of nature. **childhood** n. **childish** adj. **1.** of or like a child. **2.** immature or silly. **childishly** adv. **childless** adj. **childlike** adj. simple or innocent. **childbirth** n. giving birth to a child. **child's play** very easy task.

▷ Note that childish has overtones of foolish while childlike suggests an innocent quality.

chill n. **1.** unpleasant coldness. **2.** feverish

cold. 3. depressing influence. *—adj.* **4.** cold. *—v.* **5.** make or become cold. **6.** cool (something). **7.** depress. **chilly** *adj.* **chillier, chilliest. 1.** cold. **2.** unfriendly. **chilliness** *n.*

chilli *n.* small hot-tasting red or green pepper used in cooking.

chime *n.* **1.** bell or set of bells. **2.** sound of this. *—v.* **3.** ring or be rung. **4.** produce (sounds) or indicate (the time) by chiming. **5.** be in agreement.

chimera [kime-**meer**-a] *n.* **1.** illusory hope. **2.** fabled monster with a lion's head, goat's body, and serpent's tail. **chimerical** *adj.*

chimney *n.* hollow vertical structure for carrying away smoke or steam. **chimney breast** walls surrounding the base of a chimney or fireplace. **chimneypot** *n.* short pipe on the top of a chimney. **chimney sweep** person who cleans soot from chimneys.

chimp *n.* *Informal* short for CHIMPANZEE.

chimpanzee *n.* intelligent ape of central W Africa.

chin *n.* part of the face below the mouth. **chinwag** *n.* *Informal* chat.

china *n.* **1.** fine earthenware or porcelain. **2.** cups, saucers, etc. **china clay** same as KAOLIN.

chinchilla *n.* **1.** S American rodent with soft grey fur. **2.** its fur.

chine *n.* **1.** cut of meat including part of the backbone. **2.** ridge of land. *—v.* **3.** cut (meat) along the backbone.

Chinese *adj.* **1.** of China or its people. *—n.* **2.** *pl.* **-ese.** person from China. **3.** any of the languages of China. **Chinese chequers** game played with marbles or pegs on a star-shaped board. **Chinese lantern** collapsible lantern made of thin paper.

chink[1] *n.* cleft or crack.

chink[2] *n.* **1.** light ringing sound. *—v.* **2.** make this sound.

chintz *n.* printed cotton fabric with a glazed finish.

chip *n.* **1.** strip of potato, fried. **2.** tiny wafer of a semiconductor forming an integrated circuit. **3.** small piece broken off. **4.** mark left where a small piece has broken off. **5.** counter used to represent money in gambling. *—v.* **chipping, chipped. 6.** break small pieces from. **have a chip on one's shoulder** *Informal* bear a grudge. **chip in** *v.*

1. *Informal* contribute (money). **2.** interrupt with a remark.

chipboard *n.* thin board made of compressed wood particles.

chipmunk *n.* small striped N American squirrel.

chipolata *n.* small sausage.

chiropodist [kir-**rop**-pod-ist] *n.* person who treats minor foot complaints. **chiropody** *n.*

chiropractic [kire-oh-**prak**-tik] *n.* system of treating bodily disorders by manipulation of the spine. **chiropractor** *n.*

chirp, chirrup *v.* **1.** (of a bird or insect) make a short high-pitched sound. **2.** speak in a lively fashion. *—n.* **3.** this sound. **chirpy** *adj.* **chirpier, chirpiest.** *Informal* cheerful and lively.

chisel *n.* **1.** metal tool with a sharp end for shaping wood or stone. *—v.* **-elling, -elled. 2.** carve or form with a chisel. **3.** *Slang* cheat.

chit[1] *n.* note or memorandum.

chit[2] *n.* pert young girl.

chitchat *n.* chat or gossip.

chitterlings *pl. n.* pig's intestines cooked as food.

chivalry *n.* **1.** courteous and considerate behaviour, esp. towards women. **2.** medieval system and principles of knighthood. **chivalrous** *adj.*

chive *n.* herb with a mild onion flavour.

chivvy *v.* **-vying, -vied.** *Informal* urge to do something.

chlorine *n.* yellowish-green pungent gaseous element. **chlorinate** *v.* disinfect or purify (esp. water) with chlorine. **chlorination** *n.* **chloride** *n.* compound of chlorine.

chlorofluorocarbon *n.* any of various gaseous compounds of chlorine, fluorine, and carbon, used in refrigerators and aerosol propellants, some of which cause a breakdown of ozone in the earth's atmosphere.

chloroform *n.* **1.** strong-smelling liquid formerly used as an anaesthetic. *—v.* **2.** make unconscious with chloroform.

chlorophyll *n.* green colouring matter in plants, which helps them convert sunlight into energy.

chock *n.* **1.** block or wedge used to prevent a heavy object from moving. *—v.* **2.** secure by a chock. **chock-full, chock-a-block** *adj.* completely full.

chocolate n. 1. food made from cacao seeds. 2. sweet or drink made from this. —adj. 3. dark brown.

choice n. 1. choosing. 2. opportunity or power of choosing. 3. thing or person chosen. 4. possibilities from which to choose. —adj. 5. of superior quality.

choir n. 1. organized group of singers, esp. in church. 2. part of a church occupied by the choir.

choke v. 1. hinder or stop the breathing of (a person) by squeezing or blocking the windpipe. 2. have trouble in breathing. 3. block or clog up. —n. 4. device controlling the amount of air that is mixed with the fuel in a petrol engine. **choker** n. tight-fitting necklace. **choke back** v. suppress (anger, tears, etc.).

choler [kol-ler] n. anger or bad temper. **choleric** adj.

cholera [kol-ler-a] n. dangerous infectious disease characterized by vomiting and diarrhoea.

cholesterol [kol-lest-er-oll] n. fatty substance found in animal tissue.

chomp v. chew noisily.

choose v. choosing, chose, chosen. 1. select from a number of alternatives. 2. decide (to do something). 3. like or please. **choosy** adj. choosier, choosiest. Informal fussy, hard to please.

chop[1] v. chopping, chopped. 1. cut with a blow from an axe or knife. 2. cut into pieces. 3. hit (an opponent) with a sharp blow. —n. 4. sharp blow. 5. slice of meat, usu. with a rib. **chopper** n. 1. small axe. 2. cleaver. 3. Informal helicopter. **choppy** adj. -pier, -piest. (of the sea) fairly rough.

chop[2] v. chopping, chopped. **chop and change** change one's mind repeatedly.

chops pl. n. Informal jaws or cheeks.

chopsticks pl. n. pair of thin sticks used to eat with by the Chinese and Japanese.

chop suey n. Chinese dish of chopped meat and vegetables fried in soy sauce.

choral adj. of or for a choir.

chorale [kor-rahl] n. slow stately hymn tune.

chord n. 1. simultaneous sounding of three or more musical notes. 2. Maths straight line joining two points on a curve.

chore n. 1. routine task. 2. unpleasant task.

chorea [kor-ree-a] n. disorder of the nervous system characterized by uncontrollable brief jerky movements.

choreography n. composition of steps and movements for ballet and other dancing. **choreographer** n. **choreographic** adj.

chorister n. singer in a choir.

chortle v. 1. chuckle gleefully. —n. 2. gleeful chuckle.

chorus n., pl. -ruses. 1. large choir. 2. group of singers or dancers who perform together. 3. part of a song repeated after each verse. 4. something expressed by many people at once. —v. chorusing, chorused. 5. sing or say together. **in chorus** in unison.

chose v. past tense of CHOOSE. **chosen** v. past participle of CHOOSE.

chough [chuff] n. large black bird of the crow family.

choux pastry [shoo] n. very light pastry made with eggs.

chow[1] n. thick-coated dog with a curled tail, orig. from China.

chow[2] n. Informal food.

chowder n. thick soup containing clams or fish.

chow mein n. Chinese-American dish consisting of chopped meat or vegetables fried with noodles.

chrism n. consecrated oil used for sacramental anointing.

Christ n. Jesus, regarded by Christians as the Messiah.

christen v. 1. baptize. 2. give a name to. 3. use for the first time. **christening** n.

Christendom n. all Christian people or countries.

Christian n. 1. person who believes in and follows Christ. —adj. 2. relating to Christ or Christianity. 3. kind or good. **Christianity** n. religion based on the life and teachings of Christ. **Christian name** person's first name. **Christian Science** religious system which emphasizes spiritual healing.

Christmas n. 1. annual festival on Dec. 25 commemorating the birth of Christ. 2. period around this time. **Christmassy** adj. **Christmas box** tip given at Christmas. **Christmas Day** Dec. 25. **Christmas Eve** Dec. 24. **Christmas tree** evergreen tree or imitation of one, decorated as part of Christmas celebrations.

chromatic adj. 1. of colour or colours. 2. *Music* (of a scale) proceeding by semitones. **chromatically** adv.

chromatography n. separation and analysis of the components of a substance by slowly passing it through an adsorbing material.

chrome, chromium n. metallic element used in steel alloys and for electroplating.

chromosome n. microscopic gene-carrying body in the nucleus of a cell.

chronic adj. 1. lasting a long time. 2. habitual, e.g. *a chronic smoker.* 3. *Informal* very bad. **chronically** adv.

chronicle n. 1. record of events in chronological order. —v. 2. record in or as if in a chronicle. **chronicler** n.

chronology n., pl. **-gies.** list or arrangement of events in order of occurrence. **chronological** adj. **chronologically** adv.

chronometer n. timepiece designed to be accurate in all conditions.

chrysalis [kriss-a-liss] n. insect in the stage between larva and adult, when it is in a cocoon.

chrysanthemum n. garden plant with bright showy flowers.

chub n. freshwater fish of the carp family.

chubby adj. **-bier, -biest.** plump. **chubbiness** n.

chuck[1] v. 1. *Informal* throw. 2. *Informal* give up, reject. 3. touch (someone) affectionately under the chin.

chuck[2] n. 1. cut of beef from the neck to the shoulder. 2. device that holds a workpiece in a lathe or a tool in a drill.

chuckle v. 1. laugh softly. —n. 2. soft laugh.

chuff n. 1. puffing sound as of a steam engine. —v. 2. move while emitting such sounds.

chuffed adj. *Informal* pleased, delighted.

chug n. 1. short dull sound, as of an engine. —v. **chugging, chugged.** 2. operate or move with this sound.

chukker, chukka n. period of play in polo.

chum n. 1. *Informal* close friend. —v. **chumming, chummed.** 2. **chum up with** form a close friendship with. **chummy** adj. **-mier, -miest.**

chump n. 1. *Informal* stupid person. 2. thick piece of meat. 3. thick block of wood.

chunk n. 1. thick solid piece. 2. considerable amount. **chunky** adj. **chunkier, chunkiest.** 1. thick and short. 2. with thick pieces.

church n. 1. building for public Christian worship. 2. clergy. 3. (C-) Christians collectively. 4. particular Christian denomination. **churchgoer** n. person who attends church regularly. **churchwarden** n. 1. lay assistant of a parish priest. 2. long clay pipe. **churchyard** n. grounds round a church, used as a graveyard.

churlish adj. surly and rude.

churn n. 1. machine in which cream is shaken to make butter. 2. large container for milk. —v. 3. stir (cream) vigorously or make butter in a churn. 4. move about violently. **churn out** v. *Informal* produce (things) rapidly in large numbers.

chute [shoot] n. 1. steep channel down which things may be slid. 2. *Informal* short for PARACHUTE.

chutney n. pickle made from fruit, vinegar, and spices.

chyle n. milky fluid formed in the small intestine during digestion.

chyme n. thick fluid mass of partially digested food that leaves the stomach.

CIA *US* Central Intelligence Agency.

cicada [sik-kah-da] n. large insect that makes a high-pitched drone.

cicatrix [sik-a-trix] n., pl. **-trices.** scar.

CID Criminal Investigation Department.

cider n. alcoholic drink made from fermented apple juice.

cigar n. roll of cured tobacco leaves for smoking.

cigarette n. shredded tobacco in a thin paper cylinder for smoking.

cilium n., pl. **cilia.** 1. short thread projecting from a cell, whose rhythmic beating causes movement. 2. eyelash.

cinch [sinch] n. 1. *Informal* easy task. 2. certainty.

cinchona [sing-kone-a] n. 1. S American tree with medicinal bark. 2. (drug made from) the dried bark of this tree, which yields quinine.

cincture n. something that encircles, esp. a belt or girdle.

cinder n. piece of incombustible material left after burning coal.

Cinderella n. poor, neglected, or unsuccessful person or thing.

cine camera n. camera for taking moving pictures.

cinema n. 1. place for showing films. 2. films collectively. **cinematic** adj. **cinematograph** n. combined camera, printer, and projector. **cinematography** n. technique of making films. **cinematographer** n.

cineraria n. garden plant with daisy-like flowers.

cinerarium n., pl. **-raria**. place for keeping the ashes of the dead after cremation. **cinerary** adj.

cinnabar n. 1. heavy red mineral containing mercury. —adj. 2. bright red.

cinnamon n. 1. spice obtained from the bark of an Asian tree. —adj. 2. yellowish-brown.

cinquefoil n. plant with five-lobed leaves.

cipher [sife-er] n. 1. system of secret writing. 2. unimportant person. 3. Obs. numeral zero.

circa [sir-ka] prep. Latin about, approximately.

circle n. 1. perfectly round geometric figure, line, or shape. 2. group of people sharing an interest or activity. 3. Theatre section of seats above the main level of the auditorium. —v. 4. move in a circle. 5. surround.

circlet n. circular ornament worn on the head.

circular adj. 1. round. 2. moving in a circle. —n. 3. letter or notice for general distribution. **circularity** n.

circulate v. send, go, or move around. **circulation** n. 1. flow of blood around the body. 2. sending or moving around. 3. number of copies of a newspaper or magazine sold. **circulatory** adj.

circuit n. 1. complete round or course. 2. complete path through which an electric current can flow. 3. periodical journey around a district, as made by judges. 4. series of sports tournaments. 5. motor-racing track. **circuitous** [sir-kew-it-uss] adj. roundabout, indirect. **circuitry** [sir-kit-tree] n. electrical circuit(s).

circum- prefix around, on all sides, as in circumlocution.

circumcise v. 1. cut off the foreskin of. 2. incise or cut off the clitoris of. **circumcision** n.

circumference n. 1. boundary of a specified area or shape, esp. of a circle. 2. distance round this.

circumflex n. accent (ˆ) over a vowel to show that it is pronounced in a particular way.

circumlocution n. indirect expression. **circumlocutory** adj.

circumnavigate v. sail right round. **circumnavigation** n.

circumscribe v. 1. restrict. 2. draw a line round. **circumscription** n.

circumspect adj. cautious, prudent. **circumspectly** adv. **circumspection** n.

circumstance n. (usu. pl.) occurrence or condition that accompanies or influences a person or event. **pomp and circumstance** formal display or ceremony. **circumstantial** adj. 1. (of evidence) strongly suggesting something but not proving it. 2. detailed. **circumstantiate** v. prove by giving details.

circumvent v. 1. avoid or get round (a difficulty etc.). 2. outwit. **circumvention** n.

circus n., pl. **-cuses**. 1. (performance given by) a travelling company of acrobats, clowns, performing animals, etc. 2. open place in a town where several streets converge.

cirque n. steep-sided semicircular depression found in mountainous regions.

cirrhosis [sir-roh-siss] n. liver disease.

cirrus n., pl. **-ri**. high wispy cloud.

Cistercian n., adj. (monk or nun) of a strict Benedictine order.

cistern n. water tank.

citadel n. fortress in a city.

cite v. 1. quote. 2. bring forward as proof. 3. summon to appear before a court of law. **citation** n. 1. quoting. 2. commendation for bravery.

citizen n. 1. native or naturalized member of a state or nation. 2. inhabitant of a city or town. **citizenship** n. **Citizens' Band** range of radio frequencies for private communication by the public.

citric acid n. weak acid found in citrus fruits.

citron n. lemon-like fruit of a small Asian tree.

citrus fruit n. juicy, sharp-tasting fruit such as an orange, lemon, or lime.

city n., pl. **-ties. 1.** large or important town. **2.** town that has received this title from the Crown. **the City** area of London as a financial centre.

civet [siv-vit] n. **1.** spotted catlike African mammal. **2.** musky fluid from its glands used in perfume.

civic adj. of a city or citizens. **civics** n. study of the rights and responsibilities of citizenship.

civil adj. **1.** relating to the citizens of a state as opposed to the armed forces or the Church. **2.** polite. **civilly** adv. **civility** n. politeness. **civilian** n., adj. (person) not belonging to the armed forces. **civil law** law relating to private and civilian affairs. **civil service** service responsible for the administration of the government. **civil servant** member of the civil service. **civil war** war between people of the same country.

civilize v. **1.** bring out of barbarism into a state of civilization. **2.** refine. **civilization** n. **1.** high level of human cultural and social development. **2.** particular society which has reached this level.

civvies pl. n. Slang civilian clothes.

cl centilitre.

Cl Chem. chlorine.

clack n. **1.** sound made by two hard objects striking together. —v. **2.** (cause to) make this sound.

clad v. a past of CLOTHE.

cladding n. material used for the outside facing of a building etc.

claim v. **1.** demand as a right. **2.** assert. **3.** call for or demand. —n. **4.** demand for something as due. **5.** assertion. **6.** right. **7.** thing claimed. **claimant** n.

clairvoyance n. power of perceiving things beyond the natural range of the senses. **clairvoyant** n., adj.

clam n. **1.** edible shellfish with a hinged shell. —v. **clamming, clammed. 2. clam up** Informal refuse to talk.

clamber v. climb awkwardly or with difficulty.

clammy adj. **-mier, -miest.** unpleasantly moist and sticky. **clamminess** n.

clamour n. **1.** loud protest. **2.** loud persistent outcry or noise. —v. **3.** make a loud outcry or noise. **clamorous** adj. **clamour for** v. demand noisily.

clamp[1] n. **1.** tool with movable jaws for holding things together tightly. —v. **2.** fasten with a clamp. **clamp down on** v. **1.** become stricter about. **2.** suppress.

clamp[2] n. mound of a harvested root crop, covered with straw and earth.

clan n. **1.** group of families with a common ancestor. **2.** close group. **clannish** adj. (of a group) tending to exclude outsiders.

clandestine adj. secret, furtive.

clang n. **1.** loud ringing sound. —v. **2.** (cause to) make this sound. **clanger** n. Informal conspicuous mistake.

clangour n. loud continuous clanging sound. **clangorous** adj.

clank n. **1.** harsh metallic sound. —v. **2.** (cause to) make this sound.

clap[1] v. **clapping, clapped. 1.** applaud by striking the palms of one's hands together. **2.** put quickly or forcibly. **3.** strike (a person) lightly with an open hand as in greeting. —n. **4.** act or sound of clapping. **5.** sharp abrupt sound, esp. of thunder. **clapped out** Slang worn out.

clap[2] n. Slang gonorrhoea.

clapper n. piece of metal inside a bell, which causes it to sound when struck against the side. **clapperboard** n. pair of hinged boards clapped together during filming to aid synchronizing sound and picture.

claptrap n. empty words.

claque n. group of people hired to applaud.

claret [klar-rit] n. dry red wine from Bordeaux.

clarify v. **-fying, -fied. 1.** make or become clear. **2.** make or become free of impurities, esp. by heating. **clarification** n.

clarinet n. keyed woodwind instrument with a single reed. **clarinettist** n.

clarion n. **1.** obsolete high-pitched trumpet. **2.** its sound. **clarion call** rousing appeal.

clarity n. clearness.

clash v. **1.** come into conflict. **2.** (of events) coincide. **3.** (of colours) look unattractive together. **4.** (cause to) make a clashing sound. —n. **5.** conflict. **6.** loud harsh noise, esp. of things striking together.

clasp n. **1.** device for fastening things. **2.** firm grasp or embrace. —v. **3.** grasp or embrace firmly. **4.** fasten with a clasp.

clasp knife knife whose blade folds into the handle.

class n. 1. group of people or things sharing a common characteristic. 2. social group of a particular rank. 3. system of dividing society into such groups. 4. group of pupils or students taught together. 5. standard of quality. 6. Informal excellence or elegance. —v. 7. place in a class.

classic adj. 1. of the highest class, esp. in art or literature. 2. typical. 3. characterized by simplicity and purity of form. —n. 4. author, artist, or work of art of recognized excellence. —pl. 5. study of ancient Greek and Roman literature and culture. **classical** adj. 1. traditional and standard. 2. Music denoting serious art music. 3. of or influenced by ancient Greek and Roman culture. **classically** adv. **classicism** n. artistic style showing regularity of form and emotional restraint. **classicist** n.

▷ Classic and classical are synonyms except in the context of Greek and Roman culture, which is called classical, or highly rated art and literature, which is called classic.

classify v. -fying, -fied. 1. arrange in classes. 2. designate (information) as officially secret. **classifiable** adj. **classification** n.

classy adj. **classier, classiest.** Informal stylish, elegant.

clatter n. 1. rattling noise. —v. 2. (cause to) make a rattling noise.

clause n. 1. part of a sentence, containing a verb. 2. section in a legal document.

claustrophobia n. abnormal fear of confined spaces. **claustrophobic** adj.

clavichord n. early keyboard instrument.

clavicle n. collarbone.

claw n. 1. sharp hooked nail of a bird or beast. 2. similar part, such as a crab's pincer. —v. 3. tear with claws or nails.

clay n. fine-grained earth, soft when moist and hardening when baked, used to make bricks and pottery. **clayey** adj. **clay pigeon** baked clay disc hurled into the air as a target for shooting.

claymore n. two-edged broadsword formerly used by Scottish Highlanders.

clean adj. 1. free from dirt or impurities. 2. not yet used. 3. morally sound. 4. smooth and regular. 5. without obscenity. 6. complete, e.g. a clean break. —adv. 7. in a clean way. —v. 8. free from dirt. **come clean** Informal confess. **cleaner** n. **cleanly** adv. **cleanliness** n. **clean-cut** adj. 1. clearly outlined. 2. wholesome in appearance.

cleanse v. make clean. **cleanser** n.

clear adj. 1. transparent. 2. free from darkness or obscurity, bright. 3. (of weather) free from clouds. 4. plain, distinct. 5. free from doubt or confusion. 6. without blemish or defect. 7. free from obstruction. 8. (of money) net. —adv. 9. clearly. 10. completely. 11. out of the way, e.g. stand clear of the gates. —v. 12. make or become clear. 13. acquit. 14. pass by or over without touching. 15. make as profit. **clearly** adv. **clearness** n. **clearance** n. 1. clearing. 2. official permission. 3. space between two parts in motion. **clear-cut** adj. definite, not vague. **clearing** n. area cleared of trees. **clear off** v. Informal go away. **clear out** v. 1. empty. 2. Informal go away. **clear-sighted** adj. perceptive. **clearway** n. stretch of road on which motorists may stop only in an emergency.

cleat n. 1. wedge. 2. piece of wood or iron with two projecting ends round which ropes are fastened.

cleave[1] v. **cleaving; cleft, cleaved,** or **clove; cleft, cleaved,** or **cloven.** split apart. **cleavage** n. 1. space between a woman's breasts, as revealed by a low-cut dress. 2. division, split. **cleaver** n. heavy butcher's knife.

cleave[2] v. cling or adhere.

clef n. Music symbol at the beginning of a stave to show the pitch.

cleft n. 1. split or indentation. —v. 2. a past of CLEAVE[1]. **in a cleft stick** in a very difficult position.

clematis n. climbing plant with showy flowers.

clement adj. 1. (of weather) mild. 2. merciful. **clemency** n. mercy.

clementine n. small orange citrus fruit.

clench v. 1. close or squeeze (one's teeth or fist) firmly together. 2. grasp firmly.

clerestory [clear-store-ee] n., pl. -ries. row of windows at the top of a wall above an adjoining roof.

clergy n. priests and ministers as a group. **clergyman** n.

cleric n. member of the clergy.

clerical *adj.* **1.** of clerks or office work. **2.** of the clergy.

clerk *n.* employee in an office, bank, or court who keeps records, files, and accounts.

clever *adj.* **1.** intelligent, quick at learning. **2.** showing skill. **cleverly** *adv.* **cleverness** *n.*

cliché [klee-shay] *n.* hackneyed expression or idea. **clichéd** *adj.*

click *n.* **1.** short slight sound. —*v.* **2.** (cause to) make this sound. **3.** *Slang* be a success. **4.** *Informal* become suddenly clear. **5.** *Informal* (of two people) get on well.

client *n.* **1.** person who uses the services of a professional. **2.** customer. **clientele** [klee-on-**tell**] *n.* clients collectively.

cliff *n.* steep rock face, esp. along the sea shore. **cliffhanger** *n.* film, game, etc. which is exciting and full of suspense because its outcome is uncertain.

climacteric *n.* **1.** same as MENOPAUSE. **2.** period in the life of a man corresponding to the menopause, characterized by a diminished sex drive.

climate *n.* **1.** prevalent weather conditions of an area. **2.** prevailing trend. **climatic** *adj.* **climatically** *adv.*

climax *n.* **1.** most intense point of an experience, series of events, or story. **2.** orgasm. —*v.* **3.** reach a climax. **climactic** *adj.*

climb *v.* **1.** go up or ascend. **2.** rise. **3.** (of plants) grow upwards by twining. —*n.* **4.** climbing. **5.** place to be climbed. **climber** *n.* **climb down** *v.* retreat from an opinion or position.

clime *n. Lit.* region or its climate.

clinch *v.* **1.** settle (an argument or agreement) decisively. **2.** secure (a nail) by bending the point over. **3.** engage in a clinch. —*n.* **4.** clinching. **5.** *Boxing, wrestling* movement in which a competitor holds on to the other to avoid punches. **clincher** *n. Informal* something decisive.

cling *v.* **clinging, clung.** hold fast or stick closely. **clingfilm** *n.* thin polythene wrapping.

clinic *n.* **1.** place in which outpatients receive medical advice or treatment. **2.** private or specialized hospital. **clinical** *adj.* **1.** of a clinic. **2.** scientifically detached. **clinically** *adv.*

clink[1] *n.* **1.** light sharp metallic sound. —*v.* **2.** (cause to) make such a sound.

clink[2] *n. Slang* prison.

clinker *n.* fused coal residues from a fire or furnace.

clinker-built *adj.* (of a boat) made of overlapping planks.

clip[1] *v.* **clipping, clipped. 1.** cut with shears or scissors. **2.** shorten (a word). **3.** *Informal* hit sharply. —*n.* **4.** short extract of a film. **5.** *Informal* sharp blow. **clippers** *pl. n.* tool for clipping. **clipping** *n.* something cut out, esp. an article from a newspaper.

clip[2] *n.* **1.** device for attaching or holding things together. —*v.* **clipping, clipped. 2.** attach or hold together with a clip.

clipper *n.* fast commercial sailing ship.

clique [kleek] *n.* small exclusive group. **cliquey, cliquish** *adj.*

clitoris [**klit**-or-iss] *n.* small sexually sensitive part of the female genitals. **clitoral** *adj.*

cloak *n.* **1.** loose sleeveless outer garment. **2.** something that covers or conceals. —*v.* **3.** cover or conceal with or as if with a cloak. **cloakroom** *n.* room where coats may be left temporarily.

clobber *Informal* —*v.* **1.** batter. **2.** defeat utterly. —*n.* **3.** belongings.

cloche [klosh] *n.* **1.** cover to protect young plants. **2.** woman's close-fitting hat.

clock *n.* **1.** instrument for showing the time. **2.** device with a dial for recording or measuring. —*v.* **3.** record (time) with a stopwatch. **clockwise** *adv., adj.* in the direction in which the hands of a clock rotate. **clock in** *or* **on, out** *or* **off** *v.* register arrival at or departure from work on an automatic time recorder. **clock up** *v.* reach (a total). **clockwork** *n.* mechanism similar to that of a clock, as in a wind-up toy. **like clockwork** with complete regularity and precision.

clod *n.* **1.** lump of earth. **2.** stupid person. **cloddish** *adj.* **clodhopper** *n. Informal* clumsy person.

clog *v.* **clogging, clogged. 1.** block. **2.** hinder. —*n.* **3.** wooden-soled shoe.

cloisonné [klwah-**zon**-nay] *n.* design made by filling in a wire outline with coloured enamel.

cloister *n.* **1.** covered pillared arcade, usu. in a monastery. **2.** place of religious seclusion. **cloistered** *adj.* sheltered.

clone *n.* **1.** group of organisms or cells reproduced asexually from a single plant or animal. **2.** *Informal* person who closely

resembles another. —v. **3.** produce as a clone.

close¹ adj. **1.** near. **2.** intimate. **3.** careful, thorough. **4.** oppressive or stifling. **5.** secretive. **6.** compact, dense. —adv. **7.** closely or tightly. —n. **8.** street closed at one end. **9.** courtyard or quadrangle. **closely** adv. **closeness** n. **close season** period when it is illegal to kill certain kinds of game and fish. **close shave** Informal narrow escape. **close-up** n. photograph or film taken at very close range.

close² v. **1.** shut. **2.** prevent access to. **3.** finish. **4.** bring or come nearer together. —n. **5.** end. **closed-circuit television** television system used within a limited area such as a building. **closed shop** place of work in which all workers must belong to a particular trade union.

closet n. **1.** US cupboard. **2.** small private room. —adj. **3.** private or secret. —v. **closeting, closeted. 4.** shut away in private, esp. for conference.

closure n. **1.** closing or being closed. **2.** ending of a debate by immediate vote.

clot n. **1.** soft thick lump formed from liquid. **2.** Informal fool. —v. **clotting, clotted. 3.** form clots.

cloth n. **1.** (piece of) woven fabric. **2.** (usu. preceded by the) the clergy.

clothe v. **clothing, clothed** or **clad. 1.** put clothes on. **2.** provide with clothes. **clothes** pl. n. **1.** articles of dress. **2.** bed coverings. **clothier** n. maker or seller of clothes or cloth. **clothing** n. clothes collectively.

cloud n. **1.** mass of condensed water vapour floating in the sky. **2.** floating mass of smoke, dust, etc. **3.** large number of insects etc. in flight. **4.** something that threatens or carries gloom. —v. **5.** make or become cloudy. **6.** confuse. **7.** make gloomy or depressed. **cloudless** adj. **cloudy** adj. **1.** full of clouds. **2.** (of liquid) opaque. **cloudburst** n. heavy fall of rain.

clout Informal —n. **1.** blow. **2.** influence, power. —v. **3.** hit.

clove¹ n. **1.** dried flower bud of a tropical tree, used as a spice. **2.** segment of a bulb of garlic.

clove² v. a past tense of CLEAVE¹. **clove hitch** knot used to fasten a rope to a spar.

cloven v. a past participle of CLEAVE¹. **cloven hoof** divided hoof of a sheep, goat, etc.

clover n. plant with three-lobed leaves. **in clover** in luxury.

clown n. **1.** comic entertainer in a circus. **2.** amusing person. **3.** stupid person. —v. **4.** perform as a clown. **5.** behave foolishly. **clownish** adj.

cloy v. sicken by an excess of something sweet or pleasurable. **cloying** adj.

club n. **1.** association of people with common interests. **2.** building used by such a group. **3.** thick stick used as a weapon. **4.** bat or stick used in some games. **5.** playing card of the suit marked with black three-leafed symbols. —v. **clubbing, clubbed. 6.** strike with a club. **club together** v. combine resources for a common purpose.

club foot n. congenitally deformed foot.

cluck n. **1.** low clicking noise made by a hen. —v. **2.** make this noise.

clue n. **1.** something that helps to solve a mystery or puzzle. —v. **cluing, clued. 2.** (usu. foll. by in or up) provide with helpful information. **not have a clue** be completely baffled. **clueless** adj. stupid.

clump¹ n. **1.** cluster or mass. —v. **2.** form into a clump.

clump² v. **1.** walk or tread heavily. —n. **2.** dull heavy tread.

clumsy adj. **-sier, -siest. 1.** lacking skill or physical coordination. **2.** badly made or done. **clumsily** adv. **clumsiness** n.

clung v. past of CLING.

clunk n. **1.** dull metallic sound. —v. **2.** make such a sound.

cluster n. **1.** small close group. —v. **2.** (cause to) form a cluster.

clutch¹ v. **1.** grasp tightly. **2.** try to seize. —n. **3.** tight grasp. **4.** device enabling two revolving shafts to be connected and disconnected.

clutch² n. **1.** set of eggs laid at the same time. **2.** brood of chickens.

clutter v. **1.** strew objects about (a place) in disorder. —n. **2.** disordered heap or mass of objects.

Clydesdale n. heavy powerful carthorse, orig. from Scotland.

cm centimetre.

Cm Chem. curium.

CND Campaign for Nuclear Disarmament.

Co Chem. cobalt.

CO 1. Colorado. **2.** Commanding Officer.

Co. 1. Company. **2.** County.

co- *prefix* **1.** together. **2.** joint or jointly, e.g. *coproduction*.

c/o 1. care of. **2.** *Book-keeping* carried over.

coach *n.* **1.** long-distance bus. **2.** railway carriage. **3.** large four-wheeled horse-drawn carriage. **4.** tutor, trainer. —*v.* **5.** train or teach. **coachman** *n.* driver of a horse-drawn coach or carriage.

coagulate [koh-**ag**-yew-late] *v.* change from a liquid to a semisolid mass. **coagulation** *n.* **coagulant** *n.* substance causing coagulation.

coal *n.* black rock consisting mainly of carbon, used as fuel. **coalface** *n.* exposed seam of coal. **coalfield** *n.* area rich in coal. **coal gas** mixture of gases produced from coal, used for heating and lighting. **coal tar** black tar made from coal, used for making drugs and chemical products.

coalesce [koh-a-**less**] *v.* come together, merge. **coalescence** *n.*

coalition [koh-a-**lish**-un] *n.* temporary alliance, esp. between political parties.

coaming *n.* raised frame round a ship's hatchway for keeping out water.

coarse *adj.* **1.** rough in texture. **2.** unrefined or indecent. **3.** of inferior quality. **coarse fish** any freshwater fish not of the salmon family. **coarsely** *adv.* **coarseness** *n.* **coarsen** *v.*

coast *n.* **1.** sea shore. —*v.* **2.** move by momentum, without the use of power. **3.** proceed without great effort. **coastal** *adj.* **coaster** *n.* **1.** small ship. **2.** small mat placed under a glass. **coastguard** *n.* **1.** organization which aids shipping and prevents smuggling. **2.** member of this. **coastline** *n.* outline of a coast.

coat *n.* **1.** long outer garment with sleeves. **2.** animal's fur or hair. **3.** covering layer. —*v.* **4.** cover with a layer. **coating** *n.* covering layer. **coat of arms** heraldic emblem of a family or institution.

coax *v.* **1.** persuade gently. **2.** manipulate carefully and patiently.

coaxial [koh-**ax**-ee-al] *adj.* (of a cable) transmitting by means of two concentric conductors separated by an insulator.

cob *n.* **1.** thickset type of horse. **2.** male swan. **3.** stalk of an ear of maize. **4.** round loaf of bread.

cobalt *n.* **1.** metallic element. **2.** deep blue pigment made from it.

cobble *v.* **1.** make or mend (shoes). **2.** put together roughly. —*n.* (also **cobblestone**) **3.** round stone used for paving. **cobbler** *n.* shoe mender.

cobblers *pl. n. Taboo slang* nonsense.

COBOL high-level computer programming language for general commercial use.

cobra *n.* venomous hooded snake of Asia and Africa.

cobweb *n.* spider's web.

coca *n.* dried leaves of a S American shrub which contain cocaine.

Coca-Cola *n.* ® carbonated soft drink.

cocaine *n.* addictive drug used as a narcotic and local anaesthetic.

coccus *n., pl.* **cocci.** spherical bacterium.

coccyx [**kok**-six] *n., pl.* **coccyges** [kok-**sije**-eez] bone at the base of the spinal column.

cochineal *n.* scarlet dye obtained from a Mexican insect.

cochlea [**kok**-lee-a] *n., pl.* **-leae** [-li-ee] spiral tube in the internal ear, which converts sound vibrations into nerve impulses.

cock *n.* **1.** male bird, esp. of domestic fowl. **2.** stopcock. **3.** *Taboo slang* penis. **4.** hammer of a gun. —*v.* **5.** draw back (the hammer of a gun) to firing position. **6.** lift and turn (part of the body). **cockerel** *n.* young cock. **cock-a-hoop** *adj.* in high spirits. **cock-and-bull story** improbable story.

cockade *n.* rosette or feather worn on a hat as a badge.

cockatoo *n.* crested parrot of Australia or the East Indies.

cockatrice [**kok**-a-triss] *n.* mythical animal like a small dragon.

cockchafer *n.* large flying beetle.

cocker spaniel *n.* small breed of spaniel.

cockeyed *adj.* **1.** *Informal* askew. **2.** absurd.

cockle *n.* edible bivalve mollusc. **cockle-shell** *n.* **1.** shell of the cockle. **2.** small light boat.

Cockney *n.* **1.** native of the East End of London. **2.** Cockney dialect.

cockpit *n.* **1.** pilot's compartment in an aircraft. **2.** driver's compartment in a racing car. **3.** site of many battles or conflicts.

cockroach n. beetle-like insect which is a household pest.

cockscomb n. **1.** comb of a domestic cock. **2.** Informal conceited dandy.

cocksure adj. overconfident, arrogant.

cocktail n. **1.** mixed alcoholic drink. **2.** appetizer of seafood or mixed fruits.

cocky adj. **cockier, cockiest.** conceited and overconfident. **cockily** adv. **cockiness** n.

coco n. coconut palm.

cocoa n. **1.** powder made from the seed of the cacao tree. **2.** drink made from this powder.

coconut n. **1.** large hard fruit of a type of palm tree. **2.** edible flesh of this fruit. **coconut matting** coarse matting made from the fibrous husk of the coconut.

cocoon n. **1.** silky sheath of a chrysalis. **2.** protective covering. — v. **3.** wrap or protect as if in a cocoon.

cocotte n. small fireproof dish in which individual portions of food are cooked and served.

cod n. large food fish of the North Atlantic. **cod-liver oil** oil extracted from fish, rich in vitamins A and D.

COD cash on delivery.

coda [kode-a] n. final part of a musical composition.

coddle v. **1.** overprotect or pamper. **2.** cook (eggs) in water just below boiling point.

code n. **1.** system of letters, symbols, or prearranged signals by which messages can be communicated secretly or briefly. **2.** set of principles or rules. — v. **3.** put into code. **codify** [kode-if-fie] v. **-fying, -fied.** organize (rules or procedures) systematically. **codification** n.

codeine [kode-een] n. drug used as a painkiller.

codex n., pl. **codices.** volume of manuscripts of an ancient text.

codger n. Informal old man.

codicil [kode-iss-ill] n. addition to a will.

codpiece n. Hist. bag covering the male genitals, attached to breeches.

codswallop n. Slang nonsense.

coeducation n. education of boys and girls together. **coeducational** adj.

coefficient n. **1.** Maths number or constant placed before and multiplying a quantity. **2.** Physics number or constant used to calculate the behaviour of a substance under specified conditions.

coelacanth [seel-a-kanth] n. primitive marine fish.

coeliac disease [seel-ee-ak] n. disease which hampers digestion of food.

coenobite [seen-oh-bite] n. member of a religious order in a monastic community.

coequal adj., n. equal.

coerce [koh-urss] v. compel or force. **coercion** n. **coercive** adj.

coeval [koh-eev-al] adj., n. contemporary.

coexist v. exist together, esp. peacefully despite differences. **coexistence** n.

coextend v. (cause to) extend equally in space or time. **coextension** n. **coextensive** adj.

C of E Church of England.

coffee n. **1.** drink made from the roasted and ground seeds of a tropical shrub. **2.** beanlike seeds of this shrub. —adj. **3.** light brown. **coffee bar** café, snack bar. **coffee table** small low table. **coffee-table book** large expensive illustrated book.

coffer n. **1.** chest for valuables. —pl. **2.** store of money.

cofferdam n. watertight enclosure pumped dry to enable construction work to be done.

coffin n. box in which a corpse is buried or cremated.

cog n. **1.** one of a series of teeth on the rim of a gearwheel. **2.** unimportant person in a big organization.

cogent [koh-jent] adj. forcefully convincing. **cogency** n. **cogently** adv.

cogitate [koj-it-tate] v. think deeply, ponder. **cogitation** n.

cognac [kon-yak] n. French brandy.

cognate adj. **1.** related, akin. —n. **2.** word descended from a common language.

cognition n. act or experience of knowing or acquiring knowledge. **cognitive** adj.

cognizance n. knowledge, perception. **cognizant** adj.

cognomen [kog-noh-men] n., pl. **-nomens, -nomina** [-nom-min-a] **1.** nickname. **2.** surname.

cognoscenti [kon-yo-**shen**-tee] pl. n. connoisseurs.

cohabit v. live together as husband and wife without being married. **cohabitation** n.

cohere v. **1.** stick together. **2.** be logically connected and consistent. **coherence** n. **coherent** adj. **1.** capable of intelligible speech. **2.** logical and consistent. **3.** sticking together. **coherently** adv. **cohesion** n. tendency to unite. **cohesive** adj.

cohort n. **1.** band of associates. **2.** tenth part of a Roman legion.

coif n. close-fitting cap worn in the Middle Ages.

coiffure n. hairstyle. **coiffeur, coiffeuse** n. hairdresser.

coil v. **1.** wind or be wound in loops. **2.** move in a winding course. —n. **3.** something coiled. **4.** single loop of this. **5.** contraceptive device inserted in the womb. **6.** electrical conductor wound into a spiral.

coin n. **1.** piece of metal money. **2.** metal currency collectively. —v. **3.** make or stamp (coins). **4.** invent (a word or phrase). **coin it in** Informal make money rapidly. **coinage** n. **1.** coining. **2.** coins collectively. **3.** word or phrase coined.

coincide v. **1.** happen at the same time. **2.** agree or correspond exactly. **coincidence** n. **1.** occurrence of simultaneous or apparently connected events. **2.** coinciding. **coincident** adj. **coincidental** adj. **coincidentally** adv.

coir n. coconut husk fibre.

coition [koh-**ish**-un], **coitus** [koh-it-uss] n. sexual intercourse. **coital** adj.

coke¹ n. solid fuel left after gas has been distilled from coal.

coke² n. Slang cocaine.

Coke n. ® short for COCA-COLA.

col n. high mountain pass.

Col. Colonel.

cola n. soft drink flavoured with an extract from the nuts of a tropical tree.

colander n. perforated bowl for straining or rinsing foods.

cold adj. **1.** lacking heat. **2.** lacking affection or enthusiasm. **3.** (of a colour) giving an impression of coldness. **4.** (of a scent in hunting) faint. **5.** Slang unconscious, e.g. out cold. —n. **6.** lack of heat. **7.** illness characterized by catarrh and sneezing. **coldly** adv. **coldness** n. **cold-blooded** adj. **1.** having a body temperature that varies with that of the surroundings. **2.** callous or cruel. **cold cream** creamy preparation for softening and cleansing the skin. **cold feet** Slang fear. **cold-shoulder** v. treat (someone) with indifference. **cold sore** cluster of blisters near the lips, caused by a virus. **cold war** political hostility between countries without actual warfare.

coleslaw n. salad dish of shredded raw cabbage in a dressing.

coley n. codlike food fish of the N Atlantic.

colic n. severe pains in the stomach and bowels. **colicky** adj.

colitis [kol-**lie**-tiss] n. inflammation of the colon.

collaborate v. **1.** work with another on a project. **2.** cooperate with an enemy invader. **collaboration** n. **collaborative** adj. **collaborator** n.

collage [kol-**lahzh**] n. **1.** art form in which various materials or objects are glued onto a surface. **2.** picture made in this way.

collapse v. **1.** fall down or in suddenly. **2.** fail completely. **3.** fold compactly. —n. **4.** act of collapsing. **5.** sudden failure or breakdown. **collapsible** adj.

collar n. **1.** part of a garment round the neck. **2.** band put round an animal's neck. **3.** cut of meat from an animal's neck. **4.** band round a pipe, rod, or shaft. —v. **5.** Informal seize, arrest. **6.** catch in order to speak to. **7.** take for oneself. **collarbone** n. bone joining the shoulder blade to the breast bone.

collate v. **1.** compare carefully. **2.** gather together and put in order. **collation** n. **1.** collating. **2.** light meal. **collator** n.

collateral n. **1.** security pledged for the repayment of a loan. —adj. **2.** descended from a common ancestor but through different lines. **3.** additional but subordinate.

colleague n. fellow worker, esp. in a profession.

collect¹ v. **1.** gather or be gathered together. **2.** accumulate (stamps etc.) as a hobby. **3.** fetch. **4.** receive payments of (taxes etc.). **5.** regain control of (one's emotions). **collected** adj. calm and controlled. **collection** n. **1.** collecting. **2.** things collected. **3.** sum of money collected. **collector** n.

collect² n. short prayer.

collective n. **1.** group of people working together on an enterprise and sharing the benefits from it. —adj. **2.** of or done by a group. **collective bargaining** negotiation between a trade union and an employer on the wages etc. of the employees. **collectively** adv. **collectivism** n. theory that the state should own all means of production. **collectivize** v. organize according to the theory of collectivism.

colleen n. Irish girl.

college n. 1. place of higher education. 2. group of people of the same profession or with special duties. 3. Brit. name given to some secondary schools. **collegian** n. member of a college. **collegiate** adj.

collide v. 1. crash together violently. 2. conflict. **collision** n.

collie n. silky-coated sheepdog.

colliery n., pl. **-lieries.** coal mine. **collier** n. 1. coal miner. 2. coal ship.

collocate v. (of words) occur together regularly. **collocation** n.

colloid n. suspension of particles in a solution. **colloidal** adj.

collop n. small slice of meat.

colloquial adj. suitable for informal speech or writing. **colloquialism** n. colloquial expression.

colloquium n., pl. **-quiums, -quia.** academic seminar.

colloquy n., pl. **-quies.** conversation or conference.

collusion n. secret agreement for a fraudulent purpose. **collude** v. act in collusion.

collywobbles pl. n. 1. Slang nervousness. 2. upset stomach.

cologne n. perfumed toilet water.

colon[1] n. punctuation mark (:).

colon[2] n. part of the large intestine connected to the rectum. **colonic** adj.

colonel n. senior commissioned army or air-force officer.

colonnade n. row of columns.

colony n., pl. **-nies.** 1. group of people who settle in a new country but remain subject to their parent state. 2. territory occupied by a colony. 3. group of people or animals of the same kind living together. **colonial** n., adj. (inhabitant) of a colony. **colonialism** n. policy of acquiring and maintaining colonies. **colonist** n. settler in a colony. **colonize** v. make into a colony. **colonization** n.

colophon n. publisher's emblem.

Colorado beetle n. black-and-yellow beetle that is a serious pest of potatoes.

coloration n. colouring.

coloratura n. Music 1. complicated vocal passage. 2. soprano who specializes in such music.

colossal adj. huge.

colossus n., pl. **-si, -suses.** 1. huge statue. 2. huge or important person or thing.

colostomy n., pl. **-mies.** operation to form an opening from the colon onto the surface of the body, for emptying the bowel.

colour n. 1. appearance of things as a result of reflecting light. 2. paint or pigment. 3. complexion. 4. vividness or authenticity. —pl. 5. flag. 6. Sport badge or symbol denoting membership of a team. —v. 7. apply or give colour to. 8. influence or distort. 9. blush. **Coloured** adj. 1. (c-) possessing colour. 2. non-White. 3. in S Africa, of mixed race. **colourful** adj. 1. with bright or varied colours. 2. vivid or distinctive. **colourfully** adv. **colouring** n. 1. application of colour. 2. something added to give colour. 3. complexion. **colourless** adj. **colour-blind** adj. unable to distinguish between certain colours.

colt n. young male horse.

coltsfoot n., pl. **-foots.** weed with yellow flowers and heart-shaped leaves.

columbine n. garden flower with five spurred petals.

column n. 1. pillar. 2. vertical arrangement of numbers. 3. long narrow formation of troops. 4. vertical division of a newspaper page. 5. regular feature in a newspaper. **columnist** n. journalist writing a regular feature for a newspaper.

com-, con- prefix together, jointly, e.g. commingle.

coma n. state of deep unconsciousness. **comatose** adj. 1. in a coma. 2. sound asleep.

comb n. 1. toothed implement for arranging the hair. 2. cock's crest. 3. honeycomb. 4. tool for cleaning wool or cotton. —v. 5. use a comb on. 6. search with great care.

combat v. **-bating, -bated,** n. fight, struggle. **combatant** n. 1. fighter. —adj. 2. fighting. **combative** adj.

combe n. same as COOMB.

combine v. 1. join together. 2. form a chemical compound. —n. 3. association of people or firms for a common purpose.

combination n. 1. combining. 2. people or things combined. 3. set of numbers that opens a special lock. —pl. 4. one-piece undergarment with long sleeves and legs. **combine harvester** machine which reaps and threshes grain in one operation.

combo n., pl. **-bos**. small group of jazz musicians.

combustion n. process of burning. **combustible** adj. burning easily.

come v. **coming, came, come**. 1. move towards a place, arrive. 2. occur. 3. be available. 4. reach a specified point or condition. 5. originate (from). 6. become. **come across** v. 1. meet or find by accident. 2. (foll. by as) give an impression (of being). **comeback** n. Informal 1. return to a former position. 2. retort. **come by** v. find or obtain. **comedown** n. 1. decline in status. 2. disappointment. **come into** v. 1. enter. 2. inherit. **come of** v. result from. **come to** v. 1. regain consciousness. 2. amount to (a total figure). **come up** v. be mentioned or arise. **come-uppance** n. Informal deserved punishment.

comedy n., pl. **-dies**. 1. humorous play, film, or programme. 2. humorous aspects of events. **comedian, comedienne** n. 1. entertainer who tells jokes. 2. person who performs in comedy.

comely adj. **-lier, -liest**. Old-fashioned good-looking.

comestibles pl. n. food.

comet n. heavenly body with a long luminous tail.

comfit n. sugar-coated sweet.

comfort n. 1. physical ease or wellbeing. 2. consolation. 3. means of consolation. —v. 4. give comfort to. **comfortable** adj. 1. giving comfort. 2. free from pain. 3. Informal well-off financially. **comfortably** adv. **comforter** n. 1. person or thing that comforts. 2. baby's dummy. 3. Brit. woollen scarf.

comfrey n. tall plant with bell-shaped flowers.

comfy adj. **-fier, -fiest**. Informal comfortable.

comic adj. 1. humorous, funny. 2. relating to comedy. —n. 3. comedian. 4. Brit. magazine consisting of strip cartoons. **comical** adj. amusing. **comically** adv.

comma n. punctuation mark (,).

command v. 1. order. 2. have authority over. 3. deserve and get. 4. look down over. —n. 5. authoritative instruction that something must be done. 6. authority to command. 7. knowledge, mastery. 8. military or naval unit with a specific function. 9. instruction given to a computer. **commandant** n. officer commanding a military group. **commandeer** v. 1. seize for military use. 2. take arbitrarily. **commander** n. 1. military officer in command of a group or operation. 2. middle-ranking naval officer. **commander-in-chief** n., pl. **commanders-in-chief**. supreme commander. **commandment** n. divine command.

commando n., pl. **-dos, -does**. (member of) a military unit trained for swift raids in enemy territory.

commemorate v. honour or keep alive the memory of. **commemoration** n. **commemorative** adj.

commence v. begin. **commencement** n. 1. start. 2. US graduation ceremony.

commend v. 1. praise. 2. recommend. 3. entrust. **commendable** adj. **commendably** adv. **commendation** n.

commensurable adj. measurable by the same standard. **commensurability** n.

commensurate adj. corresponding in degree, size, or value.

comment n. 1. remark. 2. gossip. 3. explanatory note. —v. 4. make a comment or comments. **commentary** n., pl. **-taries**. 1. spoken accompaniment to a broadcast or film. 2. explanatory notes. **commentate** v. provide a commentary. **commentator** n.

commerce n. 1. buying and selling, trade. 2. dealings. **commercial** adj. 1. of commerce. 2. (of television or radio) paid for by advertisers. 3. having profit as the main aim. —n. 4. television or radio advertisement. **commercialize** v. make commercial. **commercialization** n. **commercial traveller** sales representative.

commie n. adj. Informal offens. communist.

commingle v. mix or be mixed.

commis n., pl. **-mis**. apprentice waiter or chef.

commiserate v. (foll. by with) express pity or sympathy (for). **commiseration** n.

commissar n. official responsible for political education in Communist countries.

commissariat n. military department in charge of food supplies.

commissary n., pl. **-saries**. 1. US shop supplying food or equipment, as in a military camp. 2. representative or deputy.

commission n. 1. duty or task given to someone. 2. delegated authority. 3. group of people appointed to perform certain duties. 4. percentage paid to a salesperson for each sale made. 5. Mil. rank or authority officially given to an officer. 6. committing. —v. 7. grant authority to. 8. Mil. give a commission to. 9. place an order for. **out of commission** not working. **commissioner** n. 1. appointed official in a government department. 2. member of a commission.

commissionaire n. uniformed doorman at a hotel, theatre, etc.

commit v. **-mitting, -mitted**. 1. perform (a crime or error). 2. pledge to a cause or course of action. 3. send (someone) to prison or hospital. 4. hand over, entrust. **committal** n. sending of someone for trial, etc. **commitment** n. 1. dedication to a cause. 2. responsibility or promise that hinders freedom of action.

committee n. group of people appointed to perform a specified service or function.

commode n. 1. seat with a compartment holding a chamber pot. 2. chest of drawers.

commodious adj. roomy.

commodity n., pl. **-ities**. article of trade.

commodore n. 1. senior naval or air-force officer. 2. president of a yacht club.

common adj. 1. occurring often. 2. belonging to two or more people. 3. public, general. 4. low-class. —n. 5. area of grassy land belonging to a community. —pl. 6. ordinary people. 7. shared food. 8. (C-) House of Commons. **in common** shared, in joint use. **commonly** adv. **commoner** n. person who does not belong to the nobility. **common-law** adj. (of a relationship) regarded as marriage through being long-standing. **Common Market** European Community. **commonplace** adj. 1. ordinary, everyday. —n. 2. trite remark. **common room** sitting room for students and staff in colleges. **common sense** sound practical understanding.

commonwealth n. 1. republic. 2. (C-) federation of independent states that used to be ruled by Britain.

commotion n. noisy disturbance.

commune[1] n. 1. group of people living together, sharing property and responsibil-

ities. 2. smallest district of local government in some countries. **communal** adj. shared. **communally** adv.

commune[2] v. (foll. by with) 1. experience strong emotion (for). 2. talk intimately. **communion** n. 1. sharing of thoughts or feelings. 2. (C-) Christian ritual of sharing consecrated bread and wine. 3. religious group with shared beliefs and practices.

communicate v. 1. make known, reveal (information, thoughts, or feelings). 2. (of rooms) have a connecting door. 3. receive Communion. **communicable** adj. (of a disease) able to be passed on. **communicant** n. person who receives Communion. **communication** n. 1. communicating. 2. thing communicated. —pl. 3. means of travelling or sending messages. **communicative** adj. willing to talk.

communiqué [kom-**mune**-ik-kay] n. official announcement.

communism n. 1. doctrine that all property and means of production should be shared by the people. 2. (C-) system of state control of the economy and society in some countries. **communist** n., adj. **communistic** adj.

community n., pl. **-ties**. 1. all the people living in one district. 2. group having shared interests or origins. 3. society, the public. **community centre** building used by a community for activities. **community charge** tax levied per head of adult population, to fund local government.

commute v. 1. travel daily to and from work. 2. reduce (a sentence) to a less severe one. 3. substitute. **commuter** n. person who commutes to and from work. **commutator** n. device used to change alternating electric current into direct current.

compact[1] adj. 1. closely packed. 2. neatly arranged. 3. concise, brief. —n. 4. small flat case containing a mirror and face powder. —v. 5. pack closely together. **compactly** adv. **compactness** n. **compact disc** small digital audio disc on which the sound is read by an optical laser system.

compact[2] n. agreement, contract.

companion n. 1. person who associates with or accompanies another. 2. woman paid to live with another. **companionable** adj. friendly. **companionship** n.

companionway n. ladder linking the decks of a ship.

company n., pl. **-nies. 1.** business firm. **2.** small unit of troops. **3.** group of actors. **4.** crew of a ship. **5.** companionship. **6.** associates. **7.** guest or guests. **8.** gathering of people.

compare v. **1.** examine (things) to find the resemblances or differences. **2.** declare to be like. **3.** be worthy of comparison. **comparable** adj. **1.** worthy of comparison. **2.** able to be compared. **comparability** n. **comparative** adj. **1.** relative. **2.** involving comparison. **3.** Grammar denoting the form of an adjective or adverb indicating more. —n. **4.** Grammar comparative form of a word. **comparatively** adv. **comparison** n. **1.** comparing. **2.** likeness.

compartment n. **1.** separate section. **2.** section of a railway carriage.

compass n. **1.** instrument for showing direction, with a needle that points north. **2.** range. —pl. **3.** hinged instrument for drawing circles.
▷ The drawing instrument is technically a pair of compasses and some people insist on this usage.

compassion n. pity, sympathy. **compassionate** adj.

compatible adj. able to exist, work, or be used together. **compatibility** n.

compatriot n. fellow countryman or countrywoman.

compeer n. equal, companion.

compel v. **-pelling, -pelled.** force (to be or do). **compelling** adj. arousing strong interest.

compendium n., pl. **-diums, -dia. 1.** selection of different table games in one container. **2.** concise summary. **compendious** adj. brief but inclusive.

compensate v. **1.** make amends to (someone), esp. for injury or loss. **2.** (foll. by for) cancel out a bad effect. **compensation** n. payment made as reparation for loss or injury. **compensatory** adj.

compère n. **1.** person who presents a stage, radio, or television show. —v. **2.** be the compère of.

compete v. take part in (a contest or competition). **competition** n. **1.** competing. **2.** event in which people compete. **3.** people against whom one competes. **competitive** adj. **1.** involving rivalry. **2.** good enough to be successful against commercial rivals. **competitor** n.

competent adj. having sufficient skill or knowledge. **competently** adv. **competence** n. **1.** ability. **2.** sufficient income to live on.

compile v. collect and arrange (information), esp. to form a book. **compilation** n. **compiler** n.

complacent adj. self-satisfied. **complacently** adv. **complacency** n.

complain v. **1.** express resentment or displeasure. **2.** state that one is suffering from pain or illness. **complaint** n. **1.** complaining. **2.** mild illness. **complainant** n. plaintiff.

complaisant [kom-play-zant] adj. obliging, willing to please. **complaisance** n.

complement n. **1.** thing that completes something. **2.** complete amount or number. **3.** Grammar word or words added after a verb to complete the meaning. **4.** Maths angle added to a specified angle to produce a right angle. —v. **5.** make complete. **complementary** adj.

complete adj. **1.** thorough. **2.** whole. **3.** finished. **4.** having all the necessary parts. —v. **5.** finish. **6.** make whole or perfect. **completely** adv. **completeness** n. wholeness. **completion** n. finishing.

complex adj. **1.** made up of parts. **2.** complicated. —n. **3.** whole made up of parts. **4.** group of unconscious feelings that influences behaviour. **complexity** n.

complexion n. **1.** natural appearance of the skin of the face. **2.** character or nature.

compliance n. **1.** complying. **2.** tendency to do what others want. **compliant** adj.

complicate v. make or become complex or difficult to deal with. **complication** n. **1.** complicating factor. **2.** medical condition arising as a result of another.

complicity n. fact of being an accomplice, esp. in a crime.

compliment n. **1.** expression of praise. —pl. **2.** formal greetings. —v. **3.** praise. **complimentary** adj. **1.** expressing praise. **2.** free of charge.

compline n. last service of the day in the Roman Catholic Church.

comply v. **-plying, -plied.** act in accordance (with a rule, order, or request).

component n. **1.** part of a whole. —adj. **2.** being a component.

comport v. behave (oneself) in a specified way.

compose v. **1.** put together. **2.** be the component parts of. **3.** create (music or literature). **4.** arrange in order. **5.** calm (oneself). **composed** adj. calm. **composer** n.
▷ For sense 2 the usual idiom is: *it is/was composed of.*

composite n., adj. (thing) made up of separate parts.

composition n. **1.** way that something is put together or arranged. **2.** musical work. **3.** essay. **4.** act of composing. **5.** parts which make up a whole.

compositor n. person who arranges type for printing.

compos mentis adj. *Latin* sane.

compost n. decayed plants used as a fertilizer.

composure n. calmness.

compote n. fruit stewed in syrup.

compound[1] n., adj. **1.** (thing, esp. chemical) made up of two or more combined parts or elements. —v. **2.** combine or make by combining. **3.** intensify, make worse. **compound fracture** fracture in which broken bone pierces the skin. **compound interest** interest paid on a sum and its accumulated interest.

compound[2] n. fenced area containing buildings.

comprehend v. **1.** understand. **2.** include. **comprehensible** adj. **comprehension** n. **comprehensive** adj. **1.** of broad scope, fully inclusive. —n. **2.** comprehensive school. **comprehensive school** secondary school for children of all abilities.

compress v. **1.** squeeze together. **2.** condense. —n. **3.** pad applied to stop bleeding or cool inflammation. **compressible** adj. **compression** n. **compressor** n. device that compresses a gas.

comprise v. be made up of, constitute.
▷ *Comprise* is not followed by of but directly by its object.

compromise [kom-prom-mize] n. **1.** settlement reached by concessions on each side. —v. **2.** settle a dispute by making concessions. **3.** put in a dishonourable position.

comptroller n. in titles, financial controller.

compulsion n. **1.** irresistible impulse. **2.** compelling or being compelled. **compulsive** adj. **compulsively** adv. **compulsory** adj. required by rules or laws, obligatory.

compunction n. feeling of guilt or remorse.

compute v. calculate, esp. using a computer. **computation** n. **computer** n. electronic machine that stores and processes data. **computerize** v. **1.** equip with a computer. **2.** perform or operate by computer. **computerization** n.

comrade n. **1.** companion. **2.** fellow member of a union or socialist political party. **comradeship** n.

con[1] *Informal* —v. **conning, conned. 1.** deceive or swindle (someone) by gaining his or her trust. —n. **2.** such a deception or swindle.

con[2] n. pros and cons see PRO[1].

con[3] n. *Slang* convict.

con[4], **conn** v. direct the steering of (a ship).

concatenation n. linked series of events.

concave adj. curving inwards. **concavity** n.

conceal v. **1.** cover and hide. **2.** keep secret. **concealment** n.

concede v. **1.** admit to be true. **2.** grant as a right. **3.** acknowledge defeat in (a contest or argument).

conceit n. **1.** too high an opinion of oneself. **2.** *Lit.* far-fetched or clever comparison. **conceited** adj.

conceive v. **1.** imagine or think. **2.** form in the mind. **3.** become pregnant. **conceivable** adj. imaginable or possible. **conceivably** adv.

concentrate v. **1.** fix one's attention or efforts (on). **2.** make (a substance) stronger. **3.** bring or come together in large numbers in one place. —n. **4.** concentrated substance. **concentration** n. **1.** concentrating. **2.** concentrated substance. **concentration camp** prison camp for civilian prisoners, esp. in Nazi Germany.

concentric adj. having the same centre.

concept n. abstract or general idea. **conceptual** adj. of or based on concepts. **conceptualize** v. form a concept of.

conception n. **1.** general idea. **2.** act of conceiving. **3.** origin or beginning.

concern v. **1.** worry. **2.** involve or interest. **3.** be relevant or important to. —n. **4.** anxiety. **5.** something that concerns a person. **6.** business or firm. **concerned** adj. **1.** interested or involved. **2.** anxious. **concerning** prep. about, regarding.

concert n. musical entertainment. in concert 1. working together. 2. (of musicians) performing live. concerted adj. done together.

concertina n. 1. small musical instrument similar to an accordion. —v. -naing, -naed. 2. collapse or fold up like a concertina.

concerto [kon-**chair**-toe] n., pl. -tos, -ti. large-scale composition for a solo instrument and orchestra.

concession n. 1. grant. 2. reduction in price for a specified category of people. 3. conceding. 4. thing conceded. concessionary adj.

conch n. 1. marine mollusc with a large spiral shell. 2. its shell.

concierge [kon-see-**airzh**] n. in France, caretaker of a block of flats.

conciliate v. overcome the hostility of. conciliation n. conciliator n. conciliatory adj.

concise adj. brief and to the point. concisely adv. conciseness n.

conclave n. 1. secret meeting. 2. private meeting of cardinals to elect a new pope.

conclude v. 1. end, finish. 2. decide by reasoning. 3. arrange or settle finally. conclusion n. 1. ending. 2. outcome. 3. decision or opinion. conclusive adj. ending doubt, convincing. conclusively adv.

concoct v. 1. make by combining ingredients. 2. make up (a story or plan). concoction n.

concomitant adj. 1. accompanying. —n. 2. concomitant thing.

concord n. 1. state of peaceful agreement, harmony. 2. harmonious combination of musical notes. concordance n. 1. similarity or consistency. 2. index of words in a book. concordant adj. agreeing.

concordat n. pact or treaty.

concourse n. 1. large open public place where people can gather. 2. crowd.

concrete n. 1. mixture of sand, gravel, and cement, used in building. —adj. 2. made of concrete. 3. particular, specific. 4. real or solid, not abstract. —v. 5. cover with concrete.

concubine [kon-**kew**-bine] n. 1. woman living with a man as his wife, but not married to him. 2. secondary wife in polygamous societies. concubinage n.

concupiscence [kon-**kew**-piss-enss] n. lust. concupiscent adj.

concur v. -curring, -curred. agree, be in accord. concurrence n. concurrent adj. 1. happening at the same time or place. 2. in agreement. concurrently adv. at the same time.

concussion n. 1. brain injury caused by a blow or fall. 2. violent shaking. concuss v. affect with concussion.

condemn v. 1. express disapproval of. 2. sentence. 3. doom. 4. declare unfit for use. condemnation n. condemnatory adj.

condense v. 1. express in fewer words. 2. concentrate, make more dense. 3. turn from gas into liquid. condensation n. condenser n. Electricity capacitor.

condescend v. 1. behave patronizingly towards. 2. do something as if it were beneath one's dignity. condescension n.

condiment n. relish or seasoning for food.

condition n. 1. particular state of being. 2. necessary prerequisite for something else to happen. 3. restriction or qualification. 4. state of health, physical fitness. 5. ailment. —pl. 6. circumstances. —v. 7. accustom. 8. make fit or healthy. 9. subject to a condition. on condition that only if. conditional adj. dependent on circumstances. conditioner n. thick liquid used when washing to make hair or clothes feel softer.

condole v. express sympathy (with someone). condolence n.

condom n. rubber sheath worn on the penis during sexual intercourse to prevent conception or infection.

condominium n. US apartment building in which each apartment is individually owned.

condone v. overlook or forgive (an offence or wrongdoing).

condor n. large vulture of S America.

conducive adj. (foll. by to) likely to produce (a result).

conduct n. 1. behaviour. 2. management. —v. 3. behave (oneself). 4. manage. 5. transmit (heat or electricity). 6. direct (musicians) by moving the hands or a baton. 7. lead, guide. conduction n. transmission of heat or electricity. conductive adj. able to conduct heat or electricity. conductivity n. conductor n. 1. person who conducts musicians. 2. (fem. conductress) official on a bus who collects fares. 3. US guard on a train. **4.** something that conducts electricity or heat.

conduit [kon-dew-it] *n.* channel or tube for fluid or cables.

cone *n.* **1.** hollow or solid object with a circular base, tapering to a point. **2.** scaly fruit of a conifer tree. **3.** plastic cone used as a traffic marker on the roads. **4.** cone-shaped wafer shell for holding ice cream.

coney *n.* same as CONY.

confabulation, *Informal* **confab** *n.* conversation.

confection *n.* **1.** any sweet food. **2.** elaborate article of clothing. **confectioner** *n.* maker or seller of confectionery. **confectionery** *n.* sweets and cakes.

confederate *n.* **1.** member of a confederacy. **2.** accomplice. —*v.* **3.** unite in a confederacy. —*adj.* **4.** united, allied. **confederacy** *n., pl.* **-cies.** union of states or people for a common purpose. **confederation** *n.* alliance of political units.

confer *v.* **-ferring, -ferred. 1.** discuss together. **2.** give. **conference** *n.* meeting for discussion. **conferment** *n.* formal giving.

confess *v.* **1.** admit (a fault or crime). **2.** admit to be true. **3.** declare (one's sins) to God or a priest, in hope of forgiveness. **confession** *n.* **1.** confessing. **2.** thing confessed. **confessional** *n.* small stall in which a priest hears confessions. **confessor** *n.* priest who hears confessions.

confetti *n.* small bits of coloured paper thrown at weddings.

confidant *n.* person confided in. **confidante** *n. fem.*

confide *v.* **1.** (foll. by *in*) tell (something) in confidence (to). **2.** entrust. **confidence** *n.* **1.** trust. **2.** self-assurance. **3.** something confided, secret. **in confidence** as a secret. **confidence trick** same as CON[1]. **confident** *adj.* feeling or showing self-assurance. **confidently** *adv.* **confidential** *adj.* **1.** private or secret. **2.** entrusted with another's secret affairs. **confidentially** *adv.* **confidentiality** *n.*

configuration *n.* **1.** arrangement of parts. **2.** shape.

confine *v.* **1.** keep within bounds. **2.** restrict the free movement of. **confines** *pl. n.* boundaries, limits. **confinement** *n.* **1.** being confined. **2.** period of childbirth.

confirm *v.* **1.** prove to be true. **2.** reaffirm or strengthen. **3.** administer the rite of confirmation to. **confirmation** *n.* **1.** confirming. **2.** something that confirms. **3.** *Christianity* rite which admits a baptized person to full church membership. **confirmed** *adj.* long-established in a habit or condition.

confiscate *v.* seize (property) by authority. **confiscation** *n.*

conflagration *n.* great destructive fire.

conflate *v.* combine or blend into a whole. **conflation** *n.*

conflict *n.* **1.** struggle or fight. **2.** disagreement. —*v.* **3.** be incompatible.

confluence *n.* **1.** place where two rivers join. **2.** gathering. **confluent** *adj.*

conform *v.* **1.** comply with accepted standards, rules, or customs. **2.** be like or in accordance with. **conformist** *n.* person who conforms, esp. excessively. **conformity** *n.* **1.** compliance. **2.** likeness.

confound *v.* **1.** astound, bewilder. **2.** confuse. **confounded** *adj. Informal* damned.

confront *v.* come or bring face to face with. **confrontation** *n.*

confuse *v.* **1.** mix up, mistake (one thing) for another. **2.** perplex or disconcert. **3.** make unclear. **confusion** *n.*

confute *v.* prove wrong. **confutation** *n.*

conga *n.* **1.** dance performed by a number of people in single file. **2.** large single-headed drum played with the hands.

congeal *v.* (of a liquid) coagulate, solidify.

congenial *adj.* **1.** pleasant, agreeable. **2.** of similar disposition or tastes. **congenially** *adv.* **congeniality** *n.*

congenital *adj.* (of a condition) existing from birth. **congenitally** *adv.*

conger *n.* large sea eel.

congested *adj.* **1.** too full. **2.** clogged or blocked. **congestion** *n.*

conglomerate *n.* **1.** large corporation comprising many companies. **2.** mass composed of several different things. —*v.* **3.** form into a mass. —*adj.* **4.** made up of several different things. **conglomeration** *n.*

congratulate *v.* express one's pleasure to (a person) at his or her good fortune or success. **congratulation** *n.* **congratulatory** *adj.*

congregate *v.* gather together in or as a crowd. **congregation** *n.* assembled group of worshippers. **congregational** adj. **Congregationalism** n. Protestant denomination in which each church is self-governing. **Congregationalist** n., adj.

congress n. 1. formal meeting for discussion. 2. (C-) federal parliament of the US. **congressional** adj. **congressman, congresswoman** n. member of the US Congress.

congruent adj. 1. agreeing or corresponding. 2. Geom. identical in shape and size. **congruence** n.

conic adj. of a cone. **conical** adj. cone-shaped.

conifer n. cone-bearing tree, such as the fir or pine. **coniferous** adj.

conjecture n., v. guess. **conjectural** adj.

conjugal [kon-jew-gal] adj. of marriage.

conjugate v. [kon-jew-gate] 1. give the inflections of (a verb). —adj. [kon-jew-git] 2. joined together. **conjugation** n. complete set of inflections of a verb.

conjunction n. 1. combination. 2. simultaneous occurrence of events. 3. part of speech joining words, phrases, or clauses. **conjunctive** adj.

conjunctivitis n. inflammation of the membrane covering the eyeball and inner eyelid. **conjunctiva** n. this membrane.

conjuncture n. combination of events.

conjure v. 1. perform tricks that appear to be magic. 2. summon (a spirit) by magic. **conjure up** v. produce as if by magic. **conjurer, conjuror** n.

conk n. Slang head or nose. **conk out** v. Informal (of a machine) break down.

conker n. Informal horse chestnut. **conkers** n. game played with conkers tied on strings.

connect v. 1. join together. 2. associate in the mind. 3. put into telephone communication with. **connection, connexion** n. 1. association. 2. link or bond. 3. opportunity to transfer from one public vehicle to another. 4. influential acquaintance. **connective** adj.

conning tower n. raised observation tower containing the periscope on a submarine.

connive v. 1. (foll. by at) give assent to (wrongdoing) by ignoring it. 2. conspire. **connivance** n.

connoisseur [kon-noss-sir] n. person with special knowledge of the arts, food, or drink.

connote v. imply in addition to the literal meaning. **connotation** n.

connubial [kon-new-bee-al] adj. of marriage.

conquer v. 1. defeat. 2. overcome. 3. take (a place) by force. **conqueror** n. **conquest** n. 1. conquering. 2. person or thing conquered. 3. person whose affections have been won.

consanguineous adj. related by birth. **consanguinity** n.

conscience n. sense of right or wrong as regards thoughts and actions. **conscience-stricken** adj. feeling anxious or guilty.

conscientious adj. 1. painstaking. 2. governed by conscience. **conscientious objector** person who refuses to serve in the armed forces on moral or religious grounds. **conscientiously** adv. **conscientiousness** n.

conscious adj. 1. alert and awake. 2. aware. 3. deliberate, intentional. 4. of the part of the mind that determines the choices of action. **consciously** adv. **consciousness** n.

conscript v. 1. enrol (someone) for compulsory military service. —n. 2. conscripted person. **conscription** n.

consecrate v. 1. make sacred. 2. dedicate to a specific purpose. **consecration** n.

consecutive adj. in unbroken succession. **consecutively** adv.

consensus n. general agreement.
▷ Note the spelling of this word, often confused with that of census. In view of its meaning, it is redundant to say 'a consensus of opinion'.

consent v. 1. permit, agree (to). —n. 2. permission, agreement.

consequence n. 1. result, effect. 2. importance. **consequent** adj. resulting. **consequently** adv. 1. therefore. 2. as a result. **consequential** adj. 1. important. 2. following as a result.

conservative adj. 1. opposing change. 2. cautious. 3. conventional in style. 4. (C-) of or supporting the Conservative Party, the British right-wing political party which believes in private enterprise and capitalism. —n. 5. conservative person. 6. (C-) supporter or member of the Conservative Party. **conservatism** n.

conservatoire [kon-serv-a-twahr] n. school of music.

conservatory n., pl. **-ries. 1.** greenhouse. **2.** conservatoire.

conserve v. **1.** protect from harm, decay, or loss. **2.** preserve (fruit) with sugar. —n. **3.** fruit preserved by cooking in sugar. **conservancy** n. environmental conservation. **conservation** n. **1.** conserving. **2.** protection of natural resources and the environment. **conservationist** n.

consider v. **1.** be of the opinion that. **2.** think about. **3.** be considerate of. **4.** discuss. **5.** examine. **considerable** adj. **1.** fairly large. **2.** much. **considerably** adv. **considerate** adj. thoughtful towards others. **considerately** adv. **consideration** n. **1.** careful thought. **2.** fact that must be considered. **3.** kindness. **4.** payment for a service. **considered** adj. thought out with care. **considering** prep. taking (a specified fact) into account.

consign v. **1.** deposit. **2.** entrust. **3.** address or deliver (goods). **consignee** n. **consignor** n. **consignment** n. shipment of goods.

consist v. **1. consist in** have as its main or only feature. **2. consist of** be made up of.

consistency n., pl. **-cies. 1.** degree of thickness or smoothness. **2.** being consistent. **consistent** adj. **1.** unchanging, constant. **2.** in agreement. **consistently** adv.

console¹ v. comfort in distress. **consolation** n. **1.** consoling. **2.** person or thing that consoles.

console² n. **1.** panel of controls for electronic equipment. **2.** cabinet for a television or audio equipment. **3.** ornamental wall bracket. **4.** part of an organ containing the pedals, stops, and keys.

consolidate v. **1.** make or become stronger or more stable. **2.** combine into a whole. **consolidation** n.

consommé [kon-**som**-may] n. thin clear meat soup.

consonant n. **1.** speech sound made by partially or completely blocking the breath stream. **2.** letter representing this. —adj. **3.** (foll. by with) agreeing (with). **consonance** n. harmony or agreement.

consort v. **1.** (foll. by with) keep company (with). —n. **2.** husband or wife of a monarch.

consortium n., pl. **-tia.** association of business firms.

conspectus n. survey or summary.

conspicuous adj. **1.** clearly visible. **2.** striking. **conspicuously** adv.

conspire v. **1.** plan a crime together in secret. **2.** act together as if by design. **conspiracy** n. **1.** conspiring. **2.** pl. **-cies.** plan made by conspiring. **conspirator** n. **conspiratorial** adj.

constable n. police officer of the lowest rank. **constabulary** n., pl. **-laries.** police force of an area.

constant adj. **1.** continuous. **2.** unchanging. **3.** faithful. —n. **4.** unvarying quantity. **5.** something unchanging. **constantly** adv. **constancy** n.

constellation n. group of stars.

consternation n. anxiety, dismay, or confusion.

constipation n. difficulty in defecating. **constipated** adj. having constipation.

constituent adj. **1.** forming part of a whole. **2.** having the power to make or alter the constitution of a state. —n. **3.** member of a constituency. **4.** component part. **constituency** n., pl. **-cies. 1.** area represented by a Member of Parliament. **2.** voters in such an area.

constitute v. **1.** form, compose. **2.** establish. **constitution** n. **1.** principles on which a state is governed. **2.** physical condition. **3.** structure. **constitutional** adj. **1.** of a constitution. **2.** in accordance with a political constitution. **3.** inherent in the nature. —n. **4.** walk taken for exercise. **constitutionally** adv.

constrain v. **1.** force, compel. **2.** restrain or confine. **constrained** adj. embarrassed or forced. **constraint** n. **1.** compulsion or restraint. **2.** forced unnatural manner.

constrict v. **1.** make narrower or tighter, esp. by squeezing. **2.** restrict. **constriction** n. **constrictive** adj. **constrictor** n. **1.** large snake that squeezes its prey to death. **2.** muscle that constricts.

construct v. **1.** build or put together. **2.** Geom. draw (a figure). **construction** n. **1.** constructing. **2.** thing constructed. **3.** interpretation. **4.** Grammar way in which words are arranged in a sentence, clause, or phrase. **constructive** adj. (of advice, criticism, etc.) useful and helpful. **constructively** adv.

construe v. **-struing, -strued. 1.** interpret. **2.** analyse grammatically. **3.** Old-fashioned translate.

consul n. 1. official representing a state in a foreign country. 2. one of the two chief magistrates in ancient Rome. **consular** adj. **consulate** n. position or offices of a consul. **consulship** n.

consult v. go to for information or advice. **consultant** n. 1. specialist doctor with a senior position in a hospital. 2. specialist who gives professional advice. **consultancy** n., pl. **-cies**. work or position of a consultant. **consultation** n. (meeting for) consulting. **consultative** adj. giving advice.

consume v. 1. eat or drink. 2. use up. 3. destroy. 4. obsess. **consumer** n. person who buys goods or uses services. **consumerism** n. protection of the rights of consumers. **consumption** n. 1. consuming. 2. purchase of goods and services. 3. amount consumed. 4. Old-fashioned tuberculosis. **consumptive** n., adj. (person) having tuberculosis.

consummate [**kon**-sume-mate] v. 1. make (a marriage) legal by sexual intercourse. 2. complete or fulfil. —adj. [kon-**sum**-mit] 3. supremely skilled. 4. perfect. **consummation** n.

cont. continued.

contact n. 1. communicating. 2. touching. 3. useful acquaintance. 4. connection between two electrical conductors in a circuit. 5. person who has been exposed to a contagious disease. —v. 6. get in touch with. **contact lens** lens fitting over the eyeball to correct defective vision.

contagion n. 1. passing on of disease by contact. 2. contagious disease. 3. spreading of a harmful influence. **contagious** adj. spreading by contact, catching.

contain v. 1. hold or be capable of holding. 2. consist of. 3. control, restrain. **container** n. 1. receptacle used to hold something. 2. large standard-sized box for transporting cargo by lorry or ship. **containerize** v. pack (cargo) into large containers. **containment** n. prevention of the spread of something harmful.

contaminate v. 1. pollute, make impure. 2. make radioactive. **contaminant** n. contaminating substance. **contamination** n.

contemn v. Formal regard with contempt.

contemplate v. 1. think deeply (about). 2. consider as a possibility. 3. gaze at. **contemplation** n. **contemplative** adj. of or given to contemplation. **contemplatively** adv.

contemporary adj. 1. present-day, modern. 2. living or occurring at the same time. 3. of roughly the same age. —n., pl. **-raries**. 4. person or thing living or occurring at the same time as another. **contemporaneous** adj. happening at the same time.

contempt n. 1. attitude of scornful disregard. 2. open disrespect for the authority of a court. **contemptible** adj. deserving contempt. **contemptuous** adj. showing contempt. **contemptuously** adv.

contend v. 1. (foll. by with) deal with. 2. assert. 3. compete. **contender** n. competitor.

content¹ n. 1. meaning or substance of a book etc. 2. amount of a substance in a mixture. —pl. 3. what something contains. 4. list of chapters at the front of a book.

content² adj. 1. satisfied with things as they are. 2. willing to accept a proposed course of action. —v. 3. make (someone) content. —n. 4. peace of mind. **contented** adj. **contentment** n.

contention n. 1. disagreement or dispute. 2. point asserted in argument. **contentious** adj. 1. causing dispute. 2. quarrelsome.

contest n. 1. competition or struggle. —v. 2. dispute. 3. fight or compete for. **contestant** n.

context n. 1. words before and after a word or passage that contribute to its meaning. 2. circumstances of an event or fact. **contextual** adj.

contiguous adj. very near or touching. **contiguity** n.

continent¹ n. one of the earth's large masses of land. **the Continent** Brit. mainland of Europe. **continental** adj. **continental breakfast** light breakfast of rolls, coffee, etc. **continental quilt** duvet.

continent² adj. 1. able to control one's urination and defecation. 2. sexually chaste. **continence** n.

contingent adj. 1. (foll. by on) dependent on (something uncertain). 2. accidental. —n. 3. group of people, esp. soldiers, that is part of a larger group. **contingency** n., pl. **-cies**. something that may happen.

continue v. **-tinuing, -tinued**. 1. (cause to) remain in a condition or place. 2. carry on (doing something). 3. resume. 4. prolong. **continual** adj. 1. constant. 2. frequently recurring. **continually** adv. **continuance** n. continuing. **continuation** n. 1. continuing.

2. part added. **continuity** n., pl. **-ties. 1.** smooth development or sequence. **2.** arrangement of scenes in a film so that they follow each other logically and without breaks. **continuous** adj. continuing uninterrupted. **continuously** adv.

continuo n., pl. **-tinuos.** Music continuous bass part, usually played on a keyboard instrument.

continuum n., pl. **-tinua, -tinuums.** continuous series.

contort v. twist out of normal shape. **contortion** n. **contortionist** n. performer who contorts his or her body to entertain.

contour n. **1.** outline. **2.** (also **contour line**) line on a map joining places of the same height.

contra- prefix against or contrasting, e.g. contraflow.

contraband adj., n. smuggled (goods).

contraception n. prevention of pregnancy by artificial means. **contraceptive** n. **1.** device used or pill taken to prevent pregnancy. —adj. **2.** preventing pregnancy.

contract v. **1.** make or become smaller or shorter. **2.** make a formal agreement (to do something). **3.** catch (an illness). **4.** draw (muscles) together or (of muscles) be drawn together. —n. **5.** formal agreement. **contraction** n. **1.** contracting. **2.** shortened word. **contractor** n. firm that supplies materials or labour, esp. for building. **contractual** adj.

contradict v. **1.** declare the opposite of (a statement) to be true. **2.** be at variance with. **contradiction** n. **contradictory** adj.

contradistinction n. distinction made by contrasting different qualities.

contraflow n. flow of traffic going alongside but in an opposite direction to the usual flow.

contralto n., pl. **-tos.** (singer with) the lowest female voice.

contraption n. strange-looking device.

contrapuntal adj. Music of or in counterpoint.

contrary adj. **1.** opposed, completely different. **2.** perverse, obstinate. —n. **3.** complete opposite. —adv. **4.** in opposition. **contrarily** adv. **contrariness** n. **contrariwise** adv. conversely.

contrast v. **1.** compare or be compared in order to show differences. —n. **2.** striking

difference. **3.** something showing this. **4.** degree of difference between colours in a photograph or television picture. **contrastive** adj.

contravene v. break (a rule or law). **contravention** n.

contretemps [kon-tra-tahn] n., pl. **-temps.** embarrassing minor disagreement.

contribute v. **1.** give to a common purpose or fund. **2.** (foll. by to) help (something) to occur. **3.** write (an article) for a publication. **contribution** n. **contributor** n. **contributory** adj.

contrite adj. guilty and regretful. **contritely** adv. **contrition** n.

contrive v. **1.** make happen. **2.** invent and construct. **contrivance** n. **1.** device. **2.** plan. **3.** contriving. **contrived** adj. planned, artificial.

control v. **-trolling, -trolled. 1.** have power over. **2.** curb or check. **3.** regulate. —n. **4.** power to direct something. **5.** curb or check. **6.** standard of comparison in an experiment. —pl. **7.** instruments used to operate a machine. **controllable** adj. **controller** n.

controversy n., pl. **-sies.** fierce argument or debate. **controversial** adj. causing controversy.

▷ Note that the stress used always to be on the first syllable, 'kon', but is now more often on the second syllable, 'trov'.

contumacy [kon-tume-mass-ee] n. obstinate disobedience. **contumacious** [kon-tume-may-shuss] adj.

contumely [kon-tume-mill-ee] n. scornful or insulting treatment.

contuse v. bruise. **contusion** n.

conundrum n. riddle.

conurbation n. large urban area formed by the growth and merging of towns.

convalesce v. recover health after an illness or operation. **convalescence** n. **convalescent** adj., n.

convection n. transmission of heat in liquids or gases by the circulation of currents. **convector** n. heater which emits hot air.

convene v. gather or summon for a formal meeting. **convener, convenor** n. person who calls a meeting.

convenient adj. **1.** suitable or opportune. **2.** easy to use. **3.** nearby. **conveniently** adv. **convenience** n. **1.** quality of being convenient. **2.** convenient thing. **3.** public toilet.

convent *n.* **1.** building where nuns live. **2.** school run by nuns.

conventicle *n.* secret or unauthorized religious meeting.

convention *n.* **1.** widely accepted view of proper behaviour. **2.** assembly or meeting. **3.** formal agreement. **conventional** *adj.* **1.** (slavishly) following the accepted customs. **2.** customary. **3.** (of weapons or warfare) not nuclear. **conventionally** *adv.* **conventionality** *n.*

converge *v.* move towards the same point. **convergence** *n.* **convergent** *adj.*

conversant *adj.* **conversant with** having knowledge or experience of.

converse[1] *v.* have a conversation. **conversation** *n.* informal talk. **conversational** *adj.* **conversationalist** *n.* person with a specified ability at conversation.

converse[2] *adj.*, *n.* opposite or contrary. **conversely** *adv.*

convert *v.* **1.** change in form, character, or function. **2.** cause to change in opinion or belief. **3.** *Rugby* make a conversion. **4.** change (money) into a different currency. —*n.* **5.** converted person. **conversion** *n.* **1.** (thing resulting from) a converting or being converted. **2.** *Rugby* score made after a try by kicking the ball over the crossbar. **converter, convertor** *n.* **convertible** *adj.* **1.** capable of being converted. —*n.* **2.** car with a folding or removable roof.

convex *adj.* curving outwards. **convexity** *n.*

convey *v.* **1.** communicate (information). **2.** carry, transport. **3.** transmit. **4.** transfer (the title to property). **conveyance** *n.* **1.** *Old-fashioned* vehicle. **2.** transfer of the legal title to property. **conveyancing** *n.* branch of law dealing with the transfer of ownership of property. **conveyor belt** continuous moving belt for transporting things, esp. in a factory.

convict *v.* **1.** declare guilty. —*n.* **2.** person serving a prison sentence. **conviction** *n.* **1.** instance of being convicted. **2.** firm belief.

convince *v.* persuade by evidence or argument. **convincing** *adj.* **convincingly** *adv.*

convivial *adj.* sociable, lively. **conviviality** *n.*

convoke *v.* call together. **convocation** *n.* **1.** convoking. **2.** large formal meeting.

convoluted *adj.* **1.** coiled, twisted. **2.** (of an argument or sentence) complex and hard to understand. **convolution** *n.*

convolvulus *n.* twining plant with funnel-shaped flowers.

convoy *n.* group of vehicles or ships travelling together.

convulse *v.* **1.** (of muscles) undergo violent spasms. **2.** *Informal* be overcome (with laughter or rage). **3.** shake violently. **convulsion** *n.* **1.** violent muscular spasm. —*pl.* **2.** uncontrollable laughter. **convulsive** *adj.* **convulsively** *adv.*

cony *n.*, *pl.* **conies.** **1.** rabbit. **2.** rabbit fur.

coo *v.* **cooing, cooed.** **1.** (of a dove or pigeon) make a soft murmuring sound. —*n.* **2.** cooing sound.

cooee *interj.* call to attract attention.

cook *v.* **1.** prepare (food) by heating. **2.** (of food) be cooked. **3.** *Informal* falsify (accounts etc.). —*n.* **4.** person who cooks food. **cooker** *n.* **1.** apparatus for cooking heated by gas or electricity. **2.** apple suitable for cooking. **cookery** *n.* art of cooking. **cookie** *n.* *US* biscuit. **cook up** *v.* *Informal* devise (a story or scheme).

cool *adj.* **1.** moderately cold. **2.** calm and unemotional. **3.** indifferent or unfriendly. **4.** *Informal* sophisticated or excellent. **5.** *Informal* (of a large sum of money) without exaggeration, e.g. *a cool ten thousand.* —*v.* **6.** make or become cool. —*n.* **7.** coolness. **8.** *Slang* calmness, composure. **coolly** *adv.* **coolness** *n.* **coolant** *n.* fluid used to cool machinery while it is working. **cooler** *n.* **1.** container for making or keeping things cool. **2.** *Slang* prison.

coolie *n.* *Old-fashioned offens.* unskilled Oriental labourer.

coomb, coombe *n.* valley.

coop[1] *n.* cage or pen for poultry. **coop up** *v.* confine in a restricted place.

coop[2] [koh-op] *n.* **1.** cooperative society. **2.** shop run by one.

cooper *n.* person who makes or repairs barrels or casks.

cooperate *v.* work or act together. **cooperation** *n.* **cooperative** *adj.* **1.** willing to cooperate. **2.** (of an enterprise) owned and managed collectively. —*n.* **3.** cooperative organization.

coopt [koh-opt] *v.* add (someone) to a group by the agreement of the existing members. **cooption** *n.*

coordinate *v.* **1.** bring together and cause to work together efficiently. —*n.* **2.** *Maths* any of a set of numbers defining the location of a point. —*pl.* **3.** garments designed to be worn together. **coordination** *n.* **coordinator** *n.*

coot *n.* **1.** small black water bird. **2.** foolish person.

cop *Slang* —*n.* **1.** policeman. —*v.* **copping, copped. 2.** take or seize. **cop it** get into trouble or be punished. **cop out** *v.* avoid taking responsibility or committing oneself.

copal *n.* resin used in varnishes.

cope[1] *v.* **1.** deal successfully (with). **2.** contend against.

cope[2] *n.* large ceremonial cloak worn by some Christian priests.

cope[3] *v.* provide with a coping.

copier *n.* see COPY.

copilot *n.* second pilot of an aircraft.

coping *n.* sloping top row of a wall. **coping stone**

copious [kope-ee-uss] *adj.* abundant, plentiful. **copiously** *adv.*

copper[1] *n.* **1.** soft reddish-brown metal. **2.** copper or bronze coin. **3.** large metal container used to boil water. —*adj.* **4.** reddish-brown. **copper-bottomed** *adj.* financially reliable. **copperplate** *n.* **1.** (print taken from) an engraved copper plate. **2.** fine handwriting style.

copper[2] *n. Slang* policeman.

coppice, copse *n.* dense growth of small trees and undergrowth.

copra *n.* dried oil-yielding kernel of the coconut.

copula *n., pl.* **-las, -lae.** verb used to link the subject and complement of a sentence.

copulate *v.* have sexual intercourse. **copulation** *n.*

copy *n., pl.* **copies. 1.** thing made to look exactly like another. **2.** single specimen of a book etc. **3.** material for printing. **4.** suitable material for a newspaper article. —*v.* **copying, copied. 5.** make a copy of. **6.** act or try to be like another. **copier** *n.* person or machine that copies. **copybook** *n.* book of handwriting specimens for imitation. **copyright** *n.* **1.** exclusive legal right to reproduce and control a book, work of art, etc. —*v.* **2.** take out a copyright on. —*adj.* **3.** protected by copyright. **copywriter** *n.* person who writes advertising copy.

coquette *n.* woman who flirts. **coquettish** *adj.* **coquetry** *n.*

coracle *n.* small round boat of wicker covered with skins.

coral *n.* **1.** hard substance formed from the skeletons of very small sea animals. —*adj.* **2.** made of coral. **3.** orange-pink.

cor anglais *n., pl.* **cors anglais.** woodwind instrument similar to the oboe.

corbel *n.* stone or timber support projecting from a wall.

corbie *n. Scot.* raven or crow.

cord *n.* **1.** thin rope or thick string. **2.** cordlike structure in the body. **3.** *US* electrical flex. **4.** corduroy. —*pl.* **5.** corduroy trousers. —*adj.* **6.** (of fabric) ribbed. —*v.* **7.** bind with cords.

cordate *adj.* heart-shaped.

cordial *adj.* **1.** warm and friendly. **2.** strong, e.g. *cordial dislike.* —*n.* **3.** drink with a fruit base. **cordially** *adv.* **cordiality** *n.*

cordite *n.* explosive used in guns and bombs.

cordon *n.* **1.** chain of police, soldiers, etc. guarding an area. **2.** fruit tree grown as a single stem. **3.** ornamental braid or ribbon. **cordon off** *v.* form a cordon round.

cordon bleu [bluh] *adj.* (of cookery or cooks) of the highest standard.

corduroy *n.* cotton fabric with a velvety ribbed surface.

core *n.* **1.** central part of certain fruits, containing the seeds. **2.** central or essential part. **3.** region of a nuclear reactor that contains fissionable material. —*v.* **4.** remove the core from.

co-respondent *n.* person with whom someone being sued for divorce is claimed to have committed adultery.

corgi *n.* short-legged sturdy dog.

coriander *n.* plant with aromatic seeds and leaves used for flavouring.

cork *n.* **1.** thick light bark of a Mediterranean oak. **2.** piece of this used as a stopper. —*v.* **3.** stop up with a cork. **corked** *adj.* (of wine) spoiled through having a decayed cork. **corkage** *n.* restaurant's charge for serving wine bought elsewhere. **corkscrew** *n.* **1.** spiral metal tool for extracting corks from bottles. —*adj.* **2.** resembling a corkscrew in shape.

corm *n.* bulblike underground stem of certain plants.

cormorant *n.* large dark-coloured long-necked sea bird.

corn[1] *n.* **1.** cereal plant. **2.** grain of such plants. **3.** *US* maize. **4.** *Slang* something unoriginal or oversentimental. **corny** *adj.* **cornier, corniest.** *Slang* unoriginal or oversentimental. **corncob** *n.* core of an ear of maize with kernels attached. **cornflakes** *pl. n.* breakfast cereal of toasted maize flakes. **cornflour** *n.* finely ground maize. **cornflower** *n.* plant with blue flowers.

corn[2] *n.* painful hard skin on the foot or toe.

corncrake *n.* brown bird with a harsh cry.

cornea [**korn**-ee-a] *n., pl.* **-neas, -neae.** transparent membrane covering the eyeball. **corneal** *adj.*

corned beef *n.* beef preserved in salt.

cornelian *n.* same as CARNELIAN.

corner *n.* **1.** area or angle where two converging lines or surfaces meet. **2.** place where two streets meet. **3.** sharp bend in a road. **4.** remote or inaccessible place. **5.** *Sport* free kick or shot from the corner of the field. —*v.* **6.** (of a vehicle) turn a corner. **7.** force into a difficult or inescapable position. **8.** obtain a monopoly of. **cornerstone** *n.* **1.** indispensable part or basis. **2.** stone at the corner of a wall.

cornet *n.* **1.** brass instrument similar to the trumpet. **2.** cone-shaped ice-cream wafer.

cornice [**korn**-iss] *n.* decorative moulding round the top of a wall.

Cornish *adj.* **1.** of Cornwall or its inhabitants. —*n.* **2.** Celtic language of Cornwall. **Cornish pasty** pastry case with a filling of meat and vegetables.

cornucopia [korn-yew-**kope**-ee-a] *n.* **1.** great abundance. **2.** symbol of plenty, consisting of a horn overflowing with fruit and flowers.

corolla *n.* petals of a flower collectively.

corollary [kor-**oll**-a-ree] *n., pl.* **-laries.** idea, fact, or proposition which is the natural result of something else.

corona [kor-**rone**-a] *n., pl.* **-nas, -nae. 1.** ring of light round the moon or sun. **2.** long cigar with blunt ends.

coronary [**kor**-ron-a-ree] *adj.* **1.** of the arteries surrounding the heart. —*n., pl.* **-naries. 2.** coronary thrombosis. **coronary thrombosis** condition in which the flow of blood to the heart is blocked by a blood clot.

coronation *n.* ceremony of crowning a monarch.

coroner *n.* official responsible for the investigation of violent, sudden, or suspicious deaths.

coronet *n.* small crown.

corpora *n.* plural of CORPUS.

corporal[1] *adj.* of the body. **corporal punishment** physical punishment, such as caning.

corporal[2] *n.* noncommissioned officer below sergeant.

corporation *n.* **1.** large business or company. **2.** city or town council. **3.** *Informal* large paunch. **corporate** *adj.* **1.** relating to business corporations. **2.** shared by a group. **corporative** *adj.*

corporeal [kore-**pore**-ee-al] *adj.* physical or tangible.

corps [kore] *n., pl.* **corps. 1.** military unit with a specific function. **2.** organized body of people.

corpse *n.* dead body.

corpulent *adj.* fat or plump. **corpulence** *n.*

corpus *n., pl.* **corpora.** collection of writings, esp. by a single author.

corpuscle *n.* **1.** red or white blood cell. **2.** minute particle.

corral *US* —*n.* **1.** enclosure for cattle or horses. —*v.* **-ralling, -ralled. 2.** put in a corral.

correct *adj.* **1.** free from error, true. **2.** in accordance with accepted standards. —*v.* **3.** put right. **4.** indicate the errors in. **5.** rebuke or punish. **6.** make conform to a standard. **correctly** *adv.* **correctness** *n.* **correction** *n.* **1.** correcting. **2.** alteration correcting something. **3.** punishment. **corrective** *n., adj.* (thing) intended or tending to correct.

correlate *v.* **1.** place or be placed in a mutual relationship. —*n.* **2.** either of two things mutually related. **correlation** *n.* **correlative** *adj., n.*

correspond *v.* **1.** be consistent or compatible (with). **2.** be similar (to). **3.** communicate (with) by letter. **corresponding** *adj.* **correspondingly** *adv.* **correspondence** *n.* **1.** communication by letters. **2.** letters so exchanged. **3.** relationship or similarity. **correspondence course** study conducted by post. **correspondent** *n.* **1.** writer of letters. **2.** person employed by a newspaper etc. to report on a special subject or from a foreign country.

corridor n. 1. passage in a building or train. 2. strip of land or air space providing access through foreign territory.

corrie n. Scot. circular hollow on a hillside.

corrigendum [kor-rij-end-um] n., pl. -da. thing to be corrected.

corroborate v. support (a fact or opinion) by giving proof. **corroboration** n. **corroborative** adj.

corrode v. 1. eat or be eaten away by chemical action. 2. destroy gradually. **corrosion** n. **corrosive** adj.

corrugate v. fold into alternate grooves and ridges. **corrugated** adj. **corrugation** n.

corrupt adj. 1. open to or involving bribery. 2. morally wrong, depraved. 3. (of a text, data, etc.) unreliable through errors or alterations. —v. 4. make corrupt. **corruptly** adv. **corruption** n. **corruptible** adj.

corsage [kor-sahzh] n. small bouquet worn on the bodice of a dress.

corsair n. 1. pirate. 2. pirate ship.

corselet n. 1. one-piece undergarment with a corset and bra. 2. piece of armour to cover the trunk.

corset n. close-fitting undergarment worn to support or shape the torso.

cortege [kor-tayzh] n. funeral procession.

cortex n., pl. -tices. Anat. outer layer of the brain or other internal organ. **cortical** adj.

cortisone n. steroid hormone used to treat various diseases.

corundum n. hard mineral used as an abrasive.

coruscate v. sparkle. **coruscation** n.

corvette n. lightly armed escort warship.

cos¹, cos lettuce n. long crisp-leaved lettuce.

cos² Maths cosine.

cosh n. 1. heavy blunt weapon. —v. 2. hit with a cosh.

cosine [koh-sine] n. in trigonometry, ratio of the length of the adjacent side to that of the hypotenuse in a right-angled triangle.

cosmetic n. 1. preparation used to improve the appearance of a person's skin. —adj. 2. improving the appearance only.

cosmic adj. of the whole universe. **cosmic rays** electromagnetic radiation from outer space.

cosmonaut n. Soviet astronaut.

cosmopolitan adj. 1. composed of people or elements from many countries. 2. having lived and travelled in many countries. —n. 3. cosmopolitan person. **cosmopolitanism** n.

cosmos n. the universe. **cosmogony** n. study of the origin of the universe. **cosmology** n. study of the origin and nature of the universe. **cosmological** adj.

Cossack n. member of a S Russian people famous as horsemen.

cosset v. cosseting, cosseted. pamper or pet.

cost n. 1. amount of money, time, labour, etc. required for something. —pl. 2. expenses of a lawsuit. —v. costing, cost. 3. have as its cost. 4. involve the loss or sacrifice of. 5. estimate the cost of. **costly** adj. -lier, -liest. 1. expensive. 2. involving great loss or sacrifice. **costliness** n. **cost of living** average cost of the basic necessities of life.

costal adj. of the ribs.

costermonger n. person who sells fruit and vegetables from a barrow in the street.

costive adj. having or causing constipation.

costume n. 1. style of dress of a particular place or time, or for a particular activity. 2. clothes worn by an actor or performer. **costumier** n. maker or seller of costumes. **costume jewellery** inexpensive artificial jewellery.

cosy adj. -sier, -siest. 1. snug and warm. 2. intimate, friendly. —n. 3. cover to keep a teapot etc. hot. **cosily** adv. **cosiness** n.

cot¹ n. 1. child's bed with high sides. 2. small portable bed. **cot death** unexplained death of a baby while asleep.

cot² n. 1. Lit. small cottage. 2. cote.

cote n. shelter for animals or birds.

coterie [kote-er-ee] n. exclusive group, clique.

cotoneaster [kot-tone-ee-ass-ter] n. garden shrub with red berries.

cottage n. small house in the country. **cottager** n. **cottage cheese** soft mild white cheese. **cottage industry** craft industry in which employees work at home. **cottage pie** dish of minced meat topped with mashed potato.

cotter n. pin or wedge used to secure machine parts.

cotton n. **1.** white downy fibre covering the seeds of a tropical plant. **2.** thread or cloth made of this. **cottony** adj. **cotton on (to)** v. Informal understand. **cotton wool** fluffy cotton used for surgical dressings etc.

cotyledon [kot-ill-ee-don] n. first leaf of a plant embryo.

couch n. **1.** piece of upholstered furniture for seating more than one person. —v. **2.** express in a particular way. **3.** Old-fashioned (of an animal) crouch, as when preparing to leap.

couchette [koo-shett] n. bed converted from seats on a train or ship.

couch grass n. quickly spreading grassy weed.

cougar [koo-gar] n. puma.

cough v. **1.** expel air from the lungs abruptly and noisily. —n. **2.** act or sound of coughing. **3.** illness which causes coughing. **cough up** v. Informal give up (money or information).

could v. past tense of CAN¹.

couldn't could not.

coulomb [koo-lom] n. unit of electric charge.

coulter [kole-ter] n. blade at the front of a ploughshare.

council n. **1.** group meeting for discussion or consultation. **2.** local governing body of a town or county. —adj. **3.** of or provided by a council. **councillor** n. member of a council.

counsel n. **1.** advice or guidance. **2.** discussion or consultation. **3.** barrister or barristers. —v. **-selling, -selled. 4.** give guidance to. **5.** urge or recommend. **counsellor** n.

count¹ v. **1.** say numbers in order. **2.** find the total of. **3.** be important. **4.** regard as. **5.** take into account. —n. **6.** number reached by counting. **7.** counting. **8.** Law one of a number of charges. **countless** adj. too many to be counted. **count on** v. **1.** expect. **2.** rely on. **count out** v. **1.** exclude. **2.** declare (a boxer) defeated when he has not risen from the floor within ten seconds.

count² n. European nobleman.

countdown n. counting backwards to zero of the seconds before an event.

countenance n. **1.** (expression of) the face. —v. **2.** support or tolerate.

counter¹ n. **1.** long flat surface in a bank or shop, on which business is transacted. **2.**

small flat disc used in board games. **3.** apparatus for counting things.

counter² adv. **1.** in the opposite direction. **2.** in direct contrast. —v. **3.** oppose, retaliate against. —n. **4.** opposing or retaliatory action.

counter- prefix **1.** against, opposite, e.g. counterbalance. **2.** retaliatory, rival, e.g. counter-revolution.

counteract v. neutralize or act against. **counteraction** n.

counterattack v., n. attack in response to an attack.

counterbalance n. **1.** weight or force balancing or neutralizing another. —v. **2.** act as a counterbalance to.

counterblast n. aggressive response to a verbal attack.

counterclockwise adv., adj. US anticlockwise.

counterespionage n. activities to counteract enemy espionage.

counterfeit adj. **1.** fake, forged. **2.** pretended. —n. **3.** fake, forgery. —v. **4.** fake, forge. **5.** feign.

counterfoil n. part of a cheque or receipt kept as a record.

counterintelligence n. activities designed to frustrate enemy espionage.

countermand v. cancel (a previous order).

counterpane n. bed covering.

counterpart n. **1.** person or thing complementary to or corresponding to another. **2.** duplicate document.

counterpoint n. Music **1.** technique of combining melodies. **2.** part or melody so combined.

counterpoise n., v. counterbalance.

counterproductive adj. having an effect opposite to the one intended.

countersign v. sign (a document already signed by another) as confirmation.

countersink v. drive (a screw) into a shaped hole so that its head is below the surface.

countertenor n. male alto.

countess n. **1.** wife or widow of a count or earl. **2.** woman holding the rank of count or earl in her own right.

country n., pl. **-tries. 1.** nation. **2.** nation's territory. **3.** nation's people. **4.** rural areas as opposed to town. **5.** person's native land. **countrified** *adj.* rustic in manner or appearance. **country and western, country music** popular music based on American White folk music. **country dancing** traditional dancing in rows or circles. **countryman, countrywoman** *n.* **1.** compatriot. **2.** person who lives in the country. **countryside** *n.* rural areas.

county *n.*, *pl.* **-ties. 1.** division of a country. —*adj.* **2.** *Informal* upper-class.

coup [koo] *n.* **1.** successful action. **2.** coup d'état.

coup de grace [koo de **grahss**] *n.* final or decisive action.

coup d'état [koo day-**tah**] *n.* sudden violent overthrow of a government.

coupé [**koo**-pay] *n.* sports car with two doors and a sloping fixed roof.

couple *n.* **1.** two people who are married or romantically involved. **2.** two partners in a dance or game. —*v.* **3.** connect, associate. **4.** *Lit.* have sexual intercourse. **a couple 1.** a pair. **2.** *Informal* a few. **couplet** *n.* two consecutive lines of verse, usu. rhyming and of the same metre. **coupling** *n.* device for connecting things, such as railway carriages.

coupon *n.* **1.** piece of paper entitling the holder to a discount or gift. **2.** detachable order form. **3.** football pools entry form.

courage *n.* ability to face danger or pain without fear. **courageous** *adj.* **courageously** *adv.*

courgette *n.* type of small vegetable marrow.

courier *n.* **1.** person who looks after and guides travellers. **2.** person paid to deliver urgent messages.

course *n.* **1.** onward movement in space or time. **2.** direction or route of movement. **3.** natural development of events. **4.** mode of conduct or action. **5.** series of lessons or medical treatment. **6.** any of the successive parts of a meal. **7.** area where golf is played or a race is run. **8.** continuous layer of masonry at one level in a building. —*v.* **9.** (of liquid) run swiftly. **10.** hunt with hounds that follow the quarry by sight and not scent. **of course** naturally. **courser** *n.* *Lit.* swift horse.

court *n.* **1.** body which decides legal cases. **2.** place where it meets. **3.** marked area for playing a racket game. **4.** courtyard. **5.**

residence, household, or retinue of a sovereign. —*v.* **6.** *Old-fashioned* try to win (someone) as a spouse. **7.** try to win (someone's favour). **8.** invite, e.g. *court disaster*. **courtier** *n.* attendant at a royal court. **courtly** *adj.* **-lier, -liest.** ceremoniously polite. **courtliness** *n.* **courtship** *n.* courting of an intended spouse or mate. **court martial** *n.*, *pl.* **courts martial.** court for trying naval or military offences. **court shoe** woman's low-cut shoe without straps or laces. **courtyard** *n.* paved space enclosed by buildings or walls.

courtesan [kor-tiz-**zan**] *n.* *Hist.* mistress or high-class prostitute.

courtesy *n.*, *pl.* **-sies. 1.** politeness, good manners. **2.** courteous act. **by courtesy of** by permission of. **courteous** *adj.* polite. **courteously** *adv.*

cousin *n.* child of one's uncle or aunt.

couture [koo-**toor**] *n.* high-fashion designing and dressmaking. **couturier** *n.* person who designs women's fashion clothes.

cove *n.* small bay or inlet.

coven [**kuv**-ven] *n.* meeting of witches.

covenant [**kuv**-ven-ant] *n.* **1.** formal agreement, esp. to make an annual (charitable) payment. —*v.* **2.** agree (to pay) by a covenant.

Coventry *n.* **send someone to Coventry** punish someone by refusing to speak to him or her.

cover *v.* **1.** place or spread or be placed or spread over. **2.** screen or conceal. **3.** protect from loss or risk by insurance. **4.** travel over. **5.** include. **6.** be enough to pay for. **7.** report (an event) for a newspaper. **8.** keep a gun aimed at. —*n.* **9.** anything which covers. **10.** outside of a book or magazine. **11.** shelter or protection. **12.** insurance. **13.** pretext or disguise. **14.** individual table setting. **coverage** *n.* amount or extent covered. **coverlet** *n.* bed cover. **cover charge** fixed service charge in a restaurant.

covert *adj.* **1.** secret, concealed. —*n.* **2.** thicket giving shelter to game birds or animals. **covertly** *adv.*

covet *v.* **coveting, coveted.** long to possess (what belongs to someone else). **covetous** *adj.* **covetousness** *n.*

covey [**kuv**-vee] *n.* small flock of grouse or partridge.

cow[1] *n.* mature female of cattle and of certain other animals, such as the elephant or whale. **cowboy** *n.* **1.** ranch worker who herds and tends cattle, usu. on horseback. *Informal* irresponsible or unscrupulous worker. **cowhide** *n.* leather made from the skin of a cow. **cowpat** *n.* pool of cow dung. **cowpox** *n.* disease of cows, the virus of which is used in the smallpox vaccine.

cow² *v.* intimidate, subdue.

coward *n.* person who lacks courage. **cowardly** *adj.* **cowardice** *n.* lack of courage.

cower *v.* cringe or shrink in fear.

cowl *n.* **1.** loose hood. **2.** monk's hooded robe. **3.** cover on a chimney to increase ventilation.

cowling *n.* cover on an engine.

cowrie *n.* brightly-marked sea shell.

cowslip *n.* fragrant wild primrose.

cox *n.* **1.** coxswain. —*v.* **2.** act as cox of (a boat).

coxcomb *n.* **1.** same as COCKSCOMB. **2.** *Obs.* medieval jester's cap.

coxswain [kok-sn] *n.* person who steers a rowing boat.

coy *adj.* affectedly shy or modest. **coyly** *adv.* **coyness** *n.*

coyote [koy-**ote**-ee] *n.* prairie wolf of N America.

coypu *n.* beaver-like aquatic rodent, bred for its fur.

cozen *v.* cheat or trick.

CPU *Computers* central processing unit.

Cr *Chem.* chromium.

crab *n.* **1.** edible shellfish with ten legs, the first pair modified into pincers. **2.** crab louse. **crab louse** parasitic louse living in the pubic regions of humans.

crab apple *n.* small sour apple.

crabbed *adj.* **1.** (of handwriting) hard to read. **2.** (also **crabby**) bad-tempered.

crack *v.* **1.** break or split partially. **2.** break with a sharp noise. **3.** (cause to) make a sharp noise. **4.** break down or yield under strain. **5.** hit suddenly. **6.** tell (a joke). **7.** solve (a code or problem). **8.** (of the voice) become harsh or change pitch suddenly. **9.** break into or force open. —*n.* **10.** narrow gap. **11.** sudden sharp noise. **12.** sharp blow. **13.** *Informal* gibe or joke. **14.** *Slang* pure highly addictive form of cocaine. —*adj.* **15.** *Informal* excellent, first-rate, e.g. *a crack shot.* **cracking** *adj.* first-class. **crackdown** *n.* severe disciplinary or repressive measure. **crack down on** *v.* take severe meas-

ures against. **crack up** *v. Informal* have a physical or mental breakdown.

cracker *n.* **1.** thin dry biscuit. **2.** decorated cardboard tube, pulled apart with a bang, containing a paper hat and a motto or toy. **3.** small explosive firework.

crackers *adj. Slang* crazy.

crackle *v.* **1.** make small sharp popping noises. —*n.* **2.** crackling sound. **crackling** *n.* **1.** crackle. **2.** crisp skin of roast pork.

crackpot *adj., n. Informal* eccentric (person).

cradle *n.* **1.** baby's bed on rockers. **2.** place where something originated. **3.** supporting structure. —*v.* **4.** hold gently as if in a cradle.

craft¹ *n.* **1.** skill or ability. **2.** skilled trade. **3.** cunning. **crafty** *adj.* **craftier, craftiest.** skilled in deception. **craftily** *adv.* **craftiness** *n.* **craftsman, craftswoman** *n.* skilled worker. **craftsmanship** *n.*

craft² *n., pl.* **craft.** boat, ship, aircraft, or spaceship.

crag *n.* steep rugged rock. **craggy** *adj.*

cram *v.* **cramming, crammed. 1.** force into too small a space. **2.** fill too full. **3.** study hard just before an examination.

cramp *n.* **1.** painful muscular contraction. **2.** clamp for holding masonry or timber together. —*v.* **3.** confine or restrict. **4.** affect with a cramp. **cramped** *adj.* **1.** closed in. **2.** (of handwriting) small and irregular.

crampon *n.* spiked plate strapped to a boot for climbing on ice.

cranberry *n.* sour edible red berry.

crane *n.* **1.** machine for lifting and moving heavy weights. **2.** wading bird with long legs, neck, and bill. —*v.* **3.** stretch (one's neck) to see something.

crane fly *n.* long-legged insect with slender wings.

cranesbill *n.* plant with pink or purple flowers.

cranium *n., pl.* **-niums, -nia. 1.** skull. **2.** part of the skull enclosing the brain. **cranial** *adj.*

crank *n.* **1.** arm projecting at right angles from a shaft, for transmitting or converting motion. **2.** *Informal* eccentric person. —*v.* **3.** turn with a crank. **4.** start (an engine) with a crank. **cranky** *adj.* **crankier, crankiest. 1.** eccentric. **2.** *US* bad-tempered. **crankshaft** *n.* shaft driven by a crank.

cranny n., pl. **-nies**. small opening, chink.

crap Slang —n. 1. nonsense. 2. Taboo faeces. —v. **crapping, crapped**. 3. Taboo defecate.

crape n. same as CREPE.

craps n. gambling game played with two dice.

crapulent, crapulous adj. given to or resulting from intemperance. **crapulence** n.

crash v. 1. (cause to) collide violently with a vehicle, a stationary object, or the ground. 2. (cause to) make a loud smashing noise. 3. (cause to) fall with a crash. 4. collapse or fail financially. 5. Informal gate-crash. —n. 6. collision involving a vehicle or vehicles. 7. sudden loud smashing noise. 8. financial collapse. —adj. 9. requiring or using great effort to achieve results quickly, e.g. a crash course. **crash barrier** safety barrier along a road, motorway, or racetrack. **crash-dive** v. (of a submarine) perform a sudden steep dive. **crash helmet** protective helmet worn by a motorcyclist. **crash-land** v. land (an aircraft) in an emergency, causing it damage. **crash-landing** n.

crass adj. grossly stupid. **crassly** adv. **crassness** n.

crate n. 1. large wooden container for packing goods. —v. 2. put in a crate.

crater n. 1. bowl-shaped cavity made by the impact of a meteorite or an explosion. 2. mouth of a volcano.

cravat n. man's scarf worn like a tie.

crave v. 1. desire intensely. 2. beg or plead for. **craving** n.

craven adj. 1. cowardly. —n. 2. coward.

craw n. 1. bird's crop. 2. animal's stomach.

crawfish n. same as CRAYFISH.

crawl v. 1. move on one's hands and knees. 2. move very slowly. 3. act in a servile manner. 4. be or feel as if covered with crawling creatures. —n. 5. crawling motion or pace. 6. overarm swimming stroke. **crawler** n.

crayfish n. edible freshwater shellfish like a lobster.

crayon n. 1. stick or pencil of coloured wax or clay. —v. 2. draw or colour with a crayon.

craze n. 1. short-lived fashion or enthusiasm. —v. 2. make mad. **crazed** adj. 1. demented. 2. (of porcelain) having fine

cracks. **crazy** adj. **crazier, craziest**. 1. ridiculous. 2. (foll. by about) very fond (of). 3. insane. **craziness** n. **crazy paving** paving made of irregularly shaped slabs of stone.

creak v., n. (make) a harsh squeaking sound. **creaky** adj. **creakier, creakiest**.

cream n. 1. fatty part of milk. 2. something, esp. a food or cosmetic, resembling cream in consistency. 3. best part (of something). —adj. 4. yellowish-white. —v. 5. remove the cream from. 6. beat to a creamy consistency. 7. (foll. by off) take the best part from. **creamer** n. powdered milk substitute for coffee. **creamery** n., pl. **-eries**. place where dairy products are made or sold. **creamy** adj. **creamier, creamiest**. **cream cheese** rich soft white cheese. **cream of tartar** purified tartar used in baking powder.

crease n. 1. line made by folding or pressing. 2. wrinkle or furrow. 3. Cricket line marking the bowler's and batsman's positions. —v. 4. crush.

create v. 1. bring into being. 2. appoint to a new rank or position. 3. Slang make an angry fuss. **creation** n. **creative** adj. imaginative or inventive. **creativity** n. **creator** n. 1. person who creates. 2. (C-) God.

creature n. 1. person, animal, or being. 2. person controlled by another.

crèche n. day nursery for very young children.

credence [kreed-enss] n. belief in the truth or accuracy of a statement.

credentials pl. n. document giving evidence of the bearer's identity or qualifications.

credible adj. 1. believable. 2. trustworthy. **credibly** adv. **credibility** n.

credit n. 1. system of allowing customers to take goods and pay later. 2. reputation for trustworthiness in paying debts. 3. money at one's disposal in a bank account. 4. side of an account book on which such sums are entered. 5. (source or cause of) praise or approval. 6. influence or reputation based on the good opinion of others. 7. belief or trust. —pl. 8. list of people responsible for the production of a film, programme, or record. —v. **crediting, credited**. 9. enter as a credit in an account. 10. (foll. by with) attribute (to). 11. believe. **creditable** adj. praiseworthy. **creditably** adv. **creditor** n. person to whom money is owed. **credit card** card allowing a person to buy on credit.

credo n., pl. **-dos**. creed.

credulous adj. too willing to believe. **credulity** n.

creed n. statement or system of (Christian) beliefs or principles.

creek n. **1**. narrow inlet or bay. **2**. US small stream.

creel n. wicker basket used by anglers.

creep v. **creeping, crept**. **1**. crawl with the body near to the ground. **2**. move with stealthy slow movements. **3**. (of a plant) grow along the ground or over a surface. **4**. have a crawling sensation on the skin, as from disgust. —n. **5**. creeping movement. **6**. Slang obnoxious or servile person. —pl. **7**. feeling of fear or disgust. **creeper** n. creeping plant. **creepy** adj. **creepier, creepiest**. Informal causing a feeling of fear or disgust. **creepy-crawly** n., pl. **-crawlies**. Informal small crawling creature.

cremate v. burn (a corpse) to ash. **cremation** n. **crematorium** n. building where corpses are cremated.

crème de menthe n. liqueur flavoured with peppermint.

crenellated adj. having battlements. **crenellation** n.

creole n. **1**. language developed from a mixture of languages. **2**. (C-) native-born W Indian or Latin American of mixed European and African descent.

creosote n. **1**. dark oily liquid distilled from coal tar and used for preserving wood. —v. **2**. treat with creosote.

crepe [krayp] n. **1**. fabric or rubber with a crinkled texture. **2**. very thin pancake. **crepe paper** paper with a crinkled texture.

crepitate v. make a rattling or crackling sound.

crept v. past of CREEP.

crepuscular adj. **1**. of or like twilight. **2**. (of animals) active at twilight.

Cres. Crescent.

crescendo [krish-end-oh] n., pl. **-dos**. **1**. gradual increase in loudness, esp. in music. —adv. **2**. gradually getting louder.

crescent n. **1**. (shape of) the moon as seen in its first or last quarter. **2**. crescent-shaped street. —adj. **3**. crescent-shaped.

cress n. plant with strong-tasting leaves, used in salads.

crest n. **1**. top of a mountain, hill, or wave.

2. tuft or growth on a bird's or animal's head. **3**. heraldic device used on a coat of arms, notepaper, and elsewhere. —v. **4**. come to or be at the top of. **crested** adj. **crestfallen** adj. disheartened.

cretaceous adj. chalky.

cretin n. **1**. person afflicted with physical and mental retardation caused by a thyroid deficiency. **2**. Informal stupid person. **cretinism** n. **cretinous** adj.

cretonne n. heavy printed cotton fabric used in furnishings.

crevasse n. deep open chasm, esp. in a glacier.

crevice n. narrow fissure or crack.

crew[1] n. **1**. people who man a ship or aircraft. **2**. group of people working together. **3**. Informal any group of people. —v. **4**. serve as a crew member on. **crew cut** man's closely cropped haircut.

crew[2] v. Old-fashioned past tense of CROW.

crewel n. fine worsted yarn used in embroidery.

crib n. **1**. piece of writing stolen from elsewhere. **2**. translation or list of answers used by students, often illicitly. **3**. baby's cradle. **4**. rack for fodder. **5**. short for CRIBBAGE. —v. **cribbing, cribbed**. **6**. copy (someone's work) dishonestly.

cribbage n. card game for two to four players.

crick n. **1**. muscle spasm or cramp, esp. in the back or neck. —v. **2**. cause a crick in.

cricket[1] n. outdoor game played with bats, a ball, and wickets by two teams of eleven. **cricketer** n.

cricket[2] n. chirping insect like a grasshopper.

cried v. past of CRY.

crier n. official who makes public announcements.

crime n. **1**. unlawful act. **2**. unlawful acts collectively. **3**. Informal disgraceful act. **criminal** n. **1**. person guilty of a crime. —adj. **2**. of crime. **3**. Informal deplorable. **criminally** adv. **criminality** n. **criminology** n. study of crime. **criminologist** n.

crimp v. **1**. fold or press into ridges. **2**. curl (hair) tightly.

crimson adj. deep red.

cringe v. **1**. flinch or shrink. **2**. behave in a servile or timid way.

crinkle v., n. wrinkle, twist, or fold. **crinkly** adj.

crinoline n. hooped petticoat.

cripple n. **1.** person who is lame or disabled. —v. **2.** make a cripple of (someone). **3.** damage (something).

crisis n., pl. **-ses. 1.** crucial stage, turning point. **2.** time of acute trouble or danger.

crisp adj. **1.** dry and brittle. **2.** fresh and firm. **3.** (of weather) cold but invigorating. **4.** brisk and lively. **5.** clear and sharp. **6.** clean and neat. —n. **7.** thin slice of potato fried till crunchy. —v. **8.** make or become crisp. **crisply** adv. **crispness** n. **crispy** adj. **crispier**, **crispiest**. **crispbread** n. thin dry biscuit.

crisscross v. **1.** move in, mark with, or consist of a crosswise pattern. —adj. **2.** (of lines) crossing in different directions.

criterion n., pl. **-ria.** standard of judgment.
▷ It is incorrect to use *criteria* as a singular, though this use is often found.

critic n. **1.** professional judge of any of the arts. **2.** person who finds fault. **critical** adj. **1.** very important or dangerous. **2.** seriously ill or injured. **3.** fault-finding. **4.** discerning. **5.** of a critic or criticism. **critically** adv. **criticism** n. **1.** fault-finding. **2.** evaluation of a work of art. **criticize** v. **1.** find fault with. **2.** evaluate. **critique** n. critical essay.

croak v. **1.** (of a frog or crow) give a low hoarse cry. **2.** utter or speak with a croak. **3.** *Slang* die. —n. **4.** low hoarse cry. **croaky** adj. **croakier**, **croakiest**. hoarse.

crochet [kroh-shay] n. **1.** handicraft like knitting, done with a single hooked needle. —v. **-cheting**, **-cheted. 2.** do or make such work.

crock n. **1.** earthenware jar or pot. **2.** *Informal* old or decrepit person or thing. **crockery** n. earthenware or china dishes.

crocodile n. **1.** large amphibious tropical reptile. **2.** line of children walking two by two. **crocodile tears** insincere grief.

crocus n., pl. **-cuses.** small plant with yellow, white, or purple flowers in spring.

croft n. small farm worked by the occupier in Scotland. **crofter** n.

croissant [krwah-son] n. rich flaky crescent-shaped roll.

cromlech n. circle of prehistoric standing stones.

crone n. witchlike old woman.

crony n., pl. **-nies.** close friend.

crook n. **1.** *Informal* criminal. **2.** bent or curved part. **3.** hooked pole. —v. **4.** bend or curve. **crooked** adj. **1.** bent or twisted. **2.** set at an angle. **3.** *Informal* dishonest.

croon v. hum, sing, or speak in a soft low tone. **crooner** n.

crop n. **1.** cultivated plant. **2.** season's total yield of produce. **3.** group of things appearing at one time. **4.** short haircut. **5.** pouch in a bird's gullet. **6.** (handle of) a hunting whip. —v. **cropping**, **cropped. 7.** cut short. **8.** produce or harvest as a crop. **9.** (of animals) feed on (grass etc.). **cropper** n. **come a cropper** *Informal* have a disastrous failure or heavy fall. **crop up** v. *Informal* happen unexpectedly.

croquet [kroh-kay] n. game in which balls are hit through hoops.

croquette [kroh-kett] n. fried cake of potato, meat, or fish.

crosier n. same as CROZIER.

cross n. **1.** structure, symbol, or mark of two intersecting lines. **2.** such structure of wood as a means of execution. **3.** representation of the Cross as an emblem of Christianity. **4.** affliction. **5.** mixture of two things. **6.** hybrid. —v. **7.** move or go across (something). **8.** meet and pass. **9.** mark with lines across. **10.** draw a cross or lines through (something). **11.** place (one's arms or legs) crosswise. **12.** make the sign of the cross on (oneself). **13.** interbreed or cross-fertilize. **14.** thwart or oppose. —adj. **15.** angry, in a bad mood. **16.** lying or placed across. **17.** transverse. **the Cross** *Christianity* the cross on which Christ was crucified. **crossing** n. **1.** place where a street etc. may be crossed. **2.** place where things cross. **3.** journey across water. **crossly** adv. **crossness** n. **crossbar** n. horizontal bar across goalposts or on a bicycle. **cross-bench** n. seat in Parliament for a member belonging to neither the government nor the opposition. **crossbow** n. bow fixed across a wooden stock. **crossbred** adj. bred from two different types of animal or plant. **crossbreed** n. crossbred animal or plant. **crosscheck** v. check using a different method. **cross-country** adj., adv. by way of open country or fields. **cross-examine** v. question (a witness in court) to check his or her testimony. **cross-examination** n. **cross-eyed** adj. with eyes turning inwards. **cross-fertilize** v. fertilize (an animal or plant) from one of a different kind. **cross-fertilization** n. **crossfire** n. gunfire crossing another line of fire. **cross-ply** adj. (of a tyre) having the fabric cords in the outer casing running diagonally. **cross-purposes** pl. n. at cross-purposes misunderstanding each other. **crossreference** n. reference within a text to another part. **crossroads** n. place where roads intersect. **cross section 1.** (diagram of) a surface made by cutting across something. **2.** representative sample. **crosswise** adj., adv. **1.** transverse(ly). **2.** in the shape of a cross. **crossword puzzle, crossword** n. puzzle in which words suggested by clues are written into a grid of squares.

crotch n. fork between the legs.

crotchet n. musical note half the length of a minim.

crotchety adj. Informal bad-tempered.

crouch v. **1.** bend low with the legs and body close. —n. **2.** this position.

croup[1] [kroop] n. throat disease of children, with a cough.

croup[2] [kroop] n. hind quarters of a horse.

croupier [kroop-ee-ay] n. person who collects bets and pays out winnings at a gambling table.

crouton n. small piece of fried or toasted bread served in soup.

crow[1] n. large black bird with a harsh call. **as the crow flies** in a straight line. **crow's feet** wrinkles at the corners of the eyes. **crow's nest** lookout platform high on a ship's mast.

crow[2] v. **1.** (of a cock) utter a shrill squawking sound. **2.** boast of one's superiority. **3.** (of a baby) utter cries of pleasure. —n. **4.** cock's cry.

crowbar n. iron bar used as a lever.

crowd n. **1.** large group of people or things. **2.** particular group of people. —v. **3.** flock together. **4.** press together in a confined space. **5.** fill or occupy fully.

crown n. **1.** monarch's headdress. **2.** wreath for the head. **3.** highest point of something arched or curved. **4.** former British coin worth twenty-five pence. **5.** artificial cover for a broken tooth. **6.** outstanding achievement. —v. **7.** put a crown on (someone's head) to proclaim him or her monarch. **8.** form or put on the top of. **9.** put the finishing touch to (a series of events). **10.** Informal hit on the head. **the Crown** power of the monarchy. **Crown Court** local criminal court in England and Wales. **crown jewels** jewellery used by a sovereign on state occasions. **crown prince, crown princess** heir to the throne.

crozier n. bishop's hooked staff.

CRT cathode-ray tube.

cruces n. a plural of CRUX.

crucial adj. very important, critical. **crucially** adv.

crucible n. pot in which metals are melted.

crucify v. **-fying, -fied. 1.** put to death by fastening to a cross. **2.** treat cruelly. **3.** Informal ridicule publicly. **crucifix** n. model of Christ on the Cross. **crucifixion** n. crucifying. **the Crucifixion 1.** Christianity crucifying of Christ. **2.** representation of this. **cruciform** adj. cross-shaped.

crude adj. **1.** tasteless or vulgar. **2.** in a natural or raw state. **3.** rough, unfinished. **crude oil** unrefined petroleum. **crudely** adv. **crudity** n.

cruel adj. **1.** delighting in others' pain. **2.** causing pain or suffering. **cruelly** adv. **cruelty** n.

cruet n. small container for salt, pepper, etc. at table.

cruise v. **1.** sail about for pleasure. **2.** (of a vehicle, aircraft, or ship) travel at a moderate and economical speed. —n. **3.** voyage for pleasure. **cruiser** n. **1.** motorboat with a cabin. **2.** fast warship. **cruiserweight** n. same as LIGHT HEAVYWEIGHT. **cruise missile** low-flying guided missile.

crumb n. **1.** small fragment of bread or other dry food. **2.** small bit. **crumby** adj. **crumbier, crumbiest.**

crumble v. **1.** break into fragments. **2.** fall apart or decay. —n. **3.** pudding of stewed fruit with a crumbly topping. **crumbly** adj. **-blier, -bliest.**

crummy adj. **-mier, -miest. 1.** Slang inferior. **2.** squalid.

crumpet n. **1.** round soft yeast cake eaten buttered. **2.** Slang sexually attractive women collectively.

crumple v. **1.** crush and crease. **2.** collapse. **crumpled** adj.

crunch v. **1.** crush (food) noisily with the teeth. **2.** (cause to) make a crisp or brittle sound. —n. **3.** crunching sound. **4.** Informal critical moment. **crunchy** adj. **crunchier, crunchiest.**

crupper n. strap that passes from the back of a saddle under a horse's tail.

crusade n. **1.** medieval Christian war to recover the Holy Land from the Muslims. **2.** vigorous campaign in favour of a cause. —v. **3.** take part in a crusade. **crusader** n.

cruse n. small earthenware jug or pot.

crush v. **1.** compress so as to break, injure, or crumple. **2.** break into small pieces. **3.** defeat utterly. —n. **4.** dense crowd. **5.** Informal infatuation. **6.** drink made by crushing fruit.

crust n. **1.** hard outer part of something, esp. bread. **2.** solid outer shell of the earth. —v. **3.** cover with or form a crust. **crusty** adj. **crustier**, **crustiest**. **1.** having a crust. **2.** irritable.

crustacean n. hard-shelled, usu. aquatic animal with several pairs of legs, such as the crab or lobster.

crutch n. **1.** staff with a rest for the armpit, used by a lame person. **2.** support. **3.** crotch.

crux n., pl. **cruxes**, **cruces**. crucial or decisive point.

cry v. **crying**, **cried**. **1.** shed tears. **2.** call or utter loudly. **3.** appeal urgently (for). —n., pl. **cries**. **4.** fit of weeping. **5.** loud utterance. **6.** urgent appeal. **crying** adj. **a crying shame** something demanding immediate attention. **crybaby** n. person who cries too readily. **cry off** v. Informal withdraw from an arrangement.

cryogenics n. branch of physics concerned with very low temperatures. **cryogenic** adj.

crypt n. vault, esp. one under a church.

cryptic adj. **1.** obscure in meaning. **2.** secret. **cryptically** adv. **cryptogram** n. message in code. **cryptography** n. art of writing in and deciphering codes.

cryptogam n. plant that reproduces by spores, not seeds.

crystal n. **1.** glasslike mineral. **2.** very clear and brilliant glass. **3.** tumblers, vases, etc. made of such glass. **4.** (single grain of a) symmetrically shaped solid formed naturally by some substances. —adj. **5.** bright and clear. **crystalline** adj. **1.** of or like crystal or crystals. **2.** clear. **crystallize** v. **1.** make or become definite. **2.** form into crystals. **3.** preserve (fruit) in sugar. **crystallization** n.

Cs Chem. caesium.

CSE Certificate of Secondary Education.

CS gas n. gas causing tears and painful breathing, used to control civil disturbances.

CT Connecticut.

Cu Chem. copper.

cu. cubic.

cub n. **1.** young of certain mammals, such as the lion. **2.** young or inexperienced person. **3.** (C-) Cub Scout. —v. **cubbing**, **cubbed**. **4.** give birth to (cubs). **Cub Scout** member of the junior branch of the Scout Association.

cubbyhole n. small enclosed space or room.

cube n. **1.** solid with six equal square sides. **2.** product obtained by multiplying a number by itself twice. —v. **3.** find the cube of (a number). **4.** cut into cubes. **cubic** adj. **1.** having three dimensions. **2.** cube-shaped. **3.** involving the cubes of numbers. **cubism** n. style of art in which objects are represented by geometrical shapes. **cubist** n., adj. **cube root** number whose cube is a given number.

cubicle n. enclosed part of a large room, screened for privacy.

cubit n. old measure of length based on the length of the forearm.

cuckold n. **1.** man whose wife has committed adultery. —v. **2.** make a cuckold of.

cuckoo n. **1.** migratory bird with a characteristic two-note call, which lays its eggs in the nests of other birds. —adj. **2.** Informal crazy. **cuckoo spit** white frothy mass produced on plants by larvae.

cucumber n. long green-skinned fleshy fruit used in salads.

cud n. partially digested food which a ruminant brings back into its mouth to chew again. **chew the cud** reflect or ponder.

cuddle v. **1.** hug fondly. **2.** nestle. —n. **3.** fond hug. **cuddly** adj. **-dlier**, **-dliest**.

cudgel n. short thick stick used as a weapon.

cue¹ n. **1.** signal to an actor or musician to begin speaking or playing. **2.** signal or reminder. —v. **cueing**, **cued**. **3.** give a cue to (someone).

cue² n. **1.** long tapering stick used in billiards, snooker, or pool. —v. **cueing**, **cued**. **2.** strike (a ball) with a cue.

cuff¹ n. end of a sleeve. **off the cuff** Informal impromptu. **cuff link** one of a pair of decorative fastenings for shirt cuffs.

cuff² v. 1. strike with an open hand. —n. 2. blow with an open hand.

cuisine [quiz-**zeen**] n. style of cooking.

cul-de-sac n. road with one end blocked off.

culinary adj. of the kitchen or cookery.

cull v. 1. gather, select. 2. remove or kill (inferior or surplus animals) from a herd. —n. 3. culling.

culminate v. reach the highest point or climax. **culmination** n.

culottes pl. n. women's flared trousers cut to look like a skirt.

culpable adj. deserving blame. **culpability** n.

culprit n. person guilty of an offence or misdeed.

cult n. 1. specific system of worship. 2. devotion to a person, idea, or activity. 3. popular fashion.

cultivate v. 1. prepare (land) to grow crops. 2. grow (plants). 3. develop or improve (something). 4. try to develop a friendship with (someone). **cultivated** adj. cultured or well-educated. **cultivation** n. **cultivator** n. farm implement for breaking up soil.

culture n. 1. ideas, customs, and art of a particular society. 2. particular society. 3. developed understanding of the arts. 4. development by special training. 5. cultivation of plants or rearing of animals. 6. growth of bacteria for study. —v. 7. grow (bacteria). **cultural** adj. **cultured** adj. showing culture. **cultured pearl** pearl artificially grown in an oyster shell.

culvert n. drain under a road or railway.

cum prep. with, e.g. *kitchen-cum-dining room*.

cumbersome, cumbrous adj. 1. awkward or unwieldy. 2. difficult because of complexity.

cummerbund n. broad sash worn round the waist.

cumin, cummin n. aromatic seeds of a Mediterranean plant, used in cooking.

cumquat n. same as KUMQUAT.

cumulative [kew-myew-la-tiv] adj. increasing steadily.

cumulus [kew-myew-luss] n., pl. -li. cloud shaped in heaped-up rounded masses.

cuneiform [kew-nif-form] n. 1. ancient sys-

tem of writing using wedge-shaped characters. —adj. 2. written in cuneiform.

cunning adj. 1. clever at deceiving. 2. ingenious. —n. 3. cleverness at deceiving. 4. ingenuity. **cunningly** adv.

cup n. 1. small bowl-shaped drinking container with a handle. 2. contents of a cup. 3. (competition with) a cup-shaped trophy given as a prize. 4. hollow rounded shape. 5. mixed drink with fruit juice or wine as a base. —v. **cupping, cupped.** 6. form (one's hands) into the shape of a cup. 7. hold in cupped hands. **cupful** n. **cup tie** eliminating match between two teams in a cup competition.

cupboard n. piece of furniture or recess with a door, for storage.

Cupid n. Roman god of love, shown as a winged boy with a bow and arrow.

cupidity [kew-**pid**-it-ee] n. greed for wealth or possessions.

cupola [kew-pol-la] n. domed roof or ceiling.

cupreous adj. of or containing copper.

cur n. 1. mongrel dog. 2. contemptible person.

curaçao [kew-rah-so] n. orange-flavoured liqueur.

curare [kew-rah-ree] n. poisonous resin of a S American tree, used as a muscle relaxant in medicine.

curate n. clergyman who assists a parish priest. **curacy** [kew-rah-see] n., pl. -cies. work or position of a curate.

curative adj. 1. able to cure. —n. 2. something curative.

curator n. person in charge of a museum or art gallery. **curatorship** n.

curb n. 1. check or restraint. 2. strap under a horse's jaw, used to check it. —v. 3. restrain.

curd n. coagulated milk. **curdle** v. turn into curd, coagulate.

cure v. 1. heal (an ailment or problem). 2. restore to health. 3. preserve by salting, smoking, or drying. —n. 4. restoration to health. 5. medical treatment. 6. remedy or solution. **curable** adj.

curet, curette n. 1. surgical instrument for scraping tissue from body cavities. —v. -**retting, -retted.** 2. scrape with a curet. **curettage** n.

curfew n. 1. law ordering people to stay

indoors after a specific time at night. **2.** time set as a deadline by such a law.

Curia *n., pl.* **-riae.** court and government of the Roman Catholic church.

curie *n.* standard unit of radioactivity.

curio [**kew-ree-oh**] *n., pl.* **-rios.** strange or rare thing valued as a collector's item.

curious *adj.* **1.** eager to know. **2.** eager to find out private details. **3.** unusual or peculiar. **curiously** *adv.* **curiosity** *n.* **1.** eagerness to know. **2.** eagerness to find out private details. **3.** *pl.* **-ties.** strange or rare thing.

curium [**kew-ree-um**] *n.* artificial radioactive element produced from plutonium.

curl *v.* **1.** twist (hair) or (of hair) be twisted into coils. **2.** twist into a spiral or curve. **3.** play at curling. —*n.* **4.** coil of hair. **5.** spiral or curved shape. **curly** *adj.* **curlier, curliest. curler** *n.* pin or small tube for curling hair. **curling** *n.* game like bowls, played with heavy stones on ice.

curlew *n.* long-billed wading bird.

curlicue *n.* ornamental curl or twist.

curmudgeon *n.* bad-tempered or mean person.

currant *n.* **1.** dried grape. **2.** small round berry, such as a redcurrant.

current *adj.* **1.** of the immediate present. **2.** most recent, up-to-date. **3.** commonly accepted. —*n.* **4.** flow of water or air in one direction. **5.** flow of electricity. **6.** general trend. **currently** *adv.* **currency** *n., pl.* **-cies. 1.** money in use in a particular country. **2.** state of being current. **current account** bank account from which money may be drawn at any time by cheque or computerized card.

curriculum *n., pl.* **-la, -lums.** specified course of study. **curriculum vitae** [**vee-tie**] outline of someone's educational and professional history, prepared for job applications.

curry[1] *n., pl.* **-ries. 1.** dish of meat or vegetables in a hot spicy sauce. —*v.* **-rying, -ried. 2.** prepare (food) with curry powder. **curry powder** mixture of spices for making curry.

curry[2] *v.* **-rying, -ried. 1.** groom (a horse) with a currycomb. **2.** dress (leather). **curry favour** ingratiate oneself, esp. with one's superiors. **currycomb** *n.* ridged comb for grooming a horse.

curse *n.* **1.** profane or obscene expression,

usu. of anger. **2.** call to a supernatural power for harm to come to a person. **3.** affliction, misfortune. —*v.* **4.** say profane or obscene things (to). **5.** utter a curse against. **cursed** *adj.* **1.** under a curse. **2.** hateful.

cursive *n., adj.* (handwriting) done with joined letters.

cursor *n.* movable point of light that shows a specific position on a visual display unit.

cursory *adj.* hasty and superficial. **cursorily** *adv.*

curt *adj.* (of speech) impolitely brief. **curtly** *adv.* **curtness** *n.*

curtail *v.* **1.** cut short. **2.** restrict. **curtailment** *n.*

curtain *n.* **1.** piece of cloth hung at a window or opening as a screen. **2.** hanging cloth separating the audience and the stage in a theatre. **3.** fall or closing of the curtain at the end, or the rise or opening of the curtain at the start of a theatrical performance. **4.** thing(s) forming a barrier or screen. —*pl.* **5.** *Informal* death, the end. —*v.* **6.** provide with curtains. **7.** conceal with a curtain. **curtain call** return to the stage by performers to receive applause.

curtsy, curtsey *n., pl.* **-sies, -seys. 1.** woman's gesture of respect made by bending the knees and bowing the head. —*v.* **-sying, -sied** *or* **-seying, -seyed. 2.** make a curtsy.

curve *n.* **1.** continuously bending line with no straight parts. **2.** something that curves or is curved. —*v.* **3.** bend into or move in a curve. **curvy** *adj.* **curvier, curviest. curvaceous** *adj. Informal* (of a woman) having a shapely body. **curvature** *n.* state or degree of being curved. **curvilinear** *adj.* consisting of or bounded by a curve.

cushion *n.* **1.** bag filled with soft material, to make a seat more comfortable. **2.** something that provides comfort or absorbs shock. **3.** resilient rim of a billiard table. —*v.* **4.** protect from injury or shock. **5.** lessen the effects of.

cushy *adj.* **cushier, cushiest.** *Informal* easy, e.g. *a cushy job.*

cusp *n.* **1.** pointed end, esp. on a tooth. **2.** *Astrol.* division between houses or signs of the zodiac.

cuss *Informal* —*n.* **1.** curse, oath. **2.** annoying person. —*v.* **3.** swear (at). **cussed** [**kuss-id**] *adj. Informal* obstinate.

custard n. dish or sauce made of sweetened milk thickened with eggs or cornflour.

custody n. **1.** guardianship. **2.** imprisonment prior to being tried. **custodial** adj. **custodian** n. person in charge of a public building or museum collection.

custom n. **1.** usual habit. **2.** long-established activity or action. **3.** regular use of a shop or business. —pl. **4.** duty charged on imports or exports. **5.** government department which collects these. **6.** area at a port, airport, or border where baggage and freight are examined for dutiable goods. —adj. **7.** made to the specifications of an individual customer. **customary** adj. **1.** usual. **2.** established by custom. **customarily** adv. **customer** n. **1.** person who buys goods or services. **2.** Informal person with whom one has to deal.

cut v. **cutting**, **cut**. **1.** open up, penetrate, wound, or divide with a sharp instrument. **2.** trim or shape by cutting. **3.** divide. **4.** intersect. **5.** reduce. **6.** abridge. **7.** hit (a ball) so that it spins. **8.** Informal snub (a person). **9.** Informal absent oneself from (classes). **10.** call a halt to a shooting sequence in a film. **11.** move quickly to (another scene) in a film. **12.** divide (a pack of cards) at random. —n. **13.** act of cutting. **14.** stroke or incision made by cutting. **15.** piece cut off. **16.** reduction. **17.** abridgment. **18.** style in which hair or a garment is cut. **19.** Informal share, esp. of profits. **cut and dried** Informal settled in advance. **cut back** v. **1.** shorten by cutting. **2.** make a reduction in. **cut in** v. **1.** interrupt. **2.** obstruct another vehicle in overtaking it. **cut off** v. **1.** separate. **2.** stop the supply of. **cut out** v. **1.** shape by cutting. **2.** remove. **3.** (of an engine) cease to operate suddenly. **4.** Informal stop doing (something). **cut-price** adj. at a reduced price. **cut up** v. **1.** cut into pieces. **2.** be cut up Informal be very upset.

cutaneous [kew-**tane**-ee-uss] adj. of the skin.

cute adj. **1.** appealing or attractive. **2.** Informal clever or shrewd. **cutely** adv. **cuteness** n.

cuticle [**kew**-tik-kl] n. skin at the base of a fingernail or toenail.

cutlass n. short curved one-edged sword.

cutlery n. knives, forks, and spoons, used for eating. **cutler** n. maker of cutlery.

cutlet n. **1.** small piece of meat from the neck. **2.** flat croquette of chopped meat or fish.

cutter n. **1.** person or tool that cuts. **2.** any of various small fast boats.

cutthroat adj. **1.** fierce or relentless. —n. **2.** murderer. **3.** razor with a long blade.

cutting n. **1.** piece cut from a plant for rooting or grafting. **2.** article cut from a newspaper or magazine. **3.** passage cut through high ground for a road or railway. —adj. **4.** keen, piercing. **5.** (of a remark) hurtful.

cuttlefish n. sea mollusc like a squid.

CV curriculum vitae.

cwm [koom] n. in Wales, valley.

cwt hundredweight.

cyanide n. extremely poisonous chemical compound.

cyanosis n. blueness of the skin, caused by a deficiency of oxygen in the blood.

cybernetics n. branch of science in which electronic and mechanical systems are studied and compared to biological systems.

cyclamen [**sik**-la-men] n. plant with red, pink, or white flowers having turned-back petals.

cycle n. **1.** bicycle. **2.** motorcycle. **3.** recurrent series of events. **4.** time taken for one such series. **5.** single complete movement in an electrical, electronic, or mechanical process. **6.** set of plays, songs, or poems about a figure or event. —v. **7.** ride a cycle. **8.** occur in cycles. **cyclic**, **cyclical** adj. occurring in cycles. **cyclist** n. person who rides a cycle.

cyclone n. violent wind moving clockwise round a central area. **cyclonic** adj.

cyclotron n. apparatus which accelerates charged particles by means of a strong vertical magnetic field.

cygnet n. young swan.

cylinder n. **1.** solid or hollow body with straight sides and circular ends. **2.** chamber within which the piston moves in an internal-combustion engine. **cylindrical** adj.

cymbal n. percussion instrument consisting of a brass plate which is struck against another or hit with a stick.

Cymric [**kim**-rik] adj. Welsh.

cynic [**sin**-ik] n. person who believes that people always act selfishly. **cynical** adj. **cynically** adv. **cynicism** n.

cynosure [**sin**-oh-zyure] *n.* centre of attention.

cypher *n.* same as CIPHER.

cypress *n.* evergreen tree with very dark foliage, symbolizing mourning.

Cypriot *n.* **1.** native of Cyprus. —*adj.* **2.** relating to Cyprus.

cyst [**sist**] *n.* (abnormal) sac in the body containing fluid or soft matter. **cystic** *adj.* **cystitis** [siss-**tite**-iss] *n.* inflammation of the bladder.

cytology [site-**ol**-a-jee] *n.* study of plant and animal cells. **cytological** *adj.* **cytologist** *n.*

cytoplasm *n.* protoplasm of a cell excluding the nucleus.

czar [**zahr**] *n.* same as TSAR.

Czech *n.* **1.** person from Czechoslovakia. **2.** one of the two official languages of Czechoslovakia. —*adj.* **3.** of Czechoslovakia or its people.

D

d 1. *Physics* density. **2.** the Roman numeral for 500.

D *Chem.* deuterium.

d. 1. died. **2.** *Brit.* old penny.

dab[1] *v.* **dabbing, dabbed. 1.** pat lightly. **2.** apply with short tapping strokes. —*n.* **3.** small amount of something soft or moist. **4.** light tap or stroke. **dab hand** *Informal* person who is particularly good at something.

dab[2] *n.* small flatfish.

dabble *v.* **1.** deal in something superficially. **2.** splash about. **dabbler** *n.*

dabchick *n.* type of small grebe.

dace *n.* small freshwater fish.

dacha *n.* Russian country cottage.

dachshund *n.* dog with a long body and short legs.

Dacron *n. US* ® Terylene.

dactyl *n.* metrical foot of three syllables, one long followed by two short. **dactylic** *adj.*

dad *n. Informal* father.

Dada, Dadaism *n.* early 20th-century artistic movement, founded on the principles of incongruity, irrationality, and irreverence. **Dadaist** *n., adj.*

daddy *n., pl.* **-dies.** *Informal* father.

daddy-longlegs *n. Informal* crane fly.

dado [day-doe] *n., pl.* **-does, -dos.** lower part of an interior wall that is decorated differently from the upper part.

daffodil *n.* spring plant with yellow trumpet-shaped flowers.

daft *adj. Brit. informal* foolish or crazy.

dagger *n.* short stabbing weapon with a pointed blade.

daglock *n.* dung-caked lock of wool around the hindquarters of a sheep.

daguerreotype [dag-**gair**-oh-type] *n.* type of early photograph produced on chemically treated silver.

dahlia [day-lya] *n.* garden plant with showy flowers.

Dáil Éireann [doil **air**-in], **Dáil** *n.* lower chamber of parliament in the Irish Republic.

daily *adj.* **1.** occurring every day or every weekday. —*adv.* **2.** every day. —*n., pl.* **-lies. 3.** daily newspaper. **4.** *Brit. informal* charwoman.

dainty *adj.* **-tier, -tiest. 1.** delicate or elegant. —*n., pl.* **-ties. 2.** small choice cake or sweet. **daintily** *adv.* **daintiness** *n.*

daiquiri [dak-eer-ee] *n.* iced drink containing rum, lime juice, and sugar.

dairy *n., pl.* **dairies. 1.** place for the processing or sale of milk and its products. —*adj.* **2.** of milk or its products. **dairy cattle** cows kept mainly for their milk. **dairy farm** farm where cows are kept mainly for their milk. **dairymaid** *n.* esp. formerly, woman employed to milk cows. **dairyman** *n.* man employed to look after cows.

dais [day-iss] *n.* raised platform in a hall.

daisy *n., pl.* **-sies.** flower with a yellow centre and white petals. **daisy chain** string of daisies made by linking their stems together. **daisywheel** *n.* flat disc in a word processor with radiating spokes for printing letters.

Dalai Lama *n.* chief lama and (until 1959) ruler of Tibet.

dale *n.* open valley, esp. one in N England or SE Scotland.

dally *v.* **-lying, -lied. 1.** dawdle. **2.** (foll. by *with*) amuse oneself (with). **dalliance** *n.* flirtation.

Dalmatian *n.* large dog with a white coat and black spots.

dam[1] *n.* **1.** barrier built across a river to create a lake. **2.** lake created by this. —*v.* **damming, dammed. 3.** restrict by a dam.

dam[2] *n.* female parent of an animal.

damage *v.* **1.** harm. —*n.* **2.** injury or harm to a person or thing. **3.** *Informal* cost, e.g. *what's the damage?* —*pl.* **4.** money to be paid as compensation for injury or loss.

damask *n.* fabric with a pattern woven into it, used for tablecloths etc.

dame *n.* **1.** *Slang* woman. **2.** (D-) title of a

woman who has been awarded the OBE or another order of chivalry.

damn interj. **1.** Slang exclamation of annoyance. —adv., adj. (also **damned**) **2.** Slang extreme or extremely. —v. **3.** declare to be bad or worthless. **4.** swear (at). **5.** (of God) condemn to hell. **6.** prove (someone) guilty, e.g. damning evidence. **damnable** adj. annoying. **damnably** adv. **damnation** n.

damp adj. **1.** slightly wet. —n. **2.** slight wetness, moisture. —v. **3.** make damp. **4.** (foll. by down) reduce the force of (feelings or actions). **damply** adv. **dampness** n. **damp course, damp-proof course** layer of water-resistant material built into the foot of a wall to stop moisture rising. **dampen** v. damp. **damper** n. **1.** depressing influence. **2.** movable plate to regulate the draught in a fire or furnace. **3.** pad in a piano that deadens the vibration of each string.

damsel n. Obs. young woman.

damson n. small blue-black plumlike fruit.

dan n. **1.** Judo, Karate any one of 10 black-belt grades of proficiency. **2.** competitor entitled to a dan grading.

dance v. **1.** move the feet and body rhythmically in time to music. **2.** perform (a particular kind of dance). **3.** skip or leap. **4.** move rhythmically. —n. **5.** social meeting arranged for dancing. **6.** series of steps and movements in time to music. **dance attendance on someone** be prepared to carry out someone's slightest wish. **dancer** n.

D and C Surgery dilat(at)ion and curettage: an operation in which the neck of the womb is stretched and the lining of the womb is scraped, for example to remove diseased tissue.

dandelion n. yellow-flowered wild plant.

dander n. **get one's dander up** Slang become angry.

dandle v. move (a child) up and down on one's knee.

dandruff n. loose scales of dry dead skin shed from the scalp.

dandy n., pl. **-dies. 1.** man who is greatly concerned with the elegance of his appearance. —adj. **-dier, -diest. 2.** Informal very good or fine. **dandified** adj.

dandy-brush n. stiff brush used for grooming a horse.

Dane n. person from Denmark. **Danish** adj. **1.** of Denmark, its people, or their language.

—n. **2.** language of Denmark. **Danish blue** white cheese with blue veins and a strong flavour. **Danish pastry** cake made from rich puff pastry filled with fruit, almond paste, etc.

danger n. **1.** state of being vulnerable to injury or loss. **2.** person or thing that may cause injury. **3.** likelihood that something unpleasant will happen. **danger money** extra money paid for doing dangerous work. **dangerous** adj. **dangerously** adv.

dangle v. **1.** hang freely. **2.** display as an enticement.

dank adj. unpleasantly damp and chilly.

danseuse [dahn-**serz**] n. female dancer.

daphne n. shrub with small bell-shaped flowers.

dapper adj. (of a man) neat in appearance and slight in build.

dapple v. mark with spots. **dappled** adj. **1.** marked with spots of a different colour. **2.** covered in patches of light and shadow. **dapple-grey** n. horse having a grey coat with spots of a different colour.

Darby and Joan n. elderly married couple living in domestic harmony. **Darby and Joan Club** club for elderly people.

dare v. **1.** be courageous enough to try (to do something). **2.** challenge to do something risky. —n. **3.** challenge. **I dare say 1.** it may be (that). **2.** probably. **daring** adj. **1.** willing to take risks. —n. **2.** courage to do dangerous things. **daringly** adv. **daredevil** adj., n. reckless (person).
▷ When dare is used in a question or as a negative, it does not take an -s: he dare not come.

dark adj. **1.** having little or no light. **2.** (of a colour) reflecting little light. **3.** (of hair or skin) brown or black. **4.** gloomy or sinister. **5.** secret, e.g. keep it dark. —n. **6.** absence of light. **7.** night. **in the dark** having no knowledge or information. **darkly** adv. **darkness** n. **darken** v. **dark age** period of ignorance or barbarism. **Dark Ages** period of European history between 500 and 1000 A.D. **dark horse** person who reveals unexpected talents. **darkroom** n. darkened room for processing film.

darling n. **1.** much-loved person. **2.** favourite, e.g. the darling of the gossip columns. —adj. **3.** beloved.

darn[1] v. **1.** mend (a garment) with a series of

interwoven stitches. —*n.* 2. patch of darned work.

darn[2] *interj., adv., adj., v. Euphemistic* damn.

dart *n.* 1. small narrow pointed missile that is thrown or shot, esp. in the game of darts. 2. sudden quick movement. 3. tuck made in dressmaking. —*pl.* 4. indoor game in which darts are thrown at a circular numbered board (**dartboard**). —*v.* 5. move or throw quickly and suddenly.

Darwinism *n.* theory of the origin of animal and plant species by evolution. **Darwinian, Darwinist** *adj., n.*

dash *v.* 1. move hastily. 2. throw or strike violently. 3. frustrate (someone's hopes). —*n.* 4. sudden quick movement. 5. small amount. 6. mixture of style and courage. 7. punctuation mark (–) showing a change of subject. 8. longer symbol used in Morse code. **dashing** *adj.* 1. lively. 2. stylish. **dashboard** *n.* instrument panel in a car, boat, or aircraft. **dash off** *v.* write or produce hastily.

dastardly *adj.* mean and cowardly.

data *n.* 1. series of observations, measurements, or facts. 2. numbers, digits, etc. operated on by a computer. **data base** store of information that can be easily handled by a computer. **data capture** process for converting information into a form that can be handled by a computer. **data processing** series of operations performed on data, esp. by a computer, to extract or interpret information.

▷ *Data* is a Latin plural word but it is generally used as a singular word in English.

date[1] *n.* 1. specified day of the month. 2. particular day or year when an event happened. 3. *Informal* appointment, esp. with a person of the opposite sex. 4. *US informal* this person. —*v.* 5. mark with the date. 6. assign a date of occurrence to. 7. (foll. by *from*) originate from (a date), e.g. *this house dates from the 16th century*. 8. make or become old-fashioned. **dated** *adj.* old-fashioned. **dateline** *n. Journalism* information about the place and time a story was written, placed at the top of the article. **Date Line** (sometimes d- l-) line, approx. equal to 180°, on the east side of which the date is one day earlier than on the west.

date[2] *n.* dark-brown sweet-tasting fruit of the date palm. **date palm** tall palm grown in tropical regions for its fruit.

dative *n.* in certain languages, the form of the noun that expresses the indirect object.

datum *n., pl.* **data.** thing given, known, or assumed as a basis for reckoning, reasoning etc.

daub *v.* 1. smear or spread quickly or clumsily. —*n.* 2. unskilful or crude painting.

daughter *n.* 1. female child. 2. woman who comes from a certain place or is connected with a certain thing, e.g. *daughter of the church*. **daughterly** *adj.* **daughter-in-law** *n., pl.* **daughters-in-law.** son's wife.

daunt *v.* intimidate or dishearten. **daunting** *adj.* **dauntless** *adj.* fearless.

dauphin [daw-fin] *n.* (formerly) eldest son of the king of France.

davenport *n.* 1. small writing table with drawers. 2. *US* large couch.

davit [dav-vit] *n.* crane, usu. one of a pair, at a ship's side, for lowering and hoisting boats.

Davy Jones's locker *n.* the sea, considered as a grave for sailors.

Davy lamp *n.* miner's lamp designed to prevent it from igniting gas.

dawdle *v.* 1. be slow or lag behind. 2. waste time. **dawdler** *n.*

dawn *n.* 1. daybreak. 2. beginning (of something). —*v.* 3. begin to grow light. 4. begin to develop or appear. 5. (foll. by *on* or *upon*) become apparent (to).

day *n.* 1. period of 24 hours. 2. period of light between sunrise and sunset. 3. part of a day occupied with regular activity, esp. work. 4. period or point in time. 5. day of special observance. 6. time of success. **daybreak** *n.* time in the morning when light first appears. **day centre** place providing meals, etc., where elderly or handicapped people can spend the day. **daydream** *n.* 1. pleasant fantasy indulged in while awake. —*v.* 2. indulge in idle fantasy. **daydreamer** *n.* **daylight** *n.* light from the sun. **daylight robbery** *Informal* blatant overcharging. **daylight-saving time** time set one hour ahead of the local standard time to provide an extra hour of light in the evening. **day release** system in which workers go to college one day a week. **day return** reduced price ticket for a journey to a place and back again on the same day. **day room** communal living-room in a hospital or similar institution. **day-to-day** *adj.* routine.

daze v. 1. stun, esp. by a blow or shock. —n. 2. state of confusion or shock. **dazed** adj.

dazzle v. 1. blind temporarily by sudden excessive light. 2. impress greatly. —n. 3. bright light that dazzles. **dazzling** adj. **dazzlingly** adv.

dB, db decibel(s).

DBE Dame Commander of the British Empire.

DC 1. direct current. 2. District of Columbia.

DCM Distinguished Conduct Medal.

DD Doctor of Divinity.

D-day n. day selected for the start of some operation, esp. the Allied invasion of Europe in 1944.

DDT kind of insecticide.

DE Delaware.

de- prefix indicating: 1. removal, e.g. deforest. 2. reversal, e.g. decode. 3. departure, e.g. decamp.

deacon n. 1. Christianity ordained minister ranking immediately below a priest. 2. in some Protestant churches, lay official who assists the minister. **deaconess** n. fem.

deactivate v. make (a bomb etc.) harmless or inoperative.

dead adj. 1. no longer alive. 2. no longer in use. 3. numb, e.g. my leg has gone dead. 4. complete, e.g. a dead stop. 5. Informal very tired. 6. (of a place) lacking activity. —n. 7. period during which coldness or darkness is most intense, e.g. the dead of night. —adv. 8. extremely. 9. suddenly, e.g. stop dead. **the dead** dead people. **dead set against** completely opposed to. **deadbeat** n. Informal lazy useless person. **dead beat** Informal exhausted. **dead end** 1. road with one end blocked off. 2. situation in which further progress is impossible. **dead heat** tie for first place between two participants in a contest. **dead letter** law or rule that is no longer enforced. **deadline** n. time limit. **deadlock** n. 1. point in a dispute at which further progress is impossible. —v. 2. bring to a deadlock. **dead loss** Informal useless person or thing. **dead man's handle, pedal** safety device which only allows equipment to operate when a handle or pedal is being pressed. **dead nettle** plant which resembles a nettle but has no stinging hairs on its leaves. **deadpan** adj., adv. showing no emotion or expression. **dead reckoning** method of establishing one's position using the distance and direction travelled. **dead weight** heavy weight. **dead wood** Informal useless person, thing, etc.

deaden v. 1. make less sensitive or lively. 2. make less resonant.

deadly adj. -lier, -liest. 1. likely to cause death. 2. Informal extremely boring. —adv. 3. extremely. **deadly nightshade** plant with poisonous black berries.

deaf adj. unable to hear. **deaf to** refusing to listen to or take notice of. **deafen** v. make deaf, esp. temporarily. **deafness** n. **deaf-mute** n. person who is unable to hear or speak.

deal[1] v. **dealing, dealt** [delt] 1. distribute. 2. inflict (a blow) on. 3. Cards give out (cards) to the players. 4. Slang sell any illegal drug. —n. 5. transaction or agreement. 6. treatment, e.g. a fair deal. 7. large amount. **dealer** n. **dealings** pl. n. transactions or business relations. **deal in** v. engage in commercially. **deal with** v. 1. take action on. 2. be concerned with.

deal[2] n. plank of fir or pine wood.

dean n. 1. chief administrative official of a college or university faculty. 2. chief administrator of a cathedral. **deanery** n., pl. -eries. 1. office or residence of a dean. 2. parishes of a dean.

dear adj. 1. beloved. 2. costly. —n. 3. someone regarded with affection. **dearly** adv. **dearness** n.

dearth [dirth] n. inadequate amount, scarcity.

death n. 1. permanent end of all functions of life in a person or animal. 2. instance of this. 3. ending, destruction. **deathly** adj., adv. like death, e.g. deathly quiet, deathly pale. **deathless** adj. immortal, esp. because of greatness. **deathbed** n. bed in which a person is about to die or has just died. **deathblow** n. thing or event that destroys hope. **death certificate** document issued by a doctor certifying the death of a person and giving the cause of death if known. **death duty** tax paid on property left at death. **death knell** something that heralds death or destruction. **death mask** cast taken from the face of a person who has recently died. **death row** US part of a prison where convicts awaiting execution are imprisoned. **death's-head** n. human skull or a representation of one. **deathtrap** n. place or vehicle considered very unsafe. **death warrant** official document authorizing the carrying out of an execution. **deathwatch beetle** beetle that bores into wood and makes a tapping sound.

deb n. Informal debutante.

debacle [day-bah-kl] n. disastrous collapse or defeat.

debar v. exclude or bar.

debase v. lower in value, quality, or character. **debasement** n.

debate n. 1. a discussion. 2. a formal discussion of a proposition, at the end of which people vote on whether to accept it. —v. 3. discuss, esp. in a formal assembly. 4. consider (a course of action). **in debate** in doubt, uncertain. **debatable** adj. not absolutely certain.

debauch [dib-bawch] v. 1. make someone immoral, esp. sexually. 2. bout of extreme dissipation. **debauched** adj. immoral, sexually corrupt. **debauchee** n. dissipated person. **debauchery** n.

debenture n. long-term bond, bearing fixed interest, issued by a company or a government agency.

debilitate v. weaken, make feeble. **debilitation** n. **debility** n. weakness, infirmity.

debit n. 1. acknowledgment of a sum owing by entry on the left side of an account. —v. **debiting, debited.** 2. record as a debit. 3. charge a debt.

debonair adj. 1. suave or refined. 2. carefree.

debouch v. move out from a narrow place to a wider one. **debouchment** n.

debrief v. receive a report from (a soldier, diplomat, etc.) after an event. **debriefing** n.

debris [deb-ree] n. fragments of something destroyed.

debt n. 1. something owed, esp. money. 2. state of owing something. **bad debt** a debt that is unlikely ever to be repaid. **debt of honour** a debt that is morally but not legally binding. **debtor** n.

debug v. -bugging, -bugged. 1. Informal find and remove defects in (a device, computer program, etc.). 2. remove concealed microphones from (a room etc.).

debunk v. Informal expose the pretensions or falseness of.

debut [day-byoo] n. first public appearance of a performer. **debutante** [day-byoo-tont] n. young upper-class woman making her first formal appearance in society.

Dec. December.

deca- combining form ten.

decade n. period of ten years.

decadence [dek-a-denss] n. state of deterioration of morality or culture. **decadent** adj.

decaffeinated [dee-kaf-fin-ate-id] adj. (of coffee, tea, etc.) with caffeine removed.

decagon n. geometric figure with ten sides. **decagonal** adj.

decahedron [deck-a-heed-ron] n. solid figure with ten sides.

Decalogue n. the Ten Commandments.

decamp v. depart secretly or suddenly.

decanal [dee-kay-nal] adj. of a dean or deanery.

decant v. 1. pour (a liquid) from one container to another. 2. rehouse (people) while their homes are being refurbished. **decanter** n. stoppered bottle for wine or spirits.

decapitate v. behead. **decapitation** n.

decapod n. 1. creature, such as a crab or shrimp, which has five pairs of walking limbs. 2. creature, such as a squid, which has eight short tentacles and two longer ones.

decarbonize v. remove carbon from (an internal-combustion engine). **decarbonization** n.

decathlon n. athletic contest with ten events.

decay v. 1. rot. 2. become weaker or more corrupt. —n. 3. process of decaying. 4. state brought about by this process.

decease n. Formal death. **deceased** adj. Formal dead. **the deceased** person who has recently died.

deceive v. 1. mislead by lying. 2. be unfaithful to (one's sexual partner). **deceiver** n. **deceit** n. behaviour intended to deceive. **deceitful** adj.

decelerate v. slow down. **deceleration** n.

December n. twelfth month of the year.

decennial adj. 1. lasting for ten years. 2. happening every ten years.

decent adj. 1. (of people) polite and morally acceptable. 2. fitting or proper. 3. conforming to conventions of sexual behaviour. 4. Informal kind. **decently** adv. **decency** n., pl. -cies.

decentralize v. reorganize into smaller local units. **decentralization** n.

deception n. **1.** deceiving. **2.** something that deceives, trick. **deceptive** adj. likely or designed to deceive. **deceptively** adv. **deceptiveness** n.

deci- combining form one tenth.

decibel n. unit for measuring the intensity of sound.

decide v. **1.** (cause to) reach a decision. **2.** settle (a contest or question). **decided** adj. **1.** unmistakable. **2.** determined. **decidedly** adv.

deciduous adj. **1.** (of a tree) shedding its leaves annually. **2.** (of teeth, antlers, etc.) being shed at the end of a period of growth.

decimal n. **1.** fraction written in the form of a dot followed by one or more numbers. —adj. **2.** relating to or using powers of ten. **3.** expressed as a decimal. **decimalize** v. change (a system or number) to the decimal system. **decimalization** n. **decimal currency** system of currency in which the units are parts or powers of ten. **decimal point** dot between the unit and the fraction of a number in the decimal system. **decimal system** number system with a base of ten, in which numbers are expressed by combinations of the digits 0 to 9.

decimate v. destroy or kill a large proportion of. **decimation** n.

decipher v. **1.** decode. **2.** make out the meaning of (poor handwriting). **decipherable** adj.

decision n. **1.** judgment, conclusion, or resolution. **2.** act of making up one's mind. **3.** firmness of purpose. **decisive** adj. **1.** indisputable, e.g. a decisive win. **2.** having the ability to make (quick) decisions. **decisively** adv. **decisiveness** n.

deck n. **1.** area of a ship that forms a floor. **2.** similar area in a bus. **3.** platform that supports the turntable and pick-up of a record player. **4.** US pack (of cards). —v. **5.** decorate. **deck chair** folding chair made of canvas over a wooden frame. **deck hand** sailor assigned duties on the deck of a ship. **deck out** v. dress (oneself) or decorate (a room).

deckle edge n. rough edge on paper, often left as ornamentation.

declaim v. **1.** speak loudly and dramatically. **2.** protest loudly. **declamation** n. **declamatory** adj.

declare v. **1.** state firmly and forcefully. **2.** announce officially. **3.** acknowledge for tax purposes. **4.** Cricket bring an innings to an end before the last batsman is out. **declaration** n. **declaratory** adj.

declassify v. officially state (information or a document) to be no longer secret. **declassification** n.

declension n. Grammar changes in the form of nouns, pronouns, or adjectives to show case, number, and gender.

decline v. **1.** say that one is unwilling to give, accept, or do (something). **2.** become smaller, weaker, or less important. **3.** Grammar list the inflections of (a noun, pronoun, or adjective). —n. **4.** gradual deterioration. **5.** movement downwards. **6.** diminution. **declination** n. Astronomy distance (measured in degrees) by which a star is above or below the celestial equator.

declivity n., pl. **-ties.** downward slope. **declivitous** adj.

declutch v. disengage the clutch of a motor vehicle.

decoct v. extract the essence from (a substance) by boiling. **decoction** n.

decode v. convert from code into ordinary language. **decoder** n.

decoke v. same as DECARBONIZE.

décolleté [day-kol-tay] adj. (of a woman's garment) having a low neckline. **décolletage** [day-kol-tazh] n. low neckline on a woman's dress or blouse.

decommission v. dismantle (an industrial plant or nuclear reactor) to an extent such that it can be safely abandoned.

decompose v. be broken down through chemical or bacterial action. **decomposition** n.

decompress v. **1.** free from pressure. **2.** return to normal atmospheric pressure from a state of higher pressure. **decompression** n. **decompression sickness** disorder characterized by severe pain etc., caused by sudden change in atmospheric pressure.

decongestant n., adj. (drug) that relieves nasal congestion.

decontaminate v. render harmless by the removal of poisons, radioactivity, etc. **decontamination** n.

decor, décor [day-core] n. decorative scheme of a room or house.

decorate v. **1.** ornament. **2.** paint or wallpaper (a room). **3.** award a (military) medal to. **decoration** n. **decorative** adj. **decorator** n.

decorous [dek-a-russ] adj. polite, calm, and sensible in behaviour. **decorously** adv. **decorousness** n.

decorum [dik-**core**-um] n. polite and socially correct behaviour.

decoy n. 1. person or thing used to lure someone into danger. 2. image of a bird or animal, used to lure game within shooting range. —v. 3. lure into danger by means of a decoy.

decrease v. 1. diminish. —n. 2. lessening. 3. amount by which something has been diminished.

decree n. 1. law made by someone in authority. 2. court judgment. —v. 3. order by decree. **decree absolute** final court order in a divorce case, which leaves the parties free to remarry. **decree nisi** court order in a divorce case, which will become absolute unless valid reasons are produced to oppose it.

decrepit adj. weakened or worn out by age or long use. **decrepitude** n.

decretal n. R.C. Church papal decree.

decriminalize v. to make (a formerly illegal act) no longer a crime. **decriminalization** n.

decry v. -**crying**, -**cried**. express disapproval of.

dedicate v. 1. commit (oneself or one's time) wholly to a special purpose or cause. 2. inscribe or address (a book etc.) to someone as a tribute. **dedicated** adj. devoted to a particular purpose or cause. **dedication** n.

deduce v. reach (a conclusion) by reasoning from evidence. **deducible** adj.

deduct v. subtract. **deductible** adj.

deduction n. 1. deducting. 2. something that is deducted. 3. deducing. 4. conclusion reached by deducing. **deductive** adj.

deed n. 1. something that is done. 2. legal document. **deed box** strong box in which legal documents are stored. **deed poll** Law deed made by one party only, esp. one to change one's name.

deejay n. Informal disc jockey.

deem v. have as an opinion.

deep adj. 1. extending or situated far down, inwards, backwards, or sideways. 2. of a specified dimension downwards, inwards, or backwards. 3. coming from or penetrating to a great depth. 4. difficult to understand. 5. of great intensity. 6. (foll. by in) immersed (in). 7. (of a colour) strong or dark. 8. low in pitch. **the deep** Poetic the sea. **deeply** adv. profoundly or intensely. **deepen** v. **deep-freeze** n. same as FREEZER. **deep-fry** v. cook in hot oil deep enough to completely cover the food. **deep-rooted**, **deep-seated** adj. (of ideas, beliefs, etc.) firmly fixed or held.

deer n., pl. **deer**. hoofed mammal with antlers in the male. **deerstalker** n. cloth hat with peaks back and front and earflaps.

deface v. spoil the surface or appearance of. **defacement** n.

de facto adv. 1. in fact. —adj. 2. existing in fact, whether legally recognized or not.

defalcate v. Law embezzle funds entrusted to one.

defame v. attack the good reputation of. **defamation** n. **defamatory** [dif-**fam**-a-tree] adj.

default n. 1. failure to do something. 2. option which a computer system will carry out unless instructed to do otherwise. —v. 3. fail to fulfil an obligation. **by default** because of lack of opposition or prevention. **in default of** in the absence of. **defaulter** n.

defeat v. 1. overcome. 2. thwart. —n. 3. defeating or being defeated. **defeatism** n. ready acceptance or expectation of defeat. **defeatist** n., adj.

defecate v. discharge waste from the body through the anus. **defecation** n.

defect n. 1. imperfection. —v. 2. desert one's cause or country to join the opposing forces. **defective** adj. having a flaw. **defection** n. **defector** n.

defence n. 1. resistance to attack. 2. plea in support of something. 3. a country's military resources. 4. defendant's case in a court of law. 5. Sport players whose chief task is to stop the opposition scoring. **defenceless** adj.

defend v. 1. protect from harm or danger. 2. support in the face of criticism, esp. by argument. 3. represent (a defendant) in court. 4. protect (a title) against a challenge. **defendant** n. person accused of a crime. **defender** n. **defensible** adj. capable of being defended because believed to be right. **defensibility** n. **defensive** adj. 1. intended for defence. 2. overanxious to protect oneself against (threatened) criticism. **defensively** adv.

defer[1] v. **-ferring, -ferred.** delay (something) until a future time. **deferment, deferral** n.

defer[2] v. **-ferring, -ferred.** (foll. by to) comply with the wishes (of). **deference** n. 1. compliance with the wishes of another. 2. respect. **deferential** adj. **deferentially** adv.

defiance n. see DEFY.

deficient adj. 1. lacking some essential. 2. inadequate in quality or quantity. **deficiency** n., pl. **-cies.** 1. lack. 2. state of being deficient. **deficiency disease** condition, such as scurvy, caused by a shortage of vitamins or other nutrients. **deficit** n. amount by which a sum of money is too small.

defile[1] v. desecrate. **defilement** n.

defile[2] n. narrow pass or valley.

define v. 1. state precisely the meaning of. 2. show clearly the outline of. **definable** adj. **definite** adj. 1. clear in meaning. 2. having precise limits. 3. known for certain. **definite article** the word *the*. **definitely** adv. **definition** n. 1. statement of the meaning of a word or phrase. 2. quality of being clear and distinct. **definitive** adj. 1. providing an unquestionable conclusion. 2. being the best example of something. **definitively** adv.

deflate v. 1. (cause to) collapse through the release of gas. 2. take away the self-esteem or conceit from. 3. *Economics* cause deflation of (an economy). **deflation** n. 1. *Economics* reduction in economic activity resulting in lower output and investment. 2. feeling of sadness following excitement. **deflationary** adj.

deflect v. (cause to) turn aside from a course. **deflection** n. **deflector** n.

deflower v. *Lit.* deprive (a woman) of her virginity.

defoliate v. deprive (a plant) of its leaves. **defoliant** n. **defoliation** n.

deforest v. clear of trees. **deforestation** n.

deform v. 1. cause to be misshapen. 2. make ugly. **deformation** n. **deformed** adj. **deformity** n., pl. **-ties.** 1. *Med.* distortion of an organ or part. 2. state of being deformed.

defraud v. take away or withhold money, rights, etc. from (a person) by fraud.

defray v. provide money for (costs or expenses).

defrock v. deprive (a priest) of priestly status.

defrost v. 1. make or become free of frost or ice. 2. to thaw, esp. by removal from a freezer.

deft adj. quick and skilful in movement. **deftly** adv. **deftness** n.

defunct adj. no longer existing or operative.

defuse v. 1. remove the triggering device from (an explosive device). 2. remove the tension from (a situation).

defy v. **-fying, -fied.** 1. resist openly and boldly. 2. elude, esp. in a baffling way, e.g. *defy description.* **defiance** n. open resistance or disobedience. **defiant** adj.

degenerate adj. 1. having deteriorated to a lower mental, moral, or physical level. —n. 2. degenerate person. —v. 3. become degenerate. **degeneracy** n. **degenerate** behaviour. **degeneration** n. **degenerative** adj. (of a disease or condition) getting steadily worse.

degrade v. 1. reduce to dishonour or disgrace. 2. reduce in status or quality. 3. *Chem.* decompose into smaller molecules. **degrading** adj. **degradation** n.

degree n. 1. stage in a scale of relative amount or intensity. 2. academic award given by a university or college on successful completion of a course. 3. unit of measurement for temperature, angles, or latitude and longitude.

dehisce v. (of the seed capsules of some plants) burst open spontaneously. **dehiscence** n. **dehiscent** adj.

dehumanize v. 1. deprive of human qualities. 2. make (an activity) mechanical or routine. **dehumanization** n.

dehumidify v. extract moisture from (something, esp. the air). **dehumidifier** n.

dehydrate v. 1. cause to lose water. 2. deprive (the body) of water. **dehydration** n.

de-ice v. free of ice. **de-icer** n.

deify [day-if-fie] v. **-fying, -fied.** treat or worship as a god. **deification** n.

deign [dane] v. think it worthy of oneself (to do something), condescend.

deism [dee-iz-zum] n. belief in god but not in divine revelation. **deist** n. **deistic** adj.

deity [dee-it-ee] n., pl. **-ties.** 1. god or goddess. 2. state of being divine.

déjà vu [day-zhah voo] n. feeling of having

experienced before something that is actually happening now.

dejected adj. in low spirits. **dejectedly** adv. **dejection** n.

de jure adv., adj. according to law.

dekko n. Brit. slang have a dekko have a look.

delay v. **1.** put off to a later time. **2.** slow up or cause to be late. —n. **3.** act of delaying. **4.** interval of time between events.

delectable adj. delightful or very attractive. **delectation** n. Formal great pleasure.

delegate n. **1.** person chosen to act for others, esp. at a meeting. —v. **2.** entrust (duties or powers) to another person. **3.** appoint as a delegate. **delegation** n. **1.** group of people appointed as delegates. **2.** delegating.

delete v. remove (something written or printed). **deletion** n.

deleterious [del-lit-**eer**-ee-uss] adj. harmful, injurious.

Delft n. type of earthenware, orig. from the town of Delft in the Netherlands, usu. with blue decoration on a white background (also **delftware**).

deli n. Informal delicatessen.

deliberate adj. **1.** carefully thought out in advance. **2.** careful and unhurried. —v. **3.** consider (something) deeply. **deliberately** adv. **deliberation** n. **deliberative** adj. for the purpose of deliberating, e.g. a deliberative assembly.

delicate adj. **1.** fine or subtle in quality or workmanship. **2.** having a fragile beauty. **3.** (of a taste etc.) pleasantly subtle. **4.** easily damaged. **5.** requiring tact. **delicately** adv. **delicacy** n. **1.** being delicate. **2.** pl. **-cies.** something particularly good to eat.

delicatessen n. shop selling imported or unusual foods, often already cooked or prepared.

delicious adj. very appealing, esp. to taste or smell. **deliciously** adv.

delight v. **1.** please greatly. **2.** (foll. by in) take great pleasure (in). —n. **3.** great pleasure. **delightful** adj. **delightfully** adv.

delimit v. mark or prescribe the limits of. **delimitation** n.

delineate [dill-**lin**-ee-ate] v. **1.** show by drawing. **2.** describe in words. **delineation** n.

delinquent n. **1.** someone, esp. a young person, who repeatedly breaks the law. —adj. **2.** repeatedly breaking the law. **delinquency** n., pl. **-cies.**

deliquesce v. become liquid. **deliquescence** n. **deliquescent** adj.

delirium n. **1.** state of excitement and mental confusion, often with hallucinations. **2.** violent excitement. **delirium tremens** [**treh**-menz] trembling and hallucinations caused by acute alcoholism. **delirious** adj. **deliriously** adv.

deliver v. **1.** carry (goods etc.) to a destination. **2.** hand over. **3.** release or rescue. **4.** aid in the birth of. **5.** present (a speech etc.). **6.** strike (a blow) suddenly. **deliverance** n. rescue from danger or captivity. **delivery** n., pl. **-eries. 1.** act of delivering. **2.** something that is delivered. **3.** act of giving birth to a child. **4.** style, esp. in public speaking.

dell n. small wooded hollow.

Delphic adj. ambiguous, like the ancient Greek oracle at Delphi.

delphinium n. plant with spikes of blue flowers.

delta n. **1.** fourth letter of the Greek alphabet. **2.** flat area at the mouth of some rivers where the main stream splits up into several branches. **delta wing** triangular aircraft wing.

delude v. deceive.

deluge [**del**-lyooj] n. **1.** great flood of water. **2.** torrential rain. **3.** overwhelming number. —v. **4.** flood. **5.** overwhelm.

delusion n. **1.** mistaken idea or belief. **2.** state of being deluded. **delusive** adj.

de luxe adj. **1.** rich or sumptuous. **2.** superior in quality.

delve v. **1.** research deeply (for information). **2.** Old-fashioned dig.

demagnetize v. remove magnetic properties from.

demagogue n. political agitator who appeals to the prejudice and passions of the mob. **demagogic** adj. **demagogy** n.

demand v. **1.** ask for forcefully. **2.** require as just, urgent, etc. **3.** claim as a right. —n. **4.** forceful request. **5.** Economics willingness and ability to purchase goods and services. —pl. **6.** something that requires special effort or sacrifice. **demanding** adj. requiring a lot of time or effort.

▷ The verb **demand** is followed by either of

or *from: demand too much of them; demand an explanation from you.*

demarcate *v. Formal* establish limits or boundaries, esp. between the work performed by different trade unions. **demarcation** *n.*

demean *v.* lower (someone) in dignity, character, or status.

demeanour *n.* way a person behaves.

demented *adj.* mad. **dementedly** *adv.* **dementia** [dim-**men**-sha] *n.* state of serious mental deterioration.

demerara sugar *n.* brown crystallized cane sugar.

demerger *n.* separation of two or more companies which have previously been merged.

demerit *n.* flaw, disadvantage.

demesne [dim-**mane**] *n.* **1.** land surrounding a house. **2.** *Law* possession of one's own property or land.

demi- *combining form* half.

demigod *n.* **1.** being who is part mortal, part god. **2.** godlike person.

demijohn *n.* large bottle with a short neck, often encased in wicker.

demilitarize *v.* remove the military forces from. **demilitarization** *n.*

demimonde *n.* **1.** esp. in the 19th century, class of women considered to be outside respectable society, because of promiscuity. **2.** group considered not wholly respectable.

demise *n.* **1.** *Formal* death. **2.** eventual failure (of something successful).

demisemiquaver *n. Music* note with the time value of one thirty-second of a semibreve.

demist *v.* make or become free of condensation. **demister** *n.*

demo *n., pl.* **demos.** *Informal* **1.** demonstration, organized expression of public opinion. **2.** demonstration record or tape.

demob *v. Informal* demobilize.

demobilize *v.* release from the armed forces. **demobilization** *n.*

democracy *n., pl.* **-cies. 1.** government by the people or their elected representatives. **2.** state governed in this way. **3.** social equality. **democrat** *n.* **1.** advocate of democracy. **2.** (D-) member or supporter of the Democratic Party in the US. **democratic** *adj.* **1.** connected with democracy. **2.**

upholding democracy. **3.** (D-) of the Democratic Party, the more liberal of the two main political parties in the US. **democratically** *adv.*

demography *n.* study of population statistics, such as births and deaths. **demographer** *n.* **demographic** *adj.*

demolish *v.* **1.** tear down or break up (buildings). **2.** put an end to (an argument etc.). **demolisher** *n.* **demolition** *n.*

demon *n.* **1.** evil spirit. **2.** person extremely skilful in or devoted to a given activity. **demonic** *adj.* **demoniacal, demoniac** *adj.* **1.** appearing to be possessed by a devil. **2.** frenzied. **demoniacally** *adv.* **demonology** *n.* study of demons.

demonetize *v.* withdraw (a coin etc.) from use as currency. **demonetization** *n.*

demonstrate *v.* **1.** show or prove by reasoning or evidence. **2.** reveal the existence of. **3.** display and explain the workings of. **4.** show support or protest by public parades or rallies. **demonstrable** *adj.* able to be proved. **demonstrably** *adv.* **demonstration** *n.* **1.** organized expression of public opinion. **2.** proof. **3.** explanation or experiment showing how something works. **4.** show of emotion. **demonstrative** *adj.* tending to express one's feelings unreservedly. **demonstratively** *adv.* **demonstrator** *n.* **1.** person who demonstrates machines, products, etc. **2.** person who takes part in a public demonstration.

demoralize *v.* undermine the morale of. **demoralization** *n.*

demote *v.* reduce in status or rank. **demotion** *n.*

demotic *adj.* **1.** of the common people; popular. **2.** (*sometimes* D-) in or denoting the everyday as distinct from literary form of various languages, e.g. *Demotic Greek.*

demur *v.* **-murring, -murred. 1.** show reluctance. —*n.* **2.** without demur without objecting.

demure *adj.* quiet, reserved, and rather shy. **demurely** *adv.* **demureness** *n.*

demystify *v.* remove the mystery from; make clear. **demystification** *n.*

den *n.* **1.** home of a wild animal. **2.** small secluded room in a home. **3.** place where people indulge in criminal or immoral activities, e.g. *den of iniquity.*

denarius *n., pl.* **-narii.** ancient Roman silver coin, often called a penny in translation.

denationalize v. transfer (an industry) from public to private ownership. **denationalization** n.

denature v. 1. change the nature of. 2. make (alcohol) unfit to drink.

dendrology n. study of trees.

dene, dean n. valley.

dengue [deng-gee] n. infectious tropical fever.

denial n. see DENY.

denier [den-yer] n. unit of weight used to measure the fineness of silk and man-made fibres.

denigrate v. criticize unfairly. **denigration** n. **denigrator** n.

denim n. 1. hard-wearing cotton fabric. —pl. 2. jeans made of denim.

denizen n. inhabitant.

denominate v. give a specific name to. **denomination** n. 1. group having a distinctive interpretation of a religious faith. 2. grade or unit of value, measure, etc. **denominational** adj. **denominator** n. number below the line in a fraction.

denote v. 1. be a sign of. 2. have as a literal meaning. **denotation** n.

denouement, dénouement [day-noo-mon] n. final outcome or solution, esp. in a play or book.

denounce v. 1. speak violently against. 2. give information against. **denunciation** n. open condemnation. **denunciatory** adj.

dense adj. 1. closely packed. 2. difficult to see through. 3. stupid. **densely** adv. **density** n., pl. -ties. 1. degree to which something is filled or occupied. 2. measure of the compactness of a substance, expressed as its mass per unit volume.

dent n. 1. hollow in a surface, as made by a blow. —v. 2. make a dent in.

dental adj. of or relating to the teeth or dentistry. **dental floss** waxed thread used to remove food particles from between the teeth. **dental surgeon** dentist. **dentate** adj. having teeth or teethlike features. **dentifrice** [den-tif-riss] n. paste or powder for cleaning the teeth. **dentine** [den-teen] n. hard dense tissue forming the bulk of a tooth. **dentition** n. 1. typical arrangement of teeth in a species. 2. Formal teething. **denture** n. 1. artificial tooth. —pl. 2. set of artificial teeth.

dentist n. person qualified to practise dentistry. **dentistry** n. branch of medicine concerned with the teeth and gums.

denude v. (foll. by of) remove the covering or protection from. **denudation** n.

denunciation n. see DENOUNCE.

deny v. -nying, -nied. 1. declare to be untrue. 2. refuse to give or allow. 3. refuse to acknowledge. **deniable** adj. **denial** n. 1. denying. 2. statement that something is not true.

deodorize v. remove or disguise the smell of. **deodorization** n. **deodorant** n. substance applied to the body to mask the smell of perspiration.

deoxyribonucleic acid n. same as DNA.

dep. 1. department. 2. departure.

depart v. 1. leave. 2. differ. **departed** adj. Euphemistic dead. **the departed** a dead person or dead people. **departure** n.

department n. 1. specialized division of a large organization. 2. major subdivision of the administration of a government. 3. administrative division of France and some other countries. 4. Informal area or subject a person has an interest in or responsibility for. **departmental** adj. **department store** large shop selling many kinds of goods.

depend v. 1. (foll. by on or upon) put trust (in). 2. be influenced or determined (by). 3. rely (on) for income or support. **dependable** adj. **dependably** adv. **dependability** n. **dependant** n. person who depends on another for financial support. **dependence** n. state of being dependent. **dependency** n., pl. -cies. 1. territory subject to a state on which it does not border. 2. overreliance on another person or a drug. **dependent** adj. depending on a person or thing for support.

depict v. 1. give a picture of. 2. describe in words. **depiction** n.

depilate [dep-pill-ate] v. remove hair from. **depilation** n. **depilatory** [dip-pill-a-tree] n., pl. -tories, adj. (substance) designed to remove unwanted hair.

deplete v. 1. use up. 2. reduce in number. **depletion** n.

deplore v. express or feel strong disapproval of. **deplorable** adj. very bad.

deploy v. organize (troops or resources) into a position ready for immediate action. **deployment** n.

deponent *n. Law* person who makes a statement on oath.

depopulate *v.* cause to be reduced in population. **depopulation** *n.*

deport *v.* remove forcibly from a country. **deport oneself** behave oneself in a specified manner. **deportation** *n.* **deportee** *n.*

deportment *n.* manner in which a person behaves.

depose *v.* **1.** remove from an office or position of power. **2.** *Law* make a statement on oath.

deposit *v.* **1.** put down. **2.** entrust for safekeeping, esp. to a bank. **3.** lay down naturally. —*n.* **4.** entrusting of money to a bank. **5.** money entrusted. **6.** money given in part payment or as security. **7.** accumulation of sediments, minerals, etc. **deposit account** bank account on which interest is paid, but from which money cannot be paid by cheque. **depositary** *n., pl.* -taries. person to whom something is entrusted for safety. **depositor** *n.* **depository** *n., pl.* -tories. store for furniture etc.

deposition *n.* **1.** *Law* sworn statement of a witness used in court in his or her absence. **2.** deposing. **3.** depositing. **4.** something deposited.

depot [dep-oh] *n.* **1.** building used for storage. **2.** *Brit.* building for the storage and servicing of buses or railway engines. **3.** *US* bus or railway station.

deprave *v.* make morally bad. **depraved** *adj.* **depravity** *n.* moral corruption.

deprecate *v.* express disapproval of, protest against. **deprecation** *n.* **deprecatory** *adj.*

depreciate *v.* **1.** decline in value or price. **2.** criticize. **depreciation** *n.* **depreciatory** *adj.*

depredation *n.* plundering.

depress *v.* **1.** lower the spirits of (someone). **2.** lower (prices or wages). **3.** push down. **depressing** *adj.* **depressingly** *adv.* **depressant** *n.* drug which reduces nervous activity. **depression** *n.* **1.** mental state in which a person has feelings of gloom and inadequacy. **2.** economic condition in which there is high unemployment, low output and investment. **3.** area of low air pressure. **4.** hollow or other sunken place. **the Depression** the worldwide economic depression of the early 1930s. **depressive** *adj.* **1.**

tending to cause depression. —*n.* **2.** person who tends to suffer from depression.

deprive *v.* (foll. by *of*) prevent from (possessing or enjoying). **deprivation** *n.* **deprived** *adj.* lacking adequate living conditions, education, etc.

dept department.

depth *n.* **1.** distance downwards, backwards, or inwards. **2.** intensity of emotion. **3.** profundity of character or thought. **4.** intensity of colour. —*pl.* **5.** remote inaccessible place, e.g. *the depths of the forest.* **6.** most severe part, e.g. *the depths of winter.* **7.** depressed emotional state. **depth charge** bomb used to attack submarines by exploding at a preset depth of water.

depute *v.* **1.** appoint (someone) to act on one's behalf. —*n.* **2.** *Scot.* assistant or deputy. **deputation** *n.* body of people appointed to represent others. **deputize** *v.* act as a deputy. **deputy** *n., pl.* -ties. person appointed to act on behalf of another.

derail *v.* cause (a train) to go off the rails. **derailment** *n.*

derailleur [dee-rail-yer] *n.* a type of gearchange mechanism for bicycles.

derange *v.* **1.** make insane. **2.** throw into disorder. **derangement** *n.*

derby *n., pl.* -bies. **1.** sporting event between teams from the same area. **2.** *US* bowler hat. **the Derby** annual horse race run at Epsom Downs.

deregulate *v.* remove regulations or controls from. **deregulation** *n.*

derelict *adj.* **1.** deserted or abandoned. **2.** falling into ruins. —*n.* **3.** social outcast, vagrant. **dereliction** *n.* **1.** wilful neglect (of duty). **2.** state of being abandoned.

derestrict *v.* make (a road) free from speed limits.

deride *v.* speak of or treat with contempt or ridicule. **derision** *n.* **derisive** *adj.* mocking or scornful. **derisory** *adj.* so small or inadequate that it is not worth serious consideration.

de rigueur [de rig-gur] *adj.* required by fashion.

derive *v.* (foll. by *from*) draw or be drawn (from) in origin. **derivation** *n.* **derivative** *adj.* **1.** not original but based on other sources. —*n.* **2.** word, idea, etc. derived from another. **3.** *Maths* rate of change of one quantity in relation to another.

dermatitis *n.* inflammation of the skin.

dermatology *n.* branch of medicine concerned with the skin. **dermatologist** *n.*

derogate *v.* (usu. foll. by *from*) cause to seem inferior; detract from. **derogation** *n.*

derogatory [dir-**rog**-a-tree] *adj.* intentionally offensive.

derrick *n.* **1.** simple crane. **2.** framework erected over an oil well.

derring-do *n.* *Old-fashioned or literary* spirited bravery, boldness.

derringer *n.* small pistol with a large bore.

derv *n.* diesel oil, when used for road transport.

dervish *n.* member of a Muslim religious order noted for a frenzied whirling dance.

desalination *n.* process of removing salt, esp. from sea water.

descale *v.* remove the hard coating which sometimes forms inside kettles, pipes, etc.

descant *n.* **1.** *Music* tune played or sung above a basic melody. —*adj.* **2.** being the highest-pitched of certain families of musical instruments, as in *descant recorder*.

descend *v.* **1.** move down (a slope etc.). **2.** move to a lower level, pitch, etc. **3.** (foll. by *to*) stoop to (unworthy behaviour). **4.** (foll. by *on*) visit unexpectedly. **be descended from** be connected by a blood relationship to. **descendant** *n.* person or animal descended from an individual, race, or species. **descendent** *adj.* descending. **descent** *n.* **1.** act of descending. **2.** downward slope. **3.** derivation from an ancestor.

describe *v.* **1.** give an account of (something or someone) in words. **2.** trace the outline of (a circle etc.). **description** *n.* **1.** statement that describes something or someone. **2.** sort, e.g. *reptiles of every description.* **descriptive** *adj.* **descriptively** *adv.*

descry *v.* **-scrying, -scried. 1.** catch sight of. **2.** discover by looking carefully.

desecrate *v.* violate the sacred character of (an object or place). **desecration** *n.*

desegregate *v.* end racial segregation in. **desegregation** *n.*

deselect *v.* *Brit. politics* refuse to select (an MP) for re-election. **deselection** *n.*

desensitize *v.* make insensitive or less sensitive.

desert[1] *n.* region that has little or no vegeta-

tion because of low rainfall. **desert island** small uninhabited island in the tropics.

desert[2] *v.* **1.** abandon (a person or place) without intending to return. **2.** *Mil.* abscond from (a post or duty) with no intention of returning. **deserter** *n.* **desertion** *n.*

deserts *pl. n.* **get one's just deserts** get the punishment one deserves.

deserve *v.* be entitled to or worthy of. **deserved** *adj.* rightfully earned. **deservedly** [dee-**zerv**-id-lee] *adv.* **deserving** *adj.* worthy, esp. of praise or help.

deshabille [day-zab-**beel**] *n.* same as DISHABILLE.

desiccate *v.* remove most of the water from. **desiccation** *n.*

design *v.* **1.** work out the structure or form of (something), as by making a sketch or plans. **2.** plan and make artistically. **3.** intend for a specific purpose. —*n.* **4.** preliminary drawing. **5.** arrangement or features of an artistic or decorative work. **6.** art of designing. **7.** intention, e.g. *by design.* **designedly** [dee-**zine**-id-lee] *adv.* by intention. **designer** *n.* **1.** person who draws up original sketches or plans from which things are made. —*adj.* **2.** designed by a well-known designer. **designing** *adj.* crafty, cunning.

designate [**dez**-zig-nate] *v.* **1.** give a name to. **2.** select (someone) for an office or duty. —*adj.* **3.** appointed but not yet in office. **designation** *n.* name.

desire *v.* **1.** long for. —*n.* **2.** strong feeling of wanting something. **3.** sexual appetite. **4.** person or thing desired. **desirable** *adj.* **1.** worth having. **2.** arousing sexual desire. **desirability** *n.* **desirous of** having a desire for.

desist *v.* (foll. by *from*) stop or abstain (from).

desk *n.* **1.** piece of furniture with a writing surface and usually drawers. **2.** service counter in a public building. **3.** section of a newspaper covering a specific subject, e.g. *the news desk.* **desktop** *adj.* denoting a computer system small enough to use at a desk.

desolate *adj.* **1.** uninhabited and bleak. **2.** without hope. —*v.* **3.** lay waste. **4.** make (a person) very sad. **desolation** *n.*

despair *v.* **1.** lose hope. —*n.* **2.** total loss of hope.

despatch *v., n.* same as DISPATCH.

desperado *n., pl.* **-does, -dos.** reckless person ready to commit any violent illegal act.

desperate *adj.* **1.** careless of danger, as from despair. **2.** (of an action) undertaken as a last resort. **3.** having a great need or desire. **desperately** *adv.* **desperation** *n.*

despise *v.* look down on with contempt. **despicable** *adj.* worthy of being despised. **despicably** *adv.*

despite *prep.* in spite of.

despoil *v. Formal* plunder. **despoliation** *n.*

despondent *adj.* dejected or depressed. **despondently** *adv.* **despondency** *n.*

despot *n.* person in power who acts tyrannically. **despotic** *adj.* **despotically** *adv.* **despotism** *n.* tyrannical government or behaviour.

dessert *n.* sweet course served at the end of a meal. **dessertspoon** *n.* spoon between a tablespoon and a teaspoon in size.

destabilize *v.* make (a country or government) politically or economically unstable. **destabilization** *n.*

destination *n.* place to which someone or something is going.

destine [**dess**-tin] *v.* set apart (for a certain purpose).

destiny *n., pl.* **-nies. 1.** future destined for a person or thing. **2.** (**D-**) the power that predetermines the course of events.

destitute *adj.* **1.** totally impoverished. **2.** (foll. by *of*) totally lacking. **destitution** *n.*

destroy *v.* **1.** ruin. **2.** put an end to. **3.** kill (an animal). **destroyer** *n.* **1.** small heavily armed warship. **2.** person or thing that destroys.

destruction *n.* **1.** destroying or being destroyed. **2.** cause of ruin. **destructible** *adj.* able to be destroyed. **destructive** *adj.* **1.** causing destruction. **2.** intending to discredit someone, without positive suggestions, e.g. *destructive criticism.* **destructively** *adv.* **destructiveness** *n.*

desuetude [diss-**syoo**-it-tude] *n.* condition of not being in use.

desultory [**dez**-zl-tree] *adj.* **1.** changing fitfully from one thing to another. **2.** random. **desultorily** *adv.*

detach *v.* disengage and separate. **detachable** *adj.* **detached** *adj.* **1.** standing apart. **2.** showing no emotional involvement. **detachment** *n.* **1.** aloofness. **2.** small group of soldiers.

detail *n.* **1.** item that is considered separately. **2.** unimportant item. **3.** treatment of particulars. **4.** *Chiefly mil.* personnel assigned a specific duty. — *v.* **5.** list fully. **6.** assign to a specific duty.

detain *v.* **1.** delay (someone). **2.** hold (someone) in custody. **detainee** *n.* **detainment** *n.*

detect *v.* **1.** notice. **2.** discover the existence or presence of. **detectable** *adj.* **detection** *n.* **detective** *n.* policeman or private agent who investigates crime. **detector** *n.* instrument used to find something, e.g. *smoke detector.*

detente, détente [day-**tont**] *n.* easing of tension between nations.

detention *n.* **1.** imprisonment. **2.** form of punishment in which a pupil is detained after school.

deter *v.* **-terring, -terred.** discourage (someone) from doing something by instilling fear or doubt. **deterrent** *n.* **1.** something that deters. **2.** weapon, esp. nuclear, to deter attack by another nation. —*adj.* **3.** tending to deter. **deterrence** *n.*

detergent *n.* **1.** chemical cleansing agent. —*adj.* **2.** having cleansing power.

deteriorate *v.* become worse. **deterioration** *n.*

determine *v.* **1.** settle (an argument or a question) conclusively. **2.** find out the facts about (something). **3.** make a decision to do something. **determinable** *adj.* able to be determined or found out. **determinant** *n.* factor that determines. **determinate** *adj.* definitely limited or fixed. **determination** *n.* **1.** condition of being determined or resolute. **2.** act of determining. **determined** *adj.* firmly decided, unable to be persuaded. **determinedly** *adv.* **determiner** *n. Grammar* word that determines the object to which a noun phrase refers, e.g. *all.* **determinism** *n.* theory that human choice is not free, but decided by past events. **determinist** *n., adj.* **deterministic** *adj.*

detest *v.* dislike intensely. **detestable** *adj.* **detestation** *n.*

dethrone *v.* remove from a throne or deprive of high position.

detonate *v.* cause (an explosive device) to explode or (of an explosive device) explode. **detonation** *n.* **detonator** *n.* small amount of explosive, or a device, used to set off an explosion.

detour n. deviation from a direct route or course of action.

detoxify v. **-fying, -fied.** remove poison from. **detoxification** n.

detract v. (foll. by from) lessen the value of, diminish. **detractor** n. **detraction** n.

detriment n. disadvantage or damage. **detrimental** adj. **detrimentally** adv.

detritus [dit-**trite**-uss] n. **1.** loose mass of stones or silt worn away from rocks. **2.** debris. **detrital** adj.

de trop [de **troh**] adj. French **1.** not wanted. **2.** in the way.

detumescence n. subsidence of swelling. **detumescent** adj.

deuce [**dyewss**] n. **1.** playing card or dice with two spots. **2.** Tennis score of forty all.

deus ex machina n. Latin unlikely development introduced into a play, film, etc. to resolve the plot.

deuterium n. isotope of hydrogen twice as heavy as the normal atom.

Deutschmark [**doytch**-mark], **Deutsche Mark** [**doytch**-a] n. monetary unit of Germany.

deutzia [**dyewt**-see-a] n. shrub with white or pink flower clusters.

devalue v. **-valuing, -valued. 1.** reduce the exchange value of (a currency). **2.** reduce the value of (something or someone). **devaluation** n.

Devanagari n. alphabet used in various Indian languages including Hindi.

devastate v. **1.** destroy. **2.** upset greatly. **devastation** n.

develop v. **1.** grow or bring to a later, more elaborate, or more advanced stage. **2.** come or bring into existence. **3.** improve the value or change the use of (land). **4.** treat (a photographic plate or film) to produce a visible image. **developer** n. **1.** person who develops property. **2.** chemical used to develop photographs or films. **development** n. **1.** process of growing or developing. **2.** product of developing. **3.** fact or event that changes a situation. **4.** area of land that has been developed. **developmental** adj. **developing country** poor or nonindustrial country that is seeking to develop its resources by industrialization.

deviate v. **1.** differ from others in belief or

thought. **2.** turn aside from a course of action. **deviation** n. **deviant** n., adj. (person) deviating from what is considered acceptable behaviour. **deviance** n.

device n. **1.** machine or tool used for a specific task. **2.** scheme or trick. **3.** design or emblem. **leave someone to his, her own devices** let someone do as he or she wishes.

devil n. **1.** evil spirit. **2.** person regarded as wicked. **3.** person, e.g. poor devil. **4.** person regarded as daring. **5.** Informal something difficult or annoying. —v. **-illing, -illed. 6.** prepare (food) with a highly flavoured spiced mixture. **7.** do routine literary work, esp. for a lawyer or author. **the Devil** Christianity chief spirit of evil and enemy of God. **devilish** adj. **1.** of or like the devil. —adv. **2.** (also **devilishly**) Informal extremely. **devilment** n. mischievous conduct. **devilry** n. **1.** reckless fun. **2.** wickedness. **devil-may-care** adj. happy-go-lucky. **devil's advocate** person who takes an opposing or unpopular point of view for the sake of argument.

devious adj. **1.** not sincere or straightforward. **2.** indirect. **deviously** adv. **deviousness** n.

devise v. work out (something) in one's mind.

devoid adj. (foll. by of) destitute (of) or free (from).

devolve v. (foll. by on, upon, or to) pass (power or duties) or (of power or duties) be passed to a successor or substitute. **devolution** n. transfer of authority from a central government to regional governments.

devote v. apply or dedicate to some cause. **devoted** adj. feeling loyalty or devotion. **devotedly** adv. **devotee** [dev-vote-tee] n. **1.** person ardently enthusiastic about something. **2.** zealous follower of a religion. **devotion** n. **1.** strong affection for or loyalty to a cause or person. **2.** religious zeal or piety. —pl. **3.** prayers. **devotional** adj.

devour v. **1.** eat up greedily. **2.** engulf and destroy. **3.** read or look at avidly. **devouring** adj.

devout adj. deeply religious. **the devout** people who are strong believers in a religion. **devoutly** adv.

dew n. drops of water condensed on a cool surface at night from vapour in the air. **dewy** adj. **dewier, dewiest. dewy-eyed** adj. naive, innocent, and trusting.

dewberry n. type of bramble with blue-black fruits.

dewclaw n. nonfunctional claw on a dog's leg.

dewlap n. loose fold of skin hanging under the throat in dogs, cattle, etc.

dexterity n. **1.** skill in using one's hands. **2.** mental quickness. **dexterous** adj. **dexterously** adv.

dextrin, dextrine n. sticky substance obtained from starch, used as a thickening agent in foods.

dextrose n. glucose occurring in fruit, honey, and the blood of animals.

DF Defender of the Faith.

dg decigram.

DH Department of Health.

dhal, dal n. **1.** nutritious pea-like seed of a tropical shrub. **2.** curry made from lentils or other pulses.

dharma n. **1.** Hinduism moral law or behaviour. **2.** Buddhism ideal truth.

dhoti n., pl. **-tis.** long loincloth worn by men in India.

dhow n. type of Arab sailing vessel.

DHSS formerly, Department of Health and Social Security.

DI donor insemination: method of making a woman pregnant by transferring sperm from a man other than her husband or regular partner using artificial means.

di- prefix **1.** twice; two; double, e.g. dicotyledon. **2.** containing two specified atoms or groups of atoms, e.g. carbon dioxide.

diabetes [die-a-**beet**-eez] n. disorder in which an abnormal amount of urine containing an excess of sugar is excreted. **diabetic** n. **1.** person who has diabetes. —adj. **2.** of or having diabetes. **3.** suitable for people with diabetes.

diabolic adj. **1.** of the devil. **2.** extremely cruel. **diabolical** adj. Informal extremely bad. **diabolically** adv. **diabolism** n. witchcraft, devil worship.

diachronic adj. of the study of the development of a phenomenon through time.

diaconate n. position or period of office of a deacon. **diaconal** adj.

diacritic n. sign above or below a letter or character to indicate phonetic value or stress.

diadem n. Old-fashioned crown.

diaeresis n., pl. **-ses.** same as DIERESIS.

diagnosis [die-ag-**no**-siss] n., pl. **-ses** [-seez] discovery and identification of diseases from the examination of symptoms. **diagnose** v. **diagnostic** adj.

diagonal adj. **1.** from corner to corner. **2.** slanting. —n. **3.** diagonal line. **diagonally** adv.

diagram n. sketch demonstrating the form or workings of something. **diagrammatic** adj. **diagrammatically** adv.

dial n. **1.** face of a clock or watch. **2.** graduated disc on a measuring instrument. **3.** control on a radio or television used to change the station. **4.** numbered disc on the front of some telephones. —v. **dialling, dialled. 5.** try to establish a telephone connection with (someone) by operating the dial or buttons on a telephone. **dialling tone** continuous sound heard on picking up a telephone, indicating that a number can be dialled.

dialect n. form of a language spoken in a particular area. **dialectal** adj.

dialectic n. logical debate by question and answer to resolve differences between two views. **dialectical** adj.

dialogue n. **1.** conversation between two people. **2.** discussion between representatives of two nations or groups.

dialysis [die-**al**-iss-iss] n. Med. filtering of blood through a membrane to remove waste products.

diamagnetism n. phenomenon exhibited by substances that are repelled by both poles of a magnet.

diamanté [die-a-**man**-tee] adj. decorated with artificial jewels or sequins.

diameter n. (length of) a straight line through the centre of a circle or sphere. **diametric, diametrical** adj. **1.** of a diameter. **2.** completely opposed, e.g. diametrical opposites. **diametrically** adv.

diamond n. **1.** exceptionally hard, usually colourless, precious stone. **2.** Geom. figure with four sides of equal length forming two acute and two obtuse angles. **3.** playing card marked with red diamond-shaped symbols. **4.** Baseball the playing field. **diamond jubilee** sixtieth anniversary of an event. **diamond wedding** sixtieth anniversary of a wedding.

diapason [die-a-**pay**-zon] n. 1. either of two stops found throughout the entire range of a pipe organ. 2. range of a voice or instrument.

diaper n. US nappy.

diaphanous [die-**af**-fan-ous] adj. fine and almost transparent.

diaphoretic n. 1. drug causing sweating. —adj. 2. relating to or causing sweating.

diaphragm [die-a-fram] n. 1. muscular partition that separates the abdominal cavity and chest cavity. 2. contraceptive device placed over the neck of the womb. 3. circular device for controlling the amount of light entering the lens of a camera. 4. thin vibrating disc which converts sound to electricity or vice-versa, as in a loudspeaker or microphone.

diapositive n. positive transparency; slide.

diarrhoea [die-a-**ree**-a] n. frequent discharge of abnormally liquid faeces.

diary n., pl. -**ries**. (book for a) record of daily events, appointments, or observations. **diarist** n. person who writes a diary.

Diaspora [die-**ass**-spore-a] n. 1. dispersion of the Jews after the Babylonian conquest of Palestine. 2. (oft. d-) dispersion, as of people originally of one nation.

diastase [die-a-stayss] n. enzyme that converts starch into sugar.

diastole [die-**ass**-stoh-lee] n. dilation of the chambers of the heart.

diatom n. type of microscopic alga.

diatomic adj. containing two atoms.

diatonic adj. Music 1. of or relating to a regular major or minor scale. 2. (of a melody) composed in such a scale.

diatribe n. bitter critical attack.

dibble n. small hand tool used to make holes in the ground for seeds or plants.

dice n., pl. **dice**. 1. small cube each of whose sides has a different number of spots (1 to 6), used in games of chance. 2. any of various games played with dice. 3. small cube of food. —v. 4. cut (food) into small cubes. **dice with death** take a risk. **dicey** adj. **dicier, diciest**. Informal dangerous or risky.

dichotomy [die-**kot**-a-mee] n., pl. -**mies**. division into two opposed groups or parts.

dichromatic adj. having two colours.

dick n. Taboo slang penis. **clever dick** obnoxiously smart or opinionated person.

Dickensian adj. denoting poverty, distress, and exploitation as depicted in Dickens's novels.

dicky[1] n., pl. **dickies**. false shirt front. **dicky-bird** n. child's word for a bird.

dicky[2] adj. **dickier, dickiest**. Informal shaky or weak, e.g. a dicky heart.

dicotyledon [die-kot-ill-**leed**-on] n. flowering plant with two embryonic seed leaves.

Dictaphone n. ® tape recorder for recording dictation for subsequent typing.

dictate v. 1. say aloud for another person to transcribe. 2. give (commands) authoritatively. —n. 3. authoritative command. 4. guiding principle. 5. seek to impose one's will on others. **dictation** n. **dictator** n. 1. ruler who has complete power. 2. tyrannical person. **dictatorship** n. **dictatorial** adj. like a dictator, tyrannical. **dictatorially** adv.

diction n. manner of pronouncing words and sounds.

dictionary n., pl. -**aries**. 1. book that consists of an alphabetical list of words with their meanings. 2. similar book giving equivalent words in two languages. 3. reference book listing terms and giving information about a particular subject.

dictum n., pl. -**tums**, -**ta**. 1. formal statement. 2. popular saying.

did v. past tense of DO.

didactic adj. 1. intended to instruct. 2. trying too hard to be instructive. **didactically** adv.

diddle v. Brit. informal swindle.

didgeridoo n. Music Australian Aboriginal deep-toned wind instrument.

didn't did not.

die[1] v. **dying, died**. 1. (of a person, animal, or plant) cease all biological activity permanently. 2. (of something inanimate) cease to exist or function. **be dying for** Informal be eager for. **die down** v. lose strength or power by degrees. **die-hard** n. person who resists change.

die[2] n. 1. shaped block used to cut or form metal. 2. casting mould. **die-cast** v. make or shape an object by pouring molten metal or plastic into a reusable mould.

die[3] n. same as DICE (sense 1).

dieldrin n. highly toxic crystalline insecticide.

dielectric n. 1. substance which does not

conduct electricity well, insulator. —*adj.* 2. not conducting electricity well.

dieresis [die-**air**-iss-iss] *n., pl.* **-ses** [-seez] mark (¨) placed over a vowel to show that it is pronounced separately from the preceding one, as in *Noël.*

diesel *n.* 1. diesel engine. 2. *Informal* diesel oil. 3. vehicle driven by a diesel engine. **diesel engine** internal-combustion engine in which oil is ignited by compression. **diesel oil** fuel obtained from petroleum distillation.

diet[1] *n.* 1. food that a person or animal regularly eats. 2. specific allowance of food, to control weight or for health reasons. —*v.* 3. follow a special diet so as to lose weight. **dietary** *adj.* **dietary fibre** fibrous substances in fruit and vegetables that aid digestion. **dieter** *n.* **dietetic** *adj.* prepared for special dietary requirements. **dietetics** *pl. n.* study of food intake and preparation. **dietician** *n.* person who specializes in dietetics.

diet[2] *n.* parliament of some countries.

differ *v.* 1. be unlike. 2. disagree. **difference** *n.* 1. state or quality of being unlike. 2. disagreement. 3. remainder left after subtraction. **different** *adj.* 1. unlike. 2. unusual. **differently** *adv.*
▷ The accepted idiom is *different from* but *different to* is also used. *Different than* is an Americanism.

differential *adj.* 1. of or using a difference. 2. *Maths* involving differentials. —*n.* 3. factor that differentiates between two comparable things. 4. *Maths* minute difference between values in a scale. 5. difference between rates of pay for different types of labour. **differential calculus** branch of calculus concerned with derivatives and differentials. **differential gear** mechanism in a road vehicle that allows one driving wheel to rotate faster than the other when cornering. **differentiate** *v.* 1. perceive or show the difference (between). 2. make (one thing) distinct from other such things. 3. *Maths* determine the derivative of (a function or variable). **differentiation** *n.*

difficult *adj.* 1. requiring effort or skill to do or understand. 2. not easily pleased. **difficulty** *n., pl.* **-ties.**

diffident *adj.* lacking self-confidence. **diffidence** *n.* **diffidently** *adv.*

diffract *v.* cause to undergo diffraction. **diffraction** *n.* 1. *Physics* deviation in the direction of a wave at the edge of an obstacle in its path. 2. formation of light and dark fringes by the passage of light through a small aperture.

diffuse *v.* 1. spread in all directions. —*adj.* 2. widely spread. 3. lacking conciseness. **diffusely** *adv.* **diffusion** *n.*

dig *v.* **digging, dug.** 1. (often foll. by *up*) cut into, break up, and turn over or remove (earth etc.), esp. with a spade. 2. excavate (a hole or tunnel) by digging. 3. (foll. by *out* or *up*) find by effort or searching. 4. (foll. by *in* or *into*) thrust or jab. —*n.* 5. act of digging. 6. thrust or poke. 7. cutting remark. 8. archaeological excavation. —*pl.* 9. *Informal* lodgings. **digger** *n.* machine used for digging.

digest *v.* 1. subject to a process of digestion. 2. absorb mentally. —*n.* 3. methodical compilation of information, often a condensed one. **digestible** *adj.* **digestion** *n.* process of breaking down food into easily absorbed substances. **digestive** *adj.* **digestive biscuit** biscuit made from wholemeal flour.

digit [**dij**-it] *n.* 1. finger or toe. 2. numeral from 0 to 9. **digital** *adj.* displaying information as numbers rather than with a dial, e.g. *digital clock.* **digital recording** sound-recording process that converts audio or analogue signals into a series of pulses. **digitally** *adv.* **digitate** *adj.* (of animals) having digits.

digitalis *n.* drug made from foxglove leaves, used as a heart stimulant.

dignity *n., pl.* **-ties.** 1. serious, calm, and controlled behaviour or manner. 2. quality of being worthy of honour. 3. sense of self-importance. **dignify** *v.* **-fying, -fied.** give dignity to. **dignitary** *n., pl.* **-taries.** person of high official position.

digraph *n.* combination of two letters used to represent a single sound, e.g. *gh* in *tough.*

digress *v.* depart from the main subject in speech or writing. **digression** *n.* **digressive** *adj.*

dihedral *adj.* having or formed by two intersecting planes.

dike *n.* same as DYKE.

diktat *n.* dictatorial decree.

dilapidated *adj.* (of a building) having fallen into ruin. **dilapidation** *n.*

dilate *v.* make or become wider or larger. **dilation, dilatation** *n.*

dilatory [**dill**-a-tree] *adj.* tending or intended to waste time. **dilatoriness** *n.*

dildo *n., pl.* **-dos.** object used as a substitute for an erect penis.

dilemma *n.* situation offering a choice between two equally undesirable alternatives.
▷ If a difficult choice involves more than two courses of action, it is preferable to speak of a *problem* or *difficulty.*

dilettante [dill-it-**tan**-tee] *n., pl.* **-tantes, -tanti.** person whose interest in a subject, esp. art, is superficial rather than serious. **dilettantism** *n.*

diligent *adj.* **1.** careful and persevering in carrying out duties. **2.** carried out with care and perseverance. **diligently** *adv.* **diligence** *n.*

dill *n.* sweet-smelling herb used for flavouring.

dilly-dally *v.* **-lying, -lied.** *Informal* dawdle or waste time.

dilute *v.* **1.** make (a liquid) less concentrated, esp. by adding water. **2.** make (a quality etc.) weaker in force. **dilution** *n.*

diluvial, diluvian *adj.* of a flood, esp. the great Flood described in the Old Testament.

dim *adj.* **dimmer, dimmest. 1.** badly illuminated. **2.** not clearly seen. **3.** mentally dull. —*v.* **dimming, dimmed. 4.** make or become dim. **take a dim view** of disapprove of. **dimly** *adv.* **dimness** *n.* **dimmer** *n.* device for dimming an electric light.

dime *n.* coin of the US and Canada, worth ten cents.

dimension *n.* **1.** measurement of the size of something in a particular direction. **2.** scope.

diminish *v.* make or become smaller, fewer, or less. **diminished responsibility** *Law* mental derangement which makes a person unaware that he or she is committing a crime. **diminution** *n.* **diminutive** *adj.* **1.** very small. —*n.* **2.** word or affix which implies smallness or unimportance. **diminutiveness** *n.*

diminuendo *n. Music* gradual decrease in loudness.

dimple *n.* **1.** small natural dent, esp. in the cheeks or chin. —*v.* **2.** produce dimples by smiling. **dimpled** *adj.*

dimwit *n. Informal* stupid person. **dimwitted** *adj.*

din *n.* **1.** loud discordant confused noise. —*v.* **dinning, dinned. 2.** (foll. by *into*) instil (something) into someone by constant repetition.

dinar [**dee**-nahr] *n.* monetary unit of Yugoslavia and various Middle Eastern and North African countries.

dine *v.* eat dinner. **diner** *n.* **1.** person eating a meal. **2.** *US* small cheap restaurant. **dining car** railway coach in which meals are served. **dining room** room where meals are eaten.

ding-dong *n.* **1.** sound of a bell. **2.** *Informal* violent exchange of blows or words.

dinghy [**ding**-ee] *n., pl.* **-ghies.** small boat, powered by sails, oars, or an outboard motor.

dingle *n.* small wooded dell.

dingo *n., pl.* **-goes.** wild dog of Australia.

dingy [**din**-jee] *adj.* **-gier, -giest.** dirty-looking, dull. **dinginess** *n.*

dinkum *adj. Aust. & NZ informal* genuine or right.

dinky *adj.* **-kier, -kiest.** *Brit. informal* small and neat.

dinner *n.* **1.** main meal of the day, taken either in the evening or at midday. **2.** official banquet. **dinner jacket** man's semiformal evening jacket, usu. black.

dinosaur *n.* extinct prehistoric reptile, often of gigantic size.

dint *n.* **by dint of** by means of.

diocese [**die**-a-siss] *n.* district under the jurisdiction of a bishop. **diocesan** *adj.*

diode *n.* semiconductor device for converting alternating current to direct current.

dioecious [die-**eesh**-uss] *adj.* (of plants) having the male and female reproductive organs on separate plants.

Dionysian [die-on-**niz**-zee-an] *adj.* **1.** of Dionysus, the ancient Greek god of wine and revelry. **2.** (*often* d-) wild or orgiastic.

dioptre [die-**op**-ter] *n.* unit for measuring the refractive power of a lens.

diorama *n.* miniature three-dimensional scene, in which models, stuffed animals, etc. are seen set in a three-dimensional background.

dioxide *n.* oxide containing two oxygen atoms per molecule.

dioxin *n.* very poisonous by-product of the manufacture of certain herbicides.

dip *v.* **dipping, dipped. 1.** plunge quickly or briefly into a liquid. **2.** slope downwards. **3.**

switch (car headlights) from the main to the lower beam. **4.** lower briefly. —*n.* **5.** act of dipping. **6.** brief swim. **7.** liquid chemical in which farm animals are dipped to rid them of insects. **8.** depression, esp. in a landscape. **9.** creamy mixture into which pieces of food are dipped before being eaten. **dip into** *v.* read passages at random from (a book or journal).

DipEd Diploma in Education.

diphtheria [dif-**theer**-ya] *n.* contagious disease producing fever and difficulty in breathing and swallowing.

diphthong *n.* union of two vowel sounds in a single compound sound.

diploma *n.* document conferring a qualification or recording successful completion of a course of study.

diplomacy *n.* **1.** conduct of the relations between nations by peaceful means. **2.** tact or skill in dealing with people. **diplomat** *n.* official engaged in diplomacy. **diplomatic** *adj.* **1.** of or relating to diplomacy. **2.** tactful in dealing with people. **diplomatic immunity** freedom from legal action and taxation which diplomats have in the country where they are working. **diplomatically** *adv.*

dipper *n.* **1.** ladle used for dipping. **2.** kind of river bird.

dipsomania *n.* compulsive craving for alcohol. **dipsomaniac** *n., adj.*

dipterous *adj.* having two wings or winglike parts.

dipstick *n.* notched rod dipped into a container to measure the level of a liquid.

diptych [**dip**-tik] *n.* painting on two hinged panels.

dire *adj.* **1.** desperate or urgent. **2.** indicating disaster.

direct *v.* **1.** conduct or control the affairs of. **2.** give orders with authority to (a person or group). **3.** tell (someone) the way to a place. **4.** address (a letter, package, remarks, etc.). **5.** provide guidance to (actors, cameramen, etc.) in (a play or film). —*adj.* **6.** without evasion, straightforward. **7.** (of a route) shortest, straight. **8.** without anyone or anything intervening. **9.** honest, frank. —*adv.* **10.** in a direct manner. **directly** *adv.* **1.** in a direct manner. **2.** at once. —*conj.* **3.** as soon as. **directness** *n.* **direct current** electric current which flows in one direction only. **direct debit** order given to a bank etc. by an account-holder which allows an organization

to obtain money for the payment of bills etc. directly from that person's account. **direct object** noun or pronoun receiving the direct action of the verb, e.g. *a book* in *I bought Jo a book.* **direct speech** reporting of what someone has said by quoting his or her exact words. **direct tax** tax paid by the person or organization on which it is levied.

direction *n.* **1.** course or line along which a person or thing moves, points, or lies. **2.** management or guidance. —*pl.* **3.** instructions for doing something or for reaching a place. **directional** *adj.*

directive *n.* instruction, order.

director *n.* **1.** person or thing that directs or controls. **2.** member of the governing board of a business etc. **3.** person responsible for the artistic and technical aspects of the making of a film etc. **directorial** *adj.* **directorship** *n.* **directorate** *n.* **1.** board of directors. **2.** position of director. **director-general** *n., pl.* **directors-general.** person in overall charge of certain large organizations.

directory *n., pl.* **-tories.** book listing names, addresses, and telephone numbers of individuals and firms.

dirge *n.* slow sad song of mourning.

dirigible [**dir**-rij-jib-bl] *adj.* **1.** able to be steered. —*n.* **2.** airship.

dirk *n.* dagger, formerly worn by Scottish Highlanders.

dirndl *n.* (dress with) full gathered skirt.

dirt *n.* **1.** unclean substance, filth. **2.** loose earth or soil. **3.** obscene speech or behaviour. **4.** *Informal* scandal, harmful gossip. **dirt-cheap** *adj., adv.* at a very cheap price. **dirt track** racetrack made of packed earth or cinders.

dirty *adj.* **dirtier, dirtiest. 1.** covered or marked with dirt. **2.** obscene. **3.** unfair or dishonest. **4.** displaying dislike or anger, e.g. *dirty look.* —*v.* **dirtying, dirtied. 5.** make dirty. **dirtiness** *n.*

dis- *prefix* indicating: **1.** reversal, e.g. *disconnect.* **2.** negation or lack, e.g. *dissimilar, disgrace.* **3.** removal or release, e.g. *disembowel.*

disable *v.* make ineffective, unfit, or incapable, as by crippling. **disablement** *n.* **disability** *n., pl.* **-ties. 1.** condition of being physically or mentally impaired. **2.** something that disables someone.

disabuse v. (foll. by of) rid (someone) of a mistaken idea.

disadvantage n. unfavourable circumstance, thing, or situation. **disadvantageous** adj. **disadvantaged** adj. socially or economically deprived.

disaffected adj. having lost loyalty to or affection for someone or something. **disaffection** n.

disagree v. **-greeing, -greed. 1.** have different opinions. **2.** fail to correspond. **3.** (foll. by with) cause physical discomfort (to), e.g. curry disagrees with me. **disagreement** n. **disagreeable** adj. **1.** (of a person) bad-tempered or disobliging. **2.** unpleasant. **disagreeably** adv.

disallow v. reject as untrue or invalid.

disappear v. **1.** cease to be visible. **2.** cease to exist. **disappearance** n.

disappoint v. fail to meet the expectations or hopes of. **disappointment** n. **1.** feeling of being disappointed. **2.** person or thing that disappoints.

disapprobation n. disapproval.

disapprove v. (foll. by of) consider wrong or bad. **disapproval** n.

disarm v. **1.** deprive of weapons. **2.** win the confidence or affection of. **3.** (of a nation) decrease the size of one's armed forces. **disarmament** n. **disarming** adj. removing hostility or suspicion. **disarmingly** adv.

disarrange v. throw into disorder. **disarrangement** n.

disarray n. **1.** confusion and lack of discipline. **2.** extreme untidiness.

disassociate v. same as DISSOCIATE.

disaster n. **1.** occurrence that causes great distress or destruction. **2.** project etc. that fails. **disastrous** adj. **disastrously** adv.

disavow v. deny connection with or responsibility for (something). **disavowal** n.

disband v. (cause to) cease to function as a group or unit.

disbelieve v. **1.** reject as false. **2.** (foll. by in) have no faith (in). **disbelief** n.

disburse v. pay out. **disbursement** n.

disc n. **1.** flat circular object. **2.** gramophone record. **3.** Anat. circular flat structure in the body, esp. between the vertebrae. **4.** Computers same as DISK. **disc brake** brake in which two plates rub against a flat disc. **disc jockey** person who introduces and plays pop records on a radio programme or at a disco.

discard v. get rid of (something or someone) as useless or undesirable.

discern v. see or be aware of (something) clearly. **discernible** adj. **discernibly** adv. **discerning** adj. having or showing good judgment. **discernment** n.

discharge v. **1.** release, allow to go. **2.** dismiss (someone) from duty or employment. **3.** fire (a gun). **4.** pour forth, emit. **5.** meet the demands of (an obligation etc.). **6.** relieve oneself of (a responsibility or debt). **7.** remove the cargo from (a boat etc.). —n. **8.** something that is discharged. **9.** dismissal from duty or employment. **10.** pouring forth of a fluid, emission.

disciple [diss-**sipe**-pl] n. follower of the doctrines of a teacher, esp. Jesus Christ.

discipline n. **1.** training imposed for the improvement of physical powers, self-control, etc. **2.** state of improved behaviour resulting from such training. **3.** punishment. **4.** branch of learning. —v. **5.** (attempt to) improve the behaviour of (oneself or another) by training or rules. **6.** punish. **disciplinarian** n. person who practises strict discipline. **disciplinary** adj.

disclaim v. deny (responsibility for or knowledge of something). **disclaimer** n. repudiation, denial.

disclose v. **1.** make known. **2.** allow to be seen. **disclosure** n.

disco n., pl. **-cos. 1.** occasion at which people dance to pop records. **2.** place where such dances are held. **3.** mobile equipment for providing music for a disco.

discography n., pl. **-phies.** classified list of gramophone records.

discolour v. change in colour, stain. **discoloration** n.

discomfit v. make uneasy or confused. **discomfiture** n.

discomfort n. inconvenience, distress, or mild pain.

discommode v. cause inconvenience to. **discommodious** adj.

discompose v. disturb the composure of. **discomposure** n.

disconcert v. disturb the confidence or self-possession of.

disconnect v. **1.** undo or break the connection between (two things). **2.** stop the supply of (electricity or gas) of. **disconnected** *adj.* (of speech or ideas) not logically connected. **disconnection** *n.*

disconsolate *adj.* sad beyond comfort. **disconsolately** *adv.*

discontent *n.* lack of contentment, as with one's lot in life. **discontented** *adj.* **discontentedly** *adv.*

discontinue *v.* come or bring to an end. **discontinuous** *adj.* characterized by interruptions. **discontinuity** *n.* lack of smooth or unbroken development.

discord *n.* **1.** lack of agreement or harmony between people. **2.** harsh confused sounds. **discordant** *adj.* **discordance** *n.*

discotheque *n.* full name for DISCO.

discount *v.* **1.** leave (something) out of account as being unreliable, prejudiced, or irrelevant. **2.** deduct (an amount) from the price of something. — *n.* **3.** deduction from the full price of something.

discountenance *v.* make (someone) ashamed or confused.

discourage *v.* **1.** deprive of the will to persist in something. **2.** oppose by expressing disapproval. **discouraging** *adj.* **discouragement** *n.*

discourse *n.* **1.** conversation. **2.** formal treatment of a subject in speech or writing. — *v.* **3.** (foll. by *on*) speak or write (about) at length.

discourteous *adj.* showing bad manners. **discourteously** *adv.* **discourtesy** *n.*

discover *v.* **1.** be the first to find or to find out about. **2.** learn about for the first time. **3.** find after study or search. **discoverer** *n.* **discovery** *n., pl.* **-eries**. **1.** act of discovering. **2.** person, place, or thing that has been discovered.

discredit *v.* **1.** damage the reputation of (someone). **2.** cause (an idea) to be disbelieved or distrusted. — *n.* **3.** (something that causes) damage to someone's reputation. **discreditable** *adj.* bringing discredit.

discreet *adj.* **1.** careful to avoid embarrassment, esp. by keeping confidences secret. **2.** unobtrusive. **discreetly** *adv.*

discrepancy *n., pl.* **-cies.** conflict or variation between facts, figures, or claims. **discrepant** *adj.*

discrete *adj.* separate or distinct.

discretion [diss-**kresh**-on] *n.* **1.** quality of behaving in a discreet way. **2.** freedom or authority to make judgments and to act as one sees fit. **discretionary** *adj.*

discriminate *v.* **1.** (foll. by *against* or *in favour of*) single out a particular person or group for special disfavour or favour. **2.** (foll. by *between* or *among*) recognize or understand the difference (between). **discriminating** *adj.* showing good taste and judgment. **discrimination** *n.* **discriminatory** *adj.* based on prejudice.

discursive *adj.* passing from one topic to another.

discus *n.* disc-shaped object with a heavy middle, thrown in sports competitions.

discuss *v.* **1.** consider (something) by talking it over. **2.** treat (a subject) in speech or writing. **discussion** *n.*

disdain *n.* **1.** feeling of superiority and dislike. — *v.* **2.** refuse with disdain. **disdainful** *adj.* **disdainfully** *adv.*

disease *n.* illness, sickness. **diseased** *adj.*

diseconomy *n. Economics* disadvantage resulting from the scale on which a business operates.

disembark *v.* (cause to) land from a ship, aircraft, or bus. **disembarkation** *n.*

disembodied *adj.* **1.** lacking a body. **2.** seeming not to be attached to or coming from anyone.

disembowel *v.* **-elling, -elled.** remove the entrails of.

disenchanted *adj.* disappointed and disillusioned (with something). **disenchantment** *n.*

disenfranchise *v.* deprive (a person) of the right to vote or of other rights of citizenship.

disengage *v.* release from a connection. **disengagement** *n.*

disentangle *v.* release from entanglement or confusion. **disentanglement** *n.*

disequilibrium *n.* loss or absence of stability or balance.

disestablish *v.* remove state support from (a church etc.). **disestablishment** *n.*

disfavour *n.* disapproval or dislike.

disfigure *v.* spoil the appearance or shape of. **disfigurement** *n.*

disfranchise *v.* same as DISENFRANCHISE.

disgorge *v.* **1.** vomit. **2.** discharge (contents).

disgrace *n.* **1.** condition of shame, loss of

reputation, or dishonour. **2.** shameful person or thing. —*v.* **3.** bring shame upon (oneself or others). **disgraceful** *adj.* **disgracefully** *adv.*

disgruntled *adj.* sulky or discontented. **disgruntlement** *n.*

disguise *v.* **1.** change the appearance or manner in order to conceal the identity of (someone or something). **2.** misrepresent (something) in order to obscure its actual nature or meaning. —*n.* **3.** mask, costume, or manner that disguises. **4.** state of being disguised.

disgust *v.* **1.** sicken, fill with loathing. —*n.* **2.** great loathing or distaste. **disgusted** *adj.* feeling disgust. **disgusting** *adj.* causing disgust. **disgustingly** *adv.*

dish *n.* **1.** shallow container used for holding or serving food. **2.** portion or variety of food. **3.** *Informal* attractive person. **dish aerial** aerial consisting of a concave disc-shaped reflector. **dishcloth** *n.* cloth for washing dishes. **dish out** *v. Informal* distribute. **dish up** *v. Informal* serve (food).

dishabille [diss-a-beel] *n.* state of being partly dressed.

disharmony *n.* lack of agreement, discord.

dishearten *v.* weaken or destroy the hope, courage, or enthusiasm of.

dishevelled *adj.* (of a person's hair, clothes, or general appearance) disordered and untidy.

dishonest *adj.* not honest or fair. **dishonestly** *adv.* **dishonesty** *n.*

dishonour *v.* **1.** treat with disrespect. **2.** refuse to pay the money promised by (a cheque etc.). —*n.* **3.** lack of respect. **4.** state of shame or disgrace. **5.** something that causes a loss of honour. **dishonourable** *adj.* **dishonourably** *adv.*

disillusion *v.* **1.** destroy the illusions or false ideas of. —*n.* (also **disillusionment**) **2.** state of being disillusioned.

disincentive *n.* something that acts as a deterrent.

disinclined *adj.* unwilling. **disinclination** *n.*

disinfect *v.* rid of harmful germs, esp. by chemical means. **disinfectant** *n.* substance that destroys harmful germs. **disinfection** *n.*

disinformation *n.* false information intended to mislead.

disingenuous *adj.* not sincere. **disingenuously** *adv.*

disinherit *v. Law* deprive (an heir) of inheritance. **disinheritance** *n.*

disintegrate *v.* break up into fragments. **disintegration** *n.*

disinter *v.* **-terring, -terred. 1.** dig up. **2.** reveal, make known. **disinterment** *n.*

disinterested *adj.* free from bias or involvement. **disinterest** *n.*
▷ Distinguish *disinterested* from *uninterested*, meaning 'apathetic, not caring': *We asked him to decide because he was a disinterested observer.*

disjointed *adj.* **1.** having no coherence. **2.** disconnected.

disjunction *n.* disconnection or separation. **disjunctive** *adj.*

disk *n. Computers* storage device, consisting of a stack of plates coated with a magnetic layer, which rotates rapidly as a single unit.

dislike *v.* **1.** consider unpleasant or disagreeable. —*n.* **2.** feeling of not liking something or someone.

dislocate *v.* **1.** displace (a bone or joint) from its normal position. **2.** disrupt or shift out of place. **dislocation** *n.*

dislodge *v.* remove (something) from a previously fixed position.

disloyal *adj.* not loyal, deserting one's allegiance. **disloyalty** *n.*

dismal *adj.* **1.** causing gloom or depression. **2.** *Informal* of poor quality. **dismally** *adv.*

dismantle *v.* take apart piece by piece.

dismay *v.* **1.** fill with alarm or depression. —*n.* **2.** alarm mixed with sadness.

dismember *v.* **1.** remove the limbs of. **2.** cut to pieces. **dismemberment** *n.*

dismiss *v.* **1.** remove (an employee) from a job. **2.** allow (someone) to leave. **3.** put out of one's mind. **4.** (of a judge) state that (a case) will not be brought to trial. **5.** *Cricket* to bowl (a side) out for a particular number of runs. **dismissal** *n.* **dismissive** *adj.* scornful, contemptuous.

dismount *v.* get off a horse or bicycle.

disobey *v.* neglect or refuse to obey. **disobedient** *adj.* **disobedience** *n.*

disobliging *adj.* unwilling to help.

disorder *n.* **1.** state of untidiness and disorganization. **2.** public violence or rioting. **3.** an illness. **disordered** *adj.* untidy. **disorderly** *adj.* **1.** very untidy, disorganized. **2.** uncontrolled, unruly.

disorganize v. disrupt the arrangement or system of. disorganization n.

disorientate, disorient v. cause (someone) to lose his or her bearings. disorientation n.

disown v. deny any connection with (someone).

disparage v. speak contemptuously of. disparagement n.

disparate adj. utterly different in kind. disparity n., pl. **-ties**. inequality or difference.

dispassionate adj. uninfluenced by emotion. dispassionately adv.

dispatch v. 1. send off to a destination or to perform a task. 2. carry out (a duty or a task) with speed. 3. Old-fashioned kill. —n. 4. official communication or report, sent in haste. 5. report sent to a newspaper by a correspondent. dispatch rider motorcyclist who carries dispatches.

dispel v. **-pelling, -pelled**. disperse or drive away.

dispense v. 1. distribute in portions. 2. prepare and distribute (medicine). 3. administer (the law etc.). dispensable adj. not essential. dispensation n. 1. act of dispensing. 2. exemption from an obligation. 3. administrative system. dispenser n. dispensary n., pl. **-saries**. place where medicine is dispensed. dispense with v. 1. do away with. 2. manage without.

disperse v. 1. scatter over a wide area. 2. (cause to) leave a gathering. 3. separate (light) into its different wavelengths. dispersal, dispersion n.

dispirit v. make downhearted. dispirited adj. dispiritedly adv. dispiriting adj.

displace v. 1. move from the usual location. 2. remove from office. displacement n. displaced person person forced from his or her home or country, esp. by war or revolution.

display v. 1. make visible or noticeable. —n. 2. act of displaying. 3. something displayed. 4. exhibition. 5. showiness, ostentation. 6. electronic device for presenting information visually. 7. Zoology pattern of behaviour an animal uses to draw attention to itself when courting, defending its territory, etc.

displease v. annoy. displeasure n.

disport v. disport oneself indulge oneself in pleasure.

dispose v. 1. make willing or receptive. 2. place in a certain order. disposable adj. 1. designed to be thrown away after use. 2. available for use if needed, e.g. disposable assets. disposal n. getting rid of something. at one's disposal available for use. disposition n. 1. person's usual temperament. 2. tendency. 3. arrangement. dispose of v. 1. deal with (a problem etc.). 2. get rid of. 3. kill.

dispossess v. (foll. by of) deprive (someone) of (a possession). dispossessed adj. dispossession n.

disproportion n. lack of proportion or equality. disproportionate adj. disproportionately adv.

disprove v. show (an assertion or claim) to be incorrect.

dispute v. 1. argue about (something). 2. doubt the validity of. 3. fight over possession of. —n. 4. argument. disputation n. Formal argument.

disqualify v. 1. debar from a contest. 2. make ineligible. disqualification n.

disquiet n. 1. feeling of anxiety. —v. 2. make (someone) anxious. disquietude n. anxiety, uneasiness.

disquisition n. learned or elaborate treatise or essay.

disregard v. 1. give little or no attention to. —n. 2. lack of attention or respect.

disrepair n. condition of being worn out or in poor working order.

disrepute n. loss or lack of good reputation. disreputable adj. having or causing a bad reputation.

disrespect n. lack of respect. disrespectful adj. disrespectfully adv.

disrobe v. undress.

disrupt v. interrupt the progress of. disruption n. disruptive adj.

dissatisfy v. fail to satisfy, disappoint. dissatisfied adj. dissatisfaction n.

dissect v. 1. cut open (a dead body) to examine it. 2. examine critically and minutely. dissection n.

dissemble v. conceal one's real motives or emotions by pretence.

disseminate v. scatter about. dissemination n.

dissent v. 1. disagree. 2. *Christianity* reject the doctrines of an established church. —n. 3. disagreement. 4. *Christianity* separation from an established church. dissension n. dissenter n. dissentient adj. dissenting.

dissertation n. 1. written thesis, usu. required for a higher university degree. 2. long formal speech.

disservice n. bad turn or wrong.

dissident adj. 1. disagreeing. —n. 2. person who disagrees, esp. with the government. dissidence n.

dissimilar adj. not alike, different. dissimilarity n.

dissimulate v. conceal one's real feelings by pretence. dissimulation n.

dissipate v. 1. waste or squander. 2. scatter. dissipated adj. showing signs of overindulging in alcohol and other pleasures. dissipation n.

dissociate v. regard or treat as separate. dissociate oneself from deny or break a connection with. dissociation n.

dissolute adj. leading an immoral life.

dissolution n. 1. destruction by breaking up and dispersing. 2. termination of a meeting, assembly, or legal relationship.

dissolve v. 1. (cause to) become liquid. 2. bring to an end. 3. dismiss (a meeting, Parliament, etc.). 4. collapse emotionally.

dissonance n. 1. discordant combination of sounds. 2. lack of agreement or consistency. dissonant adj.

dissuade v. deter (someone) by persuasion from a course of action, policy, etc. dissuasion n.

distaff n. rod on which wool, flax, etc. is wound for spinning. distaff side female side of a family.

distance n. 1. space between two points. 2. state of being apart. 3. distant place. 4. remoteness in manner. distance oneself from separate oneself mentally from. distant adj. 1. far apart. 2. separated by a specified distance. 3. remote in manner. distantly adv.

distaste n. dislike, aversion. distasteful adj. unpleasant or offensive. distastefully adv.

distemper[1] n. highly contagious disease of animals, esp. dogs.

distemper[2] n. 1. paint mixed with water, glue, etc., which is used for painting walls. —v. 2. paint with distemper.

distend v. expand by pressure from within. distensible adj. distension n.

distich [diss-stick] n. unit of two verse lines.

distil v. -tilling, -tilled. 1. subject to or obtain by distillation. 2. give off (a substance) in drops. 3. extract the essence of. distillation n. 1. process of evaporating a liquid and condensing its vapour. 2. (also distillate) concentrated essence. distiller n. person or company that makes spirits. distillery n., pl. -leries. place where alcoholic drinks are made by distillation.

distinct adj. 1. easily sensed or understood. 2. different. 3. sharp or clear. distinctly adv. distinction n. 1. act of distinguishing. 2. distinguishing feature. 3. state of being different. 4. special honour, recognition, or fame. distinctive adj. easily recognizable. distinctively adv. distinctiveness n.

distinguish v. 1. (foll. by *between* or *among*) make, show, or recognize a difference (between or among). 2. be a distinctive feature of. 3. perceive. distinguishable adj. distinguished adj. 1. noble or dignified in appearance. 2. highly respected.

distort v. 1. twist out of shape. 2. alter or misrepresent (facts). 3. *Electronics* reproduce or amplify a signal inaccurately. distortion n.

distract v. 1. draw the attention of (a person) away from something. 2. confuse, trouble. 3. entertain. distraction n.

distrain v. *Law* seize (goods) to enforce payment of a debt. distraint n.

distrait [diss-tray] adj. absent-minded or abstracted.

distraught [diss-trawt] adj. extremely anxious or agitated.

distress v. 1. cause mental pain to, upset badly. —n. 2. mental pain. 3. physical or financial trouble. distressed adj. 1. much troubled. 2. in financial difficulties. distressing adj. distressingly adv.

distribute v. 1. give out in shares. 2. hand out or deliver. distribution n. 1. act of distributing. 2. arrangement or location. distributor n. 1. wholesaler who distributes goods to retailers in a specific area. 2. device in a petrol engine that sends the electric current to the spark plugs. distributive adj.

district n. area of land regarded as an

administrative or geographical unit. **district nurse** nurse who attends to patients at their homes.

distrust v. 1. regard as untrustworthy. —n. 2. suspicion or doubt. **distrustful** adj.

disturb v. 1. intrude on. 2. disarrange. 3. worry, make anxious. **disturbance** n. **disturbing** adj. **disturbingly** adv. **disturbed** adj. Psychiatry emotionally upset, troubled, or maladjusted.

disunite v. cause disagreement among. **disunity** n.

disuse n. condition of being unused. **disused** adj.

ditch n. 1. narrow channel dug in the earth for drainage or irrigation. —v. 2. Slang abandon.

dither v. 1. Brit. be uncertain or indecisive. —n. 2. state of indecision or agitation. **ditherer** n. **dithery** adj.

dithyramb n. 1. in ancient Greece, passionate choral hymn in honour of Dionysus. 2. song or piece of writing resembling this. **dithyrambic** adj.

ditto n., pl. -**tos.** 1. the same. —adv. 2. in the same way.

ditty n., pl. -**ties.** short simple poem or song.

diuretic [die-yoor-et-ik] n. drug that increases the flow of urine.

diurnal [die-urn-al] adj. happening during the day or daily.

diva n. distinguished female singer.

divan n. 1. backless sofa or couch. 2. low backless bed.

dive v. diving, dived. 1. plunge headfirst into water. 2. (of a submarine or diver) submerge under water. 3. fly in a steep nose-down descending path. 4. move quickly in a specified direction. 5. (foll. by in or into) start (doing something) enthusiastically. —n. 6. act of diving. 7. steep nose-down descent. 8. Slang disreputable bar or club. **diver** n. 1. person who works or explores underwater. 2. person who dives for sport. 3. water bird that swims and dives. **dive bomber** military aircraft designed to release bombs during a dive. **diving bell** diving vehicle with an open bottom, supplied with compressed air from above. **diving board** platform or springboard from which swimmers may dive. **diving suit** diver's waterproof costume, with a helmet and air supply.

diverge v. 1. separate and go in different directions. 2. deviate (from a prescribed course). **divergence** n. **divergent** adj.

divers adj. Old-fashioned various.

diverse adj. 1. having variety. 2. different in kind. **diversity** n., pl. -**ties.** 1. quality of being different or varied. 2. range of difference. **diversify** v. -**fying,** -**fied.** **diversification** n.

divert v. 1. deflect. 2. entertain, distract the attention of. **diversion** n. 1. act of diverting. 2. Brit. official detour used by traffic when a main route is closed. 3. something that distracts from business etc. 4. an entertainment. **diversionary** adj.

divertimento n., pl. -**ti.** piece of entertaining music in several movements.

divest v. 1. strip (of clothes). 2. dispossess or deprive.

divide v. 1. separate into parts. 2. share or be shared out in parts. 3. (cause to) disagree. 4. keep apart, be a boundary between. 5. calculate how many times (one number) can be contained in (another). —n. 6. division, split. **dividend** n. 1. sum of money representing part of the profit made, paid by a company to its shareholders. 2. bonus. 3. number to be divided by another number. **divider** n. 1. screen used to divide a room into separate areas. 2. anything which separates (something) into parts or forms a barrier. —pl. 3. compasses with two pointed arms, used for measuring or dividing lines.

divine adj. 1. of God or a god. 2. godlike. 3. Informal splendid. —v. 4. discover (something) by intuition or guessing. **divinely** adv. **divination** n. art of discovering future events, as though by supernatural powers. **divinity** n. 1. theology. 2. state of being divine. 3. pl. -**ties.** god. **divining rod** forked twig said to move when held over ground in which water or metal is to be found.

division n. 1. act of dividing or sharing out. 2. one of the parts into which something is divided. 3. difference of opinion. 4. mathematical operation of dividing. **divisional** adj. of a division in an organization. **divisible** adj. **divisibility** n. **divisive** [div-vice-iv] adj. tending to cause disagreement. **divisor** n. number to be divided into another number.

divorce n. 1. legal ending of a marriage. 2. separation, esp. one that is total. —v. 3.

separate or be separated by divorce. **4.** remove or separate. **divorcé,** (*fem.*) **divorcée** *n.* person who is divorced.

divot *n.* small piece of turf.

divulge *v.* make known, disclose. **divulgence** *n.*

divvy *Informal* —*v.* **-vying, -vied. 1.** (esp. with *up*) divide and share. —*n., pl.* **-vies. 2.** dividend.

Diwali *n.* major Hindu festival, marked by feasting, giving gifts, and lighting lamps.

dixie *n. Chiefly mil.* large metal cooking pot.

Dixie *n.* southern states of the US.

DIY *Brit.* do-it-yourself.

dizzy *adj.* **-zier, -ziest. 1.** having or causing a whirling sensation. **2.** mentally confused. —*v.* **-zying, -zied. 3.** make dizzy. **dizzily** *adv.* **dizziness** *n.*

DJ 1. disc jockey. **2.** dinner jacket.

djellaba *n.* same as JELLABA.

djinni *n., pl.* **djinn.** same as JINNI.

dl decilitre.

dm decimetre.

DM Deutschmark.

DNA *n.* deoxyribonucleic acid, the main constituent of the chromosomes of all living things.

D-notice *n. Brit.* official notice sent to newspapers etc. prohibiting publication of certain security information.

do[1] *v.* **does, doing, did, done. 1.** perform or complete (a deed or action). **2.** be suitable, suffice. **3.** provide, serve, e.g. *this place doesn't do lunch on Sundays.* **4.** make tidy, elegant, or ready, e.g. *do one's hair.* **5.** improve, e.g. *that hat does nothing for you.* **6.** find the answer to (a problem or puzzle). **7.** cause or produce, e.g. *complaints do nothing to help.* **8.** give or render, e.g. *do me a favour.* **9.** work at, esp. as a course of study or a job. **10.** travel (a distance). **11.** *Informal* cheat or rob. **12.** used to form questions, e.g. *do you agree?* **13.** used to intensify positive statements and commands, e.g. *I do like your new house, do hurry!* **14.** used to form negative statements and commands, e.g. *do not leave me here alone!* **15.** used to replace an earlier verb, e.g. *he likes you as much as I do.* —*n., pl.* **dos, do's. 16.** *Informal* festive gathering or party. **do away with** *v.* **1.** kill. **2.** get rid of. **do down** *v.* belittle or humiliate. **do for** *v. Informal* **1.** cause the death or ruin of. **2.** do

housework for. **do-gooder** *n. Informal* well-intentioned but naive or impractical person. **do in** *v. Slang* **1.** kill. **2.** exhaust. **do-it-yourself** *n.* practice of constructing and repairing things oneself, esp. as a hobby. **do up** *v.* **1.** fasten. **2.** renovate. **do with** *v.* find useful or benefit from. **do without** *v.* manage without.

do[2] *n., pl.* **dos.** same as DOH.

do. ditto.

Doberman pinscher, Doberman *n.* large dog with a glossy black-and-tan coat.

docile *adj.* (of a person or animal) easily managed. **docilely** *adv.* **docility** *n.*

dock[1] *n.* **1.** enclosed area of water where ships are loaded, unloaded, or repaired. —*v.* **2.** moor or be moored at a dock. **3.** link (two spacecraft) or (of two spacecraft) be linked together in space. **docker** *n.* person employed in the loading or unloading of ships. **dockyard** *n.* place with docks and equipment where ships are built or repaired.

dock[2] *v.* **1.** remove part of (an animal's tail) by cutting through the bone. **2.** deduct (an amount) from (a person's wages).

dock[3] *n.* enclosed space in a court of law where the accused person sits or stands.

dock[4] *n.* weed with broad leaves.

docket *n.* **1.** piece of paper accompanying a package or other delivery, stating contents, delivery instructions, etc. —*v.* **-eting, -eted. 2.** fix a docket to (a package etc.).

doctor *n.* **1.** person licensed to practise medicine. **2.** person who has been awarded a doctorate. —*v.* **3.** make different in order to deceive. **4.** poison or drug (food or drink). **5.** *Informal* castrate or sterilize (a cat, dog, etc.). **doctoral** *adj.* **doctorate** *n.* highest academic degree in any field of knowledge.

doctrine [dock-trin] *n.* **1.** body of teachings of a religious, political, or philosophical group. **2.** principle or body of principles that is taught or advocated. **doctrinal** *adj.* of or related to doctrine. **doctrinaire** *adj.* stubbornly insistent on the application of a theory without regard to practicality.

document *n.* **1.** piece of paper, booklet, etc. providing information, esp. of an official nature. —*v.* **2.** record or report (something) in detail. **3.** support (a claim) with evidence. **documentation** *n.*

documentary *n., pl.* **-ries. 1.** film or television programme presenting the facts about a particular subject. —*adj.* 2. of or based on documents.

dodder *v.* move unsteadily. **dodderer** *n.* **doddery** *adj.*

doddle *n. Informal* something easily accomplished.

dodecagon [doe-**deck**-a-gon] *n.* geometric figure with twelve sides.

dodecahedron [doe-deck-a-**heed**-ron] *n.* solid figure with twelve faces.

dodge *v.* 1. avoid (a blow, being seen, etc.) by moving suddenly. 2. evade by cleverness or trickery. —*n.* 3. plan contrived to deceive. 4. sudden evasive movement. **dodger** *n.* **dodgy** *adj.* **dodgier, dodgiest.** *Informal* 1. difficult or dangerous. 2. untrustworthy.

Dodgem *n.* ® electrically propelled vehicle driven and bumped against similar cars in a rink at a funfair.

dodo *n., pl.* **dodos, dodoes.** large flightless extinct bird.

doe *n.* female deer, hare, or rabbit.

does *v.* third person singular of the present tense of DO.

doesn't does not.

doff *v.* take off or lift (one's hat) as a mark of respect.

dog *n.* 1. domesticated four-legged meat-eating mammal occurring in many different breeds. 2. any other member of the dog family, such as the dingo or coyote. 3. male of animals of the dog family. 4. *Informal* fellow, chap, e.g. *you lucky dog!* 5. mechanical device for gripping. —*v.* **dogging, dogged.** 6. follow (someone) closely. 7. trouble or plague. **the dogs** *Brit. Informal* greyhound racing. **go to the dogs** go to ruin physically or morally. **let sleeping dogs lie** leave things undisturbed. **dogcart** *n.* light horse-drawn two-wheeled vehicle. **dog collar** 1. collar for a dog. 2. *Informal* clerical collar. **dog days** hottest part of the summer. **dog-eared** *adj.* 1. (of a book) having pages folded down at the corner. 2. shabby or worn. **dog-end** *n. Informal* cigarette end. **dogfight** *n.* 1. close-quarters combat between fighter aircraft. 2. any rough fight. **dogfish** *n.* small shark. **doghouse** *n. US* kennel. **in the doghouse** *Informal* in disfavour. **dogleg** *n.* sharp bend. **dog paddle** simple swimming stroke in which the hands are paddled in imitation of a swimming dog. **dog rose** wild rose with pink or white flowers. **dog-tired** *adj. Informal* exhausted.

doge [doje] *n.* formerly, chief magistrate of Venice or Genoa.

dogged [dog-gid] *adj.* obstinately determined. **doggedly** *adv.* **doggedness** *n.*

doggerel *n.* poorly written, usually comic verse.

doggo *adv.* lie doggo *Informal* hide and keep quiet.

doggy, doggie *n., pl.* **-gies.** child's word for a dog. **doggy bag** bag in which leftovers from a meal may be taken away.

dogma *n.* doctrine or system of doctrines proclaimed by authority as true. **dogmatic** *adj.* 1. (of a statement or opinion) forcibly asserted as if unchallengeable. 2. (of a person) prone to making such statements. **dogmatically** *adv.* **dogmatism** *n.* **dogmatize** *v.* speak or write in a dogmatic manner.

dogsbody *n., pl.* **-bodies.** *Informal* person who carries out menial tasks for others.

doh *n. Music* in tonic sol-fa, first degree of any major scale.

doily *n., pl.* **-lies.** decorative mat of lace or lacelike paper, laid on plates.

Dolby *n.* ® system used in tape recorders which reduces noise level on recorded or broadcast sound.

doldrums *pl. n.* 1. depressed state of mind. 2. state of inactivity. 3. belt of sea along the equator noted for lack of wind.

dole *n.* 1. *Brit. informal* money received from the state while out of work. —*v.* 2. (foll. by *out*) distribute (something), esp. in small portions. **on the dole** *Brit. informal* unemployed and receiving money from the state.

doleful *adj.* dreary or mournful. **dolefully** *adv.* **dolefulness** *n.*

doll *n.* 1. small model of a human being, used as a toy. 2. *Slang* girl or young woman, esp. a pretty one. **doll up** *v. Slang* dress up smartly or showily.

dollar *n.* standard monetary unit of the US, Australia, Canada, and various other countries.

dollop *n. Informal* semisolid lump.

dolly *n., pl.* **-lies.** 1. child's word for a doll. 2. wheeled support on which a camera may be moved.

dolman sleeve *n.* sleeve that is very wide at the armhole and tapers to a tight wrist.

dolmen *n.* prehistoric monument consisting

of a horizontal stone supported by vertical stones.

dolomite n. mineral consisting of calcium magnesium carbonate.

dolorous adj. causing or involving pain or sorrow.

dolphin n. sea mammal of the whale family, with a beaklike snout. **dolphinarium** n. aquarium for dolphins, esp. one in which they give public displays.

dolt n. stupid person. **doltish** adj.

-dom n. suffix **1.** state, condition, e.g. freedom. **2.** rank, office, or domain of, e.g. earldom. **3.** collection of persons, e.g. officialdom.

domain n. **1.** field of knowledge or activity. **2.** land under one ruler or government.

dome n. **1.** rounded roof built on a circular base. **2.** something shaped like this. **domed** adj.

domestic adj. **1.** of the home or family. **2.** home-loving. **3.** (of an animal) bred or kept as a pet or for the supply of food. **4.** of one's own country or a specific country, e.g. domestic and foreign affairs. —n. **5.** household servant. **domestically** adv. **domesticity** n. **domesticate** v. **1.** bring or keep (wild animals or plants) under control or cultivation. **2.** accustom (someone) to home life. **domestication** n. **domestic science** study of household skills.

domicile [dom-miss-ile] n. person's regular dwelling place. **domiciliary** adj.

dominant adj. **1.** having authority or influence. **2.** predominant. **dominance** n.

dominate v. **1.** control or govern. **2.** tower above (surroundings). **3.** predominate in. **domination** n.

domineering adj. acting arrogantly or tyrannically.

Dominican n. **1.** friar or nun of an order founded by Saint Dominic. —adj. **2.** of the Dominican order.

dominion n. **1.** rule or authority. **2.** land governed by one ruler or government. **3.** (formerly) self-governing division of the British Empire.

domino n., pl. **-noes. 1.** small rectangular block marked with dots, used in dominoes. —pl. **2.** game in which dominoes with matching halves are laid together.

don[1] v. donning, donned. put on (clothing).

don[2] n. **1.** Brit. member of the teaching staff

at a university or college. **2.** Spanish gentleman or nobleman. **donnish** adj. resembling a university don.

donate v. give (something), esp. to a charity. **donation** n. **1.** act of donating. **2.** a contribution. **donor** n. **1.** person who makes a donation. **2.** Med. person who gives blood, organs, etc. for use in the treatment of another person.

done v. **1.** past participle of DO. —adj. **2.** completed. **3.** used up. **4.** socially acceptable. **5.** Informal cheated or tricked.

doner kebab n. grilled minced lamb served in a split slice of unleavened bread.

Don Juan n. successful seducer of women.

donkey n. long-eared member of the horse family. **donkey jacket** man's thick hiplength jacket with a waterproof panel across the shoulders. **donkey's years** Informal a long time. **donkey-work** n. **1.** groundwork. **2.** drudgery.

Don Quixote [don kee-hoe-tee] n. impractical idealist.

don't do not.

doodle v. **1.** scribble or draw aimlessly. —n. **2.** shape or picture drawn aimlessly.

doom n. **1.** death or a terrible fate. —v. **2.** destine or condemn to death or a terrible fate. **doomsday** n. **1.** Christianity day on which the Last Judgment will occur. **2.** any dreaded day.

door n. **1.** hinged or sliding panel for closing the entrance to a room, cupboard, etc. **2.** entrance. **doorjamb, doorpost** n. vertical post forming one side of a door frame. **doorman** n. person employed to be on duty at the doors of certain public buildings. **doormat** n. **1.** mat, placed at an entrance, for wiping dirt from shoes. **2.** Informal person who offers little resistance to illtreatment. **door-to-door** adj. **1.** (of selling) from one house to the next. **2.** (of a journey) direct. **doorway** n. opening into a building or room.

dope n. **1.** Slang illegal drug, usu. cannabis. **2.** drug, esp. one administered to a racehorse etc. to affect its performance. **3.** Informal slow-witted person. **4.** confidential information. —v. **5.** administer a drug to. **dopey, dopy** adj. **1.** half-asleep. **2.** Slang silly.

Doppelgänger n. Legend ghostly double of a living person.

Doppler effect n. change in the apparent

Doric n. **1.** style of ancient Greek architecture. **2.** rustic dialect, esp. a Scots one.

dormant adj. temporarily quiet, inactive, or not being used. **dormancy** n.

dormer, dormer window n. window that projects from a sloping roof.

dormitory n., pl. **-ries. 1.** large room, esp. at a school, containing several beds. —adj. **2.** (of a town or suburb) having most of its inhabitants travel to work in a nearby city or large town.

dormouse n., pl. **-mice.** small rodent resembling a mouse with a furry tail.

dorsal adj. of or on the back.

dory, John Dory n., pl. **-ries.** spiny-finned edible sea fish.

dose n. **1.** specific quantity of a medicine taken at one time. **2.** Informal something unpleasant to experience. —v. **3.** administer a dose to (someone). **dosage** n. size of a dose.

dosh n. Slang money, esp. cash.

doss v. **doss down** Brit. slang sleep, esp. on a makeshift bed. **dosshouse** n. Brit. slang cheap lodging house for homeless people.

dossier [doss-ee-ay] n. collection of papers with information about a subject or person.

dot n. **1.** small round mark. **2.** shorter symbol used in Morse code. —v. **dotting, dotted. 3.** mark with a dot. **4.** scatter or intersperse. **on the dot** at exactly the arranged time. **dotty** adj. **-tier, -tiest.** Slang slightly mad. **dottiness** n.

dote v. **dote on** love to an excessive or foolish degree. **dotage** n. feebleness of mind as a result of old age. **dotard** n. person who is feeble-minded through old age. **doting** adj. fond of someone to an excessive or foolish degree.

dotterel n. plover with white bands around the head and neck.

dottle n. tobacco left in a pipe after smoking.

double adj. **1.** as much again in size, strength, number, etc. **2.** composed of two equal or similar parts. **3.** designed for two users, e.g. double bed. **4.** folded in two. —adv. **5.** twice over, twofold. —n. **6.** twice the number, amount, size, etc. **7.** duplicate or counterpart, esp. a person who closely

resembles another. —pl. **8.** game between two pairs of players. —v. **9.** make or become twice as much. **10.** bend or fold (material etc.). **11.** play two parts. **12.** turn sharply. **at the double** quickly or immediately. **doubly** adv. **double agent** spy employed simultaneously by two opposing sides. **double bass** stringed instrument, largest and lowest member of the violin family. **double-barrelled** adj. **1.** (of a gun) having two barrels. **2.** (of a surname) having two hyphenated parts. **double-breasted** adj. (of a garment) having overlapping fronts. **double-check** v. make certain by checking again. **double chin** fold of fat under the chin. **double cream** thick cream with a high fat content. **double-cross** v. **1.** cheat or betray. —n. **2.** instance of double-crossing. **double-dealing** n. treacherous or deceitful behaviour. **double-decker** n. **1.** bus with two passenger decks one on top of the other. **2.** Informal sandwich made from three slices of bread with two fillings. **double Dutch** Informal incomprehensible talk, gibberish. **double-edged** adj. **1.** (of a remark) malicious in intent though apparently complimentary. **2.** (of a knife) having a cutting edge on either side of the blade. **double glazing** two panes of glass in a window, fitted to reduce heat loss. **double-jointed** adj. (of a person) having unusually flexible joints. **double-park** v. park (a car etc.) alongside or directly opposite another, thus causing an obstruction. **double standard** set of principles that allows greater freedom to one person or group than to another. **double take** esp. in comedy, delayed reaction by a person to a remark or situation. **double talk** deceptive or ambiguous talk.

double entendre [doob-bl on-tond-ra] n. word or phrase that can be interpreted in two ways, esp. with one meaning that is rude.

doublet [dub-lit] n. (formerly) man's close-fitting jacket, with or without sleeves.

doubloon n. former Spanish gold coin.

doubt n. **1.** uncertainty about the truth, facts, or existence of something. **2.** unresolved difficulty or point. —v. **3.** be inclined to disbelieve (a fact or story). **4.** distrust or be suspicious of (a person). **doubter** n. **doubtful** adj. **1.** unlikely. **2.** feeling doubt. **doubtfully** adv. **doubtless** adv. **1.** certainly. **2.** probably.

▷ If doubt is followed by a clause it is

connected by *whether: I doubt whether she means it.* If it is used with a negative it is followed by *that: I don't doubt that he is sincere.*

douche [doosh] *n.* **1.** (instrument for applying) a stream of water directed onto or into the body for cleansing or medical purposes. —*v.* **2.** cleanse or treat by means of a douche.

dough *n.* **1.** thick mixture of flour and water or milk, used for making bread. **2.** *Slang* money. **doughy** *adj.* **doughier, doughiest. doughnut** *n.* small cake of sweetened dough cooked in hot fat.

doughty [dowt-ee] *adj.* -tier, -tiest. hardy or resolute.

dour [doo-er] *adj.* sullen and unfriendly. **dourness** *n.*

douse [rhymes with **mouse**] *v.* **1.** drench with water or other liquid. **2.** put out (a light).

dove *n.* **1.** bird with a heavy body, small head, and short legs. **2.** *Politics* person opposed to war. **dovecote, dovecot** *n.* structure for housing pigeons. **dovetail** *n.* **1.** joint containing wedge-shaped tenons. —*v.* **2.** fit together neatly.

dowager *n.* widow possessing property or a title obtained from her husband.

dowdy *adj.* -dier, -diest. shabby or old-fashioned. **dowdily** *adv.* **dowdiness** *n.*

dowel *n.* wooden or metal peg that fits into two corresponding holes to join two adjacent parts.

dower *n.* life interest in a part of her husband's estate allotted to a widow by law.

down[1] *prep.* **1.** from a higher to a lower position in or on. **2.** at a lower or further level or position on, in, or along. —*adv.* **3.** at or to a lower position or level. **4.** used to indicate lowering or destruction, e.g. *knock down.* **5.** used with several verbs to indicate intensity or completion, e.g. *calm down.* **6.** immediately, e.g. *cash down.* **7.** on paper, e.g. *write this down.* **8.** lower in price. **9.** from an earlier to a later time. —*adj.* **10.** depressed, sad. —*v.* **11.** *Informal* drink, esp. quickly. **have a down on** *Informal* bear ill will towards. **down under** *Informal* Australia or New Zealand. **downward** *adj.* **1.** descending from a higher to a lower level, condition, or position. —*adv.* **2.** downwards. **downwards** *adv.* from a higher to a lower place, level, etc. **down-and-out** *adj.* **1.** without any means of livelihood. —*n.* **2.** person who is destitute and, often, homeless. **down-to-earth** *adj.* sensible or practical.

down[2] *n.* soft fine feathers or hair. **downy** *adj.* **downier, downiest.**

downbeat *adj.* **1.** *Informal* gloomy. **2.** relaxed.

downcast *adj.* **1.** dejected. **2.** (of the eyes) directed downwards.

downfall *n.* **1.** sudden loss of position or reputation. **2.** cause of this.

downgrade *v.* reduce in importance or value.

downhearted *adj.* sad and discouraged.

downhill *adj.* **1.** going or sloping down. —*adv.* **2.** towards the bottom of a hill.

Downing Street *n.* **1.** street in London containing the official residences of the prime minister of Great Britain and the chancellor of the exchequer. **2.** *Informal* British prime minister or Government.

downpour *n.* heavy fall of rain.

downright *adj., adv.* extreme(ly).

downs *pl. n.* rolling upland, esp. in the chalk areas of S England.

Down's syndrome *n.* genetic disorder characterized by a flat face, slanting eyes, and mental retardation.

downstage *adj.* at the front part of the stage.

downstairs *adv.* **1.** to or on a lower floor. —*n.* **2.** lower or ground floor.

downtrodden *adj.* oppressed and lacking the will to resist.

dowry *n., pl.* -ries. property brought by a woman to her husband at marriage.

dowse [rhymes with **cows**] *v.* search for underground water or minerals using a divining rod. **dowser** *n.*

doxology *n., pl.* -gies. short hymn of praise to God.

doyen [doy-en] *n.* senior member of a group or society. **doyenne** [doy-en] *n. fem.*

doyley *n.* same as DOILY.

doz. dozen.

doze *v.* **1.** sleep lightly or intermittently. —*n.* **2.** short sleep. **dozy** *adj.* **dozier, doziest. 1.** drowsy. **2.** *Informal* stupid. **doze off** *v.* fall into a light sleep.

dozen *adj., n.* twelve. **dozenth** *adj.*

DPP Director of Public Prosecutions.

Dr 1. Doctor. **2.** Drive.

drab adj. **drabber, drabbest. 1.** dull or dingy. **2.** cheerless or dreary. **drabness** n.

drachm [dram] n. Brit. one eighth of a fluid ounce.

drachma n., pl. **-mas, -mae.** standard monetary unit of Greece.

draconian adj. harsh or severe.

draft n. **1.** plan, sketch, or drawing of something. **2.** preliminary outline of a book, speech, etc. **3.** written order for payment of money by a bank. **4.** US selection for compulsory military service. —v. **5.** draw up an outline or plan of. **6.** detach (personnel) from one place to another. **7.** US select for compulsory military service.

drag v. **dragging, dragged. 1.** pull with force, esp. along the ground. **2.** trail on the ground. **3.** (foll. by along or to) bring (oneself or someone else) with effort or difficulty. **4.** (foll. by on or out) last, prolong, or be prolonged tediously. **5.** search (a river) with a dragnet or hook. —n. **6.** person or thing that slows up progress. **7.** Informal tedious person or thing. **8.** Slang women's clothes worn by a man. **9.** resistance to the motion of a body passing through air or a liquid. **dragnet** n. net used to scour the bottom of a pond or river, when searching for something. **drag race** race in which specially built cars or motorcycles are timed over a measured course.

draggle v. make or become wet or dirty by trailing on the ground.

dragoman n., pl. **-s, -men.** in some Middle Eastern countries, professional interpreter or guide.

dragon n. **1.** mythical fire-breathing monster with a scaly body, wings and claws, and a long tail. **2.** Informal fierce woman. **dragonfly** n. brightly coloured insect with a long slender body and two pairs of wings.

dragoon n. **1.** heavily armed cavalryman. —v. **2.** coerce or force.

drain n. **1.** pipe or channel that carries off water or sewage. **2.** cause of continuous diminution of resources or energy. —v. **3.** draw off or remove liquid from. **4.** flow away or filter off. **5.** drink the entire contents of (a glass or cup). **6.** make constant demands on (resources, energy, etc.). **7.** exhaust (someone) physically and emotionally. **drainage** n. **1.** process or method of draining. **2.** system of drains. **draining**

board sloping grooved board at the side of a sink, where washed plates are placed to dry. **drainpipe** n. **1.** pipe for carrying off rainwater or sewage. —pl. **2.** very narrow trousers.

drake n. male duck.

dram n. **1.** small amount of spirits, esp. whisky. **2.** one sixteenth of an ounce.

drama n. **1.** a work to be performed by actors. **2.** art of the writing or production of plays. **3.** situation that is highly emotional, turbulent, or tragic. **dramatic** adj. **1.** of or like drama. **2.** striking or effective. **dramatically** adv. **dramatist** n. playwright. **dramatize** v. **1.** put into dramatic form. **2.** express (something) in a dramatic or exaggerated way. **dramatization** n.

dramatis personae [drah-mat-tiss per-soh-nigh] n. characters in a play.

dramaturgy n. art and technique of the theatre. **dramaturgic, dramaturgical** adj. **dramaturgist** n. **1.** (also **dramaturge**) playwright. **2.** (also **dramaturg**) literary adviser to a theatre, film company, etc.

drank v. past tense of DRINK.

drape v. **1.** cover with material, usu. in folds. **2.** place casually and loosely. —n. **1.** US curtain. **draper** n. Brit. dealer in fabrics and sewing materials. **drapery** n., pl. **-eries. 1.** fabric or clothing arranged and draped. **2.** fabrics and cloth collectively. —pl. **3.** curtains.

drastic adj. sudden and extreme. **drastically** adv.

draught n. **1.** current of air, esp. in an enclosed space. **2.** act of pulling a load by a vehicle or animal. **3.** portion of liquid to be drunk, esp. medicine. **4.** instance of drinking. **5.** one of the flat discs used in the game of draughts. —pl. **6.** game for two players using a chessboard and twelve draughts each. **draughty** adj. **draughtier, draughtiest.** exposed to draughts of air. **draughtiness** n. **draughtsman** n. person employed to prepare detailed scale drawings of machinery, buildings, etc. **draughtsmanship** n. **draught beer** beer stored in a cask.

draw v. **drawing, drew, drawn. 1.** depict or sketch (a figure, picture, etc.) in lines, with a pencil or pen. **2.** cause (a person or thing) to move out, as from a drawer, holster, etc. **3.** move in a specified direction. **4.** arouse the interest or attention of. **5.** formulate or derive, e.g. draw conclusions. **6.** take from a source, e.g. *draw money from the bank.* **7.** (of two teams or contestants) finish a game with an equal number of points. —*n.* **8.** raffle or lottery. **9.** contest or game ending in a tie. **10.** event, act, etc., that attracts a large audience. **drawing** *n.* **1.** picture or plan made by means of lines on a surface. **2.** art of making drawings. **drawing pin** short tack with a broad smooth head. **drawing room** *Old-fashioned* room where visitors are received and entertained. **drawback** *n.* disadvantage. **drawbridge** *n.* bridge that may be raised to prevent access or to enable vessels to pass. **draw out** *v.* **1.** extend. **2.** encourage (a person) to talk freely. **drawstring** *n.* cord run through a hem around an opening, so that when it is pulled tighter, the opening closes. **draw up** *v.* **1.** (of a vehicle) come to a halt. **2.** formulate and write out (a contract).

drawer *n.* **1.** boxlike container in a chest, table, etc., made for sliding in and out. —*pl.* **2.** *Old-fashioned* undergarment worn below the waist.

drawl *v.* **1.** speak slowly, esp. prolonging the vowel sounds. —*n.* **2.** drawling manner of speech.

drawn *v.* **1.** past participle of DRAW. —*adj.* **2.** haggard, tired, or tense in appearance.

dray *n.* low cart used for carrying heavy loads.

dread *v.* **1.** anticipate with apprehension or terror. —*n.* **2.** great fear. **dreadful** *adj.* **1.** extremely disagreeable, shocking, or bad. **2.** extreme. **dreadfully** *adv.*

dreadlocks *pl. n.* hair worn in the Rastafarian style of tightly curled strands.

dream *n.* **1.** mental activity, usu. an imagined series of events, occurring during sleep. **2.** cherished hope. **3.** *Informal* something wonderful. —*v.* **dreaming, dreamt** *or* **dreamed. 4.** experience (a dream). **5.** (foll. by *of* or *about*) have an image (of) or fantasy (about). **6.** (foll. by *of*) consider the possibility (of). —*adj.* **7.** ideal, e.g. *a dream holiday.* **dreamer** *n.* **dreamy** *adj.* **dreamier, dreamiest. 1.** vague or impractical. **2.** *Informal* wonderful. **dreamily** *adv.* **dream up** *v.* invent by imagination and ingenuity.

dreary *adj.* **drearier, dreariest.** dull or boring. **drearily** *adv.* **dreariness** *n.*

dredge[1] *v.* remove (silt or mud) from (a river bed etc.). **dredger** *n.* boat fitted with machinery for dredging. **dredge up** *v. Infor-*mal remember (something) obscure or half-forgotten.

dredge[2] *v.* sprinkle (food) with flour etc.

dregs *pl. n.* **1.** solid particles that settle at the bottom of some liquids. **2.** most despised elements, e.g. *the dregs of society.*

drench *v.* **1.** make completely wet. **2.** give medicine to (an animal). —*n.* **3.** dose of medicine given to an animal. **drenching** *n.*

Dresden, Dresden china *n.* delicate and decorative porcelain ware made near Dresden in Germany.

dress *v.* **1.** put clothes on. **2.** put on formal clothes. **3.** apply protective covering to (a wound). **4.** arrange or prepare. —*n.* **5.** one-piece garment for a woman or girl, consisting of a skirt and bodice and sometimes sleeves. **6.** complete style of clothing. **dressing** *n.* **1.** sauce for salad. **2.** covering for a wound. **dressing-down** *n. Informal* severe scolding. **dressing gown** robe worn before dressing. **dressing room** room used for changing clothes, esp. backstage in a theatre. **dressing table** piece of bedroom furniture with a mirror and drawers. **dressy** *adj.* **dressier, dressiest.** (of clothes) elegant. **dressiness** *n.* **dress circle** first gallery in a theatre. **dressmaker** *n.* person who makes clothes for women. **dressmaking** *n.* **dress rehearsal** last rehearsal of a play, using costumes, lighting, etc., as for the first night. **dress up** *v.* **1.** attire (oneself or another) in glamorous or stylish clothes. **2.** put fancy dress on. **3.** improve the appearance or impression of, e.g. *to dress up the facts.*

dressage [**dress**-ahzh] *n.* training of a horse to perform manoeuvres in response to the rider's body signals.

dresser[1] *n.* set of shelves, usu. with cupboards, for storing or displaying dishes.

dresser[2] *n. Theatre* person employed to assist actors with their costumes.

drew *v.* past tense of DRAW.

drey *n.* squirrel's nest.

dribble *v.* **1.** (allow to) flow in drops. **2.** allow saliva to trickle from the mouth. **3.** propel (a ball) by repeatedly tapping it with the foot, hand, or a stick. —*n.* **4.** small quantity of liquid falling in drops. **5.** act or instance of dribbling. **dribbler** *n.*

driblet, dribblet *n.* small amount.

dribs and drabs *pl. n. Informal* small occasional amounts.

dried v. past of DRY.

drier adj. **1.** comparative of DRY. —n. **2.** same as DRYER.

driest adj. superlative of DRY.

drift v. **1.** be carried along by currents of air or water. **2.** move aimlessly from one place or activity to another. **3.** (of snow) to pile up in heaps. —n. **4.** something piled up by the wind or current, such as a snowdrift. **5.** tendency or meaning. **6.** general movement or development. **drifter** n. **1.** person who moves aimlessly from place to place or job to job. **2.** fishing boat equipped with drift nets. **drift net** fishing net which is allowed to drift with the tide. **driftwood** n. wood floating on or washed ashore by the sea.

drill¹ n. **1.** tool or machine for boring holes. **2.** strict and often repetitious training. **3.** Informal correct procedure. —v. **4.** pierce, bore, or cut (a hole) in (material) (as if) with a drill. **5.** teach by rigorous exercises and training.

drill² n. hard-wearing cotton cloth.

drill³ n. **1.** machine for sowing seed in rows. **2.** small furrow for seed. —v. **3.** sow (seed) in drills or furrows.

drill⁴ n. W African monkey.

drily adv. same as DRYLY.

drink v. drinking, drank, drunk. **1.** swallow (a liquid). **2.** consume alcohol, esp. to excess. —n. **3.** liquid suitable for drinking. **4.** portion of liquid for drinking. **5.** alcohol or its habitual or excessive consumption. **drinkable** adj. **drinker** n. **drink-driving** adj. relating to driving a car after drinking alcohol, e.g. a drink-driving charge. **drink in** v. pay close attention to. **drink to** v. drink a toast to.

drip v. dripping, dripped. **1.** fall or let fall in drops. —n. **2.** falling of drops of liquid. **3.** sound made by falling drops. **4.** Informal inane insipid person. **5.** Med. apparatus for the administration of a solution drop by drop into a vein. **drip-dry** adj. denoting clothing that will dry free of creases if hung up when wet. **drip-feed** v. feed (someone) a liquid drop by drop, usu. through a vein.

dripping n. fat that comes from meat while it is being roasted or fried.

drive v. driving, drove, driven. **1.** guide the movement of (a vehicle). **2.** transport or be transported in a vehicle. **3.** goad into a specified state. **4.** push or propel. **5.** Sport hit (a ball) very hard and straight. —n. **6.** journey in a driven vehicle. **7.** road for vehicles, esp. a private road leading to a house. **8.** united effort towards a common goal, e.g. an investment drive. **9.** energy, ambition, or initiative. **10.** Psychol. motive or interest, e.g. sex drive. **11.** means by which force, motion, etc. is transmitted in a mechanism. **driver** n. **1.** person who drives a vehicle. **2.** Golf club used for tee shots. **drive at** v. Informal intend or mean, e.g. what are you driving at? **drive-in** adj., n. (denoting) a public facility used by patrons in their cars. **driveway** n. path for vehicles connecting a building to a public road. **driving licence** official document permitting a person to drive a motor vehicle.

drivel n. **1.** foolish talk. —v. **-elling, -elled. 2.** speak foolishly.

drizzle n. **1.** very light rain. —v. **2.** rain lightly. **drizzly** adj. **-zlier, -zliest.**

drogue n. **1.** small parachute. **2.** windsock. **3.** object towed behind an aircraft as a target for firing practice.

droll adj. quaintly amusing. **drolly** adv. **drollery** n.

dromedary [drom-mid-er-ee] n., pl. **-daries.** camel with a single hump.

drone¹ n. male bee.

drone² v., n. (make) a monotonous low dull sound. **drone on** v. talk for a long time in a monotonous tone.

drool v. **1.** (foll. by over) show excessive enthusiasm (for) or pleasure (in). **2.** allow saliva to flow from the mouth.

droop v. sag, as from weakness. **droopy** adj. **droopier, droopiest.**

drop v. **1.** small quantity of liquid forming a round shape. **2.** very small quantity of liquid. **3.** act of falling. **4.** decrease in amount or value. **5.** vertical distance that anything may fall. —pl. **6.** liquid medication applied drop by drop. —v. **7.** (allow to) fall in globules. **8.** (allow to) fall vertically. **9.** decrease in amount, strength, or value. **10.** mention casually. **11.** discontinue (an activity). **droplet** n. **droppings** pl. n. faeces of certain animals, such as rabbits or birds. **drop in, by** v. pay someone a casual visit. **drop kick** in rugby etc., kick in which the ball is dropped from the hands and kicked before it hits the ground. **drop off** v. **1.** grow smaller or less. **2.** Informal fall asleep. **dropout** n. **1.** person who fails to complete a course of study. **2.** person who

dropsy *n.* illness in which watery fluid collects in the body. **dropsical** *adj.*

droshky, drosky *n.*, *pl.* **-ies.** open four-wheeled carriage, formerly used in Russia.

dross *n.* 1. scum formed on the surfaces of molten metals. 2. worthless matter.

drought *n.* prolonged shortage of rainfall.

drove[1] *v.* past tense of DRIVE.

drove[2] *n.* 1. moving herd of livestock. 2. moving crowd of people. **drover** *n.* person who drives sheep or cattle.

drown *v.* 1. die or kill by immersion in liquid. 2. forget (one's sorrows) temporarily by drinking alcohol. 3. drench thoroughly. 4. render (a sound) inaudible by making a loud noise.

drowse *v.* be sleepy, dull, or sluggish. **drowsy** *adj.* **drowsier, drowsiest. drowsily** *adv.* **drowsiness** *n.*

drubbing *n.* utter defeat, as in a contest.

drudge *n.* 1. person who works hard at wearisome menial tasks. —*v.* 2. toil at such tasks. **drudgery** *n.*

drug *n.* 1. substance used in the treatment or prevention of disease. 2. chemical substance, esp. a narcotic, taken for the effect it produces. —*v.* **drugging, drugged.** 3. mix a drug with (food or drink). 4. administer a drug to (a person or animal) in order to induce sleepiness or unconsciousness. **druggist** *n.* US pharmacist. **drugstore** *n.* US pharmacy where a wide variety of goods is available.

drugget *n.* coarse woollen fabric, usu. used for carpeting.

Druid *n.* member of an ancient order of Celtic priests. **Druidic, Druidical** *adj.*

drum *n.* 1. percussion instrument sounded by striking a skin stretched across the opening of a hollow cylinder. 2. cylindrical object or container. —*v.* **drumming, drummed.** 3. play (music) on a drum. 4. tap rhythmically or regularly. **drummer** *n.* **drum into** *v.* instil into (someone) by constant repetition. **drum machine** a synthesizer programmed to reproduce the sound of percussion instruments. **drum major** person in charge of a marching band. **drum majorette** girl who marches at the head of a procession, twirl-

ing a baton. **drum out** *v.* expel (from an organization). **drumstick** *n.* 1. stick used for playing a drum. 2. lower joint of the leg of a cooked fowl. **drum up** *v.* obtain (support) by making requests or canvassing.

drunk *v.* 1. past participle of DRINK. —*adj.* 2. intoxicated with alcohol to the extent of losing control over normal functions. 3. overwhelmed by a strong influence or emotion. —*n.* 4. person who is drunk. **drunkard** *n.* person who is frequently or habitually drunk. **drunken** *adj.* 1. drunk. 2. caused by or relating to alcoholic intoxication. **drunkenly** *adv.* **drunkenness** *n.*

drupe *n.* fleshy fruit with a stone, such as a peach, plum, or cherry.

dry *adj.* **drier, driest** *or* **dryer, dryest.** 1. lacking moisture. 2. having little or no rainfall. 3. *Informal* thirsty. 4. (of wine) not sweet. 5. uninteresting, e.g. *a dry book.* 6. (of humour) subtle and sarcastic. 7. prohibiting the sale of alcohol, e.g. *a dry area.* —*v.* **drying, dried.** 8. make or become dry. 9. preserve (food) by removing the moisture. **dryly** *adv.* **dryness** *n.* **dryer** *n.* apparatus for removing moisture. **dry battery** battery in which the electrolyte is in the form of a paste to prevent spilling. **dry-clean** *v.* clean (clothes) with a solvent other than water. **dry-cleaner** *n.* **dry-cleaning** *n.* **dry dock** dock that can be pumped dry to permit work on a ship's bottom. **dry ice** solid carbon dioxide. **dry out** *v.* 1. make or become dry. 2. (cause to) undergo treatment for alcoholism or drug addiction. **dry rot** crumbling and drying of timber, caused by certain fungi. **dry run** *Informal* rehearsal. **dry-stone** *adj.* (of a wall) made without mortar. **dry up** *v.* 1. become unproductive. 2. to dry (plates, cutlery, etc.) with a tea towel. 3. *Informal* stop speaking.

dryad *n.* wood nymph.

DSc Doctor of Science.

DSS Department of Social Security.

DT's *Informal* delirium tremens.

dual *adj.* 1. relating to or denoting two. 2. twofold. **duality** *n.* **dualism** *n.* state of having or being believed to have two distinct parts or aspects. **dual carriageway** *Brit.* road on which traffic travelling in opposite directions is separated by a central strip of turf or concrete.

dub[1] *v.* **dubbing, dubbed.** give (a person or place) a name or nickname.

dub² v. **dubbing, dubbed. 1.** provide (a film) with a new soundtrack, esp. in a different language. **2.** provide (a film or tape) with a soundtrack. —n. **3.** style of reggae record production involving exaggeration of instrumental parts, echo, etc.

dubbin n. Brit. greasy preparation applied to leather to soften and waterproof it.

dubious [dew-bee-uss] adj. feeling or causing doubt. **dubiously** adv. **dubiety** [dew-by-it-ee] n.

ducal [duke-al] adj. of a duke.

ducat [duck-it] n. former European gold or silver coin.

duchess n. **1.** woman who holds the rank of duke in her own right. **2.** wife or widow of a duke.

duchy n., pl. **duchies.** territory of a duke or duchess.

duck¹ n. **1.** water bird with short legs, webbed feet, and a broad blunt bill. **2.** female of this bird. **3.** flesh of this bird, used as food. **4.** Cricket score of nothing. **duckling** n. young duck. **duckboard** n. board laid to form a path over muddy ground. **duck-billed platypus** see PLATYPUS.

duck² v. **1.** move (the head or body) quickly downwards, to escape observation or to dodge a blow. **2.** plunge suddenly into water. **3.** Informal dodge or escape (a duty etc.).

duct n. **1.** tube, pipe, or canal by means of which a fluid or gas is conveyed. **2.** bodily passage conveying secretions or excretions. **ductless gland** gland which secretes hormones directly into the bloodstream (also **endocrine gland**).

ductile adj. **1.** (of metal) able to be shaped into sheets or wires. **2.** easily influenced. **ductility** n.

dud n. **1.** Informal person or thing that proves ineffectual. —adj. **2.** bad or useless.

dude n. US informal **1.** man, chap. **2.** Old-fashioned dandy.

dudgeon n. **in high dudgeon** angry or resentful.

duds pl. n. Old-fashioned informal clothes.

due adj. **1.** expected or scheduled to be present or arrive. **2.** owed as a debt. **3.** fitting, proper. —n. **4.** something that is owed, required, or due. —pl. **5.** charges for membership of a club or organization. —adv. **6.** directly or exactly, e.g. due north. **due to** attributable to or caused by.

▷ **Due to** is not synonymous with because of or owing to. If the words due to can be replaced by attributable to, it is generally appropriate to use due to.

duel n. **1.** formal prearranged combat with deadly weapons between two people, to settle a quarrel. —v. **duelling, duelled. 2.** fight in a duel. **duellist** n.

duenna n. esp. in Spain, elderly woman acting as chaperone to a young woman.

duet n. piece of music for two performers. **duettist** n.

duff¹ adj. Brit. informal bad or useless. **duff up** v. Brit. informal beat (a person) severely.

duff² n. kind of boiled pudding.

duffel, duffle n. short for DUFFEL COAT. **duffel bag, duffle bag** cylindrical canvas bag fastened with a drawstring. **duffel coat, duffle coat** coat made of heavy woollen cloth.

duffer n. Informal dull or incompetent person.

dug¹ v. past of DIG.

dug² n. teat or udder.

dugong n. whalelike mammal found in tropical waters.

dugout n. **1.** canoe made by hollowing out a log. **2.** Mil. covered excavation dug to provide shelter. **3.** at a sports ground, covered bench where managers and substitutes sit.

duke n. **1.** nobleman of the highest rank. **2.** prince or ruler of a small principality or duchy. **dukedom** n.

dulcet [dull-sit] adj. (of a sound) soothing or pleasant.

dulcimer n. tuned percussion instrument consisting of a set of strings stretched over a sounding board and struck with hammers.

dull adj. **1.** uninteresting. **2.** stupid. **3.** (of a blade) lacking sharpness. **4.** (of a pain) not acute or intense. **5.** (of weather) not bright or clear. **6.** lacking in spirit. —v. **7.** make or become dull. **dullness** n. **dully** adv. **dullard** n. dull or stupid person.

dulse n. seaweed with large red edible fronds.

duly adv. **1.** in a proper manner. **2.** at the proper time.

dumb adj. **1.** lacking the power to speak. **2.** silent. **3.** Informal stupid. **dumbly** adv. **dumbness** n. **dumbbell** n. exercising weight consisting of a short bar with a heavy ball or disc at either end. **dumbfound** v. strike dumb with astonishment. **dumb show** meaningful gestures without speech. **dumbwaiter** n. **1.** lift for carrying food etc. between floors. **2.** stand or revolving tray for holding food at a dining table.

dumdum n. soft-nosed bullet that expands on impact and inflicts extensive wounds.

dummy n., pl. **-mies. 1.** figure representing the human form, used for displaying clothes etc. **2.** copy of an object, often lacking some essential feature of the original. **3.** Brit. rubber teat for a baby to suck. **4.** Slang stupid person. —adj. **5.** sham or counterfeit. **dummy run** practice, rehearsal.

dump v. **1.** drop or let fall heavily or in a mass. **2.** Informal dispose of (something or someone) carelessly. **3.** market (goods) in bulk and at low prices, esp. abroad. —n. **4.** place where waste materials are dumped. **5.** Informal dirty unattractive place. **6.** Mil. place where weapons or supplies are stored. **down in the dumps** in a state of depression.

dumpling n. **1.** small ball of dough cooked and served with stew. **2.** round pastry case filled with fruit.

dumpy adj. **dumpier, dumpiest.** short and plump.

dun[1] adj. brownish-grey.

dun[2] v. **dunning, dunned. 1.** press (a debtor) for payment. —n. **2.** demand for payment.

dunce n. person who is stupid or slow to learn.

dunderhead n. slow-witted person.

dune n. mound or ridge of drifted sand.

dung n. excrement of animals.

dungarees pl. n. trousers with a bib attached.

dungeon n. underground prison cell.

dunk v. **1.** dip (a biscuit etc.) into liquid before eating it. **2.** submerge (something) in liquid.

dunlin n. small sandpiper with a brown back.

duo n., pl. **duos. 1.** pair of performers. **2.** Informal pair of closely connected people.

duodecimal adj. reckoned in twelves or twelfths.

duodenum [dew-oh-**deen**-um] n., pl. **-na, -nums.** first part of the small intestine, just below the stomach. **duodenal** adj.

duologue n. in drama, conversation between only two speakers.

dupe v. **1.** deceive or cheat. —n. **2.** person who is easily deceived.

duple adj. Music having two beats in a bar.

duplex n. **1.** US apartment on two floors. **2.** US semi-detached house. —adj. **3.** having two parts.

duplicate adj. **1.** copied exactly from an original. —n. **2.** exact copy. —v. **3.** make a replica of. **4.** do again (something that has already been done). **duplication** n. **duplicator** n.

duplicity n. deception or double-dealing.

durable adj. long-lasting. **durables, durable goods** pl. n. goods that require infrequent replacement. **durability** n.

duration n. length of time that something lasts.

durbar n. (formerly) court of a native ruler or a governor in India or a reception at such a court.

duress n. compulsion by use of force or threats.

during prep. throughout or within the limit of (a period of time).

dusk n. time just before nightfall, when it is almost dark. **dusky** adj. **duskier, duskiest. 1.** dark in colour. **2.** shadowy. **duskiness** n.

dust n. **1.** dry fine powdery material, such as particles of dirt. —v. **2.** remove dust from (furniture) by wiping. **3.** sprinkle (something) with dust or some other powdery substance. **duster** n. cloth used for dusting. **dusty** adj. **dustier, dustiest.** covered with dust. **dustbin** n. large usu. cylindrical container for household rubbish. **dustbowl** n. dry area in which the surface soil is exposed to wind erosion. **dustcart** n. road vehicle for collecting refuse. **dust jacket, cover** removable paper cover used to protect a book. **dustman** n. Brit. man whose job is to collect household rubbish. **dustpan** n. short-handled hooded shovel into which dust is swept from floors. **dustsheet, dust cover** Brit. large cloth to protect furniture from dust. **dust-up** n. Informal fight or argument.

Dutch adj. of the Netherlands, its inhabitants, or their language. **go Dutch** Informal share the expenses on an outing. **Dutch auction** auction in which the price is gradually lowered until a buyer is found. **Dutch barn** farm building consisting of a steel roof on a curved frame. **Dutch courage** false courage gained from drinking alcohol. **Dutch elm disease** fungal disease of elm trees. **Dutch uncle** *Informal* person who criticizes or scolds frankly and severely.

duty *n., pl.* **-ties. 1.** task that a person is bound to perform for moral or legal reasons. **2.** government tax, esp. on imports. **on duty** at work. **dutiable** *adj.* (of goods) requiring payment of duty. **dutiful** *adj.* showing or resulting from a sense of duty. **dutifully** *adv.* **duty-bound** *adj.* morally obliged. **duty-free** *adj., adv.* with exemption from customs or excise duties.

duvet [**doo**-vay] *n.* quilt filled with down or artificial fibre.

dux *n. Scot.* top pupil in a school or class.

dwarf *n., pl.* **dwarfs, dwarves. 1.** under-sized person. **2.** in folklore, small ugly man-like creature, often possessing magical pow-ers. —*adj.* **3.** denoting an animal or plant much below the average size for a species. —*v.* **4.** cause (someone or something) to seem small by being much larger.

dwell *v.* **dwelling, dwelt** *or* **dwelled.** live as a permanent resident. **dweller** *n.* **dwelling** *n.* place of residence. **dwell on, upon** *v.* think, speak, or write at length about.

dwindle *v.* grow less in size, intensity, or number.

Dy *Chem.* dysprosium.

dye *n.* **1.** staining or colouring substance. **2.** colour produced by dyeing. —*v.* **dyeing, dyed. 3.** colour or stain (fabric, hair, etc.) by the application of dye. **dyer** *n.* **dyed-in-the-wool** *adj.* uncompromising or unchanging in attitude or opinion.

dying *v.* present participle of DIE[1].

dyke *n.* **1.** wall built to prevent flooding. **2.** ditch. **3.** *Slang* lesbian.

dynamic *adj.* **1.** characterized by force of personality, ambition, and energy. **2.** of or concerned with energy or forces that pro-duce motion. **dynamically** *adv.* **dynamism** *n.* forcefulness of an energetic personality.

dynamics *n.* **1.** branch of mechanics con-cerned with the forces that change or pro-duce the motions of bodies. **2.** *Music* the various degrees of loudness called for in a performance.

dynamite *n.* **1.** high-explosive mixture con-taining nitroglycerin. **2.** *Informal* spectacu-lar or potentially dangerous person or thing. —*v.* **3.** mine or blow (something) up with dynamite.

dynamo *n., pl.* **-mos.** device for converting mechanical energy into electrical energy.

dynasty *n., pl.* **-ties.** sequence of hereditary rulers. **dynastic** *adj.* **dynast** *n.* hereditary ruler.

dyne *n.* old-fashioned unit of force.

dysentery *n.* infection of the intestine caus-ing severe diarrhoea.

dysfunction *n. Med.* disturbance or abnor-mality in the function of an organ or part.

dyslexia *n.* disorder causing impaired abil-ity to read. **dyslexic** *adj.*

dysmenorrhoea *n.* painful menstruation.

dyspepsia *n.* indigestion. **dyspeptic** *adj.*

dysprosium *n.* metallic element of the lanthanide series.

dystopia *n.* imaginary place where every-thing is as bad as it can be.

dystrophy [**diss**-trof-fee] *n.* wasting of the body tissues, esp. the muscles.

E

E East(ern).

each *adj., pron.* every (one) taken separately.

▷ The expressions *each other* and *one another* are interchangeable.

eager *adj.* showing or feeling great desire, keen. **eagerly** *adv.* **eagerness** *n.*

eagle *n.* **1.** large bird of prey with keen eyesight. **2.** *Golf* score of two strokes under par for a hole. **eaglet** *n.* young eagle.

ear[1] *n.* **1.** organ of hearing, esp. the external part of it. **2.** sensitivity to musical or other sounds. **earache** *n.* pain in the ear. **eardrum** *n.* thin piece of skin inside the ear which enables one to hear sounds. **earmark** *v.* **1.** set (something) aside for a specific purpose. —*n.* **2.** distinguishing mark. **earphone** *n.* receiver for a radio etc., held to or put in the ear. **ear-piercing** *adj.* deafening. **earplug** *n.* piece of soft material placed in the ear to keep out water or noise. **earring** *n.* ornament for the lobe of the ear. **earshot** *n.* hearing range.

ear[2] *n.* head of corn.

earl *n.* British nobleman ranking next below a marquess. **earldom** *n.*

early *adj., adv.* **-lier, -liest. 1.** before the expected or usual time. **2.** in the first part of a period. **3.** in a period far back in time.

earn *v.* **1.** obtain by work or merit. **2.** (of investments etc.) gain (interest). **earnings** *pl. n.* money earned.

earnest[1] *adj.* serious and sincere. **in earnest** seriously. **earnestly** *adv.*

earnest[2] *n.* part payment given in advance, esp. to confirm a contract.

earth *n.* **1.** planet that we live on. **2.** land, the ground. **3.** soil. **4.** fox's hole. **5.** wire connecting an electrical apparatus with the earth. —*v.* **6.** connect (a circuit) to earth. **run to earth** find after a long search. **earthen** *adj.* made of baked clay or earth. **earthenware** *n.* pottery made of baked clay. **earthly** *adj.* conceivable or possible, e.g. *no earthly reason.* **earthy** *adj.* **1.** coarse or crude. **2.** of or like earth. **earthquake** *n.* violent vibration of the earth's surface. **earthwork** *n.* fortification made of earth.

earthworm *n.* worm which burrows in the soil.

earwig *n.* small insect with a pincer-like tail.

ease *n.* **1.** freedom from difficulty, discomfort, or worry. **2.** rest or leisure, e.g. *at one's ease.* —*v.* **3.** give bodily or mental ease to. **4.** lessen (severity, tension, pain, etc.). **5.** move carefully or gradually. **ease off** *v.* become less severe.

easel *n.* frame to support an artist's canvas or a blackboard.

east *n.* **1.** part of the horizon where the sun rises. **2.** eastern lands or the orient. —*adj.* **3.** on, in, or near the east. **4.** (of the wind) from the east. —*adv.* **5.** in, to, or towards the east. **easterly** *adj., adv.* **1.** to the east. **2.** (of a wind) from the east. **eastern** *adj.* of, in, or from the east. **eastward** *adj., adv.* **eastwards** *adv.*

Easter *n.* Christian spring festival commemorating the Resurrection of Jesus Christ. **Easter egg** chocolate egg given at Easter.

easy *adj.* **easier, easiest. 1.** not needing much work or effort. **2.** free from pain, care, or anxiety. **3.** easy-going. **easily** *adv.* **easiness** *n.* **easy chair** comfortable armchair. **easy-going** *adj.* relaxed in attitude, tolerant.

▷ *Easy* may be used as an adverb in set phrases like *take it easy.*

eat *v.* **eating, ate, eaten. 1.** take (food) into the mouth and swallow it. **2.** (foll. by *away* or *up*) destroy. —*n.* **3.** have a meal. **eatable** *adj.* fit or suitable for eating.

eau de Cologne [oh de kol-**lone**] *n. French* light perfume.

eaves *pl. n.* overhanging edges of a roof.

eavesdrop *v.* **-dropping, -dropped.** listen secretly to a private conversation. **eavesdropper** *n.* **eavesdropping** *n.*

ebb *v.* **1.** (of tide water) flow back. **2.** become weaker. —*n.* **3.** flowing back of the tide. **at a low ebb** in a state of weakness.

ebony *n., pl.* **-onies. 1.** hard black wood. —*adj.* **2.** deep black.

ebullient *adj.* overflowing with enthusiasm and excitement. **ebullience** *n.*

EC European Community.

eccentric adj. **1.** odd or unconventional. **2.** (of circles) not having the same centre. —n. **3.** eccentric person. **eccentrically** adv. **eccentricity** n.

ecclesiastic adj. (also **ecclesiastical**) **1.** of the Christian Church or clergy. —n. **2.** clergyman.

ECG **1.** electrocardiogram. **2.** electrocardiograph.

echelon [esh-a-lon] n. **1.** level of power or responsibility. **2.** Mil. formation in which units follow one another but are spaced out sideways to allow each a line of fire ahead.

echidna [ik-kid-na] n., pl. **-s**, **-nae** [-nee] mammal with a protective layer of spines, found in Aust. and New Guinea (also **spiny anteater**).

echo n., pl. **-oes**. **1.** repetition of sounds by reflection of sound waves off a surface. **2.** close imitation. —v. **-oing**, **-oed**. **3.** repeat or be repeated as an echo. **4.** imitate closely. **echo sounder** sonar. **echo sounding** use of sonar to navigate.

éclair n. finger-shaped pastry filled with cream and covered with chocolate.

éclat [ake-lah] n. **1.** brilliant success. **2.** splendour.

eclectic adj. selecting from various ideas or sources. **eclecticism** n.

eclipse n. **1.** temporary obscuring of one heavenly body by another. —v. **2.** surpass or outclass. **ecliptic** n. apparent path of the sun.

eclogue n. short poem on a rural theme.

eco- combining form ecology; ecological, as in ecosystem.

ecology n. study of the relationships between living things and their environment. **ecological** adj. **ecologically** adv. **ecologist** n.

economy n., pl. **-mies**. **1.** system of interrelationship of money, industry, and employment in a country. **2.** careful management of resources to avoid waste. **economic** adj. **1.** of economics. **2.** profitable. **economics** n. **1.** social science concerned with the production and consumption of goods and services. —pl. **2.** financial aspects. **economical** adj. not wasteful, thrifty. **economically** adv. **economist** n. specialist in economics. **economize** v. limit or reduce waste.

ecosystem n. system involving interactions between a community and its environment.

ecru adj. greyish-yellow.

ecstasy n. **1.** state of intense delight. **2.** Slang powerful drug that can produce hallucinations. **ecstatic** adj. **ecstatically** adv.

ECT electroconvulsive therapy.

ecto- combining form outer, outside, as in ectoplasm.

-ectomy n. combining form surgical excision of a part, e.g. appendectomy.

ectoplasm n. Spiritualism substance that supposedly is emitted from the body of a medium during a trance.

ECU European Currency Unit.

ecumenical adj. of the Christian Church throughout the world, esp. with regard to its unity.

eczema [ek-sim-a] n. skin disease causing intense itching.

ed. **1.** edited. **2.** edition. **3.** editor.

Edam n. round Dutch cheese with a red rind.

EDC European Defence Community.

eddy n., pl. **eddies**. **1.** small whirling movement in air, water, etc. —v. **eddying**, **eddied**. **2.** move in eddies.

edelweiss [ade-el-vice] n. alpine plant with white flowers.

Eden n. **1.** Bible garden in which Adam and Eve were placed at the Creation. **2.** place of delight or contentment.

edge n. **1.** border or line where something ends or begins. **2.** cutting side of a blade. **3.** sharpness of tone. —v. **4.** provide an edge or border for. **5.** push (one's way) gradually. **have the edge on** have an advantage over. **on edge** nervous or irritable. **edgeways** adv. with the edge forwards or uppermost. **edging** n. anything placed along an edge to finish it. **edgy** adj. nervous or irritable.

edible adj. fit to be eaten. **edibility** n.

edict [ee-dikt] n. order issued by an authority.

edifice [ed-if-iss] n. large building.

edify [ed-if-fie] v. **-fying**, **-fied**. improve morally by instruction. **edification** n.

edit v. prepare (a book, film, etc.) for publication or broadcast. **edition** n. **1.** form in which something is published. **2.** number of copies of a new publication printed at one time. **editor** n. 1. person who edits. 2. person in overall charge of a newspaper or periodical. **editorial** adj. 1. of editing or editors. —n. 2. newspaper article stating the opinion of the editor.

educate v. 1. teach. 2. provide schooling for. **education** n. **educational** adj. **educationally** adv. **educationalist** n. expert in the theory of education. **educative** adj. educating.

Edwardian adj. of the reign of King Edward VII of Great Britain and Ireland (1901–10).

EEG electroencephalogram.

eel n. snakelike fish.

eerie adj. uncannily frightening or disturbing. **eerily** adv.

efface v. 1. remove by rubbing. 2. make (oneself) inconspicuous. **effacement** n.

effect n. 1. change or result caused by someone or something. 2. overall impression. 3. condition of being operative, e.g. the law comes into effect next month. —pl. 4. property. 5. lighting, sounds, etc. to accompany a film or a broadcast. —v. 6. cause to happen, accomplish. **effective** adj. 1. producing a desired result. 2. impressive. 3. operative. **effectively** adv. **effectual** adj. successful in producing a desired result. **effectually** adv.
▷ Note the difference between effect meaning 'accomplish' and affect meaning 'influence'.

effeminate adj. (of a man) displaying characteristics thought to be typical of a woman. **effeminacy** n.

effervesce v. 1. (of a liquid) give off bubbles. 2. (of a person) be in high spirits. **effervescence** n. **effervescent** adj.

effete [if-**feet**] adj. powerless, feeble.

efficacious adj. producing the intended result, effective. **efficacy** n.

efficient adj. functioning effectively with little waste of effort. **efficiently** adv. **efficiency** n.

effigy [**ef**-fij-ee] n., pl. -**gies** image or likeness of a person.

efflorescence n. flowering.

effluent n. liquid discharged as waste. **effluence** n. something that flows out. **effluvium** n., pl. -**via**. unpleasant smell, as decaying matter or gaseous waste.

effort n. 1. physical or mental exertion. 2. attempt. **effortless** adj. **effortlessly** adv.

effrontery n. brazen impudence.

effulgence n. brightness of light, radiance.

effusion n. 1. sudden pouring out of light or liquid. 2. unrestrained outburst. **effusive** adj. openly emotional, demonstrative. **effusively** adv. **effusiveness** n.

EFTA European Free Trade Association.

EFTPOS electronic funds transfer at point of sale.

e.g. for example.

egalitarian adj. 1. upholding the equality of all people. —n. 2. person who holds egalitarian beliefs. **egalitarianism** n.

egg[1] n. 1. oval or round object laid by the females of birds and other creatures, containing a developing embryo. 2. hen's egg used as food. 3. (also **egg cell**) ovum. **egghead** n. Informal intellectual person. **eggplant** n. US aubergine. **eggshell** n. hard covering round the egg of a bird or animal. **egg timer** n. device used for measuring the time needed to boil an egg.

egg[2] v. **egg on** encourage or incite, esp. to do wrong.

eglantine n. sweetbrier.

ego n., pl. **egos**. 1. self-esteem. 2. the conscious mind of an individual. **egoism, egotism** n. 1. excessive concern for one's own interests. 2. excessively high opinion of oneself. **egoist, egotist** n. **egoistic, egotistic** adj. **egocentric** adj. self-centred.

egregious [ig-**greej**-uss] adj. outstandingly bad.

egress [**ee**-gress] n. 1. way out. 2. departure.

egret [**ee**-grit] n. lesser white heron.

Egyptian adj. 1. relating to Egypt. —n. 2. person from Egypt.

Egyptology n. study of the culture of ancient Egypt.

eh interj. exclamation of surprise or inquiry, or to seek confirmation of a statement or question.

eider n. Arctic duck. **eiderdown** n. quilt (orig. stuffed with eider feathers).

eight adj., n. 1. one more than seven. —n. 2. eight-oared boat. 3. its crew. **eighth** adj., n. (of) number eight in a series. **eighteen** adj., n. eight and ten. **eighteenth** adj., n. **eighty** adj., n. eight times ten. **eightieth** adj., n.

einsteinium n. radioactive element artificially produced from plutonium.

Eire n. the Republic of Ireland.

eisteddfod [ice-sted-fod] n. Welsh festival with competitions in music and other performing arts.

either adj., pron. 1. one or the other (of two). 2. each of two. —conj. 3. used preceding two or more possibilities joined by or. —adv. 4. likewise, e.g. I don't eat meat and he doesn't either.
▷ When either is followed by a plural noun it is acceptable to make the verb plural too: Either of these books are useful.

ejaculate v. 1. eject (semen). 2. utter abruptly. **ejaculation** n.

eject v. force out, expel. **ejection** n. **ejector** n. **ejector seat** n. seat in an aircraft that ejects the occupant in an emergency.

eke v. **eke out 1.** make (a supply) last by frugal use. 2. make (a living) with difficulty.

elaborate adj. 1. with a lot of fine detail. —v. 2. expand upon. **elaborately** adv. **elaboration** n.

élan [ale-an] n. style and vigour.

eland [eel-and] n. large antelope of southern Africa.

elapse v. (of time) pass by.

elastic adj. 1. resuming normal shape after distortion. 2. adapting easily to change. —n. 3. tape or fabric containing interwoven strands of flexible rubber. **elasticity** n.

elate v. fill with high spirits or pride. **elation** n.

elbow n. 1. joint between the upper arm and the forearm. 2. part of a garment that covers this. —v. 3. shove or strike with the elbow. **elbow grease** vigorous physical labour. **elbowroom** n. sufficient room to move freely.

elder[1] adj. 1. older. —n. 2. older person. 3. in certain Protestant Churches, lay officer. **elderly** adj. (fairly) old. **eldest** adj. oldest.
▷ Elder (eldest) is used for age comparison in families, older for other age comparisons.

elder[2] n. small tree with white flowers and black berries.

El Dorado [el dor-rah-doe] n. fictitious country rich in gold.

eldritch adj. Scot. weird, uncanny.

elect v. 1. choose by voting. 2. decide (to do something). —adj. 3. appointed but not yet in office, e.g. president elect. **election** n. 1. choosing of representatives by voting. 2. act of choosing. **electioneer** v. be active in a political election. **elective** adj. 1. chosen by election. 2. optional. **elector** n. someone who has the right to vote in an election. **electoral** adj. **electorate** n. people who have the right to vote.

electricity n. 1. form of energy associated with stationary or moving electrons or other charged particles. 2. electric current or charge. **electric** adj. 1. produced by, producing, transmitting, or powered by electricity. 2. exciting or tense. **electrical** adj. using or concerning electricity. **electrician** n. person trained to install and repair electrical equipment. **electrics** pl. n. electric appliances. **electric chair** US chair in which criminals who have been sentenced to death are electrocuted. **electric shock** effect of an electric current passing through the body.
▷ Note that electric is an adjective. Avoid its use as a noun: The electricity (not the electric) has failed.

electrify v. -fying, -fied. 1. adapt for operation by electric power. 2. charge with electricity. 3. startle or excite intensely. **electrification** n.

electro- combining form operated by or caused by electricity.

electrocardiograph n. instrument for recording the electrical activity of the heart. **electrocardiogram** n. tracing produced by this.

electroconvulsive therapy n. treatment of severe mental disorders by passing an electric current through the brain.

electrocute v. kill or injure by electricity. **electrocution** n.

electrode n. conductor through which an electric current enters or leaves a battery, vacuum tube, etc.

electrodynamics n. branch of physics concerned with the interactions between electrical and mechanical forces.

electroencephalograph [ill-lek-tro-en-sef-a-loh-graf] n. instrument for recording the electrical activity of the brain. **electroencephalogram** n. tracing produced by this.

electrolysis [ill-lek-troll-iss-iss] n. 1. conduction of electricity by an electrolyte, esp. to induce chemical change. 2. destruction of living tissue such as hair roots by an electric current.

electrolyte n. solution or molten substance that conducts electricity. **electrolytic** adj.

electromagnet n. magnet containing a coil of wire through which an electric current is passed. **electromagnetic** adj. **electromagnetism** n.

electron n. elementary particle in all atoms that has a negative electrical charge. **electron microscope** microscope that uses electrons, rather than light, to produce a magnified image. **electron volt** unit of energy used in nuclear physics.

electronic adj. **1.** (of a device) dependent on the action of electrons. **2.** (of a process) using electronic devices. **electronics** n. technology concerned with the development of electronic devices and circuits.

electroplate v. coat with silver etc. by electrolysis.

elegant adj. **1.** tasteful in dress, style, or design. **2.** graceful. **elegance** n. **elegantly** adv.

elegy [el-lij-ee] n., pl. -egies. mournful poem, esp. a lament for the dead. **elegiac** adj. mournful or plaintive.

element n. **1.** component part. **2.** small amount. **3.** section of people within a larger group, e.g. the rowdy element. **4.** substance which cannot be separated into other substances by ordinary chemical techniques. **5.** heating wire in an electric kettle, stove, etc. —pl. **6.** basic principles of something. **7.** weather conditions, esp. wind, rain, and cold. **in one's element** in a situation where one is happiest. **elemental** adj. **1.** fundamental. **2.** of primitive natural forces or passions. **elementary** adj. simple and straightforward. **elementary particle** entity that is less complex than an atom.

elephant n. huge four-footed thick-skinned animal with ivory tusks and a long trunk. **elephantine** adj. unwieldy, clumsy. **elephantiasis** [el-lee-fan-tie-a-siss] n. disease with hardening of the skin and enlargement of the legs etc.

elevate v. **1.** raise in rank or status. **2.** lift up. **elevated** adj. (of ideas or pursuits) dignified or of a high rank. **elevation** n. **1.** raising. **2.** scale drawing of one side of a building. **3.** height above sea level. **elevator** n. US lift for carrying people.

eleven adj., n. one more than ten. —n. **2.** Sport team of eleven people. **eleventh** adj., n. (of) number eleven in a series. **elevenses**

n. Informal light mid-morning snack. **eleventh hour** the last moment.

elf n., pl. **elves.** in folklore, small mischievous fairy. **elfin** adj. small and delicate.

elicit v. draw out (information) from someone.

elide v. omit (a vowel or syllable) from a spoken word. **elision** n.

eligible adj. **1.** qualified to be chosen. **2.** desirable as a spouse. **eligibility** n.

eliminate v. get rid of. **elimination** n.

elision n. see ELIDE.

elite [ill-eet] n. most powerful, rich, or gifted members of a group. **elitism** n. belief that society should be governed by a small group of superior people. **elitist** n., adj.

elixir [ill-ix-er] n. imaginary liquid that can prolong life or turn base metals into gold.

Elizabethan adj. of the reign of Elizabeth I of England (1558–1603).

elk n. large deer of N Europe and Asia.

ellipse n. oval shape. **elliptical** adj. **1.** oval-shaped. **2.** (of speech or writing) obscure or ambiguous.

ellipsis [ill-lip-siss] n., pl. -ses. omission of letters or words in a sentence.

elm n. tree with serrated leaves.

elocution n. art of speaking clearly in public. **elocutionist** n. teacher of elocution.

elongate [eel-long-gate] v. make or become longer. **elongation** n.

elope v. run away secretly to get married. **elopement** n.

eloquence n. fluent powerful use of language. **eloquent** adj. **eloquently** adv.

else adv. **1.** otherwise. **2.** besides. **3.** instead. **elsewhere** adv. in or to another place.

elucidate v. make (something difficult) clear, explain. **elucidation** n.

elude v. **1.** baffle. **2.** escape from by cleverness or quickness. **elusive** adj. difficult to catch or remember.

elver n. young eel.

elves n. plural of ELF.

Elysium [ill-liz-zee-um] n. **1.** Greek myth (also **Elysian fields**) dwelling place of the blessed after death. **2.** state or place of perfect bliss.

em n. Printing the square of any size of type.

emaciated [im-mace-ee-ate-id] adj. abnormally thin. **emaciate** v. **emaciation** n.

emanate [em-a-nate] *v.* issue, proceed from a source. **emanation** *n.*

emancipate *v.* free from social, political, or legal restraints. **emancipation** *n.*

emasculate *v.* deprive of power. **emasculation** *n.*

embalm *v.* preserve (a corpse) from decay by the use of chemicals etc. **embalmment** *n.*

embankment *n.* man-made ridge that carries a road or railway or holds back water.

embargo *n., pl.* **-goes. 1.** order stopping the movement of ships. **2.** legal stoppage of trade. **3.** ban. —*v.* **-going, -goed. 4.** put an embargo on.

embark *v.* **1.** board a ship or aircraft. **2.** (foll. by *on* or *upon*) begin (a new project). **embarkation** *n.*

embarrass *v.* cause to feel self-conscious or ashamed. **embarrassing** *adj.* **embarrassment** *n.*

embassy *n., pl.* **-sies. 1.** offices or official residence of an ambassador. **2.** ambassador and his staff.

embattled *adj.* having a lot of difficulties.

embed *v.* **-bedding, -bedded.** fix firmly in something solid.

embellish *v.* **1.** decorate. **2.** embroider (a story). **embellishment** *n.*

ember *n.* glowing piece of wood or coal in a dying fire.

embezzle *v.* steal money that has been entrusted to one. **embezzlement** *n.* **embezzler** *n.*

embitter *v.* make (a person) feel bitter. **embittered** *adj.* **embitterment** *n.*

emblazon [im-blaze-on] *v.* **1.** decorate with bright colours. **2.** proclaim or publicize.

emblem *n.* object or representation that symbolizes a quality, type, or group. **emblematic** *adj.*

embody *v.* **-bodying, -bodied. 1.** be an example or expression of. **2.** comprise, include. **embodiment** *n.*

embolden *v.* encourage (someone).

embolism *n.* blocking of a blood vessel by a blood clot or air bubble. **embolus** *n., pl.* **-li.** material, such as a blood clot, that blocks a blood vessel.

emboss *v.* mould or carve a raised design on. **embossed** *adj.*

embrace *v.* **1.** clasp in the arms, hug. **2.**

accept (an idea) eagerly. **3.** comprise. —*n.* **4.** act of embracing.

embrasure *n.* **1.** door or window having splayed sides so that the opening is larger on the inside. **2.** opening like this in a fortified wall, for shooting through.

embrocation *n.* lotion for rubbing into the skin to relieve pain.

embroider *v.* **1.** decorate with needlework. **2.** make (a story) more interesting with fictitious detail. **embroidery** *n.*

embroil *v.* involve (a person) in problems. **embroilment** *n.*

embryo [em-bree-oh] *n., pl.* **-bryos. 1.** unborn creature in the early stages of development. **2.** something at an undeveloped stage. **embryonic** *adj.* at an early stage. **embryology** *n.* scientific study of embryos.

emend *v.* remove errors from. **emendation** *n.*

emerald *n.* **1.** bright green precious stone. —*adj.* **2.** bright green.

emerge *v.* **1.** come into view. **2.** (foll. by *from*) come out of. **3.** become known. **emergence** *n.* **emergent** *adj.*

emergency *n., pl.* **-cies.** sudden unforeseen occurrence needing immediate action.

emeritus [im-mer-rit-uss] *adj.* retired, but retaining an honorary title, e.g. *emeritus professor.*

emery *n.* hard mineral used for smoothing and polishing. **emery board** cardboard strip coated with crushed emery, for filing the nails.

emetic [im-met-ik] *n.* **1.** substance that causes vomiting. —*adj.* **2.** causing vomiting.

emf electromotive force.

emigrate *v.* go and settle in another country. **emigrant** *n.* **emigration** *n.*

émigré [em-mig-gray] *n.* someone who has left his native country for political reasons.

eminent *adj.* distinguished, well-known. **eminently** *adv.* **eminence** *n.* **1.** position of superiority or fame. **2.** (E-) title of a cardinal.

emir [em-meer] *n.* Muslim ruler. **emirate** *n.* his country.

emissary *n., pl.* **-saries.** agent sent on a mission by a government.

emit *v.* **emitting, emitted. 1.** give out (heat, light, or a smell). **2.** utter. **emission** *n.*

emollient *adj.* **1.** softening, soothing. —*n.* **2.**

substance which softens or soothes something.

emolument *n. Formal* payment for work, salary.

emotion *n.* strong feeling. **emotional** *adj.* readily affected by or appealing to the emotions. **emotionally** *adv.* **emotive** *adj.* tending to arouse emotion.

empathy *n.* power of imaginatively entering into and understanding another's feelings. **empathize** *v.*

emperor *n.* ruler of an empire. **empress** *n. fem.*

emphasis *n., pl.* **-ses. 1.** special importance or significance. **2.** stress on a word or phrase in speech. **3.** intensity of expression. **emphasize** *v.* **emphatic** *adj.* showing emphasis. **emphatically** *adv.*

emphysema [em-fiss-**see**-ma] *n.* condition in which the air sacs of the lungs are grossly enlarged, causing breathlessness.

empire *n.* **1.** group of territories under the rule of one state or person. **2.** large organization that is directed by one person or group.

empirical *adj.* relying on experiment or experience, not on theory. **empirically** *adv.* **empiricism** *n.* doctrine that all knowledge derives from experience. **empiricist** *n.*

emplacement *n.* prepared position for a gun.

employ *v.* **1.** hire (a person). **2.** provide work or occupation for. **3.** use. —*n.* **4.** state of being employed, e.g. *in someone's employ.* **employee** *n.* **employer** *n.* **employment** *n.* **1.** state of being employed. **2.** work done by a person to earn money.

emporium *n., pl.* **-riums, -ria.** *Old-fashioned* large general shop.

empower *v.* enable, authorize.

empress *n.* see EMPEROR.

empty *adj.* **-tier, -tiest. 1.** containing nothing. **2.** unoccupied. **3.** without purpose or value. **4.** (of words) insincere. —*v.* **-tying, -tied. 5.** make or become empty. **empties** *pl. n.* empty boxes, bottles, etc. **emptiness** *n.*

empyrean [em-pie-**ree**-an] *n. Poetic* heavens; sky.

EMS European Monetary System.

emu *n.* large Aust. flightless bird with long legs.

emulate *v.* attempt to equal or surpass by imitating. **emulation** *n.*

emulsion *n.* **1.** light-sensitive coating on photographic film. **2.** type of water-based paint. —*v.* **3.** paint with emulsion paint. **emulsify** *v.* **-fying, -fied.** make into an emulsion. **emulsifier** *n.*

en *n. Printing* unit of measurement, half an em.

enable *v.* provide (a person) with the means, opportunity, or authority (to do something). **enabling act** legislative act conferring certain powers on a person or organization.

enact *v.* **1.** establish by law. **2.** represent as in a play. **enactment** *n.*

enamel *n.* **1.** glasslike coating applied to metal etc. to preserve the surface. **2.** hard white coating on a tooth. —*v.* **-elling, -elled. 3.** cover with enamel.

enamoured *adj.* inspired with love.

en bloc *adv. French* as a whole, all together.

encamp *v.* set up in a camp. **encampment** *n.*

encapsulate *v.* **1.** abridge. **2.** enclose as in a capsule.

encase *v.* place or enclose as in a case. **encased** *adj.*

encephalitis [en-sef-a-**lite**-iss] *n.* inflammation of the brain.

encephalogram *n.* short for ELECTROENCEPHALOGRAM.

enchain *v.* **1.** bind with chains. **2.** hold fast or captivate (someone's) attention.

enchant *v.* bewitch or delight. **enchanting** *adj.* **enchantment** *n.* **enchanter** *n.* **enchantress** *n. fem.*

enchilada *n.* Mexican dish of tortilla filled with meat, served with chilli sauce.

encircle *v.* form a circle around. **encirclement** *n.*

enclave *n.* part of a country entirely surrounded by foreign territory.

enclose *v.* **1.** surround completely. **2.** include along with something else. **enclosure** *n.* **enclosed order** Christian religious order whose members do not go into the outside world.

encomium *n., pl.* **-miums, -mia.** formal expression of praise.

encompass *v.* **1.** surround. **2.** include comprehensively.

encore *interj.* **1**. again, once more. —*n.* **2**. extra performance due to enthusiastic demand.

encounter *v.* **1**. meet unexpectedly. **2**. be faced with. —*n.* **3**. unexpected meeting. **4**. contest.

encourage *v.* **1**. inspire with confidence. **2**. spur on. **encouraging** *adj.* **encouragement** *n.*

encroach *v.* intrude gradually on a person's rights or land. **encroachment** *n.*

encrust *v.* cover with a layer of something.

encumber *v.* hamper or burden. **encumbrance** *n.* impediment.

encyclical [en-**sik**-lik-kl] *n.* letter sent by the Pope to all bishops.

encyclopedia, encyclopaedia *n.* book or set of books containing facts about many subjects, usually in alphabetical order. **encyclopedic, encyclopaedic** *adj.* comprehensive.

end *n.* **1**. furthest point or part. **2**. limit. **3**. last part of something. **4**. fragment. **5**. *Lit.* death. **6**. destruction. **7**. purpose. **8**. *Sport* either of the two defended areas of a playing field. —*v.* **9**. bring or come to a finish. **make ends meet** have just enough money for one's needs. **ending** *n.* **endless** *adj.* **endways** *adv.* having the end forwards or upwards. **end product** final result of a process, esp. in manufacturing.

endanger *v.* put in danger.

endear *v.* cause to be liked. **endearing** *adj.* **endearment** *n.* affectionate word or phrase.

endeavour *v.* **1**. try. —*n.* **2**. effort.

endemic *adj.* present within a localized area or peculiar to a particular group of people.

endive *n.* curly-leaved plant used in salads.

endocardium *n.* lining membrane of the heart.

endocrine *adj.* relating to the glands which secrete hormones directly into the bloodstream.

endogenous [en-**dodge**-in-uss] *adj.* originating from within.

endorphin *n.* chemical occurring in the brain, which has a similar effect to morphine.

endorse *v.* **1**. give approval to. **2**. sign the back of (a cheque). **3**. record a conviction on (a driving licence). **endorsement** *n.*

endow *v.* provide permanent income for. **endowed with** provided with. **endowment** *n.*

endure *v.* **1**. bear (hardship) patiently. **2**. last for a long time. **endurable** *adj.* **endurance** *n.* act or power of enduring. **enduring** *adj.* long-lasting.

enema [en-im-a] *n.* medicine injected into the rectum to empty the bowels.

enemy *n., pl.* **-mies**. hostile person or nation, opponent.

energy *n., pl.* **-gies**. **1**. capacity for intense activity. **2**. capacity to do work and overcome resistance. **3**. source of power, such as electricity. **energetic** *adj.* **energetically** *adv.* **energize** *v.* give vigour to.

enervate *v.* weaken, deprive of vigour. **enervated** *adj.* **enervation** *n.*

enfant terrible [on-fon ter-**reeb**-la] *n., pl.* **enfants terribles**. *French* clever but unconventional or indiscreet person.

enfeeble *v.* weaken. **enfeebled** *adj.* **enfeeblement** *n.*

enfold *v.* **1**. cover by wrapping something around. **2**. embrace.

enforce *v.* **1**. impose obedience (to a law etc.). **2**. impose (a condition). **enforceable** *adj.* **enforcement** *n.*

enfranchise *v.* grant (a person) the right to vote. **enfranchised** *adj.* **enfranchisement** *n.*

engage *v.* **1**. take part, participate. **2**. involve (a person or his or her attention) intensely. **3**. employ (a person). **4**. bring (a mechanism) into operation. **5**. begin a battle with.

engaged *adj.* **1**. pledged to be married. **2**. in use. **engagement** *n.*

engaging *adj.* charming.

engender *v.* produce, cause to occur.

engine *n.* **1**. any machine which converts energy into mechanical work. **2**. railway locomotive.

engineer *n.* **1**. person trained in any branch of engineering. —*v.* **2**. plan in a clever manner. **3**. design or construct as an engineer.

engineering *n.* profession of applying scientific principles to the design and construction of engines, cars, buildings, or machines.

English *n.* **1**. language of Britain, the US, most parts of the Commonwealth, and certain other countries. —*adj.* **2**. relating to

England. the English the people of England.

engorge v. *Pathology* congest with blood. **engorgement** n.

engraft v. 1. graft on. 2. plant deeply. 3. incorporate.

engrave v. 1. carve (a design) onto a hard surface. 2. fix deeply in the mind. **engraver** n. **engraving** n. print made from an engraved plate.

engross [en-**groce**] v. occupy the attention of (a person) completely. **engrossing** adj.

engulf v. cover or surround completely.

enhance v. increase in quality, value, or attractiveness. **enhancement** n.

enigma n. puzzling thing or person. **enigmatic** adj. **enigmatically** adv.

enjambment, enjambement n. in verse, continuation of a sentence beyond the end of the line.

enjoin v. order (someone) to do something.

enjoy v. 1. take joy in. 2. have the benefit of. 3. experience. **enjoyable** adj. **enjoyment** n.

enlarge v. 1. make or grow larger. 2. (foll. by *on* or *upon*) speak or write about in greater detail. **enlargement** n.

enlighten v. give information to. **enlightened** adj. 1. guided by rational thought. 2. tolerant and free from prejudice. **enlightenment** n.

enlist v. 1. enter the armed forces. 2. obtain the support of. **enlistment** n.

enliven v. make lively or cheerful.

en masse adv. *French* in a group, all together.

enmesh v. entangle. **enmeshed** adj.

enmity n., pl. -**ties**. ill will, hatred.

ennoble v. make noble, elevate. **ennoblement** n.

ennui [on-**nwee**] n. boredom, dissatisfaction.

enormous adj. very big, vast. **enormously** adv. **enormity** n., pl. -**ties**. 1. great wickedness. 2. gross offence. 3. *Informal* great size.

enough adj. 1. as much or as many as necessary. —n. 2. sufficient quantity. —adv. 3. sufficiently. 4. just adequately.

en passant [on **pass**-on] adv. *French* in passing, by the way.

enquire v. same as INQUIRE. **enquiry** n.

enrapture v. fill with delight. **enraptured** adj.

enrich v. 1. improve in quality. 2. make rich. **enriched** adj. **enrichment** n.

enrol v. -**rolling**, -**rolled**. (cause to) become a member. **enrolment** n.

en route adv. *French* on the way.

ensconce v. settle firmly or comfortably.

ensemble [on-**som**-bl] n. 1. all the parts of something taken together. 2. complete outfit of clothes. 3. company of actors or dancers. 4. *Music* group of musicians playing together.

enshrine v. cherish or treasure.

enshroud v. cover or hide as with a shroud.

ensign n. 1. naval flag. 2. banner. 3. *US* naval officer.

ensilage n. 1. process of storing green fodder in a silo. 2. silage.

enslave v. make a slave of (someone). **enslavement** n.

ensnare v. catch in or as if in a snare.

ensue v. come next, result. **ensuing** adj.

en suite adv. *French* as part of a set or single unit.

ensure v. 1. make certain or sure. 2. make safe or secure.

ENT *Med.* ear, nose and throat.

entablature n. *Archit.* part of a classical temple above the columns, with an architrave, frieze and cornice.

entail v. 1. bring about or impose inevitably. 2. *Law* restrict (ownership of property) to a designated line of heirs.

entangle v. catch or involve in or as if in a tangle. **entanglement** n.

entente [on-**tont**] n. friendly understanding between nations.

enter v. 1. come or go in. 2. join. 3. become involved in, take part in. 4. record (an item) in a journal etc. 5. begin. **entrance** n. 1. way into a place. 2. act of entering. 3. right of entering. **entrant** n. person who enters a university, contest, etc. **entry** n., pl. -**tries**. 1. entrance. 2. entering. 3. item entered in a journal etc.

enteric [en-**ter**-ik] adj. intestinal. **enteritis** [en-ter-**rite**-iss] n. inflammation of the intestine, causing diarrhoea.

enterprise n. 1. company or firm. 2. bold or difficult undertaking. 3. boldness and energy. **enterprising** adj. full of boldness and initiative.

entertain v. 1. amuse. 2. receive as a guest. 3. consider (an idea). **entertainer** n. **entertaining** adj. **entertainment** n.

enthral [en-**thrawl**] v. **-thralling, -thralled.** hold the attention of. **enthralment** n.

enthrone v. 1. place (someone) on a throne. 2. praise or honour (something). **enthronement** n.

enthusiasm n. ardent interest, eagerness. **enthuse** v. (cause to) show enthusiasm. **enthusiast** n. ardent supporter of something. **enthusiastic** adj. **enthusiastically** adv.

entice v. attract by exciting hope or desire, tempt. **enticing** adj. **enticement** n.

entire adj. 1. complete. 2. unbroken or undivided. **entirely** adv. **entirety** n.

entitle v. 1. give a right to. 2. give a title to. **entitlement** n.

entity n., pl. **-ties.** separate distinct thing.

entomb v. 1. place a (corpse) in a tomb. 2. serve as a tomb for. **entombment** n.

entomology n. study of insects. **entomological** adj. **entomologist** n.

entourage [on-**toor**-ahzh] n. group of people who assist an important person.

entozoon [en-toe-**zoe**-on] n., pl. **-zoa** [-**zoe**-a] internal parasite. **entozoic** adj.

entr'acte [on-**tract**] n. interval between acts of a play etc.

entrails pl. n. 1. intestines. 2. innermost parts of something.

entrance[1] n. see ENTER.

entrance[2] v. 1. delight. 2. put into a trance. **entrancing** adj.

entrap v. 1. catch in a trap, or catch as if in a trap. 2. trick into difficulty etc. **entrapment** n.

entreat v. ask earnestly. **entreaty** n., pl. **-ties.** earnest request.

entrecôte [on-tra-**coat**] n. beefsteak cut from between the ribs.

entrée [on-**tray**] n. 1. main course of a meal. 2. right of admission.

entrench v. 1. establish firmly. 2. establish in a fortified position with trenches. **entrenchment** n. **entrenched** adj.

entrepreneur n. business person who at-

tempts to make a profit by risk and initiative.

entropy [en-trop-ee] n. 1. Formal lack of organization. 2. Physics unavailability of the heat energy of a system for mechanical work.

entrust v. put into the care or protection of.

entwine v. twist together or around.

E number n. any of a series of numbers with the prefix E indicating a specific food additive recognized by the EC.

enumerate v. name one by one. **enumeration** n.

enunciate v. 1. pronounce clearly. 2. proclaim. **enunciation** n.

enuresis [en-yoo-**reece**-iss] n. involuntary discharge of urine, esp. during sleep. **enuretic** adj.

envelop v. **enveloping, enveloped.** wrap up, enclose. **envelopment** n.

envelope n. folded gummed paper cover for a letter.

environment [en-**vire**-on-ment] n. external conditions and surroundings in which people, animals, or plants live. **environmental** adj. **environmentalist** n. person concerned with the protection of the natural environment.

▷ Note the 'n' before the 'm' in the spelling of environment.

environs pl. n. surrounding area, esp. of a town.

envisage v. 1. visualize. 2. conceive of as a possibility.

envoy n. 1. messenger. 2. diplomatic minister ranking below an ambassador.

envy v. **-vying, -vied. 1.** grudge (another's good fortune, success, or qualities). —n. 2. bitter contemplation of another's good fortune. **enviable** adj. arousing envy, fortunate. **envious** adj. full of envy.

enzyme n. any of a group of complex proteins that act as catalysts in specific biochemical reactions.

Eolithic adj. of the early part of the Stone Age.

EP extended-play.

epaulette n. shoulder ornament on a uniform.

ephedrine [**eff**-fid-dreen] n. alkaloid used for treatment of asthma and hay fever.

ephemeral adj. short-lived.

epic *n.* **1.** long poem, book, or film about heroic events or actions. —*adj.* **2.** very impressive or ambitious.

epicene *adj.* **1.** common to both sexes. **2.** effeminate.

epicentre *n.* point on the earth's surface immediately above the origin of an earthquake.

epicure *n.* person who enjoys good food and drink. **epicurism** *n.* **epicurean** *adj.* **1.** devoted to sensual pleasures. *esp.* food and drink. —*n.* **2.** epicure. **epicureanism** *n.*

epidemic *n.* **1.** widespread occurrence of a disease. **2.** rapid spread of something.

epidermis *n.* outer layer of the skin.

epidiascope *n.* optical device for projecting a magnified image on to a screen.

epidural [ep-**pid**-dure-al] *adj., n.* (of) spinal anaesthetic injected to relieve pain during childbirth.

epiglottis *n.* thin flap that covers the opening of the larynx during swallowing.

epigram *n.* short witty remark or poem. **epigrammatic** *adj.*

epigraph *n.* **1.** quotation at the start of a book. **2.** inscription.

epilepsy *n.* disorder of the nervous system causing loss of consciousness and sometimes convulsions. **epileptic 1.** person who has epilepsy. —*adj.* **2.** of or having epilepsy.

epilogue *n.* short speech or poem at the end of a literary work, esp. a play.

Epiphany *n.* Christian festival held on January 6 commemorating the manifestation of Christ to the Magi.

episcopal [ip-**piss**-kop-al] *adj.* of or governed by bishops. **episcopalian** *n.* **1.** member of an episcopal Church. —*adj.* **2.** advocating Church government by bishops.

episode *n.* **1.** incident in a series of incidents. **2.** section of a serialized book, television programme, etc. **episodic** *adj.* occurring at irregular intervals.

epistemology [ip-iss-stem-**ol**-a-jee] *n.* study of the source, nature, and limitations of knowledge. **epistemological** *adj.* **epistemologist** *n.*

epistle *n.* letter, esp. of an apostle. **epistolary** *adj.*

epitaph *n.* **1.** commemorative inscription on a tomb. **2.** commemorative speech or passage.

epithet *n.* descriptive word or name.

epitome [ip-**pit**-a-mee] *n.* typical example. **epitomize** *v.* be the epitome of. ▷ Avoid the use of *epitome* to mean 'the peak' of something.

epoch [**ee**-pok] *n.* period of notable events. **epoch-making** *adj.* extremely important.

eponymous [ip-**pon**-im-uss] *adj.* after whom a book, play, etc. is named. **eponymously** *adv.*

Epsom salts *pl. n.* medicinal preparation of magnesium sulphate and water, used to empty the bowels.

equable [**ek**-wab-bl] *adj.* even-tempered. **equably** *adv.*

equal *adj.* **1.** identical in size, quantity, degree, etc. **2.** having identical rights or status. **3.** evenly balanced. **4.** (foll. by *to*) having the necessary ability (for). —*n.* **5.** person or thing equal to another. —*v.* **equalling, equalled. 6.** be equal to. **equally** *adv.*

equality *n.* state of being equal.

equalize *v.* **1.** make or become equal. **2.** reach the same score as one's opponent. **equalization** *n.*

equal opportunity nondiscrimination as to sex, race, etc. in employment.

equanimity *n.* calmness of mind.

equate *v.* make or regard as equivalent. **equation** *n.* **1.** mathematical statement that two expressions are equal. **2.** act of equating. **3.** representation of a chemical reaction using symbols of the elements.

equator *n.* imaginary circle round the earth, equidistant from the poles. **equatorial** *adj.*

equerry [**ek**-kwer-ee] *n., pl.* **-ries.** officer who acts as an attendant to a member of a royal family.

equestrian *adj.* of horses and riding.

equiangular *adj.* having equal angles.

equidistant *adj.* equally distant.

equilateral *adj.* having equal sides.

equilibrium *n., pl.* **-ria.** steadiness or stability.

equine *adj.* of or like a horse.

equinox *n.* time of year when day and night are of equal length. **equinoctial** *adj.*

equip *v.* **equipping, equipped.** provide with what is needed. **equipment** *n.* **1.** set of tools or devices used for a particular purpose. **2.** equipping.

equipoise n. perfect balance.

equitation n. study and practice of riding and horsemanship.

equity n., pl. **-ties. 1.** fairness. **2.** legal system, founded on the principles of natural justice, that supplements common law. —pl. **3.** interest of ordinary shareholders in a company. **equitable** adj. fair, just. **equitably** adv.

equivalent adj. **1.** equal in value. **2.** having the same meaning or result. —n. **3.** something that is equivalent. **equivalence** n.

equivocal adj. **1.** ambiguous. **2.** deliberately misleading. **3.** of doubtful character or sincerity. **equivocally** adv. **equivocate** v. use equivocal words to mislead people. **equivocation** n.

er interj. sound made when hesitating in speech.

Er Chem. erbium.

ER Queen Elizabeth.

era n. period of time considered as distinctive.

eradicate v. destroy completely. **eradication** n.

erase v. **1.** rub out. **2.** remove. **eraser** n. object for erasing something written. **erasure** n. **1.** erasing. **2.** place or mark where something has been erased.

erbium n. metallic element of the lanthanide series.

ere prep., conj. Poetic before.

erect adj. **1.** upright. **2.** (of the penis, clitoris, or nipples) rigid as a result of sexual excitement. —v. **3.** build. **4.** set up. **erectile** adj. capable of becoming erect from sexual excitement. **erection** n.

erg n. unit of work or energy.

ergo adv. therefore.

ergonomics n. study of the relationship between workers and their environment. **ergonomic** adj. **1.** of or relating to ergonomics. **2.** designed to minimize effort.

ergot n. **1.** fungal disease of cereal. **2.** dried fungus used in medicine.

erica n. genus of plants including heathers.

ermine n. **1.** stoat in northern regions. **2.** its white winter fur.

erne, ern n. fish-eating sea eagle.

Ernie n. Brit. computer that randomly selects winning numbers of Premium Bonds (Electronic Random Number Indicating Equipment).

erode v. wear away. **erosion** n.

erogenous [ir-roj-in-uss] adj. sexually sensitive or arousing.

erotic adj. relating to sexual pleasure or desire. **eroticism** n. **erotica** n. sexual literature or art.

err v. Formal make a mistake. **erratum** n., pl. **-ta.** error in writing or printing. **erroneous** adj. incorrect, mistaken. **erroneously** adv. **error** n. something considered to be wrong or incorrect.

errand n. short trip to do something for someone.

errant adj. behaving in a manner considered to be unacceptable.

erratic adj. irregular or unpredictable. **erratically** adv.

ersatz [air-zats] adj. made in imitation, e.g. ersatz coffee.

Erse n. **1.** Gaelic. —adj. **2.** of or relating to the Gaelic language.

erstwhile adj. former.

erudite [air-rude-ite] adj. having great academic knowledge. **erudition** n.

erupt v. **1.** eject (steam, water, or volcanic material) violently. **2.** (of a blemish) appear on the skin. **3.** burst forth suddenly and violently. **eruption** n.

erysipelas [err-riss-sip-pel-ass] n. acute skin infection causing purplish patches.

erythema [err-rith-theme-a] n. patchy inflammation of the skin.

erythrocyte [ir-rith-roe-site] n. red blood cell of vertebrates that transports oxygen and carbon dioxide.

Es Chem. einsteinium.

escalate v. increase in extent or intensity. **escalation** n.

escalator n. moving staircase.

escalope [ess-kal-lop] n. thin slice of meat, esp. veal.

escapade n. mischievous adventure.

escape v. **1.** get free (of). **2.** avoid, e.g. escape attention. **3.** (of a gas, liquid, etc.) leak gradually. **4.** be forgotten by, e.g. the figure escapes me. —n. **5.** act of escaping. **6.** means of distraction.

escapee n. person who has escaped.

escapism n. taking refuge in fantasy to avoid unpleasant reality.

escapologist n. entertainer who specializes in freeing himself from confinement. **escapology** n.

escarpment n. steep face of a ridge or mountain.

eschatology [ess-cat-tol-loh-jee] n. branch of theology concerned with the end of the world. **eschatological** adj.

escheat [iss-**cheat**] Law —n. **1.** private possessions that become state property in the absence of an heir. —v. **2.** attain such property.

eschew [iss-**chew**] v. abstain from, avoid.

eschscholtzia [iss-**kol**-sha] n. garden plant with bright flowers, California poppy.

escort n. **1.** people or vehicles accompanying another person for protection or as an honour. **2.** person who accompanies a person of the opposite sex to a social event. —v. **3.** act as an escort to.

escritoire [ess-kree-**twahr**] n. type of writing desk.

escudo [ess-**kyoo**-doe] n., pl. **-dos.** monetary unit of Portugal.

escutcheon n. shield with a coat of arms. **blot on one's escutcheon** stain on one's honour.

Eskimo n. **1.** member of the aboriginal race inhabiting N Canada, Greenland, Alaska, and E Siberia. **2.** their language.

ESN educationally subnormal.

esoteric [ee-so-**ter**-rik] adj. understood by only a small number of people with special knowledge.

ESP extrasensory perception.

esp. especially.

espadrille [**ess**-pad-drill] n. light canvas shoe with a braided cord sole.

espalier [ess-**pal**-yer] n. **1.** shrub or fruit tree trained to grow flat. **2.** trellis for this.

esparto n., pl. **-tos.** grass used for making rope etc.

especial adj. Formal special. **especially** adv. particularly.
▷ Special(ly) is more common than especial(ly) and is always used in preference to especial when the sense is 'out of the ordinary'.

Esperanto n. universal artificial language.

espionage [**ess**-pyon-ahzh] n. spying.

esplanade n. wide open road used as a public promenade.

espouse v. adopt or give support to (a cause etc.). **espousal** n.

espresso n., pl. **-sos.** strong coffee made by forcing steam or boiling water through ground coffee beans.
▷ Note that the second letter is 's' not 'x'.

esprit [ess-**pree**] n. spirit, liveliness. **esprit de corps** [de **core**] pride in and loyalty to a group.

espy v. **espying, espied.** catch sight of.

Esq. esquire.

esquire n. courtesy title placed after a man's name.

ESRO European Space Research Organization.

essay n. **1.** short literary composition. —v. **2.** attempt. **essayist** n.

essence n. **1.** most important feature of a thing which determines its identity. **2.** concentrated extract obtained by distillation, e.g. vanilla essence. **essential** adj. **1.** vitally important. **2.** fundamental. —n. **3.** something essential. **essentially** adv.

est. 1. established. **2.** estimate(d).

establish v. **1.** set up on a permanent basis. **2.** make secure or permanent in a certain place, job, etc. **3.** prove. **4.** cause to be accepted. **establishment** n. **1.** act of establishing. **2.** commercial or other institution. **the Establishment** group of people having authority within a society.

estate n. **1.** landed property. **2.** large area of property development, esp. of new houses or factories. **3.** property of a deceased person. **estate agent** agent concerned with the valuation, lease, and sale of property. **estate car** car with a rear door and luggage space behind the rear seats.

esteem v. **1.** think highly of. **2.** judge or consider. —n. **3.** high regard.

ester n. Chem. compound produced by the reaction between an acid and an alcohol.

estimate v. **1.** calculate roughly. **2.** form an opinion about. —n. **3.** approximate calculation. **4.** opinion. **5.** statement from a workman etc. of the likely charge for a job. **estimable** adj. worthy of respect. **estimation** n. judgment, opinion.

estrange v. lose the affection of (someone). **estranged** adj. no longer living with one's spouse. **estrangement** n.

estuary n., pl. **-aries.** mouth of a river.

ETA estimated time of arrival.

et al. Latin et alii: and others.

etc. et cetera.
▷ Etc. means 'and the rest' so it is redundant to write and etc. Note the spelling; it comes from the Latin et cetera.

et cetera [et set-ra] n., v. **1.** and the rest, and others. **2.** or the like. **etceteras** pl. n. miscellaneous extra things or people.

etch v. **1.** wear away or cut the surface of (metal, glass, etc.) with acid. **2.** imprint vividly (on someone's mind). **etching** n. picture printed from an etched metal plate.

eternal adj. **1.** without beginning or end. **2.** unchanging. **eternally** adv. **eternity** n. **1.** infinite time. **2.** timeless existence after death. **eternity ring** ring given as a token of lasting affection.

ethane n. odourless flammable gas obtained from natural gas and petroleum.

ether n. **1.** colourless sweet-smelling liquid used as an anaesthetic. **2.** region above the clouds. **ethereal** [eth-**eer**-ee-al] adj. extremely delicate.

ethic n. moral principle. **ethical** adj. **ethically** adv. **ethics** n. **1.** study of morals. **2.** code of behaviour.

Ethiopian adj. **1.** of Ethiopia, its people, or their languages. —n. **2.** person from Ethiopia.

ethnic adj. **1.** relating to a people or group that shares a culture, religion, or language. **2.** belonging or relating to such a group, esp. one that is a minority group in a particular place. **ethnology** n. study of human races. **ethnological** adj. **ethnologist** n.

ethos [**eeth**-oss] n. distinctive spirit and attitudes of a people, culture, etc.

ethyl [**eth**-ill] adj. of, consisting of, or containing the monovalent group C_2H_5. **ethylene** n. poisonous gas used as an anaesthetic and as fuel.

etiolate [**ee**-tee-oh-late] v. **1.** become pale and weak. **2.** Botany whiten through lack of sunlight.

etiology n. study of the causes of diseases.

etiquette n. conventional code of conduct.

Eton crop n. short mannish hair style worn by women, esp. in the 1920s.

étude [ay-tewd] n. short musical composition for a solo instrument, esp. intended as a technical exercise.

etymology n., pl. **-gies.** study of the sources and development of words. **etymological** adj. **etymologist** n.

Eu Chem. europium.

eucalyptus, eucalypt n. tree, mainly grown in Australia, that provides timber, gum, and medicinal oil from the leaves.

Eucharist [**yew**-kar-ist] n. **1.** Christian sacrament commemorating Christ's Last Supper. **2.** consecrated elements of bread and wine. **Eucharistic** adj.

eugenics [yew-**jen**-iks] n. study of methods of improving the human race.

eulogy n., pl. **-gies.** speech or writing in praise of a person. **eulogize** v. praise (a person or thing) highly in speech or writing. **eulogist** n. **eulogistic** adj.

eunuch n. castrated man, esp. (formerly) a guard in a harem.

euphemism n. inoffensive word or phrase substituted for one considered offensive or upsetting. **euphemistic** adj. **euphemistically** adv.

euphony n., pl. **-nies.** pleasing sound. **euphonious** adj. pleasing to the ear. **euphonium** n. brass musical instrument, tenor tuba.

euphoria n. sense of elation. **euphoric** adj.

Eurasian adj. **1.** of Europe and Asia. **2.** of mixed European and Asian parentage. —n. **3.** person of Eurasian parentage.

Euratom n. European Atomic Energy Commission.

eureka [yew-**reek**-a] interj. exclamation of triumph at finding something.

Eurodollar n. US dollar as part of a European holding.

European n., adj. (person) from Europe. **European Community** association of a number of European nations for trade.

europium n. silvery-white element of the lanthanide series.

Eustachian tube n. passage leading from the ear to the throat.

euthanasia n. act of killing someone painlessly, esp. to relieve his or her suffering.

eV electronvolt.

evacuate v. 1. send (someone) away from a place of danger. 2. empty. **evacuation** n. **evacuee** n.

evade v. 1. get away from or avoid. 2. elude. **evasion** n. **evasive** adj. not straightforward, e.g. an evasive answer. **evasively** adv.

evaluate v. find or judge the value of. **evaluation** n.

evanescent adj. quickly fading away. **evanescence** n.

evangelical adj. 1. of or according to gospel teaching. 2. of certain Protestant sects which maintain the doctrine of salvation by faith. —n. 3. member of an evangelical sect. **evangelicalism** n.

evangelist n. 1. writer of one of the four gospels. 2. travelling preacher. **evangelism** n. teaching and spreading of the Christian gospel. **evangelize** v. preach the gospel. **evangelization** n.

evaporate v. 1. change from a liquid or solid to a vapour. 2. disappear. **evaporation** n. **evaporated milk** thick unsweetened tinned milk.

eve n. 1. evening or day before some special event. 2. period immediately before an event. **evensong** n. evening prayer.

even adj. 1. flat or smooth. 2. (foll. by with) on the same level (as). 3. constant. 4. calm. 5. equally balanced. 6. divisible by two. —adv. 7. equally. 8. simply. 9. nevertheless. —v. 10. make even.

evening n. 1. end of the day or early part of the night. 2. concluding period. **evening class** educational class for adults, held during the evening. **evening dress** attire for a formal occasion during the evening.

event n. 1. anything that takes place. 2. actual outcome. 3. contest in a sporting programme. **eventful** adj. full of exciting incidents.

eventing n. riding competitions, usually involving cross-country, jumping, and dressage.

eventual adj. ultimate. **eventually** adv. **eventuality** n. possible event.

ever adv. 1. at any time. 2. always.

evergreen n., adj. (tree or shrub) having leaves throughout the year.

everlasting adj. 1. eternal. 2. lasting for an indefinitely long period.

evermore adv. all time to come.

every adj. 1. each without exception. 2. all possible. **everybody** pron. every person. **everyday** adj. usual or ordinary. **everyone** pron. every person. **everything** pron. **everywhere** adv. in all places.

▷ Everybody and everyone are interchangeable. Although strict usage treats these pronouns as singular, modern practice is to use a plural after them: Everyone nodded their head.

evict v. legally expel (someone) from his or her home. **eviction** n.

evidence n. 1. ground for belief. 2. sign, indication. 3. matter produced before a lawcourt to prove or disprove a point. —v. 4. demonstrate, prove. in **evidence** conspicuous. **evident** adj. easily noticed or understood. **evidently** adv. **evidential** adj. of, serving as, or based on evidence. **evidentially** adv.

evil adj. 1. morally bad. 2. harmful. 3. very unpleasant. —n. 4. wickedness. 5. wicked deed. **evilly** adv. **evildoer** n. wicked person. **evil eye** 1. look superstitiously supposed to have the power of inflicting harm. 2. power to inflict harm by such a look.

evince v. make evident.

eviscerate v. disembowel. **evisceration** n.

evoke v. call or summon up (a memory, feeling, etc.). **evocation** n. **evocative** adj.

evolve v. 1. develop gradually. 2. (of an animal or plant species) undergo evolution. **evolution** n. 1. gradual change in the characteristics of living things over successive generations, esp. to a more complex form. 2. gradual development. **evolutionary** adj.

ewe n. female sheep.

ewer n. large jug with a wide mouth.

ex n. Informal former wife or husband.

ex- prefix 1. out of, outside, from, e.g. exodus. 2. former, e.g. ex-wife.

exacerbate [ig-**zass**-er-bate] v. make (pain, emotion, or a situation) worse. **exacerbation** n.

exact adj. 1. correct and complete in every detail. 2. precise, as opposed to approximate. —v. 3. demand (payment or obedience). **exactly** adv. precisely, in every respect. **exactness**, **exactitude** n. **exacting** adj. making rigorous or excessive demands.

exaggerate v. 1. regard or represent as greater than is true. 2. make greater or more noticeable. **exaggeratedly** adv. **exaggeration** n.

exalt v. 1. praise highly. 2. elevate in rank. **exaltation** n. 1. feeling of great joy. 2. act of praising highly.

exam n. short for EXAMINATION.

examine v. 1. look at closely. 2. test the knowledge of. 3. ask questions of. **examination** n. 1. examining. 2. test of a candidate's knowledge or skill. **examinee** n. person who sits an exam. **examiner** n. person who sets or marks an exam.

example n. 1. specimen typical of its group. 2. person or thing worthy of imitation. 3. punishment regarded as a warning to others. 4. instance that illustrates a fact or opinion.

exasperate v. cause great irritation to. **exasperation** n.

excavate v. 1. unearth buried objects from (a piece of land) methodically to learn about the past. 2. make (a hole) in solid matter by digging. **excavation** n. **excavator** n. large machine used for digging.

exceed v. 1. be greater than. 2. go beyond (a limit). **exceedingly** adv. very.

excel v. **-celling, -celled.** 1. be superior to. 2. be outstandingly good at something. **excellent** adj. very good. **excellence** n.

Excellency n. title used to address a high-ranking official, such as an ambassador.

except prep. 1. (sometimes foll. by for) other than, not including. —v. 2. not include. **except that** with the exception that. **excepting** prep. except. **exception** n. 1. excepting. 2. thing that is excluded from or does not conform to the general rule. **exceptionable** adj. causing offence. **exceptional** adj. 1. not ordinary. 2. much above the average. **exceptionally** adv.

excerpt n. passage taken from a book, speech, etc.

excess n. 1. state or act of exceeding the permitted limits. 2. immoderate amount. 3. amount by which a thing exceeds the permitted limits. **excessive** adj. **excessively** adv.

exchange v. 1. give or receive (something) in return for something else. —n. 2. act of exchanging. 3. thing given or received in place of another. 4. centre in which telephone lines are interconnected. 5. Finance place where securities or commodities are traded. 6. transfer of sums of money of equal value between different currencies. **exchangeable** adj. **exchange rate** rate at which the currency unit of one country may be exchanged for that of another.

Exchequer n. Brit. government department in charge of state money.

excise[1] n. tax on goods produced for the home market.

excise[2] v. cut out or away. **excision** n.

excite v. 1. arouse to strong emotion. 2. arouse or evoke (an emotion). 3. arouse sexually. **excitement** n. **excitable** adj. easily excited. **excitability** n. **exciting** adj.

exclaim v. speak suddenly, cry out. **exclamation** n. **exclamation mark** punctuation mark (!) used after exclamations. **exclamatory** adj.

exclude v. 1. leave out of consideration. 2. keep out, leave out. **exclusion** n. **exclusive** adj. 1. catering for a privileged minority. 2. not shared. 3. excluding everything else. —n. 4. story reported in only one newspaper. **exclusively** adv. **exclusiveness, exclusivity** n.

excommunicate v. exclude from membership and the sacraments of the Church. **excommunication** n.

excoriate v. 1. censure severely. 2. strip skin from. **excoriation** n.

excrement n. waste matter discharged from the body.

excrescence n. lump or growth on the surface of an animal or plant. **excrescent** adj.

excrete v. discharge (waste matter) from the body. **excretion** n. **excreta** [ik-skree-ta] n. excrement. **excretory** adj.

excruciating adj. 1. agonizing. 2. very intense. **excruciatingly** adv.

exculpate v. free from blame or guilt.

excursion n. short journey, esp. for pleasure.

excuse v. 1. put forward a reason or justification for (a fault etc.). 2. forgive (a person) or overlook (a fault etc.). 3. make allowances for. 4. exempt. 5. allow to leave. —n. 6. explanation offered to excuse (a fault etc.). **excusable** adj.

ex-directory adj. not listed in a telephone directory by request.

execrable [eks-sik-rab-bl] adj. of very poor quality.

execute v. **1.** put (a condemned person) to death. **2.** perform (a plan or action). **3.** produce (a work of art). **4.** render (a legal document) effective, as by signing. **execution** n. **executioner** n.

executive n. **1.** person or group in an administrative position. **2.** branch of government responsible for carrying out laws etc. —adj. **3.** having the function of carrying out plans, orders, laws, etc.

executor, executrix n. person appointed to perform the instructions of a will.

exegesis [eks-sij-**jee**-siss] n., pl. **-ses** [-seez] explanation of a text, esp. of the Bible.

exemplar n. **1.** example. **2.** person or thing to be copied, model. **exemplary** adj. **1.** being a good example. **2.** serving as a warning.

exemplify v. **-fying, -fied. 1.** be an example of. **2.** show an example of. **exemplification** n.

exempt adj. **1.** not subject to an obligation etc. —v. **2.** release from an obligation etc. **exemption** n.

exequies [**eks**-sik-wiz] pl. n. funeral rites.

exercise n. **1.** activity to train the body or mind. **2.** set of movements or tasks designed to improve or test a person's ability. **3.** performance of a function. —v. **4.** take exercise or perform exercises. **5.** make use of, e.g. to exercise one's rights.

exert v. use (influence, authority, etc.) forcefully or effectively. **exert oneself** make a special effort. **exertion** n.

exeunt [**eks**-see-unt] Latin they go out: used as a stage direction.

exfoliate v. peel in scales or layers.

ex gratia [eks **gray**-sha] adj. given as a favour where no legal obligation exists.

exhale v. breathe out. **exhalation** n.

exhaust v. **1.** tire out. **2.** use up. **3.** discuss (a subject) thoroughly. —n. **4.** gases ejected from an engine as waste products. **5.** pipe through which an engine's exhaust fumes pass. **exhaustible** adj. **exhaustion** n. **1.** extreme tiredness. **2.** exhausting. **exhaustive** adj. comprehensive. **exhaustively** adv.

exhibit v. **1.** show (a quality). **2.** display to the public. —n. **3.** object exhibited to the public. **4.** Law document or object produced in court as evidence. **exhibitor** n. **exhibition** n. **1.** public display of art, skills, etc. **2.** exhibiting. **exhibitionism** n. **1.** compulsive

desire to draw attention to oneself. **2.** compulsive desire to display one's genitals in public. **exhibitionist** n.

exhilarate v. make lively and cheerful. **exhilaration** n.

exhort v. urge earnestly. **exhortation** n.

exhume [ig-**zyume**] v. dig up (something buried, esp. a corpse). **exhumation** n.

exigency n., pl. **-cies.** urgent demand or need. **exigent** adj.

exiguous adj. scanty, meagre.

exile n. **1.** prolonged, usu. enforced, absence from one's country. **2.** person banished or living away from his or her country. —v. **3.** expel from one's country.

exist v. **1.** have being or reality. **2.** eke out a living. **3.** live. **existence** n. **existent** adj.

existential adj. of or relating to existence, esp. human existence. **existentialism** n. philosophical movement stressing the personal experience and responsibility of the individual, who is seen as a free agent. **existentialist** adj., n.

exit n. **1.** way out. **2.** going out. **3.** actor's going off stage. —v. **4.** go out. **5.** go offstage: used as a stage direction.

exocrine adj. relating to a gland, such as the sweat gland, that secretes externally through a duct.

exodus [**eks**-so-duss] n. departure of a large number of people. **the Exodus** departure of the Israelites from Egypt.

ex officio [eks off-**fish**-ee-oh] adv., adj. Latin by right of position or office.

exonerate v. free from blame or a criminal charge. **exoneration** n.

exorbitant adj. (of prices, demands, etc.) excessive, immoderate. **exorbitantly** adv.

exorcize v. expel (evil spirits) by prayers and religious rites. **exorcism** n. **exorcist** n.

exotic adj. **1.** having a strange allure or beauty. **2.** originating in a foreign country. —n. **3.** exotic plant. **exotically** adv. **exotica** pl. n. (collection of) exotic objects.

expand v. **1.** make or become larger. **2.** spread out. **3.** (foll. by on) enlarge (on). **4.** become more relaxed, friendly, and talkative. **expansion** n. **expansionism** n. policy of expanding the economy or territory of a country. **expansionist** adj. **expanse** n. uninterrupted wide area. **expansive** adj. **1.** friendly and talkative. **2.** wide or extensive.

expatiate [iks-**pay**-shee-ate] v. (foll. by *on*) speak or write at great length (on). **expatiation** n.

expatriate [eks-**pat**-ree-it] n. **1.** person living outside his or her native country. —*adj.* **2.** living outside one's native country. **expatriation** n.

expect v. **1.** regard as probable. **2.** look forward to, await. **3.** require as an obligation. **expectancy** n. **1.** something expected on the basis of an average, e.g. *life expectancy.* **2.** feeling of anticipation. **expectant** adj. **1.** expecting or hopeful. **2.** pregnant. **expectantly** adv. **expectation** n. **1.** act or state of expecting. **2.** something looked forward to. **3.** attitude of anticipation or hope.

expectorate v. spit out (phlegm etc.). **expectoration** n. **expectorant** n. medicine that helps to bring up phlegm from the respiratory passages.

expedient [iks-**pee**-dee-ent] n. **1.** something that achieves a particular purpose. —*adj.* **2.** suitable to the circumstances, appropriate. **expediency** n.

expedite v. hasten the progress of. **expedition** n. **1.** organized journey, esp. for exploration. **2.** people and equipment comprising an expedition. **expeditionary** adj. relating to an expedition, esp. a military one. **expeditious** adj. prompt, speedy.

expel v. **-pelling, -pelled. 1.** dismiss from a school etc. permanently. **2.** drive out with force. **expulsion** n.

expend v. spend, use up. **expendable** adj. able to be sacrificed to achieve an objective. **expenditure** n. **1.** something expended, esp. money. **2.** amount expended. **expense** n. **1.** cost. **2.** (cause of) spending. —*pl.* **3.** charges, outlay incurred. **expense account** arrangement by which an employee's expenses are refunded by the employer. **expensive** adj. high-priced.

experience n. **1.** direct personal participation. **2.** particular incident, feeling, etc. that a person has undergone. **3.** accumulated knowledge. —v. **4.** participate in. **5.** be affected by (an emotion). **experienced** adj. skilful from extensive participation.

experiment n. **1.** test to provide evidence to prove or disprove a theory. **2.** attempt at something new. —v. **3.** make an experiment. **experimental** adj. **experimentally** adv. **experimentation** n.

expert n. **1.** person with extensive skill or knowledge in a particular field. —*adj.* **2.** skilful or knowledgeable. **expertise** [eks-per-**teez**] n. special skill or knowledge. **expertly** adv.

expiate v. make amends for. **expiation** n.

expire v. **1.** finish or run out. **2.** *Lit.* die. **3.** breathe out. **expiration** n. **expiry** n. end, esp. of a contract period.

explain v. **1.** make clear and intelligible. **2.** account for. **explanation** n. **explanatory** adj.

expletive [iks-**plee**-tiv] n. swearword.

explicable adj. able to be explained. **explicate** v. *Formal* explain. **explication** n.

explicit adj. **1.** precisely and clearly expressed. **2.** shown in realistic detail. **explicitly** adv.

explode v. **1.** burst with great violence, blow up. **2.** react suddenly with emotion. **3.** increase rapidly. **4.** show (a theory etc.) to be baseless. **explosion** n. **explosive** adj. **1.** tending to explode. —n. **2.** substance that causes explosions.

exploit n. **1.** notable feat or deed. —v. **2.** take advantage of for one's own purposes. **3.** make the best use of. **exploitation** n. **exploiter** n.

explore v. **1.** travel into (unfamiliar regions), esp. for scientific purposes. **2.** investigate. **exploration** n. **exploratory** adj. **explorer** n.

expo n., pl. **expos.** *Informal* exposition, large public exhibition.

exponent n. **1.** person who advocates an idea, cause, etc. **2.** skilful performer, esp. a musician.

exponential adj. very rapid. **exponentially** adv.

export n. **1.** selling or shipping of goods to a foreign country. **2.** product shipped or sold to a foreign country. —v. **3.** sell or ship (goods) to a foreign country. **exporter** n.

expose v. **1.** uncover or reveal. **2.** make vulnerable, leave unprotected. **3.** subject (a photographic film) to light. **expose oneself** display one's sexual organs in public. **exposure** n. **1.** exposing. **2.** lack of shelter from the weather, esp. the cold. **3.** appearance before the public, as on television. **4.** *Photog.* act of exposing film or plates to light. **5.** *Photog.* intensity of light falling on a film or plate multiplied by the time of the exposure.

exposé [iks-**pose**-ay] *n.* bringing of a crime, scandal, etc. to public notice.

exposition *n.* see EXPOUND.

expostulate *v.* (foll. by *with*) reason (with), esp. to dissuade. **expostulation** *n.*

expound *v.* explain in detail. **exposition** *n.* 1. explanation. 2. large public exhibition.

express *v.* 1. put into words. 2. show (an emotion). 3. indicate by a symbol or formula. 4. squeeze out (juice etc.). —*adj.* 5. explicitly stated. 6. (of a purpose) particular. 7. of or for rapid transportation of people, mail, etc. —*n.* 8. fast train or bus stopping at only a few stations. —*adv.* 9. by express delivery. **expression** *n.* 1. expressing. 2. word or phrase. 3. showing or communication of emotion. 4. look on the face that indicates mood. 5. *Maths* variable, function, or some combination of these. **expressionless** *adj.* **expressive** *adj.* **expressiveness** *n.*

expressionism *n.* early 20th-century artistic movement which sought to express emotions rather than represent the physical world. **expressionist** *n., adj.*

expresso *n.* same as ESPRESSO.

expropriate *v.* deprive an owner of (property). **expropriation** *n.*

expulsion *n.* see EXPEL.

expunge [iks-**sponge**] *v.* delete, erase, blot out.

expurgate [**eks**-per-gate] *v.* remove objectionable parts from (a book etc.).

exquisite *adj.* 1. of extreme beauty or delicacy. 2. intense in feeling. **exquisitely** *adv.*

ex-serviceman *n.* man who has served in the armed forces.

extant *adj.* still existing.
▷ *Extant* suggests that something still exists because it has survived: *The only example of this fossil extant.*

extemporize *v.* speak, perform, or compose without preparation.

extend *v.* 1. draw out or be drawn out, stretch. 2. last for a certain time. 3. (foll. by *to*) include. 4. increase in size or scope. 5. offer, e.g. *extend one's sympathy.* **extendable** *adj.* **extension** *n.* 1. continuation or additional part of a building etc. 2. additional telephone connected to the same line as

another. 3. extending. **extensive** *adj.* having a large extent, widespread. **extensor** *n.* muscle that extends a part of the body. **extent** *n.* range over which something extends, area.

extenuate *v.* make (an offence or fault) less blameworthy. **extenuating** *adj.* **extenuation** *n.*

exterior *n.* 1. part or surface on the outside. 2. outward appearance. —*adj.* 3. of, on, or coming from the outside.

exterminate *v.* destroy (animals or people) completely. **extermination** *n.* **exterminator** *n.*

external *adj.* of, situated on, or coming from the outside. **externally** *adv.*

externalize *v.* express (feelings) in words or actions.

extinct *adj.* 1. having died out. 2. (of a volcano) no longer liable to erupt. **extinction** *n.*

extinguish *v.* 1. put out (a fire or light). 2. remove or destroy entirely. **extinguisher** *n.*

extirpate [**eks**-ter-pate] *v.* destroy utterly.

extol *v.* -**tolling**, -**tolled**. praise highly.

extort *v.* get (something) by force or threats. **extortion** *n.* **extortionate** *adj.* (of prices) excessive.

extra *adj.* 1. additional. 2. more than usual. —*n.* 3. additional person or thing. 4. something for which an additional charge is made. 5. *Films* actor hired for crowd scenes. 6. *Cricket* run not scored off the bat. —*adv.* 7. unusually or exceptionally.

extra- *prefix* outside or beyond an area or scope, e.g. *extrasensory, extraterritorial.*

extract *v.* 1. pull out by force. 2. remove. 3. derive. 4. copy out (an article, passage, etc.) from a publication. —*n.* 5. something extracted, such as a passage from a book etc. 6. preparation containing the concentrated essence of a substance, e.g. *beef extract.* **extraction** *n.* **extractor** *n.* **extractor fan** device for removing stale air or fumes from a room.

extracurricular *adj.* 1. taking place outside the normal school timetable. 2. beyond regular duties.

extradite *v.* send (an accused person) back to his or her own country for trial. **extradition** *n.*

extramural *adj.* connected with but outside

the normal courses of a university or college.

extraneous [iks-**train**-ee-uss] *adj.* irrelevant.

extraordinary *adj.* **1.** very unusual. **2.** (of a meeting) unscheduled, arranged to deal with a particular subject. **extraordinarily** *adv.*

extrapolate [iks-**trap**-a-late] *v.* **1.** infer (something not known) from the known facts. **2.** *Maths* estimate (a value of a function or measurement) beyond the known values by the extension of a curve. **extrapolation** *n.*

extrasensory *adj.* extrasensory perception supposed ability to obtain information other than through the normal senses.

extraterrestrial *adj.* of or from outside the earth's atmosphere.

extravagant *adj.* **1.** spending money excessively. **2.** going beyond reasonable limits. **extravagance** *n.* **extravaganza** *n.* elaborate and lavish entertainment, display, etc.

extreme *adj.* **1.** of a high or the highest degree or intensity. **2.** immoderate. **3.** severe. **4.** farthest or outermost. —*n.* **5.** either of the two limits of a scale or range. **extremely** *adv.* **extremism** *n.* behaviour or beliefs that are immoderate. **extremist** *n.* **1.** person who favours immoderate methods. —*adj.* **2.** holding extreme opinions. **extremity** *n.,* *pl.* **-ties.** **1.** farthest point. **2.** extreme condition, as of misfortune. —*pl.* **3.** hands and feet.

extricate *v.* free from complication or difficulty. **extrication** *n.*

extrinsic *adj.* not contained or included within. **extrinsically** *adv.*

extrovert *adj.* **1.** lively and outgoing. **2.** concerned more with external reality than inner feelings. —*n.* **3.** extrovert person. **extroversion** *n.*

extrude *v.* squeeze or force out. **extrusion** *n.*

exuberant *adj.* **1.** high-spirited. **2.** growing luxuriantly. **exuberance** *n.* **exuberantly** *adv.*

exude *v.* **1.** make apparent by mood or behaviour, e.g. *exude confidence.* **2.** ooze out as sweat or sap.

exult *v.* be joyful or jubilant. **exultation** *n.* **exultant** *adj.*

eye *n.* **1.** organ of sight. **2.** (often *pl.*) ability to see. **3.** external part of an eye. **4.** attention, e.g. *his new shirt caught my eye.* **5.** ability to judge or appreciate, e.g. *a good eye for detail.* **6.** one end of a sewing needle. **7.** dark spot on a potato from which a stem grows. **8.** small area of calm at the centre of a hurricane. —*v.* **eyeing** *or* **eying,** **eyed.** **9.** look at carefully or warily. **eyeless** *adj.* **eyelet** *n.* **1.** small hole for a lace or cord to be passed through. **2.** ring that strengthens this. **eyeball** *n.* ball-shaped part of the eye. **eyebrow** *n.* line of hair on the bony ridge above the eye. **eye-catching** *adj.* attracting attention. **eyeful** *n. Informal* **1.** view. **2.** attractive sight, esp. a woman. **eyeglass** *n.* lens for aiding defective vision. **eyelash** *n.* short hair that grows out from the eyelid. **eyelid** *n.* fold of skin that covers the eye when it is closed. **eyeliner** *n.* cosmetic used to outline the eyes. **eye-opener** *n. Informal* something startling or revealing. **eye shadow** coloured cosmetic worn on the upper eyelids. **eyesight** *n.* ability to see. **eyesore** *n.* ugly object. **eyetooth** *n.* canine tooth. **eyewash** *n. Informal* nonsense. **eyewitness** *n.* person who was present at an event and can describe what happened.

eyrie *n.* **1.** nest of an eagle. **2.** high isolated place.

F

f *Music* forte.

F 1. Fahrenheit. **2.** farad. **3.** *Chem.* fluorine. **4.** franc(s).

f. and the following (page).

fa *n.* same as FAH.

FA Football Association.

fable *n.* **1.** story with a moral. **2.** legend. **3.** false or fictitious account. **fabled** *adj.* made famous in legend.

fabric *n.* **1.** knitted or woven cloth. **2.** framework or structure.

fabricate *v.* **1.** make or build. **2.** make up (a story or lie). **fabrication** *n.* **fabricator** *n.*

fabulous *adj.* **1.** *Informal* excellent. **2.** astounding. **3.** told of in fables. **fabulously** *adv.*

façade [fas-**sahd**] *n.* **1.** front of a building. **2.** (false) outward appearance.

face *n.* **1.** front of the head. **2.** facial expression. **3.** distorted expression. **4.** outward appearance. **5.** front or main side. **6.** dial of a clock. **7.** exposed area of coal or ore in a mine. **8.** dignity, self-respect. —*v.* **9.** look or turn towards. **10.** be opposite. **11.** be confronted by. **12.** provide with a surface. **on the face of it** to all appearances, apparently. **set one's face against** oppose determinedly. **faceless** *adj.* impersonal, anonymous. **face-lift** *n.* operation to tighten facial skin, to remove wrinkles. **face-saving** *adj.* maintaining dignity or self-respect. **face up to** *v.* accept (an unpleasant fact or reality). **face value** apparent worth or meaning.

facet *n.* **1.** surface of a cut gem. **2.** aspect.

facetious [fas-**see**-shuss] *adj.* funny or trying to be funny, esp. at inappropriate times. **facetiously** *adv.* **facetiousness** *n.*

facia *n., pl.* **-ciae.** same as FASCIA.

facial *adj.* **1.** of the face. —*n.* **2.** beauty treatment for the face.

facile [fas-sile] *adj.* **1.** (of a remark, argument, etc.) superficial and showing lack of real thought. **2.** easily performed or achieved. **3.** working or moving easily or smoothly.

facilitate *v.* make easy. **facilitation** *n.*

facility *n., pl.* **-ties. 1.** skill. **2.** easiness. —*pl.* **3.** means or equipment for an activity.

facing *n.* **1.** lining or covering for decoration or reinforcement. —*pl.* **2.** contrasting collar and cuffs on a jacket.

facsimile [fak-**sim**-ill-ee] *n.* exact copy. **facsimile transmission** same as FAX (sense 1).

fact *n.* **1.** event or thing known to have happened or existed. **2.** provable truth. **fact of life** inescapable, often unpleasant, truth. **facts of life** details of sex and reproduction. **factual** *adj.*

faction[1] *n.* **1.** (dissenting) minority group within a larger body. **2.** dissension. **factious** *adj.* of or producing factions.

faction[2] *n.* dramatized presentation of a factual event.

factitious *adj.* artificial.

factor *n.* **1.** element contributing to a result. **2.** *Maths* one of the integers multiplied together to give a given number. **3.** *Scot.* property manager. **factorial** *n.* product of all the integers from one to a given number. **factorize** *v.* calculate the factors of (a number).

factory *n., pl.* **-ries.** building where goods are manufactured. **factory farm** farm on which animals are reared using modern industrial methods. **factory ship** ship that processes fish caught by a fleet.

factotum *n.* person employed to do all sorts of work.

faculty *n., pl.* **-ties. 1.** physical or mental ability. **2.** department in a university or college.

fad *n.* **1.** short-lived fashion. **2.** whim. **faddy, faddish** *adj.*

fade *v.* **1.** (cause to) lose brightness, colour, or strength. **2.** vanish slowly. **fade-in, -out** *n.* gradual increase or decrease, as of vision or sound in a film or broadcast.

faeces [**fee**-seez] *pl. n.* waste matter discharged from the anus. **faecal** [**fee**-kl] *adj.*

faff *v.* (often foll. by *about*) *Brit. informal* dither or fuss.

fag[1] *n. Slang* cigarette. **fag end 1.** cigarette stub. **2.** last and worst part.

fag[2] *n.* **1.** *Informal* boring task. **2.** young public schoolboy who does menial chores for a senior boy. —*v.* **3.** (often foll. by *out*) *Informal* tire. **4.** do menial chores in a public school.

fag[3] *n.* *US offens.* male homosexual.

faggot[1] *n.* **1.** ball of chopped liver, herbs, and bread. **2.** bundle of sticks for fuel.

faggot[2] *n.* *US offens.* male homosexual.

fah *n.* *Music* in tonic sol-fa, fourth degree of any major scale.

Fahrenheit [far-ren-hite] *adj.* of a temperature scale with the freezing point of water at 32° and the boiling point at 212°.

faïence [fie-ence] *n.* tin-glazed earthenware.

fail *v.* **1.** be unsuccessful. **2.** stop operating. **3.** be or judge to be below the required standard in a test. **4.** disappoint or be useless to (someone). **5.** omit or be unable to do (something). **6.** go bankrupt. —*n.* **7.** instance of not passing an exam or test. **without fail 1.** definitely. **2.** regularly. **failing** *n.* **1.** weak point. —*prep.* **2.** in the absence of. **failure** *n.* **1.** act or instance of failing. **2.** unsuccessful person or thing. **failsafe** *adj.* designed to return to a safe condition if something goes wrong.

fain *adv. Obs.* gladly.

faint *adj.* **1.** lacking clarity, brightness, or volume. **2.** lacking conviction or force. **3.** feeling dizzy or weak. —*v.* **4.** lose consciousness temporarily. —*n.* **5.** temporary loss of consciousness. **faint-hearted** *adj.* timid.

fair[1] *adj.* **1.** unbiased and reasonable. **2.** light in colour. **3.** beautiful. **4.** quite good. **5.** unblemished. **6.** (of weather) fine. —*adv.* **7.** fairly. **8.** absolutely. **fairly** *adv.* **1.** as deserved, reasonably. **2.** moderately. **3.** to a great degree or extent. **fairness** *n.* **fair copy** neat copy, without mistakes or alterations, of a piece of writing. **fair game** person regarded as a justifiable target for criticism or ridicule. **fair play** conventional standard of honourable behaviour. **fairway** *n. Golf* smooth area between the tee and the green. **fair-weather** *adj.* not reliable in a difficult situation, e.g. *a fair-weather friend.*

fair[2] *n.* **1.** travelling entertainment with stalls and machines to ride on, etc. **2.** exhibition of commercial or industrial products. **fairground** *n.* open space used for a fair.

fairing *n.* curved metal structure fitted round part of a car, aircraft, etc. to reduce drag.

Fair Isle *n.* intricate multicoloured knitted pattern.

fairy *n., pl.* **fairies**. **1.** imaginary small creature with magic powers. **2.** *Offens.* male homosexual. **fairy godmother** person who helps in time of trouble. **fairyland** *n.* **fairy light** small coloured light used as decoration. **fairy ring** ring of dark grass caused by fungi. **fairy tale, story 1.** story about fairies or magic. **2.** unbelievable story or explanation.

fait accompli [fate ak-kom-plee] *n. French* something already done that cannot be altered.

faith *n.* **1.** strong belief, esp. without proof. **2.** religion. **3.** complete confidence or trust. **4.** allegiance to a person or cause. **faithful** *adj.* **1.** loyal. **2.** firm in support. **3.** accurate. **faithfully** *adv.* **faithless** *adj.* disloyal or dishonest. **faith-healing** *n.* healing of bodily ailments by religious rather than medical means. **faith-healer** *n.*

fake *v.* **1.** cause (something) to appear real or more valuable by fraud. **2.** pretend to have (an illness, emotion, etc.). —*n.* **3.** person, thing, or act that is not genuine. —*adj.* **4.** not genuine. **faker** *n.*

fakir [fay-keer] *n.* **1.** member of any Islamic religious order. **2.** Hindu holy man.

falcon *n.* small bird of prey. **falconry** *n.* **1.** art of training falcons. **2.** sport of hunting with falcons. **falconer** *n.*

fall *v.* **falling, fell, fallen. 1.** drop from a higher to a lower place through the force of gravity. **2.** collapse to the ground. **3.** decrease in number or quality. **4.** slope downwards. **5.** die in battle. **6.** be captured. **7.** pass into a specified condition. **8.** (of the face) take on a sad expression. **9.** yield to temptation. **10.** occur. —*n.* **11.** falling. **12.** thing or amount that falls. **13.** decrease in value or number. **14.** decline in power or influence. **15.** *US* autumn. **16.** capture or overthrow. —*pl.* **17.** waterfall. **fall flat** fail utterly. **fall behind** *v.* **1.** fail to keep up. **2.** be in arrears with a payment etc. **fall for** *v.* **1.** *Informal* fall in love with. **2.** be taken in by. **fall guy 1.** *Informal* victim of a confidence trick. **2.** scapegoat. **fall in** *v.* **1.** collapse. **2.** (of a soldier etc.) take his or her place in a formation. **fall in with** *v.* **1.** meet with and join. **2.** agree with or support a person or idea. **fallout** *n.* radioactive particles spread as a result of a nuclear explosion. **fall out** v. **1.** Informal stop being friendly, disagree. **2.** (of a soldier etc.) leave his or her place in a formation. **fall through** v. fail. **fall to** v. **1.** to begin some activity. **2.** (of a task or duty) to become (someone's) responsibility.

fallacy n., pl. **-cies. 1.** false belief. **2.** unsound reasoning. **fallacious** adj.

fallen v. past participle of FALL. **fallen arch** collapse of the arch formed by the instep of the foot, resulting in flat feet.

fallible adj. liable to error. **fallibility** n.

Fallopian tube n. either of a pair of tubes through which egg cells pass from the ovary to the womb.

fallow[1] adj. (of land) ploughed but left unseeded to regain fertility.

fallow[2] adj. light yellowish-brown. **fallow deer** reddish-brown deer with white spots in summer.

false adj. **1.** not true or correct. **2.** artificial, fake. **3.** deceptive. **4.** treacherous. **falsely** adv. **falseness** n. **falsity** n., pl. **-ties. 1.** state of being false. **2.** lie. **falsehood** n. **1.** quality of being untrue. **2.** lie.

falsetto n., pl. **-tos.** voice pitched higher than one's natural range.

falsify v. **-fying, -fied.** alter fraudulently. **falsification** n.

falter v. **1.** lose power momentarily. **2.** be unsure. **3.** utter hesitantly. **4.** move unsteadily. **faltering** adj. **falteringly** adv.

fame n. state of being widely known or recognized. **famed** adj. **famous.**

familiar adj. **1.** well-known. **2.** acquainted. **3.** too friendly. **4.** intimate, friendly. —n. **5.** friend. **6.** demon supposed to attend a witch. **familiarly** adv. **familiarity** n., pl. **-ties. familiarize** v. acquaint fully with a particular subject. **familiarization** n.

family n., pl. **-lies. 1.** group of parents and their children. **2.** one's spouse and children. **3.** one's children. **4.** group descended from a common ancestor. **5.** group of related objects or beings. —adj. **6.** suitable for parents and children together. **familial** adj. **family doctor** Informal same as GENERAL PRACTITIONER. **family name** surname, esp. when seen as a symbol of family honour. **family planning** control of the number of children in a family, esp. through contraception. **family tree** chart showing how the members

of a family, going back over many generations, are related to one another.

famine n. severe shortage of food.

famished adj. very hungry.

famous adj. very well-known. **famously** adv. Informal excellently.

fan[1] n. **1.** hand-held or mechanical object used to create a current of air for ventilation or cooling. —v. **fanning, fanned. 2.** blow or cool with a fan. **3.** spread out like a fan. **fan belt** belt that drives a cooling fan in a car engine. **fan heater** heater which uses a fan to spread warmed air through a room. **fanlight** n. semicircular window over a door or window.

fan[2] n. Informal devotee of a pop star, sport, or hobby.

fanatic n. person who is excessively enthusiastic about something. **fanatical** adj. **fanatically** adv. **fanaticism** n.

fancy adj. **-cier, -ciest. 1.** elaborate, not plain. **2.** (of prices) higher than usual. —n., pl. **-cies. 3.** sudden irrational liking or desire. **4.** uncontrolled imagination. —v. **-cying, -cied. 5.** Informal have a wish for. **6.** Informal be sexually attracted to. **7.** picture in the imagination. **8.** suppose. **fancy oneself** Informal have a high opinion of oneself. **fancier** n. person who is interested in and often breeds plants or animals, e.g. a pigeon fancier. **fanciful** adj. **1.** not based on fact. **2.** excessively elaborate. **fancifully** adv. **fancy dress** party costume representing a historical figure, animal, etc. **fancy-free** adj. not in love. **fancy goods** pl. n. small decorative gifts.

fandango n., pl. **-gos.** lively Spanish dance.

fanfare n. short loud tune played on brass instruments.

fang n. **1.** snake's tooth which injects poison. **2.** long pointed tooth.

fanny n., pl. **-nies.** Slang **1.** Brit. taboo female genitals. **2.** US buttocks.

fantasia n. musical composition of an improvised nature.

fantastic adj. **1.** Informal very good. **2.** strange or difficult to believe. **3.** unrealistic or absurd. **fantastically** adv.

fantasy n., pl. **-sies. 1.** imagination unrestricted by reality. **2.** far-fetched notion. **3.** daydream. **4.** fiction with a large fantasy content. **fantasize** v. indulge in daydreams.

fanzine [fan-zeen] n. magazine produced for

and by devotees of a particular interest, football team, etc.

far _farther or further, farthest or furthest._ —_adv._ **1.** at, to, or from a great distance. **2.** at or to a remote time. **3.** very much. —_adj._ **4.** remote in space or time. **faraway** _adj._ **1.** very distant. **2.** absent-minded. **Far East** East Asia. **far-fetched** _adj._ hard to believe. **far-flung** _adj._ **1.** distributed over a wide area. **2.** very distant. **far-reaching** _adj._ extensive in influence, effect, or range. **far-sighted** _adj._ having or showing foresight and wisdom.

▷ _Farther_ is often used, rather than _further_, when distance, not time or effort, is involved.

farad _n._ unit of electrical capacitance.

farce _n._ **1.** boisterous comedy. **2.** ludicrous situation. **farcical** _adj._ ludicrous. **farcically** _adv._

fare _n._ **1.** charge for a passenger's journey. **2.** passenger. **3.** food provided. —_v._ **4.** get on (as specified), e.g. _we fared badly._ **fare stage 1.** section of a bus journey for which a set charge is made. **2.** bus stop marking the end of such a section.

farewell _interj._ **1.** goodbye. —_n._ **2.** act of saying goodbye and leaving.

farinaceous _adj._ mealy, starchy.

farm _n._ **1.** area of land for growing crops or rearing livestock. **2.** area of land or water for growing or rearing a specified animal or plant, e.g. _fish farm._ —_v._ **3.** cultivate (land). **4.** rear (stock). **farmer** _n._ **farm hand** person employed to work on a farm. **farmhouse** _n._ **farm out v.** send (work) to be done by others. **farmstead** _n._ farm and its buildings. **farmyard** _n._

farrago [far-**rah**-go] _n., pl._ **-gos, -goes.** jumbled mixture of things.

farrier _n._ person who shoes horses.

farrow _n._ **1.** litter of pigs. —_v._ **2.** (of a sow) give birth.

fart _Taboo_ —_n._ **1.** emission of gas from the anus. —_v._ **2.** emit gas from the anus.

farther, farthest _adv., adj._ see FAR.

farthing _n._ former British coin equivalent to a quarter of a penny.

farthingale _n. Obs._ hoop worn under skirts.

fascia [**fay**-shya] _n., pl._ **-ciae, -cias. 1.** flat surface above a shop window. **2.** outer surface of a dashboard.

fascinate _v._ **1.** attract and interest strongly.

2. make motionless from fear or awe. **fascinating** _adj._ **fascination** _n._

fascism [**fash**-iz-zum] _n._ right-wing totalitarian political system characterized by state control and extreme nationalism. **fascist** _adj., n._

fashion _n._ **1.** style in clothes, esp. the latest style. **2.** manner of doing something. —_v._ **3.** form or make into a particular shape. **fashionable** _adj._ currently popular. **fashionably** _adv._

fast[1] _adj._ **1.** (capable of) acting or moving quickly. **2.** done in or lasting a short time. **3.** allowing rapid movement. **4.** (of a clock) showing a time later than the correct time. **5.** dissipated. **6.** firmly fixed. **7.** steadfast. —_adv._ **8.** quickly. **9.** tightly, firmly. **10.** soundly, deeply. **pull a fast one** _Informal_ trick or deceive someone. **fast food** food, such as hamburgers, prepared and served very quickly. **fast lane 1.** outside lane on a motorway. **2.** quickest but most competitive route to success. **fast-track** _adj._ taking the quickest but most competitive route to success, e.g. _fast-track executives._

fast[2] _v._ **1.** go without food, esp. for religious reasons. —_n._ **2.** period of fasting.

fasten _v._ **1.** make or become firmly fixed or joined. **2.** close by fixing in place or locking. **3.** (foll. by _on_) direct (one's attention) towards. **fastener, fastening** _n._ device that fastens.

fastidious _adj._ **1.** very fussy about details. **2.** easily disgusted. **fastidiously** _adv._ **fastidiousness** _n._

fastness _n._ fortress, safe place.

fat _n._ **1.** extra flesh on the body. **2.** oily substance obtained from animals or plants. —_adj._ **fatter, fattest. 3.** having excess flesh on the body. **4.** containing much fat. **5.** thick. **6.** profitable. **fatness** _n._ **fatten** _v._ (cause to) become fat. **fatted** _adj._ fattened for slaughter. **fatty** _adj._ **fattier, fattiest.** containing fat. **fathead** _n. Informal_ fool. **fat-headed** _adj._ **fat stock** cows, sheep, etc. fattened and ready for market.

fatal _adj._ causing death or ruin. **fatally** _adv._ **fatality** _n., pl._ **-ties.** death caused by an accident or disaster.

fatalism _n._ belief that all events are predetermined and people are powerless to change their destinies. **fatalist** _n._ **fatalistic** _adj._

fate _n._ **1.** power supposed to predetermine

events. **2.** inevitable fortune that befalls a person or thing. **fated** adj. **1.** destined. **2.** doomed to death or destruction. **fateful** adj. having important, usu. disastrous, consequences.

father n. **1.** male parent. **2.** man who originates or founds something. **3.** title of some priests. **4.** (F-) God. —pl. **5.** ancestors. —v. **6.** be the father of (offspring). **fatherhood** n. **fatherless** adj. **fatherly** adj. **father-in-law** n., pl. **fathers-in-law.** father of one's husband or wife. **fatherland** n. one's native country.

fathom n. **1.** unit of measurement of the depth of water, equal to six feet. —v. **2.** understand. **fathomable** adj. **fathomless** adj. too deep or difficult to fathom.

fatigue [fat-eeg] n. **1.** physical or mental exhaustion caused by exertion. **2.** weakening of a material due to stress. **3.** soldier's nonmilitary duty. —pl. **4.** soldier's clothing for nonmilitary or battlefield duty. —v. **5.** tire out.

fatuous adj. foolish. **fatuously** adv. **fatuousness** n. **fatuity** n., pl. **-ties. 1.** complacent silliness. **2.** fatuous remark.

faucet [faw-set] n. US tap.

fault n. **1.** responsibility for something wrong. **2.** mistake. **3.** defect or flaw. **4.** Geology break in layers of rock. **5.** Tennis, squash etc. invalid serve. —v. **6.** criticize or find mistakes in. **at fault** guilty of error. **find fault** seek out minor imperfections in. **to a fault** excessively. **faulty** adj. **faultily** adv. **faultless** adj. **faultlessly** adv.

faun n. in Roman legend, rural god with goat's horns and legs.

fauna n., pl. **-nas, -nae.** animals of a given place or time.

faux pas [foe pah] n., pl. **faux pas.** social blunder.

favour n. **1.** goodwill, approval. **2.** act of goodwill or generosity. **3.** partiality. —v. **4.** prefer. **5.** support or advocate. **6.** regard or treat with especial kindness. **7.** Informal resemble.

favourable adj. **1.** giving consent. **2.** encouraging. **3.** useful or beneficial. **favourably** adv.

favourite n. **1.** preferred person or thing. **2.** Sport competitor expected to win. —adj. **3.** most liked. **favouritism** n. practice of unfairly favouring one person or group.

fawn[1] n. **1.** young deer. —adj. **2.** light yellowish-brown.

fawn[2] v. **1.** (foll. by on) seek attention from (someone) by being obsequious. **2.** (of a dog) try to please by a show of extreme affection.

fax n. **1.** electronic system for sending facsimiles of documents by telephone. **2.** document sent by this system. —v. **3.** send by this system.

faze v. Informal disconcert or fluster.

FBI US Federal Bureau of Investigation.

FC Football Club.

Fe Chem. iron.

fealty n. Obs. subordinate's loyalty to his ruler or lord.

fear n. **1.** distress or alarm caused by impending danger or pain. **2.** cause of this. —v. **3.** feel anxiety about (something). **4.** be afraid of (something or someone). **fearful** adj. **1.** feeling fear. **2.** causing fear. **3.** Informal very unpleasant. **fearfully** adv. **fearless** adj. **fearlessly** adv. **fearsome** adj. terrifying.

feasible adj. able to be done, possible. **feasibly** adv. **feasibility** n.

feast n. **1.** lavish meal. **2.** periodic religious celebration. **3.** something extremely pleasing. —v. **4.** eat a feast. **5.** (foll. by on) enjoy eating (something). **6.** give a feast to. **7.** delight.

feat n. remarkable, skilful, or daring action.

feather n. **1.** one of the barbed shafts forming the plumage of birds. —v. **2.** fit or cover with feathers. **3.** turn (an oar) edgeways. **feather in one's cap** achievement one can be pleased with. **feather one's nest** make one's life comfortable. **feathered** adj. **feathery** adj. **featherbedding** n. overprotection. **featherweight** n. **1.** boxer weighing up to 126lb (professional) or 57kg (amateur). **2.** insignificant person or thing.

feature n. **1.** prominent or distinctive part. **2.** part of the face, such as the eyes. **3.** special article in a newspaper or magazine. **4.** main film in a cinema programme. —v. **5.** have as a feature or be a feature in. **6.** give prominence to. **featureless** adj.

Feb. February.

febrile [fee-brile] adj. feverish.

February n. second month of the year.

feckless adj. ineffectual or irresponsible.

feculent *adj.* muddy, filthy, or foul. **feculence** *n.*

fecund *adj.* fertile. **fecundity** *n.*

fed *v.* past of FEED. **fed up** *Informal* bored, dissatisfied.

federal *adj.* **1.** of a system in which power is divided between one central government and several regional governments. **2.** of the central government of a federation. **federalism** *n.* **federalist** *n.* **federate** *v.* unite in a federation. **federation** *n.* **1.** union of several states, provinces, etc. **2.** association.

fedora [fid-**or**-a] *n.* man's soft hat with a brim.

fee *n.* **1.** payment for professional services. **2.** charge paid to be allowed to do something.

feeble *adj.* **1.** lacking physical or mental power. **2.** unconvincing. **feebleness** *n.* **feebly** *adv.* **feeble-minded** *adj.* mentally deficient.

feed *v.* **feeding, fed. 1.** give food to. **2.** give (something) as food. **3.** eat. **4.** supply or prepare food for. **5.** supply (what is needed). —*n.* **6.** act of feeding. **7.** food, esp. for babies or animals. **8.** *Informal* meal. **feeder** *n.* **1.** baby's bib. **2.** road or railway line linking outlying areas to the main traffic network. **feedback** *n.* **1.** information received in response to something done. **2.** return of part of the output of an electrical circuit or loudspeaker to its source.

feel *v.* **feeling, felt. 1.** have a physical or emotional sensation of. **2.** become aware of or examine by touch. **3.** believe. —*n.* **4.** act of feeling. **5.** way something feels. **6.** impression. **7.** sense of touch. **8.** instinctive aptitude. **feeler** *n.* **1.** organ of touch in some animals. **2.** remark made to test others' opinion. **feeling** *n.* **1.** emotional reaction. **2.** intuitive understanding. **3.** opinion. **4.** sympathy, understanding. **5.** ability to experience physical sensations. **6.** sensation experienced. —*pl.* **7.** emotional sensitivities. **feel like** wish for, want. **feel for** *v.* **1.** attempt to find by touch alone. **2.** have sympathy or compassion for someone in trouble. **feel up to** *v.* be fit or energetic enough to.

▷ *Feel* is followed by an adjective when it refers back to the subject: *I feel sick.* Otherwise it is followed by an adverb: *She feels strongly about it.*

feet *n.* plural of FOOT.

feign [fane] *v.* pretend. **feigned** *adj.*

feint[1] [faint] *n.* **1.** sham attack or blow meant to distract an opponent. —*v.* **2.** make a feint.

feint[2] [faint] *n.* narrow lines on ruled paper.

feldspar *n.* hard mineral that is the main constituent of igneous rocks.

felicity *n., pl.* **-ties. 1.** happiness. **2.** appropriate expression or style. **felicitate** *v.* congratulate. **felicitation** *n.* **felicitous** *adj.*

feline *adj.* **1.** of cats. **2.** catlike. —*n.* **3.** animal of the cat family.

fell[1] *v.* past tense of FALL.

fell[2] *v.* **1.** knock down. **2.** cut down (a tree).

fell[3] *adj. Old-fashioned* fierce, terrible. **one fell swoop** single action or occurrence.

fell[4] *n.* in N England, a mountain, hill, or moor.

fell[5] *n.* animal's skin or hide with its hair.

felloe *n.* (segment of) the rim of a wheel.

fellow *n.* **1.** *Informal* man or boy. **2.** comrade or associate. **3.** person in the same group or condition. **4.** member of a learned society or the governing body of a college. —*adj.* **5.** in the same group or condition. **fellowship** *n.* **1.** sharing of aims or interests. **2.** group with shared aims or interests. **3.** feeling of friendliness. **4.** paid research post in a college or university. **fellow feeling** sympathy between people who have undergone the same experience. **fellow traveller** Communist sympathizer who is not a Communist Party member.

felon *n.* person guilty of a felony. **felony** *n., pl.* **-nies.** serious crime. **felonious** *adj.*

felspar *n.* same as FELDSPAR.

felt[1] *v.* past of FEEL.

felt[2] *n.* **1.** matted fabric made by bonding fibres by pressure. —*v.* **2.** make into or cover with felt. **3.** become matted. **felt-tip pen** pen with a writing point made from pressed fibres.

fem. feminine.

female *adj.* **1.** of the sex which bears offspring. **2.** (of plants) producing fruits. —*n.* **3.** female person or animal.

feminine *adj.* **1.** of women. **2.** having qualities traditionally regarded as suitable for, or typical of, women. **3.** belonging to a particular class of grammatical inflection in some languages. **femininity** *n.* **feminism** *n.* advocacy of equal rights for women. **feminist** n., adj.

femme fatale [fam fat-tahl] n., pl. **femmes fatales.** alluring woman who causes men distress.

femur [fee-mer] n. thighbone. **femoral** adj. of the thigh.

fen n. low-lying flat marshy land. **fenland** n. **fenny** adj.

fence n. **1.** barrier of posts linked by wire or wood, enclosing an area. **2.** Slang dealer in stolen property. **3.** obstacle for a horse to jump in steeplechasing or showjumping. —v. **4.** enclose with or as if with a fence. **5.** fight with swords as a sport. **6.** avoid a question. **fencing** n. **1.** sport of fighting with swords. **2.** material for making fences. **fencer** n.

fend v. **fend for oneself** provide for oneself. **fend off** v. ward off.

fender n. **1.** low metal frame in front of a fireplace. **2.** soft but solid object hung over a ship's side to prevent damage when docking. **3.** US wing of a car.

Fenian [feen-yan] n. member of a 19th-century Irish revolutionary organization founded to fight for an independent Ireland.

fennel n. fragrant plant whose seeds, leaves, and root are used in cookery.

fenugreek n. Mediterranean plant grown for its pungent seeds.

feoff [feef] n. Hist. same as FIEF.

feral adj. wild.

ferment n. **1.** commotion, unrest. —v. **2.** undergo or cause to undergo fermentation. **fermentation** n. reaction in which an organic molecule splits into simpler substances, esp. the conversion of sugar to alcohol.

fermium n. element artificially produced by neutron bombardment of plutonium.

fern n. flowerless plant with fine fronds.

ferocious adj. fierce, violent. **ferocity** n.

ferret n. **1.** tamed polecat used to catch rabbits or rats. —v. **ferreting, ferreted. 2.** hunt with ferrets. **3.** search around. **ferret out** v. find by searching.

ferric, ferrous adj. of or containing iron.

ferris wheel n. large vertical fairground wheel with hanging seats for riding in.

ferrule n. metal cap to strengthen the end of a stick.

ferry n., pl. **-ries. 1.** boat for transporting people and vehicles. **2.** route or service operated by such a boat. —v. **-rying, -ried. 3.** carry by ferry. **4.** convey (goods or people). **ferryboat** n. **ferryman** n.

fertile adj. **1.** capable of producing young, crops, or vegetation. **2.** highly productive, e.g. a fertile mind. **fertility** n. **fertilize** v. **1.** provide (an animal or plant) with sperm or pollen to bring about fertilization. **2.** supply (soil) with nutrients. **fertilization** n. **fertilizer** n. substance added to the soil to increase its productivity.

fervent, fervid adj. intensely passionate and sincere. **fervently** adv. **fervour, fervency** n. intensity of feeling.

fescue n. pasture and lawn grass with stiff narrow leaves.

festal adj. festive.

fester v. **1.** form or cause to form pus. **2.** rot, decay. **3.** become worse.

festival n. **1.** organized series of special events or performances. **2.** day or period of celebration. **festive** adj. of or like a celebration. **festivity** n., pl. **-ties. 1.** joyful celebration, merriment. —pl. **2.** celebrations.

festoon v. hang decorations in loops.

feta n. white salty Greek cheese.

fetal adj. see FETUS.

fetch v. **1.** go after and bring back. **2.** be sold for. **3.** Informal deal (a blow). **fetching** adj. attractive. **fetch up** v. Informal arrive or end up.

fete, fête [fate] n. **1.** gala, bazaar, etc., usu. held outdoors. —v. **2.** honour or entertain regally.

fetid adj. stinking.

fetish n. **1.** form of behaviour in which sexual pleasure is derived from looking at or handling an inanimate object. **2.** thing with which one is excessively concerned. **3.** object believed to have magical powers. **fetishism** n. **fetishist** n.

fetlock n. projection behind and above a horse's hoof.

fetter n. **1.** chain or shackle for the foot. —pl. **2.** restrictions. —v. **3.** restrict. **4.** bind in fetters.

fettle n. state of health or spirits.

fetus [fee-tuss] n., pl. **-tuses.** embryo of a mammal in the later stages of development. **fetal** adj.

feu *n.* in Scotland, right of use of land in return for a fixed annual payment.

feud *n.* **1.** long bitter hostility between two people or groups. —*v.* **2.** carry on a feud.

feudalism *n.* medieval system in which people held land from a lord, and in return worked and fought for him. **feudal** *adj.* of or like feudalism.

fever *n.* **1.** (illness causing) high body temperature. **2.** nervous excitement. **fevered** *adj.* **feverish** *adj.* **1.** suffering from fever. **2.** in a state of nervous excitement. **feverishly** *adv.* **fever pitch** state of great excitement.

few *adj.* not many. **a few** a small number. **good few, quite a few** several.
▷ *Few(er)* is used of things that can be counted: *Fewer than five visits.* Compare *less*, which is used for quantity: *It uses less sugar.*

fey *adj.* **1.** whimsically strange. **2.** clairvoyant.

fez *n., pl.* **fezzes.** brimless tasselled cap, orig. from Turkey.

ff *Music* fortissimo.

ff. and the following (pages).

fiancé [fee-on-say] *n.* man engaged to be married. **fiancée** *n. fem.*

fiasco *n., pl.* **-cos, -coes.** ridiculous or humiliating failure.

fiat [fee-at] *n.* **1.** arbitrary order. **2.** official permission.

fib *n.* **1.** trivial lie. —*v.* **fibbing, fibbed. 2.** tell a fib. **fibber** *n.*

fibre *n.* **1.** thread that can be spun into yarn. **2.** threadlike animal or plant tissue. **3.** essential substance or nature. **4.** strength of character. **5.** fibrous material in food. **fibrous** *adj.* **fibreboard** *n.* board made of compressed plant fibres. **fibreglass** *n.* material made of fine glass fibres. **fibre optics** transmission of information by light along very thin flexible fibres of glass.

fibrillation *n.* uncontrollable twitching of muscles, esp. those in the heart.

fibroid [fibe-royd] *adj.* benign tumour derived from fibrous connective tissue. **fibrositis** [fibe-roh-site-iss] *n.* inflammation of the tissues of muscle sheaths.

fibula [fib-yew-la] *n., pl.* **-lae, -las.** slender outer bone of the lower leg. **fibular** *adj.*

fiche [feesh] *n.* sheet of film for storing publications in miniaturized form.

fickle *adj.* changeable, inconstant. **fickleness** *n.*

fiction *n.* **1.** literary works of the imagination, such as novels. **2.** invented story. **fictional** *adj.* **fictionalize** *v.* turn into fiction. **fictitious** *adj.* **1.** not genuine. **2.** of or in fiction.

fiddle *n.* **1.** violin. **2.** *Informal* dishonest action or scheme. —*v.* **3.** play the violin. **4.** move or touch something restlessly. **5.** falsify (accounts). **fiddling** *adj.* trivial. **fiddly** *adj.* **-lier, -liest.** awkward to do or use. **fiddlesticks** *interj.* nonsense.

fidelity *n.* **1.** faithfulness. **2.** accuracy in detail. **3.** quality of sound reproduction.

fidget *v.* **1.** move about restlessly. —*n.* **2.** person who fidgets. —*pl.* **3.** restlessness. **fidgety** *adj.*

fiduciary [fid-yew-she-er-ee] *adj.* **1.** relating to a trust or trustee. —*n., pl.* **-aries. 2.** trustee.

fie *interj. Obs.* or *jocular* exclamation of distaste or mock dismay.

fief [feef] *n. Hist.* land granted by a lord in return for war service.

field *n.* **1.** enclosed piece of agricultural land. **2.** marked off area for sports. **3.** area rich in a specified natural resource. **4.** sphere of knowledge or activity. **5.** place away from the laboratory or classroom where practical work is done. **6.** all the competitors in a competition. **7.** all the competitors except the favourite. **8.** battlefield. **9.** area over which electric, gravitational, or magnetic force is exerted. **10.** background, as of a flag. —*v.* **11.** *Sport* catch and return (a ball). **12.** send (a player or team) on to the field. **13.** play as a fielder. **14.** deal with (a question) successfully. **fielder** *n. Sport* player whose task is to field the ball. **field day** day or time of exciting activity. **field events** throwing and jumping events in athletics. **fieldfare** *n.* type of large thrush. **field glasses** binoculars. **field hockey** *US* hockey played on grass, as distinguished from ice hockey. **field marshal** army officer of the highest rank. **fieldmouse** *n., pl.* **-mice.** nocturnal mouse that lives in fields and woods. **field sports** hunting, shooting, and fishing. **fieldwork** *n.* investigation made in the field as opposed to the classroom or the laboratory.

fiend [feend] *n.* **1.** evil spirit. **2.** cruel or wicked person. **3.** *Informal* person devoted to something, e.g. *fresh-air fiend*. **fiendish** *adj*. **1**. cruel. **2**. *Informal* cunning. **3**. *Informal* very difficult. **fiendishly** *adv*.

fierce *adj*. **1**. wild or aggressive. **2**. turbulent. **3**. intense. **fiercely** *adv*. **fierceness** *n*.

fiery [fire-ee] *adj*. **fierier, fieriest**. **1**. consisting of or like fire. **2**. easily angered. **3**. (of food) very spicy.

fiesta *n*. religious festival, carnival.

FIFA [fee-fa] Fédération Internationale de Football Association (International Association Football Federation).

fife *n*. small high-pitched flute.

fifteen *adj., n*. **1**. five and ten. —*n*. **2**. Rugby Union team. **fifteenth** *adj., n*.

fifth *adj., n*. **1**. (of) number five in a series. —*n*. **2**. one of five equal parts of something. **fifth column** group secretly helping the enemy.

fifty *adj., n., pl*. **-ties**. five times ten. **fifty-fifty** *Informal* —*adv*. **1**. equally divided, e.g. *they split the profits fifty-fifty*. —*adj*. **2**. having an equal chance of happening or not happening, e.g. *a fifty-fifty chance of success*. **fiftieth** *adj., n*.

fig *n*. **1**. soft pear-shaped fruit. **2**. tree bearing it. **fig leaf 1**. representation of the leaf of a fig tree, used to cover the genitals of a nude statue or painting. **2**. anything used to conceal something thought to be shameful.

fig. 1. figurative(ly). **2**. figure.

fight *v*. **fighting, fought**. **1**. struggle (against) in battle or physical combat. **2**. struggle to overcome someone or obtain something. **3**. carry on (a battle or struggle). **4**. make (a way) by fighting. —*n*. **5**. aggressive conflict between two (groups of) people. **6**. quarrel or contest. **7**. resistance. **8**. boxing match. **fighter** *n*. **1**. boxer. **2**. determined person. **3**. aircraft designed to destroy other aircraft. **fight off** *v*. **1**. repulse. **2**. struggle to avoid.

figment *n*. **figment of one's imagination** imaginary thing.

figure *n*. **1**. numerical symbol. **2**. amount expressed in numbers. **3**. bodily shape. **4**. well-known person. **5**. representation in painting or sculpture of a human form. **6**. diagram or illustration. **7**. set of movements in dancing or skating. **8**. *Maths* any combination of lines, planes, points, or curves. —*v*. **9**. *US* consider, conclude. **10**. (usu. foll. by *in*) be included (in). **11**. calculate. **figure of**

speech expression in which words do not have their literal meaning. **figurative** *adj*. (of language) abstract, imaginative, or symbolic. **figuratively** *adv*. **figurine** *n*. statuette. **figurehead** *n*. **1**. nominal leader. **2**. carved bust at the bow of a ship. **figure out** *v*. solve or understand.

filament *n*. **1**. fine wire in a light bulb that gives out light. **2**. fine thread.

filbert *n*. hazelnut.

filch *v*. steal (small amounts).

file[1] *n*. **1**. box or folder used to keep documents in order. **2**. documents in a file. **3**. information about a person or subject. **4**. line of people one behind the other. **5**. *Computers* organized collection of related material. —*v*. **6**. place (a document) in a file. **7**. place (a legal document) on official record. **8**. bring a lawsuit, esp. for divorce. **9**. walk or march in a line. **filing cabinet** piece of office furniture with deep drawers used for storing documents.

file[2] *n*. **1**. tool with a roughened blade for smoothing or shaping. —*v*. **2**. shape or smooth with a file. **filings** *pl. n*. shavings removed by a file.

filial *adj*. of or befitting a son or daughter.

filibuster *v*. **1**. obstruct legislation by making long speeches. —*n*. **2**. act of filibustering. **3**. person who filibusters.

filigree *n*. **1**. delicate ornamental work of gold or silver wire. —*adj*. **2**. made of filigree.

Filipino [fill-lip-pee-no] *n*. **1**. (*fem*. **Filipina**) person from the Philippines. —*adj*. **2**. of the Philippines.

fill *v*. **1**. make or become full. **2**. occupy completely. **3**. plug (a gap). **4**. satisfy (a need). **5**. hold and perform the duties of (a position). **6**. appoint to (a job or position). **one's fill** sufficient for one's needs or wants. **filler** *n*. substance that fills a gap or increases bulk. **fill in** *v*. **1**. complete (a form or drawing). **2**. act as a substitute. **3**. *Informal* give (a person) fuller details. **filling** *n*. **1**. substance that fills a gap or cavity, esp. in a tooth. —*adj*. **2**. (of food) substantial and satisfying. **filling station** garage selling petrol, oil, etc.

fillet *n*. **1**. boneless piece of meat or fish. —*v*. **filleting, filleted**. **2**. remove the bones from.

fillip *n*. something that adds stimulation or enjoyment.

filly n., pl. **-lies.** young female horse.

film n. **1.** sequence of images projected on a screen, creating the illusion of movement. **2.** story told in such a sequence of images. **3.** thin strip of light-sensitive cellulose used to make photographic negatives and transparencies. **4.** thin sheet or layer. —v. **5.** photograph with a movie or video camera. **6.** make a film of (a scene, story, etc.). **7.** cover or become covered with a thin layer. —adj. **8.** connected with cinema. **filmy** adj. **filmier, filmiest.** very thin, delicate. **film strip** set of pictures on a strip of film, projected separately as slides.

filter n. **1.** material or device permitting fluid to pass but retaining solid particles. **2.** device that blocks certain frequencies of sound or light. **3.** traffic signal that allows vehicles to turn either left or right while the main signals are at red. —v. **4.** pass slowly or faintly. **5.** remove impurities from (a substance) with a filter. **filter tip** (cigarette with) a built-in filter to reduce the amount of nicotine etc. inhaled by a smoker.

filth n. **1.** disgusting dirt. **2.** offensive material or language. **filthy** adj. **filthier, filthiest.** **filthily** adv. **filthiness** n.

filtrate n. **1.** filtered gas or liquid. —v. **2.** remove impurities with a filter. **filtration** n.

fin n. **1.** projection from a fish's body enabling it to balance and swim. **2.** vertical tailplane of an aircraft.

finagle [fin-**nay**-gl] v. get or achieve by craftiness or trickery.

final adj. **1.** at the end. **2.** having no possibility of further change, action, or discussion. —n. **3.** deciding contest between winners of previous rounds in a competition. —pl. **4.** last examinations in an educational course. **finally** adv. **finality** n. **finalist** n. competitor in a final. **finalize** v. put into final form. **finale** [fin-**nah**-lee] n. concluding part of a dramatic performance or musical work.

finance n. **1.** management of money. **2.** (provision of) funds. —pl. **3.** money resources. —v. **4.** provide funds for. **financial** adj. **financially** adv. **financier** n. person involved in large-scale financial business. **financial year** twelve-month period used for financial calculations.

finch n., pl. **finches.** small songbird with a stout bill.

find v. **finding, found. 1.** discover by chance. **2.** discover by search or effort. **3.**

become aware of. **4.** consider to have a particular quality. **5.** experience (a particular feeling). **6.** Law pronounce (the defendant) guilty or not guilty. **7.** provide, esp. with difficulty. —n. **8.** person or thing found, esp. when valuable. **finder** n. **finding** n. conclusion from an investigation. **find out** v. **1.** gain knowledge of. **2.** detect (a crime, deception, etc.).

fine[1] adj. **1.** very good. **2.** in good health. **3.** acceptable. **4.** thin or slender. **5.** in small particles. **6.** subtle or abstruse, e.g. a fine distinction. **7.** of delicate workmanship. **8.** (of weather) clear and dry. **finely** adv. **fineness** n. **finery** n. showy clothing. **fine art** produced to appeal to the sense of beauty. **fine-tune** v. make small adjustments to (something) so that it works really well.

fine[2] n. **1.** payment imposed as a penalty. —v. **2.** impose a fine on.

finesse [fin-**ness**] n. **1.** delicate skill. **2.** subtlety and tact.

finger n. **1.** one of the four long jointed parts of the hand. **2.** part of a glove that covers a finger. **3.** quantity of liquid in a glass as deep as a finger is wide. —v. **4.** touch or handle with the fingers. **fingering** n. technique of using the fingers in playing a musical instrument. **fingerboard** n. part of a stringed instrument against which the strings are pressed. **finger bowl** small bowl of water for diners to rinse their hands in at the table. **fingerprint** n. **1.** impression of the ridges on the tip of the finger. —v. **2.** take the fingerprints of (someone). **fingerstall** n. cover to protect an injured finger.

finial n. Archit. ornament at the apex of a gable or spire.

finicky adj. **1.** excessively particular, fussy. **2.** overelaborate.

finis n. Latin end: used at the end of a book.

finish v. **1.** bring to an end, stop. **2.** use up. **3.** bring to a desired or completed condition. **4.** put a surface texture on (wood, cloth, or metal). **5.** defeat or destroy. —n. **6.** end, last part. **7.** death or defeat. **8.** surface texture. **finishing school** private school for girls that teaches social graces.

finite [**fine**-ite] adj. having limits in space, time, or size.

Finn n. native of Finland. **Finnish** adj. **1.** of Finland. —n. **2.** official language of Finland.

finnan haddock, haddie *n.* smoked haddock.

fiord *n.* same as FJORD.

fipple flute *n.* end-blown flute with a plug (**fipple**) at the mouthpiece, such as a recorder.

fir *n.* pyramid-shaped tree with needle-like leaves and erect cones.

fire *n.* **1.** state of combustion producing heat, flames, and smoke. **2.** uncontrolled destructive burning. **3.** burning coal or wood, or a gas or electric device, used to heat a room. **4.** shooting of guns. **5.** intense passion, ardour. —*v.* **6.** operate (a weapon) so that a bullet or missile is released. **7.** *Informal* dismiss from employment. **8.** excite. **9.** bake (ceramics etc.) in a kiln. **10.** (of an internal-combustion engine) start. **firearm** *n.* rifle, pistol, or shotgun. **fireball** *n.* **1.** ball of fire at the centre of an explosion. **2.** *Slang* energetic person. **3.** large bright meteor. **firebrand** *n.* person who causes unrest. **firebreak** *n.* strip of cleared land to stop the advance of a fire. **firebrick** *n.* heat-resistant brick used for lining furnaces, fireplaces, etc. **fire brigade** organized body of people whose job is to put out fires. **firecracker** *n.* firework which produces a loud bang. **firedamp** *n.* explosive gas, composed mainly of methane, formed in mines. **fire drill** rehearsal of procedures for escape from a fire. **fire engine** vehicle with apparatus for extinguishing fires. **fire escape** metal staircase or ladder down the outside of a building for escape in the event of fire. **firefighter** *n.* same as FIREMAN. **firefly** *n., pl.* **-flies.** beetle that glows in the dark. **fireguard** *n.* protective grating in front of a fire. **fire irons** tongs, poker, and shovel for tending a domestic fire. **fireman** *n., pl.* **-men.** member of a fire brigade. **fireplace** *n.* recess in a room for a fire. **firepower** *n. Mil.* amount a weapon or unit can fire. **fireraiser** *n.* person who deliberately starts fires. **fire station** headquarters of a fire brigade. **fire trap** building which could easily catch fire or which would be difficult to escape from if it did. **firework** *n.* **1.** device containing chemicals that is ignited to produce spectacular explosions and coloured sparks. —*pl. n.* **2.** show of fireworks. **3.** *Informal* outburst of temper. **firing line** leading or most vulnerable position. **firing squad** group of soldiers ordered to execute an offender by shooting.

firkin *n.* small cask.

firm[1] *adj.* **1.** not soft or yielding. **2.** securely in position. **3.** definite. **4.** determined, resolute. —*adv.* **5.** in an unyielding manner, e.g. *hold firm.* —*v.* **6.** make or become firm. **firmly** *adv.* **firmness** *n.*

firm[2] *n.* business company.

firmament *n. Lit.* sky, heavens.

first *adj.* **1.** earliest in time or order. **2.** graded or ranked above all others. —*n.* **3.** person or thing coming before all others. **4.** outset, beginning. **5.** first-class honours degree at university. **6.** lowest forward gear in a motor vehicle. —*adv.* **7.** before anything else. **8.** for the first time. **firstly** *adv.* **first aid** immediate medical assistance given in an emergency. **first-class** *adj.* **1.** of the highest quality. **2.** excellent. **first-foot** *Scot.* —*n., pl.* **first-foots. 1.** first person to enter a house in the New Year. —*v.* **2.** visit (someone) as a first-foot. **first-footing** *n.* **firsthand** *adj., adv.* (obtained) directly from the original source. **first mate, officer** officer of a merchant ship second in command to the captain. **first person** *Grammar* category of verbs and pronouns used by a speaker to refer to himself or herself. **first-rate** *adj.* excellent. **first refusal** right to buy something before it is offered to others. **first-strike** *adj.* (of a nuclear missile) for use in an opening attack to destroy enemy weapons.

firth *n.* narrow inlet of the sea.

fiscal *adj.* of government finances, esp. taxes.

fish *n., pl.* **fish, fishes. 1.** cold-blooded vertebrate with gills, that lives in water. **2.** its flesh as food. —*v.* **3.** try to catch fish. **4.** try to catch fish in (a specified place). **5.** (foll. by *for*) grope for and find with difficulty. **6.** (foll. by *for*) seek indirectly. **fisherman** *n., pl.* **-men.** person who catches fish for a living or for pleasure. **fishery** *n., pl.* **-eries.** area of the sea used for fishing. **fishing** *n.* job or pastime of catching fish. **fishy** *adj.* **fishier, fishiest. 1.** of or like fish. **2.** *Informal* suspicious or questionable. **fish finger** oblong piece of fish covered in breadcrumbs. **fish meal** dried ground fish used as animal feed or fertilizer. **fishmonger** *n.* seller of fish. **fishnet** *n.* open mesh fabric resembling netting. **fishwife** *n., pl.* **-wives.** coarse scolding woman.

fishplate *n.* metal plate holding rails together.

fission *n.* **1.** splitting. **2.** *Biol.* asexual reproduction involving a division into two or more equal parts. **3.** splitting of an atomic nucleus with the release of a large amount of energy. **fissionable** adj. **fissile** adj. **1.** capable of undergoing nuclear fission. **2.** tending to split.

fissure [fish-er] n. long narrow cleft or crack.

fist n. clenched hand. **fisticuffs** pl. n. fighting with the fists.

fistula [fist-yew-la] n. long narrow ulcer.

fit[1] v. **fitting, fitted. 1.** be appropriate or suitable for. **2.** be of the correct size or shape (for). **3.** adjust so as to make appropriate. **4.** try (clothes) on and note any adjustments needed. **5.** make competent or ready. **6.** correspond with the facts or circumstances. —adj. **7.** appropriate. **8.** in good health. **9.** worthy or deserving. —n. **10.** way in which something fits. **fitness** n. **fitted** adj. **1.** (of a carpet) covering a floor completely. **2.** (of a kitchen, bathroom, etc.) having equipment and furniture built or selected to suit the measurements of the room. **fitter** n. **1.** person skilled in the installation and adjustment of machinery. **2.** person who fits garments. **fitting** adj. **1.** appropriate, suitable. —n. **2.** accessory or part. **3.** trying on of clothes for size. —pl. **4.** furnishings and accessories in a building. **fitment** n. detachable part of the furnishings of a room. **fit in** v. **1.** give a place or time to. **2.** belong or conform. **fit out** v. provide with the necessary equipment.

fit[2] n. **1.** sudden attack or convulsion, such as an epileptic seizure. **2.** sudden short burst or spell.

fitful adj. occurring in irregular spells. **fitfully** adv.

five adj., n. one more than four. **fiver** n. Informal five-pound note. **fives** n. ball game resembling squash but played with bats or the hands.

fix v. **1.** make or become firm, stable, or secure. **2.** place permanently. **3.** settle definitely. **4.** direct (the eyes etc.) steadily. **5.** repair. **6.** Informal unfairly influence the outcome of. —n. **7.** Informal difficult situation. **8.** ascertaining of the position of a ship by radar etc. **9.** Slang injection of a narcotic drug. **fixed** adj. **fixedly** [fix-id-lee] adv. steadily. **fixer** n. **1.** solution used to make a photographic image permanent. **2.** Slang person who arranges things. **fix up** v. **1.** arrange. **2.** provide (with).

fixation n. preoccupation, obsession. **fixated** adj. obsessed.

fixative n. liquid used to preserve or hold things in place.

fixture n. **1.** permanently fitted piece of household equipment. **2.** person whose presence seems permanent. **3.** sports match or the date fixed for it.

fizz v. **1.** give off small bubbles. **2.** make a hissing or bubbling noise. —n. **3.** hissing or bubbling noise. **4.** releasing of small bubbles of gas by a liquid. **5.** effervescent drink. **fizzy** adj. **fizzier, fizziest. fizziness** n.

fizzle v. make a weak hissing or bubbling sound. **fizzle out** v. Informal come to nothing, fail.

fjord [fee-ord] n. long narrow inlet of the sea between cliffs, esp. in Norway.

FL Florida.

flab n. Informal unsightly body fat.

flabbergast v. amaze utterly.

flabby adj. **-bier, -biest. 1.** loose or limp. **2.** having flabby flesh. **flabbiness** n.

flaccid [flas-sid] adj. soft and limp. **flaccidity** n.

flag[1] n. **1.** piece of cloth attached to a pole as an emblem or signal. —v. **flagging, flagged. 2.** mark with a flag or sticker. **3.** (often foll. by down) signal (a vehicle) to stop by waving the arm. **flag day** day on which small stickers are sold in the streets for charity. **flagpole, flagstaff** n. pole for a flag. **flagship** n. **1.** admiral's ship. **2.** most important product of an organization.

flag[2] v. **flagging, flagged.** lose enthusiasm or vigour.

flag[3], **flagstone** n. flat paving-stone. **flagged** adj. paved with flagstones.

flag[4] n. any of various plants with sword-shaped leaves, esp. the iris.

flagellate [flaj-a-late] v. **1.** whip, esp. in religious penance or for sexual pleasure. **2.** criticize severely. **flagellation** n. **flagellant** n. person who whips himself.

flagellum [flaj-jell-lum] n., pl. **-la** [-la], **-s. 1.** Biol. whiplike outgrowth from a cell that acts as an organ of movement. **2.** Botany long thin shoot.

flageolet [flaj-a-let] n. small instrument like a recorder.

flagon n. **1.** wide bottle for wine or cider. **2.** narrow-necked jug for liquid.

flagrant [flayg-rant] *adj.* openly outrageous. **flagrantly** *adv.* **flagrancy** *n.*

flail *v.* 1. wave about wildly. 2. beat or thrash. —*n.* 3. tool formerly used for threshing grain by hand.

flair *n.* 1. natural ability. 2. stylishness.

flak *n.* 1. anti-aircraft fire. 2. *Informal* adverse criticism.

flake *n.* 1. small thin piece, esp. chipped off something. —*v.* 2. peel off in flakes. **flaky** *adj.* **flakier, flakiest. flake out** *v. Informal* collapse or fall asleep from exhaustion.

flambé [flahm-bay] *v.* **flambéing, flambéed.** cook or serve (food) in flaming brandy.

flamboyant *adj.* 1. very bright and showy. 2. behaving in a very noticeable, extravagant way. **flamboyance** *n.*

flame *n.* 1. luminous burning gas coming from burning material. —*v.* 2. burn brightly. 3. become bright red. **old flame** *Informal* former sweetheart.

flamenco *n., pl.* **-cos.** 1. rhythmical Spanish dance accompanied by a guitar and vocalist. 2. music for this dance.

flamingo *n., pl.* **-gos, -goes.** large pink wading bird with a long neck and legs.

flammable *adj.* easily set on fire. **flammability** *n.*
▷ This now replaces *inflammable* in labelling and packaging because *inflammable* was often mistaken to mean 'not flammable'.

flan *n.* open sweet or savoury tart.

flange *n.* projecting rim or collar. **flanged** *adj.*

flank *n.* 1. part of the side between the hips and ribs. 2. side of a body of troops. —*v.* 3. be at or move along the side of.

flannel *n.* 1. soft woollen fabric for clothing. 2. small piece of cloth for washing the face and hands. 3. *Informal* evasive talk. —*pl.* 4. trousers made of flannel. —*v.* **-nelling, -nelled.** 5. *Informal* talk evasively. **flannelette** *n.* cotton imitation of flannel.

flap *v.* **flapping, flapped.** 1. move back and forwards or up and down. —*n.* 2. action or sound of flapping. 3. piece of something attached by one edge only. 4. hinged section of an aircraft's wing, the angle of which can be altered to assist with take-off and landing. 5. *Informal* state of excitement or panic.

flapjack *n.* chewy biscuit made with oats.

flare *v.* 1. blaze with a sudden unsteady flame. 2. *Informal* (of temper, violence, or trouble) break out suddenly. 3. (of a skirt or trousers) become wider towards the hem. —*n.* 4. sudden unsteady flame. 5. signal light. —*pl.* 6. flared trousers. **flared** *adj.* (of a skirt or trousers) becoming wider towards the hem.

flash *n.* 1. sudden burst of light or flame. 2. sudden occurrence (of intuition or emotion). 3. very short time. 4. brief unscheduled news announcement. 5. *Photog.* small bulb that produces an intense flash of light. —*v.* 6. (cause to) burst into flame. 7. (cause to) emit light suddenly or intermittently. 8. move very fast. 9. come rapidly (to mind or view). 10. *Informal* display ostentatiously. 11. *Slang* expose oneself indecently. —*adj.* (also **flashy**) 12. vulgarly showy. **flasher** *n. Slang* man who exposes himself indecently. **flashback** *n.* scene in a book, play, or film, that shows earlier events. **flash flood** sudden short-lived flood. **flashlight** *n. US* torch. **flash point** 1. critical point beyond which a situation will inevitably erupt into violence. 2. lowest temperature at which vapour given off by a liquid can ignite.

flashing *n.* watertight material used to cover joins in a roof.

flask *n.* 1. vacuum flask. 2. flat bottle for carrying alcoholic drink in the pocket. 3. narrow-necked bottle.

flat[1] *adj.* **flatter, flattest.** 1. level and horizontal. 2. even, smooth. 3. (of a tyre) deflated. 4. outright. 5. fixed. 6. without variation or emotion. 7. (of a battery) with no electrical charge. 8. (of a drink) no longer fizzy. 9. *Music* below the true pitch. —*adv.* 10. in or into a flat position. 11. exactly. 12. completely, absolutely. 13. *Music* too low in pitch. —*n.* 14. flat surface. 15. *Music* symbol lowering the pitch of a note by a semitone. 16. punctured car tyre. 17. level ground. 18. mudbank exposed at low tide. **flat out** with maximum speed or effort. **flatly** *adv.* **flatness** *n.* **flatten** *v.* **flatfish** *n.* sea fish, such as the sole, which has a flat body. **flat-footed** *adj.* 1. having a less than usually arched instep. 2. clumsy or insensitive. **flat racing** horse racing over level ground with no jumps.

flat[2] *n.* set of rooms for living in which are part of a larger building. **flatlet** *n.* small flat. **flatmate** *n.* person one shares a flat with.

flatter *v.* 1. praise insincerely. 2. show to

advantage. **3.** make (a person) appear more attractive in a picture than in reality. **flatterer** n. **flattery** n.

flatulent adj. suffering from, or caused by, excess gas in the intestines. **flatulence** n.

flaunt v. display (oneself or one's possessions) arrogantly.
▷ Be careful not to confuse this with *flout* meaning 'disobey'.

flautist [flaw-tist] n. flute player.

flavour n. **1.** distinctive taste. **2.** distinctive characteristic or quality. —v. **3.** give flavour to. **flavouring** n. substance used to flavour food. **flavourless** adj.

flaw n. **1.** imperfection or blemish. **2.** mistake that makes a plan or argument invalid. **flawed** adj. **flawless** adj.

flax n. **1.** plant grown for its stem fibres and seeds. **2.** its fibres, spun into linen thread. **flaxen** adj. (of hair) pale yellow.

flay v. **1.** strip the skin off. **2.** criticize severely.

flea n. small wingless jumping bloodsucking insect. **flea market** market for cheap goods. **fleapit** n. *Informal* shabby cinema or theatre.

fleck n. **1.** small mark, streak, or speck. —v. **2.** speckle.

fled v. past of FLEE.

fledged adj. **1.** (of young birds) able to fly. **2.** (of people) fully trained. **fledgling, fledgeling** n. **1.** young bird. —adj. **2.** new, inexperienced.

flee v. **fleeing, fled.** run away (from).

fleece n. **1.** sheep's coat of wool. **2.** sheepskin used as a lining for coats etc. —v. **3.** defraud or overcharge. **fleecy** adj. made of or like fleece.

fleet[1] n. **1.** number of warships organized as a unit. **2.** number of vehicles under the same ownership.

fleet[2] adj. swift in movement. **fleeting** adj. rapid and soon passing. **fleetingly** adv.

Fleet Street n. **1.** street in London where many newspaper offices were formerly situated. **2.** British national newspapers collectively.

Flemish n. **1.** one of two official languages of Belgium. —adj. **2.** of Flanders, an area in Belgium, northern France and the southern Netherlands.

flesh n. **1.** soft part of a human or animal body. **2.** *Informal* excess fat. **3.** meat of animals as opposed to fish or fowl. **4.** thick soft part of a fruit or vegetable. **5.** human body as opposed to the soul. —adj. **6.** yellowish-pink. **in the flesh** in person, actually present. **one's own flesh and blood** one's family. **fleshly** adj. **1.** carnal. **2.** worldly. **fleshy** adj. **fleshier, fleshiest. 1.** plump. **2.** like flesh. **flesh wound** wound affecting only superficial tissue.

fleur-de-lis, fleur-de-lys [flur-de-lee] n., pl. **fleurs-de-lis, fleurs-de-lys.** heraldic lily with three petals.

flew v. past tense of FLY[1].

flex n. **1.** flexible insulated electric cable. —v. **2.** bend. **flexible** adj. **1.** easily bent. **2.** adaptable. **flexibly** adv. **flexibility** n. **flexitime** n. system permitting variation in starting and finishing times of work.

flibbertigibbet n. flighty gossiping person.

flick v. **1.** touch or strike quickly and lightly with or as if with a finger. **2.** move with a short sudden movement, often repeatedly, e.g. *the windscreen wipers flicked back and forth.* —n. **3.** tap or quick stroke. —pl. **4.** *Slang* the cinema. **flick knife** knife with a spring-loaded blade which shoots out when a button is pressed. **flick through** v. look at (a book or magazine) quickly or idly.

flicker v. **1.** shine unsteadily or intermittently. **2.** move quickly to and fro. —n. **3.** unsteady brief light. **4.** brief faint indication.

flier n. **1.** see FLY[1]. **2.** small advertising leaflet.

flight[1] n. **1.** act or manner of flying through the air. **2.** journey by air. **3.** group of birds or aircraft flying together. **4.** aircraft flying on a scheduled journey. **5.** set of stairs between two landings. **6.** mental soaring above the everyday world, e.g. *a flight of fancy.* **7.** stabilizing feathers or plastic fins on an arrow or dart. **flightless** adj. (of certain birds or insects) unable to fly. **flight deck 1.** crew compartment in an airliner. **2.** runway deck on an aircraft carrier. **flight lieutenant** junior commissioned officer in an air force. **flight recorder** electronic device in an aircraft storing information about its flight.

flight[2] n. act of running away.

flighty adj. **flightier, flightiest.** frivolous and fickle.

flimsy adj. **-sier, -siest. 1.** not strong or

substantial. **2.** thin. **3.** unconvincing, weak. **flimsily** *adv.* **flimsiness** *n.*

flinch *v.* draw back or wince, as from pain. **flinch from** *v.* shrink from, avoid.

fling *v.* **flinging, flung. 1.** throw, send, or move forcefully or hurriedly. —*n.* **2.** spell of self-indulgent enjoyment. **3.** brief romantic or sexual relationship. **fling oneself into** (start to) do with great vigour.

flint *n.* **1.** hard grey stone. **2.** piece of this. **3.** small piece of an iron alloy producing a spark when struck, as in a cigarette lighter. **flinty** *adj.* **1.** cruel. **2.** of or like flint. **flintlock** *n.* obsolete gun in which the powder was lit by a spark from a flint.

flip *v.* **flipping, flipped. 1.** throw (something small or light) carelessly. **2.** turn (something) over. **3.** throw (a coin) so that it turns over in the air. **4.** (also **flip one's lid**) *Slang* fly into an emotional state. —*n.* **5.** snap or tap. **6.** alcoholic drink containing beaten egg. —*adj.* **7.** *Informal* flippant. **flipper** *n.* **1.** limb of a sea animal adapted for swimming. **2.** one of a pair of paddle-like rubber devices worn on the feet to help in swimming. **flipchart** *n.* large pad of paper mounted on a stand, used in giving lectures etc. **flip-flop** *n.* rubber-soled sandal held on by a thong between the big toe and the next toe. **flip side** less important side of a record. **flip through** *v.* look at (a book or magazine) quickly or idly.

flippant *adj.* treating serious things lightly. **flippantly** *adv.* **flippancy** *n.*

flirt *v.* **1.** behave amorously without emotional commitment. **2.** consider lightly, toy (with). —*n.* **3.** person who flirts. **flirtation** *n.* **flirtatious** *adj.*

flit *v.* **flitting, flitted. 1.** move lightly and rapidly. **2.** *Scot.* move house. **3.** *Informal* depart hurriedly and secretly. —*n.* **4.** act of flitting.

flitch *n.* side of bacon.

flitter *v., n.* same as FLUTTER.

float *v.* **1.** rest on the surface of a liquid. **2.** move lightly and freely. **3.** move about aimlessly. **4.** launch (a company). **5.** offer for sale on the stock market. **6.** allow (a currency) to fluctuate against other currencies. —*n.* **7.** light object on a fishing line that moves when a fish bites. **8.** light object used to help someone or something float. **9.** small delivery vehicle. **10.** motor vehicle carrying a tableau in a parade. **11.** sum of money

used for minor expenses or to provide change. **floating** *adj.* **1.** moving about, changing, e.g. *floating population.* **2.** (of a voter) not committed to one party.

flocculent *adj.* like tufts of wool.

flock[1] *n.* **1.** number of animals of one kind together. **2.** large group of people. **3.** *Christianity* congregation. —*v.* **4.** gather in a crowd.

flock[2] *n.* **1.** very small tufts of wool giving a raised pattern on wallpaper. **2.** wool or cotton waste used as stuffing.

floe *n.* sheet of floating ice.

flog *v.* **flogging, flogged. 1.** beat with a whip, stick, etc. **2.** *Slang* sell. **flogging** *n.*

flood *n.* **1.** overflow of water onto a normally dry area. **2.** large amount of water. **3.** rising of the tide. —*v.* **4.** cover or become covered with water. **5.** fill to overflowing. **6.** come in large numbers or quantities. **7.** supply excess petrol to (an engine) so that it does not work properly. **floodgate** *n.* gate used to control the flow of water. **floodlight** *n.* **1.** lamp that casts a broad intense beam of light. —*v.* **-lighting, -lit. 2.** illuminate by floodlight.

floor *n.* **1.** lower surface of a room. **2.** level of a building. **3.** flat bottom surface. **4.** (right to speak in) a legislative hall. —*v.* **5.** *Informal* disconcert or defeat. **6.** knock down. **7.** cover with a floor. **flooring** *n.* material for floors. **floorboard** *n.* long plank used for making floors. **floor show** entertainment in a nightclub.

floozy *n., pl.* **-zies.** *Slang* disreputable woman.

flop *v.* **flopping, flopped. 1.** bend, fall, or collapse loosely or carelessly. **2.** *Informal* fail. —*n.* **3.** flopping movement. **4.** *Informal* failure. **floppy** *adj.* **floppier, floppiest.** hanging downwards, loose. **floppiness** *n.* **floppy disk** *Computers* flexible magnetic disk that stores information.

flora *n.* plants of a given time or place.

floral *adj.* consisting of or decorated with flowers.

floret [flaw-ret] *n.* small flower forming part of a composite flower head.

floribunda *n.* type of rose whose flowers grow in large clusters.

florid *adj.* **1.** with a red or flushed complexion. **2.** ornate.

florin n. former British coin equivalent to ten pence.

florist n. seller of flowers.

floss n. fine silky fibres. **flossy** adj.

flotation n. launching or financing of a business enterprise.

flotilla n. **1.** fleet of small ships. **2.** small fleet.

flotsam n. floating wreckage. **flotsam and jetsam 1.** odds and ends. **2.** homeless or vagrant people.

flounce[1] v. **1.** go with emphatic movements. —n. **2.** flouncing movement.

flounce[2] n. ornamental ruffle on a garment.

flounder[1] v. **1.** move with difficulty, as in mud. **2.** behave or speak in a bungling or hesitating manner.

flounder[2] n. edible flatfish.

flour n. **1.** powder made by grinding grain, esp. wheat. —v. **2.** sprinkle with flour. **floury** adj. **flouriness** n.

flourish v. **1.** be active, successful, or widespread. **2.** be at the peak of development. **3.** wave (something) dramatically. —n. **4.** dramatic waving motion. **5.** ornamental curly line in writing. **6.** fanfare. **flourishing** adj.

flout [rhymes with **out**] v. deliberately disobey (a rule, law, etc.).
▷ Be careful not to confuse this with *flaunt* meaning 'display'.

flow v. **1.** (of liquid) move in a stream. **2.** (of blood or electricity) circulate. **3.** proceed smoothly. **4.** hang loosely. **5.** be abundant. —n. **6.** act, rate, or manner of flowing. **7.** continuous stream or discharge. **flow chart** diagram showing a sequence of operations in a process.

flower n. **1.** part of a plant that produces seeds. **2.** plant grown for its colourful flowers. **3.** best or finest part. —v. **4.** produce flowers, bloom. **5.** come to prime condition. **in flower** with flowers open. **flowered** adj. decorated with a floral design. **flowery** adj. **1.** decorated with a floral design. **2.** (of language or style) elaborate. **flowerbed** n. piece of ground for growing flowers on.

flown v. past participle of FLY[1].

fl. oz. fluid ounce(s).

flu n. short for INFLUENZA.

fluctuate v. change frequently and erratically. **fluctuation** n.

flue n. passage or pipe for smoke or hot air.

fluent adj. **1.** able to speak or write with ease. **2.** spoken or written with ease. **fluently** adv. **fluency** n.

fluff n. **1.** soft fibres. **2.** down. **3.** *Informal* mistake. —v. **4.** make or become soft and light. **5.** *Informal* make a mistake. **fluffy** adj. **fluffier**, **fluffiest**.

fluid n. **1.** substance able to flow and change its shape; a liquid or a gas. —adj. **2.** able to flow or change shape easily. **fluidity** n. **fluid ounce** one twentieth of a pint.

fluke[1] n. accidental stroke of luck. **fluky** adj.

fluke[2] n. **1.** flat triangular point of an anchor. **2.** lobe of a whale's tail.

fluke[3] n. parasitic worm.

flume n. **1.** narrow sloping channel for water. **2.** enclosed water slide at a swimming pool.

flummox v. perplex or bewilder.

flung v. past of FLING.

flunk v. *US & NZ informal* fail.

flunky, flunkey n., pl. **flunkies, flunkeys.** **1.** manservant who wears a livery. **2.** servile person.

fluorescence n. emission of light from a substance bombarded by particles, such as electrons, or by radiation. **fluorescent** adj. **fluorescent lamp** lamp in which ultraviolet radiation causes the chemical lining of a glass tube to glow. **fluoresce** v. exhibit fluorescence.

fluoride n. compound containing fluorine. **fluoridate** v. add fluoride to (water) as protection against tooth decay. **fluoridation** n.

fluorine n. toxic yellow gas, most reactive of all the elements.

fluorspar n. mineral consisting of calcium fluoride.

flurry n., pl. **-ries. 1.** sudden commotion. **2.** squall or gust of rain, wind, or snow. —v. **-rying, -ried. 3.** fluster.

flush[1] v. **1.** blush or cause to blush. **2.** send water through (a toilet or pipe) so as to clean it. **3.** elate. —n. **4.** blush. **5.** rush of water. **6.** excitement or elation. **flushed** adj.

flush[2] adj. **1.** level with the surrounding surface. **2.** *Informal* having plenty of money.

flush[3] n. in card games, hand all of one suit.

flush[4] v. drive out of a hiding place.

fluster v. **1.** make nervous or upset. —n. **2.** nervous or upset state.

flute n. **1.** wind instrument consisting of a tube with sound holes and a mouth hole in the side. **2.** decorative groove. **fluted** adj. having decorative grooves. **fluting** n. **flutist** n. US flautist.

flutter v. **1.** wave rapidly. **2.** flap the wings. **3.** move quickly and irregularly. **4.** (of the heart) beat abnormally quickly. —n. **5.** flapping movement. **6.** nervous agitation. **7.** Informal small bet. **8.** abnormally fast heartbeat.

fluvial [flew-vee-al] adj. of rivers.

flux n. **1.** constant change or instability. **2.** flow or discharge. **3.** substance mixed with metal to assist in fusion. **4.** Physics strength of a field in a given area.

fly¹ v. **flying, flew, flown. 1.** move through the air on wings or in an aircraft. **2.** control the flight of. **3.** float, flutter, display, or be displayed in the air. **4.** transport or be transported by air. **5.** move quickly or suddenly. **6.** (of time) pass rapidly. **7.** flee. —n., pl. **flies. 8.** (often pl.) fastening at the front of trousers. **9.** flap forming the entrance to a tent. —pl. **10.** space above a stage, used for storage. **flyer, flier** n. aviator. **fly-by-night** adj. Informal unreliable or untrustworthy. **flyleaf** n. blank leaf at the beginning or end of a book. **flyover** n. road passing over another by a bridge. **flywheel** n. heavy wheel regulating the speed of a machine.

fly² n., pl. **flies.** two-winged insect, esp. the housefly. **blyblown** adj. covered with blue-bottle eggs. **flycatcher** n. small insect-eating songbird. **fly-fishing** n. fishing with an artificial fly as a lure. **flypaper** n. paper with a sticky poisonous coating, used to kill flies. **flyweight** n. boxer weighing up to 112lb (professional) or 51kg (amateur).

fly³ adj. Slang sharp and cunning.

flying adj. hurried, brief. **flying boat** aircraft fitted with floats instead of landing wheels. **flying buttress** Archit. buttress supporting a wall by an arch. **flying colours** conspicuous success, e.g. pass with flying colours. **flying fish** fish with winglike fins used for gliding above the water. **flying fox** large fruit-eating bat. **flying officer** junior officer in an air force. **flying saucer** unidentified disc-shaped flying object, supposedly from outer space. **flying squad** small group

of police, soldiers, etc., ready to act quickly. **flying start** very good start.

Fm Chem. fermium.

FM frequency modulation.

f-number n. Photog. ratio of the effective diameter of a lens to its focal length.

foal n. **1.** young of a horse or related animal. —v. **2.** give birth to a foal.

foam n. **1.** mass of small bubbles on a liquid. **2.** frothy saliva. **3.** light spongelike solid used for insulation, packing, etc. —v. **4.** produce foam. **5.** become furious, esp. in foam at the mouth. **foamy** adj. **foamier, foamiest.**

fob¹ n. **1.** short watch chain. **2.** small pocket in a waistcoat.

fob² v. **fobbing, fobbed. 1.** (foll. by off) pretend to satisfy (a person) with lies or excuses. **2.** sell or pass off (something inferior) as valuable.

fo'c's'le n. same as FORECASTLE.

focus n., pl. **-cuses, -ci** [-sye] **1.** point at which light or sound waves converge. **2.** state of an optical image when it is clearly defined. **3.** state of an instrument producing such an image. **4.** centre of interest or activity. —v. **-cusing, -cused** or **-cussing, -cussed. 5.** bring or come into focus. **6.** concentrate (on). **focal** adj. of or at a focus. **focal length** distance from a lens or a mirror to its focal point. **focal point 1.** point where the object seen in a lens or a mirror is in perfect focus. **2.** centre of interest or attention.

fodder n. feed for livestock.

foe n. enemy, opponent.

foetid adj. same as FETID.

foetus n., pl. **-tuses.** same as FETUS.

fog n. **1.** mass of condensed water vapour in the lower air, often greatly reducing visibility. **2.** blurred area on a developed photograph. —v. **fogging, fogged. 3.** cover with steam. **foggy** adj. **foggier, foggiest. fog-bound** adj. prevented from operating by fog. **foghorn** n. large horn sounded to warn ships in fog.

fogy, fogey n., pl. **-gies, -geys.** old-fashioned person.

foible n. minor weakness, idiosyncrasy.

foil¹ v. ruin (someone's plan).

foil² n. **1.** metal in a thin sheet. **2.** anything which sets off another thing to advantage.

foil³ n. light slender flexible sword tipped with a button.

foist v. (usu. foll. by on) force or impose on.

fold¹ v. **1.** bend so that one part covers another. **2.** interlace (the arms). **3.** clasp (in the arms). **4.** Cooking mix gently. **5.** Informal fail. —n. **6.** folded piece or part. **7.** mark, crease, or hollow made by folding. **folder** n. piece of folded cardboard for holding loose papers.

fold² n. **1.** enclosure for sheep. **2.** church or its members.

foliage n. leaves. **foliaceous** adj. of or like leaves. **foliate** adj. **1.** having leaves. **2.** leaflike. **foliation** n. process of producing leaves.

folio n., pl. -lios. **1.** sheet of paper folded in half to make two leaves of a book. **2.** book made up of such sheets. **3.** page number.

folk n. **1.** people in general. **2.** race of people. **3.** Informal folk music. —pl. **4.** relatives. **folksy** adj. simple and unpretentious. **folk dance** traditional country dance. **folklore** n. traditional beliefs and stories of a people. **folk music 1.** music handed down from generation to generation. **2.** piece written in the style of such music. **folk song 1.** song handed down among the common people. **2.** modern song like this. **folk singer** n.

follicle n. small cavity in the body, esp. one from which a hair grows.

follow v. **1.** go or come after. **2.** be a logical or natural consequence of. **3.** keep to the course or track of. **4.** act in accordance with. **5.** accept the ideas or beliefs of. **6.** understand. **7.** have a keen interest in. **follower** n. disciple or supporter. **following** adj. **1.** about to be mentioned. **2.** next in time. —n. **3.** group of supporters. —prep. **4.** as a result of. **follow-on** n. Cricket immediate second innings forced on a team scoring a set number of runs fewer than its opponents in the first innings. **follow through** v. **1.** continue an action or series of actions until finished. **2.** Sport continue a stroke, kick, etc. after striking the ball. **follow up** v. **1.** investigate. **2.** do a second, often similar, thing after (a first). **follow-up** n. something done to reinforce an initial action.

folly n., pl. -lies. **1.** foolishness. **2.** foolish action or idea. **3.** useless extravagant building.

foment [foam-ent] v. encourage or stir up (trouble). **fomentation** n.

fond adj. **1.** tender, loving. **2.** unlikely to be realized, e.g. a fond hope. **3.** indulgent. **fond of having a liking for. fondly** adv. **fondness** n.

fondant n. (sweet made from) flavoured paste of sugar and water.

fondle v. caress.

fondue n. Swiss dish typically of a hot melted cheese sauce into which pieces of bread are dipped.

font n. bowl in a church for baptismal water.

fontanelle n. soft membranous gap between the bones of a baby's skull.

food n. what one eats, solid nourishment. **foodie** n. Informal gourmet. **food chain** Ecology series of living organisms each member of which feeds on another in the chain and is in turn eaten. **food poisoning** illness caused by eating contaminated food. **food processor** machine for chopping, liquidizing, or mixing food. **foodstuff** n. substance used as food.

fool¹ n. **1.** person lacking sense or judgment. **2.** person made to appear ridiculous. **3.** Hist. jester, clown. —v. **4.** deceive (someone). **foolish** adj. unwise, silly, or absurd. **foolishly** adv. **foolishness** n. **foolery** n. foolish behaviour. **fool around** v. act or play irresponsibly or aimlessly. **foolproof** adj. unable to fail. **fool's paradise** state of illusory happiness and security.

fool² n. dessert of puréed fruit mixed with cream.

foolhardy adj. recklessly adventurous. **foolhardily** adv. **foolhardiness** n.

foolscap n. size of paper, 13.5 by 17 inches.

foot n., pl. **feet. 1.** part of the leg below the ankle. **2.** unit of length of twelve inches (0.3048 metre). **3.** lowest part of anything. **4.** unit of poetic rhythm. **5.** Obs. infantry. **foot it** Informal walk. **foot the bill** pay the entire cost. **footage** n. amount of film used. **foot-and-mouth disease** infectious viral disease of sheep, cattle, etc. **footbridge** n. bridge for pedestrians. **footfall** n. sound of a footstep. **foothills** pl. n. hills at the foot of a mountain. **foothold** n. **1.** small place giving a secure grip for the foot. **2.** secure position from which progress may be made. **footlights** pl. n. lights across the front of a stage. **footloose** adj. free from ties. **footman** n. male servant in livery. **footnote** n. note printed at the foot of a page. **footpath** n. narrow path for walkers only. **footplate** n. platform in the cab of a locomotive for the driver. **footprint** n. mark left by a foot. **footsore** adj. having sore or tired feet. **footstep** n. 1. step in walking. 2. sound made by walking. **footstool** n. low stool used to rest the feet on while sitting. **footwear** n. anything worn to cover the feet. **footwork** n. skilful use of the feet, as in sport or dancing.

football n. 1. game played by two teams of eleven players kicking a ball in an attempt to score goals, soccer. 2. any of various similar games, such as rugby. 3. ball used for this. **footballer** n. **football pools** form of gambling on the results of football matches.

footing n. 1. secure grip by or for the feet. 2. basis, foundation. 3. relationship between people.

footle v. (often foll. by around or about) Informal loiter aimlessly. **footling** adj. trivial.

footsie n. Informal flirtation involving the touching together of feet.

fop n. man excessively concerned with fashion. **foppery** n. **foppish** adj.

for prep. 1. intended to be received or used by. 2. in order to help or benefit. 3. representing, e.g. speaking for the opposition. 4. because of, e.g. I could not see for the fog. 5. over a span of (time or distance). 6. in the direction of, e.g. heading for the border. 7. at a cost of. 8. in favour of, e.g. vote for me. —conj. 9. because. **for it** Informal liable for punishment or blame.

forage [for-ridge] v. 1. search about (for). —n. 2. food for cattle or horses.

foray n. 1. brief raid or attack. 2. first attempt or new undertaking.

forbear[1] v. cease or refrain (from doing something). **forbearance** n. tolerance, patience. **forbearing** adj.

forbear[2] n. same as FOREBEAR.

forbid v. prohibit, refuse to allow. **forbidden** adj. **forbidden fruit** anything attractive because prohibited. **forbidding** adj. severe, threatening.

force n. 1. strength or power. 2. compulsion. 3. Physics influence tending to produce a change in a physical system. 4. mental or moral strength. 5. person or thing with strength or influence. 6. vehemence or intensity. 7. group of people organized for a particular task or duty. 8. body of troops, police, etc. —v. 9. compel, make (someone) do something. 10. acquire or produce

through effort, strength, etc. 11. propel or drive. 12. break open. 13. impose or inflict. 14. cause to grow at an increased rate. 15. strain to the utmost. **in force** 1. having legal validity. 2. in great numbers. **forced** adj. 1. compulsory. 2. false or unnatural. 3. due to an emergency. **force-feed** v. -**feeding**, -**fed** compel (a person or animal) to swallow food. **forceful** adj. 1. emphatic. 2. effective. **forcefully** adv. **forcefulness** n. **forcible** adj. 1. involving physical force or violence. 2. strong and emphatic. **forcibly** adv.

forcemeat n. mixture of chopped ingredients used for stuffing.

forceps pl. n. surgical pincers.

ford n. 1. shallow place where a river may be crossed. —v. 2. cross (a river) at a ford. **fordable** adj.

fore adj. 1. in, at, or towards the front. —n. 2. front part. —interj. 3. golfer's shouted warning to a person in the path of a ball. **to the fore** in a conspicuous position.

fore- prefix 1. before in time or rank, e.g. forefather. 2. at the front, e.g. forecourt.

fore-and-aft adj. located at both ends of a ship.

forearm[1] n. arm from the wrist to the elbow.

forearm[2] v. prepare beforehand.

forebear n. ancestor.

foreboding n. feeling that something bad is about to happen.

forecast v. -**casting**, -**cast** or -**casted**. 1. predict (weather, events, etc.). —n. 2. prediction.

forecastle [foke-sl] n. raised front part of a ship.

foreclose v. take possession of (property bought with borrowed money which has not been repaid). **foreclosure** n.

forecourt n. courtyard or open space in front of a building.

forefather n. ancestor.

forefinger n. finger next to the thumb.

forefoot n. either of the front feet of an animal.

forefront n. 1. most active or conspicuous position. 2. very front.

foregather v. same as FORGATHER.

forego v. same as FORGO.

foregoing adj. going before, preceding. **foregone conclusion** inevitable result.

foreground n. part of a view, esp. in a picture, nearest the observer.

forehand adj. **1.** (of a stroke in tennis, squash, etc.) made with the palm of the hand forward. —n. **2.** such a stroke.

forehead n. part of the face above the eyebrows.
▷ The pronunciation 'for-rid' is traditional but 'for-hed' is also acceptable.

foreign adj. **1.** not of, or in, one's own country. **2.** relating to or connected with other countries. **3.** unfamiliar, strange. **4.** in an abnormal place or position, e.g. foreign matter. **foreigner** n. **foreign secretary, minister** government minister who deals with other countries.

foreknowledge n. knowledge of something before it actually happens.

foreland n. headland.

foreleg n. either of the front legs of a horse or other animal.

forelock n. lock of hair over the forehead. **tug the forelock** behave servilely or obsequiously.

foreman n. **1.** person in charge of a group of workers. **2.** leader of a jury.

foremast n. mast nearest the bow of a ship.

foremost adj., adv. first in time, place, or importance.

forename n. first name.

forenoon n. morning.

forensic [for-ren-sik] adj. used in or connected with courts of law. **forensic medicine** use of medical knowledge for the purposes of the law.

foreordain v. determine events in the future. **foreordination** n.

forepaw n. either of the front feet of a land mammal that does not have hooves.

foreplay n. sexual stimulation before intercourse.

forerunner n. person or thing that goes before, precursor.

foresail n. main sail on the foremast of a ship.

foresee v. see or know beforehand. **foreseeable** adj.

foreshadow v. show or indicate beforehand.

foreshore n. part of the shore between high- and low-tide marks.

foreshorten v. represent (an object) in a picture as shorter than it really is, in accordance with perspective.

foresight n. ability to anticipate and provide for future needs.

foreskin n. fold of skin covering the tip of the penis.

forest n. large area with a thick growth of trees. **forested** adj. **forestry** n. **1.** science of planting and caring for trees. **2.** management of forests. **forester** n. person skilled in forestry.

forestall v. prevent or guard against in advance.

foretaste n. early limited experience of something to come.

foretell v. tell or indicate beforehand.

forethought n. thoughtful planning for future events.

forever adv. **1.** without end. **2.** at all times. **3.** Informal for a long time.

forewarn v. warn beforehand.

foreword n. introduction to a book.

forfeit [for-fit] n. **1.** thing lost or given up as a penalty for a fault or mistake. —v. **2.** lose as a forfeit. —adj. **3.** lost as a forfeit. **forfeiture** n.

forgather v. meet together, assemble.

forgave v. past tense of FORGIVE.

forge[1] n. **1.** place where metal is worked, smithy. **2.** furnace for melting metal. —v. **3.** make a fraudulent imitation of (something). **4.** shape (metal) by heating and hammering it. **5.** create (an alliance etc.).

forge[2] v. advance steadily. **forge ahead** increase speed or take the lead.

forgery n., pl. -ries. **1.** fraudulent imitation of something. **2.** act of making a fraudulent imitation. **forger** n.

forget v. -getting, -got, -gotten. **1.** fail to remember. **2.** neglect. **3.** leave behind by mistake. **forgetful** adj. tending to forget. **forgetfulness** n. **forget-me-not** n. plant with clusters of small blue flowers.

forgive v. -giving, -gave, -given. cease to blame or hold resentment against, pardon. **forgiveness** n. **forgivable** adj. able to be forgiven. **forgivably** adv. **forgiving** adj. willing to forgive.

forgo v. do without, give up.

forgot v. past tense of FORGET. **forgotten** v. past participle of FORGET.

fork *n.* **1.** tool for eating food, with prongs and a handle. **2.** large similarly-shaped tool for digging or lifting. **3.** point where a road, river, etc. divides into branches. **4.** one of the branches. —*v.* **5.** branch. **6.** take one or other branch at a fork in the road. **7.** pick up, dig, etc. with a fork. **forked** *adj.* **fork-lift truck** vehicle with a forklike device at the front which can be raised or lowered to move loads. **fork out** *v. Informal* pay.

forlorn *adj.* forsaken and unhappy. **forlorn hope** hopeless enterprise. **forlornly** *adv.*

form *n.* **1.** shape or appearance. **2.** mode in which something appears. **3.** type or kind. **4.** printed document with spaces for details. **5.** physical or mental condition. **6.** previous record of an athlete, racehorse, etc. **7.** class in school. **8.** procedure or etiquette. **9.** bench. **10.** hare's nest. —*v.* **11.** give a (particular) shape to or take a (particular) shape. **12.** come or bring into existence. **13.** make or be made. **14.** train. **15.** acquire or develop. **16.** be an element in. **formless** *adj.*

formal *adj.* **1.** of or characterized by established conventions of ceremony and behaviour. **2.** of or for formal occasions. **3.** stiff in manner. **4.** organized. **5.** symmetrical. **formally** *adv.* **formalism** *n.* concern with outward appearances and structure at the expense of content. **formalist** *n., adj.* **formality** *n., pl.* **-ties. 1.** requirement of custom or etiquette. **2.** necessary procedure without real importance. **formalize** *v.* make official or formal.

formaldehyde [for-mal-de-hide] *n.* colourless pungent gas used to make formalin. **formalin** *n.* solution of formaldehyde in water, used as a disinfectant or a preservative for biological specimens.

format *n.* **1.** size and shape of a publication. **2.** style in which something is arranged. —*v.* **-matting, -matted. 3.** arrange in a format.

formation *n.* **1.** forming. **2.** thing formed. **3.** structure or shape. **4.** arrangement of people or things acting as a unit.

formative *adj.* **1.** shaping. **2.** of or relating to development.

former *adj.* of an earlier time, previous. **the former** first mentioned of two. **formerly** *adv.*

Formica *n.* ® kind of laminated sheet used to make heat-resistant surfaces.

formic acid *n.* acid derived from ants.

formidable *adj.* **1.** arousing fear or dread. **2.** difficult to overcome or manage. **formidably** *adv.*

formula *n., pl.* **-las, -lae. 1.** group of numbers, letters, or symbols expressing a scientific or mathematical rule. **2.** set form of words used in religion, law, etc. **3.** method or rule for doing or producing something. **4.** specific category of car in motor racing. **5.** *US* powder used to produce a milky drink for babies. **formulaic** *adj.* **formulate** *v.* plan or describe precisely and clearly. **formulation** *n.*

fornicate *v.* have sexual intercourse without being married. **fornication** *n.* **fornicator** *n.*

forsake *v.* **-saking, -sook, -saken. 1.** withdraw support or friendship from. **2.** give up, renounce.

forsooth *adv. Obs.* indeed.

forswear *v.* **-swearing, -swore, -sworn.** renounce or reject.

forsythia [for-syth-ee-a] *n.* shrub with yellow flowers in spring.

fort *n.* fortified building or place. **hold the fort** *Informal* keep things going during someone's absence.

forte[1] [for-tay] *n.* thing at which a person excels.

forte[2] [for-tay] *adv. Music* loudly.

forth *adv.* forwards, out, or away.

forthcoming *adj.* **1.** about to appear or happen. **2.** available. **3.** (of a person) communicative.

forthright *adj.* direct and outspoken.

forthwith *adv.* at once.

fortieth *adj., n.* see FORTY.

fortify *v.* **-fying, -fied. 1.** make (a place) defensible, as by building walls. **2.** strengthen. **3.** add alcohol to (wine) to make sherry or port. **4.** add vitamins etc. to (food). **fortification** *n.*

fortissimo *adv. Music* very loudly.

fortitude *n.* courage in adversity or pain.

fortnight *n.* two weeks. **fortnightly** *adv., adj.*

FORTRAN *n. Computers* programming language for mathematical and scientific purposes.

fortress *n.* large fort or fortified town.

fortuitous [for-**tyew**-it-uss] *adj.* happening by (lucky) chance. **fortuitously** *adv.*

fortunate *adj.* **1.** having good luck. **2.** occurring by good luck. **fortunately** *adv.*

fortune *n.* **1.** luck, esp. when favourable. **2.** power regarded as influencing human destiny. **3.** wealth, large sum of money. —*pl.* **4.** person's destiny. **fortune-teller** *n.* person who claims to predict the future of others.

forty *adj., n., pl.* **-ties.** four times ten. **fortieth** *adj., n.* **forty winks** short sleep, nap.

forum *n.* meeting or medium for open discussion or debate.

forward *adj.* **1.** directed or moving ahead. **2.** in, at, or near the front. **3.** presumptuous. **4.** well developed or advanced. **5.** relating to the future. —*n.* **6.** attacking player in various team games, such as football or hockey. —*v.* **7.** send (a letter etc.) on to an ultimate destination. **8.** advance or promote. —*adv.* **9.** forwards. **forwardly** *adv.* **forwardness** *n.* **forwards** *adv.* **1.** towards or at a place further ahead in space or time. **2.** towards the front.

forwent *v.* past tense of FORGO.

fosse *n.* ditch or moat.

fossil *n.* **1.** hardened remains of a prehistoric animal or plant preserved in rock. —*adj.* **2.** of, like, or being a fossil. **fossil fuel** fuel such as coal or oil that is formed from the decayed remains of prehistoric animals or plants. **fossilize** *v.* **1.** turn into a fossil. **2.** become out-of-date or inflexible. **fossilization** *n.*

foster *v.* **1.** promote the growth or development of. **2.** bring up (a child not one's own). —*adj.* **3.** of or involved in fostering a child, e.g. *foster parents.* **fostering** *n.*

fought *v.* past of FIGHT.

foul *adj.* **1.** loathsome or offensive. **2.** stinking or dirty. **3.** (of language) obscene or vulgar. **4.** unfair. —*n.* **5.** *Sport* violation of the rules. —*v.* **6.** make dirty or polluted. **7.** make or become entangled or clogged. **8.** *Sport* commit a foul against (an opponent). **fall foul of** come into conflict with. **foully** *adv.* **foulness** *n.* **foul-mouthed** *adj.* (habitually) using foul language. **foul play** unfair conduct, esp. involving violence.

foulard [foo-**lard**] *n.* soft light fabric of silk or rayon.

found[1] *v.* past of FIND.

found[2] *v.* **1.** establish or bring into being. **2.** lay the foundation of. **3.** (foll. by *on* or *upon*) have a basis (in). **founder** *n.* **founder member** one of the original members of a club or organization, often someone involved in setting it up.

found[3] *v.* **1.** cast (metal or glass) by melting and setting in a mould. **2.** make (articles) by this method. **founder** *n.*

foundation *n.* **1.** basis or base. **2.** act of founding. **3.** institution supported by an endowment. **4.** cosmetic used as a base for make-up. —*pl.* **5.** part of a building or wall below the ground.

founder *v.* **1.** break down or fail. **2.** (of a ship) sink. **3.** stumble or fall.

foundling *n.* abandoned infant.

foundry *n., pl.* **-ries.** place where metal is melted and cast.

fount[1] *n.* **1.** *Lit.* fountain. **2.** source.

fount[2] *n.* set of printing type of one style and size.

fountain *n.* **1.** jet of water. **2.** structure from which such a jet spurts. **3.** source. **fountainhead** *n.* source. **fountain pen** pen supplied with ink from a container inside it.

four *adj., n.* **1.** one more than three. —*n.* **2.** (crew of) four-oared rowing boat. **on all fours** on hands and knees. **four-poster** *n.* bed with four posts supporting a canopy. **four-letter word** short obscene word referring to sex or excrement. **foursome** *n.* group of four people. **foursquare** *adv.* **1.** squarely or firmly. —*adj.* **2.** solid and strong. **3.** forthright.

fourteen *adj., n.* four and ten. **fourteenth** *adj., n.*

fourth *adj., n.* **1.** (of) number four in a series. —*n.* **2.** quarter. **fourthly** *adv.* **fourth dimension** time. **fourth estate** the press.

fowl *n.* **1.** domestic cock or hen. **2.** any bird used for food or hunted as game. —*v.* **3.** hunt or snare wild birds. **fowler** *n.*

fox *n.* **1.** reddish-brown bushy-tailed animal of the dog family. **2.** its fur. **3.** cunning person. —*v.* **4.** *Informal* perplex or deceive. **foxy** *adj.* **foxier, foxiest.** of or like a fox, esp. in craftiness. **foxglove** *n.* tall plant with purple or white flowers. **foxhole** *n.* *Mil.* small pit dug for protection. **foxhound** *n.* dog bred for hunting foxes. **fox terrier** small short-haired terrier. **foxtrot** *n.* **1.** ballroom dance with slow and quick steps. **2.** music for this.

foyer [**foy**-ay] n. entrance hall in a theatre, cinema, or hotel.

Fr Chem. francium.

Fr. 1. Father. **2.** Franc. **3.** French.

fracas [**frak**-ah] n., pl. **-cas.** noisy quarrel.

fraction n. **1.** numerical quantity that is not a whole number. **2.** fragment, piece. **3.** Chem. substance separated by distillation. **fractional** adj. **fractionally** adv.

fractious adj. peevishly irritable.

fracture n. **1.** breaking, esp. of a bone. —v. **2.** break.

fragile adj. **1.** easily broken or damaged. **2.** in a weakened physical state. **fragility** n.

fragment n. **1.** piece broken off. **2.** incomplete piece. —v. **3.** break into pieces. **fragmentary** adj. **fragmentation** n.

fragrant adj. sweet-smelling. **fragrantly** adv. **fragrance** n. **1.** pleasant smell. **2.** perfume, scent.

frail adj. **1.** physically weak. **2.** easily damaged. **frailty** n., pl. **-ties.** physical or moral weakness.

frame n. **1.** structure giving shape or support. **2.** enclosing case or border, as round a picture. **3.** person's build. **4.** individual exposure on a strip of film. **5.** individual game of snooker in a match. —v. **6.** put into a frame. **7.** put together, construct. **8.** put into words. **9.** Slang incriminate (a person) on a false charge. **frame of mind** mood, attitude. **frame-up** n. Slang false incrimination. **framework** n. supporting structure.

franc n. monetary unit of France, Switzerland, Belgium, and various African countries.

franchise n. **1.** right to vote. **2.** authorization to sell a company's goods.

Franciscan n., adj. (friar or nun) of the order founded by St. Francis of Assisi.

francium n. radioactive metallic element.

Franco- combining form of France or the French.

frangipani [fran-jee-**pah**-nee] n. fragrant tropical American shrub.

frank adj. **1.** honest and straightforward. **2.** outspoken or blunt. —n. **3.** official mark on a letter permitting delivery. —v. **4.** put such a mark on (a letter). **frankly** adv. **frankness** n.

Frankenstein's monster, Frankenstein n. creation or monster that brings

disaster and is beyond the control of its creator.

frankfurter n. smoked sausage.

frankincense n. aromatic gum resin burned as incense.

frantic adj. **1.** distracted with rage, grief, joy, etc. **2.** hurried and disorganized. **frantically** adv.

frappé adj. (esp. of drinks) chilled.

fraternal adj. of a brother, brotherly. **fraternally** adv. **fraternity** n., pl. **-ties. 1.** group of people with shared interests, aims, etc. **2.** brotherhood. **3.** US male social club at college. **fraternize** v. associate on friendly terms. **fraternization** n. **fratricide** n. **1.** crime of killing one's brother. **2.** person who does this.

Frau [rhymes with **how**] n., pl. **Fraus, Frauen.** German title, equivalent to Mrs. **Fräulein** [**froy**-line] n., pl. **-leins, -lein.** German title, equivalent to Miss.

fraud n. **1.** (criminal) deception, swindle. **2.** person who acts in a deceitful way. **fraudulent** adj. **fraudulence** n.

fraught [**frawt**] adj. tense or anxious. **fraught with** involving, filled with.

fray[1] v. **1.** make or become ragged at the edge. **2.** become strained.

fray[2] n. noisy quarrel or conflict.

frazzle n. Informal exhausted state.

freak n. **1.** abnormal person or thing. **2.** person who is excessively enthusiastic about something. —adj. **3.** abnormal. **freakish** adj. **freak out** v. Slang (cause to) be in a heightened emotional state. **freaky** adj. **freakier, freakiest.** Informal weird, peculiar.

freckle n. small brown spot on the skin. **freckled** adj. marked with freckles.

free adj. **freer, freest. 1.** able to act at will, not compelled or restrained. **2.** not subject (to). **3.** independent. **4.** provided without charge. **5.** generous, lavish. **6.** not in use. **7.** (of a person) not busy. **8.** not fixed or joined. **9.** (of a translation) not exact or literal. —v. **10.** freeing, freed. **10.** release, liberate. **11.** remove (obstacles, pain, etc.) from. **12.** make available or usable. **a free hand** unrestricted freedom to act. **freely** adv. **free-and-easy** adj. casual and tolerant. **freebooter** n. pirate. **free enterprise** economic system in which businesses compete for profit with little state control. **free fall** part of a parachute descent before the parachute opens. **free-for-all** *n. Informal* brawl. **freehand** *adj.* drawn without guiding instruments. **freehold** *n.* tenure of land for life without restrictions. **freeholder** *n.* **free house** public house not bound to sell only one brewer's products. **freelance** *adj., n.* (of) self-employed person doing specific pieces of work for various employers. **freeloader** *n. Slang* habitual scrounger. **freeman** *n., pl.* **-men.** 1. person who is not a slave. 2. person who has been given the freedom of a city. **free-market** *adj.* denoting an economic system in which supply and demand regulate prices, wages, etc. **freerange** *adj.* kept or produced in natural conditions. **free space** region with no gravitational or electromagnetic fields. **freestanding** *adj.* not attached to or supported by another object. **free-style** *n.* competition, esp. in swimming, in which each participant uses the style of his or her choice. **freethinker** *n.* person who forms his or her ideas independently of authority, esp. on religious matters. **free verse** unrhymed verse without a fixed rhythm. **freeway** *n. US* motorway. **freewheel** *v.* travel downhill on a bicycle without pedalling. **free will** 1. ability to make choices that are not externally determined. 2. ability to make a decision without outside coercion, e.g. *she left of her own free will.*

▷ *Free of* means 'not subject to': *free of charge. Free from* suggests a change of circumstances: *They were free from danger.*

-free *adj. combining form* without, e.g. *a trouble-free journey.*

freedom *n.* 1. being free. 2. (often foll. by *from*) exemption or immunity, e.g. *freedom from hunger.* 3. right or privilege of unlimited access, e.g. *the freedom of the city.*

Freemason *n.* member of a secret fraternity pledged to help each other. **Freemasonry** *n.*

freesia *n.* plant with fragrant tubular flowers.

freeze *v.* **freezing, froze, frozen.** 1. change from a liquid to a solid by the reduction of temperature, as water to ice. 2. preserve (food etc.) by extreme cold. 3. (cause to be) very cold. 4. become motionless with fear, shock, etc. 5. fix (prices or wages) at a particular level. 6. ban the exchange or collection of (loans, assets, etc.). —*n.* 7. period of very cold weather. 8. freezing of prices or wages. **freezer** *n.* insulated cabinet

for cold-storage of perishable foods. **freezedry** *v.* preserve (food) by rapid freezing and drying in a vacuum. **freeze-frame** *n.* single frame from a film or video recording shown as a still photograph. **freezing point** temperature below which a liquid turns into a solid.

freight [frate] *n.* 1. commercial transport of goods. 2. cargo transported. 3. cost of this. —*v.* 4. send by freight. **freighter** *n.* ship or aircraft for transporting goods.

French *n.* 1. language of France, also spoken in parts of Belgium, Canada, and Switzerland. —*adj.* 2. of France, its people, or their language. **French beans** green bean whose pods are eaten. **French bread** white bread in a long thin crusty loaf. **French-Canadian** *adj.* of or from the part of Canada where French is spoken. **French dressing** salad dressing of oil and vinegar. **French fries** potato chips. **French horn** brass wind instrument with a coiled tube. **French leave** unauthorized absence or departure. **French letter** *Slang* condom. **French polish** shellac varnish for wood. **French window** window extending to floor level, used as a door.

frenetic [frin-net-ik] *adj.* uncontrolled, excited. **frenetically** *adv.*

frenzy *n., pl.* **-zies.** 1. violent mental derangement. 2. wild excitement. **frenzied** *adj.* **frenziedly** *adv.*

frequent *adj.* 1. happening often. 2. habitual. —*v.* 3. visit habitually. **frequently** *adv.* **frequency** *n., pl.* **-cies.** 1. rate of occurrence. 2. *Physics* number of times a wave repeats itself in a given time.

fresco *n., pl.* **-coes, -cos.** watercolour painting done on wet plaster on a wall.

fresh *adj.* 1. newly made, acquired, etc. 2. novel, original. 3. most recent. 4. further, additional. 5. (of food) not preserved. 6. (of water) not salty. 7. (of weather) brisk or invigorating. 8. not tired. 9. *Informal* impudent. **freshly** *adv.* **freshness** *n.* **freshen** *v.* 1. make or become fresh or fresher. 2. (often foll. by *up*) refresh oneself, esp. by washing. 3. (of the wind) increase. **freshman, fresher** *n., pl.* **-men, freshers.** first-year student. **freshwater** *adj.* of or living in fresh water.

fret[1] *v.* **fretting, fretted.** 1. be worried. 2. rub or wear away. —*n.* 3. worried state. **fretful** *adj.* irritable.

fret[2] *n.* small bar on the fingerboard of a guitar etc.

fret[3] n. repetitive geometrical figure used for ornamentation. **fret saw** fine saw with a narrow blade, used for fretwork. **fretwork** n. decorative carving in wood.

Freudian [froy-dee-an] adj. of or relating to the psychoanalyst Sigmund Freud or his theories. **Freudian slip** action or error which may reveal an unconscious wish.

Fri. Friday.

friable [fry-a-bl] adj. easily crumbled. **friability** n.

friar n. member of a male Roman Catholic religious order. **friary** n., pl. **-ries**. house of friars.

fricassee n. stewed meat served in a thick white sauce.

fricative n. **1**. consonant produced by friction of the breath through a partially open mouth, such as (f) or (z). —adj. **2**. relating to or being a fricative.

friction n. **1**. rubbing. **2**. resistance met with by a body moving over another. **3**. clash of wills or personalities. **frictional** adj.

Friday n. sixth day of the week. **Good Friday** Friday before Easter.

fridge n. short for REFRIGERATOR.

fried v. past of FRY[1].

friend n. **1**. person whom one knows well and likes. **2**. supporter or ally. **3**. (F-) Quaker. **friendly** adj. **-lier, -liest. 1**. showing or expressing liking. **2**. not hostile, on the same side. —n., adj. **-lies. 3**. Sport match played for its own sake and not as part of a competition. **-friendly** adj. combining form good or easy for the person or thing specified, e.g. user-friendly. **friendly society** association of people who pay regular dues in return for pensions, sickness benefits, etc. **friendliness** n. **friendless** adj. **friendship** n.

fries pl. n. see FRY[1].

Friesian [free-zhan] n. breed of black-and-white dairy cattle.

frieze [freeze] n. ornamental band on a wall.

frigate [frig-it] n. medium-sized fast warship.

fright n. **1**. sudden fear or alarm. **2**. sudden alarming shock. **3**. Informal grotesque person. **frighten** v. **1**. scare or terrify. **2**. force (someone) to do something from fear. **frightening** adj. **frighteningly** adv. **frightful** adj. **1**. horrifying. **2**. Informal very great. **frightfully** adv.

frigid [frij-id] adj. **1**. (of a woman) sexually

unresponsive. **2**. very cold. **3**. excessively formal. **frigidly** adv. **frigidity** n.

frill n. **1**. gathered strip of fabric attached at one edge. —pl. **2**. superfluous decorations or details. **frilled** adj. **frilly** adj.

fringe n. **1**. hair cut short and hanging over the forehead. **2**. ornamental edge of hanging threads, tassels, etc. **3**. outer edge. —v. **4**. decorate with a fringe. **5**. be a fringe for, border. —adj. **6**. (of theatre etc.) unofficial or unconventional. **fringe benefit** benefit given in addition to a regular salary.

frippery n., pl. **-peries. 1**. useless ornamentation. **2**. trivia.

Frisian n. **1**. language spoken in the NW Netherlands and adjacent islands. **2**. speaker of this language. —adj. **3**. of this language or its speakers.

frisk v. **1**. move or leap playfully. **2**. Informal search (a person) for concealed weapons etc. —n. **3**. playful movement. **4**. Informal instance of searching a person. **frisky** adj. **friskier, friskiest**. lively or high-spirited. **friskily** adv.

frisson [frees-sonn] n. shiver of fear or excitement.

fritillary n., pl. **-laries**. plant with purple or white bell-shaped flowers.

fritter n. piece of food fried in batter.

fritter away v. waste.

frivolous adj. **1**. not serious or sensible. **2**. enjoyable but trivial. **frivolously** adv. **frivolity** n., pl. **-ties**.

frizz v. form (hair) into stiff wiry curls. **frizzy** adj. **frizzier, frizziest**.

frizzle v. cook or heat until crisp and shrivelled.

fro adv. away, only in to and fro.

frock n. dress. **frock coat** man's skirted coat as worn in the 19th century.

frog[1] n. smooth-skinned tailless amphibian with long back legs used for jumping. **frog in one's throat** phlegm on the vocal cords, hindering speech. **frogman** n., pl. **-men**. swimmer with a rubber suit and breathing equipment for working underwater. **frogmarch** v. force (a resisting person) to move by holding his arms. **frogspawn** n. jelly-like substance containing frog's eggs.

frog[2] n. military-style fastening on a coat consisting of a button and loop. **frogging** n. set of such fastenings on a coat.

frolic v. **-icking, -icked. 1**. run and play in a

lively way. —*n.* **2.** lively and merry behaviour. **frolicsome** *adj.* playful.

from *prep.* indicating the point of departure, source, distance, cause, change of state, etc. ▷ The use of *off* to mean *from* is very informal: *They bought milk from* (rather than *off*) *a farmer.*

frond *n.* long leaf or leaflike part of a fern, palm, or seaweed.

front *n.* **1.** fore part. **2.** position directly before or ahead. **3.** seaside promenade. **4.** battle line or area. **5.** *Meteorol.* dividing line between two different air masses. **6.** outward aspect. **7.** *Informal* cover for another, usu. criminal, activity. **8.** group with a common goal. **9.** a particular field of activity, e.g. *on the purely intellectual front.* —*v.* **10.** face (onto). **11.** be a front of or for. **12.** be the presenter of (a television show). —*adj.* **13.** of or at the front. **frontal** *adj.* **frontage** *n.* façade of a building. **front bench** parliamentary leaders of the government or opposition. **front-bencher** *n.* **frontrunner** *n.* *Informal* person regarded as most likely to win a race, election, etc.

frontier *n.* **1.** area of a country bordering on another. **2.** edge of the settled area of a country. **3.** (often *pl.*) limit of knowledge in a particular field.

frontispiece *n.* illustration facing the title page of a book.

frost *n.* **1.** white frozen dew or mist. **2.** atmospheric temperature below freezing point. —*v.* **3.** become covered with frost. **frosted** *adj.* **1.** (of glass) having a rough surface to make it opaque. **2.** covered with frosting. **frosting** *n.* *US* sugar icing. **frosty** *adj.* **frostier, frostiest. 1.** characterized by or covered with frost. **2.** unfriendly. **frostily** *adv.* **frostiness** *n.* **frostbite** *n.* destruction of tissue, esp. of the fingers or ears, by cold. **frostbitten** *adj.*

froth *n.* **1.** mass of small bubbles. **2.** trivial but superficially attractive ideas or entertainment. —*v.* **3.** foam. **frothy** *adj.* **frothier, frothiest.**

frown *v.* **1.** wrinkle one's brows in worry, anger, or thought. **2.** look disapprovingly (on). —*n.* **3.** frowning expression.

frowsty *adj.* stale or musty.

frowsy, frowzy *adj.* **-sier, -siest** *or* **-zier, -ziest.** dirty or unkempt.

froze *v.* past tense of FREEZE. **frozen** *v.* past participle of FREEZE.

FRS Fellow of the Royal Society.

fructify *v.* **-fying, -fied.** (cause to) bear fruit. **fructification** *n.*

fructose *n.* crystalline sugar occurring in many fruits.

frugal [froo-gl] *adj.* **1.** thrifty, sparing. **2.** meagre and inexpensive. **frugally** *adv.* **frugality** *n.*

fruit *n.* **1.** part of a plant containing seeds, esp. if edible. **2.** any plant product useful to man. **3.** (often *pl.*) result of an action or effort. —*v.* **4.** bear fruit. **fruiterer** *n.* person who sells fruit. **fruitful** *adj.* useful or productive. **fruitfully** *adv.* **fruitless** *adj.* useless or unproductive. **fruitlessly** *adv.* **fruity** *adj.* **fruitier, fruitiest. 1.** of or like fruit. **2.** (of a voice) mellow. **3.** *Informal* mildly bawdy. **fruitcake** *n.* cake containing dried fruit. **fruit machine** coin-operated gambling machine. **fruit salad, cocktail** dish consisting of pieces of different kinds of fruit.

fruition [froo-**ish**-on] *n.* fulfilment of something worked for or desired.

frump *n.* dowdy woman. **frumpy** *adj.* **frumpier, frumpiest.**

frustrate *v.* **1.** hinder or prevent. **2.** upset or anger. **frustrated** *adj.* **frustrating** *adj.* **frustration** *n.*

frustum *n., pl.* **-s, -ta.** *Geom.* part of a cone or pyramid contained between the base and a plane parallel to the base that intersects the solid.

fry[1] *v.* **frying, fried. 1.** cook or be cooked in fat or oil. —*n., pl.* **fries. 2.** (also **fry-up**) dish of fried food. —*pl.* **3.** potato chips. **frying pan** shallow pan used for frying food. **out of the frying pan into the fire** from a bad situation into a worse one.

fry[2] *pl. n.* young fishes. **small fry** young or insignificant people.

ft. 1. foot. **2.** feet.

fuchsia [**fyew**-sha] *n.* ornamental shrub with hanging flowers.

fuck *Taboo* —*v.* **1.** have sexual intercourse (with). —*n.* **2.** act of sexual intercourse. —*interj.* **3.** expression of strong disgust or anger. **fuck off** *v. Taboo slang* go away. **fuck up** *v. Taboo slang* make a mess of (something).

fuddle *v.* **1.** cause to be intoxicated or confused. —*n.* **2.** confused state. **fuddled** *adj.*

fuddy-duddy n., pl. **-dies**, adj. Informal old-fashioned (person).

fudge[1] n. soft caramel-like sweet.

fudge[2] v. avoid making a firm statement or decision.

fuel n. **1.** substance burned for heat or power. **2.** something that intensifies (a feeling etc.). —v. **fuelling, fuelled. 3.** provide with fuel.

fug n. hot stale atmosphere. **fuggy** adj. **fuggier, fuggiest.**

fugitive [fyew-jit-iv] n. **1.** person who flees, esp. from arrest or pursuit. —adj. **2.** fleeing. **3.** transient.

fugue [fyewg] n. musical composition in which a theme is repeated in different parts.

Führer n. German leader; title used by Hitler as Nazi dictator.

-ful adj. suffix **1.** full of; characterized by, as in painful, restful. **2.** able or tending to, as in useful. —n. suffix **3.** as much as will fill the thing specified, as in mouthful.

fulcrum n., pl. **-crums, -cra.** pivot about which a lever turns.

fulfil v. **-filling, -filled. 1.** bring about the achievement of (a desire or promise). **2.** carry out (a request or order). **3.** do what is required. **fulfilment** n. **fulfil oneself** v. achieve one's potential.

full[1] adj. **1.** containing as much or as many as possible. **2.** abundant in supply. **3.** having had enough to eat. **4.** plump. **5.** complete, whole. **6.** (of a garment) of ample cut. **7.** (of a sound or flavour) rich and strong. —adv. **8.** completely. **9.** directly. **10.** very. **fully** adv. **fullness** n. **full back** defensive player in various sports. **fullblooded** adj. vigorous or enthusiastic. **full board** provision by a hotel of a bed and all meals. **full-bodied** adj. having a full rich flavour or quality. **full-blown** adj. fully developed. **full house 1.** theatre filled to capacity. **2.** in bingo, set of numbers needed to win. **full-length** adj. **1.** (of a mirror, portrait, etc.) showing the whole human body. **2.** not abridged. **full moon** phase of the moon when it is visible as a fully illuminated disc. **full-scale** adj. **1.** (of a plan) of actual size. **2.** using all resources. **full stop** punctuation mark (.) at the end of a sentence and after abbreviations. **full time** in football, rugby, etc., end of the game. **full-time** adj. for all of the normal working week. **full up** filled to capacity.

full[2] v. clean, shrink, and press cloth. **fuller**

n. **fuller's earth** absorbent clay used for clarifying olive oils and fats, fulling cloth etc.

fulmar n. Arctic sea bird.

fulminate v. (foll. by against) criticize or denounce angrily. **fulmination** n.

fulsome adj. distastefully excessive or insincere.

fumble v. **1.** handle awkwardly. **2.** say awkwardly. —n. **3.** act of fumbling.

fume v. **1.** be very angry. **2.** give out smoke or vapour. **3.** treat with fumes. —n. **4.** (usu. pl.) pungent smoke or vapour.

fumigate [fyew-mig-gate] v. disinfect with fumes. **fumigation** n.

fun n. enjoyment or amusement. **make fun of** mock or tease. **funny** adj. **funnier, funniest. 1.** comical, humorous. **2.** odd. **funny bone** part of the elbow where the nerve is near the surface. **funnily** adv.

function n. **1.** purpose something exists for. **2.** way something works. **3.** large or formal social event. **4.** Maths quantity whose value depends on the varying value of another. —v. **5.** operate or work. **6.** (foll. by as) fill the role of another. **functional** adj. **1.** of or as a function. **2.** practical rather than decorative. **3.** in working order. **functionally** adv. **functionary** n., pl. **-aries.** official.

fund n. **1.** stock of money for a special purpose. **2.** supply or store. —pl. **3.** money resources. —v. **4.** provide money to. **funding** n.

fundamental adj. **1.** essential or primary. **2.** basic. —n. **3.** basic rule or fact. **fundamentally** adv. **fundamentalism** n. literal or strict interpretation of a religion. **fundamentalist** n., adj.

funeral n. ceremony of burying or cremating a dead person. **funeral director** undertaker. **funeral parlour** place where the dead are prepared for burial or cremation.

funerary adj. of or for a funeral.

funereal [fyew-**neer**-ee-al] adj. gloomy or sombre.

funfair n. entertainment with machines to ride on and stalls.

fungus n., pl. **-gi, -guses.** plant without leaves, flowers, or roots, such as a mushroom or mould. **fungal, fungous** adj. **fungicide** n. substance that destroys fungi.

funicular [fyew-**nik**-yew-lar] n. cable railway on a mountainside or cliff.

funk[1] n. style of dance music with a strong

beat. **funky** *adj.* **funkier, funkiest.** (of music) passionate or soulful.

funk² *Informal* —*n.* **1.** nervous or fearful state. —*v.* **2.** avoid (doing something) through fear.

funnel *n.* **1.** cone-shaped tube for pouring liquids into a narrow opening. **2.** chimney of a ship or locomotive. —*v.* **-nelling, -nelled. 3.** move through or as if through a funnel.

funny *adj.* see FUN.

fur *n.* **1.** soft hair of a mammal. **2.** animal skin with the fur left on. **3.** garment made of this. **4.** whitish coating on the tongue or inside a kettle. —*v.* **5.** cover or become covered with fur. **furry** *adj.* **furrier, furriest. furrier** *n.* dealer in furs.

furbelow *n.* **1.** flounce or ruffle. **2.** (often pl.) showy ornamentation.

furcate *v.* **1.** divide into two parts. —*adj.* **2.** forked, branching.

furious *adj.* **1.** very angry. **2.** violent or unrestrained. **furiously** *adv.*

furl *v.* roll up and fasten (a sail, umbrella, or flag). **furled** *adj.*

furlong *n.* eighth of a mile.

furlough [**fur**-loh] *n.* leave of absence from military duty.

furnace *n.* **1.** enclosed chamber containing a very hot fire. **2.** *Informal* very hot place.

furnish *v.* **1.** fit up (a house or room) with furniture. **2.** (foll. by *with*) supply, provide. **furnishings** *pl. n.* furniture, carpets, and fittings. **furniture** *n.* large movable articles such as chairs and wardrobes.

furore [fyew-**ror**-ee] *n.* very excited or angry reaction.

furrow *n.* **1.** trench made by a plough. **2.** groove, esp. a wrinkle on the forehead. —*v.* **3.** make or become wrinkled.

further *adv.* **1.** in addition. **2.** to a greater distance or extent. —*adj.* **3.** additional. **4.** more distant. —*v.* **5.** assist the progress of. **further education** education beyond school other than at a university or polytechnic. **furthest** *adv.* **1.** to the greatest distance or extent. —*adj.* **2.** most distant. **furtherance** *n.* **furthermore** *adv.* besides. **furthermost** *adj.* most distant.

furtive *adj.* sly and secretive. **furtively** *adv.*

fury *n.,* *pl.* **-ries. 1.** wild anger. **2.** uncontrolled violence. **3.** person with a violent temper.

furze *n.* gorse.

fuse¹ *n.* cord containing an explosive for detonating a bomb.

fuse² *v.* **1.** join or combine. **2.** melt with heat. **3.** unite by melting. **4.** (cause to) fail as a result of a blown fuse. —*n.* **5.** safety device for electric circuits, containing a wire that melts and breaks the connection when the circuit is overloaded.

fuselage [**fyew**-zill-lahzh] *n.* body of an aircraft.

fusible *adj.* capable of being melted.

fusilier [fyew-zill-**leer**] *n.* soldier of certain regiments.

fusillade [fyew-zill-**lade**] *n.* **1.** continuous discharge of firearms. **2.** outburst of criticism, questions, etc.

fusion *n.* **1.** melting. **2.** product of fusing. **3.** (also **nuclear fusion**) combination of the nucleus of two atoms with the release of energy. **4.** something new created by a mixture of qualities, ideas, or things. **5.** popular music blending esp. jazz and funk.

fuss *n.* **1.** needless activity or worry. **2.** complaint or objection. **3.** great display of attention. —*v.* **4.** make a fuss. **fussy** *adj.* **fussier, fussiest. 1.** inclined to fuss. **2.** overparticular. **3.** overelaborate. **fussily** *adv.* **fussiness** *n.*

fustian *n.* **1.** thick cotton cloth. **2.** pompous language.

fusty *adj.* **-tier, -tiest. 1.** stale-smelling. **2.** behind the times. **fustiness** *n.*

futile [**fyew**-tile] *adj.* unsuccessful or useless. **futility** *n.*

futon [**foo**-tonn] *n.* Japanese padded quilt, laid on the floor as a bed.

future *n.* **1.** time to come. **2.** what will happen. **3.** prospects. —*adj.* **4.** yet to come or be. **5.** of or relating to time to come. **6.** (of a verb tense) indicating that the action specified has not yet taken place. **futurism** *n.* early 20th-century artistic movement making use of the characteristics of the machine age. **futurist** *n.,* *adj.* **futuristic** *adj.* of a design appearing to belong to some future time.

fuzz¹ *n.* mass of fine or curly hairs or fibres. **fuzzy** *adj.* **fuzzier, fuzziest. 1.** of, like, or covered with fuzz. **2.** blurred. **3.** (of hair) tightly curled. **fuzzily** *adv.* **fuzziness** *n.*

fuzz² *n.* *Slang* police(man).

G

g 1. gram(s). 2. (acceleration due to) gravity.

G *Slang* grand (a thousand pounds or dollars).

Ga *Chem.* gallium.

GA Georgia.

gab *n., v.* **gabbing, gabbed.** *Informal* talk or chatter. **gift of the gab** eloquence. **gabby** *adj.* **-bier, -biest.** *Informal* talkative.

gabardine, gaberdine *n.* strong twill cloth used esp. for raincoats.

gabble *v.* 1. speak rapidly and indistinctly. —*n.* 2. rapid indistinct speech.

gable *n.* triangular upper part of a wall between sloping roofs. **gabled** *adj.*

gad *v.* **gadding, gadded. gad about, around** go around in search of pleasure. **gadabout** *n.* pleasure-seeker.

gadfly *n.* 1. fly that bites cattle. 2. constantly annoying person.

gadget *n.* small mechanical device or appliance. **gadgetry** *n.* gadgets.

gadoid [gay-doid] *adj.* 1. of the cod family of marine fishes. —*n.* 2. gadoid fish.

gadolinium *n.* silvery-white metallic element.

gadwall *n.* duck related to the mallard.

Gael [gayl] *n.* Gaelic-speaker. **Gaelic** [gah-lik, gay-lik] *n.* 1. Celtic language of Ireland and the Scottish Highlands. —*adj.* 2. of the Gaels or their language.

gaff[1] *n.* 1. stick with an iron hook for landing large fish. —*v.* 2. hook or land (a fish) with a gaff.

gaff[2] *n.* **blow the gaff** *Slang* divulge a secret.

gaffe *n.* social blunder.

gaffer *n.* 1. old man. 2. *Informal* foreman or boss.

gag[1] *v.* **gagging, gagged.** 1. stop up the mouth of (a person) with cloth etc. 2. deprive of free speech. 3. retch. 4. choke. —*n.* 5. cloth etc. put into or tied across the mouth.

gag[2] *n.* *Informal* joke.

gaga [gah-gah] *adj. Slang* 1. senile. 2. crazy.

gage[1] *n.* 1. thing given as security. 2. formerly, something thrown down as a challenge to combat.

gage[2] *n.* short for GREENGAGE.

gage[3] *n., v. US* gauge.

gaggle *n.* 1. flock of geese. 2. *Informal* disorderly crowd.

gaiety *n.* 1. cheerfulness. 2. merrymaking. **gaily** *adv.* 1. merrily. 2. colourfully.

gain *v.* 1. acquire or obtain. 2. win in competition. 3. increase or improve. 4. reach. 5. (of a watch or clock) be or become too fast. —*n.* 6. profit. 7. increase or improvement. **gainful** *adj.* useful or profitable. **gainfully** *adv.* **gain on, upon** *v.* get nearer to or catch up with.

gainsay *v.* **-saying, -said.** deny or contradict.

gait *n.* manner of walking.

gaiter *n.* cloth or leather covering for the lower leg.

gal *n. Slang* girl.

gal. gallon.

gala [gah-la] *n.* 1. festival. 2. competitive sporting event.

galantine *n.* dish of white meat served in a cold jelly.

galaxy *n., pl.* **-axies.** 1. system of stars. 2. gathering of famous people. 3. (G-) Milky Way. **galactic** *adj.*

gale *n.* 1. strong wind. 2. *Informal* loud outburst.

gall[1] [gawl] *n.* 1. *Informal* impudence. 2. bitter feeling. 3. bile. **gall bladder** sac attached to the liver, storing bile. **gallstone** *n.* hard growth in the gall bladder or its ducts.

gall[2] [gawl] *n.* 1. sore caused by chafing. —*v.* 2. make sore by rubbing. 3. annoy.

gall[3] [gawl] *n.* abnormal outgrowth on a tree or plant.

gallant *adj.* 1. brave and noble. 2. (of a man) attentive to women. 3. imposing and stately. —*n.* 4. fashionable young man who pursues women. **gallantly** *adv.* **gallantry** *n.* 1. bravery. 2. polite behaviour and speech.

galleon n. large three-masted sailing ship of the 15th–17th centuries.

gallery n., pl. **-ries. 1.** room or building for displaying works of art. **2.** balcony in a church, theatre, etc. **3.** long narrow room for a specific purpose, e.g. *shooting gallery.* **4.** covered walk with side openings. **5.** passage in a mine.

galley n. **1.** kitchen of a ship or aircraft. **2.** *Hist.* ship propelled by oars, usu. rowed by slaves. **3.** short for GALLEY PROOF. **galley proof** printer's proof in long slip form. **galley slave 1.** slave forced to row in a galley. **2.** *Informal* drudge.

Gallic adj. **1.** French. **2.** of ancient Gaul. **Gallicism** n. French word or idiom.

gallinaceous adj. of an order of birds including poultry, pheasants, and grouse.

gallium n. soft grey metallic element used in semiconductors.

gallivant v. go about in search of pleasure.

gallon n. liquid measure of eight pints, equal to 4.55 litres.

gallop n. **1.** horse's fastest pace. **2.** galloping. —v. **galloping, galloped. 3.** go or ride at a gallop. **4.** move or progress rapidly.

gallows n. wooden structure used for hanging criminals.

Gallup poll n. public opinion poll carried out by questioning a cross section of the population.

galore adv. in plenty, e.g. *presents galore.*

galoshes pl. n. waterproof overshoes.

galumph v. *Informal* leap or move about clumsily.

galvanic adj. **1.** of or producing an electric current generated by chemical means. **2.** *Informal* stimulating or startling. **galvanize** v. **1.** stimulate into action. **2.** coat (metal) with zinc. **galvanometer** n. instrument for measuring small electric currents.

gambit n. **1.** opening line or move intended to secure an advantage. **2.** *Chess* opening move involving the sacrifice of a pawn.

gamble v. **1.** play games of chance to win money. **2.** act on the expectation of something. —n. **3.** risky undertaking. **4.** bet or wager. **gambler** n. **gambling** n.

gamboge [gam-**boje**] n. gum resin used as a yellow pigment and purgative.

gambol v. **-bolling, -bolled. 1.** jump about playfully, frolic. —n. **2.** frolic.

game[1] n. **1.** amusement or pastime. **2.** contest for amusement. **3.** single period of play in a contest. **4.** score needed to win a contest. **5.** scheme or trick. **6.** animals or birds hunted for sport or food. **7.** their flesh. —pl. **8.** athletic contests. —v. **9.** gamble. —adj. **10.** brave. **11.** willing. **gamely** adv. **gaming** n. gambling. **gamy, gamey** adj. **gamier, gamiest.** having the smell or flavour of game. **gamecock** n. cock bred for fighting. **gamekeeper** n. person employed to breed game and prevent poaching. **gamesmanship** n. art of winning by cunning practices without actually cheating.

game[2] adj. lame, crippled.

gamete n. *Biol.* reproductive cell.

gamin n. street urchin.

gamine [gam-een] n. slim boyish young woman.

gamma n. third letter of the Greek alphabet. **gamma ray** electromagnetic ray of shorter wavelength and higher energy than an x-ray.

gammon n. **1.** cured or smoked ham. **2.** hindquarter of a side of bacon.

gammy adj. **-mier, -miest.** same as GAME[2].

gamp n. *Informal* umbrella.

gamut n. whole range or scale (of music, emotions, etc.).

gander n. **1.** male goose. **2.** *Informal* quick look.

gang n. **1.** (criminal) group. **2.** organized group of workmen. **gangland** n. criminal underworld. **gang up** v. form an alliance (against).

gangling adj. lanky and awkward.

ganglion n. **1.** group of nerve cells. **2.** small harmless tumour.

gangplank n. portable bridge for boarding or leaving a ship.

gangrene n. decay of body tissue as a result of disease or injury. **gangrenous** adj.

gangster n. member of a criminal gang.

gangue n. valueless material in an ore.

gangway n. **1.** passage between rows of seats. **2.** gangplank. **3.** opening in a ship's side for a gangplank.

gannet n. **1.** large sea bird. **2.** *Slang* greedy person.

gantry n., pl. **-tries.** structure supporting something such as a crane or rocket.

gaol [jayl] *n.* same as JAIL.

gap *n.* **1.** break or opening. **2.** interruption or interval. **3.** divergence or difference. **gappy** *adj.*

gape *v.* **1.** stare in wonder. **2.** open the mouth wide. **3.** be or become wide open. —*n.* **4.** wide opening. **5.** astonished stare. **gaping** *adj.*

garage *n.* **1.** building used to house cars. **2.** place for the refuelling, sale, and repair of cars. —*v.* **3.** put or keep a car in a garage.

garb *n.* **1.** clothes. —*v.* **2.** clothe.

garbage *n.* rubbish.

garble *v.* jumble or distort (a story etc.).

garden *n.* **1.** piece of land for growing flowers, fruit, or vegetables. —*pl.* **2.** ornamental park. —*v.* **3.** cultivate a garden. **gardener** *n.* **gardening** *n.* **garden centre** place selling plants and gardening equipment.

gardenia [gar-**deen**-ya] *n.* **1.** large fragrant white waxy flower. **2.** shrub bearing this.

gargantuan *adj.* huge.

gargle *v.* **1.** wash the throat with (a liquid) by breathing out slowly through the liquid. —*n.* **2.** act or sound of gargling. **3.** liquid used for gargling.

gargoyle *n.* waterspout carved in the form of a grotesque face, esp. on a church.

garish *adj.* crudely bright or colourful. **garishly** *adv.* **garishness** *n.*

garland *n.* **1.** wreath of flowers worn or hung as a decoration. —*v.* **2.** decorate with garlands.

garlic *n.* pungent bulb of a plant of the onion family, used in cooking.

garment *n.* **1.** article of clothing. —*pl.* **2.** clothes.

garner *v.* collect or store.

garnet *n.* red semiprecious stone.

garnish *v.* **1.** decorate (food). —*n.* **2.** decoration for food.

garret *n.* attic in a house.

garrison *n.* **1.** troops stationed in a town or fort. **2.** fortified place. —*v.* **3.** station troops in.

garrotte, garotte *n.* **1.** Spanish method of execution by strangling. **2.** cord or wire used for this. —*v.* **3.** kill by this method. **4.** strangle.

garrulous *adj.* talkative. **garrulously** *adv.* **garrulity** *n.*

garter *n.* band worn round the leg to hold up a sock or stocking. **the Garter** highest order of British knighthood.

gas *n., pl.* **gases, gasses. 1.** airlike substance that is not liquid or solid. **2.** fossil fuel in the form of a gas, used for heating. **3.** gaseous anaesthetic. **4.** *US* petrol. **5.** poisonous gas used in warfare. **6.** *Informal* idle talk, boasting. —*v.* **gassing, gassed. 7.** poison or render unconscious with gas. **8.** *Informal* talk idly or boastfully. **gassy** *adj.* **-sier, -siest. 1.** filled with gas. **2.** full of idle talk. **gaseous** *adj.* of or like gas. **gasbag** *n. Informal* person who talks too much. **gas chamber** airtight room which is filled with poison gas to kill people or animals. **gasholder, gasometer** [gas-**som**-it-er] *n.* large tank for storing gas. **gasify** *v.* **-fying, -fied.** change into a gas. **gasification** *n.* **gas mask** mask with a chemical filter to protect the wearer against poison gas. **gasworks** *n.* plant where coal gas is made.

gash *v.* **1.** make a long deep cut in. —*n.* **2.** long deep cut.

gasket *n.* piece of rubber etc. placed between two metal surfaces to act as a seal.

gasoline *n. US* petrol.

gasp *v.* **1.** draw in breath sharply or with difficulty. **2.** utter breathlessly. **3.** (foll. by *for*) crave. —*n.* **4.** convulsive intake of breath.

gastric *adj.* of the stomach. **gastritis** *n.* inflammation of the stomach.

gastroenteritis *n.* inflammation of the stomach and intestines.

gastronomy *n.* art of good eating. **gastronomic** *adj.*

gastropod *n.* mollusc, such as a snail, with a single flattened muscular foot.

gate *n.* **1.** movable barrier, usu. hinged, in a wall or fence. **2.** opening with a gate. **3.** any entrance or way in. **4.** (entrance money paid by) those attending a sporting event. **gate-crash** *v.* enter (a party) uninvited. **gatehouse** *n.* building at or above a gateway. **gateway** *n.* **1.** entrance with a gate. **2.** means of access, e.g. *Bombay, gateway to India.*

gâteau [**gat**-toe] *n., pl.* **-teaux** [-toes] rich elaborate cake.

gather *v.* **1.** assemble. **2.** collect gradually.

3. increase gradually. **4.** learn from information given. **5.** pick or harvest. **6.** draw (material) into small tucks or folds. **7.** (of a boil etc.) form pus. **gathers** *pl. n.* gathered folds in material. **gathering** *n.* assembly.

GATT General Agreement on Tariffs and Trade.

gauche [gohsh] *adj.* socially awkward. **gaucheness** *n.* **gaucherie** *n.* **1.** awkwardness. **2.** gauche act.

gaucho [gow-choh] *n., pl.* **-chos.** S American cowboy.

gaudy *adj.* **gaudier, gaudiest.** vulgarly bright or colourful. **gaudily** *adv.* **gaudiness** *n.*

gauge [gayj] *v.* **1.** measure the amount or condition of. **2.** estimate or judge. —*n.* **3.** scale or standard of measurement. **4.** measuring instrument. **5.** distance between the rails of a railway track. **6.** capacity or extent.

Gaul *n.* **1.** native of ancient Gaul. **2.** Frenchman.

gaunt *adj.* **1.** lean and haggard. **2.** (of a place) desolate or bleak. **gauntness** *n.*

gauntlet¹ *n.* **1.** heavy glove with a long cuff. **2.** medieval armoured glove. **throw down the gauntlet** offer a challenge.

gauntlet² *n.* **run the gauntlet** **1.** be forced to run between, and be struck by, two rows of men, as a former military punishment. **2.** be exposed to criticism or unpleasant treatment.

gauze *n.* **1.** transparent loosely-woven fabric. **2.** fine wire mesh. **gauzy** *adj.*

gave *v.* past tense of GIVE.

gavel [gahv-el] *n.* small hammer banged on a table by a judge, auctioneer, or chairman to call for attention.

gavotte *n.* **1.** old formal dance. **2.** music for this.

gawk *v.* **1.** stare stupidly. —*n.* **2.** clumsy awkward person. **gawky** *adj.* **gawkier, gawkiest.** clumsy or awkward. **gawkiness** *n.*

gawp *v. Slang* stare stupidly.

gay *adj.* **1.** homosexual. **2.** carefree and merry. **3.** colourful. —*n.* **4.** homosexual. **gayness** *n.* homosexuality.
▷ The meaning 'homosexual' is now the most frequent use of *gay*, which retains the meaning 'happy' only in older books.

gaze *v.* **1.** look fixedly. —*n.* **2.** fixed look.

gazebo [gaz-zee-boh] *n., pl.* **-bos, -boes.** summerhouse with a good view.

gazelle *n.* small graceful antelope.

gazette *n.* **1.** official publication containing announcements. —*v.* **2.** announce in a gazette. **gazetteer** *n.* (part of) a book that lists and describes places.

gazump *v.* raise the price of a house after verbally agreeing it with (a prospective buyer).

gazunder *v. Brit.* reduce an offer on a property immediately before exchanging contracts having earlier agreed a higher price with the seller.

GB Great Britain.

GBH grievous bodily harm.

GC George Cross.

GCE General Certificate of Education.

GCSE General Certificate of Secondary Education.

Gd *Chem.* gadolinium.

Ge *Chem.* germanium.

gear *n.* **1.** set of toothed wheels connecting with another or with a rack to change the direction or speed of transmitted motion. **2.** mechanism for transmitting motion by gears. **3.** setting of a gear to suit engine speed, e.g. *first gear*. **4.** clothing or belongings. **5.** equipment. —*v.* **6.** adapt (one thing) to fit in with another. **7.** equip with or connect by gears. **in, out of gear** with the gear mechanism engaged or disengaged. **gearbox** *n.* case enclosing a set of gears in a motor vehicle. **gear lever** lever for changing gears in a motor vehicle. **gear up** *v.* prepare for an activity.

gecko *n., pl.* **geckos, geckoes.** small tropical lizard.

gee *interj. US informal* mild exclamation.

geese *n.* plural of GOOSE.

geezer *n. Informal* (old or eccentric) man.

Geiger counter [guy-ger] *n.* instrument for detecting and measuring radiation.

geisha [gay-sha] *n., pl.* **-sha, -shas.** in Japan, professional female companion for men.

gel [jell] *n.* **1.** jelly-like substance. —*v.* **gelling, gelled.** **2.** form a gel. **3.** *Informal* take on a definite form.

gelatin [jel-at-tin], **gelatine** *n.* **1.** substance made by boiling animal bones. **2.** edible jelly made of this. **gelatinous**[jel-**at**-in-uss] *adj.* of or like jelly.

geld *v.* castrate. **gelding** *n.* castrated horse.

gelid [**jel**-lid] *adj.* very cold.

gelignite *n.* type of dynamite used for blasting.

gem *n.* **1.** precious stone or jewel. **2.** highly valued person or thing.

Gemini *n.* (the twins) third sign of the zodiac.

gen *n. Informal* information. **gen up on** *v.* **genning, genned.** *Informal* make or become fully informed about.

gendarme [**zhahn**-darm] *n.* member of the French police force.

gender *n.* **1.** state of being male or female, sex. **2.** *Grammar* classification of nouns in certain languages as masculine, feminine, or neuter.

gene [jean] *n.* part of a cell which determines inherited characteristics.

genealogy [jean-ee-al-a-gee] *n., pl.* **-gies.** (study of) the history and descent of a family or families. **genealogical** *adj.* **genealogist** *n.*

genera [**jen**-er-a] *n.* plural of GENUS.

general *adj.* **1.** common or widespread. **2.** of or affecting all or most. **3.** not specific. **4.** including or dealing with various or miscellaneous items. **5.** highest in authority or rank, e.g. *general manager.* **6.** true in most cases. —*n.* **7.** very senior army officer. **generally** *adv.* **generality** *n., pl.* **-ties. 1.** general principle. **2.** state of being general. **generalize** *v.* **1.** draw general conclusions. **2.** speak in generalities. **3.** make widely known or used. **generalization** *n.* **general election** election in which representatives are chosen for every constituency. **general practitioner** nonspecialist doctor serving a local area.

generalissimo *n., pl.* **-mos.** supreme commander of combined armed forces.

generate *v.* produce or bring into being. **generative** *adj.* capable of producing. **generator** *n.* **1.** machine for converting mechanical energy into electrical energy. **2.** device for producing a gas.

generation *n.* **1.** generating. **2.** all the people born about the same time. **3.** average time between two generations (about 30 years). **4.** successive stage in descent of people or animals.

generic [jin-**ner**-ik] *adj.* of a class, group, or genus. **generically** *adv.*

generous *adj.* **1.** free in giving. **2.** free from pettiness. **3.** plentiful. **generously** *adv.* **generosity** *n.*

genesis [**jen**-iss-iss] *n., pl.* **-eses** [-iss-eez] beginning or origin.

genetic [jin-**net**-tik] *adj.* of genes or genetics. **genetics** *n.* study of heredity and variation in organisms. **geneticist** *n.* **genetic engineering** alteration of the genetic structure of an organism for a particular purpose. **genetic fingerprinting** use of a person's unique DNA pattern for identification.

Geneva Convention *n.* international agreement establishing a code for wartime treatment of the sick, wounded, and prisoners of war.

genial [**jean**-ee-al] *adj.* cheerful and friendly. **genially** *adv.* **geniality** *n.*

genie [**jean**-ee] *n.* in fairy tales, a servant who appears by magic and grants wishes.

genital *adj.* of the sexual organs or reproduction. **genitals, genitalia** [jen-it-**ail**-ya] *pl. n.* external sexual organs.

genitive *adj.* (of) the grammatical case indicating possession or association.

genius [**jean**-yuss] *n.* **1.** (person with) exceptional ability in a particular field. **2.** guardian spirit of a person or place.

genocide [**jen**-no-side] *n.* murder of a race of people.

genre [**zhahn**-ra] *n.* style of literary, musical, or artistic work.

gent *Informal* —*n.* **1.** gentleman. —*pl. n.* men's public toilet.

genteel *adj.* affectedly proper and polite. **genteelly** *adv.*

gentian [**jen**-shun] *n.* mountain plant with deep blue flowers. **gentian violet** violet dye used as an antiseptic.

gentile *adj., n.* non-Jewish (person).

gentle *adj.* **1.** mild or kindly. **2.** not rough or severe. **3.** gradual. **4.** easily controlled, tame. **5.** noble or well-born. **gentleness** *n.* **gently** *adv.* **gentility** *n.* **1.** noble birth or ancestry. **2.** polite and well-mannered behaviour. **gentlefolk, gentlefolks** *pl. n.* people of good breeding. **gentleman** *n.* **1.** polite well-bred man. **2.** man of high social position. **3.** polite name for a man. **gentlemanly** *adj.* **gentlewoman** *n. fem.*

gentry n. people just below the nobility in social rank. **gentrification** n. taking-over of a traditionally working-class area by middle-class incomers. **gentrify** v. -**fying**, -**fied**.

genuflect v. bend the knee as a sign of reverence or deference. **genuflection**, **genuflexion** n.

genuine adj. **1**. not fake, authentic. **2**. sincere. **genuinely** adv. **genuineness** n.

genus [jean-uss] n., pl. **genera**. **1**. group into which a family of animals or plants is divided. **2**. kind, type.

geocentric adj. **1**. having the earth as a centre. **2**. measured as from the earth's centre.

geode n. cavity lined with crystals within a rock.

geodesic adj. **1**. of the geometry of curved surfaces. —n. **2**. shortest line between two points on a curve.

geodesy n. study of the shape and size of the earth.

geography n. **1**. study of the earth's physical features, climate, population, etc. **2**. physical features of a region. **geographer** n. **geographical**, **geographic** adj. **geographically** adv.

geology n. **1**. study of the earth's origin, structure, and composition. **2**. geological features of an area. **geological** adj. **geologically** adv. **geologist** n.

geometry n. branch of mathematics dealing with points, lines, curves, and surfaces. **geometric**, **geometrical** adj. **geometrically** adv. **geometrician** n.

Geordie n. person from, or dialect of, Tyneside.

George Cross n. British award for bravery.

georgette [jor-jet] n. fine silky fabric.

Georgian adj. **1**. of the time of any of the kings of Britain called George, esp. 1714–1830. **2**ₐ of or from Georgia.

geostationary adj. (of a satellite) orbiting so as to remain over the same point of the earth's surface.

geothermal adj. of or using the heat in the earth's interior.

geranium n. cultivated plant with red, pink, or white flowers.

gerbil [jer-bill] n. burrowing desert rodent of Asia and Africa.

geriatrics n. branch of medicine dealing with old age and its diseases. **geriatric** adj., n. old (person). **geriatrician** n.

germ n. **1**. microbe, esp. one causing disease. **2**. beginning from which something may develop. **3**. simple structure that can develop into a complete organism. **germicide** n. substance that kills germs. **germicidal** adj.

german adj. **1**. having the same parents, e.g. brother-german. **2**. being a first cousin, e.g. cousin-german.

German n. **1**. language of Germany, Austria, and part of Switzerland. **2**. person from Germany. —adj. **3**. of Germany or its language. **Germanic** adj., n. **German measles** contagious disease accompanied by a cough, sore throat, and red spots. **German shepherd dog** Alsatian.

germander n. European plant having two-lipped flowers with a very small upper lip.

germane adj. **germane to** relevant to.

germanium n. brittle grey element that is a semiconductor.

germinate v. (cause to) sprout or begin to grow. **germination** n. **germinal** adj. **1**. of or in the earliest stage of development. **2**. of germs.

gerontology n. study of ageing and the problems of elderly people. **gerontologist** n.

gerrymander v. manipulate political boundaries so as to favour one party.

gerund [jer-rund] n. noun formed from a verb, such as living.

Gestapo n. secret state police of Nazi Germany.

gestation n. **1**. (period of) carrying of young in the womb between conception and birth. **2**. developing of a plan or idea in the mind.

gesticulate v. make expressive movements of the hands and arms. **gesticulation** n.

gesture n. **1**. movement to convey meaning. **2**. thing said or done to show one's feelings. —v. **3**. gesticulate.

get v. **getting**, **got**. **1**. obtain or receive. **2**. bring or fetch. **3**. contract (an illness). **4**. capture or seize. **5**. (cause to) become as specified, e.g. get wet. **6**. prepare (a meal) **7**. understand. **8**. (often foll. by to) come (to) or arrive (at). **9**. go on board (a plane bus, etc.). **10**. persuade. **11**. receive a broadcast signal. **12.** *Informal* annoy. **13.** *Informal* have the better of. **14.** be revenged on. **get across** *v.* (cause to) be understood. **get at** *v.* **1.** gain access to. **2.** criticize. **3.** influence. **getaway** *adj., n.* (used in) escape. **get by** *v.* manage in spite of difficulties. **get off** *v.* (cause to) avoid the consequences of, or punishment for, an action. **get off with** *v. Informal* start a romantic or sexual relationship with. **get on** *v.* **1.** be friends with. **2.** (foll. by *with*) continue to do. **3.** grow old. **get over** *v.* recover from. **get through** *v.* **1.** (cause to) succeed. **2.** contact by telephone. **3.** use up (money or supplies). **get through to** *v.* make (a person) understand. **get-up** *n. Informal* costume. **get-up-and-go** *n. Informal* energy. **get up to** *v.* be involved in.

geyser[geez-er] *n.* **1.** spring that discharges steam and hot water. **2.** domestic gas water heater.

ghastly *adj.* **-lier, -liest. 1.** *Informal* unpleasant. **2.** deathly pale. **3.** *Informal* unwell. **4.** *Informal* horrible. **ghastliness** *n.*

ghat *n.* **1.** in India, steps leading down to a river. **2.** mountain pass.

ghee [gee] *n.* in Indian cookery, clarified butter.

gherkin *n.* small pickled cucumber.

ghetto *n., pl.* **-tos, -toes. 1.** slum area inhabited by a deprived minority. **2.** area in a city to which Jews were formerly restricted. **ghetto-blaster** *n. Informal* large portable cassette-recorder.

ghillie *n.* same as GILLIE.

ghost *n.* **1.** disembodied spirit of a dead person. **2.** faint trace. **3.** faint secondary image on a television screen. —*v.* **4.** ghostwrite. **ghostly** *adj.* **ghost town** deserted town. **ghostwrite** *v.* write (a book or article) on behalf of another person who is credited as the author. **ghostwriter** *n.*

ghoul [gool] *n.* **1.** person with morbid interests. **2.** demon that eats corpses. **ghoulish** *adj.*

GHQ *Mil.* General Headquarters.

GI *Informal* —*n.* **1.** US soldier. —*adj.* **2.** of the US armed forces.

giant *n.* **1.** mythical being of superhuman size. **2.** very large person or thing. **3.** person of exceptional ability or importance. —*adj.* **4.** huge. **giantess** *n. fem.*

gibber [jib-ber] *v.* speak or utter rapidly and

unintelligibly. **gibberish** *n.* rapid unintelligible talk.

gibbet [jib-bit] *n.* gallows for displaying executed criminals.

gibbon [gib-bon] *n.* agile tree-dwelling ape of S Asia.

gibbous *adj.* (of the moon) more than half but less than fully illuminated.

gibe [jibe] *v., n.* taunt or jeer.

giblets [jibl-lets] *pl. n.* gizzard, liver, heart, and neck of a fowl.

giddy *adj.* **-dier, -diest. 1.** having or causing a feeling of dizziness. **2.** scatter-brained. **giddily** *adv.* **giddiness** *n.*

gift *n.* **1.** present. **2.** natural talent. —*v.* **3.** present with. **gifted** *adj.* talented.

gig[1] *n.* **1.** single performance by pop or jazz musicians. —*v.* **gigging, gigged. 2.** play a gig or gigs.

gig[2] *n.* **1.** light two-wheeled horse-drawn carriage. **2.** long light rowing boat.

giga- *prefix* **1.** denoting 10^9, e.g. *gigavolt.* **2.** *Computers* denoting 2^{30}, e.g. *gigabyte.*

gigantic *adj.* enormous.

giggle *v.* **1.** laugh nervously or foolishly. —*n.* **2.** such a laugh. **3.** *Informal* amusing person or thing. **giggly** *adj.*

gigolo [jig-a-lo] *n., pl.* **-los.** man paid by an older woman to be her escort or lover.

gigot *n.* leg of lamb or mutton.

gild[1] *v.* **gilding, gilded** *or* **gilt. 1.** put a thin layer of gold on. **2.** make falsely attractive.

gild[2] *n.* same as GUILD.

gill[1] [gill] *n.* **1.** (usu. pl.) breathing organ in most aquatic animals. **2.** radiating structure beneath the cap of a mushroom.

gill[2] [jill] *n.* liquid measure of quarter of a pint, equal to 0.142 litres.

gillie *n.* in Scotland, attendant for hunting or fishing.

gillyflower *n.* fragrant flower.

gilt[1] *v.* **1.** past of GILD[1]. —*adj.* **2.** gilded. —*n.* **3.** thin layer of gold used as decoration. **gilt-edged** *adj.* denoting government stocks on which interest payments and final repayments are guaranteed.

gilt[2] *n.* young female pig.

gimbals *pl. n.* set of pivoted rings which allow nautical instruments to remain horizontal at sea.

gimcrack [jim-krak] *adj.* **1.** showy but cheap. **2.** shoddy.

gimlet [gim-let] *n.* small tool with a screw-like tip for boring holes in wood. **gimlet-eyed** *adj.* having a piercing glance.

gimmick *n.* something designed to attract attention or publicity. **gimmickry** *n.* **gimmicky** *adj.*

gin[1] *n.* alcoholic drink flavoured with juniper berries.

gin[2] *n.* **1.** machine for separating seeds from raw cotton. **2.** wire noose used to trap small animals.

ginger *n.* **1.** root of a tropical plant, used as a spice. **2.** light orange-brown colour. **3.** vigour. **gingery** *adj.* **ginger ale, beer** fizzy ginger-flavoured soft drink. **gingerbread** *n.* moist cake flavoured with ginger. **ginger group** group within a larger group that agitates for a more active policy. **ginger nut, snap** crisp ginger-flavoured biscuit.

gingerly *adv.* **1.** cautiously. —*adj.* **2.** cautious.

gingham *n.* cotton cloth, usu. checked or striped.

gingivitis [jin-jiv-vite-iss] *n.* inflammation of the gums.

ginkgo [gink-go] *n.*, *pl.* -**goes.** ornamental Chinese tree.

ginseng [jin-seng] *n.* (root of) a plant believed to have tonic and energy-giving properties.

Gipsy *n.*, *pl.* -**sies.** same as GYPSY.

giraffe *n.* African ruminant mammal with a spotted yellow skin and long neck and legs.

gird *v.* **girding, girded** *or* **girt. 1.** put a belt round. **2.** secure with or as if with a belt. **3.** surround. **gird, gird up one's loins** prepare for action.

girder *n.* large metal beam.

girdle[1] *n.* **1.** woman's elastic corset. **2.** belt. **3.** *Anat.* encircling structure or part. —*v.* **4.** surround or encircle.

girdle[2] *n. Scot.* griddle.

girl *n.* **1.** female child. **2.** young woman. **3.** girlfriend. **4.** *Informal* any woman. **girlhood** *n.* **girlish** *adj.* **girlie** *adj. Informal* featuring photographs of naked or scantily clad women. **girlfriend** *n.* **1.** girl or woman with whom a person is romantically or sexually involved. **2.** female friend. **Girl Guide** same as GUIDE.

giro [jire-oh] *n.*, *pl.* -**ros. 1.** system of transferring money within a post office or bank directly from one account to another. **2.** *Informal* social security payment by giro cheque.

girt *v.* past of GIRD.

girth *n.* **1.** measurement round something. **2.** band round a horse to hold the saddle in position.

gist [jist] *n.* substance or main point of a matter.

give *v.* **giving, gave, given. 1.** present (something) to another person. **2.** transfer in exchange or payment. **3.** hand over temporarily. **4.** impart. **5.** attribute. **6.** administer. **7.** be a source of. **8.** utter or emit. **9.** concede. **10.** sacrifice or devote. **11.** organize or host. **12.** yield or break under pressure. **13.** resilience or elasticity. **give away** *v.* **1.** donate as a gift. **2.** reveal. **3.** hand over (a bride) formally to her husband in a marriage ceremony. **give-away** *n.* **1.** usu. unintentional disclosure. —*adj.* **2.** very cheap or free. **give in** *v.* admit defeat. **give off** *v.* emit. **give out** *v.* **1.** distribute. **2.** emit. **3.** come to an end or fail. **give over** *v.* **1.** set aside for a specific purpose. **2.** *Informal* cease. **give up** *v.* **1.** acknowledge defeat. **2.** abandon.

gizzard *n.* part of a bird's stomach.

glacé [glass-say] *adj.* **1.** crystallized or candied. **2.** glossy.

glacier *n.* slow-moving mass of ice formed by accumulated snow. **glacial** *adj.* **1.** of ice or glaciers. **2.** very cold. **3.** unfriendly. **glaciated** *adj.* covered with or affected by glaciers. **glaciation** *n.*

glad *adj.* **gladder, gladdest. 1.** pleased and happy. **2.** causing happiness. **glad to** very willing to (do something). **the glad eye** *Informal* an inviting or seductive glance. **gladly** *adv.* **gladness** *n.* **gladden** *v.* make glad. **gladsome** *adj. Old-fashioned* cheerful. **glad rags** *Informal* best clothes.

glade *n.* open space in a forest.

gladiator *n.* in ancient Rome, man trained to fight in arenas to provide entertainment.

gladiolus *n.*, *pl.* -**lus, -li, -luses.** garden plant with sword-shaped leaves.

glair *n.* **1.** white of an egg. **2.** any similar sticky substance.

glamour *n.* alluring charm or fascination. **glamorous** *adj.* alluring. **glamorize** *v.*

glance v. **1.** look rapidly or briefly. **2.** glint or gleam. —n. **3.** brief look. **glancing** adj. hitting at an oblique angle. **glance off** v. strike and be deflected off (an object) at an oblique angle.

gland n. **1.** organ that produces and secretes substances in the body. **2.** similar organ in a plant. **glandular** adj. **glandular fever** infectious viral disease characterized by fever and swollen lymph nodes.

glanders n. contagious disease of horses.

glare v. **1.** stare angrily. **2.** be unpleasantly bright. —n. **3.** angry stare. **4.** unpleasant brightness. **glaring** adj. **1.** conspicuous. **2.** unpleasantly bright. **glaringly** adv.

glasnost n. policy of openness and accountability, esp. in the USSR.

glass n. **1.** hard brittle, usu. transparent substance made by melting sand. **2.** objects made of glass. **3.** tumbler. **4.** its contents. **5.** mirror. **6.** barometer. —pl. **7.** spectacles. **glassy** adj. **1.** like glass. **2.** expressionless. **glassiness** n. **glasshouse** n. **1.** greenhouse. **2.** Informal army prison. **glass wool** fine glass fibres used for insulating.

glaucoma n. eye disease.

glaze v. **1.** fit or cover with glass. **2.** cover with a glassy substance. **3.** become glassy. —n. **4.** transparent coating. **5.** substance used for this. **glazier** n. person who fits windows with glass.

gleam n. **1.** small beam or glow of light. **2.** brief or faint indication. —v. **3.** emit a gleam. **gleaming** adj.

glean v. **1.** gather (facts etc.) bit by bit. **2.** gather (the useful remnants of a crop) after harvesting. **gleaner** n.

glebe n. land belonging to a parish church.

glee n. **1.** triumph and delight. **2.** musical composition for three or more unaccompanied voices. **gleeful** adj. **gleefully** adv.

glen n. deep narrow valley.

glengarry n., pl. **-ries.** brimless Scottish cap with a crease down the crown.

glib adj. **glibber, glibbest.** fluent but insincere or superficial. **glibly** adv. **glibness** n.

glide v. **1.** move easily and smoothly. **2.** (of an aircraft) move without the use of engines. **3.** pass gradually and imperceptibly. —n. **4.** smooth easy movement. **glider** n. aircraft without an engine which floats on air currents. **gliding** n. sport of flying gliders.

glimmer v. **1.** shine faintly, flicker. —n. **2.** faint gleam. **3.** faint indication.

glimpse n. **1.** brief or incomplete view. **2.** vague indication. —v. **3.** catch a glimpse of.

glint v. **1.** gleam brightly. —n. **2.** bright gleam.

glissade n. **1.** gliding step in ballet. **2.** controlled slide down a snow slope. —v. **3.** perform a glissade.

glissando n. Music slide between two notes in which all intermediate notes are played.

glisten v. gleam by reflecting light.

glitch n. sudden malfunction in an electronic system.

glitter v. **1.** shine with bright flashes. **2.** be showy. —n. **3.** sparkle or brilliance. **4.** shiny powder used as decoration.

glitzy adj. **glitzier, glitziest.** Slang showily attractive.

gloaming n. twilight.

gloat v. (often foll. by over) look (at) or think (of) with smug or malicious pleasure.

glob n. rounded mass of thick fluid.

globe n. **1.** sphere with a map of the earth on it. **2.** spherical object. **the globe** the earth. **global** adj. **1.** worldwide. **2.** total or comprehensive. **globally** adv. **globetrotter** n. habitual worldwide traveller. **globetrotting** n., adj.

globule n. small round drop. **globular** adj.

globulin n. simple protein found in living tissue.

glockenspiel n. percussion instrument consisting of small metal bars played with hammers.

gloom n. **1.** darkness. **2.** melancholy or depression. **gloomy** adj. **gloomier, gloomiest. gloomily** adv.

glory n., pl. **-ries. 1.** praise or honour. **2.** praiseworthy thing. **3.** splendour. **4.** heavenly bliss. **5.** halo of a saint. —v. **-rying, -ried. 6.** (foll. by in) triumph or exalt. **glorify** v. **-fying, -fied. 1.** make glorious. **2.** praise. **3.** make (something) seem more worthy than it is. **glorification** n. **glorious** adj. **1.** full of or conferring glory. **2.** brilliantly beautiful. **3.** delightful. **gloriously** adv. **glory hole** Informal untidy cupboard or storeroom.

gloss[1] n. **1.** surface shine or lustre. **2.** paint or cosmetic giving a shiny finish. **3.** superficially attractive appearance. —v. **4.** make glossy. **glossy** adj. **-sier, -siest. 1.** smooth and shiny. **2.** (of a magazine) printed on shiny paper. **glossily** *adv.* **glossiness** *n.* **gloss over** *v.* (try to) cover up or pass over (a fault or error).

gloss² *n.* **1.** explanatory comment added to the text of a book. —*v.* **2.** add glosses to.

glossary *n., pl.* **-ries.** list of special or technical words with definitions.

glottis *n., pl.* **-tises, -tides.** vocal cords and the space between them. **glottal** *adj.* **glottal stop** speech sound made by closing and then opening the glottis.

glove *n.* **1.** covering for the hand with individual sheaths for each finger and the thumb. —*v.* **2.** cover with or as if with a glove. **glove compartment** small storage area in the dashboard of a car.

glow *v.* **1.** emit light and heat without flames. **2.** shine. **3.** have a feeling of wellbeing or satisfaction. **4.** (of a colour) look warm. **5.** be hot. —*n.* **6.** glowing light. **7.** warmth of colour. **8.** feeling of wellbeing. **glow-worm** *n.* insect giving out a green light.

glower [rhymes with **power**] *v., n.* scowl.

gloxinia *n.* tropical plant with large bellshaped flowers.

glucose *n.* kind of sugar found in fruit.

glue *n.* **1.** natural or synthetic sticky substance used as an adhesive. —*v.* **2.** fasten with glue. **3.** (foll. by *to*) pay full attention to, e.g. *her eyes were glued to the TV.* **gluey** *adj.* **gluesniffing** *n.* inhaling of glue fumes for intoxicating or hallucinatory effects.

glum *adj.* **glummer, glummest.** sullen or gloomy. **glumly** *adv.*

glut *n.* **1.** excessive supply. —*v.* **glutting, glutted. 2.** feed or fill to excess. **3.** oversupply.

gluten [gloo-ten] *n.* protein found in cereal grain.

glutinous [gloo-tin-uss] *adj.* sticky or gluey.

glutton¹ *n.* **1.** greedy person. **2.** person with a great capacity for something. **gluttonous** *adj.* **gluttony** *n.*

glutton² *n.* wolverine.

glycerin, glycerine [gliss-ser-in] *n.* colourless sweet liquid used widely in chemistry and industry.

glycerol [gliss-ser-ol] *n.* technical name for GLYCERIN.

gm gram.

G-man *n., pl.* **G-men.** *US slang* FBI agent.

GMT Greenwich Mean Time.

gnarled *adj.* rough, twisted, and knobbly.

gnash *v.* grind (the teeth) together in anger or pain.

gnat *n.* small biting two-winged fly.

gnaw *v.* **gnawing, gnawed, gnawed** or **gnawn. 1.** bite or chew steadily. **2.** erode. **3.** (foll. by *at*) cause constant distress (to).

gneiss *n.* coarse-grained metamorphic rock.

gnome *n.* **1.** imaginary creature like a little old man. **2.** international banker or financier.

gnomic [no-mik] *adj.* of pithy sayings.

Gnosticism *n.* religious movement believing in intuitive spiritual knowledge. **Gnostic** *n., adj.*

GNP Gross National Product.

gnu [noo] *n.* oxlike S African antelope.

go *v.* **going, went, gone. 1.** move to or from a place. **2.** depart. **3.** make regular journeys. **4.** function. **5.** be, do, or become as specified. **6.** contribute to a result, e.g. *it just goes to show.* **7.** be allotted to a specific purpose or recipient. **8.** be sold. **9.** blend or harmonize. **10.** fail or break down. **11.** elapse. **12.** be got rid of. **13.** attend. **14.** reach or exceed certain limits, e.g. *she's gone too far this time.* **15.** be acceptable. **16.** carry authority. —*n.* **17.** attempt. **18.** verbal attack. **19.** turn. **20.** *Informal* energy or vigour. **make a go of** be successful at. **on the go** active and energetic. **go-ahead** *adj.* enterprising or ambitious. **go back on** *v.* break (a promise etc.). **go-between** *n.* intermediary. **go for** *v.* **1.** *Informal* choose. **2.** attack. **3.** apply to equally. **go-getter** *n.* energetically ambitious person. **go-go dancer** scantily dressed erotic dancer. **go off** *v.* **1.** explode. **2.** ring or sound. **3.** *Informal* stop liking. **4.** *Informal* become stale or rotten. **go out** *v.* **1.** be romantically involved (with). **2.** be extinguished. **3.** cease to be fashionable or popular. **go over** *v.* examine or check. **go-slow** *n.* deliberate slowing of work-rate as an industrial protest. **go through** *v.* **1.** examine or search. **2.** suffer or undergo.

goad *n.* **1.** spiked stick for driving cattle. **2.** spur or incentive. —*v.* **3.** urge on with or as if with a goad.

goal n. **1.** aim or purpose. **2.** objective. **3.** *Sport* posts through which the ball or puck has to be propelled to score. **4.** score so made. **goalie** n. *Informal* goalkeeper. **goalkeeper** n. player whose task is to stop shots entering the goal. **goalpost** n. one of the two posts supporting the crossbar of a goal. **move the goalposts** change the aims of an activity to ensure the desired result.

goat n. **1.** sure-footed ruminant animal. **2.** *Informal* lecherous man. **3.** foolish person. **get someone's goat** *Slang* annoy someone. **goatee** n. pointed tuftlike beard.

gob n. **1.** lump of a soft substance. **2.** *Slang* mouth.

gobbet n. lump, esp. of food.

gobble¹ v. eat hastily and greedily.

gobble² n. **1.** rapid gurgling cry of the male turkey. —v. **2.** make this noise.

gobbledegook, gobbledygook n. unintelligible (official) language or jargon.

goblet n. drinking cup.

goblin n. in folklore, small malevolent creature.

goby n., pl. **-by, -bies.** small spiny-finned fish.

god n. **1.** spirit or being worshipped as having supernatural power. **2.** object of worship, idol. **3.** (G-) in monotheistic religions, the Supreme Being, creator and ruler of the universe. **goddess** n. fem. **the gods** top balcony in a theatre. **godlike** adj. **godly** adj. devout or pious. **godliness** n. **godfearing** adj. pious and devout. **godforsaken** adj. desolate or dismal. **godsend** n. something unexpected but welcome.

godetia n. garden plant with showy flowers.

godparent n. person who promises at a child's baptism to bring the child up as a Christian. **godchild** n. child for whom a person stands as godparent. **goddaughter** n. **godfather** n. **1.** male godparent. **2.** head of a criminal, esp. Mafia, organization. **godmother** n.

godwit n. shore bird with long legs and an upturned bill.

goer n. person who attends something regularly, e.g. *film-goer.*

goggle v. **1.** (of the eyes) bulge. **2.** stare. **goggles** pl. n. protective spectacles. **gogglebox** n. *Slang* television set.

Goidelic adj., n. (of) the group of Celtic languages consisting of Scottish Gaelic, Irish Gaelic, and Manx.

going n. **1.** departure. **2.** condition of the ground for walking or riding over. **3.** rate of travel. —adj. **4.** thriving. **5.** current or accepted. **6.** available. **going-over** n., pl. **goings-over. 1.** *Informal* investigation or examination. **2.** scolding or thrashing. **goings-on** pl. n. mysterious or unacceptable events.

goitre [goy-ter] n. swelling of the thyroid gland in the neck.

go-kart n. small low-powered racing car.

gold n. **1.** yellow precious metal. **2.** coins or articles made of this. **3.** colour of gold. **4.** wealth. —adj. **5.** made of gold. **6.** gold-coloured. **goldcrest** n. small bird with a yellow crown. **gold-digger** n. **1.** person who digs for gold. **2.** *Informal* woman who uses her sexual attractions to get money from a man. **goldfinch** n. kind of finch, the male of which has yellow-and-black wings. **goldfish** n. orange fish kept in ponds or aquariums. **gold leaf** thin gold sheet used for gilding. **gold medal** medal given to the winner of a competition or race. **gold rush** migration of people to a territory where gold has been found. **goldsmith** n. dealer in or maker of gold articles.

golden adj. **1.** made of gold. **2.** gold-coloured. **3.** very successful or promising. **golden eagle** large mountain eagle of the N hemisphere. **golden handshake** *Informal* payment to a departing employee. **golden mean** middle course between extremes. **golden rule** important principle. **golden wedding** fiftieth wedding anniversary.

golf n. **1.** outdoor game in which a ball is struck with clubs into a series of holes. —v. **2.** play golf. **golfer** n.

golliwog n. soft black-faced male doll.

golly interj. exclamation of mild surprise.

goloshes pl. n. same as GALOSHES.

gonad n. organ producing reproductive cells, such as a testicle or ovary.

gondola n. **1.** long narrow boat used in Venice. **2.** suspended cabin of a cable car, airship, etc. **gondolier** n. person who rows a gondola.

gone v. past participle of GO. **goner** n. *Informal* person or thing beyond help or recovery.

gong n. **1.** rimmed metal disc that produces a note when struck. **2.** *Slang* medal.

gonorrhoea [gon-or-**ree**-a] n. venereal disease with a discharge from the genitals.

good adj. **better, best. 1.** giving pleasure. **2.** kindly. **3.** commendable. **4.** morally excellent. **5.** talented. **6.** well-behaved. **7.** beneficial. **8.** valid. **9.** reliable. **10.** financially sound. **11.** complete or full. —n. **12.** benefit. **13.** positive moral qualities. —pl. **14.** property. **15.** merchandise. **as good as** virtually. **for good** permanently. **goodness** n. **goodly** adj. considerable. **goody** n., pl. **-dies. 1.** enjoyable thing. **2.** Informal hero in a book or film. **goody-goody** adj., n. smugly virtuous (person). **good-for-nothing** adj., n. irresponsible or worthless (person). **Good Friday** Friday before Easter, observed by Christians as a commemoration of the Crucifixion. **good-natured** adj. tolerant and kindly. **Good Samaritan** person who helps another in distress. **goodwill** n. **1.** kindly feeling. **2.** value of a business in reputation etc. over and above its tangible assets.
▷ Note that *good* is an adjective. To modify a verb, use *well: She did well.*

goodbye interj., n. expression used on parting.

gooey adj. **gooier, gooiest.** Informal sticky and soft.

goof Informal —n. **1.** mistake. **2.** stupid person. —v. **3.** make a mistake. **goofy** adj. **goofier, goofiest.**

googly n., pl. **-lies.** Cricket ball which changes direction unexpectedly on the bounce.

goon n. **1.** Informal stupid person. **2.** US hired thug.

goosander n. type of duck.

goose n., pl. **geese. 1.** web-footed bird like a large duck. **2.** female of this bird. **3.** silly person. **goose flesh, pimples** bristling of the skin due to cold or fright. **goose step** march step in which the leg is swung rigidly.

gooseberry n. **1.** edible yellowy-green berry. **2.** Informal unwanted third person accompanying a couple.

gopher [**go**-fer] n. American burrowing rodent.

gore[1] n. blood from a wound.

gore[2] v. pierce with horns.

gore[3] n. tapering piece of material in a garment, sail, or umbrella.

gorge n. **1.** deep narrow valley. **2.** contents of the stomach. —v. **3.** eat greedily. **make one's gorge rise** cause feelings of disgust.

gorgeous adj. **1.** strikingly beautiful or attractive. **2.** Informal very pleasant. **gorgeously** adv.

gorgon n. terrifying or repulsive woman.

Gorgonzola n. sharp-flavoured blue-veined Italian cheese.

gorilla n. largest of the apes, found in Africa.

gormandize v. eat (food) hurriedly or like a glutton.

gormless adj. Informal stupid.

gorse n. prickly yellow-flowered shrub.

gory adj. **gorier, goriest. 1.** horrific or bloodthirsty. **2.** involving bloodshed.

gosh interj. exclamation of mild surprise or wonder.

goshawk n. large hawk.

gosling n. young goose.

gospel n. **1.** unquestionable truth. **2.** (G-) any of the first four books of the New Testament. **3.** Black religious music originating in the churches of the Southern US.

gossamer n. **1.** filmy cobweb. **2.** very fine fabric.

gossip n. **1.** idle talk, esp. about other people. **2.** person who engages in gossip. —v. **gossiping, gossiped. 3.** engage in gossip. **gossipy** adj.

got v. past of GET. **have got** possess. **have got to** need or be required to.

Goth n. member of an East Germanic people who invaded the Roman Empire. **Gothic** adj. **1.** (of architecture) of or in the style common in Europe from the 12th–16th centuries, with pointed arches. **2.** of or in an 18th-century literary style characterized by gloom and the supernatural. **3.** barbarous. **4.** (of print) using a heavy ornate typeface.

gotten v. US past participle of GET.

gouache n. (painting using) watercolours mixed with glue.

Gouda n. mild-flavoured Dutch cheese.

gouge [gowj] v. **1.** scoop or force out. **2.** cut (a hole or groove) in (something). —n. **3.** chisel with a curved cutting edge. **4.** hole or groove.

goulash [**goo**-lash] n. rich stew seasoned with paprika.

gourd [goord] n. **1.** fleshy fruit of a climbing plant. **2.** its dried shell, used as a container.

gourmand [goor-mand] *n.* person who is very keen on food and drink.

gourmet [goor-may] *n.* connoisseur of food and drink.

gout [gowt] *n.* **1.** disease causing inflammation of the joints. **2.** drop or splash. **gouty** *adj.*

govern *v.* **1.** rule, direct, or control. **2.** exercise restraint over (temper etc.). **3.** decide or determine. **governable** *adj.* **governance** *n.* governing. **governess** *n.* woman teacher in a private household. **government** *n.* **1.** executive policy-making body of a state. **2.** exercise of political authority over a country or state. **3.** system by which a country or state is ruled. **governmental** *adj.* **governor** *n.* **1.** official governing a province or state. **2.** senior administrator of a society, institution, or prison. **3.** chief executive of a US state. **4.** device that controls the speed of an engine. **5.** *Informal* person's father or employer. **governor general** representative of the Crown in a Commonwealth dominion.

gown *n.* **1.** woman's long formal dress. **2.** surgeon's overall. **3.** official robe worn by judges, clergymen, etc.

goy *n., pl.* **goyim, goys.** *Slang* Jewish word for a non-Jew.

GP general practitioner.

GPO General Post Office.

grab *v.* **grabbing, grabbed. 1.** grasp suddenly, snatch. **2.** seize illegally. **3.** take (food, drink, or rest) hurriedly. —*n.* **4.** sudden snatch. **5.** mechanical device for gripping.

grace *n.* **1.** beauty and elegance. **2.** polite, kind behaviour. **3.** goodwill or favour. **4.** delay granted. **5.** courtesy or decency. **6.** free favour of God shown towards man. **7.** short prayer of thanks for a meal. **8.** (**G-**) title of a duke, duchess, or archbishop. —*pl.* **9.** (**G-**) in Greek mythology, three sister goddesses, givers of charm and beauty. —*v.* **10.** add grace to. **11.** honour. **graceful** *adj.* **gracefully** *adv.* **graceless** *adj.* **gracious** *adj.* **1.** kind and courteous. **2.** condescendingly polite. **3.** elegant. **graciously** *adv.* **grace note** *Music* note ornamenting a melody.

grade *n.* **1.** place on a scale of quality, rank, or size. **2.** mark or rating. **3.** *US* class in school. —*v.* **4.** arrange in grades. **5.** assign a grade to. **6.** level (a road etc.) to a suitable gradient. **make the grade** succeed. **grada-**

tion *n.* **1.** (stage in) a series of degrees or steps. **2.** arrangement in stages. **gradate** *v.* **gradational** *adj.*

gradient *n.* (degree of) slope.

gradual *adj.* occurring, developing, or moving in small stages. **gradually** *adv.*

graduate *v.* **1.** receive a degree or diploma. **2.** (often foll. by *to*) change by degrees. **3.** group by type or quality. **4.** mark (a container etc.) with units of measurement. —*n.* **5.** holder of a degree. **graduation** *n.*

graffiti [graf-**fee**-tee] *pl. n.* words or drawings scribbled or sprayed on walls etc.
▷ English does not have a singular form for this word and tends to use *graffiti* for both singular and multiple examples.

graft[1] *n.* **1.** shoot of a plant set in the stalk of another. **2.** surgical transplant of skin or tissue. —*v.* **3.** insert (a plant shoot) in another stalk. **4.** transplant (living tissue) surgically.

graft[2] *Informal* —*n.* **1.** hard work. **2.** obtaining of money by misusing one's position. —*v.* **3.** work hard. **grafter** *n.*

grail *n.* same as HOLY GRAIL.

grain *n.* **1.** seedlike fruit of a cereal plant. **2.** cereal plants in general. **3.** small hard particle. **4.** small unit of weight, 0.0648 gram. **5.** arrangement of fibres, as in wood. **6.** texture or pattern resulting from this. **7.** very small amount. —*v.* **8.** paint in imitation of the grain of wood or leather. **go against the grain** be contrary to one's natural inclination. **grainy** *adj.*

gram, gramme *n.* metric unit of mass equal to one thousandth of a kilogram.

gramineous *adj.* of or like grass (also **graminaceous**).

graminivorous *adj.* (of animals) feeding on grass.

grammar *n.* **1.** branch of linguistics dealing with the form, function, and order of words. **2.** book on the rules of grammar. **3.** use of words. **grammarian** *n.* **grammatical** *adj.* according to the rules of grammar. **grammatically** *adv.* **grammar school** esp. formerly, a secondary school providing an education with a strong academic bias.

gramme *n.* same as GRAM.

gramophone *n.* record player.

grampus *n., pl.* **-puses.** sea mammal.

gran *n. Informal* grandmother.

granary *n., pl.* **-ries. 1.** storehouse for grain.

2. region that produces a large amount of grain.

grand adj. 1. large or impressive, imposing. 2. dignified or haughty. 3. *Informal* excellent. 4. (of a total) final. 5. chief. —n. 6. grand piano. 7. *Slang* thousand pounds or dollars. **grandchild** n. child of one's child. **granddaughter** n. female grandchild. **grandfather** n. male grandparent. **grandfather clock** tall standing clock with a pendulum and wooden case. **grandmother** n. female grandparent. **grandparent** n. parent of one's parent. **grand piano** large harpshaped piano with the strings set horizontally. **grand slam** winning of all the games or major tournaments in a sport in one season. **grandson** n. male grandchild. **grandstand** n. terraced block of seats giving the best view at a sports ground.

grandee n. 1. Spanish nobleman of the highest rank. 2. person of high station.

grandeur n. 1. magnificence. 2. nobility or dignity.

grandiloquent adj. using pompous language. **grandiloquently** adv. **grandiloquence** n.

grandiose adj. 1. imposing. 2. pretentiously grand. **grandiosity** n.

Grand Prix [gron **pree**] n. international formula motor race.

grange n. country house with farm buildings.

granite [**gran**-nit] n. very hard igneous rock often used in building.

granivorous adj. feeding on grain or seeds.

granny, grannie n., pl. **-nies.** *Informal* grandmother. **granny flat** flat in or added to a house, suitable for an elderly parent.

grant v. 1. consent to fulfil (a request). 2. admit. 3. give formally. —n. 4. sum of money provided by a government for a specific purpose, such as education. **take for granted** 1. accept as true without proof. 2. take advantage of without due appreciation.

granule n. small grain. **granular** adj. of or like grains. **granulate** v. 1. make into grains. 2. give a rough surface to. **granulation** n.

grape n. small juicy green or purple berry, eaten raw or used to produce wine, raisins, currants, or sultanas. **grapeshot** n. bullets which scatter when fired. **grapevine** n. 1.

grape-bearing vine. 2. *Informal* unofficial way of spreading news.

grapefruit n. large round yellow citrus fruit.

graph n. drawing showing the relation of different numbers or quantities plotted against a set of axes.

graphic adj. 1. vividly descriptive. 2. of or using drawing, painting, etc. **graphics** pl. n. diagrams, graphs, etc., esp. as used on a television programme or computer screen. **graphically** adv.

graphite n. soft black form of carbon, used in pencil leads.

graphology n. study of handwriting. **graphologist** n.

grapnel n. 1. tool with several hooks, used to grasp or secure things. 2. small anchor with many hooks.

grapple v. 1. come to grips with (a person). 2. try to cope with (something difficult). —n. 3. grapnel. **grappling iron** grapnel.

grasp v. 1. grip something firmly. 2. try to seize. 3. understand. —n. 4. grip or clasp. 5. total rule or possession. 6. understanding. **grasping** adj. greedy or avaricious.

grass n. 1. common type of plant with jointed stems and long narrow leaves, including cereals and bamboo. 2. lawn. 3. pasture land. 4. *Slang* marijuana. 5. *Slang* person who informs, esp. on criminals. —v. 6. cover with grass. 7. *Slang* inform on. **grassy** adj. **-sier, -siest. grasshopper** n. jumping insect with long hind legs. **grass roots** 1. ordinary members of a group, as distinct from its leaders. 2. essentials. **grassroots** adj. **grass snake** harmless European snake. **grass widow** wife whose husband is absent for a time.

grate[1] n. framework of metal bars for holding fuel in a fireplace. **grating** n. framework of metal bars covering an opening.

grate[2] v. 1. rub into small bits on a rough surface. 2. scrape with a harsh rasping noise. 3. annoy. **grater** n. **grating** adj. 1. harsh or rasping. 2. annoying.

grateful adj. feeling or showing gratitude. **gratefully** adv. **gratefulness** n.

gratify v. **-fying, -fied.** 1. satisfy or please. 2. indulge (a desire or whim). **gratification** n.

gratis adv., adj. free, for nothing.

gratitude n. feeling of being thankful for a favour or gift.

gratuitous [grat-**tyoo**-it-uss] *adj*. 1. given free. 2. uncalled for. **gratuitously** *adv*.

gratuity [grat-**tyoo**-it-ee] *n.*, *pl.* **-ties**. money given for services rendered, tip.

grave[1] *n*. hole for burying a corpse. **the grave** death. **gravestone** *n*. stone marking a grave. **graveyard** *n*. cemetery.

grave[2] *adj*. 1. serious and solemn. 2. causing concern. 3. important. **gravely** *adv*.

grave[3] [rhymes with **halve**] *n*. accent (`) over a vowel to indicate a special pronunciation.

gravel *n*. 1. mixture of small stones and coarse sand. 2. small rough stones in the kidneys or bladder. —*v*. **-elling**, **-elled**. 3. cover with gravel. 4. perplex. **gravelled** *adj*. covered with gravel. **gravelly** *adj*. 1. covered with gravel. 2. rough-sounding.

graven [**grave**-en] *adj*. carved or engraved.

gravid [**grav**-id] *adj. Med*. pregnant.

gravitate *v*. 1. be influenced or drawn towards. 2. *Physics* move by gravity. **gravitation** *n*. **gravitational** *adj*.

gravity *n.*, *pl.* **-ties**. 1. force of attraction of one object for another, esp. of objects to the earth. 2. seriousness or importance. 3. solemnity.

gravy *n.*, *pl.* **-vies**. 1. juices from meat in cooking. 2. sauce made from these.

gray *adj. US* grey.

grayling *n*. fish of the salmon family.

graze[1] *v*. feed on grass. **grazier** *n*. person who feeds cattle for market. **grazing** *n*. land on which grass for livestock is grown.

graze[2] *v*. 1. touch lightly in passing. 2. scratch or scrape the skin. —*n*. 3. slight scratch or scrape.

grease *n*. 1. soft melted animal fat. 2. any thick oily substance. —*v*. 3. apply grease to. **greasy** *adj*. **greasier**, **greasiest**. 1. covered with or containing grease. 2. unctuous in manner. **greasiness** *n*. **grease gun** appliance for injecting oil or grease into machinery. **greasepaint** *n*. theatrical make-up.

great *adj*. 1. large in size or number. 2. important. 3. extreme or more than usual. 4. pre-eminent. 5. *Informal* excellent. —*n*. 6. very successful, talented, or important person. **great-** *prefix* one generation older or younger than, e.g. *great-grandfather*. **greatly** *adv*. **greatness** *n*. **greatcoat** *n*. heavy overcoat. **Great Dane** very large graceful dog.

greave *n*. piece of armour for the shin.

grebe *n*. diving water bird.

Grecian [**gree**-shan] *adj*. of ancient Greece.

greed *n*. excessive desire for food, wealth, etc. **greedy** *adj*. **greedier**, **greediest**. **greedily** *adv*. **greediness** *n*.

Greek *n*. 1. language of Greece. 2. person from Greece. —*adj*. 3. of Greece, the Greeks, or the Greek language.

green *adj*. 1. of a colour between blue and yellow. 2. unripe. 3. characterized by green plants or foliage. 4. (**G-**) of or concerned with environmental issues. 5. envious or jealous. 6. immature or gullible. 7. (of bacon) unsmoked. —*n*. 8. colour between blue and yellow. 9. area of grass kept for a special purpose. 10. (**G-**) person concerned with environmental issues. —*pl.* 11. green vegetables. —*v*. 12. make or become green. **greenness** *n*. **greenish**, **greeny** *adj*. **greenery** *n*. vegetation. **green belt** protected area of open country around a town. **greenfinch** *n*. European finch with dull green plumage in the male. **green fingers** skill in gardening. **greenfly** *n*. green aphid, a common garden pest. **greengage** *n*. sweet green plum. **greengrocer** *n*. shopkeeper selling vegetables and fruit. **greenhorn** *n*. novice. **greenhouse** *n*. glass building for rearing plants. **greenhouse effect** rise in the temperature of the earth caused by heat absorbed from the sun being unable to leave the atmosphere. **green light** 1. signal to go. 2. permission to proceed with something. **greenroom** *n*. room for actors when offstage. **greenshank** *n*. large European sandpiper.

Greenwich Mean Time *n*. local time of the 0° meridian passing through Greenwich, England: the basis for calculating times throughout the world.

greet *v*. 1. meet with expressions of welcome. 2. receive in a specified manner. 3. be immediately noticeable to. **greeting** *n*.

gregarious *adj*. 1. fond of company. 2. (of animals) living in flocks or herds.

Gregorian calendar *n*. calendar introduced by Pope Gregory XIII and still widely used.

Gregorian chant *n*. same as PLAINSONG.

gremlin *n*. imaginary being blamed for mechanical malfunctions.

grenade *n*. small bomb thrown by hand or fired from a rifle. **grenadier** *n*. soldier of a regiment formerly trained to throw grenades.

grenadine [gren-a-deen] *n.* syrup made from pomegranates.

grew *v.* past tense of GROW.

grey *adj.* **1.** of a colour between black and white. **2.** (of hair) partly turned white. **3.** dismal or dark. **4.** dull or boring. —*n.* **5.** grey colour. **6.** grey or white horse. —*v.* **7.** make or become grey. **grey matter** *Informal* brains. **greyish** *adj.* **greyness** *n.*

greyhound *n.* swift slender dog used in racing.

greylag *n.* large grey goose.

grid *n.* **1.** network of horizontal and vertical lines, bars, etc. **2.** national network of electricity supply cables.

griddle *n.* flat iron plate for cooking.

gridiron *n.* **1.** frame of metal bars for grilling food. **2.** American football pitch.

grief *n.* deep sadness. **come to grief** end unsuccessfully. **grieve** *v.* (cause to) feel grief. **grievance** *n.* real or imaginary cause for complaint. **grievous** *adj.* **1.** very severe or painful. **2.** very serious.

griffin *n.* mythical monster with an eagle's head and wings and a lion's body.

grill *n.* **1.** device on a cooker that radiates heat downwards. **2.** grilled food. **3.** gridiron. **4.** grillroom. —*v.* **5.** cook under a grill. **6.** question relentlessly. **grilling** *n.* relentless questioning. **grillroom** *n.* restaurant serving grilled foods.

grille, grill *n.* grating over an opening.

grilse [grillss] *n.* salmon on its first return from the sea to fresh water.

grim *adj.* **grimmer, grimmest. 1.** stern. **2.** harsh or forbidding. **3.** very unpleasant. **4.** harshly ironic or sinister. **grimly** *adv.* **grimness** *n.*

grimace *n.* **1.** ugly or distorted facial expression of pain, disgust, etc. —*v.* **2.** make a grimace.

grimalkin *n.* old female cat.

grime *n.* **1.** ingrained dirt. —*v.* **2.** make very dirty. **grimy** *adj.* **griminess** *n.*

grin *v.* **grinning, grinned. 1.** smile broadly, showing the teeth. —*n.* **2.** broad smile.

grind *v.* **grinding, ground. 1.** crush or rub to a powder. **2.** smooth or sharpen by friction. **3.** scrape together with a harsh noise. **4.** oppress. **5.** *Informal* work or study hard.

—*n.* **6.** *Informal* hard work. **7.** act or sound of grinding. **grind out** *v.* produce in a routine or uninspired manner. **grindstone** *n.* stone used for grinding.

grip *n.* **1.** firm hold or grasp. **2.** way in which something is grasped. **3.** mastery or understanding. **4.** handle. **5.** *US* travelling bag. —*v.* **gripping, gripped. 6.** grasp or hold tightly. **7.** hold the interest or attention of. **gripping** *adj.*

gripe *v.* **1.** *Informal* complain persistently. —*n.* **2.** sudden intense bowel pain. **3.** *Informal* complaint.

grisly *adj.* **-lier, -liest.** horrifying or ghastly.

grist *n.* grain for grinding. **grist to one's mill** something which can be turned to advantage.

gristle *n.* cartilage in meat. **gristly** *adj.*

grit *n.* **1.** rough particles of sand. **2.** courage. **3.** coarse sandstone. —*pl.* **4.** coarsely ground grain. —*v.* **gritting, gritted. 5.** clench or grind (the teeth). **6.** spread grit on (an icy road etc.). **gritty** *adj.* **-tier, -tiest. grittiness** *n.*

grizzle *v.* *Informal* whine or complain.

grizzled *adj.* grey-haired.

grizzly *adj.* **-zlier, -zliest. 1.** greyish. —*n., pl.* **-zlies. 2.** (also **grizzly bear**) large American bear.

groan *n.* **1.** deep sound of grief or pain. **2.** *Informal* complaint. —*v.* **3.** utter a groan. **4.** (usu. foll. by *beneath* or *under*) be weighed down (by). **5.** *Informal* complain.

groat *n.* *Hist.* fourpenny piece.

groats *pl. n.* hulled and crushed grain of various cereals.

grocer *n.* shopkeeper selling foodstuffs. **grocery** *n., pl.* **-ceries. 1.** business or premises of a grocer. —*pl.* **2.** goods sold by a grocer.

grog *n.* spirit, usu. rum, and water.

groggy *adj.* **-gier, -giest.** *Informal* faint, shaky, or dizzy.

grogram *n.* coarse fabric of silk mixed with wool or mohair.

groin *n.* **1.** place where the legs join the abdomen. **2.** edge made by the intersection of two vaults.

grommet *n.* ring or eyelet.

groom *n.* **1.** person who looks after horses. **2.** bridegroom. **3.** officer in a royal household. —*v.* **4.** make or keep one's clothes and appearance neat and tidy. **5.** brush or clean a horse. **6.** train (someone) for a future role.

groove n. **1.** long narrow channel in a surface. **2.** spiral channel in a gramophone record. **3.** routine. —v. **4.** cut groove(s) in. **groovy** adj. **groovier, grooviest.** Dated slang attractive or exciting.

grope v. feel about or search uncertainly. **groping** v.

grosbeak n. finch with a large powerful bill.

grosgrain [grow-grain] n. heavy ribbed silk or rayon fabric.

gross adj. **1.** repulsively fat. **2.** total, without deductions. **3.** vulgar. **4.** flagrant. **5.** thick and luxuriant. —n. **6.** twelve dozen. —v. **7.** make as total revenue before deductions. **grossly** adv. **grossness** n.

grotesque [grow-tesk] adj. **1.** strangely distorted. **2.** absurd. —n. **3.** artistic style mixing distorted human, animal, and plant forms. **4.** grotesque person or thing. **grotesquely** adv.

grotto n., pl. **-toes, -tos.** **1.** small picturesque cave. **2.** construction imitating a cave.

grotty adj. **-tier, -tiest.** Informal nasty or in bad condition.

grouch Informal —v. **1.** grumble. —n. **2.** grumble. **3.** persistent grumbler. **grouchy** adj.

ground[1] n. **1.** surface of the earth. **2.** soil. **3.** area used for a specific purpose, e.g. rugby ground. **4.** position in an argument or controversy. **5.** background colour of a painting. —pl. **6.** enclosed land round a house. **7.** reason or motive. **8.** coffee dregs. —adj. **9.** on or of the ground. —v. **10.** base. **11.** instruct in the basics. **12.** ban an aircraft or pilot from flying. **13.** run (a ship) aground. **14.** place on the ground. **groundless** adj. without reason. **grounding** n. basic knowledge of a subject. **ground floor** floor of a building level with the ground. **groundnut** n. peanut. **groundsheet** n. waterproof sheet put on the ground under a tent. **groundsman** n. person employed to maintain a sports ground or park. **groundswell** n. smooth heavy waves. **groundwork** n. preliminary work.

ground[2] v. past of GRIND. **ground beef** finely chopped beef used in beefburgers etc.

groundsel [grounce-el] n. yellow-flowered weed.

group n. **1.** number of people or things regarded as a unit. **2.** small band of musicians or singers. —v. **3.** place or form into a group. **group captain** middle-ranking air force officer.

grouper n. large edible sea fish.

grouse[1] n. **1.** stocky game bird. **2.** its flesh.

grouse[2] v. **1.** grumble or complain. —n. **2.** complaint.

grout n. **1.** thin mortar. —v. **2.** fill up with grout.

grove n. small group of trees.

grovel [grov-el] v. **-elling, -elled.** **1.** humble oneself. **2.** lie or crawl face down.

grow v. **growing, grew, grown.** **1.** develop physically. **2.** (of a plant) exist. **3.** originate. **4.** increase in size or degree. **5.** become gradually, e.g. it was growing dark. **6.** cultivate (plants). **growth** n. **1.** growing. **2.** increase. **3.** something grown or growing. **4.** tumour. **grown** adj. developed or advanced. **grown-up** adj., n. adult. **grow on** v. become more acceptable to. **grow up** v. mature.

growl v. **1.** make a low rumbling sound. **2.** utter with a growl. —n. **3.** growling sound.

groyne n. wall built out from the shore to control erosion.

grub n. **1.** legless insect larva. **2.** Slang food. —v. **grubbing, grubbed.** **3.** dig out or uproot. **4.** dig up the surface of (soil). **5.** search.

grubby adj. **-bier, -biest.** dirty. **grubbiness** n.

grudge v. **1.** be unwilling to give or allow. —n. **2.** resentment. **grudging** adj. **grudgingly** adv.

gruel n. thin porridge.

gruelling adj. exhausting or severe.

gruesome adj. causing horror and disgust.

gruff adj. rough or surly in manner or voice. **gruffly** adv. **gruffness** n.

grumble v. **1.** complain. **2.** rumble. —n. **3.** complaint. **4.** rumble. **grumbler** n. **grumbling** adj., n.

grumpy adj. **grumpier, grumpiest.** bad-tempered. **grumpily** adv. **grumpiness** n.

grunt v. **1.** (esp. of pigs) make a low short gruff sound. —n. **2.** pig's sound. **3.** gruff noise.

Gruyère [grew-yair] n. hard yellow Swiss cheese with holes.

gryphon n. same as GRIFFIN.

G-string *n.* small strip of cloth covering the genitals and attached to a waistband.

G-suit *n.* close-fitting pressurized garment worn by the crew of high-speed aircraft.

GT gran turismo, used of a sports car.

guanaco [gwah-nah-koh] *n., pl.* **-s.** S American animal related to the llama.

guano [gwah-no] *n.* dried sea-bird manure.

guarantee *n.* **1.** formal assurance, esp. in writing, that a product will meet certain standards. **2.** something that makes a specified condition or outcome certain. **3.** guarantor. **4.** guaranty. —*v.* **-teeing, -teed. 5.** give a guarantee. **6.** secure against risk etc. **7.** ensure. **guarantor** *n.* person who gives or is bound by a guarantee. **guaranty** *n., pl.* **-ties. 1.** pledge of responsibility for fulfilling another person's obligations in case of default. **2.** thing given as security for a guaranty.

guard *v.* **1.** watch over to protect or to prevent escape. **2.** control. —*n.* **3.** person or group that guards. **4.** official in charge of a train. **5.** protection. **6.** screen for enclosing anything dangerous. **7.** posture of defence in sports such as boxing or fencing. —*pl.* **8.** (G-) regiment with ceremonial duties. **guarded** *adj.* cautious or noncommittal. **guardedly** *adv.* **guard against** *v.* take precautions against. **guardhouse, guardroom** *n.* military police office for holding prisoners. **guardsman** *n.* member of the Guards.

guardian *n.* **1.** keeper or protector. **2.** person legally responsible for a child, mentally ill person, etc. **guardianship** *n.*

guava [gwah-va] *n.* yellow-skinned tropical American fruit.

gubernatorial *adj. US* of or relating to a governor.

gudgeon¹ *n.* small freshwater fish.

gudgeon² *n.* socket for a hinge or rudder.

guelder-rose [geld-er-rose] *n.* shrub with clusters of white flowers.

Guernsey [gurn-zee] *n.* **1.** breed of dairy cattle. **2.** (g-) seaman's knitted sweater.

guerrilla, guerilla *n.* member of an unofficial armed force fighting regular forces.

guess *v.* **1.** estimate or draw a conclusion without proper knowledge. **2.** estimate correctly by guessing. **3.** *US* suppose. —*n.* **4.** estimate or conclusion reached by guessing. **guesswork** *n.* process or results of guessing.

guest *n.* **1.** person entertained at another's house or at another's expense. **2.** invited performer or speaker. **3.** customer at a hotel or restaurant. **guesthouse** *n.* boarding house.

guff *n. Slang* nonsense.

guffaw *n.* **1.** crude noisy laugh. —*v.* **2.** laugh in this way.

guide *n.* **1.** person who conducts tour expeditions. **2.** person who shows the way. **3.** adviser. **4.** book of instruction or information. **5.** model for behaviour. **6.** device for directing motion. **7.** (G-) member of an organization for girls equivalent to the Scouts. —*v.* **8.** act as a guide for. **9.** control, supervise, or influence. **guidance** *n.* leadership, instruction, or advice. **guidebook** *n.* handbook with information for visitors to a place. **guided missile** missile whose flight is controlled electronically. **guide dog** dog trained to lead a blind person. **guideline** *n.* set principle for doing something.

guild *n.* **1.** organization or club. **2.** *Hist.* society of men in the same trade or craft.

guilder *n.* monetary unit of the Netherlands.

guile [gile] *n.* cunning or deceit. **guileful** *adj.* **guileless** *adj.*

guillemot [gil-lee-mot] *n.* black-and-white diving sea bird.

guillotine *n.* **1.** machine for beheading people. **2.** device for cutting paper or sheet metal. **3.** method of preventing lengthy debate in parliament by fixing a time for taking the vote. —*v.* **4.** behead by guillotine. **5.** limit debate by the guillotine.

guilt *n.* **1.** fact or state of having done wrong. **2.** remorse for wrongdoing. **guiltless** *adj.* innocent. **guilty** *adj.* **guiltier, guiltiest. 1.** responsible for an offence or misdeed. **2.** feeling or showing guilt. **guiltily** *adv.*

guinea *n.* **1.** former British monetary unit worth 21 shillings (1.05 pounds). **2.** former gold coin of this value. **guinea fowl** bird related to the pheasant. **guinea pig 1.** tailless S American rodent. **2.** *Informal* person used for experimentation.

guipure [geep-pure] *n.* heavy lace with the pattern connected by threads.

guise [rhymes with **size**] *n.* **1.** false appearance. **2.** external appearance.

guitar *n.* six-stringed instrument played by plucking or strumming. **guitarist** *n.*

Gulag *n.* department of the Soviet security

service in charge of prisons and labour camps.

gulch *n. US* deep narrow valley.

gulf *n.* **1.** large deep bay. **2.** chasm. **3.** large difference in opinion or understanding. **Gulf Stream** warm ocean current flowing from the Gulf of Mexico towards NW Europe.

gull[1] *n.* long-winged sea bird.

gull[2] *v.* cheat or deceive.

gullet *n.* muscular tube through which food passes from the mouth to the stomach.

gullible *adj.* easily tricked. **gullibility** *n.*

gully *n., pl.* **-lies.** channel cut by running water.

gulp *v.* **1.** swallow hastily. **2.** gasp. —*n.* **3.** gulping. **4.** thing gulped.

gum[1] *n.* firm flesh in which the teeth are set. **gummy** *adj.* **-mier, -miest.** toothless. **gumboil** *n.* abscess on the gum.

gum[2] *n.* **1.** sticky substance obtained from certain trees. **2.** adhesive. **3.** gumdrop. **4.** chewing gum. **5.** gumtree. —*v.* **gumming, gummed.** **6.** stick with gum. **gummy** *adj.* **-mier, -miest.** **gumboots** *pl. n.* Wellington boots. **gumdrop** *n.* hard jelly-like sweet. **gumtree** *n.* eucalypt tree.

gumption *n.* **1.** *Informal* resourcefulness. **2.** *Informal* courage.

gun *n.* **1.** weapon with a metal tube from which missiles are fired by explosion. **2.** device from which a substance is ejected under pressure. **3.** member of a shooting party. —*v.* **gunning, gunned.** **4.** cause (an engine) to run at high speed. **jump the gun** act prematurely. **gunner** *n.* artillery soldier. **gunnery** *n.* use or science of large guns. **gunboat** *n.* small warship. **guncotton** *n.* form of cellulose nitrate used as an explosive. **gun dog** dog used to retrieve game. **gun down** *v.* shoot (a person). **gun for** *v.* seek or pursue vigorously. **gunman** *n.* armed criminal. **gunmetal** *n.* **1.** alloy of copper, tin, and zinc. —*adj.* **2.** dark grey. **gunpowder** *n.* explosive mixture of potassium nitrate, sulphur, and charcoal. **gunrunning** *n.* smuggling of guns and ammunition. **gunrunner** *n.* **gunshot** *n.* shot or range of a gun.

gunge *n. Informal* sticky unpleasant substance. **gungy** *adj.* **-gier, -giest.**

gunk *n. Informal* slimy or filthy substance.

gunny *n.* strong coarse fabric used for sacks.

gunwale, gunnel [gun-nel] *n.* top of a ship's side.

guppy *n., pl.* **-pies.** small colourful aquarium fish.

gurgle *v., n.* (make) a bubbling noise.

Gurkha *n.* person, esp. a soldier, belonging to a Hindu people of Nepal.

gurnard *n.* spiny armour-headed sea fish.

guru *n.* **1.** Indian spiritual teacher. **2.** leader or adviser.

gush *v.* **1.** flow out suddenly and profusely. **2.** express admiration effusively. —*n.* **3.** sudden copious flow. **4.** effusiveness. **gusher** *n.* spurting oil well. **gushing** *adj.*

gusset *n.* piece of material sewn into a garment to strengthen it.

gust *n.* **1.** sudden blast of wind. **2.** sudden burst of rain, anger, etc. —*v.* **3.** blow in gusts. **gusty** *adj.*

gustation *n.* act of tasting or the faculty of taste. **gustatory** *adj.*

gusto *n.* enjoyment or zest.

gut *n.* **1.** intestine. **2.** short for CATGUT. **3.** *Informal* fat stomach. —*pl.* **4.** internal organs. **5.** *Informal* courage. **6.** *Informal* essential part. —*v.* **gutting, gutted.** **7.** remove the guts from. **8.** (of a fire) destroy the inside of (a building). —*adj.* **9.** basic or instinctive, e.g. *a gut reaction.* **gutless** *adj. Informal* cowardly. **gutsy** *adj.* **-sier, -siest.** *Informal* **1.** greedy. **2.** courageous.

gutta-percha *n.* whitish rubbery substance obtained from an Asian tree.

gutter *n.* **1.** shallow trough for carrying off water from a roof or roadside. —*v.* **2.** (of a candle) burn unsteadily, with wax running down the sides. **the gutter** degraded or criminal environment. **guttering** *n.* material for gutters. **gutter press** newspapers that rely on sensationalism. **guttersnipe** *n.* neglected slum child.

guttural [gut-ter-al] *adj.* **1.** (of a sound) produced at the back of the throat. **2.** (of a voice) harsh-sounding.

guy[1] *n.* **1.** effigy of Guy Fawkes burnt on Nov. 5th (**Guy Fawkes Day**). **2.** *Informal* man or boy. —*v.* **3.** make fun of.

guy[2] *n.* **1.** rope or chain to steady or secure something. —*v.* **2.** secure or guide with a guy. **guyrope** *n.*

guzzle *v.* eat or drink greedily.

gybe [jibe] *v.* **1.** (of a fore-and-aft sail) swing

suddenly from one side to the other. **2.** (of a boat) change course by gybing.

gym n. **1.** gymnasium. **2.** gymnastics. **gymslip** n. tunic or pinafore worn by schoolgirls.

gymkhana [jim-**kah**-na] n. horse-riding competition.

gymnasium n. large room with equipment for physical training. **gymnast** n. expert in gymnastics. **gymnastic** adj. **gymnastics** pl. n. exercises to develop strength and agility.

gynaecology [guy-nee-**kol**-la-jee] n. branch of medicine dealing with diseases and conditions specific to women. **gynaecological** adj. **gynaecologist** n.

gyp n. **give someone gyp** Slang cause someone severe pain.

gypsophila n. garden plant with small white flowers.

gypsum n. chalklike mineral used to make plaster of Paris.

Gypsy n., pl. **-sies.** member of a travelling people found throughout Europe.

gyrate [jire-**rate**] v. rotate or spiral about a point or axis. **gyration** n. **gyratory** adj. gyrating.

gyrfalcon [jur-fawl-kon] n. large rare falcon.

gyro n., pl. **-ros.** short for GYROSCOPE.

gyrocompass n. compass using a gyroscope.

gyroscope [jire-oh-skohp] n. disc rotating on an axis that can turn in any direction, used to keep navigation instruments steady. **gyroscopic** adj.

H

H *Chem.* hydrogen.

Ha *Chem.* hahnium.

habeas corpus [**hay**-bee-ass **kor**-puss] *n.* writ ordering a prisoner to be brought before a court.

haberdasher *n. Brit.* dealer in small articles used for sewing. **haberdashery** *n.*

habiliments *pl. n.* clothes.

habit *n.* **1.** established way of behaving. **2.** costume of a monk or nun. **3.** woman's riding costume.

habitable *adj.* fit to be lived in. **habitat** *n.* natural home of an animal or plant. **habitation** *n.* **1.** dwelling place. **2.** occupation of a dwelling place.

habitual *adj.* done regularly and repeatedly. **habitually** *adv.*

habituate *v.* accustom. **habituation** *n.* **habitué** [hab-**it**-yew-ay] *n.* frequent visitor to a place.

hacienda [hass-ee-**end**-a] *n.* ranch or large estate in Latin America.

hack[1] *v.* **1.** cut or chop (at) violently. **2.** utter a harsh dry cough.

hack[2] *n.* **1.** horse kept for riding. **2.** *Informal* (inferior) writer or journalist. **hackwork** *n.* dull repetitive work.

hacker *n. Slang* computer enthusiast, esp. one who breaks into the computer system of a company or government.

hackles *pl. n.* hairs or feathers on the back of the neck of some animals and birds, which are raised in anger.

hackney carriage *n.* **1.** taxi. **2.** coach or carriage for hire.

hackneyed [**hak**-need] *adj.* (of language) stale or trite because of overuse.

hacksaw *n.* small saw for cutting metal.

had *v.* past of HAVE.

haddock *n.* large edible sea fish.

hadedah [**hah**-dee-dah] *n.* large grey-green S Afr. ibis.

Hades [**hay**-deez] *n. Greek myth* underworld home of the dead.

hadj *n.* same as HAJJ.

haematic [hee-**mat**-ik] *adj.* relating to or containing blood.

haematite [**hee**-ma-tite] *n.* an iron ore, reddish-brown when powdered.

haematology *n.* study of blood. **haematologist** *n.*

haemo- *combining form* blood.

haemoglobin [hee-moh-**globe**-in] *n.* protein found in red blood cells which carries oxygen.

haemophilia [hee-moh-**fill**-lee-a] *n.* hereditary illness in which the blood does not clot. **haemophiliac** *n.*

haemorrhage [**hem**-or-ij] *n.* **1.** heavy bleeding. —*v.* **2.** bleed heavily.

haemorrhoids [**hem**-or-oydz] *pl. n.* swollen veins in the anus (also **piles**).

hafnium *n.* metallic element found in zirconium ores.

haft *n.* handle of an axe, knife, or dagger.

hag *n.* **1.** ugly old woman. **2.** witch. **hagridden** *adj.* distressed or worried.

haggard *adj.* looking tired and ill.

haggis *n.* Scottish dish made from sheep's offal, oatmeal, suet, and onion.

haggle *v.* bargain or wrangle over a price.

hagiology *n., pl.* **-gies.** literature about the lives of the saints. **hagiography** *n.* writing of this. **hagiographer** *n.*

ha-ha[1] *interj.* representation of the sound of laughter.

ha-ha[2] *n.* sunken fence bordering a garden or park, that allows an uninterrupted view from within.

hahnium [**hah**-nee-um] *n.* artificially produced radioactive element.

haiku [**hie**-koo] *n., pl.* **-ku.** Japanese verse form in 17 syllables.

hail[1] *n.* **1.** (shower of) small pellets of ice. **2.** large amount of words, missiles, blows, etc. —*v.* **3.** fall as or like hail. **hailstone** *n.*

hail[2] *v.* **1.** greet. **2.** call (out to). **3.** acclaim, acknowledge. **hail from** *v.* come originally from. **Hail Mary** *RC Church* prayer to the Virgin Mary.

hair n. **1.** threadlike growth on the skin. **2.** such growths collectively, esp. on the head. **hairy** adj. **hairier, hairiest. 1.** covered with hair. **2.** Slang dangerous or exciting. **hairiness** n. **hairless** adj. **hairdo** n. Informal hairstyle. **hairdresser** n. person who cuts and styles hair. **hairdressing** n. **hairgrip** n. small, tightly bent metal hairpin. **hairline** n. **1.** margin of hair at the top of the forehead. —adj. **2.** very fine or narrow. **hairpiece** n. section of false hair added to a person's real hair. **hairpin** n. U-shaped wire used to hold the hair in place. **hairpin bend** U-shaped bend in the road. **hair-raising** adj. terrifying. **hair's-breadth** n. extremely small margin or distance. **hair shirt** shirt made of horsehair cloth worn against the skin as a penance. **hairsplitting** n. making of petty distinctions. **hairspring** n. very fine spring in a watch or clock. **hairstyle** n. cut and arrangement of a person's hair.

hajj n. pilgrimage a Muslim makes to Mecca. **hajji** n. Muslim who has made a pilgrimage to Mecca.

hake n. edible fish of the cod family.

halal n. meat from animals slaughtered according to Muslim law.

halberd n. spear with an axe blade.

halcyon [hal-see-on] adj. peaceful and happy. **halcyon days** time of peace and happiness.

hale adj. robust, healthy, e.g. hale and hearty.

half n., pl. **halves. 1.** either of two equal parts. **2.** Informal half-pint. **3.** half-price ticket. —adj. **4.** incomplete. —adv. **5.** to the extent of half. **6.** partially. **half-and-half** adj. half one thing and half another thing. **halfback** n. Sport player positioned immediately behind the forwards. **half-baked** adj. Informal poorly planned. ·**half board** (in a hotel), bed, breakfast, and evening meal. **half-breed** n. **half-caste. half-brother, -sister** n. brother or sister related through one parent only. **half-caste** n. person with parents of different races. **half-cocked** adj. go off **half-cocked** fail because of inadequate preparation. **half-day** n. day when a person works only in the morning or only in the afternoon. **half-hearted** adj. unenthusiastic. **half-heartedly** adv. **half-life** n. time taken for half the atoms in radioactive material to decay. **half-mast** n. halfway position of a flag on a mast as a sign of mourning. **half-moon** n. moon when half its face is illuminated. **half-nelson** n. hold in wrestling in which one wrestler's arm is pinned behind his back by his opponent. **half-term** n. short holiday midway through a school term. **half-timbered** adj. having an exposed wooden frame filled in with plaster. **half-time** n. Sport interval between two halves of a game. **halftone** n. illustration showing lights and shadows by means of very small dots. **halfway** adv., adj. at or to half the distance. **halfwit** n. foolish or feeble-minded person. **halfwitted** adj.

halfpenny [hayp-nee] n. former British coin worth half an old penny.

halibut n. large edible flatfish.

halitosis n. bad-smelling breath.

hall n. **1.** (also **hallway**) (entrance) passage. **2.** large room or building belonging to a particular group or used for a particular purpose. **3.** large country house.

hallelujah [hal-ee-loo-ya] interj. exclamation of praise to God.

hallmark n. **1.** mark indicating the standard of tested gold and silver. **2.** distinguishing feature. —v. **3.** stamp with a hallmark.

hallo interj. same as HELLO.

halloo interj. shout used to call hounds at a hunt.

hallowed adj. regarded as holy.

Hallowe'en n. October 31, celebrated by children by dressing up as ghosts, witches, etc.

hallucinate v. seem to see something that is not really there. **hallucination** n. experience of seeming to see something that is not really there. **hallucinatory** adj. **hallucinogen** n. drug that causes hallucinations. **hallucinogenic** adj.

halo [hay-loh] n., pl. **-loes, -los. 1.** disc of light round the head of a sacred figure. **2.** ring of light round the sun or moon.

halogen [hal-oh-jen] n. Chem. any of a group of nonmetallic elements including chlorine and iodine.

halt n. **1.** temporary stop. **2.** minor railway station without a building. —v. **3.** stop. **halting** adj. hesitant, e.g. halting speech. **haltingly** adv.

halter n. strap around a horse's head with a rope to lead it with. **halterneck** n. top or dress with a strap fastened at the back of the neck.

halve v. 1. cut in half. 2. reduce to half. 3. share.

halves n. plural of HALF.

halyard n. rope for raising a ship's sail or flag.

ham n. 1. smoked or salted meat from a pig's thigh. 2. Informal actor who overacts. 3. Informal amateur radio operator. —v. hamming, hammed. 4. ham it up Informal overact. ham-fisted adj. clumsy.

hamburger n. flat round piece of minced beef, often served in a bread roll.

hamlet n. small village.

hammer n. 1. tool with a heavy head, used to drive in nails, beat metal, etc. 2. metal ball on a wire, thrown as a sport. 3. part of a gun which causes the bullet to be fired. 4. auctioneer's mallet. 5. striking mechanism in a piano. —v. 6. strike (as if) with a hammer. 7. Informal defeat. hammer and tongs with great effort or energy. hammerhead n. shark with a wide flattened head. hammer out v. settle (differences) with great effort. hammertoe n. condition in which the toe is permanently bent at the joint.

hammock n. hanging bed made of canvas or net.

hamper¹ v. make it difficult for (someone or something) to move or progress.

hamper² n. 1. large basket with a lid. 2. selection of food and drink packed as a gift.

hamster n. small rodent with a short tail and cheek pouches.
▷ Note the spelling. There is no 'p'.

hamstring n. 1. tendon at the back of the knee. —v. 2. make it difficult for someone to take any action. hamstrung adj.

hand n. 1. end of the arm beyond the wrist. 2. style of writing. 3. applause. 4. manual worker. 5. pointer on a dial. 6. cards dealt to a player in a card game. 7. unit of four inches used to measure horses. —v. 8. pass or give. hand in glove in close association. hands down easily. have a hand in be involved in. lend a hand help. at hand, on hand nearby. out of hand beyond control. handbag n. small bag in which a person carries personal articles. handbill n. small printed notice. handbook n. small reference or instruction book. handcuff n. 1. one of a linked pair of metal rings used for securing a prisoner. —v. 2. put handcuffs on. hand-me-downs pl. n. Informal clothes

that someone has finished with and passed on to someone else. hand-out n. 1. thing given free. 2. written information given out at a talk etc. hand-picked adj. (of a person) carefully chosen for a particular purpose. handrail n. rail alongside a stairway, to provide support. handset n. telephone mouthpiece and earpiece mounted as a single unit. hands-on adj. involving practical experience of equipment. handstand n. act of supporting the body on the hands in an upside-down position. hand-to-hand adj. (of combat) at close quarters. hand-to-mouth adj. having barely enough food or money to live on. handwriting n. (style of) writing by hand. handwritten adj.

h & c hot and cold (water).

handful n. 1. the amount that can be held in the hand. 2. small quantity or number. 3. Informal person or thing that is difficult to control.

handicap n. 1. any physical or mental disability. 2. something that makes progress difficult. 3. contest in which the competitors are given advantages or disadvantages in an attempt to equalize their chances. 4. disadvantage or advantage given. —v. 5. make it difficult for (someone) to do something. handicapped adj. physically or mentally disabled.

handicraft n. objects made by hand.

handiwork n. something done or made by a person himself or herself, e.g. I'm just admiring my handiwork.

handkerchief n. small square of fabric used to wipe the nose.

handle n. 1. part of an object that is held so that it can be used. —v. 2. hold, feel, or move with the hands. 3. control or deal with. handler n. person who controls an animal. handlebars pl. n. curved metal bar used to steer a cycle.

handsome adj. 1. attractive in appearance. 2. large or generous, e.g. a handsome reward. handsomely adv.

handy adj. handier, handiest. 1. convenient, useful. 2. good at manual work. handily adv. handiness n. handyman n. man skilled at odd jobs.

hang v. hanging, hung. 1. attach or be attached at the top with the lower part free. 2. past hanged. suspend or be suspended by the neck until dead. 3. fasten to a wall. 4. droop. get the hang of Informal understand. **hanger** n. curved piece of wood or hook for hanging clothes on. **hanger-on** n., pl. **hangers-on.** unwanted follower. **hanging** n. 1. execution by hanging. 2. decorative drapery hung on a wall. **hang about, around** v. stay in the same place doing nothing, usually while waiting for someone or something. **hang back** v. hesitate. **hangman** n. person who executes people by hanging. **hangover** n. aftereffects of drinking too much alcohol. **hang-up** n. Informal emotional or psychological problem.

hangar n. large shed for storing aircraft.

hangdog adj. sullen, dejected.

hang-glider n. glider with a light framework from which the pilot hangs in a harness. **hang-gliding** n.

hank n. coil or skein, esp. of yarn.

hanker v. (foll. by after) crave, long for. **hankering** n.

hanky, hankie n., pl. **hankies.** Informal handkerchief.

hanky-panky n. Informal illicit sexual relations.

hansom n. formerly, a two-wheeled horse-drawn cab for hire.

haphazard adj. not organized or planned. **haphazardly** adv.

hapless adj. unlucky.

happen v. 1. occur, take place. 2. do by chance. **happening** n. occurrence, event.

happy adj. -**pier**, -**piest.** 1. glad or content. 2. lucky or fortunate. 3. suitable. **happily** adv. **happiness** n. **happy-go-lucky** adj. carefree and cheerful.

hara-kiri n. Japanese ritual suicide by disembowelling.

harangue v. 1. address angrily or forcefully. —n. 2. angry or forceful speech.

harass v. annoy or trouble constantly. **harassed** adj. **harassment** n.

harbinger [har-binge-er] n. person or thing that announces the approach of something.

harbour n. 1. sheltered port. —v. 2. give shelter or protection to. 3. maintain secretly in the mind.

hard adj. 1. firm, solid, or rigid. 2. difficult. 3. requiring a lot of effort. 4. unkind or unfeeling. 5. difficult to bear. 6. (of water) containing calcium salts that stop soap lathering freely. 7. (of a drug) strong and addictive. —adv. 8. with great energy or effort. 9. carefully. 10. intensely. **hard of hearing** slightly deaf. **hard up** Informal short of money. **harden** v. **hardness** n. **hardship** n. 1. suffering. 2. difficult circumstances. **hard-and-fast** adj. (of rules) invariable or strict. **hard-bitten** adj. tough. **hard-boiled** adj. 1. (of eggs) boiled until solid. 2. Informal tough, unemotional. **hard cash** notes and coins, as opposed to cheques or credit cards. **hard copy** computer output printed on paper. **hard core** the members of a group who most resist change. **hard-core** adj. **hard disk** Computers inflexible disk in a sealed container. **hard-headed** adj. shrewd, practical. **hard-hearted** adj. unfeeling, unkind. **hard line** uncompromising policy. **hard-line** adj. **hard-liner** n. **hard sell** aggressive sales technique. **hard shoulder** surfaced verge at the motorway edge for emergency stops.

hardback n. book with a stiff cover.

hardboard n. thin stiff board made of compressed sawdust and woodchips.

hardly adv. 1. scarcely or not at all. 2. with difficulty.
▷ Hardly already has a negative sense and is not used with no or not.

hardware n. 1. metal tools or implements. 2. machinery used in a computer system. 3. military weapons.

hardwood n. wood of a deciduous tree such as oak or ash.

hardy adj. **hardier, hardiest.** able to stand difficult conditions. **hardiness** n.

hare n. 1. animal like a large rabbit, with longer legs and ears. —v. 2. run fast. **harebell** n. blue bell-shaped flower. **harebrained** adj. foolish or impractical. **harelip** n. split in the upper lip.

harem n. (apartments of) a Muslim man's wives and concubines.

haricot [har-rik-oh] n. white bean which can be dried.

hark v. Old-fashioned listen. **hark back** v. return (to an earlier subject).

harlequin n. 1. stock comic character, with a diamond-patterned costume and mask. —adj. 2. in many colours.

harlot n. Obs. prostitute.

harm n. 1. physical, mental, or moral injury. —v. 2. injure physically, mentally, or morally. **harmful** adj. **harmless** adj.

harmonica n. mouth organ.

harmonium n. small organ.

harmony n., pl. **-nies. 1.** peaceful agreement and cooperation. **2.** combination of notes to make a pleasing sound. **harmonious** adj. **harmoniously** adv. **harmonic** adj. **1.** of harmony. **2.** harmonious. **harmonics** n. science of musical sounds. **harmonize** v. fit in or go well with each other. **harmonization** n.

harness n. **1.** equipment for attaching a horse to a cart or plough. **2.** set of straps fastened round someone's body to attach something, e.g. *a parachute harness.* —v. **3.** put a harness on. **4.** control (something) in order to use its energy.

harp n. large triangular stringed instrument played with the fingers. **harpist** n. **harp on about** v. talk about continuously.

harpoon n. **1.** barbed spear attached to a rope used for hunting whales. —v. **2.** spear with a harpoon.

harpsichord n. stringed keyboard instrument.

harpy n., pl. **-pies.** cruel or grasping woman.

harridan n. shrewish (old) woman.

harrier n. cross-country runner.

harrow n. **1.** implement used to break up clods of soil. —v. **2.** draw a harrow over.

harrowing adj. very distressing.

harry v. **-rying, -ried.** keep asking (someone) to do something, pester.

harsh adj. **1.** unpleasant to the senses. **2.** severe or cruel. **harshly** adv. **harshness** n.

hart n. adult male deer.

hartebeest n. large African antelope.

harum-scarum adj. reckless.

harvest n. **1.** (season for) the gathering of crops. **2.** crops gathered. —v. **3.** gather (a ripened crop). **harvester** n.

has v. third person singular of the present tense of HAVE. **has-been** n. *Informal* person who is no longer popular or successful.

hash n. **1.** dish of diced meat and vegetables. **2.** *Informal* hashish. **make a hash of** *Informal* mess up or destroy.

hashish [hash-eesh] n. drug made from the hemp plant, taken for its intoxicating effects.

hasp n. clasp which fits over a staple and is secured by a bolt or padlock, used as a fastening.

hassle *Informal* —n. **1.** trouble or difficulty. **2.** nuisance. —v. **3.** cause annoyance or trouble to.

hassock n. cushion for kneeling on in church.

haste n. speed or hurry. **make haste** hurry or rush. **hasten** v. (cause to) hurry, increase speed. **hasty** adj. **hastier, hastiest.** (too) quick. **hastily** adv.

hat n. covering for the head, often with a brim, usually given to give protection from the weather. **keep something under one's hat** keep something secret. **hat trick** any three successive achievements, esp. in sport.

hatch¹ v. **1.** (cause to) emerge from an egg. **2.** devise (a plot or plan).

hatch² n. **1.** (hinged door covering) an opening in a floor or wall. **2.** opening in the wall between a kitchen and a dining area. **3.** door in an aircraft or spacecraft. **hatchback** n. car with a single lifting door in the rear. **hatchway** n. opening in the deck of a ship.

hatchet n. small axe. **bury the hatchet** make peace. **hatchet job** malicious verbal or written attack. **hatchet man** *Informal* person carrying out unpleasant tasks for an employer.

hate v. **1.** dislike intensely. **2.** be unwilling (to do something). —n. **3.** intense dislike. **4.** object of hatred. **hateful** adj. causing or deserving hate. **hatred** n. intense dislike.

haughty adj. **-tier, -tiest.** proud, arrogant. **haughtily** adv. **haughtiness** n.

haul v. **1.** pull or drag with effort. —n. **2.** amount gained by effort or theft. **long haul** something that takes a lot of time and effort to achieve. **haulage** n. (charge for) transporting goods. **haulier** n. firm or person that transports goods by road.

haulm [hawm] n. stalks of beans, potatoes, grasses, etc., collectively.

haunch n. human hip or fleshy hindquarter of an animal.

haunt v. **1.** visit in the form of a ghost. **2.** remain in the thoughts or memory of. —n. **3.** place visited frequently. **haunted** adj. **1.** visited by ghosts. **2.** worried. **haunting** adj. extremely beautiful or sad. **hauntingly** adv.

hautboy [oh-boy] n. *Old-fashioned* oboe.

haute couture [oat koo-ture] n. *French* high fashion.

hauteur [oat-ur] n. haughtiness.

Havana n. fine quality of cigar.

have v. **has**, **having**, **had**. 1. hold, possess. 2. experience or be affected with. 3. be obliged (to do). 4. *Slang* cheat or outwit. 5. receive, take, or obtain. 6. cause to be done. 7. give birth to. 8. used to form past tenses (with a past participle), e.g. *I have gone, I had gone*. **have it out** *Informal* settle by argument. **haves and have-nots** *Informal* rich people and poor people. **have on** v. 1. wear. 2. *Informal* trick or tease. **have up** v. bring to trial.

haven n. place of safety.

haver v. 1. *Dialect* talk nonsense. 2. dither. **havers** pl. n. *Scot.* nonsense.

haversack n. canvas bag carried on the back or shoulder.

havoc n. disorder and confusion.

haw n. hawthorn berry.

hawk[1] n. 1. bird of prey with short rounded wings and a long tail. 2. supporter or advocate of warlike policies. **hawkish**, **hawklike** adj. **hawk-eyed** adj. having extremely good eyesight.

hawk[2] v. offer (goods) for sale in the street or door-to-door. **hawker** n.

hawk[3] v. cough noisily.

hawser n. large rope used on a ship.

hawthorn n. thorny shrub or tree.

hay n. grass cut and dried as fodder. **hay fever** allergic reaction to pollen or dust. **haystack** n. large pile of stored hay. **haywire** adj. **go haywire** *Informal* not function properly.

hazard n. 1. risk, danger. —v. 2. put at danger. 3. venture (a guess). **hazardous** adj.

haze n. mist, often caused by heat. **hazy** adj. **hazier**, **haziest**. 1. misty. 2. vague.

hazel n. 1. bush producing nuts. —adj. 2. (of eyes) greenish-brown. **hazelnut** n.

HB on pencils, hard black.

H-bomb n. hydrogen bomb.

he pron. refers to: 1. a male person or animal. 2. a person or animal of unspecified sex.
▷ Try to avoid the use of *he* as a pronoun of general reference. It can appear sexist if the reference is to both men and women.

He *Chem.* helium.

HE Her (or His) Excellency.

head n. 1. upper or front part of the body, containing the sense organs and the brain. 2. upper or most forward part of anything. 3. chief of a group, organization, or school. 4. aptitude. 5. intellect. 6. headline or title. 7. person or animal considered as a unit. 8. white froth on beer. 9. *Informal* headache. —adj. 10. chief, principal. —v. 11. lead, direct. 12. move (in a particular direction). 13. be at the top or front of. 14. provide with a heading. 15. hit (a ball) with the head. **go to someone's head** make someone drunk or conceited. **head over heels** very much in love. **not make head nor tail of** not understand. **off one's head** *Slang* insane. **heads** adv. *Informal* with the side of a coin which has a portrait of a head on it uppermost. **header** n. 1. action of striking a ball with the head. 2. headlong dive. **heading** n. title written or printed at the top of a page. **heady** adj. **headier**, **headiest**. intoxicating or exciting. **headache** n. 1. continuous pain in the head. 2. cause of worry or annoyance. **headboard** n. vertical board at the head of a bed. **headdress** n. any head covering, esp. an ornate one. **head-hunter** n. person who sets out to recruit someone from another company for a particular job. **head-hunting** n. **headland** n. area of land jutting out into the sea. **headlight** n. powerful light on the front of a vehicle. **headline** n. 1. news summary in large type in a newspaper. —pl. 2. main points of a news broadcast. **headlong** adv., adj. 1. head foremost. 2. with haste. **head-on** adj. front foremost, e.g. *a head-on collision*. **headphones** pl. n. two small loudspeakers held against the ears by a strap. **headquarters** pl. n. centre from which operations are directed. **head start** advantage in a competition. **headstone** n. gravestone. **headstrong** adj. 1. self-willed. 2. obstinate. **head teacher** principal of a school. **headway** n. progress. **headwind** n. wind blowing against the course of an aircraft or ship.

heal v. make or become well. **healer** n. **healing** n.

health n. 1. normal good condition of someone's body. 2. toast drunk in someone's honour. **health centre** surgery and offices of the doctors in a district. **health food** natural food, organically grown and free from additives. **health visitor** nurse who visits elderly people and mothers of newborn babies in their homes. **healthy** adj.

healthier, healthiest. 1. having good health. **2.** of or producing good health. **3.** functioning well, sound. **healthily** *adv.*

heap *n.* **1.** pile of things lying one on top of another. **2.** large quantity. — *v.* **3.** gather into a pile. **4.** (foll. by *on*) give abundantly (to).

hear *v.* **hearing, heard. 1.** perceive (a sound) by ear. **2.** listen to. **3.** learn or be informed. **4.** *Law* try (a case). **hear! hear!** exclamation of approval or agreement. **hearing** *n.* **1.** ability to hear. **2.** trial of a case. **within hearing** close enough to be heard.

hearken *v. Obs.* listen.

hearsay *n.* **1.** gossip. **2.** rumour.

hearse *n.* funeral car used to carry a coffin.

heart *n.* **1.** organ which pumps blood round the body. **2.** centre of emotions and affections. **3.** tenderness. **4.** enthusiasm or courage. **5.** central or most important part. **6.** figure representing a heart. **7.** playing card of the suit marked with the figure of a heart. **break someone's heart** cause someone great grief. **by heart** from memory. **set one's heart on something** greatly desire something. **take to heart** get upset about. **hearten** *v.* make cheerful, encourage. **heartening** *adj.* **heartless** *adj.* cruel. **heartlessly** *adv.* **hearty** *adj.* **heartier, heartiest. 1.** friendly, enthusiastic. **2.** substantial, nourishing. **heartily** *adv.* **heart attack** sudden severe malfunction of the heart. **heart failure** sudden stopping of the heartbeat. **heart-rending** *adj.* causing great sorrow. **heart-throb** *n. Slang* very attractive person. **heart-to-heart** *n.* an intimate conversation.

heartache *n.* intense anguish.

heartbeat *n.* one complete pulsation of the heart.

heartbreak *n.* intense grief. **heartbreaking** *adj.* **heartbroken** *adj.*

heartburn *n.* pain in the chest caused by indigestion.

heartfelt *adj.* felt sincerely or strongly.

hearth *n.* floor of a fireplace.

heat *n.* **1.** state of being hot. **2.** energy transferred as a result of a difference in temperature. **3.** hot weather. **4.** intensity of feeling. **5.** preliminary eliminating contest in a competition. **6.** readiness to mate in some female animals. — *v.* **7.** make hot. **heated** *adj.* angry. **heatedly** *adv.* **heater** *n.* **heating** *n.* **heatstroke** *n.* same as SUN-STROKE. **heat wave** spell of unusually hot weather.

heath *n.* **1.** area of open uncultivated land. **2.** low-growing evergreen shrub.

heathen *n.* **1.** person not believing in an established religion, pagan. — *adj.* **2.** of or relating to heathen peoples.

heather *n.* shrub with small bell-shaped flowers growing on heaths and mountains.

heave *v.* **1.** lift with effort. **2.** throw (something heavy). **3.** utter (a sigh). **4.** rise and fall. **5.** vomit. **6.** (**heaving, hove**) *Naut.* move in a specified direction. — *n.* **7.** act of heaving. **heave to** *v.* (of a ship) stop moving.

heaven *n.* **1.** home of God. **2.** place or state of bliss. **the heavens** sky. **heavenly** *adj.* **1.** wonderful or divine. **2.** of or like heaven. **3.** of or occurring in space.

heavy *adj.* **heavier, heaviest. 1.** of great weight. **2.** great in degree or amount. **3.** dense. **4.** difficult or severe. **5.** sorrowful. **6.** (of a situation) serious. **heavily** *adv.* **heaviness** *n.* **heavy-duty** *adj.* made to withstand hard wear. **heavy industry** large-scale production of raw material or machinery. **heavy metal** very loud rock music featuring guitar riffs. **heavy water** water formed of oxygen and deuterium. **heavyweight** *n.* boxer weighing over 175lb (professional) or 81kg (amateur).

Hebrew *n.* **1.** ancient language of the Hebrews. **2.** its modern form, used in Israel. **3.** member of an ancient Semitic people. — *adj.* **4.** of either of the Hebrew languages or the Hebrew people.

heckle *v.* interrupt (a public speaker) with questions, taunts, and comments. **heckler** *n.*

hectare *n.* one hundred ares or 10 000 square metres (2.471 acres).

hectic *adj.* rushed or busy.

hector *v.* bully.

hedge *n.* **1.** row of bushes forming a barrier or boundary. — *v.* **2.** be evasive or noncommittal. **3.** (foll. by *against*) protect oneself from (loss). **hedgerow** *n.* bushes forming a hedge. **hedge sparrow** small brownish songbird.

hedgehog *n.* small mammal with a protective covering of spines.

hedonism *n.* doctrine that pleasure is the most important thing in life. **hedonist** *n.* **hedonistic** *adj.*

heed n. **1.** careful attention. —v. **2.** pay careful attention to. **heedless** adj. **heedless of** taking no notice of.

heel[1] n. **1.** back part of the foot. **2.** part of a shoe supporting the heel. **3.** Slang contemptible person. —v. **4.** make or replace the heel of.

heel[2] v. lean to one side.

hefty adj. **heftier, heftiest.** large, heavy, or strong.

hegemony [hig-**em**-on-ee] n. political domination.

Hegira n. Mohammed's flight from Mecca to Medina in 622 A.D.

heifer [**hef**-fer] n. young cow.

height n. **1.** distance from base to top. **2.** distance above sea level. **3.** highest degree or topmost point. **heighten** v. make or become higher or more intense.

heinous adj. evil and shocking.

heir n. person entitled to inherit property or rank. **heiress** n. fem. **heirloom** n. object that has belonged to a family for generations.

held v. past of HOLD[1].

helical adj. spiral.

helices [**hell**-iss-seez] n. plural of HELIX.

helicopter n. aircraft lifted and propelled by rotating overhead blades. **heliport** n. airport for helicopters.

heliograph n. signalling apparatus that uses a mirror to reflect the sun's rays.

heliotrope n. **1.** plant with purple flowers. —adj. **2.** light purple.

helium [**heel**-ee-um] n. very light colourless odourless gas.

helix [**heel**-iks] n., pl. **helices, helixes.** spiral.

hell n. **1.** home of the wicked after death. **2.** place or state of wickedness, suffering, or punishment. **hell for leather** at great speed. **hellish** adj. **hell-bent** adj. intent.

hellebore n. plant with white flowers that bloom in winter.

Hellenic adj. of the (ancient) Greeks or their language.

hello interj. expression of greeting or surprise.

helm n. tiller or wheel for steering a ship. **at the helm** in a position of leadership or control.

helmet n. hard hat worn for protection.

help v. **1.** make something easier, better, or quicker for (someone). **2.** improve (a situation). **3.** refrain from, e.g. I can't help laughing. **help oneself 1.** serve oneself. **2.** Informal steal something. **helper** n. **helpful** adj. **helpfully** adv. **helpfulness** n. single portion of food. **helpless** adj. weak or incapable. **helplessly** adv. **helplessness** n. **helpline** n. telephone line set aside for callers to contact an organization for help with a problem. **helpmate** n. **1.** companion and helper. **2.** husband or wife.

helter-skelter adj. **1.** haphazard and careless. —adv. **2.** in a haphazard and careless manner. —n. **3.** high spiral slide at a fairground.

hem n. **1.** border of cloth, folded under and stitched down. —v. **hemming, hemmed. 2.** provide with a hem. **hem in** v. surround and prevent from moving. **hemline** n. level to which the hem of a skirt hangs.

he-man n. Informal strong virile man.

hemisphere n. half of a sphere, esp. the earth. **hemispherical** adj.

hemlock n. poison derived from a plant with spotted stems and small white flowers.

hemp n. **1.** Asian plant with tough fibres. **2.** its fibre, used to make canvas and rope. **3.** narcotic drug obtained from hemp.

hen n. **1.** female domestic fowl. **2.** female of any bird. **hen party** party for women only. **henpecked** adj. (of a man) dominated by his wife.

henbane n. poisonous plant with sticky hairy leaves.

hence adv. **1.** for this reason. **2.** from this time. **henceforward, henceforth** adv. from now on.

henchman n. attendant or follower.

henna n. **1.** reddish dye made from a shrub or tree. —v. **2.** dye the hair with henna.

henry n., pl. **-ry, -ries, -rys.** unit of electrical inductance.

hepatitis n. inflammation of the liver.

hepta- combining form seven, e.g. heptameter.

heptagon n. figure with seven sides. **heptagonal** adj.

heptathlon n. athletic contest involving seven events.

her pron. **1.** refers to a female person or animal or anything personified as feminine when the object of a sentence or clause. —adj. **2.** of, belonging to, or associated with her.

herald n. **1.** person who announces important news. **2.** forerunner. —v. **3.** announce or signal the approach of. **heraldry** n. study of coats of arms and the histories of families. **heraldic** adj.

herb n. plant that is used for flavouring in cookery, and in medicine. **herbal** adj. **herbalist** n. person who grows or specializes in the use of medicinal herbs. **herbaceous** adj. (of a plant) soft-stemmed. **herbaceous border** flower bed that contains perennials rather than annuals. **herbicide** n. chemical which destroys plants. **herbivore** n. animal that feeds on plants. **herbivorous** [her-biv-or-uss] adj.

herculean [her-kew-lee-an] adj. requiring great strength or effort.

herd n. **1.** group of animals feeding and living together. **2.** large crowd of people. —v. **3.** collect into a herd. **herdsman** n. man who looks after a herd of animals.

here adv. in, at, or to this place or point. **hereabouts** adv. near here. **hereafter** n. **1.** life after death. —adv. **2.** in the future. **hereby** adv. by means of or as a result of this. **herein** adv. in this place, matter, or document. **hereinafter** adv. Law from this point on in this document, matter, or case. **heretofore** adv. Law until now. **herewith** adv. with this.

heredity [hir-red-it-ee] n. passing on of characteristics from one generation to another. **hereditary** adj. **1.** passed on genetically from one generation to another. **2.** passed on by inheritance.

heresy [herr-iss-ee] n., pl. **-sies.** opinion contrary to accepted opinion or belief. **heretic** [herr-it-ik] n. person who holds unorthodox opinions. **heretical** [hir-ret-ik-al] adj.

heritage n. **1.** thing that may be or is inherited. **2.** anything from the past, considered as the inheritance of present-day society.

hermaphrodite [her-maf-roe-dite] n. person, animal, or plant that has both male and female reproductive organs.

hermetic adj. sealed so as to be airtight. **hermetically** adv.

hermit n. person living in solitude, esp. for religious reasons. **hermitage** n. dwelling of

a hermit. **hermit crab** small crab that lives in shells of other shellfish.

hernia n. protrusion of (part of) an organ through the lining of the surrounding body cavity.

hero n., pl. **heroes. 1.** principal character in a film, book, play, etc. **2.** man greatly admired for exceptional qualities or achievements. **heroine** n. fem. **heroic** adj. **1.** of, like, or befitting a hero. **2.** courageous. **heroics** pl. n. extravagant behaviour. **heroically** adv. **heroism** [herr-oh-izz-um] n.

heroin n. highly addictive drug derived from morphine.

heron n. long-legged wading bird. **heronry** n., pl. **-ries.** place where herons breed.

herpes [her-peez] n. any of several inflammatory skin diseases, including shingles and cold sores.

Herr [hair] n., pl. **Herren.** German title of address equivalent to Mr.

herring n. important food fish of northern seas. **herringbone** n. pattern of zigzag lines.

hers pron. something belonging to her.

herself pron. emphatic or reflexive form of SHE or HER.

hertz n., pl. **hertz.** Physics unit of frequency.

hesitate v. **1.** be slow or uncertain in acting. **2.** be reluctant (to do something). **hesitation** n. **hesitant** adj. undecided or wavering. **hesitantly** adv. **hesitancy** n.

hessian n. coarse jute cloth.

hetero- combining form other; different, e.g. heterosexual.

heterodox adj. not orthodox. **heterodoxy** n.

heterogeneous [het-er-oh-jean-ee-uss] adj. composed of diverse elements. **heterogeneity** n.

heterosexual n., adj. (person) sexually attracted to members of the opposite sex. **heterosexuality** n.

het up adj. Informal agitated or excited.

heuristic [hew-rist-ik] adj. involving learning by investigation.

hew v. **hewing, hewed, hewed** or **hewn. 1.** chop or cut with an axe. **2.** carve from a substance.

hexa- combining form six, e.g. hexameter.

hexagon n. figure with six sides. **hexagonal** adj.

hexagram n. star formed by extending the

sides of a regular hexagon to meet at six points.

hey *interj.* expression of surprise or for catching attention. **hey presto!** exclamation used by conjurers at the climax of a trick.

heyday *n.* time of greatest success, prime.

Hf *Chem.* hafnium.

HF high frequency.

Hg *Chem.* mercury.

HGV heavy goods vehicle.

hi *interj. Informal* hello.

HI Hawaii.

hiatus [hie-**ay**-tuss] *n., pl.* **-tuses, -tus.** break or interruption in continuity.

hibernate *v.* (of an animal) pass the winter as if in a deep sleep. **hibernation** *n.*

Hibernian *adj. Poetic* Irish.

hibiscus *n., pl.* **-cuses.** tropical plant with large brightly coloured flowers.

hiccup, hiccough *n.* 1. spasm of the breathing organs with a sharp coughlike sound. —*v.* 2. make a hiccup or hiccups.

hick *n. US informal* unsophisticated country person.

hickory *n., pl.* **-ries.** 1. N American nut-bearing tree. 2. its tough wood.

hide[1] *v.* **hiding, hid, hidden.** 1. conceal or obscure (oneself or an object). 2. keep secret. —*n.* 3. place of concealment, esp. for a bird-watcher. **hiding** *n.* state of concealment, e.g. *in hiding.* **hideaway** *n.* hiding place or secluded spot. **hide-out** *n.* hiding place.

hide[2] *n.* skin of an animal. **hiding** *n. Slang* thrashing. **hidebound** *adj.* restricted by petty rules.

hideous [**hid**-ee-uss] *adj.* ugly, revolting. **hideously** *adv.*

hie *v.* **hying** *or* **hieing, hied.** *Obsolete* hurry.

hierarchy [**hire**-ark-ee] *n., pl.* **-chies.** system of people or things arranged in a graded order. **hierarchical** *adj.*

hieroglyphic [hire-oh-**gliff**-ik] *adj.* 1. of a form of writing using picture symbols, as used in ancient Egypt. —*n.* (also **hieroglyph**) 2. symbol representing an object, idea, or sound. 3. symbol that is difficult to decipher.

hi-fi *n.* 1. set of high-quality sound-reproducing equipment. —*adj.* 2. short for HIGH-FIDELITY.

higgledy-piggledy *adv., adj.* in confusion.

high *adj.* 1. tall, of greater than average height. 2. far above ground or sea level. 3. being at its peak. 4. greater than usual in intensity or amount. 5. of great importance, quality, or rank. 6. (of a sound) acute in pitch. 7. *Informal* under the influence of alcohol or drugs. 8. (of food) slightly decomposed. —*adv.* 9. at or to a high level. —*n.* 10. on a high *Informal* in an excited and happy state, (as if) intoxicated by alcohol or drugs. **highly** *adv.* **highly strung** nervous and easily upset. **Highness** *n.* title used to address or refer to a royal person. **High Church** belonging to a section within the Church of England stressing the importance of ceremony and ritual. **high commissioner** senior diplomatic representative sent by one Commonwealth country to another. **higher education** education at colleges, universities, and polytechnics. **high explosive** extremely powerful chemical explosive, such as TNT. **high-fidelity** *adj.* able to reproduce sound with little or no distortion. **high-flown** *adj.* (of ideas or speech) grand and elaborate. **high-handed** *adj.* overbearing and dogmatic. **high jump** athletic event in which competitors attempt to jump over a high bar. **high-minded** *adj.* having high moral principles. **high-powered** *adj.* dynamic and energetic. **high priest** head of a cult. **high priestess** *n. fem.* **high-rise** *adj.* (of a building) having many storeys. **high school** secondary school. **high-spirited** *adj.* vivacious, bold, or lively. **high tea** early evening meal consisting of a cooked dish, bread, cakes, and tea. **high time** latest possible time.

highball *n. US* long iced drink of whiskey with soda water or ginger ale.

highbrow *n.* 1. intellectual or scholar. —*adj.* 2. appealing to highbrows.

highchair *n.* long-legged chair with a tray attached, used for a young child at mealtimes.

highfalutin [hie-fa-**loot**-in] *adj. Informal* pompous or pretentious.

Highland *adj.* of the Highlands, a mountainous region of NW Scotland. **Highlander** *n.*

highlands *pl. n.* area of relatively high ground.

highlight *n.* 1. outstanding part or feature. 2. light-toned area in a painting or photograph. 3. lightened streak in the hair. —*v.* 4. give emphasis to.

highway *n. US* main road. **Highway Code**

regulations and recommendations applying to all road users. **highwayman** *n.* formerly, a robber, usually on horseback, who robbed travellers at gunpoint.

hijack *v.* seize control of (a vehicle or aircraft) while travelling. **hijacker** *n.*

hike *v.* **1.** walk a long way (for pleasure) in the country. **2.** (foll. by *up*) pull (up) or raise. **hiker** *n.*

hilarious *adj.* very funny. **hilariously** *adv.* **hilarity** *n.*

hill *n.* **1.** raised part of the earth's surface, less high than a mountain. **2.** incline or slope. **hilly** *adj.* **hillier, hilliest.** **hillock** *n.* small hill. **hillbilly** *n., pl.* **-billies.** *US* unsophisticated country person.

hilt *n.* handle of a sword or knife. **to the hilt,** up to the hilt to the full.

him *pron.* refers to a male person or animal when the object of a sentence or clause. **himself** *pron.* emphatic or reflexive form of HE OR HIM.

hind[1] *adj.* **hinder, hindmost.** situated at the back. **hindsight** *n.* ability to understand, after something has happened, what should have been done.

hind[2] *n.* female deer.

hinder *v.* obstruct the progress of. **hindrance** *n.*

Hinduism *n.* dominant religion of India which involves the worship of many gods and a belief in reincarnation. **Hindu** *n.* **1.** person who practises Hinduism. —*adj.* **2.** of Hinduism. **Hindi** *n.* language of N central India. **Hindustani** *n.* group of N Indian languages that includes Hindi and Urdu.

hinge *n.* **1.** device for holding together two parts so that one can swing freely. —*v.* **2.** fit a hinge to. **3.** (foll. by *on*) depend (on).

hinny *n., pl.* **-nies.** offspring of a male horse and a female donkey.

hint *n.* **1.** indirect suggestion. **2.** piece of advice. **3.** small amount. —*v.* **4.** suggest indirectly.

hinterland *n.* land lying behind a coast or near a city, esp. a port.

hip[1] *n.* either side of the body below the waist and above the thigh.

hip[2] *n.* fruit of the rose bush.

hip[3] *adj.* **hipper, hippest.** *Slang* aware of or following the latest trends.

hip-hop *n.* US pop-culture movement originating in the 1980s, comprising rap music, graffiti, and break dancing.

hippie *n.* esp. in the late 1960s, person whose behaviour and dress imply a rejection of conventional values.

hippo *n., pl.* **-pos.** *Informal* hippopotamus.

Hippocratic oath *n.* oath taken by doctors to observe a code of medical ethics.

hippodrome *n.* music hall, variety theatre, or circus.

hippopotamus *n., pl.* **-muses, -mi.** large African mammal with thick wrinkled skin, living in rivers.

hippy *n., pl.* **-pies.** same as HIPPIE.

hire *v.* **1.** obtain temporary use of by payment. **2.** employ for wages. —*n.* **3.** act of hiring. **4.** payment for the use of something. **hireling** *n.* person who works only for wages. **hire-purchase** *n.* system of purchase by which the buyer pays for goods by instalments.

hirsute [her-suit] *adj.* hairy.

his *pron., adj.* (something) belonging to him.

Hispanic *adj.* of Spain or a Spanish-speaking country.

hiss *n.* **1.** sound like that of a long *s* (as an exclamation of contempt). —*v.* **2.** utter a hiss. **3.** show derision or anger towards.

histamine [hiss-ta-meen] *n.* substance released by the body tissues, causing allergic reactions.

histogram *n.* statistical graph in which the frequency of values is represented by vertical bars of varying heights and widths.

histology *n.* study of the tissues of an animal or plant. **histological** *adj.*

history *n., pl.* **-ries.** **1.** (record or account of) past events and developments. **2.** study of these. **3.** record of someone's past. **4.** play that depicts historical events. **historian** *n.* writer of history. **historic** *adj.* famous or significant in history. **historical** *adj.* **1.** based on history. **2.** occurring in the past. **historically** *adv.*

histrionic *adj.* excessively dramatic. **histrionics** *pl. n.* melodramatic behaviour.

hit *v.* **hitting, hit.** **1.** strike, touch forcefully. **2.** come into violent contact with. **3.** affect adversely. **4.** reach (a point or place). —*n.* **5.** impact or blow. **6.** success. **hit it off** *Informal* get on well together. **hit the road** *Informal* set out on a journey. **hit-and-run** *adj.* denoting a motor-vehicle accident in which the driver does not stop to give assistance or inform the police. **hit man** hired assassin. **hit on** v. think of (an idea). **hit-or-miss, hit-and-miss** adj. haphazard.

hitch v. **1.** fasten with a loop or hook. **2.** pull up with a jerk. **3.** *Informal* obtain (a lift) by hitchhiking. —n. **4.** slight difficulty. **hitchhike** v. travel by obtaining free lifts. **hitchhiker** n.

hi-tech adj. using sophisticated technology.

hither adv. *Old-fashioned* to or towards this place. **hitherto** adv. until this time.

HIV human immunodeficiency virus.

hive n. structure in which bees live. **hive of activity** place where people are very busy. **hive off** v. separate from a larger group.

hives n. disease causing itchy red or whitish patches on the skin.

HM Her (or His) Majesty.

HMI Her (or His) Majesty's Inspector (of schools).

HMS Her (or His) Majesty's Service or Ship.

HMSO Her (or His) Majesty's Stationery Office.

HNC Higher National Certificate.

HND Higher National Diploma.

Ho *Chem.* holmium.

hoard n. **1.** store hidden away for future use. —v. **2.** gather or accumulate. **hoarder** n.

hoarding n. large board for displaying advertisements.

hoarfrost n. white ground frost.

hoarse adj. **1.** (of a voice) rough and unclear. **2.** having a rough and unclear voice. **hoarsely** adv. **hoarseness** n.

hoary adj. **hoarier, hoariest. 1.** grey or white (with age). **2.** very old.

hoax n. deception or trick. —v. **2.** deceive or play a trick upon. **hoaxer** n.

hob n. flat top part of a cooker.

hobble v. **1.** walk lamely. **2.** tie the legs of (a horse) together.

hobby n., pl. **-bies.** activity pursued in one's spare time. **hobbyhorse** n. **1.** favourite topic. **2.** toy horse.

hobgoblin n. mischievous goblin.

hobnail n. large-headed nail for boot soles. **hobnailed** adj.

hobnob v. **-nobbing, -nobbed.** (foll. by *with*) socialize (with).

hobo n., pl. **-bos.** *US* tramp or vagrant.

Hobson's choice n. the choice of taking what is offered or nothing at all.

hock¹ n. joint in the leg of a horse or similar animal corresponding to the human ankle.

hock² n. white German wine.

hock³ v. *Informal* pawn. **in hock 1.** pawned. **2.** in debt.

hockey n. **1.** team game played on a field with a ball and curved sticks. **2.** *US* ice hockey.

hocus-pocus n. trickery.

hod n. open wooden box attached to a pole, for carrying bricks or mortar.

hoe n. **1.** long-handled tool used to loosen soil or to weed. —v. **2.** scrape or weed using a hoe.

hog n. **1.** castrated male pig. **2.** *Informal* greedy person. —v. **hogging, hogged. 3.** *Informal* take more than one's share of. **go the whole hog** *Slang* do something thoroughly or unreservedly. **hogshead** n. large cask. **hogwash** n. *Informal* nonsense.

Hogmanay n. in Scotland, New Year's Eve.

ho-ho interj. representation of the sound of a deep laugh.

hoick v. raise abruptly and sharply.

hoi polloi n. the ordinary people.

hoist v. **1.** raise or lift up. —n. **2.** device for lifting things.

hoity-toity adj. *Informal* arrogant or haughty.

hokum n. *US slang* **1.** rubbish, nonsense. **2.** stereotyped sentimentality in a film or play.

hold¹ v. **holding, held. 1.** keep or support in or using the hands or arms. **2.** maintain in a specified position or state. **3.** have the capacity for. **4.** own, possess. **5.** keep possession of. **6.** reserve (a room etc.). **7.** restrain or keep back. **8.** not use. **9.** cause to take place, e.g. *hold a meeting.* **10.** (cause to) remain committed to (a promise etc.). **11.** believe. —n. **12.** act or method of holding. **13.** influence. **14.** something held onto for support. **holder** n. **holding** n. property, such as land or stocks and shares. **holdall** n. large strong travelling bag. **hold forth** v. speak for a long time. **hold-up** n. **1.** armed robbery. **2.** delay. **hold up** v. **hold with** v. approve of, e.g. *I don't hold with capital punishment.*

hold[2] n. cargo compartment in a ship or aircraft.

hole n. 1. area hollowed out in a solid. 2. opening or hollow. 3. animal's burrow. 4. Informal unattractive place. 5. Informal difficult situation. —v. 6. make holes in. 7. hit (a golf ball) into a hole. **holed up** in hiding. **holey** adj.

holiday n. 1. day or other period of rest from work or studies. 2. time spent away from home for rest or recreation.

holiness n. state of being holy. **His Holiness** title used to refer to the Pope.

holism n. consideration of the complete person in the treatment of disease. **holistic** adj.

holler v., n. Informal shout or yell.

hollow adj. 1. having a hole or space inside. 2. without any real value or worth. 3. (of sounds) as if echoing in a hollow place. —n. 4. cavity or space. 5. dip in the land. —v. 6. form a hollow in. **hollowly** adv. **hollowness** n.

holly n. evergreen tree with prickly leaves and red berries.

hollyhock n. tall garden plant with spikes of colourful flowers.

holmium n. silver-white metallic element the compounds of which are highly magnetic.

holm oak n. evergreen Mediterranean oak tree.

holocaust n. destruction or loss of life on a massive scale.

hologram n. three-dimensional photographic image.

holograph n. document handwritten by the author.

holography n. science of using lasers to produce holograms. **holographic** adj.

holster n. leather case for a pistol, hung from a belt.

holt n. otter's lair.

holy adj. **-lier, -liest. 1.** of or associated with God or a deity. **2.** devout or virtuous. **holier-than-thou** adj. self-righteous. **Holy Communion** Christianity service in remembrance of the death and resurrection of Jesus Christ. **Holy Grail** in medieval legend, the bowl used by Jesus Christ at the Last Supper. **holy orders** status of an ordained Christian minister. **Holy Spirit, Ghost**

Christianity one of the three aspects of God. **Holy Week** Christianity week before Easter.

homage n. show of respect or honour towards something or someone.

homburg n. man's soft felt hat with a dented crown and a stiff upturned brim.

home n. 1. place where one lives. 2. institution for the care of the elderly, infirm, etc. —adj. 3. of one's home, birthplace, or native country. 4. Sport played on one's own ground. —adv. 5. to or at home. —v. 6. (foll. by in on) direct or be directed onto (a point or target). **at home** at ease. **bring home to** make clear to. **home and dry** Informal safe or successful. **homeless** adj. **homelessness** n. **homely** adj. 1. simple, ordinary, and comfortable. 2. US unattractive. **homeliness** n. **homeward** adj., adv. **homewards** adv. **home-brew** n. beer made at home. **home economics** study of diet, budgeting, child care, and other subjects concerned with running a home. **home help** person employed by a local authority to do housework for a person who is too ill or too old to do his or her own housework. **home-made** adj. made at home or on the premises. **Home Office** government department responsible for law and order, immigration, and other domestic matters. **Home Secretary** head of the Home Office. **home truths** unpleasant facts told to a person about himself or herself.

homeland n. country from which a person's ancestors came.

homeopathy [home-ee-op-ath-ee] n. treatment of disease by small doses of a drug that produces symptoms of the disease in healthy people. **homeopath** n. person who practises homeopathy. **homeopathic** [home-ee-oh-path-ik] adj.

homesick adj. depressed by absence from home. **homesickness** n.

homestead n. farmhouse plus the adjoining land.

homework n. school work done at home.

homicide n. 1. killing of a human being. 2. person who kills another. **homicidal** adj.

homily n., pl. **-lies.** speech telling people how they should behave.

homing pigeon n. pigeon trained to return home after travelling great distances, kept for racing.

hominid n. man or any extinct forerunner of man.

hominoid *adj., n.* manlike (animal).

homo- *combining form* same, e.g. *homosexual.*

homogeneous [home-oh-**jean**-ee-uss] *adj.* formed of similar parts. **homogeneity** *n.* **homogenize** *v.* 1. make homogeneous. 2. break up fat globules in (milk or cream) to distribute them evenly.

homograph *n.* word spelt the same as another.

homologous [hom-**ol**-log-uss] *adj.* having a related or similar position or structure.

homonym *n.* word with the same spelling or pronunciation as another, but with a different meaning.

homophobia *n.* hatred or fear of homosexuals. **homophobic** *adj.*

homophone *n.* word with the same pronunciation as another.

Homo sapiens [hoe-moh **sap**-ee-enz] *n.* human beings as a species.

homosexual *n., adj.* (person) sexually attracted to members of the same sex. **homosexuality** *n.*

Hon. Honourable.

hone *v.* sharpen.

honest *adj.* 1. not cheating, lying, or stealing. 2. genuine or sincere. 3. just or fair. **honestly** *adv.* **honesty** *n.* 1. quality of being honest. 2. plant with silvery seed pods.

honey *n.* 1. sweet edible fluid made by bees from nectar. 2. term of endearment. **honeyed** *adj. Poetic* flattering or soothing, e.g. *honeyed words.* **honeycomb** *n.* waxy structure of hexagonal cells in which honey is stored. **honeydew melon** melon with yellow skin and sweet pale flesh. **honeymoon** *n.* holiday taken by a newly married couple. **honeysuckle** *n.* climbing shrub with sweet-smelling flowers.

honk *n.* 1. sound made by a car horn. 2. sound made by a goose. —*v.* 3. (cause to) make this sound.

honky-tonk *n. US slang* 1. cheap disreputable nightclub. 2. style of ragtime piano-playing, esp. on a tinny-sounding piano.

honour *n.* 1. personal integrity. 2. (award given out of) respect. 3. pleasure or privilege. —*pl.* 4. rank or mark of the highest academic standard in a university degree course. —*v.* 5. give praise and attention to. 6. give an award to (someone) out of respect. 7. keep (a promise). 8. accept or pay (a cheque or bill). **do the honours** act as host or hostess by pouring drinks or giving out food. **honourable** *adj.* 1. worthy of respect or esteem. 2. (H-) denoting a title of respect placed before the names of some members of the nobility, judges, etc. **honourably** *adv.* **honorary** *adj.* 1. held or given only as an honour. 2. holding a position or giving one's services without pay. **honorific** *adj.* showing respect.

hooch [rhymes with **smooch**] *n. US slang* alcoholic drink, esp. illicitly distilled spirits.

hood[1] *n.* 1. head covering, often part of a coat etc. 2. folding roof of a convertible car or a pram. 3. *US* car bonnet. —*v.* 4. cover (as if) with a hood. **hooded** *adj.* 1. (of a garment) having a hood. 2. (of eyes) having heavy eyelids that appear to be half closed.

hood[2] *n. Slang* hoodlum.

hoodlum *n. Slang* gangster, lawless youth.

hoodoo *n., pl.* -**doos.** (cause of) bad luck.

hoodwink *v.* trick or deceive.

hooey *n. Slang* nonsense.

hoof *n., pl.* **hooves, hoofs.** horny casing of the foot of a horse, deer, etc. **hoof it** *Informal* walk.

hoo-ha *n.* fuss or commotion.

hook *n.* 1. curved piece of metal used to hang, hold, or pull something. 2. short swinging punch. —*v.* 3. fasten or catch (as if) with a hook. **hooked** *adj.* 1. shaped like a hook. 2. caught. 3. (foll. by *on*) *Slang* addicted (to). **hooker** *n.* 1. *Slang* prostitute. 2. *Rugby* player who uses his feet to get the ball in a scrum. **hook-up** *n.* linking of radio or television stations. **hookworm** *n.* parasitic worm with hooked mouth parts.

hookah *n.* oriental pipe in which smoke is drawn through water and a long tube.

hooligan *n.* rowdy young person. **hooliganism** *n.*

hoop *n.* rigid circular band, used esp. as a child's toy or for animals to jump through in the circus. **be put through the hoops** go through an ordeal or test.

hoopla *n.* fairground game in which hoops are thrown over objects in an attempt to win them.

hoopoe [**hoop**-oo] *n.* bird with a pinkish-brown plumage and a fanlike crest.

hooray *interj.* same as HURRAH.

hoot *n.* 1. owl's cry or similar sound. 2. cry of derision. 3. *Informal* amusing person or thing. —v. **4.** jeer or yell contemptuously at (someone). **5.** sound (a car horn). **hooter** n. **1.** device that hoots. **2.** Slang nose.

Hoover n. **1.** ® vacuum cleaner. —v. **2.** (h-) vacuum.

hooves n. a plural of HOOF.

hop[1] v. **hopping, hopped. 1.** jump on one foot. **2.** move in short jumps. **3.** Informal move quickly. —n. **4.** instance of hopping. **5.** short journey, esp. by air. **6.** Informal dance. **hop it** Slang go away. **on the hop** Informal **1.** unawares, e.g. caught on the hop. **2.** active or busy.

hop[2] n. **1.** climbing plant with green conelike flowers used to give beer a bitter flavour. —pl. **2.** the dried flowers.

hope n. **1.** expectation of something desired. **2.** thing that gives cause for hope or is desired. —v. **3.** want (something) to happen or be true. **hopeful** adj. **1.** having, expressing, or inspiring hope. —n. **2.** person considered to be on the brink of success. **hopefully** adv. **1.** in a hopeful manner. **2.** it is hoped. **hopefulness** n. **hopeless** adj. **hopelessly** adv. **hopelessness** n.

▷ Although many people dislike the use of hopefully as in I'll see you in June, hopefully, it is now well established.

hopper n. container for storing things such as grain or sand.

hopscotch n. children's game of hopping in a pattern drawn on the ground.

horde n. large crowd.

horizon n. **1.** apparent line that divides the earth and the sky. —pl. **2.** limits of scope, interest, or knowledge.

horizontal adj. **1.** parallel to the horizon. **2.** level, flat. **horizontally** adv.

hormone n. **1.** substance secreted by certain glands which stimulates certain organs of the body. **2.** synthetic substance with the same effect. **hormonal** adj.

horn n. **1.** one of a pair of bony growths on the heads of animals such as cows and antelopes. **2.** substance of which this is made. **3.** wind instrument with a tube or pipe of brass fitted with a mouthpiece. **4.** device on a vehicle sounded as a warning. **horned** adj. **horny** adj. **hornier, horniest. 1.** of or like horn. **2.** Slang sexually aroused. **hornbeam** n. tree with smooth grey bark. **hornbill** n. bird with a bony growth on its large beak. **hornpipe** n. (music for) a lively

solo dance, traditionally associated with sailors.

hornblende n. mineral containing aluminium, calcium, sodium, magnesium, and iron.

hornet n. large wasp with a severe sting.

horology n. art or science of clock-making and measuring time. **horological** adj.

horoscope n. **1.** prediction of a person's future based on the positions of the planets, sun, and moon at his or her birth. **2.** diagram of the positions of these at a particular time and place.

horrendous adj. horrific. **horrendously** adv.

horrible adj. **1.** disagreeable. **2.** causing horror. **horribly** adv.

horrid adj. **1.** unpleasant or disagreeable. **2.** Informal unkind.

horrify v. **-fying, -fied. 1.** cause feelings of horror in. **2.** shock. **horrifying** adj. **horrifyingly** adv. **horrific** adj. particularly horrible. **horrifically** adv.

horror n. (thing or person causing) terror or hatred.

hors d'oeuvre [or durv] n. appetizer served before a main meal.

horse n. **1.** four-footed animal with hooves, a mane, and a tail, used for riding and pulling carts, etc. **2.** piece of gymnastic equipment used for vaulting over. **straight from the horse's mouth** from the most reliable source. **horsy, horsey** adj. **horsier, horsiest. 1.** devoted to horses. **2.** like a horse. **horse about, around** v. Informal play roughly or boisterously. **horsebox** n. trailer used for transporting horses. **horse chestnut** tree with broad leaves, white or pink flowers, and large brown shiny nuts. **horsefly** n. large bloodsucking fly. **horsehair** n. hair from the tail or mane of a horse. **horse laugh** harsh boisterous laugh. **horseman, horsewoman** n. **1.** rider on a horse. **2.** person who is skilled in riding. **horsemanship** n. **horseplay** n. rough or rowdy behaviour. **horsepower** n. unit of power (equivalent to 745.7 watts), used to measure the power of an engine. **horseradish** n. plant with a strong-tasting root, used to make a sauce. **horse sense** common sense. **horseshoe** n. protective U-shaped piece of iron nailed to a horse's hoof, often regarded as a symbol of good luck.

horticulture n. art or science of cultivating gardens. **horticultural** adj. **horticulturist** n.

hosanna *interj.* exclamation of praise to God.

hose[1] *n.* **1.** flexible tube for conveying liquid. —*v.* **2.** water with a hose.

hose[2] *n.* stockings, socks, and tights. **hosiery** *n.* stockings, socks, etc., collectively.

hospice [**hoss**-piss] *n.* nursing home for the terminally ill.

hospital *n.* institution for the care and treatment of sick or injured people. **hospitalize** *v.* send or admit for care in a hospital. **hospitalization** *n.*

hospitality *n.* friendliness in welcoming strangers or guests. **hospitable** *adj.* welcoming.

host[1] *n.* **1.** person who entertains another as a guest. **2.** compère of a show. **3.** animal or plant on which a parasite lives. —*v.* **4.** be the host of. **hostess** *n.* woman who welcomes guests or visitors.

host[2] *n.* large number.

Host *n. Christianity* bread used in Holy Communion.

hostage *n.* person who is illegally held prisoner until certain demands are met by other people.

hostel *n.* building providing accommodation at a low cost for particular categories of people, such as homeless people.

hostelry *n., pl.* **-ries.** *Obs.* inn.

hostile *adj.* **1.** unfriendly. **2.** of an enemy. **3.** (foll. by *to*) opposed (to). **hostility** *n., pl.* **-ties. 1.** unfriendly and aggressive feelings or behaviour. —*pl.* **2.** acts of warfare.

hot *adj.* **hotter, hottest. 1.** having a high temperature. **2.** giving or feeling heat. **3.** (of a temper) quick to flare up. **4.** (of a competition) intense. **5.** recent or new. **6.** liked very much, e.g. *a hot favourite.* **7.** spicy. **8.** *Slang* stolen. **in hot water** *Informal* in trouble. **in the hot seat** *Informal* in a difficult and responsible position. **hotly** *adv.* **hot air** *Informal* empty talk. **hot-blooded** *adj.* passionate or excitable. **hot dog** hot sausage (esp. a frankfurter) in a bread roll. **hot-headed** *adj.* having a hot temper. **hot line** direct telephone link for emergency use. **hot-water bottle** rubber container filled with hot water and used for warming a bed.

hotbed *n.* any place encouraging a particular activity, e.g. *a hotbed of vice.*

hotchpotch *n.* jumbled mixture.

hotel *n.* commercial establishment providing lodging and meals. **hotelier** *n.* owner or manager of a hotel.

hotfoot *v., adv. Informal* (go) as fast as possible.

hothouse *n.* heated greenhouse.

hotplate *n.* **1.** heated metal surface on an electric cooker. **2.** portable device for keeping food warm.

hotpot *n.* casserole of meat and vegetables, topped with potatoes.

Hottentot *n.* member of a race of people of southern Africa, now nearly extinct.

hound *n.* **1.** hunting dog. —*v.* **2.** pursue relentlessly.

hour *n.* **1.** twenty-fourth part of a day. **2.** sixty minutes. **3.** time of day. **4.** appointed time. —*pl.* **5.** period regularly appointed for work or business. **hourly** *adj., adv.* **1.** (happening) every hour. **2.** frequent(ly). **hourglass** *n.* device with two glass compartments, containing a quantity of sand that takes an hour to trickle from the top section to the bottom one.

houri *n. Islam* any of the beautiful nymphs of paradise.

house *n.* **1.** building used as a dwelling. **2.** building for some specific purpose, e.g. *schoolhouse.* **3.** law-making body or the hall where it meets. **4.** family or dynasty. **5.** business firm. **6.** theatre audience or performance. —*v.* **7.** give accommodation to. **8.** cover or contain. **get on like a house on fire** *Informal* get on very well together. **on the house** *Informal* provided free by the management. **housing** *n.* **1.** (providing of) houses. **2.** protective case or covering of a machine. **house arrest** confinement to one's home rather than to prison. **houseboat** *n.* stationary boat used as a home. **housebound** *adj.* unable to leave one's house, usually because of illness. **housebreaker** *n.* burglar. **house-breaking** *n.* **housecoat** *n.* woman's long loose robelike garment for casual wear. **household** *n.* all the people living in a house. **household name** very well-known person. **householder** *n.* person who owns or rents a house. **housekeeper** *n.* person employed to run someone else's household. **housekeeping** *n.* (money for) running a household. **housemaid** *n.* female servant who does housework. **houseman** *n.* junior hospital doctor. **house-proud** *adj.* excessively concerned with the appearance of one's house. **house-train** v. train (a domestic animal) to urinate and defecate outside. **house-warming** n. party to celebrate moving into a new home. **housewife** n. woman who runs her own household. **housewifely** adj. **housework** n. work of running a house, such as cleaning, cooking, and shopping.

House music, House n. kind of disco music based on funk, with fragments of other recordings edited in electronically.

hove v. Naut. past of HEAVE.

hovel n. small dirty dwelling.

hover v. 1. (of a bird etc.) remain suspended in one place in the air. 2. loiter. 3. be in a state of indecision. **hovercraft** n. vehicle which can travel over both land and sea on a cushion of air.

how adv. 1. in what way. 2. by what means. 3. in what condition. 4. to what degree. **however** adv. 1. nevertheless. 2. by whatever means. 3. no matter how.

howdah n. canopied seat on an elephant's back.

howitzer n. cannon firing shells at a steep angle.

howl v. 1. utter a long loud cry. —n. 2. such a cry. 3. loud burst of laughter. **howler** n. Informal stupid mistake.

hoyden n. wild or boisterous girl, tomboy.

HP, hp 1. hire-purchase. 2. horsepower.

HQ headquarters.

hr hour.

HRH Her (or His) Royal Highness.

HRT hormone replacement therapy.

hub n. 1. centre of a wheel, through which the axle passes. 2. central point of activity.

hubble-bubble n. same as HOOKAH.

hubbub n. confused noise of many voices, uproar.

hubby n., pl. **-bies**. Informal husband.

hubris [hew-briss] n. pride, arrogance.

huckster n. person using aggressive methods of selling.

huddle n. 1. small group. 2. Informal impromptu conference. —v. 3. heap or crowd closely together. 4. hunch (oneself) through cold or fear.

hue n. colour.

hue and cry n. public outcry.

huff n. 1. passing mood of anger or resent-

ment. —v. 2. blow or puff heavily. **huffy** adj. **huffier, huffiest. huffily** adv.

hug v. **hugging, hugged**. 1. clasp tightly in the arms, usually with affection. 2. keep close to. —n. 3. tight or fond embrace.

huge adj. very big. **hugely** adv. very much.

huggermugger Old-fashioned —n. 1. confusion or secrecy. —adj., adv. 2. in confusion.

huh interj. exclamation of derision, bewilderment, or inquiry.

hula n. native dance of Hawaii. **Hula-Hoop** n. ® plastic hoop swung round the body by wriggling the hips.

hulk n. 1. body of an abandoned ship. 2. Offens. large or unwieldy person or thing. **hulking** adj. bulky or unwieldy.

hull n. 1. main body of a boat. 2. leaves round the stem of a strawberry, raspberry, or similar fruit. 3. shell or husk of a fruit or seed. —v. 4. remove the hulls from (fruit or seeds).

hullabaloo n., pl. **-loos**. loud confused noise or clamour.

hullo interj. same as HELLO.

hum v. **humming, hummed**. 1. make a low continuous vibrating sound. 2. sing with closed lips. 3. Slang be very active. —n. 4. humming sound. **humming** n. **hummingbird** n. very small American bird whose powerful wings make a humming noise as they vibrate.

human adj. 1. of, concerning, or typical of people. 2. human being. **humanly** adv. by human powers or means. **human being** man, woman, or child. **human nature** ordinary human behaviour, esp. when less than perfect. **human race** mankind. **human rights** basic rights of people to liberty, justice, etc.

humane adj. kind or merciful. **humanely** adv.

humanism n. belief in human effort rather than religion. **humanist** n. **humanistic** adj.

humanitarian n., adj. (person) with the interest of mankind at heart. **humanitarianism** n.

humanity n., pl. **-ties**. 1. the quality of being human. 2. mankind. 3. kindness or mercy. —pl. 4. study of literature, philosophy, and the arts.

humanize v. make human or humane. **humanization** n.

humankind n. mankind.

humanoid *adj., n.* (robot or creature) resembling a human being in appearance.

humble *adj.* **1.** conscious of one's failings. **2.** modest, unpretentious. **3.** unimportant. —*v.* **4.** cause to become humble. **5.** humiliate. **humbly** *adv.*

humbug *n.* **1.** boiled sweet flavoured with peppermint. **2.** nonsense. **3.** person or thing that deceives people.

humdinger *n. Slang* excellent person or thing.

humdrum *adj.* commonplace and dull.

humerus [hew-mer-uss] *n., pl.* **-meri** [-mer-rye] bone from the shoulder to the elbow.

humid *adj.* (of the weather) damp and warm. **humidity** *n.* **humidify** *v.* **-fying, -fied. humidifier** *n.* device for increasing the amount of water vapour in the air in a room.

humiliate *v.* lower the dignity or hurt the pride of. **humiliating** *adj.* **humiliation** *n.*

humility *n.* quality of being humble.

hummock *n.* hillock.

humour *n.* **1.** ability to say or perceive things that are amusing. **2.** situations, speech, or writings that are humorous. **3.** state of mind, mood. **4.** *Obs.* fluid in the body. —*v.* **5.** be kind and indulgent to. **humorous** *adj.* **humorously** *adv.* **humorist** *n.* person who acts, speaks, or writes in a humorous way. **humourless** *adj.*

hump *n.* **1.** normal or deforming lump, esp. on the back. **2.** hillock. **3.** *Informal* fit of sulking. —*v.* **4.** *Slang* carry or heave. **humpback** *n.* person with an abnormal curvature of the spine. **humpbacked** *adj.* **hump-back bridge** road bridge with a sharp slope on either side.

humus [hew-muss] *n.* decomposing vegetable and animal mould in the soil.

Hun *n.* **1.** member of any of several Asiatic peoples who invaded the Roman Empire in the 4th and 5th centuries A.D. **2.** *Informal offens.* in World War 1, German.

hunch *n.* **1.** *Informal* feeling or suspicion not based on facts. —*v.* **2.** draw (one's shoulders) up or together. **hunchback** *n.* humpback. **hunchbacked** *adj.*

hundred *adj., n.* ten times ten. **hundredth** *adj., n.* (of) number one hundred in a series. **hundredfold** *adj., adv.* **hundredweight** *n.* unit of weight of 112 lbs. (50.8 kg).

hung *v.* **1.** past of HANG. —*adj.* **2.** (of a jury) unable to decide. **3.** (of a parliament) with no clear majority. **hung over** *Informal* suffering the effects of a hangover.

Hungarian *n.* **1.** language of Hungary. **2.** person from Hungary. —*adj.* **3.** of Hungary or its language.

hunger *n.* **1.** discomfort or weakness from lack of food. **2.** desire or craving. —*v.* **3.** (foll. by *for*) want very much. **hunger strike** refusal of all food, as a means of protest.

hungry *adj.* **hungrier, hungriest.** desiring food. **hungrily** *adv.*

hunk *n.* **1.** large piece. **2.** *Slang* sexually attractive man.

hunt *v.* **1.** seek out (animals) to kill or capture for sport or food. **2.** search (for). —*n.* **3.** act or instance of hunting. **4.** (party organized for) hunting wild animals for sport. **hunter** *n.* **1.** man or animal that seeks out and kills or captures game. **2.** horse or dog bred for hunting. **huntress** *n. Obs.* woman who seeks out and kills or captures game. **hunting** *n.* **huntsman** *n.* **1.** man in charge of a pack of hounds. **2.** man who hunts.

hurdle *n.* **1.** light barrier for jumping over. **2.** problem or difficulty. —*pl.* **3.** race involving hurdles. —*v.* **4.** jump over (something). **hurdler** *n.* person who races over hurdles.

hurdy-gurdy *n., pl.* **-dies.** mechanical musical instrument, such as a barrel organ.

hurl *v.* throw or utter violently.

hurling, hurley *n.* Irish game resembling hockey.

hurly-burly *n.* loud confusion.

hurrah, hurray *interj.* exclamation of joy or applause.

hurricane *n.* very strong, often destructive, wind or storm. **hurricane lamp** paraffin lamp with a glass covering.

hurry *v.* **-rying, -ried.** **1.** (cause to) move or act in great haste. —*n.* **2.** haste. **3.** eagerness. **hurried** *adj.* **hurriedly** *adv.*

hurt *v.* **hurting, hurt.** **1.** cause physical or mental pain to. **2.** wound the feelings of. **3.** *Informal* feel pain. —*n.* **4.** physical or mental pain or suffering. **hurtful** *adj.*

hurtle *v.* move rapidly or violently.

husband *n.* **1.** woman's partner in marriage. —*v.* **2.** use economically. **husbandry** *n.* **1.** farming. **2.** management of resources.

hush *v.* **1.** make or be silent. —*n.* **2.** stillness or quietness. **hushed** *adj.* **hush-hush** *adj.*

Informal secret. **hush money** *Slang* money given to someone to ensure that something is kept secret. **hush up** *v.* suppress information about.

husk *n.* **1.** outer covering of certain seeds and fruits. —*v.* **2.** remove the husk from.

husky¹ *adj.* **huskier, huskiest. 1.** hoarse or dry in the throat. **2.** *Informal* big and strong. **huskily** *adv.*

husky² *n., pl.* **huskies.** Arctic sledge dog with a thick coat and a curled tail.

hussar [hoo-zar] *n.* lightly armed cavalry soldier.

hussy *n., pl.* **-sies.** brazen or promiscuous woman.

hustings *pl. n.* proceedings at a parliamentary election.

hustle *v.* **1.** push about, jostle. **2.** *US slang* (of a prostitute) solicit. —*n.* **3.** lively activity or bustle.

hut *n.* small house or shelter.

hutch *n.* cage for small pet animals.

hyacinth *n.* sweet-smelling spring flower which grows from a bulb.

hyaena *n.* same as HYENA.

hybrid *n.* **1.** offspring of two plants or animals of different species. **2.** anything of mixed ancestry. —*adj.* **3.** of mixed ancestry.

hydatid disease [hide-at-id] *n.* condition caused by the presence of bladder-like cysts (**hydatids**) in the liver, lungs, or brain.

hydra *n.* **1.** mythical many-headed water serpent. **2.** any persistent problem. **3.** freshwater polyp.

hydrangea *n.* ornamental shrub with clusters of pink, blue, or white flowers.

hydrant *n.* outlet from a water main with a nozzle for a hose.

hydrate *n.* **1.** chemical compound of water with another substance. —*v.* **2.** treat or impregnate with water.

hydraulic *adj.* operated by pressure forced through a pipe by a liquid such as water or oil. **hydraulics** *n.* study of the mechanical properties of fluids as they apply to practical engineering. **hydraulically** *adv.*

hydro¹ *n., pl.* **hydros.** hotel offering hydropathy.

hydro² *adj.* short for HYDROELECTRIC.

hydro- *combining form* **1.** water. **2.** hydrogen.

hydrocarbon *n.* compound of hydrogen and carbon.

hydrocephalus *n.* accumulation of fluid within the cavities of the brain, causing enlargement of the head in children. **hydrocephalic** *adj.*

hydrochloric acid *n.* strong colourless acid used in many industrial and laboratory processes.

hydrodynamics *n.* science concerned with the mechanical properties of fluids.

hydroelectric *adj.* of the generation of electricity by the use of water.

hydrofoil *n.* fast light vessel with its hull raised out of the water on one or more pairs of fins.

hydrogen *n.* light flammable colourless gaseous element which combines with oxygen to form water. **hydrogen bomb** atom bomb of enormous power in which energy is released by the fusion of hydrogen nuclei to give helium nuclei. **hydrogen peroxide** colourless liquid used as a hair bleach and as an antiseptic.

hydrology *n.* study of the distribution, conservation, and use of the water of the earth and its atmosphere. **hydrological** *adj.*

hydrolysis [hie-drol-iss-iss] *n.* decomposition of a chemical compound reacting with water.

hydrometer [hie-drom-it-er] *n.* device for measuring the relative density of a liquid.

hydropathy *n.* method of treating disease by the use of large quantities of water both internally and externally.

hydrophobia *n.* **1.** fear of water. **2.** rabies.

hydroplane *n.* light motorboat which skims the water.

hydroponics *n.* science of cultivating plants in water without using soil.

hydrostatics *n.* branch of science concerned with the mechanical properties and behaviour of fluids that are not in motion. **hydrostatic** *adj.*

hydrotherapy *n. Med.* treatment of certain diseases by exercise in water.

hydrous *adj.* containing water.

hyena *n.* scavenging doglike mammal of Africa and S Asia.

hygiene *n.* **1.** principles and practice of health and cleanliness. **2.** study of these principles. **hygienic** *adj.* **hygienically** *adv.*

hymen n. membrane covering the opening of a girl's vagina, which breaks before puberty or at the first occurrence of sexual intercourse.

hymn n. Christian song of praise sung to God or a saint. **hymnal** n. book of hymns (also **hymn book**).

hype n. **1.** intensive or exaggerated publicity or sales promotion. — v. **2.** promote (a product) using intensive or exaggerated publicity.

hyper adj. Informal overactive or overexcited.

hyper- prefix over, above, excessively, e.g. hyperactive.

hyperbola [hie-per-bol-a] n. curve produced when a cone is cut by a plane at a steeper angle to its base than its side. **hyperbolic** adj.

hyperbole [hie-per-bol-ee] n. deliberate exaggeration for effect. **hyperbolic** adj.

hypermarket n. huge self-service store.

hypersensitive adj. unduly vulnerable emotionally or physically.

hypersonic adj. having a speed of at least five times the speed of sound.

hypertension n. abnormally high blood pressure.

hyperventilation n. increase in the rate of breathing, sometimes resulting in cramp and dizziness. **hyperventilate** v.

hyphen n. punctuation mark (-) indicating that two words or syllables are connected. **hyphenate** v. join with a hyphen. **hyphenated** adj. having two words or syllables joined by a hyphen. **hyphenation** n.

hypnosis n. artificially induced state of relaxation in which the mind is more than usually receptive to suggestion. **hypnotic** adj. of or (as if) producing hypnosis. **hypnotically** adv. **hypnotism** n. **hypnotist** n. **hypnotize** v. induce hypnosis in (someone).

hypo- prefix below, less than, e.g. hypocrite, hypodermic.

hypoallergenic adj. (of cosmetics) not likely to cause an allergic reaction.

hypochondria n. undue preoccupation with one's health. **hypochondriac** n.

hypocrisy [hip-ok-rass-ee] n., pl. -sies. (instance of) pretence of having standards or beliefs that are contrary to one's real character or actual behaviour. **hypocrite** [hip-oh-krit] n. person who pretends to be what he or she is not. **hypocritical** adj. **hypocritically** adv.

hypodermic adj., n. (denoting) a syringe or needle used to inject a drug beneath the skin.

hypotension n. abnormally low blood pressure.

hypotenuse [hie-pot-a-news] n. side of a right-angled triangle opposite the right angle.

hypothermia n. condition in which a person's body temperature is reduced to a dangerously low level.

hypothesis [hie-poth-iss-iss] n., pl. -ses [-seez] suggested but unproved explanation of something. **hypothesize** v. **hypothetical** adj. based on assumption rather than fact or reality. **hypothetically** adv.

hyrax n., pl. -es, hyraces. genus of hoofed but rodent-like animals.

hyssop n. aromatic herb used in folk medicine.

hysterectomy n., pl. -mies. surgical removal of the womb.

hysteria n. state of uncontrolled excitement, anger, or panic. **hysteric** n. **1.** hysterical person. —pl. **2.** attack of hysteria. **hysterical** adj. **1.** indicating hysteria. **2.** Informal wildly funny. **hysterically** adv.

Hz hertz.

I

I¹ *pron.* used by a speaker or writer to refer to himself or herself as the subject of a verb.

I² **1.** *Chem.* iodine. **2.** the Roman numeral for one.

IA Iowa.

iambic *adj.* (of poetry) written in metrical units of one long and one short syllable.

IBA Independent Broadcasting Authority.

Iberian *adj.* of Iberia, the peninsula of Spain and Portugal.

ibex [**ibe**-eks] *n.* wild goat with large backward-curving horns.

ibid. (referring to a book, passage, etc. already mentioned) in the same place.

ibis [**ibe**-iss] *n.* wading bird with long legs.

-ible *adj. suffix* same as -ABLE. **-ibility** *n. suffix* **-ibly** *adv. suffix*

-ic *adj. suffix* **1.** (also **-ical**) of, relating to, or resembling, e.g. *periodic.* **2.** *Chem.* indicating that an element is chemically combined in the higher of two possible valence states, e.g. *ferric.*

ICBM intercontinental ballistic missile.

ice *n.* **1.** frozen water. **2.** portion of ice cream. **—v. 3.** become covered with ice. **4.** cool with ice. **5.** cover with icing. **break the ice** create a relaxed atmosphere, esp. between people meeting for the first time. **iced** *adj.* **1.** served very cold. **2.** covered with icing. **icy** *adj.* **icier, iciest. 1.** covered with ice. **2.** cold. **3.** aloof and unfriendly. **icily** *adv.* **iciness** *n.* **ice age** period when much of the earth's surface was covered in glaciers. **iceberg** *n.* large floating mass of ice. **icebox** *n. US* refrigerator. **icebreaker** *n.* ship designed to break a channel through ice. **ice cap** mass of ice permanently covering an area. **ice cream** sweet creamy frozen food. **ice cube** small square block of ice added to a drink to cool it. **ice floe** sheet of floating ice. **ice hockey** team game like hockey played on ice with a puck. **ice lolly** flavoured ice on a stick. **ice pick** axe-like tool for breaking ice. **ice skate** boot with a steel blade fixed to the sole, to enable the wearer to glide over ice. **ice-skate** *v.* **ice-skater** *n.*

Icelandic *adj.* **1.** of Iceland, its people, or their language. **—n. 2.** official language of Iceland.

ichneumon [ik-**new**-mon] *n.* greyish-brown mongoose.

ichthyology [ik-thi-**ol**-a-jee] *n.* scientific study of fish. **ichthyological** *adj.* **ichthyologist** *n.*

ICI Imperial Chemical Industries.

icicle *n.* tapering spike of ice hanging where water has dripped.

icing *n.* mixture of sugar and water etc. used to cover and decorate cakes. **icing sugar** finely ground sugar for making icing.

icon *n.* **1.** picture of Christ or another religious figure, venerated in the Orthodox Church. **2.** picture on a computer screen representing a computer function that can be activated by moving the cursor over it.

iconoclast *n.* person who attacks established principles or ideas. **iconoclastic** *adj.* **iconoclasm** *n.*

id *n. Psychoanalysis* the mind's instinctive unconscious energies.

ID 1. identification. **2.** Idaho.

idea *n.* **1.** plan or thought formed in the mind. **2.** thought of something, e.g. *the idea horrified her.* **3.** belief or opinion.

ideal *n.* **1.** conception of something that is perfect. **2.** perfect person or thing. **—adj. 3.** most suitable. **4.** perfect. **ideally** *adv.* **idealism** *n.* tendency to seek perfection in everything. **idealist** *n.* **idealistic** *adj.* **idealize** *v.* regard or portray as perfect. **idealization** *n.*

idem *pron., adj. Latin* the same: used to refer to a book, article, etc. already quoted.

identical *adj.* exactly the same. **identically** *adv.*

identify *v.* **-fying, -fied. 1.** prove or recognize as being a certain person or thing. **2.** treat as being the same. **3.** understand and sympathize with a person or group because one regards oneself as being similar or similarly situated. **identifiable** *adj.* **identification** *n.*

Identikit *n.* ® set of pictures of parts of

faces that can be built up to form a likeness of a person wanted by the police.

identity n., pl. **-ties. 1.** state of being a specified person or thing. **2.** individuality or personality. **3.** state of being the same.

ideogram, ideograph n. picture, symbol, etc. representing an object rather than the sounds of its name.

ideology n., pl. **-gies.** body of ideas and beliefs of a group, nation, etc. **ideological** adj. **ideologist** n.

ides n. the 15th of March, May, July and Oct. and the 13th of other months of the Ancient Roman calendar.

idiocy n. utter stupidity.

idiom n. **1.** group of words which when used together have a different meaning from the component words, e.g. *raining cats and dogs.* **2.** way of expression natural or peculiar to a language or group. **idiomatic** adj. **idiomatically** adv.

idiosyncrasy n., pl. **-sies.** personal peculiarity of mind, habit, or behaviour. **idiosyncratic** adj.

idiot n. **1.** foolish person. **2.** mentally retarded person. **idiotic** adj. utterly stupid. **idiotically** adv.

idle adj. **1.** not doing anything. **2.** not being used. **3.** lazy. **4.** useless, e.g. *idle thoughts.* —v. **5.** be idle. **6.** (of an engine) run slowly with the gears disengaged. **7.** (esp. foll. by *away*) waste (time). **idleness** n. **idler** n. **idly** adv.

idol [ide-ol] n. **1.** image of a god as an object of worship. **2.** object of excessive devotion. **idolatry** [ide-ol-a-tree] n. **1.** worship of idols. **2.** excessive devotion or reverence. **idolater** n. **idolatrous** adj. **idolize** v. love or admire excessively. **idolization** n.

idyll [id-ill] n. **1.** scene or time of peace and happiness. **2.** description in literature of a picturesque or charming scene or episode, esp. of country life. **idyllic** adj. **idyllically** adv.

i.e. that is to say.

if conj. **1.** on the condition or supposition that. **2.** whether. **3.** even though. —n. **4.** uncertainty or doubt, e.g. *I won't have any ifs or buts.* **iffy** adj. *Informal* doubtful, uncertain.

igloo n., pl. **-loos.** dome-shaped Eskimo house of snow and ice.

igneous [ig-nee-uss] adj. (of rocks) formed as molten rock cools and hardens.

ignite v. catch fire or set fire to.

ignition n. **1.** system that ignites the fuel-air mixture to start an engine. **2.** igniting.

ignoble adj. dishonourable. **ignobly** adv.

ignominy [ig-nom-in-ee] n. humiliating disgrace. **ignominious** adj. **ignominiously** adv.

ignoramus n., pl. **-muses.** ignorant person.

ignorant adj. **1.** lacking knowledge. **2.** rude through lack of knowledge of good manners. **ignorantly** adv. **ignorance** n. lack of knowledge.

ignore v. refuse to notice, disregard deliberately.

iguana n. large tropical American lizard.

iguanodon n. large plant-eating dinosaur.

ikebana [eek-a-bah-na] n. Japanese decorative art of flower arrangement.

ikon n. same as ICON.

IL Illinois.

ileum n. lower part of the small intestine. **ileac** adj.

ilex n. any of a genus of trees or shrubs such as holly.

ilium n., pl. **-ia.** uppermost and widest of the three sections of the hipbone. **iliac** adj.

ilk n. of that ilk of the same type.

ill adj. **1.** not in good health. **2.** bad, evil. **3.** unfavourable, e.g. *an ill omen.* —n. **4.** evil, harm. —adv. **5.** badly. **6.** hardly, with difficulty, e.g. *I can ill afford the expense.* **ill at ease** uncomfortable, unable to relax. **illness** n. **ill-advised** adj. **1.** badly thought out. **2.** unwise. **ill-bred** adj. lacking good manners, rude. **ill-disposed** adj. (often foll. by *towards*) unfriendly or unsympathetic. **ill-fated** adj. doomed to end unhappily. **ill-favoured** adj. ugly or unattractive. **ill-gotten** adj. obtained dishonestly. **ill-health** n. condition of being unwell. **ill-mannered** adj. rude. **ill-starred** adj. very unlucky. **ill-tempered** adj. having a bad temper. **ill-timed** adj. done or happening at an unsuitable time. **ill-treat** v. treat cruelly. **ill-treatment** n. **ill will** unkind feeling, hostility.

illegal adj. against the law. **illegally** adv. **illegality** n., pl. **-ties.**

illegible adj. unable to be read or deciphered. **illegibility** n.

illegitimate *adj.* **1.** born to parents not married to each other. **2.** unlawful. **illegitimacy** *n.*

illiberal *adj.* **1.** narrow-minded or intolerant. **2.** not generous, mean. **3.** lacking in culture or refinement. **illiberality** *n.*

illicit *adj.* **1.** illegal. **2.** forbidden or disapproved of by society.

illiterate *adj.* **1.** unable to read or write. **2.** uneducated, ignorant. **illiteracy** *n.*

illogical *adj.* **1.** unreasonable. **2.** not logical. **illogicality** *n.*

illuminate *v.* **1.** light up. **2.** make clear, explain. **3.** decorate with lights. **4.** (also **illumine**) *Hist.* decorate (a manuscript) with designs of gold and bright colours. **illumination** *n.* **illuminating** *adj.* helping to explain.

illusion *n.* deceptive appearance or belief. **illusionist** *n.* conjurer. **illusory** *adj.* false.

illustrate *v.* **1.** explain by use of examples. **2.** provide (a book or text) with pictures. **3.** be an example of. **illustration** *n.* **1.** picture or diagram. **2.** example. **illustrative** *adj.* **illustrator** *n.*

illustrious *adj.* famous and distinguished.

image *n.* **1.** representation or likeness of a person or thing. **2.** optical counterpart, as in a mirror. **3.** double, copy. **4.** impression people have of a politician, organization, etc. **5.** simile or metaphor. —*v.* **6.** make an image of. **7.** reflect. **imagery** *n., pl.* **-ries.** images collectively, esp. in literature.

imagine *v.* **1.** form a mental image of. **2.** think, believe, or guess. **imaginable** *adj.* **imaginary** *adj.* existing only in the imagination. **imagination** *n.* **1.** ability to make mental images of things not present. **2.** creative mental ability. **imaginative** *adj.* **imaginatively** *adv.*

imago [im-**may**-go] *n., pl.* **imagoes, imagines** [im-**maj**-in-ees] sexually mature adult insect.

imam *n.* **1.** leader of prayers in a mosque. **2.** title of some Islamic leaders.

imbalance *n.* lack of proportion.

imbecile [**imb**-ess-eel] *n.* **1.** idiot. —*adj.* **2.** idiotic. **imbecilic** *adj.* **imbecility** *n., pl.* **-ties.**

imbed *v.* same as EMBED.

imbibe *v.* **1.** drink (esp. alcohol). **2.** *Lit.* absorb (ideas etc.).

imbroglio [imb-**role**-ee-oh] *n., pl.* **-ios.** confusing and complicated situation.

imbue *v.* **-buing, -bued.** (usu. foll. by *with*) fill or inspire with (ideals or principles).

IMF International Monetary Fund.

imitate *v.* **1.** take as a model. **2.** mimic or copy. **imitation** *n.* **1.** imitating. **2.** copy of an original. **imitative** *adj.* **imitator** *n.*

immaculate *adj.* **1.** completely clean or tidy. **2.** completely flawless. **immaculately** *adv.*

immanent *adj.* present within and throughout something. **immanence** *n.*

immaterial *adj.* not important, not relevant.

immature *adj.* **1.** not fully developed. **2.** lacking wisdom or stability because of youth. **immaturity** *n.*

immeasurable *adj.* incapable of being measured, limitless. **immeasurably** *adv.*

immediate *adj.* **1.** occurring at once. **2.** next or nearest in time, space, or relationship. **immediately** *adv.* **immediacy** *n.*

immemorial *adj.* having existed or happened for longer than anyone can remember. **immemorially** *adv.*

immense *adj.* huge or vast. **immensely** *adv.* **immensity** *n., pl.* **-ties.**

immerse *v.* **1.** plunge (something) into liquid. **2.** involve deeply, e.g. *I immersed myself in my work.* **immersion** *n.* **immersing. immersion heater, immerser** *n.* electric heater contained in a domestic hot-water tank.

immigrant *n.* person who comes into a country to live there.

immigrate *v.* come to a foreign country in order to settle there. **immigration** *n.*

imminent *adj.* about to happen. **imminently** *adv.* **imminence** *n.*

immobile *adj.* **1.** unable to move. **2.** not moving. **immobility** *n.* **immobilize** *v.* make unable to move or work.

immoderate *adj.* excessive or unreasonable.

immodest *adj.* **1.** behaving in an indecent or improper manner. **2.** behaving in a boastful or conceited manner. **immodestly** *adv.* **immodesty** *n.*

immolate *v.* kill as a sacrifice. **immolation** *n.*

immoral *adj.* **1.** morally wrong, corrupt. **2.**

sexually depraved or promiscuous. **immorality** n., pl. **-ties**.

▷ Do not confuse *immoral* with *amoral*, which means 'having no moral standards'.

immortal adj. **1**. living forever. **2**. famous for all time. —n. **3**. immortal being. **4**. person whose fame will last for all time. **immortality** n. **immortalize** v.

immovable, immoveable adj. **1**. unable to be moved. **2**. unwilling to change one's opinions or beliefs. **3**. not affected by feeling, emotionless. **immovability, immoveability** n. **immovably, immoveably** adv.

immune adj. **1**. protected against a specific disease. **2**. secure (against). **3**. exempt (from). **immunity** n., pl. **-ties**. **1**. ability to resist disease. **2**. freedom from prosecution, tax, etc. **immunize** v. make immune to a disease. **immunization** n.

immunodeficiency n. deficiency in or breakdown of a person's immune system.

immunology n. study of immunity. **immunological** adj. **immunologist** n.

immure v. *Lit.* imprison.

immutable [im-**mute**-a-bl] adj. unchangeable. **immutability** n.

imp n. **1**. demon. **2**. mischievous child.

impact n. **1**. collision. **2**. strong effect. —v. **3**. press firmly against or into. **impaction** n.

impair v. weaken or damage. **impairment** n.

impala [imp-**ah**-la] n. southern African antelope.

impale v. pierce with a sharp object. **impalement** n.

impalpable adj. **1**. imperceptible to the touch. **2**. difficult to understand.

impart v. **1**. communicate (information). **2**. give, e.g. *impart flavour*.

impartial adj. not favouring one side or the other. **impartially** adv. **impartiality** n.

impassable adj. (of a road etc.) impossible to travel over or through.

impasse [am-**pass**] n. situation in which progress is impossible.

impassible adj. **1**. *rare* not susceptible to pain or injury. **2**. impassive; unmoved. **impassibility, impassibleness** n.

impassioned adj. full of emotion.

impassive adj. showing no emotion, calm. **impassivity** n.

impasto n. **1**. paint applied thickly, so that

brush marks are evident. **2**. technique of painting in this way.

impatient adj. **1**. irritable at any delay or difficulty. **2**. restless to have or do something. **impatiently** adv. **impatience** n.

impeach v. charge with a serious crime against the state. **impeachment** n.

impeccable adj. without fault, excellent. **impeccably** adv.

impecunious adj. penniless.

impedance [imp-**eed**-anss] n. *Electricity* measure of the opposition to the flow of an alternating current.

impede v. hinder in action or progress. **impediment** n. something that makes action, speech, or progress difficult. **impedimenta** pl. n. objects impeding progress, esp. baggage or equipment.

impel v. **-pelling, -pelled**. drive (a person) to do something.

impending adj. (esp. of something bad) about to happen.

impenetrable adj. **1**. impossible to get through. **2**. impossible to understand.

imperative adj. **1**. extremely urgent, vital. **2**. *Grammar* denoting a mood of verbs used in commands. —n. **3**. *Grammar* imperative mood.

imperceptible adj. too slight or gradual to be noticed. **imperceptibly** adv.

imperfect adj. **1**. having faults or mistakes. **2**. not complete. **3**. *Grammar* denoting a tense of verbs describing continuous, incomplete, or repeated past actions. —n. **4**. *Grammar* imperfect tense. **imperfection** n.

imperial adj. **1**. of an empire or emperor. **2**. majestic. **3**. denoting weights and measures formerly official in Britain. **imperialism** n. rule by one country over many others. **imperialist** n., adj.

imperil v. **-illing, -illed**. endanger.

imperious adj. used to being obeyed, domineering.

impersonal adj. **1**. not influenced by emotion. **2**. lacking human warmth or personality. **3**. *Grammar* (of a verb) without a personal subject, as in *it is snowing*. **impersonality** n.

impersonate v. **1**. pretend to be (another person). **2**. imitate the mannerisms of (someone). **impersonation** n. **impersonator** n.

impertinent adj. disrespectful or rude. **impertinently** adv. **impertinence** n.

imperturbable adj. calm, not excitable. **imperturbability** n.

impervious adj. 1. not letting (water etc.) through. 2. not influenced by (a feeling, argument, etc.).

impetigo [imp-it-**tie**-go] n. contagious skin disease.

impetuous adj. done or acting without thought, rash. **impetuously** adv. **impetuosity** n.

impetus [imp-it-uss] n., pl. **-tuses.** 1. force with which a body moves. 2. impulse.

impinge v. encroach (upon), affect or restrict.

impious [imp-ee-uss] adj. showing a lack of respect or reverence.

impish adj. mischievous.

implacable adj. 1. not to be appeased. 2. unyielding. **implacably** adv. **implacability** n.

implant v. 1. fix firmly in the mind. 2. insert or embed. —n. 3. Med. anything implanted in the body, such as a tissue graft. **implantation** n.

implement n. 1. tool or instrument. —v. 2. carry out (instructions etc.). **implementation** n.

implicate v. show to be involved, esp. in a crime. **implication** n. something implied.

implicit adj. 1. expressed indirectly. 2. absolute, e.g. implicit belief. **implicitly** adv.

implode v. collapse inwards.

implore v. beg desperately.

imply v. **-plying, -plied.** 1. indicate by hinting, suggest. 2. mean.

impolite adj. rude, discourteous.

impolitic adj. unwise, ill-advised.

imponderable n., adj. (something) impossible to assess.

import v. 1. bring in (goods) from another country. —n. 2. something imported. 3. meaning. 4. importance. **importation** n. **importer** n.

important adj. 1. of great significance or value. 2. famous, powerful. **importance** n.

importunate adj. persistent in making demands. **importune** v. persist in demands. **importunity** n., pl. **-ties.**

impose v. 1. force the acceptance of. 2.

take unfair advantage of. **imposing** adj. impressive. **imposition** n. unreasonable demand, burden.

impossible adj. 1. incapable of being done or experienced. 2. absurd or unreasonable. **impossibly** adv. **impossibility** n., pl. **-ties.**

impostor n. person who cheats or swindles by pretending to be someone else.

imposture n. deception, esp. by assuming a false identity.

impotent [imp-a-tent] adj. 1. powerless. 2. (of a man) incapable of sexual intercourse. **impotence** n. **impotently** adv.

impound v. take legal possession of, confiscate.

impoverish v. make poor or weak. **impoverishment** n.

impracticable adj. incapable of being put into practice.

impractical adj. not sensible.

imprecation n. curse.

impregnable adj. impossible to break into. **impregnability** n.

impregnate v. 1. saturate, spread all through. 2. make pregnant. **impregnation** n.

impresario n., pl. **-ios.** person who runs theatre performances, concerts, etc.

impress v. 1. affect strongly, usu. favourably. 2. imprint or stamp. 3. stress or emphasize. **impression** n. 1. strong or favourable effect. 2. vague idea. 3. mark made by pressing. 4. impersonation for entertainment. **impressionable** adj. easily influenced.

impressionism n. art style that gives a general effect or mood rather than form or structure. **impressionist** n. **impressionistic** adj.

impressive adj. making a strong impression, esp. through size, importance, or quality.

imprimatur [imp-rim-**ah**-ter] n. official approval to print a book.

imprint n. 1. mark made by printing or stamping. 2. publisher's name and address on a book. —v. 3. produce (a mark) by printing or stamping.

imprison v. put in prison. **imprisonment** n.

improbable adj. unlikely. **improbability** n., pl. **-ties.**

improbity n. dishonesty or wickedness.

impromptu *adv., adj.* without preparation, improvised.

improper *adj.* 1. indecent. 2. incorrect or irregular. 3. (of a fraction) with a denominator larger than the numerator, as in 5/3.

impropriety [imp-roe-**pry**-a-tee] *n., pl.* **-ties.** unsuitable or slightly improper behaviour.

improve *v.* make or become better. **improvement** *n.*

improvident *adj.* not planning for future needs. **improvidence** *n.*

improvise *v.* 1. make use of materials at hand. 2. make up (a piece of music, speech, etc.) as one goes along. **improvisation** *n.*

imprudent *adj.* rash, heedless, or indiscreet. **imprudence** *n.*

impudent *adj.* cheeky. **impudently** *adv.* **impudence** *n.*

impugn [imp-**yoon**] *v.* call in question, cast doubt on.

impulse *n.* 1. sudden urge to do something. 2. short electrical signal passing along a wire or nerve or through the air. **on impulse** suddenly and without planning. **impulsive** *adj.* tending to act without thinking first. **impulsively** *adv.*

impunity [imp-**yoon**-it-ee] *n.* **with impunity** without punishment or unpleasant consequences.

impure *adj.* 1. having unwanted substances mixed in. 2. immoral or obscene. **impurity** *n., pl.* **-ties.**

impute *v.* attribute responsibility to. **imputation** *n.*

in *prep.* 1. inside, within. 2. during. 3. at the end of (a period of time). 4. indicating a state, situation, or manner. 5. into. —*adv.* 6. in or into a particular place. 7. at one's home or place of work. 8. in office or power. 9. in fashion. —*adj.* 10. fashionable.

In *Chem.* indium.

IN Indiana.

in. inch(es).

in-[1] *prefix* 1. not; non-, e.g. *incredible.* 2. lack of, e.g. *inexperience.*

in-[2] *prefix* 1. in; into; towards; within; on, e.g. *infiltrate.* 2. having an intensive or causative function, e.g. *inflame.*

inability *n.* lack of means or skill to do something.

inaccessible *adj.* 1. impossible or very difficult to reach. 2. (of a person) unapproachable. **inaccessibility** *n.*

inaccurate *adj.* not correct. **inaccuracy** *n., pl.* **-cies.**

inaction *n.* lack of action, inertia.

inadequate *adj.* 1. not enough. 2. not good enough. **inadequacy** *n., pl.* **-cies.**

inadmissible *adj.* not allowable or acceptable.

inadvertent *adj.* done unintentionally.

inalienable *adj.* not able to be taken away, e.g. *an inalienable right.*

inamorata, (*masc.*) **inamorato** *n., pl.* **-s.** person with whom one is in love, lover.

inane *adj.* senseless or silly. **inanity** *n., pl.* **-ties.**

inanimate *adj.* not living.

inanition *n.* exhaustion or weakness, as from lack of food.

inapplicable *adj.* not suitable or relevant.

inappropriate *adj.* not suitable.

inapt *adj.* 1. not apt or fitting. 2. lacking skill. **inaptitude** *n.*

inarticulate *adj.* unable to express oneself clearly or well.

inasmuch as *conj.* seeing that, because.

inattentive *adj.* not paying attention.

inaudible *adj.* not loud enough to be heard. **inaudibly** *adv.*

inaugurate *v.* 1. open or begin the use of, esp. with ceremony. 2. formally establish (a new leader) in office. **inaugural** *adj.* **inauguration** *n.*

inauspicious *adj.* unlucky, suggesting an unfavourable outcome.

inboard *adj.* (of a boat's engine) inside the hull.

inborn *adj.* existing from birth, natural.

inbred *adj.* 1. produced as a result of inbreeding. 2. inborn or ingrained.

inbreeding *n.* breeding from closely related individuals.

inbuilt *adj.* present from the start.

Inc. *US* (of a company) incorporated.

incalculable *adj.* impossible to estimate, very great.

in camera *adv.* in private session.

incandescent *adj.* 1. glowing with heat. 2. (of artificial light) produced by a glowing filament. **incandescence** *n.*

incantation n. ritual chanting of magic words or sounds. **incantatory** adj.

incapable adj. **1.** (foll. by of) lacking the ability to. **2.** helpless.

incapacitate v. deprive of strength or ability, disable. **incapacity** n.

incarcerate v. imprison. **incarceration** n.

incarnate adj. **1.** possessing human form. **2.** typified, e.g. *stupidity incarnate.* **incarnation** n. **Incarnation** n. *Christianity* God's coming to earth in human form as Jesus Christ.

incendiary [in-**send**-ya-ree] adj. **1.** (of bombs etc.) designed to cause fires. —n. **2.** bomb designed to cause fires. **3.** fire raiser or arsonist.

incense[1] v. make very angry.

incense[2] n. **1.** substance that gives off a sweet perfume when burned. **2.** its smoke.

incentive n. something that encourages effort or action.

inception n. beginning.

incessant adj. never stopping. **incessantly** adv.

incest n. sexual intercourse between two people too closely related to marry. **incestuous** adj.

inch n. **1.** unit of length equal to one twelfth of a foot or 2.54 centimetres. —v. **2.** move very slowly.

inchoate [in-**koe**-ate] adj. just begun and not yet properly developed.

incidence n. extent or frequency of occurrence.

incident n. **1.** (memorable) event. **2.** event involving violence.

incidental adj. **1.** occurring as a minor part of or accompaniment to something else. **2.** happening by chance. **incidentally** adv. **incidental music** background music for a film or play.

incinerate v. burn to ashes. **incineration** n. **incinerator** n. furnace for burning rubbish.

incipient adj. just starting to appear or happen.

incise v. cut into with a sharp tool. **incision** n. **incisive** adj. direct and forceful. **incisor** n. cutting tooth.

incite v. stir up or provoke. **incitement** n.

incivility n., pl. **-ties.** rudeness.

inclement adj. (of weather) bad. **inclemency** n.

incline v. **1.** lean, slope. **2.** (cause to) have a certain disposition or tendency. —n. **3.** slope. **inclination** n. **1.** liking, tendency, or preference. **2.** slope. **3.** degree of deviation from the horizontal or vertical.

include v. **1.** have as (part of) the contents. **2.** put in as part of a set or group. **inclusion** n. **inclusive** adj. including everything. **inclusively** adv.

incognito [in-kog-**nee**-toe] adv., adj. **1.** under an assumed identity. —n., pl. **-tos. 2.** false identity.

incoherent adj. (of speech) unclear and impossible to understand. **incoherence** n. **incoherently** adv.

income n. amount of money earned from work, investments, etc. **income support** in Britain, allowance paid by the government to the very poor. **income tax** personal tax levied on annual income.

incoming adj. **1.** about to arrive. **2.** about to come into office.

incommode v. inconvenience.

incommodious adj. cramped.

incommunicado adj., adv. deprived of communication with other people.

incomparable adj. beyond comparison, unequalled. **incomparably** adv.

incompatible adj. inconsistent or conflicting. **incompatibility** n.

incompetent adj. **1.** not possessing the necessary ability or skill to do something. **2.** *Law* not legally qualified. —n. **3.** incompetent person. **incompetence** n.

inconceivable adj. impossible to imagine.

inconclusive adj. not giving a final decision or result.

incongruous adj. inappropriate or out of place. **incongruously** adv. **incongruity** n., pl. **-ties.**

inconsequential, inconsequent adj. unimportant or irrelevant.

inconsiderable adj. **1.** relatively small. **2.** insignificant.

inconsiderate adj. lacking in care or thought for others, thoughtless.

inconsistent adj. **1.** changeable in behaviour or mood. **2.** containing contradictory elements, e.g. *her account of the robbery was inconsistent.* **3.** not in accordance with, e.g. *actions inconsistent with high office.* **inconsistency** *n., pl.* **-cies.**

inconsolable *adj.* impossible to comfort, broken-hearted. **inconsolably** *adv.*

inconspicuous *adj.* not easily noticed or seen. **inconspicuously** *adv.*

inconstant *adj.* liable to change one's loyalties or opinions.

incontestable *adj.* impossible to deny or argue with.

incontinent *adj.* not able to control one's bladder or bowels. **incontinence** *n.*

incontrovertible *adj.* impossible to deny or disprove.

inconvenience *n.* **1.** trouble or difficulty. —*v.* **2.** cause trouble or difficulty to. **inconvenient** *adj.*

incorporate *v.* include or be included as part of a larger unit. **incorporation** *n.*

incorporeal *adj.* without bodily existence.

incorrigible *adj.* beyond correction or reform. **incorrigibility** *n.*

incorruptible *adj.* **1.** impossible to bribe or corrupt, honest. **2.** not subject to decay.

increase *v.* **1.** make or become greater in size, number, etc. —*n.* **2.** rise in number, size, etc. **3.** amount by which something increases. **on the increase** becoming more common. **increasingly** *adv.* more and more.

incredible *adj.* **1.** unbelievable. **2.** *Informal* marvellous, amazing. **incredibly** *adv.*

incredulous *adj.* not willing or able to believe something. **incredulity** *n.*

increment *n.* increase in money or value, esp. a regular salary increase. **incremental** *adj.*

incriminate *v.* make (someone) seem guilty of a crime. **incriminating** *adj.* **incrimination** *n.*

incubate [in-cube-ate] *v.* **1.** (of birds) hatch eggs by sitting on them. **2.** grow (bacteria). **3.** (of bacteria) remain inactive in an animal or person before causing disease. **incubation** *n.* **incubator** *n.* **1.** heated enclosed apparatus for rearing premature babies. **2.** apparatus for artificially hatching eggs.

incubus [in-cube-uss] *n., pl.* **-bi, -buses.** **1.** demon believed to have sex with sleeping women. **2.** nightmarish burden or worry.

inculcate *v.* fix in someone's mind by constant repetition. **inculcation** *n.*

inculpate *v.* cause blame to be laid on, incriminate.

incumbent *adj.* **1.** **it is incumbent on** it is the duty of. —*n.* **2.** person holding a particular office or position. **incumbency** *n., pl.* **-cies.**

incur *v.* **-curring, -curred.** bring (something unpleasant) upon oneself.

incurable *adj.* **1.** not able to be cured. —*n.* **2.** person with an incurable disease. **incurably** *adv.*

incurious *adj.* showing no curiosity or interest.

incursion *n.* sudden brief invasion.

indebted *adj.* **1.** owing gratitude for help or favours. **2.** owing money. **indebtedness** *n.*

indecent *adj.* **1.** morally or sexually offensive. **2.** unsuitable or unseemly, e.g. *indecent haste.* **indecently** *adv.* **indecency** *n., pl.* **-cies.** **indecent assault** sexual attack which does not include rape. **indecent exposure** showing of one's genitals in public.

indecipherable *adj.* impossible to read.

indecisive *adj.* unable to make decisions, wavering. **indecision** *n.*

indeed *adv.* **1.** really, certainly. —*interj.* **2.** showing surprise, doubt, etc.

indefatigable *adj.* never getting tired. **indefatigably** *adv.*

indefensible *adj.* **1.** not justifiable. **2.** impossible to defend. **indefensibly** *adv.*

indefinable *adj.* impossible to be fully described or explained.

indefinite *adj.* **1.** without exact limits, e.g. *an indefinite period.* **2.** vague. **indefinite article** *Grammar* the word *a* or *an.* **indefinitely** *adv.*

indelible *adj.* **1.** impossible to erase or remove. **2.** producing indelible marks. **indelibly** *adv.*

indelicate *adj.* embarrassing, tasteless. **indelicacy** *n.*

indemnify *v.* **-ifying, -ified. 1.** give indemnity to. **2.** compensate. **indemnification** *n.*

indemnity *n., pl.* **-ties. 1.** insurance against loss or damage. **2.** compensation for loss or damage suffered.

indent *v.* **1.** start (a line of writing) further from the margin than the other lines. **2.** order (goods) using a special order form. **indentation** *n.* dent in a surface or edge.

indenture *n.* **1.** contract, esp. one binding

an apprentice to his employer. —v. **2.** bind (an apprentice) by indenture.

independent adj. **1.** free from the control or influence of others. **2.** separate. **3.** financially self-reliant. **4.** capable of acting for oneself or on one's own. —n. **5.** politician who does not belong to any party. **independently** adv. **independence** n.

in-depth adj. carefully worked out, detailed, thorough.

indescribable adj. too intense or extreme for words. **indescribably** adv.

indestructible adj. not able to be destroyed.

indeterminate adj. uncertain in extent, amount, or nature. **indeterminacy** n.

index n., pl. **indexes,** (Maths) **indices** [in-diss-eez] **1.** alphabetical list of names or subjects dealt with in a book. **2.** file or catalogue used to find things. **3.** pointer or indicator. **4.** Maths exponent. —v. **5.** provide (a book) with an index. **6.** enter in an index. **7.** make index-linked. **index finger** finger next to the thumb. **index-linked** adj. (of pensions, wages, etc.) rising or falling in line with the cost of living.

Indian n., adj. **1.** (person) from India. **2.** (person) descended from the original inhabitants of the American continent. **Indian summer** period of warm sunny weather in autumn.

indicate v. **1.** be a sign or symptom of. **2.** point out. **3.** state briefly. **4.** (of a measuring instrument) show a reading of. **indication** n. **indicative** [in-**dik**-a-tiv] adj. **1.** suggesting, e.g. clouds indicative of rain. **2.** Grammar denoting a mood of verbs used to make a statement. **indicator** n. **1.** something acting as a sign or indication. **2.** flashing light on a vehicle showing the driver's intention to turn. **3.** dial or gauge.

indices n. plural of INDEX.

indict [in-**dite**] v. formally accuse of a crime. **indictable** adj. **indictment** n.

indifferent adj. **1.** showing no interest or concern. **2.** of poor quality or low standard. **indifference** n. **indifferently** adv.

indigenous [in-**dij**-in-uss] adj. born in or natural to a country.

indigent adj. so poor as to lack necessities. **indigence** n.

indigestion n. (discomfort or pain caused by) difficulty in digesting food. **indigestible** adj.

indignation n. anger caused by something unfair or wrong. **indignant** adj. feeling or showing indignation. **indignantly** adv.

indignity n., pl. **-ties.** embarrassing or humiliating treatment.

indigo n. **1.** deep violet-blue. **2.** dye of this colour.

indirect adj. **1.** done or caused by someone or something else. **2.** not by a straight route. **indirect object** Grammar person or thing indirectly affected by an action, such as Sue in I bought Sue a book. **indirect speech** report that gives the content of what someone said but not the actual words. **indirect tax** tax, such as VAT, added to the price of something.

indiscernible adj. not able or scarcely able to be seen.

indiscreet adj. incautious or tactless in revealing secrets. **indiscreetly** adv. **indiscretion** n.

indiscriminate adj. chosen or choosing without thought or care.

indispensable adj. impossible to do without.

indisposed adj. **1.** unwell or ill. **2.** unwilling. **indisposition** n.

indisputable adj. without doubt. **indisputably** adv.

indissoluble adj. permanent.

indistinct adj. impossible to be seen or heard clearly.

indium n. soft silver-white metallic element.

individual adj. **1.** characteristic of or meant for a single person or thing. **2.** separate or distinct. **3.** distinctive, unusual. —n. **4.** single person or thing. **individually** adv. singly. **individualism** n. principle of living one's life in one's own way. **individualist** n. **individualistic** adj. **individuality** n. distinctive character or personality.

indoctrinate v. teach (someone) to accept a doctrine or belief uncritically. **indoctrination** n.

Indo-European adj., n. (of) a family of languages spoken in most of Europe and much of Asia, including English, Russian, and Hindi.

indolent adj. lazy. **indolence** n.

indomitable adj. too strong to be defeated or discouraged. **indomitably** adv.

indoor adj. inside a building. **indoors** adv.

indubitable [in-**dew**-bit-a-bl] adj. beyond doubt, certain. **indubitably** adv.

induce v. **1.** persuade. **2.** cause. **3.** Med. bring on (labour) by the use of drugs etc. **inducement** n. something that encourages someone to do something.

induct v. formally install someone, esp. a clergyman, in office.

induction n. **1.** reasoning process by which general conclusions are drawn from particular instances. **2.** process by which electrical or magnetic properties are produced by the proximity of an electrified or magnetic object. **3.** formal installing of a person into office. **inductance** n. **inductive** adj. **induction coil transformer** for producing high voltage from a low voltage. **induction course training** course to help familiarize someone with a new job.

indulge v. **1.** allow (someone) to have or do everything he or she wants. **2.** allow oneself pleasure, e.g. *indulge in daydreaming.* **indulgence** n. **1.** something allowed because it gives pleasure. **2.** act of indulging oneself or someone else. **3.** favourable or tolerant treatment. **indulgent** adj. **indulgently** adv.

industrial adj. of, used in, or employed in industry. **industrialize** v. develop large-scale industry in (a country or region). **industrialism** n. social organization characterized by large-scale manufacturing industry rather than trade or farming. **industrialist** n. person who owns or controls large amounts of money or property in industry. **industrial action** action such as a strike or work-to-rule, by which workers can protest about their conditions. **industrial estate** area of land set aside for factories and warehouses. **industrial relations** relations between management and workers.

industry n., pl. **-tries. 1.** manufacture of goods. **2.** branch of this, e.g. *the publishing industry.* **3.** quality of working hard. **industrious** adj. hard-working.

inebriate n., adj. (person who is) drunk habitually. **inebriated** adj. drunk. **inebriation** n. drunkenness.

inedible adj. not fit to be eaten.

ineducable [in-**ed**-yuke-a-bl] adj. incapable of being educated, esp. through mental retardation.

ineffable adj. too great for words. **ineffably** adv.

ineffectual adj. having no effect or an inadequate effect.

inefficient adj. unable to perform a task or function to the best advantage. **inefficiency** n.

inelegant adj. lacking elegance or refinement. **inelegance** n. **inelegantly** adv.

ineligible adj. not qualified for or entitled to something.

ineluctable adj. impossible to avoid.

inept adj. clumsy, lacking skill. **ineptitude** n.

inequality n., pl. **-ties. 1.** state or quality of being unequal. **2.** lack of smoothness or regularity of a surface. **3.** Maths statement indicating that the value of one quantity or expression is not equal to another; relation of being unequal.

inequitable adj. unfair.

ineradicable adj. impossible to remove.

inert adj. **1.** without the power of motion or resistance. **2.** chemically unreactive. **inertly** adv. **inertness** n.

inertia n. **1.** feeling of unwillingness to do anything. **2.** Physics property by which a body remains still or continues to move unless a force is applied to it. **inertial** adj. **inertia reel seat belt car seat belt in which the belt is free to unwind from a metal drum except when the drum locks because of sudden braking. **inertia selling practice of sending householders unrequested goods followed by a bill if the goods are not returned.

inescapable adj. unavoidable.

inestimable adj. too great to be estimated. **inestimably** adv.

inevitable adj. **1.** unavoidable, sure to happen. —n. **2.** something inevitable. **inevitably** adv. **inevitability** n., pl. **-ties.**

inexorable adj. **1.** relentless. **2.** unavoidable. **inexorably** adv.

inexperienced adj. having no knowledge or experience of a particular situation, activity, etc. **inexperience** n.

inexpert adj. lacking skill.

inexplicable adj. impossible to explain. **inexplicably** adv.

in extremis adv. Latin **1.** in great difficulty. **2.** at the point of death.

inextricable adj. **1.** impossible to escape

from. **2.** impossible to disentangle or separate.

infallible *adj.* **1.** never wrong. **2.** always successful. **infallibly** *adv.* **infallibility** *n.*

infamous [in-fam-uss] *adj.* well-known for something bad. **infamously** *adv.* **infamy** *n.*

infant *n.* very young child. **infancy** *n.* **1.** early childhood. **2.** early stage of development. **infantile** *adj.* childish.

infanta *n.* **1.** formerly, daughter of a king of Spain or Portugal. **2.** wife of any son of a king of Spain or Portugal, except the heir to the throne.

infanticide *n.* **1.** murder of an infant. **2.** person guilty of this.

infantry *n.* foot soldiers.

infatuate *v.* inspire with intense unreasonable passion. **infatuated** *adj.* **infatuation** *n.*

infect *v.* affect with a disease. **infection** *n.* **infectious** *adj.* **1.** (of a disease) spreading without actual contact. **2.** spreading from person to person, e.g. *infectious laughter.*

infer *v.* **-ferring, -ferred.** work out from evidence. **inference** *n.*
▷ Someone *infers* something by 'reading between the lines' of a remark. Do not confuse with *imply*, which means 'to hint'.

inferior *adj.* **1.** lower in position, status, or quality. —*n.* **2.** person of lower position or status. **inferiority** *n.* **inferiority complex** *Psychiatry* a disorder arising from a feeling of inferiority to others, characterized by aggressiveness or extreme shyness.

infernal *adj.* **1.** of hell. **2.** *Informal* irritating. **infernally** *adv.*

inferno *n., pl.* **-nos.** intense raging fire.

infertile *adj.* **1.** unable to produce offspring. **2.** (of soil) barren, not productive. **infertility** *n.*

infest *v.* inhabit or overrun in unpleasantly large numbers. **infestation** *n.*

infidel *n.* **1.** person with no religion. **2.** person who rejects a particular religion, esp. Christianity or Islam.

infidelity *n., pl.* **-ties.** sexual unfaithfulness to one's husband, wife, or lover.

infield *n.* **1.** *Cricket* area of the field near the pitch. **2.** *Baseball* area of the playing field enclosed by base lines.

infighting *n.* quarrelling within a group.

infiltrate *v.* enter gradually and secretly. **infiltration** *n.* **infiltrator** *n.*

infinite [in-fin-it] *adj.* without any limit or end. **infinitely** *adv.*

infinitesimal *adj.* extremely small.

infinitive [in-**fin**-it-iv] *n. Grammar* form of a verb not showing tense, person, or number, such as *to sleep.*

infinity *n.* endless space, time, or number.

infirm *adj.* physically or mentally weak. **infirmity** *n., pl.* **-ties.**

infirmary *n., pl.* **-ries.** hospital.

in flagrante delicto [in flag-**grant**-ee dee-**lick**-toe] while committing the offence.

inflame *v.* make angry or excited. **inflamed** *adj.* (of part of the body) red and swollen because of infection. **inflammation** *n.* inflamed part of the body.

inflammable *adj.* easily set on fire. **inflammability** *n.*
▷ *Inflammable* means the same as *flammable* but is falling out of general use as it was often mistaken to mean 'not flammable'. It is still used in metaphors: *an inflammable situation.*

inflammatory *adj.* likely to provoke anger.

inflate *v.* **1.** expand by filling with air or gas. **2.** cause economic inflation in. **inflatable** *adj.* **1.** able to be inflated. —*n.* **2.** plastic or rubber object which can be inflated.

inflation *n.* **1.** inflating. **2.** increase in prices and fall in the value of money. **inflationary** *adj.*

inflection, inflexion *n.* **1.** change in the pitch of the voice. **2.** *Grammar* change in the form of a word to show grammatical use.

inflexible *adj.* **1.** unwilling to be persuaded, obstinate. **2.** (of a rule, etc.) firmly fixed, unalterable. **3.** incapable of being bent. **inflexibly** *adv.* **inflexibility** *n.*

inflict *v.* impose (something unpleasant) on. **Infliction** *n.*

inflorescence *n. Botany* arrangement of flowers on a stem.

inflow *n.* **1.** something, such as liquid or gas, that flows in. **2.** act of flowing in; influx.

influence *n.* **1.** effect of one person or thing on another. **2.** (person with) the power to have such an effect. —*v.* **3.** have an effect on. **influential** *adj.* **influentially** *adv.*

influenza *n.* viral disease causing muscle pains, fever, and catarrh.

influx n. 1. arrival or entry of many people or things. 2. a flowing in.

info n. *Informal* information.

inform v. 1. tell. 2. give incriminating information to the police. **informant** n. person who gives information. **information** n. what is told, knowledge. **informative** adj. giving useful information. **information technology** use of computers and electronic technology to store and communicate information. **informer** n. person who informs to the police.

informal adj. 1. relaxed and friendly. 2. appropriate for everyday life or use. **informally** adv. **informality** n.

infra dig adj. *Informal* beneath one's dignity.

infrared adj. of or using rays below the red end of the visible spectrum.

infrastructure n. basic facilities, services, and equipment needed for a country or organization to function properly.

infrequent adj. not happening often. **infrequently** adv.

infringe v. break (a law or agreement). **infringement** n.

infuriate v. make very angry.

infuse v. 1. fill with (an emotion or quality). 2. soak to extract flavour. **infusion** n. 1. infusing. 2. liquid obtained by infusing.

ingenious [in-**jean**-ee-uss] adj. showing cleverness and originality. **ingeniously** adv. **ingenuity** [in-jen-**new**-it-ee] n.

ingénue [**an**-jay-new] n. naive young woman, esp. a role played by an actress.

ingenuous [in-**jen**-new-uss] adj. unsophisticated and trusting. **ingenuously** adv.

ingest v. take (food or drink) into the body. **ingestion** n.

inglenook n. warm seat in a large open fireplace.

inglorious adj. dishonourable or shameful.

ingot n. oblong block of cast metal.

ingrained adj. 1. (of a habit etc.) deep-rooted. 2. (of dirt) deeply fixed.

ingratiate v. bring (oneself) into favour (with). **ingratiating** adj. **ingratiatingly** adv.

ingratitude n. lack of gratitude or thanks.

ingredient n. component of a mixture or compound.

ingress n. act or right of entering.

ingrowing adj. (of a toenail) growing abnormally into the flesh.

inhabit v. -**habiting**, -**habited**. live in. in**habitable** adj. **inhabitant** n.

inhale v. breathe in (air, smoke, etc.). **inhalation** n. **inhalant** [in-**hale**-ant] n. medical preparation inhaled to help breathing problems. **inhaler** n. container for an inhalant.

inherent adj. existing as an inseparable part. **inherently** adv.

inherit v. -**heriting**, -**herited**. 1. receive (money etc.) from someone who has died. 2. receive (a characteristic) from parents etc. 3. receive from predecessors. **inheritance** n. **inheritor** n.

inhibit v. -**hibiting**, -**hibited**. 1. restrain (an impulse or desire). 2. hinder or prevent (action). **inhibition** n. feeling of fear or embarrassment that stops one from behaving naturally. **inhibited** adj.

inhospitable adj. 1. not welcoming, unfriendly. 2. difficult to live in, harsh.

inhuman adj. 1. cruel or brutal. 2. not human.

inhumane adj. cruel or brutal. **inhumanity** n.

inimical adj. unfavourable or hostile. **inimically** adv.

inimitable adj. impossible to imitate, unique. **inimitably** adv.

iniquity n., pl. -**ties**. 1. great injustice. 2. wickedness. 3. sin. **iniquitous** adj.

initial adj. 1. first, at the beginning. —n. 2. first letter, esp. of someone's name. —v. -**tialling**, -**tialled**. 3. sign with one's initials. **initially** adv. first, originally.

initiate v. 1. begin or set going. 2. admit (someone) into a closed group. 3. instruct in the basics of something. —n. 4. initiated person. **initiation** n. **initiator** n. **initiatory** adj.

initiative n. 1. first step, commencing move. 2. ability to act independently.

inject v. 1. put (a fluid) into the body with a syringe. 2. introduce (a new element), e.g. *he injected some humour into the scene.* **injection** n.

injudicious adj. showing poor judgment, unwise.

injunction n. court order not to do something.

injure v. 1. hurt physically or mentally. 2.

damage. **injury** n., pl. **-ries. 1.** physical hurt. **2.** damage. **injury time** Sport time added at the end of a match to compensate for time spent treating injured players. **injurious** adj.

injustice n. **1.** unfairness. **2.** unfair treatment or action.

ink n. **1.** coloured liquid used for writing or printing. —v. **2.** mark or cover with ink. **inky** adj. **inkier, inkiest. 1.** dark or black. **2.** stained with ink.

inkling n. slight idea or suspicion.

inlaid adj. **1.** set in another material so that the surface is smooth. **2.** made like this, e.g. an inlaid table.

inland adj., adv. in or towards the interior of a country, away from the sea. **Inland Revenue** government department that collects taxes.

in-laws pl. n. relatives by marriage.

inlay n. inlaid substance or pattern.

inlet n. **1.** narrow piece of water extending from the sea into the land. **2.** valve etc. through which liquid or gas enters.

in loco parentis [par-rent-iss] Latin in place of a parent.

inmate n. person living in an institution such as a prison.

inmost adj. furthest inside, most secret.

inn n. pub or small hotel, esp. in the country. **innkeeper** n.

innards pl. n. **1.** Informal internal organs. **2.** working parts.

innate adj. being part of someone's nature, inborn.

inner adj. **1.** happening or located within. **2.** of the mind or spirit, e.g. inner peace. **innermost** adj. **inner city** parts of a city near the centre, esp. when seen as poor or violent.

innings n. **1.** Sport player's or side's turn of batting. **2.** spell or turn.

innocent adj. **1.** not guilty of a crime. **2.** without experience of evil. **3.** trustful or naive. —n. **4.** innocent person, esp. a child. **innocently** adv. **innocence** n.

innocuous adj. harmless. **innocuously** adv.

innovate v. introduce new ideas or methods. **innovation** n. **innovative** adj. **innovator,** n.

innuendo n., pl. **-does.** indirect accusation.

innumerable adj. too many to be counted. **innumerably** adv.

innumerate adj. having no understanding of mathematics or science. **innumeracy** n.

inoculate v. protect against disease by injecting with a vaccine. **inoculation** n.

inoffensive adj. causing no harm or annoyance.

inoperable adj. Med. that cannot safely be operated on.

inoperative adj. not in force, effect, or operation.

inopportune adj. badly timed.

inordinate adj. excessive.

inorganic adj. **1.** not having the characteristics of living organisms. **2.** of or denoting chemical substances that do not contain carbon. **inorganically** adv.

inpatient n. patient who stays in a hospital for treatment.

input n. **1.** resources put into a project etc. **2.** data fed into a computer. —v. **-putting, -put. 3.** enter (data) in a computer.

inquest n. official inquiry into a sudden death.

inquietude n. restlessness, uneasiness, or anxiety.

inquire v. seek information or ask about. **inquirer** n. **inquiry** n., pl. **-ries. 1.** question. **2.** investigation.

inquisition n. **1.** thorough investigation. **2.** Hist. (I-) organization within the Catholic Church for suppressing heresy. **inquisitor** n. **inquisitorial** adj.

inquisitive adj. too curious about other people's business. **inquisitively** adv.

inquorate adj. without enough people present to make a quorum.

inroads pl. n. **make inroads into** start affecting or reducing, e.g. my gambling has made inroads into my savings.

ins. inches.

insalubrious adj. likely to cause ill-health.

insane adj. **1.** mentally ill. **2.** stupidly irresponsible. **insanely** adv. **insanity** n.

insanitary adj. dirty or unhealthy.

insatiable [in-saysh-a-bl] adj. impossible to satisfy.

inscribe v. write or carve words on. **inscription** n. words inscribed.

inscrutable adj. **1.** mysterious or enigmatic. **2.** incomprehensible. **inscrutably** adv. **inscrutability** n.

insect n. small invertebrate animal with six legs, a segmented body, and usu. two or four wings. **insecticide** n. substance for killing insects. **insectivorous** adj. insect-eating.

insecure adj. 1. not safe or firm. 2. anxious, not confident.

inseminate v. implant semen into. **insemination** n.

insensate adj. 1. without sensation, unconscious. 2. unfeeling.

insensible adj. 1. unconscious. 2. without feeling. 3. not aware. 4. imperceptible. **insensibility** n.

insensitive adj. unaware of or ignoring other people's feelings. **insensitivity** n.

inseparable adj. impossible to be separated or divided.

insert v. 1. put inside or between. —n. 2. something inserted. **insertion** n.

inset adj. 1. decorated with something inserted. —n. 2. small map or diagram within a larger one.

inshore adj. 1. close to the shore. —adj., adv. 2. towards the shore.

inside n. 1. inner side, surface, or part. —prep. 2. in or to the inside of. —adj. 3. of or on the inside. 4. by or from someone within an organization, e.g *inside information*. —adv. 5. in or into the inside. 6. *Slang* in prison. **inside out** 1. with the interior facing outwards. 2. thoroughly. **insider** n. member of a group who has exclusive knowledge about it.
▷ Avoid using the expression *inside of*, as the second preposition of is superfluous.

insidious adj. subtle or unseen but dangerous. **insidiously** adv.

insight n. clear understanding.

insignia [in-**sig**-nee-a] n., pl. **-nias**, **-nia**. badge or emblem of honour or office.

insignificant adj. not important. **insignificance** n.

insincere adj. pretending what one does not feel. **insincerely** adv. **insincerity** n., pl. **-ties**.

insinuate v. 1. suggest indirectly. 2. work oneself into a position by gradual manoeuvres. **insinuation** n.

insipid adj. lacking interest, spirit, or flavour. **insipidity** n.

insist v. demand or state firmly. **insistent** adj. 1. making persistent demands. 2. demanding attention. **insistently** adv. **insistence** n.

in situ adv., adj. *Latin* in its original position.

insofar as prep. to the extent that.

insole n. inner sole of a shoe or boot.

insolent adj. rude and disrespectful. **insolence** n. **insolently** adv.

insoluble adj. 1. incapable of being solved. 2. incapable of being dissolved.

insolvent adj. unable to pay one's debts. **insolvency** n.

insomnia n. sleeplessness. **insomniac** n.

insomuch adv. to such an extent.

insouciant adj. carefree and unconcerned. **insouciance** n.

inspect v. check closely or officially. **inspection** n. **inspector** n. 1. person who inspects. 2. high-ranking police officer.

inspire v. 1. fill with enthusiasm, stimulate. 2. arouse (an emotion). **inspiration** n. 1. good idea. 2. creative influence or stimulus. **inspirational** adj.

inst. instant (this month).

instability n. lack of steadiness or reliability.

install v. 1. put in and prepare (equipment) for use. 2. formally place (a person) in a position or rank. **installation** n. 1. installing. 2. equipment installed. 3. place containing equipment for a particular purpose, e.g. *radar installation*.

instalment n. any of the portions of a thing presented or a debt paid in successive parts.

instance n. 1. particular example. —v. 2. mention as an example. **for instance** for example.

instant n. 1. very brief time. 2. particular moment. —adj. 3. immediate. 4. (of foods) requiring little preparation. **instantly** adv. at once.

instantaneous adj. happening at once. **instantaneously** adv.

instead adv. as a replacement or substitute.

instep n. 1. part of the foot forming the arch between the ankle and toes. 2. part of a shoe etc. covering this.

instigate v. cause to happen, bring about. **instigation** n. **instigator** n.

instil v. **-stilling**, **-stilled**. introduce (an idea etc.) gradually in someone's mind.

instinct n. inborn tendency to behave in a

certain way. **instinctive** adj. **instinctively** adv.

institute n. **1.** organization set up for a specific purpose, esp. teaching or research. —v. **2.** start or establish.

institution n. **1.** long-established custom. **2.** large important organization such as a university or bank. **3.** hospital etc. for people with special needs. **institutional** adj. **institutionalize** v. make unable to cope with life outside an institution.

instruct v. **1.** order to do something. **2.** teach (someone) how to do something. **3.** brief (a solicitor or barrister). **instruction** n. **1.** teaching. **2.** order. —pl. **3.** information on how to do or use something. **instructive** adj. informative or helpful. **instructor** n.

instrument n. **1.** tool used for particular work. **2.** object played to produce a musical sound. **3.** measuring device to show height, speed, etc. **4.** Informal person used by another. **instrumental** adj. **1.** helping to cause. **2.** played by or composed for musical instruments. **instrumentalist** n. player of a musical instrument. **instrumentation** n. **1.** set of instruments in a car etc. **2.** arrangement of music for instruments.

insubordinate adj. not submissive to authority. **insubordination** n.

insubstantial adj. **1.** flimsy, fine, or slight. **2.** imaginary or unreal.

insufferable adj. unbearable.

insular adj. **1.** not open to new ideas, narrow-minded. **2.** of or like an island. **insularity** n.

insulate v. **1.** prevent or reduce the transfer of electricity, heat, sound, etc. by surrounding or lining with nonconductive material. **2.** isolate or set apart. **insulation** n. **insulator** n.

insulin [in-syoo-lin] n. hormone produced by the pancreas which controls the amount of sugar in the blood.

insult v. **1.** behave rudely to, offend. —n. **2.** insulting remark or action. **insulting** adj.

insuperable adj. impossible to overcome. **insuperability** n. **insuperably** adv.

insupportable adj. **1.** impossible to tolerate. **2.** impossible to be upheld or justified.

insurance n. **1.** agreement by which one makes regular payments to a company who pay an agreed sum if damage, loss, or death occurs. **2.** money paid by or for insurance.

3. means of protection. **insure** v. protect by insurance. **insurance policy** contract of insurance.

insurgent adj. **1.** in revolt. —n. **2.** rebel. **insurgency** n.

insurmountable adj. impossible to overcome, e.g. insurmountable problems.

insurrection n. rebellion.

intact adj. **1.** untouched. **2.** left complete or unharmed.

intaglio [in-tah-lee-oh] n., pl. -lios, -li. (gem carved with) an engraved design.

intake n. **1.** thing or quantity taken in. **2.** opening through which fluid or gas enters an engine, pipe, etc.

intangible adj. **1.** difficult for the mind to grasp, e.g. intangible ideas. **2.** incapable of being felt by touch.

integer n. positive or negative whole number or zero.

integral adj. **1.** being an essential part of a whole. —n. **2.** Maths sum of a large number of very small quantities.

integrate v. **1.** combine into a whole. **2.** amalgamate (a religious or racial group) into a community. **integration** n. **integrated circuit** tiny electronic circuit on a silicon chip.

integrity n. **1.** honesty. **2.** quality of being sound or whole.

integument n. natural covering such as skin or rind.

intellect n. power of thinking and reasoning. **intellectual** adj. **1.** of or appealing to the intellect. **2.** clever or intelligent. —n. **3.** intellectual person. **intellectually** adv. **intellectualism** n.

intelligent adj. **1.** able to understand, learn, and think things out quickly. **2.** (of a computerized device) able to initiate or modify action in the light of ongoing events. **intelligence** n. **1.** quality of being intelligent. **2.** information or news, esp. military information. **3.** people or department collecting military information. **intelligently** adv. **intelligence quotient** a measure of the intelligence of a person calculated by dividing the person's mental age by his or her actual age and multiplying the result by 100.

intelligentsia n. intellectual or cultured classes.

intelligible adj. understandable; **intelligibility** n.

intemperate adj. 1. extreme. 2. uncontrolled. 3. drinking alcohol to excess. **intemperance** n.

intend v. 1. propose or plan (something or to do something). 2. have as one's purpose. **intended** adj. 1. planned or future. —n. 2. Informal a person whom one is to marry.

intense adj. 1. of great strength or degree. 2. deeply emotional. **intensity** n.

intensify v. **-fying, -fied.** make or become more intense. **intensification** n.

intensive adj. using or needing concentrated effort or resources. **intensively** adv. **intensive care** thorough supervised treatment of an acutely ill patient in a hospital.

intent n. 1. intention. —adj. 2. paying close attention. **intently** adv. **intentness** n. **intent on** determined to. **to all intents and purposes** in almost every respect, virtually.

intention n. something intended. **intentional** adj. deliberate. **intentionally** adv.

inter [in-**ter**] v. **-terring, -terred.** bury (a corpse). **interment** n. burial (of a corpse).

inter- prefix between or among, e.g. intercontinental.

interact v. act on or in close relation with each other. **interaction** n. **interactive** adj.

interbreed v. breed within a related group.

intercede v. 1. plead in favour of. 2. mediate. **intercession** n. **intercessor** n.

intercept v. seize or stop in transit. **interception** n. **interceptor** n.

interchange v. 1. (cause to) exchange places. —n. 2. motorway junction. **interchangeable** adj.

inter-city adj. (of a passenger service) travelling fast between cities.

intercom n. internal communication system with loudspeakers.

intercommunion n. association between Churches, involving esp. mutual reception of Holy Communion.

intercontinental adj. travelling between or linking continents.

intercourse n. 1. act of having sex. 2. communication or dealings between people or groups.

interdenominational adj. among or involving more than one denomination of the Christian Church.

interdict, interdiction n. formal order forbidding something.

interdisciplinary adj. involving more than one branch of learning.

interest n. 1. desire to know or hear more about something. 2. hobby or subject that one enjoys. 3. (often pl.) advantage, e.g. in one's own interests. 4. sum paid for use of borrowed money. 5. right or share. —v. 6. arouse the interest of. **interested** adj. 1. feeling or showing interest. 2. involved in or affected by. **interesting** adj. **interestingly** adv.

interface n. 1. area where two things interact or link. 2. circuit linking a computer and another device.

interfere v. 1. try to influence other people's affairs where one is not involved or wanted. 2. clash (with). 3. Euphemistic abuse sexually. **interfering** adj. **interference** n. 1. interfering. 2. Radio interruption of reception by atmospherics or unwanted signals.

interferon n. protein that stops the development of an invading virus.

interim adj. temporary or provisional.

interior adj. 1. inside, inner. 2. mental or spiritual. —n. 3. inside. 4. inland region.

interject v. make (a remark) suddenly or as an interruption. **interjection** n.

interlace v. join by lacing or weaving together.

interlay v. insert (layers) between.

interleave v. insert, as blank leaves in a book, between other leaves. **interleaf** n. extra leaf.

interlink v. connect together.

interlock v. 1. join firmly together. —adj. 2. (of fabric) closely knitted.

interlocutor [in-ter-**lok**-yew-ter] n. person who takes part in a conversation.

interloper [in-ter-**lope**-er] n. person in a place or situation where he or she has no right to be.

interlude n. short rest or break in an activity or event.

intermarry v. (of families, races, or religions) become linked by marriage. **intermarriage** n.

intermediary n., pl. **-ries.** 1. person trying to create agreement between others. 2. messenger.

intermediate adj. coming between two points or extremes.

intermezzo [in-ter-**met**-so] n., pl. -zos, -zi. short piece of music, esp. one performed between the acts of an opera.

interminable adj. seemingly endless because boring. interminably adv.

intermingle v. mix together.

intermission n. interval between parts of a play, film, etc.

intermittent adj. occurring at intervals. intermittently adv.

intern v. 1. imprison, esp. during a war. —n. 2. US trainee doctor in a hospital. internment n. internee n. person who has been interned.

internal adj. 1. of or on the inside. 2. within a country or organization. 3. spiritual or mental. internally adv. internal-combustion engine engine powered by the explosion of a fuel-and-air mixture within the cylinders.

international adj. 1. of or involving two or more countries. —n. 2. game or match between teams of different countries. 3. player in such a match. internationally adv.

internecine adj. mutually destructive.

interplanetary adj. of or linking planets.

interplay n. action and reaction of two things upon each other.

Interpol International Criminal Police Organization.

interpolate [in-**ter**-pole-ate] v. insert (a comment or passage) in (a conversation or text). interpolation n.

interpose v. 1. insert between or among things. 2. say as an interruption. interposition n.

interpret v. 1. explain the meaning of. 2. translate orally from one language into another. 3. convey the meaning of (a poem, song, etc.) in performance. interpretation n. interpreter n.

interregnum n., pl. -nums, -na. interval between reigns.

interrelate v. connect (two or more things) to each other. interrelation n.

interrogate v. question closely. interrogation n. interrogative adj. 1. questioning. —n. 2. word used in asking a question, such as how or why. interrogator n.

interrupt v. 1. break into (a conversation etc.). 2. temporarily stop (a process or activity). interruption n.

intersect v. 1. divide by passing across or through. 2. (of roads) meet and cross. intersection n.

interspersed adj. scattered among, between, or on.

interstellar adj. between or among stars.

interstice [in-**ter**-stiss] n. small crack or gap between things.

intertwine v. twist together or entwine.

interval n. 1. time between two particular moments or events. 2. break between parts of a play, concert, etc. 3. difference in pitch between musical notes. at intervals 1. repeatedly. 2. with spaces left between.

intervene v. 1. involve oneself in a situation, esp. to prevent conflict. 2. happen so as to stop something. intervention n.

interview n. 1. formal discussion, esp. between a job-seeker and employer. 2. questioning of a well-known person about his or her career, views, etc., by a reporter. —v. 3. have an interview with. interviewee n. interviewer n.

interweave v. weave together.

intestate adj. not having made a will. intestacy n.

intestine n. (usu. pl.) lower part of the alimentary canal between the stomach and the anus. intestinal adj.

intimate[1] adj. 1. having a close personal relationship. 2. private. 3. (of knowledge) extensive and detailed. 4. Euphemistic having sexual relations. 5. having a friendly quiet atmosphere. —n. 6. intimate friend. intimately adv. intimacy n., pl. -cies.

intimate[2] v. 1. hint or suggest. 2. announce. intimation n.

intimidate v. subdue or influence by frightening. intimidation n. intimidating adj.

into prep. 1. to the inner part of. 2. to the middle of. 3. (up) against. 4. used to indicate the result of a change, e.g. he turned into a monster. 5. Maths used to indicate division, e.g. three into six is two. 6. Informal interested in.

intolerable adj. more than can be endured. intolerably adv.

intolerant adj. refusing to accept practices and beliefs that differ from one's own. intolerance n.

intonation n. sound pattern produced by variations in the voice.

intone v. speak or recite in an unvarying tone of voice.

in toto adv. Latin totally, entirely.

intoxicate v. 1. make drunk. 2. excite to excess. **intoxicant** n., adj. (drink) capable of intoxicating. **intoxication** n.

intractable adj. 1. (of a person) difficult to influence. 2. (of a problem or illness) hard to solve or cure.

intransigent adj. refusing to change one's attitude. **intransigence** n.

intransitive adj. (of a verb) not taking a direct object.

intrauterine adj. within the womb.

intravenous [in-tra-**vee**-nuss] adj. into a vein. **intravenously** adv.

intrepid adj. fearless or bold. **intrepidity** n.

intricate adj. 1. involved or complicated. 2. full of fine detail. **intricately** adv. **intricacy** n., pl. **-cies**.

intrigue v. 1. make interested or curious. 2. plot secretly. —n. 3. secret plotting. 4. secret love affair. **intriguing** adj.

intrinsic adj. part of the basic nature of. **intrinsically** adv.

introduce v. 1. present (someone) by name (to another person). 2. present (a radio or television programme). 3. bring forward for discussion. 4. bring into use. 5. insert. **introduction** n. 1. presentation of one person to another. 2. preliminary part or treatment. **introductory** adj. preliminary.

introspection n. examination of one's own thoughts and feelings. **introspective** adj.

introvert n. person concerned more with his or her thoughts and feelings than with external reality. **introverted** adj. **introversion** n.

intrude v. come in or join in without being invited. **intruder** n. **intrusion** n. **intrusive** adj.

intuition n. instinctive knowledge or insight without conscious reasoning. **intuitive** adj. **intuitively** adv.

Inuit n. Eskimo of North America or Greenland.

inundate v. 1. flood. 2. overwhelm. **inundation** n.

inure v. accustom, esp. to hardship or danger.

invade v. 1. enter (a country) by military force. 2. enter in large numbers. 3. disturb (privacy etc.). **invader** n.

invalid[1] n. 1. disabled or chronically ill person. —v. 2. dismiss from active service because of illness etc. **invalidity** n.

invalid[2] adj. 1. having no legal force. 2. (of an argument etc.) not valid because based on a mistake. **invalidate** v. make or show to be invalid.

invaluable adj. priceless.

invasion n. 1. act of invading. 2. intrusion.

invective n. abusive speech or writing.

inveigh [in-**vay**] v. (foll. by against) criticize (something) harshly.

inveigle v. coax or entice. **inveiglement** n.

invent v. 1. think up or create (something new). 2. make up (an excuse, lie, etc.). **invention** n. 1. something invented. 2. ability to invent. **inventive** adj. 1. resourceful. 2. creative. **inventiveness** n. **inventor** n.

inventory [in-ven-tree] n., pl. -tories. detailed list of goods or furnishings.

inverse adj. 1. opposite, inverted. 2. Maths linking two variables in such a way that one increases as the other decreases. **inversely** adv.

invert v. turn upside down or inside out. **inversion** n. **inverted commas** raised commas in writing to show where speech begins and ends.

invertebrate n. animal with no backbone.

invest v. spend (money, time, etc.) on something with the expectation of profit. **investment** n. 1. money invested. 2. something invested in. **investor** n. **invest in** v. buy. **invest with** v. give (power or rights) to.

investigate v. 1. inquire into. 2. examine. **investigation** n. **investigative** adj. **investigator** n.

investiture n. formal installation of a person in an office or rank.

inveterate adj. 1. deep-rooted. 2. confirmed in a habit or practice. **inveteracy** n.

invidious adj. likely to cause resentment. **invidiously** adv.

invigilate [in-**vij**-il-late] v. supervise examination candidates. **invigilator** n.

invigorate v. give energy to or refresh.

invincible adj. unconquerable. **invincibly** adv. **invincibility** n.

inviolable adj. that must not be broken or violated.

inviolate *adj.* unharmed, unaffected.

invisible *adj.* not able to be seen. **invisibly** *adv.* **invisibility** *n.*

invite *v.* 1. request the company of. 2. ask politely for. 3. attract, e.g. *the plan invited criticism.* —*n.* 4. *Informal* invitation. **inviting** *adj.* tempting, attractive. **invitation** *n.*

in vitro *adj.* (of a biological process) happening outside the body in an artificial environment.

invoice *v., n.* (send) a bill for goods or services supplied.

invoke *v.* 1. call on (a god) for help, inspiration, etc. 2. put (a law or penalty) into operation. 3. summon (a spirit). **invocation** *n.*

involuntary *adj.* 1. not done consciously. 2. unintentional. **involuntarily** *adv.*

involve *v.* 1. include as a necessary part. 2. affect. 3. implicate (a person). 4. make complicated. **involved** *adj.* 1. complicated. 2. concerned in. **involvement** *n.*

invulnerable *adj.* not able to be wounded or harmed.

inward *adj.* 1. internal. 2. situated within. 3. spiritual or mental. —*adv.* (also **inwards**) 4. towards the inside or middle. **inwardly** *adv.*

iodine *n.* bluish-black element used in medicine, photography, and dyeing. **iodize** *v.* treat with iodine.

ion *n.* electrically charged atom. **ionic** *adj.* **ionize** *v.* change into ions. **ionization** *n.* **ionosphere** *n.* region of ionized air in the upper atmosphere which reflects radio waves.

iota [eye-**oh**-ta] *n.* 1. ninth letter in the Greek alphabet. 2. very small amount.

IOU *n.* signed paper acknowledging debt.

IPA International Phonetic Alphabet.

ipecac [**ip**-pee-kak], **ipecacuanha** [ip pee-kak-yoo-**an**-na] *n.* S Amer. plant yielding an emetic.

ipso facto *adv. Latin* by that very fact.

IQ intelligence quotient.

Ir *Chem.* iridium.

IRA Irish Republican Army.

Iranian *n.* 1. person from Iran. —*adj.* 2. of Iran, its people, or their language.

Iraqi *n.* 1. person from Iraq. —*adj.* 2. of Iraq, its people, or their language.

irascible *adj.* easily angered. **irascibly** *adv.* **irascibility** *n.*

irate *adj.* very angry.

ire *n. Lit.* anger.

iridescent *adj.* having shimmering changing colours like a rainbow. **iridescence** *n.*

iridium *n.* very hard corrosion-resistant metal.

iris *n.* 1. circular membrane of the eye containing the pupil. 2. plant with sword-shaped leaves and showy flowers.

Irish *adj.* of Ireland. **Irish coffee** hot coffee mixed with whiskey and topped with cream.

irk *v.* irritate or annoy. **irksome** *adj.* tiresome.

iron *n.* 1. metallic element widely used for structural and engineering purposes. 2. tool made of iron. 3. appliance used, when heated, to press clothes or fabric. 4. metal-headed golf club. —*pl.* 5. fetters or chains. —*adj.* 6. made of iron. 7. inflexible, e.g. *an iron will.* —*v.* 8. smooth (clothes or fabric) with an iron. **iron out** *v.* settle (a problem) through discussion. **Iron Age** era when iron tools were used. **ironing** *n.* clothes to be ironed. **ironing board** long cloth-covered board, usu. with folding legs, on which to iron clothes.

ironic, ironical *adj.* using irony. **ironically** *adv.*

ironmonger *n.* shopkeeper or shop dealing in hardware. **ironmongery** *n.*

ironstone *n.* 1. rock consisting mainly of iron ore. 2. tough durable earthenware.

irony *n., pl.* **-nies.** 1. mildly sarcastic use of words to imply the opposite of what is said. 2. event or situation the opposite of that expected.

irradiate *v.* subject to or treat with radiation. **irradiation** *n.*

irrational *adj.* not based on logical reasoning. **irrational number** *Maths* any real number that cannot be expressed as the ratio of two integers, such as π.

irreconcilable *adj.* not able to be resolved or settled, e.g. *irreconcilable disagreement.* **irreconcilability** *n.*

irrecoverable *adj.* not able to be recovered, remedied, or rectified.

irredeemable *adj.* 1. not able to be reformed, improved, or corrected. 2. not able to be recovered, bought back, or converted into coin.

irreducible adj. impossible to put in a reduced or simpler form.

irrefutable adj. impossible to deny or disprove.

irregular adj. **1.** not regular or even. **2.** unconventional. **3.** (of a word) not following the typical pattern of formation in a language. irregularly adv. irregularity n., pl. -ties.

irrelevant adj. not connected with the matter in hand. irrelevantly adv. irrelevance n.

irreparable adj. not able to be repaired or put right. irreparably adv.

irreplaceable adj. impossible to replace.

irrepressible adj. not capable of being repressed, controlled, or restrained. irrepressibly adv.

irreproachable adj. blameless, faultless. irreproachably adv.

irresistible adj. too attractive or strong to resist. irresistibly adv.

irresolute adj. unable to make decisions, hesitating. irresolutely adv.

irrespective of prep. without taking account of.

irresponsible adj. **1.** not showing or done with due care for the consequences of one's actions or attitudes. **2.** not capable of bearing responsibility. irresponsibly adv.

irretrievable adj. impossible to put right or make good. irretrievably adv.

irreverence n. **1.** lack of due respect. **2.** disrespectful remark or act. irreverent adj.

irreversible adj. not able to be reversed or put right again, e.g. *the damage may be irreversible*. irreversibly adv.

irrevocable adj. not possible to change or undo. irrevocably adv.

irrigate v. water by artificial channels or pipes. irrigation n.

irritate v. **1.** annoy or anger. **2.** cause (a body part) to itch or become inflamed. irritable adj. easily annoyed. irritability n. irritably adv. irritant n., adj. irritation n. (person or thing) causing irritation. irritation n.

irrupt v. enter forcibly or suddenly. irruption n.

is v. third person singular present tense of BE.

isinglass [ize-ing-glass] n. kind of gelatin obtained from some freshwater fish.

Islam n. **1.** Muslim religion teaching that there is one God and that Mohammed is his prophet. **2.** Muslim countries and civilization. Islamic adj.

island n. piece of land surrounded by water. islander n. person who lives on an island.

isle n. island. islet n. little island.

-ism n. suffix indicating: **1.** political or religious belief, e.g. *socialism, Judaism.* **2.** characteristic quality, e.g. *heroism.* **3.** an action, e.g. *exorcism.* **4.** prejudice on the basis specified, e.g. *sexism.*

isobar [ice-oh-bar] n. line on a map connecting places of equal barometric pressure. isobaric adj.

isolate v. **1.** place apart or alone. **2.** Chem. obtain (a substance) in uncombined form. isolation n. isolationism n. policy of not participating in international affairs. isolationist n., adj.

isomer [ice-oh-mer] n. substance whose molecules contain the same atoms as another but in a different arrangement. isomeric adj. isomerism n.

isometric adj. **1.** having equal dimensions. **2.** relating to muscular contraction without movement. **3.** (of a three-dimensional drawing) having three equally inclined axes and drawn to scale in every direction. isometrics pl. n. system of isometric exercises.

isomorphism n. **1.** Biol. similarity of form. **2.** Chem. existence of two or more substances of different composition in similar crystalline form. **3.** Maths one-to-one correspondence between elements of two or more sets. isomorphic, isomorphous adj.

isosceles triangle [ice-soss-ill-eez] n. triangle with two sides of equal length.

isotherm [ice-oh-therm] n. line on a map connecting points of equal mean temperature.

isotope [ice-oh-tope] n. one of two or more atoms with the same number of protons in the nucleus but a different number of neutrons.

isotropic, isotropous adj. having uniform physical properties in all directions. isotropy n.

Israeli n., pl. -lis, -li. **1.** person from Israel, in SW Asia. —adj. **2.** of Israel or its people.

issue n. **1.** topic of interest or discussion. **2.**

particular edition of a magazine or news-paper. **3.** question requiring a decision. **4.** outcome or result. **5.** *Law* children. —*v.* **6.** make (a statement etc.) publicly. **7.** official-ly supply (with). **8.** send out or distribute. **9.** publish. **take issue** disagree.

-ist *n. suffix* indicating: **1.** person who per-forms a particular action, e.g. *exorcist.* **2.** person who does a particular type of work, e.g. *physicist.* —*n. suffix, adj. suffix* indicat-ing: **3.** (of) a person who holds a particular political or religious belief, e.g. *socialist, Buddhist.* **4.** (of) a person who is prejudiced on the basis specified, e.g. *sexist.*

isthmus [**iss**-muss] *n., pl.* **-muses.** narrow strip of land connecting two areas of land.

it *pron.* **1.** refers to a nonhuman, animal, plant, or inanimate object. **2.** thing men-tioned or being discussed. **3.** used as the subject of impersonal verbs, e.g. *it is snow-ing.* **4.** *Informal* crucial or ultimate point. **its** *adj.* belonging to it. **it's** it is. **itself** *pron.* emphatic form of IT.
▷ Beware of mistaking the possessive *its* (no apostrophe) as in *The cat has hurt its paw*, for the abbreviation *it's* meaning *it is* or *it has: It's been a long time.*

IT information technology.

Italian *n.* **1.** official language of Italy and one of the official languages of Switzerland. **2.** person from Italy. —*adj.* **3.** of Italy, its people, or their language.

italic *adj.* (of printing type) sloping to the right. **italics** *pl. n.* this type, now used for emphasis etc. **italicize** *v.* put in italics.

itch *n.* **1.** skin irritation causing a desire to scratch. **2.** restless desire. —*v.* **3.** have an itch. **itchy** *adj.* **itchier, itchiest.**

item *n.* **1.** single thing in a list or collection. **2.** piece of information. **itemize** *v.* **1.** put on a list. **2.** make a list of.

iterate *v.* repeat. **iteration** *n.*

itinerant *adj.* travelling from place to place.

itinerary *n., pl.* **-aries. 1.** detailed plan of a journey. **2.** route.

ITV Independent Television.

IUD intrauterine device: coil-shaped contra-ceptive fitted into the womb.

IVF in vitro fertilization.

ivory *n.* **1.** hard white bony substance form-ing the tusks of elephants. —*adj.* **2.** yellowish-white. **ivory tower** remoteness from the realities of everyday life.

ivy *n., pl.* **ivies.** climbing evergreen plant.

J

J joule(s).

jab v. **jabbing, jabbed. 1.** poke roughly. —n. **2.** poke. **3.** Informal injection.

jabber v. **1.** talk rapidly or incoherently. —n. **2.** rapid or incoherent talk.

jabot [zhab-oh] n. frill or ruffle on the front of a blouse or shirt.

jacaranda n. tropical tree with sweet-smelling wood.

jacinth n. reddish-orange precious stone.

jack n. **1.** device for raising a motor-car or other heavy object. **2.** playing card with a picture of a pageboy. **3.** Bowls small white ball aimed at by the players. **4.** socket in electrical equipment into which a plug fits. **5.** flag flown at the bow of a ship, showing nationality. **6.** piece used in the game of jacks. —pl. **7.** game in which metal pieces are thrown and picked up between bounces of a ball. **jack in** v. Informal abandon. **jack-in-the-box** n. toy consisting of a figure on a spring in a box. **jack of all trades** person who can do many kinds of work. **jack up** v. lift with a jack.

jackal n. doglike wild animal of Asia and Africa.

jackanapes n. impertinent person.

jackass n. **1.** male of the ass. **2.** fool. **laughing jackass** same as KOOKABURRA.

jackboot n. **1.** high military boot. **2.** oppressive military rule.

jackdaw n. black-and-grey bird of the crow family.

jacket n. **1.** short coat. **2.** outer paper cover on a hardback book. **3.** skin of a baked potato.

jackknife n. **1.** large clasp knife. **2.** dive with a sharp bend at the waist in mid-air. —v. **3.** (of an articulated lorry) go out of control so that the trailer swings round at a sharp angle to the cab.

jackpot n. large prize or accumulated stake that may be won in a game. **hit the jackpot** be very successful through luck.

jack rabbit n. American hare with long ears.

Jacobean [jak-a-**bee**-an] adj. of the reign of James I of England.

Jacobite n. supporter of the exiled Stuarts after the overthrow of James II of England.

Jacquard [jak-ard] n. fabric in which the design is incorporated into the weave.

Jacuzzi [jak-oo-zee] n. ® circular bath with a device that swirls the water.

jade¹ n. **1.** ornamental semiprecious stone, usu. dark green. —adj. **2.** bluish-green.

jade² n. **1.** disreputable woman. **2.** worn-out old horse.

jaded adj. tired and unenthusiastic.

Jaffa n. large orange with a thick skin.

jag¹ n. **1.** sharp or ragged projection. **2.** Informal injection. **jagged** [**jag**-gid] adj.

jag² n. spree or drinking bout.

jaguar n. large S American spotted cat.

jail n. **1.** building for confinement of criminals or suspects. —v. **2.** send to jail. **jailer** n. **jailbird** n. Informal hardened criminal.

jalopy [jal-**lop**-ee] n., pl. **-lopies**. Informal old car.

jalousie [zhal-loo-zee] n. blind or shutter made of horizontal slats of wood.

jam¹ n. spread made from fruit boiled with sugar.

jam² v. **jamming, jammed. 1.** pack tightly into a place. **2.** crowd or congest. **3.** make or become stuck. **4.** Radio block (another station) with impulses of equal wavelength. **5.** play a jam session. —n. **6.** hold-up of traffic. **7.** Informal awkward situation. **jam on** v. apply (brakes) fiercely. **jam-packed** adj. filled to capacity. **jam session** informal rock or jazz performance.

jamb n. side post of a door or window frame.

jamboree n. **1.** large rally of Scouts. **2.** large celebration.

jammy adj. **-mier, -miest**. Slang lucky.

Jan. January.

jangle v. **1.** (cause to) make a harsh ringing noise. **2.** (of nerves) be upset or irritated. —n. **3.** jangling noise.

janitor *n.* caretaker of a school or other building.

January *n.* first month of the year.

japan *n.* **1.** very hard varnish, usu. black. —*v.* **-panning, -panned. 2.** cover with this varnish.

Japanese *n., adj.* (native or language) of Japan.

jape *n.* joke or prank.

japonica *n.* shrub with red flowers.

jar[1] *n.* **1.** wide-mouthed container, usu. cylindrical and made of glass. **2.** *Informal* glass of beer.

jar[2] *v.* **jarring, jarred. 1.** have a disturbing or unpleasant effect on. **2.** (cause to) vibrate suddenly or violently. **3.** clash. —*n.* **4.** jolt or shock.

jardinière *n.* ornamental plant pot.

jargon *n.* **1.** specialized technical language of a particular subject. **2.** pretentious language.

jasmine *n.* shrub with sweet-smelling yellow or white flowers.

jasper *n.* red, yellow, dark green, or brown variety of quartz.

jaundice *n.* disease marked by yellowness of the skin. **jaundiced** *adj.* **1.** (of an attitude or opinion) bitter or cynical. **2.** having jaundice.

jaunt *n.* **1.** short journey for pleasure. —*v.* **2.** make such a journey.

jaunty *adj.* **-tier, -tiest. 1.** sprightly and cheerful. **2.** smart. **jauntily** *adv.*

javelin *n.* light spear thrown in sports competitions.

jaw *n.* **1.** one of the bones in which the teeth are set. **2.** gripping part of a vice etc. —*pl.* **3.** mouth. **4.** narrow opening of a gorge or valley. —*v.* **5.** *Slang* talk lengthily. **jawbone** *n.* lower jaw of a person or animal.

jay *n.* bird with a pinkish body and blue-and-black wings.

jaywalking *n.* crossing the road in a careless or dangerous manner. **jaywalker** *n.*

jazz *n.* **1.** rhythmic music of Black American origin. **2.** *Slang* other related things, e.g. *legal papers and all that jazz.* **jazzy** *adj.* **-zier, -ziest. 1.** flashy or showy. **2.** of or like jazz. **jazz up** *v.* make more lively.

JCB *n.* ® construction machine with a shovel at the front and an excavator at the rear.

jealous *adj.* **1.** fearful of losing a partner or possession to a rival. **2.** envious. **3.** suspiciously watchful. **jealously** *adv.* **jealousy** *n., pl.* **-sies.**

jeans *pl. n.* casual denim trousers.

Jeep *n.* ® four-wheel-drive motor vehicle.

jeer *v.* **1.** scoff or deride. —*n.* **2.** cry of derision.

Jehovah *n.* God. **Jehovah's Witness** member of a Christian sect believing that the end of the world is near.

jejune *adj.* **1.** simple or naive. **2.** dull or boring.

jell *v.* **1.** congeal. **2.** *Informal* assume a definite form.

jellaba, jellabah *n.* loose cloak with a hood, worn by Arab men.

jelly *n., pl.* **-lies. 1.** soft food made of liquid set with gelatin. **2.** jam made from fruit juice and sugar.

jellyfish *n.* small jelly-like sea animal.

jemmy *n., pl.* **-mies.** short steel crowbar used by burglars.

jenny *n., pl.* **-nies. 1.** female ass. **2.** female wren.

jeopardy *n.* danger. **jeopardize** *v.* place in danger.

jerboa *n.* small mouselike African rodent with long hind legs.

jeremiad *n.* long lamenting complaint.

jerk[1] *n.* **1.** sharp or abruptly stopped movement. **2.** sharp pull. **3.** *Slang* contemptible person. —*v.* **4.** move or throw with a jerk. **jerky** *adj.* **jerkier, jerkiest.** sudden or abrupt. **jerkily** *adv.* **jerkiness** *n.*

jerk[2] *v.* preserve (beef) by slicing it and drying it in the sun.

jerkin *n.* sleeveless jacket.

Jerry *n.* *Brit. slang* German or Germans collectively.

jerry-built *adj.* built badly using flimsy materials. **jerry-builder** *n.*

jerry can *n.* flat-sided can for carrying petrol etc.

jersey *n.* **1.** knitted jumper. **2.** machine-knitted fabric. **3.** (J-) breed of cow.

Jerusalem artichoke *n.* small yellowish-white root vegetable.

jest *n., v.* joke. **jester** *n.* **1.** joker. **2.** *Hist.* professional clown at court.

Jesuit [**jezz**-yoo-it] *n.* member of the Society

of Jesus, a Roman Catholic order. **jesuitical** *adj*. crafty through using oversubtle reasoning.

Jesus *n*. **1**. (also **Jesus Christ, Jesus of Nazareth**) ?4 B.C.–?29 A.D., founder of Christianity, believed by Christians to be the Son of God. —*interj*. **2**. used to express intense surprise, dismay, etc.

jet[1] *n*. **1**. stream of liquid or gas, esp. one forced from a small hole. **2**. nozzle from which gas or liquid is forced. **3**. burner on a gas fire. **4**. aircraft driven by jet propulsion. —*v*. **jetting, jetted**. **5**. shoot forth as a jet. **6**. fly by jet aircraft. **jet lag** fatigue caused by crossing time zones in an aircraft. **jet propulsion** propulsion by thrust provided by a jet of gas or liquid. **jet-propelled** *adj*. **jet set** rich and fashionable people who travel the world for pleasure.

jet[2] *n*. hard black mineral. **jet-black** *adj*. glossy black.

jetsam *n*. goods thrown overboard to lighten a ship.

jettison *v*. **-soning, -soned**. **1**. abandon. **2**. throw overboard.

jetty *n*., *pl*. **-ties**. **1**. small pier. **2**. structure built from a shore to protect a harbour.

Jew *n*. **1**. person whose religion is Judaism. **2**. descendant of the ancient Hebrews. **Jewess** *n. fem. now oft. offens*. **Jewish** *adj*. **Jewry** *n*. Jews collectively. **jew's-harp** *n*. musical instrument held between the teeth and played by plucking a metal strip with one's finger.

jewel *n*. **1**. precious stone. **2**. ornament containing one. **3**. precious person or thing. **jeweller** *n*. dealer in jewels. **jewellery** *n*.

Jezebel *n*. shameless or scheming woman.

jib[1] *v*. **jibbing, jibbed**. (of a horse, person, etc.) stop and refuse to go on. **jib at** *v*. object to (a proposal etc.).

jib[2] *n*. **1**. projecting arm of a crane or derrick. **2**. triangular sail set in front of a mast.

jibe *v., n*. **1**. same as GIBE. —*v*. **2**. same as GYBE.

jiffy *n., pl*. **-fies**. *Informal* very short period of time.

jig *n*. **1**. type of lively dance. **2**. music for it. **3**. device that holds a component in place for cutting etc. —*v*. **jigging, jigged**. **4**. make jerky up-and-down movements. **5**. dance a jig.

jigger *n*. small glass for spirits.

jiggery-pokery *n. Informal* trickery or mischief.

jiggle *v*. move up and down with short jerky movements.

jigsaw *n*. **1**. machine fretsaw. **2**. (also **jigsaw puzzle**) picture cut into interlocking pieces, which the user tries to fit together again.

jihad *n*. Islamic holy war against unbelievers.

jilt *v*. leave or reject (one's lover).

jingle *n*. **1**. gentle ringing noise, as of a shaken chain. **2**. catchy rhythmic verse or song, as on a television advert. —*v*. **3**. (cause to) make a jingling sound.

jingoism *n*. aggressive nationalism. **jingoist** *n*. **jingoistic** *adj*.

jinks *pl. n*. **high jinks** boisterous merry-making.

jinni *n., pl*. **jinn**. spirit in Muslim mythology.

jinx *n*. **1**. person or thing bringing bad luck. —*v*. **2**. be or put a jinx on.

jitters *pl. n*. worried nervousness. **jittery** *adj*. nervous.

jiujitsu *n*. same as JUJITSU.

jive *n*. **1**. lively dance of the 1940s and '50s. —*v*. **2**. dance the jive.

job *n*. **1**. task to be done. **2**. occupation or paid employment. **3**. *Informal* difficult task. **4**. *Informal* crime, esp. robbery. —*v*. **jobbing, jobbed**. **5**. do casual jobs. **6**. buy and sell (goods etc.) as a middleman. **jobbing** *adj*. doing individual jobs for payment. **jobless** *adj., pl. n*. unemployed (people). **jobcentre** *n*. government office displaying information about available jobs. **job lot** assortment sold together. **job sharing** splitting of one post between two people working part-time.

Job's comforter *n*. person who adds to distress while pretending to give sympathy.

jockey *n*. **1**. (professional) rider of race-horses. —*v*. **2**. ride (a horse) in a race. **jockey for position** manoeuvre to obtain an advantage.

jockstrap *n*. belt with a pouch to support the genitals, worn by male athletes.

jocose [joke-**kohss**] *adj*. playful or humorous. **jocosely** *adv*.

jocular *adj*. **1**. joking. **2**. fond of joking. **jocularly** *adv*. **jocularity** *n*.

jocund [jok-kund] adj. Lit. merry or cheerful.

jodhpurs pl. n. riding breeches, stretchy or loose-fitting above the knee but tight below.

jog v. **jogging, jogged. 1.** run at a gentle pace, esp. for exercise. **2.** nudge slightly. —n. **3.** jogging. **4.** slight nudge. **jog someone's memory** remind someone of something. **jogger** n. **jogging** n.

joggle v. **1.** move to and fro in jerks. **2.** shake.

john n. US slang toilet.

joie de vivre [jwah de **veev**-ra] n. French enjoyment of life.

join v. **1.** come or bring together. **2.** become a member (of). **3.** come into someone's company. **4.** take part (in). **5.** unite in marriage. **6.** connect (two points). —n. **7.** place of joining. **join in** v. take part in. **join up** v. enlist in the armed services.

joiner n. maker of finished woodwork. **joinery** n. joiner's work.

joint n. **1.** junction of two or more parts or objects. **2.** place where bones meet but can move. **3.** piece of meat for roasting. **4.** Slang house or place, esp. a disreputable bar or nightclub. **5.** Slang marijuana cigarette. —adj. **6.** shared by two or more. —v. **7.** divide meat into joints. **8.** provide with a joint. **out of joint 1.** dislocated. **2.** disorganized. **jointed** adj. **jointly** adv. **joint-stock company** firm whose capital is jointly owned by shareholders.

jointure n. property settled on a wife for her use after her husband's death.

joist n. horizontal beam that helps support a floor or ceiling.

jojoba [hoe-**hoe**-ba] n. shrub whose seeds yield oil used in cosmetics.

joke n. **1.** thing said or done to cause laughter. **2.** amusing or ridiculous person or thing. —v. **3.** make jokes. **jokey** adj. **jokingly** adv. **joker** n. **1.** person who jokes. **2.** Slang fellow. **3.** extra card in a pack, counted as any other in some games.

jolly adj. **-lier, -liest. 1.** happy and cheerful. **2.** merry and festive. —adv. **3.** Informal extremely. —v. **-lying, -lied. 4.** jolly along try to keep (someone) cheerful by flattery or coaxing. **jolliness** n. **jollity** n. **jollification** n. merrymaking.

jolt n. **1.** sudden jerk or bump. **2.** unpleasant surprise or shock. —v. **3.** move or shake with jolts. **4.** surprise or shock.

Jonah n. person believed to bring bad luck to those around him or her.

jonquil n. fragrant narcissus.

josh US slang —v. **1.** tease. —n. **2.** teasing joke.

joss n. Chinese idol. **joss stick** n. stick of incense giving off a sweet smell when burnt.

jostle v. **1.** knock or push against. **2.** compete with someone.

jot n. **1.** very small amount. —v. **jotting, jotted. 2.** write briefly. **3.** make a note of. **jotter** n. notebook.

joule [jool] n. Physics unit of work or energy.

journal n. **1.** daily newspaper or other periodical. **2.** daily record of events. **journalese** n. superficial and clichéd writing, as found in some newspapers. **journalism** n. writing on or editing of periodicals. **journalist** n. **journalistic** adj.

journey n. **1.** act or process of travelling from one place to another. **2.** time taken or distance travelled in a journey. —v. **3.** travel.

journeyman n. qualified craftsman employed by another.

joust Hist. —n. **1.** combat with lances between two mounted knights. —v. **2.** fight on horseback using lances.

jovial adj. happy and cheerful. **jovially** adv. **joviality** n.

jowl n. **1.** lower jaw. **2.** fatty flesh hanging from the lower jaw. —pl. **3.** cheeks.

joy n. **1.** feeling of great delight or pleasure. **2.** cause of this feeling. **joyful** adj. **joyless** adj. **joyous** adj. **joy ride** pleasure trip, esp. in a stolen car. **joystick** n. Informal control device for an aircraft or computer.

JP Justice of the Peace.

Jr Junior.

jubilant adj. feeling or expressing great joy. **jubilantly** adv. **jubilation** n.

jubilee n. **1.** special anniversary, esp. 25th (**silver jubilee**) or 50th (**golden jubilee**). **2.** time of rejoicing.

Judaism n. religion of the Jews, having only one God and based on the teachings of the Old Testament and the Talmud. **Judaic** adj.

Judas n. person who betrays a friend.

judder v. **1.** vibrate violently. —n. **2.** violent vibration.

judge n. **1.** public official who tries cases and passes sentence in a court of law. **2.** person who decides the outcome of a contest. **3.** person of reliable opinion on a subject. —v. **4.** act as a judge. **5.** appraise critically. **6.** consider something to be the case. **judgment, judgement** n. **1.** faculty of judging. **2.** sentence of a court. **3.** opinion reached after careful thought. **Judgment Day** occasion of the Last Judgment by God at the end of the world. **judgmental, judgemental** adj.
▷ The alternative spellings with or without an 'e' between 'g' and 'm' are equally acceptable.

judicature n. **1.** administration of justice. **2.** body of judges.

judicial adj. **1.** of or by a court or judge. **2.** showing or using judgment. **judicially** adv.

judiciary n. system of courts and judges.

judicious adj. well-judged, sensible. **judiciously** adv.

judo n. modern sport derived from jujitsu, where the opponent must be defeated using the minimum physical effort.

jug n. **1.** container for liquids, with a handle and small spout. **2.** its contents. **3.** Slang prison. **jugged hare** hare stewed in an earthenware pot.

juggernaut n. **1.** large heavy lorry. **2.** any irresistible destructive force.

juggle v. **1.** throw and catch (several objects) so that most are in the air at the same time. **2.** manipulate (figures, situations, etc.) to suit one's purposes. **juggler** n.

jugular vein n. one of three large veins of the neck returning blood from the head.

juice n. **1.** liquid part of vegetables, fruit, or meat. **2.** fluid secreted by an organ of the body. **3.** Informal petrol. **juicy** adj. **juicier, juiciest. 1.** succulent. **2.** interesting.

jujitsu n. Japanese art of wrestling and self-defence.

juju n. W African magic charm or fetish.

jujube n. chewy sweet of flavoured gelatin.

jukebox n. automatic coin-operated record player.

Jul. July.

julep n. sweet alcoholic drink.

Julian calendar n. calendar introduced by Julius Caesar, in which leap years occurred every fourth year.

julienne adj. **1.** cut into thin shreds. —n. **2.** clear soup containing thinly shredded vegetables.

July n. seventh month of the year.

jumble v. **1.** mix in a disordered way. —n. **2.** confused heap or state. **3.** articles for a jumble sale. **jumble sale** sale of miscellaneous second-hand items.

jumbo adj. Informal very large. **jumbo jet** large jet airliner.

jump v. **1.** leap or spring into the air using the leg muscles. **2.** leap over (an obstacle). **3.** move quickly and suddenly. **4.** jerk with surprise. **5.** increase suddenly. **6.** pass over or miss out (intervening material). **7.** change the subject abruptly. **8.** come off (tracks, rails, etc.). **9.** Informal attack without warning. **10.** Informal pass through (a red traffic light). —n. **11.** jumping. **12.** obstacle to be jumped. **13.** sudden nervous jerk. **14.** sudden rise in prices. **15.** break in continuity. **jump the gun** act prematurely. **jump the queue** not wait one's turn. **jumpy** adj. **jumpier, jumpiest.** nervous. **jump at** v. accept (a chance etc.) gladly. **jumped-up** adj. arrogant because of recent promotion. **jump jet** fixed-wing jet that can take off and land vertically. **jump leads** electric cables to connect a discharged car battery to an external battery to aid starting an engine. **jump on** v. criticize suddenly and forcefully. **jump suit** one-piece garment of trousers and top.

jumper[1] n. sweater or pullover.

jumper[2] n. person or animal that jumps.

Jun. 1. June. **2.** Junior.

junction n. **1.** place where routes, railway lines, or roads meet. **2.** point where traffic can leave or enter a motorway. **3.** join.

juncture n. point in time, esp. a critical one.

June n. sixth month of the year.

jungle n. **1.** tropical forest of dense tangled vegetation. **2.** tangled mass. **3.** place of intense struggle for survival.

junior adj. **1.** younger. **2.** of lower standing. —n. **3.** junior person. **junior school** school for children between seven and eleven.

juniper n. evergreen shrub with berries yielding oil.

junk[1] n. **1.** discarded or useless objects. **2.** Informal rubbish. **3.** Slang narcotic drug.

esp. heroin. **junkie, junky** *n., pl.* **junkies.** *Slang* drug addict. **junk food** snack food of low nutritional value.

junk² *n.* flat-bottomed Chinese sailing vessel.

junket *n.* **1.** sweetened milk set with rennet. **2.** excursion by public officials paid for from public funds. **3.** feast. —*v.* **4.** feast. **junketing** *n.*

junta *n.* group of military officers holding power in a country, esp. after a coup.

Jupiter *n.* **1.** Roman chief of the gods. **2.** largest of the planets.

juridical *adj.* of law or the administration of justice.

jurisdiction *n.* **1.** right or power to administer justice and apply laws. **2.** extent of this right or power.

jurisprudence *n.* science or philosophy of law.

jurist *n.* expert in law.

jury *n., pl.* **-ries. 1.** group of people sworn to deliver a verdict in a court of law. **2.** judges of a competition. **juror, juryman, jurywoman** *n.*

just *adv.* **1.** very recently. **2.** exactly. **3.** barely. **4.** at this instant. **5.** merely, only. **6.** really. —*adj.* **7.** fair or impartial in action or judgment. **8.** proper or right. **9.** well-founded. **justly** *adv.* **justness** *n.*

justice *n.* **1.** quality of being just. **2.** fairness. **3.** judicial proceedings. **4.** judge or magistrate. **justiciary** *n., pl.* **-aries.** judge. **justice of the peace** person who is authorized to act as a judge in a local court of law.

justify *v.* **-fying, -fied. 1.** prove right or reasonable. **2.** show to be free from blame or guilt. **3.** align (text) so the margins are straight. **justifiable** *adj.* **justifiably** *adv.* **justification** *n.*

jut *v.* **jutting, jutted.** project or stick out.

jute *n.* fibre of certain plants, used for rope, canvas, etc.

juvenile *adj.* **1.** young. **2.** suitable for young people. **3.** immature and rather silly. —*n.* **4.** young person or child. **5.** actor who performs youthful roles. **juvenilia** *pl. n.* works produced in an author's youth. **juvenile delinquent** young person guilty of a crime.

juxtapose *v.* put side by side. **juxtaposition** *n.*

K

K 1. *Chem.* potassium. 2. *Informal* thousand(s).

Kaffir [**kaf**-fer] *n. S Afr. offens. obs.* a Black African.

kaftan *n.* 1. long loose Eastern garment. 2. woman's dress resembling this.

kai *n. NZ* food.

kail *n.* same as KALE.

kaiser [**kize**-er] *n. Hist.* German or Austro-Hungarian emperor.

Kalashnikov *n.* Russian-made automatic rifle.

kale *n.* cabbage with crinkled leaves.

kaleidoscope *n.* tube-shaped toy containing loose pieces of coloured glass reflected by mirrors so that various symmetrical patterns form when the tube is twisted. **kaleidoscopic** *adj.*

kalends *pl. n.* same as CALENDS.

kamikaze [kam-mee-**kah**-zee] *n.* 1. in World War II, Japanese pilot who performed a suicide mission. —*adj.* 2. (of an action) undertaken in the knowledge that it will kill or injure the person performing it.

kangaroo *n., pl.* **-roos.** *Aust.* marsupial which moves by jumping with its powerful hind legs. **kangaroo court** unofficial court set up by a group to discipline its members.

kaolin *n.* fine white clay used to make porcelain and in some medicines.

kapok *n.* fluffy fibre from a tropical tree, used to stuff cushions etc.

kaput [kap-**poot**] *adj. Informal* ruined or broken.

karate *n.* Japanese system of unarmed combat using blows with the feet, hands, elbows, and legs.

karma *n. Buddhism, Hinduism* person's actions affecting his or her fate for his or her next reincarnation.

karoo *n. S Afr.* high arid plateau.

kasbah *n.* citadel of a N African town.

katydid *n.* large green grasshopper of N Amer.

kauri *n.* large NZ conifer grown for its valuable timber and resin.

kayak *n.* 1. Inuit canoe made of sealskins stretched over a frame. 2. fibreglass or canvas-covered canoe of this design.

kazoo *n., pl.* **-zoos.** cigar-shaped metal musical instrument that produces a buzzing sound when the player hums into it.

KBE Knight Commander of the Order of the British Empire.

kbyte *Computers* kilobyte.

kcal kilocalorie.

kea *n.* large brownish-green parrot of NZ.

kebab *n.* dish of small pieces of meat grilled on skewers.

kedge *n.* 1. small anchor. —*v.* 2. move (a ship) by hauling on a cable attached to a kedge.

kedgeree *n.* dish of fish with rice and eggs.

keel *n.* main lengthways timber or steel support along the base of a ship. **keel over** *v.* 1. turn upside down. 2. *Informal* collapse suddenly. **on an even keel** well balanced, steady.

keen[1] *adj.* 1. eager or enthusiastic. 2. intense or strong. 3. (of the senses) capable of recognizing small distinctions. 4. intellectually acute. 5. competitive. 6. cold and penetrating. 7. sharp. **keenly** *adv.* **keenness** *n.*

keen[2] *v.* 1. wail over the dead. —*n.* 2. funeral lament.

keep *v.* **keeping, kept.** 1. stay (in, on, or at a place or position). 2. have or retain possession of. 3. take temporary charge of. 4. look after or maintain. 5. detain (someone). 6. store. 7. continue or persist. 8. support financially. 9. remain good. —*n.* 10. cost of food and everyday expenses. 11. central tower of a castle. **keeper** *n.* 1. person who looks after animals in a zoo. 2. person in charge of a museum or collection. 3. short for GOALKEEPER. **keeping** *n.* care or charge. **in, out of keeping with** appropriate or inappropriate for. **keep fit** exercises designed to promote physical fitness. **keepsake** *n.* gift treasured for the sake of the giver. **keep up** *v.* maintain at the current level. **keep up with** *v.* maintain a pace set by (someone). **keep up with the Joneses**

Informal compete with friends or neighbours in material possessions.

keg *n.* small metal beer barrel.

kelp *n.* large brown seaweed.

kelvin *n.* SI unit of temperature. **Kelvin scale** temperature scale starting at absolute zero (−273.15° Celsius).

ken *n.* **1.** range of knowledge. —*v.* **kenning, kenned** *or* **kent. 2.** *Scot.* know.

kendo *n.* Japanese sport of fencing using wooden staves.

kennel *n.* **1.** hutlike shelter for a dog. —*pl.* **2.** place for breeding, boarding, or training dogs.

kepi *n.* French military cap with a flat top and horizontal peak.

kept *v.* past of KEEP.

keratin *n.* fibrous protein found in the hair and nails.

kerb *n.* stone edging to a footpath. **kerb crawling** act of driving slowly beside a pavement to pick up a prostitute.

kerchief *n.* piece of cloth worn over the head or round the neck.

kerfuffle *n. Informal* commotion or disorder.

kermes [**kur**-meez] *n.* red dyestuff obtained from dried insects.

kernel *n.* **1.** inner seed of a nut or fruit stone. **2.** central and essential part of something.

kerosene *n. US* paraffin.

kestrel *n.* small falcon.

ketch *n.* two-masted sailing ship.

ketchup *n.* thick cold sauce, usu. made of tomatoes.

kettle *n.* container with a spout and handle used for boiling water. **a fine kettle of fish** an awkward situation. **kettledrum** *n.* large metal drum with a brass bottom.

key[1] *n.* **1.** device for operating a lock by moving a bolt. **2.** device turned to wind a clock, operate a machine, etc. **3.** any of a set of levers or buttons pressed to operate a typewriter, computer, or musical keyboard instrument. **4.** *Music* set of related notes. **5.** list of explanations of codes, symbols, etc. **6.** something crucial in providing an explanation or interpretation. **7.** means of achieving a desired end. —*v.* **8.** (foll. by *to*) adjust to. **9.** (also **key in**) keyboard. —*adj.* **10.** of great

importance. **keyed up** very excited or nervous.

key[2] *n.* same as CAY.

keyboard *n.* **1.** set of keys on a piano, typewriter, etc. **2.** musical instrument played using a keyboard. —*v.* **3.** enter (text) using a keyboard.

keyhole *n.* opening for inserting a key into a lock.

keynote *n.* **1.** dominant idea of a speech etc. **2.** basic note of a musical key.

keyring *n.* decorative metal ring for keeping keys on.

keystone *n.* central stone of an arch which locks the others in position.

kg kilogram(s).

KG Knight of the Order of the Garter.

KGB *n.* Soviet secret police.

khaki *adj.* **1.** dull yellowish-brown. —*n.* **2.** hard-wearing fabric of this colour used for military uniforms.

khan *n.* title of respect in Afghanistan and central Asia.

kHz kilohertz.

kibbutz *n., pl.* **kibbutzim.** communal farm or factory in Israel.

kibosh *n.* **put the kibosh on** *Slang* put a stop to.

kick *v.* **1.** drive, push, or strike with the foot. **2.** score with a kick. **3.** (of a gun) recoil when fired. **4.** *Informal* object or resist. **5.** *Informal* free oneself of (an addiction). —*n.* **6.** thrust or blow with the foot. **7.** recoil. **8.** *Informal* excitement or thrill. **kickback** *n.* money paid illegally for favours done. **kick off** *v.* **1.** start a game of football. **2.** *Informal* begin. **kickoff** *n.* **kick out** *v.* dismiss or expel forcibly. **kick-start** *n.* **1.** (also **kick-starter**) pedal on a motorcycle that is kicked downwards to start the engine. —*v.* **2.** start (a motorcycle) by kicking this pedal. **kick up** *v. Informal* create (a fuss).

kid[1] *n.* **1.** young goat. **2.** leather made from the skin of a kid. **3.** *Informal* child.

kid[2] *v.* **kidding, kidded.** *Informal* tease or deceive (someone).

kidnap *v.* **-napping, -napped.** seize and hold (a person) to ransom. **kidnapper** *n.*

kidney *n.* **1.** either of the pair of organs that filter waste products from the blood to produce urine. **2.** animal kidney used as food. **kidney bean** reddish-brown kidney-shaped bean, edible when cooked.

kill v. **1.** cause the death of. **2.** put an end to. **3.** pass (time). **4.** *Informal* cause (someone) pain or discomfort. —n. **5.** act of killing. **6.** animals or birds killed in a hunt. **killer** n. **killing** *Informal* —adj. **1.** very tiring. **2.** very funny. —n. **3.** sudden financial success. **killjoy** n. person who spoils others' pleasure.

kiln n. oven for baking, drying, or processing pottery, bricks, etc.

kilo n. short for KILOGRAM.

kilo- *combining form* one thousand, e.g. *kilolitre.*

kilobyte n. *Computers* 1000 or 1024 units of information.

kilocalorie n. one thousand calories.

kilogram, kilogramme n. one thousand grams.

kilohertz n. one thousand hertz.

kilojoule n. one thousand joules.

kilometre n. one thousand metres.

kilowatt n. *Electricity* one thousand watts. **kilowatt-hour** n. unit of energy equal to the work done by a power of one thousand watts in an hour.

kilt n. knee-length pleated tartan skirt worn orig. by Scottish Highlanders. **kilted** adj.

kimono [kim-**moan**-no] n., pl. **-nos. 1.** loose wide-sleeved Japanese robe, fastened with a sash. **2.** European dressing gown resembling this.

kin n. person's relatives collectively.

-kin n. suffix small, e.g. *lambkin.*

kind[1] adj. considerate, friendly, and helpful. **kindness** n. **kindly** adj. **-lier, liest. 1.** having a warm-hearted nature. **2.** pleasant or agreeable. —adv. **3.** in a considerate way. **4.** please, e.g. *will you kindly be quiet!* **kindliness** n. **kind-hearted** adj.

kind[2] n. **1.** class or group with common characteristics. **2.** essential nature or character. **in kind 1.** (of payment) in goods rather than money. **2.** with something similar. **kind of** to a certain extent.
▷ Note the singular/plural usage: *this* (or *that*) *kind of dog; these* (or *those*) *kinds of dog.* In the second, plural example, you can also say *these kinds of dogs.*

kindergarten n. class or school for children of about four to six years old.

kindle v. **1.** set (a fire) alight. **2.** (of a fire)

start to burn. **3.** arouse or be aroused. **kindling** n. dry wood or straw for starting fires.

kindred adj. **1.** having similar qualities. **2.** related. —n. **3.** person's relatives collectively.

kine pl. n. *Obs.* cows or cattle.

kinetic [kin-**net**-ik] adj. relating to or caused by motion.

king n. **1.** male ruler of a monarchy. **2.** ruler or chief. **3.** best or most important of its kind. **4.** most important piece in chess. **5.** playing card with a picture of a king on it. **kingly** adj. **-lier, -liest. kingship** n. **kingdom** n. **1.** state ruled by a king or queen. **2.** division of the natural world. **king-size, king-sized** adj. *Informal* larger than standard size.

kingfisher n. small bird with a bright greenish-blue and orange plumage, that dives for fish.

kingpin n. most important person in an organization.

kink n. **1.** twist or bend in rope, wire, hair, etc. **2.** *Informal* quirk in someone's personality. **kinky** adj. **kinkier, kinkiest. 1.** full of kinks. **2.** *Slang* given to deviant or unusual sexual practices.

kinsfolk pl. n. same as KIN.

kinship n. **1.** blood relationship. **2.** state of having common characteristics.

kinsman, kinswoman n. relative.

kiosk n. **1.** small booth selling drinks, cigarettes, newspapers, etc. **2.** public telephone box.

kip n., v. **kipping, kipped.** *Informal* sleep.

kipper n. cleaned, salted, and smoked herring.

kirk n. *Scot.* church.

Kirsch n. brandy made from cherries.

kismet n. fate or destiny.

kiss v. **1.** touch with the lips in affection or greeting. **2.** join lips with a person in love or desire. —n. **3.** touch with the lips. **kisser** n. *Slang* mouth or face. **kissagram** n. greetings service in which a messenger kisses the person celebrating. **kiss of life** mouth-to-mouth resuscitation.

kit n. **1.** outfit or equipment for a specific purpose. **2.** set of pieces of equipment sold ready to be assembled. **kitbag** n. bag for a soldier's or traveller's belongings. **kit out** v.

kitting, kitted. provide with clothes or equipment needed for a particular activity.

kitchen *n.* room used for cooking. **kitchenette** *n.* small kitchen. **kitchen garden** garden for growing vegetables, herbs, etc.

kite *n.* 1. light frame covered with a thin material flown on a string in the wind. 2. large hawk with a forked tail. **Kite mark** official mark on articles approved by the British Standards Institution.

kith *n.* **kith and kin** friends and relatives.

kitsch *n.* vulgarized or pretentious art or literature with popular sentimental appeal.

kitten *n.* young cat. **kittenish** *adj.* lively and flirtatious.

kittiwake *n.* type of seagull.

kitty *n.*, *pl.* **-ties.** 1. pool in certain gambling games. 2. communal fund for buying drinks etc.

kiwi *n.* 1. NZ flightless bird with a stout beak and no tail. 2. *Informal* a New Zealander. **kiwi fruit** edible fruit with a fuzzy brownish-skin and green flesh.

kJ kilojoule(s).

klaxon *n.* loud horn used on emergency vehicles as a warning signal.

kleptomania *n.* compulsive tendency to steal. **kleptomaniac** *n.*

km kilometre(s).

knack *n.* 1. skilful way of doing something. 2. innate ability.

knacker *n.* 1. buyer of old horses for killing. —*v.* 2. *Slang* exhaust. **knackered** *adj.*

knapsack *n.* soldier's or traveller's bag worn strapped on the back.

knave *n.* 1. jack at cards. 2. *Obs.* rogue. **knavery** *n.* dishonest behaviour.

knead *v.* 1. work (flour) into dough using the hands. 2. squeeze or press with the hands.

knee *n.* 1. joint between thigh and lower leg. 2. part of a garment covering the knee. 3. lap. —*v.* 4. *kneeing, kneed.* 4. strike or push with the knee. **kneecap** *n.* 1. bone in front of the knee. —*v.* 2. shoot in the kneecap. **kneejerk** *adj.* (of a reply or reaction) automatic and predictable. **knees-up** *n.* *Informal* party.

kneel *v.* **kneeling, kneeled** *or* **knelt.** fall or rest on one's knees.

knell *n.* 1. sound of a bell, esp. at a funeral or death. 2. portent of doom.

knew *v.* past tense of KNOW.

knickerbockers *pl. n.* loose-fitting short trousers gathered in at the knee.

knickers *pl. n.* woman's or girl's undergarment covering the lower trunk and having legs or legholes.

knick-knack *n.* trifle or trinket.

knife *n.*, *pl.* **knives.** 1. cutting tool or weapon consisting of a sharp-edged blade with a handle. —*v.* 2. cut or stab with a knife. **knife edge** critical point in the development of a situation.

knight *n.* 1. honorary title given to a man by the British sovereign. 2. *Hist.* man who served his lord as a mounted armoured soldier. 3. chess piece shaped like a horse's head. —*v.* 4. award a knighthood to. **knighthood** *n.* **knightly** *adj.*

knit *v.* **knitting, knitted** *or* **knit.** 1. make (a garment) by interlocking a series of loops in wool or other yarn. 2. draw (one's eyebrows) together. 3. join closely together. **knitter** *n.* **knitting** *n.* **knitwear** *n.* knitted clothes, such as sweaters.

knives *n.* plural of KNIFE.

knob *n.* 1. rounded projection, such as a switch on a radio. 2. rounded handle on a door or drawer. 3. small amount of butter. **knobbly** *adj.* covered with small bumps.

knock *v.* 1. give a blow or push to. 2. rap audibly with the knuckles. 3. make or drive by striking. 4. *Informal* criticize adversely. 5. (of an engine) make a regular banging noise as a result of a fault. —*n.* 6. blow or rap. 7. knocking sound. **knocker** *n.* metal fitting for knocking on a door. **knock about, around** *v.* 1. travel or wander. 2. hit or kick brutally. **knockabout** *adj.* (of comedy) boisterous. **knock back** *v.* *Informal* 1. drink quickly. 2. cost. 3. reject or refuse. **knock down** *v.* reduce the price of. **knockdown** *adj.* (of a price) very low **knock-knees** *pl. n.* legs that curve in at the knees. **knock-kneed** *adj.* **knock off** *v.* 1. take (a specified amount) off a price. 2. *Informal* make or do (something) hurriedly or easily. 3. *Informal* cease work. 4. *Informal* steal. **knock-on effect** indirect result of an action or decision. **knock out** *v.* 1. render (someone) unconscious. 2. *Informal* overwhelm or amaze. 3. defeat in a knockout competition. **knockout** *n.* 1. blow that renders an opponent unconscious. 2. competition from which competitors are progressively eliminated. **3.** *Informal* overwhelmingly attractive person or thing. **knock up** *v.* **1.** assemble (something) quickly. **2.** *Informal* waken. **3.** *Slang* make pregnant. **knock-up** *n.* practice session at tennis, squash, or badminton.

knoll *n.* small rounded hill.

knot *n.* **1.** fastening made by looping and pulling tight strands of string, cord, or rope. **2.** tangle, e.g. of hair. **3.** small cluster or huddled group. **4.** round lump or spot in timber. **5.** unit of speed used by ships, equal to one nautical mile per hour. —*v.* **knotting, knotted. 6.** tie with or into a knot. **knotty** *adj.* **-tier, -tiest. 1.** full of knots. **2.** puzzling or difficult.

know *v.* **knowing, knew, known. 1.** be aware of. **2.** be or feel certain of the truth of (information etc.). **3.** be acquainted with. **4.** have a grasp of or understand (a skill or language). **in the know** *Informal* informed or aware. **knowable** *adj.* **knowing** *adj.* cunning or shrewd. **knowingly** *adv.* **1.** shrewdly. **2.** deliberately. **know-all** *n.* *Offens.* person who acts as if knowing more than other people. **know-how** *n.* *Informal* ingenuity, aptitude, or skill.

knowledge *n.* **1.** facts or experiences known by a person. **2.** state of knowing. **3.** specific information on a subject. **knowledgeable, knowledgable** *adj.* intelligent or well-informed. **knowledgeably, knowledgably** *adv.*

knuckle *n.* **1.** bone at the finger joint. **2.** knee joint of a calf or pig. **near the knuckle** *Informal* rather rude or offensive. **knuckleduster** *n.* metal appliance worn on the knuckles to add force to a blow. **knuckle under** *v.* yield or submit.

KO knockout.

koala *n.* tree-dwelling Aust. marsupial with dense grey fur.

kohl *n.* cosmetic powder used to darken the edges of the eyelids.

kohlrabi [kole-**rah**-bee] *n.* type of cabbage with an edible stem.

kook *n.* *US informal* eccentric person. **kooky** *adj.* **kookier, kookiest.**

kookaburra *n.* large Aust. kingfisher with a cackling cry.

kopeck *n.* Soviet monetary unit, one hundredth of a rouble.

kopje, koppie *n.* *S Afr.* small hill.

Koran *n.* sacred book of Islam.

Korean *n.* **1.** language of North and South Korea. **2.** person from North or South Korea. —*adj.* **3.** of North or South Korea or their language.

kosher [**koh**-sher] *adj.* **1.** conforming to Jewish religious law, esp. (of food) to Jewish dietary law. **2.** *Informal* legitimate or authentic. —*n.* **3.** kosher food.

kowtow *v.* **1.** touch one's forehead to the ground in deference. **2.** be servile (towards).

kph kilometres per hour.

Kr *Chem.* krypton.

kraal *n.* *S Afr.* village surrounded by a strong fence.

kraken *n.* mythical Norwegian sea monster.

Kremlin *n.* central government of the Soviet Union.

krill *n.,* *pl.* **krill.** small shrimplike sea creature.

kris *n.* Malayan or Indonesian knife with a scalloped edge.

krona *n.,* *pl.* **krona.** standard monetary unit of Sweden.

krone [**kroh**-na] *n.,* *pl.* **-ner** [-ner] standard monetary unit of Norway and Denmark.

krypton *n.* colourless gas present in the atmosphere and used in fluorescent lights.

KS Kansas.

kudos [**kyoo**-doss] *n.* fame or credit.

kudu *n.* Afr. antelope with spiral horns.

Ku Klux Klan *n.* secret organization of White Protestant Americans who use violence against African Americans and Jews.

kukri *n.* heavy curved Gurkha knife.

kulak *n.* *Hist.* independent well-to-do Russian peasant.

kümmel *n.* German liqueur flavoured with caraway seeds.

kumquat [**kumm**-kwott] *n.* citrus fruit resembling a tiny orange.

kung fu *n.* Chinese martial art combining techniques of judo and karate.

kW kilowatt.

kWh kilowatt-hour.

KY Kentucky.

L

l litre.

L 1. large. **2.** Latin. **3.** learner (driver). **4.** the Roman numeral for fifty.

L., l. lake.

la n. Music same as LAH.

La Chem. lanthanum.

LA Louisiana.

lab n. Informal short for LABORATORY.

Lab. Labour.

label n. **1.** piece of card or other material fixed to an object to show its ownership, destination, etc. **2.** brief descriptive term. —v. **labelling, labelled. 3.** give a label to. **4.** describe in a phrase.

labia pl. n., sing. **labium.** four liplike folds of skin forming part of the female genitals. **labial** [lay-bee-al] adj. **1.** of the lips. **2.** pronounced with the lips. —n. **3.** labial sound.

laboratory n., pl. **-ries.** building or room designed for scientific research or for the teaching of practical science.

laborious adj. involving great prolonged effort. **laboriously** adv.

labour n. **1.** physical work or exertion. **2.** final stage of pregnancy, leading to child-birth. **3.** workers in industry. —v. **4.** work hard. **5.** be at a disadvantage because of a mistake or false belief. **6.** stress to excess or too persistently. **7.** make one's way with difficulty. **laboured** adj. uttered or done with difficulty. **labourer** n. person who labours, esp. someone doing manual work for wages. **Labour Party** major British left-wing political party advocating democratic socialism and social equality.

labrador n. large retriever dog with a yellow or black coat.

laburnum n. ornamental tree with yellow hanging flowers.

labyrinth [lab-er-inth] n. **1.** network of tortuous passages, maze. **2.** interconnecting cavities in the internal ear. **3.** complex system. **labyrinthine** adj.

lac n. resinous substance secreted by some insects.

lace n. **1.** delicate decorative fabric made from threads woven into an open weblike pattern. **2.** cord drawn through eyelets and tied. —v. **3.** fasten with laces. **4.** thread a cord or string through holes in something. **5.** add a small amount of alcohol, a drug, etc. to (food or drink). **lacy** adj. fine, like lace. **lace-ups** pl. n. shoes which fasten with laces.

lacerate [lass-er-rate] v. **1.** tear (flesh) jaggedly. **2.** wound (feelings). **laceration** n.

lachrymal adj. same as LACRIMAL.

lachrymose adj. **1.** tearful. **2.** sad.

lack n. **1.** shortage or absence of something needed or wanted. —v. **2.** need or be short of (something).

lackadaisical adj. **1.** lacking vitality and purpose. **2.** lazy and careless in a dreamy way.

lackey n. **1.** servile follower. **2.** uniformed male servant.

lacklustre adj. lacking brilliance or vitality.

laconic adj. using only a few words, terse. **laconically** adv.

lacquer n. **1.** hard varnish for wood or metal. **2.** clear sticky substance sprayed onto the hair to hold it in place. —v. **3.** apply lacquer to.

lacrimal [lack-rim-al] adj. of tears or the glands which produce them.

lacrosse n. sport in which teams catch and throw a ball using long sticks with a pouched net at the end, in an attempt to score goals.

lactation n. secretion of milk by female mammals to feed young. **lacteal** adj. **1.** of milk. **2.** containing chyle. **lactic** adj. of or derived from milk. **lactose** n. white crystalline sugar found in milk.

lacuna [lak-kew-na] n., pl. **-nae, -nas.** gap or missing part, esp. in a document or series.

lad n. boy or young fellow.

ladder n. **1.** frame of two poles connected by horizontal steps used for climbing. **2.** line of stitches that have come undone in a stocking or tights. **3.** system with ascending stages, e.g. the social ladder. —v. **4.** have or cause to have such a line of undone stitches.

laden *adj.* **1.** loaded. **2.** burdened.

la-di-da, lah-di-dah *adj. Informal* affected or pretentious.

ladle *n.* **1.** spoon with a long handle and a large bowl, used for serving soup etc. —*v.* **2.** serve out liquid with a ladle.

lady *n.*, *pl.* **-dies. 1.** woman regarded as having characteristics of good breeding or high rank. **2.** polite term of address for a woman. **3.** (L-) title of some women of rank. Our Lady the Virgin Mary. Lady Day Feast of the Annunciation, March 25. **lady-in-waiting** *n.*, *pl.* **ladies-in-waiting.** female servant of a queen or princess. **ladykiller** *n. Informal* man who is or thinks he is irresistible to women. **ladylike** *adj.* polite, well-mannered. **Ladyship** *n.* title of address for a Lady.

ladybird *n.* small red beetle with black spots.

lag[1] *v.* **lagging, lagged. 1.** go too slowly, fall behind. —*n.* **2.** delay between events. **laggard** *n.* person who lags behind.

lag[2] *v.* **lagging, lagged.** wrap (a boiler, pipes, etc.) with insulating material. **lagging** *n.* insulating material.

lag[3] *n.* old lag *Slang* convict.

lager *n.* light-bodied type of beer.

lagoon *n.* saltwater lake enclosed by an atoll or separated by a sandbank from the sea.

lah *n. Music* in tonic sol-fa, sixth degree of any major scale.

laid *v.* past of LAY[1]. **laid-back** *adj. Informal* relaxed.

lain *v.* past participle of LIE[2]

lair *n.* **1.** resting place of an animal. **2.** *Informal* hiding place.

laird *n.* Scottish landowner.

laissez-faire [less-ay-**fair**] *n.* principle of nonintervention, esp. by a government in commercial affairs.

laity [**lay**-it-ee] *n.* people who are not members of the clergy.

lake[1] *n.* expanse of water entirely surrounded by land. **lakeside** *n.*

lake[2] *n.* red pigment.

lam *v.* **lamming, lammed.** *Slang* beat or hit.

lama *n.* Buddhist priest in Tibet or Mongolia. **lamasery** *n.* monastery of lamas.

lamb *n.* **1.** young of sheep. **2.** its meat. **3.** innocent or helpless creature. —*v.* **4.** (of sheep) give birth to a lamb or lambs. **lambskin** *n.* **lambswool** *n.*

lambaste, lambast *v.* **1.** beat or thrash. **2.** reprimand severely.

lambent *adj. Lit.* (of a flame) flickering softly.

lame *adj.* **1.** having an injured or disabled leg or foot. **2.** (of an excuse) unconvincing. —*v.* **3.** make lame. **lamely** *adv.* **lameness** *n.* **lame duck** person or thing unable to cope without help.

lamé [**lah**-may] *n.*, *adj.* (fabric) interwoven with gold or silver thread.

lament *v.* **1.** feel or express sorrow (for). —*n.* **2.** passionate expression of grief. **3.** song of grief. **lamentable** *adj.* deplorable. **lamentation** *n.* **lamented** *adj.* grieved for.

laminate *v.* **1.** make (a sheet of material) by bonding together two or more thin sheets. **2.** cover with a thin sheet of material. **3.** split or beat into thin sheets. —*n.* **4.** laminated sheet. **laminated** *adj.* **lamination** *n.*

Lammas *n.* August 1st, formerly a harvest festival.

lamp *n.* device which produces light from electricity, oil, or gas. **lampblack** *n.* pigment made from soot. **lamppost** *n.* post supporting a lamp in the street. **lampshade** *n.*

lampoon *n.* **1.** humorous satire ridiculing someone. —*v.* **2.** satirize or ridicule.

lamprey *n.* eel-like fish with a round sucking mouth.

lance *n.* **1.** long spear used by a mounted soldier. —*v.* **2.** pierce (a boil or abscess) with a lancet. **lancer** *n.* formerly, cavalry soldier armed with a lance. —*pl.* **2.** square dance. **lance corporal** lowest noncommissioned rank in the army.

lanceolate *adj.* narrow and tapering to a point at each end.

lancet *n.* **1.** pointed two-edged surgical knife. **2.** narrow window in the shape of a pointed arch.

land *n.* **1.** solid part of the earth's surface. **2.** ground, esp. with reference to its type or use. **3.** rural or agricultural area. **4.** property consisting of land. **5.** country or region. —*v.* **6.** come or bring to earth after a flight, jump, or fall. **7.** go or take from a ship at the end of a voyage. **8.** come to or touch shore.

9. come or bring to some point or condition. **10.** *Informal* obtain. **11.** take (a hooked fish) from the water. **12.** *Informal* deliver (a punch). **landed** *adj.* possessing or consisting of lands. **landless** *adj.* **landward** *adj.* **1.** nearest to or facing the land. —*adv.* **2.** (also **landwards**) towards land. **land mine** explosive device laid in the ground. **land up** *v.* arrive at a final point or condition.

landau [lan-daw] *n.* four-wheeled carriage with a folding hood.

landfall *n.* ship's first landing after a voyage.

landing *n.* **1.** floor area at the top of a flight of stairs. **2.** bringing or coming to land. **3.** (also **landing stage**) place where people or goods go onto or come off a boat. **landing gear** undercarriage of an aircraft.

landlocked *adj.* completely surrounded by land.

landlord, landlady *n.* **1.** person who rents out land, houses, etc. **2.** owner or manager of a pub or boarding house.

landlubber *n.* person who is not experienced at sea.

landmark *n.* **1.** prominent object in or feature of a landscape. **2.** event, decision, etc. considered as an important development.

landscape *n.* **1.** extensive piece of inland scenery seen from one place. **2.** picture of it. —*v.* **3.** improve natural features of (a piece of land).

landslide *n.* **1.** (also **landslip**) falling of soil, rock, etc. down the side of a mountain. **2.** overwhelming electoral victory.

lane *n.* **1.** narrow road. **2.** area of road for one stream of traffic. **3.** specified route followed by ships or aircraft. **4.** strip of a running track or swimming pool for use by one competitor.

language *n.* **1.** system of sounds, symbols, etc. for communicating thought. **2.** particular system used by a nation or people. **3.** style or method of expression. **4.** system of words and symbols for computer programming.

languid *adj.* **1.** lacking energy or enthusiasm. **2.** sluggish. **languidly** *adv.*

languish *v.* **1.** suffer neglect or hardship. **2.** lose or diminish in strength or vigour. **3.** pine (for). **languishing** *adj.*

languor [lang-ger] *n.* **1.** laziness or weariness. **2.** dreamy relaxation. **3.** oppressive stillness. **languorous** *adj.*

lank *adj.* **1.** (of hair) greasy and limp. **2.** lean and tall. **lanky** *adj.* ungracefully tall and thin. **lankiness** *n.*

lanolin *n.* grease from sheep's wool used in ointments etc.

lantern *n.* **1.** light in a transparent protective case. **2.** structure on top of a dome for admitting light. **3.** chamber in a lighthouse that houses the light. **lantern jaw** long thin jaw. **lantern-jawed** *adj.*

lanthanum *n.* silvery-white metallic element. **lanthanide series** class of 15 elements chemically related to lanthanum.

lanyard *n.* **1.** short cord worn round the neck to hold a knife or whistle. **2.** *Naut.* short rope.

lap[1] *n.* part between the waist and knees of a person when sitting. **lapdog** *n.* small pet dog. **laptop** *adj.* (of a computer) small enough to fit on a user's lap.

lap[2] *n.* **1.** single circuit of a racecourse or track. **2.** stage of a journey. **3.** overlap. —*v.* **lapping, lapped. 4.** overtake an opponent so as to be one or more circuits ahead. **5.** enfold or wrap around.

lap[3] *v.* **lapping, lapped.** (of waves) beat softly against (a shore etc.). **lap up** *v.* **1.** drink by scooping up with the tongue. **2.** accept (information or attention) eagerly.

lapel [lap-pel] *n.* part of the front of a coat or jacket folded back towards the shoulders.

lapidary *adj.* **1.** of stones, esp. gemstones. —*n.* **2.** cutter of or dealer in gemstones.

lapis lazuli [lap-iss lazz-yoo-lie] *n.* bright blue gemstone.

Lapp *n., adj.* (member or language) of a people living chiefly in N Scandinavia.

lapse *n.* **1.** temporary drop in a standard, esp. through forgetfulness or carelessness. **2.** instance of bad behaviour by someone usually well-behaved. **3.** break in occurrence or usage. —*v.* **4.** drop in standard. **5.** end or become invalid, esp. through disuse. **6.** (of time) slip away. **7.** abandon religious faith. **lapsed** *adj.*

lapwing *n.* plover with a tuft of feathers on the head.

larboard *n., adj. Old-fashioned* port (side of a ship).

larceny *n., pl.* **-nies.** theft.

larch *n.* deciduous coniferous tree.

lard *n.* **1.** soft white fat obtained from a pig. —*v.* **2.** insert strips of bacon in (meat) before cooking. **3.** decorate (speech or writing) with strange words unnecessarily.

larder *n.* storeroom for food.

large *adj.* **1.** great in size, number, or extent. **2.** comprehensive. **at large 1.** free, not confined. **2.** in general. **3.** fully. **largely** *adv.* **largish** *adj.* **large-scale** *adj.* wide-ranging or extensive.

largesse, largess [lar-**jess**] *n.* generous giving, esp. of money.

largo *n., pl.* **-gos,** *adv. Music* (piece to be played) in a slow and dignified manner.

lariat *n.* **1.** lasso. **2.** rope for tethering animals.

lark[1] *n.* small brown songbird, skylark.

lark[2] *n. Informal* **1.** harmless piece of mischief. **2.** unnecessary activity or job. **lark about** *v.* play pranks.

larkspur *n.* plant with spikes of blue, pink, or white flowers with spurs.

larva *n., pl.* **-vae.** insect in an immature stage, often resembling a worm. **larval** *adj.*

larynx *n., pl.* **larynges.** part of the throat containing the vocal cords. **laryngeal** *adj.* **laryngitis** *n.* inflammation of the larynx.

lasagne, lasagna [laz-**zan**-ya] *n.* **1.** pasta in wide flat sheets. **2.** dish made from layers of lasagne, meat, vegetables, etc.

lascar *n.* E Indian seaman.

lascivious [lass-**iv**-ee-uss] *adj.* lustful. **lasciviously** *adv.*

laser [**lay**-zer] *n.* device for concentrating light of mixed frequencies into an intense narrow beam.

lash[1] *n.* **1.** sharp blow with a whip. **2.** flexible end of a whip. **3.** eyelash. —*v.* **4.** hit with a whip. **5.** (of rain or waves) beat forcefully against. **6.** attack verbally, scold. **7.** flick or wave sharply to and fro. **8.** urge as with a whip. **lash out** *v.* **1.** make a sudden physical or verbal attack. **2.** *Informal* spend (money) extravagantly.

lash[2] *v.* fasten or bind tightly with cord etc.

lashings *pl. n. Informal* large amount.

lass, lassie *n.* girl.

Lassa fever *n.* serious African disease with high fever and muscular pains.

lassitude *n.* physical or mental weariness.

lasso [lass-**oo**] *n., pl.* **-sos, -soes. 1.** rope with a noose for catching cattle and horses. —*v.* **-soing, -soed. 2.** catch with a lasso.

last[1] *adj., adv.* **1.** coming at the end or after all others. **2.** most recent(ly). —*adj.* **3.** only remaining. —*n.* **4.** last person or thing. **lastly** *adv.* finally. **last-ditch** *adj.* done as a final resort. **Last Judgment** God's verdict on the destinies of all humans at the end of the world. **last post** army bugle-call played at sunset or funerals. **last straw** small irritation or setback that, coming after others, is too much to bear. **last thing** at the end of the day. **last word 1.** final comment in an argument. **2.** most recent or best example of something.

last[2] *v.* **1.** continue. **2.** be sufficient for (a specified amount of time). **3.** remain fresh, uninjured, or unaltered. **lasting** *adj.*

last[3] *n.* model of a foot on which shoes and boots are made or repaired.

lat. latitude.

latch *n.* **1.** fastening for a door with a bar and lever. **2.** lock which can only be opened from the outside with a key. —*v.* **3.** fasten with a latch. **latchkey** *n.* key for a latch. **latch onto** *v.* become attached to (a person or idea).

late *adj.* **1.** arriving or occurring after the normal or expected time. **2.** towards the end of (a period of time). **3.** recently dead. **4.** recent. **5.** former. —*adv.* **6.** after the normal or expected time. **7.** recently. **8.** at a relatively advanced age. **lately** *adv.* not long since. **lateness** *n.* **latish** *adj., adv.* **latecomer** *n.*

lateen sail *n.* triangular sail on a long yard hoisted to the head of a mast.

latent *adj.* hidden and not yet developed. **latency** *n.*

lateral [**lat**-ter-al] *adj.* of, at, to, or from the side. **laterally** *adv.* **lateral thinking** way of solving problems by apparently illogical methods.

latex *n.* milky sap found in some plants, esp. the rubber tree, used in making rubber and glue.

lath *n.* thin strip of wood used to support plaster, tiles, etc.

lathe *n.* machine for turning wood or metal while it is being shaped.

lather *n.* **1.** froth of soap and water. **2.** frothy sweat. **3.** *Informal* state of agitation. —*v.* **4.** make frothy. **5.** rub with soap until lather appears.

Latin n. 1. language of the ancient Romans. —adj. 2. of or in Latin. 3. of a people whose language derives from Latin. 4. of the Roman Catholic Church. **Latin America** parts of South and Central America whose official language is Spanish or Portuguese. **Latin American** n., adj.

latitude n. 1. angular distance measured in degrees N or S of the equator. 2. scope for freedom of action or thought. —pl. 3. regions considered in relation to their distance from the equator. **latitudinal** adj.

latitudinarian adj. liberal, esp. in religious matters.

latrine n. toilet in a barracks or camp.

latter adj. 1. second of two. 2. later. 3. more recent. **latterly** adv. **latter-day** adj. modern.
▷ *Latter* is used for the last mentioned of two items. When there are more, use *last-named*.

lattice [lat-iss] n. 1. framework of intersecting strips of wood, metal, etc. 2. gate, screen, etc. formed of such a framework. **latticed** adj.

laud v. praise or glorify. **laudable** adj. praiseworthy. **laudably** adv. **laudatory** adj. praising or glorifying.

laudanum [lawd-a-num] n. opium-based sedative.

laugh v. 1. make inarticulate sounds with the voice expressing amusement, merriment, or scorn. 2. utter or express with laughter. —n. 3. laughing. 4. manner of laughing. 5. *Informal* person or thing causing amusement. **laughable** adj. ludicrous. **laughter** n. sound or action of laughing. **laughing gas** nitrous oxide as an anaesthetic. **laughing stock** object of general derision. **laugh off** v. treat (something serious or difficult) lightly.

launch[1] v. 1. put (a ship or boat) into the water, esp. for the first time. 2. send a missile or spacecraft) into space or the air. 3. begin (a campaign, project, etc.). 4. put a new product on the market. —n. 5. launching. **launcher** n. **launch into** v. start doing something enthusiastically. **launch out** v. start doing something new.

launch[2] n. large open motorboat.

launder v. 1. wash and iron (clothes and linen). 2. make (illegally obtained money) seem legal by passing it through foreign banks or legitimate businesses. **laundry** n.,

pl. **-dries**. 1. place for washing clothes and linen, esp. as a business. 2. clothes etc. for washing or which have recently been washed. **Launderette** n. ® shop with coin-operated washing and drying machines.

laureate [lor-ee-at] adj. crowned with laurel leaves as a sign of honour. **poet laureate** see POET.

laurel n. 1. glossy-leaved shrub, bay tree. —pl. 2. wreath of laurel, an emblem of victory or merit.

lava n. molten rock thrown out by volcanoes, which hardens as it cools.

lavatory n., pl. **-ries**. toilet.

lavender n. 1. shrub with fragrant flowers. —adj. 2. bluish-purple. **lavender water** light perfume made from lavender.

lavish adj. 1. great in quantity or richness. 2. giving or spending generously. 3. extravagant. —v. 4. give or spend generously. **lavishly** adv.

law n. 1. rule binding on a community. 2. system of such rules. 3. *Informal* police. 4. general principle deduced from facts. 5. invariable sequence of events in nature. **lawful** adj. allowed by law. **lawfully** adv. **lawless** adj. breaking the law, esp. in a violent way. **lawlessly** adv. **law-abiding** adj. adhering to the laws. **law-breaker** n. **Law Lords** members of the House of Lords who sit as the highest court of appeal. **lawsuit** n. court case brought by one person or group against another.

lawn[1] n. area of tended and mown grass. **lawn mower** machine for cutting grass. **lawn tennis** tennis, esp. when played on a grass court.

lawn[2] n. fine linen or cotton fabric.

lawrencium n. element artificially produced from californium.

lawyer n. professionally qualified legal expert.

lax adj. not strict. **laxity** n. **laxly** adv.

laxative n., adj. (medicine) having a loosening effect on the bowels.

lay[1] v. **laying, laid.** 1. cause to lie. 2. set in a particular place or position. 3. arrange (a table) for a meal. 4. put forward (a plan, argument, etc.). 5. attribute (blame). 6. (of a bird or reptile) produce eggs. 7. devise or prepare. 8. place (a bet). **lay waste** devastate. **lay-by** n. stopping place for traffic beside a road. **lay down** v. 1. set down. 2.

sacrifice. **3.** formulate (a rule). **4.** store (wine). **lay in** v. accumulate and store. **lay into** v. *Informal* attack or scold severely. **lay off** v. dismiss staff during a slack period. **lay-off** n. **lay on** v. provide or supply. **lay out** v. **1.** arrange or spread out. **2.** prepare (a corpse) for burial. **3.** *Informal* spend money, esp. lavishly. **4.** *Slang* knock unconscious. **layout** n. arrangement, esp. of matter for printing or of a building. **lay up** v. **1.** *Informal* confine through illness. **2.** store for future use.

▷ *Lay* and *lie* are often confused. Lay takes an object: *He laid down his weapon; lie* does not take an object: *I'm going to lie down.*

lay² v. past tense of **LIE²**. **layabout** n. lazy person, loafer.

lay³ adj. **1.** of or involving people who are not clergymen. **2.** nonspecialist. **layman, laywoman** n. **1.** person without specialist knowledge. **2.** person who is not a member of the clergy.

lay⁴ n. short narrative poem designed to be sung.

layer n. **1.** single thickness of some substance, as a stratum or coating on a surface. **2.** laying hen. **3.** shoot of a plant pegged down or partly covered with earth to encourage root growth. —v. **4.** form a layer. **5.** propagate plants by layers. **layered** adj.

layette n. clothes for a newborn baby.

lay figure n. **1.** jointed figure of the body used by artists. **2.** nonentity.

laze v. **1.** be idle or lazy. —n. **2.** lazing.

lazy adj. **lazier, laziest. 1.** not inclined to work or exert oneself. **2.** done in a relaxed manner without much effort. **3.** (of movement) slow and gentle. **lazily** adv. **laziness** n. **lazybones** n. *Informal* lazy person.

lb pound (weight).

lbw *Cricket* leg before wicket.

lc *Printing* lower case.

lea n. *Poetic* meadow.

leach v. remove or be removed from a substance by a liquid passing through it.

lead¹ v. **leading, led. 1.** guide or conduct. **2.** cause to feel, think, or behave in a certain way. **3.** (of a road, path, etc.) go towards. **4.** control or direct. **5.** be, go, or play first. **6.** be the most important person or thing in. **7.** result in. **8.** pass or spend (one's life). —n. **9.** first or most prominent place. **10.** example or leadership. **11.** clue. **12.** amount by

which a person or group is ahead of another. **13.** length of leather or chain attached to a dog's collar to control it. **14.** principal role or actor in a film, play, etc. **15.** cable bringing current to an electrical device. —adj. **16.** acting as a leader or lead. **leading** adj. **1.** principal. **2.** in the first position. **leading light** important person in an organization. **leading question** question worded to prompt the answer desired. **lead-in** n. introduction to a subject. **lead on** v. lure or entice, esp. into wrongdoing. **lead up to** v. act as a preliminary to.

lead² n. **1.** soft heavy grey metal. **2.** in a pencil, graphite. **3.** lead weight on a line, used for sounding depths of water. **4.** thin strip of metal used to widen spaces in printing. —pl. **5.** strips of lead used as a roof covering. —v. **6.** cover or secure with lead. **leaded** adj. (of windows) made from many small panes of glass held together by lead strips. **leaden** adj. **1.** heavy or sluggish. **2.** made from lead. **3.** dull grey.

leader n. **1.** person who leads. **2.** principal first violinist of an orchestra. **3.** (also **leading article**) article in a newspaper expressing editorial views. **leadership** n.

leaf n., pl. **leaves. 1.** flat usu. green blade attached to the stem of a plant. **2.** single sheet of paper in a book. **3.** very thin sheet of metal. **4.** extending flap on a table. **leafy** adj. **leafless** adj. **leaf mould** rich soil composed of decayed leaves. **leaf through** v. turn pages without reading them.

leaflet n. **1.** sheet of printed matter for distribution. **2.** small leaf.

league¹ n. **1.** association promoting the interests of its members. **2.** association of sports clubs organizing competitions between its members. **3.** *Informal* class or level.

league² n. *Obs.* measure of distance, about three miles.

leak n. **1.** hole or defect that allows the escape or entrance of liquid, gas, radiation, etc. **2.** liquid etc. that escapes or enters. **3.** disclosure of secrets. —v. **4.** let fluid etc. in or out. **5.** (of fluid etc.) find its way through a leak. **6.** disclose secret information. **leakage** n. **1.** leaking. **2.** gradual escape or loss. **leaky** adj.

lean¹ v. **leaning, leant** or **leaned. 1.** rest against. **2.** bend or slope from an upright position. **3.** tend (towards). **leaning** n. tendency. **lean on** v. **1.** *Informal* threaten or intimidate. **2.** depend on for help or advice. **lean-to** n. shed built against an existing wall.

lean[2] adj. **1.** thin but healthy-looking. **2.** (of meat) lacking fat. **3.** unproductive. —n. **4.** lean part of meat. **leanness** n.

leap v. **leaping, leapt** or **leaped. 1.** make a sudden powerful jump. —n. **2.** sudden powerful jump. **3.** abrupt increase, as in costs or prices. **leapfrog** n. game in which a player vaults over another bending down. **leap year** year with February 29th as an extra day.

learn v. **learning, learnt** or **learned. 1.** gain skill or knowledge by study, practice, or teaching. **2.** memorize (something). **3.** find out or discover. **learned** adj. **1.** erudite, deeply read. **2.** showing much learning. **learner** n. **learning** n. knowledge got by study.

lease n. **1.** contract by which land or property is rented for a stated time by the owner to a tenant. **2.** prospect of renewed energy or happiness, e.g. a new lease of life. —v. **3.** let or rent on lease. **leasehold** adj. held on lease. **leaseholder** n.

leash n. lead for a dog.

least adj. **1.** smallest. **2.** superlative of LITTLE. —n. **3.** smallest one. —adv. **4.** in the smallest degree.

leather n. **1.** material made from specially treated animal skins. —v. **2.** beat or thrash. **leathery** adj. like leather, tough. **leatherjacket** n. tough-skinned larva of certain craneflies.

leave[1] v. **leaving, left. 1.** go away from. **2.** allow to remain, accidentally or deliberately. **3.** cause to be or remain in a specified state. **4.** discontinue membership of. **5.** permit. **6.** deposit. **7.** entrust. **8.** bequeath. **leavings** pl. n. something remaining, such as refuse. **leave out** v. exclude or omit.

leave[2] n. **1.** permission to be absent from work or duty. **2.** period of such absence. **3.** permission to do something. **4.** formal parting.

leaven [lev-ven] n. **1.** yeast. **2.** influence that produces a gradual change. —v. **3.** raise with leaven. **4.** spread through and influence (something).

lecher n. lecherous man. **lechery** n.

lecherous [letch-er-uss] adj. (of a man) having or showing excessive sexual desire. **lecherously** adv. **lecherousness** n.

lectern n. sloping reading desk, esp. in a church.

lecture n. **1.** informative talk to an audience on a subject. **2.** lengthy rebuke or scolding. —v. **3.** give a talk. **4.** reprove. **lecturer** n. **lectureship** n. appointment as a lecturer.

led v. past of LEAD[1].

LED light-emitting diode.

ledge n. **1.** narrow shelf sticking out from a wall. **2.** shelflike projection from a cliff etc.

ledger n. book of debit and credit accounts of a firm. **ledger line** short line above or below the staff for notes outside the range of the staff.

lee n. **1.** sheltered part or side. **2.** side away from the wind. **leeward** adj., n. **1.** (on) the lee side. —adv. **2.** towards this side. **leeway** n. **1.** room for free movement within limits. **2.** sideways drift of a boat or plane.

leech n. **1.** species of bloodsucking worm. **2.** person who lives off others.

leek n. vegetable of the onion family with a long bulb and thick stem.

leer v. **1.** look or grin at in a sneering or suggestive manner. —n. **2.** sneering or suggestive look or grin.

leery adj. **1.** Informal suspicious or wary (of). **2.** sly.

lees pl. n. sediment of wine.

leet n. Scot. list of candidates for a job.

left[1] adj. **1.** denotes the side that faces west when the front faces north. **2.** opposite to right. —n. **3.** left hand or part. **4.** Politics people supporting socialism rather than capitalism. —adv. **5.** on or towards the left. **leftist** n., adj. (person) of the political left. **left-handed** adj. **1.** more adept with the left hand than with the right. **2.** ambiguous or insincere. **left-wing** adj. **1.** socialist. **2.** belonging to the more radical part of a political party. **left-winger** n.

left[2] v. past of LEAVE[1].

leftover n. unused portion of food or material.

leg n. **1.** one of the limbs on which a person or animal walks, runs, or stands. **2.** part of a garment covering the leg. **3.** structure that supports, such as one of the legs of a table. **4.** stage of a journey. **5.** Sport (part of) one game or race in a series. **6.** Cricket part of the field to the left of a right-handed batsman. **pull someone's leg** tease someone. **leggy** adj. long-legged. **legless** adj. **1.** without legs. **2.** *Slang* very drunk. **leggings** *pl. n.* covering of leather or other material for the legs.

legacy *n., pl.* **-cies**. **1.** thing left in a will. **2.** thing handed down to a successor.

legal *adj.* **1.** established or permitted by law. **2.** relating to law or lawyers. **legally** *adv.* **legalism** *n.* strict adherence to the letter of the law. **legalistic** *adj.* **legalize** *v.* make legal. **legalization** *n.* **legality** *n.*

legate *n.* messenger or representative, esp. from the Pope. **legation** *n.* **1.** diplomatic minister and his staff. **2.** official residence of a diplomatic minister.

legatee *n.* recipient of a legacy.

legato [leg-**ah**-toe] *n., pl.* **-tos**, *adv. Music* (piece to be played) smoothly.

legend *n.* **1.** traditional story or myth. **2.** traditional literature. **3.** famous person or event. **4.** stories about such a person or event. **5.** inscription. **6.** explanation of symbols on a map etc. **legendary** *adj.* **1.** of or in legend. **2.** famous.

legerdemain [lej-er-de-**main**] *n.* **1.** sleight of hand. **2.** cunning deception.

leger line *n.* same as LEDGER LINE.

Leghorn *n.* breed of domestic fowl.

legible *adj.* easily read. **legibility** *n.* **legibly** *adv.*

legion *n.* **1.** large military force. **2.** large number. **3.** association of veterans. **4.** infantry unit in the Roman army. **legionary** *adj., n.* **legionnaire** *n.* member of a legion. **legionnaire's disease** serious bacterial disease similar to pneumonia.

legislate *v.* make laws. **legislation** *n.* **1.** legislating. **2.** laws made. **legislative** *adj.* **legislator** *n.* maker of laws. **legislature** *n.* body of people that makes, amends, or repeals the laws of a state.

legitimate *adj.* **1.** authorized by or in accordance with law. **2.** fairly deduced. **3.** born to parents married to each other. —*v.* **4.** make legitimate. **legitimately** *adv.* **legitimacy** *n.* **legitimize** *v.* make legitimate, legalize. **legitimization** *n.*

Lego *n.* ® construction toy of plastic bricks fitted together by studs.

leguaan *n.* large S African lizard.

legume *n.* **1.** pod of a plant of the pea or bean family. —*pl.* **2.** peas or beans. **leguminous** *adj.* (of plants) pod-bearing.

lei *n.* in Hawaii, garland of flowers.

leisure *n.* time for relaxation or hobbies. **at one's leisure** when one has time. **leisurely** *adj.* **1.** deliberate, unhurried. —*adv.* **2.** slowly. **leisured** *adj.* with plenty of spare time. **leisure centre** building with facilities such as a swimming pool, gymnasium, and café.

leitmotif [lite-mote-eef] *n. Music* recurring theme associated with a person, situation, or thought.

lemming *n.* rodent of arctic regions, reputed to run into the sea and drown during mass migrations.

lemon *n.* **1.** yellow acid fruit that grows on trees. **2.** *Slang* useless or defective person or thing. —*adj.* **3.** pale-yellow. **lemonade** *n.* lemon-flavoured soft drink, often fizzy. **lemon curd** creamy spread made of lemons, butter, etc. **lemon sole** edible flatfish.

lemur *n.* nocturnal animal like a small monkey, found on Madagascar.

lend *v.* **lending, lent**. **1.** give the temporary use of. **2.** provide (money) temporarily, often for interest. **3.** add (a quality or effect), e.g. *her presence lent beauty to the scene*. **lend itself to** be suitable for. **lender** *n.*

length *n.* **1.** quality of being long. **2.** extent or measurement from end to end. **3.** duration. **4.** piece of something narrow and long. **at length 1.** in full detail. **2.** at last. **lengthy** *adj.* very long or tiresome. **lengthily** *adv.* **lengthen** *v.* make or become longer. **lengthways, lengthwise** *adj., adv.*

lenient [lee-nee-ent] *adj.* tolerant, not strict or severe. **leniency** *n.* **leniently** *adv.*

lenity *n., adj.* **-ties**. mercy or clemency.

lens *n., pl.* **lenses**. **1.** piece of glass or similar material with one or both sides curved, used to converge or diverge light rays in cameras, spectacles, telescopes, etc. **2.** transparent structure in the eye that focuses light.

lent *v.* past of LEND.

Lent *n.* period from Ash Wednesday to Easter Eve. **Lenten** *adj.* of, in, or suitable to Lent.

lentil *n.* edible seed of a leguminous Asian plant.

lento *n., pl.* **-tos**, *adv. Music* (piece to be played) slowly.

Leo *n.* (the lion) fifth sign of the zodiac.

leonine *adj.* like a lion.

leopard n. large spotted carnivorous animal of the cat family. **leopardess** n. fem.

leotard n. tight-fitting garment covering most of the body, worn by acrobats, dancers, etc.

leper n. 1. person suffering from leprosy. 2. ignored or despised person.

lepidoptera pl. n. order of insects with four wings covered with fine gossamer scales, as moths and butterflies. **lepidopterous** adj. **lepidopterist** n. person who studies or collects butterflies or moths.

leprechaun n. mischievous elf of Irish folklore.

leprosy n. disease attacking the nerves and skin, resulting in loss of feeling in the affected parts. **leprous** adj.

lesbian n. 1. homosexual woman. —adj. 2. of homosexual women. **lesbianism** n.

lese-majesty [lezz-**maj**-est-ee] n. 1. treason. 2. taking of liberties against people in authority.

lesion n. 1. injury or wound. 2. structural change in an organ of the body caused by illness or injury.

less adj. 1. smaller in extent, degree, or duration. 2. not so much. 3. comparative of LITTLE. —n. 4. smaller part or quantity. 5. lesser amount. —adv. 6. to a smaller extent or degree. —prep. 7. after deducting, minus. **lessen** v. make or become smaller or not as much. **lesser** adj. not as great in quantity, size, or worth.

▷ Avoid confusion with few(er). Less is used with amounts that cannot be counted: less time; less fuss. Few(er) is used of things that can be counted.

lessee n. person to whom a lease is granted.

lesson n. 1. single period of instruction in a subject. 2. content of this. 3. experience that teaches. 4. portion of Scripture read in church.

lessor n. person who grants a lease.

lest conj. 1. so as to prevent any possibility that. 2. for fear that.

let[1] v. **letting, let. 1.** allow, enable, or cause. 2. allow to escape. 3. grant use of for rent, lease. 4. used as an auxiliary to express a proposal, command, threat, or assumption. —n. 5. act of letting property. **let alone** not to mention. **let down** v. 1. disappoint. 2. lower. 3. deflate. **letdown** n. disappointment. **let off** v. 1. excuse from (a duty or

punishment). 2. fire or explode (a weapon). 3. emit (gas, steam, etc.). **let on** v. Informal reveal (a secret). **let out** v. 1. emit. 2. release. 3. rent out. **let up** v. diminish or stop. **let-up** n. lessening.

let[2] n. 1. hindrance. 2. Tennis minor infringement or obstruction of the ball requiring a replay of the point.

lethal adj. deadly.

lethargy n. 1. sluggishness or dullness. 2. abnormal lack of energy. **lethargic** adj. **lethargically** adv.

letter n. 1. alphabetical symbol. 2. written message, usu. sent by post. 3. strict meaning (of a law etc.). —pl. n. 4. literary knowledge or ability. **lettered** adj. learned. **lettering** n. **letter bomb** explosive device in a parcel or letter that explodes when it is opened. **letter box 1.** slot in a door through which letters are delivered. 2. box in a street or post office where letters are posted. **letterhead** n. printed heading on stationery giving the sender's name and address.

lettuce n. plant with large green leaves used in salads.

leucocyte [loo-koh-site] n. white blood corpuscle.

leukaemia [loo-**kee**-mee-a] n. disease caused by uncontrolled overproduction of white blood corpuscles.

Levant n. area of the E Mediterranean now occupied by Lebanon, Syria, and Israel.

levee[1] n. 1. US natural or artificial river embankment. 2. landing-place.

levee[2] n. Hist. reception held by the sovereign on rising.

level adj. 1. horizontal. 2. having an even surface. 3. of the same height as something else. 4. equal to or even with (someone or something else). 5. not going above the top edge of (a spoon etc.). 6. not irregular. —v. -elling, -elled. 7. make even or horizontal. 8. make equal in position or status. 9. direct (a gun, accusation, etc.) at. 10. raze to the ground. —n. 11. horizontal line or surface. 12. device for showing or testing if something is horizontal. 13. position on a scale. 14. standard or grade. 15. flat area of land. **on the level** Informal honest or trustworthy. **level crossing** point where a railway line and road cross. **level-headed** adj. not apt to be carried away by emotion.

lever n. 1. rigid bar pivoted about a fulcrum to transfer a force with mechanical advantage. **2.** bar used to move a heavy object or to open something. **3.** handle pressed, pulled, etc. to operate machinery. **4.** means of exerting pressure to achieve an aim. —*v.* **5.** prise or move with a lever. **leverage** *n.* **1.** action or power of a lever. **2.** influence or strategic advantage.

leveret [lev-ver-it] *n.* young hare.

leviathan [lev-vie-ath-an] *n.* **1.** sea monster. **2.** anything huge or formidable.

Levis *pl. n.* ® denim jeans.

levitation *n.* raising of a solid body into the air supernaturally. **levitate** *v.* rise or cause to rise into the air.

levity *n., pl.* **-ties.** inclination to make a joke of serious matters.

levy [lev-vee] *v.* **levying, levied. 1.** impose and collect (a tax). **2.** raise (troops). —*n., pl.* **levies. 3.** imposition or collection of taxes. **4.** enrolling of troops. **5.** amount or number levied.

lewd *adj.* lustful or indecent. **lewdly** *adv.* **lewdness** *n.*

lexicon *n.* **1.** dictionary. **2.** vocabulary of a language. **lexical** *adj.* relating to the vocabulary of a language. **lexicographer** *n.* writer of dictionaries. **lexicography** *n.*

ley *n.* land temporarily under grass.

Li *Chem.* lithium.

liable *adj.* **1.** legally obliged or responsible. **2.** given to or at risk from a condition. **liability** *n.* **1.** state of being liable. **2.** financial obligation. **3.** hindrance or disadvantage.

▷ The use of *liable* to mean 'likely' is informal. It generally means 'responsible for': *He was liable for any damage.*

liaise *v.* establish and maintain communication (with). **liaison** *n.* **1.** communication and contact between groups. **2.** secret or adulterous relationship.

liana *n.* climbing plant in tropical forests.

liar *n.* person who tells lies.

lib *n. Informal* short for LIBERATION.

Lib. Liberal.

libation [lie-bay-shun] *n.* drink poured as an offering to the gods.

libel *n.* **1.** published statement falsely damaging a person's reputation. —*v.* **-belling, -belled. 2.** defame falsely. **libellous** *adj.* defamatory.

liberal *adj.* **1.** (also L-) of a political party

favouring progress and reform. **2.** generous in behaviour or temperament. **3.** tolerant. **4.** abundant. **5.** (of education) designed to develop general cultural interests. —*n.* **6.** person who has liberal ideas or opinions. **liberally** *adv.* **liberalism** *n.* belief in democratic reforms and individual freedom. **liberality** *n.* **1.** generosity. **2.** quality of being broad-minded. **liberalize** *v.* make (laws, a country, etc.) less restrictive. **liberalization** *n.*

liberate *v.* set free. **liberation** *n.* **liberator** *n.*

libertarian *n.* **1.** believer in freedom of thought and action. —*adj.* **2.** having such a belief.

libertine [lib-er-teen] *n.* morally dissolute person.

liberty *n., pl.* **-ties. 1.** freedom. **2.** act or comment regarded as forward or socially unacceptable. **at liberty 1.** free. **2.** having the right. **take liberties** be presumptuous.

libido [lib-ee-doe] *n., pl.* **-dos. 1.** life force. **2.** emotional drive, esp. of sexual origin. **libidinal** *adj.* **libidinous** *adj.* lustful.

Libra *n.* (the balance) seventh sign of the zodiac.

library *n., pl.* **-braries. 1.** room or building where books are kept. **2.** collection of books, records, etc. for consultation or borrowing. **3.** set of books published in a series. **librarian** *n.* keeper of or worker in a library. **librarianship** *n.*

libretto *n., pl.* **-tos, -ti.** words of an opera. **librettist** *n.*

Librium *n.* ® drug used as a tranquillizer.

lice *n.* a plural of LOUSE.

licence *n.* **1.** document giving official permission to do something. **2.** formal permission. **3.** excessive liberty. **4.** disregard of conventions for effect, e.g. *poetic licence.* **license** *v.* grant a licence to. **licensed** *adj.* **licensee** *n.* holder of a licence, esp. to sell alcohol.

▷ Note the *-ce* ending for the noun *licence*, with *-se* for the verb *license.*

licentiate *n.* person licensed as competent to practise a profession.

licentious *adj.* sexually immoral, dissolute. **licentiously** *adv.*

lichee *n.* same as LYCHEE.

lichen *n.* small flowerless plant forming a crust on rocks, trees, etc.

lichgate, lychgate n. roofed gate to a churchyard.

licit adj. lawful, permitted.

lick v. **1.** pass the tongue over. **2.** touch lightly or flicker round. **3.** Slang defeat. **4.** Slang thrash. —n. **5.** licking. **6.** small amount (of paint etc.). **7.** Informal fast pace. **8.** Informal blow.

licorice n. same as LIQUORICE.

lid n. **1.** movable cover. **2.** short for EYELID.

lido [lee-doe] n., pl. -dos. pleasure centre with swimming and water sports.

lie[1] v. **lying, lied. 1.** make a deliberately false statement. **2.** give a false impression. —n. **3.** deliberate falsehood. **white lie** untruth said without evil intent.

lie[2] v. **lying, lay, lain. 1.** place oneself or be in a horizontal position. **2.** be situated. **3.** be or remain in a certain state or position. **4.** exist or be found. —n. **5.** way something lies. **lie-down** n. rest. **lie in** v. remain in bed late into the morning. **lie-in** n. long stay in bed in the morning.
▷ Note that the past of *lie* is *lay*: *She lay on the beach all day.* Do not confuse with the main verb *lay* meaning 'put'.

lied [leed] n., pl. **lieder.** Music setting for voice and piano of a romantic poem.

lief adv. Obs. gladly, willingly.

liege [leej] n. **1.** lord. **2.** vassal or subject. —adj. **3.** bound to give or receive feudal service. **4.** faithful.

lien n. right to hold another's property until a debt is paid.

lieu [lyew] n. in lieu of instead of.

lieutenant [lef-ten-ant] n. **1.** junior officer in the army or navy. **2.** main assistant.

life n., pl. **lives. 1.** state of living beings, characterized by growth, reproduction, and response to stimuli. **2.** period between birth and death or between birth and the present time. **3.** amount of time something is active or continues. **4.** biography. **5.** way of living. **6.** liveliness or high spirits. **7.** living beings collectively. **8.** sentence of imprisonment for life. **lifeless** adj. **1.** dead. **2.** inert. **3.** dull. **lifer** n. Informal prisoner sentenced to imprisonment for life. **lifelike** adj. **lifelong** adj. lasting all of a person's life. **life belt, jacket** buoyant device to keep afloat a person in danger of drowning. **lifeblood** n. **1.** blood vital to life. **2.** vital thing for success or development. **lifeboat** n. boat used for rescuing people at sea. **life cycle** series of changes undergone by each generation of an animal or plant. **lifeguard** n. person who saves people from drowning. **lifeline** n. **1.** means of contact or support. **2.** rope used in rescuing a person in danger. **life science** any science concerned with living organisms, such as biology, botany, or zoology. **life-size, life-sized** adj. representing actual size. **lifestyle** n. particular attitudes, habits, etc. **life-support** adj. (of equipment or treatment) necessary to keep a person alive. **lifetime** n. length of time a person is alive.

lift v. **1.** move upwards in position, status, volume, etc. **2.** revoke or cancel. **3.** take (plants) out of the ground for harvesting. **4.** disappear. **5.** make or become more cheerful. **6.** Informal plagiarize (music or writing). —n. **7.** lifting. **8.** cage raised and lowered in a vertical shaft to transport people or goods. **9.** ride in a car etc. as a passenger. **10.** Informal feeling of cheerfulness. **liftoff** n. moment a rocket leaves the ground.

ligament n. band of tissue joining bones.

ligature n. **1.** thread for tying, esp. as used in surgery. **2.** Printing two or more joined letters.

light[1] n. **1.** electromagnetic radiation by which things are visible. **2.** source of this, lamp. **3.** anything that lets in light, such as a window. **4.** aspect or view. **5.** mental vision. **6.** brightness of countenance. **7.** light part of a photograph etc. **8.** means of setting fire to. **9.** understanding. —pl. **10.** traffic lights. —adj. **11.** bright. **12.** (of a colour) pale. —v. **lighting, lighted** or **lit. 13.** ignite. **14.** illuminate or cause to illuminate. **15.** guide by a light. **lighten** v. make less dark. **lighting** n. **1.** apparatus for supplying artificial light. **2.** use of artificial light in theatres, films, etc. **lighthouse** n. tower with a light to guide ships. **lightship** n. moored ship used as a lighthouse. **light up** v. **1.** illuminate. **2.** make or become cheerful. **light year** Astronomy distance light travels in one year, about six million million miles.

light[2] adj. **1.** not heavy, weighing relatively little. **2.** relatively low in strength, amount, density, etc. **3.** not serious or profound. **4.** not clumsy. **5.** free from care, cheerful. **6.** easily digested. **7.** carrying light arms or equipment. **8.** (of industry) producing small goods, using light machinery. —adv. **9.** with little equipment or luggage. —v. **lighting**, **lighted** or **lit. 10.** esp. of birds, settle after flight. **11.** come (upon) by chance. **lightly** adv. **lightness** n. **lighten** v. **1.** make less heavy or burdensome. **2.** make more cheerful or lively. **light-fingered** adj. liable to steal. **light-headed** adj. **1.** feeling faint, dizzy. **2.** frivolous. **light-hearted** adj. carefree. **light heavyweight** boxer weighing up to 176lb (professional) or 81kg (amateur). **lightweight** n., adj. **1.** (person) of little importance. —n. **2.** boxer weighing up to 135lb (professional) or 60kg (amateur).

lighter[1] n. device for lighting cigarettes etc.

lighter[2] n. flat-bottomed boat for unloading ships.

lightning n. **1.** visible discharge of electricity in the atmosphere. —adj. **2.** fast and sudden. **lightning conductor** metal rod attached to the top of a building to divert lightning safely to earth.

lights pl. n. lungs of animals as animal food.

ligneous adj. of or like wood.

lignite [lig-nite] n. woody textured rock used as fuel.

like[1] adj. **1.** resembling. **2.** similar. **3.** characteristic of. —prep. **4.** in the manner of. **5.** such as. —adv. **6.** in the manner of. —pron. **7.** similar thing. **liken** v. compare. **likeness** n. **1.** resemblance. **2.** portrait. **likewise** adv. in a similar manner.

like[2] v. **1.** find enjoyable. **2.** be fond of. **3.** prefer, choose, or wish. **likeable**, **likable** adj. **liking** n. **1.** fondness. **2.** preference.

likely adj. **1.** probable. **2.** tending or inclined. **3.** hopeful, promising. —adv. **4.** probably. **not likely** Informal definitely not. **likelihood** n. probability.

lilac n. **1.** shrub bearing pale mauve or white flowers. —adj. **2.** light-purple.

Lilliputian [lil-lip-pew-shun] adj. tiny.

Lilo n., pl. **-los.** ® inflatable rubber mattress.

lilt n. **1.** pleasing musical quality in speaking. **2.** jaunty rhythm. **3.** graceful rhythmic motion. —v. **4.** speak with a lilt. **lilting** adj.

lily n., pl. **lilies.** plant which grows from a bulb and has large, often white, flowers. **lily of the valley** small plant with fragrant white flowers.

limb[1] n. **1.** arm or leg. **2.** wing. **3.** main branch of a tree. **out on a limb** in a dangerous or isolated position.

limb[2] n. outer edge of the sun, a moon, or a planet.

limber adj. pliant or supple. **limber up** v. loosen stiff muscles by exercising.

limbo[1] n., pl. **-bos. 1.** supposed region intermediate between Heaven and Hell for the unbaptized. **2.** unknown intermediate place or state.

limbo[2] n., pl. **-bos.** West Indian dance in which dancers lean backwards to pass under a bar.

lime[1] n. **1.** calcium compound used as a fertilizer or in making cement. —v. **2.** treat (land) with lime. **limelight** n. glare of publicity. **limestone** n. sedimentary rock used in building.

lime[2] n. small green citrus fruit. **lime-green** adj. greenish-yellow.

lime[3] n. linden tree.

limerick [lim-mer-ik] n. nonsensical humorous verse of five lines.

limey n. US slang British person.

limit n. **1.** ultimate extent, degree, or amount of something. **2.** boundary or edge. —v. **-iting, -ited. 3.** restrict or confine. **limitation** n. **limitless** adj. **limited company** company whose shareholders' liability is restricted.

limn v. represent in drawing or painting.

limousine n. large luxurious car.

limp[1] adj. **1.** without firmness or stiffness. **2.** lacking strength or energy. **limply** adv.

limp[2] v. **1.** walk lamely. **2.** proceed with difficulty. —n. **3.** limping gait.

limpet n. shellfish which sticks tightly to rocks.

limpid adj. **1.** clear or transparent. **2.** easy to understand. **limpidity** n.

linchpin n. **1.** pin to hold a wheel on its axle. **2.** essential person or thing.

linctus n., pl. **-tuses.** syrupy cough medicine.

linden n. deciduous tree with heart-shaped leaves and fragrant flowers, the lime.

line n. **1.** long narrow mark. **2.** indented mark or wrinkle. **3.** continuous length without breadth. **4.** row of words. **5.** queue of people. **6.** boundary or limit. **7.** mark on a sports ground showing divisions of a pitch or track. **8.** string or wire for a particular use. **9.** telephone connection. **10.** wire or cable for transmitting electricity. **11.** shipping company. **12.** railway track. **13.** course or direction of movement. **14.** class of goods. **15.** prescribed way of thinking. **16.** course or method of action. **17.** field of interest or activity. **18.** ancestors collectively. **19.** unit of verse. —*pl.* **20.** words of a theatrical part. **21.** school punishment of writing out a sentence a specified number of times. **22.** protected boundary of an area occupied by an army. —*v.* **23.** mark with lines. **24.** bring into line. **25.** be or form a border or edge. **26.** give a lining to. **27.** cover the inside of. **28.** fill. **in line** for candidate for. **in line with** in accordance with. **line-up** *n.* people or things assembled for a particular purpose. **line up** *v.* form or organize a line-up.

lineage [lin-ee-ij] *n.* descent from or descendants of an ancestor. **lineal** *adj.* in direct line of descent.

lineament *n.* facial feature.

linear [lin-ee-er] *adj.* of or in lines.

linen *n.* **1.** cloth or thread made from flax. **2.** sheets, tablecloths, etc.

liner *n.* **1.** large passenger ship or aircraft. **2.** something used as a lining.

linesman *n.* **1.** in some sports, an official who helps the referee or umpire. **2.** person who maintains railway, electricity, or telephone lines.

ling[1] *n.* slender food fish.

ling[2] *n.* heather.

linger *v.* **1.** delay or prolong departure. **2.** continue in a weakened state for a long time before dying or disappearing. **3.** spend a long time doing something. **lingering** *adj.*

lingerie [lan-zher-ee] *n.* women's underwear or nightwear

lingo *n.*, *pl.* **-goes.** *Informal* foreign or unfamiliar language or jargon.

lingua franca *n.*, *pl.* **lingua francas, linguae francae.** language used for communication between people of different mother tongues.

lingual *adj.* **1.** of the tongue. **2.** made by the tongue.

linguist *n.* **1.** person skilled in foreign languages. **2.** person who studies linguistics. **linguistic** *adj.* of languages. **linguistics** *n.* scientific study of language.

liniment *n.* medicated liquid rubbed on the skin to relieve pain or stiffness.

lining *n.* **1.** layer of cloth attached to the inside of a garment etc. **2.** inner covering of anything.

link *n.* **1.** any of the rings forming a chain. **2.** person or thing forming a connection. —*v.* **3.** connect with or as if with links. **4.** connect by association. **linkage** *n.* **link-up** *n.* joining together of two systems or groups.

links *pl. n.* golf course, esp. one by the sea.

linnet *n.* songbird of the finch family.

lino *n.* short for LINOLEUM.

linocut *n.* **1.** design cut in relief on a block of linoleum. **2.** print from such a block.

linoleum *n.* floor covering of hessian or jute with a smooth decorative coating of powdered cork.

Linotype *n.* ® typesetting machine which casts lines of words in one piece.

linseed *n.* seed of the flax plant.

linsey-woolsey *n.* rough fabric of linen and wool or cotton.

lint *n.* soft material for dressing a wound.

lintel *n.* horizontal beam at the top of a door or window.

lion *n.* **1.** large animal of the cat family, the male of which has a shaggy mane. **2.** courageous person. **lioness** *n. fem.* **the lion's share** the biggest part. **lionize** *v.* treat as a celebrity. **lion-hearted** *adj.* brave.

lip *n.* **1.** either of the fleshy edges of the mouth. **2.** rim of a jug etc. **3.** *Slang* impudence. **lip-reading** *n.* method of understanding speech by interpreting lip movements. **lip-read** *v.* **lip service** insincere tribute or respect. **lipstick** *n.* cosmetic in stick form, for colouring the lips.

liquefy *v.* **-fying, -fied.** make or become liquid. **liquefaction** *n.*

liqueur [lik-cure] *n.* flavoured and sweetened alcoholic spirit

liquid *n.* **1.** substance in a physical state which can change shape but not size. —*adj.* **2.** of or being a liquid. **3.** flowing smoothly. **4.** transparent and shining. **5.** (of assets) in the form of money or easily converted into money. **liquidize** *v.* make or become liquid. **liquidizer** *n.* kitchen appliance that liquidizes food. **liquidity** *n.* state of being able to meet financial obligations.

liquidate *v.* **1.** pay (a debt). **2.** dissolve a company and share its assets between creditors. **3.** wipe out or kill. **liquidation** *n.* **liquidator** *n.* official appointed to liquidate a business.

liquor *n*. **1**. alcoholic drink, esp. spirits. **2**. liquid in which food has been cooked.

liquorice [lik-ker-iss] *n*. black substance used in medicine and as a sweet.

lira *n*., *pl*. **-re**, **-ras**. monetary unit of Italy and Turkey.

lisle [rhymes with **mile**] *n*. strong fine cotton thread or fabric.

lisp *n*. **1**. speech defect in which *s* and *z* are pronounced *th*. —*v*. **2**. speak or utter with a lisp.

lissom, **lissome** *adj*. supple, agile.

list[1] *n*. **1**. item-by-item record of names or things, usu. written one below another. —*pl*. **2**. field of combat in a tournament. —*v*. **3**. make a list of. **4**. include in a list. **listed building** building protected from demolition or alteration because of its historical or architectural interest. **enter the lists** engage in a conflict.

list[2] *v*. **1**. (of a ship) lean to one side. —*n*. **2**. leaning to one side.

listen *v*. **1**. concentrate on hearing something. **2**. heed or pay attention to. **listener** *n*. **listen in** *v*. listen secretly, eavesdrop.

listeriosis *n*. dangerous form of food poisoning.

listless *adj*. lacking interest or energy. **listlessly** *adv*.

lit *v*. past of LIGHT[1], LIGHT[2].

litany *n*., *pl*. **-nies**. **1**. prayer with responses from the congregation. **2**. any tedious recital.

litchi *n*. same as LYCHEE.

literacy *n*. ability to read and write.

literal *adj*. **1**. according to the explicit meaning of a word or text, not figurative. **2**. (of a translation) word for word. **3**. actual, true. **literally** *adv*.
▷ Note that *literally* means much the same as 'actually'. It is very loosely used to mean 'just about' but this can be ambiguous.

literary *adj*. **1**. of or learned in literature. **2**. (of a word) formal, not colloquial. **literariness** *n*.

literate *adj*. **1**. able to read and write. **2**. educated. **literati** *pl. n*. literary people.

literature *n*. **1**. written works such as novels, plays, and poetry. **2**. books and writings of a country, period, or subject. **3**. printed matter on a subject.

lithe *adj*. flexible or supple, pliant.

lithium *n*. chemical element, the lightest known metal.

litho *n*., *pl*. **-thos**. **1**. short for LITHOGRAPH. —*adj*. **2**. short for LITHOGRAPHIC.

lithography [lith-og-ra-fee] *n*. method of printing from a metal or stone surface in which the printing areas are made receptive to ink. **lithograph** *n*. **1**. print made by lithography. —*v*. **2**. reproduce by lithography. **lithographer** *n*. **lithographic** *adj*.

litigate *v*. **1**. bring or contest a law suit. **2**. engage in legal action. **litigant** *n*. person involved in a lawsuit. **litigation** *n*. lawsuit. **litigious** [lit-ij-uss] *adj*. frequently going to law.

litmus *n*. blue dye turned red by acids and restored to blue by alkali. **litmus paper** paper impregnated with litmus.

litotes *n*. ironical understatement for rhetorical effect.

litre *n*. unit of liquid measure equal to 1.76 pints.

litter *n*. **1**. untidy rubbish dropped in public places. **2**. group of young animals produced at one birth. **3**. straw etc. as bedding for an animal. **4**. dry material to absorb a cat's excrement. **5**. bed or seat on parallel sticks for carrying people. —*v*. **6**. strew with litter. **7**. scatter or be scattered about untidily. **8**. give birth to young.

little *adj*. **1**. small or smaller than average. **2**. young. —*n*. **3**. small amount, extent, or duration. —*adv*. **4**. not a lot. **5**. hardly. **6**. not much or often. **little by little** by small degrees.

littoral *adj*. **1**. of or by the seashore. —*n*. **2**. coastal district.

liturgy *n*., *pl*. **-gies**. prescribed form of public worship. **liturgical** *adj*.

live[1] *v*. **1**. be alive. **2**. remain in life or existence. **3**. exist in a specified way, e.g. *we live well*. **4**. reside. **5**. continue or last. **6**. subsist. **7**. enjoy life to the full. **liver** *n*. person who lives in a specified way. **live down** *v*. wait till people forget a past mistake or misdeed. **live-in** *adj*. sharing a house with one's sexual partner. **live together** *v*. (of an unmarried couple) share a house and have a sexual relationship. **live up to** *v*. meet (expectations). **live with** *v*. tolerate.

live[2] *adj*. **1**. living, alive. **2**. current. **3**. glowing or burning. **4**. capable of exploding. **5**. (of a wire, circuit, etc.) carrying an electric current. **6**. (of a broadcast) transmitted during the actual performance. —*adv.* **7.** in the form of a live performance. **lively** *adj.* **1.** full of life or vigour. **2.** animated. **3.** vivid. **liveliness** *n.* **liven up** *v.* make (more) lively. **live wire 1.** *Informal* energetic person. **2.** wire carrying an electric current.

livelihood *n.* occupation or employment.

livelong [liv-long] *adj. Lit.* long.

liver *n.* **1.** organ secreting bile. **2.** animal liver as food. **liverish** *adj.* **1.** unwell. **2.** touchy or irritable.

liverwort *n.* plant resembling seaweed or leafy moss.

livery *n., pl.* **-eries. 1.** distinctive dress, esp. of a servant or servants. **2.** distinctive design or colours of a company. **liveried** *adj.* **livery stable** stable where horses are kept at a charge or hired out.

lives *n.* plural of LIFE.

livestock *n.* farm animals.

livid *adj.* **1.** *Informal* angry or furious. **2.** bluish-grey.

living *adj.* **1.** possessing life, not dead or inanimate. **2.** currently in use or existing. **3.** of everyday life, e.g. *living conditions.* —*n.* **4.** condition of being alive. **5.** manner of life. **6.** financial means. **7.** church benefice. **living-room** *n.* room in a house used for relaxation and entertainment. **living wage** wage adequate for a worker to live on in reasonable comfort.

lizard *n.* four-footed reptile with a long body and tail.

llama *n.* woolly animal of the camel family used as a beast of burden in S America.

LLB Bachelor of Laws.

lo *interj. Lit.* look!

loach *n.* carplike freshwater fish.

load *n.* **1.** burden or weight. **2.** amount carried. **3.** amount of electrical energy drawn from a source. **4.** source of worry. —*pl.* **5.** *Informal* lots. —*v.* **6.** put a load on or into. **7.** burden or oppress. **8.** supply in abundance. **9.** cause to be biased. **10.** put ammunition into a weapon. **11.** put film into a camera. **12.** transfer (a program) into computer memory. **a load of** *Informal* a quantity of. **loaded** *adj.* **1.** (of a question) containing a hidden trap or implication. **2.** *Slang* wealthy. **3.** (of dice) dishonestly weighted. **4.** *Slang* drunk.

loadstar *n.* same as LODESTAR.

loadstone *n.* same as LODESTONE.

loaf[1] *n., pl.* **loaves. 1.** shaped mass of baked bread. **2.** shaped mass of food. **3.** *Slang* common sense, e.g. *use your loaf.*

loaf[2] *v.* idle, loiter. **loafer** *n.*

loam *n.* fertile soil.

loan *n.* **1.** money borrowed at interest. **2.** lending. **3.** thing lent. —*v.* **4.** lend, grant a loan of.

loath, loth [rhymes with **both**] *adj.* unwilling or reluctant (to). ▷ Distinguish between *loath* 'reluctant' and *loathe* 'be disgusted by'.

loathe *v.* hate, be disgusted by. **loathing** *n.* **loathsome** *adj.*

loaves *n.* plural of LOAF[1].

lob *Sport* —*n.* **1.** ball struck or thrown high in the air. —*v.* **lobbing, lobbed. 2.** strike or throw (a ball) high in the air.

lobby *n., pl.* **-bies. 1.** corridor into which rooms open. **2.** hall in a legislative building to which the public has access. **3.** group which tries to influence legislators. —*v.* **-bying, -bied. 4.** try to influence (legislators) in the formulation of policy. **lobbyist** *n.*

lobe *n.* **1.** rounded projection. **2.** soft hanging part of the ear. **3.** subdivision of a body organ. **lobed** *adj.* **lobar** [loh-ber] *adj.* of or affecting a lobe. **lobate** *adj.* with or like lobes.

lobelia *n.* garden plant with blue, red, or white lobed flowers.

lobotomy *n., pl.* **-mies.** surgical incision into a lobe of the brain to treat mental disorders.

lobster *n.* shellfish with a long tail and claws, which turns red when boiled. **lobster pot** basket-like trap for catching lobsters.

local *adj.* **1.** of or existing in a particular place. **2.** confined to a particular place. —*n.* **3.** person belonging to a particular district. **4.** *Informal* (nearby) pub. **locally** *adv.* **locality** *n.* **1.** neighbourhood or area. **2.** site. **localize** *v.* restrict to a definite place. **locale** [loh-kahl] *n.* scene of an event. **local anaesthetic** anaesthetic which produces insensibility in one part of the body. **local authority** governing body of a county or district. **local government** government of towns, counties, and districts by locally elected political bodies.

locate *v.* **1.** discover the whereabouts of. **2.** situate or place. **location** *n.* **1.** site or position. **2.** site of a film production away from the studio. **3.** *S Afr.* Black African or coloured township.

loch *n.* **1.** *Scot.* lake. **2.** long narrow bay.

loci *n.* plural of LOCUS.

lock[1] *n.* **1.** appliance for fastening a door, case, etc. **2.** section of a canal shut off by gates between which the water level can be altered to aid boats moving from one level to another. **3.** extent to which a vehicle's front wheels will turn. **4.** interlocking of parts. **5.** mechanism for firing a gun. **6.** wrestling hold. —*v.* **7.** fasten or become fastened securely. **8.** become or cause to become immovable. **9.** become or cause to become fixed or united. **10.** embrace closely. **lockout** *n.* exclusion of workers by an employer as a means of coercion. **locksmith** *n.* person who makes and mends locks. **lockup** *n.* **1.** prison. **2.** garage or storage place away from the main premises. **lock up** *v.* **1.** imprison. **2.** secure (a building) by locking.

lock[2] *n.* tress of hair.

locker *n.* small cupboard with a lock.

locket *n.* small hinged pendant for a portrait etc.

lockjaw *n.* tetanus.

locomotive *n.* **1.** self-propelled engine for pulling trains. —*adj.* **2.** of locomotion. **locomotion** *n.* action or power of moving.

locum *n.* temporary stand-in for a doctor or clergyman.

locus [**loh**-kuss] *n., pl.* **loci** [**loh**-sigh] **1.** area or place where something happens. **2.** *Maths* set of points or lines satisfying one or more specified conditions.

locust *n.* **1.** destructive African insect that flies in swarms and eats crops. **2.** N American tree with prickly branches.

locution *n.* **1.** style of speech. **2.** word or phrase.

lode *n.* vein of ore. **lodestar** *n.* Pole Star. **lodestone** *n.* magnetic iron ore.

lodge *n.* **1.** house or cabin used occasionally by hunters, skiers, etc. **2.** gatekeeper's house. **3.** porters' room in a university or college. **4.** local branch of some societies. **5.** beaver's home. —*v.* **6.** live in another's house at a fixed charge. **7.** stick or become stuck (in a place). **8.** make (a complaint etc.) formally. **9.** deposit for safety or storage. **lodger** *n.* **lodging** *n.* **1.** temporary

residence. —*pl.* **2.** rented room or rooms in another person's house.

loft *n.* **1.** space between the top storey and roof of a building. **2.** gallery in a church etc. **3.** room over a stable used for storing hay. —*v.* **4.** *Sport* strike, throw, or kick (a ball) high into the air.

lofty *adj.* **loftier, loftiest.** **1.** of great height. **2.** exalted or noble. **3.** haughty. **loftily** *adv.* haughtily. **loftiness** *n.*

log[1] *n.* **1.** portion of a felled tree stripped of branches. **2.** detailed record of a journey of a ship, aircraft, etc. —*v.* **logging, logged.** **3.** record in a log. **4.** saw logs from a tree. **logging** *n.* work of cutting and transporting logs. **logbook** *n.* book recording the details about a car or a ship's journeys. **log in, out** *v.* gain entrance to *or* leave a computer system by keying in a special command.

log[2] *n.* short for LOGARITHM.

loganberry *n.* purplish-red fruit, a cross between a raspberry and a blackberry.

logarithm *n.* one of a series of arithmetical functions used to make certain calculations easier. **logarithmic** *adj.*

loggerheads *pl. n.* **at loggerheads** quarrelling, disputing.

loggia [**loj**-ya] *n.* covered gallery at the side of a building.

logic *n.* **1.** philosophy of reasoning. **2.** reasoned thought or argument. **logical** *adj.* **1.** of logic. **2.** reasonable. **3.** capable of or using clear valid reasoning. **logically** *adv.* **logician** *n.*

logistics *n.* detailed planning and organization of a large, esp. military, operation. **logistical, logistic** *adj.* **logistically** *adv.*

logo [**loh**-go] *n., pl.* **-os.** company emblem or similar device.

loin *n.* **1.** part of the body between the ribs and the hips. **2.** cut of meat from this part of an animal. —*pl.* **3.** hips and inner thighs. **4.** *Old-fashioned* genitals. **loincloth** *n.* piece of cloth covering the loins only.

loiter *v.* stand or wait aimlessly or idly. **loiterer** *n.*

loll *v.* **1.** lounge lazily. **2.** (esp. of the tongue) hang out.

lollipop *n.* boiled sweet on a small wooden stick. **lollipop man, lady** *Informal* person holding a circular sign on a pole, who controls traffic so that children may cross the road safely.

lollop v. run clumsily.

lolly n., pl. **-ies. 1.** *Informal* lollipop or ice lolly. **2.** *Slang* money.

lone adj. **1.** solitary. **2.** isolated. **lonely** adj. **1.** sad because alone. **2.** unfrequented. **3.** resulting from being alone. **loneliness** n. **loner** n. *Informal* person who prefers to be alone. **lonesome** adj. lonely.

long[1] adj. **1.** having length, esp. great length, in space or time. —adv. **2.** for a long time. **3.** for a certain time. **longways, longwise** adv. lengthways. **longboat** n. largest boat carried on a ship. **longbow** n. large powerful bow. **long-distance** adj. going between places far apart. **long-drawn-out** adj. lasting too long. **long face** glum expression. **longhand** n. ordinary writing, not shorthand or typing. **long johns** *Informal* long underpants. **long jump** contest of jumping the farthest distance from a fixed mark. **long-life** adj. (of milk, batteries, etc.) lasting longer than the regular kind. **long-lived** adj. living or lasting for a long time. **long-range** adj. **1.** (of weapons) designed to hit a distant target. **2.** into the future. **long shot** competitor, undertaking, or bet with little chance of success. **long-sighted** adj. able to see distant objects in focus but not nearby ones. **long-standing** adj. existing for a long time. **long-suffering** adj. enduring trouble or unhappiness without complaint. **long-term** adj. lasting or effective for a long time. **long wave** radio wave with a wavelength of over 1000 metres. **long-winded** adj. speaking or writing at tedious length.

long[2] v. (foll. by *for*) have a strong desire for. **longing** n. yearning. **longingly** adv.

long. longitude.

longevity [lon-jev-it-ee] n. long existence or life.

longitude n. distance east or west from a standard meridian. **longitudinal** adj. **1.** of length or longitude. **2.** lengthwise.

longshoreman n. *US* docker.

loo n. *Informal* toilet.

loofah n. dried pod of a gourd, used as a sponge.

look v. **1.** direct the eyes or attention (towards). **2.** seem. **3.** face in a particular direction. **4.** search (for). **5.** hope (for). —n. **6.** looking. **7.** search. **8.** view or sight. **9.** (often pl.) appearance. **look after** v. take care of. **lookalike** n. person who is the double of another. **look down on** v. treat as inferior or unimportant. **look forward to** v. anticipate with pleasure. **look-in** n. *Informal* chance to participate. **look in** v. *Informal* pay a short visit. **looking glass** mirror. **look on** v. **1.** be an onlooker. **2.** consider or regard. **lookout** n. **1.** guard. **2.** place for watching. **3.** chances or prospect. **4.** *Informal* worry or concern. **look up** v. **1.** discover or confirm by checking in a book. **2.** visit. **3.** improve. **look up to** v. respect.

loom[1] n. machine for weaving cloth.

loom[2] v. **1.** appear dimly. **2.** seem ominously close. **3.** assume great importance.

loon n. diving bord.

loony *Slang* —n., pl. **loonies. 1.** foolish or insane person. —adj. **loonier, looniest. 2.** foolish or insane. **loony bin** *Slang* mental hospital.

loop n. **1.** rounded shape made by a curved line or rope crossing itself. **2.** set of instructions to be repeatedly performed in a computer program. **3.** continuous strip of film or tape. —v. **4.** form or fasten with a loop. **loop the loop** fly or be flown in a complete vertical circle. **loophole** n. means of evading a rule without breaking it.

loose adj. **1.** not tight, fastened, fixed, or tense. **2.** slack. **3.** vague. **4.** dissolute or promiscuous. —v. **5.** free. **6.** unfasten. **7.** slacken. **8.** let fly (an arrow, bullet, etc.). **at a loose end** bored, with nothing to do. **on the loose** free from confinement. **loosely** adv. **looseness** n. **loosen** v. make loose. **loosen up** v. relax, stop worrying. **looseleaf** adj. allowing the addition or removal of pages.

▷ *Loose* and *lose* are often confused in spelling but rarely in meaning.

loot n., v. **1.** plunder. —n. **2.** *Informal* money. **looter** n. **looting** n.

lop v. **lopping, lopped. 1.** cut away twigs and branches. **2.** chop off.

lope v. **1.** run with long easy strides. —n. **2.** loping stride.

lop-eared adj. having drooping ears.

lopsided adj. greater in height, weight, or size on one side.

loquacious adj. talkative. **loquacity** n.

lord n. **1.** person with power over others, such as a monarch or master. **2.** male member of the nobility. **3.** *Hist.* feudal superior. **4.** (L-) God or Jesus. **5.** title given to certain male officials and peers. **House of Lords** unelected upper chamber of the British parliament. **lord it over** act in a superior manner towards. **the Lord's Prayer** prayer taught by Christ to his disciples. **lordly** *adj.* imperious, proud. **Lordship** *n.* title of some male officials and peers.

lore *n.* body of traditions on a subject.

lorgnette [lor-**nyet**] *n.* pair of spectacles mounted on a long handle.

lorry *n., pl.* **-ries.** large vehicle for transporting loads by road.

lose *v.* **losing, lost. 1.** come to be without, as by accident or carelessness. **2.** fail to keep or maintain. **3.** be deprived of. **4.** get rid of. **5.** fail to get or make use of. **6.** have an income less than one's expenditure. **7.** fail to perceive or understand. **8.** be defeated in a competition etc. **9.** be or become engrossed, e.g. *lost in thought*. **10.** go astray or allow to go astray. **11.** die or be destroyed. **12.** (of a clock etc.) run slow (by a specified amount). **loser** *n.* **1.** person or thing that loses. **2.** *Informal* person who seems destined to fail. ▷ *Lose* and *loose* are often confused in spelling but rarely in meaning.

loss *n.* **1.** losing. **2.** that which is lost. **3.** damage resulting from losing. **at a loss 1.** confused or bewildered. **2.** not earning enough to cover costs. **loss leader** item sold at a loss to attract customers.

lost *v.* **1.** past of LOSE. —*adj.* **2.** unable to find one's way. **3.** unable to be found. **4.** bewildered or confused. **5.** no longer possessed or existing. **6.** (foll. by *on*) not used, noticed, or understood by.

lot *pron.* **1.** great number. —*n.* **2.** collection of people or things. **3.** large quantity. **4.** *US* area of land. **5.** fate or destiny. **6.** item at auction. **7.** one of a set of objects drawn at random to make a selection or choice. —*pl.* **8.** *Informal* great numbers or quantities. **a lot** *adv.* *Informal* a great deal. **bad lot** disreputable person. **the lot** entire amount or number.

loth *adj.* same as LOATH.

lotion *n.* medical or cosmetic liquid for use on the skin.

lottery *n., pl.* **-teries. 1.** method of raising funds by selling tickets that win prizes by chance. **2.** gamble.

lotto *n.* game of chance like bingo.

lotus *n.* **1.** legendary plant whose fruit induces forgetfulness. **2.** Egyptian water lily.

loud *adj.* **1.** relatively great in volume. **2.** capable of making much noise. **3.** insistent and emphatic. **4.** unpleasantly patterned or colourful. **loudly** *adv.* **loudness** *n.* **loudspeaker** *n.* instrument for converting electrical signals into sound.

lough *n. Irish* loch.

lounge *v.* **1.** sit, lie, or stand in a relaxed manner. —*n.* **2.** living room in a private house. **3.** area for waiting in an airport. **4.** more expensive bar in a pub. **lounge suit** man's suit for daytime wear.

lour *v.* same as LOWER².

louse *n.* **1.** *pl.* **lice.** wingless parasitic insect. **2.** *pl.* **louses.** unpleasant person. **lousy** *adj.* **lousier, lousiest. 1.** *Slang* mean or unpleasant. **2.** bad, inferior. **3.** unwell. **4.** infested with lice.

lout *n.* crude, oafish, or aggressive person. **loutish** *adj.*

louvre [**loo**-ver] *n.* one of a set of parallel slats slanted to admit air but not rain. **louvred** *adj.*

lovage *n.* European plant used for flavouring food.

love *n.* **1.** warm affection. **2.** sexual passion. **3.** wholehearted liking for something. **4.** beloved person. **5.** *Tennis, squash etc.* score of nothing. —*v.* **6.** have a great affection for. **7.** feel sexual passion for. **8.** enjoy (something) very much. **fall in love** become in love. **in love (with)** feeling a strong emotional (and sexual) attraction (for). **make love (to)** have sexual intercourse (with). **lovable** *adj.* **loveless** *adj.* **lover** *n.* **1.** person having a sexual relationship outside marriage. **2.** person in love. **3.** someone who loves a specified person or thing. **loving** *adj.* affectionate, tender. **lovingly** *adv.* **love affair** romantic or sexual relationship between two people who are not married to each other. **lovebird** *n.* small parrot. **love child** *Euphemistic* child of an unmarried couple. **love life** person's romantic or sexual relationships. **lovelorn** *adj.* forsaken by or pining for a lover. **lovemaking** *n.*

low¹ *adj.* **1.** not tall, high, or elevated. **2.** of little or less than the usual amount, degree, quality, or cost. **3.** coarse or vulgar. **4.** dejected. **5.** ill. **6.** not loud. **7.** deep in pitch. **8.** (of a gear) providing a relatively low speed. —*n.* **9.** low position, level, or degree. **10.** area of low atmospheric pressure, depression. —*adv.* **11.** in or to a low position, level, or degree. **lowly** *adj.* modest, humble. **lowliness** *n.* **lowbrow** *n., adj.* (person) with nonintellectual tastes and interests. **Low**

Church section of the Anglican Church stressing evangelical beliefs and practices. **lowdown** *n. Informal* inside information. **low-down** *adj. Informal* mean, shabby, or dishonest. **low-key** *adj.* subdued, restrained, not intense. **lowland** *n.* **1.** low-lying country. —*pl.* **2.** (L-) less mountainous parts of Scotland. **low profile** position or attitude avoiding prominence or publicity. **low-spirited** *adj.* depressed.

low² *n.* **1.** cry of cattle, moo. —*v.* **2.** moo.

lower¹ *v.* **1.** cause or allow to move down. **2.** diminish or degrade. **3.** lessen. —*adj.* **4.** below one or more other things. **5.** smaller or reduced in amount or value. **lower case** small, as distinct from capital, letters.

lower², **lour** *v.* (of the sky or weather) look gloomy or threatening. **lowering** *adj.*

loyal *adj.* faithful to one's friends, country, or government. **loyally** *adv.* **loyalty** *n.* **loyalist** *n.*

lozenge *n.* **1.** medicated tablet held in the mouth until it dissolves. **2.** four-sided diamond-shaped figure.

LP *n.* record playing approximately 20–25 minutes each side.

L-plate *n.* sign on a car being driven by a learner driver.

Lr *Chem.* lawrencium.

LSD lysergic acid diethylamide, a hallucinogenic drug.

Lt Lieutenant.

Ltd Limited (Liability).

Lu *Chem.* lutetium.

lubber *n.* clumsy person.

lubricate [**loo**-brik-ate] *v.* oil or grease to lessen friction. **lubricant** *n.* lubricating substance such as oil. **lubrication** *n.*

lubricious [loo-**brish**-uss] *adj. Lit.* lewd.

lucerne *n.* fodder plant like clover, alfalfa.

lucid *adj.* **1.** clear and easily understood. **2.** able to think clearly. **3.** bright and clear. **lucidly** *adv.* **lucidity** *n.*

Lucifer *n.* Satan.

luck *n.* **1.** fortune, good or bad. **2.** good fortune. **3.** chance. **lucky** *adj.* having or bringing good luck. **lucky dip** game in which prizes are picked from a tub at random. **luckily** *adv.* fortunately. **luckless** *adj.* having bad luck.

lucrative *adj.* very profitable.

lucre [**loo**-ker] *n.* filthy lucre *Informal, usu. facetious* money.

Luddite *n.* person opposed to change in industrial methods.

ludicrous *adj.* absurd or ridiculous. **ludicrously** *adv.*

ludo *n.* game played with dice and counters on a board.

luff *v.* sail (a ship) towards the wind.

lug¹ *v.* **lugging, lugged.** carry or drag with great effort.

lug² *n.* **1.** projection serving as a handle. **2.** *Informal* ear.

luggage *n.* traveller's cases, bags, etc.

lugger *n.* working boat rigged with an oblong sail.

lugubrious [loo-**goo**-bree-uss] *adj.* mournful, gloomy. **lugubriously** *adv.*

lugworm *n.* large worm used as bait.

lukewarm *adj.* **1.** moderately warm, tepid. **2.** indifferent or half-hearted.

lull *n.* **1.** brief time of quiet in a storm etc. —*v.* **2.** soothe (someone) by soft sounds or motions. **3.** calm (fears or suspicions) by deception.

lullaby *n., pl.* **-bies.** quiet song to send a child to sleep.

lumbago [lum-**bay**-go] *n.* pain in the lower back. **lumbar** *adj.* relating to the lower back.

lumber¹ *n.* **1.** useless disused articles, such as old furniture. **2.** *US* sawn timber. —*v.* **3.** *Informal* burden with something unpleasant. **lumberjack** *n. US* man who fells trees and prepares logs for transport.

lumber² *v.* move heavily and awkwardly. **lumbering** *adj.*

luminous *adj.* reflecting or giving off light. **luminosity** *n.* **luminary** *n.* **1.** famous person. **2.** *Lit.* heavenly body giving off light. **luminescence** *n.* emission of light at low temperatures by any process other than burning. **luminescent** *adj.*

lump¹ *n.* **1.** shapeless piece or mass. **2.** swelling. **3.** *Informal* awkward or stupid person. —*v.* **4.** consider as a single group. **lump in one's throat** tight dry feeling in one's throat, usu. caused by great emotion. **lumpish** *adj.* stupid or clumsy. **lumpy** *adj.* **lump sum** relatively large sum of money paid at one time.

lump[2] v. **lump it** *Informal* tolerate or put up with it.

lunar adj. relating to the moon. **lunar month**, **lunation** n. time taken for the moon to go once round the earth, approx. 29½ days.

lunatic adj. **1.** foolish and irresponsible. —n. **2.** foolish or annoying person. **3.** *Old-fashioned* insane person. **lunacy** n.

lunch n. **1.** meal taken in the middle of the day. —v. **2.** eat lunch. **luncheon** n. formal lunch. **luncheon meat** tinned ground mixture of meat and cereal. **luncheon voucher** voucher for a certain amount, given to an employee and accepted by some restaurants as payment for a meal.

lung n. organ that allows an animal or bird to breathe air: humans have two lungs in the chest.

lunge n. **1.** sudden forward motion. **2.** thrust with a sword. —v. **3.** move with or make a lunge.

lupin n. garden plant with tall spikes of flowers.

lupine adj. like a wolf.

lupus n. ulcerous skin disease.

lurch[1] v. **1.** tilt or lean suddenly to one side. **2.** stagger. —n. **3.** lurching movement.

lurch[2] n. **leave someone in the lurch** abandon someone in difficulties.

lurcher n. crossbred dog trained to hunt silently.

lure v. **1.** tempt or attract by the promise of reward. —n. **2.** person or thing that lures. **3.** brightly-coloured artificial angling bait. **4.** feathered decoy for attracting a falcon.

lurid adj. **1.** vivid in shocking detail, sensational. **2.** glaring in colour. **luridly** adv.

lurk v. **1.** lie hidden or move stealthily, esp. for sinister purposes. **2.** be latent.

luscious [**lush**-uss] adj. **1.** extremely pleasurable to taste or smell. **2.** very attractive.

lush[1] adj. **1.** (of grass etc.) growing thickly and healthily. **2.** opulent. **lushly** adv. **lushness** n.

lush[2] n. *US slang* alcoholic.

lust n. **1.** strong sexual desire. **2.** any strong desire. —v. **3.** have passionate desire (for). **lustful** adj. **lusty** adj. vigorous, healthy. **lustily** adv.

lustre n. **1.** gloss, sheen. **2.** splendour or glory. **3.** metallic pottery glaze. **lustrous** adj. shining, luminous.

lute n. ancient guitar-like musical instrument with a body shaped like a half pear. **lutenist** n. person who plays a lute.

lutetium [loo-**tee**-shee-um] n. silvery-white metallic element.

Lutheran adj. of Martin Luther (1483–1546), German Reformation leader, his doctrines, or a Church following these doctrines.

lux n., pl. **lux.** unit of illumination.

luxuriant adj. **1.** rich and abundant. **2.** very elaborate. **luxuriantly** adv. **luxuriance** n.

luxuriate v. **1.** take self-indulgent pleasure (in). **2.** flourish.

luxury n., pl. **-ries. 1.** enjoyment of rich, very comfortable living. **2.** enjoyable but not essential thing. —adj. **3.** of or providing luxury. **luxurious** adj. full of luxury, sumptuous. **luxuriously** adv.

LV luncheon voucher.

lychee [lie-**chee**] n. Chinese fruit with a whitish juicy pulp.

lychgate n. same as LICHGATE.

Lycra n. ® elastic fabric used for tight-fitting garments, such as swimming costumes.

lye n. water made alkaline with wood ashes etc., esp. as formerly used for washing.

lying v. present participle of LIE[1], LIE[2]. **lying-in** n. *Old-fashioned* period of confinement during childbirth.

lymph n. colourless bodily fluid consisting mainly of white blood cells. **lymphatic** adj. **lymph node** mass of tissue that helps to fight infection in the body.

lymphocyte n. type of white blood cell.

lynch v. put to death without a trial.

lynx n. animal of the cat family with tufted ears and a short tail.

lyre n. ancient musical instrument like a U-shaped harp. **lyrebird** n. Aust. bird, the male of which spreads its tail into the shape of a lyre.

lyric n. **1.** short poem expressing personal emotion in a songlike style. —pl. **2.** words of a popular song. —adj. **3.** of such poems. **4.** in the style of a song. **lyrical** adj. **1.** lyric. **2.** enthusiastic. **lyricism** n. **lyricist** n. person who writes the words of songs or musicals.

M

m 1. metre(s). **2.** mile(s). **3.** minute(s).

M 1. mega-. **2.** *pl.* **MM.** Monsieur. **3.** Motorway. **4.** the Roman numeral for 1000.

m. 1. male. **2.** married. **3.** masculine. **4.** meridian. **5.** month.

ma *n. Informal* mother.

MA 1. Master of Arts. **2.** Massachusetts.

ma'am *n.* madam.

mac *n. Informal* mackintosh.

macabre [mak-**kahb**-ra] *adj.* strange and horrible, gruesome.

macadam *n.* road surface of pressed layers of small broken stones. **macadamize** *v.* pave (a road) with macadam.

macaque [mac-**kahk**] *n.* monkey of Asia and Africa with cheek pouches and either a short tail or no tail.

macaroni *n.* pasta in short tube shapes.

macaroon *n.* small biscuit or cake made with ground almonds.

macaw *n.* large tropical American parrot.

mace[1] *n.* **1.** ceremonial staff of office. **2.** medieval weapon with a spiked metal head.

mace[2] *n.* spice made from the dried husk of the nutmeg.

macerate [**mass**-er-ate] *v.* soften by soaking. **maceration** *n.*

Mach [mak] *n.* short for MACH NUMBER.

machete [mash-**ett**-ee] *n.* broad heavy knife used for cutting or as a weapon.

Machiavellian [mak-ee-a-**vel**-yan] *adj.* unprincipled, crafty, and opportunist.

machinations [mak-in-**nay**-shunz] *pl. n.* cunning plots and ploys.

machine *n.* **1.** apparatus, usu. powered by electricity, designed to perform a particular task. **2.** vehicle, such as a car or aircraft. **3.** controlling system of an organization. — *v.* **4.** make or produce by machine. **machinery** *n.* machines or machine parts collectively. **machinist** *n.* person who operates a machine. **machine gun** automatic gun that fires rapidly and continuously. **machine-gun** *v.* fire at with such a gun. **machine language** instructions for a computer in binary code that require no conversion or translation by the computer. **machine-readable** *adj.* (of data) in a form suitable for processing by a computer.

machismo [mak-**izz**-moh] *n.* strong or exaggerated masculinity.

Mach number [mak] *n.* ratio of the speed of a body in a particular medium to the speed of sound in that medium.

macho [**match**-oh] *adj.* strongly or exaggeratedly masculine.

mack *n. Informal* mackintosh.

mackerel *n.* edible sea fish with blue and silver stripes.

mackintosh, macintosh *n.* **1.** waterproof raincoat of rubberized cloth. **2.** any raincoat.

macramé [mak-**rah**-mee] *n.* ornamental work of knotted cord.

macro- *combining form* large, long, or great, e.g. *macroscopic*.

macrobiotics *n.* dietary system advocating whole grains and vegetables grown without chemical additives. **macrobiotic** *adj.*

macrocosm *n.* **1.** the universe. **2.** any large complete system.

mad *adj.* **madder, maddest. 1.** mentally deranged, insane. **2.** very foolish. **3.** (foll. by *about* or *on*) very enthusiastic (about). **4.** frantic. **5.** *Informal* angry. **like mad** *Informal* with great energy, enthusiasm, or haste. **madly** *adv.* **1.** with great speed and energy. **2.** *Informal* extremely or excessively. **madness** *n.* **maddening** *adj.* infuriating or irritating. **maddeningly** *adv.* **madman, madwoman** *n.*

madam *n.* **1.** polite form of address to a woman. **2.** *Informal* precocious or conceited girl.

madame [mad-**dam**] *n., pl.* **mesdames** [may-**dam**] French title equivalent to *Mrs.*

madcap *adj.* foolish or reckless.

madder *n.* **1.** climbing plant. **2.** red dye made from its root.

made *v.* past of MAKE. **have (got) it made** *Informal* be assured of success.

Madeira [mad-**deer**-a] *n.* fortified white wine. **Madeira cake** rich sponge cake.

mademoiselle [mad-mwah-**zel**] *n., pl.* **mesdemoiselles** [maid-mwah-**zel**] French title equivalent to *Miss*.

madhouse *n.* **1.** *Old-fashioned* mental hospital. **2.** *Informal* place filled with uproar or confusion.

Madonna *n.* **1.** the Virgin Mary. **2.** picture or statue of her.

madrigal *n.* 16th–17th-century part song for unaccompanied voices.

maelstrom [**male**-strom] *n.* **1.** great whirlpool. **2.** turmoil.

maestro [**my**-stroh] *n., pl.* **-tri**, **-tros**. **1.** outstanding musician or conductor. **2.** any master of an art.

mae west *n.* inflatable life jacket.

Mafia *n.* international secret criminal organization founded in Sicily. **mafioso** *n., pl.* **-sos**, **-si.** member of the Mafia.

magazine *n.* **1.** periodical publication with articles by different writers. **2.** television or radio programme made up of short nonfictional items. **3.** appliance for automatically supplying cartridges to a gun or slides to a projector. **4.** storehouse for explosives or arms.

magenta [maj-**jen**-ta] *adj.* deep purplish-red.

maggot *n.* larva of an insect, esp. the blowfly. **maggoty** *adj.*

Magi [**maje**-eye] *pl. n.* wise men from the East at the Nativity.

magic *n.* **1.** supposed art of invoking supernatural powers to influence events. **2.** conjuring tricks done to entertain. **3.** mysterious quality or power. —*adj.* **4.** (also **magical**) of, using, or like magic. **5.** *Informal* wonderful, marvellous. **magically** *adv.* **magician** *n.* **1.** conjurer. **2.** person with magic powers.

magistrate *n.* **1.** public officer administering the law. **2.** justice of the peace. **magisterial** *adj.* **1.** commanding or authoritative. **2.** of a magistrate.

magma *n.* molten rock inside the earth's crust.

magnanimous *adj.* noble and generous. **magnanimously** *adv.* **magnanimity** *n.*

magnate *n.* influential or wealthy person, esp. in industry.

magnesia *n.* white tasteless substance used as an antacid and a laxative; magnesium oxide.

magnesium *n.* silvery-white metallic element.

magnet *n.* piece of iron or steel capable of attracting iron and pointing north when suspended. **magnetic** *adj.* **1.** having the properties of a magnet. **2.** powerfully attractive. **magnetically** *adv.* **magnetism** *n.* **1.** magnetic property. **2.** science of this. **3.** powerful personal charm. **magnetize** *v.* **1.** make into a magnet. **2.** attract strongly. **magnetic field** area around a magnet in which its power of attraction is felt. **magnetic north** direction in which a compass needle points. **magnetic tape** plastic strip coated with a magnetic substance for recording sound or video signals.

magneto [mag-**nee**-toe] *n., pl.* **-tos.** apparatus for ignition in an internal-combustion engine.

magnificent *adj.* **1.** splendid or impressive. **2.** excellent. **magnificently** *adv.* **magnificence** *n.*

magnify *v.* **-fying**, **-fied**. **1.** increase in apparent size, as with a lens. **2.** exaggerate. **magnification** *n.* **magnifying glass** convex lens used to produce an enlarged image of an object.

magnitude *n.* relative importance or size.

magnolia *n.* shrub or tree with showy white or pink flowers.

magnum *n.* large wine bottle holding about 1.5 litres.

magnum opus *n.* greatest single work of art or literature of a particular artist.

magpie *n.* black-and-white bird.

Magyar *n.* **1.** member of the prevailing race in Hungary. **2.** Hungarian language. —*adj.* **3.** of the Magyars.

maharajah *n.* former title of some Indian princes. **maharanee** *n. fem.*

maharishi *n.* Hindu religious teacher or mystic.

mahatma *n. Hinduism* person revered for holiness and wisdom.

mahjong, mahjongg *n.* Chinese table game for four, played with tiles bearing different designs.

mahogany *n.* hard reddish-brown wood of several tropical trees.

mahout [ma-**howt**] *n.* in India and the East Indies, elephant driver or keeper.

maid *n.* **1.** (also **maidservant**) female servant. **2.** *Lit.* young unmarried woman.

maiden *n.* **1.** *Lit.* young unmarried woman. —*adj.* **2.** unmarried. **3.** first, e.g. *maiden voyage.* **maidenly** *adj.* modest. **maidenhair** *n.* fern with delicate fronds. **maidenhead** *n.* virginity. **maiden name** woman's surname before marriage. **maiden over** *Cricket* over in which no runs are scored.

mail[1] *n.* **1.** letters and packages transported and delivered by the post office. **2.** postal system. **3.** letters and packages conveyed at one time. **4.** train, ship, or aircraft carrying mail. —*v.* **5.** send by post. **mailing list** register of names and addresses to which information and advertising material is sent by post. **mail order** system of buying goods by post. **mailshot** *n.* posting of advertising material to many selected people at once.

mail[2] *n.* flexible armour of interlaced rings or links.

maim *v.* cripple or mutilate.

main *adj.* **1.** chief or principal. —*n.* **2.** principal pipe or line carrying water, gas, or electricity. —*pl.* **3.** main distribution network for water, gas, or electricity. **in the main** on the whole. **mainly** *adv.* for the most part, chiefly. **mainframe** *n., adj. Computers* (denoting) a high-speed general-purpose computer. **mainland** *n.* stretch of land which forms the main part of a country. **mainmast** *n.* chief mast of a ship. **mainsail** *n.* largest sail on a mainmast. **mainspring** *n.* **1.** chief spring of a watch or clock. **2.** chief cause or motive. **mainstay** *n.* **1.** rope securing a mainmast. **2.** chief support. **mainstream** *n.* prevailing cultural trend.

maintain *v.* **1.** continue or keep in existence. **2.** keep up or preserve. **3.** support financially. **4.** assert. **maintenance** *n.* **1.** maintaining. **2.** upkeep of a building, car, etc. **3.** provision of money for a separated or divorced spouse.

maisonette *n.* flat with more than one floor.

maître d'hôtel [met-ra dote-**tell**] *n. French* head waiter.

maize *n.* type of corn with spikes of yellow grains.

Maj. Major.

majesty *n., pl.* **-ties. 1.** stateliness or grandeur. **2.** supreme power. **majestic** *adj.* majestically *adv.*

majolica *n.* type of ornamented Italian pottery.

major *adj.* **1.** greater in number, quality, or extent. **2.** significant or serious. —*n.* **3.** middle-ranking army officer. **4.** scale in music. **5.** *US* principal field of study at a university etc. —*v.* **6.** (foll. by *in*) *US* do one's principal study in (a particular subject). **majorette** *n.* one of a group of girls who practise formation marching and baton twirling. **major-domo** *n., pl.* **-domos.** chief steward of a great household. **major-general** *n.* senior military officer.

▷ *Major* strictly involves the comparison of one part with another: *He found the major part of the evidence.* Its use as a rough equivalent to 'large' is very informal.

majority *n., pl.* **-ties. 1.** greater number. **2.** largest party voting together. **3.** number by which the votes on one side exceed those on the other. **4.** state of being legally an adult.

make *v.* **making, made. 1.** create, construct, or establish. **2.** cause to do or be. **3.** bring about or produce. **4.** perform (an action). **5.** amount to. **6.** earn. **7.** serve as or become. —*n.* **8.** brand, type, or style. **make do** manage with an inferior alternative. **make it** *Informal* be successful. **on the make** *Informal* out for profit or conquest. **maker** *n.* **1.** person or company that makes something. **2.** (M-) title given to God. **making** *n.* **1.** creation or production. —*pl.* **2.** necessary requirements or qualities. **make-believe** *n.* fantasy or pretence. **make for** *v.* head towards. **make off** *v.* steal or abduct. **make out** *v.* **1.** manage to see or hear (something), perceive. **2.** understand. **3.** pretend. **4.** write out (a cheque). **5.** *Informal* manage or fare, e.g. *How did you make out in the competition?* **makeshift** *adj.* serving as a temporary substitute. **make up** *v.* **1.** form or constitute. **2.** prepare. **3.** invent. **4.** supply what is lacking, complete. **5.** (foll. by *for*) compensate (for). **6.** settle a quarrel. **7.** apply cosmetics. **make-up** *n.* **1.** cosmetics. **2.** mental or physical constitution. **3.** way something is made. **makeweight** *n.* something unimportant added to make up a lack.

mako *n., pl.* **makos.** powerful shark of the Atlantic and Pacific Oceans.

mal- *combining form* bad or badly, e.g. *malformation.*

malachite [mal-a-kite] *n.* green mineral.

maladjusted *adj. Psychol.* unable to meet the demands of society. **maladjustment** *n.*

maladministration *n.* inefficient or dishonest administration.

maladroit [mal-a-droyt] *adj.* clumsy or awkward.

malady [mal-a-dee] *n., pl.* -**dies.** disease or illness.

malaise [mal-laze] *n.* vague feeling of illness or unease.

malapropism *n.* comical misuse of a word by confusion with one which sounds similar.

malaria *n.* infectious disease caused by the bite of some mosquitoes. **malarial** *adj.*

Malay *n.* **1.** member of a people of Malaysia or Indonesia. **2.** language of this people. **Malayan** *adj., n.*

malcontent *n.* discontented person.

male *adj.* **1.** of the sex which can fertilize female reproductive cells. —*n.* **2.** male person or animal. **maleness** *n.* **male chauvinism** belief, held by some men, that men are superior to women. **male chauvinist** (characteristic of) a man who believes that men are superior to women.

malediction [mal-lid-**dik**-shun] *n.* curse.

malefactor [mal-if-act-or] *n.* criminal or wrongdoer.

malevolent [mal-lev-a-lent] *adj.* wishing evil to others. **malevolently** *adv.* **malevolence** *n.*

malfeasance [mal-fee-zanss] *n.* misconduct, esp. by a public official.

malformed *adj.* misshapen or deformed. **malformation** *n.*

malfunction *v.* **1.** function imperfectly or fail to function. —*n.* **2.** defective functioning or failure to function.

malice [mal-iss] *n.* desire to cause harm to others. **malice aforethought** *Law* deliberate intention to do something unlawful. **malicious** *adj.* **maliciously** *adv.*

malign [mal-line] *v.* **1.** slander or defame. —*adj.* **2.** evil in influence or effect. **malignity** [mal-lig-nit-tee] *n.* evil disposition.

malignant [mal-lig-nant] *adj.* **1.** seeking to harm others. **2.** (of a tumour) harmful and uncontrollable. **malignancy** *n.*

malinger [mal-ling-ger] *v.* feign illness to avoid work. **malingerer** *n.*

mall [mawl] *n.* street or shopping area closed to vehicles.

mallard *n.* wild duck.

malleable [mal-lee-a-bl] *adj.* **1.** capable of being hammered or pressed into shape. **2.** easily influenced. **malleability** *n.*

mallet *n.* **1.** (wooden) hammer. **2.** stick with a head like a hammer, used in croquet or polo.

mallow *n.* plant with pink or purple flowers.

malmsey *n.* kind of strong sweet wine.

malnutrition *n.* inadequate nutrition.

malodorous [mal-**lode**-or-uss] *adj.* badsmelling.

malpractice *n.* immoral, illegal, or unethical professional conduct.

malt *n.* **1.** grain, such as barley, prepared for use in making beer or whisky. **2.** malt whisky. —*v.* **3.** make into or make with malt. **malted milk** drink made from powdered milk with malted cereals. **malt whisky** whisky made from malted barley.

Maltese *adj.* **1.** of Malta or its language. —*n.* **2.** *pl.* -**tese.** person from Malta. **3.** language of Malta. **Maltese cross** cross with triangular arms that taper towards the centre.

maltreat *v.* treat badly. **maltreatment** *n.*

mama [mam-ma] *n. Old-fashioned* mother.

mamba *n.* deadly S Afr. snake.

mamma *n.* same as MAMA.

mammal *n.* animal of the type that suckles its young. **mammalian** *adj.*

mammary *adj.* of the breasts or milk-producing glands.

mammon *n.* wealth regarded as a source of evil.

mammoth *n.* **1.** extinct elephant-like mammal. —*adj.* **2.** colossal.

man *n., pl.* **men. 1.** adult male. **2.** human being or person. **3.** mankind. **4.** manservant. **5.** (usu. pl.) member of the armed forces who is not an officer. **6.** piece used in chess etc. —*v.* **manning, manned. 7.** supply with sufficient people for operation or defence. **man in the street** average person. **manhood** *n.* **mankind** *n.* human beings collectively. **manly** *adj.* -**lier,** -**liest.** (possessing qualities) appropriate to a man. **manliness** *n.* **manned** *adj.* having a human personnel or crew. **mannish** *adj.* like a man. **manhour** *n.* work done by one person in one hour. **man-made** *adj.* synthetic.

manacle [man-a-kl] *n., v.* handcuff or fetter.

manage v. **1.** succeed in doing. **2.** be in charge of, administer. **3.** handle or control. **4.** cope with (financial) difficulties. **manageable** adj. **management** n. **1.** managers collectively. **2.** administration or organization. **manager, manageress** n. person in charge of a business, institution, actor, sports team, etc. **managerial** adj.
▷ In professional life the title *manager* is used for either men or women. Elsewhere the term *manageress* is still in use.

mañana [man-yah-na] adv., n. *Spanish* **1.** tomorrow. **2.** some later (unspecified) time.

manatee n. large tropical plant-eating aquatic mammal.

mandarin n. **1.** high-ranking government official. **2.** kind of small orange.

Mandarin Chinese, Mandarin n. official language of China.

mandate n. **1.** official or authoritative command. **2.** authorization or instruction from an electorate to its representative or government. —v. **3.** give authority to. **mandatory** adj. compulsory.

mandible n. lower jawbone or jawlike part.

mandolin n. musical instrument with four pairs of strings.

mandrake n. plant with a forked root, formerly used as a narcotic.

mandrel n. shaft on which work is held in a lathe.

mandrill n. large blue-faced baboon.

mane n. long hair on the neck of a horse, lion, etc.

manful adj. determined and brave. **manfully** adv.

manganese n. brittle greyish-white metallic element.

mange n. skin disease of domestic animals.

mangelwurzel n. variety of beet used as cattle food.

manger n. eating trough in a stable or barn.

mangetout [mawnzh-too] n. variety of pea with an edible pod.

mangle[1] v. **1.** destroy by crushing and twisting. **2.** spoil.

mangle[2] n. **1.** machine with rollers for squeezing water from washed clothes. —v. **2.** put through a mangle.

mango n., pl. **-goes, -gos.** tropical fruit with sweet juicy yellow flesh.

mangrove n. tropical tree with exposed roots, which grows beside water.

mangy adj. **mangier, mangiest. 1.** having mange. **2.** scruffy or shabby.

manhandle v. treat roughly.

manhole n. hole with a cover, through which a person can enter a drain or sewer.

manhunt n. organized search, usu. by police, for a wanted man or a fugitive.

mania n. **1.** madness. **2.** extreme enthusiasm. **maniac** n. **1.** mad person. **2.** *Informal* person who has an extreme enthusiasm for something. **maniacal** [man-eye-a-kl] adj.

manic adj. affected by mania. **manic-depressive** adj., n. *Psychiatry* (person afflicted with) a mental disorder that causes mood swings from extreme euphoria to deep depression.

manicure n. **1.** cosmetic care of the fingernails and hands. —v. **2.** care for (the fingernails and hands) in this way. **manicurist** n.

manifest adj. **1.** easily noticed, obvious. —v. **2.** show plainly. **3.** be evidence of. —n. **4.** list of cargo or passengers for customs. **manifestly** adv. **manifestation** n.

manifesto n., pl. **-toes, -tos.** declaration of policy as issued by a political party.

manifold adj. **1.** numerous and varied. —n. **2.** pipe with several outlets, esp. in an internal-combustion engine.

manikin n. **1.** little man or dwarf. **2.** model of the human body.

manila, manilla n. strong brown paper used for envelopes.

manipulate v. **1.** handle skilfully. **2.** control cleverly or deviously. **manipulation** n. **manipulative** adj. **manipulator** n.

manna n. **1.** *Bible* miraculous food which sustained the Israelites in the wilderness. **2.** windfall.

mannequin n. **1.** woman who models clothes at a fashion show. **2.** life-size dummy of the human body used to fit or display clothes.

manner n. **1.** way a thing happens or is done. **2.** person's bearing or behaviour. **3.** type or kind. **4.** custom or style. —pl. **5.** (polite) social behaviour. **mannered** adj. affected. **mannerism** n. person's distinctive habit or trait. **mannerly** adj. having good manners, polite.

mannikin n. same as MANIKIN.

manoeuvre [man-**noo**-ver] n. **1.** contrived, complicated, and possibly deceptive plan or action. **2.** skilful movement. —pl. **3.** military or naval exercises. —v. **4.** manipulate or contrive skilfully or cunningly. **5.** perform manoeuvres. **manoeuvrable** adj.

manor n. large country house and its lands. **manorial** adj.

manpower n. available number of workers.

manqué [mong-kay] adj. would-be, e.g. an actor manqué.

mansard roof n. roof with a break in its slope, the lower part being steeper than the upper.

manse n. minister's house in some religious denominations.

manservant n., pl. **menservants**. male servant, esp. a valet.

mansion n. large house.

manslaughter n. unlawful but unintentional killing of a person.

mantel n. structure round a fireplace. **mantelpiece, mantel shelf** n. shelf above a fireplace.

mantilla n. in Spain, a lace scarf covering a woman's head and shoulders.

mantis n., pl. **-tises, -tes**. carnivorous insect like a grasshopper.

mantle n. **1.** loose cloak. **2.** covering. **3.** incandescent gauze round a gas jet.

mantra n. Hinduism, Buddhism any sacred word or syllable used as an object of concentration.

manual adj. **1.** of or done with the hands. **2.** by human labour rather than automatic means. —n. **3.** handbook. **4.** organ keyboard. **manually** adv.

manufacture v. **1.** process or make (goods) on a large scale using machinery. **2.** invent or concoct (an excuse etc.). —n. **3.** process of manufacturing goods. **manufacturer** n.

manure n. **1.** animal excrement used as a fertilizer. —v. **2.** fertilize (land) with this.

manuscript n. **1.** book or document, orig. one written by hand. **2.** copy for printing.

Manx adj. **1.** of the Isle of Man or its inhabitants. —n. **2.** language of the Isle of Man. **Manx cat** tailless breed of cat.

many adj. **more, most. 1.** numerous. —n. **2.** large number.

Maoism n. form of Marxism advanced by Mao Tse-Tung in China. **Maoist** n., adj.

Maori n. **1.** member of the indigenous race of New Zealand. **2.** language of the Maoris. —adj. **3.** of the Maoris or their language.

map n. **1.** representation of the earth's surface or some part of it, showing geographical features. **2.** Maths (also **mapping**) same as FUNCTION (sense 4). —v. **mapping, mapped. 3.** make a map of. **4.** Maths represent or transform (a function, figure, or set). **map out** v. plan.

maple n. tree with broad leaves, a variety of which (**sugar maple**) yields sugar. **maple syrup** very sweet syrup made from the sap of the sugar maple.

mar v. **marring, marred.** spoil or impair.

Mar. March.

marabou n. **1.** kind of African stork. **2.** its soft white down, used to trim hats etc.

maraca [mar-**rak**-a] n. shaken percussion instrument made from a gourd containing dried seeds etc.

maraschino cherry [mar-rass-**kee**-no] n. cherry preserved in a cherry liqueur with a taste like bitter almonds.

marathon n. **1.** long-distance race of just over 26 miles. **2.** long or arduous task.

marauding adj. **1.** hunting for plunder. **2.** pillaging. **marauder** n.

marble n. **1.** kind of limestone with a mottled appearance, which can be highly polished. **2.** slab of or sculpture in this. **3.** small glass ball used in playing marbles. —pl. **4.** game of rolling these. **marbled** adj. having a mottled appearance like marble.

marcasite n. crystals of iron pyrites, used in jewellery.

march[1] v. **1.** walk with a military step. **2.** make (a person or group) proceed. **3.** progress steadily. —n. **4.** action of marching. **5.** distance covered by marching. **6.** steady progress. **7.** piece of music, as for a march. **marcher** n.

march[2] n. border or frontier.

March n. third month of the year.

marchioness [marsh-on-**ness**] n. **1.** woman holding the rank of marquis. **2.** wife or widow of a marquis.

Mardi Gras [mar-dee grah] n. festival of Shrove Tuesday, celebrated in some cities with great revelry.

mare *n.* female horse. **mare's nest** discovery which proves worthless.

margarine *n.* butter substitute made from animal or vegetable fats.

marge *n. Informal* margarine.

margin *n.* **1.** edge or border. **2.** blank space round a printed page. **3.** additional amount or one greater than necessary. **4.** limit. **marginal** *adj.* **1.** insignificant, unimportant. **2.** near a limit. **3.** *Politics* (of a constituency) won by only a small margin. —*n.* **4.** *Politics* marginal constituency. **marginally** *adv.*

marguerite *n.* large daisy.

marigold *n.* plant with yellow flowers.

marijuana [mar-ree-wah-na] *n.* dried flowers and leaves of the hemp plant, used as a drug, esp. in cigarettes.

marimba *n.* Latin American percussion instrument resembling a xylophone.

marina *n.* harbour for yachts and other pleasure boats.

marinade *n.* **1.** seasoned liquid in which fish or meat is soaked before cooking. —*v.* **2.** same as MARINATE. **marinate** *v.* soak in marinade.

marine *adj.* **1.** of the sea or shipping. **2.** used at or found in the sea. —*n.* **3.** country's shipping or fleet. **4.** soldier trained for land and sea combat. **mariner** [mar-in-er] *n.* sailor.

marionette *n.* puppet worked with strings.

marital *adj.* relating to marriage.

maritime *adj.* **1.** relating to shipping. **2.** of, near, or living in the sea.

marjoram *n.* aromatic herb used for seasoning food and in salads.

mark[1] *n.* **1.** line, dot, scar, etc. visible on a surface. **2.** distinguishing sign or symbol. **3.** written or printed symbol. **4.** letter or number used to grade academic work. **5.** indication of position. **6.** indication of some quality. **7.** target or goal. —*v.* **8.** make a mark on. **9.** be a distinguishing mark of. **10.** indicate. **11.** pay attention to. **12.** notice or watch. **13.** grade (academic work). **14.** stay close to (a sporting opponent) to hamper his or her play. **mark time 1.** move the feet up and down as if marching, without moving forward. **2.** wait for something more interesting to happen. **marked** *adj.* noticeable. **markedly** [mark-id-lee] *adv.* **marker** *n.* **1.** object used to show the position of some-

thing. **2.** (also **marker pen**) thick felt-tipped pen for drawing and colouring. **marking** *n.*

mark[2] *n.* same as DEUTSCHMARK.

market *n.* **1.** assembly or place for buying and selling. **2.** demand for goods. —*v.* **-keting, -keted. 3.** offer or produce for sale. **on the market** for sale. **marketable** *adj.* **marketing** *n.* part of a business that controls the way that goods or services are sold. **market garden** place where fruit and vegetables are grown for sale. **market maker** *Stock Exchange* person who uses a firm's money to create a market for a stock. **marketplace** *n.* **1.** market. **2.** commercial world. **market research** research into consumers' needs and purchases.

marksman *n.* person skilled at shooting. **marksmanship** *n.*

marl *n.* soil formed of clay and lime, used as fertilizer.

marlinespike, marlinspike [mar-lin-spike] *n.* pointed hook used to separate strands of rope.

marmalade *n.* jam made from citrus fruits.

marmoreal [mar-more-ee-al] *adj.* of or like marble.

marmoset *n.* small bushy-tailed monkey.

marmot *n.* burrowing rodent.

maroon[1] *adj.* reddish-purple.

maroon[2] *v.* **1.** abandon ashore, esp. on an island. **2.** isolate without resources.

marquee *n.* large tent used for a party or exhibition.

marquess [mar-kwiss] *n. Brit.* nobleman of the rank below a duke.

marquetry *n.* ornamental inlaid work of wood.

marquis *n.* in various countries, nobleman of the rank above a count.

marquise [mar-keez] *n.* same as MARCHIONESS.

marram grass *n.* grass that grows on sandy shores.

marrow *n.* **1.** fatty substance inside bones. **2.** long thick striped green vegetable with whitish flesh.

marry *v.* **-rying, -ried. 1.** take as a husband or wife. **2.** join or give in marriage. **3.** unite closely. **marriage** *n.* **1.** state of being married. **2.** wedding. **marriageable** *adj.*

Mars *n.* **1.** Roman god of war. **2.** fourth planet from the sun.

Marsala [mar-**sah**-la] *n.* dark sweet wine.

Marseillaise [mar-say-**yaze**] *n.* French national anthem.

marsh *n.* low-lying wet land. **marshy** *adj.* **marshier, marshiest.**

marshal *n.* **1.** officer of the highest rank. **2.** official who organizes ceremonies or events. **3.** *US* law officer. —*v.* -**shalling, -shalled. 4.** arrange in order. **5.** assemble. **6.** conduct with ceremony. **marshalling yard** railway depot for goods trains.

marshmallow *n.* spongy pink or white sweet.

marsupial [mar-**soop**-ee-al] *n.* animal that carries its young in a pouch, such as a kangaroo.

mart *n.* market.

Martello tower *n.* round tower for coastal defence.

marten *n.* **1.** weasel-like animal. **2.** its fur.

martial *adj.* of war, warlike. **martial art** any of various philosophies; and techniques of self-defence, orig. Eastern, such as karate. **martial law** law enforced by military authorities in times of danger or emergency.

Martian [**marsh**-an] *adj.* **1.** of Mars. —*n.* **2.** supposed inhabitant of Mars.

martin *n.* bird with a slightly forked tail.

martinet *n.* strict disciplinarian.

martingale *n.* strap from the reins to the girth of a horse, preventing it from throwing up its head.

martini *n.* cocktail of vermouth and gin.

martyr *n.* **1.** person who dies or suffers for his or her beliefs. —*v.* **2.** make a martyr of. **be a martyr to** be constantly suffering from. **martyrdom** *n.*

marvel *v.* -**velling, -velled. 1.** be filled with wonder. —*n.* **2.** wonderful thing. **marvellous** *adj.* **1.** amazing. **2.** wonderful. **marvellously** *adv.*

Marxism *n.* state socialism as conceived by Karl Marx. **Marxist** *n.,* adj.

marzipan *n.* paste of ground almonds, sugar, and egg whites.

masc. masculine.

mascara *n.* cosmetic for darkening the eyelashes.

mascot *n.* person, animal, or thing supposed to bring good luck.

masculine *adj.* **1.** relating to males. **2.** manly. **3.** *Grammar* of the gender of nouns that includes some male animate things. **masculinity** *n.*

maser *n.* device for amplifying microwaves.

mash *n.* **1.** bran or meal mixed with warm water as food for horses etc. **2.** *Informal* mashed potatoes. —*v.* **3.** crush into a soft mass.

mask *n.* **1.** covering for the face, as a disguise or protection. **2.** behaviour that hides one's true feelings. —*v.* **3.** cover with a mask. **4.** hide or disguise. **masking tape** adhesive tape used to protect surfaces surrounding an area to be painted.

masochism [**mass**-oh-kiz-zum] *n.* form of (sexual) perversion marked by love of pain or of being humiliated. **masochist** *n.* **masochistic** *adj.* **masochistically** *adv.*

mason *n.* **1.** person who works with stone. **2.** (M-) Freemason. **Masonic** *adj.* of Freemasonry. **masonry** *n.* **1.** stonework. **2.** (M-) Freemasonry.

masque [mask] *n. Hist.* 16th–17th-century form of dramatic entertainment.

masquerade [mask-er-**aid**] *n.* **1.** deceptive show or pretence. **2.** party at which masks and costumes are worn. —*v.* **3.** pretend to be someone or something else.

mass *n.* **1.** coherent body of matter. **2.** large quantity or number. **3.** *Physics* amount of matter in a body. —*adj.* **4.** large-scale. **5.** involving many people. —*v.* **6.** form into a mass. **the masses** ordinary people. **massive** *adj.* large and heavy. **massively** *adv.* **mass-market** *adj.* for or appealing to a large number of people. **mass media** means of communication to many people, such as television and newspapers. **mass-produce** *v.* manufacture (standardized goods) in large quantities. **mass production** manufacturing of standardized goods in large quantities.

Mass *n.* service of the Eucharist, esp. in the RC Church.

massacre [**mass**-a-ker] *n.* **1.** indiscriminate killing of large numbers of people. —*v.* **2.** kill in large numbers.

massage [**mass**-ahzh] *n.* **1.** rubbing and kneading of parts of the body to reduce pain or stiffness. —*v.* **2.** give a massage to. **masseur** [mass-**ur**], **masseuse** [mass-**urz**] *n.* person who gives massages.

massif [**mass**-seef] *n.* connected group of mountains.

mast[1] n. tall pole for supporting something, esp. a ship's sails. **masthead** n. 1. *Naut.* head of a mast. 2. name of a newspaper printed at the top of the front page.

mast[2] n. fruit of the beech, oak, etc., used as pig fodder.

mastectomy [mass-**tek**-tom-ee] n., pl. **-mies.** surgical removal of a breast.

master n. 1. person in control, such as an employer or an owner of slaves or animals. 2. expert. 3. great artist. 4. male teacher. 5. original thing from which copies are made. 6. (M-) title of a boy. —adj. 7. overall or controlling. 8. main or principal. —v. 9. overcome. 10. acquire knowledge of or skill in. **masterful** adj. 1. domineering. 2. showing great skill. **masterly** adj. showing great skill. **mastery** n. 1. expertise. 2. control or command. **master key** key that opens all the locks of a set. **mastermind** v. 1. plan and direct (a complex task). —n. 2. person who plans and directs a complex task. **master of ceremonies** person who presides over a public ceremony, formal dinner, or entertainment, introducing the events and performers. **masterpiece** n. outstanding work of art. **masterstroke** n. outstanding piece of strategy, skill, or talent.

mastic n. 1. gum obtained from certain trees. 2. putty-like substance used as a filler, adhesive, or seal.

masticate v. chew. **mastication** n.

mastiff n. large dog.

mastitis n. inflammation of a breast or udder.

mastodon n. extinct elephant-like mammal.

mastoid n. projection of the bone behind the ear. **mastoiditis** n. inflammation of this area.

masturbate v. stimulate the genitals (of). **masturbation** n.

mat[1] n. 1. piece of fabric used as a floor covering or to protect a surface. 2. thick tangled mass. —v. **matting, matted.** 3. form into a mat. **on the mat** *Informal* summoned for a reprimand.

mat[2] adj. same as MATT.

matador n. man who kills the bull in bullfights.

match[1] n. 1. contest in a game or sport. 2. person or thing exactly like, equal to, or in harmony with another. 3. marriage. —v. 4. be exactly like, equal to, or in harmony with. 5. put in competition (with). 6. find a match for. 7. join (in marriage). **matchless** adj. unequalled. **matchmaker** n. person who schemes to bring about a marriage. **matchmaking** n., adj.

match[2] n. small stick with a tip which ignites when scraped on a rough surface. **matchbox** n. **matchstick** n. 1. wooden part of a match. —adj. 2. (of drawn figures) thin and straight. **matchwood** n. small splinters.

mate[1] n. 1. *Informal* common Brit. and Aust. term of address between males. 2. sexual partner of an animal. 3. officer in a merchant ship. 4. tradesman's assistant. —v. 5. pair (animals) or (of animals) be paired for reproduction.

mate[2] n., v. *Chess* checkmate.

material n. 1. substance of which a thing is made. 2. cloth. 3. information on which a piece of work may be based. —pl. 4. things needed for an activity. —adj. 5. of matter or substance. 6. affecting physical wellbeing. 7. not spiritual. 8. relevant. **materially** adv. considerably. **materialism** n. 1. excessive interest in or desire for money and possessions. 2. belief that only the material world exists. **materialist** adj., n. **materialistic** adj. **materialize** v. 1. come into existence or view. 2. actually happen. **materialization** n.

maternal adj. 1. of a mother. 2. related through one's mother. **maternity** n. 1. motherhood. —adj. 2. of or for pregnant women, e.g. *maternity leave.*

matey adj. *Informal* friendly or intimate.

mathematics n. science of number, quantity, shape, and space. **mathematical** adj. **mathematically** adv. **mathematician** n.

maths n. *Informal* mathematics.

matinée [mat-in-nay] n. afternoon performance in a theatre.

matins pl. n. early morning service in various Christian Churches.

matriarch [mate-ree-ark] n. female head of a tribe or family. **matriarchal** adj. **matriarchy** n., pl. **-archies.** society with matriarchal government and descent traced through the female line.

matrices [may-triss-eez] n. plural of MATRIX.

matricide n. 1. crime of killing one's mother. 2. person who does this.

matriculate v. enrol or be enrolled in a college or university. **matriculation** n.

matrimony *n.* marriage. **matrimonial** *adj.*

matrix [**may**-trix] *n., pl.* **matrices**. **1.** substance or situation in which something originates, takes form, or is enclosed. **2.** mould for casting. **3.** *Maths* rectangular array of numbers or elements.

matron *n.* **1.** staid or dignified married woman. **2.** former name for NURSING OFFICER. **3.** woman who supervises the domestic or medical arrangements of an institution. **matronly** *adj.* (of a woman) middle-aged and plump.

matt *adj.* dull, not shiny.

matter *n.* **1.** substance of which something is made. **2.** physical substance. **3.** event, situation, or subject. **4.** written material in general. **5.** pus. —*v.* **6.** be of importance. **what's the matter?** what is wrong? **matter-of-fact** *adj.* unimaginative or emotionless. **matter-of-factly** *adv.* **matter-of-factness** *n.*

matting *n.* coarsely woven fabric used as a floor-covering and packing material.

mattock *n.* large pick with one of its blade ends flattened for loosening soil.

mattress *n.* large stuffed flat case, often with springs, used on or as a bed.

mature *adj.* **1.** fully developed or grown-up. **2.** ripe. —*v.* **3.** make or become mature. **4.** (of a bill or bond) become due for payment. **maturity** *n.* state of being mature. **maturation** *n.* process of becoming mature.

maudlin *adj.* foolishly or tearfully sentimental.

maul *v.* **1.** handle roughly. **2.** beat or tear.

maunder *v.* talk or act aimlessly or idly.

Maundy money *n.* special silver coins given to the poor in a symbolic ceremony on the Thursday before Easter (**Maundy Thursday**).

mausoleum [maw-so-**lee**-um] *n.* stately tomb.

mauve *adj.* pale purple.

maverick *n., adj.* independent and unorthodox (person).

maw *n.* animal's mouth, throat, or stomach.

mawkish *adj.* foolishly sentimental. **mawkishness** *n.*

max. maximum.

maxim *n.* general truth or principle.

maximum *adj., n., pl.* **-mums, -ma.** greatest possible (amount or number). **maximal** *adj.* maximum. **maximize** *v.* increase to a maximum. **maximization** *n.*

may *v., past tense* **might.** used as an auxiliary to express possibility, permission, opportunity, etc.
▷ In very careful usage *may* is used in preference to *can* for asking permission. *Might* is used to express a more tentative request: *May/might I ask a favour?*

May *n.* **1.** fifth month of the year. **2.** (m-) same as HAWTHORN. **mayfly** *n.* short-lived aquatic insect. **maypole** *n.* pole set up for dancing round on the first day of May (**May Day**).

maybe *adv.* perhaps, possibly.

Mayday *n.* international radiotelephone distress signal.

mayhem *n.* violent destruction or confusion.

mayonnaise *n.* creamy sauce of egg yolks, oil, and vinegar.

mayor *n.* head of a municipality. **mayoress** *n.* **1.** mayor's wife. **2.** female mayor. **mayoralty** *n., pl.* **-ties.** (term of) office of a mayor.

maze *n.* **1.** complex network of paths or lines designed to puzzle. **2.** state of confusion.

mazurka *n.* **1.** lively Polish dance. **2.** music for this.

MB 1. Bachelor of Medicine. **2.** Manitoba.

MBE Member of the Order of the British Empire.

MC Master of Ceremonies.

MCC Marylebone Cricket Club.

Md *Chem.* mendelevium.

MD 1. Doctor of Medicine. **2.** Managing Director. **3.** Maryland.

MDMA *n.* same as ECSTASY (sense 2).

me[1] *pron.* objective form of I.
▷ The use of *it's me* in preference to *it's I* is accepted as quite standard.

me[2] *n. Music* in tonic sol-fa, third degree of any major scale.

ME 1. myalgic encephalomyelitis: painful muscles and general weakness sometimes persisting long after a viral illness. **2.** Maine.

mead *n.* alcoholic drink made from honey.

meadow *n.* piece of grassland. **meadowsweet** *n.* plant with dense heads of small fragrant flowers.

meagre adj. scanty or insufficient.

meal[1] n. 1. occasion when food is served and eaten. 2. the food itself. **make a meal of** Informal perform (a task) with an unnecessary amount of effort. **meals-on-wheels** n. service taking hot meals to elderly or infirm people in their own homes. **meal ticket** Slang person or situation providing a source of livelihood or income.

meal[2] n. grain ground to powder. **mealy** adj. **mealier, mealiest. mealy-mouthed** adj. not outspoken enough.

mealie n. S Afr. maize.

mean[1] v. **meaning, meant. 1.** intend to convey or express. **2.** intend. **3.** signify, denote, or portend. **4.** have importance as specified. **meaning** n. **1.** sense, significance. —adj. **2.** expressive. **meaningful** adj. **meaningfully** adv. **meaningfulness** n. **meaningless** adj. **meaninglessly** adv. **meaninglessness** n.

mean[2] adj. **1.** miserly, ungenerous, or petty. **2.** despicable or callous. **3.** US informal bad-tempered. **meanly** adv. **meanness** n. **meanie** n. Informal unkind or miserly person.

mean[3] n. **1.** middle point between two extremes. **2.** average. —pl. **3.** method by which something is done. **4.** money. —adj. **5.** intermediate in size or quantity. **6.** average. **by all means** certainly. **by no means** not at all. **means test** inquiry into a person's means to decide on eligibility for financial aid.

meander [mee-**and**-er] v. **1.** follow a winding course. **2.** wander aimlessly. —n. **3.** winding course.

meant v. past of MEAN[1]

meantime n. **1.** intervening period. —adv. **2.** meanwhile.

meanwhile adv. **1.** during the intervening period. **2.** at the same time.

measles n. infectious disease producing red spots. **measly** adj. **-lier, -liest.** Informal meagre.

measure n. **1.** size or quantity. **2.** graduated scale etc. for measuring size or quantity. **3.** unit of size or quantity. **4.** extent. **5.** action taken. **6.** law. **7.** poetical rhythm. —v. **8.** determine the size or quantity of. **9.** be (a specified amount) in size or quantity. **measurable** adj. **measured** adj. **1.** slow and steady. **2.** carefully considered. **measure-**

ment n. **1.** measuring. **2.** size. **measure up to** v. fulfil (expectations or requirements).

meat n. animal flesh as food. **meaty** adj. **meatier, meatiest. 1.** (tasting) of or like meat. **2.** brawny. **3.** full of significance or interest.

Mecca n. **1.** holy city of Islam. **2.** place that attracts visitors.

mechanic n. person skilled in repairing or operating machinery. **mechanics** n. scientific study of motion and force. **mechanical** adj. **1.** of or done by machines. **2.** (of an action) without thought or feeling. **mechanically** adv.

mechanism n. **1.** way a machine works. **2.** piece of machinery. **3.** process or technique, e.g. defence mechanism. **mechanistic** adj. **mechanize** v. **1.** equip with machinery. **2.** make mechanical or automatic. **3.** Mil. equip (an army) with armoured vehicles. **mechanization** n.

med. 1. medical. **2.** medicine. **3.** medieval. **4.** medium.

medal n. piece of metal with an inscription etc., given as a reward or memento. **medallion** n. **1.** large medal. **2.** circular decorative device in architecture. **medallist** n. winner of a medal.

meddle v. interfere annoyingly. **meddler** n. **meddlesome** adj.

media n. **1.** a plural of MEDIUM. **2.** the mass media collectively. **media event** event that is staged for or exploited by the mass media. ▷ Media is a plural noun. There is an increasing tendency to use it also as a singular noun because of the ambiguous senses of medium.

mediaeval [med-ee-**eve**-al] adj. same as MEDIEVAL.

medial [mee-dee-al] adj. of or in the middle.

median adj., n. middle (point or line).

mediate [mee-dee-ate] v. intervene in a dispute to bring about agreement. **mediation** n. **mediator** n.

medic n. Informal doctor or medical student.

medical adj. **1.** of the science of medicine. —n. **2.** Informal medical examination. **medically** adv. **medicament** [mid-**dik**-ament] n. a medicine. **medicate** v. treat with a medicinal substance. **medication** n. (treatment with) a medicinal substance.

medicine n. **1.** substance used to treat

disease. **2.** science of preventing, diagnosing, or curing disease. **medicinal** [med-**diss**-in-al] *adj.* having therapeutic properties. **medicinally** *adv.* **medicine man** witch doctor.

medieval [med-ee-**eve**-al] *adj.* of the Middle Ages.

mediocre [mee-dee-**oak**-er] *adj.* **1.** average in quality. **2.** second-rate. **mediocrity** [mee-dee-**ok**-rit-ee] *n.* **1.** state of being mediocre. **2.** *pl.* **-rities.** mediocre person.

meditate *v.* **1.** reflect deeply, esp. on spiritual matters. **2.** think about or plan. **meditation** *n.* **meditative** *adj.* **meditatively** *adv.* **meditator** *n.*

Mediterranean *adj.* of (the area around) the Mediterranean Sea, between S Europe, N Africa, and SW Asia.

medium *adj.* **1.** midway between extremes, average. *—n., pl.* **-dia, -diums. 2.** middle state, degree, or condition. **3.** intervening substance producing an effect. **4.** means of communicating news or information to the public, such as radio or newspapers. **5.** person who can supposedly communicate with the dead. **6.** surroundings or environment. **7.** category of art according to the material used. **medium wave** radio wave with a wavelength between 100 and 1000 metres.

medlar *n.* apple-like fruit of a small tree, eaten when it begins to decay.

medley *n.* **1.** miscellaneous mixture. **2.** musical sequence of different tunes.

medulla [mid-**dull**-la] *n., pl.* **-las, -lae.** marrow, pith, or inner tissue.

meek *adj.* submissive or humble. **meekly** *adv.* **meekness** *n.*

meerkat *n.* S African mongoose.

meerschaum [**meer**-shum] *n.* **1.** white substance like clay. **2.** tobacco pipe with a bowl made of this.

meet[1] *v.* **meeting, met. 1.** come together (with). **2.** come into contact (with). **3.** be at the place of arrival of. **4.** make the acquaintance of. **5.** satisfy (a need etc.). **6.** experience. *—n.* **7.** assembly of a hunt. **8.** sports meeting. **meeting** *n.* **1.** coming together. **2.** assembly.

▷ *Meet* is only followed by *with* in the context of misfortune: *I met his son; I met with an accident.*

meet[2] *adj. Obs.* fit or suitable.

mega *adj. Slang* extremely good, great, or successful.

mega- *combining form* **1.** denoting one million, e.g. *megawatt.* **2.** very great, e.g. *megastar.*

megabyte *n. Computers* 2^{20} or 1 048 576 bytes.

megahertz *n., pl.* **-hertz.** one million hertz.

megalith *n.* great stone, esp. as part of a prehistoric monument. **megalithic** *adj.*

megalomania *n.* craving for or mental delusions of power. **megalomaniac** *adj., n.*

megaphone *n.* cone-shaped instrument used to amplify the voice.

megaton *n.* explosive power equal to that of one million tons of TNT.

meiosis [my-**oh**-siss] *n.* type of cell division in which reproductive cells are produced, each containing half the chromosome number of the parent nucleus.

melamine *n.* colourless crystalline compound used in making synthetic resins. **melamine resin** resilient kind of plastic.

melancholy [**mel**-an-kol-lee] *n.* **1.** sadness or gloom. *—adj.* **2.** sad or gloomy. **melancholia** [mel-an-**kole**-lee-a] *n.* old name for depression. **melancholic** *adj., n.*

melange [may-**lahnzh**] *n.* mixture.

melanin *n.* dark pigment found in the hair, skin, and eyes of humans and animals.

Melba toast *n.* very thin crisp toast.

mêlée [**mel**-lay] *n.* noisy confused fight or crowd.

mellifluous [mel-**lif**-flew-uss] *adj.* (of sound) smooth and sweet.

mellow *adj.* **1.** (of fruit) ripe. **2.** kindhearted, esp. through maturity. **3.** soft, not harsh. *—v.* **4.** make or become mellow.

melodrama *n.* **1.** play full of extravagant action and emotion. **2.** overdramatic behaviour or emotion. **melodramatic** *adj.*

melody *n., pl.* **-dies. 1.** series of musical notes which make a tune. **2.** sweet sound. **melodic** [mel-**lod**-ik] *adj.* **1.** of melody. **2.** melodious. **melodious** [mel-**lode**-ee-uss] *adj.* **1.** pleasing to the ear. **2.** tuneful.

melon *n.* large round juicy fruit with a hard rind.

melt *v.* **1.** (cause to) become liquid by heat. **2.** dissolve. **3.** soften through emotion. **4.** blend (into). **5.** disappear. **meltdown** *n.* in a nuclear reactor, melting of the fuel rods, with the possible release of radiation. **melting pot** place or situation in which many races, ideas, etc., are mixed.

member *n.* **1.** individual making up a body or society. **2.** limb. **membership** *n.* **Member of Parliament** person elected to parliament.

membrane *n.* thin flexible tissue in a plant or animal body. **membranous** *adj.*

memento *n., pl.* **-tos, -toes.** thing serving to remind, souvenir.

memo *n., pl.* **memos.** short for MEMORANDUM.

memoir [mem-wahr] *n.* **1.** biography or historical account based on personal knowledge. *—pl.* **2.** collection of these. **3.** autobiography.

memorable *adj.* worth remembering, noteworthy. **memorably** *adv.* **memorabilia** *pl. n.* objects connected with famous people or events.

memorandum *n., pl.* **-dums, -da. 1.** written record or communication within a business. **2.** note of things to be remembered.

memory *n., pl.* **-ries. 1.** ability to remember. **2.** sum of things remembered. **3.** particular recollection. **4.** length of time one can remember. **5.** commemoration. **6.** part of a computer which stores information. **memorize** *v.* commit to memory. **memorial** *n.* **1.** something serving to commemorate a person or thing. *—adj.* **2.** serving as a memorial.

memsahib *n.* formerly, in India, term of respect used for a European married woman.

men *n.* plural of MAN.

menace *n.* **1.** threat. **2.** *Informal* nuisance. *—v.* **3.** threaten, endanger. **menacing** *adj.* **menacingly** *adv.*

ménage [may-nahzh] *n.* household.

menagerie [min-naj-er-ee] *n.* collection of wild animals for exhibition.

mend *v.* **1.** repair or patch. **2.** make or become better. **3.** recover or heal. *—n.* **4.** mended area. **on the mend** regaining health.

mendacity *n.* (tendency to) untruthfulness. **mendacious** *adj.*

mendelevium *n.* artificially produced radioactive element.

mendicant *adj.* **1.** begging. *—n.* **2.** beggar.

menfolk *pl. n.* men collectively, esp. the men of a particular family.

menhir [men-hear] *n.* single upright prehistoric stone.

menial [mean-nee-al] *adj.* **1.** involving boring work of low status. *—n.* **2.** domestic servant.

meningitis [men-in-jite-iss] *n.* inflammation of the membranes of the brain.

meniscus *n.* **1.** curved surface of a liquid. **2.** crescent-shaped lens.

menopause *n.* time when a woman's menstrual cycle ceases. **menopausal** *adj.*

menstruation *n.* approximately monthly discharge of blood and cellular debris from the womb of a nonpregnant woman. **menstruate** *v.* **menstrual** *adj.*

mensuration *n.* measuring, esp. in geometry.

mental *adj.* **1.** of, in, or done by the mind. **2.** of or for mental illness. **3.** *Informal* insane. **mentally** *adv.* **mentality** *n., pl.* **-ties.** way of thinking.

menthol *n.* organic compound found in peppermint, used medicinally.

mention *v.* **1.** refer to briefly. **2.** acknowledge. *—n.* **3.** acknowledgment. **4.** brief reference to a person or thing.

mentor *n.* adviser or guide.

menu *n.* **1.** list of dishes to be served, or from which to order. **2.** *Computers* list of options displayed on a screen.

MEP Member of the European Parliament.

mercantile *adj.* of trade or traders.

Mercator projection [mer-kate-er] *n.* method of map-making in which latitude and longitude form a rectangular grid.

mercenary *adj.* **1.** influenced by greed. **2.** working merely for reward. *—n., pl.* **-aries. 3.** hired soldier.

mercerized *adj.* (of cotton) given lustre by treating with chemicals.

merchandise *n.* commodities.

merchant *n.* person engaged in trade, wholesale trader. **merchant bank** bank dealing mainly with businesses and investment. **merchantman** *n.* trading ship. **merchant navy** ships or crew engaged in a nation's commercial shipping.

mercury *n.* **1.** silvery liquid metal. **2.** (M-) *Roman myth* messenger of the gods. **3.** (M-)

planet nearest the sun. **mercurial** [mer-cure-ee-al] *adj.* lively, changeable.

mercy *n., pl.* **-cies. 1.** compassionate treatment of an offender or enemy who is in one's power. **2.** merciful act. **merciful** *adj.* **1.** compassionate. **2.** giving relief. **mercifully** *adv.* **merciless** *adj.* **mercilessly** *adv.*

mere¹ *adj.* nothing more than, e.g. *mere chance.* **merely** *adv.*

mere² *n. Obs.* lake.

meretricious *adj.* superficially or garishly attractive but of no real value.

merganser [mer-gan-ser] *n.* large crested diving duck.

merge *v.* combine or blend. **merger** *n.* combination of business firms into one.

meridian *n.* **1.** imaginary circle of the earth passing through both poles. **2.** peak or zenith.

meringue [mer-rang] *n.* **1.** baked mixture of egg whites and sugar. **2.** small cake of this.

merino *n., pl.* **-nos. 1.** breed of sheep with fine soft wool. **2.** this wool.

merit *n.* **1.** excellence or worth. —*pl.* **2.** admirable qualities. —*v.* **-iting, -ited. 3.** deserve. **meritorious** *adj.* deserving praise. **meritocracy** [mer-it-tok-rass-ee] *n.* rule by people of superior talent or intellect.

merlin *n.* small falcon.

mermaid *n.* imaginary sea creature with the upper part of a woman and the lower part of a fish.

merry *adj.* **-rier, -riest. 1.** cheerful or jolly. **2.** *Informal* slightly drunk. **merrily** *adv.* **merriment** *n.* **merry-go-round** *n.* roundabout. **merrymaking** *n.* revelry.

mescaline *n.* hallucinogenic drug obtained from the tops of mescals. **mescal** [mess-kal] *n.* spineless globe-shaped cactus of Mexico and the SW of the USA.

mesdames *n.* plural of MADAME.

mesdemoiselles *n.* plural of MADEMOISELLE.

mesembryanthemum *n.* low-growing plant with bright daisy-like flowers.

mesh *n.* **1.** network or net. **2.** (open space between) strands forming a network. —*v.* **3.** (of gear teeth) engage.

mesmerize *v.* **1.** hold spellbound. **2.** *Obs.* hypnotize. **mesmerizing** *adj.*

meso- *combining form* middle or intermediate, e.g. *mesosphere.*

meson [mee-zon] *n.* elementary atomic particle.

mess *n.* **1.** untidy or dirty confusion. **2.** trouble or difficulty. **3.** group of servicemen who regularly eat together. **4.** place where they eat. —*v.* **5.** muddle or dirty. **6.** (foll. by *about*) potter about. **7.** (foll. by *with*) interfere with. **8.** (of servicemen) eat in a group.

message *n.* **1.** communication sent. **2.** meaning or moral. **messenger** *n.* bearer of a message. **get the message** *Informal* understand.

Messiah *n.* **1.** Jews' promised deliverer. **2.** Christ. **Messianic** *adj.*

messieurs *n.* plural of MONSIEUR.

Messrs [mess-erz] *n.* plural of MR.

messy *adj.* **messier, messiest.** dirty, confused, or untidy. **messily** *adv.*

met *v.* past of MEET¹

Met *adj., n. Informal* Meteorological (Office).

metabolism [met-tab-oh-liz-zum] *n.* chemical processes of a living body. **metabolic** *adj.* **metabolize** *v.* produce or be produced by metabolism.

metal *n.* **1.** chemical element, such as iron or copper, that is malleable and capable of conducting heat and electricity. **2.** short for ROAD METAL. **3.** *Informal* short for HEAVY METAL. —*adj.* **4.** made of metal. **metallic** *adj.* **metallurgy** *n.* scientific study of the structure, properties, extraction, and refining of metals. **metallurgical** *adj.* **metallurgist** *n.* **metalwork** *n.* **1.** craft of making objects from metal. **2.** metal part of something.

metamorphosis [met-a-more-foss-is] *n., pl.* **-phoses** [-foss-eez] change of form or character. **metamorphic** *adj.* (of rocks) changed in texture or structure by heat and pressure. **metamorphose** *v.* transform.

metaphor *n.* figure of speech in which a term is applied to something it does not literally denote in order to imply a resemblance, e.g. *he is a lion in battle.* **metaphorical** *adj.* **metaphorically** *adv.*

metaphysics *n.* branch of philosophy concerned with being and knowing. **metaphysical** *adj.*

mete *v.* (usu. with *out*) deal out as punishment.

meteor *n.* small fast-moving heavenly body, visible as a streak of incandescence if it enters the earth's atmosphere. **meteoric** [meet-ee-or-rik] *adj.* **1.** of a meteor. **2.** brilliant and very rapid, e.g. *his meteoric rise to power*. **meteorite** *n.* meteor that has fallen to earth.

meteorology *n.* study of the earth's atmosphere, esp. for weather forecasting. **meteorological** *adj.* **meteorologist** *n.*

meter *n.* **1.** instrument for measuring and recording something, such as the consumption of gas or electricity. —*v.* **2.** measure by meter.

methane *n.* colourless inflammable gas.

methanol *n.* colourless poisonous liquid used as a solvent and fuel (also **methyl alcohol**).

methinks *v., past tense* **methought.** *Obs.* it seems to me.

method *n.* **1.** way or manner. **2.** technique. **3.** orderliness. **methodical** *adj.* orderly. **methodically** *adv.* **methodology** *n., pl.* **-gies.** particular method or procedure.

Methodist *n.* **1.** member of any of the Protestant churches originated by John Wesley and his followers. —*adj.* **2.** of Methodists or their Church. **Methodism** *n.*

meths *n. Informal* methylated spirits.

methyl *n.* (compound containing) a saturated hydrocarbon group of atoms. **methylated spirits** alcohol with methanol added, used as a solvent and for heating.

meticulous *adj.* very careful about details. **meticulously** *adv.*

métier [met-ee-ay] *n.* **1.** profession or trade. **2.** one's strong point.

metonymy [mit-on-im-ee] *n.* figure of speech in which one thing is replaced by another associated with it, such as 'the Crown' for 'the king'.

metre *n.* **1.** basic unit of length equal to about 1.094 yards. **2.** rhythm of poetry. **metric** *adj.* of the decimal system of weights and measures based on the metre. **metric ton** same as TONNE. **metrical** *adj.* **1.** of measurement. **2.** of poetic metre. **metrication** *n.* conversion to the metric system.

metro *n., pl.* **metros.** underground railway system, esp. in Paris.

metronome *n.* instrument which marks musical time by means of a ticking pendulum.

metropolis [mit-trop-oh-liss] *n.* chief city of a country or region. **metropolitan** *adj.* of a metropolis.

mettle *n.* courage or spirit. **on one's mettle** roused to making one's best efforts.

mew *n.* **1.** cry of a cat. —*v.* **2.** utter this cry.

mews *n.* yard or street orig. of stables, now often converted into houses.

Mexican *adj.* **1.** of Mexico. —*n.* **2.** person from Mexico.

mezzanine [mez-zan-een] *n.* intermediate storey, esp. between the ground and first floor.

mezzo-soprano [met-so-] *n.* voice or singer between a soprano and contralto (also **mezzo**).

mezzotint [met-so-tint] *n.* **1.** method of engraving by scraping the roughened surface of a metal plate. **2.** print so made.

mg milligram(s).

Mg *Chem.* magnesium.

Mgr 1. manager. **2.** Monseigneur. **3.** Monsignor.

MHz megahertz.

mi *n. Music* same as ME[2]

MI 1. Military Intelligence. **2.** Michigan.

MI5 Military Intelligence, section five: British Government counterintelligence agency.

MI6 Military Intelligence, section six: British Government intelligence and espionage agency.

miaow [mee-ow] *n., v.* same as MEW.

miasma [mee-azz-ma] *n.* unwholesome or foreboding atmosphere.

mica [my-ka] *n.* glasslike mineral used as an electrical insulator.

mice *n.* plural of MOUSE.

Michaelmas [mik-kl-mass] *n.* Sept. 29th, feast of St Michael the archangel. **Michaelmas daisy** garden plant with small daisy-shaped flowers.

mickey *n.* **take the mickey (out of)** *Informal* tease.

micro *n., pl.* **-cros.** short for MICROCOMPUTER, MICROPROCESSOR.

micro- *combining form* **1.** small or minute, e.g. *microcopy.* **2.** denoting a millionth part, e.g. *microsecond.*

microbe *n.* minute organism, esp. one causing disease. **microbial** *adj.*

microbiology n. branch of biology involving the study of microorganisms. **microbiological** adj. **microbiologist** n.

microchip n. small wafer of silicon containing electronic circuits.

microcircuit n. miniature electronic circuit, esp. an integrated circuit.

microcomputer n. computer with a central processing unit contained in one or more silicon chips.

microcosm n. 1. miniature representation of something. 2. man regarded as epitomizing the universe.

microdot n. photographic copy of a document reduced to pinhead size.

microelectronics n. branch of electronics concerned with microcircuits. **microelectronic** adj.

microfiche [my-kroh-feesh] n. microfilm in sheet form.

microfilm n. miniaturized recording of books or documents on a roll of film.

microlight, microlite n. very small light private aircraft with large wings.

micrometer [my-krom-it-er] n. instrument for measuring very small distances or angles.

micron [my-kron] n. one millionth of a metre.

microorganism n. organism of microscopic size.

microphone n. instrument for amplifying or transmitting sounds.

microprocessor n. integrated circuit acting as the central processing unit in a small computer.

microscope n. instrument with lens(es) which produces a magnified image of a very small object. **microscopic** adj. 1. too small to be seen except with a microscope. 2. very small. 3. of a microscope. **microscopically** adv. **microscopy** n. use of a microscope.

microstructure n. structure on a microscopic scale, esp. of a metal or a cell.

microsurgery n. intricate surgery using a special microscope and miniature precision instruments.

microwave n. 1. electromagnetic wave with a wavelength of a few centimetres, used in radar and cooking. 2. microwave oven. —v. 3. cook in a microwave oven.

microwave oven oven using microwaves to cook food quickly.

micturate v. urinate. **micturition** n.

mid adj. intermediate, middle. **mid-off** n. Cricket fielding position on the off side closest to the bowler. **mid-on** n. Cricket fielding position on the on side closest to the bowler.

midair n. some point above ground level, in the air.

midday n. noon.

midden n. dunghill or rubbish heap.

middle adj. 1. equidistant from two extremes. 2. medium, intermediate. —n. 3. middle point or part. **middle age** period of life between youth and old age. **middle-aged** adj. **Middle Ages** period from about 1000 A.D. to the 15th century. **middle class** social class of business and professional people. **middle-class** adj. **middle ear** sound-conducting part of the ear immediately inside the eardrum. **Middle East** area around the eastern Mediterranean up to and including Iran. **middleman** n. trader who buys from the producer and sells to the consumer. **middle-of-the-road** adj. 1. politically moderate. 2. (of music) generally popular. **middleweight** n. boxer weighing up to 160lb (professional) or 75kg (amateur).

middling adj. 1. mediocre. 2. moderate. —adv. 3. moderately.

midfield n. Soccer area between the two opposing defences.

midge n. small mosquito-like insect.

midget n. very small person or thing.

MIDI adj. denoting a specification for the external control of electronic musical instruments, e.g. a MIDI system.

midland n. middle part of a country. —pl. 2. (M-) central England.

midnight n. twelve o'clock at night.

midriff n. middle part of the body.

midshipman n. naval officer of the lowest commissioned rank.

midst n. **in the midst of** 1. surrounded by. 2. at a point during.

midsummer n. 1. summer solstice. 2. middle of summer. **Midsummer Day, Midsummer's Day** June 24th.

midway adj., adv. halfway.

midwife n. trained person who assists at childbirth. **midwifery** [mid-wiff-fer-ree] n.

midwinter n. **1.** middle or depth of winter. **2.** winter solstice.

mien [mean] n. Lit. person's bearing, demeanour, or appearance.

miffed adj. Informal offended or upset.

might[1] v. past tense of MAY.
▷ Both might and may can be used to express a tentative request: Might/may I ask a favour?

might[2] n. power or strength. **with might and main** energetically or forcefully. **mighty** adj. **mightier, mightiest. 1.** powerful. **2.** important. —adv. **3.** US informal very. **mightily** adv.

mignonette [min-yon-net] n. grey-green plant with sweet-smelling flowers.

migraine [mee-grain] n. severe headache, often with nausea and other symptoms.

migrate v. **1.** move from one place to settle in another. **2.** (of animals) journey between different habitats at specific seasons. **migration** n. **migrant** n. **1.** person or animal that moves from one place to another. —adj. **2.** moving from one place to another, e.g. migrant workers. **migratory** adj. (of an animal) migrating every year.

mikado n., pl. **-dos.** Old-fashioned Japanese emperor.

mike n. Informal microphone.

milch [miltch] adj. (of a cow) giving milk.

mild adj. **1.** not strongly flavoured. **2.** gentle. **3.** calm or temperate. **mildly** adv. **mildness** n.

mildew n. destructive fungus on plants or things exposed to damp. **mildewed** adj.

mile n. unit of length equal to 1760 yards or 1.609 km. **mileage** n. **1.** distance travelled in miles. **2.** miles travelled by a motor vehicle per gallon of petrol. **3.** Informal usefulness of something. **mileometer** [mile-om-it-er] n. device that records the number of miles a vehicle has travelled. **milestone** n. **1.** stone marker showing the distance to a certain place. **2.** significant event.

milieu [meal-yer] n., pl. **milieus, milieux** [meal-yerz] environment or surroundings.

militant adj. aggressive or vigorous in support of a cause. **militancy** n. **militantly** adv.

military adj. **1.** of or for soldiers, armies, or war. —n. **2.** armed services. **militarily** adv. **militarism** n. belief in the use of military force and methods. **militarist** n. **militaristic** adj.

militate v. (usu. with against or for) have a strong influence or effect.
▷ Do not confuse militate with mitigate 'make less severe'.

militia [mill-ish-a] n. military force of trained citizens for use in emergency only. **militiaman** n.

milk n. **1.** white fluid produced by female mammals to feed their young. **2.** milk of cows, goats, etc., used by humans as food. **3.** fluid in some plants. —v. **4.** draw milk from. **5.** exploit (a person or situation). **milking** n. **milky** adj. **milkier, milkiest. Milky Way** luminous band of stars stretching across the night sky. **milk float** small electrically powered vehicle used to deliver milk to houses. **milkmaid** n. esp. in former times, woman who milks cows. **milkman** n. man who delivers milk to people's houses. **milk round 1.** route along which a milkman regularly delivers milk. **2.** regular series of visits to colleges made by recruitment officers from industry. **milkshake** n. frothy flavoured cold milk drink. **milksop** n. feeble man. **milk teeth** first set of teeth in young children.

mill n. **1.** factory. **2.** machine for grinding, processing, or rolling. —v. **3.** put through a mill. **4.** cut fine grooves across the edges of (coins). **5.** move in a confused manner. **miller** n. person who works in a mill.

millennium [mill-en-nee-um] n., pl. **-niums, -nia** [-nee-a] **1.** period of a thousand years. **2.** future period of peace and happiness.

millet n. a cereal grass.

milli- combining form denoting a thousandth part, e.g. millisecond.

milliard n. Brit. one thousand millions.

millibar n. unit of atmospheric pressure.

milligram n. thousandth part of a gram.

millilitre n. thousandth part of a litre.

millimetre n. thousandth part of a metre.

milliner n. maker or seller of women's hats. **millinery** n.

million n. one thousand thousands. **millionth** adj., n. **millionaire** n. person who owns at least a million pounds, dollars, etc.

millipede n. small animal with a jointed body and many pairs of legs.

millstone n. flat circular stone for grinding corn. **millstone round one's neck** heavy burden of responsibility or obligation.

millwheel n. waterwheel that drives a mill.

milometer [mile-om-it-er] *n.* same as MILE-OMETER.

milt *n.* sperm of fish.

mime *n.* 1. acting without the use of words. 2. performer who does this. —*v.* 3. act in mime. 4. perform as if singing or playing music that is prerecorded.

mimic *v.* **-icking, -icked.** 1. imitate (a person or manner), esp. for satirical effect. —*n.* 2. person or animal that is good at mimicking. **mimicry** *n.*

mimosa *n.* shrub with fluffy yellow flowers and sensitive leaves.

min. 1. minimum. 2. minute(s).

Min. 1. Minister. 2. Ministry.

mina *n.* same as MYNA.

minaret *n.* tall slender tower of a mosque.

minatory *adj.* threatening or menacing.

mince *v.* 1. cut or grind into very small pieces. 2. soften or moderate (one's words). 3. walk or speak in an affected manner. —*n.* 4. minced meat. **mincer** *n.* machine for mincing meat. **mincing** *adj.* affected in manner. **mincemeat** *n.* sweet mixture of dried fruit and spices. **mince pie** pie containing mincemeat.

mind *n.* 1. thinking faculties. 2. memory or attention. 3. intention. 4. sanity. —*v.* 5. take offence at. 6. take care of. 7. pay attention to. 8. be cautious or careful about (something). **change one's mind** alter one's decision or opinion. **in one's mind's eye** in one's imagination. **make up one's mind** reach a decision. **minded** *adj.* having an inclination as specified, e.g. *politically minded.* **minder** *n. Informal* aide or bodyguard. **mindful** *adj.* 1. keeping aware. 2. heedful. **mindless** *adj.* 1. stupid. 2. requiring no thought. 3. careless.

mine[1] *pron.* belonging to me.

mine[2] *n.* 1. deep hole for digging coal, ores, etc. 2. bomb placed under the ground or in water. 3. profitable source, e.g. *a mine of information.* —*v.* 4. dig for minerals. 5. dig (minerals) from a mine. 6. place explosive mines in or on. **miner** *n.* person who works in a mine. **mining** *n.* **minefield** *n.* area of land or water containing mines. **minesweeper** *n.* ship for clearing away mines.

mineral *n.* 1. naturally occurring inorganic substance, such as metal. —*adj.* 2. of, containing, or like minerals. **mineralogy** [min-er-al-a-jee] *n.* study of minerals. **mineralogist** *n.* **mineral water** water containing dissolved mineral salts or gases.

minestrone [min-ness-strone-ee] *n.* soup containing vegetables and pasta.

mingle *v.* 1. mix or blend. 2. come into association (with).

mingy *adj.* **-gier, -giest.** *Informal* miserly.

mini *n., adj.* 1. (something) small or miniature. 2. short (skirt).

mini- *combining form* smaller or shorter than usual, e.g. *mini-budget, minidress.*

miniature *n.* 1. small portrait, model, or copy. —*adj.* 2. small-scale. **miniaturist** *n.* **miniaturize** *v.* make to a very small scale. **miniaturization** *n.*

minibus *n.* small bus.

minicab *n.* ordinary car used as a taxi.

minicomputer *n.* computer smaller than a mainframe but more powerful than a microcomputer.

minim *n. Music* note half the length of a semibreve.

minimum *adj., n., pl.* **-mums, -ma.** least possible (amount or number). **minimal** *adj.* minimum. **minimally** *adv.* **minimize** *v.* 1. reduce to a minimum. 2. belittle. **minimization** *n.* **minimum lending rate** minimum rate of interest at which the Bank of England will lend money.

minion *n.* servile assistant.

miniseries *n.* TV programme shown in several parts, often on consecutive days.

miniskirt *n.* very short skirt.

minister *n.* 1. head of a government department. 2. diplomatic representative. 3. clergyman. —*v.* 4. (foll. by *to*) attend to the needs of. **ministerial** *adj.* **ministration** *n.* giving of help. **ministry** *n., pl.* **-tries.** 1. profession or duties of a clergyman. 2. ministers collectively. 3. government department.

mink *n.* 1. stoatlike animal. 2. its highly valued fur.

minnow *n.* small freshwater fish.

minor *adj.* 1. lesser. 2. under age. 3. *Music* (of a scale) having a semitone above the second note. —*n.* 4. person regarded legally as a child. 5. *Music* minor scale. **minority** *n., pl.* **-ties.** 1. lesser number. 2. smaller party voting together. 3. group in a minority in any state. 4. state of being legally a child.

minster *n.* cathedral or large church.

minstrel *n.* medieval singer or musician.

mint[1] *n.* **1.** aromatic herb. **2.** peppermint. **3.** sweet flavoured with this.

mint[2] *n.* **1.** place where money is coined. —*v.* **2.** make (coins).

minuet [min-new-**wet**] *n.* **1.** stately dance. **2.** music for this.

minus *prep.* **1.** reduced by the subtraction of. **2.** *Informal* without, lacking, e.g. *minus a leg.* —*adj.* **3.** less than zero, e.g. *minus two.* **4.** denoting subtraction, e.g. *minus sign.* **5.** *Education* slightly below the standard of a particular grade, e.g. *a B minus.* —*n.* **6.** sign (−) denoting subtraction or a number less than zero.

minuscule [min-niss-skyool] *adj.* very small.

minute[1] *n.* **1.** 60th part of an hour or degree. **2.** moment. —*pl.* **3.** record of the proceedings of a meeting. —*v.* **4.** record in the minutes.

minute[2] *adj.* **1.** very small. **2.** precise. **minutely** *adv.* **minutiae** [my-**new**-shee-eye] *pl. n.* trifling or precise details.

minx *n.* bold or flirtatious girl.

miracle *n.* **1.** wonderful supernatural event. **2.** marvel. **miraculous** *adj.* **miraculously** *adv.* **miracle play** medieval play based on a sacred subject.

mirage [mir-**rahz**] *n.* optical illusion, esp. one caused by hot air.

mire *n.* **1.** swampy ground. **2.** mud.

mirror *n.* **1.** coated glass surface for reflecting images. —*v.* **2.** reflect in or as if in a mirror. **mirror image** image or object that has left and right reversed as if seen in a mirror.

mirth *n.* laughter, merriment, or gaiety. **mirthful** *adj.* **mirthless** *adj.* **mirthlessly** *adv.*

mis- *prefix* wrong(ly), bad(ly).

misadventure *n.* unlucky chance.

misanthrope [**miz**-zan-thrope] *n.* person who dislikes people in general. **misanthropic** [miz-zan-**throp**-ik] *adj.* **misanthropy** [miz-**zan**-throp-ee] *n.*

misapplication *n.* use of something for the wrong purpose.

misapprehend *v.* misunderstand. **misapprehension** *n.*

misappropriate *v.* take and use (money) dishonestly. **misappropriation** *n.*

misbehave *v.* behave badly. **misbehaviour** *n.*

miscalculate *v.* calculate or judge wrongly. **miscalculation** *n.*

miscarriage *n.* **1.** spontaneous premature expulsion of a fetus from the womb. **2.** failure, e.g. *a miscarriage of justice.* **miscarry** *v.* **1.** have a miscarriage. **2.** fail.

miscast *v.* **-casting, -cast.** cast (a role or actor) in (a play or film) inappropriately.

miscegenation [miss-ij-in-**nay**-shun] *n.* interbreeding of races.

miscellaneous [miss-sell-**lane**-ee-uss] *adj.* mixed or assorted. **miscellany** [miss-**sell**-a-nee] *n.* mixed assortment.

mischance *n.* unlucky event.

mischief *n.* **1.** annoying but not malicious behaviour. **2.** inclination to tease. **3.** harm. **mischievous** [**miss**-chiv-uss] *adj.* **1.** full of mischief. **2.** intended to cause harm. **mischievously** *adv.*

miscible [**miss**-sib-bl] *adj.* able to be mixed.

misconception *n.* wrong idea or belief. **misconceived** *adj.*

misconduct *n.* immoral or unethical behaviour.

misconstrue *v.* interpret wrongly. **misconstruction** *n.*

miscreant [**miss**-kree-ant] *n.* wrongdoer.

misdeed *n.* wrongful act.

misdemeanour *n.* minor wrongdoing.

misdirect *v.* give (someone) wrong directions or instructions. **misdirection** *n.*

miser *n.* person who hoards money and hates spending it. **miserly** *adj.*

miserable *adj.* **1.** very unhappy, wretched. **2.** causing misery. **3.** squalid. **4.** mean. **miserably** *adv.* **misery** *n.,* *pl.* **-eries.** **1.** great unhappiness. **2.** *Informal* complaining person.

misfire *v.* **1.** (of a firearm or engine) fail to fire correctly. **2.** (of a plan) fail to turn out as intended.

misfit *n.* person not suited to his or her environment.

misfortune *n.* (piece of) bad luck.

misgiving *n.* feeling of fear or doubt.

misguided *adj.* mistaken or unwise.

mishandle *v.* handle badly or inefficiently.

mishap n. minor accident.

mishear v. hear (what someone says) wrongly.

mishmash n. confused collection or mixture.

misinform v. give incorrect information to. **misinformation** n.

misinterpret v. understand or represent (something) wrongly. **misinterpretation** n.

misjudge v. judge wrongly or unfairly. **misjudgment, misjudgement** n.

mislay v. lose (something) temporarily.

mislead v. give false or confusing information to. **misleading** adj. **misleadingly** adv.

mismanage v. organize or run (something) badly. **mismanagement** n.

misnomer [miss-no-mer] n. **1.** wrongly applied name. **2.** use of this.

misogyny [miss-oj-in-ee] n. hatred of women. **misogynist** n.

misplace v. **1.** put in the wrong place. **2.** mislay. **3.** give (trust or affection) inappropriately.

misprint n. printing error.

mispronounce v. pronounce (a word) wrongly. **mispronunciation** n.

misquote v. quote inaccurately. **misquotation** n.

misread v. **1.** misinterpret (a situation etc.). **2.** read incorrectly.

misrepresent v. represent wrongly or inaccurately. **misrepresentation** n.

misrule v. **1.** govern inefficiently or unjustly. —n. **2.** inefficient or unjust government.

miss v. **1.** fail to hit, reach, find, catch, or notice. **2.** not be in time for. **3.** notice or regret the absence of. **4.** avoid. **5.** (of an engine) misfire. —n. **6.** fact or instance of missing. **missing** adj. lost or absent. **miss out** v. **1.** leave out or overlook. **2.** (foll. by on) fail to take part in (something enjoyable or beneficial).

Miss n. title of a girl or unmarried woman.

missal n. book containing the prayers and rites of the Mass.

misshapen adj. badly shaped, deformed.

missile n. object or weapon thrown, shot, or launched at a target.

mission n. **1.** specific task or duty. **2.** group of people sent on a mission. **3.** building in which missionaries work. **missionary** n., pl. -aries. person sent abroad to do religious and social work.

missive n. letter.

misspell v. spell (a word) wrongly.

misspent adj. wasted or misused.

missus, missis n. Informal one's wife or the wife of the person addressed or referred to.

mist n. **1.** thin fog. **2.** fine spray of liquid. **misty** adj. **mistier, mistiest. 1.** full of mist. **2.** dim or obscure. **mist over** v. **1.** (also **mist up**) (of glass) become covered with small drops of moisture causing a misty effect. **2.** (of eyes) fill up with tears.

mistake n. **1.** error or blunder. —v. -**taking, -took, -taken. 2.** misunderstand. **3.** confuse (a person or thing) with another. **mistaken** adj. wrong in judgment or opinion. **mistakenly** adv.

Mister n. polite form of address to a man.

mistime v. do (something) at the wrong time.

mistletoe n. evergreen plant with white berries growing as a parasite on trees.

mistral n. strong dry northerly wind of S France.

mistreat v. treat (a person or animal) badly.

mistress n. **1.** woman who is the illicit lover of a married man. **2.** woman in control of people or animals. **3.** female teacher.

mistrial n. Law trial made void because of some error.

mistrust v. **1.** not trust. —n. **2.** lack of trust. **mistrustful** adj.

misunderstand v. fail to understand properly. **misunderstanding** n.

misuse n. **1.** incorrect, improper, or careless use. —v. **2.** use wrongly. **3.** treat badly.

mite n. **1.** very small spiderlike animal. **2.** very small thing or amount.

mitigate v. make less severe. **mitigation** n. ▷ *Mitigate* is often confused with *militate* 'have an influence on'.

mitosis n. type of cell division in which the nucleus divides into two nuclei which each contain the same number of chromosomes as the original nucleus.

mitre [my-ter] n. **1.** bishop's pointed headdress. **2.** joint between two pieces of wood bevelled to meet at right angles. —v. **3.** join with a mitre joint.

mitt *n.* **1.** short for MITTEN. **2.** *Slang* hand. **3.** baseball catcher's glove.

mitten *n.* glove with one section for the thumb and one for the four fingers together.

mix *v.* **1.** combine or blend into one mass. **2.** form (something) by mixing. **3.** be sociable. —*n.* **4.** mixture. **mixed** *adj.* **mixed blessing** something that has advantages as well as disadvantages. **mixed grill** dish of several kinds of grilled meat, tomatoes, and mushrooms. **mixed up** *adj. Informal* confused. **mixer** *n.* **1.** kitchen appliance used for mixing foods. **2.** *Informal* person considered in relation to his or her ability to mix socially, e.g. *a good mixer.* **3.** nonalcoholic drink, e.g. tonic water, that is mixed with an alcoholic drink. **mixture** *n.* **1.** something mixed. **2.** combination. **mix-up** *n.* confused situation.

mizzenmast *n.* mast nearest the stern of a full-rigged ship.

mks units *pl. n.* metric system of units based on the metre, kilogram, and second.

ml millilitre(s).

Mlle *pl.* **Mlles.** Mademoiselle.

mm millimetre(s).

MM plural of M (sense 2).

Mme *pl.* **Mmes.** Madame.

Mn *Chem.* manganese.

MN Minnesota.

mnemonic [nim-on-ik] *n., adj.* (rhyme etc.) intended to help the memory.

mo *n., pl.* **mos.** *Informal* short for MOMENT.

Mo *Chem.* molybdenum.

MO 1. Medical Officer. **2.** Missouri.

moan *n.* **1.** low cry of pain. **2.** *Informal* grumble. —*v.* **3.** make or utter with a moan. **4.** *Informal* grumble. **moaner** *n.*

moat *n.* deep wide ditch, esp. round a castle.

mob *n.* **1.** disorderly crowd. **2.** *Slang* gang. —*v.* **mobbing, mobbed. 3.** surround in a mob to acclaim or attack.

mobile *adj.* **1.** able to move. —*n.* **2.** hanging structure designed to move in air currents. **mobility** *n.*

mobilize *v.* **1.** (of the armed services) prepare for active service. **2.** organize for a purpose. **mobilization** *n.*

moccasin *n.* soft leather shoe.

mocha [mock-a] *n.* **1.** kind of strong dark coffee. **2.** flavouring made from coffee and chocolate.

mock *v.* **1.** make fun of. **2.** mimic. —*n.* **3.** imitation. —*pl.* **4.** *Informal* practice exams taken before public exams. —*adj.* **5.** sham or imitation. **put the mockers on** *Informal* ruin the chances of success of. **mockery** *n.* **1.** derision. **2.** inadequate attempt. **mocking** *adj.* **mocking bird** N American bird which imitates other birds' songs. **mockingly** *adv.* **mock orange** shrub with white fragrant flowers. **mock-up** *n.* full-scale model for test or study.

mod[1] *n.* member of a group of young people, orig. in the mid-1960s, who are very clothes-conscious, ride motor scooters, and like a particular kind of pop music.

mod[2] *n.* annual Highland Gaelic meeting with musical and literary competitions.

MOD Ministry of Defence.

mod. 1. moderate. **2.** modern.

mod cons *pl. n. Informal* modern conveniences, such as heating and hot water.

mode *n.* **1.** method or manner. **2.** current fashion.

model *n.* **1.** (miniature) representation. **2.** pattern. **3.** person or thing worthy of imitation. **4.** person who poses for an artist or photographer. **5.** person who wears clothes to display them to prospective buyers. —*adj.* **6.** excellent or perfect, e.g. *a model husband.* —*v.* **-elling, -elled. 7.** make a model of. **8.** mould. **9.** display (clothing) as a model. **modelling** *n.*

modem [mode-em] *n.* device for connecting two computers by a telephone line.

moderate *adj.* **1.** not extreme. **2.** temperate. **3.** average. —*n.* **4.** person of moderate views. —*v.* **5.** make or become less violent or extreme. **moderately** *adv.* **moderation** *n.* **moderator** *n.* **1.** Presbyterian Church, minister appointed to preside over a Church court, general assembly, etc. **2.** arbitrator.

modern *adj.* **1.** of present or recent times. **2.** in current fashion. **modernity** *n.* **modernism** *n.* (support of) modern tendencies, thoughts, or styles. **modernist** *adj., n.* **modernize** *v.* bring up to date. **modernization** *n.*

modest *adj.* **1.** not vain or boastful. **2.** shy. **3.** not excessive. **4.** decorous or decent. **modestly** *adv.* **modesty** *n.*

modicum *n.* small quantity.

modify *v.* **-fying, -fied. 1.** change slightly. **2.** tone down. **3.** (of a word) qualify (another word). **modifier** *n.* word that qualifies another. **modification** *n.*

modish [mode-ish] *adj.* in fashion.

modulate *v.* 1. vary in tone. 2. adjust. 3. change the key of (music). **modulation** *n.* 1. modulating. 2. *Electronics* superimposing of a wave or signal on to another wave or signal. **modulator** *n.*

module *n.* self-contained unit, section, or component with a specific function. **modular** *adj.*

modus operandi [mode-uss op-er-**an**-die] *n. Latin* method of operating.

modus vivendi [mode-uss viv-**venn**-die] *n. Latin* working arrangement between conflicting interests.

moggy *n., pl.* **-gies.** *Slang* cat.

mogul [**moh**-gl] *n.* important or powerful person.

MOH Medical Officer of Health.

mohair *n.* 1. fine hair of the Angora goat. 2. yarn or fabric made from this.

Mohammedan *n., adj. not in Muslim use* same as MUSLIM.

mohican *n.* punk hairstyle with shaved sides and a stiff central strip of hair, often brightly coloured.

moiety [**moy**-it-ee] *n., pl.* **-ties.** half.

moiré [**mwahr**-ray] *adj.* 1. having a watered or wavelike pattern. —*n.* 2. any fabric having such a pattern.

moist *adj.* slightly wet. **moisten** *v.* make or become moist. **moisture** *n.* liquid diffused as vapour or condensed in drops. **moisturize** *v.* add moisture to (the skin etc.). **moisturizer** *n.*

moke *n. Slang* donkey.

molar *n.* large back tooth used for grinding.

molasses *n.* dark syrup, a by-product of sugar refining.

mole[1] *n.* small dark raised spot on the skin.

mole[2] *n.* 1. small burrowing mammal. 2. *Informal* spy who has infiltrated and become a trusted member of an organization. **molehill** *n.* small mound of earth thrown up by a burrowing mole. **make a mountain out of a molehill** exaggerate an unimportant matter out of all proportion.

mole[3] *n.* 1. breakwater. 2. harbour protected by this.

mole[4] *n.* unit of amount of substance.

molecule [**mol**-lik-kyool] *n.* 1. simplest freely existing chemical unit, composed of two or more atoms. 2. very small particle. **molecular** [mol-**lek**-yew-lar] *adj.*

molest *v.* 1. interfere with sexually. 2. annoy or injure. **molester** *n.* **molestation** *n.*

moll *n.* 1. *Slang* gangster's female accomplice. 2. prostitute.

mollify *v.* **-fying, -fied.** pacify or soothe. **mollification** *n.*

mollusc *n.* soft-bodied, usu. hard-shelled, animal, such as a snail or oyster.

mollycoddle *v.* pamper.

Molotov cocktail *n.* petrol bomb.

molten *adj.* liquefied or melted.

molybdenum [mol-**lib**-din-um] *n.* silver-white metallic element.

moment *n.* 1. short space of time. 2. (present) point in time. **momentary** *adj.* lasting only a moment. **momentarily** *adv.*
▷ Note that some American speakers use *momentarily* to mean 'soon' rather than 'for a moment'.

momentous [moh-**men**-tuss] *adj.* of great significance.

momentum [moh-**men**-tum] *n.* 1. product of a body's mass and velocity. 2. impetus of a moving body.

Mon. Monday.

monarch *n.* sovereign ruler of a state. **monarchical** *adj.* **monarchist** *n.* supporter of monarchy. **monarchy** *n., pl.* **-chies.** government by or a state ruled by a sovereign.

monastery *n., pl.* **-teries.** residence of a religious order. **monastic** *adj.* 1. of monks, nuns, or monasteries. 2. ascetic. **monasticism** *n.*

monatomic *adj.* consisting of single atoms.

Monday *n.* second day of the week.

monetary *adj.* of money or currency. **monetarism** *n.* theory that inflation is caused by an increase in the money supply. **monetarist** *n., adj.*

money *n.* medium of exchange, coins or banknotes. **moneyed, monied** *adj.* rich. **moneylender** *n.* person who lends money at a high rate of interest as a living.

Mongolian *n.* 1. person from Mongolia. 2. language of Mongolia. —*adj.* 3. of Mongolia or its language.

mongolism *n. Offens.* Down's syndrome.

mongol n., adj. Offens. (person) affected by this.

mongoose n., pl. -gooses. stoatlike mammal of Asia and Africa that kills snakes.

mongrel n. 1. animal, esp. a dog, of mixed breed. 2. hybrid. —adj. 3. of mixed breed.

monitor n. 1. person or device that checks, controls, warns, or keeps a record of something. 2. pupil assisting a teacher with duties. 3. television set used in a studio to check what is being transmitted. 4. type of large lizard. —v. 5. watch and check on.

monk n. member of an all-male religious community bound by vows. **monkish** adj. **monkshood** n. poisonous plant with hooded flowers.

monkey n. 1. long-tailed primate. 2. mischievous child. —v. 3. (usu. foll. by about or around) meddle or fool. **monkey nut** peanut. **monkey puzzle** coniferous tree with sharp stiff leaves. **monkey wrench** wrench with adjustable jaws.

mono adj. 1. short for MONOPHONIC. —n. 2. monophonic sound.

mono- combining form single, e.g. monolingual.

monochrome adj. 1. in only one colour. 2. black-and-white.

monocle [mon-a-kl] n. eyeglass for one eye only.

monocotyledon [mon-no-kot-ill-leed-on] n. flowering plant with a single embryonic seed leaf.

monocular adj. having or for one eye only.

monogamy n. custom of being married to one person at a time. **monogamous** adj.

monogram n. design of combined letters, esp. a person's initials. **monogrammed** adj. marked with such a design.

monograph n. book or paper on a single subject.

monolith n. large upright block of stone. **monolithic** adj.

monologue n. 1. dramatic piece for one performer. 2. long speech by one person.

monomania n. obsession with one thing. **monomaniac** n., adj.

monophonic adj. (of a system of broadcasting, recording, or reproducing sound) using only one channel between source and loudspeaker.

monoplane n. aeroplane with one pair of wings.

monopoly n. 1. pl. -lies. exclusive possession of or right to do something. 2. (M-) ® board game for four to six players who deal in 'property' as they move around the board. **monopolistic** adj. **monopolize** v. have or take exclusive possession of.

monorail n. single-rail railway.

monosodium glutamate n. white crystalline substance used as a food additive to enhance protein flavours.

monosyllable n. word of one syllable. **monosyllabic** adj.

monotheism n. belief in only one God. **monotheistic** adj.

monotone n. unvaried pitch in speech or sound. **monotonous** adj. tedious due to lack of variety. **monotonously** adv. **monotony** n. wearisome routine, dullness.

monoxide n. oxide that contains one oxygen atom per molecule.

Monseigneur [mon-sen-nyur] n., pl. **Messeigneurs** [may-sen-nyur] title of French prelates.

monsieur [muss-syur] n., pl. **messieurs** [may-syur] French title of address equivalent to sir or Mr.

Monsignor n. RC Church title attached to certain offices.

monsoon n. 1. seasonal wind of SE Asia. 2. rainy season accompanying this.

monster n. 1. imaginary, usu. frightening, beast. 2. very wicked person. 3. huge person, animal, or thing. —adj. 4. huge. **monstrosity** n., pl. -ities. large ugly thing. **monstrous** adj. 1. unnatural or ugly. 2. outrageous or shocking. 3. huge. **monstrously** adv.

monstrance n. RC Church container in which the consecrated Host is exposed for adoration.

montage [mon-tahzh] n. 1. (making of) a picture composed from pieces of others. 2. method of film editing incorporating several shots to form a single image.

month n. 1. one of the twelve divisions of the calendar year. 2. period of four weeks. **monthly** adj. 1. happening or payable once a month. —adv. 2. once a month. —n., pl. -lies. 3. monthly magazine.

monument n. something, esp. a building or statue, that commemorates something.

monumental *adj.* **1.** large, impressive, or lasting. **2.** of or being a monument. **3.** *Informal* extreme. **monumentally** *adv. Informal* extremely.

moo *n.* **1.** long deep cry of a cow. —*v.* **2.** make this noise.

mooch *v. Slang* loiter about aimlessly.

mood[1] *n.* temporary (gloomy) state of mind. **moody** *adj.* **moodier, moodiest. 1.** gloomy or sullen. **2.** changeable in mood. **moodily** *adv.* **moodiness** *n.*

mood[2] *n. Grammar* form of a verb indicating whether it expresses a fact, wish, supposition, or command.

moon *n.* **1.** natural satellite of the earth. **2.** natural satellite of any planet. —*v.* **3.** (foll. by *about* or *around*) be idle in a listless or dreamy way. **moonless** *adj.* **moony** *adj. Informal* dreamy or listless. **moonbeam** *n.* ray of moonlight. **moonlight** *n.* **1.** light from the moon. —*adj.* **2.** illuminated by the moon, e.g. *a moonlight drive.* —*v.* **3.** *Informal* work at a secondary job, esp. illegally. **moonlit** *adj.* **moonshine** *n.* **1.** illicitly distilled whisky. **2.** nonsense. **moonstone** *n.* translucent semiprecious stone. **moonstruck** *adj.* deranged.

moor[1] *n.* tract of open uncultivated ground covered with grass and heather. **moorhen** *n.* small black water bird. **moorland** *n.*

moor[2] *v.* secure (a ship) with ropes etc. **mooring** *n.* **1.** place for mooring a ship. —*pl.* **2.** ropes etc. used in mooring a ship.

Moor *n.* member of a Muslim people of NW Africa who ruled Spain between the 8th and 15th centuries. **Moorish** *adj.*

moose *n.* large N American deer.

moot *adj.* **1.** debatable, e.g. *a moot point.* —*v.* **2.** bring up for discussion.

mop *n.* **1.** long stick with twists of cotton or a sponge on the end, used for cleaning. **2.** thick mass of hair. —*v.* **mopping, mopped. 3.** clean or soak up with or as if with a mop.

mope *v.* be gloomy and apathetic.

moped *n.* light motorized cycle.

moraine *n.* accumulated mass of debris deposited by a glacier.

moral *adj.* **1.** concerned with right and wrong conduct. **2.** based on a sense of right and wrong. **3.** (of support or a victory) psychological rather than practical. —*n.* **4.** lesson to be obtained from a story or event. —*pl.* **5.** behaviour with respect to right and wrong. **morally** *adv.* **moralist** *n.* person who lives by or expresses moral principles. **moralistic** *adj.* **morality** *n.* **1.** good moral conduct. **2.** moral goodness or badness. **morality play** medieval play with a moral lesson. **moralize** *v.* make moral pronouncements.

morale [mor-**rahl**] *n.* degree of confidence or hope of a person or group.

morass *n.* **1.** marsh. **2.** mess.

moratorium *n., pl.* **-ria, -riums.** legally authorized ban or delay.

moray *n.* large voracious eel.

morbid *adj.* **1.** unduly interested in death or unpleasant events. **2.** gruesome. **morbidly** *adv.*

mordant *adj.* **1.** sarcastic or scathing. —*n.* **2.** substance used to fix dyes.

more *adj.* **1.** greater in amount or degree. **2.** comparative of MUCH and MANY. **3.** additional or further. —*adv.* **4.** to a greater extent. **5.** in addition. —*pron.* **6.** greater or additional amount or number. **moreover** *adv.* besides.

morel *n.* edible mushroom with a pitted cap.

mores [**more**-rayz] *pl. n.* customs and conventions embodying the fundamental values of a community.

morganatic marriage *n.* marriage of a person of high rank to a lower-ranking person whose status remains unchanged.

morgue *n.* mortuary.

moribund *adj.* without force or vitality.

Mormon *n.* member of a religious sect founded in the USA.

morn *n. Poetic* morning.

mornay *adj.* served with a cheese sauce, e.g. *sole mornay.*

morning *n.* part of the day before noon. **the morning after** *Informal* the aftereffects of overindulgence, hangover. **morning coat** frock coat. **morning dress** formal day dress for men, comprising a morning coat, grey trousers, and a top hat. **morning-glory** *n.* plant with trumpet-shaped flowers which close in the late afternoon. **morning sickness** nausea shortly after rising, often experienced in the first few months of pregnancy.

Moroccan *adj.* **1.** of Morocco. —*n.* **2.** person from Morocco.

morocco *n.* goatskin leather.

moron n. 1. mentally deficient person. 2. *Informal* fool. **moronic** adj.

morose [mor-**rohss**] adj. sullen or moody. **morosely** adv.

morphine, morphia n. drug extracted from opium, used as an anaesthetic and sedative.

morphology n. science of forms and structures of organisms or words. **morphological** adj.

morris dance n. traditional English folk dance performed by men.

morrow n. *Poetic* next day.

Morse n. system of signalling in which letters of the alphabet are represented by combinations of short and long signals.

morsel n. small piece, esp. of food.

mortal adj. 1. subject to death. 2. causing death. —n. 3. mortal creature. **mortally** adv. **mortality** n. 1. state of being mortal. 2. great loss of life. 3. death rate. **mortal sin** *RC Church* sin meriting damnation.

mortar n. 1. mixture of lime, sand, and water for holding bricks and stones together. 2. small cannon with a short range. 3. bowl in which substances are pounded. **mortarboard** n. square academic cap.

mortgage n. 1. conditional pledging of property, esp. a house, as security for the repayment of a loan. 2. the loan itself. —v. 3. pledge (property) as security thus. **mortgagee** n. creditor in a mortgage. **mortgagor, -ger** n. debtor in a mortgage.

mortify v. **-fying, -fied.** 1. humiliate. 2. subdue by self-denial. 3. (of flesh) become gangrenous. **mortification** n.

mortise, mortice [**more**-tiss] n. hole in a piece of wood or stone shaped to receive a matching projection on another piece. **mortise lock** lock set into a door.

mortuary n., pl. **-aries.** building where corpses are kept before burial or cremation.

mosaic [mow-**zay**-ik] n. design or decoration using small pieces of coloured stone or glass.

Mosaic adj. of Moses.

Moselle n. light white wine.

Moslem n., adj. same as MUSLIM.

mosque n. Muslim temple.

mosquito n., pl. **-toes, -tos.** blood-sucking flying insect.

moss n. small flowerless plant growing in masses on moist surfaces. **mossy** adj. **mossier, mossiest.**

most adj. 1. greatest in number or degree. 2. superlative of MUCH and MANY. —n. 3. greatest number or degree. —adv. 4. in the greatest degree. **mostly** adv. for the most part, generally.

MOT, MOT test n. compulsory annual test of the roadworthiness of vehicles over a certain age.

mote n. tiny speck.

motel n. roadside hotel for motorists.

motet [moh-**tet**] n. short sacred choral song.

moth n. nocturnal insect like a butterfly. **mothball** n. 1. small ball of camphor or naphthalene used to repel moths from stored clothes. —v. 2. store (something operational) for future use. 3. postpone (a project etc.). **motheaten** adj. 1. eaten or damaged by moth larvae. 2. decayed or scruffy.

mother n. 1. female parent. 2. head of a female religious community. —adj. 3. native or inborn, e.g. *mother wit.* —v. 4. look after as a mother. **motherhood** n. **motherly** adj. **motherless** adj. **mother country, motherland** country where one was born. **mother-in-law** n., pl. **mothers-in-law.** mother of one's husband or wife. **mother of pearl** iridescent lining of certain shells. **mother tongue** one's native language.

motif [moh-**teef**] n. (recurring) theme or design.

motion n. 1. process, action, or way of moving. 2. proposal in a meeting. 3. evacuation of the bowels. —v. 4. direct (someone) by gesture. **motionless** adj. not moving. **motion picture** *US* cinema film.

motive n. 1. reason for a course of action. —adj. 2. causing motion. **motivate** v. give incentive to. **motivation** n.

motley adj. 1. miscellaneous. 2. multicoloured. —n. 3. *Hist.* jester's costume.

motocross n. motorcycle race over a rough course.

motor n. 1. engine, esp. of a vehicle. 2. machine that converts electrical energy into mechanical energy. 3. car. —v. 4. travel by car. **motorist** n. driver of a car. **motorize** v. equip with a motor or motor transport. **motorbike** n. **motorboat** n. **motorcade** n. procession of cars carrying important people. **motorcar** n. **motorcycle** n. **motorcyclist** n. **motor scooter** light motorcycle

with small wheels and an enclosed engine.
motorway n. main road for fast-moving
traffic.

mottled adj. marked with blotches.

motto n., pl. **-toes, -tos. 1.** saying expressing an ideal or rule of conduct. **2.** verse or
maxim in a paper cracker.

mould[1] n. **1.** hollow container in which
metal is cast. **2.** shape, form, or pattern.
3. nature or character. —v. **4.** shape. **5.**
influence or direct. **moulding** n. moulded
ornamental edging.

mould[2] n. fungal growth caused by dampness. **mouldy** adj. **mouldier, mouldiest. 1.**
stale or musty. **2.** dull or boring.

mould[3] n. loose soil. **moulder** v. decay into
dust.

moult v. **1.** shed feathers, hair, or skin to
make way for new growth. —n. **2.** process of
moulting.

mound n. **1.** heap, esp. of earth or stones. **2.**
small hill.

mount v. **1.** climb or ascend. **2.** get up on (a
horse etc.). **3.** increase. **4.** fix on a support
or backing. **5.** organize, e.g. mount a campaign. —n. **6.** backing or support on which
something is fixed. **7.** horse for riding. **8.**
hill.

mountain n. **1.** hill of great size. **2.** large
heap. **mountainous** adj. **1.** full of mountains. **2.** huge. **mountaineer** n. person who
climbs mountains. **mountaineering** n.
mountain bike bicycle with straight handlebars and heavy-duty tyres, for cycling over
rough terrain. mountain lion same as PUMA.

mountebank n. charlatan or fake.

Mountie n. Informal member of the Royal
Canadian Mounted Police.

mourn v. feel or express sorrow for (a dead
person or lost thing). **mourner** n. **mournful**
adj. sad or dismal. **mournfully** adv. **mourning** n. **1.** grieving. **2.** conventional symbols
of grief for death, such as the wearing of
black.

mouse n., pl. **mice. 1.** small long-tailed
rodent. **2.** timid person. **3.** Computers hand-
held device for moving the cursor without
keying. —v. **4.** catch or hunt mice. **mouser**
n. cat used to catch mice. **mousy** adj.
mousier, mousiest. 1. like a mouse, esp. in
hair colour. **2.** meek and shy.

moussaka n. dish made with meat, auber-

gines, and tomatoes, topped with cheese
sauce.

mousse n. **1.** dish of flavoured cream
whipped and set. **2.** short for STYLING MOUSSE.

moustache n. hair on the upper lip.

mouth n. **1.** opening in the head for eating
and issuing sounds. **2.** opening. **3.** entrance.
4. point where a river enters the sea. —v. **5.**
speak or utter insincerely, esp. in public. **6.**
form (words) with the lips without speaking.
mouthful n. **1.** amount of food or drink put
into the mouth at any one time when eating
or drinking. **2.** word, phrase, or name that is
difficult to say. mouth organ small musical
instrument played by sucking and blowing.
mouthpiece n. **1.** part of a telephone into
which a person speaks. **2.** part of a wind
instrument into which the player blows. **3.**
spokesperson. **mouthwash** n. medicated
liquid for gargling and cleansing the mouth.

move v. **1.** change in place or position. **2.**
change (one's opinion etc.). **3.** take action. **4.**
stir the emotions of. **5.** incite. **6.** suggest (a
proposal) formally. —n. **7.** moving. **8.** action
towards some goal. **movable, moveable**
adj. **movement** n. **1.** action or process of
moving. **2.** moving parts of a machine. **3.**
group with a common aim. **4.** division of a
piece of music. **moving** adj. arousing or
touching the emotions. **movingly** adv.

movie n. US informal cinema film.

mow v. **mowing, mowed, mowed** or
mown. cut (grass or crops). **mower** n.
mow down v. kill in large numbers.

mozzarella [mot-sa-**rel**-la] n. moist white
cheese originally made in Italy from buffalo
milk.

MP 1. Member of Parliament. **2.** Military
Police(man).

mpg miles per gallon.

mph miles per hour.

Mr Mister.

Mrs n. title of a married woman.

Ms [mizz] n. title used instead of Miss or
Mrs.

MS 1. manuscript. **2.** multiple sclerosis. **3.**
Mississippi.

MSc Master of Science.

MSS manuscripts.

Mt Mount.

MT Montana.

much adj. **more, most. 1.** large amount or

degree of. —n. 2. large amount or degree. —adv. more, most. 3. to a great degree. 4. nearly. much of a muchness very similar.

mucilage [mew-sill-ij] n. gum or glue.

muck n. 1. dirt, filth. 2. manure. 3. Slang something of poor quality, rubbish. mucky adj. muckier, muckiest. muck about v. Slang waste time or misbehave. muck in v. Slang share a task with other people. muck out v. clean (a byre, stable, etc.). muckraking n. seeking out and exposing scandal relating to well-known people. muckraker n. muck up v. Slang ruin or spoil.

mucus [mew-kuss] n. slimy secretion of the mucous membranes. mucous adj. mucous membrane membrane lining body cavities or passages.

mud n. wet soft earth. muddy adj. -dier, -diest. 1. covered or filled with mud. 2. not clear or bright, e.g. muddy brown. —v. -dying, -dies. 3. make muddy. 4. make (a situation or issue) less clear. mud flat area of low muddy land that is covered by the sea only at high tide. mudguard n. cover over a wheel to prevent mud or water being thrown up by it. mudpack n. cosmetic paste to improve the complexion.

muddle v. 1. (often foll. by up) confuse. 2. mix up. —n. 3. state of confusion.

muesli [mewz-lee] n. mixture of grain, nuts, and dried fruit, eaten with milk.

muezzin [moo-ezz-in] n. official who summons Muslims to prayer.

muff[1] n. tube-shaped covering to keep the hands warm.

muff[2] v. bungle (an action).

muffin n. 1. light round flat yeast cake. 2. small cup-shaped sweet bread roll.

muffle v. wrap up for warmth or to deaden sound. muffler n. scarf.

mufti n. civilian clothes worn by a person who usually wears a uniform.

mug[1] n. large drinking cup.

mug[2] n. 1. Slang face. 2. Slang gullible person. —v. mugging, mugged. 3. Informal attack in order to rob. mugger n. mugging n. mug shot Informal photograph of the face of a suspect or criminal, held in a police file.

mug[3] v. mugging, mugged. (foll. by up) Informal study hard.

muggins n. Informal stupid or gullible person.

muggy adj. -gier, -giest. (of weather) damp and stifling.

mujaheddin, mujahedeen [moo-ja-hed-deen] pl. n. fundamentalist Muslim guerrillas.

mulatto [mew-lat-toe] n., pl. -tos, -toes. child of one Black and one White parent.

mulberry n. 1. tree whose leaves are used to feed silkworms. 2. purple fruit of this tree.

mulch n. 1. mixture of wet straw, leaves, etc., used to protect the roots of plants. —v. 2. cover (land) with mulch.

mulct v. fine (a person).

mule[1] n. offspring of a horse and a donkey. mulish adj. obstinate. muleteer n. mule driver.

mule[2] n. backless shoe or slipper.

mull v. 1. heat (wine) with sugar and spices. 2. think (over) or ponder.

mullah n. Muslim theologian.

mullet n. edible sea fish.

mulligatawny n. soup made with curry powder.

mullion n. upright dividing bar in a window. mullioned adj. having mullions.

multi- combining form many, e.g. multicultural, multistorey.

multicoloured adj. having many different colours.

multifarious [mull-tee-**fare**-ee-uss] adj. having many various parts.

multilateral adj. of or involving more than two nations or parties.

multilingual adj. speaking or written in more than two languages.

multimillionaire n. person who owns several million pounds, dollars, etc.

multinational adj., n. (large business company) operating in several countries.

multiple adj. 1. having many parts. —n. 2. quantity which contains another an exact number of times. multiple-choice adj. having a number of possible given answers out of which the correct one must be chosen. multiple sclerosis chronic progressive disease of the nervous system, resulting in speech and visual disorders, tremor, and partial paralysis.

multiplex n. 1. purpose-built complex containing several cinemas and usu. restaurants and bars. —*adj.* **2.** having many elements, complex.

multiplicity *n., pl.* **-ties.** large number or great variety.

multiply *v.* **-plying, -plied. 1.** (cause to) increase in number, quantity, or degree. **2.** add (a number or quantity) to itself a given number of times. **3.** increase in number by reproduction. **multiplication** *n.* **multiplicand** *n. Maths* number to be multiplied. **multiplier** *n. Maths* number by which another number is multiplied.

multipurpose *adj.* having many uses, e.g. *a multipurpose vehicle.*

multiracial *adj.* made up of people from many races, e.g. *a multiracial society.*

multitude *n.* **1.** great number. **2.** great crowd. **multitudinous** *adj.* very numerous.

mum[1] *n. Informal* mother.

mum[2] *adj.* silent, e.g. *keep mum.*

mumble *v.* speak indistinctly, mutter.

mumbo jumbo *n.* **1.** meaningless religious ritual. **2.** deliberately complicated language.

mummer *n.* actor in a folk play or mime.

mummy[1] *n., pl.* **-mies.** body embalmed and wrapped for burial in ancient Egypt. **mummify** *v.* **-fying, -fied.** preserve (a body) as a mummy.

mummy[2] *n., pl.* **-mies.** child's word for MOTHER.

mumps *n.* infectious disease with swelling in the glands of the neck.

munch *v.* chew noisily and steadily.

mundane *adj.* **1.** everyday. **2.** earthly.

municipal *adj.* relating to a city or town. **municipality** *n., pl.* **-ties. 1.** city or town with local self-government. **2.** governing body of this.

munificent [mew-niff-fiss-sent] *adj.* very generous. **munificence** *n.*

muniments [mew-nim-ments] *pl. n.* title deeds or similar documents.

munitions [mew-nish-unz] *pl. n.* military stores.

mural [myoor-al] *n.* painting on a wall.

murder *n.* **1.** unlawful intentional killing of a human being. —*v.* **2.** kill thus. **murderer, murderess** *n.* **murderous** *adj.*

murk *n.* thick darkness. **murky** *adj.* **murkier, murkiest.** dark or gloomy.

murmur *n.* **1.** continuous low indistinct sound. **2.** complaint, e.g. *she went without a murmur.* **3.** abnormal soft blowing sound heard made by the heart. —*v.* **-muring, -mured. 4.** make such a sound. **5.** complain. **6.** utter in a murmur.

murrain [murr-rin] *n.* cattle plague.

muscat *n.* sweet white grape. **muscatel** [musk-a-tell] *n.* **1.** wine from muscat grapes. **2.** muscat grape or raisin.

muscle *n.* **1.** tissue in the body which produces movement by contracting. **2.** strength or power. **muscular** *adj.* **1.** with well-developed muscles. **2.** of muscles. **muscular dystrophy** disease with wasting of the muscles. **muscle in** *v. Informal* force one's way in.

muse *v.* ponder.

Muse *n.* **1.** *Greek myth* one of nine goddesses, each of whom inspired an art or science. **2.** (m-) force that inspires a creative artist.

museum *n.* building where natural, artistic, historical, or scientific objects are exhibited and preserved. **museum piece** *Informal* very old object or building.

mush *n.* **1.** soft pulpy mass. **2.** *Informal* cloying sentimentality. **mushy** *adj.* **mushier, mushiest.**

mushroom *n.* **1.** edible fungus with a stem and cap. —*v.* **2.** grow rapidly. **mushroom cloud** large mushroom-shaped cloud produced by a nuclear explosion.

music *n.* **1.** art form using a melodious and harmonious combination of notes. **2.** written or printed form of this. **musical** *adj.* **1.** of or like music. **2.** talented in or fond of music. **3.** pleasant-sounding. —*n.* **4.** play or film with songs and dancing. **musically** *adv.* **musician** *n.* **musicianship** *n.* **musicology** *n.* scientific study of music. **musicologist** *n.* **music centre** combined record player, radio, and cassette player. **music hall** variety theatre.

musk *n.* scent obtained from a gland of the **musk deer** or produced synthetically. **musky** *adj.* **muskier, muskiest. muskrat** *n.* **1.** N American beaver-like rodent. **2.** its fur.

musket *n. Hist.* long-barrelled gun. **musketeer** *n.* **musketry** *n.* (use of) muskets.

Muslim *n.* **1.** follower of the religion of Islam. —*adj.* **2.** of or relating to Islam.

muslin *n.* fine cotton fabric.

musquash *n.* muskrat fur.

mussel *n.* kind of bivalve mollusc.

must[1] v. **1.** used as an auxiliary to express obligation, certainty, or resolution. —n. **2.** something one must do.

must[2] n. newly pressed grape juice.

mustang n. wild horse of SW USA.

mustard n. **1.** paste made from the powdered seeds of a plant, used as a condiment. **2.** the plant. **mustard gas** poisonous gas causing blistering.

muster v. **1.** summon up (strength, energy, or support). **2.** assemble. —n. **3.** assembly. **pass muster** be acceptable.

musty adj. **mustier, mustiest.** smelling mouldy and stale. **mustiness** n.

mutable [mew-tab-bl] adj. liable to change. **mutability** n.

mutation [mew-tay-shun] n. (genetic) change. **mutate** [mew-tate] v. (cause to) undergo mutation. **mutant** [mew-tant] n. mutated animal, plant, etc.

mute adj. **1.** unable to speak. **2.** silent. —n. **3.** person who is unable to speak. **4.** Music device to soften the tone of an instrument. **muted** adj. **1.** (of sound or colour) softened. **2.** (of a reaction) subdued. **mutely** adv.

mutilate [mew-till-ate] v. **1.** deprive of a limb or other part. **2.** damage (a book or text). **mutilation** n.

mutiny [mew-tin-ee] n., pl. **-nies. 1.** rebellion against authority, esp. by soldiers or sailors. —v. **-nying, -nied. 2.** commit mutiny. **mutineer** n. **mutinous** adj.

mutt n. **1.** Slang stupid person. **2.** mongrel dog.

mutter v. **1.** utter or speak indistinctly. **2.** grumble. —n. **3.** muttered sound or grumble. **muttering** n.

mutton n. flesh of sheep, used as food.

mutual [mew-chew-al] adj. **1.** felt or expressed by each of two people about the other. **2.** Informal common to both or all. **mutually** adv.
▷ The objection that something mutual holds between two people only is outdated; nowadays mutual is equivalent to 'shared, in common'.

Muzak n. ® recorded light music played in shops etc.

muzzle n. **1.** animal's mouth and nose. **2.** cover for these to prevent biting. **3.** open end of a gun. —v. **4.** put a muzzle on. **5.** force to keep silent.

muzzy adj. **-zier, -ziest. 1.** confused or muddled. **2.** blurred or hazy.

mW milliwatt(s).

MW 1. megawatt(s). **2.** medium wave.

my adj. belonging to me.

mycology n. study of fungi.

myna, mynah, mina n. Indian bird which can mimic human speech.

myopia [my-oh-pee-a] n. short-sightedness. **myopic** [my-op-ik] adj. **myopically** adv.

myriad [mir-ree-ad] adj. **1.** innumerable. —n. **2.** large indefinite number.

myrrh [mur] n. aromatic gum, formerly used in incense.

myrtle [mur-tl] n. flowering evergreen shrub.

myself pron. emphatic or reflexive form of I. or ME.

mystery n., pl. **-teries. 1.** strange or inexplicable event or phenomenon. **2.** obscure or secret thing. **3.** story or film that arouses suspense. **mysterious** adj. **mysteriously** adv.

mystic n. **1.** person who seeks spiritual knowledge. —adj. **2.** mystical. **mystical** adj. having a spiritual or religious significance beyond human understanding. **mysticism** n.

mystify v. **-fying, -fied.** bewilder or puzzle. **mystification** n.

mystique [miss-steek] n. aura of mystery or power.

myth n. **1.** tale with supernatural characters, usu. of how the world and mankind began. **2.** imaginary person or object. **mythical, mythic** adj. **mythology** n. **1.** myths collectively. **2.** study of myths. **mythological** adj.

myxomatosis [mix-a-mat-oh-siss] n. contagious fatal viral disease of rabbits.

N

n *adj.* **1.** indefinite number (of), e.g. *there are n ways of doing this.* **2.** *Maths* number whose value is not stated, e.g. *two to the power n.* **nth** *adj.*

N 1. *Chess* knight. **2.** *Chem.* nitrogen. **3.** *Physics* newton(s). **4.** north(ern). **5.** nuclear, e.g. *N waste.*

n. 1. neuter. **2.** noun. **3.** number.

Na *Chem.* sodium.

n/a, N.A. not applicable: used to indicate that a question on a form is not relevant to the person filling it in.

Naafi *n.* **1.** Navy, Army, and Air Force Institutes. **2.** canteen or shop for military personnel run by this organization.

naan *n.* same as NAN BREAD.

nab *v.* **nabbing, nabbed.** *Informal* **1.** arrest (someone). **2.** catch (someone) in wrong-doing.

nabob [**nay-bob**] *n.* *Informal* rich or important person.

nacelle [nah-**sell**] *n.* streamlined enclosure on an aircraft, esp. one housing an engine.

nacre [**nay-ker**] *n.* mother-of-pearl. **nacreous** *adj.*

nadir *n.* **1.** point in the sky opposite the zenith. **2.** lowest point.

naevus [**nee-vuss**] *n., pl.* **-vi.** birthmark or mole.

naff *adj.* *Slang* inferior or useless.

nag[1] *v.* **nagging, nagged. 1.** scold or find fault (with) constantly. **2.** be a constant source of discomfort, pain, or worry (to). —*n.* **3.** person who nags. **nagging** *adj., n.*

nag[2] *n.* *Informal* (old) horse.

naiad [**nye-ad**] *n.* *Greek myth* water nymph.

naïf *adj.* same as NAIVE.

nail *n.* **1.** hard covering of the upper tips of the fingers and toes. **2.** pointed piece of metal with a head, hit with a hammer to join two objects together. —*v.* **3.** attach (something) with nails. **4.** *Informal* catch or arrest. **hit the nail on the head** say something exactly correct. **on the nail** at once, esp. in *pay on the nail.* **nailfile** *n.* small metal file used to smooth or shape the finger or toe nails. **nail polish, varnish** cosmetic lacquer applied to the finger or toe nails.

naive, naïve [nye-**eev**] *adj.* **1.** innocent and credulous. **2.** lacking developed powers of reasoning and criticism. **naively, naïvely** *adv.* **naivety, naïvety, naiveté, naïveté** [nye-**eev**-tee] *n.*

naked *adj.* **1.** without clothes. **2.** without any covering, e.g. *naked flame.* **3.** not concealed, e.g. *naked hostility.* **the naked eye** the eye unassisted by any optical instrument. **nakedly** *adv.* **nakedness** *n.*

NALGO National and Local Government Officers' Association.

namby-pamby *adj.* sentimental or insipid.

name *n.* **1.** word by which a person or thing is known. **2.** reputation, esp. a good one. **3.** abusive word or description. **4.** famous person, e.g. *a big name in the music business.* —*v.* **5.** give a name to. **6.** refer to by name. **7.** specify. **in name only** not possessing the powers implied by his, her, or its title, e.g. *ruler in name only.* **nameless** *adj.* **1.** without a name. **2.** unspecified. **3.** too horrible to be mentioned. **namely** *adv.* that is to say. **name day** *RC Church* feast day of a saint whose name one bears. **name-drop** *v.* **-dropping, -dropped.** refer to famous people as if they were friends, in order to impress others. **name-dropper** *n.* **nameplate** *n.* small sign on or by a door giving the occupant's name and, sometimes, profession. **namesake** *n.* person with the same name as another.

nan bread *n.* slightly leavened Indian bread in a large flat leaf shape.

nancy, nancy boy *n.* effeminate or homosexual boy or man.

nankeen *n.* buff-coloured cotton fabric.

nanny *n., pl.* **-nies.** woman whose job is looking after young children. **nanny goat** female goat.

nano- *combining form* denoting one thousand millionth, e.g. *nanosecond.*

nap[1] *n.* **1.** short sleep. —*v.* **napping, napped. 2.** have a short sleep.

nap[2] *n.* raised fibres of velvet or similar cloth.

nap³ n. **1.** card game similar to whist. **2.** *Horse racing* tipster's choice for a certain winner. —v. **napping, napped. 3.** name (a horse) as a certain winner.

napalm n. **1.** highly inflammable jellied petrol, used in bombs. —v. **2.** attack (people or places) with napalm.

nape n. back of the neck.

naphtha n. liquid mixture distilled from coal tar or petroleum, used as a solvent and in petrol. **naphthalene** n. white crystalline product distilled from coal tar or petroleum, used in disinfectants, mothballs, and explosives.

napkin n. piece of cloth or paper for wiping the mouth or protecting the clothes while eating.

nappy n., pl. **-pies.** piece of absorbent material fastened round a baby's lower torso to absorb urine and faeces.

narcissism n. abnormal love and admiration for oneself. **narcissistic** adj.

narcissus n., pl. **-cissi.** yellow, orange, or white flower related to the daffodil.

narcotic n., adj. (of) a drug, such as morphine or opium, which produces numbness and drowsiness, used medicinally but addictive. **narcosis** n. effect of a narcotic.

nark *Slang* —v. **1.** annoy. —n. **2.** someone who complains in an irritating manner. **3.** informer. **narky** adj. **narkier, narkiest.** *Slang* irritable or complaining.

narrate v. **1.** tell (a story). **2.** speak the words accompanying and telling what is happening in a film or TV programme. **narration** n. **narrator** n. **narrative** n. **1.** account, story. —adj. **2.** telling a story, e.g. *a narrative poem.*

narrow adj. **1.** of little breadth in comparison to length. **2.** limited in range, extent, or outlook. **3.** with little margin, e.g. *a narrow escape.* —v. **4.** make or become narrow. **5.** (often foll. by *down*) limit or restrict. **narrows** pl. n. narrow part of a strait, river, or current. **narrowly** adv. **narrowness** n. **narrow boat** long bargelike canal boat. **narrow-gauge** adj. (of a railway) having less than the standard distance of 56½ inches between the rails. **narrow-minded** adj. intolerant or bigoted. **narrow-mindedness** n.

narwhal n. arctic porpoise with a long spiral tusk.

NASA *US* National Aeronautics and Space Administration.

nasal adj. **1.** of the nose. **2.** (of a sound) pronounced with air passing through the nose. **3.** (of a voice) characterized by nasal sounds. **nasally** adv.

nascent adj. starting to grow or develop.

nasturtium n. plant with yellow, red, or orange trumpet-shaped flowers.

nasty adj. **-tier, -tiest. 1.** unpleasant. **2.** (of an injury) dangerous or painful. **3.** spiteful or unkind. **nastily** adv. **nastiness** n.

nat. 1. national. **2.** nationalist.

natal [nay-tal] adj. of or relating to birth.

nation n. people of one or more cultures or races organized as a single state. **nationwide** adj. covering all of a nation.

national adj. **1.** of or serving a nation as a whole. **2.** characteristic of a particular nation. —n. **3.** citizen of a nation. **nationally** adv. **national anthem** official patriotic song of a nation. **national debt** total outstanding debt of a country's government. **national grid** network of high-voltage power lines linking power stations. **National Health Service** system of national medical services financed mainly by taxation. **national insurance** state insurance scheme providing payments to the unemployed, sick, and retired. **national park** area of countryside protected by a government for its natural or environmental importance. **national service** compulsory military service.

nationalism n. **1.** policy of national independence. **2.** patriotism. **nationalist** n., adj. **nationalistic** adj. fiercely or excessively patriotic.

nationality n. **1.** fact of being a citizen of a particular nation. **2.** nation.

nationalize v. put (an industry or a company) under state control. **nationalization** n.

native adj. **1.** relating to a place where a person was born. **2.** born in a specified place. **3.** (foll. by *to*) originating (in). **4.** inborn. —n. **5.** person born in a specified place. **6.** member of the original race of a country. **7.** indigenous animal or plant.

Nativity n. *Christianity* birth of Jesus Christ.

NATO North Atlantic Treaty Organization.

natter *Informal* —v. **1.** talk idly or chatter. —n. **2.** long idle chat.

natty adj. **-tier, -tiest.** *Informal* smart and spruce.

natural *adj.* **1.** normal. **2.** of, according to, existing in, or produced by nature. **3.** genuine, not affected. **4.** not created by human beings. **5.** not synthetic. **6.** (of a parent) not adoptive. **7.** (of a child) illegitimate. **8.** *Music* not sharp or flat. —*n.* **9.** person with an inborn talent or skill. **10.** *Music* symbol cancelling the effect of a previous sharp or flat. **naturally** *adv.* **1.** of course. **2.** in a natural or normal way. **3.** instinctively. **naturalness** *n.* **natural gas** gas found below the ground, used mainly as a fuel. **natural history** study of animals and plants in the wild. **natural number** positive integer, such as 1, 2, 3, etc. **natural philosophy** *Old-fashioned* physics. **natural science** science dealing with the physical world, such as physics, biology or geology. **natural selection** process by which only creatures and plants well adapted to their environment survive.

naturalism *n.* movement in art and literature advocating detailed realism. **naturalistic** *adj.*

naturalist *n.* student of natural history.

naturalize *v.* give citizenship to (a person born in another country). **naturalization** *n.*

nature *n.* **1.** whole system of the existence, forces, and events of the physical world that are not controlled by human beings. **2.** fundamental or essential qualities of a person or thing. **3.** kind or sort.

naturism *n.* nudism. **naturist** *n.*

naught *n.* **1.** *Obs.* nothing. **2.** figure 0.

naughty *adj.* **-tier, -tiest. 1.** disobedient or mischievous. **2.** mildly indecent. **naughtily** *adv.* **naughtiness** *n.*

nausea [naw-zee-a] *n.* feeling of being about to vomit. **nauseate** *v.* **1.** make (someone) feel sick. **2.** disgust. **nauseous** *adj.* **1.** as if about to vomit. **2.** sickening.

nautical *adj.* of the sea or ships. **nautical mile** 1852 metres.

nautilus *n., pl.* **-luses, -li.** shellfish with many tentacles.

naval *adj.* see NAVY.

nave[1] *n.* long central part of a church.

nave[2] *n.* hub of wheel.

navel *n.* hollow in the middle of the abdomen where the umbilical cord was attached. **navel orange** sweet orange with a navel-like hollow at the top.

navigate *v.* **1.** direct or plot the path or position of a ship, aircraft, or car. **2.** travel over or through. **navigation** *n.* **navigational** *adj.* **navigator** *n.* **navigable** *adj.* **1.** wide, deep, or safe enough to be sailed through. **2.** able to be steered.

navvy *n., pl.* **-vies.** labourer employed on a road or a building site.

navy *n., pl.* **-vies. 1.** branch of a country's armed services comprising warships with their crews and organization. **2.** warships of a nation. —*adj.* **3.** navy-blue. **naval** *adj.* of or relating to a navy or ships. **navy-blue** *adj.* very dark blue.

nay *interj. Obs.* no.

Nazi *n.* **1.** member of the National Socialist Party, which seized political control in Germany in 1933 under Adolf Hitler. —*adj.* **2.** of or relating to the Nazis. **Nazism** *n.*

Nb *Chem.* niobium.

NB 1. New Brunswick. **2.** note well.

NC North Carolina.

NCO noncommissioned officer.

Nd *Chem.* neodymium.

ND North Dakota.

Ne *Chem.* neon.

NE 1. Nebraska. **2.** northeast(ern).

Neanderthal [nee-ann-der-tahl] *adj.* of a type of primitive man that lived in Europe before 12 000 B.C.

Neapolitan *n.* **1.** person from Naples. —*adj.* **2.** of Naples.

neap tide *n.* tide at the first and last quarters of the moon when there is the smallest rise and fall in tidal level.

near *prep.* **1.** close to, not far from. —*adv.* **2.** at or to a place or time not far away. —*adj.* **3.** (situated) at or in a place or time not far away. **4.** (of people) closely related. **5.** almost being the thing specified, e.g. *a near tragedy.* —*v.* **6.** approach and be about to reach. **nearly** *adv.* almost. **nearness** *n.* **nearby** *adj.* not far away. **Near East** same as MIDDLE EAST. **nearside** *n.* side of a vehicle that is nearer the kerb. **near-sighted** *adj.* (of a person) short-sighted.

neat *adj.* **1.** tidy and clean. **2.** smoothly or competently done. **3.** undiluted. **neatly** *adv.* **neatness** *n.* **neaten** *v.* make neat.

nebula [neb-yew-la] *n., pl.* **-lae** [-lee] *Astronomy* hazy cloud of particles and gases. **nebular** *adj.* **nebulous** *adj.* vague, indistinct.

NEC National Executive Committee.

necessary adj. **1.** indispensable or required. **2.** inevitable, e.g. the necessary consequences. **necessaries** pl. n. essential items, e.g. the necessaries of life. **necessarily** adv. **necessitate** v. compel or require. **necessitous** adj. very needy. **necessity** n., pl. **-ties. 1.** something needed. **2.** circumstances that inevitably require a certain result. **3.** great poverty.

neck n. **1.** part of the body joining the head to the shoulders. **2.** part of a garment round the neck. **3.** narrow part of something such as a bottle or violin. — v. **4.** Slang kiss and cuddle. **neck and neck** absolutely level in a race or competiton. **stick one's neck out** Informal risk criticism or ridicule by speaking one's mind. **neckerchief** n. piece of cloth worn tied round the neck. **necklace** n. decorative piece of jewellery worn around the neck. **neckline** n. shape or position of the upper edge of a dress or top. **necktie** n. US same as TIE (sense 6).

necromancy [neck-rome-man-see] n. **1.** communication with the dead. **2.** sorcery. **necromancer** n.

necrophilia n. sexual attraction for or intercourse with dead bodies.

necropolis [neck-rop-pol-liss] n. cemetery.

necrosis n. Biol., Med. death of cells in the body.

nectar n. **1.** sweet liquid collected from flowers by bees. **2.** drink of the gods.

nectarine n. smooth-skinned peach.

née [nay] prep. indicating the maiden name of a married woman.

need v. **1.** want or require. **2.** be obliged (to do something). — n. **3.** condition of lacking something. **4.** requirement, necessity. **5.** poverty. **needs** adv. (preceded or foll. by must) necessarily. **needy** adj. **needier, neediest.** poor, in need of financial support. **needful** adj. necessary or required. **needless** adj. unnecessary. **needlessly** adv.

needle n. **1.** thin pointed piece of metal with an eye through which thread is passed for sewing. **2.** long pointed rod used in knitting. **3.** pointed part of a hypodermic syringe. **4.** small pointed part in a record player that touches the record and picks up the sound signals, stylus. **5.** pointer on a measuring instrument or compass. **6.** long narrow stiff leaf. **7.** Informal intense rivalry or ill-feeling, esp. in a sports match. — v. **8.** Informal goad or provoke. **needlecord** n.

finely-ribbed corduroy. **needlepoint** n. embroidery done on canvas. **needlework** n. sewing and embroidery.

ne'er adv. Lit. never. **ne'er-do-well** n. useless or lazy person.

nefarious [nif-fair-ee-uss] adj. wicked.

negate v. **1.** invalidate. **2.** deny the existence of. **negation** n.

negative adj. **1.** expressing a denial or refusal. **2.** lacking positive qualities. **3.** (of an electrical charge) having the same electrical charge as an electron. **4.** Med. indicating the absence of a condition for which a test was made. — n. **5.** negative word or statement. **6.** Photog. image with a reversal of tones or colours from which positive prints are made.

neglect v. **1.** take no care of. **2.** disregard. **3.** fail (to do something) through carelessness. — n. **4.** neglecting or being neglected. **neglectful** adj.

negligee, négligée [neg-lee-zhay] n. woman's lightweight usu. lace-trimmed dressing gown.

negligence n. neglect or carelessness. **negligent** adj. **negligently** adv.

negligible adj. so small or unimportant as to be not worth considering.

negotiate v. **1.** discuss in order to reach (an agreement). **2.** succeed in passing round or over (a place or problem). **negotiation** n. **negotiator** n. **negotiable** adj.

Negro n., pl. **-groes.** member of any of the Black peoples originating in Africa. **Negress** n. fem. **Negroid** adj. of or relating to the Negro race.

neigh n. **1.** loud high-pitched sound made by a horse. — v. **2.** make this sound.

neighbour n. one who lives or is situated near another. **neighbouring** adj. situated nearby. **neighbourhood** n. **1.** district. **2.** people of a district. **3.** surroundings. **neighbourhood watch** scheme in which the residents of an area keep an eye on each other's property as a means of preventing crime. **neighbourly** adj. kind, friendly, and helpful.

neither adj., pron. **1.** not one nor the other. — conj. **2.** not.
▷ When neither is followed by a plural noun it is acceptable to make the verb plural too: Neither of these books are useful.

nelson n. wrestling hold in which a wrestler places his arm(s) under his opponent's

arm(s) from behind and exerts pressure with his palms on the back of his opponent's neck.

nematode, nematode worm *n.* slender cylindrical unsegmented worm, such as a hookworm.

nemesis [nem-miss-iss] *n.*, *pl.* -ses. retribution or vengeance.

neo- *combining form* new, recent, or a modern form of, e.g. *neoclassicism.*

neoclassicism *n.* **1.** late 18th- and early 19th-century style of art and architecture, based on ancient Roman and Greek models. **2.** early 20th-century style of music, based on small-scale contrapuntal models from the 17th and 18th centuries. **neoclassical** *adj.*

neocolonialism *n.* political control yielded by one country over another through control of its economy. **neocolonial** *adj.*

neodymium *n.* silvery-white metallic element of lanthanide series.

neolithic *adj.* of the later Stone Age.

neologism [nee-ol-a-jiz-zum] *n.* newly-coined word or an established word used in a new sense.

neon *n.* colourless odourless gaseous element used in illuminated signs and lights.

neonatal *adj.* relating to the first few weeks of a baby's life.

neophyte *n.* **1.** beginner or novice. **2.** new convert.

nephew *n.* son of one's sister or brother.

nephritis [nif-**frite**-tiss] *n.* inflammation of a kidney.

nepotism [nep-a-tiz-zum] *n.* favouritism in business shown to relatives and friends.

Neptune *n.* **1.** Roman god of the sea. **2.** eighth planet from the sun.

neptunium *n.* synthetic radioactive metallic element.

nerve *n.* **1.** cordlike bundle of fibres that conducts impulses between the brain and other parts of the body. **2.** bravery and determination. **3.** impudence. —*pl.* **4.** anxiety or tension. **5.** ability or inability to remain calm in a difficult situation. **get on someone's nerves** irritate someone. **nerve oneself** prepare oneself (to do something difficult or unpleasant). **nerveless** *adj.* **1.** fearless. **2.** numb, without feeling. **nervy** *adj.* **nervier, nerviest.** excitable or nervous. **nerve centre** place from which a system or organization is controlled. **nerve gas** poi-

sonous gas which affects the nervous system. **nerve-racking** *adj.* very distressing or harrowing.

nervous *adj.* **1.** apprehensive or worried. **2.** of or relating to the nerves. **nervously** *adv.* **nervousness** *n.* **nervous breakdown** mental illness in which the sufferer ceases to function properly. **nervous system** brain, spinal column and nerves, which together control thought, feeling and movement.

ness *n.* headland, cape.

nest *n.* **1.** place or structure in which birds or certain animals lay eggs or give birth to young. **2.** snug retreat. **3.** set of things of graduated sizes designed to fit together. —*v.* **4.** make or inhabit a nest. **5.** (of a set of objects) fit one inside another. **nest egg** fund of money kept in reserve.

nestle *v.* **1.** snuggle. **2.** be in a sheltered position.

nestling *n.* bird too young to leave the nest.

net[1] *n.* **1.** openwork fabric of meshes of string, thread, or wire. **2.** piece of net used to protect or hold things or to trap animals. **3.** in certain sports, piece of net over which the ball or shuttlecock must be hit. **4.** goal in soccer or hockey. **5.** strategy intended to trap people, e.g. *the murderer slipped through the police net.* —*v.* **netting, netted.** **6.** cover with or catch in a net. **netting** *n.* material made of net. **netball** *n.* team game in which a ball has to be thrown through a net hanging from a ring at the top of a pole.

net[2], **nett** *adj.* **1.** left after all deductions. **2.** (of weight) excluding the wrapping or container. **3.** final, conclusive, e.g. *the net result.* —*v.* **netting, netted. 4.** yield or earn as a clear profit.

nether *adj.* lower. **nethermost** *adj.* lowest.

nettle *n.* **1.** plant with stinging hairs on the leaves. —*v.* **2.** irritate. **nettle rash** skin condition in which itchy red or white raised patches appear.

network *n.* **1.** system of intersecting lines, roads, etc. **2.** interconnecting group or system. **3.** in broadcasting, group of stations that all transmit the same programmes simultaneously. —*v.* **4.** broadcast (a programme) over a network.

neural *adj.* of a nerve or the nervous system.

neuralgia *n.* severe pain along a nerve. **neuralgic** *adj.*

neuritis [nyoor-**rite**-tiss] n. inflammation of a nerve or nerves.

neurology n. scientific study of the nervous system. **neurological** adj. **neurologist** n.

neuron, neurone n. cell specialized to conduct nerve impulses.

neurosis n., pl. **-ses**. mental disorder producing hysteria, anxiety, depression, or obsessive behaviour. **neurotic** adj. **1**. abnormally sensitive. **2**. suffering from neurosis. — n. **3**. neurotic person.

neurosurgery n. branch of surgery concerned with the nervous system. **neurosurgical** adj. **neurosurgeon** n.

neuter adj. **1**. belonging to a particular class of grammatical inflections in some languages. **2**. (of an animal) sexually underdeveloped. — v. **3**. castrate (an animal).

neutral adj. **1**. taking neither side in a war or dispute. **2**. of or belonging to a neutral party or country. **3**. (of a colour) not definite or striking. **4**. of no distinctive quality or type. — n. **5**. neutral person or nation. **6**. neutral gear. **neutrality** n. **neutralize** v. make ineffective or neutral. **neutral gear** position of the controls of a gearbox that leaves the gears unconnected to the engine.

neutrino [new-**tree**-no] n., pl. **-nos**. elementary particle with no mass or electrical charge.

neutron n. electrically neutral elementary particle of about the same mass as a proton. **neutron bomb** nuclear bomb designed to kill people and animals while leaving buildings virtually undamaged.

never adv. at no time. **never-ending** adj. long and boring. **nevermore** adv. Lit. never again. **nevertheless** adv. in spite of that.
▷ Avoid the use of never with the past tense to mean not: I didn't see her (not I never saw her).

never-never n. Informal hire-purchase. **never-never land** n. imaginary idyllic place.

new adj. **1**. not existing before. **2**. recently acquired. **3**. having lately come into some state. **4**. additional. **5**. (foll. by to) unfamiliar. — adv. **6**. recently. **newness** n. **New Age, New Age Music** style of gentle melodic largely instrumental popular music originating in the USA in the late 1980s. **newborn** adj. recently or just born. **newcomer** n. recent arrival or participant. **newfangled** adj. objectionably or unnecessarily modern. **newly** adv. **newly-wed** n., adj.

(person who is) recently married. **new moon** moon when it appears as a narrow crescent at the beginning of its cycle. **New Testament** part of Christian Bible dealing with life and teachings of Christ and his followers. **new town** town planned and built as a complete unit. **New World** the Americas; the western hemisphere. **New Year** (holiday marking) the first day or days of the year.

newel n. post at the top or bottom of a flight of stairs that supports the handrail.

news n. **1**. important or interesting recent happenings. **2**. information about such events reported in the mass media. **3**. television or radio programme presenting such information. **newsy** adj. full of news. **newsagent** n. shopkeeper who sells newspapers and magazines. **newscaster, newsreader** n. person who reads the news on the television or radio. **newsflash** n. brief important news item, which interrupts a radio or television programme. **newsletter** n. bulletin issued periodically to members of a group. **newspaper** n. weekly or daily publication containing news. **newsprint** n. inexpensive paper used for newspapers. **newsreel** n. short film giving news. **newsroom** n. room where news is received and prepared for publication or broadcasting. **newsworthy** adj. sufficiently interesting to be reported as news.

newt n. small amphibious creature with a long slender body and tail.

newton n. unit of force.

next adj., adv. **1**. immediately following. **2**. nearest. **next door** adj., adv. (often hyphenated) in, at, or to the adjacent house or flat. **next-of-kin** n. closest relative.

nexus n., pl. **nexus**. connection or link.

NF Newfoundland.

NH New Hampshire.

NHS National Health Service.

Ni Chem. nickel.

NI 1. Brit. National Insurance. **2**. Northern Ireland.

nib n. writing point of a pen.

nibble v. **1**. take little bites (of). — n. **2**. little bite. **3**. light meal.

nibs n. **his, her nibs** Slang mock title of respect.

nice adj. **1**. pleasant. **2**. kind, e.g. a nice gesture. **3**. good or satisfactory, e.g. they

made a nice job of it. **4.** subtle, e.g. *a nice distinction.* **nicely** *adv.* **niceness** *n.*
▷ It is mistaken to suggest that the adjective *nice* should never be used, but, since it has been overused, it should be used sparingly.

nicety *n.*, *pl.* **-ties. 1.** subtle point. **2.** refinement or delicacy.

niche [neesh] *n.* **1.** hollow area in a wall. **2.** suitable position for a particular person.

nick *v.* **1.** make a small cut in. **2.** *Slang* steal. **3.** *Slang* arrest. —*n.* **4.** small cut. **5.** *Slang* prison or police station. **in good nick** *Informal* in good condition. **in the nick of time** just in time.

nickel *n.* **1.** silvery-white metal often used in alloys. **2.** US coin worth five cents.

nickelodeon *n.* *US* early type of jukebox.

nicker *n.*, *pl.* **nicker.** *Brit. slang* pound sterling.

nickname *n.* **1.** familiar name given to a person or place. —*v.* **2.** call by a nickname.

nicotine *n.* poisonous substance found in tobacco.

nictitate *v.* blink. **nictitating membrane** in reptiles, birds, and some mammals, thin fold of skin that can be drawn across the eye beneath the eyelid.

niece *n.* daughter of one's sister or brother.

nifty *adj.* **-tier, -tiest.** *Informal* neat or smart.

niggard *n.* stingy person. **niggardly** *adj.*

nigger *n.* *Offens.* Black person.

niggle *v.* **1.** continually find fault (with). **2.** worry slightly. —*n.* **3.** small worry or doubt.

nigh *adv.*, *prep. Lit.* near.

night *n.* **1.** time of darkness between sunset and sunrise. **2.** nightfall or dusk. **3.** evening. **4.** period between going to bed and morning. **5.** an evening designated for a specified activity, e.g. *parents' night.* —*adj.* **6.** of, occurring, or working at night, e.g. *the night shift.* **nightly** *adj.*, *adv.* (happening) each night. **nightcap** *n.* **1.** drink taken just before bedtime. **2.** soft cap formerly worn in bed. **nightclub** *n.* establishment for dancing, music, etc., open late at night. **nightdress** *n.* woman's loose dress worn in bed. **nightgown** *n.* loose garment worn in bed; nightdress or nightshirt. **nightfall** *n.* approach of darkness. **nightie** *n. Informal* nightdress. **nightingale** *n.* small bird with a musical song usually heard at night. **nightjar** *n.*

nocturnal bird with a harsh cry. **nightlife** *n.* entertainment and social activities available at night in a town or city. **night-light** *n.* dim light left on overnight. **nightmare** *n.* **1.** very bad dream. **2.** very unpleasant experience. **nightmarish** *adj.* **night safe** safe built into the outside wall of a bank, which customers can deposit money in when the bank is closed. **night school** place where adults can attend educational courses in the evenings. **nightshade** *n.* plant with bell-shaped flowers which are often poisonous. **nightshirt** *n.* man's long loose shirt worn in bed. **nighttime** *n.* time from sunset to sunrise.

nihilism [nye-ill-liz-zum] *n.* rejection of all established authority and institutions. **nihilist** *n.* **nihilistic** *adj.*

nil *n.* nothing, zero.

nimble *adj.* **1.** agile and quick. **2.** mentally alert or acute. **nimbly** *adv.*

nimbus *n.*, *pl.* **-bi, -buses. 1.** dark grey rain cloud. **2.** halo.

nincompoop *n. Informal* stupid person.

nine *adj.*, *n.* one more than eight. **ninth** *adj.*, *n.* (of) number nine in a series. **ninepins** *n.* game of skittles.

nineteen *adj.*, *n.* ten and nine. **talk nineteen to the dozen** talk very fast. **nineteenth** *adj.*, *n.* nineteenth hole *Golf Slang* bar in a golf clubhouse.

ninety *adj.*, *n.* ten times nine. **ninetieth** *adj.*, *n.*

niobium *n.* white superconductive metallic element.

nip *v.* **nipping, nipped. 1.** pinch or squeeze. **2.** bite lightly. **3.** *Informal* hurry. **4.** (of the cold) cause pain. —*n.* **5.** pinch. **6.** light bite. **7.** small alcoholic drink. **8.** sharp coldness, e.g. *a nip in the air.* **nippy** *adj.* **-pier, -piest. 1.** frosty or chilly. **2.** *Informal* quick or nimble. **nipper** *n. Informal* small child.

nipple *n.* **1.** projection in the centre of a breast. **2.** small projection through which oil or grease can be put into a machine or component.

nirvana [near-**vah**-na] *n. Buddhism, Hinduism* absolute spiritual enlightenment and bliss.

nisi [nye-sigh] *adj.* see DECREE NISI.

Nissen hut *n.* tunnel-shaped military hut made of corrugated steel.

nit *n.* **1.** egg or larva of a louse. **2.** *Informal* short for NITWIT. **nit-picking** *adj. Informal* overconcerned with insignificant detail, esp. to find fault. **nitwit** *n. Informal* stupid person.

nitrogen [**nite**-roj-jen] *n.* colourless odourless gas that forms four fifths of the air. **nitric, nitrous, nitrogenous** *adj.* of or containing nitrogen. **nitrate** *n.* compound of nitric acid, used as a fertilizer. **nitroglycerin, nitroglycerine** *n.* explosive liquid. **nitrogen fixation** conversion of nitrogen in the air into nitrogen compounds by bacteria in the soil. **nitric acid** corrosive liquid widely used in industry. **nitrous oxide** anaesthetic gas.

nitty-gritty *n. Informal* basic facts.

NJ New Jersey.

NM New Mexico.

NNE north-northeast.

NNW north-northwest.

no *interj.* **1.** expresses denial, disagreement, or refusal. —*adj.* **2.** not any, not a. —*adv.* **3.** not at all. —*n., pl.* **noes, nos. 4.** answer or vote of 'no'. **5.** person who answers or votes 'no'. **no-ball** in cricket or rounders, improperly bowled ball. **no-claim bonus, no-claims bonus** reduction in the cost of an insurance policy made if no claims have been made in a specified period. **no-go area** district barricaded off so that the police or army can enter only by force. **no-man's-land** *n.* land between boundaries, esp. contested land between two opposing forces. **no-one, no one** *pron.* nobody.

▷ When *no-one* refers to 'people in general' it may be followed by a plural: *No-one finished their drink.*

no. number.

No[1] *n., pl.* **No.** Japanese classical drama, using music and dancing.

No[2] *Chem.* nobelium.

n.o. *Cricket* not out.

nob *n. Slang* person of wealth or social distinction.

nobble *v.* **1.** *Slang* attract the attention of (someone) in order to talk to him or her. **2.** *Slang* bribe or threaten.

nobelium *n.* artificially-produced radioactive element.

Nobel Prize [no-**bell**] *n.* prize awarded annually for outstanding achievement in various fields.

noble *adj.* **1.** showing or having high moral qualities. **2.** of the nobility. **3.** impressive and magnificent. —*n.* **4.** member of the nobility. **nobility** *n.* **1.** quality of being noble. **2.** class of people holding titles and high social rank. **nobly** *adv.* **nobleman, noblewoman** *n.* **noble gas** *Chem.* any of a group of very unreactive gases, including helium and neon.

noblesse oblige [no-**bless** oh-**bleezh**] *n. oft. ironic* supposed obligation of nobility to be honourable and generous.

nobody *pron.* **1.** no person. —*n., pl.* **-bodies. 2.** person of no importance.

▷ *Nobody* is equivalent in its uses to *no-one*.

nock *n.* notch on an arrow or a bow for the bowstring.

nocturnal *adj.* **1.** of the night. **2.** active at night.

nocturne *n.* short dreamy piece of music.

nod *v.* **nodding, nodded. 1.** lower and raise (one's head) briefly in agreement or greeting. **2.** let one's head fall forward with sleep. —*n.* **3.** act of nodding. **nod off** *v. Informal* fall asleep.

noddle *n. Informal* the head.

node *n.* **1.** point on a plant stem from which leaves grow. **2.** point at which a curve crosses itself. **nodal** *adj.*

nodule *n.* **1.** small knot or lump. **2.** rounded mineral growth on the root of a plant. **nodular** *adj.*

Noel, Noël *n.* Christmas.

nog *n.* alcoholic drink containing beaten egg.

noggin *n.* **1.** small quantity of an alcoholic drink. **2.** *Informal* head.

Noh *n., pl.* **Noh.** same as No[1]

noise *n.* sound, usually a loud or disturbing one. **be noised abroad** be rumoured. **noisy** *adj.* **noisier, noisiest. 1.** making a lot of noise. **2.** full of noise. **noisily** *adv.* **noiseless** *adj.* **noiselessly** *adv.*

noisome *adj.* **1.** (of smells) offensive. **2.** harmful or poisonous.

nomad *n.* member of a tribe with no fixed dwelling place, wanderer. **nomadic** *adj.*

nom de plume *n., pl.* **noms de plume.** pen name.

nomenclature [no-**men**-klatch-er] *n.* system of names used in a particular subject.

nominal *adj.* **1.** in name only. **2.** very small in comparison with real worth. **nominally** *adv.*

nominate v. **1.** suggest as a candidate. **2.** appoint to an office or position. **nomination** n. **nominee** n. candidate. **nominative** n. form of a noun indicating the subject of a verb.

non- prefix indicating: **1.** negation, e.g. nonexistent. **2.** refusal or failure, e.g. noncooperation. **3.** exclusion from a specified class, e.g. nonfiction. **4.** lack or absence, e.g. nonevent.

nonage n. **1.** Law state of being under full legal age for various actions. **2.** any period of immaturity.

nonagenarian n. person aged between ninety and ninety-nine.

nonaggression n. (of countries) idea or policy of not attacking.

nonagon n. geometric figure with nine sides. **nonagonal** adj.

nonalcoholic adj. containing no alcohol.

nonaligned adj. (of a country) not part of a major alliance or power bloc. **nonalignment** n.

nonbelligerent adj. (of a country) not taking part in a war.

nonce n. **for the nonce** for the present. **nonce word** word coined for a single occasion.

nonchalant [non-shall-ant] adj. casually unconcerned or indifferent. **nonchalantly** adv. **nonchalance** n.

noncombatant n. member of the armed forces whose duties do not include fighting.

noncommissioned officer n. in the armed forces, a subordinate officer, risen from the ranks.

noncommittal adj. not committing oneself to any particular opinion.

non compos mentis adj. of unsound mind.

nonconductor n. substance that is a poor conductor of heat, electricity, or sound.

nonconformist n. **1.** person who does not conform to generally accepted patterns of behaviour or thought. **2.** (N-) member of a Protestant group separated from the Church of England. —adj. **3.** (of behaviour or ideas) not conforming to accepted patterns. **nonconformity** n.

noncontributory adj. denoting a pension scheme for employees, the premiums of which are paid entirely by the employer.

non-cooperation n. refusal to do more than is legally or contractually required of one.

nondescript adj. lacking outstanding features.

none pron. **1.** not any. **2.** no-one. **nonetheless** adv. despite that, however.
▷ Although none means 'not one', and can take a singular verb, it more often takes a plural: None of them are mine.

nonentity [non-enn-tit-tee] n., pl. -ties. insignificant person or thing.

nonessential adj. not absolutely necessary.

nonevent n. disappointing or insignificant occurrence.

nonexistent adj. not existing, imaginary. **nonexistence** n.

nonferrous adj. **1.** denoting metal other than iron. **2.** not containing iron.

nonflammable adj. not easily set on fire.

nonintervention n. refusal to intervene in the affairs of others.

noniron adj. not requiring ironing.

non-nuclear adj. not involving or using nuclear power or weapons.

nonpareil [non-par-rail] n. person or thing that is unsurpassed.

nonpartisan adj. not supporting any single political party.

nonpayment n. failure to pay money owed.

nonplussed adj. perplexed.

non-profit-making adj. not run with the intention of making a profit.

nonproliferation n. limitation of the production or spread of something, such as nuclear weapons.

nonrepresentational adj. Art abstract.

nonresident n. person who does not live in a particular country, hotel, etc.

nonsectarian adj. not sectarian; not confined to any specific religion.

nonsense n. **1.** something that has or makes no sense. **2.** absurd language. **3.** foolish behaviour. **nonsensical** adj.

non sequitur [sek-wit-tur] n. statement with little or no relation to what preceded it.

nonsmoker n. **1.** person who does not smoke. **2.** train carriage or compartment in which smoking is forbidden. **nonsmoking, no-smoking** adj. denoting an area in which smoking is forbidden.

nonstandard *adj.* denoting language that is not regarded as correct by educated native speakers.

nonstarter *n.* person or idea that has little chance of success.

nonstick *adj.* coated with a substance that food will not stick to when cooked.

nonstop *adj., adv.* without a stop.

nontoxic *adj.* not poisonous.

nonunion *adj.* **1.** (of a company) not employing trade union members. **2.** (of a person) not belonging to a trade union.

nonviolence *n.* use of peaceful methods to bring about change. **nonviolent** *adj.*

nonvoting *adj.* (of shares in a company) not entitling the owner to vote at company meetings.

noodle *n.* strip of pasta.

nook *n.* **1.** corner or recess. **2.** sheltered place.

noon *n.* twelve o'clock midday. **noonday** *n. Lit.* noon.

noose *n.* loop in the end of a rope, tied with a slipknot.

nor *conj.* and not.

Nordic *adj.* of Scandinavia or its typically tall blond and blue-eyed people.

norm *n.* standard that is regarded as normal.

normal *adj.* **1.** usual, regular, or typical. **2.** free from mental or physical disorder. —*n.* **3.** usual or regular state, degree or form. **normally** *adv.* **normality**, *Formal* **normalcy** *n.* **normalize** *v.* **1.** make or become normal. **2.** make comply with a standard. **normalization** *n.* **normative** *adj.* of or setting a norm or standard.

Norman *n.* **1.** person from Normandy in N France, esp. one of the people who conquered England in 1066. **2.** (also **Norman French**) medieval Norman and English dialect of French. —*adj.* **3.** of the Normans or their dialect of French. **4.** of Normandy. **5.** of a style of architecture used in Britain from the Norman Conquest until the 12th century, characterized by massive masonry walls and rounded arches.

Norse *n., adj.* (language) of ancient and medieval Norway. **Norseman** *n.* Viking.

north *n.* **1.** direction towards the North Pole, oppposite south. **2.** area lying in or towards the north. —*adv.* **3.** in, to, or towards the north. —*adj.* **4.** to or in the north. **5.** (of a wind) from the north. **northerly** *adj.* **northern** *adj.* **northerner** *n.* person from the north of a country or area. **northwards** *adv.* **northeast** *n., adj., adv.* (in or to) direction between north and east. **northwest** *n., adj., adv.* (in or to) direction between north and west. **North Pole** northernmost point on the earth's axis.

Norwegian *adj.* **1.** of Norway, its language, or its people. —*n.* **2.** language of Norway. **3.** person from Norway.

nos. numbers.

nose *n.* **1.** organ of smell, used also in breathing. **2.** sense of smell. **3.** front part of a vehicle. **4.** distinctive smell of a wine, perfume, etc. **5.** instinctive smell in finding something, e.g. *a nose for a bargain*. —*v.* **6.** move forward slowly and carefully. **7.** pry or snoop. **nosebag** *n.* bag containing feed fastened round a horse's head. **nosebleed** *n.* bleeding from the nose. **nose dive** sudden drop. **nosegay** *n.* small bunch of flowers. **nose out** *v.* discover by searching or prying. **nosy, nosey** *adj.* **nosier, nosiest.** *Informal* prying or inquisitive. **nosiness** *n.*

nosh *Slang* —*n.* **1.** food. —*v.* **2.** eat. **nosh-up** *n.* large meal.

nostalgia *n.* sentimental longing for the past. **nostalgic** *adj.*

nostril *n.* one of the two openings at the end of the nose.

nostrum *n.* **1.** quack medicine. **2.** favourite remedy.

not *adv.* expressing negation, refusal, or denial.

nota bene [note-a bee-ni] note well, take note.

notable [note-a-bl] *adj.* **1.** worthy of being noted, remarkable. —*n.* **2.** person of distinction. **notably** *adv.* **notability** [note-a-bill-lit-tee] *n.*

notary, notary public [note-a-ree] *n., pl.* **-ries.** person authorized to witness the signing of legal documents.

notation [no-tay-shun] *n.* **1.** representation of numbers or quantities in a system by a series of symbols. **2.** set of such symbols.

notch *n.* **1.** V-shaped cut. **2.** *Informal* step or level. —*v.* **3.** make a notch in. **4.** (usu. foll. by *up*) score or achieve.

note *n.* **1.** short letter. **2.** brief comment or record. **3.** banknote. **4.** (symbol for) a musical sound. **5.** hint or mood. —*v.* **6.** notice, pay attention to. **7.** record in writing. **8.** remark upon. **noted** *adj.* well-known. **notebook** *n.* book for writing in. **notelet** *n.* small folded card with a design on the front, used for writing informal letters. **notepaper** *n.* paper used for writing letters. **noteworthy** *adj.* worth noting, remarkable.

nothing *pron.* **1.** not anything. **2.** matter of no importance. **3.** figure 0. —*adv.* **4.** not at all. **nothingness** *n.* **1.** nonexistence. **2.** insignificance.

▷ *Nothing* is usually followed by a singular verb but, if it comes before a plural noun, this can sound odd: *Nothing but books was/were on the shelf.* A solution is to rephrase the sentence: *Only books were...*

notice *n.* **1.** observation or attention. **2.** sign giving warning or an announcement. **3.** advance notification of intention to end a contract of employment. **4.** review in a newspaper of a book, play, etc. —*v.* **5.** observe, become aware of. **6.** point out or remark upon. **noticeable** *adj.* easily seen or detected, appreciable. **noticeably** *adv.* **notice board** board on which notices are displayed.

notify *v.* **-fying, -fied.** inform. **notification** *n.* **notifiable** *adj.* having to be reported to the authorities.

notion *n.* **1.** vague idea. **2.** whim. **notional** *adj.* speculative, imaginary, or unreal.

notorious *adj.* well known for something bad. **notoriously** *adv.* **notoriety** *n.*

notwithstanding *prep.* **1.** in spite of. —*adv.* **2.** nevertheless.

nougat *n.* chewy sweet containing nuts and fruit.

nought *n.* **1.** nothing. **2.** figure 0.

noun *n.* word that refers to a person, place, or thing.

nourish *v.* **1.** feed. **2.** encourage or foster (an idea or feeling). **nourishment** *n.* **nourishing** *adj.* providing the food necessary for life and growth.

nous *n. Old-fashioned Slang* common sense.

nouveau riche [noo-voh **reesh**] *n., pl.* **nouveaux riches** [noo-voh **reesh**] person who has recently become rich and is regarded as vulgar.

nouvelle cuisine [noo-**vell** kwee-**zeen**] *n.* style of preparing and presenting food with light sauces and unusual combinations of flavours.

Nov. November.

nova *n., pl.* **-vae, -vas.** star that suddenly becomes brighter and then gradually decreases to its original brightness.

novel[1] *n.* long fictitious story in book form. **novelist** *n.* writer of novels. **novelette** *n.* short novel, esp. one regarded as trivial or sentimental. **novella** *n., pl.* **-las, -lae.** short novel.

novel[2] *adj.* fresh, new, or original. **novelty** *n.* **1.** newness. **2.** something new or unusual. **3.** cheap toy or trinket.

November *n.* eleventh month of the year.

novena [no-**vee**-na] *n., pl.* **-nae.** *RC Church* set of prayers or services on nine consecutive days.

novice [**nov**-viss] *n.* **1.** beginner. **2.** person who has entered a religious order but has not yet taken vows.

novitiate, noviciate *n.* **1.** period of being a novice. **2.** part of a monastery or convent where the novices live.

now *adv.* **1.** at or for the present time. **2.** immediately. —*conj.* **3.** seeing that, since. **just now** very recently. **now and again, then** occasionally. **nowadays** *adv.* in these times.

Nowel, Nowell *n.* same as NOEL.

nowhere *adv.* not anywhere.

noxious *adj.* **1.** poisonous or harmful. **2.** extremely unpleasant.

nozzle *n.* projecting spout through which fluid is discharged.

Np *Chem.* neptunium.

nr near.

NS Nova Scotia.

NSPCC National Society for the Prevention of Cruelty to Children.

NSW New South Wales.

NT **1.** National Trust. **2.** New Testament. **3.** Northern Territory.

nuance [**new**-ahnss] *n.* subtle difference in colour, meaning, or tone.

nub *n.* point or gist (of a story etc.).

nubile [**new**-bile] *adj.* **1.** (of a young woman) sexually attractive. **2.** old enough to be married.

nuclear *adj.* **1.** of nuclear weapons or energy. **2.** of a nucleus, esp. the nucleus of an atom. **nuclear bomb** bomb whose force is due to uncontrolled nuclear fusion or fission.

nuclear energy energy released as a result of nuclear fission or fusion. **nuclear family** family consisting only of parents and their offspring. **nuclear fission** splitting of an atomic nucleus. **nuclear fusion** combination of two nuclei to form a heavier nucleus with the release of energy. **nuclear power** power produced by a nuclear reactor. **nuclear reaction** change in structure and energy content of an atomic nucleus by interaction with another nucleus or particle. **nuclear reactor** device in which a nuclear reaction is maintained and controlled to produce nuclear energy. **nuclear winter** theoretical period of low temperatures and little light after a nuclear war.

nucleic acid n. complex compound, such as DNA or RNA, found in all living cells.

nucleonics n. branch of physics dealing with the applications of nuclear energy.

nucleus n., pl. -clei. 1. centre, esp. of an atom or cell. 2. central thing around which others are grouped.

nude adj. 1. naked. —n. 2. naked figure in painting, sculpture, or photography. **nudity** n. **nudism** n. practice of not wearing clothes. **nudist** n.

nudge v. 1. push gently, esp. with the elbow. —n. 2. gentle push or touch.

nugatory [new-gat-tree] adj. 1. trifling. 2. not valid.

nugget n. 1. small lump of gold in its natural state. 2. something small but valuable.

nuisance n. something or someone that causes annoyance or bother.

nuke Slang —v. 1. attack with nuclear weapons. —n. 2. nuclear bomb.

null adj. **null and void** not legally valid. **nullity** n. **nullify** v. -fying, -fied. 1. make ineffective. 2. cancel.

numb adj. 1. without feeling, as through cold, shock, or fear. —v. 2. make numb. **numbly** adv. **numbness** n. **numbskull** n. same as NUMSKULL.

number n. 1. sum or quantity. 2. word or symbol used to express a sum or quantity, numeral. 3. one of a series, such as a copy of a magazine. 4. Grammar classification of words depending on how many persons or things are referred to. 5. song or piece of music. 6. group of people. 7. numeral or string of numerals used to identify a person or thing. —v. 8. count. 9. give a number to.

10. amount to. 11. include in a group. **numberless** adj. too many to be counted. **number crunching** Computers large-scale processing of numerical data. **number one** n. Informal 1. oneself. 2. best-selling pop record in any one week. —adj. 3. first in importance or quality. **numberplate** n. plate on a car showing the registration number.

numeral n. word or symbol used to express a sum or quantity.

numerate adj. able to do basic arithmetic. **numeracy** n.

numeration n. act or process of numbering or counting.

numerator n. Maths number above the line in a fraction.

numerical adj. measured or expressed in numbers. **numerically** adv.

numerology n. study of numbers and their supposed influence on human affairs.

numerous adj. existing or happening in large numbers.

numinous adj. 1. arousing religious or spiritual emotions. 2. mysterious or awe-inspiring.

numismatist n. coin collector. **numismatics** n. study or collection of coins. **numismatic** adj.

numskull n. stupid person.

nun n. female member of a religious order. **nunnery** n., pl. -neries. convent.

nuncio n., pl. -cios. RC Church pope's ambassador.

nuptial adj. relating to marriage. **nuptials** pl. n. wedding.

nurse n. 1. person employed to look after sick people, usu. in hospital. 2. (also **nurse-maid, nursery nurse**) woman employed to look after children. —v. 3. look after (a sick person). 4. breast-feed (a baby). 5. try to cure (an ailment). 6. harbour or foster (a feeling). **nursing home** private hospital or home for old people. **nursing officer** administrative head of the nursing staff of a hospital.

nursery n., pl. -ries. 1. room where children sleep or play. 2. place where children are taken care of while their parents are at work. 3. place where plants are grown for sale. **nurseryman** n., pl. -men. person who raises plants for sale. **nursery rhyme** short traditional verse or song for children.

nursery school school for children from 3 to 5 years old. **nursery slope** gentle ski slope for beginners.

nurture *n.* **1.** act or process of promoting the development of a child or young plant. —*v.* **2.** promote or encourage the development of.

nut *n.* **1.** fruit consisting of a hard shell and a kernel. **2.** small piece of metal that screws onto a bolt. **3.** *Slang* head. **4.** (also **nutcase**) *Slang* insane or eccentric person. **nuts** *adj. Slang* insane or eccentric. **nuts and bolts** *Informal* essential or practical details. **nutshell** *n.* **in a nutshell** in essence, briefly. **nutty** *adj.* **-tier, -tiest. 1.** containing or resembling nuts. **2.** *Slang* insane or eccentric. **nutter** *n. Slang* insane or violent person. **nutcracker** *n.* device for cracking the shells of nuts. **nuthatch** *n.* small songbird. **nutmeg** *n.* spice made from the seed of a tropical tree.

nutria [new-tree-a] *n.* fur of the coypu.

nutrient [new-tree-ent] *n.* substance that provides nourishment.

nutriment [new-tree-ment] *n.* food or nourishment required by all living things to grow and stay healthy.

nutrition [new-trish-shun] *n.* **1.** process of taking in and absorbing nutrients. **2.** process of being nourished. **3.** study of nutrition. **nutritious, nutritive** *adj.* nourishing.

nuzzle *v.* push or rub gently with the nose or snout.

NV Nevada.

NW northwest(ern).

NY New York.

nylon *n.* **1.** synthetic material used for clothing etc. —*pl.* **2.** stockings made of nylon.

nymph *n.* **1.** mythical spirit of nature, represented as a beautiful young woman. **2.** larva of certain insects, resembling the adult form.

nymphet *n.* sexually precocious young girl.

nymphomania *n.* abnormally intense sexual desire in women. **nymphomaniac** *n.* woman with an abnormally intense sexual desire.

NZ New Zealand.

O

o, O *n., pl.* **o's, O's, Os.** same as NOUGHT.

O[1] **1.** *Chem.* oxygen. **2.** Old.

O[2] *interj.* same as OH.

o' *prep. Informal* of, e.g. *a cup o' tea.*

oaf *n.* stupid or clumsy person. **oafish** *adj.*

oak *n.* **1.** deciduous forest tree. **2.** its wood, used for furniture. **oaken** *adj.* **oak apple** brownish lump found on oak trees.

oakum *n.* fibre obtained by unravelling old rope.

OAP old-age pensioner.

oar *n.* pole with a broad blade, used for rowing a boat. **oarsman, oarswoman** *n.*

oasis *n., pl.* **-ses.** fertile area in a desert.

oast *n.* kiln for drying hops. **oast-house** *n.* building containing oasts.

oath *n.* **1.** solemn promise, esp. to be truthful in court. **2.** swearword.

oats *pl. n.* grain of a cereal plant, used for food. **sow one's wild oats** have many sexual relationships when young. **oaten** *adj.* **oatcake** *n.* thin flat biscuit of oatmeal. **oatmeal** *n.* **1.** coarse flour made from oats. —*adj.* **2.** pale brownish-cream.

ob. on tombstones, he *or* she died.

obbligato [ob-lig-**gah**-toe] *n., pl.* **-tos.** *Music* essential part or accompaniment.

obdurate *adj.* **1.** hardhearted. **2.** stubborn. **obduracy** *n.*

OBE Officer of the Order of the British Empire.

obedient *adj.* obeying or willing to obey. **obediently** *adv.* **obedience** *n.*

obeisance [oh-**bay**-sanss] *n.* **1.** attitude of respect. **2.** bow or curtsy.

obelisk [**ob**-bill-isk] *n.* four-sided stone column tapering to a pyramid at the top.

obese [oh-**beess**] *adj.* very fat. **obesity** *n.*

obey *v.* **1.** carry out the instructions of (someone). **2.** comply with (instructions).

obfuscate *v.* **1.** darken. **2.** make (something) confusing. **obfuscation** *n.*

obituary *n., pl.* **-aries.** announcement of someone's death, esp. in a newspaper. **obituarist** *n.*

object[1] *n.* **1.** physical thing. **2.** focus of thoughts or action. **3.** aim or purpose. **4.** *Grammar* word that a verb or preposition affects. **no object** not a hindrance.

object[2] *v.* (foll. by *to*) oppose. **objection** *n.* **objectionable** *adj.* unpleasant. **objector** *n.*

objective *adj.* **1.** existing in the real world outside the human mind. **2.** not biased. —*n.* **3.** aim or purpose. **objectively** *adv.* **objectivity** *n.*

objet d'art [ob-zhay **dahr**] *n., pl.* **objets d'art.** small object of artistic value.

oblate *adj.* (of a sphere) flattened at the poles.

oblation *n.* religious offering.

oblige *v.* **1.** compel (someone) morally or by law to do (something). **2.** do a favour for (someone). **obliging** *adj.* ready to help other people. **obligingly** *adv.* **obligate** *v.* cause (someone) to be obliged to do (something). **obligation** *n.* **1.** duty. **2.** indebtedness for a favour. **obligatory** *adj.* required by a rule or law.

oblique [oh-**bleak**] *adj.* **1.** slanting. **2.** indirect. —*n.* **3.** the symbol (/). **obliquely** *adv.* **obliqueness** *n.* **oblique angle** angle that is not a right angle.

obliterate *v.* wipe out, destroy. **obliteration** *n.*

oblivious *adj.* (foll. by *to* or *of*) unaware (of). **oblivion** *n.* **1.** state of being forgotten. **2.** state of being unaware or unconscious.

oblong *adj.* **1.** shape with two long sides, two short sides, and four right angles. —*n.* **2.** oblong figure.

obloquy [**ob**-lock-wee] *n., pl.* **-quies. 1.** verbal abuse. **2.** discredit.

obnoxious *adj.* offensive. **obnoxiousness** *n.*

oboe *n.* double-reeded woodwind instrument. **oboist** *n.*

obscene *adj.* **1.** portraying sex offensively. **2.** disgusting. **obscenity** *n.*

obscure *adj.* **1.** not well known. **2.** hard to understand. **3.** indistinct. —*v.* **4.** make (something) obscure. **obscurity** *n.*

obsequies [**ob**-sick-weez] *pl. n.* funeral rites.

obsequious [ob-seek-wee-uss] *adj.* too eager to please in order to be liked. **obsequiousness** *n.*

observe *v.* 1. watch (someone or something) carefully. 2. perceive visually. 3. remark. 4. act according to (a law or custom). **observation** *n.* 1. action or habit of observing. 2. something observed. 3. remark. **observer** *n.* **observable** *adj.* **observably** *adv.* **observance** *n.* 1. observing of a custom. 2. ritual or ceremony. **observant** *adj.* quick to notice things. **observatory** *n.* building equipped for astronomical or meteorological observations.

obsess *v.* preoccupy (someone) compulsively. **obsessive** *adj.* **obsession** *n.* **obsessional** *adj.*

obsidian *n.* dark glassy volcanic rock.

obsolete *adj.* no longer in use. **obsolescent** *adj.* becoming obsolete. **obsolescence** *n.*

obstacle *n.* something that makes progress difficult.

obstetrics *n.* branch of medicine concerned with pregnancy and childbirth. **obstetric** *adj.* **obstetrician** *n.*

obstinate *adj.* 1. stubborn. 2. difficult to remove or change. **obstinately** *adv.* **obstinacy** *n.*

obstreperous *adj.* unruly, noisy.

obstruct *v.* 1. block with an obstacle. 2. make (progress) difficult. **obstruction** *n.* **obstructionist** *n.* person who deliberately obstructs formal proceedings. **obstructive** *adj.*

obtain *v.* 1. acquire intentionally. 2. be customary. **obtainable** *adj.*

obtrude *v.* 1. push oneself or one's ideas on others. 2. stick out noticeably. **obtrusion** *n.* **obtrusive** *adj.* unpleasantly noticeable. **obtrusively** *adv.*

obtuse *adj.* 1. mentally slow. 2. *Maths* (of an angle) between 90° and 180°. 3. not pointed. **obtusely** *adv.* **obtuseness** *n.*

obverse *n.* 1. opposite way of looking at an idea. 2. main side of a coin or medal.

obviate *v.* make unnecessary.

obvious *adj.* easy to see or understand, evident. **obviously** *adv.*

ocarina *n.* small oval wind instrument made of clay.

occasion *n.* 1. time at which a particular thing happens. 2. special event. 3. reason, e.g. *no occasion for complaint.* 4. opportunity. —*v.* 5. cause. **occasional** *adj.* 1. happening sometimes. 2. for a special event. **occasionally** *adv.*

Occident *n. Lit.* the West. **Occidental** *adj.*

occiput [ox-sip-put] *n.* back of the head.

occlude *v.* 1. obstruct. 2. close off. **occlusion** *n.* **occlusive** *adj.* **occluded front** *Meteorol.* front formed when a cold front overtakes a warm front and warm air rises.

occult *n.* 1. **the occult** knowledge or study of the supernatural. —*adj.* 2. relating to the supernatural.

occupant *n.* person occupying a specified place. **occupancy** *n.* (length of a) person's stay in a specified place.

occupation *n.* 1. profession. 2. activity that occupies one's time. 3. being occupied. 4. control of a country by a foreign military power. **occupational** *adj.* **occupational therapy** activities, esp. crafts, designed to aid recovery from illness.

occupy *v.* -pying, -pied. 1. live or work in (a building). 2. take up the attention of (someone). 3. take up (space or time). 4. take possession of (a place) by force. 5. hold (an office or position). **occupier** *n.*

occur *v.* -curring, -curred. 1. take place. 2. exist. 3. (foll. by *to*) come to the mind (of). **occurrence** *n.* 1. something that occurs. 2. occurring.
▷ Avoid the use of *occur* (or *happen*) for events that are planned. Compare *An accident occurred* with *A wedding took place.*

ocean *n.* 1. vast area of sea between continents. 2. large quantity or expanse. **oceanic** *adj.* **oceanography** *n.* scientific study of the oceans. **oceanographer** *n.* **ocean-going** *adj.* able to sail on the open sea.

ocelot [oss-ill-lot] *n.* American wild cat with a spotted coat.

oche [ok-kee] *n. Darts* mark on the floor behind which a player must stand.

ochre [oak-er] *adj., n.* brownish-yellow (earth).

o'clock *adv.* used after a number to specify an hour.

Oct. October.

octagon *n.* geometric figure with eight sides. **octagonal** *adj.*

octahedron [ok-ta-heed-ron] *n., pl.* -drons, -dra. three-dimensional geometric figure with eight faces.

octane n. hydrocarbon found in petrol. **octane rating** measure of petrol quality.

octave n. Music (interval between the first and) eighth note of a scale.

octavo n., pl. **-vos**. book size in which the sheets are folded into eight leaves.

octet n. 1. group of eight performers. 2. music for such a group.

October n. tenth month of the year.

octogenarian n. person aged between eighty and eighty-nine.

octopus n., pl. **-puses**. sea creature with a soft body and eight tentacles.

ocular adj. relating to the eyes or sight.

oculist n. Old-fashioned ophthalmologist.

OD n. 1. Med. overdose. —v. **OD'ing, OD'd**. 2. Informal take an overdose.

odd adj. 1. unusual. 2. occasional. 3. not divisible by two. 4. not part of a set. **odds** pl. n. 1. (ratio showing) the probability of something happening. 2. likelihood. **at odds** in conflict. **odds and ends** small miscellaneous items. **oddball** n. Informal eccentric person. **oddness** n. quality of being odd. **oddity** n. odd person or thing. **oddments** pl. n. things left over.

ode n. lyric poem, usu. addressed to a particular subject.

odium [oh-dee-um] n. widespread dislike. **odious** adj. offensive.

odour n. particular smell. **odorous** adj. **odourless** adj. **odoriferous** adj. giving off a pleasant smell. **odorize** v. fill (something) with scent.

odyssey [odd-iss-ee] n. long eventful journey.

OECD Organization for Economic Cooperation and Development.

oedema [id-deem-a] n., pl. **-mata**. abnormal swelling.

o'er prep., adv. Lit. over.

oesophagus [ee-soff-a-guss] n., pl. **-gi**. passage between the mouth and stomach.

oestrogen [ee-stra-jen] n. female hormone that controls the reproductive cycle.

of prep. 1. belonging to. 2. consisting of. 3. connected with. 4. characteristic of.
▷ Only when of means 'belonging to' can an apostrophe be used: Bill's dog (the dog of Bill).

off prep. 1. away from. —adv. 2. away. 3. so as to stop or disengage. —adj. 4. not operating. 5. cancelled. 6. (of food) gone bad. —n. 7. Cricket side of the field on the bowler's left. **offbeat** adj. unusual or eccentric. **off chance** slight possibility. **off colour** slightly ill. **off-line** adj. (of a computer) not directly controlled by a central processor. **offputting** adj. arousing dislike.
▷ Avoid using of after off: He got off the bus (not off of). The use of off to mean from is very informal: They brought milk from (rather than off) a farmer.

offal n. 1. edible organs of an animal, such as liver or kidneys. 2. rubbish.

offcut n. piece remaining after the required parts have been cut out.

offend v. 1. hurt the feelings of, insult. 2. commit a crime. 3. disgust. **offender** n. **offence** n. 1. (cause of) hurt feelings or annoyance. 2. illegal act. **offensive** adj. 1. insulting. 2. aggressive. 3. disagreeable. —n. 4. position or action of attack.

offer v. 1. present (something) for acceptance or rejection. 2. provide. 3. propose (a sum of money) as payment. 4. be willing (to do something). —n. 5. instance of offering something. 6. something offered. **offering** n. thing offered. **offertory** n. Christianity 1. offering of the bread and wine for Communion. 2. collection of money at Communion.

offhand adj. 1. (also **offhanded**) casual, curt. —adv. 2. without preparation.

office n. 1. room or building where people work at desks. 2. department of a commercial organization. 3. place where tickets or information can be obtained. 4. formal position of responsibility. 5. duty, function. 6. (esp. pl.) something done for another. 7. (esp. pl.) religious ceremony. **officer** n. 1. person in authority in the armed services. 2. a member of the police force. 3. person with special responsibility in an organization.

official adj. 1. approved or arranged by someone in authority. 2. of a position of authority. 3. formal. —n. 4. person who holds a position of authority. **officially** adv. **officialdom** n. Offens. officials collectively. **Official Receiver** person who deals with the affairs of a bankrupt company.

officiate v. conduct a ceremony in an official role.

officious adj. 1. giving unnecessary instructions. 2. interfering.

offing n. area of the sea visible from the shore. **in the offing** likely to happen soon.

off-licence n. shop licensed to sell alcohol.

offset v. cancel out, compensate for.

offshoot n. **1.** something developed from something else. **2.** shoot growing on the main stem of a plant.

offside adj., adv. Sport (positioned) illegally ahead of the ball.

offspring n., pl. **offspring.** one's child.

often adv. frequently, much of the time. **oft** adv. Poetic often.

ogee arch [oh-jee] n. pointed arch with an S-shaped curve on both sides.

ogle v. stare at (someone) lustfully.

ogre n. giant that eats human flesh.

oh interj. exclamation of surprise, pain, etc.

OH Ohio.

ohm n. unit of electrical resistance.

OHMS On Her or His Majesty's Service.

oil n. **1.** viscous liquid, insoluble in water and usu. flammable. **2.** same as PETROLEUM. **3.** petroleum derivative, used as a fuel or lubricant. —pl. **4.** oil-based paints used in art. —v. **5.** lubricate (a machine) with oil. **oily** adj. **oilcloth** n. waterproof material. **oilfield** n. area containing oil reserves. **oil rig** platform constructed for boring oil wells. **oilskins** pl. n. waterproof clothing.

ointment n. greasy substance used for healing skin or as a cosmetic.

OK Oklahoma.

O.K., okay Informal —interj. **1.** all right. —n. **2.** approval. —v. **3.** approve (something).

okapi [ok-kah-pee] n. African animal related to the giraffe but with a shorter neck.

okra n. tropical plant with edible green pods.

old adj. **1.** having lived or existed for a long time. **2.** of a specified age, e.g. two years old. **3.** former. **olden** adj. old, e.g. in the olden days. **oldie** n. Informal old but popular song or film. **old age pensioner** retired person receiving an allowance from the government. **old boy, girl** former pupil of a school. **old-fashioned** adj. no longer commonly used or valued. **old guard** group of people in an organization who have traditional values. **old hand** skilled and experienced person. **old hat** boring because so familiar. **old maid** elderly unmarried woman. **old master** European painter or painting from the

period 1500–1800. **Old Nick** Informal the Devil. **old school tie** system of mutual help between former pupils of a public school. **Old Testament** part of the Bible recording Hebrew history. **Old World** world as it was known before the discovery of the Americas.

oleaginous [ol-lee-aj-in-uss] adj. oily, producing oil.

oleander [ol-lee-ann-der] n. Mediterranean flowering evergreen shrub.

O level n. former basic level of the General Certificate of Education.

olfactory adj. relating to the sense of smell.

oligarchy [ol-lee-gark-ee] n., pl. **-chies. 1.** government by a small group of people. **2.** state governed this way. **oligarch** n. member of an oligarchy. **oligarchic, oligarchical** adj.

olive n. **1.** small green or black fruit used as food or pressed for its oil. **2.** tree on which this fruit grows. —adj. **3.** greyish-green. **olive branch** conciliatory gesture.

Olympiad n. staging of the Olympic Games.

Olympian adj. **1.** of Mount Olympus or the classical Greek gods. **2.** majestic or godlike.

Olympic Games pl. n. four-yearly international sports competition. **Olympic** adj.

OM Order of Merit.

ombudsman n. official who investigates complaints against government organizations.

omega n. last letter in the Greek alphabet.

omelette n. dish of eggs beaten and fried.

omen n. happening or object thought to foretell success or misfortune. **ominous** adj. worrying, seeming to foretell of misfortune.

omit v. omitting, omitted. **1.** leave out. **2.** neglect (to do something). **omission** n.

omni- combining form all, everywhere, e.g. omnidirectional.

omnibus n. **1.** Old-fashioned bus. **2.** several books or TV or radio programmes made into one.

omnipotent [om-nip-a-tent] adj. having unlimited power. **omnipotence** n.

omnipresent adj. present everywhere. **omnipresence** n.

omniscient [om-niss-ee-ent] adj. knowing everything. **omniscience** n.

omnivorous [om-niv-vor-uss] adj. **1.** eating food obtained from both animals and plants.

2. taking in everything indiscriminately. **omnivore** *n.* omnivorous animal.

on *prep.* **1.** above and touching. **2.** attached to. **3.** concerning. **4.** during, e.g. *on Monday.* **5.** through the medium of, e.g. *on television.* —*adv.* **6.** in operation. **7.** forwards. **8.** continuing. —*adj.* **9.** operating. **10.** taking place. —*n.* **11.** *Cricket* side of the field on the bowler's right.

ON Ontario.

onager *n., pl.* **-gri, -gers.** wild ass.

onanism *n.* masturbation.

ONC Ordinary National Certificate.

once *adv.* **1.** on one occasion. **2.** formerly. —*conj.* **3.** as soon as. —*n.* **4.** one occasion. **at once 1.** immediately. **2.** simultaneously. **once-over** *n.* *Informal* quick examination.

oncogene [on-koh-jean] *n.* gene that can cause cancer when abnormally activated.

oncoming *adj.* approaching from the front.

OND Ordinary National Diploma.

one *adj.* **1.** single, lone. **2.** only. —*n.* **3.** number or figure 1. **4.** single unit. —*pron.* **5.** any person. **at one** in harmony. **one by one** individually. **oneness** *n.* unity. **oneself** *pron.* reflexive form of ONE. **one-armed bandit** fruit machine operated by a lever on one side. **one-liner** *n.* witty remark. **one-night stand** sexual encounter lasting one night. **one-off** *n.* thing made or happening only once. **one-sided** *adj.* considering only one point of view. **one-way** *adj.* allowing movement in one direction only.
▷ Avoid overuse of the pronoun *one* as a substitute for *I.* Many listeners find it affected. The pronouns *I* and *one* should not be mixed within the same group of sentences. Choose one of them and continue with it.

onerous [own-er-uss] *adj.* (of a task) difficult to carry out.

ongoing *adj.* in progress, continuing.

onion *n.* strongly flavoured edible bulb.

on-line *adj.* *Computers* (of equipment) directly connected to and controlled by the computer.

onlooker *n.* person who watches something happening without taking part.

only *adj.* **1.** alone of its kind. —*adv.* **2.** exclusively. **3.** merely. **4.** no more than. —*conj.* **5.** but.
▷ The use of *only* to connect sentences is rather informal: *I would come only I'm busy.* In formal use *only* is placed directly before

the words it modifies: *The club opens only on Thursdays* but in everyday use this becomes: *The club only opens on Thursdays.*

o.n.o. or near(est) offer.

onomatopoeia [on-a-mat-a-**pee**-a] *n.* formation of a word which imitates the sound it represents, such as *hiss.* **onomatopoeic** *adj.*

onset *n.* beginning.

onslaught *n.* violent attack.

onto *prep.* **1.** to a position on. **2.** aware of, e.g. *she's onto us.*

ontology *n.* *Philosophy* study of existence. **ontological** *adj.*

onus [**own**-uss] *n., pl.* **onuses.** responsibility or burden.

onward *adj.* **1.** directed or moving forward. —*adv.* (also **onwards**) **2.** ahead, forward.

onyx *n.* type of quartz with coloured layers.

oodles *pl. n.* *Informal* great quantities.

oolite [**oh**-a-lite] *n.* limestone made up of tiny grains. **oolitic** *adj.*

ooze *v.* **1.** flow slowly. **2.** overflow with (a quality). —*n.* **3.** sluggish flow. **4.** soft mud at the bottom of a lake or river. **oozy** *adj.*

op *n.* *Informal* operation.

op. opus.

opacity [oh-**pass**-it-tee] *n.* state of being opaque.

opal *n.* iridescent precious stone. **opalescent** *adj.* iridescent like an opal.

opaque *adj.* **1.** not able to be seen through, not transparent. **2.** hard to understand.

op. cit. [op sit] in the work cited.

OPEC Organization of Petroleum Exporting Countries.

open *adj.* **1.** not closed. **2.** uncovered. **3.** unfolded. **4.** free from obstruction, accessible. **5.** unrestricted. **6.** not finalized. **7.** frank. —*v.* **8.** (cause to) become open. **9.** begin. —*n.* **10.** *Sport* competition open to everyone. **in the open** outdoors. **opener** *n.* tool for opening cans and bottles. **openly** *adv.* without concealment. **opening** *n.* **1.** beginning. **2.** hole. **3.** opportunity. —*adj.* **4.** first. **open air** outdoors. **open-and-shut case** problem that is easily solved. **open-cast mining** mining at the surface and not underground. **open day** day on which a school or college is open to the public. **open-ended** *adj.* without definite limits. **open-handed** *adj.* generous. **open-hearted** *adj.* **1.** generous. **2.** frank. **open-heart sur-**

gery surgery on the heart during which the blood circulation is maintained by machine. **open house** hospitality to visitors at any time. **open letter** letter to an individual that the writer makes public in a newspaper or magazine. **open-minded** adj. receptive to new ideas. **open-plan** adj. (of a house or office) having few interior walls. **open prison** prison with minimal security. **open verdict** coroner's verdict not stating the cause of death. **openwork** n. patterns made by leaving spaces in a design.

opera[1] n. drama in which the text is sung to an orchestral accompaniment. **operatic** adj. **operetta** n. light-hearted comic opera. **opera glasses** small binoculars used by theatre audiences.

opera[2] n. a plural of OPUS.

operate v. 1. (cause to) function. 2. direct. 3. perform an operation. **operator** n. **operation** n. 1. method or procedure of working. 2. action or series of actions. 3. medical procedure in which the body is worked on to repair a damaged part. 4. military campaign. **operational** adj. 1. relating to an operation. 2. in working order. **operative** [op-rat-tiv] adj. 1. working. 2. having particular significance. —n. 3. worker with a special skill.

ophidian n., adj. (reptile) of the snake family.

ophthalmic adj. relating to the eyes. **ophthalmia** n. inflammation of the eye. **ophthalmology** n. study of the eye and its diseases. **ophthalmologist** n. **ophthalmoscope** n. instrument for examining the interior of the eye. **ophthalmic optician** see OPTICIAN.

opiate [oh-pee-ate] n. 1. narcotic drug containing opium. 2. thing producing a stupefying effect.

opinion n. 1. personal belief or judgment. 2. judgment given by an expert. **opinion poll** same as POLL (sense 1). **opinionated** adj. having strong opinions. **opine** v. Old-fashioned express an opinion.

opium [oh-pee-um] n. addictive narcotic drug made from poppy seeds.

opossum n. small marsupial of America or Australia.

opponent n. person one is working against in a contest, battle, or argument.

opportunity n., pl. **-ties.** 1. favourable time or condition. 2. good chance. **opportune**

adj. happening at a suitable time. **opportunist** n. person who does whatever is advantageous without regard for principles. **opportunism** n.

oppose v. 1. work against. 2. contrast. 3. place opposite. **be opposed to** disagree with or disapprove of. **opposition** n. 1. obstruction or hostility. 2. largest political party not in power. 3. group opposing another.

opposite adj. 1. situated on the other side. 2. facing. 3. diametrically different. —n. 4. person or thing that is opposite. —prep., adv. 5. facing. 6. on the other side (from).

oppress v. 1. subjugate by cruelty or force. 2. depress. **oppression** n. **oppressor** n. **oppressive** adj. 1. tyrannical. 2. (of weather) hot and humid. 3. depressing. **oppressively** adv.

opprobrium [op-probe-ree-um] n. state of being criticized severely for wrong one has done. **opprobrious** adj.

oppugn [op-pewn] v. 1. dispute. 2. question.

opt v. (foll. by for) show a preference (for), choose. **opt out** v. choose not to be part (of).

optic adj. relating to the eyes or sight. **optics** n. science of sight and light. **optical** adj. **optical character reader** device that electronically reads and stores text. **optical fibre** fine glass-fibre tube used to transmit information.

optician n. person who makes or sells glasses. **dispensing optician** person who supplies and fits glasses. **ophthalmic optician** person qualified to prescribe glasses.

optimism n. tendency to always take the most hopeful view. **optimist** n. **optimistic** adj. **optimistically** adv.

optimum n., pl. **-ma, -mums.** 1. best possible conditions. —adj. 2. most favourable. **optimal** adj. **optimize** v. make the most of.

option n. 1. choice. 2. thing chosen. 3. right to choose. 4. right to buy or sell something at a specified price within a given time. **optional** adj. possible but not compulsory.

optometrist [op-tom-met-trist] n. person qualified to prescribe glasses. **optometry** n.

opulent [op-pew-lent] adj. 1. having or indicating wealth. 2. abundant. **opulence** n.

opus [oh-puss] n., pl. **opuses, opera.** artistic creation, esp. a musical work.

or conj. used to join alternatives, e.g. tea or coffee.

OR Oregon.

oracle *n.* **1.** shrine of an ancient god. **2.** prophecy, often obscure, revealed at a shrine. **3.** person believed to make infallible predictions. **4.** (**O-**) ® ITV teletext service. **oracular** *adj.*

oral *adj.* **1.** spoken. **2.** (of a drug) to be taken by mouth. **3.** of or for the mouth. —*n.* **4.** spoken examination. **orally** *adv.*

orange *adj.* **1.** reddish-yellow. —*n.* **2.** reddish-yellow citrus fruit. **orangeade** *n.* orange-flavoured, usu. fizzy drink. **orangery** *n.* greenhouse for growing orange trees.

Orangeman *n.* member of a society in Ireland for the upholding of Protestantism.

orang-utan, orang-outang *n.* large reddish-brown ape with long arms.

orator [or-rat-tor] *n.* skilful public speaker. **oration** *n.* formal speech. **oratorical** *adj.* **oratory** [or-rat-tree] *n.* **1.** art of making speeches. **2.** small private chapel.

oratorio [or-rat-tor-ee-oh] *n., pl.* -**rios.** musical composition for choir and orchestra, usu. with a religious theme.

orb *n.* **1.** ceremonial decorated sphere with a cross on top, carried by a monarch. **2.** globe.

orbit *n.* **1.** curved path of a planet, satellite, or spacecraft around another heavenly body. **2.** sphere of influence. —*v.* **orbiting, orbited. 3.** move in an orbit around. **4.** put (a satellite or spacecraft) into orbit.

Orcadian *n.* **1.** person from the Orkneys. —*adj.* **2.** of the Orkneys.

orchard *n.* area where fruit trees are grown.

orchestra *n.* **1.** large group of musicians, esp. playing a variety of instruments. **2.** orchestra pit. **orchestral** *adj.* **orchestrate** *v.* **1.** arrange (music) for orchestra. **2.** organize (something) to particular effect. **orchestration** *n.* **orchestra pit** area of a theatre in front of the stage, for the orchestra.

orchid *n.* plant with flowers that have unusual lip-shaped petals.

ordain *v.* **1.** make (someone) a member of the clergy. **2.** order or establish with authority.

ordeal *n.* painful or difficult experience.

order *n.* **1.** instruction to be carried out. **2.** request for goods to be supplied. **3.** goods so supplied. **4.** written instruction to pay money. **5.** methodical arrangement or sequence.

6. established social system. **7.** condition of a law-abiding society. **8.** social class. **9.** group of similar plants or animals. **10.** kind, sort. **11.** religious society, usu. of monks or nuns. **12.** office or rank of a Christian minister. **13.** group of people who have been awarded an honour. —*v.* **14.** give an instruction to. **15.** request (something) to be supplied. **16.** arrange methodically. **in order** so that it is possible. **orderly** *adj.* **1.** well organized. **2.** well behaved. —*n., pl.* -**lies. 3.** male hospital attendant. **4.** soldier attending an officer. **orderliness** *n.*

ordinal number *n.* number showing a position in a series, e.g. *first, second.*

ordinance *n.* official rule or order.

ordinary *adj.* **1.** usual or normal. **2.** dull or commonplace. **ordinarily** *adv.* **ordinary seaman** navy rank equivalent to an army private.

ordination *n.* ordaining.

ordnance *n.* weapons and military supplies. **ordnance survey** official map-making survey of Britain.

ordure *n.* excrement.

ore *n.* (rock containing) a mineral which yields metal.

oregano [or-rig-**gah**-no] *n.* aromatic herb used in cooking.

organ *n.* **1.** part of an animal or plant that has a particular function, such as the heart or lungs. **2.** means of conveying information, esp. a newspaper. **3.** musical keyboard instument in which notes are produced by forcing air through pipes. **organist** *n.* organ player. **organ-grinder** *n.* person who plays a barrel organ in the streets.

organdie *n.* fine cotton fabric.

organic *adj.* **1.** of or produced from animals or plants. **2.** *Chem.* relating to compounds of carbon. **3.** grown without artificial fertilizers or pesticides. **4.** organized systematically. **organically** *adv.* **organism** *n.* **1.** any living animal or plant. **2.** organized body or system.

organize *v.* **1.** make arrangements for. **2.** arrange systematically. **3.** unite (people) for a shared purpose. **organization** *n.* **1.** group of people working together. **2.** act of organizing. **3.** administrative body. **organizer** *n.*

orgasm *n.* most intense point of sexual pleasure. **orgasmic** *adj.*

orgy *n., pl.* -**gies. 1.** party involving promiscuous sexual activity. **2.** unrestrained indulgence, e.g. *an orgy of destruction*. **orgiastic** *adj.*

oriel *n.* upper window built out from a wall.

Orient *n.* **the Orient** *Lit.* East Asia. **Oriental** *adj.* **1.** of the Orient. **2.** (o-) eastern. —*n.* **3.** person from the Orient. **Orientalist** *n.* specialist in the languages and history of the Far East. **orient, orientate** *v.* **1.** position (oneself) according to one's surroundings. **2.** position (a map) in relation to the points of the compass. **orientation** *n.* **orienteering** *n.* sport in which competitors hike over a course using a compass and map.

orifice [or-rif-fiss] *n.* opening or hole.

origami [or-rig-gah-mee] *n.* Japanese decorative art of paper folding.

origin *n.* **1.** point from which something develops. —*pl.* **2.** ancestry. **original** *adj.* **1.** earliest. **2.** new, not copied or based on something else. **3.** able to think up new ideas. —*n.* **4.** first version, from which others are copied. **original sin** human imperfection and mortality as a result of Adam's disobedience. **originally** *adv.* **originality** *n.* **originate** *v.* come or bring into existence. **origination** *n.* **originator** *n.*

oriole *n.* tropical or American songbird.

ormolu *n.* gold-coloured alloy used for decoration.

ornament *n.* **1.** decorative object. **2.** decorations collectively. **3.** person regarded as an asset to a group. —*v.* **4.** decorate. **ornamental** *adj.* **ornamentation** *n.*

ornate *adj.* highly decorated, elaborate.

ornithology *n.* study of birds. **ornithological** *adj.* **ornithologist** *n.*

orotund *adj.* **1.** (of a voice) resonant. **2.** (of language) pompous.

orphan *n.* **1.** child whose parents are dead. —*v.* **2.** deprive of parents. **orphanage** *n.* children's home for orphans. **orphaned** *adj.* having no living parents.

orrery *n., pl.* **-ries.** mechanical model of the solar system.

orris *n.* **1.** kind of iris. **2.** (also **orrisroot**) fragrant root used for perfume.

orthodontics *n.* branch of dentistry concerned with correcting irregular teeth. **orthodontist** *n.*

orthodox *adj.* conforming to established views. **orthodoxy** *n.* **Orthodox Church** dominant Christian Church in Eastern Europe.

orthography *n.* correct spelling. **orthographic** *adj.*

orthopaedics *n.* branch of medicine concerned with disorders of the muscles or joints. **orthopaedic** *adj.* **orthopaedist** *n.*

ortolan *n.* small European bird eaten as a delicacy.

oryx *n.* large African antelope.

Os *Chem.* osmium.

OS 1. outsize(d). **2.** Ordnance Survey.

Oscar *n.* award in the form of a statuette given for achievements in films.

oscillate [oss-ill-late] *v.* **1.** swing back and forth. **2.** waver. **3.** (of an electric current) vary between values. **oscillation** *n.* **oscillator** *n.* **oscillatory** *adj.* **oscilloscope** [oss-sill-oh-scope] *n.* instrument that shows the shape of a wave on a cathode-ray tube.

osculate *v. jocular* kiss. **osculation** *n.*

osier [oh-zee-er] *n.* **1.** willow tree. **2.** willow branch used in basketwork.

osmium *n.* heaviest known metallic element.

osmosis *n.* **1.** movement of a liquid through a membrane from a higher to a lower concentration. **2.** process of subtle influence. **osmotic** *adj.*

osprey *n.* large fish-eating bird of prey.

osseous *adj.* made of or like bone.

ossify *v.* **-fying, -fied. 1.** (cause to) become bone, harden. **2.** become inflexible. **ossification** *n.*

ostensible *adj.* apparent, seeming. **ostensibly** *adv.*

ostentation *n.* pretentious display. **ostentatious** *adj.* **ostentatiously** *adv.*

osteopathy *n.* medical treatment involving manipulation of the joints. **osteopath** *n.*

ostler *n. Hist.* stableman at an inn.

ostracize *v.* exclude (a person) from a group. **ostracism** *n.*

ostrich *n.* large African bird that runs fast but cannot fly.

OT Old Testament.

OTC Officers' Training Corps.

other *adj.* **1.** remaining in a group of which one or some have been specified. **2.** different from the ones specified or understood. **3.** additional. —*n.* **4.** other person or thing.

otherwise adv. 1. differently, in another way. 2. in other respects. —conj. 3. or else, if not. **otherworldly** adj. concerned with spiritual rather than practical matters.

otiose [oh-tee-oze] adj. not useful, e.g. otiose language.

otter n. small brown freshwater mammal that eats fish.

ottoman n., pl. **-mans**. storage chest with a padded lid for use as a seat. **Ottoman** n., adj. Hist. (member) of the former Turkish empire.

oubliette [oo-blee-ett] n. dungeon entered only by a trapdoor.

ouch interj. exclamation of sudden pain.

ought v. (foll. by to) used to express: 1. obligation, e.g. you ought to pay. 2. advisability, e.g. you ought to diet. 3. probability, e.g. you ought to know by then.
▷ In standard English did and had are not used with ought: ought not to (not didn't/hadn't ought to).

Ouija n. ® lettered board on which supposed messages from the dead are spelt out.

ounce n. 1. unit of weight equal to one sixteenth of a pound (28.4 grams). 2. a small amount.

our adj. belonging to us. **ours** pron. thing(s) belonging to us. **ourselves** pron. emphatic and reflexive form of WE or US.

ousel n. same as DIPPER (sense 2).

oust v. force (someone) out, expel.

out adv., adj. 1. away from inside. 2. not at home. 3. revealed or made public. 4. used up. 5. not correct, e.g. the calculations were out. 6. not fashionable. 7. on strike. 8. excluded from consideration. 9. openly homosexual. 10. Sport dismissed. **out of** at or to a point outside. **out of date** old-fashioned. **out-of-the-way** adj. remote. **outer** adj. 1. on the outside. 2. further from the middle. **outermost** adj. furthest out. **outer space** space beyond the earth's atmosphere. **outing** n. leisure trip. **outward** adj. 1. apparent. 2. away from a place. 3. of the outside. —adv. 4. (also **outwards**) away from somewhere. **outwardly** adv.

out- prefix 1. surpassing, e.g. outlive, outdistance. 2. outside, away, e.g. outpatient, outgrowth.

outback n. remote bush country of Australia.

outbid v. offer a higher price than.

outboard motor n. engine externally attached to the stern of a boat.

outbreak n. sudden occurrence (of something unpleasant).

outbuilding n. outhouse.

outburst n. 1. sudden expression of emotion. 2. sudden period of violent activity.

outcast n. person rejected by a particular group.

outclass v. surpass in quality.

outcome n. result.

outcrop n. Geology area where bedrock is covered by little or no soil.

outcry n., pl. **-cries**. expression of vehement or widespread protest.

outdated adj. old-fashioned.

outdo v. surpass in performance.

outdoors adv. 1. in(to) the open air. —n. 2. the open air. **outdoor** adj.

outface v. subdue or disconcert (someone) by staring.

outfall n. mouth of a river or drain.

outfield n. Cricket area far from the pitch.

outfit n. 1. matching set of clothes. 2. Informal group of people working together. 3. kit for a job. **outfitter** n. Old-fashioned supplier of men's clothes.

outflank v. 1. get round the side of (an enemy army). 2. outdo (someone).

outgoing adj. 1. leaving. 2. sociable. **outgoings** pl. n. expenses.

outgrow v. become too large or too old for. **outgrowth** n. 1. thing growing out from a main body. 2. natural development.

outhouse n. building near a main building.

outlandish adj. extravagantly eccentric.

outlast v. last longer than.

outlaw n. 1. Hist. criminal deprived of legal protection, bandit. —v. 2. make illegal. 3. Hist. make (someone) an outlaw.

outlay n. expenditure.

outlet n. 1. means of expressing emotion. 2. market for a product. 3. place where a product is sold. 4. opening or way out.

outline n. 1. line defining the shape of something. 2. short general explanation. —v. 3. draw the outline of. 4. summarize.

outlive v. 1. live longer than. 2. live through (an unpleasant experience).

outlook n. **1.** attitude. **2.** probable outcome. **3.** view.

outlying adj. distant from the main area.

outmanoeuvre v. get an advantage over.

outmatch v. surpass.

outmoded adj. no longer fashionable or accepted.

outnumber v. exceed in number.

outpatient n. patient who does not stay in hospital overnight.

outpost n. outlying settlement.

outpouring n. **1.** amount poured out. —pl. **2.** passionate outburst.

output n. **1.** amount produced. **2.** Computers data produced. —v. **3.** Computers produce (data) at the end of a process.

outrage n. **1.** great moral indignation. **2.** gross violation of morality. —v. **3.** offend morally. **outrageous** adj. **1.** shocking. **2.** offensive. **outrageously** adv.

outré [oo-tray] adj. shockingly eccentric.

outrider n. motorcyclist acting as an escort.

outrigger n. stabilizing frame projecting from a boat.

outright adj., adv. **1.** absolute(ly). **2.** open-(ly) and direct(ly).

outrun v. **1.** run faster than. **2.** exceed.

outsell v. be sold in greater quantities than.

outset n. beginning.

outshine v. surpass (someone) in excellence.

outside prep. **1.** to the exterior of. **2.** beyond the limits of. —adv. **3.** on or to the exterior. **4.** in(to) the open air. —n. **5.** external area or surface. —adj. **6.** exterior. **7.** unlikely, e.g. an outside chance. **8.** coming from outside. **outsider** n. **1.** person outside a specific group. **2.** contestant thought unlikely to win.
▷ Outside is not followed by of in standard English.

outsize, outsized adj. larger than normal.

outskirts pl. n. outer areas, esp. of a town.

outsmart v. Informal outwit.

outspoken adj. **1.** tending to say what one thinks. **2.** said openly.

outstanding adj. **1.** excellent. **2.** still to be dealt with or paid.

outstay v. overstay.

outstretched adj. stretched out as far as possible.

outstrip v. **1.** go faster than. **2.** surpass.

outtake n. unreleased take from a recording session, film, or TV programme.

outvote v. defeat by a majority of votes.

outweigh v. **1.** be more important, significant, or influential than. **2.** be heavier than.

outwit v. **-witting, -witted**. get the better of (someone) by cunning.

outworks pl. n. secondary external defences of a fort.

outworn adj. no longer in use.

ouzel [ooze-el] n. same as DIPPER (sense 2).

ouzo [ooze-oh] n. strong aniseed-flavoured spirit from Greece.

ova n. plural of OVUM.

oval adj. **1.** egg-shaped. —n. **2.** anything that is oval in shape.

ovary n., pl. **-ries**. **1.** female egg-producing organ. **2.** part of a plant containing the ovules. **ovarian** adj.

ovation n. enthusiastic round of applause.

oven n. heated compartment or container for cooking or for drying or firing ceramics.

over prep. **1.** higher than. **2.** on or across the top of. **3.** on or to the other side of. **4.** during. **5.** more than. **6.** concerning. **7.** recovered from. —adv. **8.** above or across something. **9.** onto its side, e.g. the jug toppled over. **10.** in excess. **11.** covering the whole area. **12.** from beginning to end. —adj. **13.** finished. —n. **14.** Cricket series of six balls bowled from one end. **overly** adv. excessively.

over- prefix **1.** too much, e.g. overeat. **2.** above, e.g. overlord. **3.** on top, e.g. overshoe.

overact v. act in an exaggerated way.

overall n. **1.** coat-shaped protective garment. —pl. **2.** protective garment consisting of trousers with a jacket or bib and braces attached. —adj., adv. **3.** in total.

overarm adj., adv. (thrown) with the arm above the shoulder.

overawe v. affect (someone) with an overpowering sense of awe.

overbalance v. lose balance.

overbearing adj. domineering.

overblown adj. excessive.

overboard adv. from a boat into the water.

go overboard go to extremes, esp. in enthusiasm.

overcast *adj.* (of the sky) covered by clouds.

overcharge *v.* charge too much.

overcoat *n.* heavy coat.

overcome *v.* **1.** gain control over after an effort. **2.** (of an emotion) affect strongly.

overcrowd *v.* cause to be too crowded.

overdo *v.* **1.** do to excess. **2.** exaggerate (something). **3.** cook too long. **overdo it** do something to a greater degree than is advisable.

overdose *n.* **1.** excessive dose of a drug. —*v.* **2.** take an overdose.

overdraft *n.* **1.** overdrawing. **2.** amount overdrawn.

overdraw *v.* withdraw more money than is in (one's bank account). **overdrawn** *adj.* **1.** having overdrawn one's account. **2.** (of an account) in debit.

overdress *v.* dress too elaborately or formally.

overdrive *n.* very high gear in a motor vehicle.

overdue *adj.* still due after the time allowed.

overestimate *v.* estimate too highly.

overflow *v.* **1.** flood. **2.** be filled beyond capacity. —*n.* **3.** outlet for excess liquid. **4.** excess amount.

overgrown *adj.* thickly covered with plants and weeds.

overhang *v.* **1.** project beyond something. —*n.* **2.** overhanging part.

overhaul *v.* **1.** examine and repair. **2.** overtake. —*n.* **3.** examination and repair.

overhead *adv.* **1.** in the sky. —*adj.* **2.** over one's head. **overheads** *pl. n.* general cost of maintaining a business.

overhear *v.* hear (a speaker or remark) unintentionally or without the speaker's knowledge.

overjoyed *adj.* extremely pleased.

overkill *n.* treatment that is greater than required.

overland *adj., adv.* by land.

overlap *v.* **1.** share part of the same space or period of time (as). —*n.* **2.** area overlapping.

overlay *v.* cover with a thin layer.

overleaf *adv.* on the back of the current page.

overload *v.* **1.** put too large a load on or in. —*n.* **2.** excessive load.

overlook *v.* **1.** fail to notice. **2.** ignore. **3.** look at from above.

overman *v.* provide with too many staff.

overmuch *adv., adj.* too much.

overnight *adj., adv.* **1.** (taking place) during one night. **2.** (happening) very quickly.

overpower *v.* **1.** subdue or overcome (someone). **2.** make helpless or ineffective.

overrate *v.* have too high an opinion of.

overreach *v.* **overreach oneself** fail by trying to be too clever.

override *v.* **1.** overrule. **2.** replace.

overrule *v.* **1.** reverse the decision of (a person with less power). **2.** reverse (someone else's decision).

overrun *v.* **1.** conquer rapidly. **2.** spread over (a place) rapidly. **3.** extend beyond a set limit.

overseas *adj., adv.* to, of, or from a distant country.

oversee *v.* watch over from a position of authority. **overseer** *n.*

overshadow *v.* **1.** reduce the significance of (a person or thing) by comparison. **2.** sadden the atmosphere of.

overshoe *n.* protective shoe worn over an ordinary shoe.

overshoot *v.* go beyond (a mark or target).

oversight *n.* mistake caused by not noticing something.

oversleep *v.* sleep beyond the intended time.

overspill *n.* rehousing of people from crowded cities to smaller towns.

overstate *v.* state too strongly. **overstatement** *n.*

overstay *v.* **overstay one's welcome** stay longer than one's host or hostess would like.

overstep *v.* go beyond (a certain limit).

overt *adj.* open, not hidden. **overtly** *adv.*

overtake *v.* **1.** move past (a vehicle or person) while travelling in the same direction. **2.** come upon suddenly or unexpectedly.

overtax *v.* **1.** put too great a strain on. **2.** tax too heavily.

overthrow v. 1. defeat and replace. —n. 2. downfall, destruction.

overtime n., adv. (paid work done) in addition to one's normal working hours.

overtone n. additional meaning.

overture n. 1. *Music* orchestral introduction. 2. opening moves in a new relationship.

overturn v. 1. turn upside down. 2. overrule (a legal decision). 3. overthrow (a government).

overview n. general survey.

overweening adj. excessive or immoderate.

overweight adj. weighing more than is healthy.

overwhelm v. 1. overpower, esp. emotionally. 2. defeat by force. **overwhelming** adj. **overwhelmingly** adv.

overwork v. 1. work too much. 2. use too much. —n. 3. excessive work.

overwrought adj. nervous and agitated.

oviduct n. tube through which eggs are conveyed from the ovary.

oviform adj. egg-shaped.

ovine adj. of or like a sheep.

oviparous [oh-**vip**-par-uss] adj. producing young by laying eggs.

ovoid [**oh**-void] adj. egg-shaped.

ovulate [**ov**-yew-late] v. release an egg cell from an ovary. **ovulation** n.

ovule n. plant part that contains the egg cell and becomes the seed after fertilization.

ovum [**oh**-vum] n., pl. **ova**. unfertilized egg cell.

owe v. 1. be obliged to pay (a sum of money) to (a person). 2. have as a result of.

3. feel an obligation to do. **owing to** as result of.

owl n. night bird of prey. **owlish** adj. **owlet** n. young owl.

own adj. 1. used to emphasize possession, e.g. *my own idea.* —v. 2. possess. 3. acknowledge. **hold one's own** be able to deal successfully with a situation. **on one's own** 1. alone. 2. without help. **owner** n. **ownership** n. **own up** v. confess.

ox n., pl. **oxen**. castrated bull.

oxalic acid n. poisonous acid found in many plants.

Oxbridge n. British universities of Oxford and Cambridge.

oxeye n. plant with daisy-like flowers.

Oxfam Oxford Committee for Famine Relief.

oxide n. compound of oxygen and one other element. **oxidize** v. combine chemically with oxygen, as in burning or rusting. **oxidation** n. oxidizing.

oxygen n. gaseous element essential to life and combustion. **oxygenate** v. add oxygen to. **oxyacetylene** n. mixture of oxygen and acetylene used in high-temperature welding.

oxymoron [ox-see-**more**-on] n. figure of speech that combines two apparently contradictory ideas, e.g. *cruel kindness.*

oyez interj. Hist. shouted three times by a public crier, listen.

oyster n. edible shellfish. **oystercatcher** n. wading bird with black-and-white feathers.

oz. ounce.

ozone n. 1. highly reactive strong-smelling form of oxygen. 2. bracing seaside air. **ozone layer** layer of ozone in the upper atmosphere that filters out ultraviolet radiation.

P

p 1. page. **2.** penny or pence. **3.** *Music* piano.

P 1. (car) park. **2.** *Chem.* phosphorus.

Pa *Chem.* protactinium.

PA 1. personal assistant. **2.** public-address system. **3.** Pennsylvania.

p.a. each year.

pace¹ *n.* **1.** single step in walking. **2.** length of a step. **3.** rate of progress. —*v.* **4.** walk with regular steps. **5.** set the speed for (competitors in a race). **6.** cross or measure with steps. **put someone through his, her paces** test someone's ability. **pacemaker** *n.* **1.** person who sets the speed of a race. **2.** electronic device surgically implanted in a person with heart disease to regulate the heartbeat.

pace² *prep.* with due respect to: used to express polite disagreement.

pachyderm [**pak**-ee-durm] *n.* thick-skinned animal such as an elephant.

pacifist *n.* person who refuses on principle to take part in war. **pacifism** *n.*

pacify *v.* **-fying, -fied. 1.** soothe, calm. **2.** establish peace in. **pacification** *n.*

pack *n.* **1.** load carried on the back. **2.** set of things sold together. **3.** container for things sold. **4.** set of playing cards. **5.** group of hunting animals. —*v.* **6.** put (clothes etc.) together in a suitcase or bag. **7.** press tightly together, cram. **8.** fill with things. **packing** *n.* material, such as paper or plastic, used to cushion packed goods. **pack ice** mass of floating ice in the sea. **pack in** *v.* *Informal* stop doing. **pack off** *v.* send away. **pack up** *v.* **1.** put (one's belongings) in a case, bag, etc. before leaving. **2.** *Informal* stop doing (something). **3.** *Informal* (of a machine) break down.

package *n.* **1.** parcel. —*v.* **2.** put into packages. **packaging** *n.* **package (deal)** an offer which includes a number of items, all of which must be accepted if the offer as a whole is accepted. **package holiday** holiday in which everything is arranged by one company for a fixed price.

packet *n.* **1.** small parcel. **2.** small container (and contents). **3.** *Slang* large sum of money. **packet (boat)** *n.* *Hist.* boat that carried mail, goods, or passengers on a fixed short route.

packhorse *n.* horse for carrying goods.

pact *n.* formal agreement.

pad *n.* **1.** piece of soft material used for protection, support, absorption of liquid, etc. **2.** block of sheets of paper fastened at the edge. **3.** fleshy underpart of an animal's paw. **4.** place for launching rockets. **5.** *Slang* home. —*v.* **padding, padded. 6.** protect or fill in with soft material. **7.** walk with soft or muffled steps. **padding** *n.* **1.** soft material used to pad something. **2.** unnecessary words put into a speech or written work to make it longer.

paddle¹ *n.* **1.** short oar with a broad blade at one or each end. —*v.* **2.** move (a canoe etc.) with a paddle. **paddle steamer** ship propelled by paddle wheels. **paddle wheel** wheel with crosswise blades that strike the water successively to propel a ship.

paddle² *v.* walk with bare feet in shallow water.

paddock *n.* small field or enclosure for horses.

paddy *n.* *Informal* fit of temper.

paddy field *n.* field where rice is grown.

padlock *n.* **1.** detachable lock with a hinged hoop fastened over a ring on the object to be secured —*v.* **2.** fasten (something) with a padlock.

padre [**pah**-dray] *n.* chaplain in the armed forces.

paean [**pee**-an] *n.* song of triumph or thanksgiving.

paediatrics *n.* branch of medicine concerned with diseases of children. **paediatrician** *n.*

paedophilia *n.* condition of being sexually attracted to children. **paedophile** *n.* person who is sexually attracted to children.

paella [pie-**ell**-a] *n.* Spanish dish made of rice, chicken, shellfish, and vegetables.

pagan *adj.* **1.** not belonging to one of the world's main religions. —*n.* **2.** pagan person. **paganism** *n.*

page[1] n. (one side of) a sheet of paper forming a book etc.

page[2] n. 1. (also **pageboy**) small boy who attends a bride at her wedding. 2. *Hist.* boy in training for knighthood. —v. 3. summon (a person whose whereabouts is unknown), for example by electronic bleeper or loud-speaker announcement.

pageant n. parade or display of people in costume, usu. illustrating a scene from history. **pageantry** n.

paginate v. number the pages of (a book etc.). **pagination** n.

pagoda n. pyramid-shaped Asian temple or tower.

paid v. past of PAY. **put paid to** *Informal* end, destroy, e.g. *bad weather put paid to their chances of winning the match.*

pail n. bucket. **pailful** n.

pain n. 1. bodily or mental suffering. —pl. 2. trouble, effort. **on pain of** subject to the penalty of. **painful** adj. **painfully** adv. **painless** adj. **painlessly** adv. **painkiller** n. drug that reduces pain.

painstaking adj. thorough and careful.

paint n. 1. colouring spread on a surface with a brush or roller. —v. 2. colour or coat with paint. 3. make a picture of. **painter** n. **painting** n.

painter n. rope at the bow of a boat for tying it up.

pair n. 1. set of two things matched for use together. 2. two people, animals, or things used or grouped together. —v. 3. group or be grouped in twos.
▷ *Pair* is followed by a singular verb if it refers to a unit: *A pair of shoes was on the floor*, and by a plural verb if it refers to two individuals: *That pair are good friends.*

paisley pattern n. pattern of small curving shapes.

pajamas pl. n. *US* pyjamas.

Pakistani adj. 1. of or relating to Pakistan. —n. 2. person from Pakistan.

pal n. *Informal* friend.

palace n. 1. residence of a king, bishop, etc. 2. large grand building.

paladin n. *Hist.* knight errant.

palaeo- *combining form* old, ancient, pre-historic, e.g. *palaeography.*

palaeography [pal-ee-**og**-ra-fee] n. study of ancient writings.

palaeolithic [pal-ee-oh-**lith**-ik] adj. of the Old Stone Age.

palaeontology [pal-ee-on-**tol**-a-jee] n. study of past geological periods and fossils. **palaeontological** adj.

palatable adj. 1. pleasant to eat. 2. acceptable or satisfactory, e.g. *a palatable suggestion.*

palate n. 1. roof of the mouth. 2. sense of taste.

palatial adj. 1. like a palace. 2. magnificent.

palaver [pal-**lah**-ver] n. time-wasting fuss.

pale[1] adj. 1. light, whitish. 2. having less colour than normal. —v. 3. become pale.

pale[2] n. 1. *Hist.* fence. 2. boundary. **beyond the pale** outside the limits of social convention.

palette n. artist's flat board for mixing colours on. **palette knife** spatula with a thin flexible blade used in painting or cookery.

palindrome n. word, phrase, or sentence that reads the same backwards as forwards.

paling n. any of the upright planks in a fence.

palisade n. fence made of stakes.

pall[1] n. 1. cloth spread over a coffin. 2. depressing oppressive atmosphere. 3. dark cloud (of smoke). **pallbearer** n. person carrying a coffin at a funeral.

pall[2] v. become boring.

palladium n. silvery-white element of the platinum metal group.

pallet[1] n. portable platform for storing and moving goods.

pallet[2] n. 1. straw mattress. 2. small bed.

palliasse n. straw mattress.

palliate v. lessen the severity of (something) without curing it. **palliative** adj. 1. giving temporary or partial relief. —n. 2. something, for example a drug, that palliates.

pallid adj. pale, esp. because ill or weak. **pallor** n.

pally adj. **-lier, -liest.** *Informal* on friendly terms.

palm n. 1. inner surface of the hand. 2. tropical tree with a straight trunk crowned with long pointed leaves. **palm off** v. get rid of (an unwanted thing or person), esp. by deceit. **Palm Sunday** the Sunday before Easter.

palmistry n. fortune-telling from lines on the palm of the hand. **palmist** n.

palomino n., pl. **-nos.** gold-coloured horse with a white mane and tail.

palpable adj. **1.** obvious. **2.** able to be touched or felt. **palpably** adv.

palpate v. Med. examine (an area of the body) by touching.

palpitate v. **1.** (of the heart) beat rapidly. **2.** flutter or tremble. **palpitation** n.

palsy [**pawl**-zee] n. paralysis. **palsied** adj. affected with palsy.

paltry adj. **-trier, -triest.** worthless, insignificant.

pampas pl. n. vast grassy treeless plains in S America. **pampas grass** tall grass with feathery ornamental flower branches.

pamper v. treat (someone) with great indulgence, spoil.

pamphlet n. thin paper-covered booklet. **pamphleteer** n. writer of pamphlets.

pan[1] n. **1.** wide long-handled metal container used in cooking. **2.** bowl of a lavatory. —v. **panning, panned. 3.** sift gravel from (a riverbed) in a pan to search for gold. **4.** Informal criticize harshly. **pan out** v. result.

pan[2] v. **panning, panned.** move a film camera slowly so as to cover a whole scene or follow a moving object.

pan- combining form all, e.g. pan-African.

panacea [pan-a-**see**-a] n. remedy for all diseases or problems.

panache [pan-**ash**] n. confident elegant style.

panama n. straw hat.

panatella n. long slender cigar.

pancake n. thin flat circle of fried batter. **Pancake Day** Shrove Tuesday, when people traditionally eat pancakes. **pancake landing** a landing in which an aircraft comes down to a height of a few feet and then drops flat onto the ground. **pancake roll** small pancake filled with Chinese-style vegetables and rolled up.

panchromatic adj. Photog. sensitive to light of all colours.

pancreas [**pang**-kree-ass] n. large gland behind the stomach that produces insulin and helps digestion. **pancreatic** adj.

panda n. large black-and-white bearlike mammal from China. **panda car** police patrol car.

pandemic adj. (of a disease) occurring over a wide area.

pandemonium n. **1.** wild confusion. **2.** uproar.

pander n. person who procures a sexual partner for someone. **pander to** v. indulge (a person or his or her desires).

p & p postage and packing.

pane n. single piece of glass in a window or door.

panegyric [pan-ee-**jire**-ik] n. formal speech or piece of writing in praise of someone or something.

panel n. **1.** flat distinct section of a larger surface, such as that in a door. **2.** group of people as a team in a quiz etc. **3.** list of jurors, doctors, etc. **4.** board or surface which contains switches and controls to operate equipment. —v. **-elling, -elled. 5.** decorate or cover with panels. **panelling** n. panels collectively, such as those on a wall. **panellist** n. member of a panel. **panel beater** person who repairs damage to car bodies.

pang n. sudden sharp feeling of pain or sadness.

pangolin n. scaly anteater.

panic n. **1.** sudden overwhelming fear, often infectious. —v. **-icking, -icked. 2.** feel or cause to feel panic. **panicky** adj. **panic-stricken** adj.

panicle n. loose, irregularly branched cluster of flowers.

pannier n. **1.** bag fixed on the back of a bike or motorbike. **2.** basket carried by a beast of burden.

panoply [**pan**-a-plee] n. magnificent array.

panorama n. **1.** wide or complete view. **2.** picture of a scene unrolled so as to appear continuous. **panoramic** adj.

pansy n., pl. **-sies. 1.** garden flower with velvety petals. **2.** Offens. effeminate or homosexual man.

pant v. breathe quickly and noisily after exertion.

pantaloons pl. n. baggy trousers gathered at the ankles.

pantechnicon n. large van for furniture removals.

pantheism n. belief that God is present in everything. **pantheist** n. **pantheistic** adj.

pantheon *n.* in ancient Greece and Rome, temple to all the gods.

panther *n.* leopard, esp. a black one.

panties *pl. n.* women's underpants.

pantile *n.* roofing tile with an S-shaped cross section.

pantograph *n.* **1.** instrument for copying maps etc. to any scale. **2.** device on the roof of an electric train for picking up the electric current.

pantomime *n.* play based on a fairy tale, performed at Christmas time.

pantry *n., pl.* **-tries.** room or cupboard for storing food or cooking utensils.

pants *pl. n.* **1.** undergarment for the lower part of the body. **2.** *US* trousers.

pap[1] *n.* **1.** soft food for babies or invalids. **2.** worthless or oversimplified ideas.

pap[2] *n. Obs.* nipple.

papacy [pay-pa-see] *n., pl.* **-cies.** the position or term of office of a pope. **papal** *adj.* of the pope or papacy.

paparazzo [pap-a-rat-so] *n., pl.* **-razzi.** photographer specializing in unposed shots of famous people.

papaya [pa-pie-ya], **papaw** [pa-paw] *n.* large sweet West Indian fruit.

paper *n.* **1.** material made in sheets from wood pulp or other fibres. **2.** printed sheet of this. **3.** newspaper. **4.** article or essay. **5.** set of examination questions. —*pl.* **6.** personal documents. —*v.* **7.** cover (walls) with wallpaper. **on paper** in theory, as opposed to fact, e.g. *the project looks impressive enough on paper.* **paperback** *n.* book with flexible paper covers. **paper money** banknotes, rather than coins. **paperweight** *n.* heavy decorative object placed on top of loose papers. **paperwork** *n.* the part of a job that consists of dealing with routine letters, forms, etc.

papier-mâché [pap-yay mash-ay] *n.* material made from paper mixed with paste, shaped by moulding and dried hard.

papist *n., adj. Offens.* Roman Catholic.

papoose *n.* N American Indian child.

paprika *n.* (powdered seasoning made from) a type of red pepper.

Pap test, smear *n. Med.* examination of stained cells in a specimen taken from the neck or lining of the womb for detection of cancer.

papyrus [pap-ire-uss] *n., pl.* **-ri, -ruses. 1.** tall water plant. **2.** (manuscript written on) a kind of paper made from this plant.

par *n.* **1.** usual or average condition. **2.** face value of stocks and shares. **3.** *Golf* expected standard score. **on a par with** equal to.

para- *combining form* beside, beyond, as in *paradigm, parallel.*

parable *n.* story that illustrates a religious teaching.

parabola [par-ab-bol-a] *n.* regular curve resembling the course of an object thrown forward and up. **parabolic** *adj.*

paracetamol *n.* mild pain-relieving drug.

parachute *n.* **1.** large fabric canopy that slows the descent of a person or object from an aircraft. —*v.* **2.** land or drop by parachute. **parachutist** *n.*

parade *n.* **1.** procession. **2.** public display by soldiers. **3.** street or promenade. —*v.* **4.** march in procession. **5.** display or flaunt. **parade ground** place where soldiers assemble regularly for inspection or display.

paradigm [par-a-dime] *n.* example or model.

paradise *n.* **1.** heaven. **2.** state of bliss. **3.** Garden of Eden.

paradox *n.* statement that seems self-contradictory but may be true. **paradoxical** *adj.* **paradoxically** *adv.*

paraffin *n.* liquid mixture distilled from petroleum and used as a fuel, solvent, etc.

paragliding *n.* cross-country gliding using a parachute.

paragon *n.* model of perfection.

paragraph *n.* section of a piece of writing starting on a new line.

parakeet *n.* small long-tailed parrot.

parallax *n.* apparent difference in an object's position as viewed from different points.

parallel *adj.* **1.** separated by an equal distance at every point. **2.** precisely corresponding. —*n.* **3.** line equidistant from another at all points. **4.** thing with similar features to another. **5.** line of latitude. —*v.* **6.** be parallel to. **7.** correspond to. **parallelism** *n.*

parallelogram *n.* four-sided geometric figure with opposite sides parallel.

paralysis *n.* inability to move or feel, because of damage to the nervous system.

paralyse v. 1. affect with paralysis. 2. make immobile. **paralytic** n., adj. (person) affected with paralysis.

paramedic n. person working in support of the medical profession. **paramedical** adj.

parameter [par-**am**-it-er] n. limiting factor, boundary.

paramilitary adj. organized on military lines.

paramount adj. of the greatest importance.

paramour n. Obs. illicit lover, mistress.

paranoia n. 1. mental illness causing delusions of fame or persecution. 2. Informal intense fear or suspicion. **paranoiac, paranoid** adj., n.

paranormal adj. beyond scientific explanation.

parapet n. low wall or railing along the edge of a balcony, bridge, etc.

paraphernalia n. personal belongings or bits of equipment.

paraphrase v. express (meaning) in different words.

paraplegia [par-a-**pleej**-ya] n. paralysis of the lower half of the body. **paraplegic** n., adj.

parapsychology n. study of phenomena outside normal human ability, such as telepathy.

Paraquat n. ® very poisonous weedkiller.

parasite n. 1. animal or plant living in or on another. 2. person who lives at the expense of others, sponger. **parasitic** adj.

parasol n. umbrella-like sunshade.

paratroops, -troopers pl. n. troops trained to attack by descending by parachute.

parboil v. boil until partly cooked.

parcel n. 1. something wrapped up, package. —v. **-celling, -celled**. 2. wrap up. **parcel out** v. divide into parts.

parch v. 1. make very hot and dry. 2. make thirsty.

parchment n. thick smooth writing material made from animal skin.

pardon v. 1. forgive or excuse. —n. 2. forgiveness. 3. official release from punishment. **pardonable** adj. **pardonably** adv.

pare v. 1. peel (fruit, etc.). 2. trim or cut the edge of. **paring** n. piece pared off.

parent n. father or mother. **parental** adj.

parenthood n. **parentage** n. ancestry or family. **parenting** n. activity of bringing up children.

parenthesis [par-en-**thiss**-iss] n., pl. **-ses**. 1. word or sentence inserted in a passage, usu. marked off by brackets, dashes, or commas. —pl. 2. round brackets, ( ). **parenthetic, parenthetical** adj.

par excellence adv. beyond comparison, e.g. she is a hostess par excellence.

pargeting n. ornamental plasterwork on the outside of a house.

pariah [par-**rye**-a] n. social outcast.

parietal [par-**rye**-it-al] adj. of the walls of body cavities such as the skull.

parish n. area that has its own church and clergyman. **parishioner** n. inhabitant of a parish.

parity n. equality or equivalence.

park n. 1. area of open land for recreational use by the public. 2. area containing a number of related businesses. 3. large enclosed piece of ground attached to a country house. —v. 4. stop and leave (a vehicle) temporarily. **parking meter** coin-operated device beside a parking space that indicates how long a vehicle may be left parked. **parking ticket** notice of a fine served on a motorist for a parking offence.

parka n. warm waterproof hooded jacket.

Parkinson's disease n. progressive disorder of the central nervous system which causes impaired muscular coordination and tremor (also **Parkinsonism**).

parky adj. **parkier, parkiest**. Informal (of the weather) chilly.

parlance n. particular way of speaking, idiom.

parley n. 1. meeting between leaders or representatives of opposing forces to discuss terms. —v. 2. have a parley.

parliament n. law-making assembly of a country. **parliamentary** adj. **parliamentarian** n. expert in parliamentary procedures.

parlour n. Old-fashioned living room for receiving visitors.

parlous adj. Obs. dangerous.

Parmesan n. hard strong-flavoured Italian cheese.

parochial adj. 1. narrow in outlook, provincial. 2. of a parish. **parochialism** n.

parody n., pl. **-dies**. 1. exaggerated and

amusing imitation of someone else's style. —v. -dying, -died. 2. make a parody of.

parole n. 1. early freeing of a prisoner on condition that he or she behaves well. —v. 2. place on parole. **on parole** (of a prisoner) released on condition that he or she behaves well.

parotid gland n. large salivary gland in front of and below each ear.

paroxysm n. 1. uncontrollable outburst, as of laughter. 2. spasm or convulsion, as of pain.

parquet [par-kay] n. 1. wooden blocks arranged in a pattern and forming a floor. —v. 2. cover (a floor) with parquet. **parquetry** n.

parricide n. 1. person who kills one of his or her parents. 2. act of killing either of one's parents.

parrot n. 1. tropical bird with a short hooked beak, some varieties of which can imitate speaking. —v. -roting, -roted. 2. repeat (words) without thinking.

parry v. -rying, -ried. 1. ward off (an attack). 2. cleverly avoid (an awkward question).

parse [parz] v. analyse (a sentence) in terms of grammar.

parsec n. unit of length used in expressing the distance of stars.

parsimony n. stinginess. **parsimonious** adj.

parsley n. herb used for seasoning and decorating food.

parsnip n. long tapering cream-coloured root vegetable.

parson n. parish priest in the Church of England. **parsonage** n. parson's house. **parson's nose** rump of a cooked fowl.

part n. 1. piece or portion. 2. one of several equal divisions. 3. actor's role. 4. (often pl.) region, area. 5. component of a vehicle or machine. —v. 6. divide. 7. (of people) leave each other. **part and parcel of** necessary part of. **take someone's part** support someone in an argument etc. **take something in good part** respond (to criticism etc.) with good humour. **parting** n. 1. division between sections of hair on the head. 2. separation. 3. leave-taking. **partly** adv. not completely. **part of speech** particular grammatical class of words, such as noun or verb. **part song** song for several voices singing in harmony. **part-time** adj. occupy-

ing or working less than the full working week. **part with** v. give up ownership of.

partake v. -taking, -took, -taken. 1. (foll. by of) take food or drink. 2. (foll. by in) take part in.

parterre n. formally patterned flower garden.

partial adj. 1. not general or complete. 2. prejudiced. **partial to** very fond of. **partiality** n. 1. favouritism. 2. fondness for. **partially** adv.

participate v. become actively involved in. **participant** n. **participation** n. **participator** n.

participle n. form of a verb used in compound tenses or as an adjective, e.g. *worried, worrying.* **participial** adj.

particle n. 1. extremely small piece or amount. 2. *Physics* minute piece of matter, such as a proton or electron.

parti-coloured adj. differently coloured in different parts.

particular adj. 1. relating to one person or thing, not general. 2. exceptional or special. 3. very exact. 4. not easily satisfied, fastidious. —n. 5. detail. 6. item of information. **particularly** adv. **particularize** v. give details about. **particularity** n.

partisan n. 1. strong supporter of a party or group. 2. guerrilla, member of a resistance movement. —adj. 3. prejudiced or one-sided.

partition n. 1. screen or thin wall that divides a room. 2. division of a country into independent parts. —v. 3. divide with a partition.

partner n. 1. either member of a couple in a relationship or activity. 2. member of a business partnership. —v. 3. be the partner of (someone). **partnership** n. joint business venture between two or more people.

partridge n. game bird of the grouse family.

parturition n. act of giving birth.

party n., pl. -ties. 1. social gathering for pleasure. 2. group of people travelling or working together. 3. group of people with a common political aim. 4. person or people forming one side in a lawsuit etc. **party line** 1. telephone line shared by two or more subscribers. 2. official view of a political party. **party wall** common wall separating adjoining buildings.

parvenu [par-ven-new] n. person newly risen to a position of power or wealth, upstart.

pascal n. unit of pressure.

paschal [**pass**-kal] adj. of the Passover or Easter.

pass v. **1.** go by, beyond, through, etc. **2.** exceed. **3.** be accepted. **4.** be successful in a test etc. **5.** examine and declare satisfactory. **6.** spend (time) or (of time) elapse. **7.** transfer. **8.** exchange. **9.** change or move from one state or person to another. **10.** bring (a law) into force. **11.** come to an end. **12.** choose not to take one's turn in a game or quiz. **13.** discharge (urine, etc.) from the body. **14.** Sport hit, kick, or throw (the ball) to another player. —n. **15.** successful result in a test. **16.** Sport transfer of a ball. **17.** permit or licence. **18.** narrow gap through mountains. **make a pass at** Informal make amorous advances to. **passable** adj. (just) acceptable. **passing** adj. **1.** brief or transitory. **2.** cursory or casual. **pass away** v. die. **pass out** v. Informal faint. **pass over** v. take no notice of, disregard. **pass up** v. Informal ignore or reject.

passage n. **1.** channel or opening providing a way through etc. **2.** hall or corridor. **3.** section of a book etc. **4.** journey by sea. **5.** right or freedom to pass. **passageway** n. passage or corridor.

passbook n. book issued by a bank, etc. for keeping a record of deposits and withdrawals.

passé [**pass**-say] adj. out-of-date.

passenger n. **1.** person travelling in a vehicle driven by someone else. **2.** one of a team who does not pull his or her weight.

passer-by n., pl. **passers-by.** person who is walking past something or someone.

passerine adj. belonging to the order of perching birds.

passim adv. Latin everywhere, throughout.

passion n. **1.** intense sexual love. **2.** any strong emotion. **3.** great enthusiasm. **4.** (P-) Christianity the suffering of Christ. **passionate** adj. **passionately** adv. **passionflower** n. tropical American plant. **passion fruit** edible fruit of the passionflower. **Passion play** play about Christ's suffering.

passive adj. **1.** not playing an active part. **2.** submissive and receptive to outside forces. **3.** denoting a form of verbs indicating that the subject receives the action, such as was jeered in He was jeered by the crowd. **passively** adv. **passivity** n. **passive resistance** resistance to a government, law,

etc. by nonviolent acts. **passive smoking** inhalation of smoke from others' cigarettes by a nonsmoker.

Passover n. Jewish festival commemorating the sparing of the Jews in Egypt.

passport n. official document granting permission to travel abroad.

password n. secret word or phrase that ensures admission.

past adj. **1.** of the time before the present. **2.** ended, gone by. **3.** (of a verb tense) indicating that the action specified took place earlier. —n. **4.** bygone times. **5.** person's past life, esp. an earlier, disreputable period. **6.** past tense. —adv. **7.** by. **8.** along. —prep. **9.** beyond. **past it** Informal unable to do the things one could do when younger. **past master** person with great talent or experience in a particular subject.

pasta n. type of food, such as spaghetti, that is made in different shapes from flour and water.

paste n. **1.** moist soft mixture, such as toothpaste. **2.** adhesive, esp. for paper. **3.** pastry dough. **4.** shiny glass used to make imitation jewellery. **5.** smooth preparation of fish, etc. for spreading on bread. —v. **6.** fasten with paste. **pasting** n. **1.** Slang defeat. **2.** strong criticism. **pasteboard** n. stiff thick paper.

pastel n. **1.** coloured chalk crayon for drawing. **2.** picture drawn in pastels. **3.** pale delicate colour. —adj. **4.** pale and delicate in colour.

pasteurize v. sterilize by heat. **pasteurization** n.

pastiche [pass-**teesh**] n. work of art that mixes styles or copies the style of another artist.

pastille n. small fruit-flavoured and sometimes medicated sweet.

pastime n. activity that makes time pass pleasantly.

pastor n. clergyman in charge of a congregation. **pastoral** adj. **1.** of or depicting country life. **2.** of a clergyman or his duties. —n. **3.** poem or picture portraying country life.

pastrami n. highly seasoned smoked beef.

pastry n., pl. **-ries. 1.** baking dough made of flour, fat, and water. **2.** cake or pie.

pasture n. **1.** grassy land for farm animals

to graze on. —v. 2. (cause to) graze. **pasturage** n. (right to) pasture.

pasty[1] [pay-stee] adj. **pastier, pastiest**. (of a complexion) pale and unhealthy.

pasty[2] [pass-tee] n., pl. **pasties**. round of pastry folded over a savoury filling.

pat v. **patting, patted. 1.** tap lightly. —n. **2.** gentle tap or stroke. **3.** small shaped mass of butter etc. —adj. **4.** quick, ready, or glib. **off pat** learned thoroughly.

patch n. **1.** piece of material sewn on a garment. **2.** small contrasting section. **3.** plot of ground. **4.** protecting pad for the eye. —v. **5.** mend with a patch. **6.** repair clumsily. **patchy** adj. **patchier, patchiest**. of uneven quality or intensity. **patch up** v. make up (a quarrel). **patchwork** n. needlework made of pieces of different materials sewn together.

pate n. Old-fashioned head.

pâté [pat-ay] n. spread of finely minced liver etc.

patella n., pl. **-lae**. kneecap.

paten [pat-in] n. plate for bread in Communion.

patent n. **1.** document giving the exclusive right to make or sell an invention. —adj. **2.** open to public inspection, e.g. **letters patent. 3.** obvious. **4.** protected by a patent. —v. **5.** obtain a patent for. **patently** adv. obviously. **patent leather** leather processed to give a hard glossy surface.

paternal adj. **1.** fatherly. **2.** related through one's father. **paternity** n. **1.** relation of a father to his offspring. **2.** fatherhood. **paternalism** n. authority exercised in a way that limits individual responsibility. **paternalistic** adj.

Paternoster n. RC Church the Lord's Prayer.

path n. **1.** surfaced walk or track. **2.** course of action.

pathetic adj. **1.** causing feelings of pity or sadness. **2.** distressingly inadequate. **pathetically** adv.

pathogenic adj. producing disease.

pathology n. scientific study of diseases. **pathological** adj. **1.** of pathology. **2.** Informal compulsively motivated. **pathologist** n.

pathos n. power of arousing pity or sadness.

patient adj. **1.** enduring difficulties calmly. —n. **2.** person receiving medical treatment.

patience n. **1.** quality of being patient. **2.** card game for one.

patina n. **1.** fine layer on a surface. **2.** sheen of age on woodwork.

patio n., pl. **-tios**. paved area adjoining a house.

patois [pat-wah] n., pl. **patois** [pat-wahz] regional dialect.

patriarch n. **1.** male head of a family or tribe. **2.** highest-ranking bishop in Orthodox Churches. **patriarchal** adj. **patriarchy** n., pl. **-chies**. society in which men have most of the power.

patrician n. **1.** member of the nobility, esp. of ancient Rome. —adj. **2.** of noble birth.

patricide n. **1.** crime of killing one's father. **2.** person who does this.

patrimony n., pl. **-nies**. property inherited from ancestors.

patriot n. person who loves his or her country and supports its interests. **patriotic** adj. **patriotism** n.

patrol n. **1.** regular circuit by a guard. **2.** person or small group patrolling. **3.** unit of Scouts or Guides. —v. **-trolling, -trolled. 4.** go round on guard, or reconnoitring. **patrol car** police car used for patrolling streets.

patron n. **1.** person who gives (financial) support to charities, artists, etc. **2.** regular customer of a shop, pub, etc. **patronage** n. support given by a patron. **patronize** v. **1.** treat in a condescending way. **2.** be a patron of. **patron saint** saint regarded as the guardian of a country or group.

patronymic n. name derived from one's father or a male ancestor.

patten n. Hist. type of clog.

patter v. **1.** make repeated soft tapping sounds. —n. **2.** quick succession of taps. **3.** glib rapid speech.

pattern n. **1.** arrangement of repeated parts or decorative designs. **2.** diagram or shape used as a guide to make something. —v. **3.** (foll. by on) make or do on the model of. **patterned** adj. decorated with a pattern.

patty n., pl. **-ties. 1.** small pie. **2.** minced meat formed into a small disc.

paucity n. **1.** scarcity. **2.** smallness of amount or number.

paunch n. protruding belly.

pauper n. very poor person. **pauperism** n.

pause v. **1.** stop for a time. **2.** hesitate. —n.

3. stop or rest in speech or action. **4.** *Music* continuation of a note or rest beyond its normal length.

pave *v.* form (a surface) with stone or brick. **pavement** *n.* paved path for pedestrians.

pavilion *n.* **1.** clubhouse on a playing field etc. **2.** building for housing an exhibition etc.

pavlova *n.* meringue cake topped with whipped cream and fruit.

paw *n.* **1.** animal's foot with claws and pads. —*v.* **2.** scrape with the paw or hoof. **3.** handle roughly. **4.** stroke in an overfamiliar way.

pawl *n.* pivoted lever shaped to engage with a ratchet wheel to prevent motion in a particular direction.

pawn[1] *v.* deposit (an article) as security for money borrowed. **in pawn** deposited as security with a pawnbroker. **pawnbroker** *n.* lender of money on goods deposited.

pawn[2] *n.* **1.** chessman of the lowest value. **2.** person manipulated by someone else.

pawpaw *n.* same as PAPAYA.

pay *v.* **paying, paid. 1.** give money etc. in return for goods or services. **2.** settle a debt or obligation. **3.** compensate (for). **4.** give, bestow. **5.** be profitable to. —*n.* **6.** wages or salary. **payment** *n.* **1.** act of paying. **2.** money paid. **payable** *adj.* due to be paid. **payee** *n.* person to whom money is paid or due. **paying guest** lodger. **pay off** *v.* **1.** pay (debt) in full. **2.** turn out successfully. **pay out** *v.* **1.** spend. **2.** release (a rope) bit by bit.

PAYE pay as you earn: system by which income tax is paid by an employer straight to the government.

payload *n.* **1.** passengers or cargo of an aircraft. **2.** explosive power of a missile etc.

payola *n. Informal* bribe to get special treatment, esp. to promote a commercial product.

payroll *n.* list of employees who receive regular pay.

Pb *Chem.* lead.

pc 1. per cent. **2.** postcard.

PC 1. personal computer. **2.** Police Constable. **3.** Privy Councillor.

Pd *Chem.* palladium.

PE 1. physical education. **2.** Prince Edward Island.

pea *n.* **1.** climbing plant with seeds growing in pods. **2.** its seed, eaten as a vegetable.

pea-green *adj.* yellowish-green. **peasouper** *n. Informal* thick fog.

peace *n.* **1.** calm, quietness. **2.** absence of anxiety. **3.** freedom from war. **4.** harmony between people. **peaceable** *adj.* inclined towards peace. **peaceably** *adv.* **peaceful** *adj.* **peacefully** *adv.*

peacemaker *n.* person who brings about peace, esp. between others.

peach *n.* **1.** soft juicy fruit with a stone and a downy skin. **2.** *Informal* very pleasing person or thing. —*adj.* **3.** pinkish-orange.

peacock *n.* large male bird with a brilliantly coloured fanlike tail. **peahen** *n. fem.* **peafowl** *n.* peacock or peahen.

peak *n.* **1.** pointed top, esp. of a mountain. **2.** point of greatest development etc. **3.** projecting piece on the front of a cap. —*adj.* **4.** of or at the point of greatest demand. —*v.* **5.** (cause to) form or reach peaks. **peaked** *adj.* **peaky** *adj.* **peakier, peakiest.** *Informal* looking pale and sickly.

peal *n.* **1.** long loud echoing sound, esp. of bells or thunder. —*v.* **2.** sound with a peal or peals.

peanut *n.* **1.** pea-shaped nut that ripens underground. —*pl.* **2.** *Informal* trifling amount of money.

pear *n.* sweet juicy fruit with a narrow top and rounded base.

pearl *n.* hard round lustrous object found inside some oyster shells and used as a jewel. **pearly** *adj.* **pearlier, pearliest. pearl barley** barley ground into small round grains.

peasant *n.* in some countries, farmer or farmworker of a low social class. **peasantry** *n.* peasants collectively.

pease pudding *n.* dish of boiled split peas.

peat *n.* decayed vegetable material found in bogs, used as fertilizer or fuel.

pebble *n.* small roundish stone. **pebbly** *adj.* **pebblier, pebbliest. pebble dash** coating for exterior walls consisting of small stones set in plaster.

pecan [pee-kan] *n.* edible nut of a N American tree.

peccadillo *n., pl.* **-los, -loes.** trivial misdeed.

peccary *n., pl.* **-ries.** wild pig of American forests.

peck[1] *v.* **1.** strike or pick up with the beak. **2.** *Informal* kiss quickly. —*n.* **3.** pecking movement. **peckish** *adj. Informal* hungry. **peck at** *v.* nibble, eat reluctantly.

peck[2] *n.* fourth part of bushel, 2 gallons.

pectin *n.* substance in fruit that makes jam set.

pectoral *adj.* 1. of the chest or thorax. —*n.* 2. pectoral muscle or fin.

peculation *n.* embezzlement, theft.

peculiar *adj.* 1. strange. 2. distinct, special. 3. belonging exclusively to. **peculiarity** *n.*, *pl.* -**ties**. 1. oddity, eccentricity. 2. characteristic.

pecuniary *adj.* relating to, or consisting of, money.

pedagogue *n.* schoolteacher, esp. a pedantic one.

pedal *n.* 1. foot-operated lever used to control a vehicle or machine, or to modify the tone of a musical instrument. —*v.* -**alling**, -**alled**. 2. propel (a bicycle) by using its pedals.

pedant *n.* person who is overconcerned with details and rules, esp. in academic work. **pedantic** *adj.* **pedantry** *n.*

peddle *v.* sell (goods) from door to door. **peddler** *n.* person who sells illegal drugs.

pederast *n.* man who has homosexual relations with boys. **pederasty** *n.*

pedestal *n.* base supporting a column, statue, etc.

pedestrian *n.* 1. person who is walking, esp. in a street. —*adj.* 2. dull, uninspiring. **pedestrian crossing** place marked where pedestrians may cross a road. **pedestrian precinct** (shopping) area for pedestrians only.

pedicel *n.* small short stalk of a leaf, flower, or fruit.

pedicure *n.* medical or cosmetic treatment of the feet.

pedigree *n.* register of ancestors, esp. of a purebred animal.

pediment *n.* triangular part over a door etc.

pedlar *n.* person who sells goods from door to door.

pedometer [pid-**dom**-it-er] *n.* instrument which measures the distance walked.

peduncle *n.* 1. flower stalk. 2. *Anat.* stalk-like structure.

pee *Informal* —*v.* **peeing, peed.** 1. urinate. —*n.* 2. urine.

peek *v., n.* peep or glance.

peel *v.* 1. remove the skin or rind of (a vegetable or fruit). 2. (of skin or a surface) come off in flakes. —*n.* 3. rind or skin. **peelings** *pl. n.*

peep[1] *v.* 1. look slyly or quickly. —*n.* 2. peeping look. **Peeping Tom** man who furtively watches women undressing.

peep[2] *v.* 1. make a small shrill noise. —*n.* 2. small shrill noise.

peer[1] *n.* 1. nobleman (*fem.* **peeress**). 2. person of the same status, age, etc. **peerage** *n.* 1. whole body of peers. 2. rank of a peer. **peerless** *adj.* unequalled, unsurpassed. **peer group** group of people of similar age, status, etc.

peer[2] *v.* look closely and intently.

peeved *adj. Informal* annoyed.

peevish *adj.* 1. fretful. 2. irritable. **peevishly** *adv.* **peevishness** *n.*

peewit *n.* same as LAPWING.

peg *n.* 1. pin or clip for joining, fastening, marking, etc. 2. hook or knob for hanging things on. —*v.* **pegging, pegged.** 3. fasten with pegs. 4. stabilize (prices). **off the peg** (of clothes) ready-to-wear, not tailor-made.

peignoir [pay-**nwahr**] *n.* woman's light dressing gown.

pejorative [pij-**jor**-a-tiv] *adj.* (of words etc.) with an insulting or critical connotation.

Pekingese, Pekinese *n., pl.* -**ese**. small dog with a short wrinkled muzzle.

pelargonium *n.* plant with red, white, or pink flowers.

pelican *n.* large water bird with a pouch beneath its bill for storing fish. **pelican crossing** a pedestrian crossing with pedestrian-operated traffic lights.

pellagra *n.* disease caused by lack of vitamin B.

pellet *n.* small ball of something.

pell-mell *adv.* in utter confusion, headlong.

pellucid *adj.* very clear.

pelmet *n.* ornamental drapery or board, concealing a curtain rail.

pelt[1] *v.* 1. throw missiles at. 2. run fast, rush. 3. rain heavily. **at full pelt** at top speed.

pelt[2] *n.* skin of a fur-bearing animal.

pelvis *n.* framework of bones at the base of the spine, to which the hips are attached. **pelvic** *adj.*

pen[1] *n*. **1.** instrument for writing in ink. —*v.* **penning, penned. 2.** write or compose. **pen friend** friend with whom a person corresponds without meeting. **penknife** *n*. small knife with blade(s) that fold into the handle. **pen name** name used by an author instead of his or her real name.

pen[2] *n*. **1.** small enclosure for domestic animals. —*v.* **penning, penned. 2.** put or keep in a pen.

pen[3] *n*. female swan.

Pen. Peninsula.

penal [pee-nal] *adj*. of or used in punishment. **penalize** *v*. **1.** impose a penalty on. **2.** handicap, hinder. **penalty** *n., pl*. **-ties. 1.** punishment for a crime or offence. **2.** *Sports* handicap or disadvantage imposed for an infringement of a rule.

penance *n*. voluntary self-punishment to make amends for wrongdoing.

pence *n*. a plural of PENNY.

penchant [pon-shon] *n*. inclination or liking.

pencil *n*. **1.** thin cylindrical instrument containing graphite, for writing or drawing. —*v.* **-cilling, -cilled. 2.** draw, write, or mark with a pencil.

pendant *n*. ornament worn on a chain round the neck.

pendent *adj*. hanging.

pending *prep*. **1.** while waiting for. —*adj*. **2.** not yet decided or settled.

pendulous *adj*. hanging, swinging.

pendulum *n*. suspended weight swinging to and fro, esp. as a regulator for a clock.

penetrate *v*. **1.** find or force a way into or through. **2.** arrive at the meaning of. **penetrable** *adj*. capable of being penetrated. **penetrating** *adj*. **1.** quick to understand. **2.** (of a sound) loud and unpleasant. **penetration** *n*.

penguin *n*. flightless black-and-white Antarctic sea bird.

penicillin *n*. antibiotic drug effective against a wide range of diseases and infections.

peninsula *n*. strip of land nearly surrounded by water. **peninsular** *adj*.

penis *n*. organ of copulation and urination in male mammals.

penitent *adj*. **1.** feeling sorry for having done wrong. —*n*. **2.** someone who is penitent. **penitence** *n*. **penitentiary** *n., pl*. **-ries.**

1. *US* prison. —*adj*. (also **penitential**) **2.** relating to penance.

pennant *n*. long narrow flag.

pennon *n*. small triangular or swallow-tailed flag.

penny *n., pl*. **pence, pennies. 1.** Brit. bronze coin worth one hundredth of a pound. **2.** former Brit. coin worth one twelfth of a shilling. **penniless** *adj*. **1.** having no money. **2.** poor. **penny-pinching** *adj*. excessively careful with money.

penology [pee-nol-a-jee] *n*. study of punishment and prison management.

pension[1] *n*. regular payment to people above a certain age, retired employees, widows, etc. **pensionable** *adj*. **pensioner** *n*. person receiving a pension. **pension off** *v*. force (someone) to retire from a job and pay him or her a pension.

pension[2] [pon-syon] *n*. boarding house in Europe.

pensive *adj*. deeply thoughtful, often with a tinge of sadness.

pentacle, pentagram *n*. five-pointed star.

pentagon *n*. **1.** geometric figure with five sides. **2.** (P-) headquarters of the US military. **pentagonal** *adj*.

pentameter [pen-tam-it-er] *n*. line of poetry with five metrical feet.

Pentateuch [pent-a-tyuke] *n*. first five books of the Old Testament.

pentathlon *n*. athletic event consisting of five sports.

Pentecost *n*. **1.** Christian festival celebrating the descent of the Holy Spirit to the apostles, Whitsuntide. **2.** Jewish harvest festival fifty days after Passover.

penthouse *n*. flat built on the roof or top floor of a building.

pent-up *adj*. (of an emotion) not released, repressed.

penultimate *adj*. second last.

penumbra *n., pl*. **-brae, -bras. 1.** partial shadow. **2.** in an eclipse, the partially shadowed region which surrounds the full shadow. **penumbral** *adj*.

penury *n*. extreme poverty. **penurious** *adj*.

peony *n., pl*. **-nies.** garden plant with showy red, pink, or white flowers.

people *pl. n*. **1.** persons generally. **2.** the community. **3.** one's family. —*n*. **4.** race or nation. —v. 5. stock with inhabitants. 6. populate.

pep n. Informal high spirits, energy or enthusiasm. **pep pill** Informal tablet containing a stimulant drug. **pep talk** Informal talk designed to increase enthusiasm. **pep up** v. **pepping, pepped.** stimulate, invigorate.

pepper n. 1. sharp hot condiment made from the fruit of an East Indian climbing plant. 2. colourful tropical fruit used as a vegetable, capsicum. —v. 3. season with pepper. 4. sprinkle, dot. 5. pelt with missiles. **peppery** adj. 1. tasting of pepper. 2. irritable. **peppercorn** n. dried berry of the pepper plant. **peppercorn rent** low or nominal rent. **pepper mill** small hand mill used to grind peppercorns.

peppermint n. 1. plant that yields an oil with a strong sharp flavour. 2. sweet flavoured with this.

peptic adj. relating to digestion or the digestive juices. **peptic ulcer** ulcer in the stomach or duodenum.

per prep. 1. for each. 2. in the manner of.

perambulate v. walk through or about (a place). **perambulation** n. **perambulator** n. pram.

per annum adv. Latin in each year.

percale n. woven cotton used esp. for sheets.

per capita adj., adv. Latin of or for each person.

perceive v. 1. become aware of (something) through the senses. 2. understand.

percentage n. proportion or rate per hundred. **per cent** in each hundred.

perceptible adj. discernible, recognizable. **perceptibly** adv.

perception n. 1. act of perceiving. 2. intuitive judgment. **perceptive** adj.

perch[1] n. 1. resting place for a bird. —v. 2. alight, rest, or place on or as if on a perch.

perch[2] n. edible freshwater fish.

perchance adv. Old-fashioned perhaps.

percipient adj. quick to notice things, observant. **percipience** n.

percolate v. 1. pass or filter through small holes. 2. permeate. 3. make (coffee) or (of coffee) be made in a percolator. **percolation** n. **percolator** n. coffeepot in which boiling water is forced through a tube and filters down through coffee.

percussion n. striking of one thing against another. **percussion instrument** musical instrument played by being struck, such as drums or cymbals.

perdition n. spiritual ruin.

peregrination n. travels, roaming.

peregrine n. falcon with dark upper parts and a light underside.

peremptory adj. authoritative, imperious.

perennial adj. 1. lasting through the years. 2. recurring perpetually. —n. 3. plant lasting more than two years. **perennially** adv.

perestroika n. policy of restructuring the Soviet economy and political system.

perfect adj. 1. having all the essential elements, complete. 2. unspoilt. 3. faultless. 4. correct, precise. 5. excellent. —n. 6. tense of verb describing an action that has been completed. —v. 7. improve. 8. make skilful. **perfectly** adv. **perfection** n. state of being perfect. **perfectionist** n. person who demands the highest standards of excellence. **perfectionism** n.

perfidy n., pl. **-dies.** treachery, disloyalty. **perfidious** adj.

perforate v. make holes in. **perforation** n.

perforce adv. of necessity.

perform v. 1. carry out (an action). 2. fulfil (a request etc.). 3. act, sing, or present a play before an audience. 4. work or function. **performance** n. **performer** n.

perfume n. 1. liquid cosmetic worn for its pleasant smell. 2. fragrance. —v. 3. give a pleasant smell to. **perfumery** n. perfumes in general.

perfunctory adj. done only as a matter of routine, superficial. **perfunctorily** adv.

pergola n. arch or framework of trellis supporting climbing plants.

perhaps adv. it may be (so), possibly.

pericardium n., pl. **-dia.** membrane enclosing the heart.

perigee n. point in its orbit around the earth when the moon or a satellite is nearest the earth.

perihelion n., pl. **-lia.** point in the orbit of a planet or comet nearest to the sun.

peril n. great danger. **perilous** adj. **perilously** adv.

perimeter [per-rim-it-er] n. (length of) the outer edge of an area.

perinatal *adj.* of or in the weeks shortly before or after birth.

period *n.* **1.** particular portion of time. **2.** series of years. **3.** single occurrence of menstruation. **4.** same as FULL STOP. —*adj.* **5.** (of furniture, dress, a play, etc.) dating from or in the style of an earlier time in history. **periodic** *adj.* recurring at intervals. **periodic table** chart of the elements, arranged to show their relationship to each other. **periodical** *n.* **1.** magazine issued at regular intervals. —*adj.* **2.** periodic.

peripatetic [per-rip-a-**tet**-ik] *adj.* travelling about from place to place.

periphery [per-**if**-er-ee] *n., pl.* -**eries. 1.** circumference. **2.** fringes of a field of activity. **peripheral** [per-**if**-er-al] *adj.* **1.** unimportant, not central. **2.** of or on the periphery. —*n.* **3.** any extra device that can be attached to or put in a computer.

periphrasis [per-**if**-ra-siss] *n., pl.* -**rases** [-ra-seez] roundabout speech or expression. **periphrastic** *adj.*

periscope *n.* instrument used, esp. in submarines, for giving a view of objects on a different level.

perish *v.* **1.** be destroyed or die. **2.** decay, rot. **perishable** *adj.* liable to rot quickly. **perishing** *adj. Informal* very cold.

peritoneum [per-rit-toe-**nee**-um] *n., pl.* -**nea,** -**neums.** membrane lining the internal surface of the abdomen. **peritonitis** [per-rit-tone-**ite**-iss] *n.* inflammation of the peritoneum.

periwig *n. Hist.* wig.

periwinkle[1] *n.* small edible shellfish, the winkle.

periwinkle[2] *n.* plant with trailing stems and blue flowers.

perjury [**per**-jer-ee] *n., pl.* -**juries.** act or crime of lying while under oath in a court. **perjure** *v.* perjure oneself commit perjury.

perk *n. Informal* incidental benefit gained from a job, such as a company car.

perk up *v.* cheer up. **perky** *adj.* **perkier, perkiest.** lively or cheerful.

perm *n.* **1.** long-lasting curly hairstyle produced by treating the hair with chemicals. —*v.* **2.** give (hair) a perm.

permafrost *n.* permanently frozen ground.

permanent *adj.* lasting forever. **permanently** *adv.* **permanence** *n.*

permanganate *n.* a salt of an acid of manganese.

permeate *v.* pervade or pass through the whole of (something). **permeable** *adj.* able to be permeated, esp. by liquid.

permit *v.* -**mitting,** -**mitted. 1.** give permission. **2.** allow, agree to. —*n.* **3.** document giving permission to do something. **permission** *n.* authorization to do something. **permissible** *adj.* **permissive** *adj.* (excessively) tolerant, esp. in sexual matters.

permutation *n.* **1.** any of the ways a number of things can be arranged or combined. **2.** *Maths* arrangement of a number of quantities in every possible order. **3.** fixed combinations for selections of results on football pools.

pernicious *adj.* **1.** wicked. **2.** extremely harmful, deadly.

pernickety *adj. Informal* (excessively) fussy about details.

peroration *n.* concluding part of a speech, usu. summing up the main points.

peroxide *n.* **1.** oxide of a given base containing a high proportion of oxygen. **2.** short for HYDROGEN PEROXIDE.

perpendicular *adj.* **1.** at right angles to a line or surface. **2.** upright or vertical. —*n.* **3.** line at right angles to another line or plane.

perpetrate *v.* commit or be responsible for (a wrongdoing). **perpetration** *n.* **perpetrator** *n.*

perpetual *adj.* **1.** lasting forever. **2.** continually repeated. **perpetually** *adv.* **perpetuate** *v.* cause to continue or be remembered. **perpetuation** *n.* **perpetuity** *n.* eternity. **in perpetuity** forever.

perplex *v.* puzzle, bewilder. **perplexity** *n., pl.* -**ties.**

perquisite *n.* same as PERK.

perry *n., pl.* -**ries.** alcoholic drink made from fermented pears.

per se [per **say**] *adv. Latin* in itself.

persecute *v.* **1.** treat cruelly because of race, religion, etc. **2.** subject to persistent harassment. **persecution** *n.* **persecutor** *n.*

persevere *v.* keep making an effort despite difficulties. **perseverance** *n.*

Persian *adj.* **1.** of ancient Persia or modern Iran, their people, or their languages. —*n.* **2.** person from modern Iran, Iranian. **Persian carpet, rug** hand-made carpet or rug with flowing or geometric designs in rich colours. **Persian cat** long-haired domestic cat.

persiflage [per-sif-flahzh] n. light frivolous talk or writing.

persimmon n. sweet red tropical fruit.

persist v. 1. continue in spite of obstacles or objections. 2. continue to be or happen, last. **persistent** adj. **persistently** adv. **persistence** n.

person n. 1. human being. 2. body of a human being. 3. Grammar form of pronouns and verbs that shows if a person is speaking, spoken to, or spoken of. **in person** actually present.
▷ Person is generally used in the singular and people is used to indicate more than one. The plural persons is restricted to formal notices.

persona [per-soh-na] n., pl. **-nae** [-nee] someone's personality as presented to others.

personable adj. pleasant in appearance and personality.

personage n. important person.

personal adj. 1. individual or private. 2. of the body, e.g. personal hygiene. 3. (of a remark etc.) offensive. **personally** adv. 1. in one's own opinion. 2. directly, not by delegation to others. **personal column** newspaper column containing personal messages and advertisements. **personal computer** small computer used for word processing or computer games. **personal pronoun** pronoun like I or she that stands for a definite person. **personal stereo** very small portable cassette player with headphones.

personality n., pl. **-ties**. 1. person's distinctive characteristics. 2. celebrity. —pl. 3. personal remarks, e.g. the discussion degenerated into personalities.

personify v. **-fying**, **-fied**. 1. give human characteristics to. 2. be an example of, typify. **personification** n.

personnel n. people employed in an organization.

perspective n. 1. mental view. 2. method of drawing that gives the effect of solidity and relative distances and sizes.

Perspex n. ® transparent acrylic substitute for glass.

perspicacious adj. having quick mental insight. **perspicacity** n.

perspire v. sweat. **perspiration** n.

persuade v. 1. make (someone) do something by argument, charm, etc. 2. convince. **persuasion** n. 1. act of persuading. 2. way of thinking or belief. **persuasive** adj.

pert adj. saucy and cheeky.

pertain v. belong or be relevant (to).

pertinacious adj. very persistent and determined. **pertinacity** n.

pertinent adj. relevant. **pertinence** n.

perturb v. 1. disturb greatly. 2. alarm. **perturbation** n.

peruke n. Hist. wig.

peruse v. read in a careful or leisurely manner. **perusal** n.

pervade v. spread right through (something). **pervasive** adj.

perverse adj. deliberately doing something different from what is thought normal or proper. **perversely** adv. **perversity** n.

pervert v. 1. use or alter for a wrong purpose. 2. lead into abnormal (sexual) behaviour. —n. 3. person who practises sexual perversion. **perversion** n. 1. sexual act or desire considered abnormal. 2. act of perverting.

pervious adj. able to be penetrated, permeable.

peseta [pa-say-ta] n. monetary unit of Spain.

peso [pay-so] n., pl. **pesos**. standard monetary unit of Argentina, Mexico, etc.

pessary n., pl. **-ries**. 1. appliance worn in the vagina, either to prevent conception or to support the womb. 2. medicated suppository.

pessimism n. tendency to expect the worst in all things. **pessimist** n. **pessimistic** adj. **pessimistically** adv.

pest n. 1. annoying person. 2. insect or animal that damages crops. **pesticide** n. chemical for killing insect pests.

pester v. annoy or nag continually.

pestilence n. deadly epidemic disease. **pestilential** adj. 1. annoying, troublesome. 2. deadly.

pestle n. club-shaped implement for grinding things to powder in a mortar.

pet n. 1. animal kept for pleasure and companionship. 2. person favoured or indulged. —v. **petting**, **petted**. 3. treat as a pet. 4. pat or stroke affectionately. 5. Informal kiss and caress erotically.

petal n. one of the white or coloured outer parts of a flower. **petalled** adj.

petard n. Hist. explosive device. **hoist with one's own petard** being the victim of one's own schemes.

peter out v. gradually come to an end.

petersham n. thick corded ribbon used to stiffen belts, etc.

petite adj. (of a woman) small and dainty.

petition n. 1. formal request, esp. one signed by many people and presented to parliament. —v. 2. present a petition to. **petitioner** n.

petrel n. long-winged dark-coloured sea bird.

petrify v. **-fying, -fied. 1.** frighten severely. **2.** turn to stone. **petrification** n.

petrochemical n. a substance, such as acetone, obtained from petroleum.

petrodollar n. money earned by a country by exporting petroleum.

petrol n. inflammable liquid obtained from petroleum, used as fuel in internal-combustion engines. **petrol bomb** home-made incendiary device consisting of a bottle filled with petrol.

petroleum n. crude oil found underground.

petticoat n. woman's skirt-shaped undergarment.

pettifogging adj. overconcerned with unimportant detail.

pettish adj. fretful, irritable.

petty adj. **-tier, -tiest. 1.** unimportant, trivial. **2.** small-minded. **3.** on a small scale, e.g. petty crime. **pettiness** n. **petty cash** cash kept by a firm to pay minor expenses. **petty officer** noncommissioned officer in the navy.

petulant adj. childishly irritable or peevish. **petulantly** adv. **petulance** n.

petunia n. garden plant with funnel-shaped flowers.

pew n. **1.** fixed benchlike seat in a church. **2.** Informal chair, seat.

pewter n. greyish metal made of tin and lead.

phalanger n. long-tailed Aust. tree-dwelling marsupial.

phalanx n., pl. **phalanxes, phalanges.** closely grouped mass of people.

phallus n., pl. **-li, -luses.** penis, esp. as a symbol of reproductive power in primitive rites. **phallic** adj.

phantasm n. unreal vision, illusion. **phantasmal** adj.

phantasmagoria n. shifting medley of dreamlike figures.

phantasy n., pl. **-sies.** same as FANTASY.

phantom n. **1.** ghost. **2.** unreal vision.

Pharaoh [fare-oh] n. title of the ancient Egyptian kings.

Pharisee n. **1.** member of an ancient Jewish sect teaching strict observance of Jewish traditions. **2.** self-righteous hypocrite. **Pharisaic, Pharisaical** adj.

pharmaceutical adj. of pharmacy.

pharmacology n. study of drugs. **pharmacological** adj. **pharmacologist** n.

pharmacopoeia [far-ma-koh-pee-a] n. a book with a list of and directions for the use of drugs.

pharmacy n., pl. **-cies. 1.** preparation and dispensing of drugs and medicines. **2.** pharmacist's shop. **pharmacist** n. person qualified to prepare and sell drugs and medicines.

pharynx [far-rinks] n., pl. **pharynges, pharynxes.** cavity forming the back part of the mouth. **pharyngeal** adj. **pharyngitis** [farrin-jite-iss] n. inflammation of the pharynx.

phase n. **1.** any distinct or characteristic stage in a development or chain of events. —v. **2.** arrange or carry out in stages or to coincide with something else. **phase in** or **out** v. introduce or discontinue gradually.

PhD Doctor of Philosophy.

pheasant n. game bird with bright plumage.

phenobarbitone n. drug inducing sleep or relaxation.

phenol n. chemical used in disinfectants and antiseptics.

phenomenon n., pl. **-ena. 1.** anything appearing or observed. **2.** remarkable person or thing. **phenomenal** adj. extraordinary, outstanding. **phenomenally** adv.
▷ Avoid using phenomena as a singular.

phew interj. exclamation of relief, surprise, etc.

phial n. small bottle for medicine etc.

philadelphus n. shrub with sweet-scented flowers.

philanderer n. man who flirts or has many casual love affairs. **philandering** n.

philanthropy n. practice of helping people less well-off than oneself. **philanthropic** adj. **philanthropist** n.

philately [fill-**lat**-a-lee] n. stamp collecting. **philatelic** adj. **philatelist** n.

philharmonic adj. in names of orchestras etc., music-loving.

philippic n. bitter or impassioned speech of denunciation, invective.

philistine adj., n. boorishly uncultivated (person). **philistinism** n.

philology n. science of the structure and development of languages. **philological** adj. **philologist** n.

philosophy n., pl. **-phies**. 1. study of the meaning of life, knowledge, thought, etc. 2. theory or set of ideas held by a particular philosopher. 3. person's outlook on life. **philosopher** n. person who studies philosophy. **philosophical**, **philosophic** adj. 1. of philosophy. 2. calm in the face of difficulties or disappointments. **philosophically** adv. **philosophize** v. talk in a boring and pretentious manner about basic things.

philtre n. magic drink supposed to arouse love in the person who drinks it.

phlebitis [fleb-**bite**-iss] n. inflammation of a vein.

phlegm [**flem**] n. thick yellowish substance formed in the nose and throat during a cold.

phlegmatic [fleg-**mat**-ik] adj. not easily excited, unemotional. **phlegmatically** adv.

phlox n., pl. **phlox**, **phloxes**. flowering garden plant.

phobia n. intense and unreasoning fear or dislike. **phobic** adj.

phoenix n. legendary bird said to set fire to itself and rise anew from its ashes.

phone n., v. Informal telephone. **phonecard** n. 1. public telephone operated by a special card. 2. the card itself. **phone-in** n. broadcast in which telephone comments or questions from the public are transmitted live.

phonetic adj. 1. of speech sounds. 2. (of spelling) written as it is sounded. **phonetics** n. science of speech sounds. **phonetically** adv.

phonic adj. of speech sounds.

phonograph n. US Old-fashioned record player.

phonology n. study of the speech sounds in a language. **phonological** adj.

phony, phoney Informal —adj. **phonier**, **phoniest**. 1. not genuine. 2. false. 3. insincere. —n., pl. **phonies**. 4. phony person or thing.

phosgene [**foz**-jean] n. poisonous gas used in warfare.

phosphorescence n. faint glow in the dark. **phosphorescent** adj.

phosphorus n. toxic flammable nonmetallic element which appears luminous in the dark. **phosphate** n. 1. compound of phosphorus. 2. fertilizer containing phosphorus.

photo n., pl. **photos**. short for PHOTOGRAPH. **photo finish** finish of a race in which the contestants are so close that a photo is needed to decide the result.

photo- combining form light, as in photometer.

photocell n. cell which produces a current or voltage when exposed to light or other electromagnetic radiation.

photocopy n., pl. **-copies**. 1. photographic reproduction. —v. **-copying**, **-copied**. 2. make a photocopy of.

photoelectric adj. using or worked by electricity produced by the action of light. **photoelectric cell** same as PHOTOCELL.

photogenic adj. always looking attractive in photographs.

photograph n. 1. picture made by the chemical action of light on sensitive film. —v. 2. take a photograph of. **photographer** n. **photographic** adj. **photography** n. art of taking photographs.

photogravure n. process in which an etched metal plate for printing is produced by photography.

photolithography n. lithographic printing process using photographically made plates.

photometer [foe-**tom**-it-er] n. instrument for measuring the intensity of light.

photon n. quantum of electromagnetic radiation energy, such as light, having both particle and wave behaviour.

Photostat n. 1. ® type of photocopying machine. 2. copy made by it.

photosynthesis n. process by which a green plant uses sunlight to build up carbohydrate reserves.

phrase n. 1. group of words forming a unit

of meaning, esp. within a sentence. **2.** short effective expression. —v. **3.** express in words. **phrasal verb** phrase consisting of a verb and an adverb or preposition, with a meaning different from the parts, such as *take in* meaning *deceive.*

phraseology n., pl. **-gies.** way in which words are used.

phrenology n. formerly, the study of the shape and size of the skull as a means of finding out a person's character and mental ability. **phrenologist** n.

phut adv. **go phut** Informal (of a machine) break down.

phylactery n., pl. **-teries.** leather case containing religious texts, worn by Jewish men.

phylum n., pl. **-la.** major taxonomic division of animals and plants that contain one or more classes.

physical adj. **1.** of the body, as contrasted with the mind or spirit. **2.** of material things or nature. **3.** of physics. **physically** adv. **physical geography** branch of geography dealing with the features of the earth's surface.

physician n. doctor of medicine.

physics n. science of the properties of matter and energy. **physicist** n. person skilled in, or studying, physics.

physiognomy [fiz-ee-on-om-ee] n., pl. **-mies.** face.

physiography n. science of the earth's surface. **physiographer** n.

physiology n. science of the normal function of living things. **physiological** adj. **physiologist** n.

physiotherapy n. treatment of disease or injury by physical means such as massage, rather than by drugs. **physiotherapist** n.

physique n. person's bodily build and muscular development.

pi n. **1.** sixteenth letter in the Greek alphabet. **2.** Maths ratio of the circumference of a circle to its diameter.

pianissimo adv. Music very quietly.

piano[1] n., pl. **pianos.** (orig. **pianoforte**) musical instrument with strings which are struck by hammers worked by a keyboard. **pianist** n. **Pianola** n. ® mechanically played piano.

piano[2] adv. Music quietly.

piazza n. square or marketplace, esp. in Italy.

pibroch [**pee**-brok] n. form of bagpipe music.

pic n., pl. **pics, pix.** Informal photograph or illustration.

pica [**pie**-ka] n. **1.** printing type of 6 lines to the inch. **2.** typewriter typesize of 10 letters to the inch.

picador n. mounted bullfighter with a lance.

picaresque adj. denoting a type of fiction in which the hero, a rogue, has a series of adventures.

piccalilli n. pickle of vegetables in mustard sauce.

piccaninny n., pl. **-nies.** Offens. Black child.

piccolo n., pl. **-los.** small flute.

pick[1] v. **1.** choose. **2.** remove (flowers or fruit) from a plant. **3.** remove loose particles from. **4.** take hold of and move with the fingers. **5.** provoke (a fight etc.) deliberately. **6.** open (a lock) by means other than a key. —n. **7.** choice, e.g. *take your pick.* **8.** best part. **pick-me-up** n. **1.** Informal tonic. **2.** stimulating drink. **pick on** v. find fault with. **pick out** v. recognize, distinguish. **pick up** v. **1.** raise, lift. **2.** collect. **3.** improve, get better. **4.** become acquainted with for a sexual purpose. **5.** accelerate. **pick-up** n. **1.** device for conversion of mechanical energy into electric signals, as in a record player. **2.** small truck. **3.** casual acquaintance made for a sexual purpose.

pick[2] n. tool with a curved iron crossbar and wooden shaft, for breaking up hard ground or masonry.

pickaback n. same as PIGGYBACK.

pickaxe n. large pick.

picket n. **1.** person or group standing outside a workplace to deter would-be workers during a strike. **2.** sentry or sentries posted to give warning of an attack. **3.** pointed stick used as part of a fence. —v. **4.** form a picket outside (a workplace). **picket line** line of people acting as pickets.

pickings pl. n. money easily acquired.

pickle n. **1.** food preserved in vinegar or salt water. **2.** Informal awkward situation. —v. **3.** preserve in vinegar or salt water. **pickled** adj. Informal drunk.

pickpocket n. thief who steals from someone's pocket.

picnic *n.* **1.** informal meal out of doors. —*v.* **-nicking, -nicked. 2.** have a picnic.

picot [**peek**-oh] *n.* any of pattern of small loops, as on lace.

Pict *n.* member of an ancient race of N Britain. **Pictish** *adj.*

pictograph *n.* picture or symbol standing for word or group of words, as in written Chinese.

pictorial *adj.* **1.** of or in painting or pictures. **2.** illustrated. —*n.* **3.** newspaper etc. with many pictures. **pictorially** *adv.*

picture *n.* **1.** drawing or painting. **2.** photograph. **3.** mental image. **4.** beautiful or picturesque object. **5.** image on a TV screen. —*pl.* **6.** cinema. —*v.* **7.** visualize, imagine. **8.** represent in a picture. **picturesque** *adj.* **1.** (of a place or view) pleasant to look at. **2.** (of language) forceful, vivid. **picture rail** narrow piece of wood near the top of a wall from which pictures are hung. **picture window** large window made of a single sheet of glass.

piddle *v. Informal* urinate.

piddling *adj. Informal* small or unimportant.

pidgin *n.* language, not a mother tongue, made up of elements of two or more other languages.

pie *n.* dish of meat, fruit, etc. baked in pastry. **pie chart** circular diagram with sectors representing quantities.

piebald *n., adj.* (horse) with irregular black-and-white markings.

piece *n.* **1.** separate bit or part. **2.** instance, e.g. *a piece of luck.* **3.** example, specimen. **4.** coin. **5.** literary or musical composition. **6.** small object used in draughts, chess, etc. **piece together** *v.* make or assemble bit by bit.

pièce de résistance [pyess de ray-**ziss**-tonss] *n. French* most impressive item.

piecemeal *adv.* a bit at a time.

piecework *n.* work paid for according to the quantity produced.

pied *adj.* having markings of two or more colours.

pied-à-terre [pyay da **tair**] *n., pl.* **pieds-à-terre** [pyay da **tair**] small flat or house for occasional use.

pie-eyed *adj. Slang* drunk.

pier *n.* **1.** platform on stilts sticking out into

the sea. **2.** pillar, esp. one supporting a bridge.

pierce *v.* **1.** make a hole in or through with a sharp instrument. **2.** make a way through. **piercing** *adj.* **1.** (of a sound) shrill and high-pitched. **2.** (of wind or cold) fierce, penetrating.

pierrot [**pier**-roe] *n.* pantomime character, clown.

piety *n., pl.* **-ties.** deep devotion to God and religion.

piffle *n. Informal* nonsense.

pig *n.* **1.** animal kept and killed for pork, ham, and bacon. **2.** *Informal* greedy, dirty, or rude person. **piglet** *n.* young pig. **piggish, piggy** *adj.* **1.** *Informal* dirty. **2.** greedy. **3.** stubborn. **piggery** *n., pl.* **-geries.** place for keeping and breeding pigs. **pig-headed** *adj.* obstinate. **piggy bank** child's bank shaped like a pig with a slot for coins. **pig iron** crude iron produced in a blast furnace.

pigeon *n.* **1.** bird with a heavy body and short legs, sometimes trained to carry messages. **2.** *Informal* concern or responsibility. **pigeonhole** *n.* **1.** compartment for papers in a desk etc. —*v.* **2.** classify. **3.** put aside and do nothing about. **pigeon-toed** *adj.* with the feet or toes turned inwards.

piggyback *n.* **1.** ride on someone's shoulders. —*adv.* **2.** carried on someone's shoulders.

pigment *n.* colouring matter, paint or dye. **pigmentation** *n.*

Pigmy *n., pl.* **-mies,** *adj.* same as PYGMY.

pigsty *n., pl.* **-sties. 1.** pen for pigs. **2.** an untidy place.

pigtail *n.* plait of hair hanging from the back or either side of the head.

pike[1] *n.* large predatory freshwater fish.

pike[2] *n. Hist.* long-handled spear.

pilaster *n.* square column, usu. set in a wall.

pilau, pilaf, pilaff *n.* Middle Eastern dish of meat or poultry boiled with rice, spices, etc.

pilchard *n.* small edible sea fish of the herring family.

pile[1] *n.* **1.** number of things lying on top of each other. **2.** *Informal* large amount. **3.** large building. —*v.* **4.** collect into a pile. **5.** (foll. by *in, out, off,* etc.) move in a group. **pile-up** *n. Informal* traffic accident involving several vehicles.

pile² n. beam driven into the ground, esp. as a foundation for building in water or wet ground.

pile³ n. fibres of a carpet or a fabric, esp. velvet, that stand up from the weave.

piles pl. n. swollen veins in the rectum, haemorrhoids.

pilfer v. steal in small quantities.

pilgrim n. person who journeys to a holy place. **pilgrimage** n.

pill n. small ball of medicine swallowed whole. **the pill** pill taken by a woman to prevent pregnancy. **pillbox** n. **1.** small box for pills. **2.** small concrete fort.

pillage v. **1.** steal property by violence in war. —n. **2.** violent seizure of goods, esp. in war.

pillar n. **1.** slender upright post, usu. supporting a roof. **2.** strong supporter. **pillar box** red pillar-shaped letter box in the street.

pillion n. seat for a passenger behind the rider of a motorcycle.

pillory n., pl. -ries. **1.** Hist. frame with holes for the head and hands in which an offender was locked and exposed to public abuse. —v. -rying, -ried. **2.** ridicule publicly.

pillow n. **1.** stuffed cloth bag for supporting the head in bed. —v. **2.** rest as if on a pillow. **pillowcase, pillowslip** n. removable cover for a pillow.

pilot n. **1.** person qualified to fly an aircraft or spacecraft. **2.** person employed to steer a ship entering or leaving a harbour. —adj. **3.** experimental and preliminary. —v. **4.** act as the pilot of. **5.** guide, steer. **pilot light** small flame lighting the main one in a gas appliance. **pilot officer** most junior commissioned rank in certain air forces.

pimento n., pl. -tos. mild-tasting red pepper.

pimp n. **1.** man who gets customers for a prostitute in return for a share of his or her earnings. —v. **2.** act as a pimp.

pimpernel n. wild plant with small flowers that close in dull weather.

pimple n. small pus-filled spot on the skin. **pimply** adj.

pin n. **1.** short thin piece of stiff wire with a point and head, for fastening things. **2.** wooden or metal peg or stake. —v. **pinning, pinned. 3.** fasten with a pin. **4.** seize and hold fast. **pin down** v. **1.** force (someone) to make a decision, take action, etc. **2.** define

clearly. **pin money** small amount earned to buy small luxuries. **pin tuck** narrow ornamental fold in shirt, etc. **pin-up** n. picture of a sexually attractive person, esp. (partly) naked.

pinafore n. **1.** apron. **2.** dress with a bib top.

pinball n. electrically operated table game, in which a small ball is shot through various hazards.

pince-nez [panss-nay] n., pl. **pince-nez**. glasses kept in place only by a clip on the bridge of the nose.

pincers pl. n. **1.** tool consisting of two hinged arms, for gripping. **2.** claws of a lobster etc.

pinch v. **1.** squeeze between finger and thumb. **2.** cause pain by being too tight. **3.** Informal steal. **4.** Informal arrest. —n. **5.** act of pinching. **6.** as much as can be taken up between the finger and thumb. **at a pinch** if absolutely necessary. **feel the pinch** have to economize.

pinchbeck n. alloy of zinc and copper, used as imitation gold.

pincushion n. small cushion in which pins are stuck ready for use.

pine¹ n. **1.** evergreen coniferous tree. **2.** its wood. **pine cone** woody cone-shaped fruit of the pine tree. **pine marten** wild mammal of the coniferous forests of Europe and Asia.

pine² v. **1.** (foll. by for) feel great longing (for). **2.** become thin and ill through grief etc.

pineal gland [pin-ee-al] n. small cone-shaped gland at the base of the brain.

pineapple n. large tropical fruit with juicy yellow flesh and a hard skin.

ping v., n. (make) a short high-pitched sound. **pinger** n. device, esp. a timer, that makes a pinging sound.

Ping-Pong n. ® table tennis.

pinion¹ n. **1.** bird's wing. —v. **2.** immobilize (someone) by tying or holding his or her arms.

pinion² n. small cogwheel.

pink n. **1.** pale reddish colour. **2.** fragrant garden plant. —adj. **3.** of the colour pink. —v. **4.** (of an engine) make a metallic noise because not working properly, knock. **in the pink** in good health.

pinking shears pl. n. scissors with a serrated edge that give a wavy edge to material to prevent fraying.

pinnace *n.* ship's tender.

pinnacle *n.* **1.** highest point of success etc. **2.** mountain peak. **3.** small slender spire.

pinnate *adj.* (of compound leaves) having leaflets growing opposite each other in pairs.

pinpoint *v.* locate or identify exactly.

pinprick *n.* small irritation or annoyance.

pinstripe *n.* **1.** very narrow stripe in fabric. **2.** the fabric itself.

pint *n.* liquid measure, half a quart, ⅛ gallon (.568 litre).

Pinyin *n.* system for representing Chinese in Roman letters.

pioneer *n.* **1.** explorer or early settler of a new country. **2.** originator or developer of something new. —*v.* **3.** be the pioneer or leader of.

pious *adj.* deeply religious, devout.

pip¹ *n.* small seed in a fruit.

pip² *n.* **1.** high-pitched sound used as a time signal on radio. **2.** *Informal* star on a junior army officer's shoulder showing rank.

pip³ *n.* **give someone the pip** *Slang* annoy someone.

pipe *n.* **1.** tube for conveying liquid or gas. **2.** tube with a small bowl at the end for smoking tobacco. **3.** tubular musical instrument. —*pl.* **4.** bagpipes. —*v.* **5.** play on a pipe. **6.** utter in a shrill tone. **7.** convey by pipe. **8.** decorate with piping. **piper** *n.* player on a pipe or bagpipes. **piping** *n.* **1.** system of pipes. **2.** decoration of icing on a cake etc. **3.** fancy edging on clothes. **piping hot** extremely hot. **pipe cleaner** piece of wire coated with tiny tufts of yarn for cleaning the stem of a tobacco pipe. **piped music** recorded music played as background music in public places. **pipe down** *v. Informal* stop talking. **pipe dream** fanciful impossible plan etc. **pipeline** *n.* **1.** long pipe for transporting oil, water, etc. **2.** means of communication. **in the pipeline** in preparation. **pipe up** *v.* speak up shrilly.

pipette *n.* slender glass tube used to transfer or measure fluids.

pipit *n.* small brownish bird.

pippin *n.* type of eating apple.

piquant [pee-kant] *adj.* **1.** having a pleasant spicy taste. **2.** mentally stimulating. **piquancy** *n.*

pique [peek] *n.* **1.** feeling of hurt pride, baffled curiosity, or resentment. —*v.* **2.** hurt the pride of. **3.** arouse (curiosity).

piqué [pee-kay] *n.* stiff ribbed cotton fabric.

piquet [pik-ket] *n.* card game for two.

piranha *n.* small fierce freshwater fish of tropical America.

pirate *n.* **1.** sea robber. **2.** person who illegally publishes or sells work owned by someone else. **3.** person or company that broadcasts illegally. —*v.* **4.** sell or reproduce (artistic work etc.) illegally. **piracy** *n.* **piratical** *adj.*

pirouette *v., n.* (make) a spinning turn balanced on the toes of one foot.

piscatorial *adj.* of fishing or fishes.

Pisces *pl. n.* (the fishes) twelfth sign of the zodiac.

piss *Taboo* —*v.* **1.** urinate. —*n.* **2.** act of urinating. **3.** urine.

pistachio *n., pl.* **-os.** edible nut of a Mediterranean tree.

piste [peest] *n.* ski slope.

pistil *n.* seed-bearing part of a flower.

pistol *n.* short-barrelled handgun.

piston *n.* cylindrical part in an engine that slides to and fro in a cylinder.

pit *n.* **1.** deep hole in the ground. **2.** coal mine. **3.** dent or depression. **4.** servicing and refuelling area on a motor-racing track. **5.** same as ORCHESTRA PIT. —*v.* **pitting, pitted. 6.** mark with small dents or scars. **pit one's wits against** compete against in a test or contest. **pit bull terrier** strong, muscular terrier with a short coat.

pitapat *adv.* **1.** with quick light taps. —*n.* **2.** such taps.

pitch¹ *v.* **1.** throw, hurl. **2.** set up (a tent). **3.** fall headlong. **4.** (of a ship or plane) move with the front and back going up and down alternately. **5.** set the level or tone of. —*n.* **6.** area marked out for playing sport. **7.** degree or angle of slope. **8.** degree of highness or lowness of a (musical) sound. **9.** place where a street or market trader regularly sells. **10.** *Informal* persuasive sales talk. **pitcher** *n.* **pitched battle** fierce and violent fight. **pitch in** *v.* join in enthusiastically. **pitch into** *v. Informal* attack.

pitch² *n.* dark sticky substance obtained from tar. **pitch-black, -dark** *adj.* very dark.

pitchblende *n.* mineral composed largely of uranium oxide, yielding radium.

pitcher n. large jug with a narrow neck.

pitchfork n. 1. large long-handled fork for lifting hay. —v. 2. thrust abruptly or violently.

pitfall n. hidden difficulty or danger.

pith n. 1. soft white lining of the rind of oranges etc. 2. soft tissue in the stems of certain plants. 3. essential part. **pithy** adj. **pithier, pithiest.** short and full of meaning.

pithead n. top of a mine shaft and the buildings and hoisting gear around it.

piton [peet-on] n. metal spike used in climbing to secure a rope.

pitta bread n. flat, slightly leavened bread orig. from the Middle East.

pittance n. very small allowance of money.

pitter-patter n. 1. sound of light rapid taps or pats, as of raindrops. —v. 2. make such a sound.

pituitary n., pl. -taries. (also **pituitary gland**) gland at the base of the brain, that helps to control growth.

pity n., pl. **pities.** 1. sympathy or sorrow for others' suffering. 2. regrettable fact. —v. 3. feel pity for. **piteous, pitying, pitied.** 3. feel pity for. **piteous, pitiable** adj. arousing pity. **pitiful** adj. 1. arousing pity. 2. woeful, contemptible. **pitifully** adv. **pitiless** adj. feeling no pity, hard, merciless.

pivot n. 1. central shaft on which something turns. —v. 2. provide with or turn on a pivot. **pivotal** adj. of crucial importance.

pix n. Informal a plural of PIC.

pixie n. in folklore, fairy.

pizza n. flat disc of dough covered with a wide variety of savoury toppings and baked.

pizzazz n. Informal attractive combination of energy and style.

pizzicato [pit-see-kah-toe] adj. Music played by plucking the string of a violin etc. with the finger.

pl. 1. place. 2. plural.

placard n. large board with a slogan on it that is carried or displayed in public.

placate v. make (someone) stop feeling angry or upset. **placatory** adj.

place n. 1. particular part of an area or space. 2. particular town, building, etc. 3. position or point reached. 4. usual position. 5. duty or right. 6. position of employment. 7. seat or space. —v. 8. put in a particular place. 9. identify, put in context. 10. make

(an order, bet, etc.). **be placed** (of a competitor in a race) be among the first three. **take place** happen, occur. **placement** n. 1. arrangement or employment. 2. process of finding someone a job or a home. **place setting** cutlery, crockery, and glassware laid for one person at a meal.

placebo [plas-see-bo] n., pl. -bos, -boes. sugar pill etc. given to an unsuspecting patient as an active drug.

placenta [plass-ent-a] n., pl. -tas, -tae. organ formed in the womb during pregnancy, providing nutrients for the fetus. **placental** adj.

placid adj. calm, not easily excited or upset. **placidity** n.

placket n. opening at the top of a skirt etc. fastened with buttons or a zip.

plagiarize [play-jer-ize] v. steal ideas, passages, etc. from (someone else's work) and present them as one's own. **plagiarism** n. **plagiarist** n.

plague n. 1. fast-spreading fatal disease. 2. Hist. bubonic plague. 3. widespread infestation. —v. **plaguing, plagued.** 4. trouble or annoy continually.

plaice n. edible European flatfish.

plaid n. 1. long piece of tartan cloth worn as part of Highland dress. 2. tartan cloth or pattern.

plain adj. 1. obvious, unmistakable. 2. easy to see or understand. 3. simple, ordinary. 4. without decoration or pattern. 5. expressed honestly and clearly. 6. not beautiful. —n. 7. large stretch of level country. **plainly** adv. **plainness** n. **plain clothes** ordinary clothes, as opposed to uniform. **plain sailing** easy progress. **plain speaking** saying exactly what one thinks.

plainsong n. unaccompanied singing, esp. in a medieval church.

plaintiff n. person who sues in a court of law.

plaintive adj. sad, mournful. **plaintively** adv.

plait [platt] v. 1. intertwine separate strands to form one ropelike length. —n. 2. length of hair that has been plaited.

plan n. 1. way thought out to do or achieve something. 2. diagram showing the layout or design of something. —v. **planning, planned.** 3. arrange beforehand. 4. make a diagram of.

planchette *n.* small board used in spiritualism.

plane[1] *n.* **1.** an aircraft. —*v.* **2.** (of a boat) rise and partly skim over water.

plane[2] *n.* **1.** *Maths* flat surface. **2.** level of attainment etc. **3.** tool for smoothing wood. —*v.* **4.** smooth (wood) with a plane. —*adj.* **5.** perfectly flat or level.

plane[3] *n.* tree with broad leaves.

planet *n.* large body in space that revolves round the sun or another star. **planetary** *adj.*

planetarium *n., pl.* **-iums, -ia.** building where the movements of the stars, planets, etc. are shown by projecting lights on the inside of a dome.

plangent [plan-jent] *adj.* (of sounds) mournful and resounding.

plank *n.* long flat piece of sawn timber.

plankton *n.* minute animals and plants floating in the surface water of a sea or lake.

plant *n.* **1.** living organism that grows in the ground and has no power to move. **2.** equipment or machinery used in industrial processes. **3.** factory or other industrial premises. —*v.* **4.** put in the ground to grow. **5.** place firmly in position. **6.** *Informal* hide (stolen goods etc.) on a person to make him or her seem guilty. **7.** *Informal* put (a person) secretly in an organization to spy. **planter** *n.* **1.** ornamental pot for house plants. **2.** owner of a plantation.

plantain[1] *n.* low-growing wild plant with broad leaves.

plantain[2] *n.* tropical fruit like a green banana.

plantation *n.* **1.** estate for the cultivation of tea, tobacco, etc. **2.** wood of cultivated trees.

plaque *n.* **1.** inscribed commemorative stone or metal plate fixed to a wall. **2.** filmy deposit on teeth that causes decay.

plasma *n.* **1.** clear liquid part of blood. **2.** *Physics* hot ionized gas containing positive ions and free electrons.

plaster *n.* **1.** mixture of lime, sand, etc. for coating walls. **2.** adhesive strip of material for dressing cuts. —*v.* **3.** cover with plaster. **4.** coat thickly. **plastered** *adj. Slang* drunk. **plasterboard** *n.* thin rectangular sheets of cardboard held together with plaster, used to cover interior walls, etc. **plaster of Paris** white powder which dries to form a

hard solid when mixed with water, used for sculptures and casts for broken limbs.

plastic *n.* **1.** synthetic material that can be moulded when soft but sets in a hard long-lasting shape. —*adj.* **2.** made of plastic. **3.** easily moulded, pliant. **plasticity** *n.* ability to be moulded. **plastic bullet** solid PVC cylinder fired by police in riot control. **plastic surgery** repair or reconstruction of missing or malformed parts of the body for medical or cosmetic reasons.

Plasticine *n.* ® soft coloured modelling material used esp. by children.

plate *n.* **1.** shallow round dish for holding food. **2.** flat thin sheet of metal, glass, etc. **3.** thin coating of metal on another metal. **4.** dishes or cutlery made of gold or silver. **5.** illustration, usu. on fine quality paper, in a book. **6.** *Informal* set of false teeth. —*v.* **7.** cover with a thin coating of gold, silver, or other metal. **plateful** *n.* **plate glass** kind of thick glass used for mirrors and windows. **plate tectonics** study of the structure of the earth's crust, esp. the movement of layers of rocks.

plateau *n., pl.* **-teaus, -teaux. 1.** area of level high land. **2.** stage when there is no change or development.

platelet *n.* minute particle occurring in blood of vertebrates and involved in clotting of blood.

platen *n.* **1.** roller of a typewriter, against which the paper is held. **2.** plate in a printing press by which the paper is pressed against the type.

platform *n.* **1.** raised floor for speakers. **2.** raised area in a station from which passengers board trains. **3.** programme of a political party. **4.** structure in the sea which holds machinery, stores, etc. for drilling an oil well.

platinum *n.* very valuable silvery-white metal. **platinum blonde** woman with silvery-blonde hair.

platitude *n.* remark that is true but not interesting or original. **platitudinous** *adj.*

platonic *adj.* friendly or affectionate but not sexual.

platoon *n.* subunit of a company of soldiers.

platteland *n. S Afr.* rural district.

platter *n.* large dish.

platypus *n.* (also **duck-billed platypus**)

Aust. egg-laying amphibious mammal, with dense fur, webbed feet, and a ducklike bill.

plaudit n. expression of approval.

plausible adj. **1.** apparently true or reasonable. **2.** persuasive but insincere. **plausibly** adv. **plausibility** n.

play v. **1.** occupy oneself in (a game or recreation). **2.** compete against in a game or sport. **3.** behave carelessly. **4.** act (a part) on the stage. **5.** perform on (a musical instrument). **6.** cause (a radio, record player, etc.) to give out sound. **7.** move lightly or irregularly, flicker. —n. **8.** story performed on stage or broadcast. **9.** activities children take part in for amusement. **10.** playing of a game. **11.** conduct, e.g. fair play. **12.** (scope for) freedom of movement. **player** n. **playful** adj. lively. **play back** v. listen to or watch (something recorded). **play down** v. minimize the importance of. **playing card** one of a set of 52 cards used in card games. **playing fields** extensive piece of ground for open-air games. **play off** v. set (two people) against each other for one's own ends. **play on** v. exploit or encourage (someone's sympathy or weakness). **play up** v. **1.** cause trouble. **2.** give prominence to.

playboy n. rich man who lives only for pleasure.

playground n. outdoor area children to play on, esp. one with swings, etc. or adjoining a school.

playgroup n. regular meeting of very young children for supervised play.

playhouse n. theatre.

playpen n. small portable enclosure with bars or a net round the sides in which a young child can safely be left to play.

playschool n. nursery group for young children.

plaything n. **1.** toy. **2.** person regarded or treated as a toy.

playwright n. author of plays.

plaza n. **1.** modern shopping complex. **2.** open space or square.

PLC, plc Public Limited Company.

plea n. **1.** serious or urgent request, entreaty. **2.** statement of a prisoner or defendant. **3.** excuse.

plead v. **1.** ask urgently or with deep feeling. **2.** give as an excuse. **3.** Law declare oneself to be guilty or innocent of a charge made against one.

pleasant adj. pleasing, enjoyable. **pleasantly** adv. **pleasantry** n., pl. **-tries.** polite or joking remark.

please v. **1.** give pleasure or satisfaction to. —adv. **2.** polite word of request. **please oneself** do as one likes. **pleased** adj. **pleasing** adj. giving pleasure or satisfaction.

pleasure n. **1.** feeling of happiness and satisfaction. **2.** something that causes this. **pleasurable** adj. giving pleasure. **pleasurably** adv.

pleat n. **1.** fold made by doubling material back on itself. —v. **2.** arrange (material) in pleats.

plebeian [pleb-ee-an] adj. **1.** of the lower social classes. **2.** vulgar or rough. —n. **3.** (also (Offens.) **pleb**) member of the lower social classes.

plebiscite [pleb-iss-ite] n. decision by direct voting of the people of a country.

plectrum n., pl. **-trums, -tra.** small implement for plucking the strings of a guitar etc.

pledge n. **1.** solemn promise. **2.** something valuable given as a guarantee that a promise will be kept or a debt paid. —v. **3.** promise solemnly. **4.** bind by or as if by a pledge, e.g. pledge to secrecy.

plenary adj. (of a meeting) attended by all members.

plenipotentiary n., pl. **-aries. 1.** diplomat or representative having full powers. —adj. **2.** having full powers.

plenitude n. completeness, abundance.

plenteous adj. plentiful.

plentiful adj. existing in large amounts or numbers. **plentifully** adv.

plenty n. **1.** large amount or number. **2.** quite enough.

pleonasm n. use of more words than necessary. **pleonastic** adj.

plethora n. oversupply.

pleurisy n. inflammation of the membrane lining the chest and covering the lungs.

pliable adj. **1.** easily bent. **2.** easily influenced. **pliability** n.

pliant adj. pliable. **pliancy** n.

pliers pl. n. tool with hinged arms and jaws for gripping.

plight[1] n. difficult or dangerous situation.

plight[2] v. **plight one's troth** Old-fashioned promise to marry.

Plimsoll line n. mark on a ship showing the level the water should reach when the ship is fully loaded.

plimsolls pl. n. rubber-soled canvas shoes.

plinth n. slab forming the base of a column etc.

PLO Palestine Liberation Organization.

plod v. **plodding, plodded. 1.** walk with slow heavy steps. **2.** work slowly but determinedly. **plodder** n.

plonk[1] v. put (something) down heavily and carelessly.

plonk[2] n. Informal cheap inferior wine.

plop n. **1.** sound of an object falling into water without a splash. —v. **plopping, plopped. 2.** make this sound.

plot[1] n. **1.** secret plan to do something illegal or wrong. **2.** sequence of events on which a film, novel, etc. is based. —v. **plotting, plotted. 3.** plan secretly, conspire. **4.** mark the position or course of (a ship or aircraft) on a map. **5.** mark and join up (points on a graph).

plot[2] n. small piece of land.

plough n. **1.** agricultural tool for turning over soil. —v. **2.** turn over (earth) with a plough. **3.** move or work through slowly and laboriously. **ploughman** n. **ploughshare** n. blade of a plough.

plover n. shore bird with a straight bill and long pointed wings.

ploy n. manoeuvre designed to gain an advantage.

pluck v. **1.** pull or pick off. **2.** pull out the feathers of (a bird for cooking). **3.** sound the strings of (a guitar etc.) with the fingers or a plectrum. —n. **4.** courage. **plucky** adj. **pluckier, pluckiest.** brave. **pluckily** adv. **pluck up** v. summon up (courage).

plug n. **1.** thing fitting into and filling a hole. **2.** device connecting an appliance to an electricity supply. **3.** Informal favourable mention of a product etc., designed to encourage people to buy it. —v. **plugging, plugged. 4.** block or seal (a hole or gap) with a plug. **5.** Informal advertise (a product etc.) by constant repetition. **plug away** v. Informal work steadily. **plug in** v. connect (an electrical appliance) to a power source by pushing a plug into a socket.

plum n. **1.** oval usu. dark red fruit with a stone in the middle. —adj. **2.** dark purplish-red. **3.** very desirable.

plumage n. bird's feathers.

plumb v. **1.** understand (something obscure). **2.** test with a plumb line. —adv. **3.** exactly. **plumb the depths of** experience the worst extremes of (an unpleasant quality or emotion). **plumber** n. person who fits and repairs pipes and fixtures for water and drainage systems. **plumbing** n. pipes and fixtures used in water and drainage systems. **plumb in** v. connect (an appliance such as a washing machine) to a water supply. **plumb line** string with a weight at the end, used to test the depth of water or to test whether something is vertical.

plume n. feather, esp. one worn as an ornament. **plume oneself on** be proud of oneself because of.

plummet v. **-meting, -meted.** plunge downward.

plump[1] adj. moderately or attractively fat. **plumpness** n. **plump up** v. make (a pillow) fuller or rounded.

plump[2] v. **1.** sit or fall heavily and suddenly. —adv. **2.** suddenly and heavily. **3.** directly. **plump for** v. choose, vote only for.

plunder v. **1.** take by force, esp. in time of war. —n. **2.** things plundered, spoils.

plunge v. **1.** put or throw forcibly or suddenly (into). —n. **2.** plunging, dive. **take the plunge** Informal. **1.** embark on a risky enterprise. **2.** get married. **plunger** n. rubber suction cup used to clear blocked pipes. **plunging** adj. (of the neckline of a dress) cut low so as to show the top of the breasts. **plunge into** v. become deeply involved in.

plunk v. pluck the strings of (a banjo etc.) to produce a twanging sound.

pluperfect adj., n. Grammar (tense) expressing an action completed before a past time, such as had gone in his wife had gone already.

plural adj. **1.** of or consisting of more than one. —n. **2.** a word in its plural form.

pluralism n. existence and toleration of a variety of peoples, opinions, etc. in a society. **pluralist** n. **pluralistic** adj.

plus prep. **1.** with the addition of: usu. indicated by the sign (+). —adj. **2.** more than zero or the number already mentioned. **3.** positive. **4.** advantageous. —n. **5.** plus sign. **6.** advantage.
▷ Avoid using plus to mean 'additionally' except in very informal contexts.

plus fours *pl. n.* trousers gathered in at the knee.

plush *n.* **1.** fabric with long velvety pile. —*adj.* (also **plushy**) **2.** luxurious.

Pluto *n.* **1.** Greek god of the underworld. **2.** farthest planet from the sun.

plutocrat *n.* person who is powerful because of being very rich. **plutocratic** *adj.*

plutonium *n.* radioactive metallic element used esp. in nuclear reactors and weapons.

pluvial *adj.* of or caused by the action of rain.

ply[1] *v.* **plying, plied. 1.** work at (a job or trade). **2.** use (a tool). **3.** (of a ship) travel regularly along or between. **ply with** *v.* supply with or subject to persistently.

ply[2] *n.* thickness of wool, fabric, etc.

plywood *n.* board made of thin layers of wood glued together.

pm, PM 1. after noon. **2.** postmortem.

Pm *Chem.* promethium.

PM prime minister.

PMS premenstrual syndrome.

PMT premenstrual tension.

pneumatic *adj.* worked by or inflated with wind or air.

pneumonia *n.* inflammation of the lungs.

Po *Chem.* polonium.

PO 1. postal order. **2.** Post Office.

poach[1] *v.* **1.** catch (animals) illegally on someone else's land. **2.** encroach on or steal something belonging to someone else. **poacher** *n.*

poach[2] *v.* simmer (food) gently in liquid.

pocket *n.* **1.** small bag sewn into clothing for carrying things. **2.** pouchlike container, esp. for catching balls at the edge of a snooker table. **3.** isolated or distinct group or area. —*v.* **pocketing, pocketed. 4.** put into one's pocket. **5.** take secretly or dishonestly. —*adj.* **6.** small. **in, out of pocket** having made a profit *or* loss. **pocket money 1.** small regular allowance given to children by parents. **2.** allowance for small personal expenses.

pockmarked *adj.* (of the skin) marked with hollow scars where diseased spots have been.

pod *n.* long narrow seed case of peas, beans, etc.

podgy *adj.* **podgier, podgiest.** short and fat.

podium *n., pl.* **-diums, -dia.** small raised platform for a conductor or speaker.

poem *n.* imaginative piece of writing in rhythmic lines.

poesy *n.* *Obs.* poetry.

poet *n.* writer of poems. **poet laureate** poet appointed by the British sovereign to write poems on important occasions. **poetry** *n.* **1.** poems. **2.** art of writing poems. **3.** beautiful or pleasing quality. **poetic** *adj.* (also **poetical**) of or like poetry. **poetically** *adv.* **poetic justice** suitable reward or punishment for someone's past actions. **poetic licence** freedom from the normal rules of language and truth, as in poetry. **poetaster** *n.* would-be or inferior poet.

po-faced *adj.* wearing a disapproving stern expression.

pogo stick *n.* pole with steps for the feet and a spring at the bottom, so that the user can bounce up, down, and along on it.

pogrom *n.* organized persecution and massacre.

poignant *adj.* sharply painful to the feelings. **poignancy** *n.*

poinsettia *n.* Central American shrub widely cultivated for its clusters of scarlet leaves, which resemble petals.

point *n.* **1.** single idea in a discussion, argument, etc. **2.** main or essential aspect. **3.** aim or purpose. **4.** detail or item. **5.** characteristic. **6.** particular position, stage; or time. **7.** unit for recording a value or score. **8.** dot indicating decimals. **9.** full stop. **10.** sharp end. **11.** headland. **12.** one of the direction marks of a compass. **13.** movable rail used to change a train to other rails. **14.** electrical socket. —*pl.* **15.** electrical contacts in the distributor of an engine. —*v.* **16.** show the direction or position of something or draw attention to it by extending a finger or other pointed object towards it. **17.** direct (a gun etc.) towards. **18.** finish or repair the joints in brickwork with mortar. **19.** (of a gun dog) show where game is by standing rigidly with the muzzle towards it. **on the point of** very shortly going to. **pointed** *adj.* **1.** having a sharp end. **2.** (of a remark) obviously directed at a particular person. **pointedly** *adv.* **pointer** *n.* **1.** indicator on a measuring instrument. **2.** breed of gundog. **3.** helpful hint. **pointless** *adj.* meaningless, irrelevant. **point-blank** *adj., adv.* **1.** fired at a very close target. **2.** (of a remark or question) direct, blunt. **point duty** policeman's position at a road junction to control traffic. **point of view** way of considering something. **point-to-point** n. horse race across open country.

poise n. calm dignified manner. **poised** adj. 1. absolutely ready. 2. behaving with or showing poise.

poison n. 1. substance that kills or injures when swallowed or absorbed. —v. 2. give poison to. 3. have a harmful or evil effect on, spoil. **poisoner** n. **poisonous** adj. **poison-pen letter** malicious anonymous letter.

poke v. 1. jab or prod with one's finger, a stick, etc. 2. thrust forward or out. —n. 3. poking. **poky** adj. **pokier, pokiest.** *Informal* small and cramped.

poker¹ n. metal rod for stirring a fire to make it burn more brightly.

poker² n. card game involving bluff. **poker-faced** adj. expressionless.

polar adj. of or near either of the earth's poles. **polar bear** white bear that lives in the regions around the North Pole.

polarize v. 1. form or cause to form into groups with directly opposite views. 2. *Physics* restrict (light waves) to certain directions of vibration. **polarization** n.

Polaroid n. ® 1. plastic which polarizes light and so reduces glare. 2. camera that develops a print very quickly inside itself.

polder n. land reclaimed from the sea.

pole¹ n. long rounded piece of wood etc.

pole² n. 1. point furthest north (**North Pole**) or furthest south (**South Pole**) on the earth's axis of rotation. 2. either of the opposite ends of a magnet or electric cell. **Pole Star** star nearest to the North Pole in the northern hemisphere.

poleaxe v. hit or stun with a heavy blow.

polecat n. small animal of the weasel family.

polemic [pol-em-ik] n. fierce attack on or defence of a particular opinion, belief, etc. **polemical** adj.

police n. 1. organized force in a state which keeps law and order. —v. 2. control or watch over with police or a similar body. **policeman, policewoman** n. member of a police force. **police dog** dog trained to help the police. **police state** state or country in which the government controls people's

freedom by means of esp. secret police. **police station** office of the police force of a district.

policy¹ n., pl. **-cies.** plan of action adopted by a person, group, or state.

policy² n., pl. **-cies.** document containing an insurance contract.

polio n. (also **poliomyelitis**) disease affecting the spinal cord, which often causes paralysis.

polish v. 1. make smooth and shiny by rubbing. 2. make more nearly perfect. —n. 3. liquid, aerosol, etc. for polishing. 4. pleasing elegant style. **polished** adj. 1. (of a person) socially sophisticated in manner. 2. done or performed well or professionally. **polish off** v. finish completely, dispose of.

Polish adj. 1. of Poland, its people, or their language. —n. 2. official language of Poland.

Politburo n. decision-making committee in a Communist country.

polite adj. 1. showing consideration for others in one's manners, speech, etc. 2. socially correct or refined. **politely** adv. **politeness** n.

politic adj. wise and likely to prove advantageous.

politics n. 1. winning and using of power to govern society. 2. person's beliefs about how a country should be governed. 3. (study of) the art of government. **political** adj. of the state, government, or public administration. **politically** adv. **political prisoner** person imprisoned because of his or her political beliefs. **politician** n. person actively engaged in politics, esp. a member of parliament.

polka n. 1. lively 19th-century dance. 2. music for this. **polka dots** pattern of bold spots on fabric.

poll n. 1. (also **opinion poll**) questioning of a random sample of people to find out general opinion. 2. voting. 3. number of votes recorded. —v. 4. receive (votes). 5. question in an opinion poll. **pollster** n. person who conducts opinion polls. **polling station** building where people vote in an election. **poll tax** (also **community charge**) tax levied on every adult person.

pollarded adj. (of a tree) growing very bushy because its top branches have been cut short.

pollen n. fine dust produced by flowers that fertilizes other flowers. **pollinate** v. fertilize with pollen. **pollen count** measure of the amount of pollen in the air, esp. as a warning to people with hay fever.

pollute v. contaminate with something poisonous or harmful. **pollution** n. **pollutant** n. something that pollutes.

polo n. game like hockey played by teams of players on horseback. **polo neck** sweater with tight turned-over collar. **polo shirt** cotton short-sleeved shirt with a collar and three-button opening at the neck.

polonaise n. 1. old stately dance. 2. music for this.

polonium n. radioactive element that occurs in trace amounts in uranium ores.

poltergeist n. spirit believed to move furniture and throw objects around.

poltroon n. Obs. utter coward.

poly n., pl. **polys.** Informal polytechnic.

poly- combining form many, much.

polyandry n. practice of having more than one husband at the same time.

polyanthus n. garden primrose.

polychromatic adj. many-coloured.

polyester n. synthetic material used to make plastics and textile fibres.

polygamy [pol-ig-a-mee] n. practice of having more than one husband or wife at the same time. **polygamous** adj. **polygamist** n.

polyglot adj., n. (person) able to speak or write several languages.

polygon n. geometrical figure with three or more angles and sides. **polygonal** adj.

polygraph n. instrument for recording pulse rate and perspiration, used esp. as a lie detector.

polygyny n. practice of having more than one wife at the same time.

polyhedron n., pl. **-drons, -dra.** solid figure with four or more sides.

polymath n. person of great and varied learning.

polymer n. chemical compound with large molecules made of simple molecules of the same kind. **polymerize** v. form into polymers. **polymerization** n.

polynomial adj. 1. of two or more names or terms. —n. 2. mathematical expression consisting of a sum of terms each of which is the product of a constant and one or more variables raised to a positive or zero integral power. 3. (also **multinomial**) any mathematical expression consisting of the sum of a number of terms.

polyp n. 1. small simple sea creature with a hollow cylindrical body. 2. small growth on a mucous membrane.

polyphonic adj. Music consisting of several melodies played simultaneously.

polystyrene n. synthetic material used esp. as white rigid foam for packing and insulation.

polytechnic n. college offering courses in many subjects at and below degree level.

polytheism n. belief in many gods. **polytheist** n. **polytheistic** adj.

polythene n. light plastic used for many everyday articles.

polyunsaturated adj. of a group of fats that do not form cholesterol in the blood.

polyurethane n. synthetic material used esp. in paints.

polyvinyl chloride n. same as PVC.

pomade n. perfumed oil or ointment applied to the hair to make it smooth and shiny.

pomander n. (container for) a mixture of sweet-smelling petals, herbs, etc.

pomegranate n. round tropical fruit with a thick rind containing many seeds in a red pulp.

Pomeranian n. small dog with long straight hair.

pommel n. 1. raised part on the front of a saddle. 2. knob at the top of a sword hilt.

pommy n., pl. **-mies.** Aust. & NZ slang (also **pom**) person from Britain.

pomp n. stately display or ceremony.

pompom n. decorative ball of tufted wool, silk, etc.

pompous adj. foolishly serious and grand, self-important. **pompously** adv. **pomposity** n.

ponce n. Offens. 1. effeminate man. 2. pimp. **ponce around** v. act stupidly, waste time.

poncho n., pl. **-chos.** loose circular cloak with a hole for the head.

pond n. small area of still water. **pondweed** n. plant that grows in ponds.

ponder v. think thoroughly or deeply (about).

ponderous adj. 1. serious and dull. 2.

heavy and unwieldy. **3.** (of movement) slow and clumsy. **ponderously** adv.

pong n., v. Informal (give off) a strong unpleasant smell.

pontiff n. the Pope. **pontifical** adj. pompous and dogmatic. **pontificate** v. **1.** state one's opinions as if they were the only possible correct ones. —n. **2.** period of office of a Pope.

pontoon[1] n. floating platform supporting a temporary bridge.

pontoon[2] n. gambling card game.

pony n., pl. **ponies.** small horse. **ponytail** n. **1.** long hair tied in one bunch at the back of the head. **pony trekking** pastime of riding ponies cross-country.

poodle n. dog with curly hair often clipped fancifully.

poof n. Offens. homosexual man.

pooh interj. exclamation of disdain, contempt or disgust. **pooh-pooh** v. express disdain or scorn for.

pool[1] n. **1.** small body of still water. **2.** puddle of spilt liquid. **3.** swimming pool.

pool[2] n. **1.** shared fund or group of workers or resources. **2.** game like snooker. —pl. **3.** short for FOOTBALL POOLS. —v. **4.** put in a common fund.

poop n. raised part at the back of a sailing ship.

poor adj. **1.** having little money and few possessions. **2.** less, smaller, or weaker than is needed or expected. **3.** unproductive. **4.** unlucky, pitiable. **poorly** adv. **1.** in a poor manner. —adj. **2.** not in good health. **poorness** n.

pop[1] v. **popping, popped. 1.** make or cause to make a small explosive sound. **2.** Informal go, put, or come unexpectedly or suddenly. —n. **3.** small explosive sound. **4.** nonalcoholic fizzy drink. **popcorn** n. maize kernels heated until they puff up and burst.

pop[2] n. **1.** music of general appeal, esp. to young people. —adj. **2.** popular. **pop art** movement in modern art that uses the styles and themes of popular culture and mass media.

pop[3] n. Informal father.

Pope n. head of the Roman Catholic Church. **popish** adj. Offens. Roman Catholic.

popeyed adj. staring in astonishment.

popinjay n. **1.** conceited or talkative person. **2.** Obs. parrot.

poplar n. tall slender tree.

poplin n. ribbed cotton material.

poppadom n. thin round crisp Indian bread.

poppet n. term of affection for a small child or sweetheart.

poppy n., pl. **-pies. 1.** plant with a large delicate red flower. **2.** artificial red poppy worn to mark Remembrance Sunday.

poppycock n. Informal nonsense.

populace n. **1.** the ordinary people. **2.** the masses.

popular adj. **1.** widely liked and admired. **2.** of or for the public in general. **popularly** adv. **popularity** n. **popularize** v. **1.** make popular. **2.** make (something technical or specialist) easily understood.

populate v. fill with inhabitants. **population** n. **1.** all the people who live in a particular place. **2.** the number of people living in a particular place. **populous** adj. thickly populated.

porbeagle n. kind of shark.

porcelain n. **1.** fine china. **2.** objects made of it.

porch n. covered approach to the entrance of a building.

porcine adj. of or like a pig.

porcupine n. animal covered with long pointed quills.

pore[1] n. tiny opening in the skin or in the surface of a plant.

pore[2] v. (foll. by over) make a careful study or examination of (a book, map, etc.).

pork n. pig meat. **porker** n. pig raised for food.

porn, porno n., adj. Informal short for PORNOGRAPHY or PORNOGRAPHIC.

pornography n. writing, films, or pictures designed to be sexually exciting. **pornographer** n. producer of pornography. **pornographic** adj.

porous adj. allowing liquid to pass through gradually. **porosity** n.

porphyry [por-fir-ee] n. reddish rock with large crystals in it.

porpoise n. fish-like sea mammal.

porridge n. **1.** breakfast food made of oatmeal cooked in water or milk. 2. *Slang* prison term.

porringer n. small dish for soup or porridge.

port[1] n. 1. harbour. 2. town with a harbour.

port[2] n. left side of a ship or aircraft when facing the front of it.

port[3] n. strong sweet wine, usu. red.

port[4] n. 1. opening in the side of a ship. 2. porthole.

portable adj. easily carried. **portability** n.

portage n. (cost of) transporting boats and supplies overland between navigable waterways.

portal n. large imposing doorway or gate.

portcullis n. grating suspended above a castle gateway, that can be lowered to block the entrance.

portend v. be a sign of.

portent n. sign of a future event. **portentous** adj. 1. of great or ominous significance. 2. pompous, self-important.

porter n. 1. man on duty at the entrance to a hotel etc. 2. man who carries luggage. 3. hospital worker who transfers patients between rooms etc.

portfolio n., pl. -os. 1. (flat case for carrying) examples of an artist's work. 2. area of responsibility of a minister of state. 3. list of investments held by an investor.

porthole n. small round window in a ship or aircraft.

portico n., pl. -cos, -coes. porch or covered walkway with columns supporting the roof.

portion n. 1. part or share. 2. helping of food for one person. 3. destiny or fate. **portion out** v. divide into shares.

portly adj. -lier, -liest. rather fat.

portmanteau n., pl. -teaus, -teaux. 1. *Old-fashioned* large suitcase that opens into two compartments. —adj. 2. combining aspects of different things.

portrait n. 1. picture of a person. 2. lifelike description.

portray v. describe or represent by artistic means, as in writing or film. **portrayal** n.

Portuguese adj. 1. of Portugal, its people, or their language. —n. 2. person from Portugal. 3. language of Portugal and Brazil. **Portuguese man-of-war** sea creature resembling a jellyfish, with stinging tentacles.

pose v. 1. place in or take up a particular position to be photographed or drawn. 2. ask (a question). 3. raise (a problem). —n. 4. position while posing. 5. behaviour adopted for effect. **pose as** pretend to be. **poser** n. 1. puzzling question. 2. *Informal* person who likes to be seen in trendy clothes in fashionable places. 3. poseur. **poseur** n. person who behaves in an affected way to impress others.

posh adj. 1. *Informal* smart, luxurious. 2. affectedly upper-class.

posit [pozz-it] v. lay down as a basis for argument.

position n. 1. place. 2. usual or expected place. 3. way in which something is placed or arranged. 4. attitude, point of view. 5. social standing. 6. state of affairs. 7. job. —v. 8. place.

positive adj. 1. feeling no doubts, certain. 2. helpful, providing encouragement. 3. confident, hopeful. 4. absolute, downright. 5. *Med.* indicating the presence of a condition for which a test was made. 6. *Maths* greater than zero. 7. *Electricity* having a deficiency of electrons. **positively** adv. **positive discrimination** provision of special opportunities for a disadvantaged group.

positivism n. philosophical system which accepts only things that can be seen or proved. **positivist** n., adj.

positron n. positive electron.

posse [poss-ee] n. 1. *US* group of men organized to maintain law and order. 2. *Informal* group or gang.

possess v. 1. have as one's property. 2. (of a feeling, belief, etc.) have complete control of, dominate. **possessor** n. **possession** n. 1. state of possessing, ownership. —pl. 2. things a person possesses. **possessive** adj. 1. wanting all the attention or love of another person. 2. (of a word) indicating the person or thing that something belongs to. **possessiveness** n.

possible adj. 1. able to exist, happen, or be done. 2. worthy of consideration. —n. 3. person or thing that might be suitable or chosen. **possibility** n., pl. -ties. **possibly** adv. perhaps, not necessarily.

possum n. same as OPOSSUM. **play possum** pretend to be dead or asleep to deceive an opponent.

post[1] n. 1. official system of carrying and delivering letters and parcels. 2. (single collection or delivery of) letters and parcels sent by this system. —v. **3.** send by post. **keep someone posted** supply someone regularly with the latest information. **postage** n. charge for sending a letter or parcel by post. **postal** adj. **postal order** written money order sent by post and cashed at a post office by the person who receives it. **post office** place where postal business is conducted.

post[2] n. **1.** length of wood, concrete, etc. fixed upright to support or mark something. —v. **2.** put up (a notice) in a public place.

post[3] n. **1.** job. **2.** position to which someone, esp. a soldier, is assigned for duty. **3.** military establishment. —v. **4.** send (a person) to a new place to work. **5.** put (a guard etc.) on duty.

post- prefix after, later than, e.g. postwar.

postbag n. **1.** postman's bag. **2.** post received by a magazine, famous person, etc.

postbox n. same as LETTER BOX (sense 2).

postcard n. card for sending a message by post without an envelope.

postcode n. system of letters and numbers used to aid the sorting of mail.

postdate v. write a date on (a cheque) that is later than the actual date.

poster n. large picture or notice stuck on a wall.

poste restante n. French post-office department where a traveller's letters are kept until called for.

posterior n. **1.** buttocks. —adj. **2.** behind, at the back of.

posterity n. future generations, descendants.

postern n. small back door or gate.

postgraduate n. person with a degree who is studying for a more advanced qualification.

posthaste adv. with great speed.

posthumous [poss-tume-uss] adj. **1.** occurring after one's death. **2.** born after one's father's death. **3.** published after the author's death. **posthumously** adv.

postilion, postillion n. Hist. person riding one of a pair of horses drawing a carriage.

postman n. man who collects and delivers post.

postmark n. official mark stamped on letters showing place and date of posting.

postmaster, postmistress n. official in charge of a post office.

postmortem n. medical examination of a body to establish the cause of death.

postnatal adj. occurring after childbirth.

postpone v. put off to a later time. **postponement** n.

postprandial adj. after dinner.

postscript n. passage added at the end of a letter.

postulant n. candidate for admission to a religious order.

postulate v. assume to be true as the basis of an argument or theory. **postulation** n.

posture n. **1.** position or way in which someone stands, walks, etc. —v. **2.** behave in an exaggerated way to get attention.

posy n., pl. **-sies.** small bunch of flowers.

pot n. **1.** round deep container. **2.** teapot. **3.** Slang cannabis. —pl. **4.** Informal a lot. —v. **potting, potted. 5.** plant in a pot. **6.** Snooker hit (a ball) into a pocket. **potted** adj. **1.** grown in a pot. **2.** (of meat or fish) preserved in a pot. **3.** Informal abridged. **potbelly** n. bulging belly. **potluck** n. whatever is available. **potsherd** n. broken fragment of pottery. **pot shot** shot taken without aiming carefully. **potting shed** shed where plants are potted.

potable [pote-a-bl] adj. drinkable.

potash n. white powdery substance obtained from ashes and used as fertilizer.

potassium n. white metallic element.

potato n., pl. **-toes.** roundish starchy vegetable that grows underground.

poteen n. in Ireland, illicitly distilled alcoholic drink.

potent adj. **1.** having great power or influence. **2.** (of a male) capable of having sexual intercourse. **potency** n.

potentate n. ruler or monarch.

potential adj. **1.** possible but not yet actual. —n. **2.** ability or talent not yet fully used. **3.** Electricity level of electric pressure. **potentially** adv. **potentiality** n., pl. **-ties.**

pothole n. **1.** hole in the surface of a road. **2.** deep hole in a limestone area. **potholing** n. sport of exploring underground caves. **potholer** n.

potion n. dose of medicine or poison.

potpourri [po-poor-ee] n. **1.** fragrant mixture of dried flower petals. **2.** musical or literary medley.

pottage n. thick soup or stew.

potter[1] n. person who makes pottery.

potter[2] v. be busy in a pleasant but aimless way.

pottery n., pl. **-ries. 1.** articles made from baked clay. **2.** place where they are made.

potty[1] adj. **-tier, -tiest.** Informal crazy or silly.

potty[2] n., pl. **-ties.** bowl used by a small child as a toilet.

pouch n. **1.** small bag. **2.** baglike pocket of skin on an animal.

pouf, pouffe [poof] n. large solid cushion used as a seat.

poulterer n. person who sells poultry.

poultice [pole-tiss] n. moist dressing, often heated, applied to inflamed skin.

poultry n. domestic fowls.

pounce v. **1.** spring upon suddenly to attack or capture. —n. **2.** pouncing.

pound[1] n. **1.** monetary unit of Britain and some other countries. **2.** unit of weight equal to 0.454 kg.

pound[2] v. **1.** hit heavily and repeatedly. **2.** crush to pieces or powder. **3.** (of the heart) throb heavily. **4.** run heavily.

pound[3] n. enclosure for stray animals or officially removed vehicles.

poundage n. charge of so much per pound of weight or sterling.

pour v. **1.** flow or cause to flow out in a stream. **2.** rain heavily. **3.** come or go in large numbers.

pout v. **1.** thrust out one's lips, look sulky. —n. **2.** pouting look.

pouter n. pigeon that can puff out its crop.

poverty n. **1.** state of being without enough food or money. **2.** lack of, scarcity. **poverty-stricken** adj. very poor. **poverty trap** situation of being unable to raise one's living standard because any extra income would result in state benefits being reduced.

POW prisoner of war.

powder n. **1.** substance in the form of tiny loose particles. **2.** medicine or cosmetic in this form. —v. **3.** apply powder to. **powdered** adj. in the form of a powder, e.g. powdered milk. **powdery** adj. **powder puff**

soft pad used to apply cosmetic powder to the skin. **powder room** ladies' toilet.

power n. **1.** ability to do or act. **2.** strength. **3.** position of authority or control. **4.** person or thing having authority. **5.** particular form of energy, e.g. nuclear power. **6.** electricity supply. **7.** Physics rate at which work is done. **8.** Maths product from continuous multiplication of a number by itself. **powered** adj. having or operated by mechanical or electrical power. **powerful** adj. **powerless** adj. **power cut** temporary interruption in the supply of electricity. **power point** socket on a wall for plugging in electrical appliances. **power station** installation for generating and distributing electric power. **power steering** type of steering on vehicles in which the turning of the steering wheel is assisted by power from the engine.

powwow n. talk, conference.

pox n. **1.** disease in which skin pustules form. **2.** Informal syphilis.

pp 1. past participle. **2.** in signing a document, for and on behalf of. **3.** Music pianissimo.

▷ The original meaning of pp (Latin per procurationem) is 'by delegation to', so traditionally pp is written before the name of the typist to show that she or he has signed the letter on behalf of someone else. Nowadays the meaning has been overtaken by the sense of 'on behalf of' and pp is often written before the name of the person who composed the letter.

pp. pages.

PQ Quebec.

Pr Chem. praseodymium.

PR 1. proportional representation. **2.** public relations.

practicable adj. capable of being carried out successfully. **practicability** n.

practical adj. **1.** involving experience or actual use rather than theory. **2.** sensible. **3.** adapted for use. **4.** good at making or doing things. **5.** in effect though not in name. —n. **6.** examination in which something has to be done or made. **practically** adv. **practicality** n., pl. **-ties. practical joke** trick intended to make someone look foolish.

practice n. **1.** something done regularly or habitually. **2.** repetition of something so as to gain skill. **3.** doctor's or lawyer's place of work. **in practice** what actually happens as distinct from what is supposed to happen.

put into **practice** carry out, do.

▷ Note the *-ice* ending for the noun, with *-ise* for the verb (*practise*).

practise *v.* **1.** do repeatedly so as to gain skill. **2.** take part in, follow (a religion etc.). **3.** work at, e.g. *practise medicine*. **4.** do habitually.

▷ Note the *-ise* ending for the verb, with *-ice* for the noun (*practice*).

practitioner *n.* person who practises a profession.

pragmatic *adj.* concerned with practical consequences rather than theory. **pragmatism** *n.* **pragmatist** *n.*

prairie *n.* large treeless area of grassland, esp. in N America and Canada. **prairie dog** rodent that lives in burrows in the N American prairies.

praise *v.* **1.** express approval or admiration of (someone or something). **2.** express honour and thanks to (God). —*n.* **3.** something said or written to show approval or admiration. **sing someone's praises** praise someone highly. **praiseworthy** *adj.*

praline [**prah**-leen] *n.* sweet made of nuts and caramelized sugar.

pram *n.* four-wheeled carriage for a baby, pushed by hand.

prance *v.* walk with exaggerated bouncing steps.

prang *n. Old-fashioned slang* crash (a car or aircraft).

prank *n.* mischievous trick or escapade, frolic.

prat *n. Offens.* stupid person.

prattle *v.* **1.** chatter in a childish or foolish way. —*n.* **2.** childish or foolish talk. **prattler** *n.*

prawn *n.* edible shellfish like a large shrimp.

praxis *n.* practice as opposed to theory.

pray *v.* **1.** say prayers. **2.** ask earnestly, entreat. **prayer** *n.* **1.** thanks or appeal addressed to God. **2.** set form of words used in praying. **3.** earnest request.

pre- *prefix* before, beforehand, e.g. *prenatal, prerecorded, preshrunk.*

preach *v.* **1.** give a talk on a religious theme as part of a church service. **2.** speak in support of (an idea, principle, etc.). **preacher** *n.*

preamble *n.* introductory part to something said or written.

prearranged *adj.* arranged beforehand.

prebendary *n., pl.* **-daries.** clergyman who is a member of the chapter of a cathedral.

precarious *adj.* insecure, unsafe, likely to fall or collapse. **precariously** *adv.*

precaution *n.* action taken in advance to prevent something bad happening. **precautionary** *adj.*

precede *v.* go or be before. **precedence** [**press**-ee-denss] *n.* formal order of rank or position. **take precedence over** be more important than. **precedent** *n.* previous case or occurrence regarded as an example to be followed.

precentor *n.* person who leads the singing in a church.

precept *n.* rule of behaviour.

precession *n.* **precession of the equinoxes** slightly earlier occurrence of the equinoxes each year.

precinct *n.* **1.** area in a town closed to traffic. **2.** enclosed area round a building, e.g. *cathedral precinct.* **3.** *US* administrative area of a city. —*pl.* **4.** surrounding region.

precious *adj.* **1.** of great value and importance. **2.** loved and treasured. **3.** (of behaviour) affected, unnatural. **precious metal** gold, silver, or platinum. **precious stone** rare mineral, such as a ruby, valued as a gem.

precipice *n.* very steep cliff or rockface. **precipitous** *adj.* sheer.

precipitant *adj.* hasty or rash.

precipitate *v.* **1.** cause to happen suddenly. **2.** throw headlong. **3.** *Chem.* cause to be deposited in solid form from a solution. —*adj.* **4.** done rashly or hastily. —*n.* **5.** *Chem.* substance precipitated from a solution. **precipitately** *adv.* **precipitation** *n.* **1.** precipitating. **2.** rain, snow, etc.

précis [**pray**-see] *n., pl.* **précis. 1.** short written summary of the main points of a longer piece. —*v.* **2.** make a précis of.

precise *adj.* **1.** exact, accurate in every detail. **2.** strict in observing rules or standards. **precisely** *adv.* **precision** *n.*

preclude *v.* make impossible to happen.

precocious *adj.* having developed or matured early or too soon. **precocity, precociousness** *n.*

precognition n. alleged ability to foretell the future.

preconceived adj. (of an idea) formed without real experience or reliable information. **preconception** n.

precondition n. something that must happen or exist before something else can.

precursor n. something that precedes and is a signal of something else, forerunner.

predate v. write a date on (a document) that is earlier than the actual date.

predatory [pred-a-tree] adj. habitually hunting and killing other animals for food. **predator** n. predatory animal.

predecease v. die before (someone else).

predecessor n. 1. person who precedes another in an office or position. 2. ancestor.

predestination n. belief that future events have already been decided by God. **predestined** adj.

predetermined adj. decided in advance.

predicament n. embarrassing or difficult situation.

predicate n. 1. part of a sentence in which something is said about the subject, e.g. *went home* in *I went home*. —v. 2. declare or assert. **predicative** adj. of or in the predicate of a sentence.

predict v. tell about in advance, prophesy. **predictable** adj. **prediction** n.

predilection n. preference or liking.

predispose v. 1. influence (someone) in favour of something. 2. make (someone) susceptible to something. **predisposition** n.

predominate v. be the main or controlling element. **predominance** n. **predominant** adj. **predominantly** adv.

pre-eminent adj. excelling all others, outstanding. **pre-eminently** adv. **pre-eminence** n.

pre-empt v. get or do in advance of or to the exclusion of others. **pre-emption** n. **pre-emptive** adj.

preen v. (of a bird) clean or trim (its feathers) with its beak. **preen oneself 1.** smarten oneself. **2.** show self-satisfaction.

prefab n. prefabricated house.

prefabricated adj. (of a building) manufactured in shaped sections for rapid assembly on site.

preface [pref-iss] n. 1. introduction to a book. —v. 2. serve as an introduction to (a book, speech, etc.). **prefatory** adj.

prefect n. 1. senior pupil in a school, with limited power over others. 2. senior administrative officer in some countries. **prefecture** n. office or area of authority of a prefect.

prefer v. -ferring, -ferred. 1. like better. 2. *Law* bring (charges) before a court. **preferable** adj. more desirable. **preferably** adv. **preference** n. **preferential** adj. showing preference. **preferment** n. promotion or advancement.

prefigure v. represent or suggest in advance.

prefix n. 1. letter or group of letters put at the beginning of a word to make a new word, such as *un-* in *unhappy*. —v. 2. put as an introduction or prefix (to).

pregnant adj. 1. carrying a fetus in the womb. 2. full of meaning or significance, as in *pregnant pause*. **pregnancy** n., pl. -cies.

prehensile adj. capable of grasping. **prehensility** n.

prehistoric adj. of the period before written history begins. **prehistory** n.

prejudge v. judge beforehand without sufficient evidence.

prejudice n. 1. unreasonable or unfair dislike or preference. —v. 2. cause (someone) to have a prejudice. 3. harm, cause disadvantage to. **prejudicial** adj. harmful, disadvantageous.

prelate [prel-it] n. bishop or other churchman of high rank. **prelacy** n.

preliminary adj. 1. happening before and in preparation, introductory. —n., pl. -naries. 2. preliminary remarks, contest, etc.

prelude [prel-yewd] n. 1. introductory movement in music. 2. event preceding and introducing something else.

premarital adj. occurring before marriage.

premature adj. 1. happening or done before the normal or expected time. 2. (of a baby) born before the end of the normal period of pregnancy. **prematurely** adv.

premedication n. drugs given to prepare a patient for a general anaesthetic.

premeditated adj. planned in advance. **premeditation** n.

premenstrual adj. occurring or experienced before a menstrual period, e.g. *premenstrual tension*.

premier n. **1.** prime minister. —adj. **2.** chief, leading. **premiership** n.

première n. first performance of a play, film, etc.

premise, premiss n. statement assumed to be true and used as the basis of reasoning.

premises pl. n. house or other building and its land.

premium n. **1.** additional sum of money, as on a wage or charge. **2.** (regular) sum paid for insurance. **at a premium** in great demand because scarce. **Premium (Savings) Bond** savings certificate issued by the government, on which no interest is paid but cash prizes can be won.

premonition n. feeling that something unpleasant is going to happen. **premonitory** adj.

prenatal adj. **1.** before birth. **2.** during pregnancy.

preoccupy v. **-pying, -pied.** fill the thoughts or attention of (someone) to the exclusion of other things. **preoccupation** n.

preordained adj. decreed or determined in advance.

prep n. Informal preparation for schoolwork.

prep. **1.** preparatory. **2.** preposition.

prepacked adj. sold already wrapped.

prepaid adj. paid for in advance.

prepare v. make or get ready. **prepared** adj. **1.** willing. **2.** ready. **preparation** n. **1.** preparing. **2.** something done in readiness for something else. **3.** mixture prepared for use as a cosmetic, medicine, etc. **preparatory** [prip-par-a-tree] adj. preparing for. **preparatory school** private school for children going on to public school.

preponderant adj. greater in amount, force, or influence. **preponderantly** adv. **preponderance** n.

preposition n. word used before a noun or pronoun to show its relationship with other words, such as by in go by bus. **prepositional** adj.

prepossessing adj. making a favourable impression, attractive.

preposterous adj. utterly absurd.

prep school n. short for PREPARATORY SCHOOL.

prepuce [pree-pyewss] n. retractable fold of skin covering the tip of the penis, foreskin.

prerecorded adj. recorded in advance to be played or broadcast later.

prerequisite n., adj. (something) that must happen or exist before something else is possible.

prerogative n. special power or privilege.

presage [press-ij] v. be a sign or warning of.

presbyopia n. inability of the eye to focus on nearby objects.

Presbyterian adj., n. (member) of a Protestant church governed by lay elders. **Presbyterianism** n.

presbytery n., pl. **-teries.** **1.** Presbyterian Church local church court. **2.** RC Church priest's house.

prescience [press-ee-enss] n. knowledge of events before they happen. **prescient** adj.

prescribe v. **1.** recommend the use of (a medicine). **2.** lay down as a rule. **prescription** n. written instructions from a doctor for the making up and use of a medicine. **prescriptive** adj. laying down rules.

presence n. **1.** fact of being in a specified place. **2.** impressive dignified appearance. **presence of mind** ability to act sensibly in a crisis.

present[1] adj. **1.** being in a specified place. **2.** existing or happening now. **3.** (of a verb tense) indicating that the action specified is taking place now. —n. **4.** present time or tense. **presently** adv. **1.** soon. **2.** US & Scot. now.

present[2] n. **1.** something given to bring pleasure to another person. —v. **2.** introduce formally or publicly. **3.** introduce and compère (a TV or radio show). **4.** cause, e.g. present a difficulty. **5.** give, award. **presentation** n. **presentable** adj. attractive, neat, fit for people to see. **presenter** n. person introducing a TV or radio show.

presentiment [pree-zen-tim-ent] n. sense of something usu. unpleasant about to happen.

preserve v. **1.** keep from being damaged, changed, or ended. **2.** treat (food) to prevent it decaying. —n. **3.** area of interest restricted to a particular person or group. **4.** fruit preserved by cooking in sugar. **5.** area where game is kept for private fishing or shooting. **preservation** n. **preservative** n. chemical that prevents decay.

preshrunk adj. (of fabric or a garment) having been shrunk during manufacture so that further shrinkage will not occur when washed.

preside v. be in charge, esp. of a meeting.

president n. **1.** head of state in countries without a king or queen. **2.** head of a society, institution, etc. **presidential** adj. **presidency** n., pl. **-cies.**

press[1] v. **1.** apply force or weight to. **2.** squeeze. **3.** smooth by applying pressure or heat. **4.** crowd, push. **5.** urge insistently. —n. **6.** printing machine. **pressed** for short of, as in *pressed for time*. **the press 1.** news media collectively, esp. newspapers. **2.** reporters, journalists. **pressing** adj. urgent. **press box** room at a sports ground reserved for reporters. **press conference** interview for reporters given by a celebrity. **press release** official announcement or account of a news item supplied to the press. **press stud** fastener in which one part with a projecting knob snaps into a hole on another part.

press[2] v. press into service force to be involved or used. **press gang** Hist. group of men who captured men and boys and forced them to join the navy.

press-up n. exercise in which the body is raised from and lowered to the floor by straightening and bending the arms.

pressure n. **1.** force produced by pressing. **2.** urgent claims or demands, e.g. *working under pressure.* **3.** Physics force applied to a surface per unit of area. **bring pressure to bear on** use influence or authority to persuade. **pressurize** v. **pressure cooker** airtight pot which cooks food quickly by steam under pressure. **pressure group** group that tries to influence policies, public opinion, etc.

prestidigitation n. skilful quickness with the hands, conjuring.

prestige n. high status or respect resulting from success or achievements. **prestigious** adj.

presto adv. Music very quickly.

prestressed adj. (of concrete) containing stretched steel wires to strengthen it.

presume v. **1.** suppose to be the case. **2.** (foll. by to) dare (to), take the liberty (of). **presumably** adv. one supposes (that). **presumption** n. **1.** bold insolent behaviour. **2.** strong probability. **presumptuous** adj. doing things one has no right or authority to do. **presumptuously** adv. **presumptive** adj.

assumed to be true or valid until the contrary is proved. **heir presumptive** heir whose right may be defeated by the birth of a closer relative.

presuppose v. need as a previous condition in order to be true. **presupposition** n.

pretend v. claim or give the appearance of (something untrue) to deceive or in play. **pretender** n. person who makes a false or disputed claim to a position of power. **pretence** n. behaviour intended to deceive, pretending. **pretentious** adj. making (unjustified) claims to special merit or importance. **pretension** n.

preterite [pret-er-it] adj., n. Grammar (expressing) a past tense, such as *jumped, swam.*

preternatural adj. beyond what is natural, supernatural.

pretext n. false reason given to hide the real one.

pretty adj. **-tier, -tiest. 1.** pleasing to look at. —adv. **2.** fairly, moderately, as in *I'm pretty certain.* **prettily** adv. **prettiness** n. **sitting pretty** in a favourable state.

pretzel n. brittle salted biscuit.

prevail v. **1.** gain mastery. **2.** be generally established. **prevailing** adj. **1.** widespread. **2.** predominant. **prevalence** n. **prevalent** adj. widespread, common.

prevaricate v. be evasive, avoid giving a direct or truthful answer. **prevarication** n.

prevent v. keep from happening or doing. **preventable** adj. **prevention** n. **preventive** adj., n.

preview n. advance showing of a film or exhibition before it is shown to the public.

previous adj. coming or happening before. **previously** adv.

prey n. **1.** animal hunted and killed for food by another animal. **2.** victim. **bird of prey** bird that kills and eats other birds or animals. **prey on** v. **1.** hunt and kill for food. **2.** worry, obsess.

price n. **1.** amount of money for which a thing is bought or sold. **2.** unpleasant thing that must be endured to get something desirable. —v. **3.** fix or ask the price of. **priceless** adj. **1.** very valuable. **2.** Informal very funny. **pricey, pricy** adj. **pricier, priciest.** Informal expensive.

prick v. **1.** pierce slightly with a sharp point. **2.** cause to feel mental pain. **3.** (of an animal) make (the ears) stand erect. —*n.* **4.** sudden sharp pain caused by pricking. **5.** mark made by pricking. **6.** remorse. **7.** *Taboo slang* penis. **prick up one's ears** listen intently.

prickle *n.* **1.** thorn or spike on a plant. —*v.* **2.** have a tingling or pricking sensation. **prickly** *adj.* **prickly heat** itchy rash occurring in hot moist weather.

pride *n.* **1.** feeling of pleasure and satisfaction when one has done well. **2.** too high an opinion of oneself. **3.** something that causes one to feel pride. **4.** group of lions. **pride of place** most important position. **pride oneself on** feel pride about.

prie-dieu [pree-dyur] *n.* upright frame with a ledge for kneeling upon, for use when praying.

priest *n.* **1.** in the Christian church, a person who can administer the sacraments and preach. **2.** in some other religions, an official who performs religious ceremonies. **priestess** *fem.* woman priest. **priesthood** *n.* **priestly** *adj.*

prig *n.* self-righteous person who acts as if superior to others. **priggish** *adj.* **priggishness** *n.*

prim *adj.* **primmer, primmest.** formal, proper, and rather prudish. **primly** *adv.* **primness** *n.*

prima ballerina *n.* leading female ballet dancer.

primacy *n., pl.* **-cies. 1.** state of being first in rank, grade, etc. **2.** office of an archbishop.

prima donna *n.* **1.** leading female opera singer. **2.** *Informal* temperamental person.

primaeval *adj.* same as PRIMEVAL.

prima facie [prime-a fay-shee] *adv. Latin* as it seems at first.

primal *adj.* of basic causes or origins.

primary *adj.* chief, most important. **primarily** *adv.* **primary colours** (in physics) red, green, and blue or (in art) red, yellow, and blue, from which all other colours can be produced by mixing. **primary school** school for children from five to eleven years.

primate[1] *n.* archbishop.

primate[2] *n.* member of an order of mammals including monkeys and humans.

prime *adj.* **1.** main, most important. **2.** of the highest quality. —*n.* **3.** time when some-

one is at his or her best or most vigorous. —*v.* **4.** give (someone) information in advance to prepare them for something. **5.** prepare (a surface) for painting. **6.** prepare (a gun, pump, etc.) for use. **Prime Minister** leader of a government. **prime number** number that can be divided exactly only by itself and one. **prime time** peak viewing time on television.

primer *n.* **1.** special paint applied to bare wood etc. before the main paint. **2.** beginners' school book or manual.

primeval [prime-ee-val] *adj.* of the earliest age of the world.

primitive *adj.* **1.** of an early simple stage of development. **2.** basic, crude, e.g. *a primitive hut.*

primogeniture *n.* system under which the eldest son inherits all his parents' property.

primordial *adj.* existing at or from the beginning.

primrose *n.* pale yellow spring flower.

primula *n.* type of primrose with brightly coloured flowers.

Primus *n.* ® portable cooking stove used esp. by campers.

prince *n.* **1.** male member of a royal family, esp. the son of the king or queen. **2.** male ruler of a small country. **princely** *adj.* **1.** of or like a prince. **2.** generous, lavish, or magnificent. **prince consort** husband of a reigning queen. **Prince of Wales** eldest son of the British sovereign. **princess** *n.* female member of a royal family, esp. the daughter of the king or queen. **Princess Royal** title sometimes given to the eldest daughter of the British sovereign.

principal *adj.* **1.** main, most important. —*n.* **2.** head of a school or college. **3.** person taking a leading part in something. **4.** sum of money lent on which interest is paid. **principally** *adv.* **principal boy** leading male role in pantomime, played by a woman. ▷ Distinguish the spellings of *principal* and *principle*. These are different words but often confused.

principality *n., pl.* **-ties.** territory ruled by a prince.

principle *n.* **1.** moral rule guiding behaviour. **2.** general or basic truth, e.g. *the principle of equality.* **3.** scientific law concerning the working of something. **in principle** in theory but not always in practice. **on principle** because of one's beliefs.

▷ Distinguish the spellings of *principle* and *principal*. These are different words but often confused.

print v. **1.** reproduce (a newspaper, book, etc.) in large quantities by mechanical or electronic means. **2.** reproduce (text or pictures) by pressing ink onto paper etc. **3.** write in letters that are not joined up. **4.** *Photog.* produce (pictures) from negatives. **5.** stamp (fabric) with a design. —n. **6.** printed words etc. **7.** printed lettering. **8.** photograph. **9.** printed copy of a painting. **10.** mark left on a surface by something that has pressed against it. **11.** printed fabric. **out of print** no longer available from a publisher. **printer** n. **1.** person or company engaged in printing. **2.** machine that prints. **printed circuit** electronic circuit with wiring printed on an insulating base. **print-out** n. printed information from a computer.

prior¹ adj. earlier. **prior to** before.

prior² n. head monk in a priory. **prioress** n. deputy head nun in a convent. **priory** n., pl. -ries. place where certain orders of monks or nuns live.

priority n., pl. -ties. **1.** most important thing that must be dealt with first. **2.** right to be or go before others.

prise v. force open by levering.

prism n. transparent block usu. with triangular ends and rectangular sides, used to disperse light into a spectrum or refract it in optical instruments. **prismatic** adj. **1.** of or shaped like a prism. **2.** (of colour) as if produced by refraction through a prism, rainbow-like.

prison n. building where criminals and accused people are held. **prisoner** n. person held captive. **prisoner of war** serviceman captured by an enemy in wartime.

prissy adj. -sier, -siest. prim, correct, and easily shocked. **prissily** adv.

pristine adj. clean, new, and unused.

private adj. **1.** for the use of one person or group only. **2.** secret. **3.** owned or paid for by individuals rather than by the government. **4.** quiet, not likely to be disturbed. **5.** personal, unconnected with one's work. —n. **6.** soldier of the lowest rank. **privately** adv. **privacy** n. **private company** limited company that does not issue shares for public subscription. **private detective** person hired by a client to do detective work.

private member's bill law proposed by a Member of Parliament who is not a government minister. **private parts** *Euphemistic* genitals. **private sector** part of a country's economy not controlled or financially supported by the government.

privateer n. **1.** *Hist.* privately owned armed vessel authorized by the government to take part in a war. **2.** captain of such a ship.

privation n. loss or lack of the necessities of life.

privatize v. sell (a publicly owned company) to individuals or a private company. **privatization** n.

privet n. bushy evergreen shrub used for hedges.

privilege n. advantage or favour that only some people have. **privileged** adj. enjoying a special right or immunity.

privy adj. **1.** sharing knowledge of something secret. —n., pl. **privies. 2.** *Obs.* toilet, esp. an outside one. **privy council** council of state of a monarch.

prize¹ n. **1.** reward given for success in a competition etc. —adj. **2.** winning or likely to win a prize. —v. **3.** value highly. **prizefighter** n. boxer who fights for money. **prizefight** n.

prize² v. same as PRISE.

pro¹ adj., adv. in favour of. **pros and cons** arguments for and against.

pro² n., pl. **pros.** *Informal* **1.** professional. **2.** prostitute.

pro- prefix **1.** in favour of, e.g. *pro-Russian.* **2.** instead of, e.g. *pronoun.*

probable adj. likely to happen or be true. **probably** adv. **probability** n., pl. -ties.

probate n. **1.** process of proving the authenticity of a will. **2.** certificate of this.

probation n. **1.** system of dealing with law-breakers, esp. juvenile ones, by placing them under supervision. **2.** period when someone is assessed for suitability for a job etc. **probationer** n. person on probation. **probationary** adj.

probe v. **1.** search into or examine closely. —n. **2.** surgical instrument used to examine a wound, cavity, etc.

probity n. honesty, integrity.

problem n. **1.** something difficult to deal with or solve. **2.** question or puzzle set for solution. **problematical** adj.

proboscis [pro-**boss**-iss] *n.* **1.** elephant's trunk. **2.** long snout. **3.** elongated mouthpart of some insects.

procedure *n.* way of doing something, esp. the correct or usual one.

proceed *v.* **1.** start or continue doing. **2.** *Formal* walk, go. **3.** start a legal action. **4.** arise from. **proceeds** *pl. n.* money obtained from an event or activity. **proceedings** *pl. n.* **1.** organized or related series of events. **2.** minutes of a meeting. **3.** legal action.

process *n.* **1.** series of actions or changes. **2.** method of doing or producing something. —*v.* **3.** handle or prepare by a special method of manufacture. **4.** treat (food) to prevent it decaying. **processor** *n. Computers* same as CENTRAL PROCESSING UNIT.

procession *n.* line of people or vehicles moving forward together in order.

proclaim *v.* declare publicly. **proclamation** *n.*

proclivity *n., pl.* **-ties.** inclination, tendency.

proconsul *n. Hist.* governor of a province, esp. of the Roman Empire.

procrastinate *v.* put off taking action, delay. **procrastination** *n.* **procrastinator** *n.*

procreate *v. Formal* produce offspring. **procreation** *n.*

Procrustean *adj.* ruthlessly enforcing uniformity.

procurator fiscal *n.* in Scotland, law officer who acts as public prosecutor and coroner.

procure *v.* **1.** get, provide. **2.** obtain (people) to act as prostitutes. **procurement** *n.* **procurer, procuress** *n.* person who obtains people to act as prostitutes.

prod *v.* **prodding, prodded.** **1.** poke with something pointed. **2.** goad (someone) to take action. —*n.* **3.** prodding.

prodigal *adj.* recklessly extravagant, wasteful. **prodigality** *n.*

prodigy *n., pl.* **-gies.** **1.** person with some marvellous talent. **2.** wonderful thing. **prodigious** *adj.* **1.** very large, immense. **2.** wonderful. **prodigiously** *adv.*

produce *v.* **1.** bring into existence. **2.** present to view, show. **3.** make, manufacture. **4.** present on stage, film, or television. —*n.* **5.** food grown for sale. **producer** *n.* **1.** person with financial and administrative control of a film etc. **2.** person or company that produces something.

product *n.* **1.** something produced. **2.** number resulting from multiplication. **production** *n.* **1.** producing. **2.** things produced. **productive** *adj.* **1.** producing large quantities. **2.** useful, profitable. **productivity** *n.*

profane *adj.* **1.** showing disrespect for religion or holy things. **2.** (of language) coarse, blasphemous. —*v.* **3.** treat (something sacred) irreverently, desecrate. **profanation** *n.* act of profaning. **profanity** *n.* profane talk or behaviour, blasphemy.

profess *v.* **1.** state or claim (something as true), sometimes falsely. **2.** have as one's belief or religion. **professed** *adj.* supposed.

profession *n.* **1.** type of work, such as being a doctor, that needs special training. **2.** all the people employed in a profession, e.g. *the legal profession.* **3.** declaration of a belief or feeling. **professional** *adj.* **1.** working in a profession. **2.** taking part in an activity, such as sport or music, for money. **3.** very competent. —*n.* **4.** person who works in a profession. **5.** person paid to take part in sport, music, etc. **professionally** *adv.* **professionalism** *n.*

professor *n.* teacher of the highest rank in a university. **professorial** *adj.* **professorship** *n.*

proffer *v.* offer.

proficient *adj.* skilled, expert. **proficiency** *n.*

profile *n.* **1.** outline, esp. of the face, as seen from the side. **2.** brief biographical sketch.

profit *n.* **1.** money gained. **2.** benefit obtained. —*v.* **3.** gain or benefit. **profitable** *adj.* making profit. **profitably** *adv.* **profitability** *n.* **profiteer** *n.* person who makes excessive profits at the expense of the public. **profiteering** *n.*

profligate *adj.* **1.** recklessly extravagant. **2.** shamelessly immoral. —*n.* **3.** dissolute person. **profligacy** *n.*

pro forma *adj. Latin* prescribing a set form.

profound *adj.* **1.** showing or needing great knowledge. **2.** strongly felt, intense. **profundity** *n., pl.* **-ties.**

profuse *adj.* plentiful. **profusion** *n.*

progeny [**proj**-in-ee] *n., pl.* **-nies.** children. **progenitor** [pro-**jen**-it-er] *n.* ancestor.

progesterone *n.* hormone which prepares the womb for pregnancy and prevents further ovulation.

prognathous *adj.* having a projecting lower jaw.

prognosis *n., pl.* **-noses. 1.** doctor's forecast about the progress of an illness. **2.** any forecast.

prognostication *n.* forecast or prediction.

program *n.* **1.** sequence of coded instructions for a computer. —*v.* **-gramming, -grammed. 2.** arrange (data) so that it can be processed by a computer. **3.** feed a program into (a computer). **programmer** *n.* **programmable** *adj.*

programme *n.* **1.** planned series of events. **2.** broadcast on radio or television. **3.** list of items or performers in an entertainment.

progress *n.* **1.** improvement, development. **2.** movement forward. —*v.* **3.** become more advanced or skilful. **4.** move forward. **in progress** taking place. **progression** *n.* **1.** act of progressing, advance. **2.** sequence of numbers in which each differs from the next by a fixed ratio. **progressive** *adj.* **1.** favouring political or social reform. **2.** happening gradually. **progressively** *adv.*

prohibit *v.* forbid or prevent from happening. **prohibition** *n.* **1.** act of forbidding. **2.** ban on the sale or drinking of alcohol. **prohibitive** *adj.* (of prices) too high to be affordable. **prohibitively** *adv.*
▷ The idiom is *prohibit* someone *from* doing something.

project *n.* **1.** planned scheme to do or examine something over a period. —*v.* **2.** make a forecast based on known data. **3.** make (a film or slide) appear on a screen. **4.** communicate (an impression). **5.** stick out beyond a surface or edge. **projector** *n.* apparatus for projecting photographic images, films, or slides on a screen. **projection** *n.* **projectionist** *n.* person who operates a projector.

projectile *n.* object thrown as a weapon or fired from a gun.

prolapse *n.* slipping down of an internal organ of the body from its normal position.

prole *adj., n. Offens.* proletarian.

proletariat [pro-lit-**air**-ee-at] *n.* working class. **proletarian** *adj., n.*

proliferate *v.* grow or reproduce rapidly. **proliferation** *n.*

prolific *adj.* very productive. **prolifically** *adv.*

prolix *adj.* (of speech or a piece of writing) overlong and boring. **prolixity** *n.*

prologue *n.* introduction to a play or book.

prolong *v.* make (something) last longer. **prolongation** *n.*

prom *n.* short for PROMENADE or PROMENADE CONCERT.

promenade *n.* **1.** paved walkway along the seafront at a holiday resort. —*v., n.* **2.** *Old-fashioned* (take) a leisurely walk. **promenade concert** concert at which part of the audience stands rather than sits.

prominent *adj.* **1.** very noticeable. **2.** famous, widely known. **prominently** *adv.* **prominence** *n.*

promiscuous *adj.* having many casual sexual relationships. **promiscuity** *n.*

promise *v.* **1.** say that one will definitely do or not do something. **2.** show signs of, seem likely. —*n.* **3.** undertaking to do or not to do something. **4.** indication of future success. **show promise** seem likely to succeed. **promising** *adj.* likely to succeed or turn out well. **promissory note** written promise to pay a sum of money to a certain person on a certain date or on demand.

promo *n., pl.* **-mos.** *Informal* short video film made to promote a pop record.

promontory *n., pl.* **-ries.** point of high land jutting out into the sea.

promote *v.* **1.** help to make (something) happen or increase. **2.** raise to a higher rank or position. **3.** encourage the sale of by advertising. **promoter** *n.* person who organizes or finances an event etc. **promotion** *n.* **promotional** *adj.*

prompt *v.* **1.** cause (an action). **2.** remind (an actor or speaker) of words that he or she has forgotten. —*adj.* **3.** done without delay. —*adv.* **4.** exactly, e.g. *six o'clock prompt.* **promptly** *adv.* immediately, without delay. **promptness** *n.* **prompter** *n.* person offstage who prompts actors.

promulgate *v.* **1.** put (a law etc.) into effect by announcing it officially. **2.** make widely known. **promulgation** *n.* **promulgator** *n.*

prone *adj.* **1.** (foll. by *to*) likely to do or be affected by (something). **2.** lying face downwards.

prong *n.* one spike of a fork or similar instrument. **pronged** *adj.*

pronoun *n.* word, such as *she, it,* used to replace a noun. **pronominal** *adj.*

pronounce v. 1. form the sounds of (words or letters), esp. clearly or in a particular way. 2. declare formally or officially. **pronounceable** adj. **pronounced** adj. very noticeable. **pronouncement** n. formal announcement. **pronunciation** n. way in which a word or language is pronounced.
▷ Note the difference in spelling between *pronounce* and *pronunciation*. The pronunciation also changes from 'nown' to 'nun'.

pronto adv. Informal at once.

proof n. 1. evidence that shows that something is true or has happened. 2. copy of something printed, such as the pages of a book, for checking before final production. 3. Photog. trial print from a negative. —adj. 4. able to withstand, e.g. proof against criticism. 5. denoting the strength of an alcoholic drink, e.g. seventy proof. **proofread** v. read and correct (printer's proofs). **proofreader** n.

prop[1] v. **propping, propped. 1.** support (something) so that it stays upright or in place. —n. 2. pole, beam, etc. used as a support.

prop[2] n. movable object used on the set of a film or play.

prop[3] n. Informal propeller.

propaganda n. (organized promotion of) information to assist or damage the cause of a government or movement. **propagandist** n.

propagate v. 1. reproduce, breed, or grow. 2. spread (information and ideas). **propagation** n.

propane n. flammable gas found in petroleum and used as a fuel.

propel v. **-pelling, -pelled.** cause to move forward. **propellant** n. 1. something that provides or causes propulsion. 2. gas used in an aerosol spray. **propeller** n. revolving shaft with blades for driving a ship or aircraft. **propulsion** n. 1. propelling or being propelled. 2. method by which something is propelled.

propensity n., pl. **-ties.** natural tendency.

proper adj. 1. real or genuine. 2. appropriate. 3. suited to a particular purpose. 4. correct in behaviour. 5. excessively moral. 6. Informal complete. **properly** adv. **proper noun** name of a person or place, as in David or Iceland.

property n., pl. **-ties. 1.** something owned. 2. possessions collectively. 3. land or build-

ings owned by somebody. 4. quality or attribute.

prophet n. 1. person supposedly chosen by God to spread His word. 2. person who predicts the future. **prophetic** adj. **prophetically** adv. **prophecy** n., pl. **-cies. 1.** prediction. 2. message revealing God's will. **prophesy** v. **-sying, -sied.** foretell.
▷ Note the difference in spelling between the noun (*prophecy*) and the verb (*prophesy*).

prophylactic n., adj. (drug) used to prevent disease.

propinquity n. nearness in time, place, or relationship.

propitiate v. appease, win the favour of. **propitiation** n. **propitiatory** adj. intended to appease someone. **propitious** adj. favourable or auspicious.

proponent n. person who argues in favour of something.

proportion n. 1. relative size or extent. 2. correct relation between connected parts. 3. part considered with respect to the whole. —pl. 4. dimensions or size. —v. 5. adjust in relative amount or size. **in proportion 1.** comparable in size, rate of increase, etc. 2. without exaggerating. **proportional, proportionate** adj. being in proportion. **proportionally** adv. **proportional representation** representation of political parties in parliament in proportion to the votes they win.

propose v. 1. put forward for consideration. 2. nominate. 3. intend or plan (to do). 4. make an offer of marriage. **proposal** n. **proposition** n. 1. offer. 2. statement or assertion. 3. Maths theorem. 4. Informal thing to be dealt with. —v. 5. Informal ask (someone) to have sexual intercourse with one.

propound v. put forward for consideration.

proprietor n. owner of a business establishment. **proprietress** n. fem. **proprietary** adj. 1. made and distributed under a trade name. 2. denoting or suggesting ownership.

propriety n., pl. **-ties.** correct conduct.

propulsion n. see PROPEL.

pro rata adv., adj. Latin in proportion.

prorogue v. suspend (parliament) without dissolving it. **prorogation** n.

prosaic [pro-zay-ik] adj. lacking imagination, dull. **prosaically** adv.

proscenium *n., pl.* **-niums, -nia.** arch in a theatre separating the stage from the auditorium.

proscribe *v.* prohibit, outlaw. **proscription** *n.* **proscriptive** *adj.*

prose *n.* ordinary speech or writing in contrast to poetry.

prosecute *v.* **1.** bring a criminal charge against. **2.** continue to do. **prosecution** *n.* **prosecutor** *n.*

proselyte [**pross-ill-ite**] *n.* recent convert. **proselytize** [**pross-lll-lt-ize**] *v.* attempt to convert.

prosody [**pross-a-dee**] *n.* study of poetic metre and techniques. **prosodic** *adj.* **prosodist** *n.*

prospect *n.* **1.** something anticipated, e.g. *the prospect of defeat.* **2.** *Old-fashioned* view from a place. —*v.* **3.** probability of future success. —*v.* **4.** explore, esp. for gold. **prospective** *adj.* **1.** expected. **2.** future. **prospector** *n.* **prospectus** *n.* booklet giving details of a university, company, etc.

prosper *v.* be successful. **prosperity** *n.* success and wealth. **prosperous** *adj.*

prostate *n.* gland in male mammals that surrounds the neck of the bladder.

prosthesis [**pross-theess-iss**] *n., pl.* **-ses** [-seez] artificial body part, such as a limb or breast. **prosthetic** *adj.*

prostitute *n.* **1.** person who offers sexual intercourse in return for payment. —*v.* **2.** make a prostitute of. **3.** offer (oneself or one's talents) for unworthy purposes. **prostitution** *n.*

prostrate *adj.* **1.** lying face downwards. **2.** physically or emotionally exhausted. —*v.* **3.** lie face downwards. **4.** exhaust physically or emotionally. **prostration** *n.*

protagonist *n.* **1.** leading character in a play or a story. **2.** supporter of a cause.

protea [**pro-tee-a**] *n.* African shrub with showy flowers.

protean [**pro-tee-an**] *adj.* constantly changing.

protect *v.* defend from trouble, harm, or loss. **protection** *n.* **protectionism** *n.* policy of protecting industries by taxing competing imports. **protectionist** *n.* **protective** *adj.* **1.** giving protection, e.g. *protective clothing.* **2.** tending or wishing to protect someone. **protector** *n.* **1.** person or thing that protects. **2.** regent. **protectorate** *n.* **1.** territory largely controlled by a stronger state. **2.** (period of) rule of a regent.

protégé [**pro-ti-zhay**] *n.* person who is protected and helped by another. **protégée** *n. fem.*

protein *n.* any of a group of complex organic compounds that are essential for life.

pro tempore *adv., adj.* (*often shortened to* **pro tem**) for the time being.

protest *n.* **1.** declaration or demonstration of objection. —*v.* **2.** object, disagree. **3.** assert formally. **protester** *n.* **protestation** *n.* strong declaration.

▷ The verb *protest* is followed by *against* and then the noun. In American English it can be directly followed by a noun.

Protestant *adj.* **1.** of or relating to any of the Christian churches that split from the Roman Catholic Church in the sixteenth century. —*n.* **2.** member of a Protestant church. **Protestantism** *n.*

protium *n.* most common isotope of hydrogen.

proto- *combining form* first, e.g. *protohuman.*

protocol *n.* rules of behaviour for formal occasions.

proton *n.* positively charged particle in the nucleus of an atom.

protoplasm *n.* substance forming the living contents of a cell.

prototype *n.* original or model after which something is copied.

protozoan [**pro-toe-zoe-an**] *n., pl.* **-zoa.** microscopic one-celled creature.

protract *v.* lengthen or extend. **protracted** *adj.* **protraction** *n.* **protractor** *n.* instrument for measuring angles.

protrude *v.* stick out, project. **protrusion** *n.*

protuberant *adj.* swelling out, bulging. **protuberance** *n.*

proud *adj.* **1.** feeling pleasure and satisfaction. **2.** feeling honoured. **3.** thinking oneself superior to other people. **4.** dignified. **proudly** *adv.* **proud flesh** flesh growing around a healing wound.

prove *v.* **proving, proved, proved** *or* **proven. 1.** establish the validity of. **2.** demonstrate, test. **3.** be found to be. **proven** *adj.* known from experience to work.

provenance [**prov-in-anss**] *n.* place of origin.

provender n. Old-fashioned fodder.

proverb n. short saying that expresses a truth or gives a warning. **proverbial** adj.

provide v. 1. make available. 2. (foll. by for) take precautions (against). 3. support financially. **provider** n. **provided that, providing on condition that.**
▷ The usage is either providing on its own or provided that (not providing that).

providence n. God or nature seen as a protective force that arranges people's lives. **provident** adj. 1. thrifty. 2. showing foresight. **providential** adj. lucky. **providentially** adv.

province n. 1. area governed as a unit of a country or empire. 2. area of learning, activity, etc. —pl. 3. any part of a country outside the capital. **provincial** adj. 1. of a province or the provinces. 2. unsophisticated and narrow-minded. —n. 3. unsophisticated person. 4. person from a province or the provinces. **provincialism** n. narrow-mindedness and lack of sophistication.

provision n. 1. act of supplying something. 2. something supplied. 3. Law condition incorporated in a document. —pl. 4. food. —v. 5. supply with food. **provisional** adj. 1. temporary. 2. conditional. **provisionally** adv.

proviso [pro-vize-oh] n., pl. -sos, -soes. condition, stipulation.

provoke v. 1. deliberately anger. 2. cause (an adverse reaction). **provocation** n. **provocative** adj.

provost n. 1. head of certain university colleges. 2. chief councillor of a Scottish town. **provost marshal** head of military police.

prow n. bow of a vessel.

prowess n. 1. superior skill or ability. 2. bravery, fearlessness.

prowl v. 1. move stealthily around a place as if in search of prey or plunder. —n. 2. prowling. **prowler** n.

proximity n. 1. nearness in space or time. 2. nearness or closeness in a series. **proximate** adj.

proxy n., pl. **proxies**. 1. person authorized to act on behalf of someone else. 2. authority to act on behalf of someone else.

prude n. person who is excessively modest, prim, or proper. **prudish** adj. **prudery** n.

prudent adj. cautious, discreet, and sensible.

prudence n. **prudential** adj. Old-fashioned prudent.

prune[1] n. dried plum.

prune[2] v. 1. cut out dead parts or excessive branches from (a tree or plant). 2. shorten, reduce.

prurient adj. excessively interested in sexual matters. **prurience** n.

pry v. **prying, pried.** make an impertinent or uninvited inquiry into a private matter.

PS postscript.

psalm n. sacred song. **psalmist** n. writer of psalms. **psalmody** n. singing of sacred music.

Psalter n. book containing (a version of) psalms from the Bible. **psaltery** n., pl. -ries. ancient instrument played by plucking strings.

PSBR public sector borrowing requirement.

psephology [sef-fol-a-jee] n. statistical study of elections.

pseud n. Informal pretentious person.

pseudo- combining form false, pretending, or unauthentic, e.g. pseudo-intellectual.

pseudonym n. fictitious name adopted esp. by an author. **pseudonymous** adj.

psittacosis n. disease of parrots that can be transmitted to humans.

psoriasis [so-rye-a-siss] n. skin disease with reddish spots and patches covered with silvery scales.

psyche n. human mind or soul.

psychedelic adj. 1. denoting a drug that causes hallucinations. 2. having vivid colours and complex patterns similar to those experienced during hallucinations.

psychiatry n. branch of medicine concerned with mental disorders. **psychiatric** adj. **psychiatrist** n.

psychic adj. (also **psychical**) 1. having mental powers which cannot be explained by natural laws. 2. relating to the mind. —n. 3. person with psychic powers.

psycho n., pl. -chos. Informal psychopath.

psycho- combining form mind, mental processes, as in psychology, psychosomatic.

psychoanalysis n. method of treating mental and emotional disorders by discussion and analysis of one's thoughts and feelings. **psychoanalyse** v. **psychoanalyst** n.

psychology n., pl. **-gies. 1.** study of human and animal behaviour. **2.** *Informal* person's mental make-up. **psychologist** n. **psychological** adj. **1.** of psychology. **2.** of or affecting the mind. **psychological moment** most appropriate time for producing a desired effect. **psychological warfare** military application of psychology, esp. to influence morale in time of war.

psychopath n. person afflicted with a personality disorder causing him or her to commit antisocial or violent acts. **psychopathic** adj.

psychosis n., pl. **-choses.** severe mental disorder in which the sufferer's contact with reality becomes distorted. **psychotic** adj., n.

psychosomatic adj. (of a physical disorder) thought to have psychological causes.

psychotherapy n. treatment of nervous disorders by psychological methods. **psychotherapeutic** adj. **psychotherapist** n.

psych up v. prepare (oneself) mentally for a contest or task.

pt 1. part. **2.** past tense. **3.** point. **4.** port. **5.** pro tempore.

Pt *Chem.* platinum.

PT *Old-fashioned* physical training.

pt. pint.

PTA Parent-Teacher Association.

ptarmigan [tar-mig-an] n. bird of the grouse family which turns white in winter.

pterodactyl [terr-roe-dak-til] n. extinct flying reptile with batlike wings.

PTO please turn over.

ptomaine [toe-main] n. any of a group of poisonous alkaloids found in decaying matter.

Pu *Chem.* plutonium.

pub n. building with a bar licensed to sell alcoholic drinks.

puberty [pew-ber-tee] n. sexual maturity. **pubertal** adj.

pubescent adj. **1.** arriving or having arrived at puberty. **2.** covered with fine short hairs or down, as some plants and animals. **pubescence** n.

pubic [pew-bik] adj. of the lower abdomen, as in *pubic hair*.

pubis n., pl. **-bes.** one of the three sections of the hipbone that forms part of the pelvis.

public n. **1.** the community, people in gener-al. —adj. **2.** of or concerning the people as a whole. **3.** for use by everyone. **4.** well-known. **5.** performed or made openly. **publicly** adv. **publican** n. person who owns or runs a pub. **public company** limited company whose shares may be purchased by the public. **public house** pub. **public lending right** right of authors to receive payment when their books are borrowed from public libraries. **public relations** promotion of a favourable opinion towards an organization among the public. **public school** private fee-paying school in England. **public sector** part of a country's economy controlled and financially supported by the government. **public-spirited** adj. having or showing an active interest in the good of the community.

publicity n. **1.** process or information used to arouse public attention. **2.** public interest aroused. **publicize** v. advertise. **publicist** n. person who publicizes something, such as a press agent or journalist.

publish v. **1.** produce and issue (printed matter) for sale. **2.** announce formally or in public. **publication** n. **publisher** n.

puce adj. purplish-brown.

puck[1] n. small rubber disc used in ice hockey.

puck[2] n. mischievous or evil spirit. **puckish** adj.

pucker v. **1.** gather into wrinkles. —n. **2.** wrinkle or crease.

pudding n. **1.** dessert, esp. a cooked one served hot. **2.** savoury dish with pastry or batter, e.g. *steak-and-kidney pudding*. **3.** sausage-like mass of meat, e.g. *black pudding*.

puddle n. small pool of water, esp. of rain.

pudenda pl. n. human external genital organs, esp. of a female.

puerile adj. silly and childish.

puerperium [pure-peer-ee-um] n. period following childbirth. **puerperal** [pure-per-al] adj.

puff n. **1.** (sound of) a short blast of breath, wind, etc. **2.** instance of breathing in and out. **3.** act of inhaling cigarette smoke. —v. **4.** blow or breathe in short quick draughts. **5.** take draws at (a cigarette). **6.** send out in small clouds. **7.** swell. **out of puff** out of breath. **puffy** adj. **puffier, puffiest. puff adder** large venomous African viper. **puff-**

ball n. ball-shaped fungus. **puff pastry** light flaky pastry.

puffin n. black-and-white sea bird with a large brightly-coloured beak.

pug n. small snub-nosed dog. **pug nose** short stubby upturned nose.

pugilism [pew-jil-iz-zum] n. boxing. **pugilist** n. **pugilistic** adj.

pugnacious adj. ready and eager to fight. **pugnacity** n.

puissant [pew-iss-sant] adj. Poetic powerful. **puissance** n. showjumping competition that tests a horse's ability to jump large obstacles.

puke Slang —v. 1. vomit. —n. 2. act of vomiting. 3. vomited matter.

pukka, pucka adj. Anglo-Indian 1. properly done, constructed, etc. 2. genuine, real.

pulchritude n. Lit. beauty.

pule v. whine or whimper.

pull v. 1. exert force on (an object) to move it towards the source of the force. 2. move in a specified direction. 3. strain or stretch. 4. remove or extract. 5. attract. —n. 6. pulling. 7. force used in pulling. 8. act of taking in drink or smoke. 9. Informal power, influence. **pull oneself together** Informal regain one's self-control. **pull in** v. 1. (of a vehicle or driver) draw in to the side of the road or stop. 2. reach a destination. 3. attract in large numbers. 4. Slang arrest. **pull off** v. Informal succeed in performing. **pull out** v. 1. (of a vehicle or driver) move away from the side of the road or move out to overtake. 2. (of a train) depart. 3. withdraw. 4. remove by pulling. **pull through** v. survive or recover, esp. after a serious illness. **pull up** v. 1. (of a vehicle or driver) stop. 2. remove by the roots. 3. reprimand.

pullet n. young hen.

pulley n. wheel with a grooved rim in which a belt, chain, or piece of rope runs in order to lift weights by a downward pull.

Pullman n., pl. **-mans.** luxurious railway coach.

pullover n. sweater that is pulled on over the head.

pulmonary adj. of the lungs.

pulp n. 1. soft moist plant tissue, such as the material used to make paper. 2. flesh of a fruit. 3. any soft soggy mass. 4. poor-quality books and magazines. —v. 5. reduce to pulp.

pulpit n. raised platform for a preacher.

pulsar n. small dense star which emits regular bursts of radio waves.

pulse[1] n. 1. regular beating of blood through the arteries at each heartbeat which can be felt at the wrists and elsewhere. 2. any regular beat or vibration. **pulsate** v. throb, quiver. **pulsation** n.

pulse[2] n. edible seed of a pod-bearing plant such as a bean or pea.

pulverize v. 1. reduce to fine pieces. 2. destroy completely. **pulverization** n.

puma n. large American wild cat with a greyish-brown coat.

pumice [pumm-iss] n. light porous stone used for scouring.

pummel v. **-melling, -melled.** strike repeatedly with or as if with the fists.

pump[1] n. 1. machine used to force a liquid or gas to move in a particular direction. —v. 2. raise or drive with a pump. 3. supply in large amounts. 4. extract information from. 5. operate or work in the manner of a pump.

pump[2] n. light flat-soled shoe.

pumpernickel n. sour black bread made of coarse rye flour.

pumpkin n. large round fruit with an orange rind, soft flesh, and many seeds.

pun n. 1. use of words to exploit double meanings for humorous effect. —v. **punning, punned.** 2. make puns. **punster** n. person fond of making puns.

punch[1] v. 1. strike with a clenched fist. —n. 2. blow with a clenched fist. 3. Informal effectiveness or vigour. **punchy** adj. **punchier, punchiest.** **punch-drunk** adj. dazed by or as if by repeated blows to the head. **punch line** line of a joke or funny story that gives it its point. **punch-up** n. Informal fight or brawl.

punch[2] n. 1. tool or machine for shaping, piercing, or engraving. —v. 2. pierce, cut, stamp, shape, or drive with a punch.

punch[3] n. drink made from a mixture of wine, spirits, fruit, sugar, and spices.

punctilious adj. 1. paying great attention to correctness in etiquette. 2. careful about small details.

punctual adj. arriving or taking place at the correct time. **punctuality** n. **punctually** adv.

punctuate v. 1. put punctuation marks in. 2. interrupt at frequent intervals. **punctua-**

tion *n*. (use of) marks such as commas, colons, etc. in writing, to assist in making the sense clear.

puncture *n*. **1.** small hole made by a sharp object, esp. in a tyre. —*v*. **2.** pierce a hole in.

pundit *n*. expert who speaks publicly on a subject.

pungent *adj*. having a strong sharp bitter flavour. **pungency** *n*.

punish *v*. cause (someone) to suffer or undergo a penalty for some wrongdoing. **punishing** *adj*. harsh or difficult. **punishment** *n*. **punitive** [pew-nit-tiv] *adj*. relating to punishment.

punk *n*. **1.** anti-Establishment youth movement and style of rock music of the late 1970s. **2.** follower of this music. **3.** worthless person.

punkah *n*. fan made of palm leaves.

punnet *n*. small basket for fruit.

punt[1] *n*. **1.** open flat-bottomed boat propelled by a pole. —*v*. **2.** travel in a punt.

punt[2] *Sport* —*v*. **1.** kick (a ball) before it touches the ground when dropped from the hands. —*n*. **2.** such a kick.

punt[3] *n*. monetary unit of the Irish Republic.

punter *n*. **1.** person who bets. **2.** any member of the public.

puny *adj*. **-nier, -niest.** small and feeble.

pup *n*. young of certain animals, such as dogs and seals.

pupa [pew-pa] *n*., *pl*. **-pae, -pas.** insect at the stage of development between a larva and an adult. **pupal** *adj*.

pupil[1] *n*. person who is taught by a teacher.

pupil[2] *n*. round dark opening in the centre of the eye.

puppet *n*. **1.** small doll or figure moved by strings or by the operator's hand. **2.** person or country controlled by another. **puppeteer** *n*.

puppy *n*., *pl*. **-pies.** young dog. **puppy fat** fatty tissue in a child or adolescent, usu. disappearing with maturity.

purblind *adj*. partly or nearly blind.

purchase *v*. **1.** obtain by payment. —*n*. **2.** buying. **3.** what is bought. **4.** leverage, grip. **purchaser** *n*.

purdah *n*. Muslim and Hindu custom of keeping women in seclusion, with clothing that conceals them completely when they go out.

pure *adj*. **1.** unmixed, untainted. **2.** faultless. **3.** innocent. **4.** complete, e.g. *pure delight.* **5.** concerned with theory only, e.g. *pure mathematics.* **purely** *adv*. **purity** *n*. **purify** *v*. **-fying, -fied.** make or become pure. **purification** *n*. **purist** *n*. person obsessed with strict obedience to the traditions of a subject.

purée [pure-ray] *n*. **1.** pulp of cooked food. —*v*. **-réing, -réed. 2.** make into a purée.

purgatory *n*. **1.** place or state of temporary suffering. **2.** (P-) *RC Church* place where souls of the dead undergo punishment for their sins before being admitted to Heaven. **purgatorial** *adj*.

purge *v*. **1.** rid (a thing or place) of (unwanted things or people). —*n*. **2.** purging. **purgation** *n*. **purgative** *adj*., *n*. (medicine) designed to cause defecation.

Puritan *n*. **1.** *Hist*. member of the English Protestant group who wanted simpler church ceremonies. **2.** (p-) person with strict moral and religious principles. **puritanical** *adj*. **puritanism** *n*.

purl[1] *n*. **1.** stitch made by knitting a plain stitch backwards. —*v*. **2.** knit in purl.

purl[2] *v*. (of a stream) flow with a burbling sound.

purlieus [per-lyooz] *pl. n*. *Lit*. outskirts.

purloin *v*. steal.

purple *adj*. of a colour between red and blue.

purport *v*. **1.** claim (to be or do something). —*n*. **2.** apparent meaning, significance.

purpose *n*. **1.** reason for which something is done or exists. **2.** determination. **3.** practical advantage or use, e.g. *use the time to good purpose.* —*v*. **4.** *Old-fashioned* intend. **purposeful** *adj*. with a definite purpose, determined. **purposely** *adv*. (also **on purpose**) intentionally.

purr *n*. **1.** low vibrant sound that a cat makes when pleased. —*v*. **2.** make this sound.

purse *n*. **1.** small bag for money. **2.** *US* handbag. **3.** financial resources. **4.** prize money. —*v*. **5.** draw (one's lips) together into a small round shape. **purser** *n*. ship's officer who keeps the accounts.

pursue *v*. **1.** chase. **2.** follow (a goal). **3.** engage in. **4.** continue to discuss or ask about (something). **pursuer** *n*. **pursuit** *n*. **1.** pursuing. **2.** occupation. **pursuance** *n*. carrying out.

purulent [**pure**-yoo-lent] *adj.* of or containing pus. **purulence** *n.*

purvey *v.* supply (provisions). **purveyance** *n.* **purveyor** *n.*

purview *n.* scope or range of activity or outlook.

pus *n.* yellowish matter produced by infected tissue.

push *v.* **1.** move or try to move by steady force. **2.** drive or spur (oneself or another person) to do something. **3.** *Informal* sell (drugs) illegally. —*n.* **4.** pushing. **5.** special effort. **the push** *Slang* **1.** dismissal from a job. **2.** ending of a relationship. **pusher** *n.* person who sells illegal drugs. **pushy** *adj.* **pushier, pushiest.** too assertive or ambitious. **push-bike** *n. Informal* bicycle. **pushchair** *n.* collapsible chair-shaped carriage for a baby. **pushover** *n. Informal* **1.** something easily achieved. **2.** person or team easily taken advantage of or defeated.

pusillanimous *adj.* cowardly. **pusillanimity** *n.*

puss, pussy *n., pl.* **pusses, pussies.** cat.

pussyfoot *v. Informal* behave too cautiously.

pustule *n.* pimple containing pus. **pustular** *adj.*

put *v.* **putting, put. 1.** cause to be (in a position, state, or place). **2.** express. **3.** throw (the shot) in the shot put. —*n.* **4.** throw in putting the shot. **put about** *v.* make widely known. **put across** *v.* express successfully. **put down** *v.* **1.** make a written record of. **2.** repress, e.g. *put down a rebellion.* **3.** put (an animal) to death. **4.** *Slang* belittle or humiliate. **put-down** *n.* cruelly crushing remark. **put off** *v.* **1.** postpone. **2.** disconcert. **3.** repel. **put over** *v. Informal* communicate (facts or information). **put up** *v.* **1.** erect. **2.** accommodate. **3.** nominate. **put-upon** *adj.* taken advantage of.

putative [**pew**-tat-iv] *adj.* reputed, supposed.

putrid *adj.* rotten and foul-smelling. **putrefy** *v.* **-fying, -fied.** rot and produce an offensive smell. **putrefaction** *n.* **putrescent** *adj.* **1.** becoming putrid. **2.** rotting.

putsch *n.* sudden violent attempt to remove a government from power.

putt *Golf* —*n.* **1.** stroke on the green with a putter to roll the ball into or near the hole. —*v.* **2.** strike (the ball) in this way. **putter** *n.* golf club with a short shaft for putting.

puttee *n.* strip of cloth worn wound around the leg from the ankle to the knee.

putty *n.* paste used to fix glass into frames and fill cracks in woodwork.

puzzle *v.* **1.** perplex and confuse or be perplexed or confused. —*n.* **2.** problem that cannot be easily solved. **3.** toy, game, or question that requires skill or ingenuity to solve. **puzzlement** *n.* **puzzling** *adj.*

PVC polyvinyl chloride: synthetic thermoplastic material.

pyaemia, pyemia *n.* blood poisoning.

Pygmy *n., pl.* **-mies. 1.** member of one of the dwarf peoples of Equatorial Africa. —*adj.* **2.** (p-) very small.

pyjamas *pl. n.* loose-fitting trousers and top worn in bed.

pylon *n.* steel tower-like structure supporting electrical cables.

pyorrhoea [pire-**ree**-a] *n.* disease of the gums and tooth sockets which causes bleeding of the gums and the formation of pus.

pyramid *n.* **1.** solid figure with a flat base and triangular sides sloping upwards to a point. **2.** structure of this shape, esp. an ancient Egyptian one. **pyramidal** *adj.*

pyre *n.* pile of wood for burning a corpse on.

Pyrex *n.* ® heat-resistant glassware.

pyrites [pie-**rite**-eez] *n.* sulphide of a metal, esp. iron pyrites.

pyromania *n.* uncontrollable urge to set things on fire. **pyromaniac** *n.*

pyrotechnics *n.* **1.** art of making fireworks. **2.** firework display. **pyrotechnic** *adj.*

Pyrrhic victory [**pir**-ik] *n.* victory in which the victor's losses are as great as those of the defeated.

python *n.* large nonpoisonous snake that crushes its prey.

pyx *n. Christianity* vessel in which the consecrated Host is preserved.

Q

QC Queen's Counsel.

QED which was to be shown or proved.

QLD Queensland.

QM Quartermaster.

qr. 1. quarter. 2. quire.

qt. quart.

q.t. *n.* on the q.t. *Informal* secretly.

qua [kwah] *prep.* in the capacity of.

quack[1] *v.* 1. (of a duck) utter a harsh guttural sound. 2. make a noise like a duck. —*n.* 3. sound made by a duck.

quack[2] *n.* 1. unqualified person who claims medical knowledge. 2. *Informal* doctor. **quackery** *n.*

quad *n.* 1. short for QUADRANGLE. 2. *Informal* quadruplet. —*adj.* 3. short for QUADRAPHONIC.

quadrangle *n.* 1. rectangular courtyard with buildings on all four sides. 2. geometric figure consisting of four points connected by four lines. **quadrangular** *adj.*

quadrant *n.* 1. quarter of a circle. 2. quarter of a circle's circumference. 3. instrument for measuring the altitude of the stars.

quadraphonic *adj.* using four independent channels to reproduce or record sound.

quadratic *Maths* —*n.* 1. equation in which the variable is raised to the power of two, but nowhere raised to a higher power. —*adj.* 2. of the second power.

quadrennial *adj.* 1. occurring every four years. 2. lasting four years.

quadri- *combining form* four, e.g. *quadrilateral.*

quadrilateral *adj.* 1. having four sides. —*n.* 2. polygon with four sides.

quadrille *n.* square dance for four couples.

quadriplegia *n.* paralysis of all four limbs. **quadriplegic** *adj.*

quadruped [kwod-roo-ped] *n.* any animal with four legs.

quadruple *v.* 1. multiply by four. —*adj.* 2. four times as much or as many. 3. consisting of four parts.

quadruplet *n.* one of four offspring born at one birth.

quaff [kwoff] *v.* drink heartily or in one draught.

quagga *n., pl.* **-ga, -gas.** recently extinct zebra, striped only on the head and shoulders.

quagmire [kwog-mire] *n.* soft wet area of land.

quail[1] *n., pl.* **quail, quails.** small game bird of the partridge family.

quail[2] *v.* shrink back with fear.

quaint *adj.* attractively unusual, esp. in an old-fashioned style. **quaintly** *adv.* **quaintness** *n.*

quake *v.* 1. shake or tremble with or as if with fear. —*n.* 2. *Informal* earthquake.

Quaker *n.* member of a Christian sect, the Society of Friends. **Quakerism** *n.*

qualify *v.* **-fying, -fied.** 1. provide or be provided with the abilities necessary for a task, office, or duty. 2. moderate or restrict (something, esp. a statement). 3. to be classified as, e.g. *their romance hardly qualifies as news.* 4. reach the later stages of a competition, as by being successful in earlier rounds. 5. *Grammar* to modify the sense of a word. **qualified** *adj.* **qualifier** *n.* **qualification** *n.* 1. quality or skill needed for a particular activity. 2. condition that modifies or limits. 3. act of qualifying.

quality *n., pl.* **-ties.** 1. degree or standard of excellence. 2. distinguishing characteristic or attribute. 3. basic character or nature of something. —*adj.* 4. excellent or superior. 5. (of a newspaper) concentrating on detailed and serious accounts of the news, business affairs and the arts. **qualitative** *adj.* of or relating to quality. **quality control** checking of the relative quality of products, usually by testing samples.

qualm [kwahm] *n.* 1. pang of conscience. 2. sudden sensation of misgiving.

quandary *n., pl.* **-ries.** difficult situation or dilemma.

quango *n., pl.* **-gos.** quasi-autonomous nongovernmental organization: any partly independent official body set up by a government.

quanta n. plural of QUANTUM.

quantify v. -**fying**, -**fied**. discover or express the quantity of. **quantifiable** adj. **quantification** n.

quantity n., pl. -**ties**. 1. specified or definite amount or number. 2. aspect of anything that can be measured, weighed, or counted. 3. large amount. **quantitative** adj. of or relating to quantity. **quantity surveyor** person who estimates the cost of the materials and labour necessary for a construction job.

quantum n., pl. -**ta**. 1. desired or required amount, esp. a very small one. 2. Physics smallest amount of some physical property, such as energy, that a system can possess. **quantum jump, leap** Informal sudden large change, increase or advance. **quantum theory** physics theory based on the idea that energy of electrons is discharged in discrete quanta.

quarantine n. 1. period of isolation of people or animals to prevent the spread of disease. —v. 2. isolate in or as if in quarantine.

quark¹ n. Physics subatomic particle thought to be the fundamental unit of matter.

quark² n. low-fat soft cheese.

quarrel n. 1. angry disagreement. 2. cause of dispute. —v. -**relling**, -**relled**. 3. have a disagreement or dispute. **quarrelsome** adj.

quarry¹ n., pl. -**ries**. 1. place where stone is dug from the surface of the earth. —v. -**rying**, -**ried**. 2. extract (stone) from a quarry. **quarry tile** unglazed floor tile.

quarry² n., pl. -**ries**. person or animal that is being hunted.

quart n. unit of liquid measure equal to two pints.

quarter n. 1. one of four equal parts of something. 2. fourth part of a year. 3. Informal unit of weight equal to 4 ounces. 4. region or district of a town or city. 5. US 25-cent piece. 6. mercy or pity, as shown towards a defeated opponent. 7. either of two phases of the moon when it appears as a semicircle. 8. (sometimes pl.) unspecified people or group of people, e.g. the highest quarters. —pl. 9. lodgings. —v. 10. divide into four equal parts. 11. billet or be billeted in lodgings. **quarterly** adj. 1. occurring, due, or issued at intervals of three months. —n., pl. -**lies**. 2. magazine issued every three

months. —adv. 3. once every three months. **quarterback** n. player in American football who directs attacking play. **quarter day** any of the four days in the year when certain payments become due. **quarterdeck** n. Naut. rear part of the upper deck of a ship. **quarterfinal** n. round before the semifinal in a competition. **quarterlight** n. small triangular window in the door of a car. **quartermaster** n. military officer responsible for accommodation, food, and equipment.

quartet n. 1. group of four performers. 2. music for such a group. 3. any group of four people or things.

quarto n., pl. -**tos**. book size in which the sheets are folded into four leaves.

quartz n. hard glossy mineral. **quartz clock, watch** very accurate clock or watch operated by a vibrating crystal of quartz.

quasar [kway-zar] n. extremely distant starlike object that emits powerful radio waves.

quash v. 1. annul or make void. 2. subdue forcefully and completely.

quasi- [kway-zie] combining form almost but not really, e.g. quasi-religious, a quasi-scholar.

quassia [kwosh-a] n. tropical American tree, the wood of which yields a substance used in insecticides.

quaternary adj. having four parts.

quatrain n. stanza or poem of four lines.

quatrefoil n. 1. leaf composed of four leaflets. 2. Archit. carved ornament having four arcs arranged about a common centre.

quaver v. 1. (of a voice) quiver or tremble. —n. 2. Music note half the length of a crotchet. 3. tremulous sound or note.

quay [kee] n. wharf built parallel to the shore.

queasy adj. -**sier**, -**siest**. 1. having the feeling that one is about to vomit. 2. feeling or causing uneasiness. **queasily** adv. **queasiness** n.

queen n. 1. female sovereign who is the official ruler or head of state. 2. wife of a king. 3. woman, place, or thing considered to be the best of her or its kind. 4. Slang effeminate male homosexual. 5. only fertile female in a colony of bees, wasps, or ants. 6. the most powerful piece in chess. **queen it** Informal behave in an overbearing manner. **queenly** adj. **Queen Mother** widow of a former king who is also the mother of the current monarch. **Queen's Counsel** barrister or advocate appointed Counsel to the Crown.

Queensberry rules *pl. n.* **1.** code of rules followed in modern boxing. **2.** *Informal* gentlemanly conduct, esp. in a dispute.

queer *adj.* **1.** not normal or usual. **2.** dubious or suspicious. **3.** faint, giddy, or queasy. **4.** *Offens.* homosexual. —*n.* **5.** *Offens.* homosexual. **queer someone's pitch** *Informal* spoil someone's chances of something. **in queer street** *Informal* in debt or facing bankruptcy.

quell *v.* **1.** suppress. **2.** overcome.

quench *v.* **1.** satisfy (one's thirst). **2.** put out or extinguish.

quern *n.* stone hand mill for grinding corn.

querulous [**kwer**-yoo-luss] *adj.* complaining or peevish. **querulously** *adv.*

query *n., pl.* **-ries. 1.** question, esp. one raising doubt. **2.** question mark. —*v.* **-rying, -ried. 3.** express uncertainty, doubt, or an objection concerning (something).

quest *n.* **1.** long and difficult search. —*v.* **2.** (foll. by *for* or *after*) go in search of.

question *n.* **1.** form of words addressed to a person in order to obtain an answer. **2.** point at issue. **3.** difficulty or uncertainty. —*v.* **4.** put a question or questions to (a person). **5.** express uncertainty about. **in question** under discussion. **out of the question** impossible. **questionable** *adj.* of disputable value or authority. **questionably** *adv.* **questionnaire** *n.* set of questions on a form, used to collect information from people. **question mark 1.** punctuation mark (?) written at the end of questions. **2.** a doubt or uncertainty, e.g. *a question mark still hangs over the success of the project.* **question master** chairman of a radio or television quiz or panel game. **question time** in a parliament, period when MPs can question government ministers.

queue *n.* **1.** line of people or vehicles waiting for something. —*v.* **queueing** *or* **queuing, queued. 2.** (often foll. by *up*) form or remain in a line while waiting.

quibble *v.* **1.** make trivial objections. —*n.* **2.** trivial objection.

quiche [keesh] *n.* savoury flan with an egg custard filling to which vegetables etc. are added.

quick *adj.* **1.** lasting or taking a short time. **2.** speedy, fast. **3.** alert and responsive. **4.**

easily excited or aroused. —*n.* **5.** area of sensitive flesh under a nail. —*adv.* **6.** *Informal* in a rapid manner. **cut someone to the quick** hurt someone's feelings deeply. **quickly** *adv.* **quicken** *v.* **1.** make or become faster. **2.** make or become more lively. **3.** (of a fetus) reach the stage of development where its movements can be felt. **quickie** *n. Informal* anything done or made hurriedly. **quicklime** *n.* white solid used in the manufacture of glass and steel. **quicksand** *n.* deep mass of loose wet sand that sucks anything on top of it into it. **quicksilver** *n.* mercury. **quickstep** *n.* fast modern ballroom dance.

quid[1] *n., pl.* **quid.** *Brit. slang* pound (sterling).

quid[2] *n.* piece of tobacco for chewing.

quid pro quo *n., pl.* **quid pro quos.** one thing, esp. an advantage or object, given in exchange for another.

quiescent [kwee-**ess**-ent] *adj.* quiet, inactive, or dormant. **quiescence** *n.*

quiet *adj.* **1.** with little noise. **2.** calm or tranquil. **3.** untroubled. **4.** private or low-key. —*n.* **5.** quietness. —*v.* **6.** make or become quiet. **on the quiet** without other people knowing, secretly. **quietly** *adv.* **quietness** *n.* **quieten** *v.* (often foll. by *down*) make or become quiet. **quietude** *n.* quietness, peace, or tranquillity.

quietism *n.* passivity and calmness of mind towards external events. **quietist** *n., adj.*

quietus *n.* **1.** release from life; death. **2.** discharge or settlement of debts or duties.

quiff *n.* tuft of hair brushed up above the forehead.

quill *n.* **1.** pen made from the feather of a bird's wing or tail. **2.** stiff hollow spine of a hedgehog or porcupine. **3.** large stiff feather in a bird's wing or tail.

quilt *n.* padded covering for a bed. **quilted** *adj.* consisting of two layers of fabric with a layer of soft material between them.

quin *n.* short for QUINTUPLET.

quince *n.* acid-tasting pear-shaped fruit.

quinine *n.* bitter drug used as a tonic and formerly to treat malaria.

quinquennial *adj.* **1.** occurring every five years. **2.** lasting five years.

quinquereme *n.* ancient Roman galley with five banks of oars.

quinsy *n.* inflammation of the throat or tonsils.

quintessence *n.* most perfect representation of a quality or state. **quintessential** *adj.*

quintet *n.* **1.** group of five performers. **2.** music for such a group.

quintuple *v.* **1.** multiply by five. —*adj.* **2.** five times as much or as many; fivefold. **3.** consisting of five parts. —*n.* **4.** quantity or number five times as great as another.

quintuplet *n.* one of five offspring born at one birth.

quip *n.* **1.** witty saying. —*v.* **quipping, quipped. 2.** make a quip.

quire *n.* set of 24 or 25 sheets of paper.

quirk *n.* **1.** peculiarity of character. **2.** unexpected twist or turn, e.g. *a quirk of fate.* **quirky** *adj.* **quirkier, quirkiest.**

quisling *n.* traitor who aids an occupying enemy force.

quit *v.* **quitting, quit. 1.** depart from. **2.** give up (a job). **3.** *Chiefly US* stop (doing something). **quitter** *n.* person who lacks perseverance. **quits** *adj. Informal* on an equal footing.

quitch grass *n.* same as COUCH GRASS.

quite *adv.* **1.** absolutely, e.g. *you're quite right.* **2.** somewhat, e.g. *she's quite pretty.* **3.** in actuality, truly. —*interj.* **4.** expression of agreement.
▷ Note that because *quite* can mean 'extremely': *quite amazing;* or can express a reservation: *quite friendly,* it should be used carefully.

quiver[1] *v.* **1.** shake with a tremulous movement. —*n.* **2.** shaking or trembling.

quiver[2] *n.* case for arrows.

quixotic [kwik-**sot**-ik] *adj.* romantic and unrealistic. **quixotically** *adv.*

quiz *n., pl.* **quizzes. 1.** entertainment in which the knowledge of the players is tested by a series of questions. —*v.* **quizzing,**

quizzed. 2. investigate by close questioning. **quizzical** *adj.* questioning and mocking, e.g. *a quizzical look.* **quizzically** *adv.*

quod *n. Brit. slang* jail.

quoin *n.* **1.** external corner of a building. **2.** small wedge.

quoit *n.* **1.** large ring used in the game of quoits. —*pl.* **2.** game in which quoits are tossed at a stake in the ground in attempts to encircle it.

quondam *adj.* of an earlier time; former.

quorum *n.* minimum number of people required to be present at a meeting before any transactions can take place. **quorate** *adj.* having or being a quorum.

quota *n.* **1.** share that is due from, due to, or allocated to a group or person. **2.** prescribed number or quantity allowed, required, or admitted.

quote *v.* **1.** repeat (words) exactly from (an earlier work, speech, or conversation). **2.** state (a price) for goods or a job of work. —*n.* **3.** *Informal* quotation. **quotable** *adj.* **quotation** *n.* **1.** written or spoken passage repeated exactly in a later work, speech, or conversation. **2.** act of quoting. **3.** estimate of costs submitted by a contractor to a prospective client. **quotation marks** raised commas used in writing to mark the beginning and end of a quotation or passage of speech.

quoth *v. Obs.* said.

quotidian *adj.* **1.** daily. **2.** commonplace.

quotient *n.* result of the division of one number or quantity by another.

Quran *n.* same as KORAN.

q.v. used to refer a reader to another item in the same book, which (word, item, etc.) see.

qwerty, QWERTY keyboard *n.* standard English language typewriter or computer keyboard.

R

r 1. radius. **2.** ratio. **3.** right.

R 1. Queen. **2.** King. **3.** River.

Ra *Chem.* radium.

RA 1. Royal Academy. **2.** Royal Artillery.

rabbet *n.* **1.** groove cut into a piece of timber into which another piece fits —*v.* **2.** cut a rabbet in. **3.** join (pieces of wood) with a rabbet.

rabbi [rab-bye] *n., pl.* **-bis.** Jewish spiritual leader. **rabbinical** *adj.*

rabbit *n.* small burrowing mammal with long ears. **go rabbiting** hunt rabbits. **rabbit on** *v.* **rabbiting, rabbited.** *Informal* talk too much.

rabble *n.* disorderly crowd of noisy people. **rabble-rouser** *n.* person who stirs up the feelings of the mob.

Rabelaisian *adj.* characterized by broad, often bawdy humour and sharp satire.

rabid *adj.* **1.** fanatical. **2.** having rabies. **rabidly** *adv.*

rabies [ray-beez] *n.* usually fatal viral disease transmitted by dogs and certain other animals.

RAC Royal Automobile Club.

raccoon *n.* small N American mammal with a long striped tail.

race¹ *n.* **1.** contest of speed. **2.** any competition or rivalry, e.g. *the arms race.* **3.** rapid current or channel. —*pl.* **4.** meeting for horse racing. —*v.* **5.** compete with in a race. **6.** run swiftly. **7.** (of an engine) run faster than normal. **racer** *n.* **racecourse** *n.* **racehorse** *n.* **racetrack** *n.*

race² *n.* group of people of common ancestry with distinguishing physical features, such as skin colour. **racial** *adj.*

raceme [rass-eem] *n.* cluster of flowers along a central stem, as in the foxglove.

racism, racialism *n.* hostile attitude or behaviour to members of other races, based on a belief in the innate superiority of one's own race. **racist, racialist** *adj., n.*

rack¹ *n.* **1.** framework for holding particular articles, such as coats or luggage. **2.** straight bar with teeth on its edge, to work with a cogwheel. **3.** *Hist.* instrument of torture that stretched the victim's body. —*v.* **4.** cause great suffering to. **rack one's brains** try very hard to remember. **rack-rent** *n.* extortionate rent.

rack² *n.* **go to rack and ruin** be destroyed.

rack³ *v.* clear (wine, beer etc.) by siphoning it off from the dregs.

racket¹ *n.* **1.** noisy disturbance, din. **2.** occupation by which money is made illegally. **3.** *Slang* business or occupation. —*v.* **racketing, racketed.** **4.** (often foll. by *about* or *around*) make a commotion.

racket², racquet *n.* bat with strings stretched in an oval frame, used in tennis etc. **rackets** *n.* ball game played in a paved walled court.

racketeer *n.* person making illegal profits. **racketeering** *n.*

raconteur [rak-on-tur] *n.* skilled storyteller.

racoon *n.* same as RACCOON.

racy *adj.* **racier, raciest. 1.** slightly shocking. **2.** spirited or lively. **racily** *adv.* **raciness** *n.*

radar *n.* device for tracking distant objects by bouncing high-frequency radio pulses off them.

raddled *adj.* (of a person) unkempt or run-down in appearance.

radial *adj.* **1.** emanating from a common central point. **2.** of a radius. **3.** (also **radial-ply**) (of a tyre) having flexible sidewalls strengthened with radial cords.

radian *n.* unit for measuring angles, equal to 57.296°.

radiant *adj.* **1.** looking happy. **2.** shining. **3.** emitted as radiation, e.g. *radiant heat.* **4.** emitting radiation. **radiantly** *adv.* **radiance** *n.*

radiate *v.* **1.** emit or be emitted as radiation. **2.** spread out from a centre. **radiator** *n.* **1.** arrangement of pipes containing hot water or steam to heat a room. **2.** tubes containing water as cooling apparatus for a car engine.

radiation *n.* **1.** transmission of heat or light from one body to another. **2.** particles or rays emitted in nuclear decay. **3.** process of radiating. **radiation sickness** illness caused by overexposure to radioactive material or x-rays.

radical adj. **1.** fundamental. **2.** thorough. **3.** advocating fundamental change. —n. **4.** person advocating fundamental (political) change. **5.** number expressed as the root of another. **6.** group of atoms which acts as a unit during chemical reactions. **radically** adv. **radicalism** n.

radicle n. small or developing root.

radii n. a plural of RADIUS.

radio n., pl. **-dios. 1.** use of electromagnetic waves for broadcasting, communication, etc. **2.** device for receiving and amplifying radio signals. **3.** sound broadcasting. —v. **4.** transmit (a message) by radio. —adj. **5.** of, relating to, or using radio, e.g. radio drama. **radio-controlled** adj. controlled by signals sent by radio. **radio telephone** telephone which sends and receives messages using radio waves rather than wires. **radio telescope** instrument which picks up and analyses radio signals from space.

radio- combining form of rays, radiation, or radium.

radioactive adj. emitting radiation as a result of nuclear decay. **radioactivity** n.

radiocarbon n. radioactive form of carbon used in calculating the age of very old objects.

radiography [ray-dee-og-ra-fee] n. production of an image on a film or plate by radiation. **radiographer** n.

radioisotope n. radioactive isotope.

radiology [ray-dee-ol-a-jee] n. science of using x-rays in medicine. **radiologist** n.

radiotherapy n. treatment of disease, esp. cancer, by radiation. **radiotherapist** n.

radish n. small hot-flavoured root vegetable eaten raw in salads.

radium n. radioactive metallic element.

radius n., pl. **radii, radiuses. 1.** (length of) a straight line from the centre to the circumference of a circle. **2.** outer of two bones in the forearm. **3.** circular area of a specified size round a central point, e.g. police evacuated everyone within a two-mile radius.

radon [ray-don] n. radioactive gaseous element.

RAF Royal Air Force.

raffia n. prepared palm fibre for weaving mats etc.

raffish adj. disreputable.

raffle n. **1.** lottery with an article as a prize. —v. **2.** offer as a prize in a raffle.

raft n. floating platform of logs, planks, etc.

rafter n. one of the main beams of a roof.

rag^1 n. **1.** fragment of cloth. **2.** torn piece. **3.** Informal newspaper. —pl. **4.** tattered clothing. **from rags to riches** from being extremely poor to being extremely wealthy. **ragged** [rag-gid] adj. **1.** torn. **2.** dressed in shabby or torn clothes. **3.** lacking smoothness. **ragbag** n. confused assortment, jumble. **ragtime** n. style of jazz piano music.

rag^2 v. **ragging, ragged. 1.** tease. **2.** play practical jokes on. —n. **3.** carnival with processions etc., organized by students to raise money for charities.

ragamuffin n. ragged dirty child.

rage n. **1.** violent anger or passion. —v. **2.** speak or act with fury. **3.** proceed violently and without check, e.g. a storm was raging. **all the rage** very popular.

raglan adj. (of a sleeve) joined to a garment by diagonal seams from the neck to the underarm.

ragout [rag-goo] n. richly seasoned stew of meat and vegetables.

raid n. **1.** sudden surprise attack or search. —v. **2.** make a raid on. **3.** sneak into (a place) in order to steal. **raider** n.

rail^1 n. **1.** horizontal bar, esp. as part of a fence or track. **2.** railway. **go off the rails** start behaving eccentrically or improperly. **railing** n. fence made of rails supported by posts. **railcard** n. card which pensioners, young people, etc. can buy, entitling them to cheaper rail travel. **railroad** n. **1.** US railway. —v. **2.** Informal force (a person) into an action with haste or by unfair means. **railway** n. **1.** track of iron rails on which trains run. **2.** company operating a railway.

rail^2 v. (foll. by at or against) complain bitterly or loudly. **raillery** n. teasing or joking.

rail^3 n. small marsh bird.

raiment n. Obs. clothing.

rain n. **1.** water falling in drops from the clouds. **2.** large quantity of anything falling rapidly. —v. **3.** fall or pour down as rain. **the rains** season in the tropics when there is a lot of rain. **rainy** adj. **rainier, rainiest.**

rainy day future time of need, esp. financial need. **rainbow** n. arch of colours in the sky. **rainbow trout** freshwater trout with black spots and two red stripes. **raincoat** n. water-resistant overcoat. **rainfall** n. amount of rain. **rainforest** n. dense forest in the tropics.

raise v. 1. lift up. 2. set upright. 3. build. 4. increase in amount or intensity. 5. bring up (a family). 6. put forward for consideration. 7. collect or levy. 8. end, e.g. *raise a siege.* —n. 9. *US* increase in pay, rise. **raised** adj. higher than the surrounding area.

raisin n. dried grape.

raison d'être [ray-zon **det**-ra] n., pl. **raisons d'être** [ray-zon **det**-ra] *French* reason or justification for existence.

raita [rye-ta] n. Indian dish of chopped cucumber, mint, etc., in yoghurt, served with curries.

Raj n. **the Raj** former British rule in India.

rajah, raja n. *Hist.* Indian prince or ruler.

rake[1] n. 1. tool with a long handle and a crosspiece with teeth, used for smoothing earth or gathering leaves, hay, etc. —v. 2. gather or smooth with a rake. 3. search (through). 4. sweep (with gunfire). **rake it in** *Informal* make a large amount of money. **rake-off** n. *Slang* share of profits, esp. illegal. **rake up** v. revive memories of (a forgotten unpleasant event).

rake[2] n. dissolute or immoral man. **rakish** adj.

rake[3] n. 1. slope, esp. backwards, of a ship's funnel etc. —v. 2. incline from perpendicular. **raked** adj. (of the floor in a theatre etc.) sloping so that it is higher at the back than the front.

rakish [ray-kish] adj. dashing or jaunty.

rally[1] v. **-lying, -lied. 1.** bring or come together after dispersal or for a common cause. **2.** regain health or strength, revive. —n., pl. **-lies. 3.** large gathering of people for a (political) meeting. **4.** car-driving competition on public roads. **5.** *Tennis* lively exchange of strokes. **rally round** v. group together to help someone.

rally[2] v. **-lying, -lied.** mock or tease (someone) in a good-natured way.

ram n. 1. male sheep. 2. hydraulic machine. —v. **ramming, rammed. 3.** force or drive. 4. strike against with force. 5. cram or stuff. **ram (something) down someone's throat**

put forward or emphasize (an idea or argument) with excessive force.

RAM *Computers* random access memory.

Ramadan n. 1. 9th Muslim month. 2. strict fasting from dawn to dusk observed during this time.

ramble v. 1. walk without a definite route. 2. talk incoherently. —n. 3. walk, esp. in the country. **rambler** n. 1. climbing rose. 2. person who rambles. **rambling** adj. 1. (of speech or writing) confused and long-winded. 2. irregularly shaped; large and formless. —n. 3. activity of going for long walks in the country.

ramekin [ram-ik-in] n. small ovenproof dish for a single serving of food.

ramify v. **-ifying, -ified. 1.** become complex. 2. spread in branches, subdivide. **ramification** n. consequence.

ramp n. 1. slope joining two level surfaces. 2. place where the level of a road surface changes because of road works. 3. mobile stairs by which passengers enter or leave an aircraft.

rampage v. dash about violently. **on the rampage** behaving violently or destructively.

rampant adj. 1. unrestrained in growth or spread, rife. 2. (of a heraldic beast) on its hind legs.

rampart n. mound or wall for defence.

ramrod n. 1. long thin rod used for cleaning the barrel of a gun or forcing gunpowder into an old-fashioned gun. —adj. 2. (of someone's posture) very straight and upright.

ramshackle adj. tumbledown, rickety, or makeshift.

ran v. past tense of RUN.

ranch n. large cattle farm in the American West. **rancher** n.

rancid adj. (of butter, bacon, etc.) stale and having an offensive smell. **rancidity** n.

rancour n. deep bitter hate. **rancorous** adj.

rand n. monetary unit of S Africa.

R & B rhythm and blues.

R & D research and development.

random adj. made or done by chance or without plan. **at random** haphazard(ly). **randomly** adv.

randy adj. **randier, randiest.** *Informal* sexually aroused. **randiness** n.

ranee n. same as RANI.

rang v. past tense of RING[2].

range n. 1. limits of effectiveness or variation. 2. whole set of related things. 3. distance that a missile or plane can travel. 4. distance of a mark shot at. 5. place for shooting practice or rocket testing. 6. chain of mountains. 7. kitchen stove. 8. difference in pitch between the highest and lowest note a voice or instrument can make. —v. 9. vary between one point and another. 10. cover or extend over. 11. roam. **ranger** n. 1. official in charge of a nature reserve etc. 2. (R-) member of the senior branch of Guides. **rangefinder** n. instrument for finding how far away an object is.

rangy [rain-jee] adj. **rangier, rangiest.** having long slender limbs.

rani n. wife or widow of a rajah.

rank[1] n. 1. status. 2. relative place or position. 3. social class. 4. order. 5. row or line. 6. Brit. place where taxis wait to be hired. —v. 7. have a specific rank or position. 8. arrange in rows or lines. **rank and file** ordinary people or members. **the ranks** common soldiers.

rank[2] adj. 1. smelling offensively strong. 2. complete or absolute, e.g. *rank favouritism*. 3. growing too thickly. **rankly** adv.

rankle v. continue to cause resentment or bitterness.

ransack v. 1. search thoroughly. 2. pillage, plunder.

ransom n. 1. money demanded in return for the release of someone who has been kidnapped. —v. 2. pay money to obtain the release of a captive. 3. release a captive in return for money.

rant v. talk in a loud and excited way. **ranter** n. **ranting** n., adj.

ranunculus n., pl. **-luses, -li.** genus of plants including the buttercup.

rap n. 1. quick slight blow. 2. rhythmic monologue performed to music. —v. **rapping, rapped.** 3. give a rap to. 4. utter (a command) abruptly. 5. perform a rhythmic monologue with musical backing. **take the rap** Slang suffer punishment for something whether guilty or not. **rapper** n.

rapacious adj. greedy or grasping. **rapacity** n.

rape[1] v. 1. force to submit to sexual intercourse. —n. 2. act of raping. 3. any violation or abuse. **rapist** n.

rape[2] n. plant with oil-yielding seeds, also used as fodder.

rapid adj. quick, swift. **rapids** pl. n. stretch of a river with a fast turbulent current. **rapidly** adv. **rapidity** n.

rapier [ray-pyer] n. fine-bladed sword.

rapine [rap-pine] n. pillage or plundering.

rapport [rap-pore] n. harmony or agreement.

rapprochement [rap-prosh-mong] n. reestablishment of friendly relations, esp. between nations.

rapscallion n. Old-fashioned rascal or rogue.

rapt adj. engrossed or spellbound. **rapture** n. ecstasy. **rapturous** adj.

raptor n. any bird of prey. **raptorial** adj. 1. predatory. 2. of birds of prey.

rare[1] adj. 1. uncommon. 2. infrequent. 3. of uncommonly high quality. 4. (of air at high altitudes) having low density, thin. **rarely** adv. seldom. **rarity** n., pl. **-ities.**

rare[2] adj. (of meat) lightly cooked.

rarebit n. see WELSH RABBIT.

rarefied [rare-if-ide] adj. 1. highly specialized, exalted. 2. (of air) thin.

raring adj. **raring to go** enthusiastic, willing, or ready.

rascal n. 1. rogue. 2. naughty (young) person. **rascally** adj.

rase v. same as RAZE.

rash[1] adj. hasty, reckless, or incautious. **rashly** adv.

rash[2] n. 1. eruption of spots or patches on the skin. 2. outbreak of (unpleasant) occurrences.

rasher n. thin slice of bacon.

rasp n. 1. harsh grating noise. 2. coarse file. —v. 3. speak in a grating voice. 4. make a scraping noise.

raspberry n. 1. red juicy edible berry. 2. plant which bears it. 3. Informal spluttering noise made with the tongue and lips, to show contempt.

Rastafarian n., adj. (member) of a cult originating in Jamaica and regarding Haile Selassie as God (also **Rasta**).

rat n. 1. small rodent. 2. Informal contemptible person, esp. a deserter or informer. —v. **ratting, ratted.** 3. Informal inform (on). 4. hunt rats. **smell a rat** detect something suspicious. **ratty** adj. **-tier, -tiest.** Slang bad-tempered, irritable. **rat race** continual hectic competitive activity.

ratafia [rat-a-**fee**-a] n. **1.** liqueur made from fruit. **2.** almond-flavoured biscuit.

ratatouille [rat-a-**twee**] n. vegetable casserole of tomatoes, aubergines, etc.

ratchet n. set of teeth on a bar or wheel allowing motion in one direction only.

rate[1] n. **1.** degree of progress or speed. **2.** proportion between two things. **3.** charge. —pl. **4.** local tax on business (and formerly also domestic) property. —v. **5.** consider or value. **6.** estimate the value of. **7.** be worthy of; deserve. **at any rate** in any case. **rateable, ratable** adj. **1.** able to be rated. **2.** (of property) liable to payment of rates. **ratepayer** n.

rate[2] v. scold or criticize severely.

rather adv. **1.** to some extent. **2.** more truly or appropriately. **3.** more willingly.

ratify v. **-ifying, -ified.** give formal approval to. **ratification** n.

rating n. **1.** valuation or assessment. **2.** classification. **3.** noncommissioned sailor. —pl. **4.** size of the audience for a TV programme.

ratio n., pl. **-tios.** relationship between two numbers or amounts expressed as a proportion.

ratiocinate [rat-ee-**oss**-in-nate] v. reason or think out. **ratiocination** n.

ration n. **1.** fixed allowance of food etc. —v. **2.** limit to a certain amount per person. **3.** (often foll. by out) distribute a fixed amount of food etc. to each person in a group.

rational adj. **1.** reasonable, sensible. **2.** capable of reasoning. **3.** Maths (of a number) able to be expressed as a ratio of two integers. **rationally** adv. **rationality** n. **rationale** [rash-a-**nahl**] n. reason for an action or decision. **rationalism** n. philosophy that regards reason as the only basis for beliefs or actions. **rationalist** n., adj. **rationalistic** adj. **rationalize** v. **1.** justify by plausible reasoning. **2.** reorganize to improve efficiency or profitability. **rationalization** n.

rattan n. **1.** climbing palm with jointed stems. **2.** cane from this.

rattle v. **1.** give out a succession of short sharp sounds. **2.** send, move or drive with such a sound. **3.** shake briskly causing sharp sounds. **4.** Informal confuse or fluster. **5.** (often foll. by off or out) recite perfunctorily or rapidly. **6.** (often foll. by on or away) talk quickly and at length about something unimportant. —n. **7.** short sharp sound. **8.** instrument for making it. **rattling** adj. **1.** Informal, old-fashioned exceptionally; very. —n. **2.** succession of short sharp sounds. **rattlesnake** n. poisonous snake with loose horny segments on the tail that make a rattling sound. **rattle through** v. do very quickly.

raucous adj. hoarse or harsh.

raunchy adj. **raunchier, raunchiest.** Slang earthy, sexy.

ravage v. Lit. lay waste or plunder. **ravages** pl. n. destruction.

rave v. **1.** talk wildly or with enthusiasm. —n. **2.** Informal enthusiastically good review. **3.** Slang (Acid House) party. **raving** adj. **1.** delirious. **2.** Informal exceptional, e.g. a raving beauty.

ravel v. **-elling, -elled.** tangle or become entangled.

raven n. **1.** black bird like a large crow. —adj. **2.** (of hair) shiny black.

ravening adj. (of animals) hungrily searching for prey.

ravenous adj. very hungry.

ravine [rav-**veen**] n. narrow steep-sided valley worn by a stream.

ravioli pl. n. small squares of pasta with a savoury filling.

ravish v. **1.** enrapture. **2.** Lit. rape. **ravishing** adj. lovely or entrancing.

raw adj. **1.** uncooked. **2.** not manufactured or refined. **3.** inexperienced, e.g. raw recruits. **4.** chilly. **5.** (of the skin or a wound) painful, with the surface scraped away. **raw deal** unfair or dishonest treatment. **rawhide** n. untanned hide.

ray[1] n. **1.** single line or narrow beam of light. **2.** any of a set of radiating lines. **3.** slight indication of something desirable, e.g. a ray of hope.

ray[2] n. large sea fish with a flat body and a whiplike tail.

ray[3] n. Music in tonic sol-fa, second note of any major scale.

rayon n. (fabric made of) a synthetic fibre.

raze v. destroy (buildings or a town) completely.

razor n. sharp instrument for shaving. **razorbill** n. N Atlantic auk. **razor shell** (shell of) a burrowing shellfish with a long narrow shell. **razor wire** strong wire with pieces of sharp metal set across it at intervals.

razzle-dazzle, razzmatazz n. 1. *Slang* showy activity. 2. spree.

Rb *Chem.* rubidium.

RC 1. Roman Catholic. 2. Red Cross.

Rd Road.

re[1] *prep.* with reference to, concerning.
▷ In commercial correspondence the use of *re* is becoming less frequent in favour of *with reference to* or *about*.

re[2] n. same as RAY[3]

Re *Chem.* rhenium.

RE religious education.

re- *prefix* again, e.g. *re-enter, retrial*.

reach v. 1. arrive at. 2. extend to. 3. succeed in touching. 4. make contact or communication with. —n. 5. distance that one can reach. 6. range of influence. 7. stretch of a river between two bends. **reachable** adj.

react v. 1. act in response (to). 2. (foll. by *against*) act in an opposing or contrary manner. 3. undergo a chemical reaction. **reaction** n. 1. physical or emotional response to a stimulus. 2. any action resisting another. 3. opposition to change. 4. chemical or nuclear change, combination, or decomposition. **reactionary** adj., n., pl. **-aries.** (person) opposed to change, esp. in politics. **reactance** n. *Electricity* resistance to the flow of an alternating current caused by the inductance or capacitance of the circuit. **reactive** adj. chemically active. **reactor** n. apparatus in which a nuclear reaction is maintained and controlled to produce nuclear energy.

read v. **reading, read.** 1. look at and understand or take in (written or printed matter). 2. look at and say aloud. 3. study. 4. understand (an indicating instrument). 5. (of an instrument) register. 6. make out the true mood of. 7. to have a certain wording, e.g. *the statement reads as follows.* —n. 8. matter suitable for reading, e.g. *a good read.* 9. spell of reading. **reading** n. **reader** n. 1. person who reads. 2. senior university lecturer. 3. textbook. **readership** n. readers of a publication collectively. **readable** adj. 1. enjoyable to read. 2. legible. **readability** n.

readjust v. adapt to a new situation. **readjustment** n.

readmit v. **-mitting, -mitted.** let (a person, country, etc.) back in to a place or organization.

ready adj. **readier, readiest.** 1. prepared for use or action. 2. willing, prompt. **readily** adv. **readiness** n. **ready-made** adj. for immediate use by any customer. **ready money, the ready, the readies** cash for immediate use.

reaffirm v. state again; confirm. **reaffirmation** n.

reafforest v. plant new trees in (an area that was formerly forested). **reafforestation** n.

reagent [ree-age-ent] n. chemical substance that reacts with another, used to detect the presence of the other.

real adj. 1. existing in fact. 2. happening. 3. actual. 4. genuine. 5. (of property) consisting of land and houses. **really** adv. 1. very. 2. truly. —*interj.* 3. indeed! **reality** n. real existence. **real ale** beer allowed to ferment in the barrel. **real estate** landed property. **real number** any rational or irrational number. **real tennis** old form of tennis played in a four-walled indoor court. **real-time** adj. (of a computer system) processing data as it is received.
▷ To intensify an adjective, use the adverb form *really,* not *real: He's really strong.*

realistic adj. seeing and accepting things as they really are, practical. **realistically** adv. **realism** n. 1. awareness or acceptance of things as they are. 2. style in art or literature that attempts to portray the world as it really is. **realist** n.

realize v. 1. become aware or grasp the significance of. 2. achieve (a plan, hopes, etc.). 3. convert into money. **realization** n.

realm n. 1. kingdom. 2. sphere of interest.

ream n. 1. twenty quires of paper, generally 500 sheets. —pl. 2. *Informal* large quantity (of written matter).

reap v. 1. cut and gather (harvest). 2. receive as the result of a previous activity. **reaper** n.

reappear v. appear again. **reappearance** n.

reappraise v. consider or review to see if changes are needed. **reappraisal** n.

rear[1] n. 1. back part. 2. part of an army, procession, etc. behind the others. **bring up the rear** come last. **rearmost** adj. **rearward** adj., adv. **rear admiral** high-ranking naval officer. **rearguard** *n.* troops protecting the rear of an army. **rear-view mirror** mirror inside a vehicle which allows the driver to see out of the rear window.

rear² *v.* **1.** care for and educate (children). **2.** breed (animals). **3.** (of a horse) rise on its hind feet.

rearm *v.* **1.** arm again. **2.** equip with better weapons. **rearmament** *n.*

rearrange *v.* organize differently, alter. **rearrangement** *n.*

reason *n.* **1.** ground or motive. **2.** faculty of rational thought. **3.** sanity. —*v.* **4.** think logically in forming conclusions. **5.** (usu. foll. by *with*) persuade by logical argument into doing something. **reasonable** *adj.* **1.** sensible. **2.** not excessive. **3.** suitable. **4.** logical. **reasonably** *adv.*

reassess *v.* reconsider the value or importance of.

reassure *v.* restore confidence to. **reassurance** *n.* **reassuring** *adj.*

rebate¹ *n.* discount or refund.

rebate² *n., v.* same as RABBET.

rebel *v.* **-belling, -belled. 1.** revolt against the ruling power. **2.** reject accepted conventions. —*n.* **3.** person who rebels. **rebellion** *n.* **1.** organized open resistance to authority. **2.** rejection of conventions. **rebellious** *adj.*

rebirth *n.* revival or renaissance. **reborn** *adj.* active again after a period of inactivity.

rebore, reboring *n.* boring of a cylinder to restore its true shape.

rebound *v.* **1.** spring back. **2.** misfire so as to hurt the perpetrator of a plan or deed. **on the rebound** *Informal* while recovering from rejection.

rebuff *v.* **1.** reject or snub. —*n.* **2.** blunt refusal, snub.

rebuke *v.* **1.** scold sternly. —*n.* **2.** stern scolding.

rebus [**ree-buss**] *n., pl.* **-buses.** puzzle consisting of pictures and symbols representing words or syllables.

rebut *v.* **-butting, -butted.** refute or disprove. **rebuttal** *n.*

recalcitrant *adj.* wilfully disobedient. **recalcitrance** *n.*

recall *v.* **1.** recollect or remember. **2.** order to return. **3.** annul or cancel. —*n.* **4.** order to return. **5.** ability to remember.

recant *v.* withdraw (a statement or belief) publicly. **recantation** *n.*

recap *Informal* —*v.* **-capping, -capped. 1.** recapitulate. —*n.* **2.** recapitulation.

recapitulate *v.* state again briefly, repeat. **recapitulation** *n.*

recapture *v.* **1.** experience again. **2.** capture again.

recast *v.* **-casting, -cast. 1.** organize or set out in a different way. **2.** assign a part in a play or film to an actor other than the one originally intended.

recce *Slang* —*v.* **-ceing, -ced** *or* **-ceed. 1.** reconnoitre. —*n.* **2.** reconnaissance.

recede *v.* **1.** become distant. **2.** (of the hair) stop growing at the front.

receipt *n.* **1.** written acknowledgment of money or goods received. **2.** receiving or being received.

receive *v.* **1.** take, accept, or get. **2.** experience. **3.** greet (guests). **4.** have (an honour) bestowed. **5.** convert radio or television signals into sound or vision. **6.** be accepted as a member of, e.g. *received into the priesthood.* **7.** support or sustain (the weight of something). **received** *adj.* generally accepted. **receiver** *n.* **1.** equipment in a telephone, radio, or television that converts electrical signals into sound. **2.** person appointed by a court to manage the property of a bankrupt. **3.** person who handles stolen goods knowing they have been stolen. **receivership** *n.*

recent *adj.* **1.** having happened lately. **2.** new. **recently** *adv.*

receptacle *n.* object used to contain something.

reception *n.* **1.** area for receiving guests, clients, etc. **2.** formal party. **3.** manner of receiving. **4.** welcome. **5.** in broadcasting, quality of signals received. **receptionist** *n.* person who receives guests, clients, etc. **reception room** esp. in property advertisements, room in a house suitable for entertaining guests.

receptive *adj.* willing to receive new ideas, suggestions, etc. **receptivity, receptiveness** *n.*

recess *n.* **1.** niche or alcove. **2.** secret hidden place. **3.** holiday between sessions of work. **recessed** *adj.* hidden or placed in a recess.

recession *n.* period of economic difficulty

when little is being bought or sold. **recessive** adj. receding.

recharge v. cause (a battery etc.) to take in and store electricity again. **rechargeable** adj.

recherché [rish-**air**-shay] adj. **1**. of studied elegance. **2**. choice or rare.

recidivist n. person who relapses into crime. **recidivism** n.

recipe n. **1**. directions for cooking a dish. **2**. method for achieving something.

recipient n. person who receives something.

reciprocal [ris-**sip**-pro-kal] adj. **1**. mutual. **2**. given or done in return. —n. **3**. Maths number or quantity that gives a product of one when multiplied by a given number or quantity, e.g. 0.25 is the reciprocal of 4. **reciprocally** adv. **reciprocity** n.

reciprocate v. give or feel in return. **2**. (of a machine part) move backwards and forwards. **reciprocation** n.

recite v. **1**. repeat (a poem etc.) aloud to an audience. **2**. give a detailed account of. **recital** [ris-**site**-al] n. **1**. musical performance by a soloist or soloists. **2**. act of reciting. **recitation** n. recital, usu. from memory, of poetry or prose. **recitative** [ress-it-a-**teev**] n. speechlike style of singing, used esp. for narrative passages in opera.

reckless adj. heedless of danger. **recklessly** adv. **recklessness** n.

reckon v. **1**. expect. **2**. consider or think. **3**. make calculations, count. **4**. (foll. by with or without) take into account or fail to take into account. **5**. (foll. by on or upon) rely on. **reckoner** n. **reckoning** n.

reclaim v. **1**. regain possession of. **2**. make fit for cultivation. **3**. recover (useful substances) from waste. **reclamation** n.

recline v. rest in a leaning position. **reclining** adj.

recluse n. **1**. person avoiding society. **2**. hermit. **reclusive** adj.

recognize v. **1**. identify as (a person or thing) already known. **2**. accept as true or existing. **3**. treat as valid. **4**. notice, show appreciation of. **recognition** n. **recognizable** adj. **recognizance** [rik-**og**-nizz-anss] n. undertaking before a court to observe some condition.

recoil v. **1**. jerk or spring back. **2**. draw back in horror. **3**. (of an action) go wrong so as to

hurt the perpetrator. —n. **4**. backward jerk. **5**. recoiling.

recollect v. call back to mind, remember. **recollection** n.

recommend v. **1**. advise or counsel. **2**. praise or commend. **3**. make acceptable. **recommendation** n.

recompense v. **1**. pay or reward. **2**. compensate or make up for. —n. **3**. compensation. **4**. reward or remuneration.

reconcile v. **1**. harmonize (conflicting beliefs etc.). **2**. bring back into friendship. **3**. accept or cause to accept (an unpleasant situation). **reconcilable** adj. **reconciliation** n.

recondite adj. difficult to understand, abstruse.

recondition v. restore to good condition or working order.

reconnaissance [rik-**kon**-iss-anss] n. survey for military or engineering purposes.

reconnoitre [rek-a-**noy**-ter] v. make a reconnaissance of.

reconsider v. think about again, consider changing.

reconstitute v. **1**. restore (food) to its former state, esp. by the addition of water to a concentrate. **2**. reorganize. **reconstitution** n.

reconstruct v. **1**. use evidence to re-create. **2**. rebuild. **reconstruction** n.

record n. [**rek**-ord] **1**. document or other thing that preserves information. **2**. disc with indentations which a record player transforms into sound. **3**. best recorded achievement. **4**. known facts about a person's past. —v. [re-**kord**] **5**. put in writing. **6**. preserve (sound, TV programmes, etc.) on plastic disc, magnetic tape, etc., for reproduction on a playback device. **7**. show or register. **off the record** not for publication. **recorder** n. **1**. person or machine that records, esp. a video, cassette, or tape recorder. **2**. type of flute, blown at one end. **3**. judge in certain courts. **recording** n. **record player** instrument for reproducing sound on records. **recorded delivery** postal service by which an official receipt is obtained for the posting and delivery of a letter or parcel.

recount v. tell in detail.

re-count v. **1**. count again. —n. **2**. second or subsequent count, esp. of votes.

recoup [rik-koop] v. **1.** regain or make good (a loss). **2.** recompense or compensate.

recourse n. **1.** (resorting to) a source of help. **2.** Law right of action or appeal.

recover v. **1.** become healthy again. **2.** get back (a loss or expense). **3.** obtain (useful substances) from waste. **recovery** n. **recoverable** adj.

recreant n. Old-fashioned cowardly or disloyal person.

re-create v. make happen or exist again. **re-creation** n.

recreation n. agreeable or refreshing occupation, relaxation or amusement. **recreational** adj.

recrimination n. mutual blame. **recriminatory** adj.

recrudesce v. break out again. **recrudescence** n. **recrudescent** adj.

recruit n. **1.** newly enlisted soldier. **2.** new member or supporter. —v. **3.** enlist (new soldiers, members, etc.). **recruitment** n.

rectal adj. see RECTUM.

rectangle n. oblong four-sided figure with four right angles. **rectangular** adj.

rectify v. **-fying, -fied. 1.** put right, correct. **2.** purify by distillation. **3.** Electricity convert (alternating current) into direct current. **rectification** n. **rectifier** n.

rectilinear [rek-tee-lin-ee-er] adj. **1.** in a straight line. **2.** characterized by straight lines.

rectitude n. moral correctness.

recto n., pl. **-tos. 1.** right-hand page of a book. **2.** front of a sheet of paper.

rector n. **1.** clergyman in charge of a parish. **2.** head of certain academic institutions. **rectory** n., pl. **-ories.** rector's house.

rectum n., pl. **-ta.** final section of the large intestine. **rectal** adj.

recumbent adj. lying down.

recuperate v. recover from illness. **recuperation** n. **recuperative** adj.

recur v. **-curring, -curred.** happen again. **recurrence** n. repetition. **recurrent** adj. **recurring decimal** number in which a pattern of digits is repeated indefinitely after the decimal point.

recusant [rek-yew-zant] n. **1.** Hist. person who refused to obey the Church of England. **2.** person refusing to obey authority.

recycle v. reprocess (used materials) for further use. **recyclable, recycleable** adj.

red adj. **redder, reddest. 1.** of a colour varying from crimson to orange and seen in blood, fire, etc. **2.** flushed in the face from anger, shame, etc. —n. **3.** red colour. **4.** (R-) Informal communist. **in the red** Informal in debt. **see red** Informal be angry. **redness** n. **redden** v. make or become red. **reddish** adj. **red blood cell** same as ERYTHROCYTE. **red-blooded** adj. **1.** Informal vigorous. **2.** virile. **redbrick** adj. (of a university) founded in the late 19th or early 20th century. **red card** Soccer piece of red pasteboard shown by a referee to indicate that a player has been sent off. **red carpet** very special welcome for an important guest. **redcoat** n. **1.** Hist. British soldier. **2.** Canadian Informal Mountie. **Red Crescent** name and symbol used by the Red Cross in Muslim countries. **Red Cross** international organization providing help for victims of war or natural disasters. **redcurrant** n. small round edible red berry. **red flag 1.** symbol of revolution. **2.** danger signal. **red-handed** adj. Informal (caught) in the act of doing something wrong or illegal. **redhead** n. person with reddish hair. **redheaded** adj. **red herring** something which diverts attention from the main issue. **red-hot** adj. **1.** glowing red. **2.** extremely hot. **3.** very keen. **Red Indian** Offens. N American Indian. **red-letter day** memorably happy or important occasion. **red light 1.** traffic signal to stop. **2.** danger signal. **red-light district** area where prostitutes work. **red meat** dark meat, esp. beef or lamb. **red rag** something that infuriates or provokes. **redshank** n. large sandpiper with red legs. **red shift** appearance of lines in the spectrums of distant stars nearer the red end of the spectrum than on earth: used to calculate the velocity of objects in relation to the earth. **redskin** n. Informal, offens. N American Indian. **redstart** n. European bird of the thrush family, the male of which has an orange-brown tail and breast. **red tape** excessive adherence to official rules. **redwood** n. giant Californian conifer with reddish bark.

redeem v. **1.** buy back. **2.** pay off (a loan or debt). **3.** free from sin. **4.** reinstate (oneself) in someone's good opinion. **5.** make up for. **the Redeemer** Jesus Christ. **redeemable** adj. **redemption** n. **redemptive** adj.

redeploy v. assign to a new position or task. **redeployment** n.

redevelop v. rebuild or renovate (an area or building). **redevelopment** n.

redolent adj. **1**. smelling strongly (of). **2**. reminiscent (of). **redolence** n.

redouble v. increase, multiply, or intensify.

redoubt n. small fort defending a hilltop or pass.

redoubtable adj. formidable.

redound v. cause advantage or disadvantage (to).

redox n. chemical reaction in which one substance is reduced and the other is oxidized.

redress v. **1**. make amends for. —n. **2**. compensation or amends.

reduce v. **1**. bring down, lower. **2**. lessen, weaken. **3**. bring by force or necessity to some state or action. **4**. slim. **5**. simplify. **6**. make (sauce) more concentrated. **7**. Chem. separate (a substance) from others with which it is combined. **reducible** adj. **reduction** n.

redundant adj. **1**. (of a worker) no longer needed. **2**. superfluous. **redundancy** n., pl. -cies.

reduplicate v. make or become double; repeat.

re-echo v. **-echoing, -echoed**. echo over and over again; resound.

reed n. **1**. tall grass that grows in swamps and shallow water. **2**. tall straight stem of this plant. **3**. Music vibrating cane or metal strip in certain wind instruments. **reedy** adj. **reedier, reediest**. **1**. full of reeds. **2**. harsh and thin in tone.

reef[1] n. **1**. ridge of rock or coral near the surface of the sea. **2**. vein of ore.

reef[2] n. **1**. part of a sail which can be rolled up to reduce its area. —v. **2**. take in a reef of. **reefer** n. **1**. short thick jacket worn esp. by sailors. **2**. Old-fashioned slang hand-rolled cigarette containing cannabis. **reef knot** two overhand knots turned opposite ways.

reek n. **1**. strong (unpleasant) smell. —v. **2**. smell strongly. **3**. (foll. by of) be full (of).

reel[1] n. **1**. cylindrical object on which film, tape, thread, or wire is wound. **2**. winding apparatus, as of a fishing rod. —v. **3**. wind on a reel. **4**. draw in by means of a reel. **reel off** v. recite or write fluently or quickly.

reel[2] v. stagger, sway, or whirl.

reel[3] n. lively Scottish dance.

re-enter v. **1**. come back into a place, esp. a country. **2**. (of a spacecraft) return into the earth's atmosphere. **re-entry** n.

reeve n. Hist. manorial steward or official.

ref n. Informal referee in sport.

refectory n., pl. -tories. room for meals in a college etc. **refectory table** long narrow dining table supported by two trestles.

refer v. **-ferring, -ferred**. (foll by to) **1**. relate or allude (to). **2**. send (to) for information. **3**. be relevant (to). **4**. submit (to) for decision. **referable, referrable** adj. **referral** n. **reference** n. **1**. act of referring. **2**. citation or direction in a book. **3**. appeal to the judgment of another. **4**. testimonial. **5**. person to whom inquiries as to character etc. may be made. **with reference to** concerning. **reference book** book, such as an encyclopedia or dictionary, containing information or facts. **reference library** library in which books may be consulted but not borrowed.

▷ *Refer* includes the sense 'back' in its meaning. Avoid using *refer back* unless the context involves sending papers back to a committee for further consideration.

referee n. **1**. umpire in sports, esp. football or boxing. **2**. person willing to testify to someone's character etc. **3**. arbitrator. —v. **-eeing, -eed. 4**. act as referee of.

referendum n., pl. **-dums, -da**. submitting of a question to the electorate.

refill v. **1**. fill again. —n. **2**. subsequent filling. **3**. replacement supply of something in a permanent container.

refine v. **1**. purify. **2**. improve. **3**. separate (a mixture) into its components. **refined** adj. **1**. cultured or polite. **2**. purified. **refinement** n. **1**. subtlety. **2**. improvement or elaboration. **3**. fineness of taste or manners. **refinery** n., pl. -eries. place where sugar, oil, etc. is refined. **refiner** n.

refit v. **1**. make ready for use again by repairing or re-equipping. —n. **2**. repair or re-equipping for further use.

reflation n. increase in the supply of money and credit designed to encourage economic activity. **reflate** v. **reflationary** adj.

reflect v. **1**. throw back, esp. rays of light, heat, etc. **2**. form an image of. **3**. show. **4**. bring credit or discredit upon. **5**. consider at length. **reflecting telescope** telescope in which the initial image is formed by a concave mirror. **reflection** n. **1**. act of reflecting. **2.** return of rays of heat, light, etc. from a surface. **3.** image of an object given back by a mirror etc. **4.** conscious thought or meditation. **5.** attribution of discredit or blame. **reflective** *adj.* **1.** quiet, contemplative. **2.** capable of reflecting images. **reflector** *n.* **1.** polished surface for reflecting light etc. **2.** reflecting telescope.

reflex *n.* **1.** involuntary response to a stimulus or situation. —*adj.* **2.** (of a muscular action) involuntary. **3.** reflected. **4.** (of an angle) more than 180°. **reflexive** *adj. Grammar* denoting a verb whose subject is the same as its object, e.g. *to dress oneself.* **reflex camera** camera which uses a mirror to channel light from a lens to the viewfinder, so that the image seen is the same as the image photographed.

reflexology *n.* foot massage as a therapy in alternative medicine.

reform *v.* **1.** improve. **2.** abandon evil practices. —*n.* **3.** improvement. **reformative** *adj.* **reformer** *n.* **1.** person seeking reform. **2.** (R-) leader of the Reformation. **reformation** [ref-fer-**may**-shun] *n.* **1.** a reforming. **2.** (R-) religious movement in 16th-century Europe that resulted in the establishment of the Protestant Churches. **reformatory** *n., pl.* -**tories.** (formerly) institution for reforming juvenile offenders. **reformist** *n., adj.* (person) seeking the reform of something rather than its abolition or overthrow.

refract *v.* change the course of (light etc.) passing from one medium to another. **refraction** *n.* **refractive** *adj.* **refractor** *n.* **refracting telescope** telescope in which the image is formed by a series of lenses (also **refractor**).

refractory *adj.* **1.** unmanageable or rebellious. **2.** *Med.* resistant to treatment. **3.** resistant to heat.

refrain[1] *v.* (foll. by *from*) keep oneself from doing.

refrain[2] *n.* frequently repeated part of a song.

refrangible *adj.* that can be refracted. **refrangibility** *n.*

refresh *v.* **1.** revive or reinvigorate, as through food, drink, or rest. **2.** stimulate (the memory). **refresher** *n.* **refreshing** *adj.* **refreshment** *n.* something that refreshes, esp. food or drink.

refrigerate *v.* **1.** freeze. **2.** cool. **refrigeration** *n.* **refrigerator** *n.* apparatus in which

food and drinks are kept cool. **refrigerant** *n.* **1.** fluid capable of vaporizing at low temperatures used in refrigerators. —*adj.* **2.** refrigerating.

refuge *n.* (source of) shelter or protection. **refugee** *n.* person who seeks refuge, esp. in a foreign country.

refulgent *adj.* shining, radiant. **refulgence** *n.*

refund *v.* **1.** pay back. —*n.* **2.** return of money. **3.** amount returned.

refurbish *v.* renovate and brighten up. **refurbishment** *n.*

refuse[1] *v.* **1.** decline, deny, or reject. **2.** (of a horse) be unwilling to jump a fence. **refusal** *n.* denial of anything demanded or offered. **refusenik** *n.* person who refuses to obey a law or cooperate with the government because of strong beliefs.

refuse[2] *n.* rubbish or useless matter.

refute *v.* disprove. **refutable** *adj.* **refutation** *n.*
▷ *Refute* is not the same as *deny*. It means 'show evidence to disprove something', while *deny* means only 'say something is not true'.

regain *v.* **1.** get back or recover. **2.** reach again.

regal *adj.* of or like a king or queen. **regally** *adv.* **regality** *n.* **regalia** *pl. n.* ceremonial emblems of royalty, an order, etc.

regale *v.* (foll. by *with*) attempt to entertain (someone) with (stories).

regard *v.* **1.** look at. **2.** consider. **3.** relate to. **4.** heed. —*n.* **5.** look. **6.** attention. **7.** particular respect. **8.** esteem. —*pl.* **9.** expression of goodwill. **as regards, regarding** in respect of, concerning. **regardful** *adj.* (usually foll. by *of*) heedful (of); paying attention (to). **regarding** *prep.* in respect of; on the subject of. **regardless** *adj.* **1.** heedless. —*adv.* **2.** in spite of everything.

regatta *n.* meeting for yacht or boat races.

regenerate *v.* [ri-**jen**-er-ate] **1.** (cause to) undergo spiritual, moral, or physical renewal. **2.** reproduce or re-create. —*adj.* [ri-**jen**-er-it] **3.** spiritually, morally, or physically renewed. **regeneration** *n.* **regenerative** *adj.*

regent *n.* **1.** ruler of a kingdom during the absence, childhood, or illness of its monarch. —*adj.* **2.** ruling as a regent, e.g. *prince* *regent.* **regency** *n., pl.* **-cies.** status or period of office of a regent.

reggae *n.* style of Jamaican popular music with a strong beat.

regicide *n.* **1.** person who kills a king. **2.** killing of a king.

regime [ray-zheem] *n.* **1.** system of government. **2.** particular administration. **3.** *Med.* regimen.

regimen *n.* **1.** prescribed system of diet etc. **2.** rule.

regiment *n.* **1.** organized body of troops as a unit of the army. **2.** large number or group. —*v.* **3.** discipline, organize (too) rigidly. **regimental** *adj.* **regimentals** *pl. n.* military uniform. **regimentation** *n.*

region *n.* **1.** administrative division of a country. **2.** an area considered as a unit but with no definite boundaries. **3.** part of the body. **in the region of** approximately. **regional** *adj.* **regionalism** *n.* **1.** division of a country or organization into geographical regions each having some autonomy. **2.** loyalty to one's home region.

register *n.* **1.** (book containing) an official list or record of things. **2.** range of a voice or instrument. —*v.* **3.** show or be shown on a meter or the face. **4.** enter in a register, record, or set down in writing. **5.** *Informal* have an effect; make an impression. **registered** *adj.* (of mail) insured against loss by the Post Office, e.g. *a registered letter.* **registration** *n.* **registration document** document giving identification details of a vehicle, including its owner's name. **registration number** numbers and letters displayed on a vehicle to identify it. **registrar** *n.* **1.** keeper of official records. **2.** senior hospital doctor, junior to a consultant. **registry** *n., pl.* **-tries.** **1.** place where official records are kept. **2.** registration of a ship's place of origin, e.g. *a tanker of Liberian registry.* **register office,** *Informal* **registry office** place where births, marriages, and deaths are recorded.

Regius professor [reej-yuss] *n.* professor appointed by the Crown to a university chair founded by a royal patron.

regress *v.* revert to a former worse condition. **regression** *n.* **1.** act of regressing. **2.** *Psychol.* using an earlier (inappropriate) mode of behaviour. **regressive** *adj.*

regret *v.* **-gretting, -gretted.** **1.** feel sorry about. **2.** express apology or distress. —*n.* **3.** feeling of repentance, guilt, or sorrow. **regretful** *adj.* **regrettable** *adj.* **regrettably** *adv.*

regular *adj.* **1.** normal. **2.** habitual. **3.** done or occurring according to a rule. **4.** periodical. **5.** straight or level. **6.** symmetrical or even. **7.** employed continuously in the armed forces. —*n.* **8.** regular soldier. **9.** *Informal* regular customer. **regularity** *n.* **regularize** *v.* **regularly** *adv.*

regulate *v.* **1.** control, esp. by rules. **2.** adjust slightly. **regulation** *n.* **1.** rule. **2.** regulating. —*adj.* **3.** in accordance with rules or conventions. **regulator** *n.* device that automatically controls pressure, temperature, etc. **regulatory** *adj.*

regurgitate *v.* **1.** vomit. **2.** (of some birds and animals) bring back (partly digested food) into the mouth. **3.** reproduce (ideas, facts, etc.) without understanding them. **regurgitation** *n.*

rehabilitate *v.* **1.** help (a person) to readjust to society after illness, imprisonment, etc. **2.** restore to a former position or rank. **3.** restore the good reputation of. **rehabilitation** *n.*

rehash *v.* **1.** rework or reuse. —*n.* **2.** old materials presented in a new form.

rehearse *v.* **1.** practise (a play, concert, etc.). **2.** repeat aloud. **rehearsal** *n.*

rehouse *v.* provide with a new (and better) home.

Reich [ryke] *n. German* kingdom or regime. **Third Reich** Nazi dictatorship in Germany from 1933–45.

reign *n.* **1.** period of a sovereign's rule. **2.** period when a person or thing is dominant, e.g. *reign of terror.* —*v.* **3.** rule (a country). **4.** be supreme.

reimburse *v.* refund, pay back. **reimbursement** *n.*

rein *n.* (usu. pl.) **1.** narrow strap attached to a bit to guide a horse. **2.** narrow straps attached to a harness to control a young child. **3.** means of control. —*v.* **4.** check or manage with reins. **5.** control. **give (a) free rein** allow a considerable amount of freedom.

reincarnation *n.* **1.** rebirth of a soul in successive bodies. **2.** one of a series of such transmigrations. **reincarnate** *v.*

reindeer *n., pl.* **-deer, -deers.** deer of arctic regions with large branched antlers.

reinforce v. 1. strengthen with new support, material, or force. 2. strengthen with additional troops, ships, etc. **reinforcement** n. **reinforced concrete** concrete strengthened by having steel mesh or bars embedded in it.

reinstate v. 1. restore to a former position. 2. re-establish. **reinstatement** n.

reiterate v. repeat again and again. **reiteration** n.

reject v. 1. refuse to accept or believe. 2. discard as useless. 3. rebuff (a person). 4. fail to accept (a tissue graft or organ transplant). —n. 5. person or thing rejected as not up to standard. **rejection** n.

rejig v. **-jigging, -jigged.** 1. re-equip (a factory or plant). 2. rearrange.

rejoice v. feel or express great happiness. **rejoicing** n.

rejoin v. 1. reply. 2. join again.

rejoinder n. answer, retort.

rejuvenate v. restore youth or vitality to. **rejuvenation** n.

rekindle v. arouse former emotions or interests.

relapse v. 1. fall back into bad habits, illness, etc. —n. 2. return of bad habits, illness, etc.

relate v. 1. tell (a story) or describe (an event). 2. establish a relation between. 3. have reference or relation to. 4. (foll. by to) form a sympathetic relationship (with). **related** adj.

relation n. 1. connection by blood or marriage. 2. relative. 3. connection between things. 4. act of relating (a story). —pl. 5. social or political dealings. 6. family. 7. Euphemistic sexual intercourse. **relationship** n. 1. dealings and feelings between people or countries. 2. emotional or sexual affair. 3. connection between two things. 4. association by blood or marriage, kinship.

relative adj. 1. dependent on relation to something else, not absolute. 2. having reference or relation (to). 3. Grammar referring to a word or clause earlier in the sentence. —n. 4. person connected by blood or marriage. 5. Grammar relative pronoun or clause. **relatively** adv. **relativity** n. 1. state of being relative. 2. subject of two theories of Albert Einstein, dealing with relationships of space, time, and motion, and acceleration and gravity.

relax v. 1. make or become looser, less tense, or less rigid. 2. ease up from effort or attention, rest. 3. become more friendly. 4. be less strict about. **relaxed** adj. **relaxing** adj. **relaxation** n.

relay n. 1. fresh set of people or animals relieving others. 2. Electricity device for making or breaking a local circuit. 3. broadcasting station receiving and retransmitting programmes. —v. **-laying, -layed.** 4. pass on (a message). **relay race** race between teams of which each runner races part of the distance.

release v. 1. set free. 2. let go or fall. 3. permit public showing of (a film etc.). 4. emit heat, energy, etc. —n. 5. setting free. 6. written discharge. 7. statement to the press. 8. catch or handle. 9. newly issued film, record, etc.

relegate v. 1. put in a less important position. 2. demote (a sports team) to a lower league. **relegation** n.

relent v. give up a harsh intention, become less severe. **relentless** adj. 1. merciless. 2. unremitting.

relevant adj. to do with the matter in hand. **relevance** n.

reliable adj. able to be trusted, dependable. **reliably** adv. **reliability** n.

reliance n. dependence, confidence, or trust. **reliant** adj.

relic n. 1. something that has survived from the past. 2. body or possession of a saint, regarded as holy. —pl. 3. remains or traces. **relict** n. Obs. widow.

relief n. 1. gladness at the end or removal of pain, distress, etc. 2. money or food given to victims of disaster, poverty, etc. 3. release from monotony or duty. 4. person who relieves another. 5. freeing of a besieged city etc. 6. projection of a carved design from the surface. 7. distinctness or prominence, e.g. stand out in bold relief. 8. any vivid effect resulting from contrast, e.g. comic relief. **relieve** v. bring relief to. **relieve oneself** urinate or defecate. **relief map** map showing the shape and height of land by shading.

religion n. system of belief in and worship of a supernatural power or god. **religious** adj. 1. of religion. 2. pious or devout. 3. scrupulous or conscientious. **religiously** adv.

relinquish v. give up or abandon. **relinquishment** n.

reliquary [rel-lik-wer-ee] n., pl. -ries. case or shrine for holy relics.

relish v. 1. enjoy, like very much. —n. 2. liking or gusto. 3. appetizing savoury food, such as pickle. 4. zestful quality or flavour.

relive v. experience (a sensation etc.) again, esp. in the imagination.

relocate v. move to a new place to live or work. relocation n.

reluctant adj. unwilling or disinclined. reluctantly adv. reluctance n.

rely v. -lying, -lied. 1. depend (on). 2. trust.

remain v. 1. stay, be left behind. 2. continue. 3. be left (over). 4. be left to be done, said, etc. remains pl. n. 1. relics, esp. of ancient buildings. 2. dead body. remainder n. 1. part which is left. 2. amount left over after subtraction or division. 3. copy of a book sold cheaply because it has been impossible to sell at full price. —v. 4. offer (copies of a poorly selling book) at reduced prices.

remand v. send back into custody or put on bail before trial. on remand in custody or on bail before trial. remand centre place where accused people are detained awaiting trial.

remark v. 1. make casual comment (on). 2. say. 3. observe or notice. —n. 4. observation or comment. remarkable adj. 1. worthy of note or attention. 2. striking or unusual. remarkably adv.

remarry v. -rying, -ried. marry again following a divorce or the death of one's previous husband or wife.

rematch n. Sport second or return game or contest between two players.

remedy n., pl. -dies. 1. means of curing pain or disease. 2. means of solving a problem. —v. -edying, -edied. 3. put right. remediable adj. able to be put right. remedial adj. intended to correct a specific disability, handicap, etc.

remember v. 1. retain in or recall to one's memory. 2. have in mind. 3. give money to, as in a tip or through a will. 4. pass on someone's greeting (to), e.g. remember me to your mother. remembrance n. 1. memory. 2. token or souvenir. 3. honouring of the memory of a person or event. Remembrance Day Sunday closest to November 11th, on which the dead of both World Wars are commemorated.

remind v. 1. cause to remember. 2. put in mind (of). reminder n. 1. something that recalls the past. 2. note to remind a person of something not done.

reminisce v. talk or write of past times, experiences, etc. reminiscence n. 1. remembering. 2. thing recollected. —pl. 3. memoirs. reminiscent adj. reminding or suggestive (of).

remiss adj. negligent or careless.

remission n. 1. reduction in the length of a prison term. 2. pardon or forgiveness. 3. easing of intensity, as of an illness.

remit v. [re-mitt], -mitting, -mitted. 1. send (money) for goods, services, etc., esp. by post. 2. cancel (a punishment or debt). 3. refer (a decision) to a higher authority or later date. —n. [ree-mitt] 4. area of competence or authority. remittance n. 1. sending of money. 2. money sent.

remix v. 1. change the relative prominence of each performer's part of (a recording). —n. 2. remixed version of a recording.

remnant n. 1. small piece, esp. of fabric, left over. 2. surviving trace.

remonstrate v. argue in protest. remonstrance, remonstration n.

remorse n. feeling of sorrow and regret for something one did. remorseful adj. remorsefully adv. remorseless adj. 1. pitiless. 2. persistent. remorselessly adv.

remote adj. 1. far away, distant. 2. aloof. 3. slight or faint. remotely adv. remote control control of an apparatus from a distance by an electrical device.

remould v. 1. renovate (a worn tyre). —n. 2. renovated tyre.

remove v. 1. take away or off. 2. dismiss from office. 3. get rid of. —n. 4. degree of difference. removable adj. removal n. removing, esp. changing residence.

remunerate v. reward or pay. remuneration n. remunerative adj.

renaissance n. 1. revival or rebirth. 2. (R-) revival of learning in the 14th–16th centuries. —adj. 3. (R-) of the Renaissance.

renal [ree-nal] adj. of the kidneys.

renascent adj. becoming active or vigorous again. renascence n.

rend v. rending, rent. 1. tear or wrench apart. 2. (of a sound) break (the silence) violently.

render v. 1. submit or present (a bill). 2. give or provide (aid, a service, etc.). 3. cause to become. 4. portray or represent. 5. melt down (fat). 6. cover with plaster.

rendezvous [ron-day-voo] n., pl. -**vous**. 1. appointment. 2. meeting place. —v. 3. meet as arranged.

rendition n. 1. performance. 2. translation.

renegade n. person who deserts a cause.

renege [rin-**nayg**] v. (usu. foll. by *on*) go back on (a promise etc.).

renew v. 1. begin again. 2. reaffirm. 3. make valid again. 4. grow again. 5. restore to a former state. 6. replace (a worn part). **renewable** adj. **renewal** n.

rennet n. substance for curdling milk to make cheese.

renounce v. 1. give up (a belief, habit, etc.) voluntarily. 2. give up (a title or claim) formally. **renunciation** n.

renovate v. restore to good condition. **renovation** n.

renown n. widespread good reputation. **renowned** adj. famous.

rent[1] n. 1. regular payment for use of land, a building, machine, etc. —v. 2. give or have use of in return for rent. **rental** n. 1. sum payable as rent. —adj. 2. of or relating to rent.

rent[2] n. 1. tear or fissure. —v. 2. past of REND.

rentier [ron-tee-ay] n. *French* person who lives off unearned income such as rents or interest.

renunciation n. see RENOUNCE.

reorganize v. organize in a new and more efficient way. **reorganization** n.

rep[1] n. short for REPERTORY COMPANY.

rep[2] n. short for REPRESENTATIVE.

repaid v. past of REPAY.

repair[1] v. 1. restore to good condition, mend —n. 2. repaired part. 3. state or condition, e.g. *in good repair*. **repairable** adj. **reparation** n. something done or given as compensation.

repair[2] v. go (to).

repartee n. 1. witty retort. 2. interchange of witty retorts.

repast n. meal.

repatriate v. send (someone) back to his or her own country. **repatriation** n.

repay v. **repaying**, **repaid**. 1. pay back, refund. 2. make a return for. **repayable** adj. **repayment** n.

repeal v. 1. cancel (a law) officially. —n. 2. act of repealing.

repeat v. 1. say or do again. 2. happen again, recur. —n. 3. act or instance of repeating. 4. programme broadcast again. 5. *Music* passage that is identical to the one before it. **repeatedly** adv. **repeater** n. firearm that may be discharged many times without reloading.

repel v. -**pelling**, -**pelled**. 1. be disgusting to. 2. drive back, ward off. 3. resist. **repellent** adj. 1. distasteful. 2. resisting water etc. —n. 3. something that repels, esp. a chemical to repel insects.

repent v. feel regret for (a deed or omission). **repentance** n. **repentant** adj.

repercussion n. indirect effect, often unpleasant.

repertoire n. stock of plays, songs, etc. that a player or company can give.

repertory n., pl. -**ries**. repertoire. **repertory company** permanent theatre company producing a succession of plays.

repetition n. 1. act of repeating. 2. thing repeated. **repetitive**, **repetitious** adj. full of repetition.

rephrase v. express in different words.

repine v. fret or complain.

replace v. 1. substitute for. 2. put back. **replacement** n.

replay n. 1. (also **action replay**) immediate reshowing on TV of an incident in sport, esp. in slow motion. 2. second sports match, esp. one following an earlier draw. —v. 3. play (a match, recording, etc.) again.

replenish v. fill up again, resupply. **replenishment** n.

replete adj. filled or gorged. **repletion** n.

replica n. exact copy. **replicate** v. make or be a copy of. **replication** n.

reply v. -**plying**, -**plied**. 1. answer or respond. —n., pl. -**plies**. 2. answer or response.

report n. 1. account or statement. 2. written statement of a child's progress at school. 3. rumour. 4. bang. —v. 5. announce or relate. 6. give an account of. 7. make a report (on). 8. make a formal complaint about. 9. present oneself (to). 10. be responsible (to). **reportedly** adv. according to rumour. **re-**

porter *n.* person who gathers news for a newspaper, TV, etc. **reported speech** same as INDIRECT SPEECH.

repose[1] *n.* **1.** peace. **2.** composure. **3.** sleep. —*v.* **4.** lie or lay at rest. **5.** lie when dead.

repose[2] *v.* place one's trust (in).

repository *n., pl.* **-ries.** place where valuables are deposited for safekeeping, store.

repossess *v.* (of a lender) take back property from a customer who is behind with payments. **repossession** *n.*

reprehend *v.* find fault with. **reprehensible** *adj.* open to criticism, unworthy.

represent *v.* **1.** stand for. **2.** act as a delegate for. **3.** symbolize. **4.** make out to be. **5.** portray, as in art. **representation** *n.* **representational** *adj.* (of art) portraying people or things; not abstract. **representative** *n.* **1.** person chosen to stand for a group. **2.** (travelling) salesperson. —*adj.* **3.** typical. **4.** of a political system in which people choose a person to make decisions on their behalf.

repress *v.* **1.** keep (feelings) in check. **2.** subjugate. **repression** *n.* **repressive** *adj.*

reprieve *v.* **1.** postpone the execution of (a condemned person). **2.** give temporary relief to. —*n.* **3.** postponement or cancellation of a punishment. **4.** temporary relief.

reprimand *v.* **1.** blame (someone) officially for a fault. —*n.* **2.** official blame.

reprint *v.* **1.** print further copies of (a book). —*n.* **2.** reprinted copy.

reprisal *n.* retaliation.

reproach *v.* **1.** blame or rebuke. —*n.* **2.** scolding or blame. **reproachful** *adj.* **reproachfully** *adv.*

reprobate [**rep**-roh-bate] *adj., n.* depraved or disreputable (person). **reprobation** *n.* disapproval or blame.

reproduce *v.* **1.** produce a copy of. **2.** bring new individuals into existence. **3.** re-create. **reproducible** *adj.* **reproduction** *n.* **1.** process of reproducing. **2.** thing that is reproduced. **3.** facsimile, as of a painting etc. **4.** quality of sound from an audio system. —*adj.* **5.** made in imitation of an earlier style, e.g. *reproduction furniture.* **reproductive** *adj.*

reprove *v.* speak severely to (someone) about a fault. **reproof** *n.* severe blaming of someone for a fault.

reptile *n.* **1.** cold-blooded air-breathing vertebrate with horny scales or plates, such as

a snake or tortoise. **2.** contemptible grovelling person. **reptilian** *adj.*

republic *n.* **1.** form of government in which the people or their elected representatives possess the supreme power. **2.** country in which a president is the head of state. **republican** *adj.* **1.** of or supporting a republic. **2.** person who supports or advocates a republic. **republicanism** *n.* **Republican** *n., adj.* **1.** (member or supporter) of the Irish Republican Army. **2.** (member or supporter) of the Republican Party, the more conservative of the two main political parties in the US. **Republicanism** *n.*

repudiate [rip-**pew**-dee-ate] *v.* **1.** reject the authority or validity of. **2.** disown. **repudiation** *n.*

repugnant *adj.* offensive or distasteful. **repugnance** *n.*

repulse *v.* **1.** be disgusting to. **2.** drive (an army) back. **3.** rebuff or reject. —*n.* **4.** driving back. **5.** rejection. **6.** rebuff. **repulsion** *n.* **1.** distaste or aversion. **2.** *Physics* force separating two objects. **repulsive** *adj.* loathsome, disgusting.

reputation *n.* estimation in which a person is held. **reputable** [**rep**-yoo-tab-bl] *adj.* of good reputation, respectable. **repute** *n.* reputation. **reputed** *adj.* supposed. **reputedly** *adv.*

request *n.* **1.** asking. **2.** thing asked for. —*v.* **3.** ask.

Requiem [**rek**-wee-em] *n.* **1.** Mass for the dead. **2.** music for this.

require *v.* **1.** want or need. **2.** demand. **requirement** *n.* **1.** essential condition. **2.** specific need or want.
▷ *Require* suggests a demand imposed by some regulation. *Need* is usually something that comes from a person.

requisite [**rek**-wizz-it] *adj.* **1.** necessary, essential. —*n.* **2.** an essential.

requisition *n.* **1.** formal demand, such as for materials or supplies. —*v.* **2.** demand (supplies).

requite *v.* return to someone (the same treatment or feeling as received). **requital** *n.*

reredos [**rear**-doss] *n.* ornamental screen behind an altar.

rerun *v.* **1.** put on (a film or programme) again. **2.** run (a race) again. —*n.* **3.** film or programme that is broadcast again; repeat. **4.** race that is run again.

resale n. selling of something purchased earlier.

rescind v. annul or repeal.

rescue v. -cuing, -cued. 1. deliver from danger or trouble, save. —n. 2. rescuing. **rescuer** n.

research n. 1. systematic investigation to discover facts or collect information. —v. 2. carry out investigations. **researcher** n.

resemble v. be or look like. **resemblance** n.

resent v. feel indignant or bitter about. **resentful** adj. **resentment** n.

reservation n. 1. seat, room, etc. that has been reserved. 2. doubt. 3. exception or limitation. 4. area of land reserved for use by a particular group. 5. (also **central reservation**) strip of ground separating the two carriageways of a dual carriageway or motorway.

reserve v. 1. set aside, keep for future use. 2. obtain by arranging beforehand, book. 3. retain. —n. 4. something, esp. money or troops, kept for emergencies. 5. area of land reserved for a particular purpose. 6. concealment of feelings or friendliness. 7. Sport substitute. **reserved** adj. not showing one's feelings, lacking friendliness. **reservist** n. member of a military reserve. **reserve price** minimum price acceptable to the owner of property being auctioned.

reservoir n. 1. natural or artificial lake storing water for community supplies. 2. store or supply of something.

reshuffle n. 1. reorganization. —v. 2. reorganize.

reside v. dwell permanently. **residence** n. home or house. **in residence** (of an artist) working for a set period at a college, gallery, etc., e.g. writer in residence. **resident** n. 1. person who lives in a place. 2. bird or animal that does not migrate. —adj. 3. living in a place. 4. (of a bird or animal) not migrating. **residential** adj. 1. (of part of a town) consisting mainly of houses. 2. providing living accommodation.

residue n. 1. what is left, remainder. 2. Law what is left of an estate after debts have been paid and specific gifts made. **residual** adj. **residuum** n., pl. **-ua.** residue.

resign v. 1. give up office, a job, etc. 2. reconcile (oneself) to. 3. give up a right, claim, etc.; relinquish. **resigned** adj. content to endure. **resignation** n. 1. resigning. 2. passive endurance of difficulties.

resilient adj. 1. able to return to normal shape after stretching etc. 2. (of a person) recovering quickly from a shock etc. **resilience** n.

resin [rezz-in] n. 1. sticky substance from plants, esp. pines. 2. similar synthetic substance. **resinous** adj.

resist v. 1. withstand or oppose. 2. refrain from despite temptation. 3. be proof against. **resistance** n. 1. act of resisting. 2. opposition. 3. Electricity opposition offered by a circuit to the passage of a current through it. 4. any force that slows or hampers movement, e.g. wind resistance. 5. (often R-) illegal organization fighting for national liberty in a country under enemy occupation. **resistant** adj. **resistible** adj. **resistivity** n. measure of electrical resistance. **resistor** n. component of an electrical circuit producing resistance.

resit v. -sitting, -sat. 1. retake (an exam). —n. 2. exam that has to be retaken.

resolute adj. firm in purpose. **resolutely** adv. **resolution** n. 1. act of resolving. 2. firmness of conduct or character. 3. thing resolved upon. 4. decision of a court or vote of an assembly. 5. ability of a television, microscope, etc. to show fine detail.

resolve v. 1. make up one's mind. 2. decide with an effort of will. 3. form (a resolution) by a vote. 4. separate the component parts of. 5. make clear, settle. **resolved** adj. determined.

resonance n. 1. echoing, esp. with a deep sound. 2. sound produced in one object by sound waves coming from another object. **resonant** adj. **resonate** v. **resonator** n.

resort v. 1. have recourse (to) for help etc. —n. 2. place for holidays. 3. recourse.

resound [riz-zownd] v. 1. echo or ring with sound. 2. (of sounds) echo or ring. 3. be widely known, e.g. his fame resounded through the land. **resounding** adj. 1. echoing. 2. clear and emphatic.

resource n. 1. ingenuity. 2. thing resorted to for support. 3. means of achieving something. —pl. 4. sources of economic wealth. 5. stock that can be drawn on, funds. **resourceful** adj. **resourcefully** adv. **resourcefulness** n.

respect n. 1. deference or esteem. 2. point or aspect. 3. reference or relation, e.g. with respect to. 4. consideration. —pl. 5. polite greetings. —v. 6. treat with esteem. 7. show consideration for. **respecter** n. **respectful** adj. **respectfully** adv. **respecting** prep. concerning.

respectable adj. **1.** worthy of respect. **2.** fairly good. **3.** having good social standing and reputation. **respectably** adv. **respectability** n.

respective adj. relating separately to each of those in question. **respectively** adv.

respiration [ress-per-ray-shun] n. **1.** breathing. **2.** process in plants and animals of taking in oxygen and giving out carbon dioxide. **3.** breakdown of complex organic substances by living cells to produce energy and carbon dioxide. **respirator** n. apparatus worn over the mouth and breathed through as protection against dust, poison gas, etc., or to provide artificial respiration. **respiratory** adj. **respire** v. breathe.

respite n. **1.** pause, interval of rest. **2.** delay.

resplendent adj. **1.** brilliant or splendid. **2.** shining. **resplendence** n.

respond v. **1.** answer. **2.** act in answer to any stimulus. **3.** react favourably. **respondent** n. Law defendant. **response** n. **1.** answer. **2.** reaction to a stimulus. **3.** in some Christian churches, words sung or recited in reply to a priest during a service. **responsive** adj. readily reacting to some influence. **responsiveness** n.

responsible adj. **1.** having control and authority. **2.** reporting or accountable (to). **3.** sensible and dependable. **4.** involving responsibility. **responsibly** adv. **responsibility** n., pl. **-ties. 1.** state of being responsible. **2.** person or thing for which one is responsible.

respray n. new coat of paint applied to a car, van, etc.

rest[1] n. **1.** repose. **2.** freedom from exertion etc. **3.** an object used for support. **4.** pause, esp. in music. —v. **5.** take a rest. **6.** give a rest (to). **7.** be supported. **8.** place on a support. **9.** depend or rely, e.g. their hopes rested on an early end to the dispute. **10.** (of someone's gaze) settle on, e.g. her eyes rested on the dog. **restful** adj. **restless** adj.

rest[2] n. **1.** what is left. **2.** others. —v. **3.** remain, continue to be.

restaurant n. commercial establishment serving meals. **restaurateur** [rest-er-a-tur] n. person who owns or runs a restaurant. **restaurant car** railway coach where meals are served.

restitution n. **1.** giving back. **2.** reparation or compensation.

restive adj. restless or impatient.

restore v. **1.** return (a building, painting, etc.) to its original condition. **2.** re-establish. **3.** give back, return. **4.** cause to recover health or spirits. **restoration** n. **restorative** [rest-or-a-tiv] adj. **1.** restoring. —n. **2.** food or medicine to strengthen etc. **restorer** n.

restrain v. **1.** hold (someone) back from action. **2.** control or restrict. **restraint** n. **1.** restraining. **2.** control, esp. self-control. **3.** something that restrains. **restrained** adj. not displaying emotion.

restrict v. confine to certain limits. **restriction** n. **restrictive** adj. **restrictive practice** trading or industrial agreement which is against the interests of the public or other business interests.

result n. **1.** outcome or consequence. **2.** number obtained from a calculation. **3.** score. **4.** exam mark or grade. —v. **5.** (foll. by from) be the outcome or consequence (of). **6.** (foll. by in) end (in). **resultant** adj. **1.** arising as a result. —n. **2.** Maths, physics sum of two or more vectors, such as the force resulting from two or more forces acting on a single point.

resume v. **1.** begin again. **2.** occupy or take again. **resumption** n.

résumé [rez-yoo-may] n. summary.

resurgence n. rising again to vigour. **resurgent** adj.

resurrect v. **1.** restore to life. **2.** use once more (something discarded etc.), revive. **resurrection** n. **1.** rising again (esp. from the dead). **2.** revival.

resuscitate [ris-suss-it-tate] v. restore to consciousness. **resuscitation** n.

retail n. **1.** selling of goods individually or in small amounts to the public. —adj. **2.** of or engaged in such selling. —adv. **3.** by retail. —v. **4.** sell or be sold retail. **5.** recount in detail. **retailer** n.

retain v. **1.** keep in one's possession. **2.** be able to hold or contain. **3.** engage the services of. **retainer** n. **1.** fee to retain someone's services. **2.** old-established servant of a family.

retake v. **-taking, -took, -taken. 1.** take something, such as an examination, again. **2.** recapture. —n. **3.** Films rephotographed scene.

retaliate v. repay (an injury or wrong) in kind. **retaliation** n. **retaliatory** adj.

retard v. delay or slow (progress or development). **retarded** adj. underdeveloped, esp. mentally. **retardation** n.

retch v. try to vomit.

retention n. **1.** retaining. **2.** ability to remember. **3.** abnormal holding of something, esp. fluid, in the body. **retentive** adj. capable of retaining or remembering.

rethink v. consider again, esp. with a view to changing one's tactics.

reticent adj. uncommunicative, reserved. **reticence** n.

reticulate adj. made or arranged like a net. **reticulation** n.

reticule n. Old-fashioned handbag.

retina n., pl. **-nas, -nae.** light-sensitive membrane at the back of the eye.

retinue n. band of attendants.

retire v. **1.** (cause to) give up office or work, esp. through age. **2.** go away or withdraw. **3.** go to bed. **retired** adj. having retired from work etc. **retirement** n. **retirement pension** weekly pension paid by the government to retired people over a specified age. **retiring** adj. shy.

retort[1] v. **1.** reply quickly, wittily, or angrily. —n. **2.** quick, witty, or angry reply.

retort[2] n. glass container with a bent neck used for distilling.

retouch v. restore or improve by new touches, esp. of paint.

retrace v. go back over (a route etc.) again.

retract v. **1.** withdraw (a statement etc.). **2.** draw in or back. **retractable, retractile** adj. able to be retracted. **retraction** n.

retread v., n. same as REMOULD.

retreat v. **1.** move back from a position, withdraw. —n. **2.** act of or military signal for retiring or withdrawal. **3.** place to which anyone retires, refuge. **4.** period of seclusion, esp. for religious contemplation.

retrench v. reduce expenditure, cut back. **retrenchment** n.

retrial n. second trial of a case or defendant in a court of law.

retribution n. punishment or vengeance for evil deeds. **retributive** adj.

retrieve v. **1.** fetch back again. **2.** restore to a better state. **3.** recover (information) from a computer. **retrievable** adj. **retrieval** n. **retriever** n. dog trained to retrieve shot game.

retro adj. associated with or revived from the past, e.g. retro fashion.

retro- prefix back; backwards, as in retroactive.

retroactive adj. effective from a date in the past.

retroflex adj. bent or curved backwards.

retrograde adj. **1.** tending towards an earlier worse condition. **2.** moving or bending backwards.

retrogress v. go back to an earlier worse condition. **retrogression** n. **retrogressive** adj.

retrorocket n. small rocket engine used to slow a spacecraft.

retrospect n. **in retrospect** when looking back on the past. **retrospective** adj. **1.** looking back in time. **2.** applying from a date in the past. —n. **3.** exhibition of an artist's life's work.

retroussé [rit-**troo**-say] adj. (of a nose) turned upwards.

retsina n. Greek wine flavoured with resin.

return v. **1.** go or come back. **2.** give, put, or send back. **3.** repay with something of equivalent value, e.g. return the compliment. **4.** reply. **5.** elect. **6.** Sport hit, throw or play (a ball) back. —n. **7.** returning. **8.** being returned. **9.** profit. **10.** official report, as of taxable income. **11.** return ticket. —adj. **12.** of or being a return, e.g. a return visit. **returnable** adj. **returning officer** person in charge of an election. **return ticket** ticket allowing a passenger to travel to a place and back.

reunify v. bring together again something previously divided. **reunification** n.

reunion n. gathering of people who have been apart. **reunite** v. bring or come together again after a separation.

reuse v. use again. **reusable** adj.

rev Informal —n. **1.** revolution (of an engine). —v. **revving, revved. 2.** (foll. by up) increase the speed of revolution of (an engine).

Rev., Revd. Reverend.

revalue v. adjust the exchange value of (a currency) upwards. **revaluation** n.

revamp v. renovate or restore.

reveal v. 1. make known. 2. expose or show. **revelation** n.

reveille [riv-**val**-ee] n. morning bugle call to waken soldiers.

revel v. -**elling**, -**elled**. 1. take pleasure (in). 2. make merry. —n. 3. (usu. pl.) merry-making. **reveller** n. **revelry** n. festivity.

revenge n. 1. retaliation for wrong done. —v. 2. avenge (oneself or another). 3. make retaliation for. **revengeful** adj.

revenue n. 1. income, esp. of a state. —adj. 2. involved in collecting taxes. **Inland Revenue** see INLAND.

reverberate v. echo or resound. **reverberation** n.

revere v. be in awe of and respect greatly. **reverence** n. awe mingled with respect and esteem. **reverend** adj. (R- esp. as a prefix to a clergyman's name) worthy of reverence. **reverent** adj. showing reverence. **reverently** adv. **reverential** adj. marked by reverence.

reverie n. absent-minded daydream.

revers [riv-**veer**] n. turned back part of a garment, such as the lapel.

reverse v. 1. turn upside down or the other way round. 2. change completely. 3. move (a vehicle) backwards. —n. 4. opposite or contrary. 5. back side, obverse. 6. defeat. 7. reverse gear. —adj. 8. opposite or contrary. **reverse the charges** make a telephone call at the recipient's expense. **reversal** n. **reversible** adj. **reverse gear** mechanism enabling a vehicle to move backwards. **reversing light** light on the back of a motor vehicle that goes on when the vehicle is moving backwards.

revert v. 1. return to a former state. 2. come back to a subject. 3. (of property) return to its former owner. **reversion** n. 1. return to a former state, practice or belief. 2. (of property) rightful passing to the owner, designated heir, etc.

revetment n. facing of stone, sandbags, etc. for a wall.

review v. 1. hold or write a review of. 2. examine, reconsider, or look back on. 3. inspect formally. —n. 4. critical assessment of a book, concert, etc. 5. periodical with critical articles. 6. general survey. 7. inspection of troops. **reviewer** n. writer of reviews.

revile v. be abusively scornful of.

revise v. 1. look over and correct. 2. re-study (work) in preparation for an examination. 3. change or alter. **revision** n.

revive v. bring or come back to life, vigour, use, etc. **revival** n. 1. reviving or renewal. 2. new production of a play that has not been recently performed. 3. movement seeking to restore religious faith. **revivalism** n. **revivalist** n.

revoke v. cancel (a will, agreement, etc.). **revocation** n.

revolt n. 1. uprising against authority. —v. 2. rise in rebellion. 3. cause to feel disgust. **revolting** adj. disgusting, horrible.

revolution n. 1. overthrow of a government by the governed. 2. great change. 3. complete rotation. 4. spinning round. **revolutionary** adj. 1. advocating or engaged in revolution. 2. radically new or different. —n., pl. -**aries**. 3. person advocating or engaged in revolution. **revolutionize** v. change considerably.

revolve v. 1. turn round, rotate. 2. (foll. by around) be centred (on). **revolver** n. repeating pistol.

revue n. theatrical entertainment with topical sketches and songs.

revulsion n. strong disgust.

reward n. 1. something given in return for a service. 2. sum of money offered for finding a criminal or missing property. —v. 3. pay or give something to (someone) for a service, information, etc. **rewarding** adj. giving personal satisfaction, worthwhile.

rewind v. run (a tape or film) back to an earlier point in order to replay.

rewire v. provide (a house, engine, etc.) with new wiring.

rewrite v. 1. write again in a different way. —n. 2. something rewritten.

Rf Chem. rutherfordium.

Rh 1. Chem. rhodium. 2. rhesus.

rhapsody n., pl. -**dies**. 1. freely structured emotional piece of music. 2. expression of ecstatic enthusiasm. **rhapsodic** adj. **rhapsodize** v. speak or write with extravagant enthusiasm.

rhea [**ree**-a] n. S American three-toed ostrich.

rhenium n. silvery-white metallic element with a high melting point.

rheostat *n.* instrument for varying the resistance of an electric circuit.

rhesus [ree-suss] *n.* small long-tailed monkey of S Asia. **rhesus factor, Rh factor** antigen commonly found in human blood.

rhetoric [ret-a-rik] *n.* 1. art of effective speaking or writing. 2. artificial or exaggerated language. **rhetorical** [rit-tor-ik-kal] *adj.* 1. (of a question) not requiring an answer. 2. of, like, or using rhetoric. **rhetorically** *adv.*

rheum [room] *n.* watery discharge from the eyes or nose. **rheumy** *adj.* **rheumier, rheumiest.**

rheumatism *n.* painful inflammation of joints or muscles. **rheumatic** *n., adj.* (person) affected by rheumatism. **rheumaticky** *adj. Informal* affected by rheumatism. **rheumatoid** *adj.* of or like rheumatism. **rheumatoid arthritis** chronic disease characterized by inflammation and swelling of the joints.

Rh factor *n.* see RHESUS.

rhinestone *n.* imitation diamond.

rhino *n., pl.* **rhinos.** short for RHINOCEROS.

rhinoceros *n., pl.* **-oses, -os.** large thick-skinned animal with one or two horns on its nose.

rhizome *n.* thick underground stem producing new plants.

rhodium *n.* hard metal used for plating jewellery.

rhododendron *n.* evergreen flowering shrub.

rhombus *n., pl.* **-buses, -bi.** parallelogram with sides of equal length but no right angles, diamond-shaped figure. **rhomboid** *n.* parallelogram with adjacent sides of unequal length.

rhubarb *n.* garden plant of which the fleshy stalks are cooked as fruit.

rhumba *n.* same as RUMBA.

rhyme *n.* 1. sameness of the final sounds at the ends of lines of verse, or in words. 2. word identical in sound to another in its final sounds, e.g. *'seven' rhymes with 'heaven'.* 3. verse marked by rhyme. —*v.* 4. make a rhyme. **rhyming slang** slang in which a word is replaced by a word or phrase which rhymes with it.

rhythm *n.* 1. any regular movement or beat. 2. arrangement of the durations of and stress on the notes of a piece of music, usu.

grouped into a regular pattern. 3. in poetry, arrangement of words to form a regular pattern of stresses. **rhythmic, rhythmical** *adj.* **rhythmically** *adv.* **rhythm and blues** popular music, orig. Black American, influenced by the blues. **rhythm method** method of contraception in which intercourse is avoided at times when conception is most likely.

RI Rhode Island.

rib[1] *n.* 1. one of the curved bones forming the framework of the upper part of the body. 2. cut of meat including the rib(s). 3. curved supporting part, as in the hull of a boat. 4. raised series of rows in knitting. —*v.* **ribbing, ribbed.** 5. provide or mark with ribs. 6. knit to form a rib pattern. **ribbed** *adj.* **ribbing** *n.* **ribcage** *n.* bony structure of ribs enclosing the lungs.

rib[2] *v.* **ribbing, ribbed.** *Informal* tease or ridicule. **ribbing** *n.*

ribald *adj.* humorously or mockingly rude or obscene. **ribaldry** *n.*

ribbon *n.* 1. narrow band of fabric used for trimming, tying, etc. 2. any long strip, for example of inked tape in a typewriter. 3. small strip of coloured cloth worn as a badge or as the symbol of an award (also **riband, ribband**). —*pl.* 4. ragged strips or shreds.

riboflavin [rye-boe-flay-vin] *n.* form of vitamin B.

ribonucleic acid *n.* see RNA.

rice *n.* 1. cereal plant grown on wet ground in warm countries. 2. its seeds as food. **rice paper** thin edible paper.

rich *adj.* 1. owning a lot of money or property, wealthy. 2. fertile. 3. abounding. 4. valuable. 5. (of food) containing much fat or sugar. 6. mellow. 7. amusing. **riches** *pl. n.* wealth. **richly** *adv.* 1. elaborately. 2. fully. **richness** *n.*

Richter scale *n.* scale for measuring the intensity of earthquakes.

rick[1] *n.* stack of hay etc.

rick[2] *v., n.* sprain or wrench.

rickets *n.* disease of children marked by softening of the bones, bow legs, etc., caused by vitamin D deficiency.

rickety *adj.* shaky or unstable.

rickshaw *n.* light two-wheeled man-drawn Asian vehicle.

ricochet [rik-osh-ay] *v.* 1. (of a bullet) rebound from a solid surface. —*n.* 2. such a rebound.

rid *v.* **ridding, rid.** clear or relieve (of). **get rid of** free oneself of (something undesirable). **good riddance** relief at getting rid of something or someone.

ridden *v.* past participle of RIDE. —*adj.* 2. afflicted or affected by the thing specified, e.g. *disease-ridden.*

riddle¹ *n.* 1. question made puzzling to test one's ingenuity. 2. puzzling person or thing. 3. speak in riddles.

riddle² *v.* 1. pierce with many holes. —*n.* 2. coarse sieve for gravel etc. **riddled with** full of.

ride *v.* **riding, rode, ridden.** 1. sit on and control or propel (a horse, bicycle, etc.). 2. go on horseback or in a vehicle. 3. be carried on or across. 4. travel over. 5. lie at anchor. 6. (often foll. by *out*) endure successfully, survive. —*n.* 7. journey on a horse etc., or in a vehicle. 8. type of movement experienced in a vehicle. **rider** *n.* 1. person who rides. 2. supplementary clause added to a document. **ride up** *v.* (of a garment) move up from the proper position.

ridge *n.* 1. long narrow hill. 2. long narrow raised part on a surface. 3. line where two sloping surfaces meet. 4. elongated area of high pressure. **ridged** *adj.*

ridiculous *adj.* deserving to be laughed at, absurd. **ridicule** *n.* 1. treatment of a person or thing as ridiculous. —*v.* 2. laugh at, make fun of.

riding *n.* former administrative district of Yorkshire.

riesling *n.* type of white wine.

rife *adj.* widespread or common. **rife with** full of.

riff *n. Jazz, rock* short repeated melodic figure.

riffle *v.* flick through (pages etc.) quickly.

riffraff *n.* rabble, disreputable people.

rifle¹ *n.* 1. firearm with a long barrel. —*v.* 2. cut spiral grooves inside the barrel of a gun.

rifle² *v.* 1. search and rob. 2. ransack.

rift *n.* 1. break in friendly relations. 2. crack, split, or cleft. **rift valley** long narrow valley resulting from subsidence between faults.

rig *v.* **rigging, rigged.** 1. arrange in a dishonest way. 2. (often foll. by *up*) set up, esp. as a makeshift. 3. equip. 4. provide (a ship) with spars, ropes, etc. —*n.* 5. apparatus for drill-

ing for oil and gas. 6. way a ship's masts and sails are arranged. 7. (also **rigout**) *Informal* outfit of clothes. **rigging** *n.* ship's spars and ropes.

right *adj.* 1. just. 2. in accordance with truth and duty. 3. true. 4. correct. 5. proper. 6. of the side that faces east when the front is turned to the north. 7. straight. 8. upright. 9. of the outer side of a fabric. —*v.* 10. bring or come back to a vertical position. 11. bring or come back to a normal or correct state. 12. do justice to. —*n.* 13. claim, title, etc. allowed or due. 14. what is just or due. 15. conservative political party or group. —*adv.* 16. straight. 17. properly. 18. very. 19. on or to the right side. **in the right** morally or legally correct. **right away** immediately. **rightly** *adv.* **rightful** *adj.* **rightfully** *adv.* **rightist** *n., adj.* (person) on the political right. **right angle** angle of 90°. **right-handed** *adj.* using or for the right hand. **right-hand man** person's most valuable assistant. **right-minded, right-thinking** *adj.* having opinions or principles deemed acceptable by the speaker. **right of way** *n., pl.* **rights of way.** 1. *Law* right to pass over someone's land. 2. path used. **right-wing** *adj.* 1. conservative or reactionary. 2. belonging to the more conservative part of a political party. **right-winger** *n.*

righteous [*rye*-chuss] *adj.* 1. upright, godly, or virtuous. 2. morally justified. **righteousness** *n.*

rigid *adj.* 1. inflexible or strict. 2. unyielding or stiff. **rigidly** *adv.* **rigidity** *n.*

rigmarole *n.* 1. meaningless string of words. 2. long complicated procedure.

rigor mortis *n.* stiffening of the body after death.

rigour *n.* 1. harshness, severity, or strictness. 2. hardship. **rigorous** *adj.* harsh, severe, or stern.

rile *v.* anger or annoy.

rill *n.* small stream.

rim *n.* 1. edge or border. 2. outer ring of a wheel. **rimmed** *adj.*

rime *Lit.* —*n.* 1. hoarfrost. —*v.* 2. cover with rime or something resembling it.

rind *n.* tough outer coating of fruits, cheese, or bacon.

rinderpest *n.* acute infectious disease of cattle.

ring¹ *n.* 1. circle of gold etc., esp. for a finger. 2. any circular band, coil, or rim. 3. circle of people. **4.** enclosed area, esp. a circle for a circus or a roped-in square for boxing. **5.** group operating (illegal) control of a market. —*v.* **6.** put a ring round. **7.** mark a (bird) with a ring. **8.** kill (a tree) by cutting the bark round the trunk. **ringer** *n. Slang* person or thing apparently identical to another (also **dead ringer**). **ringlet** *n.* curly lock of hair. **ring binder** binder with metal rings that can be opened to insert perforated paper. **ringdove** *n.* large pigeon with white patches on the wings and neck. **ring finger** third finger, esp. of the left hand, on which the wedding ring is worn. **ringleader** *n.* instigator of a mutiny, riot, etc. **ringmaster** *n.* master of ceremonies in a circus. **ring road** main road that bypasses a town (centre). **ringside** *n.* row of seats nearest a boxing or circus ring. **ringworm** *n.* fungal skin disease in circular patches.

ring² *v.* **ringing, rang, rung. 1.** give out a clear resonant sound, as a bell. **2.** resound. **3.** cause (a bell) to sound. **4.** telephone. —*n.* **5.** ringing. **6.** telephone call. **7.** inherent quality, e.g. *the ring of truth.* **ring off** *v.* end a telephone call. **ring up** *v.* **1.** telephone. **2.** record on a cash register.

▷ The simple past is *rang: He rang the bell.* Avoid the use of the past participle *rung* for the simple past.

rink *n.* **1.** sheet of ice for skating or curling. **2.** floor for roller skating. **3.** in bowls or curling, players on one side in a game.

rinkhals *n.* S African cobra that can spit venom.

rinse *v.* **1.** remove soap from (washed clothes, hair, etc.) by applying clean water. **2.** wash lightly. —*n.* **3.** rinsing. **4.** liquid to tint hair.

riot *n.* **1.** disorderly unruly disturbance. **2.** loud revelry. **3.** *Slang* very amusing person or thing. **4.** profusion. —*v.* **5.** take part in a riot. **read the riot act** reprimand severely. **run riot 1.** behave without restraint. **2.** grow profusely. **rioter** *n.* **riotous** *adj.* **1.** unruly or rebellious. **2.** unrestrained.

rip *v.* **ripping, ripped. 1.** tear violently. **2.** tear away. **3.** *Informal* rush. —*n.* **4.** split or tear. **let rip** act or speak without restraint. **ripcord** *n.* cord pulled to open a parachute. **rip off** *v. Slang* cheat by overcharging. **rip-off** *n. Slang* cheat or swindle. **rip-roaring** *adj. Informal* boisterous and exciting.

RIP rest in peace.

riparian [rip-**pair**-ee-an] *adj.* of or on the banks of a river.

ripe *adj.* **1.** ready to be reaped, eaten, etc. **2.** matured. **3.** ready or suitable. **ripen** *v.* **1.** grow ripe. **2.** mature.

riposte [rip-**posst**] *n.* **1.** verbal retort. **2.** counterattack. —*v.* **3.** make a riposte.

ripple *n.* **1.** slight wave, ruffling of a surface. **2.** sound like ripples of water. —*v.* **3.** flow or form into little waves (on). **4.** (of sounds) rise and fall gently.

rise *v.* **rising, rose, risen. 1.** get up from a lying, sitting or kneeling position. **2.** get out of bed. **3.** move upwards. **4.** (of the sun or moon) appear above the horizon. **5.** reach a higher level. **6.** (of an amount or price) increase. **7.** rebel. **8.** (of a court) adjourn. **9.** have its source. —*n.* **10.** rising. **11.** upward slope. **12.** increase, esp. of wages. **take a rise out of** *Slang* provoke an angry reaction from. **give rise to** cause. **riser** *n.* **1.** person who rises, esp. from bed. **2.** vertical part of a step. **rising** *n.* **1.** revolt. —*adj.* **2.** increasing in rank or maturity.

risible [**riz**-zib-bl] *adj.* causing laughter, ridiculous.

risk *n.* **1.** chance of disaster or loss. **2.** person or thing considered as a potential hazard. —*v.* **3.** act in spite of the possibility of (injury or loss). **4.** expose to danger or loss. **risky** *adj.* **riskier, riskiest.** full of risk, dangerous. **riskily** *adv.*

risotto *n., pl.* **-tos.** dish of rice cooked in stock with vegetables, meat, etc.

risqué [**risk**-ay] *adj.* bordering on indecency.

rissole *n.* cake of minced meat, coated with breadcrumbs and fried.

rite *n.* formal practice or custom, esp. religious.

ritual *n.* **1.** prescribed order of rites. **2.** regular repeated action or behaviour. —*adj.* **3.** concerning rites. **ritually** *adv.* **ritualistic** *adj.* like a ritual.

ritzy *adj.* **ritzier, ritziest.** *Slang* luxurious or elegant.

rival *n.* **1.** person or thing that competes with or equals another for favour, success, etc. —*adj.* **2.** in the position of a rival. —*v.* **-valling, -valled. 3.** (try to) equal. **rivalry** *n.* keen competition.

riven *adj.* **1.** split apart. **2.** torn to shreds.

river *n.* **1.** large natural stream of water. **2.** plentiful flow.

rivet [riv-vit] n. **1.** bolt for fastening metal plates, the end being put through holes and then beaten flat. —v. **riveting, riveted. 2.** cause to be fixed, as in fascination. **3.** fasten with rivets. **riveter** n. **riveting** adj. very interesting and exciting.

rivulet n. small stream.

Rn Chem. radon.

RN Royal Navy.

RNA ribonucleic acid: substance in living cells essential for the synthesis of protein.

roach¹ n. freshwater fish.

roach² n. US same as COCKROACH.

road n. **1.** way prepared for passengers, vehicles, etc. **2.** way or course, e.g. the road to fame. **3.** street. **4.** roadstead. **on the road** travelling. **roadie** n. Informal person who transports and sets up equipment for a band. **roadblock** n. barricade across a road to stop traffic for inspection etc. **road hog** Informal selfish aggressive driver. **roadholding** n. extent to which a vehicle does not skid on bends or wet surfaces. **roadhouse** n. pub or restaurant on a country road. **road metal** broken stones used in building roads. **road show** Radio live broadcast from a radio van taking a particular programme on a tour of the country. **roadside** n., adj. **roadstead** n. Naut. partly sheltered anchorage. **road test** test of a vehicle etc. in actual use. **road-test** v. test (a vehicle etc.) in actual use. **roadway** n. the part of a road used by vehicles. **roadworks** pl. n. repairs to a road, esp. blocking part of the road. **roadworthy** adj. (of a vehicle) mechanically sound.

roam v. wander about.

roan adj. **1.** (of a horse) having a brown or black coat sprinkled with white hairs. —n. **2.** roan horse.

roar v. **1.** make or utter a loud deep hoarse sound like that of a lion. **2.** shout (something) as in anger. **3.** laugh loudly. —n. **4.** such a sound. **roaring** adj. **1.** Informal brisk and profitable. —adv. **2.** noisily.

roast v. **1.** cook by dry heat, as in an oven. **2.** make or be very hot. —n. **3.** roasted joint of meat. —adj, **4.** roasted. **roasting** Informal —adj. **1.** extremely hot. —n. **2.** severe criticism or scolding.

rob v. **robbing, robbed. 1.** steal from. **2.** deprive. **robber** n. **robbery** n., pl. -beries.

robe n. **1.** long loose outer garment. —v. **2.** put a robe on.

robin n. small brown bird with a red breast.

robot n. **1.** automated machine, esp. one performing functions in a human manner. **2.** person of machine-like efficiency. **robotic** adj. **robotics** n. science of designing and using robots.

robust adj. **1.** very strong and healthy. **2.** sturdily built. **3.** requiring physical strength, e.g. robust outdoor games. **robustly** adv. **robustness** n.

roc n. monstrous bird of Arabian mythology.

rock¹ n. **1.** hard mineral substance that makes up part of the earth's crust, stone. **2.** large rugged mass of stone. **3.** US & Aust. a stone. **4.** hard sweet in sticks. **on the rocks 1.** (of a marriage) about to end. **2.** (of an alcoholic drink) served with ice. **rocky** adj. **rockier, rockiest.** having many rocks. **rockery** n., pl. **-eries.** mound of stones in a garden for (alpine) plants. **rock bottom** lowest possible level. **rock cake** small fruit cake with a rough surface. **rock plant** any plant which grows on rocky ground. **rock salt** common salt as a naturally occurring mineral.

rock² v. **1.** (cause to) sway to and fro. **2.** (cause to) feel shock, e.g. the scandal rocked the government. —n. **3.** (also **rock music**) style of pop music with a heavy beat. —adj. **4.** of or relating to rock music. **rocky** adj. **rockier, rockiest.** shaky or unstable. **rock and roll** style of pop music blending rhythm and blues and country music.

rocker n. **1.** curved piece of wood etc. on which something may rock. **2.** rocking chair. **3.** rock music performer, fan, or song. **off one's rocker** Informal insane.

rocket n. **1.** self-propelling device powered by the burning of explosive contents (used as a firework, weapon, etc.). **2.** vehicle propelled by a rocket engine, as a weapon or carrying a spacecraft. **3.** Informal severe reprimand. —v. **rocketing, rocketed. 4.** move fast, esp. upwards, as a rocket. **rocketry** n.

rococo [rok-koe-koe] adj. (of furniture, architecture, etc.) having much elaborate decoration in an early 18th-century French style.

rod n. **1.** slender straight bar, stick. **2.** cane.

rode v. past tense of RIDE.

rodent n. animal with teeth specialized for gnawing, such as a rat, mouse, or squirrel.

rodeo *n., pl.* **-deos.** display of skill by cowboys, such as bareback riding.

rodomontade *n. Lit.* boastful words or behaviour.

roe[1] *n.* small species of deer.

roe[2] *n.* mass of eggs in a fish, sometimes eaten as food.

roentgen [ront-gən] *n.* unit measuring a radiation dose.

rogation *n.* (usu. pl.) *Christianity* solemn supplication, esp. in a form of ceremony prescribed by the Church. **Rogation Days** the three days preceding Ascension Day.

roger *interj.* used in signalling, message received and understood.

rogue *n.* **1.** dishonest or unprincipled person. **2.** mischief-loving person. **3.** inferior or defective specimen, esp. of a plant. —*adj.* **4.** (of a wild beast) having a savage temper and living apart from the herd. **roguery** *n.* **roguish** *adj.*

roister *v.* make merry noisily or boisterously. **roisterer** *n.*

role, rôle *n.* **1.** actor's part. **2.** task or function.

roll *v.* **1.** move by turning over and over. **2.** wind round. **3.** smooth out with a roller. **4.** move or sweep along. **5.** undulate. **6.** (of a ship or aircraft) turn from side to side about a line from nose to tail. **7.** (of a drum, thunder, etc.) make a continuous deep loud noise. **8.** walk with a swaying gait. **9.** (of machinery) (begin to) operate. —*n.* **10.** act of rolling over or from side to side. **11.** piece of paper etc. rolled up. **12.** list or register. **13.** small rounded individually baked piece of bread. **14.** swaying unsteady movement or gait. **15.** continuous sound, as of drums, thunder, etc. **16.** complete rotation of an aircraft about a line from nose to tail. **roll call** calling out of a list of names, as in a school or the army, to check who is present. **rolled gold** metal coated with a thin layer of gold. **rolling** *adj.* **1.** (of hills) gently sloping, undulating. **2.** (of a gait) slow and swaying. **rolling pin** cylindrical roller for pastry. **rolling stock** locomotives, carriages, etc. of a railway. **rolling stone** restless, wandering person. **rollmop** *n.* herring fillet rolled round onion slices and pickled. **roll-on/roll-off** *adj.* denoting a ship which vehicles can be driven straight onto or off. **roll-top** *adj.* (of a desk) having a flexible lid sliding in grooves. **roll up** *v. Informal* appear or arrive. **roll-up** *n. Informal* cigarette made by the smoker from loose tobacco and cigarette paper.

roller *n.* **1.** rotating cylinder used for smoothing or supporting a thing to be moved, spreading paint, etc. **2.** long wave of the sea. **roller coaster** at a funfair, narrow railway with steep slopes. **roller skate** skate with wheels. **roller towel** towel that has its ends joined and is mounted on a roller.

rollicking *adj.* boisterously carefree.

roly-poly *adj.* round or plump.

ROM *Computers* read only memory.

Roman *adj.* of Rome or the Roman Catholic Church. **Roman alphabet** alphabet used for writing W European languages, including English. **Roman candle** firework that emits a steady stream of coloured sparks. **Roman Catholic** (member) of that section of the Christian Church that acknowledges the supremacy of the Pope. **Roman nose** nose with a high prominent bridge. **Roman numerals** the letters I, V, X, L, C, D, M, used to represent numbers. **roman type** plain upright letters in printing.

romance *n.* **1.** love affair. **2.** mysterious or exciting quality. **3.** novel or film dealing with love, esp. sentimentally. **4.** story with scenes remote from ordinary life. —*v.* **5.** exaggerate or fantasize. **romancer** *n.*

Romance *adj.* (of a language) developed from Latin, such as French or Spanish.

Romanesque *adj. n.* (in) a style of architecture of the 9th–12th centuries, characterized by round arches.

romantic *adj.* **1.** of or dealing with love. **2.** idealistic but impractical. **3.** (of literature, music, etc.) displaying passion and imagination rather than order and form. —*n.* **4.** romantic person or artist. **romantically** *adv.* **romanticism** *n.* **romanticist** *n.* **romanticize** *v.* describe or regard in an idealized and unrealistic way.

Romany *n., pl.* **-nies,** *adj.* Gypsy.

Romeo *n., pl.* **Romeos.** ardent male lover.

romp *v.* **1.** play wildly and joyfully. —*n.* **2.** spell of romping. **romp home** win easily. **rompers** *pl. n.* child's overalls.

rondavel *n. S Afr.* circular building, often thatched.

rondeau *n., pl.* **-deaux.** short poem with the opening words used as a refrain.

rondo *n., pl.* **-dos.** piece of music with a leading theme continually returned to.

roo *n. Aust. Informal* kangaroo.

rood *n.* **1.** *Christianity* the Cross. **2.** crucifix. **rood screen** in a church, screen separating the nave from the choir.

roof *n., pl.* **roofs.** **1.** outside upper covering of a building, car, etc. —*v.* **2.** put a roof on. **roof rack** rack for carrying luggage attached to the roof of a car.

rook[1] *n.* **1.** bird of the crow family. —*v.* **2.** *Old-fashioned slang* swindle. **rookery** *n., pl.* **-eries.** colony of rooks, penguins, or seals.

rook[2] *n.* piece in chess.

rookie *n. Informal* recruit, esp. in the army.

room *n.* **1.** space. **2.** space enough. **3.** division of a house. **4.** scope or opportunity. —*pl.* **5.** lodgings. —*v.* **6.** *US* occupy or share a room. **roomy** *adj.* **roomier, roomiest.** spacious.

roost *n.* **1.** perch for fowls. —*v.* **2.** perch. **rooster** *n. US* domestic cock.

root[1] *n.* **1.** part of a plant that grows down into the earth obtaining nourishment. **2.** plant with an edible root, such as a carrot. **3.** source or origin. **4.** part of a tooth, hair, etc. below the skin. **5.** form of a word from which other words and forms are derived. **6.** *Maths* factor of a quantity which, when multiplied by itself the number of times indicated, gives the quantity. —*pl.* **7.** person's sense of belonging. —*v.* **8.** establish a root and start to grow. **rootless** *adj.* having no sense of belonging. **root for** *v. Informal* cheer on. **root out** *v.* get rid of completely. **rootstock** *n.* rhizome. **root up** *v.* pull up by the roots.

root[2], **rootle** *v.* **1.** dig or burrow. **2.** *Informal* search vigorously but unsystematically.

rope *n.* thick cord. **know the ropes** be thoroughly familiar with an activity. **rope in** *v.* persuade to join in. **rope off** *v.* enclose or divide with a rope.

ropy, ropey *adj.* **ropier, ropiest.** **1.** *Informal* inferior or inadequate. **2.** *Informal* not well. **ropiness** *n.*

Roquefort *n.* strong blue-veined cheese made from ewes' or goats' milk.

rorqual *n.* whalebone whale with a dorsal fin.

rosaceous *adj.* of or belonging to a family of plants typically having five-petalled flowers, including the rose, strawberry, and many fruit trees.

rosary *n., pl.* **-saries.** **1.** series of prayers. **2.** string of beads for counting these prayers.

rose[1] *n.* **1.** shrub or climbing plant with prickly stems and fragrant flowers. **2.** the flower. **3.** perforated flat nozzle for a hose. **4.** pink colour. —*adj.* **5.** pink. **roseate** [roe-zee-ate] *adj.* rose-coloured. **rose-coloured** *adj.* unjustifiably optimistic. **rose window** circular window with spokes branching from the centre. **rosewood** *n.* fragrant wood used to make furniture.

rose[2] *v.* past tense of RISE.

rosé [roe-zay] *n.* pink wine.

rosehip *n.* berry-like fruit of a rose plant.

rosemary *n.* **1.** fragrant flowering shrub. **2.** its leaves as a herb.

rosette *n.* rose-shaped ornament, esp. a circular bunch of ribbons.

Rosh Hashanah, Rosh Hashana *n.* Hebrew Jewish New Year festival.

rosin [rozz-in] *n.* **1.** resin used for treating the bows of violins etc. —*v.* **2.** apply rosin to.

roster *n.* list of people and their turns of duty.

rostrum *n., pl.* **-trums, -tra.** platform or stage.

rosy *adj.* **1.** flushed. **2.** hopeful or promising.

rot *v.* **rotting, rotted.** **1.** decompose or decay. **2.** slowly deteriorate physically or mentally. —*n.* **3.** decay. **4.** *Informal* nonsense.

rota *n.* list of people who take it in turn to do a particular task.

rotary *adj.* **1.** revolving. **2.** operated by rotation.

rotate *v.* **1.** (cause to) move round a centre or on a pivot. **2.** (cause to) follow a set sequence. **3.** plant different crops from one year to the next to maintain the fertility of the soil. **rotation** *n.*

rote *n.* mechanical repetition. **by rote** by memory.

rotisserie *n.* (electrically driven) rotating spit for cooking meat.

rotor *n.* **1.** revolving portion of a dynamo, motor, or turbine. **2.** rotating device with long blades that provides thrust to lift a helicopter.

rotten *adj.* **1.** decomposed. **2.** *Informal* very bad. **3.** corrupt. **rottenness** *n.*

rotter n. Slang despicable person.

Rottweiler [rawt-vile-er] n. large sturdy dog with a smooth black and tan coat and usu. a docked tail.

rotund [roe-tund] adj. 1. round and plump. 2. sonorous. **rotundity** n.

rotunda n. circular building or room, esp. with a dome.

rouble [roo-bl] n. monetary unit of the Soviet Union.

roué [roo-ay] n. man given to immoral living.

rouge n. 1. red cosmetic used to colour the cheeks. 2. apply rouge to.

rough adj. 1. not smooth, uneven or irregular. 2. violent, stormy, or boisterous. 3. rude. 4. lacking refinement. 5. approximate. 6. in preliminary form. —v. 7. make rough. 8. plan out approximately. —n. 9. rough state or area. 10. sketch. **rough it** live without the usual comforts etc. **roughen** v. **roughly** adv. **roughness** n. **roughage** n. indigestible constituents of food which aid digestion. **rough-and-ready** adj. hastily prepared but adequate. **rough-and-tumble** n. playful fight. **rough-hewn** adj. roughly shaped. **roughhouse** n. Slang fight. **roughneck** n. Slang 1. violent person. 2. worker on an oil rig.

roughcast n. 1. mixture of plaster and small stones for outside walls. —v. 2. coat with this.

roughshod adv. **ride roughshod over** act with total disregard for.

roulette n. gambling game played with a revolving wheel and a ball.

round adj. 1. spherical, cylindrical, circular, or curved. 2. complete or whole, e.g. round numbers. 3. plump. 4. candid, e.g. a round assertion. —adv. 5. with a circular or circuitous course. 6. on all or most sides. 7. to a specific place. —n. 8. thing round in shape. 9. recurrent duties. 10. customary course, as of a milkman. 11. stage in a competition. 12. game (of golf). 13. one of several periods in a boxing match etc. 14. bullet or shell for a gun. 15. part song in which singers join at equal intervals. 16. circular movement. 17. set of sandwiches. 18. number of drinks bought at one time. —prep. 19. surrounding or encircling. 20. on or outside the perimeter of. 21. on all sides of. —v. 22. make or become round. 23. move round. **roundly** adv. thoroughly. **rounders** n. bat-and-ball team game. **round on** v. attack angrily. **round robin** petition signed with names in a circle to conceal the order. **round table** meeting of people on equal terms for discussion. **round-the-clock** adj. throughout the day and night. **round trip** journey out and back again, esp. by a different route. **round up** v. gather (people or animals) together. **roundup** n.

roundabout n. 1. road junction at which traffic passes round a central island. 2. revolving circular platform on which people ride for amusement. —adj. 3. not straightforward.

roundel n. 1. small disc. 2. rondeau. **roundelay** n. simple song with a refrain.

Roundhead n. supporter of Parliament against Charles I in the English Civil War.

rouse v. 1. wake up. 2. provoke or excite. **rousing** adj. lively, vigorous.

roustabout n. labourer on an oil rig.

rout n. 1. overwhelming defeat. 2. disorderly retreat. —v. 3. defeat and put to flight. **rout out** v. 1. search for. 2. drive out.

route n. 1. road. 2. chosen way. —v. 3. send by a particular route. **routemarch** n. long training march.

routine n. 1. usual or regular method of procedure. 2. set sequence. —adj. 3. ordinary. 4. regular.

roux [roo] n. fat and flour cooked together as a basis for sauces.

rove v. wander. **rover** n. 1. person who roves. 2. pirate.

row[1] n. straight line of people or things. **in a row** in succession.

row[2] v. 1. propel (a boat) by oars. —n. 2. spell of rowing. **rowing boat** boat propelled by oars.

row[3] Informal —n. 1. dispute. 2. disturbance. 3. reprimand. —v. 4. quarrel noisily.

rowan n. tree producing bright red berries, mountain ash.

rowdy adj. -dier, -diest. 1. disorderly, noisy, and rough. —n., pl. -dies. 2. person like this.

rowel [rhymes with towel] n. small spiked wheel on a spur.

rowlock n. device on the gunwale of a boat that holds an oar in place.

royal adj. 1. of, befitting, or supported by a king or queen. 2. splendid. —n. 3. Informal member of a royal family. **royally** adv. **royalist** n. supporter of monarchy. **royalty**

n. **1.** royal people. **2.** rank or power. **3.** *pl.* **-ties.** payment to author, musician, inventor, etc. **royal blue** bright blue.

RPI retail price index.

rpm revolutions per minute.

RR Right Reverend.

RSI repetitive strain injury.

RSPCA Royal Society for the Prevention of Cruelty to Animals.

RSVP please reply.

Rt Hon. Right Honourable.

Ru *Chem.* ruthenium.

rub *v.* **rubbing, rubbed. 1.** apply pressure and friction to (something) with a circular or backwards-and-forwards movement. **2.** clean, polish, or dry by rubbing. **3.** remove by rubbing. **4.** chafe or fray through rubbing. —*n.* **5.** act of rubbing. **6.** difficulty. **rub it in** emphasize an unpleasant fact. **rub along** *v.* have a friendly relationship. **rub off** *v.* affect through close association. **rub out** *v.* remove with a rubber.

rubato *adv. Music* with expressive flexibility of tempo.

rubber[1] *n.* **1.** strong waterproof elastic material, orig. made from the dried sap of a tropical tree, now usually synthetic. **2.** piece of rubber used for erasing mistakes. —*adj.* **3.** made of or producing rubber. **rubberize** *v.* coat or treat with rubber. **rubbery** *adj.* like rubber, soft or elastic. **rubberneck** *v. US* stare with unthinking curiosity. **rubber plant** house plant with glossy leaves. **rubber stamp** *n.* device for imprinting the date, a name, etc. **2.** automatic authorization.

rubber[2] *n.* **1.** match consisting of three games of bridge, whist, etc. **2.** series of matches.

rubbish *n.* **1.** waste matter. **2.** anything worthless. **3.** nonsense. —*v.* **4.** *Informal* criticize. **rubbishy** *adj.*

rubble *n.* fragments of broken stone, brick, etc.

rubella [roo-**bell**-a] *n.* same as GERMAN MEASLES.

rubicund [roo-**bik**-kund] *adj.* ruddy.

rubidium [roo-**bid**-ee-um] *n.* soft highly reactive radioactive element.

rubric [roo-**brik**] *n.* **1.** heading or explanation inserted in a text. **2.** set of rules for behaviour.

ruby *n., pl.* **-bies. 1.** red precious gemstone.

—*adj.* **2.** deep red. **ruby wedding** fortieth wedding anniversary.

ruche *n.* pleat or frill of lace etc. as a decoration.

ruck[1] *n.* **1.** rough crowd of common people. **2.** *Rugby* loose scrummage.

ruck[2] *n., v.* wrinkle or crease.

rucksack *n.* large pack carried on the back.

ructions *pl. n. Informal* noisy uproar.

rudder *n.* vertical hinged piece at the stern of a boat or at the rear of an aircraft, for steering.

ruddy *adj.* **-dier, -diest. 1.** of a fresh healthy red colour. —*adv., adj.* **2.** *Informal* bloody.

rude *adj.* **1.** impolite or insulting. **2.** coarse, vulgar, or obscene. **3.** roughly made. **4.** robust. **5.** unexpected and unpleasant. **rudely** *adv.* **rudeness** *n.*

rudiments *pl. n.* simplest and most basic stages of a subject. **rudimentary** *adj.* basic, elementary.

rue[1] *v.* **ruing, rued.** feel regret for. **rueful** *adj.* regretful or sorry. **ruefully** *adv.*

rue[2] *n.* plant with evergreen bitter leaves.

ruff[1] *n.* **1.** starched and frilled collar. **2.** natural collar of feathers, fur, etc. on certain birds and animals. **3.** kind of sandpiper.

ruff[2] *n., adj., v. Cards* same as TRUMP[1]

ruffian *n.* violent lawless person.

ruffle *v.* **1.** disturb the calm of. **2.** annoy, irritate. —*n.* **3.** frill or pleat.

rufous *adj.* reddish-brown.

rug *n.* **1.** small carpet. **2.** thick woollen blanket.

rugby *n.* form of football played with an oval ball which may be handled by the players.

rugged [rug-gid] *adj.* **1.** rough. **2.** uneven and jagged. **3.** strong-featured. **4.** tough and sturdy.

rugger *n. Informal* rugby.

ruin *n.* **1.** broken-down unused building(s). **2.** destruction or decay. **3.** loss of wealth, position, etc. —*v.* **4.** reduce to ruins. **5.** spoil. **6.** impoverish. **ruination** *n.* **1.** act of ruining. **2.** state of being ruined. **3.** cause of ruin. **ruinous** *adj.* **1.** causing ruin. **2.** more expensive than is reasonable. **ruinously** *adv.*

rule *n.* **1.** statement of what is allowed, for example in a game or procedure. **2.** what is usual. **3.** government, authority, or control. **4.** measuring device with a straight edge.

—*v.* **5.** govern. **6.** restrain. **7.** give a formal decision. **8.** be pre-eminent. **9.** mark with straight line(s). **as a rule** usually. **ruler** *n.* **1.** person who governs. **2.** measuring device with a straight edge. **ruling** *n.* formal decision. **rule of thumb** practical but imprecise approach. **rule out** *v.* exclude.

rum[1] *n.* alcoholic drink distilled from sugar cane.

rum[2] *adj. Informal* odd, strange.

rumba *n.* lively ballroom dance of Cuban origin.

rumble[1] *v.* **1.** (of traffic etc.) make a low continuous noise. —*n.* **2.** such a noise.

rumble[2] *v. Informal* discover the (disreputable) truth about.

rumbustious *adj.* boisterous or unruly.

ruminate *v.* **1.** ponder or meditate. **2.** chew the cud. **ruminant** *adj., n.* cud-chewing (animal, such as a cow, sheep, or deer). **rumination** *n.* quiet meditation and reflection. **ruminative** *adj.*

rummage *v.* **1.** search untidily and at length. —*n.* **2.** untidy search through a collection of things.

rummy *n.* card game in which players try to collect sets or sequences.

rumour *n.* **1.** gossip or common talk. **2.** unproved statement. **be rumoured** be circulated as a rumour.

rump *n.* **1.** buttocks. **2.** rear of an animal.

rumple *v.* make untidy, crumpled, or dishevelled.

rumpus *n., pl.* **-puses.** noisy commotion.

run *v.* **running, ran, run. 1.** move with a more rapid pace than walking. **2.** go quickly (across). **3.** flow. **4.** compete in a race, election, etc. **5.** continue (for a specified period). **6.** function. **7.** travel according to schedule. **8.** melt. **9.** spread. **10.** (of stitches) unravel. **11.** expose oneself to (a risk). **12.** (of a newspaper) publish (a story). **13.** smuggle (goods, esp. arms). **14.** manage or be in charge of. —*n.* **15.** ride in a car. **16.** act or spell of running. **17.** rush. **18.** tendency or trend, e.g. *the run of the market.* **19.** continuous period, e.g. *a run of good luck.* **20.** sequence. **21.** heavy demand. **22.** enclosure for domestic fowls. **23.** series of unravelled stitches, ladder. **24.** score of one at cricket. **25.** steep snow-covered course for skiing. **26.** unrestricted access. **run across** *v.* meet by chance. **run away** *v.*

make one's escape, flee. **runaway** *n.* person or animal that runs away. **run down** *v.* **1.** be rude about. **2.** stop working. **3.** reduce in number or size. **rundown** *n.* **run-down** *adj.* exhausted. **run in** *v.* **1.** run (an engine) gently. **2.** *Informal* arrest. **run-in** *n. Informal* argument. **run into** *v.* meet. **run-of-the-mill** *adj.* ordinary. **run out** *v.* be completely used up. **run up** *v.* incur (a debt).

rune *n.* **1.** any character of the earliest Germanic alphabet. **2.** obscure piece of writing using mysterious symbols. **runic** *adj.*

rung[1] *n.* crossbar on a ladder.

rung[2] *v.* past participle of RING[2]

runnel *n.* small brook or rivulet.

runner *n.* **1.** competitor in a race. **2.** messenger. **3.** smuggler. **4.** part underneath an ice skate etc., on which it slides. **5.** slender horizontal stem of a plant, such as a strawberry, running along the ground and forming new roots at intervals. **6.** long strip of carpet or decorative cloth. **runner bean** seeds and pod of a climbing bean plant. **runner-up** *n.* person who comes second in a competition.

running *adj.* **1.** continuous. **2.** consecutive. **3.** (of water) flowing. —*n.* **4.** act of moving or flowing quickly. **5.** management of a business etc. **in, out of the running** having or not having a good chance in a competition.

runny *adj.* **-nier, -niest. 1.** tending to flow. **2.** exuding moisture.

runt *n.* **1.** smallest animal in a litter. **2.** undersized person.

runway *n.* hard level roadway where aircraft take off and land.

rupee *n.* monetary unit of India and Pakistan.

rupture *n.* **1.** breaking, breach. **2.** hernia. —*v.* **3.** break, burst, or sever.

rural *adj.* in or of the countryside.

ruse [rooz] *n.* stratagem or trick.

rush[1] *v.* **1.** move or do very quickly. **2.** force (someone) to act hastily. **3.** make a sudden attack upon (a person or place). —*n.* **4.** sudden quick or violent movement. **5.** sudden demand. —*pl.* **6.** first unedited prints of a scene for a film. —*adj.* **7.** done with speed, hasty. **rush hour** period at the beginning and end of the working day, when many people are travelling to or from work.

rush[2] *n.* marsh plant with a slender pithy

stem. **rushy** *adj*. **rushier, rushiest**. full of rushes.

rusk *n*. hard brown crisp biscuit, used esp. for feeding babies.

russet *adj*. **1**. reddish-brown. —*n*. **2**. the colour. **3**. apple with rough reddish-brown skin.

Russian *n*. **1**. official language of the Soviet Union. **2**. person from Russia or the Soviet Union. —*adj*. **3**. of Russia or the Soviet Union. **Russian roulette** act of bravado in which a person spins the cylinder of a revolver loaded with only one cartridge and presses the trigger with the barrel against his own head.

rust *n*. **1**. reddish-brown coating formed on iron etc. that has been exposed to moisture. **2**. disease of plants with rust-coloured spots. —*adj*. **3**. reddish-brown. —*v*. **4**. become coated with rust. **5**. deteriorate through lack of use. **rusty** *adj*. **rustier, rustiest. 1**. coated with rust. **2**. of a rust colour. **3**. out of practice. **rustproof** *adj*.

rustic *adj*. **1**. of or resembling country people. **2**. rural. **3**. crude, awkward, or uncouth. **4**. (of furniture) made of un-trimmed branches. —*n*. **5**. person from the country. **rusticity** *n*.

rusticate *v*. **1**. banish temporarily from university as a punishment. **2**. retire to the country. **rustication** *n*.

rustle[1] *v*. **1**. make a low whispering sound, as of dry leaves. —*n*. **2**. this sound.

rustle[2] *v*. *US* steal (cattle). **rustler** *n*. *US* cattle thief. **rustle up** *v*. prepare at short notice.

rut[1] *n*. **1**. furrow made by wheels. **2**. dull settled habits or way of living.

rut[2] *n*. **1**. recurrent period of sexual excitability in male deer. —*v*. **rutting, rutted. 2**. be in a period of sexual excitability.

ruthenium *n*. rare hard brittle white element.

rutherfordium *n*. artificially produced radioactive element.

ruthless *adj*. pitiless, merciless. **ruthlessly** *adv*. **ruthlessness** *n*.

rye *n*. **1**. kind of grain used for fodder and bread. **2**. *US* whiskey made from rye.

rye-grass *n*. any of several kinds of grass cultivated for fodder.

S

s 1. second(s). **2.** singular.

S 1. Saint. **2.** South(ern). **3.** *Chem.* sulphur.

SA 1. Salvation Army. **2.** South Africa.

Sabbath *n.* day of worship and rest: Saturday for Jews, Sunday for Christians. **sabbatical** *adj., n.* (denoting) leave for study.

sable *n.* **1.** dark fur from a small weasel-like Arctic animal. —*adj.* **2.** black.

sabot [**sab**-oh] *n.* wooden shoe, clog.

sabotage *n.* **1.** intentional damage done to machinery, systems, etc. —*v.* **2.** damage intentionally. **saboteur** *n.* person who commits sabotage.

sabre *n.* **1.** curved cavalry sword. **2.** light fencing sword.

sac *n.* pouchlike structure in an animal or plant.

saccharin, saccharine *n.* artificial sweetener. **saccharine** *adj.* **1.** excessively sweet. **2.** of or like sugar.

sacerdotal *adj.* of priests.

sachet *n.* **1.** small envelope or bag containing a single portion. **2.** small bag of perfumed powder for scenting clothing.

sack[1] *n.* **1.** large bag made of coarse material. **2.** plundering of a captured town. **3.** *Informal* dismissal. **4.** *Slang* bed. —*v.* **5.** plunder (a captured town). **6.** *Informal* dismiss. **sacking** *n.* rough woven material used for sacks. **sackcloth** *n.* coarse fabric used for sacks, formerly worn as a penance.

sack[2] *n. Old-fashioned* dry white wine.

sacrament *n.* ceremony of the Christian Church, esp. Communion. **sacramental** *adj.*

sacred *adj.* **1.** holy. **2.** set apart, reserved. **3.** connected with religion. **sacred cow** person, custom, etc. regarded as being beyond criticism.

sacrifice *n.* **1.** giving something up. **2.** thing given up. **3.** making of an offering to a god. **4.** thing offered. —*v.* **5.** offer as a sacrifice. **6.** give (something) up. **sacrificial** *adj.*

sacrilege *n.* misuse or desecration of something sacred. **sacrilegious** *adj.*

sacristan *n.* person in charge of the contents of a church. **sacristy** *n., pl.* **-ties.** room in a church where sacred objects are kept.

sacrosanct *adj.* regarded as sacred, inviolable.

sacrum [**say**-krum] *n., pl.* **-cra.** compound bone at the base of the spine.

sad *adj.* **sadder, saddest. 1.** sorrowful, unhappy. **2.** causing or expressing sorrow. **3.** deplorably bad. **sadden** *v.* make sad. **sadly** *adv.* **sadness** *n.*

saddle *n.* **1.** rider's seat on a horse or bicycle. **2.** joint of meat. —*v.* **3.** put a saddle on (a horse). **4.** burden (with a responsibility). **saddler** *n.* maker or seller of saddles. **saddlery** *n.*

sadism [**say**-dizz-um] *n.* gaining of (sexual) pleasure from inflicting pain. **sadist** *n.* **sadistic** *adj.* **sadistically** *adv.*

sadomasochism *n.* combination of sadism and masochism. **sadomasochist** *n.*

s.a.e. stamped addressed envelope.

safari *n., pl.* **-ris.** expedition to hunt or observe wild animals, esp. in Africa. **safari park** park where lions, elephants, etc. are kept uncaged so that people can see them from cars.

safe *adj.* **1.** secure, protected. **2.** uninjured, out of danger. **3.** not involving risk. **4.** worthy of trust. —*n.* **5.** strong lockable container. **safely** *adv.* **safe-conduct** *n.* permit allowing travel through a dangerous area. **safe deposit** place where valuables can be stored safely. **safekeeping** *n.* protection.

safeguard *n.* **1.** protection. —*v.* **2.** protect.

safety *n., pl.* **-ties.** state of being safe. **safety belt** same as SEAT BELT. **safety net** net to catch performers on a trapeze or high wire if they fall. **safety pin** pin with a spring fastening and a guard over the point when closed. **safety valve 1.** valve that allows steam etc. to escape if pressure becomes excessive. **2.** harmless outlet for emotion.

safflower *n.* thistle-like plant with flowers used for dye and oil.

saffron *n.* **1.** orange-coloured flavouring obtained from a crocus. —*adj.* **2.** orange.

sag v. **sagging, sagged. 1.** sink in the middle. **2.** tire. **3.** (of clothes) hang loosely. —n. **4.** droop.

saga [**sah**-ga] n. **1.** legend of Norse heroes. **2.** any long story.

sagacious adj. wise. **sagaciously** adv. **sagacity** n.

sage[1] n. aromatic herb with grey-green leaves.

sage[2] n. **1.** very wise man. —adj. **2.** Lit. wise. **sagely** adv.

sagebrush n. aromatic plant of West N America.

Sagittarius n. (the archer) ninth sign of the zodiac.

sago n. starchy cereal from the powdered pith of the **sago palm.**

sahib n. Indian term of address placed after a man's name as a mark of respect.

said v. past of SAY.

sail n. **1.** sheet of fabric stretched to catch the wind for propelling a sailing boat. **2.** journey by boat. **3.** arm of a windmill. —v. **4.** travel by water. **5.** move smoothly. **6.** begin a voyage. **7.** navigate a vessel. **sailor** n. **1.** member of a ship's crew. **2.** person considered as liable or not liable to seasickness, e.g. a bad sailor, a good sailor. **sailboard** n. board with a mast and single sail, used for windsurfing. **sailcloth** n. **1.** fabric for making sails. **2.** light canvas for making clothes.

saint n. **1.** Christianity person venerated after death as specially holy. **2.** exceptionally good person. **saintly** adj. **saintliness** n. **sainthood** n.

saithe n. dark-coloured edible sea fish.

sake[1] n. **1.** benefit. **2.** purpose. **for the sake of 1.** for the purpose of. **2.** to please or benefit (someone).

sake[2], **saki** [**sah**-kee] n. Japanese alcoholic drink made from fermented rice.

salaam [sal-**ahm**] n. **1.** low bow of greeting among Muslims. —v. **2.** make a salaam.

salacious adj. excessively concerned with sex.

salad n. dish of raw vegetables, eaten as a meal or part of a meal. **salad days** period of youth and inexperience. **salad dressing** sauce of oil and vinegar or mayonnaise.

salamander n. **1.** type of lizard. **2.** mythical reptile supposed to live in fire.

salami n. highly spiced sausage.

salary n., pl. **-ries.** fixed regular payment, usu. monthly, to an employee. **salaried** adj.

sale n. **1.** exchange of goods for money. **2.** amount sold. **3.** selling of goods at unusually low prices. **4.** auction. **saleable** adj. fit or likely to be sold. **saleroom** n. place where goods are sold by auction. **salesman, saleswoman, salesperson** n. person who sells goods. **salesmanship** n. skill in selling.

salient [**say**-lee-ent] adj. **1.** prominent, noticeable. —n. **2.** Mil. projecting part of a front line.

saline [**say**-line] adj. containing salt. **salinity** n.

saliva [sal-**lie**-va] n. liquid that forms in the mouth, spittle. **salivary** adj. **salivate** v. produce saliva.

sallow[1] adj. of an unhealthy pale or yellowish colour.

sallow[2] n. tree or shrub related to the willow.

sally n., pl. **-lies. 1.** sudden brief attack by troops. **2.** witty remark. —v. **-lying, -lied.** (foll. by forth) **3.** rush out. **4.** go out.

salmon n. **1.** large fish with orange-pink flesh valued as food. —adj. **2.** orange-pink.

salmonella n., pl. **-lae.** bacterium causing food poisoning.

salon n. **1.** commercial premises of a hairdresser, beautician, etc. **2.** elegant reception room for guests. **3.** informal gathering of important people.

saloon n. **1.** car with a fixed roof. **2.** large public room, as on a ship. **3.** US bar serving alcoholic drinks. **saloon bar** more expensive bar in a pub.

salsify n. plant with a long white edible root.

salt n. **1.** white crystalline substance used to season food. **2.** chemical compound of acid and metal. **3.** liveliness, wit. —pl. **4.** mineral salts used as a medicine. —v. **5.** season or preserve with salt. **6.** scatter salt over (an icy road) to melt the ice. **old salt** experienced sailor. **with a pinch, grain of salt** allowing for exaggeration. **worth one's salt** efficient. **salty** adj. **salt away** v. hoard or save. **saltcellar** n. small container for salt at table. **saltwater** adj. living in the sea.

SALT Strategic Arms Limitation Talks or Treaty.

saltpetre n. compound used in gunpowder and as a preservative.

salubrious *adj.* favourable to health. **salubrity** *n.*

Saluki *n.* tall hound with a silky coat.

salutary *adj.* producing a beneficial result.

salute *n.* **1.** motion of the arm as a formal military sign of respect. **2.** firing of guns as a military greeting of honour. —*v.* **3.** greet with a salute. **4.** make a salute. **5.** acknowledge with praise. **salutation** *n.* greeting by words or actions.

salvage *n.* **1.** saving of a ship or other property from destruction. **2.** property so saved. —*v.* **3.** save from destruction or waste. **4.** gain (something beneficial) from a failure.

salvation *n.* **1.** fact or state of being saved from harm or the consequences of sin. **2.** person or thing that preserves from harm.

salve *n.* **1.** healing or soothing ointment. —*v.* **2.** soothe or appease, e.g. *salve one's conscience.*

salver *n.* (silver) tray on which something is presented.

salvia *n.* plant with blue or red flowers.

salvo *n., pl.* **-vos, -voes. 1.** simultaneous discharge of guns etc. **2.** burst of applause or questions.

sal volatile [sal vol-**at**-ill-ee] *n.* preparation of ammonia, used to revive a person who feels faint.

SAM surface-to-air missile.

Samaritan *n.* person who helps people in distress.

samarium *n.* silvery metallic element.

samba *n., pl.* **-bas.** lively Brazilian dance.

same *adj.* **1.** identical, not different, unchanged. **2.** just mentioned. **all the same, just the same** nevertheless. **sameness** *n.*

samovar *n.* Russian tea urn.

Samoyed *n.* dog with a thick white coat and tightly curled tail.

sampan *n.* small boat with oars used in China.

samphire *n.* plant found on rocks by the seashore.

sample *n.* **1.** part taken as representative of a whole. —*v.* **2.** take and test a sample of. **sampler** *n.* piece of embroidery showing the embroiderer's skill. **sampling** *n.*

samurai *n., pl.* **-rai.** member of an ancient Japanese warrior caste.

sanatorium *n., pl.* **-riums, -ria. 1.** institution for invalids or convalescents. **2.** room for sick pupils at a boarding school.

sanctify *v.* **-fying, -fied. 1.** make holy. **2.** sanction as religiously binding. **sanctification** *n.*

sanctimonious *adj.* making a show of piety.

sanction *n.* **1.** permission, authorization. **2.** coercive measure or penalty. —*v.* **3.** allow, authorize.

sanctity *n.* sacredness, inviolability.

sanctuary *n., pl.* **-aries. 1.** place of safety for a fugitive. **2.** place where animals or birds can live undisturbed. **3.** holy place. **4.** part of a church nearest the altar.

sanctum *n., pl.* **-tums, -ta. 1.** sacred place. **2.** person's private room.

sand *n.* **1.** substance consisting of small grains of rock, esp. on a beach or in a desert. —*pl.* **2.** stretches of sand forming a beach or desert. —*v.* **3.** smooth with sandpaper. **4.** fill with sand. **sander** *n.* power tool for smoothing surfaces. **sandy** *adj.* **1.** covered with sand. **2.** (of hair) reddish-fair. **sandbag** *n.* **1.** bag filled with sand, used as protection against gunfire, floodwater, etc. —*v.* **2.** protect with sandbags. **sandbank** *n.* bank of sand below the surface of a river or sea. **sandblast** *v., n.* (clean with) a jet of sand blown from a nozzle under pressure. **sand castle** model of a castle made from sand. **sand martin** small brown songbird. **sandpaper** *n.* **1.** paper coated with sand for smoothing a surface. —*v.* **2.** smooth with sandpaper. **sandpiper** *n.* shore bird with a long bill and slender legs. **sandstone** *n.* rock composed of sand. **sandstorm** *n.* desert wind that whips up clouds of sand.

sandal *n.* light shoe consisting of a sole attached by straps.

sandalwood *n.* sweet-scented wood.

sandwich *n.* **1.** two slices of bread with a layer of food between. —*v.* **2.** insert between two other things. **sandwich board** pair of boards hung over a person's shoulders to display advertisements in front and behind. **sandwich course** course consisting of alternate periods of study and work.

sane *adj.* **1.** of sound mind. **2.** sensible, rational. **sanity** *n.*

sang *v.* past tense of SING.

sang-froid [sahng-**frwah**] *n.* composure, self-possession.

sangria *n.* Spanish drink of wine and fruit juice.

sanguinary *adj.* **1.** accompanied by bloodshed. **2.** bloodthirsty.

sanguine *adj.* **1.** cheerful, optimistic. **2.** ruddy.

Sanhedrin [**san**-id-rin] *n. Judaism* highest court of the ancient Jewish nation.

sanitary *adj.* **1.** promoting health by getting rid of dirt and germs. **2.** hygienic. **sanitation** *n.* sanitary measures, esp. drainage or sewerage. **sanitary towel** absorbent pad worn externally during menstruation.

sank *v.* past tense of SINK.

Sanskrit *n.* ancient language of India.

Santa Claus *n.* legendary patron saint of children, who brings presents at Christmas.

sap[1] *n.* **1.** moisture that circulates in plants. **2.** energy. **3.** *Informal* gullible person. **sappy** *adj.*

sap[2] *v.* **sapping, sapped. 1.** undermine. **2.** weaken. —*n.* **3.** trench dug to undermine an enemy position. **sapper** *n.* soldier in an engineering unit.

sapient [**say**-pee-ent] *adj. Lit.* wise, shrewd. **sapience** *n.*

sapling *n.* young tree.

sapphire *n.* **1.** blue precious stone. —*adj.* **2.** deep blue.

saprophyte *n.* plant that lives on dead organic matter.

saraband, sarabande *n.* slow stately Spanish dance.

Saracen *n. Hist.* Arab or Muslim who opposed the Crusades.

sarcasm *n.* (use of) bitter or wounding ironic language. **sarcastic** *adj.* **sarcastically** *adv.*

sarcoma *n., pl.* **-mata, -mas.** malignant tumour beginning in connective tissue.

sarcophagus *n., pl.* **-gi, -guses.** stone coffin.

sardine *n.* small fish of the herring family, usu. preserved in tightly packed tins.

sardonic *adj.* mocking or scornful. **sardonically** *adv.*

sardonyx *n.* brown-and-white gemstone.

sargassum, sargasso *n.* type of floating seaweed.

sari, saree *n.* long piece of cloth draped around the body and over one shoulder, worn by Hindu women.

sarong *n.* long piece of cloth tucked around the waist or under the armpits, worn esp. in Malaysia.

sarsaparilla *n.* soft drink, orig. made from the root of a tropical American plant.

sartorial *adj.* of men's clothes or tailoring.

SAS Special Air Service.

sash[1] *n.* decorative strip of cloth worn round the waist or over one shoulder.

sash[2] *n.* wooden frame containing the panes of a window. **sash window** window consisting of two sashes that can be opened by sliding one over the other.

sassafras *n.* American tree with aromatic bark used medicinally.

Sassenach *n. Scot.* English person.

sat *v.* past of SIT.

Sat. Saturday.

Satan *n.* the Devil. **satanic** *adj.* **1.** of Satan. **2.** supremely evil. **Satanism** *n.* worship of Satan.

satchel *n.* bag, usu. with a shoulder strap, for carrying school books.

sate *v.* satisfy (a desire or appetite) fully.

satellite *n.* **1.** man-made device orbiting in space. **2.** heavenly body that orbits another. **3.** country that is dependent on a more powerful one. —*adj.* **4.** of or used in the transmission of television signals from a satellite to the home.

satiate [**say**-she-ate] *v.* **1.** satisfy fully. **2.** surfeit. **satiable** *adj.* **satiety** [sat-**tie**-a-tee] *n.* feeling of having had too much.

satin *n.* silky fabric with a glossy surface on one side. **satiny** *adj.* of or like satin. **satinwood** *n.* tropical tree yielding hard wood.

satire *n.* **1.** use of ridicule to expose vice or folly. **2.** poem or other work that does this. **satirical** *adj.* **satirist** *n.* **satirize** *v.* ridicule by means of satire.

satisfy *v.* **-fying, -fied. 1.** please, content. **2.** provide amply for (a need or desire). **3.** convince, persuade. **4.** fulfil the requirements of. **satisfaction** *n.* **satisfactory** *adj.*

satsuma *n.* kind of small orange.

saturate *v.* **1.** soak thoroughly. **2.** cause to absorb the maximum of something. **saturation** *n.* **saturation point** point at which some capacity is at its fullest.

Saturday *n.* seventh day of the week.

Saturn *n.* **1.** Roman god. **2.** one of the planets. **saturnine** *adj.* gloomy in temperament or appearance. **saturnalia** *n.* wild revelry.

satyr *n.* **1.** woodland god, part man, part goat. **2.** lustful man.

sauce *n.* **1.** liquid added to food to enhance flavour. **2.** *Informal* impudence. **saucy** *adj.* **1.** impudent. **2.** pert, jaunty. **saucily** *adv.* **saucepan** *n.* cooking pot with a long handle.

saucer *n.* small round dish put under a cup.

sauerkraut *n.* shredded cabbage fermented in brine.

sauna *n.* Finnish-style steam bath.

saunter *v.* **1.** walk in a leisurely manner, stroll. —*n.* **2.** leisurely walk.

saurian *adj.* of or like a lizard.

sausage *n.* minced meat in an edible tube-shaped skin. **sausage roll** skinless sausage covered in pastry.

sauté [so-tay] *v.* **-téing** *or* **-téeing**, **-téed**. fry quickly in a little fat.

savage *adj.* **1.** wild, untamed. **2.** cruel and violent. **3.** uncivilized, primitive. —*n.* **4.** uncivilized person. —*v.* **5.** attack ferociously. **6.** criticize violently. **savagely** *adv.* **savagery** *n.*

savanna, savannah *n.* extensive open grassy plain in Africa.

savant *n.* learned person.

save *v.* **1.** rescue or preserve from harm, protect. **2.** keep for the future. **3.** set aside (money). **4.** avoid the waste or loss of. **5.** prevent the necessity for. **6.** *Sport* prevent the scoring of (a goal). —*n.* **7.** *Sport* act of preventing a goal. —*prep.* **8.** *Old-fashioned* except. **saver** *n.* **saving** *adj.* **1.** compensating, e.g. *saving grace.* —*n.* **2.** economy. —*pl.* **3.** money put by for future use. —*prep.* **4.** except.

saveloy *n.* spicy smoked sausage.

saviour *n.* **1.** person who rescues another. **2.** (S-) Christ.

savoir-faire [sav-wahr-**fair**] *n. French* ability to do and say the right thing in any situation.

savory *n.* aromatic herb used in cooking.

savour *n.* **1.** characteristic taste or odour. **2.** slight but distinctive quality. —*v.* **3.** (foll. by *of*) have a flavour or suggestion of. **4.** enjoy, relish. **savoury** *adj.* **1.** salty or spicy. **2.** not

sweet. —*n., pl.* **-vouries**. **3.** savoury dish served before or after a meal.

savoy *n.* variety of cabbage.

savvy *Slang* —*v.* **-vying**, **-vied**. **1.** understand. —*n.* **2.** understanding, intelligence.

saw[1] *n.* **1.** cutting tool with a toothed metal blade. —*v.* **sawing, sawed, sawed** *or* **sawn. 2.** cut with a saw. **3.** move (something) back and forth. **sawyer** *n.* person who saws timber for a living. **sawdust** *n.* fine wood fragments made in sawing. **sawfish** *n.* fish with a long toothed snout. **sawmill** *n.* mill where timber is sawn into planks.

saw[2] *v.* past tense of SEE[1]

saw[3] *n.* wise saying, proverb.

sax *n. Informal* short for SAXOPHONE.

saxifrage *n.* alpine rock plant with small flowers.

Saxon *n.* **1.** member of the W Germanic people who settled widely in Europe in the early Middle Ages. —*adj.* **2.** of the Saxons.

saxophone *n.* brass wind instrument with keys and a curved body. **saxophonist** *n.*

say *v.* **saying, said. 1.** speak or utter. **2.** express (an idea) in words. **3.** suppose as an example or possibility. **4.** give as one's opinion. **5.** indicate or show. —*n.* **6.** right or chance to speak. **7.** share in a decision. **saying** *n.* maxim, proverb. **say-so** *n. Informal* permission.

SAYE save as you earn: system by which regular payments are made into a savings account from a salary.

Sb *Chem.* antimony.

Sc *Chem.* scandium.

SC South Carolina.

scab *n.* **1.** crust formed over a wound. **2.** *Offens.* blackleg. **3.** disease of plants and animals. **scabby** *adj.* **1.** covered with scabs. **2.** *Informal* despicable.

scabbard *n.* sheath for a sword or dagger.

scabies [skay-beez] *n.* itchy skin disease.

scabious [skay-bee-uss] *n.* plant with globular blue flower heads.

scabrous [skay-bruss] *adj.* **1.** indecent. **2.** rough and scaly.

scaffold *n.* **1.** temporary platform for workmen. **2.** gallows. **scaffolding** *n.* (materials for building) scaffolds.

scalar *n., adj.* (variable quantity) having magnitude but no direction.

scald v. **1.** burn with hot liquid or steam. **2.** sterilize with boiling water. **3.** heat (liquid) almost to boiling point. —n. **4.** injury by scalding.

scale[1] n. **1.** one of the thin overlapping plates covering fishes and reptiles. **2.** thin flake. **3.** coating which forms in kettles etc. due to hard water. **4.** tartar formed on the teeth. —v. **5.** remove scales from. **6.** come off in scales. **scaly** adj.

scale[2] n. (often pl.) weighing instrument.

scale[3] n. **1.** graduated table or sequence of marks at regular intervals, used as a reference in making measurements. **2.** fixed series of notes in music. **3.** ratio of size between a thing and a representation of it. **4.** relative degree or extent. **5.** graded system, e.g. *a wage scale*. **6.** notation of a number system. —v. **7.** climb. **scale up, down** v. increase *or* decrease proportionately in size.

scalene adj. (of a triangle) with three unequal sides.

scallion n. spring onion.

scallop n. **1.** edible shellfish with two fan-shaped shells. **2.** one of a series of small curves along an edge. **scalloped** adj. decorated with small curves along the edge.

scallywag n. *Informal* scamp, rascal.

scalp n. **1.** skin and hair on top of the head. **2.** part of this taken as a trophy from a slain person by a N American Indian. —v. **3.** cut off the scalp of.

scalpel n. small surgical knife.

scamp n. **1.** mischievous child. —v. **2.** do carelessly.

scamper v. **1.** run about hurriedly or in play. —n. **2.** scampering.

scampi pl. n. large prawns.

scan v. **scanning, scanned. 1.** scrutinize carefully. **2.** glance over quickly. **3.** examine or search (an area) by passing a radar or sonar beam over it. **4.** (of verse) conform to metrical rules. —n. **5.** scanning. **scanner** n. electronic device used for scanning. **scansion** n. metrical scanning of verse.

scandal n. **1.** disgraceful action or event. **2.** malicious gossip. **3.** shame or outrage. **scandalize** v. shock by scandal. **scandalmonger** n. person who spreads gossip. **scandalous** adj.

Scandinavian n., adj. (inhabitant or language) of Scandinavia (Norway, Denmark, Sweden, and Iceland).

scandium n. rare silvery-white metallic element.

scant adj. barely sufficient, meagre.

scanty adj. **scantier, scantiest.** barely sufficient or not sufficient. **scantily** adv. **scantiness** n.

scapegoat n. person made to bear the blame for others.

scapula n., pl. **-lae, -las.** shoulder blade. **scapular** adj. of the scapula.

scar[1] n. **1.** mark left by a healed wound. **2.** permanent emotional damage left by an unpleasant experience. —v. **scarring, scarred.** mark or become marked with a scar.

scar[2] n. bare craggy rock formation.

scarab n. sacred beetle of ancient Egypt.

scarce adj. **1.** not common, rarely found. **2.** insufficient to meet demand. **make oneself scarce** *Informal* go away. **scarcely** adv. **1.** only just. **2.** not quite. **3.** definitely or probably not. **scarcity** n.
▷ As **scarcely** has a negative sense it is followed by *ever* or *any* (not *never* or *no*).

scare v. **1.** frighten or be frightened. **2.** (foll. by *away* or *off*) drive away by frightening. —n. **3.** fright, sudden panic. **4.** period of general alarm. **scary** adj. *Informal* frightening. **scarecrow** n. **1.** figure dressed in old clothes, set up to scare birds away from crops. **2.** raggedly dressed person. **scaremonger** n. person who spreads alarming rumours.

scarf[1] n., pl. **scarfs, scarves.** piece of material worn round the neck, head, or shoulders.

scarf[2] n. **1.** joint between two pieces of timber made by notching the ends and fastening them together. —v. **2.** join in this way.

scarify v. **-fying, -fied. 1.** scratch or cut slightly all over. **2.** break up and loosen (topsoil). **3.** criticize mercilessly. **scarification** n.

scarlatina n. scarlet fever.

scarlet adj., n. brilliant red. **scarlet fever** infectious fever with a scarlet rash.

scarp n. steep slope.

scarper v. *Slang* run away.

scat[1] v. **scatting, scatted.** *Informal* go away.

scat[2] n. jazz singing using improvised vocal sounds instead of words.

scathing *adj.* harshly critical.

scatology n. preoccupation with obscenity, esp. with references to excrement. **scatological** *adj.*

scatter v. **1.** throw about in various directions. **2.** put here and there. **3.** disperse. —n. **4.** scattering. **scatterbrain** n. empty-headed person.

scatty *adj.* **-tier, -tiest.** *Informal* empty-headed.

scavenge v. search for (anything usable) among discarded material. **scavenger** n. **1.** person who scavenges. **2.** animal that feeds on decaying matter.

SCE Scottish Certificate of Education.

scenario n., *pl.* **-rios. 1.** summary of the plot of a play or film. **2.** imagined sequence of future events.

scene n. **1.** place of action of a real or imaginary event. **2.** subdivision of a play or film in which the action is continuous. **3.** scenery. **4.** view of a place. **5.** display of emotion. **6.** *Informal* specific activity or interest, e.g. *the fashion scene.* **behind the scenes 1.** backstage. **2.** in secret. **scenery** n. **1.** natural features of a landscape. **2.** painted backcloths or screens used on stage to represent the scene of action. **scenic** *adj.* **1.** picturesque. **2.** of stage scenery.

scent n. **1.** pleasant smell. **2.** smell left in passing, by which an animal can be traced. **3.** series of clues. **4.** perfume. —v. **5.** detect by smell. **6.** suspect. **7.** fill with fragrance.

sceptic [skep-tik] n. person who habitually doubts generally accepted beliefs. **sceptical** *adj.* **sceptically** *adv.* **scepticism** n.

sceptre n. ornamental rod symbolizing royal power.

schedule n. **1.** plan of procedure for a project. **2.** timetable. **3.** list. —v. **4.** plan to occur at a certain time. **5.** make or place in a schedule.

schema n., *pl.* **-mata.** overall plan or diagram. **schematic** *adj.* presented as a plan or diagram. **schematize** v. arrange in a scheme.

scheme n. **1.** systematic plan. **2.** secret plot. **3.** systematic arrangement. —v. **4.**

plan in an underhand manner. **schemer** n. **scheming** *adj., n.*

scherzo [skairt-so] n., *pl.* **-zos, -zi.** brisk lively piece of music.

schilling n. standard monetary unit of Austria.

schism [skizz-um] n. (group resulting from) division in an organization. **schismatic** *adj., n.*

schist [skist] n. crystalline rock which splits into layers.

schizo [skit-so] *adj., n., pl.* **-os.** *Informal* schizophrenic (person).

schizoid *adj.* **1.** abnormally introverted. **2.** *Informal* contradictory. —n. **3.** schizoid person.

schizophrenia n. **1.** mental disorder involving deterioration of or confusion about the personality. **2.** *Informal* contradictory behaviour or attitudes. **schizophrenic** *adj., n.*

schmaltz n. excessive sentimentality. **schmaltzy** *adj.*

schnapps n. strong alcoholic spirit.

schnitzel n. thin slice of meat, esp. veal.

scholar n. **1.** learned person. **2.** pupil. **3.** student receiving a scholarship. **scholarly** *adj.* learned. **scholarship** n. **1.** learning. **2.** financial aid given to a student because of academic merit. **scholastic** *adj.* of schools or scholars.

school[1] n. **1.** place where children are taught or instruction is given in a subject. **2.** staff and pupils of a school. **3.** group of artists, thinkers, etc. with shared principles or methods. **4.** department specializing in a subject. —v. **5.** educate. **6.** discipline, train. **schooling** n. education. **schoolboy**, (*fem.*) **schoolgirl** n. child attending school. **schoolmaster, schoolmistress, schoolteacher** n. person who teaches in a school.

school[2] n. shoal of fish, whales, etc.

schooner n. **1.** sailing ship rigged fore-and-aft. **2.** large glass.

schottische n. type of slow polka.

sciatica n. severe pain in the large nerve in the back of the leg. **sciatic** *adj.* **1.** of the hip. **2.** of or afflicted with sciatica.

science n. **1.** systematic study and knowledge of natural or physical phenomena. **2.** branch of this knowledge. **3.** skill or technique. **scientific** *adj.* **1.** of science. **2.** systematic. **scientifically** *adv.* **scientist** n.

person who studies or practises a science. **science fiction** stories making imaginative use of scientific knowledge. **science park** area where scientific research and commercial development are carried on in co-operation.

sci-fi n. short for SCIENCE FICTION.

scimitar n. curved oriental sword.

scintillate v. 1. give off sparks. 2. be animated and witty. **scintillating** adj. **scintillation** n.

scion [sy-on] n. 1. descendant or heir. 2. shoot of a plant for grafting.

scissors pl. n. cutting instrument with two crossed pivoted blades.

sclerosis n., pl. **-ses**. abnormal hardening of body tissues.

scoff[1] v. 1. express derision. —n. 2. derisive expression.

scoff[2] v. Slang eat rapidly.

scold v. 1. find fault with, reprimand. —n. 2. person who scolds. **scolding** n.

scollop n. same as SCALLOP.

sconce n. bracket on a wall for holding candles or lights.

scone n. small plain cake baked in an oven or on a griddle.

scoop n. 1. shovel-like tool for ladling or hollowing out. 2. news story reported in one newspaper before all its rivals. —v. 3. take up or hollow out with or as if with a scoop. 4. beat (rival newspapers) in reporting a news item.

scoot v. Slang leave or move quickly. **scooter** n. 1. child's vehicle propelled by pushing on the ground with one foot. 2. light motorcycle.

scope n. 1. range of activity. 2. opportunity for using abilities.

scorch v. 1. burn on the surface. 2. parch or shrivel from heat. —n. 3. slight burn. **scorcher** n. Informal very hot day.

score n. 1. points gained in a game or competition. 2. twenty. 3. written version of a piece of music showing parts for each musician. 4. mark or cut. 5. grievance, e.g. *settle old scores*. 6. record of amounts due. 7. reason. —pl. 8. lots. —v. 9. gain points in a game. 10. mark or cut. 11. (foll. by *out*) cross out. 12. arrange music (for). 13. keep a record of points. 14. achieve a success. **score off** v. gain an advantage at someone else's expense.

scorn n. 1. contempt, derision. —v. 2. despise. 3. reject with contempt. **scornful** adj. **scornfully** adv.

Scorpio n. (the scorpion) eighth sign of the zodiac.

scorpion n. small lobster-shaped animal with a sting at the end of a jointed tail.

Scot n. person from Scotland. **Scottish** adj. of Scotland, its people, or their languages. **Scotch** n. whisky distilled in Scotland. **Scotch broth** thick soup of beef or lamb and vegetables. **Scotch egg** hard-boiled egg encased in sausage meat and breadcrumbs. **Scots** adj. 1. Scottish. —n. 2. English dialect spoken in Scotland. **Scotsman**, **Scotswoman** n.
▷ Scotch is used only in certain fixed expressions like *Scotch egg*.

scotch v. 1. put an end to. 2. wound.

scot-free adj. without harm or punishment.

Scotland Yard n. headquarters of the police force of metropolitan London.

scoundrel n. Old-fashioned villainous person.

scour[1] v. 1. clean or polish by rubbing with something rough. 2. clear or flush out. —n. 3. scouring. **scourer** n. small rough nylon pad used for cleaning pots and pans.

scour[2] v. 1. search thoroughly and energetically. 2. move swiftly over.

scourge n. 1. person or thing causing severe suffering. 2. whip. —v. 3. cause severe suffering to. 4. whip.

Scouse Informal —n. 1. (also **Scouser**) person from Liverpool. 2. dialect of Liverpool. —adj. 3. of Liverpool, its people, or their dialect.

scout n. 1. person sent out to reconnoitre. 2. (S-) member of the **Scout Association**, an organization for boys which aims to develop character and promotes outdoor activities. —v. 3. act as a scout. 4. reconnoitre. **Scouter** n. leader of a troop of Scouts.

scow n. unpowered barge.

scowl v., n. (have) an angry or sullen expression.

scrabble v. 1. scrape at with the hands, feet, or claws. —n. 2. (S-) ® board game in which words are formed by letter tiles.

scrag n. 1. lean end of a neck of mutton. 2. scrawny person or animal. **scraggy** adj. thin, bony.

scram v. **scramming, scrammed. 1.** (of a nuclear reactor) shut or be shut down in an emergency. **2.** *Informal* go away hastily. —n. **3.** emergency shutdown of a nuclear reactor.

scramble v. **1.** climb or crawl hastily or awkwardly. **2.** struggle with others (for). **3.** mix up. **4.** cook (eggs beaten up with milk). **5.** render (transmitted speech) unintelligible by an electronic device. **6.** (of an aircraft or aircrew) take off hurriedly in an emergency. —n. **7.** scrambling. **8.** rough climb. **9.** disorderly struggle. **10.** motorcycle race over rough ground. **scrambler** n. electronic device that renders transmitted speech unintelligible.

scrap n. **1.** small piece. **2.** waste metal collected for reprocessing. **3.** *Informal* fight or quarrel. —pl. **4.** leftover food. —v. **scrapping, scrapped. 5.** discard as useless. **6.** *Informal* fight or quarrel. **scrappy** adj. fragmentary, disjointed. **scrapbook** n. book with blank pages in which newspaper cuttings or pictures are stuck.

scrape v. **1.** rub with something rough or sharp. **2.** clean or smooth thus. **3.** rub with a harsh noise. **4.** economize. —n. **5.** act or sound of scraping. **6.** mark or wound caused by scraping. **7.** *Informal* awkward situation. **scraper** n. **scrape through** v. succeed in or obtain with difficulty.

scratch v. **1.** mark or cut with claws, nails, or anything rough or sharp. **2.** scrape (skin) with nails or claws to relieve itching. **3.** cross out. **4.** withdraw from a race or competition. —n. **5.** wound, mark, or sound made by scratching. —adj. **6.** put together at short notice. **7.** *Sport* with no handicap allowed. **from scratch** from the very beginning. **up to scratch** up to standard. **scratchy** adj.

scrawl v. **1.** write carelessly or hastily. —n. **2.** scribbled writing.

scrawny adj. **scrawnier, scrawniest.** thin and bony.

scream v. **1.** utter a piercing cry, esp. of fear or pain. **2.** utter with a scream. —n. **3.** shrill piercing cry. **4.** *Informal* very funny person or thing.

scree n. slope of loose shifting stones.

screech v., n. (utter) a shrill cry. **screech owl** barn owl.

screed n. long tedious piece of writing.

screen n. **1.** movable structure used to shelter, divide, or conceal something. **2.** surface of a television set, VDU, etc., on which an image is formed. **3.** white surface on which films or slides are projected. —v. **4.** shelter or conceal with or as if with a screen. **5.** show (a film). **6.** examine (a person or group) to determine suitability for a task or to detect the presence of disease or weapons. **the screen** cinema generally. **screenplay** n. script for a film.

screw n. **1.** metal pin with a spiral ridge along its length, twisted into materials to fasten them together. **2.** *Slang* prison guard. —v. **3.** turn (a screw). **4.** fasten with screw(s). **5.** twist. **6.** *Informal* extort. **screwy** adj. *Informal* crazy or eccentric. **screwdriver** n. tool for turning screws. **screw up** v. **1.** *Informal* bungle. **2.** distort. **3.** summon up (courage).

scribble v. **1.** write hastily or illegibly. **2.** make meaningless or illegible marks. —n. **3.** something scribbled.

scribe n. **1.** person who copied manuscripts before the invention of printing. **2.** *Bible* scholar of the Jewish Law. **scribal** adj.

scrimmage n. **1.** rough or disorderly struggle. —v. **2.** engage in a scrimmage.

scrimp v. be very economical.

scrip n. certificate representing a claim to stocks or shares.

script n. **1.** text of a film, play, or TV programme. **2.** particular system of writing, e.g. *Arabic script.* **3.** candidate's answer paper in an exam. **4.** handwriting. —v. **5.** write a script for.

scripture n. **1.** sacred writings of a religion. **2.** (S-) Old and New Testaments. **scriptural** adj.

scrofula n. tuberculosis of the lymphatic glands. **scrofulous** adj.

scroll n. **1.** roll of parchment or paper. **2.** ornamental carving shaped like this. **3.** ancient book in scroll form. —v. **4.** move (text) up or down on a VDU screen.

Scrooge n. miserly person.

scrotum n., pl. **-ta, -tums.** pouch of skin containing the testicles.

scrounge v. *Informal* get by cadging or begging. **scrounger** n.

scrub[1] v. **scrubbing, scrubbed. 1.** clean by rubbing, often with a hard brush and water. **2.** *Informal* delete or cancel. —n. **3.** scrubbing.

scrub² n. **1.** stunted trees. **2.** area of land covered with scrub. **scrubby** adj. **1.** covered with scrub. **2.** stunted. **3.** Informal shabby.

scruff¹ n. nape (of the neck).

scruff² n. Informal untidy person. **scruffy** adj. unkempt or shabby.

scrum, scrummage n. **1.** Rugby restarting of play in which opposing packs of forwards push against each other to gain possession of the ball. **2.** disorderly struggle.

scrump v. Brit. dialect steal (apples) from an orchard or garden.

scrumptious adj. Informal delicious.

scrumpy n. rough dry cider.

scrunch v. **1.** crumple or crunch or be crumpled or crunched. —n. **2.** act or sound of scrunching.

scrunchie n. loop of elastic covered loosely with fabric, used to hold the hair in a ponytail.

scruple n. **1.** doubt produced by one's conscience or morals. —v. **2.** have doubts on moral grounds. **scrupulous** adj. **1.** very conscientious. **2.** very careful or precise. **scrupulously** adv.

scrutiny n., pl. -nies. **1.** close examination. **2.** searching look. **scrutinize** v. examine closely.

scuba diving n. sport of swimming under water using cylinders containing compressed air attached to breathing apparatus.

scud v. **scudding, scudded. 1.** move along swiftly. **2.** run before a gale.

scuff v. **1.** drag (the feet) while walking. **2.** scrape (one's shoes) by doing so. —n. **3.** mark caused by scuffing.

scuffle v. **1.** fight in a disorderly manner. **2.** move by shuffling. —n. **3.** disorderly struggle. **4.** scuffling sound.

scull n. **1.** small oar. —v. **2.** row (a boat) using a scull.

scullery n., pl. -leries. small room where washing-up and other kitchen work is done.

sculpture n. **1.** art of making figures or designs in wood, stone, etc. **2.** product of this art. —v. (also **sculpt**) **3.** represent in sculpture. **sculptor, sculptress** n. **sculptural** adj.

scum n. **1.** impure or waste matter on the surface of a liquid. **2.** worthless people. **scummy** adj.

scupper v. **1.** Informal defeat or ruin. —n. **2.** drain in the side of a ship.

scurf n. flaky skin on the scalp. **scurfy** adj.

scurrilous adj. untrue and defamatory. **scurrility** n.

scurry v. -rying, -ried. **1.** move hastily. —n. **2.** act or sound of scurrying.

scurvy n. **1.** disease caused by lack of vitamin C. —adj. **2.** mean and despicable.

scut n. short tail of the hare, rabbit, or deer.

scuttle¹ n. fireside container for coal.

scuttle² v. **1.** run with short quick steps. —n. **2.** hurried run.

scuttle³ v. make a hole in (a ship) to sink it.

scythe n. **1.** long-handled tool with a curved blade for cutting grass. —v. **2.** cut with a scythe.

SD South Dakota.

Se Chem. selenium.

SE southeast(ern).

sea n. **1.** mass of salt water covering three quarters of the earth's surface. **2.** particular area of this. **3.** turbulence or swell. **4.** vast expanse. **at sea 1.** in a ship on the ocean. **2.** confused or bewildered. **sea anemone** sea animal with suckers like petals. **seaboard** n. coast. **sea dog** experienced sailor. **seafaring** adj. working or travelling by sea. **seafood** n. edible saltwater fish or shellfish. **seagoing** adj. built for travelling on the sea. **sea gull** gull. **sea horse** small sea fish with a plated body and horselike head. **sea legs** ability to keep one's balance at sea and resist seasickness. **sea level** average level of the sea's surface in relation to the land. **sea lion** kind of large seal. **seaman** n. sailor. **seaplane** n. aircraft designed to take off from and land on water. **seascape** n. picture of a scene at sea. **seashell** n. empty shell of a mollusc. **seasick** adj. suffering from nausea caused by the motion of a ship. **seasickness** n. **seaside** n. area, esp. a holiday resort, on the coast. **sea urchin** sea animal with a round spiky shell. **seaweed** n. plant growing in the sea. **seaworthy** adj. (of a ship) in fit condition for a sea voyage.

seal¹ n. **1.** piece of wax, lead, etc. with a special design impressed upon it, attached to a letter or document as a mark of authentication. **2.** device for making such an impression. **3.** device or material used to close an opening tightly. —v. **4.** affix a seal to or stamp with a seal. **5.** close with or as if with a seal. **6.** make airtight or watertight. **7.** decide (one's fate) irrevocably. **sealant** n. any substance used for sealing. **sealing wax** hard material which softens when heated, used to make a seal. **seal off** v. enclose or isolate (a place) completely.

seal[2] n. **1.** amphibious mammal with flippers as limbs. —v. **2.** hunt seals. **sealskin** n.

seam n. **1.** line where two edges are joined, as by stitching. **2.** thin layer of coal or ore. —v. **3.** mark with furrows or wrinkles. **seamless** adj. **seamy** adj. sordid.

seamstress n. woman who sews.

seance [say-anss] n. meeting at which spiritualists attempt to communicate with the dead.

sear v. **1.** scorch, burn the surface of. **2.** cause to wither.

search v. **1.** examine closely in order to find something. **2.** make a search. —n. **3.** searching. **searching** adj. keen or thorough, e.g. a searching look. **searchlight** n. powerful light with a beam that can be shone in any direction. **search warrant** document permitting the entry and search of premises.

season n. **1.** one of four divisions of the year, each of which has characteristic weather conditions. **2.** period during which a thing happens or is plentiful. **3.** fitting or proper time. **4.** any definite or indefinite period, e.g. the busy season. —v. **5.** flavour with salt, herbs, etc. **6.** dry (timber) till ready for use. **seasonable** adj. **1.** appropriate for the season. **2.** timely or opportune. **seasonal** adj. depending on or varying with the seasons. **seasoned** adj. experienced. **seasoning** n. salt, herbs, etc. added to food to enhance flavour. **season ticket** ticket for a series of journeys or events within a specified period.

seat n. **1.** thing designed or used for sitting on. **2.** part of a chair on which one sits. **3.** place to sit in a theatre, esp. one that requires a ticket. **4.** buttocks. **5.** part of a garment covering the buttocks. **6.** membership of a legislative or administrative body. **7.** place in which something is based. **8.** country house. —v. **9.** cause to sit. **10.** provide seating for. **seating** n. supply or arrangement of seats. **seat belt** belt worn in a car or aircraft to prevent a person being thrown forward in a crash.

sebaceous adj. of, like, or secreting fat or oil.

sec[1] adj. (of wines) dry.

sec[2] n. Informal second (of time).

sec. 1. second (of time). **2.** secondary. **3.** secretary.

secateurs pl. n. small pruning shears.

secede v. withdraw formally from a political alliance or federation. **secession** n. **secessionist** n.

seclude v. keep (a person) from contact with others. **secluded** adj. private, sheltered. **seclusion** n.

second[1] adj. **1.** coming directly after the first. **2.** alternate, additional. **3.** inferior. —n. **4.** person or thing coming second. **5.** sixtieth part of a minute of an angle or time. **6.** moment. **7.** attendant in a duel or boxing match. —pl. **8.** inferior goods. —v. **9.** express formal support for (a motion proposed in a meeting). **secondly** adv. **second-best** adj. next to the best. **second-class** adj. **1.** inferior. **2.** cheaper, slower, or less comfortable than first-class. **second-hand** adj. **1.** bought after use by another. **2.** not from an original source. **second nature** something so habitual that it seems part of one's character. **second-rate** adj. not of the highest quality. **second sight** supposed ability to predict events. **second thoughts** revised opinion on a matter already considered. **second wind** renewed ability to continue effort.

second[2] [si-**kawnd**] v. transfer (a person) temporarily to another job. **secondment** n.

secondary adj. **1.** coming after or derived from what is primary or first. **2.** of less importance. **3.** relating to the education of people between the ages of 11 and 18.

secret adj. **1.** kept from the knowledge of others. **2.** secretive. —n. **3.** something kept secret. **4.** mystery. **5.** underlying explanation, e.g. the secret of my success. **in secret** without other people knowing. **secretly** adv. **secrecy** n. **secretive** adj. inclined to keep things secret. **secretiveness** n. **secret agent** spy. **secret service** government department concerned with spying.

secretariat n. administrative office or staff of a legislative body.

secretary n., pl. **-ries. 1.** person who deals with correspondence and general clerical work. **2.** head of a state department, e.g. Home Secretary. **3.** person who keeps records for a company. **secretarial** adj. **secretary bird** large African bird of prey. **Secre-**

tary of State head of a major government department.

secrete v. 1. hide or conceal. 2. (of an organ, gland, etc.) produce and release (a substance). **secretion** n. **secretory** [sek-**reet**-or-ee] adj.

sect n. subdivision of a religious or political group, esp. one with extreme beliefs. **sectarian** adj. 1. of a sect. 2. narrow-minded. **sectarianism** n.

section n. 1. part cut off. 2. part or subdivision of something. 3. distinct part of a country or community. 4. cutting. 5. drawing of something as if cut through. —v. 6. cut or divide into sections. **sectional** adj.

sector n. 1. part or subdivision. 2. part of a circle enclosed by two radii and the arc which they cut off. 3. portion of an area for military operations.

secular adj. 1. worldly, as opposed to sacred. 2. not connected with religion or the church. 3. occurring once in an age or century. **secularism** n. belief that religion should have no place in education. **secularize** v. remove from the influence of the Church.

secure adj. 1. free from danger. 2. free from anxiety. 3. firmly fixed. 4. reliable. —v. 5. obtain. 6. make safe. 7. make firm. 8. guarantee payment of (a loan) by giving something as security. **securely** adv. **security** n., pl. **-ties** 1. state of being secure. 2. precautions against theft, espionage, or other danger. 3. something given or pledged to guarantee payment of a loan. 4. certificate of ownership of a share, stock, or bond.

sedan n. US saloon car. **sedan chair** Hist. enclosed chair for one person, carried on poles by two bearers.

sedate[1] adj. 1. calm and dignified. 2. sober or decorous. **sedately** adv.

sedate[2] v. give a sedative drug to. **sedation** n. **sedative** adj. 1. having a soothing or calming effect. —n. 2. sedative drug.

sedentary [sed-en-tree] adj. done sitting down, involving little exercise.

sedge n. coarse grasslike plant growing on wet ground. **sedgy** adj.

sediment n. 1. matter which settles to the bottom of a liquid. 2. material deposited by water, ice, or wind. **sedimentary** adj.

sedition n. speech or action encouraging rebellion against the government. **seditious** adj.

seduce v. 1. persuade into sexual intercourse. 2. tempt into wrongdoing. **seducer**, **seductress** n. **seduction** n. **seductive** adj.

sedulous adj. diligent or persevering. **sedulously** adv.

sedum n. rock plant.

see[1] v. **seeing, saw, seen**. 1. perceive with the eyes or mind. 2. understand. 3. watch. 4. find out. 5. make sure (of something). 6. consider or decide. 7. have experience of. 8. meet or visit. 9. interview. 10. frequent the company of. 11. accompany. **seeing** conj. 1. in view of the fact that. —n. 2. use of the eyes. **see about** v. attend to. **see off** v. be present at the departure of. **see through** v. 1. perceive the true nature of. 2. remain with until the end. **see-through** adj. transparent.

see[2] n. diocese of a bishop.

seed n. 1. mature fertilized grain of a plant. 2. such grains used for sowing. 3. origin. 4. Obs. offspring. 5. Sport seeded player. —v. 6. sow with seed. 7. produce seeds. 8. remove seeds from. 9. arrange (the draw of a sports tournament) so that the outstanding competitors will not meet in the early rounds. **go, run to seed** 1. (of plants) produce or shed seeds after flowering. 2. lose vigour or usefulness. **seedling** n. young plant raised from a seed. **seedy** adj. 1. shabby. 2. Informal unwell. 3. full of seeds.

seek v. **seeking, sought**. 1. try to find or obtain. 2. try (to do something).

seem v. 1. appear to be. 2. have the impression. **seeming** adj. apparent but not real. **seemingly** adv.

seemly adj. **-lier, -liest**. proper or fitting. **seemliness** n.

seen v. past participle of SEE.

seep v. trickle through slowly, ooze. **seepage** n.

seer n. prophet.

seersucker n. light cotton fabric with a slightly crinkled surface.

seesaw n. 1. plank balanced in the middle so that two people seated on either end ride up and down alternately. —v. 2. move up and down.

seethe v. **seething, seethed**. 1. be very agitated. 2. (of a liquid) boil or foam.

segment n. 1. one of several sections into which something may be divided. 2. part of a circle cut off by an intersecting line. —v. 3. divide into segments. **segregate** v. 1. set apart. 2. keep (a racial or minority group) apart from the rest of the community. **segregation** n.

seigneur n. feudal lord.

seine [sane] n. large fishing net that hangs vertically from floats.

seismic adj. relating to earthquakes. **seismology** n. study of earthquakes. **seismologic, seismological** adj. **seismologist** n. **seismograph, seismometer** n. instrument that records the strength of earthquakes.

seize v. 1. take hold of forcibly or quickly. 2. take immediate advantage of. 3. take legal possession of. 4. (usu. foll. by up) (of mechanical parts) stick tightly through overheating. **seizure** n. 1. seizing or being seized. 2. sudden violent attack of an illness.

seldom adv. not often, rarely.

select v. 1. pick out or choose. —adj. 2. chosen in preference to others. 3. restricted to a particular group, exclusive. **selection** n. 1. selecting. 2. things that have been selected. 3. range from which something may be selected. **selective** adj. chosen or choosing carefully. **selectively** adv. **selectivity** n. **selector** n.

selenium n. nonmetallic element with photoelectric properties.

self n., pl. **selves**. 1. distinct individuality or identity of a person or thing. 2. one's basic nature. 3. one's own welfare or interests. **selfish** adj. caring too much about oneself and not enough about others. **selfishly** adv. **selfishness** n. **selfless** adj. unselfish.

self- prefix used with many main words to mean: 1. of oneself or itself. 2. by, to, in, due to, for, or from the self. 3. automatic(ally). **self-addressed** adj. addressed to the sender. **self-assertion** n. putting forward one's opinions, esp. aggressively. **self-assertive** adj. **self-assured** adj. confident. **self-catering** adj. (of accommodation) for people who provide their own food. **self-centred** adj. totally preoccupied with one's own concerns. **self-certification** n. completion of a form by a worker stating that absence was due to sickness. **self-coloured** adj. having only a single colour. **self-confessed** adj. according to one's own admission. **self-confidence** n. belief in one's own abilities. **self-confident** adj. **self-conscious** adj. embarrassed at being the object of others'

attention. **self-contained** adj. 1. containing everything needed, complete. 2. (of a flat) having its own facilities. **self-control** n. ability to control one's feelings and reactions. **self-defence** n. defending of oneself or one's property. **self-determination** n. the right of a nation to decide its own form of government. **self-effacing** adj. unwilling to draw attention to oneself. **self-employed** adj. earning a living from one's own business. **self-esteem** n. favourable opinion of oneself. **self-evident** adj. obvious without evidence or proof. **self-government** n. government of a nation or community by its own people. **self-help** n. 1. use of one's own abilities to solve problems. 2. practice of solving one's problems within a group of people with similar problems. **self-important** adj. having an unduly high opinion of one's importance. **self-importance** n. **self-indulgent** adj. tending to indulge one's desires. **self-interest** n. one's own advantage. **self-made** adj. having achieved wealth or status by one's own efforts. **self-opinionated** adj. clinging stubbornly to one's own opinions. **self-possessed** adj. having control of one's emotions, calm. **self-raising** adj. (of flour) containing a raising agent. **self-respect** n. sense of one's dignity and integrity. **self-righteous** adj. thinking oneself more virtuous than others. **selfsame** adj. the very same. **self-satisfied** adj. conceited. **self-seeking** adj., n. seeking to promote only one's own interests. **self-service** adj. denoting a shop, café, or garage where customers serve themselves and then pay a cashier. **self-styled** adj. using a title or name that one has taken without right. **self-sufficient** adj. able to provide for oneself without help. **self-willed** adj. stubbornly determined to get one's own way.

sell v. **selling, sold**. 1. exchange (something) for money. 2. stock, deal in. 3. (of goods) be sold. 4. (foll. by for) have a specified price. 5. promote. 6. be in demand. 7. Informal persuade (someone) to accept (something). 8. give up for a price or reward. —n. 9. manner of selling. **seller** n. **sell-by date** date printed on packaged food specifying the date after which the food should not be sold. **past one's sell-by date** Informal beyond one's prime. **sell out** v. 1. dispose of (something) completely by selling. 2. Informal betray. **sellout** n. 1. performance of a show etc. for which all the tickets are sold. **2.** *Informal* betrayal. **sell up** *v.* sell all one's goods.

Sellotape *n.* **1.** ® type of adhesive tape. —*v.* **2.** stick with Sellotape.

selvage, selvedge *n.* edge of cloth, woven so as to prevent unravelling.

selves *n.* plural of SELF.

semantic *adj.* relating to the meaning of words. **semantics** *n.* study of linguistic meaning.

semaphore *n.* system of signalling by holding two flags in different positions to represent letters of the alphabet.

semblance *n.* outward or superficial appearance.

semen *n.* sperm-carrying fluid produced by male animals.

semester *n. US* either of two divisions of the academic year.

semi *n. Informal* semidetached house.

semi- *prefix* used with many main words to mean: **1.** half, e.g. *semicircle*. **2.** partly or almost, e.g. *semiprofessional*. **3.** occurring twice in a specified period, e.g. *semiweekly*.

semibreve *n.* musical note four beats long.

semicircle *n.* half of a circle. **semicircular** *adj.*

semicolon *n.* the punctuation mark (;).

semiconductor *n.* substance with an electrical conductivity that increases with temperature.

semidetached *adj.* (of a house) joined to another on one side.

semifinal *n.* match or round before the final. **semifinalist** *n.*

seminal *adj.* **1.** capable of developing. **2.** original and influential. **3.** of semen or seed.

seminar *n.* meeting of a group of students for discussion.

seminary *n., pl.* **-ries.** college for priests.

semiotics *n.* study of human communications, esp. signs and symbols.

semiprecious *adj.* (of gemstones) having less value than precious stones.

semiquaver *n.* musical note half the length of a quaver.

semiskilled *adj.* partly trained but not for specialized work.

Semite *n.* member of the group of peoples including Jews and Arabs. **Semitic** *adj.*

semitone *n.* smallest interval between two notes in Western music.

semolina *n.* hard grains of wheat left after the milling of flour, used to make puddings and pasta.

sempre *adv. Music* always, consistently.

SEN State Enrolled Nurse.

Senate *n.* **1.** upper house of some parliaments. **2.** governing body of some universities. **senator** *n.* member of a Senate. **senatorial** *adj.*

send *v.* **sending, sent. 1.** cause (a person or thing) to go to or be taken or transmitted to a place. **2.** bring into a specified state or condition. **3.** (foll. by *for*) issue a request for. **sender** *n.* **send down** *v.* **1.** expel from university. **2.** *Informal* send to jail. **sendoff** *n.* demonstration of good wishes at a person's departure. **send up** *v. Informal* make fun of by imitating. **send-up** *n. Informal* imitation.

senescent *adj.* growing old. **senescence** *n.*

senile *adj.* mentally or physically weak because of old age. **senility** *n.*

senior *adj.* **1.** superior in rank or standing. **2.** older. **3.** of or for older pupils. —*n.* **4.** senior person. **seniority** *n.* **senior citizen** old person, esp. a pensioner.

senna *n.* **1.** tropical plant. **2.** its dried leaves or pods used as a laxative.

señor [sen-**nyor**] *n., pl.* **-ores.** Spanish term of address equivalent to *sir* or *Mr.* **señora** [sen-**nyor**-a] *n.* Spanish term of address equivalent to *madam* or *Mrs.* **señorita** [sen-nyor-**ee**-ta] *n.* Spanish term of address equivalent to *madam* or *Miss.*

sensation *n.* **1.** ability to feel things physically. **2.** physical feeling. **3.** general feeling or awareness. **4.** state of excitement. **5.** exciting person or thing. **sensational** *adj.* **1.** causing intense shock, anger, or excitement. **2.** *Informal* very good. **sensationalism** *n.* deliberate use of sensational language or subject matter. **sensationalist** *adj., n.*

sense *n.* **1.** any of the faculties of perception or feeling (sight, hearing, touch, taste, or smell). **2.** ability to perceive. **3.** feeling perceived through one of the senses. **4.** awareness. **5.** (sometimes *pl.*) sound practical judgment or intelligence. **6.** specific meaning. **7.** moral discernment. **8.** reason or purpose. —*v.* **9.** perceive. **senseless** *adj.* **1.** foolish. **2.** unconscious.

sensible adj. 1. having or showing good sense. 2. (foll. by *of*) aware. 3. practical, e.g. *sensible shoes*. 4. capable of being perceived by the senses. **sensibly** adv. **sensibility** n. 1. ability to experience deep feelings. 2. (usu. pl.) tendency to be influenced or offended.

sensitive adj. 1. responsive to external stimuli. 2. easily hurt or offended. 3. (of an instrument) responsive to slight changes. 4. (of a subject) liable to arouse controversy or strong feelings. **sensitively** adv. **sensitivity** n. **sensitize** v. make sensitive.

sensor n. device that detects or measures the presence of something, such as radiation.

sensory adj. of the senses or sensation.

sensual adj. 1. giving pleasure to the body and senses rather than the mind. 2. having a strong liking for physical pleasures. **sensually** adv. **sensuality** n. **sensualism** n. **sensualist** n.

sensuous adj. pleasing to the senses. **sensuously** adv.

sent v. past of SEND.

sentence n. 1. sequence of words capable of standing alone as a statement, question, or command. 2. punishment passed on a criminal. —v. 3. pass sentence on (a convicted person).

sententious adj. 1. trying to sound wise. 2. pompously moralizing. **sententiously** adv. **sententiousness** n.

sentient [sen-tee-ent] adj. capable of feeling. **sentience** n.

sentiment n. 1. thought, opinion, or attitude. 2. feeling expressed in words. 3. exaggerated or mawkish emotion. 4. tendency to be influenced by emotion. **sentimental** adj. excessively romantic or nostalgic. **sentimentalism** n. **sentimentality** n. **sentimentalize** v. make sentimental.

sentinel n. sentry.

sentry n., pl. -tries. soldier on watch.

sepal n. leaflike division of the calyx of a flower.

separate v. 1. divide up into parts. 2. distinguish between. 3. (of a married couple) stop living together. 4. act as a barrier between. 5. sever or be severed. —adj. 6. set apart. 7. not the same, different. 8. not shared, individual. —pl. n. 9. clothes that only cover half the body, such as skirts and blouses. **separately** adv. **separation** n. 1. separating or being separated. 2. Law living apart of a married couple without divorce. **separable** adj. **separatist** n. person who advocates the separation of a group from an organization or country. **separatism** n.

sepia adj., n. reddish-brown (pigment).

sepoy n. formerly, Indian soldier in the service of the British.

sepsis n. poisoning caused by pus-forming bacteria.

Sept. September.

September n. ninth month of the year.

septet n. 1. group of seven performers. 2. music for such a group.

septic adj. 1. (of a wound) infected. 2. of or caused by harmful bacteria. **septic tank** tank in which sewage is decomposed by the action of bacteria.

septicaemia [sep-tis-see-mee-a] n. blood poisoning.

septuagenarian n., adj. (person) between seventy and seventy-nine years old.

septum n., pl. -ta. dividing partition between two cavities in the body.

sepulchre [sep-pull-ker] n. tomb or burial vault. **sepulchral** [sip-pulk-ral] adj. gloomy.

sequel n. 1. novel, play, or film that continues the story of an earlier one. 2. thing that follows something else. 3. consequence.

sequence n. 1. arrangement of two or more things in successive order. 2. the successive order of two or more things. 3. section of a film showing a single uninterrupted episode. **sequential** adj.

sequester v. 1. separate. 2. seclude. 3. sequestrate.

sequestrate v. confiscate (property) until its owner's debts are paid or a court order is complied with. **sequestration** n.

sequin n. small ornamental metal disc on a garment. **sequined** adj.

sequoia n. giant Californian coniferous tree.

seraglio [sir-ah-lee-oh] n., pl. -raglios. 1. harem of a Muslim palace. 2. Turkish sultan's palace.

seraph n., pl. -aphs, -aphim. member of the highest order of angels. **seraphic** adj.

Serbian adj. 1. of Serbia, its people, or their dialect of Serbo-Croatian. —n. 2. dialect of Serbo-Croatian spoken in Serbia. 3. person from Serbia. **Serbo-Croatian, Serbo-Croat**

adj., n. (of) the chief official language of Yugoslavia.

serenade n. 1. music played or sung to a woman by a lover. 2. piece of music for a small orchestra. —v. 3. sing or play a serenade to (someone).

serendipity n. gift of making fortunate discoveries by accident.

serene adj. 1. calm, peaceful. 2. (of the sky) clear. **serenely** adv. **serenity** n.

serf n. medieval farm labourer who could not leave the land he worked on. **serfdom** n.

serge n. strong woollen fabric.

sergeant n. 1. noncommissioned officer in the army. 2. police officer ranking between constable and inspector. **sergeant at arms** parliamentary or court officer with ceremonial duties. **sergeant major** highest rank of noncommissioned officer in the army.

serial n. 1. story or play produced in successive instalments. —adj. 2. of or forming a series. 3. published or presented as a serial. **serialize** v. publish or present as a serial. **serial killer** person who commits a series of murders.

seriatim [seer-ree-ah-tim] adv. one after another.

series n., pl. -**ries.** 1. group or succession of related things, usu. arranged in order. 2. set of radio or TV programmes about the same subject or characters.

serious adj. 1. giving cause for concern. 2. concerned with important matters. 3. not cheerful, grave. 4. sincere, not joking. 5. requiring concentration. **seriously** adv. **seriousness** n.

sermon n. 1. speech on a religious or moral subject by a clergyman in a church service. 2. long moralizing speech. **sermonize** v. make a long moralizing speech.

serpent n. snake. **serpentine** adj. twisting like a snake.

serrated adj. having a notched or sawlike edge. **serration** n.

serried adj. in close formation.

serum [seer-um] n. 1. watery fluid left after blood has clotted. 2. this fluid from the blood of immunized animals used for inoculation or vaccination.

serval n. feline African mammal.

servant n. person employed to do household work for another.

serve v. 1. work for (a person, community, or cause). 2. perform official duties. 3. attend to (customers). 4. provide with food or drink. 5. present (food or drink). 6. provide with a service. 7. be a member of the armed forces. 8. spend (time) in prison. 9. be useful or suitable. 10. *Tennis etc.* put (the ball) into play. 11. deliver (a legal document) to (a person). —n. 12. *Tennis etc.* act of serving the ball. **serve someone right** *Informal* be what someone deserves for doing something wrong.

service n. 1. serving. 2. system that provides something needed by the public. 3. overhaul of a machine or vehicle. 4. availability for use. 5. maintenance of goods provided by a dealer after sale. 6. department of public employment and its employees. 7. set of dishes etc. for serving a meal. 8. formal religious ceremony. 9. *Tennis etc.* act, manner, or right of serving the ball. —pl. 10. armed forces. —adj. 11. serving the public rather than producing goods, e.g. *service industry.* —v. 12. provide a service or services to. 13. overhaul (a machine or vehicle). **serviceable** adj. 1. useful or helpful. 2. able or ready to be used. **service area** area beside a motorway with garage, restaurant, and toilet facilities. **service charge** additional cost on a restaurant bill to pay for service. **service flat** flat where domestic services are provided. **serviceman, sevicewoman** n. member of the armed forces. **service road** narrow road giving access to houses and shops. **service station** garage selling fuel for motor vehicles.

serviette n. table napkin.

servile adj. 1. too eager to obey people, fawning. 2. suitable for a slave. **servility** n.

servitude n. bondage or slavery.

servomechanism n. device which converts a small force into a larger force, used esp. in steering mechanisms.

sesame [sess-am-ee] n. plant cultivated for its seeds and oil, which are used in cooking.

session n. 1. meeting of a court, parliament, or council. 2. series or period of such meetings. 3. period spent in an activity. 4. academic term or year.

set v. setting, set. 1. put in a specified position or state. 2. make ready. 3. make or become firm or rigid. 4. put (a broken bone) or (of a broken bone) be put into a normal position for healing. 5. adjust (a clock) to a particular position. **6.** establish, arrange. **7.** prescribe, assign. **8.** put to music. **9.** arrange (hair) while wet, so that it dries in position. **10.** place (a jewel) in a setting. **11.** arrange (type) for printing. **12.** (of the sun) go down. **13.** (of plants) produce (fruit or seeds). **14.** (of a gun dog) face game. —*adj.* **15.** fixed or established beforehand. **16.** rigid or inflexible. **17.** conventional or stereotyped. **18.** determined (to do something). **19.** ready. —*n.* **20.** setting or being set. **21.** number of things or people grouped or belonging together. **22.** *Maths* group of numbers or objects that satisfy a given condition or belong to a set. **23.** television or radio receiver. **24.** scenery used in a play or film. **25.** bearing or posture. **26.** *Tennis etc.* group of games in a match. **set back** *v.* **1.** hinder. **2.** cost. **setback** *n.* anything that delays progress. **set off** *v.* **1.** embark on a journey. **2.** cause to explode. **3.** cause to begin. **4.** act as a contrast to. **set square** *n.* flat right-angled triangular instrument used for drawing triangles. **set theory** branch of mathematics concerned with the properties of sets. **set to** *v.* begin working. **set-to** *n.* brief fight. **set up** *v.* arrange or establish. **setup** *n.* way in which anything is organized or arranged.

sett, set *n.* **1.** badger's burrow. **2.** small paving stone.

settee *n.* couch.

setter *n.* long-haired gun dog.

setting *n.* **1.** background or surroundings. **2.** time and place where a film, book, etc. is supposed to have taken place. **3.** music written for the words of a text. **4.** decorative metalwork in which a gem is set. **5.** plates and cutlery for a single place at table. **6.** descending below the horizon of the sun. **7.** position or level to which the controls of a machine can be adjusted.

settle[1] *v.* **1.** arrange or put in order. **2.** establish or become established as a resident. **3.** colonize. **4.** make quiet, calm, or stable. **5.** come to rest. **6.** dispose of, conclude. **7.** end (a dispute). **8.** pay (a bill). **9.** bestow (property) legally. **settlement** *n.* **1.** act of settling. **2.** place newly colonized. **3.** property bestowed legally. **4.** subsidence (of a building). **settler** *n.* colonist. **settle down** *v.* **1.** adopt a routine way of life. **2.** (foll. by *to*) concentrate on. **3.** make or become calm.

settle[2] *n.* long wooden bench with high back and arms.

seven *adj., n.* one more than six. **seventh** *adj., n.* (of) number seven in a series. **seventeen** *adj., n.* ten and seven. **seventeenth** *adj., n.* **seventy** *adj., n.* ten times seven. **seventieth** *adj., n.*

sever *v.* **1.** separate, divide. **2.** cut off. **severance** *n.* **severance pay** compensation paid by a firm to an employee who leaves because the job he or she was appointed to do no longer exists.

several *adj.* **1.** some, a few. **2.** various, separate. —*pron.* **3.** indefinite small number. **severally** *adv.* separately.

severe *adj.* **1.** strict or harsh. **2.** very intense or unpleasant. **3.** strictly restrained in appearance. **severely** *adv.* **severity** *n.*

sew *v.* **sewing, sewed, sewn** *or* **sewed. 1.** join with thread repeatedly passed through with a needle. **2.** make or fasten by sewing.

sewage *n.* waste matter or excrement carried away in sewers. **sewer** *n.* drain to remove waste water and sewage. **sewerage** *n.* system of sewers.

sewn *v.* a past participle of SEW.

sex *n.* **1.** state of being male or female. **2.** male or female category. **3.** sexual intercourse. **4.** sexual feelings or behaviour. —*v.* **5.** ascertain the sex of. **sexy** *adj.* **1.** sexually exciting or attractive. **2.** *Informal* exciting or trendy. **sexism** *n.* discrimination on the basis of a person's sex. **sexist** *adj., n.* **sexual** *adj.* **sexually** *adv.* **sexuality** *n.* **sexual intercourse** sexual act in which the male's penis is inserted into the female's vagina.

sexagenarian *n., adj.* (person) between sixty and sixty-nine years old.

sextant *n.* navigator's instrument for measuring angles, as between the sun and horizon, to calculate one's position.

sextet *n.* **1.** group of six performers. **2.** music for such a group.

sexton *n.* official in charge of a church and churchyard.

sextuplet *n.* one of six children born at one birth.

SF science fiction.

SFA Scottish Football Association.

Sgt. Sergeant.

sh *interj.* be quiet!

shabby *adj.* **-bier, -biest. 1.** worn or dilapidated in appearance. **2.** mean or unworthy, e.g. *shabby treatment.* **shabbily** *adv.* **shabbiness** *n.*

shack *n.* rough hut. **shack up with** *v. Slang* live with (one's lover).

shackle *n.* **1.** one of a pair of metal rings joined by a chain, for securing a person's wrists or ankles. **2.** anything that restricts freedom. —*v.* **3.** fasten with shackles. **4.** hinder.

shad *n.* herring-like fish.

shade *n.* **1.** relative darkness. **2.** place sheltered from sun. **3.** depth of colour. **4.** slight amount. **5.** *Lit.* ghost. **6.** screen or cover used to protect from a direct source of light. —*pl.* **7.** *Slang* sunglasses. —*v.* **8.** screen from light. **9.** darken. **10.** represent (darker areas) in drawing. **11.** change slightly or by degrees. **shady** *adj.* **1.** situated in or giving shade. **2.** of doubtful honesty or legality. **in the shade** in a position of relative obscurity.

shadow *n.* **1.** dark shape cast on a surface when something stands between a light and the surface. **2.** patch of shade. **3.** slight trace. **4.** threatening influence. **5.** inseparable companion. **6.** person who secretly trails another. —*v.* **7.** cast a shadow over. **8.** follow secretly. **shadowy** *adj.* **shadowboxing** *n.* boxing against an imaginary opponent for practice. **Shadow Cabinet** members of the main opposition party in Parliament who would be ministers if their party were in power.

shaft *n.* **1.** long narrow straight handle of a tool or weapon. **2.** ray of light. **3.** revolving rod that transmits power in a machine. **4.** vertical passageway, as for a lift or a mine. **5.** one of the bars between which an animal is harnessed to a vehicle. **6.** something directed like a missile, e.g. *shafts of wit.* **7.** middle part of a column.

shag[1] *n.* **1.** coarse shredded tobacco. **2.** tangled hair or wool. —*adj.* **3.** (of a carpet) having a long pile. **shaggy** *adj.* **1.** covered with rough hair or wool. **2.** tousled, unkempt. **shagginess** *n.* **shaggy-dog story** long anecdote with a humorous twist at the end.

shag[2] *n.* cormorant.

shagreen *n.* **1.** rough grainy untanned leather. **2.** sharkskin.

shah *n.* formerly, ruler of Iran.

shake *v.* **shaking, shook, shaken. 1.** move quickly up and down or back and forth. **2.** make unsteady. **3.** tremble. **4.** grasp (someone's hand) in greeting or agreement. **5.** shock or upset. **6.** undermine or weaken. —*n.* **7.** shaking. **8.** vibration. **9.** *Informal* short period of time. **shaker** *n.* container in which drinks are mixed or from which powder is shaken. **shaky** *adj.* **1.** unsteady. **2.** uncertain or questionable. **shakily** *adv.* **shake down** *v.* lie down on a makeshift bed. **shake up** *v.* **1.** mix by shaking. **2.** shock. **3.** reorganize drastically.

shale *n.* flaky sedimentary rock.

shall *v., past tense* **should.** used as an auxiliary to make the future tense or to indicate intention, obligation, or inevitability.

▷ The use of *shall* with *I* and *we* is a matter of preference, not rule. *Shall* is commonly used for questions in southern England but less often in the north and Scotland.

shallot [shal-**lot**] *n.* kind of small onion.

shallow *adj.* **1.** not deep. **2.** lacking depth of character or intellect. **shallows** *pl. n.* area of shallow water. **shallowness** *n.*

sham *n.* **1.** thing or person that is not genuine. —*adj.* **2.** not real or genuine. —*v.* **shamming, shammed. 3.** fake, feign.

shamble *v.* walk in a shuffling awkward way.

shambles *n.* **1.** disorderly event or place. **2.** slaughterhouse. **shambolic** *adj. Informal* completely disorganized.

shame *n.* **1.** painful emotion caused by awareness of having done something dishonourable or foolish. **2.** capacity to feel shame. **3.** disgrace. **4.** cause of shame. **5.** cause for regret. —*v.* **6.** cause to feel shame. **7.** disgrace. **8.** compel by shame, e.g. *she was shamed into helping.* **shameful** *adj.* causing or deserving shame. **shamefully** *adv.* **shameless** *adj.* with no sense of shame. **shamefaced** *adj.* looking ashamed.

shammy *n., pl.* **-mies.** *Informal* piece of chamois leather.

shampoo *n.* **1.** liquid soap for washing hair, carpets, or upholstery. **2.** process of shampooing. —*v.* **3.** wash with shampoo.

shamrock *n.* clover leaf, esp. as the Irish emblem.

shandy *n., pl.* **-dies.** drink made of beer and lemonade.

shanghai *v.* force or trick (someone) into doing something.

shank *n*. **1.** lower leg. **2.** shaft or stem.

shan't shall not.

shantung *n*. soft Chinese silk with a knobbly surface.

shanty¹ *n.*, *pl.* **-ties.** shack or crude dwelling. **shantytown** *n*. slum consisting of shanties.

shanty² *n.*, *pl.* **-ties.** sailor's traditional song.

shape *n*. **1.** outward form of an object. **2.** way in which something is organized. **3.** pattern or mould. **4.** condition or state. —*v.* **5.** form or mould. **6.** devise or develop. **shapeless** *adj*. **shapely** *adj*. having an attractive shape. **shape up** *v. Informal* develop satisfactorily.

shard *n*. broken piece of pottery.

share¹ *n*. **1.** part of something that belongs to or is contributed by a person. **2.** one of the equal parts into which the capital stock of a public company is divided. —*v.* **3.** give or take a share of (something). **4.** join with others in doing or using (something). **5.** divide and distribute. **shareholder** *n*.

share² *n*. blade of a plough.

shark *n*. **1.** large usu. predatory sea fish. **2.** person who cheats others.

sharkskin *n*. stiff glossy fabric.

sharp *adj*. **1.** having a keen cutting edge or fine point. **2.** not gradual. **3.** clearly defined. **4.** mentally acute. **5.** clever but underhand. **6.** shrill. **7.** bitter or sour in taste. **8.** (of a note) being one semitone above natural pitch. **9.** (of an instrument or voice) out of tune by being too high in pitch. —*adv.* **10.** promptly. —*n.* **11.** *Music* symbol raising a note one semitone above natural pitch. **12.** note raised in this way. **sharply** *adv*. **sharpness** *n*. **sharpen** *v*. make or become sharp or sharper. **sharpener** *n*. **sharper** *n*. person who cheats. **sharpshooter** *n*. marksman.

shatter *v*. **1.** break into pieces. **2.** destroy completely. **3.** upset (someone) greatly. **4.** *Informal* cause to be exhausted.

shave *v*. **shaving, shaved, shaved** or **shaven. 1.** remove (hair) from (the face, head, or body) with a razor or shaver. **2.** pare away. **3.** touch lightly in passing. **4.** reduce. —*n.* **5.** shaving. **close shave** *Informal* narrow escape. **shaver** *n*. electric razor. **shavings** *pl. n.* parings.

shawl *n*. piece of cloth worn over a woman's head or shoulders or wrapped around a baby.

she *pron*. **1.** female person or animal previously mentioned. **2.** something regarded as female, such as a car, ship, or nation.

sheaf *n.*, *pl.* **sheaves. 1.** bundle of papers. **2.** tied bundle of reaped corn. —*v.* **3.** tie into a sheaf.

shear *v*. **shearing, sheared, sheared** or **shorn. 1.** clip hair or wool from. **2.** cut through. **3.** cause (a part) to break or (of a part) break through strain or twisting. **4.** deprive (of). **shears** *pl. n.* large scissors or a cutting tool shaped like these. **shearer** *n*.

sheath *n*. **1.** close-fitting cover, esp. for a knife or sword. **2.** condom. **sheathe** *v*. **1.** put into a sheath. **2.** cover with a sheath.

sheaves *n*. plural of SHEAF.

shed¹ *n*. building used for storage or shelter or as a workshop.

shed² *v*. **shedding, shed. 1.** pour forth (tears). **2.** cast off (skin). **3.** lose (hair).

sheen *n*. glistening brightness on the surface of something.

sheep *n.*, *pl.* **sheep. 1.** ruminant animal bred for wool and meat. **2.** timid person. **sheep-dip** *n*. liquid disinfectant in which sheep are immersed. **sheepdog** *n*. dog used for herding sheep. **sheepskin** *n*. skin of a sheep with the fleece still on, used for clothing or rugs.

sheepish *adj*. embarrassed because of feeling foolish. **sheepishly** *adv*.

sheer¹ *adj*. **1.** absolute, complete, e.g. *sheer folly*. **2.** (of material) so fine as to be transparent. **3.** perpendicular, steep. —*adv.* **4.** steeply.

sheer² *v*. **1.** change course suddenly. **2.** avoid an unpleasant person or thing.

sheet¹ *n*. **1.** large piece of cloth used as an inner bedcover. **2.** broad thin piece of any material. **3.** large expanse. **sheet lightning** lightning that appears to flash across a large part of the sky at once.

sheet² *n*. rope for controlling the position of a sail. **sheet anchor 1.** strong anchor for use in an emergency. **2.** person or thing relied on.

sheikh, sheik [shake] *n*. Arab chief. **sheikhdom, sheikdom** *n*.

sheila *n. Aust. slang* girl or woman.

shekel *n*. **1.** monetary unit of Israel. —*pl.* **2.** *Informal* money.

shelf *n.*, *pl.* **shelves. 1.** board fixed horizontally for holding things. **2.** ledge. on the shelf past the age where marriage is likely. **shelf life** time a packaged product will remain fresh.

shell n. **1.** hard outer covering of an egg, nut, or certain animals. **2.** explosive projectile fired from a large gun. **3.** external frame of something. **4.** light rowing boat. —v. **5.** take the shell from. **6.** fire at with artillery shells. **shellfish** n. aquatic mollusc or crustacean. **shell out** v. Informal pay out or hand over (money). **shell shock** nervous disorder caused by exposure to battle conditions.

shellac n. **1.** resin used in varnishes. —v. **-lacking, -lacked. 2.** coat with shellac.

shelter n. **1.** structure providing protection from danger or the weather. **2.** protection. —v. **3.** give shelter to. **4.** take shelter.

shelve v. **1.** put aside or postpone. **2.** slope. **3.** provide with shelves. **shelving** n. (material for) shelves.

shelves n. plural of SHELF.

shenanigans pl. n. Informal **1.** mischief or nonsense. **2.** trickery.

shepherd n. **1.** person who tends sheep. —v. **2.** guide or watch over (people). **shepherdess** n. fem. **shepherd's pie** baked dish of mince covered with mashed potato.

sherbet n. fruit-flavoured fizzy powder.

sherd n. same as SHARD.

sheriff n. **1.** in the US, chief law enforcement officer of a county. **2.** in England and Wales, chief executive officer of the Crown in a county. **3.** in Scotland, chief judge of a district.

Sherpa n. member of a people of Tibet and Nepal.

sherry n., pl. **-ries.** pale or dark brown fortified wine.

Shetland pony n. very small sturdy breed of pony.

shibboleth n. slogan or principle, usu. considered outworn, characteristic of a particular group.

shied v. past of SHY.

shield n. **1.** piece of armour carried on the arm to protect the body from blows or missiles. **2.** anything that protects. **3.** sports trophy in the shape of a shield. —v. **4.** protect.

shift v. **1.** move. **2.** transfer (blame or responsibility). **3.** remove or be removed.

—n. **4.** shifting. **5.** group of workers who work during a specified period. **6.** period of time during which they work. **7.** loose-fitting straight underskirt or dress. **shiftless** adj. lacking in ambition or initiative. **shifty** adj. evasive or untrustworthy. **shiftiness** n.

shillelagh [shil-lay-lee] n. in Ireland, a cudgel.

shilling n. **1.** former British coin, replaced by the 5p piece. **2.** monetary unit in some E African countries.

shillyshally v. **-lying, -lied.** Informal be indecisive.

shimmer v., n. (shine with) a faint unsteady light.

shin n. **1.** front of the lower leg. —v. **shinning, shinned. 2.** climb by using the hands or arms and legs. **shinbone** n. tibia.

shindig n. Informal **1.** noisy party. **2.** brawl.

shine v. **shining, shone. 1.** give out or reflect light. **2.** aim (a light). **3.** polish. **4.** excel. —n. **5.** brightness or lustre. **take a shine to** Informal take a liking to (someone). **shiny** adj. **shiner** n. Informal black eye.

shingle[1] n. **1.** wooden roof tile. —v. **2.** cover (a roof) with shingles.

shingle[2] n. coarse gravel found on beaches.

shingles n. disease causing a rash of small blisters along a nerve.

Shinto n. Japanese religion in which ancestors and nature spirits are worshipped. **Shintoism** n.

shinty n. game like hockey.

ship n. **1.** large seagoing vessel. **2.** airship or spaceship. —v. **shipping, shipped. 3.** send or transport by carrier, esp. a ship. **4.** bring or go aboard a ship. **5.** Informal send away. **6.** be hired to work on a ship. **shipment** n. **1.** act of shipping cargo. **2.** consignment of goods shipped. **shipping** n. **1.** freight transport business. **2.** ships collectively. **shipmate** n. sailor serving on the same ship as another. **shipshape** adj. orderly or neat. **shipwreck** n. **1.** destruction of a ship through storm or collision. **2.** ruin or destruction. —v. **3.** cause to undergo shipwreck. **shipyard** n. place where ships are built.

shire n. county.

shire horse n. large powerful breed of horse.

shirk v. avoid (duty or work). **shirker** n.

shirt n. garment for the upper part of the body. **shirtsleeves** pl. n. in one's shirtsleeves not wearing a jacket.

shirty adj. **-tier, -tiest.** Slang bad-tempered or annoyed.

shish kebab n. meat and vegetable dish cooked on a skewer.

shit Taboo —v. **shitting, shitted** or **shit.** 1. defecate. —n. 2. excrement. 3. Slang nonsense. 4. Slang worthless person. —interj. 5. Slang exclamation of anger or disgust. **shitty** adj.

shiver[1] v. 1. tremble, as from cold or fear. —n. 2. shivering. **shivery** adj.

shiver[2] v. 1. splinter into pieces. —n. 2. splintered piece.

shoal[1] n. 1. large number of fish swimming together. 2. large group of people.

shoal[2] n. 1. stretch of shallow water. 2. sandbank.

shock[1] v. 1. horrify, disgust, or astonish. —n. 2. sudden violent emotional disturbance. 3. sudden violent blow or impact. 4. something causing this. 5. state of bodily collapse caused by physical or mental shock. 6. pain and muscular spasm caused by an electric current passing through the body. **shocker** n. **shocking** adj. 1. causing horror, disgust, or astonishment. 2. Informal very bad. **shock absorber** device on a car for reducing the effects of travelling over bumps. **shock therapy** electroconvulsive therapy.

shock[2] n. bushy mass (of hair).

shod v. past of SHOE.

shoddy adj. **-dier, -diest.** of poor quality.

shoe n. 1. outer covering for the foot, ending below the ankle. 2. horseshoe. —v. **shoeing, shod.** 3. fit with a shoe or shoes. **shoehorn** n. smooth curved implement inserted at the heel of a shoe to ease the foot into it. **shoelace** n. cord for fastening shoes. **shoestring** n. on a shoestring using a very small amount of money. **shoetree** n. piece of metal, wood, or plastic inserted in a shoe to keep its shape.

shone v. past of SHINE.

shoo interj. 1. go away! —v. 2. drive away as by saying 'shoo'.

shook v. past tense of SHAKE.

shoot v. **shooting, shot.** 1. hit, wound, or kill with a missile fired from a weapon. 2. fire (a missile from) a weapon. 3. send out or move rapidly. 4. hunt. 5. (of a plant) sprout. 6. photograph or film. 7. Sport take a shot at goal. —n. 8. new branch or sprout of a plant. 9. hunting expedition. **shooting star** meteor. **shooting stick** stick with a spike at one end and a folding seat at the other.

shop n. 1. place for sale of goods and services. 2. workshop. —v. **shopping, shopped.** 3. visit a shop or shops to buy goods. 4. Slang inform against (someone). **talk shop** discuss one's work, esp. on a social occasion. **shopper** n. **shopping** n. 1. act of going to shops and buying things. 2. things bought. **shopping centre** area or building with many shops. **shop around** v. visit various shops to compare goods and prices. **shop assistant** person serving in a shop. **shop floor** 1. production area of a factory. 2. workers in a factory. **shoplifter** n. person who steals from a shop. **shopsoiled** adj. soiled or faded from being displayed in a shop. **shop steward** trade-union official elected to represent his or her fellow workers.

shore[1] n. 1. edge of a sea or lake. 2. land.

shore[2] v. 1. (foll. by up) prop or support. —n. 2. prop set under or against something as a support.

shorn v. a past participle of SHEAR.

short adj. 1. not long. 2. not tall. 3. not lasting long, brief. 4. deficient, e.g. short of cash. 5. abrupt, rude. 6. (of a drink) consisting chiefly of a spirit. 7. (of pastry) crumbly. —adv. 8. abruptly. —n. 9. drink of spirits. 10. short film. 11. Informal short circuit. —pl. 12. short trousers. —v. 13. short-circuit. **shortage** n. deficiency. **shorten** v. make or become shorter. **shortly** adv. 1. soon. 2. rudely. **shortbread, shortcake** n. crumbly biscuit made with butter. **short change** v. 1. give (someone) less than the correct amount of change. 2. Slang swindle. **short circuit** faulty or accidental connection in a circuit, which deflects current through a path of low resistance. **short-circuit** v. 1. develop a short circuit. 2. bypass. **shortcoming** n. failing or defect. **short cut** quicker route or method. **shortfall** n. deficit. **shorthand** n. system of rapid writing using symbols to represent words. **short-handed** adj. not having enough workers. **short list** selected list of candidates for a job or prize, from which the final choice will be made. **short-list** v. put on a short list. **short-lived** adj. lasting a short time. **short shrift** brief and unsympathetic treatment. **short-sighted** adj. **1.** unable to see faraway things clearly. **2.** lacking in foresight. **short-tempered** adj. easily angered. **short-term** adj. of or lasting a short time. **short wave** radio wave with a wavelength of less than 60 metres.

shot[1] n. **1.** shooting. **2.** small lead pellets used in a shotgun. **3.** person with specified skill in shooting. **4.** Slang attempt. **5.** Sport act or instance of hitting, kicking, or throwing the ball. **6.** photograph. **7.** uninterrupted film sequence. **8.** Informal injection. **9.** Informal drink of spirits. —adj. **10.** woven so that the colour varies according to the angle of light. **shotgun** n. gun for firing a charge of shot at short range. **shotgun wedding** wedding enforced because the bride is pregnant.

shot[2] v. **1.** past of SHOOT. —adj. **2.** woven to show changing colours, e.g. shot silk. **3.** streaked with colour.

shot put n. athletic event in which contestants hurl a heavy metal ball as far as possible. **shot-putter** n.

should v. past tense of SHALL: used as an auxiliary to make the subjunctive mood or to indicate obligation or possibility.

shoulder n. **1.** part of the body to which an arm, foreleg, or wing is attached. **2.** cut of meat including the upper foreleg. **3.** part of a garment which covers the shoulder. **4.** side of a road. —v. **5.** bear (a burden or responsibility). **6.** put on one's shoulder. **7.** push with one's shoulder. **shoulder blade** large flat triangular bone at the shoulder.

shouldn't should not.

shout n. **1.** loud cry. —v. **2.** cry out loudly. **shout down** v. silence (someone) by shouting.

shove v. **1.** push roughly. **2.** Informal put. —n. **3.** rough push. **shove off** v. Informal go away.

shovel n. **1.** tool for lifting or moving loose material. —v. **2.** -**elling**, -**elled**. lift or move as with a shovel.

show v. **showing, showed, shown** or **showed. 1.** make, be, or become noticeable or visible. **2.** exhibit or display. **3.** indicate. **4.** instruct by demonstration. **5.** prove. **6.** guide. **7.** reveal or display (an emotion). —n. **8.** public exhibition. **9.** theatrical or other entertainment. **10.** mere display or pretence. **11.** Slang thing or affair. **showy** adj.

1. gaudy. **2.** ostentatious. **showily** adv. **showing** n. **1.** exhibition. **2.** manner of presentation. **show business** the entertainment industry. **showcase** n. **1.** glass case used to display objects. **2.** situation in which something is displayed to best advantage. **showdown** n. confrontation that settles a dispute. **showjumping** n. competitive sport of riding horses to demonstrate skill in jumping. **showman** n. man skilled at presenting anything spectacularly. **showmanship** n. show off v. **1.** exhibit to invite admiration. **2.** Informal behave flamboyantly in order to attract attention. **show-off** n. Informal person who shows off. **showpiece** n. excellent specimen shown for display or as an example. **showroom** n. room in which goods for sale are on display. **show up** v. **1.** reveal or be revealed clearly. **2.** expose the faults or defects of. **3.** Informal embarrass. **4.** Informal arrive.

shower n. **1.** kind of bath in which a person stands while being sprayed with water. **2.** wash in this. **3.** short period of rain, hail, or snow. **4.** sudden abundant fall of objects, e.g. shower of sparks. —v. **5.** wash in a shower. **6.** bestow (things) or present (someone) with things liberally. **7.** sprinkle with or as if with a shower. **showery** adj.

shown v. a past participle of SHOW.

shrank v. a past tense of SHRINK.

shrapnel n. **1.** artillery shell filled with pellets which scatter on explosion. **2.** fragments from this.

shred n. **1.** long narrow strip torn from something. **2.** small amount. —v. **shredding, shredded** or **shred. 3.** tear to shreds.

shrew n. **1.** small mouselike animal. **2.** bad-tempered nagging woman. **shrewish** adj.

shrewd adj. clever and perceptive. **shrewdly** adv. **shrewdness** n.

shriek n. **1.** shrill cry. —v. **2.** utter (with) a shriek.

shrike n. songbird with a heavy hooked bill.

shrill adj. **1.** (of a sound) sharp and high-pitched. —v. **2.** utter shrilly. **shrillness** n. **shrilly** adv.

shrimp n. **1.** small edible shellfish. **2.** Informal small person. **shrimping** n. fishing for shrimps.

shrine n. **1.** place of worship associated with a sacred person or object. **2.** container for holy relics.

shrink v. **shrinking, shrank** or **shrunk,**

shrunk *or* **shrunken**. **1.** become or make smaller. **2.** recoil or withdraw. —*n.* **3.** *Slang* psychiatrist. **shrinkage** *n.* decrease in size, value, or weight.

shrive *v.* **shriving**, **shrived** *or* **shrove**, **shriven**. *Old-fashioned* give absolution to after hearing confession.

shrivel *v.* **-elling**, **-elled**. shrink and wither.

shroud *n.* **1.** piece of cloth used to wrap a dead body. **2.** anything which conceals. —*v.* **3.** conceal.

Shrovetide *n.* the three days preceding Lent. **Shrove Tuesday** day before Ash Wednesday.

shrub *n.* woody plant smaller than a tree. **shrubbery** *n.* area planted with shrubs.

shrug *v.* **shrugging**, **shrugged**. **1.** raise and then drop (the shoulders) as a sign of indifference, ignorance, or doubt. —*n.* **2.** shrugging. **shrug off** *v.* dismiss as unimportant.

shrunk *v.* a past of SHRINK.

shrunken *v.* a past participle of SHRINK.

shudder *v.* **1.** shake or tremble violently, esp. with horror. —*n.* **2.** shaking or trembling.

shuffle *v.* **1.** walk without lifting the feet. **2.** rearrange. **3.** jumble together. —*n.* **4.** shuffling. **5.** rearrangement.

shun *v.* **shunning**, **shunned**. avoid.

shunt *v.* **1.** move (objects or people) to a different position. **2.** move (a train) from one track to another. —*n.* **3.** shunting. **4.** railway point.

shush *interj.* **1.** be quiet! —*v.* **2.** quiet by saying 'shush'.

shut *v.* **shutting**, **shut**. **1.** bring together or fold, close. **2.** prevent access to. **3.** (of a shop etc.) stop operating for the day. **shutter** *n.* **1.** hinged doorlike cover for closing off a window. **2.** device in a camera letting in the light required to expose a film. —*v.* **3.** close or equip with a shutter. **shut down** *v.* close or stop (a factory, machine, or business). **shutdown** *n.* **shuteye** *n.* *Slang* sleep. **shut up** *v.* **1.** *Informal* stop talking. **2.** confine.

shuttle *n.* **1.** vehicle going to and fro over a short distance. **2.** instrument which passes the weft thread between the warp threads in weaving. **3.** small thread-holding device in a sewing machine. —*v.* **4.** travel by or as if by shuttle.

shuttlecock *n.* small light cone with feathers stuck in one end, struck to and fro in badminton.

shy[1] *adj.* **1.** not at ease in company. **2.** timid. **3.** (foll. by *of*) cautious or wary. **4.** reluctant, e.g. *workshy*. —*v.* **shying**, **shied**. **5.** start back in fear. **6.** (foll. by *away from*) avoid (doing something) through fear or lack of confidence. **shyly** *adv.* **shyness** *n.*

shy[2] *v.* **shying**, **shied**. **1.** throw. —*n.*, *pl.* **shies**. **2.** throw.

shyster *n.* *US informal* unscrupulous person, esp. a lawyer.

Si *Chem.* silicon.

SI *French* Système International (d'Unités), international metric system of units of measurement.

Siamese *adj.* of Siam, former name of Thailand. **Siamese cat** breed of cat with cream fur, dark ears and face, and blue eyes. **Siamese twins** twins born joined to each other at some part of the body.

sibilant *adj.* **1.** hissing. —*n.* **2.** consonant pronounced with a hissing sound.

sibling *n.* brother or sister.

sibyl *n.* in ancient Greece and Rome, prophetess. **sibylline** *adj.*

sic *Latin* thus: used to indicate that an odd spelling or reading is in fact accurate.

sick *adj.* **1.** vomiting or likely to vomit. **2.** physically or mentally unwell. **3.** *Informal* amused by something sadistic or morbid. **4.** (foll. by *of*) *Informal* disgusted (by) or weary (of). —*n.* **5.** *Informal* vomit. **sickness** *n.* **sicken** *v.* **1.** make nauseated or disgusted. **2.** become ill. **sickly** *adj.* **1.** unhealthy, weak. **2.** causing revulsion or nausea. **3.** looking pale and ill. **sickbay** *n.* place for sick people, such as that on a ship.

sickle *n.* tool with a curved blade for cutting grass or grain.

side *n.* **1.** line or surface that borders anything. **2.** either surface of a flat object. **3.** either of two halves into which something can be divided. **4.** right or left part of the body. **5.** area immediately next to a person or thing. **6.** slope of a hill. **7.** region. **8.** aspect or part. **9.** one of two opposing groups or teams. **10.** line of descent through one parent. **11.** *Slang* conceit. —*adj.* **12.** at or on the side. **13.** subordinate. **on the side 1.** as an extra. **2.** unofficially. **siding** *n.* short stretch of railway track on which trains or wagons are shunted from the main line. **sideboard** *n.* **1.** piece of furniture for holding plates, cutlery, etc. in a dining room. —*pl.* (also **sideburns**) 2. man's side whiskers. **sidecar** *n.* small passenger car on the side of a motorcycle. **side-effect** *n.* additional undesirable effect. **sidekick** *n. Informal* close friend or associate. **sidelight** *n.* either of two small lights on the front of a vehicle. **sideline** *n.* 1. subsidiary interest or source of income. 2. *Sport* line marking the boundary of a playing area. **sidelong** *adj.* 1. sideways. 2. oblique. —*adv.* 3. obliquely. **side-saddle** *n.* saddle designed to allow a woman rider to sit with both legs on the same side of the horse. **sideshow** *n.* entertainment offered along with the main show. **sidestep** *v.* 1. dodge (an issue). 2. avoid by stepping sideways. **sidetrack** *v.* divert from the main topic. **sidewalk** *n. US* pavement. **sideways** *adv.* 1. to or from the side. 2. obliquely. **side with** *v.* support (one side in a dispute).

sidereal [side-**eer**-ee-al] *adj.* of or determined with reference to the stars.

sidle *v.* move in a furtive manner.

SIDS sudden infant death syndrome, cot death.

siege *n.* surrounding and blockading of a place.

siemens *n.* SI unit of electrical conductance.

sienna *n.* reddish- or yellowish-brown pigment made from natural earth.

sierra *n.* range of mountains in Spain or America with jagged peaks.

siesta *n.* afternoon nap, taken in hot countries.

sieve [siv] *n.* 1. utensil with mesh through which a substance is sifted or strained. —*v.* 2. sift or strain through a sieve.

sift *v.* 1. remove the coarser particles from a substance with a sieve. 2. examine (information or evidence) to select what is important.

sigh *n.* 1. long audible breath expressing sadness, tiredness, relief, or longing. —*v.* 2. utter a sigh. **sigh for** *v.* long for.

sight *n.* 1. ability to see. 2. instance of seeing. 3. range of vision. 4. thing seen. 5. thing worth seeing. 6. *Informal* unsightly thing. 7. device for guiding the eye while using a gun or optical instrument. 8. *Informal* a lot. —*v.* 9. catch sight of. 10. aim (a weapon) using a sight. **sightless** *adj.* blind. **sight-read** *v.* play or sing printed music

without previous preparation. **sightseeing** *n.* visiting places of interest. **sightseer** *n.*

sign *n.* 1. indication of something not immediately or outwardly observable. 2. notice displayed to advertise, inform, or warn. 3. gesture, mark, or symbol conveying a meaning. 4. omen. 5. visible indication. —*v.* 6. make a sign or gesture. 7. write (one's name) on (a document or letter) to show its authenticity or one's agreement. 8. communicate using sign language. 9. engage by signing a contract. **sign language** (also **signing**) system of communication by gestures, as used by deaf people. **sign on** *v.* 1. register as unemployed. 2. sign a document committing oneself to a job, course, etc. **signpost** *n.* 1. post bearing a sign that shows the way. —*v.* 2. mark with signposts.

signal *n.* 1. sign or gesture to convey information. 2. sequence of electrical impulses or radio waves transmitted or received. —*adj.* 3. remarkable or striking. —*v.* **-nalling**, **-nalled**. 4. make a signal. 5. convey (information) by signal. **signally** *adv.* **signal box** building from which railway signals are operated. **signalman** *n.* railwayman in charge of signals and points.

signatory [sig-na-tree] *n.*, *pl.* **-ries.** one of the parties who sign a document.

signature *n.* 1. person's name written by himself or herself in signing something. 2. sign at the start of a piece of music to show the key or tempo. 3. identifying characteristic. **signature tune** tune used to introduce a particular television or radio programme.

signet *n.* small seal used to authenticate documents. **signet ring** finger ring bearing a signet.

significant *adj.* 1. important. 2. having or expressing a meaning. **significantly** *adv.* **significance** *n.*

signify *v.* **-fying**, **-fied.** 1. indicate or suggest. 2. be a symbol or sign for. 3. be important. **signification** *n.* meaning.

signor [see-**nyor**] *n.* Italian term of address equivalent to *Sir* or *Mr.* **signora** [see-**nyor**-a] *n.* Italian term of address equivalent to *madam* or *Mrs.* **signorina** [see-nyor-**ee**-na] *n.* Italian term of address equivalent to *madam* or *Miss.*

Sikh [seek] *n.* member of an Indian religion having only one God.

silage [**sile**-ij] *n.* fodder crop harvested

while green and partially fermented in a silo.

silence n. **1.** absence of noise or speech. **2.** refusal or failure to speak or communicate. —v. **3.** make silent. **4.** put a stop to. **silent** adj. **silently** adv. **silencer** n. device to reduce the noise of an engine exhaust or gun.

silhouette n. **1.** outline of a dark shape seen against a light background. **2.** outline drawing of a profile. —v. **3.** show in silhouette.

silica n. hard glossy mineral found as quartz and in sandstone. **silicosis** n. lung disease caused by inhaling silica dust.

silicate n. compound of silicon, oxygen, and a metal.

silicon n. brittle nonmetallic element widely used in chemistry and industry. **silicone** n. tough synthetic substance made from silicon and used in lubricants, paints, and resins. **silicon chip** tiny wafer of silicon processed to form an integrated circuit.

silk n. **1.** fibre made by the larva (**silkworm**) of a certain moth. **2.** thread or fabric made from this. **take silk** become a Queen's (or King's) Counsel. **silky, silken** adj. of or like silk.

sill n. ledge at the bottom of a window or door.

silly adj. **-lier, -liest.** foolish. **silliness** n.

silo n., pl. **-los. 1.** pit or airtight tower for storing silage. **2.** underground structure in which nuclear missiles are kept ready for launching.

silt n. **1.** mud deposited by moving water. —v. **2.** (foll. by up) fill or be choked with silt.

silvan adj. same as SYLVAN.

silver n. **1.** white precious metal. **2.** coins or articles made of silver. —adj. **3.** made of or of the colour of silver. —v. **4.** coat with silver. **silvery** adj. **1.** like silver. **2.** having a clear ringing sound. **silver birch** tree with silvery-white bark. **silverfish** n. small wingless silver-coloured insect. **silver medal** medal given to the runner-up in a competition or race. **silver-plated** adj. covered with a thin layer of silver. **silverside** n. cut of beef from below the rump and above the leg. **silversmith** n. person who makes articles of silver. **silver wedding** twenty-fifth wedding anniversary.

silviculture n. cultivation of forest trees.

simian adj., n. (of or like) a monkey or ape.

similar adj. alike but not identical. **similarity** n. **similarly** adv.

▷ Do not confuse *similar* and *same*. *Similar* is 'alike but not identical'; *same* means 'identical'.

simile [sim-ill-ee] n. figure of speech comparing one thing to another, using 'as' or 'like'.

similitude n. similarity, likeness.

simmer v. **1.** cook gently at just below boiling point. **2.** be in a state of suppressed rage. **simmer down** v. calm down.

simnel cake n. fruit cake covered with marzipan.

simper v. **1.** smile in a silly or affected way. **2.** utter (something) with a simper. —n. **3.** simpering smile.

simple adj. **1.** easy to understand or do. **2.** plain or unpretentious. **3.** not combined or complex. **4.** sincere or frank. **5.** feeble-minded. **simply** adv. **1.** in a simple manner. **2.** merely. **3.** absolutely. **simplicity** n. **simplify** v. **-fying, -fied.** make less complicated. **simplification** n. **simplistic** adj. oversimplified or oversimplifying. **simple-minded** adj. unsophisticated. **simple fraction** fraction in which the numerator and denominator are whole numbers. **simpleton** n. foolish or half-witted person.

simulate v. **1.** make a pretence of. **2.** have the appearance of. **3.** imitate the conditions of (a particular situation). **simulation** n. **simulator** n.

simultaneous adj. occurring at the same time. **simultaneity** n. **simultaneously** adv.

sin¹ n. **1.** breaking of a religious or moral law. **2.** offence against a principle or standard. —v. **3.** commit a sin. **sinful** adj. **1.** being a sin. **2.** guilty of sin. **sinfully** adv. **sinner** n.

sin² in trigonometry, sine.

since prep. **1.** during the period of time after. —conj. **2.** from the time when. **3.** for the reason that. —adv. **4.** from that time.

▷ Avoid the use of *ago* with *since*. It is redundant: *It is ten years since he wrote his book* (not *ten years ago since*).

sincere adj. without pretence or deceit. **sincerely** adv. **sincerity** n.

sine n. in trigonometry, ratio of the length of the opposite side to that of the hypotenuse in a right-angled triangle.

sinecure [sin-ee-cure] n. paid job with minimal duties.

sine die [sin-ay dee-ay] adv. Latin with no date fixed for future action.

sine qua non [sin-ay kwah non] n. Latin essential requirement.

sinew n. 1. tough fibrous tissue joining muscle to bone. 2. muscles or strength. **sinewy** adj.

sing v. **singing, sang, sung. 1.** make musical sounds with the voice. **2.** perform (a song). **3.** make a humming or whistling sound. **singer** n. **singing telegram** service in which a messenger presents greetings to a person by singing. **singsong** n. **1.** informal singing session. —adj. **2.** (of the voice) repeatedly rising and falling in pitch.
▷ The simple past of *sing* is *sang: He sang the chorus.* Avoid the use of the past participle *sung* for the simple past.

singe v. **singeing, singed. 1.** burn the surface of. —n. **2.** superficial burn.

single adj. **1.** one only. **2.** distinct from others of the same kind. **3.** unmarried. **4.** designed for one user. **5.** formed of only one part. **6.** (of a ticket) valid for an outward journey only. —n. **7.** single thing. **8.** thing intended for one person. **9.** record with one short song or tune on each side. **10.** single ticket. —pl. **11.** game between two players. —v. **12.** (foll. by *out*) pick out from others. **singly** adv. **single-breasted** adj. (of a garment) having only slightly overlapping fronts and one row of buttons. **single file** (of people or things) arranged in one line. **single-handed** adj. without assistance. **single-minded** adj. having one aim only.

singlet n. sleeveless vest.

singular adj. **1.** (of a word or form) denoting one person or thing. **2.** remarkable, unusual. —n. **3.** singular form of a word. **singularity** n. **singularly** adv.

Sinhalese, Singhalese n., adj. (member or language) of a people living mainly in Sri Lanka.

sinister adj. threatening or suggesting evil or harm.

sink v. **sinking, sank** or **sunk, sunk** or **sunken. 1.** submerge (in liquid). **2.** descend or cause to descend. **3.** decline in value or amount. **4.** become weaker in health. **5.** seep or penetrate. **6.** dig or drill (a hole or shaft). **7.** invest (money). **8.** *Golf, snooker* hit (a ball) into a hole or pocket. —n. **9.** fixed basin with a water supply and drainage pipe. **sinker** n. weight for a fishing line. **sink in** v. penetrate the mind. **sinking fund** money set aside regularly to repay a long-term debt.

Sino- combining form Chinese.

sinuous adj. **1.** curving. **2.** lithe. **sinuously** adv. **sinuosity** n.

sinus [sine-uss] n. hollow space in a bone, esp. an air passage opening into the nose. **sinusitis** n. inflammation of a sinus membrane.

sip v. **sipping, sipped. 1.** drink in small mouthfuls. —n. **2.** amount sipped.

siphon n. **1.** bent tube which uses air pressure to draw liquid from a container. —v. **2.** draw off thus. **3.** redirect (resources).

sir n. **1.** polite term of address for a man. **2.** (S-) title of a knight or baronet.

sire n. **1.** male parent of a horse or other domestic animal. **2.** respectful term of address to a king. —v. **3.** father.

siren n. **1.** device making a loud wailing noise as a warning. **2.** dangerously alluring woman.

sirloin n. prime cut of loin of beef.

sirocco n., pl. **-cos.** hot wind blowing from N Africa into S Europe.

sisal [size-al] n. (fibre of) plant used in making ropes.

siskin n. yellow-and-black finch.

sissy adj., n., pl. **-sies.** weak or cowardly (person).

sister n. **1.** girl or woman with the same parents as another person. **2.** senior nurse. **3.** nun. **4.** female fellow-member of a group. —adj. **5.** closely related, similar. **sisterhood** n. **1.** state of being a sister. **2.** group of women united by common aims or beliefs. **sisterly** adj. **sister-in-law** n., pl. **sisters-in-law. 1.** sister of one's husband or wife. **2.** one's brother's wife.

sit v. **sitting, sat. 1.** rest one's body upright on the buttocks. **2.** cause to sit. **3.** perch. **4.** (of a bird) incubate (eggs) by sitting on them. **5.** be situated. **6.** pose for a portrait. **7.** occupy an official position. **8.** (of an official body) hold a session. **9.** take (an examination). **10.** fit or hang as specified. **sit tight** *Informal* wait patiently without taking action. **sitter** n. **1.** baby-sitter. **2.** person posing for a picture. **sitting** n. **1.** time when a meal is served. **2.** meeting of an official body. —*adj.* **3.** seated. **4.** current. **sit down** *v.* (cause to) adopt a sitting posture. **sit-in** *n.* protest in which demonstrators occupy a place and refuse to move. **sit on** *v. Informal* delay action on. **sit out** *v.* endure to the end. **sitting room** room in a house where people sit and relax.

sitar *n.* Indian stringed musical instrument.

sitcom *n. Informal* situation comedy.

site *n.* **1.** place where something is, was, or is intended to be located. —*v.* **2.** provide with a site.

situate *v.* place. **situation** *n.* **1.** location and surroundings. **2.** state of affairs. **3.** position of employment. **situation comedy** radio or television series involving the same characters in various situations.

six *adj., n.* one more than five. **sixth** *adj., n.* (of) number six in a series. **sixteen** *adj., n.* six and ten. **sixteenth** *adj., n.* **sixty** *adj., n.* six times ten. **sixtieth** *adj., n.* **sixpence** *n.* former British coin worth six pennies. **sixth sense** perception beyond the five senses.

size¹ *n.* **1.** dimensions, bigness. **2.** one of a series of standard measurements of goods. —*v.* **3.** arrange according to size. **sizeable, sizable** *adj.* quite large. **size up** *v. Informal* assess.

size² *n.* **1.** gluey substance used as a sealer. —*v.* **2.** treat with size.

sizzle *v.* **1.** make a hissing sound like frying fat. —*n.* **2.** hissing sound.

SK Saskatchewan.

skate¹ *n.* **1.** boot with a steel blade or sets of wheels attached to the sole for gliding over ice or a hard surface. —*v.* **2.** glide on or as if on skates. **skateboard** *n.* board mounted on small wheels for riding on while standing up. **skate over, round** *v.* avoid discussing or dealing with (a matter) fully.

skate² *n.* large marine flatfish.

skean-dhu *n.* dagger worn in the stocking as part of the Highland dress.

skedaddle *v. Informal* run off.

skein *n.* **1.** yarn wound in a loose coil. **2.** flock of geese in flight.

skeleton *n.* **1.** framework of bones inside a person's or animal's body. **2.** essential framework of a structure. **3.** skinny person or animal. **4.** outline of bare essentials. —*adj.* **5.** reduced to a minimum. **skeletal** *adj.* **skeleton key** key which can open many different locks.

skerry *n., pl.* **-ries.** rocky island or reef.

sketch *n.* **1.** rough drawing. **2.** brief description. **3.** short humorous play. —*v.* **4.** make a sketch (of). **sketchy** *adj.* incomplete or inadequate.

skew *v.* **1.** make slanting or crooked. —*adj.* **2.** slanting or crooked. **skewwhiff** *adj. Informal* slanting or crooked.

skewbald *n., adj.* (horse) marked with patches of white and another colour.

skewer *n.* **1.** pin to hold meat together during cooking. —*v.* **2.** fasten with a skewer.

ski *n.* **1.** one of a pair of long runners fastened to boots for gliding over snow or water. —*v.* **skiing, skied** *or* **ski'd. 2.** travel on skis. **skier** *n.*

skid *v.* **skidding, skidded. 1.** (of a moving vehicle) slide sideways uncontrollably. —*n.* **2.** skidding. **skid row** *US slang* dilapidated part of a city frequented by down-and-outs.

skiff *n.* small boat.

skill *n.* **1.** special ability or expertise. **2.** something requiring special training or expertise. **skilful** *adj.* having or showing skill. **skilfully** *adv.* **skilled** *adj.*

skillet *n.* small frying pan or shallow cooking pot.

skim *v.* **skimming, skimmed. 1.** remove floating matter from the surface of (a liquid). **2.** glide smoothly over. **3.** read quickly. **4.** throw across a surface. **skimmed, skim milk** milk from which the cream has been removed.

skimp *v.* not invest enough time, money, material, etc. **skimpy** *adj.* scanty or insufficient.

skin *n.* **1.** outer covering of the body. **2.** complexion. **3.** outer layer or covering. **4.** film on a liquid. **5.** animal skin used as a material or container. —*v.* **skinning, skinned. 6.** remove the skin of. **7.** graze. **8.** *Slang* swindle. **skinless** *adj.* **skinny** *adj.* thin. **skin-deep** *adj.* superficial. **skin diving** underwater swimming using flippers and light breathing apparatus. **skin-diver** *n.* **skinflint** *n.* miser. **skinhead** *n.* youth with very short hair. **skin-tight** *adj.* fitting tightly over the body.

skint *adj. Slang* having no money.

skip¹ *n.* **1.** leap lightly from one foot to the other. **2.** jump over a rope as it is swung under one. **3.** *Informal* pass over, omit. **4.** change quickly from one subject to another. —*n.* **5.** skipping.

skip[2] *n.* **1.** large open container for builders' rubbish. **2.** cage used as a lift in mines.

skipper *n.*, *v.* captain.

skirl *n.* sound of bagpipes.

skirmish *n.* **1.** brief or minor fight or argument. —*v.* **2.** take part in a skirmish.

skirt *n.* **1.** woman's garment hanging from the waist. **2.** part of a dress or coat below the waist. **3.** cut of beef from the flank. **4.** circular hanging part. —*v.* **5.** border. **6.** go round. **7.** avoid dealing with (an issue). **skirting board** narrow board round the bottom of an interior wall.

skit *n.* brief satirical sketch.

skittish *adj.* **1.** playful or lively. **2.** (of a horse) easily frightened.

skittle *n.* **1.** bottle-shaped object used as a target in some games. —*pl.* **2.** game in which players try to knock over skittles by rolling a ball at them.

skive *v.* *Informal* evade work or responsibility.

skivvy *n.*, *pl.* -**vies**. female servant who does menial work.

skua *n.* large predatory gull.

skulduggery *n.* *Informal* trickery.

skulk *v.* **1.** move stealthily. **2.** lurk.

skull *n.* **1.** bony framework of the head. **2.** *Informal* brain or mind. **skullcap** *n.* close-fitting brimless cap.

skunk *n.* **1.** small black-and-white N American mammal which emits an evil-smelling fluid when attacked. **2.** *Slang* despicable person.

sky *n.*, *pl.* **skies**. **1.** upper atmosphere as seen from the earth. —*v.* **2.** skying, skied. **2.** *Informal* hit high in the air. **skydiving** *n.* sport of jumping from an aircraft and performing manoeuvres before opening one's parachute. **skylark** *n.* lark that sings while soaring at a great height. **skylight** *n.* window in a roof or ceiling. **skyline** *n.* outline of buildings, trees, etc. against the sky. **skyscraper** *n.* very tall building.

slab *n.* broad flat piece.

slack[1] *adj.* **1.** not tight. **2.** negligent. **3.** not busy. **4.** (of water) moving slowly. —*n.* **5.** slack part. **6.** slack period. —*pl.* **7.** informal trousers. —*v.* **8.** neglect one's work or duty.

9. loosen or slacken. **slackness** *n.* **slacken** *v.* make or become slack. **slacker** *n.*

slack[2] *n.* coal dust or small pieces of coal.

slag *n.* **1.** waste left after metal is smelted. —*v.* **slagging, slagged. 2.** *Slang* criticize. **slag heap** pile of waste from smelting or mining.

slain *v.* past participle of SLAY.

slake *v.* **1.** satisfy (thirst or desire). **2.** combine (quicklime) with water.

slalom *n.* skiing or canoeing race over a winding course.

slam *v.* **slamming, slammed. 1.** shut, put down, or hit violently and noisily. **2.** *Informal* criticize harshly. —*n.* **3.** act or sound of slamming. **grand slam** see GRAND.

slander *n.* **1.** false and malicious statement about a person. **2.** crime of making such a statement. —*v.* **3.** utter slander about. **slanderous** *adj.*

slang *n.* very informal language. **slangy** *adj.* **slanging match** abusive argument.

slant *v.* **1.** lean at an angle. **2.** present (information) in a biased way. —*n.* **3.** slope. **4.** point of view, esp. a biased one. **slanting** *adj.*

slap *n.* **1.** blow with the open hand or a flat object. —*v.* **slapping, slapped. 2.** strike with the open hand or a flat object. **3.** *Informal* place forcefully or carelessly. **slapdash** *adj.* careless and hasty. **slaphappy** *adj.* *Informal* cheerfully careless. **slapstick** *n.* boisterous knockabout comedy. **slap-up** *adj.* (of a meal) large and luxurious.

slash *v.* **1.** gash. **2.** cut with a sweeping stroke. **3.** reduce drastically. **4.** criticize harshly. —*n.* **5.** gash. **6.** sweeping stroke.

slat *n.* narrow strip of wood or metal.

slate *n.* **1.** rock which splits easily into thin layers. **2.** piece of this for covering a roof or, formerly, for writing on. —*v.* **3.** criticize severely. **4.** *US* plan or arrange. —*adj.* **5.** dark grey.

slater *n.* woodlouse.

slattern *n.* *Old-fashioned* slovenly woman. **slatternly** *adj.*

slaughter *v.* **1.** kill (animals) for food. **2.** kill (people) savagely or indiscriminately. —*n.* **3.** slaughtering. **slaughterhouse** *n.* place where animals are killed for food.

Slav *n.* member of any of the peoples of E Europe or Soviet Asia who speak a Slavonic language. **Slavonic** *n.* **1.** language group including Russian, Polish, and Czech. —*adj.* 2. of this language group.

slave *n.* 1. person owned by another for whom he or she has to work. 2. person dominated by another or by a habit. 3. drudge. —*v.* 4. work like a slave. **slaver** *n.* person or ship engaged in the slave trade. **slavery** *n.* 1. state or condition of being a slave. 2. practice of owning slaves. **slavish** *adj.* 1. of or like a slave. 2. imitative. **slave-driver** *n.* person who makes others work very hard.

slaver *v.* 1. dribble saliva from the mouth. —*n.* 2. saliva dribbling from the mouth.

slay *v.* **slaying, slew, slain.** kill.

sleazy *adj.* **-zier, -ziest.** sordid. **sleaziness** *n.*

sledge[1] *n.* 1. carriage on runners for sliding on snow. 2. light wooden frame for sliding over snow. —*v.* 3. travel by sledge.

sledge[2], **sledgehammer** *n.* heavy hammer with a long handle.

sleek *adj.* 1. glossy, smooth, and shiny. 2. looking well-fed and well-groomed.

sleep *n.* 1. state of rest characterized by unconsciousness. 2. period of this. —*v.* **sleeping, slept.** 3. be in or as if in a state of sleep. 4. have sleeping accommodation for (a specified number). **sleeper** *n.* 1. person who sleeps. 2. beam supporting the rails of a railway. 3. railway car fitted for sleeping in. 4. ring worn in a pierced ear to stop the hole from closing up. **sleepy** *adj.* 1. needing sleep. 2. without activity or bustle. **sleepily** *adv.* **sleepiness** *n.* **sleepless** *adj.* **sleep in** *v.* sleep longer than usual. **sleeping bag** padded bag for sleeping in. **sleeping partner** business partner who does not play an active role. **sleeping sickness** African disease spread by the tsetse fly. **sleepwalk** *v.* walk while asleep. **sleepwalker** *n.* **sleep with, together** *v.* have sexual intercourse (with).

sleet *n.* 1. rain and snow or hail falling together. —*v.* 2. fall as sleet.

sleeve *n.* 1. part of a garment which covers the arm. 2. tubelike cover. 3. gramophone record cover. **up one's sleeve** secretly ready. **sleeveless** *adj.*

sleigh *n.*, *v.* sledge.

sleight of hand [**slite**] *n.* skilful use of the hands when performing conjuring tricks.

slender *adj.* 1. slim. 2. small in amount.

slept *v.* past of SLEEP.

sleuth [**slooth**] *n.* detective.

slew[1] *v.* past tense of SLAY.

slew[2] *v.* twist or swing round.

slice *n.* 1. thin flat piece cut from something. 2. share. 3. kitchen tool with a broad flat blade. 4. *Sport* hitting of a ball so that it travels obliquely. —*v.* 5. cut into slices. 6. *Sport* hit (a ball) with a slice. 7. cut (through).

slick *adj.* 1. persuasive and glib. 2. skilfully devised or carried out. 3. well-made and attractive, but superficial. —*v.* 4. make smooth or sleek. —*n.* 5. patch of oil on water.

slide *v.* **sliding, slid.** 1. slip smoothly along (a surface). 2. pass unobtrusively. 3. go into or become (something) by degrees, e.g. *he slid into loose living.* —*n.* 4. sliding. 5. surface or structure for sliding on or down. 6. piece of glass holding an object to be viewed under a microscope. 7. photographic transparency. 8. ornamental hair clip. 9. sliding curved part of a trombone. **slide rule** mathematical instrument formerly used for rapid calculations. **sliding scale** variable scale according to which things such as wages fluctuate in response to changes in other factors.

slight *adj.* 1. small in quantity or extent. 2. not important. 3. slim and delicate. —*v.*, *n.* 4. snub. **slightly** *adv.*

slim *adj.* **slimmer, slimmest.** 1. not heavy or stout, thin. 2. slight. —*v.* **slimming, slimmed.** 3. make or become slim by diet and exercise. **slimmer** *n.*

slime *n.* unpleasant thick slippery substance. **slimy** *adj.* 1. of, like, or covered with slime. 2. ingratiating.

sling[1] *n.* 1. bandage hung from the neck to support an injured hand or arm. 2. strap with a string at each end for throwing a stone. 3. rope or strap for lifting something. —*v.* **slinging, slung.** 4. throw. 5. carry, hang, or throw with or as if with a sling. **slingback** *n.* shoe with a strap that goes around the back of the heel.

sling[2] *n.* sweetened drink with a spirit base, e.g. *gin sling.*

slink *v.* **slinking, slunk.** move furtively or guiltily. **slinky** *adj.* 1. (of clothes) figure-hugging. 2. sinuously graceful.

slip[1] *v.* **slipping, slipped.** 1. lose balance by

sliding. **2.** move smoothly, easily, or quietly. **3.** (foll. by *on* or *off*) put on or take off easily or quickly. **4.** pass out of (the mind). **5.** place quickly or stealthily. **6.** become worse. **7.** dislocate (a bone). —*n.* **8.** slipping. **9.** mistake. **10.** petticoat. **11.** small piece (of paper). **12.** slender person. **13.** *Cricket* fielding position behind and to the offside of the wicketkeeper. **14.** cutting from a plant. **give someone the slip** escape from someone. **slippy** *adj. Informal* slippery. **slipknot** *n.* knot tied so that it will slip along the rope round which it is made. **slip-on** *adj.* (of a garment or shoe) made to be put on easily. **slipped disc** painful condition in which one of the discs connecting the bones of the spine becomes displaced. **slip road** narrow road giving access to a motorway. **slipshod** *adj.* (of an action) careless. **slipstream** *n.* stream of air forced backwards by a fast-moving object. **slip up** make a mistake. **slipway** *n.* launching slope on which ships are built or repaired.

slip² *n.* clay mixed with water used for decorating pottery.

slipper *n.* light shoe for indoor wear.

slippery *adj.* **1.** so smooth or wet as to cause slipping or be difficult to hold. **2.** (of a person) untrustworthy.

slit *v.* **slitting, slit. 1.** make a long straight cut in. —*n.* **2.** long narrow cut or opening.

slither *v.* **1.** slide unsteadily. **2.** move in a twisting way.

sliver [sliv-ver] *n.* **1.** small thin piece. —*v.* **2.** cut into slivers.

slob *n. Informal* lazy and untidy person. **slobbish** *adj.*

slobber *v.* **1.** dribble or drool. **2.** behave in a gushy way. **slobbery** *adj.*

sloe *n.* sour blue-black fruit.

slog *v.* **slogging, slogged. 1.** work hard and steadily. **2.** make one's way with difficulty. **3.** hit hard. —*n.* **4.** long and exhausting work or walk.

slogan *n.* catchword or phrase used in politics or advertising.

sloop *n.* small single-masted ship.

slop *v.* **slopping, slopped. 1.** splash or spill. —*n.* **2.** spilt liquid. **3.** liquid food. —*pl.* **4.** liquid refuse and waste food used to feed animals. **sloppy** *adj.* **1.** careless or untidy. **2.** gushingly sentimental.

slope *v.* **1.** slant. —*n.* **2.** sloping surface. **3.**

degree of inclination. —*pl.* **4.** hills. **slope off** *v. Informal* go furtively.

slosh *n.* **1.** splashing sound. —*v.* **2.** splash carelessly. **3.** *Slang* hit hard. **4.** pour carelessly. **sloshed** *adj. Slang* drunk.

slot *n.* **1.** narrow opening for inserting something. **2.** *Informal* place in a series or scheme. —*v.* **slotting, slotted. 3.** make a slot or slots in. **4.** fit into a slot. **slot machine** automatic machine worked by placing a coin in a slot.

sloth [rhymes with **both**] *n.* **1.** slow-moving animal of tropical America. **2.** laziness. **slothful** *adj.* lazy or idle.

slouch *v.* **1.** sit, stand, or move with a drooping posture. —*n.* **2.** drooping posture. **3.** *Informal* incompetent or lazy person.

slough¹ [rhymes with **now**] *n.* bog.

slough² [sluff] *v.* **1.** (of a snake) shed (its skin) or (of a skin) be shed. —*n.* **2.** outer covering that has been shed. **slough off** get rid of (something unwanted or unnecessary).

sloven *n.* habitually dirty or untidy person. **slovenly** *adj.* **1.** dirty or untidy. **2.** careless.

slow *adj.* **1.** taking a longer time than is usual or expected. **2.** not fast. **3.** (of a clock or watch) showing a time earlier than the correct one. **4.** stupid. **5.** dull or uninteresting. —*v.* **6.** reduce the speed (of). —*adv.* **7.** slowly. **slowly** *adv.* **slowness** *n.* **slowcoach** *n. Informal* person who moves or works slowly. **slow motion** movement on film made to appear much slower than it actually is.

slowworm *n.* small legless lizard.

sludge *n.* **1.** thick mud. **2.** sewage.

slug¹ *n.* **1.** land snail with no shell. **2.** bullet. **sluggish** *adj.* slow-moving, lacking energy. **sluggishly** *adv.* **sluggishness** *n.* **sluggard** *n.* lazy person.

slug² *v.* **slugging, slugged. 1.** hit hard. —*n.* **2.** heavy blow. **3.** *Informal* mouthful of an alcoholic drink.

sluice *n.* **1.** channel carrying water. **2.** sliding gate used to control the flow of water in this. **3.** water controlled by a sluice. —*v.* **4.** pour a stream of water over or through.

slum *n.* **1.** squalid overcrowded house or area. —*v.* **slumming, slummed. 2.** temporarily and deliberately experience poorer places or conditions than usual. **slummy** *adj.*

slumber v., n. Lit. sleep.

slump v. 1. sink or fall heavily. 2. (of prices or demand) decline suddenly. —n. 3. sudden decline in prices or demand. 4. time of substantial unemployment.

slung v. past of SLING¹

slunk v. past of SLINK.

slur v. **slurring, slurred. 1.** pronounce or utter (words) indistinctly. 2. *Music* sing or play (notes) smoothly without a break. 3. disparage. 4. treat carelessly. —n. 5. slurring of words. 6. remark intended to discredit someone. 7. *Music* slurring of notes. 8. curved line indicating notes to be slurred.

slurp *Informal* —v. 1. eat or drink noisily. —n. 2. slurping sound.

slurry n., pl. **-ries.** muddy liquid mixture.

slush n. 1. watery muddy substance. 2. sloppy sentimental talk or writing. **slushy** adj. **slush fund** fund for financing bribery or corruption.

slut n. *Offens.* dirty or immoral woman. **sluttish** adj.

sly adj. **slyer, slyest** or **slier, sliest. 1.** crafty. 2. secretive and cunning. 3. roguish. **on the sly** secretly. **slyly** adv. **slyness** n.

Sm *Chem.* samarium.

smack¹ v. 1. slap sharply. 2. open and close (the lips) loudly in enjoyment or anticipation. —n. 3. sharp slap. 4. slapping sound. 5. loud kiss. —adv. 6. *Informal* squarely or directly, e.g. *smack in the middle.* **smacker** n. *Slang* 1. loud kiss. 2. pound note or dollar bill.

smack² n. 1. slight flavour or trace. 2. *Slang* heroin. —v. 3. have a slight flavour or trace (of).

smack³ n. small single-masted fishing boat.

small adj. 1. not large in size, number, or amount. 2. unimportant. 3. mean or petty. —n. 4. narrow part of the lower back. —pl. 5. *Informal* underwear. —adv. 6. into small pieces. **smallness** n. **small change** coins of low value. **smallholding** n. small area of farming land. **small hours** hours just after midnight. **small-minded** adj. intolerant, petty. **smallpox** n. contagious disease with blisters that leave scars. **small talk** light social conversation. **small-time** adj. insignificant or minor.

smarmy adj. **smarmier, smarmiest.** *Informal* unpleasantly suave or flattering.

smart adj. 1. well-kept and neat. 2. astute.

3. witty. 4. impertinent. 5. fashionable. 6. brisk. 7. causing a stinging pain. —v. 8. feel or cause stinging pain. —n. 9. stinging pain. **smart aleck** *Informal* irritatingly clever person. **smarten** v. make or become smart. **smartly** adv. **smartness** n.

smash v. 1. break violently and noisily. 2. throw (against) violently. 3. collide forcefully. 4. destroy. —n. 5. act or sound of smashing. 6. violent collision of vehicles. 7. *Informal* popular success. 8. *Sport* powerful overhead shot. —adv. 9. with a smash. **smasher** n. *Informal* attractive person or thing. **smashing** adj. *Informal* excellent. **smash-and-grab** adj. *Informal* denoting a robbery in which a shop window is broken and the contents removed.

smattering n. slight knowledge.

smear v. 1. spread with a greasy or sticky substance. 2. rub so as to produce a dirty mark or smudge. 3. slander. —n. 4. dirty mark or smudge. 5. slander. 6. *Med.* sample of a secretion smeared on to a slide for examination under a microscope.

smell v. **smelling, smelt** or **smelled. 1.** perceive (a scent or odour) by means of the nose. 2. have or give off a smell. 3. detect by instinct. 4. have an unpleasant smell. 5. (foll. by *of*) indicate, suggest. —n. 6. odour or scent. 7. smelling. 8. ability to perceive odours by the nose. **smelly** adj. having a nasty smell. **smelling salts** preparation of ammonia used to revive a person who feels faint.

smelt¹ v. extract (a metal) from (an ore) by heating. **smelter** n.

smelt² n. small fish of the salmon family.

smelt³ v. a past of SMELL.

smile n. 1. turning up of the corners of the mouth to show pleasure, amusement, or friendliness. —v. 2. give a smile. 3. express by a smile. **smile on, upon** v. regard favourably.

smirch v., n. disgrace.

smirk n. 1. smug smile. —v. 2. give a smirk.

smite v. **smiting, smote, smitten. 1.** *Old-fashioned* strike hard. 2. affect severely.

smith n. worker in metal. **smithy** n. blacksmith's workshop.

smithereens pl. n. shattered fragments.

smitten v. 1. past participle of SMITE. —adj. 2. affected by love.

smock n. 1. loose overall. 2. woman's loose

blouselike garment. —v. **3.** gather (material) by sewing in a honeycomb pattern. **smocking** n.

smog n. mixture of smoke and fog.

smoke n. **1.** cloudy mass that rises from something burning. **2.** spell of smoking tobacco. **3.** *Informal* cigarette or cigar. —v. **4.** give off smoke. **5.** inhale and expel smoke of (a cigar, cigarette, or pipe). **6.** do this habitually. **7.** cure (meat, fish, or cheese) by treating with smoke. **smokeless** adj. **smoker** n. **smoky** adj. **smoke out** v. drive out of hiding, esp. by using smoke. **smoke screen** something said or done to hide the truth. **smokestack** n. tall chimney of a factory.

smolt n. young salmon at the stage when it migrates to the sea.

smooch *Informal* —v. **1.** kiss and cuddle. —n. **2.** smooching.

smooth adj. **1.** even in surface, texture, or consistency. **2.** without obstructions or difficulties. **3.** charming and polite but possibly insincere. **4.** free from jolts. **5.** not harsh in taste. —v. **6.** make smooth. **7.** calm. **smoothly** adv.

smorgasbord n. buffet meal of assorted dishes.

smote v. past tense of SMITE.

smother v. **1.** suffocate or stifle. **2.** cover thickly. **3.** suppress. **4.** surround or overwhelm (with).

smoulder v. **1.** burn slowly with smoke but no flame. **2.** (of feelings) exist in a suppressed state.

smudge v. **1.** make or become smeared or soiled. —n. **2.** dirty mark. **3.** blurred form. **smudgy** adj.

smug adj. **smugger, smuggest.** selfsatisfied. **smugly** adv. **smugness** n.

smuggle v. **1.** import or export (goods) secretly and illegally. **2.** take somewhere secretly. **smuggler** n.

smut n. **1.** speck of soot. **2.** mark left by this. **3.** obscene jokes, pictures, etc. **4.** fungal disease of cereals. **smutty** adj.

Sn *Chem.* tin.

snack n. light quick meal. **snack bar** place where snacks are sold.

snaffle n. **1.** jointed bit for a horse. —v. **2.** *Slang* steal.

snag n. **1.** difficulty or disadvantage. **2.** sharp projecting point. **3.** hole in fabric caused by a sharp object. —v. **snagging, snagged. 4.** catch or tear on a point.

snail n. slow-moving mollusc with a spiral shell. **snail's pace** very slow speed.

snake n. **1.** long thin scaly limbless reptile. —v. **2.** move in a winding course like a snake. **snake in the grass** treacherous person. **snaky** adj. twisted or winding.

snap v. **snapping, snapped. 1.** break suddenly. **2.** (cause to) make a sharp cracking sound. **3.** bite (at) suddenly. **4.** move suddenly. **5.** speak sharply and angrily. **6.** take a snapshot of. —n. **7.** act or sound of snapping. **8.** fastener that closes with a snapping sound. **9.** *Informal* snapshot. **10.** sudden brief spell of cold weather. **11.** thin crisp biscuit. **12.** card game in which the word 'snap' is called when two similar cards are put down. —adj. **13.** made on the spur of the moment. —adv. **14.** with a snap. **snapper** n. fish of the perch family. **snappy** adj. **1.** (also **snappish**) irritable. **2.** *Slang* quick. **3.** *Slang* smart and fashionable. **snapdragon** n. plant with flowers that can open and shut like a mouth. **snapshot** n. informal photograph. **snap up** v. take eagerly and quickly.

snare[1] n. **1.** trap with a noose. —v. **2.** catch in or as if in a snare.

snare[2] n. *Music.* set of gut strings wound with wire fitted across the bottom of a drum to increase vibration. **snare drum** cylindrical double-headed drum with snares.

snarl v. **1.** (of an animal) growl with bared teeth. **2.** speak or utter fiercely. **3.** make tangled. —n. **4.** act or sound of snarling. **5.** tangled mass. **snarl-up** n. *Informal* confused situation such as a traffic jam.

snatch v. **1.** seize or try to seize suddenly. **2.** take (food, rest, etc.) hurriedly. **3.** remove suddenly. —n. **4.** snatching. **5.** fragment.

snazzy adj. **-zier, -ziest.** *Informal* stylish and flashy.

sneak v. **1.** move furtively. **2.** bring, take, or put furtively. **3.** *Informal* tell tales. —n. **4.** cowardly or underhand person. **5.** *Informal* telltale. **sneaking** adj. **1.** secret. **2.** slight but persistent. **sneaky** adj.

sneakers pl. n. *US* canvas shoes with rubber soles.

sneer n. **1.** contemptuous expression or remark. —v. **2.** show contempt by a sneer.

sneeze v. **1.** expel air from the nose suddenly, involuntarily, and noisily. —*n.* **2.** act or sound of sneezing. **sneeze at** *v. Informal* dismiss lightly.

snib *n.* catch of a door or window.

snick *v., n.* (make) a small cut or notch.

snicker *n., v.* same as SNIGGER.

snide *adj.* maliciously derogatory.

sniff *v.* **1.** inhale through the nose in short audible breaths. **2.** smell by sniffing. —*n.* **3.** act or sound of sniffing. **sniffle** *v.* **1.** sniff repeatedly, as when suffering from a cold. —*n.* **2.** slight cold. **sniff at** *v.* express contempt for. **sniffer dog** police dog trained to detect drugs or explosives by smell.

snifter *n. Informal* small quantity of alcoholic drink.

snigger *n.* **1.** sly disrespectful laugh, esp. one partly stifled. —*v.* **2.** utter a snigger.

snip *v.* **snipping, snipped. 1.** cut in small quick strokes with scissors or shears. —*n.* **2.** act or sound of snipping. **3.** *Informal* bargain. **4.** piece snipped off. **snippet** *n.* small piece.

snipe *n.* **1.** wading bird with a long straight bill. —*v.* **2.** (foll. by *at*) shoot at (a person) from cover. **3.** make critical remarks about. **sniper** *n.*

snitch *Informal* —*v.* **1.** act as an informer. **2.** steal. —*n.* **3.** informer.

snivel *v.* **-elling, -elled. 1.** cry in a whining way. **2.** have a runny nose.

snob *n.* **1.** person who judges others by social rank. **2.** person who feels smugly superior in his or her tastes or interests. **snobbery** *n.* **snobbish** *adj.*

snog *v.* **snogging, snogged.** *Informal* kiss and cuddle.

snood *n.* pouch, often of net, loosely holding a woman's hair at the back.

snook *n.* **cock a snook at** show contempt for.

snooker *n.* **1.** game played on a billiard table. —*v.* **2.** leave (a snooker opponent) in a position such that another ball blocks the target ball. **3.** *Informal* put (someone) in a position where he or she can do nothing.

snoop *Informal* —*v.* **1.** pry. —*n.* **2.** snooping. **snooper** *n.*

snooty *adj.* **snootier, snootiest.** *Informal* haughty.

snooze *Informal* —*v.* **1.** take a brief light sleep. —*n.* **2.** brief light sleep.

snore *v.* **1.** make snorting sounds while sleeping. —*n.* **2.** sound of snoring.

snorkel *n.* **1.** tube allowing a swimmer to breathe while face down on the surface of the water. **2.** device supplying air to a submarine when under water. —*v.* **-kelling, -kelled. 3.** swim using a snorkel.

snort *v.* **1.** exhale noisily through the nostrils. **2.** express contempt or anger by snorting. **3.** say with a snort. —*n.* **4.** act or sound of snorting. **5.** *Informal* small drink of alcohol.

snot *n. Slang* mucus from the nose.

snout *n.* animal's projecting nose and jaws.

snow *n.* **1.** frozen vapour falling from the sky in flakes. **2.** *Slang* cocaine. —*v.* **3.** fall as or like snow. **be snowed under** be overwhelmed, esp. with paperwork. **snowy** *adj.* **snowball** *n.* **1.** snow pressed into a ball for throwing. —*v.* **2.** increase rapidly. **snowblind** *adj.* temporarily blinded by the brightness of the sun on snow. **snowbound** *adj.* shut in by snow. **snowdrift** *n.* bank of deep snow. **snowdrop** *n.* small white bell-shaped spring flower. **snowflake** *n.* single crystal of snow. **snow line** on a mountain, height above which there is permanent snow. **snowman** *n.* figure shaped out of snow. **snowplough** *n.* vehicle for clearing away snow. **snowshoes** *pl. n.* racket-shaped shoes for travelling on snow.

SNP Scottish National Party.

snub *v.* **snubbing, snubbed. 1.** insult deliberately. —*n.* **2.** deliberate insult. —*adj.* **3.** (of a nose) short and blunt. **snub-nosed** *adj.*

snuff[1] *n.* **1.** powdered tobacco for sniffing up the nostrils. —*v.* **2.** take in air through the nose.

snuff[2] *v.* extinguish (a candle). **snuff it** *Informal* die. **snuff out** *v. Informal* put an end to.

snuffle *v.* **1.** breathe noisily or with difficulty. **2.** speak through the nose.

snug *adj.* **snugger, snuggest. 1.** warm and comfortable. **2.** comfortably close-fitting. —*n.* **3.** small room in a pub. **snugly** *adv.*

snuggle *v.* nestle into a person or thing for warmth or for affection.

so[1] *adv.* **1.** to such an extent. **2.** in such a manner. **3.** very. **4.** also. **5.** thereupon. —*conj.* **6.** in order that. **7.** with the result that. **8.** therefore. —*interj.* **9.** exclamation of surprise, triumph, or realization. **or so**

approximately. **so-and-so** n. **1.** *Informal* person whose name is not specified. **2.** unpleasant person or thing. **so-called** adj. called (in the speaker's opinion, wrongly) by that name. **so long** goodbye. **so that** in order that.

so[2] n. *Music* same as **soh**.

soak v. **1.** make wet. **2.** put or lie in liquid so as to become thoroughly wet. **3.** (of liquid) penetrate. —n. **4.** soaking. **5.** *Slang* drunkard. **soaking** n., adj. **soak up** v. absorb.

soap n. **1.** compound of alkali and fat, used with water as a cleaning agent. **2.** *Informal* soap opera. —v. **3.** apply soap to. **soapy** adj. **soapbox** n. crate used as a platform for speech-making. **soap opera** radio or television serial dealing with domestic themes.

soapstone n. soft mineral used for making table tops and ornaments.

soar v. **1.** rise or fly upwards. **2.** increase suddenly.

sob v. **sobbing, sobbed. 1.** weep with convulsive gasps. **2.** utter with sobs. —n. **3.** act or sound of sobbing. **sob story** tale of personal distress told to arouse sympathy.

sober adj. **1.** not drunk. **2.** serious. **3.** (of colours) plain and dull. **4.** temperate. —v. **5.** make or become sober. **soberly** adv. **sobriety** n. state of being sober.

sobriquet [so-brik-ay] n. nickname.

Soc. Society.

soccer n. football played by two teams of eleven kicking a spherical ball.

sociable adj. **1.** friendly or companionable. **2.** (of an occasion) providing companionship. **sociability** n. **sociably** adv.

social adj. **1.** living in a community. **2.** of society or its organization. **3.** of the behaviour of people living in groups. **4.** sociable. —n. **5.** convivial gathering. **socially** adv. **socialize** v. **1.** meet others socially. **2.** prepare for life in society. **socialite** n. member of fashionable society. **social democrat** socialist who believes in the gradual transformation of capitalism into democratic socialism. **social science** scientific study of society and its relationships. **social security** state provision for the unemployed, aged, or sick. **social services** welfare services provided by the local authorities. **social work** work which involves helping people with serious financial or family problems.

socialism n. political system which advocates public ownership of industries, re-

sources, and transport. **socialist** n., adj. **socialistic** adj.

society n., pl. **-ties. 1.** human beings considered as a group. **2.** organized community. **3.** structure and institutions of such a community. **4.** organized group with common aims and interests. **5.** upper-class or fashionable people collectively. **6.** companionship.

sociology n. study of human societies. **sociological** adj. **sociologist** n.

sock[1] n. cloth covering for the foot.

sock[2] *Slang* —v. **1.** hit hard. —n. **2.** hard blow.

socket n. hole or recess into which something fits.

sod n. **1.** (piece of) turf. **2.** *Slang* obnoxious person.

soda n. **1.** compound of sodium. **2.** soda water. **soda fountain** *US* counter serving soft drinks and snacks. **soda water** fizzy drink made from water charged with carbon dioxide.

sodden adj. **1.** soaked. **2.** dulled, esp. by drink.

sodium n. silver-white metallic element. **sodium bicarbonate** white soluble compound used in baking powder. **sodium hydroxide** white alkaline substance used in making paper and soap.

sodomy n. anal intercourse. **sodomite** n. person who practises sodomy.

sofa n. couch.

soft adj. **1.** not hard, rough, or harsh. **2.** (of a breeze or climate) mild. **3.** (too) lenient. **4.** easily influenced or imposed upon. **5.** feeble or silly. **6.** not robust. **7.** *Informal* easy. **8.** (of water) containing few mineral salts. **9.** (of drugs) not liable to cause addiction. —adv. **10.** softly. **softly** adv. **soften** v. **1.** make or become soft or softer. **2.** make or become more gentle. **softy, softie** n. *Informal* person who is easily upset. **soft drink** nonalcoholic drink. **soft furnishings** curtains, rugs, lampshades, and furniture covers. **soft option** easiest alternative. **soft-pedal** v. deliberately avoid emphasizing something. **soft-soap** v. *Informal* flatter. **soft touch** *Informal* person easily persuaded, esp. to lend money. **software** n. computer programs. **softwood** n. wood of a coniferous tree.

soggy adj. **-gier, -giest. 1.** soaked. **2.** moist and heavy. **sogginess** n.

soh n. Music in tonic sol-fa, fifth degree of any major scale.

soigné, (fem.) **soignée** [swah-nyay] adj. well-groomed, elegant.

soil[1] n. **1.** top layer of earth. **2.** country or territory.

soil[2] v. **1.** make or become dirty. **2.** disgrace. —n. **3.** soiled spot. **4.** refuse.

soiree [swah-ray] n. evening party or gathering.

sojourn [soj-urn] v. **1.** stay temporarily. —n. **2.** temporary stay.

sol n. Music same as SOH.

solace [sol-iss] n., v. comfort in distress.

solar adj. **1.** of the sun. **2.** using the energy of the sun. **solar plexus 1.** network of nerves at the pit of the stomach. **2.** this part of the stomach. **solar system** the sun and the heavenly bodies that go round it.

solarium n., pl. **-laria, -lariums.** place with beds and ultraviolet lights used for acquiring an artificial suntan.

sold v. past of SELL.

solder n. **1.** soft alloy used to join two metal surfaces. —v. **2.** join with solder. **soldering iron** tool for melting and applying solder.

soldier n. **1.** member of an army. —v. **2.** serve in an army. **soldierly** adj. **soldier on** v. persist doggedly.

sole[1] adj. **1.** one and only. **2.** not shared, exclusive. **solely** adv. **1.** only, completely. **2.** entirely. **3.** alone.

sole[2] n. **1.** underside of the foot. **2.** underside of a shoe. **3.** lower surface of something. —v. **4.** provide (a shoe) with a sole.

sole[3] n. small edible flatfish.

solecism [sol-iss-izz-um] n. **1.** minor grammatical mistake. **2.** breach of etiquette.

solemn adj. **1.** serious, deeply sincere. **2.** formal. **3.** glum. **solemnly** adv. **solemnity** n. **solemnize** v. **1.** celebrate or perform (a ceremony). **2.** make solemn. **solemnization** n.

solenoid [sole-in-oid] n. coil of wire magnetized by passing a current through it.

sol-fa n. system of syllables used as names for the notes of a scale.

solicit v. **-iting, -ited. 1.** request. **2.** (of a prostitute) offer (a person) sex for money. **solicitation** n.

solicitor n. lawyer who advises clients and prepares documents and cases.

solicitous adj. **1.** anxious about someone's welfare. **2.** eager. **solicitude** n.

solid adj. **1.** (of a substance) keeping its shape. **2.** strong or substantial. **3.** not liquid or gas. **4.** not hollow. **5.** of the same substance throughout. **6.** sound or reliable. **7.** having three dimensions. —n. **8.** three-dimensional shape. **9.** solid substance. **solidly** adv. **solidify** v. make or become solid or firm. **solidity** n.

solidarity n. agreement in aims or interests, total unity.

solidus n., pl. **-di.** short oblique stroke (/) used to separate items in text.

soliloquy n., pl. **-quies.** speech made by a person while alone, esp. in a play. **soliloquize** v. utter a soliloquy.

solipsism n. doctrine that the self is the only thing known to exist. **solipsist** n.

solitaire n. **1.** game for one person played with pegs set in a board. **2.** gem set by itself. **3.** US card game for one person.

solitary adj. **1.** alone, single. **2.** (of a place) lonely. —n. **3.** hermit. **solitude** n. state of being solitary. **solitary confinement** isolation of a prisoner in a special cell.

solo n., pl. **-los. 1.** music for one performer. **2.** any act done without assistance. —adj. **3.** done alone. —adv. **4.** by oneself, alone. **soloist** n.

solstice n. either the shortest (in winter) or longest (in summer) day of the year.

soluble adj. **1.** able to be dissolved. **2.** able to be solved. **solubility** n.

solution n. **1.** answer to a problem. **2.** act of solving a problem. **3.** liquid with something dissolved in it. **4.** process of dissolving.

solve v. find the answer to (a problem). **solvable** adj.

solvent adj. **1.** able to meet financial obligations. —n. **2.** liquid capable of dissolving other substances. **solvency** n. **solvent abuse** deliberate inhaling of intoxicating fumes from certain solvents.

somatic adj. of the body, as distinct from the mind.

sombre adj. dark, gloomy.

sombrero n., pl. **-ros.** wide-brimmed Mexican hat.

some adj. **1.** unknown or unspecified. **2.**

unknown or unspecified quantity or number of. **3.** considerable number or amount of. **4.** a little. **5.** *Informal* remarkable. —*pron.* **6.** certain unknown or unspecified people or things. **7.** unknown or unspecified number or quantity. —*adv.* **8.** approximately. **somebody** *pron.* **1.** some person. —*n.* **2.** important person. **somehow** *adv.* in some unspecified way. **someone** *pron.* somebody. **something** *pron.* **1.** unknown or unspecified thing or amount. **2.** impressive or important thing. **sometime** *adv.* **1.** at some unspecified time. —*adj.* **2.** former. **sometimes** *adv.* from time to time, now and then. **somewhat** *adv.* to some extent, rather. **somewhere** *adv.* in, to, or at some unspecified or unknown place.

▷ *Somebody* and *someone* are singular and in formal usage are followed by a singular verb or pronoun. Informal usage favours the use of the plural *they* to avoid the use of the clumsy *he or she: If I annoy somebody, they* (rather than *he or she*) *will take it out on me.*

somersault *n.* **1.** leap or roll in which the trunk and legs are turned over the head. —*v.* **2.** perform a somersault.

somnambulist *n.* person who walks in his or her sleep. **somnambulism** *n.*

somnolent *adj.* drowsy. **somnolence** *n.*

son *n.* **1.** male offspring. **2.** man who comes from a certain place or is connected with a certain thing. **son-in-law** *n.*, *pl.* **sons-in-law.** daughter's husband.

sonar *n.* device for detecting underwater objects by the reflection of sound waves.

sonata *n.* piece of music in several movements for one instrument with or without piano. **sonatina** *n.* short sonata.

son et lumière [sawn eh **loo**-mee-er] *n.* *French* night-time entertainment with lighting and sound effects, telling the story of the place where it is staged.

song *n.* **1.** music for the voice. **2.** tuneful sound made by certain birds. **3.** singing. **for a song** very cheaply. **songster, songstress** *n.* singer. **songbird** *n.* any bird with a musical call.

sonic *adj.* of or producing sound. **sonic boom** loud bang caused by an aircraft flying faster than sound.

sonnet *n.* fourteen-line poem with a fixed rhyme scheme.

sonny *n.* *Informal* term of address to a boy.

sonorous *adj.* **1.** (of sound) deep or resonant. **2.** (of speech) pompous. **sonorously** *adv.* **sonority** *n.*

soon *adv.* in a short time. **sooner** *adv.* rather, e.g. *I'd sooner go alone.* **sooner or later** eventually.

soot *n.* black powder formed by the incomplete burning of an organic substance. **sooty** *adj.*

soothe *v.* **1.** make calm. **2.** relieve (pain etc.).

soothsayer *n.* seer or prophet.

sop *n.* **1.** concession to pacify someone. —*pl.* **2.** food soaked in liquid. —*v.* **sopping, sopped. 3.** mop up or absorb (liquid). **sopping** *adj.* completely soaked. **soppy** *adj.* *Informal* oversentimental.

sophist *n.* person who uses clever but invalid arguments. **sophism, sophistry** *n.* clever but invalid argument.

sophisticate *v.* **1.** make less natural or innocent. **2.** make more complex or refined. —*n.* **3.** sophisticated person. **sophisticated** *adj.* **1.** having or appealing to refined or cultured tastes and habits. **2.** complex and refined. **sophistication** *n.*

sophomore *n.* *US* student in second year at college.

soporific *adj.* **1.** causing sleep. —*n.* **2.** drug that causes sleep.

soprano *n.*, *pl.* **-pranos. 1.** (singer with) the highest female or boy's voice. **2.** highest pitched of a family of instruments.

sorbet *n.* flavoured water ice.

sorcerer *n.* magician. **sorceress** *n.* fem. **sorcery** *n.* witchcraft or magic.

sordid *adj.* **1.** dirty, squalid. **2.** base, vile. **3.** selfish and grasping. **sordidly** *adv.* **sordidness** *n.*

sore *adj.* **1.** painful. **2.** causing annoyance. **3.** resentful. **4.** (of need) urgent. —*adv.* **5.** *Obs.* greatly. —*n.* **6.** painful area on the body. **sorely** *adv.* **1.** greatly. **2.** grievously. **soreness** *n.*

sorghum *n.* kind of grass cultivated for grain.

sorority *n.*, *pl.* **-ties** *Chiefly US* society for female students.

sorrel *n.* **1.** bitter-tasting plant. **2.** reddish-brown colour. **3.** horse of this colour.

sorrow *n.* **1.** grief or sadness. **2.** cause of

sorrow. —v. **3.** grieve. **sorrowful** *adj.* **sorrowfully** *adv.*

sorry *adj.* **-rier, -riest. 1.** feeling pity or regret. **2.** pitiful or wretched. **3.** of poor quality.

sort *n.* **1.** group all sharing certain qualities or characteristics. **2.** *Informal* type of character. —v. **3.** arrange according to kind. **4.** mend or fix. **out of sorts** slightly unwell or bad-tempered. **sort out** v. **1.** put in order. **2.** find a solution. **3.** *Informal* scold or punish.
▷ Note the singular/plural usage: *this* (or *that*) *sort of thing*; *these* (or *those*) *sorts of thing*. In the second, plural example you can also say *these sorts of things*.

sortie *n.* **1.** sally by besieged forces. **2.** operational flight made by military aircraft.

SOS *n.* **1.** international code signal of distress. **2.** call for help.

so-so *adj.* **1.** *Informal* mediocre. —adv. **2.** in an average way.

sot *n.* habitual drunkard.

sotto voce [sot-toe **voe**-chay] *adv.* in an undertone.

sou *n.* **1.** former French coin. **2.** small amount of money.

soubriquet [so-brik-ay] *n.* same as SOBRIQUET.

soufflé [soo-flay] *n.* light fluffy dish made with beaten egg whites and other ingredients.

sough [rhymes with **now**] *v.* (of the wind) make a sighing sound.

sought [sawt] *v.* past of SEEK.

souk [sook] *n.* open-air marketplace in Muslim countries.

soul *n.* **1.** spiritual and immortal part of a human being. **2.** essential part or fundamental nature. **3.** deep and sincere feelings. **4.** person regarded as typifying some quality. **5.** person. **6.** (also **soul music**) type of Black music combining blues, pop, and gospel. **soulful** *adj.* full of emotion. **soulless** *adj.* **1.** lacking human qualities, mechanical. **2.** (of a person) lacking sensitivity. **soul-destroying** *adj.* extremely monotonous. **soul-searching** *n.* deep examination of one's actions and feelings.

sound¹ *n.* **1.** something heard, noise. **2.** vibrations travelling in waves through air, water, etc. —v. **3.** make or cause to make a sound. **4.** seem to be as specified. **5.** pronounce. **6.** announce by a sound. **sound barrier** *Informal* sudden increase in air resistance against an object as it approaches the speed of sound. **soundproof** *adj.* **1.** not penetrable by sound. —v. **2.** make soundproof. **sound track** recorded sound accompaniment to a film.

sound² *adj.* **1.** in good condition. **2.** firm, substantial. **3.** showing good judgment. **4.** ethically correct. **5.** financially reliable. **6.** thorough. **7.** (of sleep) deep. **soundly** *adv.*

sound³ *v.* **1.** find the depth of (water etc.). **2.** ascertain the views of. **3.** examine with a probe. **soundings** *pl. n.* measurements of depth taken by sounding. **sounding board** person or group used to test a new idea.

sound⁴ *n.* channel or strait.

soup *n.* liquid food made from meat, vegetables, etc. **soupy** *adj.* **soup kitchen** place where food and drink is served to needy people. **soup up** v. modify (an engine) to increase its power.

soupçon [soop-sonn] *n.* small amount.

sour *adj.* **1.** sharp-tasting. **2.** (of milk) gone bad. **3.** (of a person's temperament) sullen. —v. **4.** make or become sour. **sourly** *adv.* **sourness** *n.* **sour grapes** attitude of claiming to despise something when one cannot have it oneself. **sourpuss** *n.* *Informal* sullen person.

source *n.* **1.** origin or starting point. **2.** spring where a river or stream begins. **3.** person, book, etc. providing information.

souse v. **1.** plunge (something) into liquid. **2.** drench. **3.** pickle. **soused** *adj.* *Slang* drunk.

soutane [soo-tan] *n.* Roman Catholic priest's cassock.

south *n.* **1.** direction towards the South Pole, opposite north. **2.** area lying in or towards the south. —adj. **3.** to or in the south. **4.** (of a wind) from the south. —adv. **5.** in, to, or towards the south. **southerly** *adj.* **southern** *adj.* **southerner** *n.* person from the south of a country or area. **southward** *adj., adv.* **southwards** *adv.* **southeast** *n., adj., adv.* (in or to) direction between south and east. **southwest** *n., adj., adv.* (in or to) direction between south and west. **southpaw** *n.* *Informal* left-handed person, esp. a boxer. **South Pole** southernmost point on the earth's axis.

souvenir *n.* keepsake, memento.

sou'wester *n.* seaman's waterproof hat covering the head and back of the neck.

sovereign *n.* **1.** king or queen. **2.** former

British gold coin worth one pound. —*adj.* 3. supreme in rank or authority. 4. excellent. 5. (of a state) independent. **sovereignty** *n.*

soviet *n.* 1. elected council at various levels of government in the USSR. —*adj.* 2. (S-) of the USSR.

sow[1] *v.* **sowing, sowed, sown** *or* **sowed.** 1. scatter or plant (seed) in or on (the ground). 2. implant or introduce.

sow[2] *n.* female adult pig.

soya *n.* plant whose edible bean (**soya bean**) is used for food and as a source of oil. **soy sauce** sauce made from fermented soya beans, used in Chinese cookery.

sozzled *adj. Slang* drunk.

spa *n.* resort with a mineral-water spring.

space *n.* 1. unlimited expanse in which all objects exist and move. 2. interval. 3. blank portion. 4. unoccupied area. 5. the universe beyond the earth's atmosphere. —*v.* 6. place at intervals. **spacious** *adj.* having a large capacity or area. **spacecraft, spaceship** *n.* vehicle for travel beyond the earth's atmosphere. **space shuttle** manned reusable vehicle for repeated space flights. **space station** artificial satellite used as a base for people travelling and researching in space. **spacesuit** *n.* sealed pressurized suit worn by an astronaut.

spade[1] *n.* tool for digging. **spadework** *n.* hard preparatory work.

spade[2] *n.* playing card of the suit marked with black leaf-shaped symbols.

spaghetti *n.* pasta in the form of long strings.

span *n.* 1. space between two points. 2. complete extent. 3. distance from thumb to little finger of the expanded hand. —*v.* **spanning, spanned.** 4. stretch or extend across.

spangle *n.* 1. small shiny metallic ornament. —*v.* 2. decorate with spangles.

Spaniard *n.* person from Spain.

spaniel *n.* dog with long ears and silky hair.

Spanish *n.* 1. official language of Spain and most countries of S and Central America. —*adj.* 2. of Spain or its language or people.

spank *v.* 1. slap with the open hand, esp. on the buttocks. —*n.* 2. such a slap. **spanking** *n.* 1. series of spanks. —*adj.* 2. *Informal* quick. 3. outstandingly fine or smart.

spanner *n.* tool for gripping and turning a nut or bolt.

spar[1] *n.* pole used as a ship's mast, boom, or yard.

spar[2] *v.* **sparring, sparred.** 1. box using light blows for practice. 2. argue (with someone). —*n.* 3. an argument.

spare *v.* 1. refrain from punishing or harming. 2. protect (someone) from (something unpleasant). 3. afford to give. —*adj.* 4. extra. 5. in reserve. 6. (of a person) thin. 7. very plain or simple. 8. *Slang* upset or angry. —*n.* 9. duplicate kept in case of damage or loss. **to spare** in addition to what is needed. **sparing** *adj.* economical. **spare ribs** pork ribs with most of the meat trimmed off. **spare tyre** *Informal* roll of fat at the waist.

spark *n.* 1. fiery particle thrown out from a fire or caused by friction. 2. flash of light produced by an electrical discharge. 3. trace or hint (of a particular quality). 4. liveliness or humour. —*v.* 5. give off sparks. 6. initiate. **spark plug, sparking plug** device in an engine that ignites the fuel by producing an electric spark.

sparkle *v.* 1. glitter with many points of light. 2. be vivacious or witty. —*n.* 3. sparkling points of light. 4. vivacity or wit. **sparkler** *n.* hand-held firework that emits sparks. **sparkling** *adj.* (of wine or mineral water) slightly fizzy.

sparrow *n.* small brownish bird. **sparrowhawk** *n.* small hawk.

sparse *adj.* thinly scattered. **sparsely** *adv.* **sparseness** *n.*

spartan *adj.* 1. strict and austere. —*n.* 2. brave person.

spasm *n.* 1. involuntary muscular contraction. 2. sudden burst of activity or feeling. **spasmodic** *adj.* occurring in spasms. **spasmodically** *adv.*

spastic *n.* 1. person with cerebral palsy. —*adj.* 2. suffering from cerebral palsy. 3. affected by spasms.

spat[1] *v.* past of SPIT[1]

spat[2] *n.* slight quarrel.

spat[3] *n.* old-fashioned short gaiter.

spate *n.* sudden outpouring or flood.

spathe *n.* large sheathlike leaf enclosing a flower cluster.

spatial *adj.* of or in space.

spatter *v.* 1. scatter or be scattered in drops over (something). —*n.* 2. spattering sound. 3. something spattered.

spatula n. utensil with a broad flat blade for spreading or stirring.

spawn n. **1.** jelly-like mass of eggs of fish, frogs, or molluscs. —v. **2.** (of fish, frogs, or molluscs) lay eggs. **3.** generate.

spay v. remove the ovaries from (a female animal).

speak v. **speaking, spoke, spoken. 1.** say words, talk. **2.** communicate or express in words. **3.** give a speech or lecture. **4.** know how to talk in (a specified language). **speaker** n. **1.** person who speaks, esp. at a formal occasion. **2.** loudspeaker. **3.** (S-) official chairman of a body. **speak out, speak up** v. **1.** state one's beliefs firmly. **2.** speak more loudly.

spear n. **1.** weapon consisting of a long shaft with a sharp point. **2.** slender shoot. —v. **3.** pierce with or as if with a spear. **spearhead** n. **1.** leading force in an attack or campaign. —v. **2.** lead (an attack or campaign).

spearmint n. type of mint.

spec n. **on spec** Informal as a risk or gamble.

special adj. **1.** distinguished from others of its kind. **2.** for a specific purpose. **3.** exceptional. **4.** particular. —n. **5.** product, programme, etc. which is only available at a certain time. **specially** adv. **specialist** n. expert in a particular activity or subject. **speciality** n. **1.** special interest or skill. **2.** product specialized in. **specialize** v. be a specialist. **specialization** n. **Special Branch** British police department concerned with political security.

specie n. coins as distinct from paper money.

species n., pl. **-cies.** group of plants or animals that are related closely enough to interbreed naturally.

specific adj. **1.** particular, definite. **2.** relating to a particular thing. —n. **3.** drug used to treat a particular disease. —pl. **4.** particular details. **specifically** adv. **specification** n. detailed description of something to be made or done. **specify** v. **1.** refer to or state specifically. **2.** state as a condition. **specific gravity** ratio of the density of a substance to that of water.

specimen n. **1.** individual or part typifying a whole. **2.** sample of blood etc. taken for analysis. **3.** Informal person.

specious [spee-shuss] adj. apparently true, but actually false.

speck n. small spot or particle. **speckle** n. **1.** small spot. —v. **2.** mark with speckles.

specs pl. n. Informal short for SPECTACLES.

spectacle n. **1.** strange, interesting, or ridiculous sight. **2.** impressive public show. —pl. **3.** pair of glasses for correcting faulty vision. **spectacular** adj. **1.** impressive. —n. **2.** spectacular public show. **spectacularly** adv.

spectate v. watch. **spectator** n. person viewing anything, onlooker.

spectre n. **1.** ghost. **2.** menacing mental image. **spectral** adj.

spectrum n., pl. **-tra. 1.** range of different colours, radio waves, etc. in order of their wavelengths. **2.** entire range of anything. **spectroscope** n. instrument for producing or examining spectra.

speculate v. **1.** guess, conjecture. **2.** buy property, shares, etc. in the hope of selling them at a profit. **speculation** n. **speculative** adj. **speculator** n.

speculum n., pl. **-la, -lums.** medical instrument for examining body cavities.

sped v. a past of SPEED.

speech n. **1.** act, power, or manner of speaking. **2.** utterance. **3.** talk given to an audience. **4.** language or dialect. **speechify** v. make speeches, esp. boringly. **speechless** adj. unable to speak because of great emotion. **speech therapy** treatment of people with speech problems.

speed n. **1.** swiftness. **2.** rate at which something moves or acts. **3.** Slang amphetamine. **4.** measure of the light sensitivity of photographic film. —v. **speeding, sped** or **speeded. 5.** go quickly. **6.** drive faster than the legal limit. **speedy** adj. **1.** rapid. **2.** prompt. **speedily** adv. **speedboat** n. light fast motorboat. **speed limit** maximum legal speed for travelling on a particular road. **speedometer** n. instrument to show the speed of a vehicle. **speed up** v. accelerate. **speedway** n. track for motorcycle racing. **speedwell** n. plant with small blue flowers.

speleology n. study and exploration of caves. **speleological** adj. **speleologist** n.

spell[1] v. **spelling, spelt** or **spelled. 1.** give in correct order the letters that form (a word). **2.** (of letters) make up (a word). **3.** indicate. **spelling** n. **1.** way a word is spelt. **2.** person's ability to spell. **spell out** v. make explicit.

spell² n. 1. formula of words supposed to have magic power. 2. effect of a spell. 3. fascination. **spellbound** adj. entranced.

spell³ n. period of time of weather or activity.

spelt v. a past of SPELL¹

spend v. **spending, spent**. 1. pay out (money). 2. use or pass (time). 3. use up completely. **spendthrift** n. person who spends money wastefully.

sperm n. 1. male reproductive cell. 2. semen. **spermicide** n. substance that kills sperm. **sperm whale** large toothed whale.

spermaceti [sper-ma-**set**-ee] n. waxy solid obtained from the sperm whale.

spermatozoon [sper-ma-toe-**zoe**-on] n., pl. **-zoa**. sperm.

spew v. 1. vomit. 2. send out in a stream.

sphagnum n. moss found in bogs.

sphere n. 1. perfectly round solid object. 2. field of activity. 3. social class. **spherical** adj.

sphincter n. ring of muscle which controls the opening and closing of a hollow organ.

Sphinx n. 1. statue in Egypt with a lion's body and human head. 2. (s-) enigmatic person.

spice n. 1. aromatic substance used as flavouring. 2. something that adds zest or interest. —v. 3. flavour with spices. 4. add zest or interest to. **spicy** adj. 1. flavoured with spices. 2. Informal slightly scandalous.

spick-and-span adj. neat and clean.

spider n. small eight-legged creature which spins a web to catch insects for food. **spidery** adj.

spiel n. glib plausible talk.

spigot n. stopper for, or tap fitted to, a cask.

spike¹ n. 1. sharp point. 2. sharp pointed metal object. —pl. 3. sports shoes with spikes for greater grip. —v. 4. put spikes on. 5. pierce or fasten with a spike. 6. add alcohol to (a drink). **spike someone's guns** thwart someone. **spiky** adj.

spike² n. 1. long pointed flower cluster. 2. ear of corn.

spill¹ v. **spilling, spilt** or **spilled**. 1. pour from or as if from a container. 2. come out of a place. 3. shed (blood). —n. 4. fall. 5. amount spilt. **spill the beans** Informal give away a secret. **spillage** n.

spill² n. thin strip of wood or paper for lighting pipes or fires.

spin v. **spinning, spun**. 1. revolve or cause to revolve rapidly. 2. draw out and twist (fibres) into thread. 3. (of a spider) form (a web) from a silky fibre from the body. 4. grow dizzy. —n. 5. revolving motion. 6. continuous spiral descent of an aircraft. 7. Informal short drive for pleasure. 8. spinning motion given to a ball in sport. **spin a yarn** tell an improbable story. **spinner** n. **spin-dry** v. dry (clothes) in a spin-dryer. **spin-dryer** n. machine in which washed clothes are spun in a perforated drum to remove excess water. **spinning wheel** wheel-like machine for spinning, worked by hand or foot. **spin-off** n. incidental benefit. **spin out** v. prolong.

spina bifida n. condition in which part of the spinal cord protrudes through a gap in the backbone, often causing paralysis.

spinach n. dark green leafy vegetable.

spindle n. 1. rotating rod that acts as an axle. 2. weighted rod rotated for spinning thread by hand. **spindly** adj. long, slender, and frail.

spindrift n. spray blown along the surface of the sea.

spine n. 1. backbone. 2. sharp point on an animal or plant. 3. edge of a book, record sleeve, etc. on which the title is printed. **spinal** adj. of the spine. **spinal cord** cord of nerves inside the spine, which connects the brain to the nerves in the body. **spineless** adj. lacking courage. **spiny** adj. covered with spines. **spine-chiller** n. terrifying film or story.

spinet n. small harpsichord.

spinnaker n. large sail on a racing yacht.

spinneret n. organ through which silk threads come out of a spider.

spinney n. small wood.

spinster n. unmarried woman.

spiral n. 1. continuous curve formed by a point winding about a central axis at an ever-increasing distance from it. 2. steadily accelerating increase or decrease. —v. -ralling, -ralled. 3. move in a spiral. 4. increase or decrease with steady acceleration. —adj. 5. having the form of a spiral.

spire n. pointed part of a steeple.

spirit n. 1. force giving life to a body. 2. temperament or disposition. 3. liveliness. 4.

courage. **5.** mood or attitude. **6.** prevailing feeling. **7.** essential meaning as opposed to literal interpretation. **8.** ghost. **9.** liquid obtained by distillation. —*pl.* **10.** emotional state. **11.** strong alcoholic drink. —*v.* **-iting, -ited. 12.** carry away mysteriously. **spirited** *adj.* **1.** lively. **2.** characterized by the mood specified, e.g. *low-spirited*. **spirituous** *adj.* alcoholic. **spirit level** glass tube containing a bubble in liquid, used to check whether a surface is level.

spiritual *adj.* **1.** relating to the spirit. **2.** relating to sacred things. —*n.* **3.** type of religious folk song originating among Black slaves in America. **spiritually** *adv.* **spirituality** *n.* **spiritualism** *n.* belief that the spirits of the dead can communicate with the living. **spiritualist** *n.*

spit[1] *v.* **spitting, spat. 1.** eject (saliva or food) from the mouth. **2.** throw out particles explosively. **3.** rain slightly. **4.** utter (words) in a violent manner. —*n.* **5.** saliva. **spitting image** *Informal* person who looks very like another. **spittle** *n.* fluid produced in the mouth, saliva. **spittoon** *n.* bowl to spit into.

spit[2] *n.* **1.** sharp rod on which meat is skewered for roasting. **2.** long strip of land projecting into the sea.

spite *n.* **1.** deliberate nastiness. —*v.* **2.** annoy or hurt from spite. **in spite of** in defiance of. **spiteful** *adj.* **spitefully** *adv.*

spitfire *n.* person with a fiery temper.

spiv *n.* *Slang* smartly dressed man who makes a living by shady dealings.

splash *v.* **1.** scatter (liquid) or (of liquid) be scattered in drops. **2.** scatter liquid on (something). **3.** print (a story or photograph) prominently in a newspaper. —*n.* **4.** splashing sound. **5.** amount splashed. **6.** patch (of colour or light). **7.** extravagant display. **8.** small amount of liquid added to a drink. **splashdown** *n.* landing of a spacecraft on water. **splash out** *v.* *Informal* spend extravagantly.

splatter *v., n.* splash.

splay *v.* **1.** spread out. **2.** slant outwards. —*adj.* **3.** splayed.

spleen *n.* **1.** abdominal organ which filters bacteria from the blood. **2.** bad temper. **splenetic** *adj.* spiteful or irritable.

splendid *adj.* **1.** excellent. **2.** brilliant in appearance. **splendidly** *adv.* **splendour** *n.*

splice *v.* join by interweaving or overlapping ends. **get spliced** *Slang* get married.

splint *n.* rigid support for a broken bone.

splinter *n.* **1.** thin sharp piece broken off, esp. from wood. —*v.* **2.** break into fragments. **splinter group** group that has broken away from an organization.

split *v.* **splitting, split. 1.** break into separate pieces. **2.** separate. **3.** share. **4.** separate because of disagreement. **5.** (foll. by *on*) *Slang* inform. —*n.* **6.** splitting. **7.** dessert of sliced fruit, ice cream, and cream. **8.** crack or division caused by splitting. —*pl.* **9.** act of sitting with the legs outstretched in opposite directions. **splitting** *adj.* (of a headache) very painful. **split-level** *adj.* (of a house or room) having the ground floor on different levels. **split personality 1.** tendency to change mood rapidly. **2.** schizophrenia. **split second** very short period of time.

splotch, splodge *n., v.* splash, daub.

splurge *v.* **1.** spend money extravagantly. —*n.* **2.** bout of extravagance.

splutter *v.* **1.** make hissing spitting sounds. **2.** utter with spitting sounds. —*n.* **3.** spluttering.

spoil *v.* **spoiling, spoilt** *or* **spoiled. 1.** damage. **2.** harm the character of (a child) by giving it all it wants. **3.** go bad. **spoils** *pl. n.* **1.** booty. **2.** benefits of public office. **spoiling for** eager for. **spoiler** *n.* device on an aircraft or car to increase drag. **spoilsport** *n.* person who spoils the enjoyment of others.

spoke[1] *v.* past tense of SPEAK.

spoke[2] *n.* bar joining the hub of a wheel to the rim.

spoken *v.* past participle of SPEAK.

spokesman, spokeswoman, spokesperson *n.* person chosen to speak on behalf of a group.

spoliation *n.* plundering.

sponge *n.* **1.** sea animal with a porous absorbent skeleton. **2.** skeleton of a sponge, or a substance like it, used for cleaning. **3.** type of light cake. **4.** act of sponging. —*v.* **5.** wipe with a sponge. **6.** live at the expense of others. **sponger** *n.* *Slang* person who sponges on others. **spongy** *adj.* **sponge bag** small bag for holding toiletries.

sponsor *n.* **1.** person who promotes something. **2.** person who agrees to give money to a charity on completion of a specified activity by another. **3.** godparent. **4.** person who pays the costs of a programme in return for advertising. —v. **5.** act as a sponsor for. **sponsorship** n.

spontaneous adj. **1.** voluntary and unpremeditated. **2.** occurring through natural processes without outside influence. **spontaneously** adv. **spontaneity** n.

spoof n. **1.** mildly satirical parody. **2.** trick.

spook n. Informal ghost. **spooky** adj.

spool n. cylinder round which something can be wound.

spoon n. **1.** shallow bowl attached to a handle for eating, stirring, or serving food. —v. **2.** lift with a spoon. **spoonful** n. **spoonfeed** v. **1.** feed with a spoon. **2.** give (someone) too much help.

spoonerism n. accidental changing over of the initial sounds of a pair of words, such as half-warmed fish for half-formed wish.

spoor n. trail of an animal.

sporadic adj. intermittent, scattered. **sporadically** adv.

spore n. minute reproductive body of some plants.

sporran n. pouch worn in front of a kilt.

sport n. **1.** activity for pleasure, competition, or exercise. **2.** such activities collectively. **3.** enjoyment. **4.** playful joking. **5.** person who reacts cheerfully. —v. **6.** wear proudly. **sporting** adj. **1.** of sport. **2.** having a sportsmanlike attitude. **sporting chance** reasonable chance of success. **sporty** adj. **sportive** adj. playful. **sports car** fast low-built car, usu. open-topped. **sports jacket** man's casual jacket. **sportsman**, **sportswoman** n. **1.** person who plays sports. **2.** person who plays fair and is good-humoured when losing. **sportsmanlike** adj. **sportsmanship** n.

spot n. **1.** small mark on a surface. **2.** pimple. **3.** location. **4.** Informal awkward situation. **5.** Informal small quantity. **6.** part of a show assigned to a performer. —v. **7.** notice. **8.** watch for and take note of. **9.** mark with spots. **10.** rain lightly. **on the spot 1.** at the place in question. **2.** immediately. **3.** in an awkward predicament. **spotless** adj. absolutely clean. **spotlessly** adv. **spotted** adj. **spotty** adj. **1.** with spots. **2.** inconsistent. **spot check** random examination. **spotlight** n. **1.** powerful light illuminating a small area. **2.** centre of attention. —v. **3.** draw attention to. **spot-on** adj. Informal absolutely accurate.

spouse n. husband or wife.

spout n. **1.** projecting tube or lip for pouring liquids. **2.** stream or jet of liquid. —v. **3.** pour out in a stream or jet. **4.** Slang utter (a stream of words) lengthily. **up the spout** Slang ruined or lost.

sprain v. **1.** injure (a joint) by a sudden twist. —n. **2.** such an injury.

sprang v. a past tense of SPRING.

sprat n. small sea fish.

sprawl v. **1.** lie or sit with the limbs spread out. **2.** spread out in a straggling manner. —n. **3.** sprawling arrangement.

spray[1] n. **1.** (device for producing) fine drops of liquid. **2.** number of small objects flying through the air. —v. **3.** scatter in fine drops. **4.** cover with a spray. **spray gun** device for spraying paint etc.

spray[2] n. **1.** branch with buds, leaves, flowers, or berries. **2.** ornament like this.

spread v. **spreading, spread. 1.** open out or be displayed to the fullest extent. **2.** extend over a larger expanse. **3.** apply as a coating. **4.** send or be sent in all directions. —n. **5.** spreading. **6.** extent. **7.** Informal ample meal. **8.** soft food which can be spread. **9.** two facing pages in a magazine or book. **spread-eagled** adj. with arms and legs outstretched.

spree n. session of overindulgence, usu. in drinking or spending money.

sprig n. **1.** twig or shoot. **2.** design like this. **sprigged** adj.

sprightly adj. **-lier, -liest.** lively and brisk. **sprightliness** n.

spring v. **springing, sprang** or **sprung, sprung. 1.** move suddenly upwards or forwards in a single motion, jump. **2.** develop unexpectedly. **3.** originate (from). **4.** Informal arrange the escape of (someone) from prison. **5.** cause to happen unexpectedly. **6.** provide with springs. —n. **7.** season between winter and summer. **8.** coil which can be compressed, stretched, or bent and returns to its original shape when released. **9.** natural pool forming the source of a stream. **10.** jump. **11.** elasticity. **springy** adj. elastic. **springboard** n. **1.** flexible board used to gain height or momentum in diving or gymnastics. **2.** thing acting as an impetus. **springclean** v. clean (a house) thoroughly. **spring onion** onion with a tiny bulb and long green leaves. **spring tide** high tide at new or full moon. **springtime** n. season of spring.

springbok n. S African antelope.

springer n. small spaniel.

sprinkle v. 1. scatter (liquid or powder) in tiny drops or particles over (something). 2. distribute over. **sprinkler** n. **sprinkling** n. small quantity or number.

sprint v. 1. run a short distance at top speed. —n. 2. short race run at top speed. 3. fast run. **sprinter** n.

sprit n. small spar set diagonally across a sail to extend it. **spritsail** n. sail extended by a sprit.

sprite n. elf.

sprocket n. wheel with teeth on the rim, that drives or is driven by a chain.

sprout v. 1. put forth shoots. 2. begin to grow or develop. —n. 3. shoot. 4. short for BRUSSELS SPROUT.

spruce[1] n. kind of fir.

spruce[2] adj. neat and smart. **spruce up** v. make neat and smart.

sprung v. past of SPRING.

spry adj. **spryer, spryest** or **sprier, spriest.** active or nimble.

spud n. Informal potato.

spume n., v. froth.

spun v. past of SPIN.

spunk n. Informal courage, spirit. **spunky** adj.

spur n. 1. spiked wheel on the heel of a rider's boot used to urge on a horse. 2. stimulus or incentive. 3. projection. —v. **spurring, spurred.** 4. urge on, incite (someone). **on the spur of the moment** on impulse.

spurge n. plant with milky sap.

spurious adj. not genuine.

spurn v. reject with scorn.

spurt v. 1. gush or cause to gush out in a jet. —n. 2. short sudden burst of activity or speed. 3. sudden gush.

sputnik n. early Soviet artificial satellite.

sputter v., n. splutter.

sputum n., pl. **-ta.** spittle, usu. mixed with mucus.

spy n., pl. **spies.** 1. person employed to obtain secret information. 2. person who secretly watches others. —v. **spying, spied.** 3. act as a spy. 4. catch sight of. **spyglass** n. small telescope.

Sq. Square.

squab n. young unfledged bird.

squabble v., n. (engage in) a petty or noisy quarrel.

squad n. small group of people working or training together.

squadron n. division of an air force, fleet, or cavalry regiment.

squalid adj. 1. dirty and unpleasant. 2. morally sordid. **squalor** n. disgusting dirt and filth.

squall n. 1. sudden strong wind. 2. harsh cry. —v. 3. cry noisily, yell.

squander v. waste (money or resources).

square n. 1. geometric figure with four equal sides and four right angles. 2. open area in a town in this shape. 3. product of a number multiplied by itself. —adj. 4. square in shape. 5. denoting a measure of area. 6. straight or level. 7. fair and honest. 8. with all accounts or debts settled. 9. Informal old-fashioned. —v. 10. make square. 11. multiply (a number) by itself. 12. be or cause to be consistent. 13. settle (a debt). 14. level the score. —adv. 15. squarely, directly. **squarely** adv. 1. in a direct way. 2. in an honest and frank manner. **square dance** formation dance in which the couples form squares. **square meal** substantial meal. **square root** number of which a given number is the square. **square up to** v. prepare to confront (a person or problem).

squash v. 1. crush flat. 2. suppress. 3. humiliate with a crushing retort. 4. push into a confined space. —n. 5. sweet fruit drink diluted with water. 6. crowd of people in a confined space. 7. (also **squash rackets**) game played in an enclosed court with a rubber ball and long-handled rackets. 8. marrow-like vegetable. **squashy** adj.

squat v. **squatting, squatted.** 1. crouch with the knees bent and the weight on the feet. 2. occupy unused premises to which one has no legal right. —n. 3. place where squatters live. —adj. 4. short and broad. **squatter** n. illegal occupier of unused premises.

squaw n. Offens. native American woman.

squawk n. 1. loud harsh cry. 2. loud complaint. —v. 3. utter a squawk.

squeak n. 1. short shrill cry or sound. —v. 2. make or utter a squeak. **narrow squeak** Informal narrow escape. **squeaky** adj.

squeal n. 1. long shrill cry or sound. —v. 2.

make or utter a squeal. **3.** *Slang* inform on someone to the police.

squeamish *adj.* easily sickened or shocked.

squeegee *n.* tool with a rubber blade for clearing water from a surface.

squeeze *v.* **1.** grip or press firmly. **2.** crush or press to extract liquid. **3.** push into a confined space. **4.** hug. **5.** obtain (something) by force or great effort. —*n.* **6.** squeezing. **7.** amount extracted by squeezing. **8.** hug. **9.** crush of people in a confined space. **10.** restriction on borrowing.

squelch *v.* **1.** make a wet sucking sound, as by walking through mud. —*n.* **2.** squelching sound.

squib *n.* small firework that hisses before exploding.

squid *n.* sea creature with a torpedo-shaped body and ten tentacles.

squiffy *adj. Informal* slightly drunk.

squiggle *n.* wavy line. **squiggly** *adj.*

squint *v.* **1.** have eyes which face in different directions. **2.** glance sideways. —*n.* **3.** squinting condition of the eye. **4.** *Informal* glance. —*adj.* **5.** crooked.

squire *n.* **1.** country gentleman, usu. the main landowner in a community. **2.** *Hist.* knight's apprentice. —*v.* **3.** (of a man) escort (a woman).

squirm *v.* **1.** wriggle, writhe. **2.** feel embarrassed. —*n.* **3.** wriggling movement.

squirrel *n.* small bushy-tailed tree-living animal.

squirt *v.* **1.** force (a liquid) or (of a liquid) be forced out of a narrow opening. **2.** squirt liquid at. —*n.* **3.** jet of liquid. **4.** *Informal* small or insignificant person.

squish *v., n.* (make) a soft squelching sound. **squishy** *adj.*

Sr *Chem.* strontium.

Sr. 1. Senior. **2.** Señor.

SRN State Registered Nurse.

SS 1. Schutzstaffel: Nazi paramilitary security force. **2.** steamship.

SSE south-southeast.

SSW south-southwest.

st. stone (weight).

St. 1. Saint. **2.** Street.

stab *v.* **stabbing, stabbed. 1.** pierce with something pointed. **2.** jab (at). —*n.* **3.** stab-

bing. **4.** sudden unpleasant sensation. **5.** *Informal* attempt.

stabilize *v.* make or become stable. **stabilization** *n.* **stabilizer** *n.* device for stabilizing a child's bicycle, an aircraft, or a ship.

stable¹ *n.* **1.** building in which horses are kept. **2.** establishment that breeds and trains racehorses. **3.** establishment that manages or trains several entertainers or athletes. —*v.* **4.** put or keep (a horse) in a stable.

stable² *adj.* **1.** firmly fixed or established. **2.** firm in character. **3.** *Science* not subject to decay or decomposition. **stability** *n.*

staccato [stak-ah-toe] *adj., adv.* **1.** *Music* with the notes sharply separated. —*adj.* **2.** consisting of short abrupt sounds.

stack *n.* **1.** ordered pile. **2.** large amount. **3.** chimney. —*v.* **4.** pile in a stack. **5.** control (aircraft waiting to land) so that they fly at different altitudes.

stadium *n., pl.* **-diums, -dia.** sports arena with tiered seats for spectators.

staff¹ *n.* **1.** people employed in an organization. **2.** stick used as a weapon, support, etc. —*v.* **3.** supply with personnel.

staff² *n., pl.* **staves.** set of five horizontal lines on which music is written.

stag *n.* adult male deer. **stag beetle** beetle with large branched jaws. **stag party, night party** for men only.

stage *n.* **1.** step or period of development. **2.** platform in a theatre where actors perform. **3.** portion of a journey. **4.** scene of action. **5.** separate unit of a rocket that can be jettisoned. —*v.* **6.** put (a play) on stage. **7.** organize and carry out (an event). **the stage** theatre as a profession. **stagy** *adj.* overtheatrical. **stagecoach** *n.* large horse-drawn vehicle formerly used to carry passengers and mail. **stage door** theatre door leading backstage. **stage fright** nervousness felt by a person about to face an audience. **stagehand** *n.* person who moves props and scenery on a stage. **stage-manage** *v.* arrange from behind the scenes. **stage-manager** *n.* **stage whisper** loud whisper intended to be heard by an audience.

stagger *v.* **1.** walk unsteadily. **2.** astound. **3.** arrange in alternating positions or periods. —*n.* **4.** staggering. **staggering** *adj.*

stagnant *adj.* **1.** (of water or air) stale from

not moving. **2.** not growing or developing. **stagnate** v. be stagnant. **stagnation** n.

staid adj. sedate, serious, and rather dull.

stain v. **1.** discolour, mark. **2.** colour with a penetrating pigment. —n. **3.** discoloration or mark. **4.** moral blemish or slur. **5.** penetrating liquid used to colour things. **stainless** adj. **stainless steel** steel alloy that does not rust.

stairs pl. n. flight of steps between floors, usu. indoors. **staircase, stairway** n. flight of stairs with a handrail or banisters.

stake n. **1.** pointed stick or post driven into the ground as a support or marker. **2.** money wagered. **3.** an interest, usu. financial, held in something. —pl. **4.** prize in a race or contest. —v. **5.** support or mark out with stakes. **6.** wager, risk. **7.** support financially. **at stake** being risked. **stake a claim** to claim a right to. **stake out** v. Slang (of police) keep (a place) under surveillance.

stalactite n. lime deposit hanging from the roof of a cave.

stalagmite n. lime deposit sticking up from the floor of a cave.

stale adj. **1.** not fresh. **2.** uninteresting from overuse. **3.** lacking energy or ideas through overwork or monotony. **staleness** n.

stalemate n. **1.** Chess position in which any of a player's moves would put his king in check, resulting in a draw. **2.** deadlock, impasse.

stalk[1] n. plant's stem.

stalk[2] v. **1.** follow or approach stealthily. **2.** walk in a stiff or haughty manner. **stalking-horse** n. pretext.

stall n. **1.** small stand for the display and sale of goods. **2.** ground-floor seat in a theatre or cinema. **3.** one of a row of seats in a church for the choir or clergy. **4.** compartment in a stable. **5.** small room or compartment. —v. **6.** stop (a motor vehicle or engine) or (of a motor vehicle or engine) stop accidentally. **7.** (of an aircraft) begin to drop because the speed is too low. **8.** employ delaying tactics.

stallion n. uncastrated male horse.

stalwart [stawl-wart] adj. **1.** strong and sturdy. **2.** dependable. —n. **3.** stalwart person.

stamen n. pollen-producing part of a flower.

stamina n. enduring energy and strength.

stammer v. **1.** speak or say with involuntary pauses or repetition of syllables. —n. **2.** tendency to stammer.

stamp v. **1.** stick a postage stamp on. **2.** impress (a pattern or mark) on. **3.** bring (one's foot) down forcefully. **4.** walk with heavy footsteps. **5.** characterize. —n. **6.** (also **postage stamp**) piece of gummed paper stuck to an envelope or parcel to show that the postage has been paid. **7.** instrument for stamping a pattern or mark. **8.** pattern or mark stamped. **9.** act of stamping the foot. **10.** characteristic feature. **stamping ground** favourite meeting place. **stamp out** v. suppress by force.

stampede n. **1.** sudden rush of frightened animals or of a crowd. —v. **2.** (cause to) take part in a stampede.

stance n. **1.** manner of standing. **2.** attitude.

stanch [stahnch] v. same as STAUNCH[2]

stanchion n. upright bar used as a support.

stand v. **standing, stood. 1.** be in, rise to, or place in an upright position. **2.** be situated. **3.** be in a specified state or position. **4.** remain unchanged or valid. **5.** tolerate. **6.** offer oneself as a candidate. **7.** Informal treat. **8.** survive. —n. **9.** stall for the sale of goods. **10.** structure for spectators at a sports ground. **11.** firmly held opinion. **12.** US witness box. **13.** rack or piece of furniture on which things may be placed. **14.** act of standing. **15.** halt to counter-attack. **standing** n. **1.** reputation or status. **2.** duration. —adj. **3.** permanent, lasting. **4.** used to stand in. **stand by** v. **1.** be available and ready. **2.** watch without taking any action. **3.** be faithful to. **stand-by** n. person or thing ready to be used in an emergency. **stand down** v. resign or withdraw. **stand for** v. **1.** represent or mean. **2.** Informal tolerate. **stand in** v. act as a substitute. **stand-in** n. substitute. **standing order** instruction to a bank to pay a stated sum at regular intervals. **stand-offish** adj. reserved or haughty. **stand out** v. be distinctive. **stand up** v. **1.** rise to one's feet. **2.** withstand examination. **3.** Informal fail to keep an appointment. **stand up for** v. support or defend. **stand up to** v. **1.** confront and resist. **2.** withstand and endure.

standard n. **1.** level of quality. **2.** example against which others are judged or measured. **3.** moral principle. **4.** distinctive flag. **5.** upright pole. —adj. **6.** usual, regular, or average. **7.** accepted as correct. **8.** of recognized authority. **standardize** v. cause to

conform to a standard. **standardization** n.
standard-bearer n. leader of a movement.
standard lamp lamp attached to an upright
pole on a base.

standpipe n. tap attached to a water main
to provide a public water supply.

standpoint n. point of view.

standstill n. complete halt.

stank v. a past tense of STINK.

stanza n. verse of a poem.

staple[1] n. **1.** U-shaped piece of metal used to
fasten papers or secure things. —v. **2.** fasten
with staples. **stapler** n. small device for
fastening papers together.

staple[2] adj. **1.** of prime importance, principal. —n. **2.** main constituent of anything.

star n. **1.** hot gaseous mass in space, visible
in the night sky as a point of light. **2.** star-
shaped mark used to indicate excellence. **3.**
asterisk. **4.** celebrity in the entertainment
or sports world. —pl. **5.** astrological forecast, horoscope. —v. **starring, starred. 6.**
mark with a star or stars. **7.** feature or be
featured as a star. —adj. **8.** leading, famous.
stardom n. status of a star in the entertainment or sports world. **starlet** n. young
actress presented as a future star. **starry**
adj. full of or like stars. **starry-eyed** adj. full
of naive optimism. **starfish** n. star-shaped
sea creature. **Stars and Stripes** national
flag of America.

starboard n. **1.** right-hand side of a ship,
when facing forward. —adj. **2.** of or on this
side.

starch n. **1.** carbohydrate forming the main
food element in bread, potatoes, etc., and
used mixed with water for stiffening fabric.
—v. **2.** stiffen (fabric) with starch. **starchy**
adj. **1.** containing starch. **2.** stiff and formal.

stare v. **1.** look or gaze fixedly (at). —n. **2.**
fixed gaze.

stark adj. **1.** desolate, bare. **2.** without elaboration. **3.** absolute. —adv. **4.** completely.

starling n. songbird with glossy black speckled feathers.

start v. **1.** take the first step, begin. **2.** set or
be set in motion. **3.** establish or set up. **4.**
make a sudden involuntary movement from
fright. —n. **5.** first part of something. **6.**
place or time of starting. **7.** advantage or
lead in a competitive activity. **8.** starting
movement from fright. **starter** n. **1.** first
course of a meal. **2.** device for starting a

car's engine. **3.** person who signals the start
of a race.

startle v. slightly surprise or frighten.

starve v. **1.** die or suffer or cause to die or
suffer from hunger. **2.** deprive of something
needed. **starvation** n.

stash v. Informal store in a secret place.

state n. **1.** condition of a person or thing. **2.**
Informal excited or agitated condition. **3.**
pomp. **4.** (often S-) sovereign political power or its territory. **5.** (S-) the government.
—adj. **6.** of or concerning the State. **7.**
involving ceremony. —v. **8.** express in
words. **the States** United States of America. **stately** adj. dignified or grand. **statement** n. **1.** something stated. **2.** printed
financial account. **stateroom** n. **1.** private
cabin on a ship. **2.** large room in a palace,
used for ceremonial occasions. **statesman,
stateswoman** n. experienced and respected
political leader. **statesmanship** n.

static adj. **1.** stationary or inactive. **2.** (of a
force) acting but producing no movement.
—n. **3.** crackling sound or speckled picture
caused by interference in radio or television
reception. **4.** (also **static electricity**) electric sparks produced by friction. **statics** n.
branch of mechanics dealing with the forces
producing a state of equilibrium.

station n. **1.** place where trains stop for
passengers. **2.** headquarters of the police or
a fire brigade. **3.** building with special
equipment for a particular purpose, e.g.
power station. **4.** place or position assigned
to a person. **5.** television or radio channel.
6. large Aust. sheep or cattle ranch. **7.**
position in society. —v. **8.** assign (someone)
to a particular place. **stationmaster** n. official in charge of a railway station. **station
wagon** US estate car.

stationary adj. **1.** not moving. **2.** not changing.

stationery n. writing materials such as
paper and pens. **stationer** n. dealer in
stationery.

statistic n. numerical fact collected and
classified systematically. **statistics** n. science of classifying and interpreting numerical information. **statistical** adj. **statistical-
ly** adv. **statistician** n. person who compiles
and studies statistics.

statue n. large sculpture of a human or
animal figure. **statuary** n. statues collectively. **statuesque** [stat-yoo-**esk**] adj. (of a

woman) tall and well-proportioned. **statuette** n. small statue.

stature n. **1.** person's height. **2.** intellectual or moral greatness.

status n. **1.** social position. **2.** prestige. **3.** person's legal standing. **status quo** existing state of affairs. **status symbol** possession regarded as a sign of position or wealth.

statute n. written law. **statutory** adj. required or authorized by law.

staunch[1] adj. loyal, firm.

staunch[2], **stanch** v. stop (a flow of blood).

stave n. **1.** one of the strips of wood forming a barrel. **2.** Music same as STAFF[2]. **3.** thick stick. **4.** stanza. —v. **staving, staved** or **stove. 5.** burst a hole in. **stave off** v. ward off.

staves n. plural of STAFF[2] and STAVE.

stay[1] v. **1.** remain in a place or condition. **2.** reside temporarily. **3.** endure. —n. **4.** period of staying in a place. **5.** postponement. **staying power** stamina.

stay[2] n. **1.** rope or wire supporting a ship's mast. **2.** prop or buttress. —pl. **3.** corset.

STD 1. sexually transmitted disease. **2.** subscriber trunk dialling.

stead n. **in someone's stead** in someone's place. **stand someone in good stead** be useful to someone.

steadfast adj. firm, determined. **steadfastly** adv.

steady adj. **steadier, steadiest. 1.** not shaky or wavering. **2.** sensible and dependable. **3.** regular or continuous. —v. **steadying, steadied. 4.** make steady. —adv. **5.** in a steady manner. **steadily** adv. **steadiness** n.

steak n. **1.** thick slice of meat, esp. beef. **2.** slice of fish.

steal v. **stealing, stole, stolen. 1.** take unlawfully or without permission. **2.** move stealthily.

stealth n. secret or underhand behaviour. **stealthy** adj. **stealthily** adv.

steam n. **1.** vapour into which water changes when boiled. **2.** power, energy, or speed. —v. **3.** give off steam. **4.** (of a vehicle) move by steam power. **5.** cook or treat with steam. **steamer** n. **1.** steampropelled ship. **2.** container used to cook food in steam. **steamy** adj. **steamier, steamiest. 1.** full of steam. **2.** Informal erotic. **steam engine** engine worked by steam. **steamroller** n. **1.** steam-powered

vehicle with heavy rollers, used to level road surfaces. —v. **2.** use overpowering force to make (someone) do what one wants.

steatite [stee-a-tite] n. same as SOAPSTONE.

steed n. Lit. horse.

steel n. **1.** hard malleable alloy of iron and carbon. **2.** steel rod used for sharpening knives. **3.** hardness of character or attitude. —v. **4.** make (oneself) hard and unfeeling. **steely** adj. **steel band** band of people playing on metal drums, popular in the West Indies.

steep[1] adj. **1.** sloping sharply. **2.** Informal (of a price) unreasonably high. **steeply** adv. **steepness** n.

steep[2] v. soak or be soaked in liquid. **steeped in** filled with, e.g. steeped in history.

steeple n. church tower with a spire. **steeplejack** n. person who repairs steeples and chimneys.

steeplechase n. **1.** horse race with obstacles to jump. **2.** track race with hurdles and a water jump.

steer[1] v. **1.** direct the course of (a vehicle or ship). **2.** direct (one's course). **steerage** n. cheapest accommodation on a passenger ship. **steering wheel** wheel turned by the driver of a vehicle in order to steer it.

steer[2] n. castrated male ox.

stein [stine] n. earthenware beer mug.

stellar adj. of stars.

stem[1] n. **1.** long thin central part of a plant. **2.** long slender part, as of a wineglass. **3.** part of a word to which inflections are added. —v. **stemming, stemmed. 4.** stem from originate from.

stem[2] v. **stemming, stemmed.** stop (the flow of something).

stench n. foul smell.

stencil n. **1.** thin sheet with cut-out pattern through which ink or paint passes to form the pattern on the surface below. **2.** pattern made thus. —v. **-cilling, -cilled. 3.** make (a pattern) with a stencil.

stenography n. shorthand. **stenographer** n. US shorthand typist.

stentorian adj. (of a voice) very loud.

step v. **stepping, stepped. 1.** move and set down the foot, as when walking. **2.** walk a short distance. —n. **3.** stepping. **4.** distance covered by a step. **5.** sound made by stepping. **6.** foot movement in a dance. **7.** one of a sequence of actions taken in order to achieve a goal. **8.** degree in a series or scale. **9.** flat surface for placing the foot on when going up or down. —*pl.* **10.** stepladder. **11.** flight of stairs. **step in** *v.* intervene. **stepladder** *n.* folding portable ladder with supporting frame. **stepping stone 1.** one of a series of stones for stepping on in crossing a stream. **2.** means of progress towards a goal. **step up** *v.* increase (something) by steps.

step- *prefix* denoting a relationship created by the remarriage of a parent, e.g. *stepmother.*

steppe *n.* wide grassy treeless plain.

stereo *adj.* **1.** short for STEREOPHONIC. —*n.* **2.** stereophonic record player. **3.** stereophonic sound.

stereophonic *adj.* using two separate loudspeakers to give the effect of naturally distributed sound.

stereoscopic *adj.* having a three-dimensional effect.

stereotype *n.* **1.** standardized idea of a type of person or thing. **2.** monotonously familiar idea. —*v.* **3.** form a stereotype of.

sterile *adj.* **1.** free from germs. **2.** unable to produce offspring or seeds. **3.** lacking inspiration or vitality. **sterility** *n.* **sterilize** *v.* make sterile. **sterilization** *n.*

sterling *n.* **1.** British money system. —*adj.* **2.** genuine. **3.** reliable. **sterling silver** alloy with 92.5 per cent silver.

stern¹ *adj.* severe, strict. **sternly** *adv.* **sternness** *n.*

stern² *n.* rear part of a ship.

sternum *n., pl.* **-na, -nums.** breast bone.

steroid *n.* organic compound containing a carbon ring system, such as many hormones.

stertorous *adj.* (of breathing) laboured and noisy.

stet *v.* **stetting, stetted.** (used as an instruction) ignore alteration previously made by a proofreader.

stethoscope *n.* medical instrument for listening to sounds made inside the body.

stetson *n.* tall broad-brimmed hat, worn mainly by cowboys.

stevedore *n.* person who loads and unloads ships.

stew *n.* **1.** food cooked slowly in a closed pot. **2.** *Informal* troubled or worried state. —*v.* **3.** cook slowly in a closed pot.

steward *n.* **1.** person who looks after passengers on a ship or aircraft. **2.** official who helps at a public event such as a race. **3.** person who administers another's property. **stewardess** *n. fem.*

stick¹ *n.* **1.** long thin piece of wood. **2.** such a piece of wood shaped for a special purpose, e.g. *hockey stick.* **3.** something like a stick, e.g. *stick of celery.* **4.** *Slang* verbal abuse, criticism. **the sticks** *Informal* remote country area. **stick insect** tropical insect resembling a twig.

stick² *v.* **sticking, stuck. 1.** push (a pointed object) into (something). **2.** fasten or be fastened by or as if by pins or glue. **3.** (foll. by *out*) extend beyond something else, protrude. **4.** *Informal* put. **5.** come to a standstill. **6.** jam. **7.** remain for a long time. **8.** *Slang* tolerate, abide. **sticker** *n.* adhesive label or sign. **sticky** *adj.* **1.** covered with an adhesive substance. **2.** (of weather) warm and humid. **3.** *Informal* difficult, unpleasant. **stick around** *v. Informal* remain in a place. **stick-in-the-mud** *n.* person who does not like anything new. **stick-up** *n. Slang* robbery at gunpoint. **stick up for** *v. Informal* support or defend.

stickleback *n.* small fish with sharp spines on its back.

stickler *n.* person who insists on something, e.g. *stickler for accuracy.*

stiff *adj.* **1.** not easily bent or moved. **2.** firm in consistency. **3.** unrelaxed or awkward. **4.** severe, e.g. *stiff punishment.* **5.** strong, e.g. *a stiff drink.* **6.** moving with pain. **7.** difficult. —*n.* **8.** *Slang* corpse. **stiffly** *adv.* **stiffness** *n.* **stiffen** *v.* make or become stiff. **stiff-necked** *adj.* haughtily stubborn.

stifle *v.* **1.** suffocate. **2.** suppress. **3.** feel difficulty in breathing.

stigma *n.* **1.** mark of social disgrace. **2.** part of a plant that receives pollen. **stigmata** *pl. n.* marks resembling the wounds of the crucified Christ. **stigmatize** *v.* mark as being shameful.

stile *n.* set of steps allowing people to climb a fence.

stiletto *n., pl.* **-tos. 1.** small slender dagger. **2.** (also **stiletto heel**) high narrow heel on a woman's shoe.

still¹ *adv.* **1.** now or in the future as before.

2. up to this or that time. **3.** even or yet, e.g. *still more insults.* **4.** nevertheless. **5.** quietly or without movement. —*adj.* **6.** motionless. **7.** silent and calm, undisturbed. **8.** (of a drink) not fizzy. —*v.* **9.** make still. **10.** relieve or end. —*n.* **11.** photograph from a film scene. **12.** calmness. **stillness** *n.* **stillborn** *adj.* born dead. **still life** painting of inanimate objects.

still² *n.* apparatus for distilling alcoholic drinks.

stilted *adj.* stiff and formal in manner.

Stilton *n.* ® strong-flavoured cheese.

stilts *pl. n.* **1.** pair of poles with footrests for walking raised from the ground. **2.** long posts supporting a building above ground level.

stimulus *n., pl.* **-li.** something that rouses a person or thing to activity. **stimulant** *n.* something, such as a drug, that acts as a stimulus. **stimulate** *v.* act as a stimulus (on). **stimulation** *n.*

sting *v.* **stinging, stung. 1.** (of certain animals or plants) wound by injecting with poison. **2.** feel or cause to feel sharp physical or mental pain. **3.** *Slang* cheat (someone) by overcharging. **4.** incite. —*n.* **5.** wound or pain caused by or as if by stinging. **6.** mental pain. **7.** sharp pointed organ of certain animals or plants by which poison can be injected. **stingray** *n.* flatfish capable of inflicting painful wounds.

stingy *adj.* **-gier, -giest.** mean or miserly. **stinginess** *n.*

stink *v.* **stinking, stank** *or* **stunk, stunk. 1.** give off a strong unpleasant smell. **2.** *Slang* be very unpleasant. —*n.* **3.** strong unpleasant smell. **4.** *Slang* unpleasant fuss. **stinker** *n. Informal* difficult or unpleasant person or thing. **stinking** *Informal* —*adj.* **1.** unpleasant. —*adv.* **2.** extremely.

stint *v.* **1.** (foll. by *on*) be miserly with (something). —*n.* **2.** allotted amount of work.

stipend [sty-pend] *n.* regular allowance or salary, esp. that paid to a clergyman. **stipendiary** *n., adj.* (person) receiving a stipend.

stipple *v.* paint, draw, or engrave using dots. **stippling** *n.*

stipulate *v.* specify as a condition of an agreement. **stipulation** *n.*

stir *v.* **stirring, stirred. 1.** mix up (a liquid) by moving a spoon etc. around in it. **2.** move. **3.** excite or stimulate (a person) emotionally. —*n.* **4.** a stirring. **5.** strong reaction, usu. of excitement. **stir up** *v.* instigate.

stirrup *n.* metal loop attached to a saddle for supporting a rider's foot.

stitch *n.* **1.** link made by drawing thread through material with a needle. **2.** loop of yarn formed round a needle or hook in knitting or crochet. **3.** sharp pain in the side. —*v.* **4.** sew. **in stitches** *Informal* laughing uncontrollably. **not a stitch** *Informal* no clothes at all.

stoat *n.* small mammal of the weasel family, with brown fur that turns white in winter.

stock *n.* **1.** total amount of goods available for sale in a shop. **2.** supply stored for future use. **3.** financial shares in, or capital of, a company. **4.** lineage. **5.** livestock. **6.** handle of a rifle. **7.** liquid produced by boiling meat, fish, bones, or vegetables. **8.** fragrant flowering plant. **9.** standing or status. —*pl.* **10.** *Hist.* instrument of punishment consisting of a wooden frame with holes into which the hands and feet of the victim were locked. —*adj.* **11.** kept in stock, standard. **12.** hackneyed. —*v.* **13.** keep for sale or future use. **14.** supply (a farm) with livestock or (a lake etc.) with fish. **stockist** *n.* dealer who stocks a particular product. **stocky** *adj.* (of a person) broad and sturdy. **stockbroker** *n.* person who buys and sells stocks and shares for customers. **stock car** car modified for a form of racing in which the cars often collide. **stock exchange, market** institution for the buying and selling of shares. **stock in trade** thing constantly used as part of a profession. **stockpile** *v.* **1.** acquire and store a large quantity of (something) for future use. —*n.* **2.** accumulated store. **stock-still** *adj.* motionless. **stocktaking** *n.* counting and valuing of the goods in a shop. **stockyard** *n.* yard where farm animals are sold.

stockade *n.* enclosure or barrier made of stakes.

stockinet *n.* machine-knitted elastic fabric.

stocking *n.* close-fitting covering for the foot and leg. **stocking stitch** alternate rows of plain and purl in knitting.

stodgy *adj.* **stodgier, stodgiest. 1.** (of food) heavy and starchy. **2.** (of a person) serious and boring. **stodge** *n.* heavy starchy food.

stoic [stow-ik] *n.* **1.** person who suffers hardship without showing his or her feelings. —*adj.* **2.** (also **stoical**) suffering hardship without showing one's feelings. **stoical-ly** *adv.* **stoicism** [stow-iss-izz-um] *n.*

stoke *v.* feed and tend (a fire or furnace). **stoker** *n.*

stole[1] *v.* past tense of STEAL.

stole[2] *n.* long scarf or shawl.

stolen *v.* past participle of STEAL.

stolid *adj.* showing little emotion or interest. **stolidity** *n.* **stolidly** *adv.*

stomach *n.* **1.** organ in the body which digests food. **2.** front of the body around the waist. **3.** desire or inclination. —*v.* **4.** put up with.

stomp *v.* *US informal* tread heavily.

stone *n.* **1.** material of which rocks are made. **2.** piece of this. **3.** gem. **4.** piece of rock for a specific purpose. **5.** hard central part of a fruit. **6.** hard deposit formed in the kidney or bladder. **7.** unit of weight equal to 14 pounds. —*v.* **8.** throw stones at. **9.** remove stones from (a fruit). **stoned** *adj. Slang* under the influence of alcohol or drugs. **stony** *adj.* **1.** of or like stone. **2.** unfeeling or hard. **stony-broke** *adj. Slang* completely penniless. **stonily** *adv.* **Stone Age** prehistoric period when tools were made of stone. **stone-cold** *adj.* completely cold. **stone-deaf** *adj.* completely deaf. **stonewall** *v.* obstruct or hinder discussion. **stoneware** *n.* hard kind of pottery fired at a very high temperature. **stonework** *n.* part of a building made of stone.

stood *v.* past of STAND.

stooge *n.* **1.** actor who feeds lines to a comedian or acts as the butt of his jokes. **2.** *Slang* person taken advantage of by a superior.

stool *n.* **1.** chair without arms or back. **2.** piece of excrement.

stool pigeon *n.* informer for the police.

stoop *v.* **1.** bend (the body) forward and downward. **2.** carry oneself habitually in this way. **3.** degrade oneself. —*n.* **4.** stooping posture.

stop *v.* **stopping, stopped. 1.** bring to or come to a halt. **2.** cease or cause to cease from doing (something). **3.** prevent or restrain. **4.** withhold. **5.** block or plug. **6.** stay or rest. **7.** instruct a bank not to honour (a cheque). —*n.* **8.** place where something stops. **9.** stopping or being stopped. **10.** full stop. **11.** knob on an organ that is pulled out to allow a set of pipes to sound. **12.** device

that prevents, limits, or ends the motion of a mechanism. **stoppage** *n.* stoppage time same as INJURY TIME. **stopper** *n.* plug for closing a bottle etc. **stopcock** *n.* valve to control or stop the flow of fluid in a pipe. **stopgap** *n.* temporary substitute. **stopover** *n.* short break in a journey. **stop press** news item put into a newspaper after printing has been started. **stopwatch** *n.* watch which can be stopped instantly for exact timing of a sporting event.

store *v.* **1.** collect and keep (things) for future use. **2.** put (furniture etc.) in a warehouse for safekeeping. **3.** stock (goods). **4.** *Computers* enter or retain (data). —*n.* **5.** shop. **6.** supply kept for future use. **7.** storage place, such as a warehouse. —*pl.* **8.** stock of provisions. **in store** forthcoming or imminent. **set great store by** value greatly. **storage** *n.* **1.** storing. **2.** space for storing. **storage heater** electric device that can accumulate and radiate heat generated by off-peak electricity.

storey *n.* floor or level of a building.

stork *n.* large wading bird.

storm *n.* **1.** violent weather with wind, rain, or snow. **2.** strongly expressed reaction. **3.** heavy shower of missiles. —*v.* **4.** rush violently or angrily. **5.** rage. **6.** attack or capture (a place) suddenly. **stormy** *adj.* **1.** characterized by storms. **2.** involving violent emotions. **storm trooper** member of the Nazi militia.

story *n., pl.* **-ries. 1.** description of a series of events told or written for entertainment. **2.** plot of a book or film. **3.** newspaper report. **4.** *Informal* lie.

stoup [stoop] *n.* small basin for holy water.

stout *adj.* **1.** fat. **2.** thick and strong. **3.** brave and resolute. —*n.* **4.** strong dark beer. **stoutly** *adv.* **stoutness** *n.*

stove[1] *n.* apparatus for cooking or heating.

stove[2] *v.* a past of STAVE.

stow *v.* pack or store. **stowage** *n.* space or charge for stowing goods. **stow away** *v.* hide as a stowaway. **stowaway** *n.* person who hides on a ship or aircraft in order to travel free.

straddle *v.* have one leg or part on each side of (something).

strafe *v.* attack (an enemy) with machine guns from the air.

straggle *v.* **1.** go or spread in a rambling or

irregular way. **2.** linger behind. **straggler** n. **straggly** adj.

straight adj. **1.** not curved or crooked. **2.** level or upright. **3.** orderly. **4.** honest or frank. **5.** in continuous succession. **6.** (of spirits) undiluted. **7.** *Theatre* serious. **8.** *Slang* heterosexual. **9.** *Slang* conventional. —n. **10.** straight part, esp. of a racetrack. —adv. **11.** in a straight line. **12.** immediately. **13.** in a level or upright position. **14.** uninterruptedly. **go straight** *Informal* reform after being a criminal. **straighten** v. **straightaway** adv. immediately. **straight face** serious facial expression concealing a desire to laugh. **straightforward** adj. **1.** (of a task) easy. **2.** honest, frank.

strain[1] v. **1.** cause (something) to be used or tested beyond its limits. **2.** make an intense effort. **3.** injure by overexertion. **4.** sieve. **5.** draw or be drawn taut. —n. **6.** force exerted by straining. **7.** injury from overexertion. **8.** great demand on strength or resources. **9.** tension or tiredness. **10.** melody or theme. **strained** adj. **1.** not relaxed, tense. **2.** not natural, forced. **strainer** n. sieve.

strain[2] n. **1.** breed or race. **2.** trace or streak.

strait n. **1.** narrow channel connecting two areas of sea. —pl. **2.** position of acute difficulty. **straitjacket** n. strong jacket with long sleeves used to bind the arms of a violent person. **strait-laced** adj. prudish or puritanical.

straitened adj. in straitened circumstances not having much money.

strand[1] v. **1.** run aground. **2.** leave in difficulties. —n. **3.** *Poetic* shore.

strand[2] n. **1.** single thread of string, wire, etc. **2.** element of something.

strange adj. **1.** odd or unusual. **2.** not familiar. **3.** inexperienced (in) or unaccustomed (to). **strangely** adv. **strangeness** n. **stranger** n. person who is not known or is new to a place or experience.

strangle v. **1.** kill by squeezing the throat. **2.** prevent the development of. **strangler** n. **strangulation** n. strangling. **stranglehold** n. **1.** strangling grip in wrestling. **2.** powerful control.

strap n. **1.** strip of flexible material for lifting, fastening, or holding in place. —v. **strapping, strapped. 2.** fasten with a strap or straps. **strapping** adj. tall and sturdy.

strata n. plural of STRATUM.

stratagem n. clever plan, trick.

strategy n., pl. **-gies. 1.** overall plan. **2.** art of planning in war. **strategic** [strat-**ee**-jik] adj. **1.** advantageous. **2.** (of weapons) aimed at an enemy's homeland. **strategically** adv. **strategist** n.

strathspey n. Scottish dance with gliding steps.

stratosphere n. atmospheric layer between about 15 and 50 km above the earth.

stratum [**strah**-tum] n., pl. **strata. 1.** layer, esp. of rock. **2.** social class. **stratify** v. divide into strata. **stratification** n.

straw n. **1.** dried stalks of grain. **2.** single stalk of straw. **3.** long thin tube used to suck up liquid into the mouth. —adj. **4.** pale yellow. **straw poll** unofficial poll taken to determine general opinion.

strawberry n. sweet fleshy red fruit with small seeds on the outside. **strawberry mark** red birthmark.

stray v. **1.** wander. **2.** digress. **3.** deviate from certain moral standards. —adj. **4.** having strayed. **5.** scattered, random. —n. **6.** stray animal.

streak n. **1.** long band of contrasting colour or substance. **2.** quality or characteristic. **3.** short stretch (of good or bad luck). **4.** sudden flash. —v. **5.** mark with streaks. **6.** move rapidly. **7.** *Informal* run naked in public. **streaker** n. **streaky** adj.

stream n. **1.** small river. **2.** steady flow, as of liquid, speech, or people. **3.** schoolchildren grouped together because of similar ability. —v. **4.** flow steadily. **5.** move in unbroken succession. **6.** float in the air. **7.** group (pupils) in streams. **streamer** n. **1.** strip of coloured paper that unrolls when tossed. **2.** long narrow flag.

streamline v. **1.** give (a car, plane, etc.) a smooth even shape to offer least resistance to the flow of air or water. **2.** make more efficient by simplifying.

street n. public road, usu. lined with buildings. **streetcar** n. *US* tram. **streetwalker** n. prostitute. **streetwise** adj. knowing how to survive in big cities.

strength n. **1.** quality of being strong. **2.** quality or ability considered an advantage. **3.** degree of intensity. **4.** total number of people in a group. **on the strength of** on the basis of. **strengthen** v.

strenuous adj. requiring great energy or effort. **strenuously** adv.

streptococcus [strep-toe-**kok**-uss] n., pl. -**cocci**. bacterium occurring in chains, many species of which cause disease.

streptomycin n. antibiotic drug.

stress n. 1. emphasis. 2. tension or strain. 3. stronger sound in saying a word or syllable. 4. Physics force producing strain. —v. 5. emphasize. 6. subject to stress. 7. put stress on (a word or syllable). **stressful** adj.

stretch v. 1. extend or be extended. 2. be able to be stretched. 3. extend the limbs or body. 4. strain (resources or abilities) to the utmost. 5. pull tight. —n. 6. stretching. 7. continuous expanse. 8. period. 9. ability to be stretched. 10. Informal term of imprisonment. **stretchy** adj. **stretcher** n. frame covered with canvas, on which an injured person is carried.

strew v. **strewing, strewed, strewed** or **strewn**. scatter (things) over a surface.

striation n. 1. scratch or groove. 2. pattern of scratches or grooves. **striated** adj.

stricken adj. seriously affected by disease, grief, pain, etc.

strict adj. 1. stern or severe. 2. adhering closely to specified rules. 3. complete, absolute. **strictly** adv. **strictness** n.

stricture n. severe criticism.

stride v. **striding, strode, stridden**. 1. walk with long steps. —n. 2. long step. 3. regular pace. —pl. 4. progress.

strident adj. loud and harsh. **stridently** adv. **stridency** n.

strife n. conflict, quarrelling.

strike v. **striking, struck**. 1. cease work as a protest. 2. hit. 3. attack suddenly. 4. afflict. 5. enter the mind of. 6. affect in a particular way. 7. sound (a note) on a musical instrument. 8. agree (a bargain). 9. render. 10. ignite (a match) by friction. 11. (of a clock) indicate (a time) by sounding a bell. 12. discover (gold, oil, etc.). 13. make (a coin) by stamping it. 14. take up (a posture). —n. 15. striking. 16. stoppage of work as a protest. 17. military attack. 18. discovery of gold, oil, etc. **strike camp** dismantle and pack up tents. **strike home** have the desired effect. **striker** n. 1. striking worker. 2. attacking footballer. **striking** adj. 1. noteworthy. 2. impressive. **strikebreaker** n. person who works while others are on strike.

strike off, out v. cross out. **strike up** v. 1. begin (a conversation or friendship). 2. begin to play music.

string n. 1. thin cord used for tying. 2. set of objects threaded on a string. 3. series of things or events. 4. stretched wire or cord on a musical instrument that produces sound when vibrated. —pl. 5. restrictions or conditions. 6. section of an orchestra consisting of stringed instruments. —v. **stringing, strung**. 7. provide with a string or strings. 8. thread on a string. 9. extend in a line. **pull strings** use one's influence. **stringed** adj. (of a musical instrument) having strings that are plucked or played with a bow. **stringy** adj. 1. like string. 2. (of meat) fibrous. **string along** v. 1. Informal accompany. 2. deceive over a period of time. **string up** v. Informal kill by hanging.

stringent [**strin**-jent] adj. strictly controlled or enforced. **stringently** adv. **stringency** n.

strip v. **stripping, stripped**. 1. take (the covering or clothes) off. 2. take a title or possession away from (someone). 3. dismantle (an engine). 4. remove (paint) from (a surface). —n. 5. long narrow piece. 6. clothes a football team plays in. 7. act of stripping. **stripper** n. person who performs a striptease. **strip cartoon** sequence of drawings telling a story. **striptease** n. entertainment in which a performer undresses to music.

stripe n. 1. long narrow band of contrasting colour or substance. 2. chevron on a uniform to indicate rank. **striped, stripy** adj.

stripling n. youth.

strive v. **striving, strove, striven**. make a great effort.

strobe n. short for STROBOSCOPE.

stroboscope n. instrument producing a very bright flashing light.

strode v. past tense of STRIDE.

stroke v. 1. touch or caress lightly with the hand. —n. 2. light touch or caress with the hand. 3. rupture of a blood vessel in the brain. 4. mark made by a pen or paintbrush. 5. style or method of swimming. 6. hitting of the ball in some sports. 7. blow. 8. action or occurrence of the kind specified, e.g. a stroke of luck. 9. chime of a clock. 10. single pull on the oars in rowing.

stroll v. 1. walk in a leisurely manner. —n. 2. leisurely walk.

strong adj. 1. having physical power. 2. not

easily broken. **3.** having an extreme or drastic effect, e.g. *strong discipline*. **4.** great in degree or intensity. **5.** having moral force. **6.** (of a drink) containing a lot of alcohol. **7.** having a specified number, e.g. *twenty strong*. **going strong** *Informal* thriving. **strongly** *adv*. **strong-arm** *adj*. involving violence. **stronghold** *n*. **1.** fortress. **2.** area of predominance of a particular belief. **strong point** thing at which one excels. **strongroom** *n*. room designed for the safe-keeping of valuables.

strontium *n*. silvery-white metallic element. **strontium-90** *n*. radioactive isotope present in the fallout of nuclear explosions.

strop *n*. leather strap for sharpening razors.

stroppy *adj*. **-pier, -piest.** *Slang* angry or awkward.

strove *v*. past tense of STRIVE.

struck *v*. past of STRIKE.

structure *n*. **1.** complex construction. **2.** manner or basis of construction or organization. —*v*. **3.** give a structure to. **structural** *adj*. **structuralism** *n*. approach to literature, social sciences, etc., which sees changes in the subject as caused and organized by a hidden set of universal rules. **structuralist** *n*., *adj*.

strudel *n*. thin sheet of filled dough rolled up and baked, usu. with an apple filling.

struggle *v*. **1.** work, strive, or make one's way with difficulty. **2.** move about violently in an attempt to get free. **3.** fight (with someone). —*n*. **4.** striving. **5.** fight.

strum *v*. **strumming, strummed.** play (a guitar or banjo) by sweeping the thumb or a plectrum across the strings.

strumpet *n*. *Old-fashioned* prostitute.

strung *v*. past of STRING.

strut *v*. **strutting, strutted. 1.** walk pompously, swagger. —*n*. **2.** bar supporting a structure. **3.** strutting walk.

strychnine [**strik**-neen] *n*. very poisonous drug used in small quantities as a stimulant.

stub *n*. **1.** short piece left after use. **2.** counterfoil of a cheque or ticket. —*v*. **stubbing, stubbed. 3.** strike (the toe) painfully against an object. **4.** put out (a cigarette) by pressing the end against a surface. **stubby** *adj*. short and broad.

stubble *n*. **1.** short stalks of grain left in a field after reaping. **2.** short growth of hair on the chin of a man who has not shaved recently. **stubbly** *adj*.

stubborn *adj*. **1.** refusing to agree or give in. **2.** difficult to deal with. **stubbornly** *adv*. **stubbornness** *n*.

stucco *n*. plaster used for coating or decorating walls. **stuccoed** *adj*.

stuck *v*. past of STICK[2]. **stuck-up** *adj*. *Informal* conceited or snobbish.

stud[1] *n*. **1.** small piece of metal attached to a surface for decoration. **2.** disc-like removable fastener for clothes. **3.** one of several small round objects fixed to the sole of a football boot to give better grip. —*v*. **studding, studded. 4.** set with studs.

stud[2] *n*. **1.** male animal, esp. a stallion, kept for breeding. **2.** (also **stud farm**) place where horses are bred. **3.** *Slang* virile or sexually active man.

student *n*. person who studies a subject, esp. at university.

studio *n*., *pl*. **-dios. 1.** workroom of an artist or photographer. **2.** room or building in which television or radio programmes, records, or films are made. **studio flat** one-room flat with a small kitchen and bathroom.

study *v*. **studying, studied. 1.** be engaged in learning (a subject). **2.** investigate by observation and research. **3.** scrutinize. —*n*., *pl*. **studies. 4.** act or process of studying. **5.** room for studying in. **6.** book or paper produced as a result of study. **7.** sketch done as practice or preparation. **8.** musical composition designed to improve playing technique. **studied** *adj*. carefully practised or planned. **studious** [**styoo**-dee-uss] *adj*. **1.** fond of study. **2.** careful and deliberate. **studiously** *adv*.

stuff *v*. **1.** pack, cram, or fill completely. **2.** fill (food) with a seasoned mixture. **3.** fill (an animal's skin) with material to restore the shape of the live animal. **4.** fill with padding. —*n*. **5.** substance or material. **6.** collection of unnamed things. **7.** raw material of something. **8.** woollen fabric. **9.** subject matter. **stuff oneself** *Informal* eat large quantities. **stuffing** *n*. **1.** seasoned mixture with which food is stuffed. **2.** padding.

stuffy *adj*. **stuffier, stuffiest. 1.** lacking fresh air. **2.** *Informal* dull or conventional.

stultify *v*. **-fying, -fied.** dull the mind of (someone) by boring routine.

stumble *v*. **1.** trip and nearly fall. **2.** walk

with frequent stumbling. **3.** make frequent mistakes in speech. —**n. 4.** stumbling. **stumble across** v. discover accidentally. **stumbling block** obstacle or difficulty.

stump n. **1.** base of a tree left when the main trunk has been cut away. **2.** part of a thing left after a larger part has been removed. **3.** *Cricket* one of the three upright sticks forming the wicket. —v. **4.** baffle. **5.** *Cricket* dismiss (a batsman) by breaking his wicket with the ball. **6.** walk with heavy steps. **stumpy** *adj.* short and stubby. **stump up** v. *Informal* give (the money required).

stun v. **stunning, stunned. 1.** knock senseless. **2.** shock or overwhelm. **stunner** n. *Informal* beautiful person or thing. **stunning** *adj.* very attractive or impressive.

stung v. past of STING.

stunk v. a past of STINK.

stunt¹ v. prevent or impede the growth of. **stunted** *adj.*

stunt² n. **1.** acrobatic or dangerous action. **2.** anything spectacular done to gain publicity.

stupefy v. **-fying, -fied. 1.** make insensitive or lethargic. **2.** astound. **stupefaction** n.

stupendous *adj.* **1.** astonishing. **2.** huge. **stupendously** *adv.*

stupid *adj.* **1.** lacking intelligence. **2.** silly. **3.** in a stupor. **stupidity** n. **stupidly** *adv.*

stupor n. dazed or unconscious state.

sturdy *adj.* **-dier, -diest. 1.** healthy and robust. **2.** strongly-built. **sturdily** *adv.* **sturdiness** n.

sturgeon n. fish from which caviar is obtained.

stutter v. **1.** speak with repetition of initial consonants. —n. **2.** tendency to stutter.

sty¹ n., *pl.* **sties.** pen for pigs.

sty², **stye** n., *pl.* **sties, styes.** inflammation at the base of an eyelash.

Stygian [**stij**-jee-an] *adj. Lit.* gloomy.

style n. **1.** manner of writing, speaking, or doing something. **2.** shape or design. **3.** elegance, refinement. **4.** prevailing fashion. **5.** part of a flower that bears the stigma. —v. **6.** shape or design. **7.** name or call. **stylish** *adj.* smart, elegant, and fashionable. **stylishly** *adv.* **stylist** n. **1.** hairdresser. **2.** designer. **3.** person who writes with great attention to style. **stylistic** *adj.* of literary or artistic style. **stylize** v. cause to conform to an established stylistic form. **styling**

mousse foamy substance applied to hair before styling to hold the style.

stylus n. needle-like device on a record player that rests in the groove of the record and picks up the sound signals.

stymie v. **-mieing, -mied.** hinder or thwart.

styptic n., adj. (drug) used to stop bleeding.

suave [**swahv**] *adj.* smooth and sophisticated in manner. **suavely** *adv.* **suavity** n.

sub n. **1.** subeditor. **2.** submarine. **3.** subscription. **4.** substitute. **5.** *Informal* advance payment of wages or salary. —v. **subbing, subbed. 6.** act as a substitute. **7.** grant advance payment to. **8.** act as a subeditor.

sub- *prefix* used with many main words to mean: **1.** under or beneath, e.g. *submarine.* **2.** subordinate, e.g. *sublieutenant.* **3.** falling short of, e.g. *subnormal.* **4.** forming a subdivision, e.g. *subheading.*

subaltern n. army officer below the rank of captain.

subatomic *adj.* of or being one of the particles which make up an atom.

subcommittee n. small committee formed from some members of a larger committee.

subconscious *adj.* **1.** happening or existing without one's awareness. —n. **2.** *Psychoanalysis* that part of the mind of which one is not aware but which can influence one's behaviour. **subconsciously** *adv.*

subcontinent n. large land mass that is a distinct part of a continent.

subcontract n. **1.** secondary contract by which the main contractor for a job puts work out to others. —v. **2.** put out (work) on a subcontract. **subcontractor** n.

subcutaneous [sub-cute-**ayn**-ee-uss] *adj.* under the skin.

subdivide v. divide (a part of something) into smaller parts. **subdivision** n.

subdue v. **-duing, -dued. 1.** overcome. **2.** make less intense.

subeditor n. person who checks and edits text for a newspaper or magazine.

subhuman *adj.* less than human.

subject n. **1.** person or thing being dealt with or studied. **2.** *Grammar* word or phrase that represents the person or thing performing the action of the verb in a sentence. **3.** person under the rule of a monarch or government. **4.** figure, scene, etc. portrayed by an artist or photographer. —adj. **5.** being under the rule of a monarch or government. —v. (foll. by *to*) **6.** cause to undergo. **7.** bring under the control (of). **subject to 1.** liable to. **2.** conditional upon. **subjection** *n.*

subjective *adj.* based on personal feelings or prejudices. **subjectively** *adv.*

sub judice [sub joo-diss-ee] *adj. Latin* under judicial consideration.

subjugate *v.* bring (a group of people) under one's control. **subjugation** *n.*

subjunctive *Grammar* —*n.* **1.** mood of verbs used when the content of the clause is doubted, supposed, or wished. —*adj.* **2.** in or of that mood.

sublet *v.* **-letting**, **-let.** rent out (property rented from someone else).

sublieutenant *n.* naval officer of the lowest rank.

sublimate *v. Psychol.* direct the energy of (a primitive impulse) into socially acceptable activities. **sublimation** *n.*

sublime *adj.* **1.** of high moral, intellectual, or spiritual value. **2.** unparalleled, supreme. —*v.* **3.** *Chem.* change from a solid to a vapour without first melting. **sublimely** *adv.*

subliminal *adj.* relating to mental processes of which the individual is not aware.

sub-machine-gun *n.* portable machinegun with a short barrel.

submarine *n.* **1.** vessel which can operate below the surface of the sea. —*adj.* **2.** below the surface of the sea.

submerge *v.* **1.** put or go below the surface of water or other liquid. **2.** overwhelm. **submersion** *n.* **submersible** *n., adj.* (vehicle) able to work under water.

submit *v.* **-mitting**, **-mitted.** **1.** surrender. **2.** be (voluntarily) subjected to a process or treatment. **3.** put forward for consideration. **submission** *n.* **1.** submitting. **2.** something submitted for consideration. **3.** state of being submissive. **submissive** *adj.* meek and obedient.

subnormal *adj.* less than normal, esp. in intelligence.

subordinate *adj.* **1.** of lesser rank or importance. —*n.* **2.** subordinate person or thing. —*v.* **3.** make or treat as subordinate. **subordination** *n.*

suborn *v.* bribe or incite (a person) to commit a wrongful act.

subpoena [sub-pee-na] *n.* **1.** writ requiring a person to appear before a lawcourt. —*v.* **2.** summon (someone) with a subpoena.

sub rosa [sub rose-a] *adv. Latin* in secret.

subscribe *v.* **1.** pay (a subscription). **2.** give support or approval (to). **subscriber** *n.* **subscription** *n.* **1.** payment for issues of a publication over a period. **2.** money contributed to a charity etc. **3.** membership fees paid to a society.

subscript *n., adj.* (character) printed below the line.

subsection *n.* division of a section.

subsequent *adj.* occurring after, succeeding. **subsequently** *adv.*

subservient *adj.* submissive, servile. **subservience** *n.*

subside *v.* **1.** become less intense. **2.** sink to a lower level. **subsidence** *n.* act or process of subsiding.

subsidiary *adj.* **1.** of lesser importance. **2.** subordinate. —*n., pl.* **-aries. 3.** subsidiary person or thing.

subsidize *v.* help financially. **subsidy** *n., pl.* **-dies.** financial aid.

subsist *v.* manage to live. **subsistence** *n.*

subsoil *n.* earth just below the surface soil.

subsonic *adj.* moving at a speed less than that of sound.

substance *n.* **1.** solid, powder, liquid, or paste. **2.** physical composition of something. **3.** essential meaning of something. **4.** solid or meaningful quality. **5.** wealth. **substantial** *adj.* **1.** of considerable size or value. **2.** (of food or a meal) sufficient and nourishing. **3.** solid or strong. **4.** real. **substantially** *adv.* **substantiate** *v.* support (a story) with evidence. **substantiation** *n.* **substantive** *adj.* **1.** of or being the essential element of a thing. —*n.* **2.** noun.

substitute *v.* **1.** take the place of or put in place of another. —*n.* **2.** person or thing taking the place of (another). **substitution** *n.*

subsume *v.* incorporate (an idea, case, etc.) under a comprehensive classification.

subterfuge *n.* trick used to achieve an objective.

subterranean *adj.* underground.

subtitle *n.* **1.** secondary title of a book. —*pl.* **2.** printed translation at the bottom of the picture in a film with foreign dialogue. —*v.* **3.** provide with a subtitle or subtitles.

subtle *adj.* **1.** not immediately obvious. **2.** having or requiring ingenuity. **3.** delicate. **subtly** *adv.* **subtlety** *n.*

subtract *v.* take (one number or quantity) from another. **subtraction** *n.*

subtropical *adj.* of the regions bordering on the tropics.

suburb *n.* residential area on the outskirts of a city. **suburban** *adj.* **1.** of or inhabiting a suburb. **2.** narrow or unadventurous in outlook. **suburbanite** *n.* **suburbia** *n.* suburbs and their inhabitants.

subvention *n.* subsidy.

subvert *v.* overthrow the authority of. **subversion** *n.* **subversive** *adj.*

subway *n.* **1.** passage under a road or railway. **2.** *Scot. & US* underground railway.

succeed *v.* **1.** accomplish an aim. **2.** turn out satisfactorily. **3.** come next in order after (something). **4.** take over a position from (someone). **success** *n.* **1.** favourable outcome of an attempt. **2.** attainment of wealth, fame, or position. **3.** successful person or thing. **successful** *adj.* having success. **successfully** *adv.* **succession** *n.* **1.** series of people or things following one another in order. **2.** act or right by which one person succeeds another in a position. **successive** *adj.* consecutive. **successively** *adv.* **successor** *n.* person who succeeds someone in a position.

succinct *adj.* brief and clear. **succinctly** *adv.*

succour *v., n.* help in distress.

succubus *n., pl.* **-bi.** female demon believed to have sex with sleeping men.

succulent *adj.* **1.** juicy and delicious. **2.** (of a plant) having thick fleshy leaves. —*n.* **3.** succulent plant. **succulence** *n.*

succumb *v.* **1.** (foll. by *to*) give way (to something overpowering). **2.** die of (an illness).

such *adj.* **1.** of the kind specified. **2.** so great, so much. —*pron.* **3.** such things. **such-and-such** *adj.* specific, but not known or named. **suchlike** *adj. Informal* of the kind specified.

suck *v.* **1.** draw (liquid or air) into the mouth. **2.** take (something) into the mouth and moisten, dissolve, or roll it around with the tongue. **3.** (foll. by *in*) draw in by irresistible force. —*n.* **4.** sucking. **sucker** *n.* **1.** *Slang* person who is easily deceived or swindled. **2.** organ or device which adheres by suction. **3.** shoot coming from a plant's root or the base of its main stem. **suck up to** *v. Informal* flatter (someone) for one's own profit.

suckle *v.* feed at the breast. **suckling** *n.* unweaned baby or young animal.

sucrose [soo-kroze] *n.* chemical name for sugar.

suction *n.* **1.** sucking. **2.** force produced by drawing air out of a space to make a vacuum that will suck in a substance from another space.

sudden *adj.* done or occurring quickly and unexpectedly. **all of a sudden** quickly and unexpectedly. **suddenly** *adv.* **suddenness** *n.* **sudden death** *Sport* period of extra time in which the first competitor to score wins.

sudorific [syoo-dor-**if**-ik] *n., adj.* (drug) causing sweating.

suds *pl. n.* froth of soap and water, lather.

sue *v.* **suing, sued.** start legal proceedings against.

suede *n.* leather with a velvety finish on one side.

suet *n.* hard fat obtained from sheep and cattle, used in cooking.

suffer *v.* **1.** undergo or be subjected to. **2.** tolerate. **sufferer** *n.* **suffering** *n.* **sufferance** *n.* **on sufferance** tolerated with reluctance.

suffice [suf-**fice**] *v.* be enough for a purpose. **sufficiency** *n.* adequate amount. **sufficient** *adj.* enough, adequate. **sufficiently** *adv.*

suffix *n.* letter or letters added to the end of a word to form another word.

suffocate *v.* **1.** kill or be killed by deprivation of oxygen. **2.** feel or cause to feel discomfort from heat and lack of air. **suffocation** *n.*

suffragan *n.* bishop appointed to assist an archbishop or another bishop.

suffrage *n.* right to vote in public elections. **suffragette** *n.* in Britain in the early 20th century, a woman who campaigned militantly for the right to vote.

suffuse *v.* spread through or over (something). **suffusion** *n.*

sugar *n.* **1.** sweet crystalline carbohydrate found in many plants and used to sweeten food and drinks. —*v.* **2.** sweeten or cover with sugar. **sugary** *adj.* **sugar beet** beet cultivated for the sugar obtained from its roots. **sugar cane** tropical grass cultivated for the sugar obtained from its canes. **sugar daddy** *Slang* elderly man who gives a young woman money and gifts in return for sexual favours.

suggest *v.* **1.** put forward (an idea) for consideration. **2.** bring to mind by the association of ideas. **3.** give a hint of. **suggestible** *adj.* easily influenced. **suggestion** *n.* **1.** suggesting. **2.** thing suggested. **3.** hint or indication. **suggestive** *adj.* **1.** suggesting something indecent. **2.** conveying a hint (of). **suggestively** *adv.*

suicide *n.* **1.** killing oneself intentionally. **2.** person who kills himself intentionally. **3.** self-inflicted ruin of one's own prospects or interests. **suicidal** *adj.* liable to commit suicide. **suicidally** *adv.*

suit *n.* **1.** set of clothes designed to be worn together. **2.** outfit worn for a specific purpose. **3.** one of the four sets into which a pack of cards is divided. **4.** lawsuit. — *v.* **5.** be appropriate for. **6.** be acceptable to. **suitable** *adj.* appropriate or proper. **suitably** *adv.* **suitability** *n.* **suitcase** *n.* portable travelling case for clothing.

suite *n.* **1.** set of connected rooms in a hotel. **2.** matching set of furniture. **3.** set of musical pieces in the same key.

suitor *n.* *Old-fashioned* man who is courting a woman.

sulk *v.* **1.** be silent and sullen because of resentment or bad temper. — *n.* **2.** resentful or sullen mood. **sulky** *adj.* **sulkily** *adv.* **sulkiness** *n.*

sullen *adj.* **1.** unwilling to talk or be sociable. **2.** dark and dismal. **sullenly** *adv.* **sullenness** *n.*

sully *v.* **-lying, -lied. 1.** make dirty. **2.** ruin (someone's reputation).

sulphate *n.* salt or ester of sulphuric acid.

sulphide *n.* compound of sulphur with another element.

sulphite *n.* salt or ester of sulphurous acid.

sulphonamide [sulf-**on**-a-mide] *n.* any of a class of drugs that prevent the growth of bacteria.

sulphur *n.* pale yellow nonmetallic element. **sulphuric, sulphurous** *adj.* of or containing sulphur. **sulphuric acid** colourless corrosive liquid used for making explosives.

sultan *n.* sovereign of a Muslim country. **sultana** *n.* **1.** kind of raisin. **2.** sultan's wife, mother, or daughter. **sultanate** *n.* territory of a sultan.

sultry *adj.* **-trier, -triest. 1.** (of weather or climate) hot and humid. **2.** passionate, sensual.

sum *n.* **1.** result of addition, total. **2.** problem in arithmetic. **3.** quantity of money. **4.** gist of a matter. **sum total** complete or final total. **sum up** *v.* **summing, summed. 1.** summarize. **2.** form a quick opinion of.

summary *n., pl.* **-ries. 1.** brief account giving the main points of something. — *adj.* **2.** done quickly, without formalities. **summarily** *adv.* **summarize** *v.* make or be a summary of (something). **summation** *n.* **1.** summary. **2.** adding up.

summer *n.* warmest season of the year, between spring and autumn. **summery** *adj.* **summerhouse** *n.* small building in a garden. **summer school** academic course held during the summer. **summertime** *n.* period or season of summer. **summer time** time shown by clocks put forward in summer to give extra daylight in the evenings.

summit *n.* **1.** highest point. **2.** top of a mountain or hill. **3.** conference between heads of state.

summon *v.* **1.** order (someone) to come. **2.** send for (someone) to appear in court. **3.** call upon (someone) to do something. **4.** gather (one's courage, strength, etc.). **summons** *n.* **1.** command summoning someone. **2.** order requiring someone to appear in court. — *v.* **3.** order (someone) to appear in court.

sumo *n.* Japanese style of wrestling.

sump *n.* **1.** receptacle in an internal-combustion engine into which oil can drain. **2.** hollow into which liquid drains.

sumptuous *adj.* lavish, magnificent. **sumptuously** *adv.* **sumptuousness** *n.*

sun *n.* **1.** star around which the earth and other planets revolve. **2.** any star around which planets revolve. **3.** heat and light from the sun. — *v.* **sunning, sunned. 4.** expose (oneself) to the sun's rays. **sunless** *adj.* **sunny** *adj.* **1.** full of or exposed to sunlight. **2.** cheerful. **sunbathe** *v.* lie in the sunshine in order to get a suntan. **sunbeam** *n.* ray of sun. **sunburn** *n.* painful reddening of the skin caused by overexposure to the sun. **sunburnt, sunburned** *adj.* **sundial** *n.* device showing the time by means of a pointer that casts a shadow on a marked dial. **sundown** n. US sunset. **sunflower** n. tall plant with large golden flowers. **sunglasses** n. dark glasses to protect the eyes from the sun. **sun lamp** lamp that gives off ultraviolet rays. **sunrise** n. **1.** daily appearance of the sun above the horizon. **2.** time of this. **sunroof** n. panel in the roof of a car that opens to let in air. **sunset** n. **1.** daily disappearance of the sun below the horizon. **2.** time of this. **sunshine** n. light and warmth from the sun. **sunspot** n. dark patch appearing temporarily on the sun's surface. **sunstroke** n. illness caused by prolonged exposure to intensely hot sunlight. **suntan** n. browning of the skin caused by exposure to the sun. **sun-up** n. US sunrise.

Sun. Sunday.

sundae n. ice cream topped with fruit etc.

Sunday n. first day of the week and the Christian day of worship. **Sunday school** school for teaching children about Christianity.

sunder v. break or tear apart.

sundry adj. several, various. **sundries** pl. n. miscellaneous unspecified items. **all and sundry** everybody.

sung v. past participle of SING.

sunk v. a past of SINK.

sunken v. **1.** a past participle of SINK. —adj. **2.** unhealthily hollow. **3.** situated at a low level. **4.** underwater.

sup v. **supping, supped. 1.** take (liquid) by sips. **2.** Obs. take supper. —n. **3.** sip.

super adj. Informal excellent.

super- prefix used with many main words to mean: **1.** above or over, e.g. superimpose. **2.** outstanding, e.g. superstar. **3.** of greater size or extent, e.g. supermarket.

superannuation n. **1.** regular payment by an employee into a pension fund. **2.** pension paid from this. **superannuated** adj. discharged with a pension, owing to old age or illness.

superb adj. excellent, impressive, or splendid. **superbly** adv.

supercharged adj. (of an engine) having a supercharger. **supercharger** n. device that increases the power of an internal-combustion engine by forcing extra air into it.

supercilious adj. showing arrogant pride or scorn. **superciliousness** n.

superconductor n. substance which has almost no electrical resistance at very low temperatures. **superconductivity** n.

supererogation n. act of doing more work than is required.

superficial adj. **1.** of or on the surface. **2.** not careful or thorough. **3.** (of a person) without depth of character, shallow. **superficially** adv. **superficiality** n.

superfluous [soo-per-flew-uss] adj. more than is needed. **superfluity** n.

supergrass n. person who acts as a police informer on a large scale.

superhuman adj. beyond normal human ability or experience.

superimpose v. place (something) on or over something else.

superintend v. supervise (a person or activity). **superintendence** n. **superintendent** n. **1.** senior police officer. **2.** supervisor.

superior adj. **1.** greater in quality, quantity, or merit. **2.** higher in position or rank. **3.** believing oneself to be better than others. —n. **4.** person of greater rank or status. **superiority** n.

superlative [soo-per-lat-iv] adj. **1.** of outstanding quality. **2.** Grammar denoting the form of an adjective or adverb indicating most. —n. **3.** Grammar superlative form of a word.

superman n. man of apparently superhuman powers.

supermarket n. large self-service store selling food and household goods.

supernatural adj. of or relating to things beyond the laws of nature. **the supernatural** supernatural forces, occurrences, and beings collectively.

supernova n., pl. **-vae, -vas.** star that explodes and briefly becomes exceptionally bright.

supernumerary adj. **1.** exceeding the required or regular number. —n., pl. **-ries. 2.** supernumerary person or thing.

superphosphate n. chemical fertilizer containing phosphates.

superpower n. extremely powerful nation.

superscript adj. **1.** (of a character) printed or written above the line. —n. **2.** superscript character.

supersede v. replace, supplant.

supersonic *adj.* of or travelling at a speed greater than the speed of sound.

superstar *n.* very famous entertainer or sportsperson.

superstition *n.* **1.** belief in omens, ghosts, etc. **2.** idea or practice based on this. **superstitious** *adj.*

superstructure *n.* **1.** structure erected on something else. **2.** part of a ship above the main deck.

supertanker *n.* large fast tanker.

supertax *n.* extra tax on incomes above a certain level.

supervene *v.* occur as an unexpected development. **supervention** *n.*

supervise *v.* watch over to direct or check. **supervision** *n.* **supervisor** *n.* **supervisory** *adj.*

supine [**soo**-pine] *adj.* lying flat on one's back.

supper *n.* light evening meal.

supplant *v.* take the place of, oust.

supple *adj.* **1.** (of a person) moving and bending easily and gracefully. **2.** bending easily without damage. **suppleness** *n.* **supply** *adv.*

supplement *n.* **1.** thing added to complete something or make up for a lack. **2.** magazine inserted into a newspaper. **3.** section added to a publication to supply further information. —*v.* **4.** provide or be a supplement to (something). **supplementary** *adj.*

supplication *n.* humble petition. **supplicant** *n.* person who makes a humble request.

supply *v.* -**plying**, -**plied**. **1.** provide with something required. **2.** make available. —*n.*, *pl.* -**plies**. **3.** supplying. **4.** amount available. **5.** *Economics* willingness and ability to provide goods and services. **6.** temporary substitute. —*pl.* **7.** food or equipment. **supplier** *n.*

support *v.* **1.** bear the weight of. **2.** provide the necessities of life for. **3.** speak in favour of. **4.** give practical or emotional help to. **5.** take an active interest in (a sports team, political principle, etc.). **6.** help to prove (a theory etc.). **7.** play a subordinate part. —*n.* **8.** supporting. **9.** means of support. **supporter** *n.* person who supports a team, principle, etc. **supportive** *adj.*

suppose *v.* **1.** presume to be true. **2.**

consider as a proposal for the sake of discussion. **3.** presuppose. **supposed** *adj.* **1.** presumed to be true without proof. **2.** doubtful. **supposed** to **1.** expected or required to, e.g. *you were supposed to phone me.* **2.** permitted to, e.g. *we're not supposed to swim here.* **supposedly** *adv.* **supposition** *n.* **1.** supposing. **2.** something supposed.

suppository *n.,* *pl.* -**ries.** solid medication inserted into the rectum or vagina and left to melt.

suppress *v.* **1.** put an end to. **2.** restrain (an emotion or response). **3.** prevent publication of (information). **suppression** *n.*

suppurate *v.* (of a wound etc.) produce pus. **suppuration** *n.*

supreme *adj.* highest in authority, rank, or degree. **supremely** *adv.* extremely. **supremacy** *n.* **1.** supreme power. **2.** state of being supreme. **supremo** *n.* *Informal* person in overall authority.

surcharge *n.* additional charge.

surd *n.* *Maths* number that cannot be expressed in whole numbers.

sure *adj.* **1.** free from uncertainty or doubt. **2.** reliable. **3.** inevitable. **4.** physically secure. —*adv., interj.* **5.** *Informal* certainly. **for sure** without a doubt. **surely** *adv.* it must be true that. **sure-fire** *adj.* *Informal* certain to succeed. **sure-footed** *adj.* unlikely to slip or stumble.

surety *n.,* *pl.* -**ties.** person who takes responsibility, or thing given as a guarantee, for the fulfilment of another's obligation.

surf *n.* **1.** foam caused by waves breaking on the shore. —*v.* **2.** take part in surfing. **surfing** *n.* sport of riding towards the shore on a surfboard on the crest of a wave. **surfer** *n.* **surfboard** *n.* long smooth board used in surfing.

surface *n.* **1.** outside or top of an object. **2.** material covering the surface of an object. **3.** superficial appearance. **4.** top level of the land or sea. —*v.* **5.** rise to the surface. **6.** put a surface on. **7.** become apparent.

surfeit *n.* excessive amount.

surge *n.* **1.** sudden powerful increase. **2.** strong rolling movement, esp. of the sea. —*v.* **3.** increase suddenly. **4.** move forward strongly.

surgeon *n.* doctor who specializes in surgery. **surgery** *n.* **1.** treatment in which the patient's body is cut open in order to treat the affected part. **2.** *pl.* -**geries.** place where, or time when, a doctor, dentist, MP, etc. can be consulted. **surgical** *adj.* **surgically** *adv.* **surgical spirit** spirit used for sterilizing and cleaning.

surly *adj.* **-lier, -liest.** ill-tempered and rude. **surliness** *n.*

surmise *v., n.* guess, conjecture.

surmount *v.* **1.** overcome (a problem). **2.** be on top of (something). **surmountable** *adj.*

surname *n.* family name.

surpass *v.* be greater than or superior to.

surplice *n.* loose white robe worn by clergymen and choristers.

surplus *n.* **1.** amount left over in excess of what is required. —*adj.* **2.** extra.

surprise *n.* **1.** unexpected event. **2.** amazement and wonder. **3.** act of taking someone unawares. —*v.* **4.** cause to feel amazement or wonder. **5.** come upon, attack, or catch suddenly and unexpectedly. **take someone by surprise** catch someone unprepared.

surrealism *n.* movement in art and literature involving the combination of incongruous images, as in a dream. **surreal** *adj.* **surrealist** *n., adj.* **surrealistic** *adj.*

surrender *v.* **1.** give (something) up to another. **2.** give oneself up. **3.** yield (to a temptation or influence). —*n.* **4.** surrendering.

surreptitious *adj.* done secretly or stealthily. **surreptitiously** *adv.*

surrogate *n.* substitute. **surrogate mother** woman who gives birth to a child on behalf of a couple who cannot have children.

surround *v.* **1.** be, come, or place all around (a person or thing). —*n.* **2.** border or edging. **surroundings** *pl. n.* conditions, scenery, etc. around a person, place, or thing.

surtax *n.* extra tax on incomes above a certain level.

surveillance *n.* close observation.

survey *v.* **1.** view or consider in a general way. **2.** make a map of (an area). **3.** inspect (a building) to assess its condition and value. **4.** find out the incomes, opinions, etc. of a group of people). —*n.* **5.** surveying. **6.** report produced by a survey. **surveyor** *n.*

survive *v.* **1.** continue to live or exist after (a difficult experience). **2.** live after the death of (another). **survival** *n.* **1.** condition of having survived. **2.** thing that has survived from an earlier time. **survivor** *n.*

susceptible *adj.* liable to be influenced or affected by. **susceptibility** *n.*

suspect *v.* **1.** believe (someone) to be guilty without having any proof. **2.** think (something) to be false or questionable. **3.** believe (something) to be the case. —*adj.* **4.** not to be trusted. —*n.* **5.** person who is suspected.

suspend *v.* **1.** hang from a high place. **2.** cause to remain floating or hanging. **3.** cause to cease temporarily. **4.** remove (someone) temporarily from a job or team. **suspenders** *pl. n.* **1.** straps for holding up stockings. **2.** *US* braces. **suspended sentence** prison sentence that is not served unless the offender commits another crime during a specified period.

suspense *n.* state of uncertainty while awaiting news, an event, etc.

suspension *n.* **1.** suspending or being suspended. **2.** system of springs and shock absorbers supporting the body of a vehicle. **3.** mixture of fine particles of a solid in a fluid. **suspension bridge** bridge hanging from cables attached to towers at each end.

suspicion *n.* **1.** feeling of not trusting a person or thing. **2.** belief that something is true without definite proof. **3.** slight trace. **suspicious** *adj.* feeling or causing suspicion. **suspiciously** *adv.*

suss out *v. Slang* work out using one's intuition.

sustain *v.* **1.** maintain or prolong. **2.** suffer (an injury or loss). **3.** keep up the vitality or strength of. **4.** support. **5.** confirm. **sustenance** *n.* food.

suture [**soo**-cher] *n.* stitch joining the edges of a wound.

suzerain *n.* **1.** state or sovereign with limited authority over another self-governing state. **2.** feudal lord. **suzerainty** *n.*

svelte *adj.* attractively or gracefully slim.

SW southwest(ern).

swab *n.* **1.** small piece of cotton wool used to apply medication, clean a wound, etc. —*v.* **swabbing, swabbed.** **2.** clean (a wound) with a swab. **3.** clean (the deck of a ship) with a mop.

swaddle *v.* wrap (a baby) in swaddling clothes. **swaddling clothes** long strips of cloth formerly wrapped round a newborn baby.

swag *n.* **1.** *Slang* stolen property. **2.** *Aust. informal* bundle of belongings carried by a swagman. **swagman** n. Aust. tramp who carries his belongings in a bundle on his back.

swagger v. **1.** walk or behave arrogantly. —n. **2.** arrogant walk or manner.

swain n. **1.** Poetic suitor. **2.** country youth.

swallow[1] v. **1.** cause to pass down one's throat. **2.** make a gulping movement in the throat, as when nervous. **3.** Informal believe (something) gullibly. **4.** refrain from showing (a feeling). **5.** engulf or absorb. —n. **6.** swallowing. **7.** amount swallowed.

swallow[2] n. small migratory bird with long pointed wings and a forked tail.

swam v. past tense of SWIM.

swamp n. **1.** watery area of land, bog. —v. **2.** cause (a boat) to fill with water and sink. **3.** overwhelm. **swampy** adj.

swan n. **1.** large usu. white water bird with a long graceful neck. —v. **swanning, swanned. 2.** Informal wander about idly. **swan song** person's last performance before retirement or death.

swank Slang —v. **1.** show off or boast. —n. **2.** showing off or boasting. **swanky** adj. Slang expensive and showy, stylish.

swap v. **swapping, swapped. 1.** exchange (something) for something else. —n. **2.** exchange.

sward n. stretch of short grass.

swarm[1] n. **1.** large group of bees or other insects. **2.** large crowd. —v. **3.** move in a swarm. **4.** (of a place) be crowded or overrun.

swarm[2] v. (foll. by up) climb (a ladder or rope) by gripping with the hands and feet.

swarthy adj. **-thier, -thiest.** dark-complexioned.

swashbuckler n. daredevil adventurer. **swashbuckling** adj.

swastika n. symbol in the shape of a cross with the arms bent at right angles, used as the emblem of Nazi Germany.

swat v. **swatting, swatted. 1.** hit sharply. —n. **2.** sharp blow.

swatch n. sample of cloth.

swath [swawth] n. **1.** the width of one sweep of a scythe or mower. **2.** strip cut in one sweep.

swathe v. **1.** wrap in bandages or layers of cloth. —n. **2.** same as SWATH.

sway v. **1.** swing to and fro or from side to

side. **2.** waver or cause to waver in opinion. —n. **3.** power or influence. **4.** swaying motion.

swear v. **swearing, swore, sworn. 1.** use obscene or blasphemous language. **2.** state earnestly. **3.** state or promise on oath. **swear by** v. have complete confidence in. **swear in** v. cause to take an oath. **swearword** n. word considered obscene or blasphemous.

sweat n. **1.** salty liquid given off through the pores of the skin. **2.** Slang drudgery or hard labour. **3.** Informal state of anxiety. —v. **4.** have sweat coming through the pores. **5.** be anxious. **6.** toil. **sweaty** adj. **sweatband** n. strip of cloth tied around the forehead or wrist to absorb sweat. **sweatshirt** n. long-sleeved cotton jersey. **sweatshop** n. place where employees work long hours in poor conditions for low pay.

sweater n. (woollen) garment for the upper part of the body.

swede n. **1.** kind of turnip. **2.** (S-) person from Sweden. **Swedish** n., adj. (language) of Sweden.

sweep v. **sweeping, swept. 1.** remove dirt from (a floor) with a broom. **2.** move smoothly and quickly. **3.** spread rapidly. **4.** move majestically. **5.** carry away suddenly or forcefully. **6.** stretch in a long wide curve. —n. **7.** sweeping. **8.** sweeping motion. **9.** wide expanse. **10.** curving line. **11.** person who cleans chimneys. **12.** sweepstake. **sweeping** adj. **1.** indiscriminate. **2.** wide-ranging. **sweepstake** n. lottery in which the stakes of the participants make up the prize.

sweet adj. **1.** tasting of or like sugar. **2.** agreeable to the senses or mind. **3.** kind and charming. **4.** (of wine) with a high sugar content. —n. **5.** shaped piece of food consisting mainly of sugar. **6.** dessert. **sweetly** adv. **sweetness** n. **sweeten** v. **sweetener** n. **1.** sweetening agent that does not contain sugar. **2.** Slang bribe. **sweetie** n. Informal **1.** lovable person. **2.** a sweet. **sweetbread** n. animal's pancreas used as food. **sweetbrier** n. wild rose. **sweet corn** type of maize with sweet yellow kernels, eaten as a vegetable. **sweetheart** n. lover. **sweetmeat** n. Old-fashioned sweet delicacy such as a small cake. **sweet pea** climbing plant with bright fragrant flowers. **sweet potato** tropical root vegetable with yellow flesh. **sweet-talk** v. Informal coax or flatter. **sweet**

tooth strong liking for sweet foods. **sweet william** garden plant with flat clusters of scented flowers.

swell v. **swelling, swelled, swollen** or **swelled. 1.** expand or increase. **2.** be puffed up with pride or other emotion. **3.** (of a sound) become gradually louder. —n. **4.** swelling or being swollen. **5.** movement of waves in the sea. **6.** Old-fashioned slang fashionable person. —adj. **7.** US slang excellent or fine. **swelling** n. enlargement of part of the body, caused by injury or infection.

swelter v. be oppressed by heat.

swept v. past of SWEEP.

swerve v. **1.** turn aside from a course sharply or suddenly. —n. **2.** swerving.

swift adj. **1.** moving or able to move quickly. **2.** performed or happening quickly. —n. **3.** fast-flying bird with pointed wings. **swiftly** adv. **swiftness** n.

swig n. **1.** large mouthful of drink. —v. **swigging, swigged. 2.** drink in large mouthfuls.

swill v. **1.** drink greedily. **2.** rinse (something) in large amounts of water. —n. **3.** sloppy mixture containing waste food, fed to pigs. **4.** deep drink. **5.** rinsing.

swim v. **swimming, swam, swum. 1.** move along in water by movements of the limbs. **2.** be covered or flooded with liquid. **3.** reel, e.g. her head was swimming. **4.** float on a liquid. —n. **5.** act or period of swimming. **swimmer** n. **swimmingly** adv. successfully and effortlessly. **swimming costume, swimsuit** n. swimming garment that leaves the arms and legs bare. **swimming pool** (building containing) an artificial pond for swimming in.

swindle v. **1.** cheat (someone) out of money. —n. **2.** instance of swindling. **swindler** n.

swine n. **1.** contemptible person. **2.** pig. **swinish** adj.

swing v. **swinging, swung. 1.** move to and fro, sway. **2.** move in a curve. **3.** hit out with a sweeping motion. **4.** (of an opinion or mood) change sharply. **5.** turn, as on a hinge. **6.** Slang be hanged. **7.** Informal manipulate or influence. —n. **8.** swinging. **9.** suspended seat on which a child can swing to and fro. **10.** style of popular dance music played by big bands in the 1930s. **11.** sudden or extreme change.

swingeing [swin-jing] adj. punishing, severe.

swipe v. **1.** strike (at) with a sweeping blow. **2.** Slang steal. —n. **3.** sweeping blow.

swirl v. **1.** turn with a whirling motion. —n. **2.** whirling motion. **3.** twisting shape.

swish v. **1.** move with a whistling or hissing sound. —n. **2.** whistling or hissing sound. —adj. **3.** Informal fashionable, smart.

Swiss adj. **1.** of Switzerland or its people. —n., pl. **Swiss. 2.** person from Switzerland. **swiss roll** sponge cake spread with jam or cream and rolled up.

switch n. **1.** device for opening and closing an electric circuit. **2.** abrupt change. **3.** exchange or swap. **4.** flexible rod or twig. —v. **5.** change abruptly. **6.** exchange or swap. **switchback** n. road or railway with many sharp hills or bends. **switchboard** n. installation in a telephone exchange or office where telephone calls are connected. **switch on, off** v. turn (a device) on or off by means of a switch.

swivel n. **1.** coupling device that allows an attached object to turn freely. —v. **-elling, -elled. 2.** turn on or as if on a swivel.

swizz n. Informal swindle or disappointment.

swizzle stick n. small ornamental stick used to stir a cocktail.

swollen v. a past participle of SWELL.

swoon v., n. faint.

swoop v. **1.** sweep down or pounce on suddenly. —n. **2.** swooping.

swop v. **swopping, swopped,** n. same as SWAP.

sword n. weapon with a long sharp blade. **sword dance** Highland dance performed over swords on the ground. **swordfish** n. large fish with a very long upper jaw. **swordsman** n. person skilled in the use of a sword.

swore v. past tense of SWEAR.

sworn v. **1.** past participle of SWEAR. —adj. **2.** bound by or as if by an oath, e.g. sworn enemies.

swot Informal —v. **swotting, swotted. 1.** study hard. —n. **2.** person who studies hard.

swum v. past participle of SWIM.

swung v. past of SWING.

sybarite [sib-bar-ite] n. lover of luxury. **sybaritic** adj.

sycamore n. tree with five-pointed leaves and two-winged fruits.

sycophant *n.* person who uses flattery to win favour from people with power or influence. **sycophantic** *adj.* **sycophancy** *n.*

syllable *n.* part of a word pronounced as a unit. **syllabic** *adj.*

syllabub *n.* dessert of beaten cream, sugar, and wine.

syllabus *n., pl.* **-buses, -bi.** list of subjects for a course of study.
▷ The usual plural is *syllabuses.*

syllogism *n.* form of logical reasoning consisting of two premises and a conclusion. **syllogistic** *adj.*

sylph *n.* **1.** imaginary being supposed to inhabit the air. **2.** slender graceful girl or woman. **sylphlike** *adj.*

sylvan *adj. Lit.* relating to woods and trees.

symbiosis *n.* close association of two species living together to their mutual benefit. **symbiotic** *adj.*

symbol *n.* sign or thing that stands for something else. **symbolic** *adj.* **symbolically** *adv.* **symbolism** *n.* **1.** representation of something by symbols. **2.** movement in art and literature using ideas to express abstract and mystical ideas. **symbolist** *n., adj.* **symbolize** *v.* **1.** be a symbol of. **2.** represent with a symbol.

symmetry *n.* **1.** state of having two halves that are mirror images of each other. **2.** beauty resulting from a balanced arrangement of parts. **symmetrical** *adj.* **symmetrically** *adv.*

sympathy *n., pl.* **-thies. 1.** compassion for someone's pain or distress. **2.** agreement with someone's feelings or interests. **3.** feelings of loyalty and support for an idea. **sympathetic** *adj.* **1.** feeling or showing sympathy. **2.** likeable or appealing. **sympathetically** *adv.* **sympathize** *v.* **1.** feel or express sympathy. **2.** agree with. **sympathizer** *n.*

symphony *n., pl.* **-nies. 1.** composition for orchestra, with several movements. **2.** visually pleasing arrangement. **symphonic** *adj.*

symposium *n., pl.* **-siums, -sia. 1.** conference for discussion of a particular topic. **2.** collection of essays on a topic.

symptom *n.* **1.** sign indicating the presence of an illness. **2.** sign that something is wrong. **symptomatic** *adj.*

synagogue *n.* Jewish place of worship and religious instruction.

sync, synch *Informal* —*n.* **1.** synchronization. —*v.* **2.** synchronize.

synchromesh *adj.* (of a gearbox) having a device that synchronizes the speeds of gears before they engage.

synchronize *v.* **1.** (of two or more people) perform (an action) at the same time. **2.** match (the soundtrack and action of a film) precisely. **3.** set (watches) to show the same time. **synchronization** *n.* **synchronous, synchronic** *adj.* happening or existing at the same time.

syncopate *v. Music* stress the weak beats in (a rhythm) instead of the strong ones. **syncopation** *n.*

syncope [sing-kop-ee] *n. Med.* a faint.

syndicate *n.* **1.** group of people or firms undertaking a joint business project. **2.** agency that sells material to several newspapers. —*v.* **3.** form a syndicate. **4.** publish (material) in several newspapers. **syndication** *n.*

syndrome *n.* **1.** combination of symptoms indicating a particular disease. **2.** set of characteristics indicating a particular problem.

synod *n.* church council.

synonym *n.* word with the same meaning as another. **synonymous** *adj.*

synopsis *n., pl.* **-ses.** summary or outline.

syntax *n. Grammar* way in which words are arranged to form phrases and sentences. **syntactic** *adj.* **syntactically** *adv.*

synthesis *n., pl.* **-ses. 1.** combination of objects or ideas into a whole. **2.** artificial production of a substance. **synthesize** *v.* produce by synthesis. **synthesizer** *n.* electronic musical instrument producing a range of sounds. **synthetic** *adj.* **1.** (of a substance) made artificially. **2.** not genuine, insincere. **synthetically** *adv.*

syphilis *n.* serious sexually transmitted disease. **syphilitic** *adj.*

syphon *n., v.* same as SIPHON.

Syrian *adj.* **1.** of Syria, its people, or their dialect of Arabic. —*n.* **2.** person from Syria.

syringa *n.* same as MOCK ORANGE or LILAC.

syringe *n.* **1.** device for withdrawing or injecting fluids, consisting of a hollow cylinder, a piston, and a hollow needle. —*v.* **2.** wash out or inject with a syringe.

syrup *n.* **1.** solution of sugar in water. **2.**

thick sweet liquid. **3.** excessive sentimentality. **4.** sugar solution containing medicine. **syrupy** *adj.*

system *n.* **1.** method or set of methods. **2.** scheme of classification or arrangement. **3.** network or assembly of parts that form a whole. **4.** orderliness. **5.** body considered as a whole. **the system** society or government regarded as oppressive and exploitative. **systematic** *adj.* **systematically** *adv.* **systematize** *v.* organize using a system. **systematization** *n.* **systemic** *adj.* affecting the entire animal or body. **systemically** *adv.*

systole [**siss**-tol-ee] *n.* regular contraction of the heart as it pumps blood. **systolic** *adj.*

T

t tonne.

T *n.* **to a T 1.** in every detail. **2.** perfectly.

t. ton.

ta *interj. Informal* thank you.

Ta *Chem.* tantalum.

TA Territorial Army.

tab *n.* small flap or projecting label. **keep tabs on** *Informal* watch closely.

tabard *n.* short sleeveless tunic decorated with a coat of arms, worn in medieval times.

Tabasco *n.* ® very hot red pepper sauce.

tabby *n., pl.* **-bies,** *adj.* (cat) with dark stripes on a lighter background.

tabernacle *n.* **1.** portable shrine of the Israelites. **2.** *RC Church* receptacle for the consecrated Host. **3.** Christian place of worship not called a church.

tabla *n., pl.* **-blas, -bla.** one of a pair of Indian drums played with the hands.

table *n.* **1.** piece of furniture with a flat top supported by legs. **2.** arrangement of information in columns. —*v.* **3.** submit (a motion) for discussion by a meeting. **4.** *US* suspend discussion of (a proposal). **tablecloth** *n.* cloth for covering the top of a table, esp. during meals. **tableland** *n.* high plateau. **tablespoon** *n.* large spoon for serving food. **table tennis** game like tennis played on a table with small bats and a light ball.

tableau [tab-loh] *n., pl.* **-leaux, -leaus.** silent motionless group arranged to represent some scene.

table d'hôte [tah-bla dote] *n., pl.* **tables d'hôte,** *adj.* (meal) having a set number of dishes at a fixed price.

tablet *n.* **1.** pill of compressed medicinal substance. **2.** flattish cake of soap etc. **3.** inscribed slab of stone etc.

tabloid *n.* small-sized newspaper with many photographs and a concise, usu. sensational style.

taboo *n., pl.* **-boos. 1.** prohibition resulting from religious or social conventions. —*adj.* **2.** forbidden by a taboo.

tabor, tabour *n.* small drum, used esp. in the Middle Ages.

tabular *adj.* arranged in a table. **tabulate** *v.* arrange (information) in a table. **tabulation** *n.*

tachograph *n.* device for recording the speed and distance travelled by a motor vehicle.

tachometer *n.* device for measuring speed, esp. that of a revolving shaft.

tacit [tass-it] *adj.* implied but not spoken. **tacitly** *adv.*

taciturn [tass-it-turn] *adj.* habitually uncommunicative. **taciturnity** *n.*

tack¹ *n.* **1.** short nail with a large head. **2.** long loose stitch. —*v.* **3.** fasten with tacks. **4.** stitch with tacks. **5.** append.

tack² *n.* **1.** course of a ship sailing obliquely into the wind. **2.** course of action. —*v.* **3.** sail into the wind on a zigzag course.

tack³ *n.* riding harness for horses.

tackle *n.* **1.** set of ropes and pulleys for lifting heavy weights. **2.** equipment for a particular activity. **3.** *Sport* act of tackling an opposing player. —*v.* **4.** undertake (a task). **5.** confront (an opponent). **6.** *Sport* attempt to get the ball from (an opposing player).

tacky¹ *adj.* **tackier, tackiest.** slightly sticky. **tackiness** *n.*

tacky² *adj.* **tackier, tackiest. 1.** *Informal* vulgar and tasteless. **2.** shabby. **tackiness** *n.*

tact *n.* skill in avoiding giving offence. **tactful** *adj.* **tactfully** *adv.* **tactless** *adj.* **tactlessly** *adv.* **tactlessness** *n.*

tactics *pl. n.* **1.** art of directing military forces in battle. **2.** methods or plans to achieve an end. **tactical** *adj.* **tactically** *adv.* **tactician** *n.*

tactile *adj.* of or having the sense of touch.

tadpole *n.* limbless tailed larva of a frog or toad.

taffeta *n.* shiny silk or rayon fabric.

taffrail *n.* rail at the stern of a ship.

tag¹ *n.* **1.** label bearing information. **2.** pointed end of a cord or lace. **3.** trite quotation. —*v.* **tagging, tagged. 4.** attach a tag to. **tag along** v. accompany someone, esp. if uninvited.

tag[2] n. **1.** children's game where the person being chased becomes the chaser upon being touched. —v. **tagging, tagged. 2.** touch and catch in this game.

tagliatelle n. pasta in long narrow strips.

tail n. **1.** rear part of an animal's body, usu. forming a flexible appendage. **2.** rear or last part or parts of something. **3.** *Informal* person employed to follow and spy on another. —pl. **4.** side of a coin without a portrait of a head on it. **5.** *Informal* tail coat. —v. **6.** *Informal* follow (someone) secretly. —pl. **7.** at the rear. **turn tail** run away. **tailless** adj. **tailback** n. queue of traffic stretching back from an obstruction. **tailboard** n. removable or hinged rear board on a lorry etc. **tail coat** man's coat with a long back split into two below the waist. **tail off, away** v. diminish gradually. **tailplane** n. small stabilizing wing at the rear of an aircraft. **tailspin** n. uncontrolled spinning dive of an aircraft. **tailwind** n. wind coming from the rear.

tailor n. **1.** person who makes men's clothes. —v. **2.** adapt to suit a purpose. **tailored** adj. made to fit close to a particular person's body. **tailor-made** adj. **1.** made by a tailor. **2.** perfect for a purpose.

taint v. **1.** spoil with a small amount of decay, contamination, or other bad quality. —n. **2.** something that taints.

take v. **taking, took, taken. 1.** remove from a place. **2.** get possession of, esp. dishonestly. **3.** carry or accompany. **4.** capture. **5.** require (time, resources, or ability). **6.** use. **7.** assume. **8.** write down. **9.** accept. **10.** subtract or deduct. —n. **11.** one of a series of recordings from which the best will be used. **take place** happen. **taking** adj. charming. **takings** pl. n. money received by a shop. **take after** v. look or behave like (a parent etc.). **take away** v. subtract. **take-away** n. **1.** shop or restaurant selling meals for eating elsewhere. **2.** meal bought at a takeaway. **take in** v. **1.** understand. **2.** make (clothing) smaller. **3.** deceive or swindle. **take off** v. **1.** (of an aircraft) leave the ground. **2.** *Informal* depart. **3.** *Informal* parody. **take-off** n. **takeover** n. act of taking control of a company by buying a large number of its shares. **take up** v. **1.** occupy or fill (space or time). **2.** adopt the study or activity of. **3.** accept (an offer). **4.** shorten (a garment).

talc n. **1.** soft mineral of magnesium silicate. **2.** talcum powder. **talcum powder** powder, usu. scented, used to dry or perfume the body.

tale n. **1.** story. **2.** malicious piece of gossip.

talent n. **1.** natural ability. **2.** ancient unit of weight or money. **3.** *Informal* attractive members of the opposite sex. **talented** adj.

talisman n., pl. **-mans.** object believed to have magic power. **talismanic** adj.

talk v. **1.** express ideas or feelings by means of speech. **2.** utter. **3.** discuss, e.g. *let's talk business.* **4.** reveal information. **5.** (be able to) speak in a specified language. **talker** n. **talkative** adj. fond of talking. **talk back** v. answer impudently. **talking-to** n. *Informal* reproof. **talk into** persuade (someone) to do something by talking. **talk out of** dissuade (someone) from talking.

tall adj. **1.** higher than average. **2.** of a specified height. **tall order** difficult task. **tall story** unlikely and probably untrue tale.

tallboy n. high chest of drawers.

tallow n. hard animal fat used to make candles.

tally v. **-lying, -lied. 1.** (of two things) correspond. —n., pl. **-lies. 2.** record of a debt or score.

tally-ho interj. huntsman's cry when the quarry is sighted.

Talmud n. body of Jewish law. **Talmudic** adj.

talon n. bird's hooked claw.

tamarind n. **1.** tropical tree. **2.** its acid fruit.

tamarisk n. evergreen shrub with slender branches and feathery flower clusters.

tambour n. **1.** embroidery frame consisting of two hoops over which fabric is stretched while being worked. **2.** drum.

tambourine n. percussion instrument like a small drum with jingling metal discs attached.

tame adj. **1.** (of animals) brought under human control. **2.** (of animals) not afraid of people. **3.** meek or submissive. **4.** uninteresting. —v. **5.** make tame. **tamely** adv. **tamer** n.

Tamil n. **1.** member of a people of Sri Lanka and S India. **2.** their language.

tam-o'-shanter n. brimless wool cap with a bobble in the centre.

tamp v. pack down by repeated blows.

tamper v. (foll. by *with*) interfere.

tampon n. absorbent plug of cotton wool inserted into the vagina during menstruation.

tan v. **tanning, tanned**. **1**. (of skin) go brown from exposure to sunlight. **2**. convert (a hide) into leather. —n. **3**. brown colour of tanned skin. —adj. **4**. yellowish-brown. **tannery** n., pl. **-eries**. place where hides are tanned. **tanner** n.

tandem n. bicycle for two riders, one behind the other. **in tandem** together.

tandoor n. Indian clay oven. **tandoori** adj. cooked in a tandoor.

tang n. **1**. strong taste or smell. **2**. trace or hint. **tangy** adj. **tangier, tangiest**.

tangent n. **1**. line that touches a curve without intersecting it. **2**. in trigonometry, ratio of the length of the opposite side to that of the adjacent side of a right-angled triangle. **go off at a tangent** suddenly take a completely different line of thought or action. **tangential** adj. **1**. of a tangent. **2**. of superficial relevance only. **tangentially** adv.

tangerine n. small orange-like fruit of an Asian citrus tree.

tangible adj. **1**. able to be touched. **2**. clear and definite. **tangibly** adv. **tangibility** n.

tangle n. **1**. confused mass or situation. —v. **2**. twist together in a tangle. **3**. (often foll. by *with*) come into conflict.

tango n., pl. **-gos**. **1**. S American dance. —v. **2**. dance a tango.

tank n. **1**. container for liquids or gases. **2**. armoured fighting vehicle moving on tracks. **tanker** n. ship or lorry for carrying liquid in bulk.

tankard n. large beer-mug, often with a hinged lid.

tannic acid, tannin n. vegetable substance used in tanning.

Tannoy n. ® type of public-address system.

tansy n., pl. **-sies**. yellow-flowered plant.

tantalize v. torment by showing but withholding something desired. **tantalizing** adj. **tantalizingly** adv.

tantalum n. hard greyish-white metallic element.

tantalus n. case in which bottles of wine and spirits can be locked with their contents visible.

tantamount adj. (foll. by *to*) equivalent in effect to.

tantrum n. childish outburst of temper.

Taoism [tow-iz-zum] n. system of religion and philosophy advocating a simple, honest life and noninterference with the course of natural events. **Taoist** n., adj.

tap[1] v. **tapping, tapped**. **1**. knock lightly and usu. repeatedly. —n. **2**. light knock. **tap dance** dance in which the feet beat out an elaborate rhythm.

tap[2] n. **1**. valve to control the flow of liquid from a pipe or cask. —v. **tapping, tapped**. **2**. listen in on (a telephone) secretly by making an illegal connection. **3**. fit a tap to (a pipe etc.). **4**. draw off with or as if with a tap. **on tap 1**. *Informal* readily available. **2**. (of beer etc.) drawn from a cask.

tape n. **1**. narrow long strip of material. **2**. string stretched across a race track to mark the finish. **3**. recording made on magnetized tape. —v. **4**. bind or fasten with tape. **5**. record on magnetized tape. **have a person, situation taped** *Informal* have full understanding and control of a person *or* situation. **tape measure** tape marked off in centimetres or inches for measuring. **tape recorder** device for recording and reproducing sound on magnetized tape. **tapeworm** n. long flat parasitic worm living in the intestines of vertebrates.

taper v. **1**. become narrower towards one end. —n. **2**. long thin candle. **3**. narrowing. **taper off** v. become gradually less.

tapestry n., pl. **-tries**. fabric decorated with coloured woven designs.

tapioca n. beadlike starch made from cassava root, used in puddings.

tapir [tape-er] n. piglike mammal of tropical America and SE Asia, with a long snout.

tappet n. short steel rod in an engine, transferring motion from one part to another.

taproot n. main root of a plant, growing straight down.

tar n. **1**. thick black liquid distilled from coal etc. —v. **tarring, tarred**. **2**. coat with tar.

taramasalata n. creamy pink pâté made from fish roe.

tarantella *n.* **1.** lively Italian dance. **2.** music for this.

tarantula *n.* large hairy spider with a poisonous bite.

tarboosh *n.* felt brimless cap, usu. red and often with a silk tassel, formerly worn by Muslim men.

tardy *adj.* **tardier, tardiest.** slow or late. **tardily** *adv.* **tardiness** *n.*

tare[1] *n.* **1.** weight of the wrapping or container of goods. **2.** unladen weight of a vehicle.

tare[2] *n.* **1.** type of vetch plant. **2.** *Bible* weed.

target *n.* **1.** object or person a missile is aimed at. **2.** goal or objective. **3.** object of criticism. —*v.* **-geting, -geted. 4.** aim or direct.

tariff *n.* **1.** tax levied on imports. **2.** list of fixed prices.

Tarmac *n.* **1.** ® mixture of tar, bitumen, and crushed stones used for roads etc. **2.** (t-) airport runway.

tarn *n.* small mountain lake.

tarnish *v.* **1.** make or become stained or less bright. **2.** damage or taint. —*n.* **3.** discoloration or blemish.

taro *n.* tropical plant with edible roots.

tarot [tarr-oh] *n.* special pack of cards used mainly in fortune-telling. **tarot card**

tarpaulin *n.* (sheet of) heavy waterproof fabric.

tarragon *n.* aromatic herb.

tarry *v.* **-rying, -ried. 1.** *Old-fashioned* linger or delay. **2.** stay briefly.

tarsier *n.* monkey-like mammal of the E Indies.

tarsus *n., pl.* **-si.** bones of the heel and ankle collectively.

tart[1] *n.* pie or flan with a sweet filling.

tart[2] *adj.* sharp or bitter. **tartly** *adv.* **tartness** *n.*

tart[3] *n. Informal* sexually provocative or promiscuous woman. **tart up** *v. Informal* dress or decorate in a smart or flashy way.

tartan *n.* design of straight lines crossing at right angles, esp. one associated with a Scottish clan. **2.** cloth with such a pattern.

tartar[1] *n.* **1.** hard deposit on the teeth. **2.** deposit formed during the fermentation of wine.

tartar[2] *n.* fearsome or formidable person.

Tartar *n., adj.* same as TATAR.

tartar sauce *n.* mayonnaise sauce mixed with chopped herbs and capers, served with seafood.

tartrazine [tar-traz-zeen] *n.* artificial yellow dye used in food etc.

TAS Tasmania.

task *n.* (difficult or unpleasant) piece of work to be done. **take to task** criticize or scold. **task force** (military) group formed to carry out a specific task. **taskmaster** *n.* person who enforces hard work.

Tasmanian devil *n.* small carnivorous marsupial found in Tasmania.

Tass *n.* principal news agency of the Soviet Union.

tassel *n.* decorative fringed knot of threads. **tasselled** *adj.*

taste *n.* **1.** sense by which the flavour of a substance is distinguished in the mouth. **2.** distinctive flavour. **3.** brief experience of something. **4.** small amount tasted. **5.** liking. **6.** ability to appreciate what is beautiful or excellent. —*v.* **7.** distinguish the taste of (a substance). **8.** take a small amount of (something) into the mouth. **9.** have a specific taste. **10.** experience briefly. **tasteful** *adj.* having or showing good taste. **tastefully** *adv.* **tasteless** *adj.* **1.** bland or insipid. **2.** showing bad taste. **tastelessly** *adv.* **tasty** *adj.* pleasantly flavoured. **taste bud** small organ on the tongue which perceives flavours.

tat *n.* tatty or tasteless article(s).

Tatar, Tartar *n.* **1.** member of a Mongoloid people who established a powerful state in central Asia in the 13th century. **2.** their descendants, now living in the Soviet Union. —*adj.* **3.** of the Tatars.

tattered *adj.* ragged or torn. **tatters** *pl. n.* ragged pieces.

tattle *n., v.* gossip or chatter.

tattoo[1] *v.* **-tooing, -tooed. 1.** make (a pattern) on the skin by pricking and staining it with indelible inks. —*n.* **2.** pattern so made. **tattooist** *n.*

tattoo[2] *n.* **1.** military display or pageant. **2.** drumming or tapping.

tatty *adj.* **-tier, -tiest.** shabby or worn out. **tattiness** *n.*

taught *v.* past of TEACH.

taunt *v.* **1.** tease with jeers. —*n.* **2.** jeering remark.

taupe *adj.* brownish-grey.

Taurus *n.* (the bull) second sign of the zodiac.

taut *adj.* **1.** drawn tight. **2.** showing nervous strain. **tauten** *v.* make or become taut.

tautology *n., pl.* **-gies.** use of words which merely repeat something already stated. **tautological** *adj.*

tavern *n. Old-fashioned* pub.

tawdry *adj.* **-drier, -driest.** cheap, showy, and of poor quality. **tawdriness** *n.*

tawny *adj.* **-nier, -niest.** yellowish-brown.

tax *n.* **1.** compulsory payment levied by a government on income, property, etc. to raise revenue. **2.** heavy demand on something. —*v.* **3.** levy a tax on. **4.** make heavy demands on. **taxable** *adj.* **taxation** *n.* levying of taxes. **tax-free** *adj.* (of goods and services) not taxed. **taxpayer** *n.* **tax relief** reduction in the amount of tax a person or company has to pay. **tax return** statement of personal income for tax purposes.

taxi *n.* (also **taxicab**) **1.** car with a driver that may be hired to take people to any specified destination. —*v.* **taxiing, taxied. 2.** (of an aircraft) run along the ground before taking off or after landing. **taximeter** *n.* meter in a taxi that registers the fare. **taxi rank** place where taxis wait to be hired.

taxidermy *n.* art of stuffing and mounting animal skins to give them a lifelike appearance. **taxidermist** *n.*

taxonomy *n.* classification of plants and animals into groups. **taxonomic** *adj.* **taxonomist** *n.*

Tb *Chem.* terbium.

TB tuberculosis.

T-bone steak *n.* steak cut from the sirloin of beef, containing a T-shaped bone.

tbs., tbsp. tablespoon(ful).

Tc *Chem.* technetium.

te *n. Music* in tonic sol-fa, seventh degree of any major scale.

Te *Chem.* tellurium.

tea *n.* **1.** dried leaves of an Asian bush. **2.** drink made by infusing these leaves in boiling water. **3.** drink like tea, made from other plants. **4.** main evening meal. **5.** light afternoon meal of tea, cakes, etc. **tea bag** small porous bag of tea leaves. **tea-break** *n.*

short interruption of the working day permitted for drinking tea. **tea cosy** covering for a teapot to keep the tea warm. **teapot** *n.* container with a lid, spout, and handle for making and serving tea. **teaspoon** *n.* small spoon for stirring tea. **tea towel** towel for drying dishes.

teach *v.* **teaching, taught. 1.** tell or show (someone) how to do something. **2.** cause to learn or understand. **3.** give lessons in (a subject). **teachable** *adj.* **teacher** *n.* **teaching** *n.*

teak *n.* very hard wood of an E Indian tree.

teal *n.* kind of small duck.

team *n.* **1.** group of people forming one side in a game. **2.** group of people or animals working together. **teamster** *n. US* lorry driver. **team spirit** willingness to cooperate as part of a team. **team up** *v.* make or join a team. **teamwork** *n.* cooperative work by a team.

tear[1], **teardrop** *n.* drop of fluid appearing in and falling from the eye. **in tears** weeping. **tearful** *adj.* weeping or about to weep. **tear gas** gas that stings the eyes and causes temporary blindness. **tear-jerker** *n. Informal* excessively sentimental film or book.

tear[2] *v.* **tearing, tore, torn. 1.** rip a hole in. **2.** rip apart. **3.** become ripped. **4.** rush. —*n.* **5.** hole or split. **tearaway** *n.* wild or unruly person.

tease *v.* **1.** make fun of (someone) in a provoking or playful way. **2.** separate the fibres of. —*n.* **3.** person who teases. **teaser** *n.* annoying or difficult problem. **teasing** *adj., n.*

teasel, teazel, teazle *n.* plant with prickly leaves and flowers.

teat *n.* **1.** rubber nipple of a feeding bottle. **2.** nipple of a breast or udder.

tech *n. Informal* technical college.

technetium [tek-**neesh**-ee-um] *n.* silvery-grey metallic element, artificially produced by bombardment of molybdenum by deuterons.

technical *adj.* **1.** of or specializing in industrial, practical, or mechanical arts and applied sciences. **2.** skilled in technical subjects. **3.** relating to a particular field. **4.** according to the letter of the law. **5.** showing technique, e.g. *technical brilliance.* **technically** *adv.* **technicality** *n.* petty point based on a strict application of rules. **technician** *n.* person skilled in a particular technical field. **technical college** higher educational institution with courses in arts and technical subjects.

Technicolor *n.* ® system of colour photography used for the cinema.

technique *n.* **1.** method or skill used for a particular task. **2.** technical proficiency.

technocracy *n., pl.* **-cies.** government by technical experts. **technocrat** *n.*

technology *n.* **1.** application of practical or mechanical sciences to industry or commerce. **2.** sciences applied thus. **technological** *adj.* **technologist** *n.*

tectonics *n.* study of the earth's crust and the forces affecting it.

teddy *n., pl.* **-dies. 1.** teddy bear. **2.** combined camisole and knickers. **teddy bear** soft toy bear.

teddy boy *n. Brit.* youth who wore mock Edwardian fashions in Britain esp. in the mid-1950s.

Te Deum [tee **dee**-um] *n.* ancient Latin hymn of thanksgiving.

tedious *adj.* causing fatigue or boredom. **tediously** *adv.* **tedium** *n.* monotony.

tee *n.* **1.** small peg from which a golf ball can be played at the start of each hole. **2.** area of a golf course from which the first stroke of a hole is made. **tee off** *v.* make the first stroke of a hole in golf.

teem *v.* **1.** be full of. **2.** rain heavily.

teenage *adj.* of the period of life between the ages of 13 and 19. **teenager** *n.* person aged between 13 and 19.

teens *pl. n.* period of being a teenager.

teeny *adj. Informal* extremely small.

teepee *n.* same as TEPEE.

tee-shirt *n.* same as T-SHIRT.

teeter *v.* wobble or move unsteadily.

teeth *n.* plural of TOOTH.

teethe *v.* (of a baby) grow his or her first teeth. **teething troubles** problems during the early stages of something.

teetotal *adj.* drinking no alcohol. **teetotaller** *n.*

TEFL Teaching of English as a Foreign Language.

Teflon *n.* ® substance used for nonstick coatings on saucepans etc.

telecommunications *pl. n.* communications using telephone, radio, television, etc.

telegram *n.* formerly, a message sent by telegraph.

telegraph *n.* **1.** formerly, a system for sending messages over a distance along a cable. —*v.* **2.** communicate by telegraph. **telegraphic** *adj.* **telegraphist** *n.* person who works a telegraph. **telegraphy** *n.* science or use of a telegraph.

telekinesis *n.* movement of objects by thought or willpower.

telemeter *n.* device for recording or measuring a distant event and transmitting the data to a receiver. **telemetry** *n.* **telemetric** *adj.*

teleology *n.* belief that all things have a predetermined purpose. **teleological** *adj.*

telepathy *n.* direct communication between minds. **telepathic** *adj.* **telepathically** *adv.*

telephone *n.* **1.** device for transmitting sound over a distance along wires. —*v.* **2.** call or talk to (a person) by telephone. **telephony** *n.* **telephonic** *adj.* **telephonist** *n.* person operating a telephone switchboard.

telephoto lens *n.* camera lens producing a magnified image of a distant object.

teleprinter *n.* apparatus like a typewriter for sending and receiving typed messages by wire.

Teleprompter *n.* ® device under a television camera enabling a speaker to read the script while appearing to look at the camera.

telesales *n.* selling of a product or service by telephone.

telescope *n.* **1.** optical instrument for magnifying distant objects. —*v.* **2.** shorten by the sliding of each part over the next. **3.** shorten by crushing. **telescopic** *adj.*

teletext *n.* system which shows information and news on subscribers' television screens.

television *n.* **1.** system of producing a moving image and accompanying sound on a distant screen. **2.** device for receiving broadcast signals and converting them into sound and pictures. **3.** content of television programmes. **televise** *v.* broadcast on television. **televisual** *adj.*

telex *n.* **1.** international communication service using teleprinters. **2.** message sent by telex. —*v.* **3.** transmit by telex.

tell *v.* **telling, told. 1.** make known in words. **2.** order or instruct. **3.** give an account of. **4.**

discern or distinguish. **5.** have an effect. **6.** *Informal* reveal secrets. **teller** *n.* **1.** narrator. **2.** bank cashier. **3.** person who counts votes. **telling** *adj.* having a marked effect. **tell off** *v.* reprimand. **telling-off** *n.* **telltale** *n.* **1.** person who reveals secrets. —*adj.* **2.** revealing.

tellurian *adj.* of the earth.

tellurium *n.* brittle silvery-white nonmetallic element.

telly *n., pl.* **-lies.** *Informal* television.

temerity [tim-**merr**-it-tee] *n.* boldness or audacity.

temp *Informal* —*n.* **1.** temporary employee, esp. a secretary. —*v.* **2.** work as a temp.

temp. 1. temperature. **2.** temporary.

temper *n.* **1.** outburst of anger. **2.** tendency to become angry. **3.** calm mental condition, e.g. *I lost my temper.* **4.** frame of mind. —*v.* **5.** make less extreme. **6.** strengthen or toughen (metal).

tempera *n.* painting medium of pigment and egg yolk.

temperament *n.* person's character or disposition. **temperamental** *adj.* **1.** having changeable moods. **2.** of temperament. **3.** *Informal* erratic and unreliable. **temperamentally** *adv.*

temperate *adj.* **1.** (of climate) not extreme. **2.** self-restrained or moderate. **temperance** *n.* **1.** moderation. **2.** abstinence from alcohol.

temperature *n.* **1.** degree of heat or cold. **2.** *Informal* abnormally high body temperature.

tempest *n.* violent storm. **tempestuous** *adj.* **1.** violent or stormy. **2.** extremely emotional or passionate. **tempestuously** *adv.*

template *n.* pattern used to cut out shapes accurately.

temple[1] *n.* building for worship.

temple[2] *n.* region on either side of the forehead.

tempo *n., pl.* **-pos, -pi. 1.** speed of a piece of music. **2.** rate or pace.

temporal *adj.* **1.** of time. **2.** worldly rather than spiritual. **3.** of the temple(s) of the head.

temporary *adj.* lasting only for a short time. **temporarily** *adv.*

temporize *v.* **1.** gain time by negotiation or

evasiveness. **2.** adapt to circumstances. **temporization** *n.*

tempt *v.* **1.** (try to) entice (a person) to do something wrong. **2.** risk provoking, e.g. *you're tempting fate.* **tempter, temptress** *n.* **temptation** *n.* **1.** tempting. **2.** tempting thing. **tempting** *adj.* attractive or inviting.

ten *adj., n.* one more than nine. **tenth** *adj., n.* (of) number ten in a series.

tenable *adj.* able to be upheld or maintained.

tenacious *adj.* **1.** holding fast. **2.** stubborn. **tenaciously** *adv.* **tenacity** *n.*

tenant *n.* person who rents land or a building. **tenancy** *n.*

tench *n., pl.* **tench.** freshwater game fish of the carp family.

tend[1] *v.* **1.** be inclined. **2.** go in the direction of. **tendency** *n.* inclination to act in a certain way. **tendentious** *adj.* biased, not impartial.

tend[2] *v.* take care of.

tender[1] *adj.* **1.** not tough. **2.** gentle and affectionate. **3.** vulnerable or sensitive. **tenderly** *adv.* **tenderness** *n.* **tenderize** *v.* soften (meat) by pounding or treatment with a special substance. **tenderizer** *n.* **tenderloin** *n.* tender cut of pork from between the sirloin and the ribs.

tender[2] *v.* **1.** offer. **2.** make a tender. —*n.* **3.** formal offer to supply goods or services at a stated cost. **legal tender** currency that must, by law, be accepted as payment.

tender[3] *n.* **1.** small boat that brings supplies to a larger ship in a port. **2.** carriage for fuel and water attached to a steam locomotive.

tendon *n.* sinew attaching a muscle to a bone.

tendril *n.* slender stem by which a climbing plant clings.

tenement *n.* building divided into several flats.

tenet [**ten**-nit] *n.* doctrine or belief.

tenner *n. Informal* ten-pound note.

tennis *n.* game in which players use rackets to hit a ball back and forth over a net.

tenon *n.* projecting end on a piece of wood fitting into a slot in another.

tenor *n.* **1.** (singer with) the second highest male voice. **2.** general meaning. —*adj.* **3.** (of a voice or instrument) between alto and baritone.

tenpin bowling n. game in which players try to knock over ten skittles by rolling a ball at them.

tense[1] n. form of a verb showing the time of action.

tense[2] adj. **1.** stretched tight. **2.** emotionally strained. —v. **3.** make or become tense.

tensile adj. of tension. **tensile strength** measure of the ability of a material to withstand lengthways stress.

tension n. **1.** degree of stretching. **2.** emotional strain. **3.** hostility or suspense. **4.** Electricity voltage.

tent n. portable canvas shelter.

tentacle n. flexible organ of many invertebrates, used for grasping, feeding, etc.

tentative adj. **1.** provisional or experimental. **2.** cautious or hesitant. **tentatively** adv.

tenterhooks pl. n. **on tenterhooks** in anxious suspense.

tenuous adj. slight or flimsy. **tenuously** adv. **tenuousness** n.

tenure n. **1.** (period of) the holding of an office or position. **2.** legal right to live in a building or use land for a period of time.

tenuto adj., adv. Music (of a note) to be held for or beyond its full time value.

tepee [tee-pee] n. N American Indian cone-shaped tent.

tepid adj. **1.** slightly warm. **2.** half-hearted.

tequila n. Mexican alcoholic drink.

terbium n. rare metallic element.

tercel, tiercel n. male falcon or hawk, esp. as used in falconry.

tercentenary adj., n., pl. **-naries.** (of) a three hundredth anniversary.

term n. **1.** word or expression. **2.** fixed period. **3.** period of the year when a school etc. is open or a lawcourt holds sessions. —pl. **4.** conditions. **5.** mutual relationship. —v. **6.** name or designate. **terms of trade** Brit. economics ratio of export prices to import prices.

termagant n. rare unpleasant and bad-tempered woman.

terminable adj. capable of being terminated.

terminal adj. **1.** at or being an end. **2.** (of an illness) ending in death. —n. **3.** terminating point or place. **4.** point where current enters or leaves an electrical device. **5.** keyboard and VDU having input and output links with a computer. **6.** place where people or vehicles begin or end a journey. **terminally** adv.

terminal velocity n. Physics maximum velocity reached by a body falling under gravity through a fluid, esp. the atmosphere.

terminate v. bring or come to an end. **termination** n.

terminology n. technical terms relating to a subject. **terminological** adj.

terminus n., pl. **-ni, -nuses. 1.** final point. **2.** railway or bus station at the end of a line.

termite n. white antlike insect destructive to timber.

tern n. gull-like sea bird with a forked tail and pointed wings.

ternary adj. **1.** consisting of three parts. **2.** Maths (of a number system) to the base three.

Terpsichorean adj. of dancing.

terrace n. **1.** row of houses built as one block. **2.** paved area next to a building. **3.** level tier cut out of a hill. —pl. (also **terracing**) **4.** tiered area in a stadium where spectators stand. —v. **5.** form into or provide with a terrace.

terracotta adj., n. **1.** (made of) brownish-red unglazed pottery. —adj. **2.** brownish-red.

terra firma n. dry land or solid ground.

terrain n. area of ground, esp. with reference to its physical character.

terrapin n. kind of aquatic tortoise.

terrarium n., pl. **-rariums, -raria.** enclosed container for small plants or animals.

terrazzo n., pl. **-zos.** floor of marble chips set in mortar and polished.

terrestrial adj. **1.** of the earth. **2.** of or living on land.

terrible adj. **1.** very serious. **2.** Informal very bad. **3.** causing fear. **terribly** adv.

terrier n. any of various breeds of small active dog.

terrific adj. **1.** great or intense. **2.** Informal excellent.

terrify v. **-fying, -fied.** fill with fear. **terrifying** adj. **terrifyingly** adv.

terrine [terr-reen] n. **1.** pâté or similar food. **2.** earthenware dish with a lid.

territory n., pl. **-ries. 1.** district. **2.** area under the control of a particular government. **3.** area inhabited and defended by an animal. **4.** area of knowledge. **5.** (T-) region of a country, esp. of a federal state, that does not enjoy full rights. **territorial** *adj.* **Territorial Army** reserve army. **territorial waters** parts of the sea over which a country exercises control, esp. with regard to fishing rights.

terror *n.* **1.** great fear. **2.** terrifying person or thing. **3.** *Informal* troublesome person or thing. **terrorism** *n.* use of violence and intimidation to achieve political ends. **terrorist** *n., adj.* **terrorize** *v.* force or oppress by fear or violence.

terry *n.* fabric with small loops covering both sides, used esp. for making towels.

terse *adj.* **1.** concise. **2.** curt. **tersely** *adv.*

tertiary [tur-shar-ee] *adj.* third in degree, order, etc.

Terylene *n.* ® synthetic polyester yarn or fabric.

TESSA Tax Exempt Special Savings Account.

tessellated *adj.* paved or inlaid with a mosaic of small tiles. **tessera** *n., pl.* **-serae.** small square tile used in mosaics.

test *v.* **1.** try out to ascertain the worth, capability, or endurance of. **2.** carry out an examination on. —*n.* **3.** critical examination. **4.** method or standard of judgment. **5.** test match. **testing** *adj.* **test case** lawsuit that establishes a precedent. **test match** one of a series of international cricket or rugby matches. **test pilot** pilot who tests the performance of new aircraft. **test tube** narrow cylindrical glass vessel used in scientific experiments. **test-tube baby** baby conceived outside the mother's body.

testament *n.* **1.** *Law* will. **2.** proof or tribute. **3.** (T-) one of the two main divisions of the Bible. **testamentary** *adj.*

testate *adj.* having left a valid will. **testacy** *n.* **testator** [test-tay-tor], **testatrix** [test-tay-triks] *n.* maker of a will.

testicle *n.* either of the two male reproductive glands.

testify *v.* **-fying, -fied. 1.** give evidence under oath. **2.** (foll. by *to*) be evidence (of).

testimony *n., pl.* **-nies. 1.** declaration of truth or fact. **2.** evidence given under oath. **testimonial** *n.* **1.** recommendation of the worth of a person or thing. **2.** tribute for services or achievement.

▷ A *testimonial* is an open letter of recommendation about someone. A *reference* is a

confidential report that is not read by the person who is the subject.

testis *n., pl.* **-tes.** testicle.

testy *adj.* **testier, testiest.** irritable or touchy. **testily** *adv.* **testiness** *n.*

tetanus *n.* acute infectious disease producing muscular spasms and convulsions.

tetchy *adj.* **tetchier, tetchiest.** cross and irritable. **tetchiness** *n.*

tête-à-tête *n., pl.* **-têtes, -tête.** private conversation.

tether *n.* **1.** rope or chain for tying an animal to a spot. —*v.* **2.** tie up with rope. **at the end of one's tether** at the limit of one's endurance.

tetrad *n.* group or series of four.

tetraethyl lead *n.* colourless oily insoluble liquid used in petrol to prevent knocking.

tetragon *n.* figure with four angles and four sides. **tetragonal** *adj.*

tetrahedron [tet-ra-heed-ron] *n., pl.* **-drons, -dra.** *Geom.* solid figure with four faces.

tetralogy *n., pl.* **-gies.** series of four related works.

tetrameter [tet-tram-it-er] *n.* **1.** *Prosody* line of verse consisting of four metrical feet. **2.** verse composed of such lines.

Teutonic [tew-tonn-ik] *adj.* of or like the (ancient) Germans.

text *n.* **1.** main body of a book as distinct from illustrations etc. **2.** passage of the Bible as the subject of a sermon. **3.** novel or play needed for a course. **textual** *adj.* **textbook** *n.* **1.** standard book on a particular subject. —*adj.* **2.** perfect, e.g. *a textbook landing.*

textile *n.* **1.** fabric or cloth, esp. woven. —*adj.* **2.** of (the making of) fabrics.

texture *n.* structure, feel, or consistency. **textured** *adj.* **textural** *adj.*

Th *Chem.* thorium.

Thai *adj.* **1.** of Thailand. —*n.* **2.** *pl.* **-s, Thai.** person from Thailand. **3.** language of Thailand.

thalidomide [thal-lid-oh-mide] *n.* drug formerly used as a sedative, but found to cause abnormalities in developing fetuses.

thallium *n.* highly toxic metallic element.

than *conj.* used to introduce the second element of a comparison.

thane n. Hist. Anglo-Saxon or medieval Scottish nobleman.

thank v. 1. express gratitude to. 2. hold responsible. **thanks** pl. n. 1. words of gratitude. —interj. (also **thank you**) 2. polite expression of gratitude. **thanks to** because of. **thankful** adj. grateful. **thankless** adj. unrewarding or unappreciated. **Thanksgiving Day** autumn public holiday in Canada and the US.

▷ When *thank you* is used to express gratitude it should be written as two words: *Thank you for the gift.* When it is used as an adjective, use a hyphen: *a thank-you note.*

that adj., pron. 1. used to refer to something already mentioned or familiar, or further away. —conj. 2. used to introduce a clause. —pron. 3. used to introduce a relative clause.

▷ The relative pronoun *that* may often be used interchangeably with *which* in defining clauses: *the coat that/which you bought.* Some people, however, prefer to reserve *which* for the type of clause (called nondefining) that contains explanations and amplifications and is divided by a comma from the rest of the sentence; *he found the book, which was a start.*

thatch n. 1. roofing material of reeds or straw. —v. 2. roof (a house) with reeds or straw. **thatcher** n.

thaw v. 1. make or become unfrozen. 2. become more relaxed or friendly. —n. 3. thawing. 4. weather causing snow or ice to melt.

the adj. the definite article.

theatre n. 1. place where plays etc. are performed. 2. drama and acting in general. 3. hospital operating room. 4. region in which a war takes place. **theatrical** adj. 1. of the theatre. 2. exaggerated or affected. **theatricals** pl. n. (amateur) dramatic performances. **theatrically** adv. **theatricality** n.

thee pron. Obs. objective form of THOU.

theft n. the act or an instance of stealing.

their adj. of or associated with them. **theirs** pron. (thing or person) belonging to them.

▷ Be careful not to confuse *their* with *there*. *Their* is used for possession: *their new baby*. *There* indicates place and has a similar '-ere' spelling pattern to *here* and *where*.

theism [**thee**-iz-zum] n. belief in the creation of the universe by one God. **theist** n., adj. **theistic** adj.

them pron. refers to people or things other than the speaker or those addressed. **themselves** pron. emphatic and reflexive form of THEY and THEM.

▷ *Them* may be used after a singular to avoid the clumsy *him or her*: *If you see a person looking lost, help them*.

theme n. 1. main idea or subject being discussed. 2. recurring melodic figure in music. **thematic** adj. **thematically** adv.

theme park n. leisure area in which all the activities and displays are based on a single theme.

then adv. 1. at that time. 2. after that. 3. that being so.

thence adv. 1. from that place or time. 2. therefore.

theocracy n., pl. **-cies**. government by a god or priests. **theocratic** adj.

theodolite [thee-**odd**-oh-lite] n. surveying instrument for measuring angles.

theology n., pl. **-gies**. study of religions and religious beliefs. **theologian** n. **theological** adj. **theologically** adv.

theorem n. proposition that can be proved by reasoning.

theory n., pl. **-ries**. 1. set of ideas to explain something. 2. abstract knowledge or reasoning. 3. idea or opinion. 4. ideal or hypothetical situation. **theoretical** adj. based on theory rather than practice or fact. **theoretically** adv. **theorist** n. **theorize** v. form theories, speculate.

theosophy n. religious or philosophical system claiming to be based on intuitive insight into the divine nature. **theosophical** adj.

therapy n., pl. **-pies**. curing treatment. **therapist** n. **therapeutic** [ther-rap-**pew**-tik] adj. curing. **therapeutics** n. art of curing.

there adv. 1. in or to that place. 2. in that respect. **thereabouts** adv. near that place, time, amount, etc. **thereafter** adv. Formal from that time onwards. **thereby** adv. by that means. **therefore** adv. consequently, that being so. **thereupon** adv. immediately after that.

▷ Be careful not to confuse *there* with *their*. *There* indicates place and has a similar '-ere' spelling pattern to *here* and *where*. *Their* indicates possession: *their new baby*.

therm n. unit of measurement of heat. **thermal** adj. 1. of heat. 2. hot or warm. 3.

(of clothing) retaining heat. —*n.* **4.** rising current of warm air.

thermionic valve *n.* electronic valve in which electrons are emitted from a heated rather than a cold cathode.

thermocouple *n.* device for measuring heat, consisting of two wires of different metals joined at both ends.

thermodynamics *pl. n.* scientific study of the relationship between heat and other forms of energy.

thermoelectric, thermoelectrical *adj.* of, relating to, or operated by the conversion of heat energy to electrical energy.

thermometer *n.* instrument for measuring temperature.

thermonuclear *adj.* **1.** involving nuclear fusion. **2.** involving atomic weapons.

thermoplastic *adj.* (of a plastic) softening when heated and resetting on cooling.

Thermos *n.* ® vacuum flask.

thermosetting *adj.* (of a plastic) remaining hard when heated.

thermostat *n.* device for automatically regulating temperature. **thermostatic** *adj.* **thermostatically** *adv.*

thesaurus [thiss-sore-uss] *n., pl.* -ri, -ruses. book containing lists of synonyms and related words.

these *adj., pron.* plural of THIS.

thesis *n., pl.* **theses. 1.** written work submitted for a degree. **2.** opinion supported by reasoned argument.

Thespian *adj.* **1.** of the theatre. —*n.* **2.** actor or actress.

they *pron.* refers to: **1.** people or things other than the speaker or people addressed. **2.** people in general. **3.** *Informal* he or she.
▷ *They* may be used after a singular to avoid the clumsy *he or she*: *If a person is born gloomy, they cannot help it.*

thiamine *n.* vitamin found in the outer coat of rice and other grains.

thick *adj.* **1.** of great or specified extent from one side to the other. **2.** having a dense consistency. **3.** full of. **4.** *Informal* stupid or insensitive. **5.** (of a voice) throaty. **6.** *Informal* friendly. **a bit thick** *Informal* unfair or unreasonable. **the thick** busiest or most intense part. **thicken** *v.* make or become thick or thicker. **thickener** *n.* substance used to thicken liquids. **thickly** *adv.* **thickness** *n.* **1.** state of being thick. **2.** dimension

through an object. **3.** layer. **thickset** *adj.* **1.** stocky in build. **2.** set closely together.

thick-skinned *adj.* insensitive to criticism or hints.

thicket *n.* dense growth of small trees.

thief *n., pl.* **thieves.** person who steals. **thieve** *v.* steal. **thieving** *adj., n.*

thigh *n.* upper part of the human leg.

thimble *n.* cap protecting the end of the finger when sewing.

thin *adj.* **thinner, thinnest. 1.** not thick. **2.** slim or lean. **3.** sparse or meagre. **4.** of low density. **5.** poor or unconvincing. —*v.* **thinning, thinned. 6.** make or become thin. **thinness** *n.* **thin-skinned** *adj.* sensitive to criticism or hints.

thine *pron. Obs.* (something) of or associated with you (thou).

thing *n.* **1.** material object. **2.** object, fact, or idea considered as a separate entity. **3.** *Informal* obsession. —*pl.* **4.** possessions, clothes, etc.

think *v.* **thinking, thought. 1.** consider, judge, or believe. **2.** make use of the mind. **3.** be considerate enough or remember to do something. **thinker** *n.* **thinking** *adj., n.* **think-tank** *n.* group of experts studying specific problems. **think up** *v.* invent or devise.

third *adj.* **1.** of number three in a series. **2.** rated or graded below the second level. —*n.* **3.** one of three equal parts. **third degree** violent interrogation. **third party** (applying to) a person involved by chance or only incidentally in legal proceedings, an accident, etc.

Third World *n.* developing countries of Africa, Asia, and Latin America.

thirst *n.* **1.** desire to drink. **2.** craving or yearning. —*v.* **3.** feel thirst. **thirsty** *adj.* **thirstier, thirstiest. thirstily** *adv.*

thirteen *adj., n.* three plus ten. **thirteenth** *adj., n.*

thirty *adj., n.* three times ten. **thirtieth** *adj., n.*

this *adj., pron.* **1.** used to refer to a thing or person nearby or just mentioned. —*adj.* **2.** used to refer to the present time, e.g. *this morning.*

thistle *n.* prickly plant with dense flower heads. **thistledown** *n.* mass of feathery plumed seeds produced by thistles.

thither *adv. Obs.* to or towards that place.

tho, tho' *conj., adv.* short for THOUGH.

thole, tholepin n. wooden pin set in the side of a rowing boat to hold the oar in place.

thong n. thin strip of leather etc.

thorax n., pl. **thoraxes, thoraces.** part of the body between the neck and the abdomen. **thoracic** adj.

thorium n. radioactive metallic element.

thorn n. **1.** prickle on a plant. **2.** bush with thorns. **thorn in one's side,** flesh source of irritation. **thorny** adj. **1.** covered with thorns. **2.** (of a problem, subject) difficult or unpleasant.

thorough adj. **1.** careful or methodical. **2.** complete. **thoroughly** adv. **thoroughness** n. **thoroughbred** n., adj. (animal) of pure breed. **thoroughfare** n. way through from one place to another. **thoroughgoing** adj. extremely thorough.

those adj., pron. plural of THAT.

thou pron. Obs. singular form of YOU.

though conj. **1.** despite the fact that. —adv. **2.** nevertheless.

thought v. **1.** past of THINK. —n. **2.** thinking. **3.** concept or idea. **4.** ideas typical of a time or place. **5.** consideration. **6.** intention or expectation. **thoughtful** adj. **1.** considerate. **2.** showing careful thought. **3.** pensive or reflective. **thoughtless** adj. inconsiderate. **thoughtlessly** adv.

thousand adj., n. **1.** ten hundred. **2.** large but unspecified number. **thousandth** adj., n. (of) number one thousand in a series.

thrall, thraldom n. state of being in the power of another person.

thrash v. **1.** beat, esp. with a stick or whip. **2.** defeat soundly. **3.** move about wildly. **4.** thresh. **thrashing** n. severe beating. **thrash out** v. solve by thorough argument.

thread n. **1.** fine strand or yarn. **2.** spiral ridge on a screw, nut, or bolt. **3.** unifying theme. —v. **4.** pass thread through. **5.** fit (a film, tape, etc.) into a machine. **6.** pick (one's way etc.) with care. **threadbare** adj. **1.** (of fabric) with the nap worn off. **2.** hackneyed. **3.** shabby.

threat n. **1.** declaration of intent to harm. **2.** dangerous person or thing. **threaten** v. **1.** make or be a threat to. **2.** be a menacing indication of. **threatening** adj. **threateningly** adv.

three adj., n. one more than two. **threefold** adj., adv. (having) three times as many or as much. **threesome** n. group of three. **three-dimensional, 3-D** adj. having three dimensions. **three-ply** adj. **1.** (of wood) having three layers. **2.** (of wool) having three strands. **three-point turn** complete turn of a motor vehicle using forward and reverse gears. **three-quarter** adj. being three quarters of something.

threnody n., pl. **-dies.** lament for the dead.

thresh v. **1.** beat (wheat etc.) to separate the grain from the husks and straw. **2.** move about wildly.

threshold n. **1.** bar forming the bottom of a doorway. **2.** entrance. **3.** starting point. **4.** point at which a stimulus produces a response.

threw v. past tense of THROW.

thrice adv. Lit. three times.

thrift n. **1.** wisdom and caution with money. **2.** low-growing plant with pink flowers. **thrifty** adj. **thriftier, thriftiest. thriftily** adv. **thriftiness** n. **thriftless** adj.

thrill n. **1.** sudden feeling of excitement. —v. **2.** (cause to) feel a thrill. **thrilling** adj.

thriller n. book, film, etc. with an atmosphere of mystery or suspense.

thrive v. **thriving, thrived** or **throve, thrived** or **thriven. 1.** grow well. **2.** flourish or prosper.

throat n. **1.** front of the neck. **2.** passage from the mouth and nose to the stomach and lungs. **throaty** adj. (of the voice) hoarse.

throb v. **throbbing, throbbed. 1.** pulsate repeatedly. **2.** vibrate rhythmically. —n. **3.** throbbing.

throes pl. n. violent pangs or pains. **in the throes of** Informal struggling with difficulty with.

thrombosis n., pl. **-ses.** forming of a clot in a blood vessel or the heart.

throne n. **1.** ceremonial seat of a monarch or bishop. **2.** sovereign power.

throng n., v. crowd.

throstle n. song-thrush.

throttle n. **1.** device controlling the amount of fuel entering an engine. —v. **2.** strangle.

through prep. **1.** from end to end or side to side of. **2.** because of. **3.** during. —adj. **4.** finished. **5.** (of transport) going directly to a place. **6.** (on a telephone line) connected. **through and through** completely. **through-**

out *adv., prep.* in every part (of). **throughput** *n.* amount of material processed.

throve *v.* past tense of THRIVE.

throw *v.* **throwing, threw, thrown. 1.** hurl through the air. **2.** move or put suddenly or carelessly. **3.** bring into a specified state, esp. suddenly. **4.** direct (a look, light, etc.). **5.** give (a party). **6.** project (the voice) so that it seems to come from elsewhere. **7.** shape (pottery) on a wheel. **8.** move (a switch, lever, etc.). **9.** *Informal* baffle or disconcert. *—n.* **10.** throwing. **11.** distance thrown. **throwaway** *adj.* **1.** designed to be discarded after use. **2.** done or said casually. **throwback** *n.* person or thing that reverts to an earlier type. **throw up** *v.* vomit.

thrum *v.* **thrumming, thrummed. 1.** strum rhythmically but without expression on (a musical instrument). **2.** drum incessantly.

thrush[1] *n.* brown songbird.

thrush[2] *n.* fungal disease of the mouth or vagina.

thrust *v.* **thrusting, thrust. 1.** push forcefully. **2.** stab. *—n.* **3.** lunge or stab. **4.** force or power. **5.** intellectual or emotional drive.

thud *n.* **1.** dull heavy sound. *—v.* **thudding, thudded. 2.** make such a sound.

thug *n.* violent criminal. **thuggery** *n.* **thuggish** *adj.*

thulium *n.* malleable ductile silvery-grey element.

thumb *n.* **1.** short thick finger set apart from the others. *—v.* **2.** touch or handle with the thumb. **3.** flick through (a book or magazine). **4.** signal with the thumb for a lift in a vehicle. **thumb index** series of notches cut into the edge of a book to allow quick reference.

thump *n.* **1.** (sound of) a dull heavy blow. *—v.* **2.** strike heavily. **thumping** *adj. Informal* huge or excessive.

thunder *n.* **1.** loud noise accompanying lightning. *—v.* **2.** rumble with thunder. **3.** shout. **4.** move fast, heavily, and noisily. **thunderous** *adj.* **thundery** *adj.* **thunderbolt** *n.* **1.** lightning flash. **2.** something sudden and unexpected. **thunderclap** *n.* peal of thunder. **thunderstorm** *n.* storm with lightning and thunder. **thunderstruck** *adj.* taken aback, amazed.

Thursday *n.* fifth day of the week.

thus *adv.* **1.** in this way. **2.** therefore.

thwack *v., n.* whack.

thwart *v.* **1.** foil or frustrate. *—n.* **2.** seat across a boat.

thy *adj. Obs.* of or associated with you (thou). **thyself** *pron. Obs.* emphatic form of THOU.

thyme [time] *n.* aromatic herb.

thymol *n.* substance obtained from thyme, used as an antiseptic.

thymus *n., pl.* **-muses, -mi.** small gland at the base of the neck.

thyroid *adj., n.* (of) a gland in the neck controlling body growth.

ti *n. Music* same as TE.

Ti *Chem.* titanium.

tiara *n.* semicircular jewelled headdress.

tibia *n., pl.* **tibiae, tibias.** inner bone of the lower leg. **tibial** *adj.*

tic *n.* spasmodic muscular twitch.

tick[1] *n.* **1.** mark (✓) used to check off or indicate the correctness of something. **2.** recurrent tapping sound, as of a clock. **3.** *Informal* moment. *—v.* **4.** mark with a tick. **5.** make a ticking sound. **tick off** *v.* **1.** mark off. **2.** reprimand. **tick over** *v.* **1.** (of an engine) idle. **2.** function smoothly. **ticktack** *n.* bookmakers' sign language.

tick[2] *n.* tiny bloodsucking parasitic animal.

tick[3] *n. Informal* credit or account.

ticket *n.* **1.** card or paper entitling the holder to admission, travel, etc. **2.** label, esp. showing price. **3.** official notification of a parking or traffic offence. **4.** declared policy of a political party. *—v.* **-eting, -eted. 5.** attach or issue a ticket to.

ticking *n.* strong material for mattress covers.

tickle *v.* **1.** touch or stroke (a person) to produce laughter. **2.** please or amuse. **3.** itch or tingle. *—n.* **4.** tickling. **ticklish** *adj.* **1.** sensitive to tickling. **2.** requiring care or tact.

tiddler *n. Informal* very small fish. **tiddly** *adj.* **1.** tiny. **2.** *Informal* slightly drunk.

tiddlywinks *pl. n.* game in which players try to flip small plastic discs into a cup.

tide *n.* **1.** rise and fall of the sea caused by the gravitational pull of the sun and moon. **2.** current caused by this. **3.** widespread feeling or tendency. **tidal** *adj.* **tidal wave** huge wave produced by an earthquake. **tideline** *n.* mark left by the highest or lowest point of the tide. **tide over** *v.* help (someone) temporarily.

tidings pl. n. news.

tidy adj. **tidier, tidiest. 1.** neat and orderly. **2.** Informal considerable. —v. **tidying, tidied. 3.** put in order. **tidily** adv. **tidiness** n.

tie v. **tying, tied. 1.** fasten or be fastened with string, rope, etc. **2.** make (a knot or bow) in (something). **3.** restrict or limit. **4.** score the same as another competitor. —n. **5.** bond or fastening. **6.** long narrow piece of material worn knotted round the neck. **7.** drawn game or contest. **8.** match in an eliminating competition. **tiebreaker** n. extra game or question that decides the result of a contest ending in a draw. **tied** adj. **1.** (of a pub) allowed to sell only the beer of a particular brewery. **2.** (of a cottage etc.) rented to the tenant only as long as he or she is employed by the owner.

tier n. one of a set of rows placed one above and behind the other.

tiercel n. same as TERCEL.

tiff n. petty quarrel.

tiger n. large yellow-and-black striped Asian cat. **tigress** n. **1.** female tiger. **2.** Informal fierce woman.

tight adj. **1.** stretched or drawn taut. **2.** closely fitting. **3.** secure or firm. **4.** cramped. **5.** Informal mean. **6.** Informal drunk. **7.** (of a match or game) very close. **tights** pl. n. one-piece clinging garment covering the body from the waist to the feet. **tightly** adv. **tighten** v. make or become tight or tighter. **tightfisted** adj. very mean. **tight-lipped** adj. **1.** secretive. **2.** with lips pressed tightly together, as through anger. **tightrope** n. rope stretched taut on which acrobats perform.

tike n. Informal same as TYKE.

tilde n. accent (˜) used in Spanish to indicate that the letter 'n' is to be pronounced in a particular way.

tile n. **1.** flat piece of ceramic, plastic, etc. used to cover a roof, floor, or wall. —v. **2.** cover with tiles. **tiled** adj. **tiling** n. tiles collectively.

till[1] prep., conj. until.

till[2] v. cultivate (land). **tillage** n. **tiller** n.

till[3] n. drawer for money, usu. in a cash register.

tiller n. lever to move a rudder of a boat.

tilt v. **1.** slant at an angle. **2.** Hist. compete against in a jousting contest. —n. **3.** slope. **4.** Hist. jousting contest. **at full tilt** at full speed or force.

tilth n. **1.** tilled land. **2.** condition of land that has been tilled.

timber n. **1.** wood as a building material. **2.** trees collectively. **3.** wooden beam in the frame of a house, boat, etc. **timbered** adj. **timber line** altitude above which trees will not grow.

timbre [**tam**-bra] n. distinctive quality of sound of a voice or instrument.

time n. **1.** past, present, and future as a continuous whole. **2.** specific point in time. **3.** unspecified interval. **4.** period with specific features. **5.** instance. **6.** occasion. **7.** tempo. **8.** Slang imprisonment. —v. **9.** note the time taken by. **10.** choose a time for. **timeless** adj. **1.** unaffected by time. **2.** eternal. **timely** adj. at the appropriate time. **time-honoured** adj. sanctioned by custom. **time-lag** n. period between cause and effect. **timepiece** n. watch or clock. **timeserver** n. person who changes his or her views to gain support or favour. **time sharing 1.** system of part ownership of a holiday property for a specified period each year. **2.** system enabling users at different terminals of a computer to use it at the same time. **time signature** Music sign that indicates the tempo. **timetable** n. plan showing the times when something takes place, the departure and arrival times of trains or buses, etc. **time zone** region throughout which the same standard time is used.

timid adj. **1.** easily frightened. **2.** shy, not bold. **timidly** adv. **timidity** n. **timorous** [**tim**-mor-uss] adj. timid.

timpani [**tim**-pan-ee] pl. n. set of kettledrums. **timpanist** n.

tin n. **1.** soft metallic element. **2.** airtight metal container. **tinned** adj. (of food) preserved by being sealed in a tin. **tinny** adj. (of sound) thin and metallic. **tinpot** adj. Informal worthless or unimportant.

tincture n. medicinal extract in a solution of alcohol.

tinder n. dry easily-burning material used to start a fire. **tinderbox** n. formerly, small box for tinder, esp. one fitted with a flint and steel.

tine n. prong of a fork or antler.

ting n. high metallic sound, as of a small bell.

tinge n. **1.** slight tint. **2.** trace. —v. **tingeing**

or **tinging, tinged. 3.** give a slight tint or trace to.

tingle *v., n.* (feel) a prickling or stinging sensation.

tinker *n.* **1.** travelling mender of pots and pans. **2.** *Scot. & Irish* Gypsy. —*v.* **3.** fiddle with (an engine etc.) in an attempt to repair it.

tinkle *v.* **1.** ring with a high tinny sound like a small bell. —*n.* **2.** this sound or action.

tinsel *n.* **1.** decorative metallic strips or threads. **2.** anything cheap and gaudy.

tint *n.* **1.** (pale) shade of a colour. **2.** dye for the hair. **3.** trace. —*v.* **4.** give a tint to.

tintinnabulation *n.* the ringing or pealing of bells.

tiny *adj.* **tinier, tiniest.** very small.

tip[1] *n.* **1.** narrow or pointed end of anything. **2.** small piece forming an end. —*v.* **tipping, tipped. 3.** put a tip on.

tip[2] *n.* **1.** money given in return for service. **2.** helpful hint or warning. **3.** piece of inside information. —*v.* **tipping, tipped. 4.** give a tip to. **tipster** *n.* person who sells tips about races.

tip[3] *v.* **tipping, tipped. 1.** tilt or overturn. **2.** dump (rubbish). —*n.* **3.** rubbish dump.

tippet *n.* piece of fur worn as a scarf.

tipple *v.* **1.** drink (alcohol) habitually, esp. in small quantities. —*n.* **2.** drink. **tippler** *n.*

tipsy *adj.* **-sier, -siest.** slightly drunk.

tiptoe *v.* **-toeing, -toed.** walk quietly with the heels off the ground.

tiptop *adj.* of the highest quality or condition.

tirade *n.* long angry speech.

tire *v.* **1.** reduce the energy of, as by exertion. **2.** weary or bore. **tired** *adj.* **1.** weary. **2.** hackneyed or stale. **tiring** *adj.* **tireless** *adj.* not tiring easily. **tirelessly** *adv.* **tiresome** *adj.* boring and irritating.

tiro *n.*, *pl.* **-ros.** same as TYRO.

tissue *n.* **1.** substance of an animal body or plant. **2.** piece of thin soft paper used as a handkerchief etc. **3.** interwoven series, e.g. *a tissue of lies.*

tit[1] *n.* any of various small songbirds.

tit[2] *n. Slang* female breast.

titanic *adj.* huge or very important. **titan** *n.* person who is huge, strong or very important.

titanium *n.* strong light metallic element used to make alloys.

titbit *n.* **1.** tasty piece of food. **2.** pleasing scrap of scandal.

tit for tat *n.* equivalent given in retaliation.

tithe *Hist.* —*n.* **1.** one tenth of one's income or produce paid to the church as a tax. —*v.* **2.** charge a tithe.

Titian [**tish**-an] *adj.* (of hair) reddish-gold.

titillate *v.* excite or stimulate pleasurably. **titillating** *adj.* **titillation** *n.*

titivate *v.* smarten up. **titivation** *n.*

title *n.* **1.** name of a book, film, etc. **2.** name signifying rank or position. **3.** formal designation, such as *Mrs.* **4.** *Sport* championship. **5.** *Law* legal right of possession. **titled** *adj.* aristocratic. **title deed** legal document of ownership. **titleholder** *n.* person who holds a title, esp. a sporting championship. **title role** the role of the character after whom a film or play is named.

titration *n.* operation in which a measured amount of one solution is added to a known quantity of another solution until the reaction between the two is complete.

titter *v.* **1.** laugh in a suppressed way. —*n.* **2.** suppressed laugh.

tittle-tattle *n., v.* gossip.

titular *adj.* **1.** of a title. **2.** in name only.

tizzy *n., pl.* **-zies.** *Informal* confused or agitated state.

Tl *Chem.* thallium.

Tm *Chem.* thulium.

TNT *n.* trinitrotoluene, a powerful explosive.

to *prep.* **1.** towards. **2.** as far as. **3.** used to mark the indirect object or infinitive of a verb. **4.** used to indicate equality or comparison. **5.** before the hour of. —*adv.* **6.** to a closed position, e.g. *pull the door to.* **to and fro** back and forth.

toad *n.* animal like a large frog.

toad-in-the-hole *n.* sausages baked in batter.

toadstool *n.* poisonous fungus like a mushroom.

toady *n., pl.* **toadies. 1.** ingratiating person. —*v.* **toadying, toadied. 2.** be ingratiating.

toast *n.* **1.** slice of bread browned by heat. **2.** tribute or proposal of health or success marked by people raising glasses and drinking together. **3.** person or thing so honoured.

—*v.* **4.** brown bread by heat. **5.** drink a toast to. **6.** warm or be warmed. **toaster** *n.* electrical device for toasting bread.

tobacco *n., pl.* **-cos, -coes.** plant with large leaves dried for smoking. **tobacconist** *n.* person or shop selling tobacco, cigarettes, etc.

toboggan *n.* **1.** narrow sledge for sliding over snow. —*v.* **-ganing, -ganed. 2.** ride a toboggan.

toby jug *n.* mug in the form of a stout seated man.

toccata [tok-**kah**-ta] *n.* rapid piece of music for a keyboard instrument.

tocsin *n.* alarm signal or bell.

today *n.* **1.** this day. **2.** the present age. —*adv.* **3.** on this day. **4.** nowadays.

toddle *v.* walk with short unsteady steps. **toddler** *n.* child beginning to walk.

toddy *n., pl.* **-dies.** sweetened drink of spirits and hot water.

to-do *n., pl.* **-dos.** *Informal* fuss or commotion.

toe *n.* **1.** digit of the foot. **2.** part of a shoe or sock covering the toes. —*v.* **toeing, toed. 3.** touch or kick with the toe. **toecap** *n.* strengthened covering for the toe of a shoe. **toehold** *n.* **1.** small space on a mountain for supporting the toe of the foot in climbing. **2.** means of gaining access or advantage. **3.** small beginning, esp. in a career. **toe the line** conform.

toff *n. Slang* well-dressed or upper-class person.

toffee *n.* chewy sweet made of boiled sugar. **tofee-apple** *n.* apple fixed on a stick and coated with toffee. **toffee-nosed** *adj. Informal* snobbish.

tofu *n.* soft food made from soya-bean curd.

tog *n.* **1.** unit for measuring the insulating power of duvets. —*pl.* **2.** *Informal* clothes.

toga [**toe**-ga] *n.* garment worn by citizens of ancient Rome.

together *adv.* **1.** in company. **2.** simultaneously. —*adj.* **3.** *Informal* organized.
▷ Two nouns linked by *together* with do not make a plural subject so the following verb must be singular: *Jones, together with his partner, has had great success.*

toggle *n.* **1.** small bar-shaped button inserted through a loop for fastening. **2.** switch used to turn a machine or computer function on or off.

toil *n.* **1.** hard work. —*v.* **2.** work hard. **3.** progress with difficulty. **toilsome** *adj.* requiring hard work.

toilet *n.* **1.** (room with) a bowl connected to a drain for receiving and disposing of urine and faeces. **2.** washing and dressing. **toiletry** *n., pl.* **-ries.** object or cosmetic used to clean or groom oneself. **toilet paper** thin absorbent paper used for cleaning oneself after defecation. **toilet training** training of a young child to use the toilet.

toilet water *n.* light perfume.

token *n.* **1.** sign or symbol. **2.** memento. **3.** disc used as money in a slot machine. **4.** voucher exchangeable for goods of a specified value. —*adj.* **5.** nominal or slight. **tokenism** *n.* policy of making only a token effort, esp. to comply with a law.

told *v.* past of TELL.

tolerate *v.* **1.** put up with. **2.** permit. **toleration** *n.* **tolerable** *adj.* **1.** bearable. **2.** *Informal* quite good. **tolerably** *adv.* **tolerance** *n.* **1.** acceptance of other people's rights to their own opinions or actions. **2.** ability to endure something. **tolerant** *adj.* **tolerantly** *adv.* **toleration** *n.*

toll[1] *v.* **1.** ring (a bell) slowly and regularly, esp. to announce a death. —*n.* **2.** tolling.

toll[2] *n.* **1.** charge for the use of a bridge or road. **2.** total loss or damage from a disaster.

toluene *n.* colourless volatile flammable liquid obtained from petroleum and coal tar.

tom *n.* male cat.

tomahawk *n.* fighting axe of the N American Indians.

tomato *n., pl.* **-toes.** red fruit used in salads and as a vegetable.

tomb *n.* **1.** grave. **2.** monument over a grave. **tombstone** *n.* gravestone.

tombola *n.* lottery with tickets drawn from a revolving drum.

tomboy *n.* girl who acts or dresses like a boy.

tome *n.* large heavy book.

tomfoolery *n.* foolish behaviour.

Tommy *n., pl.* **-mies.** *Brit. informal* private soldier in the British army.

Tommy gun *n.* light sub-machine-gun.

tomorrow *adv., n.* **1.** (on) the day after today. **2.** (in) the future.

tom-tom *n.* drum beaten with the hands.

ton n. unit of weight equal to 2240 lbs or 1016 kg (**long ton**) or, in the US, 2000 lbs or 907 kg (**short ton**). **tonnage** n. weight capacity of a ship.

tone n. **1.** sound with reference to its pitch, volume, etc. **2.** *US music* note. **3.** *Music* (also **whole tone**) interval of two semitones. **4.** quality of a colour. **5.** general character. **6.** healthy bodily condition. —v. **7.** give tone to. **8.** harmonize (with). **tonal** adj. *Music* written in a key. **tonality** n. **toneless** adj. **tone-deaf** adj. unable to perceive subtle differences in pitch. **tone down** v. make or become more moderate. **tone up** v. to make or become more healthy.

tongs pl. n. large pincers for grasping and lifting.

tongue n. **1.** muscular organ in the mouth, used in speaking and tasting. **2.** animal tongue as food. **3.** language. **4.** flap of leather on a shoe. **5.** thin projecting strip. **tongue-tied** adj. speechless, esp. with shyness or embarrassment. **tongue twister** n. sentence or phrase that is difficult to say quickly.

tonguing n. technique of playing a wind instrument by obstructing and uncovering the air passage through the lips with the tongue.

tonic n. **1.** medicine to improve body tone. **2.** anything that is strengthening or cheering. **3.** *Music* first note of a scale. —adj. **4.** invigorating. **tonic (water)** n. mineral water containing quinine.

tonight adv., n. (in or during) the night or evening of this day.

tonne [tunn] n. unit of weight equal to 1000 kg.

tonsil n. small gland in the throat. **tonsillectomy** n. surgical removal of the tonsils. **tonsillitis** n. inflammation of the tonsils.

tonsure n. **1.** shaving of all or the top of the head as a religious or monastic practice. **2.** part shaved. **tonsured** adj.

too adv. **1.** also, as well. **2.** to excess. **3.** extremely.

took v. past tense of TAKE.

tool n. **1.** implement used by hand. **2.** person used by another to perform unpleasant or dishonourable tasks. —v. **3.** work on with a tool. **4.** equip with tools.

toot n. **1.** short hooting sound. —v. **2.** (cause to) make such a sound.

tooth n., pl. **teeth**. **1.** bonelike projection in the jaws of most vertebrates for biting and chewing. **2.** toothlike prong or point. **sweet tooth** liking for sweet food. **toothless** adj. **1.** lacking teeth. **2.** (of an official body) lacking power or influence. **toothpaste** n. paste used to clean the teeth. **toothpick** n. small stick for removing scraps of food from between the teeth.

top[1] n. **1.** highest point or part. **2.** lid or cap. **3.** highest rank. **4.** garment for the upper part of the body. —adj. **5.** at or of the top. —v. **topping, topped**. **6.** form a top on. **7.** be at the top of. **8.** exceed or surpass. **topping** n. sauce or garnish for food. **topless** adj. (of a costume or woman) with no covering for the breasts. **topmost** adj. highest or best. **top brass** most important officers or leaders. **top-dress** v. spread fertilizer on the surface of the land. **top-dressing** n. **top hat** man's tall cylindrical hat. **topheavy** adj. unstable through being overloaded at the top. **top-notch** adj. excellent, first-class. **top-secret** adj. (of military or government information) classified as needing the highest level of secrecy and security. **topsoil** n. surface layer of soil.

top[2] n. toy which spins on a pointed base.

topaz [toe-pazz] n. semiprecious stone in various colours.

tope n. small European shark.

topee, topi [toe-pee] n. lightweight pith hat worn in tropical countries.

topiary [tope-yar-ee] n. art of trimming trees and bushes into decorative shapes. **topiarist** n.

topic n. subject of a conversation, book, etc. **topical** adj. relating to current events. **topicality** n.

topography n., pl. **-phies**. (science of describing) the surface features of a place. **topographer** n. **topographic** adj.

topology n. geometry of the properties of a shape which are unaffected by continuous distortion. **topological** adj.

topple v. **1.** (cause to) fall over. **2.** overthrow (a government etc.).

topsy-turvy adj. **1.** upside down. **2.** in confusion.

toque [toke] n. small round hat.

tor n. high rocky hill.

Torah n. body of traditional Jewish teaching.

torch n. **1.** small portable battery-powered

lamp. **2.** wooden shaft dipped in wax and set alight. **carry a torch for** be in love with (someone).

tore v. past tense of TEAR².

toreador [torr-ee-a-dor] n. bullfighter.

torment v. **1.** cause (someone) great suffering. **2.** tease cruelly. —n. **3.** great suffering. **4.** source of suffering. **tormentor** n.

torn v. past participle of TEAR².

tornado n., pl. **-does, -dos.** violent whirlwind.

torpedo n., pl. **-does. 1.** self-propelled underwater missile. —v. **-doing, -doed. 2.** attack or destroy with or as if with torpedoes.

torpid adj. sluggish and inactive. **torpidity** n. **torpor** n. torpid state.

torque [tork] n. **1.** force causing rotation. **2.** Celtic necklace or armband of twisted metal.

torrent n. **1.** rushing stream. **2.** downpour. **torrential** adj.

torrid adj. **1.** very hot and dry. **2.** highly emotional.

torsion n. the twisting of a part by equal forces being applied at both ends but in opposite directions.

torso n., pl. **-sos. 1.** trunk of the human body. **2.** statue of a nude human trunk.

tort n. Law civil wrong or injury for which damages may be claimed.

tortilla n. thin Mexican pancake.

tortoise n. slow-moving land reptile with a dome-shaped shell. **tortoiseshell** n. **1.** mottled brown shell of a turtle, used for making ornaments. —adj. **2.** having brown, orange, and black markings.

tortuous adj. **1.** winding or twisting. **2.** not straightforward.

torture v. **1.** cause (someone) severe pain or mental anguish. —n. **2.** severe physical or mental pain. **3.** torturing. **torturer** n.

Tory n., pl. **Tories. 1.** member of the Conservative Party in Great Britain or Canada. —adj. **2.** of Tories. **Toryism** n.

toss v. **1.** throw lightly. **2.** fling or be flung about. **3.** (of a horse) throw (its rider). **4.** coat (food) by gentle stirring or mixing. **5.** throw up (a coin) to decide between alternatives by guessing which side will land uppermost. —n. **6.** tossing. **toss up** v. toss a coin. **toss-up** n. even chance or risk.

tot¹ n. **1.** small child. **2.** small drink of spirits.

tot² v. **totting, totted. tot up** add (numbers) together.

total n. **1.** whole, esp. a sum of parts. —adj. **2.** complete. **3.** of or being a total. —v. **-talling, -talled. 4.** amount to. **5.** add up. **totally** adv. **totality** n. **totalizator** n. machine operating a betting system in which money is paid out to the winners in proportion to their stakes.

totalitarian adj. of a dictatorial one-party government. **totalitarianism** n.

tote¹ n. short for TOTALIZATOR.

tote² v. haul or carry.

totem n. tribal badge or emblem. **totem pole** post carved or painted with totems by American Indians.

totter v. **1.** move unsteadily. **2.** be about to fall.

toucan n. tropical American bird with a large bill.

touch n. **1.** sense by which an object's qualities are perceived when they come into contact with part of the body. **2.** gentle tap, push, or caress. **3.** small amount. **4.** characteristic style. **5.** detail. —v. **6.** come into contact with. **7.** tap, feel, or stroke. **8.** affect. **9.** move emotionally. **10.** eat or drink. **11.** refer to in passing. **12.** equal or match. **13.** Slang ask for money. **touch and go** risky or critical. **touched** adj. **1.** emotionally moved. **2.** slightly mad. **touching** adj. emotionally moving. **touchy** adj. easily offended. **touch down** v. (of an aircraft) land.

touché [too-shay] interj. acknowledgment of the striking home of a remark or witty reply.

touchline n. side line of the pitch in some games.

touchstone n. standard by which a judgment is made.

touch-type v. type without looking at the keyboard.

touchwood n. dry wood used as tinder.

tough adj. **1.** strong or resilient. **2.** difficult to chew or cut. **3.** hardy and fit. **4.** rough and violent. **5.** difficult. **6.** firm and determined. **7.** Informal unlucky or unfair. —n. **8.** Informal rough violent person. **toughness** n. **toughen** v. make or become tough or tougher.

toupeé [too-pay] n. wig.

tour n. 1. journey visiting places of interest along the way. 2. trip to perform or play in different places. —v. 3. make a tour (of). **tourism** n. tourist travel as an industry. **tourist** n. person travelling for pleasure. **touristy** adj. Informal often derogatory full of tourists or tourist attractions.

tour de force n., pl. **tours de force.** French brilliant stroke or achievement.

tourmaline n. crystalline mineral used for optical instruments and as a gem.

tournament n. 1. sporting competition with several stages to decide the overall winner. 2. Hist. (also **tourney**) contest between knights on horseback.

tourniquet [**tour**-nick-kay] n. something twisted round a limb to stop bleeding.

tousled adj. ruffled and untidy.

tout [rhymes with **shout**] v. 1. solicit custom in a persistent manner. 2. obtain and sell information about racehorses. —n. 3. person who sells tickets for a popular event at inflated prices.

tow¹ v. 1. drag, esp. by means of a rope. —n. 2. towing. **in tow** following closely behind. **on tow** being towed. **towbar** n. metal bar on a car for towing vehicles. **towrope** n. rope or cable used for towing a vehicle or vessel. **towpath** n. path beside a canal or river, originally for horses towing boats.

tow² n. fibre of hemp or flax. **tow-headed** adj. with blond hair.

towards, toward prep. 1. in the direction of. 2. with regard to. 3. as a contribution to.
▷ *Towards* is usual. The form *toward* is chiefly American.

towel n. 1. cloth for drying things. —v. **-elling, -elled.** 2. to dry or wipe with a towel. **throw in the towel** give up completely. **towelling** n. material used for making towels.

tower n. 1. tall structure, often forming part of a larger building. —v. 2. be very tall. 3. loom (over). **tower block** tall building divided into flats or offices. **tower of strength** person who supports or comforts.

town n. 1. group of buildings larger than a village. 2. central part of this. 3. people of a town. **township** n. 1. small town. 2. in S Africa, urban settlement for Black or Coloured people only. **town hall** large building used for council meetings, concerts, etc. **town planning** comprehensive planning of the physical and social development of a town.

toxaemia [tox-**seem**-ya] n. 1. blood poisoning. 2. high blood pressure in pregnancy.

toxic adj. 1. poisonous. 2. caused by poison. **toxicity** n. **toxicology** n. study of poisons. **toxin** n. poison of bacterial origin.

toy n. 1. something designed to be played with. 2. miniature variety of a breed of dog. —adj. 3. very small. **toy with** v. play or fiddle with.

trace¹ n. 1. track left by something. 2. indication. 3. minute quantity. —v. 4. follow the course of. 5. track down and find. 6. copy exactly by drawing on a thin sheet of transparent paper set on top of the original. **traceable** adj. **tracer** n. projectile which leaves a visible trail. **tracery** n. pattern of interlacing lines. **tracing** n. traced copy. **trace element** chemical element occurring in very small amounts in soil etc.

trace² n. strap by which a horse pulls a vehicle. **kick over the traces** escape or defy control.

trachea [track-**kee**-a] n., pl. **tracheae.** windpipe. **tracheotomy** [track-ee-ot-a-mee] n. surgical incision into the trachea.

track n. 1. mark or trail left by the passage of anything. 2. rough road or path. 3. railway line. 4. course of action or thought. 5. endless band round the wheels of a tank, bulldozer, etc. 6. course for racing. 7. separate section on a record, tape, or CD. —v. 8. follow the trail or path of. **track down** v. hunt for and find. **track event** athletic sport held on a track. **track record** past accomplishments of a person or organization. **track shoe** light running shoe fitted with spikes for better grip. **tracksuit** n. warm loose-fitting suit worn by athletes etc., esp. during training.

tract¹ n. 1. wide area. 2. Anat. system of organs with a particular function.

tract² n. pamphlet, esp. a religious one.

tractable adj. easy to manage or control.

traction n. 1. pulling, esp. by engine power. 2. Med. application of a steady pull on an injured limb by weights and pulleys. 3. grip of the wheels of a vehicle on the ground. **traction engine** an old-fashioned steam-powered vehicle for pulling heavy loads.

tractor n. motor vehicle with large rear wheels for pulling farm machinery.

trad n. Brit. informal traditional jazz.

trade n. 1. buying, selling, or exchange of goods. 2. person's job or craft. 3. (people engaged in) a particular industry or business. —v. 4. buy and sell. 5. exchange. 6. engage in trade. **trader** n. **trading** n. **trade-in** n. used article given in part payment for a new one. **trademark, tradename** n. (legally registered) name or symbol used by a firm to distinguish its goods. **trade-off** n. exchange made as a compromise. **trade secret** secret formula, technique, or process known and used to advantage by only one manufacturer. **tradesman** n. 1. skilled worker. 2. shopkeeper. **trade union** society of workers for the protection of their interests. **trade wind** wind blowing steadily towards the equator.

tradescantia [trad-dess-**kan**-shee-a] n. a widely cultivated plant with striped variegated leaves.

tradition n. 1. unwritten body of beliefs, customs, etc. handed down from generation to generation. 2. custom or practice of long standing. **traditional** adj. **traditionally** adv. **traditionalist** n. person who supports established customs or beliefs. **traditionalism** n.

traduce v. slander.

traffic n. 1. vehicles coming and going on a road. 2. (illicit) trade. —v. **-ficking, -ficked.** 3. trade, usu. illicitly. **trafficker** n. **traffic lights** set of coloured lights at a junction to control the traffic flow. **traffic warden** person employed to control the movement and parking of traffic.

tragedy n., pl. **-dies.** 1. shocking or sad event. 2. serious play, film, etc. in which the hero is destroyed by a personal failing in adverse circumstances. **tragedian** [traj-jee-dee-an] n. actor in or writer of tragedies. **tragedienne** [traj-jee-dee-**enn**] n. actress in tragedies. **tragic** adj. of or like a tragedy. **tragically** adv. **tragicomedy** n. play with both tragic and comic elements.

trail v. 1. drag along the ground. 2. follow the tracks of. 3. lag behind. 4. (of plants) grow along the ground or hang loosely. —n. 5. track or trace. 6. path, track, or road. **trailer** n. 1. vehicle designed to be towed by another vehicle. 2. extract from a film or programme used to advertise it.

train v. 1. instruct in a skill. 2. cause (an animal) to perform or (a plant) to grow in a particular way. 3. aim (a gun etc.). 4. exercise in preparation for a sports event. —n. 5. line of railway coaches or wagons drawn by an engine. 6. sequence or series. 7. long trailing back section of a dress. 8. body of attendants. **trainer** n. 1. person who trains an athlete or sportsman. 2. person who trains racehorses. 3. piece of equipment employed in training, such as a simulated aircraft cockpit. 4. running shoe. **trainee** n. person being trained.

train spotter n. person who collects the numbers of railway trains.

traipse v. Informal walk wearily.

trait n. characteristic feature.

traitor n. person guilty of treason or treachery. **traitorous** adj.

trajectory n., pl. **-ries.** line of flight, esp. of a projectile.

tram n. public transport vehicle powered by an overhead wire and running on rails laid in the road. **tramlines** pl. n. track for trams.

trammel v. **-elling, -elled.** hinder or restrain.

tramp v. 1. travel on foot, hike. 2. walk heavily. —n. 3. homeless person who travels on foot. 4. hike. 5. sound of tramping. 6. cargo ship available for hire. 7. US promiscuous woman.

trample v. tread on and crush.

trampoline n. 1. tough canvas sheet attached to a frame by springs, used by acrobats etc. —v. 2. bounce on a trampoline.

trance n. 1. unconscious or dazed state. 2. state of ecstasy or total absorption.

tranquil adj. calm and quiet. **tranquilly** adv. **tranquillity** n. **tranquillize** v. make calm. **tranquillizer** n. drug which reduces anxiety or tension.

trans- prefix across, through, or beyond.

transact v. conduct or negotiate (a business deal). **transaction** n. 1. transacting. 2. business deal transacted.

transatlantic adj. on, from, or to the other side of the Atlantic.

transceiver n. combined radio transmitter and receiver.

transcend v. 1. rise above. 2. be superior to. **transcendence** n. **transcendent** adj. **transcendental** adj. 1. based on intuition rather than experience. 2. supernatural or mystical. **transcendentalism** n.

transcribe v. 1. copy out. 2. write down (something said). 3. record for a later broadcast. **4.** arrange (music) for a different instrument. **transcript** *n.* copy.

transducer *n.* device that converts one form of energy to another.

transept *n.* either of the two shorter wings of a cross-shaped church.

transfer *v.* **-ferring, -ferred. 1.** move or send from one person or place to another. **—n. 2.** transferring. **3.** design which can be transferred from one surface to another. **transferable** *adj.* **transference** *n.* transferring.

transfigure *v.* change in appearance. **transfiguration** *n.*

transfix *v.* **1.** astound or stun. **2.** pierce through.

transform *v.* change the shape or character of. **transformation** *n.* **transformer** *n.* device for changing the voltage of an alternating current.

transfusion *n.* injection of blood into the blood vessels of a patient. **transfuse** *v.* **1.** give a transfusion to. **2.** permeate or infuse.

transgress *v.* break (a moral law). **transgression** *n.* **transgressor** *n.*

transient *adj.* lasting only for a short time. **transience** *n.*

transistor *n.* **1.** semiconducting device used to amplify electric currents. **2.** portable radio using transistors. **transistorized** *adj.*

transit *n.* going from one place to another. **transition** *n.* change from one state to another. **transitional** *adj.* **transitive** *adj.* (of a verb) requiring a direct object. **transitory** *adj.* not lasting long.

translate *v.* turn from one language into another. **translatable** *adj.* **translation** *n.* **1.** piece of writing or speech translated into another language. **2.** *Maths* transformation in which the origin of a coordinate system is moved to another position so that each axis retains the same direction. **translator** *n.*

transliterate *v.* convert to the letters of a different alphabet. **transliteration** *n.*

translucent *adj.* letting light pass through, but not transparent. **translucence** *n.*

transmigrate *v.* (of a soul) pass into another body. **transmigration** *n.*

transmit *v.* **-mitting, -mitted. 1.** pass (something) from one person or place to another. **2.** send out (signals) by radio waves. **3.** broadcast (a radio or television programme). **transmission** *n.* **1.** transmitting. **2.** shafts and gears through which power passes from a vehicle's engine to its wheels. **transmittable** *adj.* **transmitter** *n.* **1.** person or thing that transmits. **2.** piece of equipment used for broadcasting radio or television programmes.

transmogrify *v.* **-fying, -fied.** *Informal* change completely.

transmute *v.* change the form or nature of. **transmutation** *n.*

transom *n.* **1.** horizontal bar across a window. **2.** bar separating a door from the window over it.

transparent *adj.* **1.** able to be seen through, clear. **2.** easily understood or recognized. **transparently** *adv.* **transparency** *n.* **1.** transparent quality. **2.** *pl.* **-cies.** colour photograph on transparent film, viewed by means of a projector.

transpire *v.* **1.** become known. **2.** *Informal* happen. **3.** give off water vapour through pores. **transpiration** *n.*
▷ *Transpire* is so often used for 'happen' or 'occur' that the objection that it should be used only for 'become known' is no longer valid.

transplant *v.* **1.** remove and transfer (a plant) to another place. **2.** transfer (an organ or tissue) surgically from one part or body to another. **—n. 3.** surgical transplanting. **4.** thing transplanted. **transplantation** *n.*

transport *v.* **1.** convey from one place to another. **2.** *Hist.* exile (a criminal) to a penal colony. **3.** enrapture. **—n. 4.** business or system of transporting. **5.** vehicle used in transport. **6.** ecstasy or rapture. **transportation** *n.* **transporter** *n.* large goods vehicle.

transpose *v.* **1.** interchange two things. **2.** put (music) into a different key. **3.** *Maths* move (a term) from one side of an equation to the other with a corresponding reversal in sign. **transposition** *n.*

transsexual *n.* person who has had a sex-change operation.

transubstantiation *n.* *Christianity* doctrine that the bread and wine consecrated in Communion changes into the substance of Christ's body.

transuranic [tranz-yoor-**ran**-ik] *adj.* (of an element) having an atomic number greater than that of uranium.

transverse *adj.* crossing from side to side.

transvestite *n.* person who seeks sexual

pleasure by wearing the clothes of the opposite sex. **transvestism** n.

trap n. **1.** device for catching animals. **2.** plan for tricking or catching a person. **3.** bend in a pipe containing liquid to prevent the escape of gas. **4.** stall in which greyhounds are enclosed before a race. **5.** Hist. two-wheeled carriage. **6.** Slang mouth. —v. **trapping, trapped.** **7.** catch. **8.** trick. **trapper** n. person who traps animals for their fur. **trapdoor** n. door in floor or roof.

trapeze n. horizontal bar suspended from two ropes, used by circus acrobats.

trapezium n., pl. **-ziums, -zia.** quadrilateral with two parallel sides of unequal length. **trapezoid** [trap-piz-zoid] n. **1.** quadrilateral with no sides parallel. **2.** US trapezium.

trappings pl. n. the accessories that symbolize an office or position.

Trappist n. member of an order of Christian monks who observe strict silence.

trash n. **1.** anything worthless. **2.** US rubbish. **trashy** adj.

trauma [traw-ma] n. **1.** emotional shock. **2.** injury or wound. **traumatic** adj. **traumatically** adv. **traumatize** v.

travail v., n. Lit. labour or toil.

travel v. **-elling, -elled. 1.** go from one place to another, through an area, or for a specified distance. —n. **2.** travelling, esp. as a tourist. —pl. **3.** (account of) travelling. **traveller** n. person who makes a journey or travels a lot. **travelogue** n. film or talk about someone's travels. **travel agency** agency that arranges holidays. **traveller's cheque** cheque sold by a bank to the bearer, who signs it on purchase and cashes it abroad by signing it again.

traverse v. **1.** move over or back and forth over. **2.** move sideways. —n. **3.** traversing. **4.** path or road across.

travesty n., pl. **-ties. 1.** grotesque imitation or mockery. —v. **-tying, -tied. 2.** make or be a travesty of.

trawl n. **1.** net dragged at deep levels behind a fishing boat. —v. **2.** fish with such a net. **trawler** n. trawling boat.

tray n. **1.** flat board, usu. with a rim, for carrying things. **2.** open receptacle for office correspondence.

treachery n., pl. **-eries.** wilful betrayal. **treacherous** adj. **1.** disloyal. **2.** unreliable or dangerous. **treacherously** adv.

treacle n. thick dark syrup produced when sugar is refined. **treacly** adj.

tread v. **treading, trod, trodden** or **trod. 1.** set one's foot on. **2.** crush by walking on. —n. **3.** way of walking or dancing. **4.** treading. **5.** upper surface of a step. **6.** part of a tyre that touches the ground. **tread water** stay afloat in an upright position by moving the legs in a walking motion. **treadmill** n. **1.** Hist. cylinder turned by treading on steps projecting from it. **2.** dreary routine.

treadle [tred-dl] n. lever worked by the foot to turn a wheel.

treason n. **1.** betrayal of one's sovereign or country. **2.** treachery or disloyalty. **treasonable, treasonous** adj.

treasure n. **1.** collection of wealth, esp. gold or jewels. **2.** valued person or thing. —v. **3.** prize or cherish. **treasurer** n. official in charge of funds. **treasury** n. **1.** storage place for treasure. **2.** government department in charge of finance. **treasure-trove** n. treasure found with no evidence of ownership.

treat n. **1.** pleasure, entertainment, etc. given or paid for by someone else. —v. **2.** deal with or regard in a certain manner. **3.** give medical treatment to. **4.** subject to a chemical or industrial process. **5.** provide (someone) with (something) as a treat. **treatment** n. **1.** way of treating a person or thing. **2.** medical care.

treatise [treat-izz] n. formal piece of writing on a particular subject.

treaty n., pl. **-ties.** signed contract between states.

treble adj. **1.** threefold, triple. **2.** Music high-pitched. —n. **3.** (singer with or part for) a soprano voice. —v. **4.** increase threefold. **trebly** adv.

tree n. large perennial plant with a woody trunk. **treeless** adj. **tree surgery** repair of damaged trees. **tree surgeon**

trefoil [tref-foil] n. **1.** plant, such as clover, with a three-lobed leaf. **2.** carved ornament like this.

trek n. **1.** long difficult journey, esp. on foot. **2.** S Afr. migration by ox wagon. —v. **trekking, trekked. 3.** make such a journey.

trellis n. framework of horizontal and vertical strips of wood.

tremble v. **1.** shake or quiver. **2.** feel fear or anxiety. —n. **3.** trembling. **trembling** adj.

tremendous adj. 1. huge. 2. Informal great in quality or amount. **tremendously** adv.

tremolo n., pl. -los. Music quivering effect in singing or playing.

tremor n. 1. involuntary shaking. 2. minor earthquake.

tremulous adj. trembling, as from fear or excitement. **tremulously** adv.

trench n. long narrow ditch, esp. one used as a shelter in war. **trench coat** double-breasted waterproof coat.

trenchant adj. 1. incisive. 2. effective.

trencher n. Hist. wooden plate for serving food. **trencherman** n. hearty eater.

trend n. 1. general tendency or direction. 2. fashion. **trendy** adj., n. Informal consciously fashionable (person). **trendiness** n. **trendsetter** n. person or thing that creates, or may create, a new fashion. **trendsetting** adj.

trepidation n. fear or anxiety.

trespass v. 1. go onto another's property without permission. —n. 2. trespassing. 3. Old-fashioned sin or wrongdoing. **trespasser** n. **trespass on** v. take unfair advantage of (someone's friendship, patience, etc.).

tress n. long lock of hair.

trestle n. board fixed on pairs of spreading legs, used as a support.

trews pl. n. close-fitting tartan trousers.

tri- combining form three.

triad n. 1. group of three. 2. (T-) Chinese criminal secret society.

trial n. 1. trying or testing. 2. Law investigation of a case before a judge. 3. thing or person straining endurance or patience. —pl. 4. sporting competition for individuals. **trial and error** method of discovery based on practical experience and experiment rather than theory.

triangle n. 1. geometric figure with three sides. 2. triangular percussion instrument. 3. situation involving three people. **triangular** adj.

tribe n. group of clans or families believed to have a common ancestor. **tribal** adj. **tribalism** n. loyalty to a tribe.

tribulation n. great distress.

tribunal n. 1. lawcourt. 2. board appointed to inquire into a specific matter.

tribune n. people's representative in ancient Rome.

tributary n., pl. -taries. 1. stream or river flowing into a larger one. —adj. 2. (of a stream or river) flowing into a larger one.

tribute n. 1. sign of respect or admiration. 2. tax paid by one state to another.

trice n. **in a trice** instantly.

triceps n. muscle at the back of the upper arm.

trichology [trick-ol-a-jee] n. study and treatment of hair and its diseases. **trichologist** n.

trichromatic adj. 1. having or involving three colours. 2. of or having normal colour vision. **trichromatism** n.

trick n. 1. deceitful or cunning action or plan. 2. joke or prank. 3. feat of skill or cunning. 4. knack. 5. mannerism. 6. cards played in one round. —v. 7. cheat or deceive. **trickery** n. **trickster** n. **tricky** adj. 1. difficult, needing careful handling. 2. crafty.

trickle v. 1. (cause to) flow in a thin stream or drops. 2. move gradually. —n. 3. gradual flow.

tricolour [trick-kol-lor] n. three-coloured striped flag.

tricot n. 1. thin rayon or nylon fabric knitted or resembling knitting. 2. ribbed dress fabric.

tricycle n. three-wheeled cycle.

trident n. three-pronged spear.

triennial adj. happening every three years.

trifle n. 1. insignificant thing. 2. small amount. 3. dessert of sponge cake, custard, etc. —v. 4. (usu. foll. by with) toy with. **trifling** adj. insignificant.

trigger n. 1. small lever releasing a catch on a gun or machine. 2. action that sets off a course of events. —v. 3. (usu. foll. by off) set (an action or process) in motion. **trigger-happy** adj. too quick to use guns.

trigonometry n. branch of mathematics dealing with relations of the sides and angles of triangles. **trigonometrical** adj.

trike n. Informal tricycle.

trilateral adj. having three sides.

trilby n., pl. -bies. man's soft felt hat.

trill n. 1. rapid alternation between two notes. 2. shrill warbling sound made by some birds. —v. 3. play or sing a trill.

trillion n. 1. Brit. one million million million, 10^{18}. 2. US one million million, 10^{12}.
▷ A trillion is what British speakers used to call 'a billion'.

trilobite [**trile**-oh-bite] *n.* small prehistoric sea animal.

trilogy [**trill**-a-jee] *n., pl.* **-gies.** series of three related books, plays, etc.

trim *adj.* **trimmer, trimmest. 1.** neat and smart. **2.** slender. **3.** in good condition. —*v.* **trimming, trimmed. 4.** cut or prune into good shape. **5.** decorate with lace, ribbons, etc. **6.** adjust the balance of (a ship or aircraft) by shifting the cargo etc. **7.** adjust the sails of a ship to take advantage of the wind. —*n.* **8.** decoration. **9.** upholstery and decorative facings in a car. **10.** trim state. **11.** haircut that neatens the existing style. **trimming** *n.* **1.** decoration. —*pl.* **2.** usual accompaniments, e.g. *turkey with all the trimmings.*

trimaran [**trime**-a-ran] *n.* three-hulled boat.

trinitrotoluene *n.* full name of TNT.

trinity *n., pl.* **-ties. 1.** group of three. **2.** (T-) *Christianity* union of three persons, Father, Son, and Holy Spirit, in one God.

trinket *n.* small or worthless ornament or piece of jewellery.

trio *n., pl.* **trios. 1.** group of three. **2.** piece of music for three performers.

triode *n. Electronics* three-electrode valve.

trip *n.* **1.** journey to a place and back, esp. for pleasure. **2.** stumble. **3.** switch on a mechanism. **4.** *Informal* hallucinogenic drug experience. —*v.* **tripping, tripped. 5.** (cause to) stumble. **6.** (often foll. by *up*) catch (someone) in a mistake. **7.** move or tread lightly. **8.** operate (a switch). **9.** *Informal* take a hallucinogenic drug. **tripper** *n.* tourist.

tripartite *adj.* involving or composed of three people or parts.

tripe *n.* **1.** stomach of a cow used as food. **2.** *Informal* nonsense.

triplane *n.* aeroplane with three wings one above another.

triple *adj.* **1.** having three parts. **2.** three times as great or as many. **3.** (of musical time or rhythm) having three beats in each bar. —*v.* **4.** increase threefold. **triplet** *n.* one of three babies born at one birth. **triple jump** athletics event in which competitors make a hop, a step, and a jump as a continuous movement.

triplicate *adj.* **1.** triple. —*n.* **2.** one of three copies. **in triplicate** in three copies.

tripod [**tripe**-pod] *n.* three-legged stand, stool, etc.

tripos [**tripe**-poss] *n.* final examinations for the degree of BA at Cambridge University.

triptych [**trip**-tick] *n.* painting or carving on three hinged panels, often forming an altarpiece.

trisect *v.* divide into three equal parts. **trisection** *n.*

trite *adj.* (of a remark or idea) commonplace and unoriginal.

tritium *n.* radioactive isotope of hydrogen.

triumph *n.* **1.** (happiness caused by) victory or success. —*v.* **2.** be victorious or successful. **3.** rejoice over a victory. **triumphal** *adj.* celebrating a triumph. **triumphant** *adj.* feeling or showing triumph. **triumphantly** *adv.*

triumvirate [try-**umm**-vir-rit] *n.* group of three people in joint control.

trivalent *adj.* **1.** *Chem.* having a valency of three. **2.** having three valencies. **trivalency** *n.*

trivet [**triv**-vit] *n.* metal stand for a pot or kettle.

trivial *adj.* **1.** of little importance. **2.** everyday, trite. **trivially** *adv.* **trivia** *pl. n.* trivial things or details. **triviality** *n.* **trivialize** *v.* make (something) seem less important or complex than it is.

trod *v.* past tense and a past participle of TREAD.

trodden *v.* a past participle of TREAD.

troglodyte *n.* cave dweller.

troika *n.* **1.** Russian vehicle drawn by three horses abreast. **2.** group of three people in authority.

Trojan *n.* **1.** person from ancient Troy. **2.** hard-working person. —*adj.* **3.** hardworking. **Trojan Horse** trap intended to undermine an enemy.

troll[1] *n.* giant or dwarf in Scandinavian folklore.

troll[2] *v.* fish for by dragging a baited hook through the water.

trolley *n.* **1.** small wheeled table for food and drink. **2.** wheeled cart for moving goods. **trolleybus** *n.* bus powered by electricity from an overhead wire but not running on rails.

trollop *n.* promiscuous or slovenly woman.

trombone *n.* brass musical instrument with a sliding tube. **trombonist** *n.*

troop n. **1.** large group. **2.** artillery or cavalry unit. **3.** Scout company. —pl. **4.** soldiers. —v. **5.** move in a crowd. **6.** Brit. mil. parade (the colour or flag of a regiment) ceremonially. **trooper** n. cavalry soldier.

trope n. figure of speech.

trophy n., pl. **-phies. 1.** cup, shield, etc. given as a prize. **2.** memento of success.

tropic n. **1.** either of two lines of latitude at 23½° N (**tropic of Cancer**) or 23½°S (**tropic of Capricorn**). —pl. **2.** part of the earth's surface between these lines. **tropical** adj. **1.** of or in the tropics. **2.** (of climate) very hot.

tropism n. tendency of a plant or animal to turn or curve in response to an external stimulus.

troposphere n. lowest layer of the earth's atmosphere.

trot v. **trotting, trotted. 1.** move or cause (a horse) to move at a medium pace, lifting the feet in diagonal pairs. **2.** (of a person) move at a steady brisk pace. —n. **3.** trotting. **trotter** n. pig's foot. **trot out** v. repeat (old ideas etc.) without fresh thought.

troth [rhymes with **growth**] n. pledge of devotion, esp. a betrothal.

Trotskyite, Trotskyist n., adj. (supporter) of the theories of Leon Trotsky, Russian communist writer.

troubadour [**troo**-bad-oor] n. medieval travelling poet and singer.

trouble n. **1.** (cause of) distress or anxiety. **2.** disease or malfunctioning. **3.** care or effort. —v. **4.** (cause to) worry. **5.** cause inconvenience to. **6.** exert oneself. **troubled** adj. **troublesome** adj. **trouble-free** adj. causing no difficulties. **troublemaker** n. person who causes trouble, esp. between people. **troubleshooter** n. person employed to locate and deal with faults or problems.

trough [troff] n. **1.** long open container, esp. for animals' food or water. **2.** narrow channel between two waves or ridges. **3.** Meteorol. area of low pressure.

trounce v. defeat utterly.

troupe [troop] n. company of performers. **trouper** n.

trousers pl. n. two-legged outer garment with legs reaching usu. to the ankles. **trouser** adj. of trousers.

trousseau [**troo**-so] n., pl. **-seaux, -seaus.** bride's collection of clothing etc. for her marriage.

trout n. game fish related to the salmon.

trowel n. hand tool with a flat wide blade for spreading mortar, lifting plants, etc.

troy weight, troy n. system of weights used for gold, silver, and jewels.

truant n. pupil who stays away from school without permission. **play truant** stay away from school without permission. **truancy** n.

truce n. temporary agreement to stop fighting.

truck¹ n. **1.** railway goods wagon. **2.** US lorry. **trucker** n. US lorry driver.

truck² n. **have no truck with** refuse to be involved with.

truckle v. (usu. foll. by to) yield weakly.

truckle bed n. low bed on wheels, stored under a larger bed.

truculent [**truck**-yew-lent] adj. aggressively defiant. **truculence** n.

trudge v. **1.** walk heavily or wearily. —n. **2.** long tiring walk.

true adj. **truer, truest. 1.** in accordance with facts. **2.** faithful. **3.** exact. **4.** genuine. **truly** adv. **truism** n. self-evident truth. **truth** n. **1.** state of being true. **2.** something true. **truthful** adj. **1.** honest. **2.** exact. **truthfully** adv.

true-blue adj. fiercely loyal. **true blue** Brit. staunch Royalist or Conservative.

truffle n. **1.** edible underground fungus. **2.** sweet flavoured with chocolate.

trug n. long shallow basket used by gardeners.

trump¹ n., adj. **1.** (card) of the suit temporarily outranking the others. —v. **2.** play a trump card on (another card). —pl. n. **3.** trump suit. **turn up trumps** turn out unexpectedly well. **trump up** v. invent or concoct.

trump² n. Lit. (sound of) a trumpet.

trumpery n. **1.** foolish talk or actions. **2.** useless or worthless article. —adj. **3.** useless or worthless.

trumpet n. **1.** valved brass instrument with a flared tube. —v. **-peting, -peted. 2.** (of an elephant) cry loudly. **3.** proclaim loudly. **trumpeter** n.

truncate v. cut short.

truncheon n. small club carried by a policeman.

trundle v. move heavily on wheels.

trunk n. **1.** main stem of a tree. **2.** person's body excluding the head and limbs. **3.** large case or box for clothes etc. **4.** elephant's long nose. **5.** US car boot. —pl. **6.** man's swimming shorts. **trunk call** long-distance telephone call. **trunk road** main road.

truss v. **1.** tie or bind up. —n. **2.** device for holding a hernia in place. **3.** framework supporting a roof, bridge, etc.

trust n. **1.** confidence in the truth, reliability, etc. of a person or thing. **2.** obligation arising from responsibility. **3.** charge or care. **4.** arrangement in which one person administers property, money, etc. on another's behalf. **5.** property held for another. **6.** group of companies joined to control a market. —v. **7.** believe in and rely on. **8.** expect or hope. **9.** consign to someone's care. **trustee** n. person holding property on another's behalf. **trusteeship** n. **trustful, trusting** adj. inclined to trust. **trustworthy** adj. reliable or honest. **trusty** adj. faithful or reliable. **trust fund** money or securities held in trust.

truth n. see TRUE.

try v. **trying, tried. 1.** make an effort or attempt. **2.** test or sample. **3.** put strain on, e.g. he tries my patience. **4.** investigate (a case). **5.** examine (a person) in a lawcourt. —n., pl. **tries. 6.** attempt or effort. **7.** Rugby score gained by touching the ball down over the opponent's goal line. **try it on** Informal try to deceive or fool someone. **trying** adj. Informal difficult or annoying.
▷ The idiom try to can be used at any time. The alternative try and is less formal and often signals a 'dare': Just try and stop me!

tryst n. Old-fashioned arrangement to meet.

tsar [zahr] n. Hist. Russian emperor.

tsetse [tset-see] n. bloodsucking African fly whose bite transmits disease, esp. sleeping sickness.

T-shirt n. short-sleeved casual shirt or top.

tsp. teaspoon.

T-square n. T-shaped ruler.

tsunami n., pl. **-mis, -mi.** tidal wave, usu. caused by an earthquake under the sea.

TT teetotal.

tub n. **1.** open, usu. round container. **2.** bath. **tubby** adj. (of a person) short and fat.

tuba [tube-a] n. valved low-pitched brass instrument.

tube n. **1.** hollow cylinder. **2.** flexible cylinder with a cap to hold pastes. **the tube** underground railway, esp. the one in London. **tubing** [tube-ing] n. **1.** length of tube. **2.** system of tubes. **tubular** [tube-yew-lar] adj. of or like a tube.

tuber [tube-er] n. fleshy underground root of a plant such as a potato. **tuberous** [tube-er-uss] adj.

tubercle [tube-er-kl] n. small rounded swelling.

tuberculosis [tube-berk-yew-lohss-iss] n. infectious disease causing tubercles, esp. in the lungs. **tubercular** [tube-berk-yew-lar] adj. of tuberculosis. **tuberculin** n. extract from a bacillus used to test for tuberculosis.

TUC Trades Union Congress.

tuck v. **1.** push or fold into a small space. **2.** stitch in folds. —n. **3.** stitched fold. **4.** Informal food. **tuck away** v. store in a safe place.

Tudor adj. **1.** of the English royal house ruling from 1485–1603. **2.** in an architectural style characterized by half-timbered buildings.

Tuesday n. third day of the week.

tufa [tew-fa] n. porous rock formed as a deposit from springs.

tuff n. hard volcanic rock consisting of consolidated fragments of lava.

tuffet n. small mound or seat.

tuft n. bunch of feathers, grass, hair, etc. held or growing together at the base. **tufted** adj.

tug v. **tugging, tugged. 1.** pull hard. —n. **2.** hard pull. **3.** (also **tugboat**) small ship used to tow other vessels. **tug of war** contest in which two teams pull against one another on a rope.

tuition n. instruction, esp. received individually or in a small group.

tulip n. plant with bright cup-shaped flowers.

tulle [tewl] n. fine net fabric of silk etc.

tumble v. **1.** (cause to) fall, esp. awkwardly or violently. **2.** roll or twist, esp. in play. **3.** rumple. —n. **4.** fall. **5.** somersault. **tumbler** n. **1.** stemless drinking glass. **2.** acrobat. **3.** spring catch in a lock. **tumbledown** adj. dilapidated. **tumble dryer, tumbler dryer** machine that dries laundry by rotating it in warm air. **tumble to** v. Informal realize, understand.

tumbrel, tumbril n. farm cart used during the French Revolution to take prisoners to the guillotine.

tumescent [tew-**mess**-ent] adj. swollen or becoming swollen. **tumescence** n.

tummy n., pl. **-mies.** Informal stomach.

tumour [**tew**-mer] n. abnormal growth in or on the body.

tumult [**tew**-mult] n. uproar or commotion. **tumultuous** [tew-**mull**-tew-uss] adj.

tumulus [**tew**-mew-luss] n., pl. **-li** [-lie] burial mound.

tun n. large beer cask.

tuna [**tune**-a] n. large marine food fish.

tundra n. vast treeless Arctic region with permanently frozen subsoil.

tune n. **1.** (pleasing) sequence of musical notes. **2.** correct musical pitch, e.g. she sang out of tune. —v. **3.** adjust (a musical instrument) so that it is in tune. **4.** adjust (a machine) to obtain the desired performance. **tuneful** adj. **tunefully** adv. **tuneless** adj. **tuner** n. part of a radio or television receiver for selecting channels. **tune in** v. adjust (a radio or television) to receive (a station or programme). **tuning fork** small steel instrument which produces a note of a fixed musical pitch when struck.

tungsten n. greyish-white metal.

tunic n. **1.** close-fitting jacket forming part of some uniforms. **2.** loose knee-length garment.

tunnel n. **1.** underground passage. —v. **-nelling, -nelled. 2.** make a tunnel (through). **tunnel vision 1.** condition in which a person is unable to see things that are not straight in front of him or her. **2.** narrowness of viewpoint caused by concentration on a single idea or opinion.

tunny n., pl. **-nies, -ny.** same as TUNA.

tup n. male sheep.

turban n. Muslim or Sikh man's head covering, made by winding cloth round the head.

turbid adj. muddy, not clear. **turbidity** n.

turbine n. machine or generator driven by gas, water, etc. turning blades.

turbo- combining form of or powered by a turbine. **turbocharger** n. device that increases the power of an internal-combustion engine by using the exhaust gases to drive a turbine. **turbofan** n. engine in which a large fan driven by a turbine forces air rearwards

around the exhaust gases to increase the thrust. **turboprop** n. gas turbine for driving an aircraft propeller.

turbot n. large European edible flatfish.

turbulence n. **1.** confusion, movement, or agitation. **2.** atmospheric instability causing gusty air currents. **turbulent** adj.

tureen n. serving dish for soup.

turf n., pl. **turfs, turves. 1.** short thick even grass. **2.** square of this with roots and soil attached. —v. **3.** cover with turf. **the turf 1.** horse racing. **2.** racecourse. **turf accountant** bookmaker. **turf out** v. Informal throw out.

turgid [**tur**-jid] adj. **1.** swollen and thick. **2.** (of language) pompous. **turgidity** n.

turkey n. large bird bred for food.

Turkish adj. **1.** of Turkey, its people, or their language. —n. **2.** Turkish language. **Turkish bath** steam bath. **Turkish delight** jelly-like sweet coated with icing sugar.

turmeric n. yellow spice obtained from the root of an Asian plant.

turmoil n. agitation or confusion.

turn v. **1.** move around an axis, rotate. **2.** change the position or direction (of). **3.** (usu. foll. by into) change in nature or character. **4.** become sour. **5.** shape on a lathe. **6.** go round (a corner). **7.** reach or pass in age, time, etc, e.g. she has just turned twenty. —n. **8.** turning. **9.** direction or drift. **10.** opportunity to do something as part of an agreed succession. **11.** period or spell. **12.** short theatrical performance. **good, bad turn** helpful or unhelpful act. **turner** n. **turning** n. road or path leading off a main route. **turncoat** n. person who deserts one party or cause to join another. **turn down** v. **1.** refuse or reject. **2.** reduce the volume or brightness (of). **turn in** v. **1.** go to bed. **2.** hand in. **turning circle** smallest circle in which a vehicle can turn. **turning point** moment when a decisive change occurs. **turn off** v. stop (something) working by using a knob etc. **turn on** v. **1.** start (something) working by using a knob etc. **2.** become aggressive towards. **3.** Informal excite, esp. sexually. **turnout** n. **1.** number of people appearing at a gathering. **2.** outfit. **turnover** n. **1.** total sales made by a business over a certain period. **2.** rate at which staff leave and are replaced. **3.** small pastry. **turnpike** n. road where a toll is collected at barriers. **turnstile** n. revolving gate for admitting one person at a time. **turntable** *n.* revolving platform. **turn up** *v.* **1.** arrive or appear. **2.** find or be found. **3.** increase the volume or brightness (of). **turn-up** *n.* **1.** turned-up fold at the bottom of a trouser leg. **2.** *Informal* unexpected event.

turnip *n.* root vegetable with orange or white flesh.

turpentine *n.* (oil made from) the resin of certain trees. **turps** *n.* turpentine oil.

turpitude *n.* depravity.

turquoise *n.* **1.** blue-green precious stone. —*adj.* **2.** blue-green.

turret *n.* **1.** small tower. **2.** revolving gun tower on a warship or tank. **turreted** *adj.*

turtle *n.* sea tortoise. **turn turtle** capsize. **turtledove** *n.* small wild dove.

turtleneck *n.* (sweater with) a round high close-fitting neck.

tusk *n.* long pointed tooth of an elephant, walrus, etc.

tussle *n., v.* fight or scuffle.

tussock *n.* tuft of grass.

tutelage [**tew**-till-lij] *n.* **1.** instruction or guidance, esp. by a tutor. **2.** state of being supervised by a guardian or tutor. **tutelary** [**tew**-till-lar-ee] *adj.*

tutor *n.* person teaching individuals or small groups. —*v.* **2.** act as a tutor to. **tutorial** *n.* period of instruction with a tutor.

tutti *adj., adv. Music* to be performed by the whole orchestra or choir.

tutti-frutti *n.* ice cream or other sweet food containing small pieces of candied or fresh fruits.

tutu *n.* short stiff skirt worn by ballerinas.

tuxedo *n., pl.* **-dos.** *US* dinner jacket.

TV television.

twaddle *n.* silly or pretentious talk or writing.

twain *n. Obs.* two.

twang *n.* **1.** sharp ringing sound. **2.** nasal speech. —*v.* **3.** (cause to) make a twang. **twangy** *adj.*

tweak *v.* **1.** pinch or twist sharply. —*n.* **2.** tweaking.

twee *adj. Informal* too sentimental, sweet, or pretty.

tweed *n.* **1.** thick woollen cloth. —*pl.* **2.** suit of tweed. **tweedy** *adj.* **1.** of or made of

tweed. **2.** showing a fondness for country life, often associated with wearers of tweed.

tweet *n., v.* chirp. **tweeter** *n.* loudspeaker reproducing high-frequency sounds.

tweezers *pl. n.* small pincer-like tool.

twelve *adj., n.* two more than ten. **twelfth** *adj., n.* (of) number twelve in a series.

twenty *adj., n.* two times ten. **twentieth** *adj., n.*

twerp *n. Informal* silly person.

twice *adv.* two times.

twiddle *v.* (foll. by *with*) fiddle (with), twirl. **twiddle one's thumbs** be bored, have nothing to do.

twig[1] *n.* small branch or shoot.

twig[2] *v.* **twigging, twigged.** *Informal* realize or understand.

twilight *n.* **1.** soft dim light just after sunset. **2.** period in which strength or importance is gradually declining. **twilit** *adj.*

twill *n.* fabric woven to produce parallel ridges.

twin *n.* **1.** one of a pair, esp. of two children born at one birth. —*v.* **twinning, twinned.** **2.** pair or be paired. **twin town** *Brit.* town that has cultural and social links with a foreign town.

twine *v.* **1.** twist or coil round. —*n.* **2.** string or cord.

twinge *n.* sudden sharp pain or emotional pang.

twinkle *v.* **1.** shine brightly but intermittently. —*n.* **2.** flickering brightness. **in the twinkling of an eye** in a very short time.

twirl *v.* **1.** turn or twist around quickly. **2.** twiddle, esp. idly.

twirp *n. Informal* same as TWERP.

twist *v.* **1.** turn out of the natural position. **2.** wind or twine. **3.** distort or pervert. —*n.* **4.** twisting. **5.** twisted thing. **6.** unexpected development in the plot of a film, book, etc. **7.** bend or curve. **8.** distortion. **twisted** *adj.* (of a person) cruel or perverted. **twister** *n. Informal* swindler. **twisty** *adj.*

twit[1] *v.* **twitting, twitted.** poke fun at (someone).

twit[2] *n. Informal* foolish person.

twitch *v.* **1.** move spasmodically. **2.** pull sharply. —*n.* **3.** nervous muscular spasm. **4.** sharp pull.

twitter *v.* **1.** (of birds) utter chirping sounds.

2. talk nervously. —*n.* **3.** act or sound of twittering.

two *adj., n.* one more than one. **two-edged** *adj.* (of a remark) having both a favourable and an unfavourable interpretation. **two-faced** *adj.* deceitful, hypocritical. **two-ply** *adj.* **1.** (of wood) having two layers. **2.** (of wool) having two strands. **two-stroke** *adj.* (of an internal combustion engine) making one explosion to every two strokes of the piston. **two-time** *v. Informal* deceive (a lover) by having an affair with someone else. **two-way** *adj.* **1.** moving in, or allowing movement in, two opposite directions. **2.** involving mutual involvement or cooperation. **3.** (of a radio or transmitter) capable of both transmission and reception of messages.

TX Texas.

tycoon *n.* powerful wealthy businessman.

tyke *n.* **1.** *Informal* small cheeky child. **2.** small mongrel dog.

tympani *pl. n.* same as TIMPANI.

tympanum *n., pl.* **-s, -na. 1.** cavity of the middle ear. **2.** tympanic membrane. **3.** *Archit.* space between the arch and the lintel above a door. **4.** *Music* drum or drumhead. **tympanic** *adj.* **tympanic membrane** thin membrane separating the external ear from the middle ear.

type *n.* **1.** class or category. **2.** *Informal* person, esp. of a specified kind. **3.** block or a raised character used for printing. **4.** printed text. —*v.* **5.** print with a typewriter. **6.** typify. **7.** classify. **typist** *n.* person who types with a typewriter. **typecast** *v.* continually cast (an actor or actress) in similar roles. **typeface** *n. Printing* style of the type. **typescript** *n.* typewritten document. **typewriter** *n.* machine which prints a character when the appropriate key is pressed.

typhoid fever *n.* acute infectious feverish disease.

typhoon *n.* violent tropical storm.

typhus *n.* infectious feverish disease.

typical *adj.* true to type, characteristic. **typically** *adv.*

typify *v.* **-fying, -fied.** be typical of.

typography *n.* art or style of printing. **typographical** *adj.* **typographer** *n.*

tyrant *n.* **1.** oppressive or cruel ruler. **2.** person who exercises authority tyrannically. **tyrannical** *adj.* like a tyrant, oppressive. **tyrannically** *adv.* **tyrannize** *v.* exert power (over) oppressively or cruelly. **tyrannous** *adj.* **tyranny** *n.* tyrannical rule.

tyre *n.* rubber ring, usu. inflated, over the rim of a vehicle's wheel to grip the road.

tyro *n., pl.* **-ros.** novice or beginner.

tzar *n.* same as TSAR.

tzetze *n.* same as TSETSE.

U

U *Chem.* uranium.

UB40 *n. Brit.* registration card issued to an unemployed person.

ubiquitous [yew-**bik**-wit-uss] *adj.* being or seeming to be everywhere at once. **ubiquity** *n.*

U-boat *n.* German submarine.

u.c. *Printing* upper case.

udder *n.* large baglike milk-producing gland of cows, sheep, or goats.

UDI Unilateral Declaration of Independence.

UEFA Union of European Football Associations.

UFO unidentified flying object.

ugh [uhh] *interj.* exclamation of disgust.

ugly *adj.* **uglier, ugliest. 1.** of unpleasant appearance. **2.** ominous or menacing. **ugliness** *n.*

UHF ultrahigh frequency.

UHT (of milk or cream) ultra-heat-treated.

UK United Kingdom.

ukulele [yew-kal-**lay**-lee] *n.* small guitar with four strings.

ulcer *n.* open sore on the surface of the skin or mucous membrane. **ulcerate** *v.* make or become ulcerous. **ulceration** *n.* **ulcerous** *adj.* of, like, or characterized by ulcers.

ulna *n., pl.* **-nae, -nas.** inner and longer of the two bones of the human forearm.

ulster *n.* man's heavy double-breasted overcoat.

ult. ultimo.

ulterior [ult-**ear**-ee-or] *adj.* lying beyond what is revealed or seen, e.g. *ulterior motives.*

ultimate *adj.* **1.** final in a series or process. **2.** highest or most significant. **ultimately** *adv.*

ultimatum [ult-im-**may**-tum] *n.* final communication stating that action will be taken unless certain conditions are met.

ultimo *adv.* in formal correspondence, of the previous month, e.g. *the 7th ultimo.*

ultra- *prefix* **1.** beyond a specified extent, range, or limit, e.g. *ultrasonic.* **2.** extremely, e.g. *ultramodern.*

ultrahigh frequency *n.* radio frequency between 3000 and 300 megahertz.

ultramarine *adj.* vivid blue.

ultrasonic *adj.* of or producing sound waves with a higher frequency than the human ear can hear.

ultrasound *n.* ultrasonic waves, used in medical diagnosis and therapy and in echo sounding.

ultraviolet *adj., n.* (of) light beyond the limit of visibility at the violet end of the spectrum.

ululate [**yewl**-yew-late] *v.* howl or wail. **ululation** *n.*

umbel *n.* umbrella-like flower cluster with the stalks springing from the central point. **umbelliferous** *adj.* denoting a plant with flowers in umbels.

umber *adj.* dark brown to greenish-brown.

umbilical [um-**bill**-ik-al] *adj.* of the navel. **umbilical cord** long flexible tube of blood vessels that connects a fetus with the placenta.

umbra *n., pl.* **-brae, -bras.** shadow, esp. the shadow cast by the moon onto the earth during a solar eclipse.

umbrage *n.* displeasure or resentment. **take umbrage** feel offended or upset.

umbrella *n.* **1.** portable device used for protection against rain, consisting of a folding frame covered in material attached to a central rod. **2.** single organization, idea, etc. that contains or covers many different organizations.

umiak [**oo**-mee-ak] *n.* Eskimo boat made of skins.

umlaut [**oom**-lowt] *n.* mark (¨) placed over a vowel, esp. in German, to indicate a change in its sound.

umpire *n.* **1.** official who rules on the playing of a game. —*v.* **2.** act as umpire in (a game).

umpteen *adj. Informal* very many. **umpteenth** *n., adj.*

UN United Nations.

un- *prefix* **1.** not, e.g. *unidentified*. **2.** denoting reversal of an action, e.g. *untie*. **3.** denoting removal from, e.g. *unthrone*.

unabated *adv.* without any reduction in force, e.g. *the storm continued unabated.*

unable *adj.* (foll. by *to*) lacking the necessary power, ability, or authority to (do something).

unaccountable *adj.* **1.** unable to be explained. **2.** (foll. by *to*) not answerable to. **unaccountably** *adv.*

unadulterated *adj.* with nothing added, pure.

unaffected *adj.* **1.** unpretentious, natural, sincere. **2.** not influenced or moved by something.

unanimous [yew-**nan**-im-uss] *adj.* **1.** in complete agreement. **2.** agreed by all. **unanimously** *adv.* **unanimity** *n.*

unannounced *adv.* without warning, e.g. *He turned up unannounced.*

unapproachable *adj.* discouraging friendliness, aloof.

unarmed *adj.* without weapons.

unassailable *adj.* unable to be attacked or disputed.

unassuming *adj.* modest or unpretentious.

unattached *adj.* **1.** not connected with any specific group or organization. **2.** not married or involved in a steady relationship.

unavailing *adj.* useless or futile.

unavoidable *adj.* unable to be avoided or prevented. **unavoidably** *adv.*

unaware *adj.* not aware or conscious. **unawares** *adv.* **1.** by surprise. **2.** without knowing.
▷ Note the difference between the adjective *unaware*, usually followed by *of* or *that*, and the adverb *unawares*.

unbalanced *adj.* **1.** mentally deranged. **2.** biased or one-sided.

unbearable *adj.* not able to be endured. **unbearably** *adv.*

unbecoming *adj.* unattractive or unsuitable.

unbeknown *adv.* (foll. by *to*) without the knowledge of (a person).

unbelievable *adj.* **1.** too unlikely to be believed. **2.** *Informal* marvellous, amazing. **3.** *Informal* terrible, shocking. **unbelievably** *adv.*

unbend *v. Informal* become less strict or more informal in one's attitudes or behaviour. **unbending** *adj.*

unbidden *adj.* not ordered or asked.

unborn *adj.* not yet born.

unbosom *v.* relieve (oneself) of (secrets or feelings) by telling someone.

unbridled *adj.* (of feelings or behaviour) not controlled in any way.

unburden *v.* relieve (one's mind or oneself) of a worry by confiding in someone.

uncalled-for *adj.* not fair or justified.

uncanny *adj.* weird or mysterious. **uncannily** *adv.*

unceremonious *adj.* **1.** without ceremony. **2.** abrupt or rude. **unceremoniously** *adv.*

uncertain *adj.* **1.** not able to be accurately known or predicted. **2.** not able to be depended upon. **3.** changeable. **uncertainty** *n.*

uncharacteristic *adj.* not typical. **uncharacteristically** *adv.*

uncharitable *adj.* unkind or harsh. **uncharitably** *adv.*

un-Christian *adj.* not in accordance with Christian principles.

uncivilized *adj.* **1.** (of a tribe or people) not yet civilized. **2.** lacking culture or sophistication.

uncle *n.* **1.** brother of one's father or mother. **2.** husband of one's aunt.

unclean *adj.* lacking moral, spiritual, or physical cleanliness.

uncomfortable *adj.* **1.** not physically relaxed. **2.** anxious or uneasy. **uncomfortably** *adv.*

uncommon *adj.* **1.** beyond normal experience. **2.** in excess of what is normal. **uncommonly** *adv.*

uncompromising *adj.* not prepared to compromise. **uncompromisingly** *adv.*

unconcerned *adj.* lacking in concern or involvement. **unconcernedly** [un-kon-**sern**-id-lee] *adv.*

unconditional *adj.* without conditions or limitations. **unconditionally** *adv.*

unconscionable *adj.* **1.** having no principles, unscrupulous. **2.** excessive in amount or degree.

unconscious *adj.* **1.** lacking normal awareness through the senses. **2.** not aware of one's actions or behaviour. **unconsciously** *adv.* **unconsciousness** *n.*

unconventional *adj.* not conforming to accepted rules or standards.

uncooperative *adj.* not willing to cooperate, not helpful.

uncouth *adj.* lacking in good manners, refinement, or grace.

uncover *v.* **1.** remove the cap, top, etc., from. **2.** reveal or disclose.

unction *n.* act of anointing with oil in sacramental ceremonies.

unctuous *adj.* pretending to be kind and concerned.

undeceive *v.* reveal the truth to (someone previously misled or deceived).

undecided *adj.* **1.** not having made up one's mind. **2.** (of an issue or problem) not agreed or decided upon.

undeniable *adj.* indisputably true. **undeniably** *adv.*

under *prep.* **1.** on, to, or beneath the underside or base of. **2.** less than. **3.** subject to the supervision, control, or influence of. **4.** subject to (conditions). —*adv.* **5.** to a position underneath.

under- *prefix* **1.** below, e.g. *underground.* **2.** insufficient or insufficiently, e.g. *underrate.*

underachieve *v.* fail to achieve a performance appropriate to one's age or talents. **underachiever** *n.*

underage *adj.* below the required or standard age.

underarm *Sport* —*adj.* **1.** denoting a style of throwing, bowling, or serving in which the hand is swung below shoulder level. —*adv.* **2.** in an underarm style.

undercarriage *n.* **1.** landing gear of an aircraft. **2.** framework supporting the body of a vehicle.

undercoat *n.* coat of paint applied before the final coat.

undercover *adj.* done or acting in secret.

undercurrent *n.* **1.** current that is not apparent at the surface. **2.** underlying opinion or emotion.

undercut *v.* charge less than (a competitor) to obtain trade.

underdeveloped *adj.* **1.** immature or undersized. **2.** (of a country) lacking the finance, industries, and organization necessary to advance.

underdog *n.* person or team in a weak or underprivileged position.

underdone *adj.* not cooked enough.

underestimate *v.* **1.** make too low an estimate of. **2.** not realize the full potential of.

underfelt *n.* thick felt laid under a carpet to increase insulation.

underfoot *adv.* under the feet.

undergarment *n.* any piece of underwear.

undergo *v.* experience, endure, or sustain.

undergraduate *n.* person studying in a university for a first degree.

underground *adj.* **1.** occurring, situated, used, or going below ground level. **2.** secret. —*n.* **3.** electric passenger railway operated in underground tunnels. **4.** movement dedicated to overthrowing a government or occupation forces.

undergrowth *n.* small trees and bushes growing beneath taller trees in a wood or forest.

underhand *adj.* sly, deceitful, and secretive.

underlay *n.* felt or rubber laid beneath a carpet to increase insulation and resilience.

underlie *v.* **1.** lie or be placed under. **2.** be the foundation, cause, or basis of. **underlying** *adj.* fundamental or basic.

underline *v.* **1.** draw a line under. **2.** state forcibly, emphasize.

underling *n.* subordinate.

undermine *v.* **1.** weaken gradually. **2.** (of the sea or wind) wear away the base of (cliffs).

underneath *prep., adv.* **1.** under or beneath. —*adj., n.* **2.** lower (part or surface).

underpants *pl. n.* man's undergarment for the lower part of the body.

underpass *n.* section of a road that passes under another road or a railway line.

underpin *v.* give strength or support to.

underprivileged *adj.* lacking the rights and advantages of other members of society.

underrate *v.* underestimate. **underrated** *adj.*

underseal *n.* coating of tar etc. applied to the underside of a motor vehicle to prevent corrosion.

undersecretary *n.* senior civil servant or

junior minister in a government department.

underside n. bottom or lower surface.

undersized adj. of less than usual size.

underskirt n. skirtlike garment worn under a skirt or dress, petticoat.

understand v. 1. know and comprehend the nature or meaning of. 2. realize or grasp (something). 3. assume, infer, or believe. **understandable** adj. **understandably** adv. **understanding** n. 1. ability to learn, judge, or make decisions. 2. personal interpretation of a subject. 3. mutual agreement, usu. an informal or private one. —adj. 4. kind and sympathetic.

understate v. 1. describe or represent (something) in restrained terms. 2. state that (something, such as a number) is less than it is. **understatement** n.

understudy n. 1. actor who studies a part in order to be able to replace the usual actor if necessary. —v. 2. act as an understudy for.

undertake v. 1. agree or commit oneself to (something) or (to do something). 2. promise. **undertaking** n. 1. task or enterprise. 2. agreement to do something.

undertaker n. person whose profession is to prepare corpses for burial and organize funerals.

undertone n. 1. quiet tone of voice. 2. underlying quality or feeling.

undertow n. strong undercurrent flowing in a different direction from the surface current.

underwater adj., adv. (situated, occurring, or for use) below the surface of the sea, a lake, or a river.

underwear n. clothing worn under the outer garments and next to the skin.

underworld n. 1. criminals and their associates. 2. Greek & Roman myth regions below the earth's surface regarded as the abode of the dead.

underwrite v. 1. accept financial responsibility for (a commercial project). 2. sign and issue (an insurance policy), thus accepting liability. **underwriter** n.

undesirable adj. 1. not desirable or pleasant, objectionable. 2. objectionable person. **undesirably** adv.

undies pl. n. Informal underwear, esp. women's.

undistinguished adj. not particularly good or bad, mediocre.

undo v. 1. open, unwrap. 2. reverse the effects of. 3. cause the downfall of. **undone** adj. **undoing** n. cause of someone's downfall.

undoubted adj. certain or indisputable. **undoubtedly** adv.

undress v. 1. take off the clothes of (oneself or another person). —n. 2. in a state of undress naked or nearly naked.

undue adj. greater than is reasonable, excessive. **unduly** adv.

undulate v. move in waves. **undulation** n.

undying adj. never ending, eternal.

unearned income n. income from property or investments rather than work.

unearth v. 1. dig up out of the earth. 2. reveal or discover.

unearthly adj. 1. ghostly or eerie. 2. ridiculous or unreasonable, e.g. an unearthly hour.

uneasy adj. 1. (of a person) anxious or apprehensive. 2. (of a condition) precarious or uncomfortable. **uneasily** adv. **uneasiness** n. **unease** n. 1. feeling of anxiety. 2. state of dissatisfaction.

unemployed adj. out of work. **unemployment** n.

unequivocal adj. completely clear in meaning. **unequivocally** adv.

unerring adj. never mistaken, consistently accurate.

UNESCO United Nations Educational, Scientific, and Cultural Organization.

uneven adj. 1. not level or flat. 2. not consistent in quality, e.g. an uneven performance. 3. not fairly matched, e.g. an uneven race.

unexceptionable adj. beyond criticism or objection.

unexceptional adj. ordinary or normal.

unexpected adj. surprising or unforeseen. **unexpectedly** adv.

unfailing adj. continuous or reliable. **unfailingly** adv.

unfair adj. not right, fair, or just. **unfairly** adv. **unfairness** n.

unfaithful adj. 1. guilty of adultery. 2. not true to a promise or vow. **unfaithfulness** n.

unfathomable adj. too strange or too complicated to be understood.

unfavourable adj. 1. adverse or inauspicious, e.g. unfavourable weather conditions. 2. disapproving, e.g. an unfavourable opinion. **unfavourably** adv.

unfeeling adj. without sympathy.

unfit adj. 1. (foll. by for) unqualified or unsuitable. 2. in poor physical condition.

unflappable adj. Informal not easily upset. **unflappability** n.

unfold v. 1. open or spread out from a folded state. 2. reveal or be revealed.

unforeseen adj. surprising because not expected.

unforgettable adj. impossible to forget, memorable. **unforgettably** adv.

unfortunate adj. 1. unlucky, unsuccessful, or unhappy. 2. regrettable or unsuitable. **unfortunately** adv.

unfounded adj. not based on facts or evidence.

unfrock v. deprive (a priest in holy orders) of his priesthood.

unfurl v. unroll or unfold.

ungainly adj. -lier, -liest. lacking grace when moving. **ungainliness** n.

ungodly adj. 1. wicked or sinful. 2. Informal unreasonable or outrageous, e.g. an ungodly hour. **ungodliness** n.

ungovernable adj. not able to be disciplined or restrained.

ungrateful adj. not grateful or thankful. **ungratefully** adv. **ungratefulness** n.

unguarded adj. 1. not protected. 2. incautious or careless.

unguent [ung-gwent] n. ointment.

unhand v. Old-fashioned or lit. release from one's grasp.

unhappy adj. 1. sad or depressed. 2. unfortunate or wretched. **unhappily** adv. **unhappiness** n.

unhealthy adj. 1. characterized by ill health, sick. 2. of, causing, or due to ill health. 3. morbid, unnatural.

unheard-of adj. 1. without precedent. 2. highly offensive or shocking.

unhinge v. derange or unbalance (a person or his or her mind).

unholy adj. 1. immoral or wicked. 2. Informal unreasonable or outrageous, e.g. an unholy hour.

uni- combining form of, consisting of, or having only one, e.g. unicellular.

UNICEF United Nations International Children's Emergency Fund.

unicorn n. imaginary horselike creature with one horn growing from its forehead.

uniform n. 1. special identifying set of clothes for the members of an organization, such as soldiers. —adj. 2. unvarying. 3. alike or like. **uniformly** adv. **uniformity** n.

unify v. -fying, -fied. make or become one. **unification** n.

unilateral adj. made or done by only one person or group. **unilaterally** adv.

unimpeachable adj. completely honest and reliable.

uninterested adj. having or showing no interest in someone or something.

union n. 1. uniting or being united. 2. association or confederation of individuals or groups for a common purpose. 3. short for TRADE UNION. **unionist** n. member or supporter of a trade union. **unionism** n. **unionize** v. organize (workers) into a trade union. **unionization** n. **Union Jack** national flag of the United Kingdom.

unique [yoo-neek] adj. 1. being the only one of a particular type. 2. without equal or like. **uniquely** adv.
▷ Because of its meaning, avoid using unique with modifiers like very and rather.

unisex adj. designed for use by both sexes.

unison n. 1. complete agreement. 2. Music singing or playing the same notes together at the same time.

unit n. 1. single undivided entity or whole. 2. group or individual regarded as a basic element of a larger whole. 3. fixed quantity etc., used as a standard of measurement. 4. piece of furniture designed to be fitted with other similar pieces, e.g. kitchen units. **unit trust** Brit. investment trust that issues units for public sale and invests the money in many different businesses.

Unitarian n. person who believes that God is one being and rejects the Trinity. **Unitarianism** n.

unitary adj. 1. of a unit or units. 2. based on or marked by unity.

unite v. 1. make or become an integrated whole. 2. (cause to) enter into an association or alliance.

unity n. 1. state of being one. 2. mutual agreement.

universe n. 1. whole of all existing matter, energy, and space. 2. the world. **universal** adj. 1. of or typical of the whole of mankind or of nature. 2. existing everywhere. **universally** adv. **universality** n.

university n., pl. **-ties**. institution of higher education having the authority to award degrees.

unkempt adj. 1. (of the hair) not combed. 2. slovenly or untidy.

unkind adj. unsympathetic or cruel. **unkindly** adv. **unkindness** n.

unknown adj. 1. not known. 2. not famous. —n. 3. unknown person, quantity, or thing.

unleaded adj. (of petrol) containing less tetraethyl lead, in order to reduce environmental pollution.

unleash v. release, as if from a leash.

unleavened [un-**lev**-vend] adj. (of bread) made without yeast.

unless conj. except under the circumstances that.

unlike adj. 1. dissimilar or different. —prep. 2. not like or typical of.

unlikely adj. improbable.

unload v. 1. remove (cargo) from (a ship, lorry, or plane). 2. get rid of. 3. remove the ammunition from (a firearm).

unlooked-for adj. unexpected or unforeseen.

unlucky adj. 1. having bad luck, unfortunate. 2. ill-omened or inauspicious.

unman v. cause to lose courage or nerve.

unmanned adj. having no personnel or crew.

unmask v. 1. remove the mask or disguise from. 2. (cause to) appear in true character.

unmentionable adj. unsuitable as a topic of conversation.

unmistakable, unmistakeable adj. not ambiguous, clear. **unmistakably, unmistakeably** adv.

unmitigated adj. 1. not reduced or lessened in severity etc. 2. total and complete.

unmoved adj. not affected by emotion, indifferent.

unnatural adj. 1. contrary to nature. 2. not in accordance with accepted standards of behaviour. **unnaturally** adv. not unnaturally as one would expect.

unnecessary adj. not essential, or more than is essential. **unnecessarily** adv.

unnerve v. cause to lose courage, confidence, or self-control. **unnerving** adj. **unnervingly** adv.

unnumbered adj. 1. countless. 2. not counted or given a number.

UNO United Nations Organization.

unobtrusive adj. not drawing attention to oneself, inconspicuous. **unobtrusively** adv.

unorthodox adj. not conventional in belief, behaviour, etc.

unpack v. 1. remove the contents of (a suitcase, trunk, etc.). 2. take (something) out of a packed container.

unpalatable adj. 1. (of food) unpleasant to taste. 2. (of a fact, idea, etc.) unpleasant and hard to accept.

unparalleled adj. not equalled, supreme.

unpick v. undo (the stitches) of (a piece of sewing).

unpleasant adj. not pleasant or agreeable. **unpleasantly** adv. **unpleasantness** n.

unpopular adj. generally disliked or disapproved of. **unpopularity** n.

unprecedented adj. never having happened before, unparalleled.

unprepossessing adj. unattractive in appearance.

unpretentious adj. without ostentation.

unprincipled adj. lacking moral principles, unscrupulous.

unprintable adj. unsuitable for printing for reasons of obscenity or libel.

unprofessional adj. 1. contrary to the accepted code of a profession. 2. not belonging to a profession. **unprofessionally** adv.

unprofitable adj. 1. not making a profit. 2. not helpful or beneficial.

unqualified adj. 1. lacking the necessary qualifications. 2. not modified.

unquestionable adj. not to be doubted, indisputable. **unquestionably** adv.

unquote interj. expression used to indicate the end of a quotation that was introduced with the word 'quote'.

unravel v. **-elling, -elled**. 1. reduce (something knitted or woven) to separate strands. 2. become unravelled. 3. explain or solve.

unreadable *adj.* **1.** unable to be read or deciphered. **2.** too difficult or dull to read.

unreal *adj.* **1.** (as if) existing only in the imagination. **2.** insincere or artificial. **unreality** *n.*

unreasonable *adj.* **1.** immoderate or excessive. **2.** refusing to listen to reason. **unreasonably** *adv.*

unremitting *adj.* never slackening or stopping. **unremittingly** *adv.*

unrequited *adj.* not returned, e.g. *unrequited love.*

unreserved *adj.* completely, without reservation. **unreservedly** [un-re-**zerv**-id-lee] *adv.*

unrest *n.* rebellious state of discontent.

unrivalled *adj.* having no equal.

unroll *v.* open out or unwind (something rolled or coiled) or (of something rolled or coiled) become opened out or unwound.

unruffled *adj.* **1.** calm and unperturbed. **2.** smooth and still.

unruly *adj.* **-lier, -liest.** given to disobedience or indiscipline.

unsaturated *adj.* **1.** (of an organic compound) containing a double or triple bond and therefore capable of combining with other substances. **2.** (of a fat, esp. a vegetable fat) containing a high proportion of fatty acids with double bonds.

unsavoury *adj.* distasteful or objectionable.

unscathed *adj.* not harmed or injured.

unscrupulous *adj.* unprincipled or without scruples.

unseasonable *adj.* inappropriate or unusual for the time of year. **unseasonably** *adv.*

unseat *v.* **1.** throw or displace from a seat or saddle. **2.** depose from an office or position.

unseemly *adj.* not polite, indecorous.

unsettled *adj.* **1.** lacking order or stability. **2.** disturbed and restless. **3.** constantly changing or moving from place to place.

unshakable, unshakeable *adj.* (of beliefs) completely firm, not wavering. **unshakably, unshakeably** *adv.*

unsightly *adj.* unpleasant to look at.

unsocial *adj.* **1.** (also **unsociable**) avoiding the company of other people. **2.** falling outside the normal working day, e.g. *unsocial hours.*

unsound *adj.* **1.** unhealthy or unstable. **2.** not based on truth or fact.

unspeakable *adj.* indescribably bad or evil. **unspeakably** *adv.*

unstable *adj.* **1.** lacking stability or firmness. **2.** having abrupt changes of mood or behaviour.

unsteady *adj.* **1.** not securely fixed. **2.** shaky or staggering. **unsteadily** *adv.*

unstinting *adj.* generous, gladly given, e.g. *unstinting praise.*

unstructured *adj.* without formal or systematic organization.

unstuck *adj.* **come unstuck** *Informal* fail badly.

unstudied *adj.* natural or spontaneous.

unsuccessful *adj.* not achieving success. **unsuccessfully** *adv.*

unsuitable *adj.* not right or appropriate for a particular purpose. **unsuitably** *adv.*

unsung *adj.* not acclaimed or honoured, e.g. *unsung heroes.*

unswerving *adj.* firm, constant, not changing.

unsympathetic *adj.* **1.** not feeling or showing sympathy. **2.** unpleasant, not likeable. **3.** (foll. by *to*) opposed to.

untapped *adj.* not yet used, e.g. *untapped reserves.*

untenable *adj.* (of a theory, idea, etc.) incapable of being defended.

unthinkable *adj.* out of the question, inconceivable.

untidy *adj.* not neat, slovenly. **untidily** *adv.* **untidiness** *n.*

untie *v.* **1.** open or free (something that is tied). **2.** free from constraint.

until *conj.* **1.** up to the time that. —*prep.* **2.** in or throughout the period before. **not until** not before (a time or event).

untimely *adj.* **1.** occurring before the expected or normal time. **2.** inappropriate to the occasion or time. **untimeliness** *n.*

unto *prep. Old-fashioned* to.

untold *adj.* **1.** incapable of description. **2.** incalculably great in number or quantity.

untouchable *adj.* **1.** above reproach or suspicion. **2.** unable to be touched. —*n.* **3.** member of the lowest Hindu caste in India.

untoward *adj.* causing misfortune or annoyance.

untrue *adj.* **1.** incorrect or false. **2.** disloyal or unfaithful. **untruth** *n.* statement that is not true, lie. **untruthful** *adj.* **untruthfully** *adv.*

unusual *adj.* uncommon or extraordinary. **unusually** *adv.*

unutterable *adj.* incapable of being expressed in words. **unutterably** *adv.*

unvarnished *adj.* not elaborated upon, e.g. *the unvarnished truth.*

unveil *v.* **1.** ceremonially remove the cover from (a new picture, plaque, etc.). **2.** make public (a secret). **unveiling** *n.*

unwarranted *adj.* not justified, not necessary.

unwell *adj.* not healthy, ill.

unwieldy *adj.* too heavy, large, or awkward to be easily handled.

unwind *v.* **1.** (cause to) slacken, undo, or unravel. **2.** relax after a busy or tense time.

unwitting *adj.* **1.** not knowing or conscious. **2.** not intentional. **unwittingly** *adv.*

unwonted *adj.* out of the ordinary.

unworthy *adj.* **1.** not deserving or worthy. **2.** (foll. by *of*) beneath the level considered befitting (to). **3.** lacking merit or value.

unwrap *v.* remove the wrapping from (something).

unwritten *adj.* **1.** not printed or in writing. **2.** operating only through custom, e.g. *an unwritten rule.*

up *prep.* **1.** indicating movement to a higher position on or in, e.g. *They went up the hill.* **2.** at a higher or further level or position in or on, e.g. *the shop up the road.* —*adv.* **3.** to an upward, higher, or erect position. **4.** indicating readiness for an activity, e.g. *up and about.* **5.** indicating intensity or completion of an action. **6.** to the place referred to or where the speaker is. —*adj.* **7.** of a high or higher position. **8.** out of bed. —*v.* **upping, upped. 9.** increase or raise. **10.** (foll. by *and*) *Informal* do something suddenly, e.g. *he upped and left.* **up against** having to cope with. **ups and downs** alternating periods of good and bad luck. **up to 1.** engaged in (usu. something shady, secretive, or mischievous). **2.** the responsibility of, e.g. *it's up to you to lock the doors.* **3.** equal to or capable of (doing something). **what's up?** *Informal* what is wrong? **upward** *adj.* **1.** directed or moving towards a higher place

or level. —*adv.* (also **upwards**) **2.** from a lower to a higher place, level, or condition.

up-and-coming *adj.* likely to be successful in the future.

upbeat *n.* **1.** *Music* unaccented beat. —*adj.* **2.** *Informal* cheerful and optimistic.

upbraid *v.* scold or reproach.

upbringing *n.* education of a person during the formative years.

update *v.* bring up to date.

upend *v.* turn or set (something) on its end.

upfront *adj.* **1.** open and frank. —*adv., adj.* **2.** (of money) paid out at the beginning of a business arrangement.

upgrade *v.* promote (a person or job) to a higher rank. **upgrading** *n.*

upheaval *n.* strong, sudden, or violent disturbance.

uphill *adj.* **1.** sloping or leading upwards. **2.** requiring a great deal of effort. —*adv.* **3.** up a slope.

uphold *v.* **1.** maintain or defend against opposition. **2.** give moral support to. **upholder** *n.*

upholster *v.* fit (a chair or sofa) with padding, springs, and covering. **upholsterer** *n.* **upholstery** *n.* soft covering on a chair or sofa.

upkeep *n.* act, process, or cost of keeping something in good repair.

upland *n.* **1.** area of high or relatively high ground. —*adj.* **2.** of or in an upland.

uplift *v.* **1.** raise or lift up. **2.** raise morally or spiritually. —*n.* **3.** act, process, or result of lifting up. **uplifting** *adj.*

up-market *adj.* expensive and of superior quality.

upon *prep.* **1.** on. **2.** up and on.

upper *adj.* **1.** higher or highest in physical position, wealth, rank, or status. —*n.* **2.** part of a shoe above the sole. **on one's uppers** destitute. **uppermost** *adj.* **1.** highest in position, power, or importance. —*adv.* **2.** in or into the highest place or position. **upper case** *n.* capital letters. **upper class** highest social class. **upper-class** *adj.* **upper crust** *Informal* upper class. **uppercut** *n.* short swinging upward punch delivered to the chin. **upper hand** position of control.

uppish, uppity *adj. Informal* snobbish, arrogant, or presumptuous.

upright *adj.* **1.** vertical or erect. **2.** honest

or just. —*adv.* **3.** vertically or in an erect position. —*n.* **4.** vertical support, such as a post. **uprightness** *n.*

uprising *n.* rebellion or revolt.

uproar *n.* disturbance characterized by loud noise and confusion. **uproarious** *adj.* **1.** very funny. **2.** (of laughter) loud and boisterous. **uproariously** *adv.*

uproot *v.* **1.** pull up by or as if by the roots. **2.** displace (a person or people) from their native or usual surroundings.

upset *v.* **1.** tip over. **2.** disturb the normal state or stability of. **3.** disturb mentally or emotionally. **4.** make physically ill. —*n.* **5.** unexpected defeat or reversal. **6.** disturbance or disorder of the emotions, mind, or body. —*adj.* **7.** emotionally or physically disturbed or distressed. **upsetting** *adj.*

upshot *n.* final result or conclusion.

upside down *adj.* **1.** turned over completely. **2.** *Informal* confused or jumbled. —*adv.* **3.** in an inverted fashion. **4.** in a chaotic manner.

upstage *adj.* **1.** at the back half of the stage. —*v.* **2.** *Informal* draw attention to oneself from (someone else).

upstairs *adv.* **1.** up the stairs. —*n.* **2.** upper floor. —*adj.* **3.** situated on an upper floor.

upstanding *adj.* of good character.

upstart *n.* person who has risen suddenly to a position of power and behaves arrogantly.

upstream *adv., adj.* in or towards the higher part of a stream.

upsurge *n.* rapid rise or swell.

uptake *n.* **quick, slow on the uptake** *Informal* quick *or* slow to understand or learn.

uptight *adj.* *Informal* nervously tense, irritable, or angry.

up-to-date *adj.* modern or fashionable.

upturn *n.* **1.** upward trend or improvement. **2.** upheaval.

uranium [yew-rain-ee-um] *n.* radioactive silvery-white metallic element, used chiefly as a source of nuclear energy.

Uranus *n.* **1.** Greek god of the sun. **2.** seventh planet from the sun.

urban *adj.* of or living in a city or town. **urbanize** *v.* make (a rural area) more industrialized and urban. **urbanization** *n.*

urbane *adj.* characterized by courtesy, elegance, and sophistication. **urbanity** *n.*

urchin *n.* mischievous child.

Urdu [oor-doo] *n.* language of Pakistan.

ureter [yew-reet-er] *n.* tube that conveys urine from the kidney to the bladder.

urethra [yew-reeth-ra] *n.* canal that carries urine from the bladder out of the body.

urge *n.* **1.** strong impulse, inner drive, or yearning. —*v.* **2.** plead with or press (a person to do something). **3.** advocate earnestly. **4.** force or drive onwards.

urgent *adj.* requiring speedy action or attention. **urgency** *n.* **urgently** *adv.*

uric acid *n.* white odourless crystalline acid present in the blood and urine.

urine *n.* pale yellow fluid excreted by the kidneys to the bladder and passed as waste from the body. **urinary** *adj.* **urinate** *v.* discharge urine. **urination** *n.* **urinal** *n.* (place with) sanitary fitting(s) used by men for urination.

urn *n.* **1.** vase used as a container for the ashes of the dead. **2.** large metal container with a tap, used for making and holding tea or coffee.

ursine *adj.* of or like a bear.

us *pron.* objective case of WE.

US, USA United States (of America).

use *v.* **1.** put into service or action. **2.** behave towards in a particular way, usu. selfishly. **3.** consume or expend. —*n.* **4.** using or being used. **5.** ability or permission to use. **6.** usefulness or advantage. **7.** purpose for which something is used. **user** *n.* **user-friendly** *adj.* easy to familiarize oneself with, understand, and use. **usable** *adj.* able to be used. **usage** *n.* **1.** act or a manner of using. **2.** constant use, custom, or habit. **used** *adj.* second-hand. **used to** *adj.* **1.** accustomed to. —*v.* **2.** used as an auxiliary to express past habitual or accustomed actions, e.g. *I used to live there.* **useful** *adj.* **1.** able to be used advantageously or for several different purposes. **2.** *Informal* commendable or capable, e.g. *a useful day's work.* **usefully** *adv.* **usefulness** *n.* **useless** *adj.* **1.** having no practical use. **2.** *Informal* ineffectual, weak, or stupid, e.g. *useless at maths.* **uselessly** *adv.* **uselessness** *n.*
▷ In the negative there are two common combinations: *didn't use to* and *used not to.* The abbreviated form is *usedn't to.*

usher *n.* **1.** official who shows people to their seats, as in a church. —*v.* **2.** conduct or escort. **usherette** *n.* female assistant in a cinema who shows people to their seats.

USSR Union of Soviet Socialist Republics.

usual *adj.* of the most normal, frequent, or regular type. **as usual** as happens normally. **usually** *adv.* most often, in most cases.

usurp [yewz-**zurp**] *v.* seize (a position or power) without authority. **usurpation** *n.* **usurper** *n.*

usury *n.* practice of lending money at an extremely high rate of interest. **usurer** [**yewz**-yoor-er] *n.*

UT Utah.

utensil *n.* tool or container for practical use.

uterus [**yew**-ter-russ] *n.* womb. **uterine** *adj.*

utilitarian *adj.* **1.** of utilitarianism. **2.** useful rather than beautiful. **utilitarianism** *n.* doctrine that the right action is the one that brings about the greatest good for the greatest number of people.

utility *n.*, *pl.* **-ties. 1.** usefulness. **2.** public service, such as electricity. —*adj.* **3.** designed for use rather than beauty. **utility room** room used for large domestic appliances and equipment.

utilize *v.* make practical use of. **utilization** *n.*

utmost *adj.*, *n.* (of the) greatest possible degree or amount.

Utopia [yew-**tope**-ee-a] *n.* any real or imaginary society, place, or state considered to be perfect or ideal. **Utopian** *adj.*

utter[1] *v.* express (something) audibly. **utterance** *n.* **1.** something uttered. **2.** act or power of uttering.

utter[2] *adj.* total or absolute. **utterly** *adv.*

uttermost *adj.*, *n.* same as UTMOST.

U-turn *n.* **1.** turn, made by a vehicle, in the shape of a U, resulting in a reversal of direction. **2.** complete change in policy.

UV ultraviolet.

uvula [**yew**-view-la] *n.* small fleshy part of the soft palate that hangs in the back of the throat.

uxorious [ux-or-ee-uss] *adj.* excessively fond of or dependent on one's wife.

V

V 1. *Chem.* vanadium. **2.** volt. **3.** the Roman numeral for five.

v. 1. versus. **2.** very.

VA Virginia.

vacant *adj.* **1.** (of a toilet, room, etc.) unoccupied. **2.** without interest or understanding. **vacantly** *adv.* **vacancy** *n., pl.* **-cies. 1.** unfilled job. **2.** unoccupied room in a guesthouse. **3.** state of being unoccupied.

vacate *v.* leave (a place or job). **vacation** *n.* **1.** time when universities and law courts are closed. **2.** *US* holiday.

vaccinate *v.* inoculate with a vaccine. **vaccination** *n.* **vaccine** *n.* substance designed to cause a mild form of a disease to make a person immune to the disease itself.

vacillate [**vass**-ill-late] *v.* waver in one's opinions. **vacillation** *n.*

vacuous *adj.* not expressing intelligent thought. **vacuity** *n.*

vacuum *n., pl.* **vacuums, vacua. 1.** empty space from which all or most air or gas has been removed. —*v.* **2.** clean with a vacuum cleaner. **vacuum cleaner** electrical appliance for removing dust by suction. **vacuum flask** double-walled flask with a vacuum between the walls that keeps drinks hot or cold. **vacuum-packed** *adj.* contained in packaging from which the air has been removed.

vagabond *n.* person with no fixed home, esp. a beggar.

vagary [**vaig**-a-ree] *n., pl.* **-garies. 1.** unpredictable change. **2.** whim.

vagina [vaj-**jine**-a] *n., pl.* **-nas, -nae.** in female mammals, passage from the womb to the external genitals. **vaginal** *adj.*

vagrant [**vaig**-rant] *n.* **1.** person with no settled home. —*adj.* **2.** wandering. **vagrancy** *n.*

vague *adj.* **1.** not clearly explained. **2.** unable to be seen or heard clearly. **3.** absent-minded. **vaguely** *adv.*

vain *adj.* **1.** excessively proud, esp. of one's appearance. **2.** bound to fail, futile. **in vain** unsuccessfully.

vainglorious *adj. Lit.* boastful. **vainglory** *n.*

valance [**val**-lenss] *n.* piece of drapery round the edge of a bed.

vale *n. Lit.* valley.

valediction [val-lid-**dik**-shun] *n.* farewell speech. **valedictory** *adj.*

valence [**vale**-ence] *n.* molecular bonding between atoms.

valency *n., pl.* **-cies.** power of an atom to make molecular bonds.

valentine *n.* (person to whom one sends) a romantic card on Saint Valentine's Day, 14th February.

valerian *n.* herb used as a sedative.

valet *n.* man's personal male servant.

valetudinarian [val-lit-yew-din-**air**-ee-an] *n.* **1.** person with a long-term illness. **2.** hypochondriac.

valiant *adj.* brave or courageous. **valiantly** *adv.*

valid *adj.* **1.** soundly reasoned. **2.** having legal force. **validate** *v.* make valid. **validation** *n.* **validity** *n.*

valise [val-**leez**] *n. Old-fashioned* travelling bag.

Valium *n.* ® drug used as a tranquillizer.

valley *n.* low area between hills, usu. with a river running through it.

valour *n. Lit.* bravery. **valorous** *adj.*

value *n.* **1.** importance, usefulness. **2.** monetary worth. **3.** satisfaction, e.g. *value for money.* **4.** *Maths* particular number represented by a figure or symbol. —*pl.* **5.** moral principles. —*v.* **valuing, valued. 6.** assess the value of. **7.** have a high regard for. **valuable** *adj.* having great worth. **valuables** *pl. n.* valuable personal property. **valuation** *n.* assessment of worth. **valueless** *adj.* **valuer** *n.* **value-added tax** *Brit.* see VAT. **value judgment** opinion based on personal belief.

valve *n.* **1.** device to control the movement of fluid through a pipe. **2.** *Anat.* flap in a part of the body allowing blood to flow in one direction only. **3.** *Physics* tube containing a vacuum, allowing current to flow from a cathode to an anode. **4.** *Zool.* one of the hinged shells of an oyster or clam. **5.** *Music* device on brass instruments to lengthen the tube. **valvular** adj. **1.** of or having valves. **2.** like valves.

vamoose v. Slang go away.

vamp[1] n. Informal woman who seduces men to her own advantage.

vamp[2] v. **1.** (foll. by up) renovate. **2.** improvise an accompaniment to (a tune).

vampire n. in folklore, a corpse that rises at night to drink the blood of the living. **vampire bat** tropical bat that feeds on blood.

van[1] n. **1.** motor vehicle for transporting goods. **2.** Brit. railway carriage for goods in which the guard travels.

van[2] n. short for VANGUARD.

vanadium n. metallic element, used in steel.

vandal n. person who deliberately damages property. **vandalism** n. **vandalize** v.

Vandyke beard n. short pointed beard (also **Vandyke**).

vane n. flat blade on a rotary device such as a weathercock or propeller.

vanguard n. **1.** unit of soldiers leading an army. **2.** most advanced group or position in a movement or activity.

vanilla n. seed pod of a tropical climbing orchid, used for flavouring.

vanish v. **1.** disappear suddenly or mysteriously. **2.** cease to exist.

vanity n., pl. **-ties.** (display of) excessive pride. **vanity case** small bag for carrying cosmetics.

vanquish v. Lit. defeat (someone) utterly. **vanquishable** adj. **vanquisher** n.

vantage n. advantage. **vantage point** position that gives one an overall view.

vapid adj. lacking character, dull. **vapidity** n.

vapour n. **1.** moisture suspended in air as steam or mist. **2.** gaseous form of something that is liquid or solid at room temperature. **vaporize** v. change into a vapour. **vaporizer** n. **vaporous** adj.

variable adj. **1.** not always the same, changeable. —n. **2.** something that is subject to variation. **3.** Maths expression with a range of values. **variability** n.

variant adj. **1.** different or alternative. —n. **2.** alternative form. **at variance** in disagreement.

variation n. **1.** extent to which something

varies. **2.** Music repetition in different forms of a basic theme. **variational** adj.

varicose veins pl. n. knotted and swollen veins, esp. in the legs.

variegated adj. having patches or streaks of different colours. **variegation** n.

variety n., pl. **-ties. 1.** state of being diverse or various. **2.** different things of the same kind. **3.** sort or kind. **4.** light entertainment composed of unrelated acts.

various adj. of several kinds. **variously** adv.

varlet n. Obs. rascal.

varnish n. **1.** solution of oil and resin, put on a surface to make it hard and glossy. —v. **2.** apply varnish to.

varsity n. Brit. informal university.

vary v. **varying, varied. 1.** change. **2.** cause differences in. **varied** adj.

vascular adj. Biol. relating to vessels.

vas deferens n., pl. **vasa deferentia.** Anat. sperm-carrying duct in each testicle.

vase n. ornamental jar, esp. for flowers.

vasectomy n., pl. **-mies.** (operation for) the removal of part of the vas deferens, as a contraceptive method.

Vaseline n. ® thick oily cream made from petroleum, used in skin care.

vassal n. **1.** Hist. man given land in return for allegiance to his lord. **2.** subordinate person or nation. **vassalage** n.

vast adj. extremely large. **vastly** adv. **vastness** n.

vat n. large container for liquids.

VAT Brit. value-added tax: tax on the difference between the cost of materials and the selling price.

Vatican n. the Pope's palace.

vaudeville n. variety entertainment of songs and comic turns.

vault[1] n. **1.** secure room for storing valuables. **2.** underground burial chamber. **vaulted** adj. having an arched roof.

vault[2] v. **1.** jump over (something) by resting one's hand(s) on it. —n. **2.** such a jump.

vaunt v. describe or display (success or possessions) boastfully. **vaunted** adj.

VC 1. Vice Chancellor. **2.** Victoria Cross.

VCR video cassette recorder.

VD venereal disease.

VDU visual display unit.

veal *n.* calf meat.

vector *n.* **1.** *Maths* quantity that has size and direction, such as force. **2.** animal, usu. an insect, that carries disease.

veer *v.* change direction suddenly.

vegan [vee-gan] *n.* **1.** person who eats no meat, eggs, or dairy products. —*adj.* **2.** suitable for a vegan. **veganism** *n.*

vegetable *n.* **1.** edible plant. **2.** *Informal* severely brain-damaged person. —*adj.* **3.** of or like plants or vegetables.

vegetarian *n.* **1.** person who eats no meat. —*adj.* **2.** suitable for a vegetarian. **vegetarianism** *n.*

vegetate *v.* live a dull uncreative life. **vegetative** *adj.* of plant life or growth.

vegetation *n.* plant life of a given place.

vehement *adj.* expressing strong feelings. **vehemence** *n.* **vehemently** *adv.*

vehicle *n.* **1.** machine, esp. with an engine and wheels, for carrying people or objects. **2.** means of conveying something. **vehicular** *adj.*

veil *n.* **1.** piece of thin cloth covering the head or face. **2.** something that masks the truth, e.g. *a veil of secrecy.* —*v.* **3.** cover with a veil. **take the veil** become a nun. **veiled** *adj.* disguised.

vein *n.* **1.** tube that takes blood to the heart. **2.** line in a leaf or an insect's wing. **3.** layer of ore or mineral in rock. **4.** streak in marble, wood, or cheese. **5.** feature of someone's writing or speech, e.g. *a vein of humour.* **6.** mood, e.g. *in a lighter vein.* **veined** *adj.*

Velcro *n.* ® fastening consisting of one piece of fabric with tiny hooked threads and another with a coarse surface that adheres to it.

veld, veldt *n.* high grassland in Southern Africa.

vellum *n.* **1.** fine calfskin parchment. **2.** type of smooth paper.

velocity [vel-loss-it-ee] *n., pl.* **-ties.** speed of movement in a given direction.

velour, velours [vel-loor] *n.* velvety fabric.

velvet *n.* fabric with a thick pile. **velvety** *adj.* soft and smooth. **velveteen** *n.* cotton velvet.

venal [vee-nal] *adj.* **1.** easily bribed. **2.** characterized by bribery. **venally** *adv.* **venality** *n.*

vend *v.* sell. **vendor** *n.* **vending machine** machine that dispenses goods when coins are inserted.

vendetta *n.* prolonged quarrel between families, esp. one involving revenge killings.

veneer *n.* **1.** thin layer of wood etc. covering a cheaper material. **2.** superficial appearance, e.g. *a veneer of sophistication.*

venerable *adj.* worthy of deep respect. **venerate** *v.* hold (a person) in deep respect. **veneration** *n.*

venereal disease [ven-ear-ee-al] *n.* disease transmitted sexually.

Venetian *adj.* **1.** of Venice, port in NE Italy. —*n.* **2.** native or inhabitant of Venice. **Venetian blind** window blind made of thin horizontal slats that turn to let in more or less light.

vengeance *n.* revenge. **with a vengeance** to an excessive degree. **vengeful** *adj.* wanting revenge. **vengefully** *adv.*

venial [veen-ee-al] *adj.* (of a sin or fault) easily forgiven. **veniality** *n.*

venison *n.* deer meat.

venom *n.* **1.** poison produced by snakes etc. **2.** malice or spite. **venomous** *adj.* **venomously** *adv.*

venous [vee-nuss] *adj. Anat.* of veins.

vent[1] *n.* **1.** outlet releasing fumes or fluid. —*v.* **2.** express (an emotion) freely.

vent[2] *n.* vertical slit in a jacket.

ventilate *v.* **1.** let fresh air into. **2.** discuss (a complaint) openly. **ventilation** *n.* **ventilator** *n.* device to let fresh air into a room or building.

ventral *adj.* relating to the front of the body.

ventricle *n. Anat.* one of the four cavities of the heart or brain.

ventriloquist *n.* entertainer who can speak without moving his or her lips, so that a voice seems to come from elsewhere. **ventriloquism** *n.*

venture *n.* **1.** risky undertaking, esp. in business. —*v.* **2.** do something risky. **3.** dare to express (an opinion). **4.** go to an unknown place. **venturesome** *adj.* daring.

venue *n.* place where an organized gathering is held.

Venus *n.* **1.** planet second nearest to the sun. **2.** Roman goddess of love. **Venus's flytrap, Venus flytrap** plant that traps and digests insects between hinged leaves.

veracious adj. habitually truthful. **veracity** n.

veranda, verandah n. open porch attached to a house.

verb n. word that expresses the idea of action, happening, or being. **verbal** adj. **1.** spoken. **2.** of a verb. **verbally** adv. **verbalize** v. express (something) in words.

verbatim [verb-**bait**-im] adv., adj. word for word.

verbena n. plant with sweet-smelling flowers.

verbiage n. excessive use of words.

verbose [verb-**bohss**] adj. long-winded. **verbosity** n.

verdant adj. Lit. covered in green vegetation.

verdict n. **1.** decision of a jury. **2.** opinion formed after examining the facts.

verdigris [**ver**-dig-riss] n. green film on copper, brass, or bronze.

verdure n. Lit. flourishing green vegetation.

verge n. grass border along a road. **on the verge of** having almost reached (a point or condition). **verge on** v. be near to (a condition).

verger n. C of E church caretaker.

verify v. **-ifying, -ified.** check the truth or accuracy of. **verifiable** adj. **verification** n.

verily adv. Obs. in truth.

verisimilitude n. appearance of being real.

veritable adj. rightly called, without exaggeration, e.g. a veritable feast. **veritably** adv.

verity n., pl. **-ties.** true statement or principle.

vermicelli [ver-me-**chell**-ee] n. **1.** fine strands of pasta. **2.** tiny strands of chocolate.

vermicide n. substance to destroy worms.

vermiform adj. shaped like a worm. **vermiform appendix** Anat. same as APPENDIX.

vermilion adj. orange-red.

vermin pl. n. animals, esp. insects and rodents, that spread disease or cause damage. **verminous** adj.

vermouth [**ver**-muth] n. wine flavoured with herbs.

vernacular [ver-**nak**-yew-lar] n. **1.** most widely spoken language of a particular people or place. —adj. **2.** in or using the vernacular.

vernal adj. occurring in spring.

vernier [**ver**-nee-er] n. movable scale on a graduated measuring instrument for taking readings in fractions.

veronica n. plant with small blue, pink, or white flowers.

verruca [ver-**roo**-ka] n. wart, usu. on the foot.

versatile adj. having many skills or uses. **versatility** n.

verse n. **1.** group of lines in a song or poem. **2.** poetry as distinct from prose. **3.** subdivision of a chapter of the Bible. **versed in** knowledgeable about. **versify** v. **-fying, -fied.** write in verse. **versification** n.

version n. **1.** form of something, such as a piece of writing, with some differences from other forms. **2.** account of an incident from a particular point of view.

verso n., pl. **-sos. 1.** left-hand page of a book. **2.** back of a sheet of paper.

versus prep. **1.** Sport, Law against. **2.** in contrast with.

vertebra [**ver**-tib-ra] n., pl. **vertebrae** [**ver**-tib-ree] one of the bones that form the spine. **vertebral** adj. **vertebrate** n., adj. (animal) having a spine.

vertex n., pl. **-toxes, -tices. 1.** Maths point on a geometric figure where the sides form an angle. **2.** highest point of a triangle.

vertical adj. **1.** straight up and down. —n. **2.** vertical direction. **vertically** adv.

vertigo n. dizziness when looking down from a high place. **vertiginous** adj.

vervain n. plant with spikes of blue, purple, or white flowers.

verve n. enthusiasm or liveliness.

very adv. **1.** more than usually, extremely. —adj. **2.** absolute, exact, e.g. the very top, the very man.

vesicle n. Biol. sac or small cavity, esp. one containing fluid.

vespers pl. n. RC Church (service of) evening prayer.

vessel n. **1.** Lit. container, esp. for liquids. **2.** ship. **3.** Biol. tubular structure in animals and plants that carries body fluids, such as blood or sap.

vest n. **1.** Brit. undergarment worn on the top half of the body. **2.** US waistcoat. —v. **3.** (foll. by in or with) give (authority) to (someone). **vested interest** interest someone has in a matter because he or she might benefit from it.

vestal *adj.* pure, chaste. **vestal virgin** in ancient Rome, one of the virgin priestesses whose lives were dedicated to Vesta and to maintaining the sacred fire in her temple.

vestibule *n.* entrance hall.

vestige [vest-ij] *n.* small amount or trace. **vestigial** [vest-ij-ee-al] *adj.*

vestments *pl. n.* priest's robes.

vestry *n.*, *pl.* **-tries**. room in a church used as an office by the priest or minister.

vet[1] *n.* **1.** short for VETERINARY SURGEON. —*v.* **vetting, vetted. 2.** check the suitability of (a candidate).

vet[2] *n. US* military veteran.

vetch *n.* climbing plant with a beanlike fruit used as fodder.

veteran *n.* **1.** person with long experience in a particular activity, esp. military service. —*adj.* **2.** long-serving. **veteran car** car built before 1919, esp. before 1905.

veterinarian *n. US* veterinary surgeon.

veterinary *adj.* concerning animal health. **veterinary surgeon** medical specialist who treats sick animals.

veto [vee-toe] *n.*, *pl.* **-toes. 1.** official power to cancel a proposal. —*v.* **-toing, -toed. 2.** enforce a veto against.

vex *v.* frustrate, annoy. **vexation** *n.* **1.** something annoying. **2.** being annoyed. **vexatious** *adj.* **vexed question** much debated subject.

VHF very high frequency: radio frequency band between 30 and 300 MHz.

VHS Video Home System: format for recording on video.

VI Vancouver Island.

via *prep.* by way of.

viable *adj.* **1.** able to be put into practice. **2.** *Biol.* able to live and grow independently. **viably** *adv.* **viability** *n.*

viaduct *n.* bridge over a valley.

vial *n.* same as PHIAL.

viands *pl. n. Obs.* food.

viaticum *n.*, *pl.* **-ca, -cums.** Holy Communion as administered to a person dying or in danger of death.

vibes *pl. n. Informal* **1.** emotional reactions between people. **2.** atmosphere of a place. **3.** short for VIBRAPHONE.

vibrant [vibe-rant] *adj.* **1.** vigorous in appearance, energetic. **2.** (of a voice) resonant. **3.** (of a colour) strong and bright. **vibrancy** *n.*

vibraphone *n.* musical instrument with metal bars that resonate electronically when hit.

vibrate *v.* **1.** move back and forth rapidly. **2.** (cause to) resonate. **vibration** *n.* **vibrator** *n.* device that produces vibratory motion, used for massage or as a sex aid. **vibratory** *adj.*

vibrato *n. Music* rapid fluctuation in the pitch of a note.

viburnum *n.* subtropical shrub with white flowers and berrylike fruits.

VIC Victoria (Aust. state).

vicar *n. C of E* clergyman in charge of a parish. **vicarage** *n.* vicar's house.

vicarious [vick-air-ee-uss] *adj.* **1.** felt indirectly by imagining what another person experiences. **2.** delegated. **vicariously** *adv.*

vice[1] *n.* **1.** immoral personal quality. **2.** criminal immorality, esp. involving sex. **3.** minor imperfection in someone's character.

vice[2] *n.* tool with a screw mechanism for holding an object while working on it.

vice[3] *adj.* serving in place of.

vice chancellor *n.* chief executive of a university.

vicegerent *n.* **1.** person appointed to exercise all or some of the authority of another. —*adj.* **2.** invested with or characterized by delegated authority. **vicegerency** *n.*

vice president *n.* officer ranking immediately below the president and serving as his deputy. **vice-presidency** *n.*

viceroy *n.* governor of a colony who represents the monarch. **viceregal** *adj.*

vice versa [vie-see ver-sa] *adv. Latin* conversely, the other way round.

Vichy water [vee-shee waw-ter] *n.* mineral water from Vichy in France, reputed to be beneficial to health.

vicinity [viss-in-it-ee] *n.* surrounding area.

vicious *adj.* cruel and violent. **viciously** *adv.* **vicious circle** sequence of problems and solutions which always leads back to the original problem.

vicissitudes [viss-iss-it-yewds] *pl. n.* changes in fortune.

victim *n.* **1.** person or thing harmed or killed. **2.** person or animal killed as a sacrifice. **victimize** *v.* **1.** punish unfairly. **2.** discriminate against. **victimization** *n.*

victor *n.* person who has defeated an opponent, esp. in war or in sport. **victorious** *adj.* **victory** *n., pl.* **-tories.** winning of a battle or contest.

victoria *n.* large sweet plum, red and yellow in colour.

Victoria Cross *n. Brit.* highest award for bravery.

Victorian *adj.* **1.** of or in the reign of Queen Victoria (1837–1901). **2.** characterized by prudery or hypocrisy. —*n.* **3.** person who lived during Victoria's reign.

victuals [**vit**-tals] *pl. n. Old-fashioned* food. **victual** *v.* **victualling, victualled.** supply with or obtain victuals. **victualler** *n.*

vicuna [vik-**koo**-nya] *n.* **1.** S American animal like the llama. **2.** fine cloth made from its wool.

vide [**vie**-dee] *Latin* see.

videlicet [vid-**deal**-ee-set] *Latin* namely.

video *n., pl.* **-os.** **1.** short for VIDEO CASSETTE (RECORDER). —*v.* **videoing, videoed.** **2.** record (a TV programme or event) on video. —*adj.* **3.** relating to or used in producing television images. **video nasty** horrific or pornographic film, usu. made for video. **videotext** *n.* means of representing on a TV screen information that is held in a computer.

video cassette *n.* cassette containing video tape. **video cassette recorder** tape recorder for recording and playing back TV programmes and films.

video tape *n.* **1.** magnetic tape used to record video-frequency signals in TV production. **2.** magnetic tape used to record programmes when they are broadcast. **videotape** *v.* record (a TV programme) on video tape. **video tape recorder** tape recorder for vision signals, used in TV production.

Videotex *n.* ® same as VIEWDATA.

vie *v.* **vying, vied.** compete (with someone).

Vietnamese *adj.* **1.** of Vietnam, in SE Asia. —*n.* **2.** *pl.* **-ese.** native of Vietnam. **3.** language of Vietnam.

view *n.* **1.** everything that can be seen from a given place. **2.** picture of this. **3.** opinion. —*v.* **4.** think of (something) in a particular way. **in view of** taking into consideration. **on view** exhibited to the public. **viewer** *n.* **1.** person who watches television. **2.** hand-held device for looking at photographic slides. **viewfinder** *n.* window on a camera showing what will appear in a photograph.

Viewdata *n.* ® videotext service linking users to a computer by telephone.

vigil [**vij**-ill] *n.* night-time period of staying awake to look after a sick person, pray, etc. **vigilant** *adj.* watchful in case of danger. **vigilance** *n.*

vigilante [vij-ill-**ant**-ee] *n.* person, esp. as one of a group, who takes it upon himself or herself to enforce the law.

vignette [vin-**yet**] *n.* **1.** concise description of the typical features of something. **2.** small decorative illustration in a book.

vigour *n.* physical or mental energy. **vigorous** *adj.* **vigorously** *adv.*

Viking *n. Hist.* seafaring raider and settler from Scandinavia.

vile *adj.* **1.** very wicked. **2.** disgusting. **vilely** *adv.* **vileness** *n.*

vilify [**vill**-if-fie] *v.* **-ifying, -ified.** unjustly attack the character of. **vilification** *n.*

villa *n.* **1.** large house with gardens. **2.** holiday home, usu. in the Mediterranean.

village *n.* **1.** small group of houses in a country area. **2.** rural community. **villager** *n.*

villain *n.* **1.** wicked person. **2.** main wicked character in a play. **villainous** *adj.* **villainy** *n.*

villein [**vill**-an] *n. Hist.* peasant bound in service to his lord.

vim *n. Informal* force, energy.

vinaigrette *n.* salad dressing of oil and vinegar.

vindicate *v.* **1.** clear (someone) of guilt. **2.** justify (someone) whose behaviour has been challenged. **vindication** *n.*

vindictive *adj.* maliciously seeking revenge. **vindictiveness** *n.* **vindictively** *adv.*

vine *n.* climbing plant, esp. one producing grapes. **vineyard** [**vinn**-yard] *n.* plantation of grape vines, esp. for making wine.

vinegar *n.* acid liquid made from wine, beer, or cider. **vinegary** *adj.*

viniculture *n.* process or business of growing grapes and making wine.

vino [**vee**-noh] *n. Informal* wine.

vintage n. **1.** wine from a particular harvest of grapes. —adj. **2.** best and most typical. **vintage car** car built between 1919 and 1930.

vintner n. dealer in wine.

vinyl [**vine**-ill] n. type of plastic, used in mock leather and records.

viol [**vie**-oll] n. early stringed instrument preceding the violin.

viola[1] [vee-**oh**-la] n. stringed instrument lower in pitch than a violin.

viola[2] [vie-**ol**-la] n. variety of pansy.

violate v. **1.** break (a law or agreement). **2.** disturb (someone's privacy). **3.** treat (a sacred place) disrespectfully. **4.** rape. **violation** n. **violator** n.

violent adj. **1.** using or marked by physical strength that is harmful or destructive. **2.** aggressively intense. **3.** using excessive force. **violence** n. **violently** adv.

violet n. **1.** plant with bluish-purple flowers. **2.** bluish-purple colour. —adj. **3.** bluish-purple.

violin n. small four-stringed musical instrument played with a bow. **violinist** n.

violoncello [vie-oll-on-**chell**-oh] n., pl. **-los**. same as CELLO.

VIP very important person.

viper n. poisonous snake.

virago [vir-**rah**-go] n., pl. **-goes, -gos**. aggressive woman.

viral [**vie**-ral] adj. of or caused by a virus.

virgin n. **1.** person, esp. a woman, who has not had sexual intercourse. —adj. **2.** not having had sexual intercourse. **3.** not yet exploited or explored. **virginal** adj. **1.** like a virgin. —n. **2.** rectangular keyboard instrument like a small harpsichord. **virginity** n. **the Virgin, the Virgin Mary** Christianity Mary, the mother of Christ.

Virginia creeper n. climbing plant that turns red in autumn.

Virgo n. (the virgin) sixth sign of the zodiac.

virile adj. having the traditional male characteristics of physical strength and a high sex drive. **virility** n.

virology n. study of viruses.

virtual adj. having the effect but not the form of something. **virtually** adv. practically, almost.

virtue n. **1.** moral goodness. **2.** positive moral quality. **3.** merit. **by virtue of** by

reason of. **virtuous** adj. morally good. **virtuously** adv.

virtuoso n., pl. **-sos, -si**. person with impressive esp. musical skill. **virtuosity** n.

virulent [**vir**-yew-lent] adj. **1.** very infectious. **2.** violently harmful. **virulently** adv. **virulence** n.

virus n. **1.** microorganism that causes disease in humans, animals, and plants. **2.** Computers program that propagates itself, via disks and electronic networks, to cause disruption.

visa n. permission to enter a country, granted by its government and shown by a stamp on one's passport.

visage [**viz**-zij] n. Lit. face.

vis-à-vis [veez-ah-**vee**] prep. in relation to, regarding.

viscera [**viss**-er-a] pl. n. large abdominal organs. **visceral** adj. **1.** instinctive. **2.** of or relating to the viscera.

viscid [**viss**-id] adj. sticky. **viscidity** n.

viscose n. synthetic fabric made from cellulose.

viscount [**vie**-count] n. British nobleman ranking between an earl and a baron. **viscountcy** n., pl. **-cies**.

viscountess [**vie**-count-iss] n. ↑. wife or widow of a viscount. **2.** woman holding the rank of viscount in her own right.

viscous adj. thick and sticky. **viscosity** n.

visible adj. **1.** able to be seen. **2.** able to be perceived by the mind. **visibly** adv. **visibility** n. range or clarity of vision.

vision n. **1.** ability to see. **2.** mental image of something. **3.** foresight. **4.** hallucination. **visionary** adj. **1.** showing foresight. **2.** idealistic but impractical. —n., pl. **-aries**. **3.** visionary person.

visit v. **-iting, -ited. 1.** go or come to see. **2.** stay temporarily with. **3.** (foll. by upon) Lit. afflict. —n. **4.** instance of visiting. **5.** official call. **visitor** n. **visitation** n. **1.** formal visit or inspection. **2.** catastrophe seen as divine punishment.

visor [**vize**-or] n. **1.** part of a helmet that moves up and down over the face. **2.** eyeshade, esp. in a car. **3.** peak on a cap.

vista n. (beautiful) extensive view.

visual adj. **1.** done by or used in seeing. **2.** designed to be looked at. **visualize** v. form a mental image of. **visualization** n. **visual**

display unit device with a screen for displaying data held in a computer.

vital adj. **1.** essential or highly important. **2.** lively. **3.** necessary to maintain life. **vitals** pl. n. body organs. **vitally** adv. **vitality** n. physical or mental energy. **vital statistics 1.** statistics of births, deaths, and marriages. **2.** Informal woman's bust, waist, and hip measurements.

vitamin n. one of a group of substances that are essential in the diet for specific body processes.

vitiate [vish-ee-ate] v. spoil the effectiveness of. **vitiation** n.

viticulture n. cultivation of grapevines.

vitreous adj. like or made from glass. **vitreous humour** gelatinous substance that fills the eyeball.

vitrify v. **-ifying, -ified.** change or be changed into glass or a glassy substance. **vitrification** n.

vitriol n. **1.** language expressing bitterness and hatred. **2.** sulphuric acid. **vitriolic** adj.

vituperative [vite-**tyew**-pra-tiv] adj. bitterly abusive. **vituperation** n.

viva[1] interj. long live (a person or thing).

viva[2] n. examination in the form of an interview.

vivace [viv-**vah**-chee] adv. Music in a lively manner.

vivacious adj. full of energy and enthusiasm. **vivacity** n.

vivarium n., pl. **-iums, -ia.** place where animals are kept in natural conditions.

viva voce [**vive**-a **voh**-chee] adv. **1.** in spoken words. —n. **2.** same as VIVA[2].

vivid adj. **1.** very bright. **2.** conveying images that are true to life. **vividly** adv. **vividness** n.

vivify v. **-ifying, -ified.** animate, inspire.

viviparous [viv-**vip**-a-russ] adj. producing live offspring.

vivisection n. performing surgical experiments on living animals. **vivisectionist** n.

vixen n. **1.** female fox. **2.** Informal spiteful woman. **vixenish** adj.

viz. (introducing specified items) namely.

vizier [viz-**zeer**] n. (formerly) Muslim high official.

vizor n. same as VISOR.

VLF, vlf Radio very low frequency.

V neck n. neck on a garment shaped like the letter 'V'. **V-neck, V-necked** adj.

vocabulary n., pl. **-aries. 1.** all the words that a person knows. **2.** all the words in a language. **3.** specialist terms used in a given subject. **4.** list of words in another language with their translation.

vocal adj. **1.** relating to the voice. **2.** outspoken. **vocals** pl. n. singing part of a piece of pop music. **vocally** adv. **vocalist** n. singer. **vocalize** v. express with or use the voice. **vocalization** n. **vocal cords** membranes in the larynx that vibrate to produce sound.

vocalic adj. of vowel(s).

vocation n. **1.** occupation that someone feels called to. **2.** profession or trade. **vocational** adj. directed towards a particular profession or trade.

vocative n. in some languages, case of nouns used in addressing a person.

vociferate v. exclaim, cry out. **vociferation** n. **vociferous** adj. shouting, noisy. **vociferously** adv.

vodka n. (Russian) spirit distilled from potatoes or grain.

vogue n. **1.** popular style. **2.** period of popularity. **in vogue** fashionable.

voice n. **1.** (quality of) sound made when speaking or singing. **2.** expression of opinion by a person or group. **3.** property of verbs that makes them active or passive. —v. **4.** express verbally. **voiceless** adj. **voice-over** n. film commentary spoken by someone off-camera.

void adj. **1.** not legally binding. **2.** empty. —n. **3.** empty space. —v. **4.** make invalid. **5.** empty.

voile [voyl] n. light semitransparent fabric.

vol. volume.

volatile [**voll**-a-tile] adj. **1.** evaporating quickly. **2.** liable to sudden change, esp. in behaviour. **volatility** n.

vol-au-vent [**voll**-oh-von] n. small puff-pastry case with a savoury filling.

volcano n., pl. **-noes, -nos** mountain with a vent through which lava is ejected. **volcanic** adj.

vole n. small rodent.

volition n. faculty of exercising the will. **of one's own volition** through one's own choice.

volley n. **1.** simultaneous discharge of ammunition. **2.** burst of questions or critical comments. **3.** *Sport* stroke or kick at a moving ball before it hits the ground. —*v.* **4.** discharge (ammunition) in a volley. **5.** hit or kick (a ball) in a volley. **volleyball** *n.* team game where a ball is hit with the hands over a high net.

volt *n.* unit of electric potential. **voltaic** *adj.* same as GALVANIC. **voltage** *n.* electric potential difference expressed in volts. **voltmeter** *n.* instrument for measuring voltage.

volte-face [volt-**fass**] *n.* reversal of opinion.

voluble *adj.* talking easily and at length. **volubility** *n.* **volubly** *adv.*

volume *n.* **1.** size of the space occupied by something. **2.** amount. **3.** loudness of sound. **4.** control on a radio or TV for adjusting this. **5.** book, esp. one of a series. **voluminous** *adj.* **1.** (of clothes) large and roomy. **2.** (of writings) extensive. **volumetric** *adj.* relating to measurement by volume.

voluntary *adj.* **1.** done by choice. **2.** done or maintained without payment. **3.** controlled by the will. —*n., pl.* **-taries. 4.** organ solo in a church service. **voluntarily** *adv.*

volunteer *n.* **1.** person who offers voluntarily to do something, esp. military service. —*v.* **2.** offer one's services. **3.** offer the services of (another person). **4.** give (information) willingly.

voluptuous *adj.* **1.** (of a woman) sexually alluring through fullness of figure. **2.** sensually pleasurable. **voluptuary** *n., pl.* **-aries.** person devoted to sensual pleasures.

vomit *v.* **-iting, -ited. 1.** eject (the contents of the stomach) through the mouth. —*n.* **2.** matter vomited.

voodoo *n.* religion involving ancestor worship and witchcraft, practised by Black people in the West Indies, esp. in Haiti.

voracious *adj.* **1.** craving great quantities of food. **2.** insatiably eager. **voraciously** *adv.* **voracity** *n.*

vortex *n., pl.* **-texes, -tices. 1.** whirlpool. **2.** whirling motion.

votary *n., pl.* **-ries.** person dedicated to religion or to a cause.

vote *n.* **1.** choice made by a participant in a shared decision, esp. in electing a candidate. **2.** right to this choice. **3.** total number of votes cast. **4.** collective voting power of a given group, e.g. *the Black vote.* —*v.* **5.** make a choice by a vote. **6.** authorize (something) by vote. **voter** *n.*

votive *adj.* done or given to fulfil a vow.

vouch *v.* **1.** (foll. by *for*) give one's personal assurance about. **2.** (foll. by *for*) be proof of.

voucher *n.* **1.** ticket used instead of money to buy specified goods. **2.** record of a financial transaction, receipt.

vouchsafe *v.* **1.** *Old-fashioned* give, entrust. **2.** agree graciously.

vow *n.* **1.** solemn promise, esp. to a god or saint. —*v.* **2.** promise solemnly.

vowel *n.* **1.** speech sound made without obstructing the flow of breath. **2.** letter representing this.

vox pop *n.* interviews with members of the public on TV or radio.

vox populi *n.* public opinion.

voyage *n.* **1.** long journey by sea or in space. —*v.* **2.** make a voyage. **voyager** *n.*

voyeur *n.* person who derives pleasure from watching people undressing or having sex. **voyeurism** *n.* **voyeuristic** *adj.*

vs versus.

V-sign *n.* **1.** offensive gesture made by sticking up the index and middle fingers with the palm inwards. **2.** similar gesture, with the palm outwards, meaning victory or peace.

VT Vermont.

VTOL vertical takeoff and landing.

VTR video tape recorder.

vulcanize *v.* strengthen (rubber) by treating it with sulphur. **vulcanization** *n.* **vulcanite** *n.* vulcanized rubber.

vulgar *adj.* showing lack of good taste, decency, or refinement. **vulgarly** *adv.* **vulgarity** *n.* **vulgarian** *n.* vulgar (rich) person. **vulgarism** *n.* coarse word or phrase. **vulgarize** *v.* make vulgar or too common. **vulgarization** *n.* **vulgar fraction** simple fraction.

Vulgate *n.* fourth-century Latin version of the Bible.

vulnerable *adj.* **1.** unprotected from physical or emotional hurt. **2.** unable to defend oneself. **vulnerability** *n.*

vulpine *adj.* of or like a fox.

vulture *n.* large bird that feeds on the flesh of dead animals.

vulva *n.* woman's external genitals.

vying *v.* present participle of VIE.

W

W 1. *Chem.* tungsten. 2. watt. 3. Wednesday. 4. Welsh. 5. west(ern).

w. 1. week. 2. weight. 3. width.

WA 1. Washington. 2. West Africa.

wacky *adj.* **wackier, wackiest.** *Informal* eccentric or funny. **wackiness** *n.*

wad *n.* 1. small mass of soft material. 2. roll or bundle, esp. of banknotes. —*v.* **wadding, wadded.** 3. make into a wad. 4. pad or stuff with wadding. **wadding** *n.* soft material used for padding or stuffing.

waddle *v.* 1. walk with short swaying steps. —*n.* 2. swaying walk.

wade *v.* 1. walk with difficulty through water or mud. 2. proceed with difficulty. **wader** *n.* 1. long-legged water bird. —*pl.* 2. angler's long waterproof boots.

wadi [wod-dee] *n., pl.* **-dies.** in N Africa and Arabia, a watercourse which is dry except in the wet season.

wafer *n.* 1. thin crisp biscuit. 2. thin disc of unleavened bread used at Communion. 3. thin slice. **wafer-thin** *adj.* extremely thin.

waffle[1] *Informal* —*v.* 1. speak or write in a vague wordy way. —*n.* 2. vague wordy talk or writing.

waffle[2] *n.* square crisp pancake with a gridlike pattern.

waft *v.* 1. drift or carry gently through air or water. —*n.* 2. something wafted.

wag *v.* **wagging, wagged.** 1. move rapidly from side to side. —*n.* 2. wagging movement. 3. *Old-fashioned* humorous witty person. **waggish** *adj.* **waggishly** *adv.* **wagtail** *n.* small long-tailed bird.

wage *n.* 1. (often *pl.*) payment for work done, esp. when paid weekly. —*v.* 2. engage in (an activity).

wager *n., v.* bet on the outcome of something.

waggle *v.* wag. **waggly** *adj.*

Wagnerian [vahg-**near**-ee-an] *adj.* of or relating to the German composer Richard Wagner, his music, or his theories.

wagon, waggon *n.* 1. four-wheeled vehi-

cle for heavy loads. 2. railway freight truck. **wagoner, waggoner** *n.*

waif *n.* homeless child.

wail *v.* 1. cry out in pain or misery. —*n.* 2. mournful cry.

wain *n.* *Poetic* farm wagon.

wainscot, wainscoting *n.* wooden lining of the lower part of the walls of a room.

waist *n.* 1. part of the body between the ribs and hips. 2. narrow middle part. **waistcoat** *n.* sleeveless garment which buttons up the front, worn under a jacket. **waistline** *n.* (size of) the waist of a person or garment.

wait *v.* 1. remain inactive in expectation (of something). 2. be ready (for something). 3. delay or be delayed. 4. serve in a restaurant etc. —*n.* 5. act or period of waiting. **waiter** *n.* man who serves in a restaurant etc. **waitress** *n. fem.* **waiting list** list of people who have applied for something that is not immediately available. **waiting-room** *n.* room for waiting in, as at a station or surgery.

waive *v.* refrain from enforcing (a law, right, etc.). **waiver** *n.* (written statement of) this act.

wake[1] *v.* **wake, woke, woken.** 1. rouse from sleep or inactivity. —*n.* 2. vigil beside a corpse the night before burial. **waken** *v.* wake. **wakeful** *adj.* **wakefulness** *n.*

wake[2] *n.* track left by a moving ship. **in the wake of** following, often as a result.

walk *v.* 1. move on foot with at least one foot always on the ground. 2. pass through or over on foot. 3. escort or accompany on foot. —*n.* 4. act or instance of walking. 5. distance walked. 6. manner of walking. 7. place or route for walking. **walk of life** occupation or career. **walker** *n.* **walkabout** *n.* informal walk among the public by royalty etc. **walkie-talkie** *n.* portable radio transmitter and receiver. **walking stick** stick used as a support when walking. **walk into** *v.* meet with unwittingly. **Walkman** *n., pl.* **-mans.** ® small portable cassette player with headphones. **walk-on** *n.* small part in a play, esp. one without lines. **walkout** *n.* 1.

strike. **2.** act of leaving as a protest. **walk-over** *n.* easy victory.

wall *n.* **1.** structure of brick, stone, etc. used to enclose, divide, or support. **2.** something having the function or effect of a wall. —*v.* **3.** enclose or seal with a wall or walls. **go to the wall** be ruined, esp. financially. **wall-to-wall** *adj.* (esp. of carpeting) completely covering a floor. **wallflower** *n.* **1.** fragrant garden plant. **2.** at a dance, a woman who remains seated for lack of a partner. **wallpaper** *n.* decorative paper to cover interior walls.

wallaby *n., pl.* **-bies.** marsupial like a small kangaroo.

wallet *n.* small folding case for paper money, documents, etc.

walleyed *adj.* having eyes with an abnormal amount of white showing.

wallop *Informal* —*v.* **-loping, -loped. 1.** hit hard. —*n.* **2.** hard blow. **walloping** *Informal* —*n.* **1.** thrashing. —*adj.* **2.** large or great.

wallow *v.* **1.** roll in liquid or mud. **2.** revel in an emotion. —*n.* **3.** act or instance of wallowing. **4.** muddy place where animals wallow.

Wall Street *n.* street in New York, where the Stock Exchange and major banks are situated.

wally *n., pl.* **-lies.** *Slang* stupid person.

walnut *n.* **1.** edible nut with a wrinkled shell. **2.** tree it grows on. **3.** its wood, used for making furniture.

walrus *n., pl.* **-ruses, -rus.** large sea mammal with long tusks.

waltz *n.* **1.** ballroom dance. **2.** music for this. —*v.* **3.** dance a waltz. **4.** move in a relaxed confident way.

wampum [**wom**-pum] *n.* shells woven together, formerly used by N American Indians for money and ornament.

wan [rhymes with **swan**] *adj.* **wanner, wannest.** pale and sickly looking.

wand *n.* thin rod, esp. one used in performing magic tricks.

wander *v.* **1.** move about without a definite destination or aim. **2.** go astray, deviate. **3.** lose concentration. —*n.* **4.** act or instance of wandering. **wanderer** *n.* **wanderlust** *n.* great desire to travel.

wane *v.* **1.** decrease gradually in size or strength. **2.** (of the moon) decrease in size. **on the wane** in decline.

wangle *v.* *Informal* get by devious methods.

want *v.* **1.** desire or wish. **2.** lack or need. —*n.* **3.** act or instance of wanting. **4.** thing wanted. **5.** lack or absence, e.g. *a want of foresight.* **6.** state of being in need, poverty. **wanted** *adj.* sought by the police. **wanting** *adj.* **1.** lacking. **2.** not good enough.

wanton *adj.* **1.** dissolute or immoral. **2.** without motive. **3.** unrestrained. **wantonly** *adv.*

wapiti [**wop**-pit-tee] *n., pl.* **-tis.** large N American and NZ deer.

war *n.* **1.** fighting between nations. **2.** conflict or contest. —*adj.* **3.** of, like, or caused by war. —*v.* **warring, warred. 4.** make war. **warring** *adj.* warlike. **on the warpath** *Informal* angry and prepared for conflict. **war crime** crime, such as killing, committed during a war in violation of accepted conventions. **war criminal** person who has committed war crimes. **war cry 1.** shout used in battle. **2.** slogan. **warfare** *n.* fighting or hostilities. **warhead** *n.* explosive front part of a missile. **warmonger** *n.* person who encourages war. **warmongering** *n., adj.* **warship** *n.* ship designed and equipped for naval combat.

warble *v.* sing with trills. **warbler** *n.* any of various small songbirds.

ward *n.* **1.** room in a hospital for patients needing a similar kind of care. **2.** electoral division of a town. **3.** child under the care of a guardian or court. **warder** *n.* prison officer. **wardress** *n. fem.* **wardship** *n.* state of being a ward. **ward off** *v.* avert or repel. **wardroom** *n.* officers' quarters on a warship.

warden *n.* **1.** person in charge of a building and its occupants. **2.** official responsible for the enforcement of regulations.

wardrobe *n.* **1.** cupboard for hanging clothes in. **2.** person's collection of clothes. **3.** costumes of a theatrical company.

ware *n.* **1.** articles of a specified type or material, e.g. *silverware.* —*pl.* **2.** goods for sale. **warehouse** *n.* building for storing goods prior to sale or distribution.

warlock *n.* sorcerer.

warm *adj.* **1.** moderately hot. **2.** providing warmth. **3.** affectionate. **4.** enthusiastic. **5.** (of a colour) predominantly yellow or red. —*v.* **6.** make or become warm. **warmly** *adv.* **warmth** *n.* **1.** mild heat. **2.** cordiality. **3.** intensity of emotion. **warm-blooded** *adj.*

1. Zool. (of mammals and birds) having a constant body temperature, usu. higher than the surroundings. **2.** passionate. **warm up** v. **1.** make or become warmer. **2.** do preliminary exercises before a race or more strenuous exercise. **3.** make or become more lively. **warm-up** n.

warn v. **1.** make aware of possible danger or harm. **2.** caution or scold. **3.** inform (someone) in advance. **warning** n. **1.** something that warns. **2.** scolding or caution. **warn off** v. advise (someone) not to become involved with.

warp v. **1.** twist out of shape. **2.** pervert. —n. **3.** state of being warped. **4.** lengthwise threads on a loom.

warrant n. **1.** (document giving) official authorization. —v. **2.** guarantee. **3.** give authority or power to. **warranty** n., pl. **-ties.** (document giving) a guarantee. **warrant officer** officer in certain armed services with a rank between a commissioned and noncommissioned officer.

warren n. **1.** series of burrows in which rabbits live. **2.** overcrowded building or part of a town.

warrior n. person who fights in a war.

wart n. small hard growth on the skin. **warty** adj. **wart hog** kind of African wild pig.

wary [**ware**-ree] adj. **warier, wariest.** watchful or cautious. **warily** adv. **wariness** n.

was v. first and third person singular past tense of BE.

wash v. **1.** clean (oneself, clothes, etc.) with water and usu. soap. **2.** be washable. **3.** flow or sweep over or against. **4.** Informal be believable or acceptable, e.g. that excuse won't wash. —n. **5.** act or process of washing. **6.** clothes washed at one time. **7.** thin coat of paint. **8.** disturbance in the water after a ship has passed by. **washable** adj. **washer** n. ring put under a nut or bolt or in a tap as a seal. **washing** n. clothes to be washed. **washing machine** electric machine for washing clothes and linen. **washing-up** n. (washing of) dishes and cutlery needing to be cleaned after a meal. **wash away** v. carry or be carried off by moving water. **washbasin** n. basin for washing the face and hands. **washout** n. Informal complete failure. **washed-out** adj. **1.** faded. **2.** tired. **wash up** v. wash dishes and cutlery after a meal.

wasp n. stinging insect with a slender black-and-yellow body. **waspish** adj. bad-tempered. **waspishness** n.

Wasp, WASP n. US derogatory person descended from N European Protestant stock.

wassail n. **1.** formerly, festivity when much drinking took place. —v. **2.** drink health of (a person) at a wassail.

waste v. **1.** use pointlessly or thoughtlessly. **2.** fail to take advantage of. **3.** (cause to) decline in health or strength. —n. **4.** act of wasting or state of being wasted. **5.** anything wasted. **6.** waste material. —pl. **7.** desert. —adj. **8.** rejected as worthless or surplus to requirements. **9.** not cultivated or inhabited. **wastage** n. **1.** loss by wear or waste. **2.** reduction in size of a workforce by not filling vacancies. **wasteful** adj. extravagant. **wastefully** adv. **waster, wastrel** n. layabout. **wasteland** n. barren or desolate area of land. **wastepaper basket** container for discarded paper.

watch v. **1.** look at closely. **2.** wait expectantly (for). **3.** guard or supervise. —n. **4.** portable timepiece for the wrist or pocket. **5.** (period of) watching. **6.** sailor's spell of duty. **watchable** adj. **watcher** n. **watchful** adj. vigilant or alert. **watchfully** adv. **watchfulness** n. **watchdog** n. **1.** dog kept to guard property. **2.** person or group guarding against inefficiency or illegality. **watchman** n., pl. **-men.** man employed to guard a building or property. **watchword** n. **1.** password. **2.** slogan.

water n. **1.** clear colourless tasteless liquid that falls as rain and forms rivers etc. **2.** body of water, such as a sea or lake. **3.** level of the tide. **4.** urine. —v. **5.** put water on or into. **6.** (of the eyes) fill with tears. **7.** (of the mouth) salivate. **watery** adj. **water buffalo** oxlike Asian animal. **water closet** (room containing) a toilet flushed by water. **watercolour** n. **1.** paint thinned with water. **2.** painting done in this. **watercourse** n. stream or river. **watercress** n. edible plant growing in clear ponds and streams. **water down** v. dilute, make less strong. **waterfall** n. place where the waters of a river drop vertically. **waterfront** n. part of a town alongside a body of water. **waterhole** n. pond or pool in a dry area where animals drink. **water ice** ice cream made from frozen fruit-flavoured syrup. **watering place 1.** place where drinking water may be obtained for people or animals. **2.** resort or spa. **water lily** water plant with large floating leaves. **waterline** *n.* level to which a ship's hull will be immersed when afloat. **waterlogged** *adj.* saturated with water. **watermark** *n.* faint translucent design in a sheet of paper. **watermelon** *n.* melon with green skin and red flesh. **water polo team** game played by swimmers with a ball. **waterproof** *adj.* **1.** not letting water through. —*v.* **2.** make waterproof. —*n.* **3.** waterproof garment. **watershed** *n.* **1.** line separating two river systems. **2.** dividing line. **water-skiing** *n.* sport of riding over water on skis towed by a speedboat. **watertight** *adj.* **1.** not letting water through. **2.** with no loopholes or weak points. **water wheel** large wheel which is turned by flowing water to drive machinery.

watt [wott] *n.* unit of power. **wattage** *n.* electrical power expressed in watts.

wattle [wott-tl] *n.* **1.** branches woven over sticks to make a fence. **2.** fold of skin hanging from the neck of certain birds.

wave *v.* **1.** move the hand to and fro as a greeting or signal. **2.** move or flap to and fro. —*n.* **3.** moving ridge on water. **4.** curve(s) in the hair. **5.** gesture of waving. **6.** vibration carrying energy through a medium. **7.** prolonged spell of something, e.g. *the recent wave of bombings.* **wavy** *adj.* **wavier, waviest. wavelength** *n.* distance between the same points of two successive waves.

waver *v.* **1.** hesitate or be irresolute. **2.** be or become unsteady. **waverer** *n.*

wax[1] *n.* **1.** solid shiny fatty or oily substance used for sealing, making candles, etc. **2.** similar substance made by bees. **3.** waxy secretion of the ear. —*v.* **4.** coat or polish with wax. **waxen** *adj.* made of or like wax. **waxy** *adj.* **waxier, waxiest. waxwing** *n.* small migratory songbird. **waxwork** *n.* **1.** lifelike wax model of a (famous) person. —*pl.* **2.** place exhibiting these.

wax[2] *v.* **1.** increase in size or strength. **2.** (of the moon) get gradually larger.

way *n.* **1.** manner or method. **2.** route or direction. **3.** track or path. **4.** room for movement or activity, e.g. *you're in the way.* **5.** distance. **6.** passage or journey. **7.** characteristic manner. **8.** *Informal* state or condition. **wayfarer** *n.* traveller. **waylay** *v.* lie in wait for and accost or attack. **way-out** *adj. Informal* extremely unconventional.

wayside *adj., n.* (situated by) the side of a road.

wayward *adj.* erratic, selfish, or stubborn. **waywardness** *n.*

Wb *Physics* weber.

WC water closet.

we *pron.* (used as the subject of a verb) **1.** the speaker or writer and one or more others. **2.** people in general. **3.** formal word for *I* used by editors and monarchs.

weak *adj.* **1.** lacking strength. **2.** liable to give way. **3.** lacking flavour. **4.** unconvincing. **weaken** *v.* make or become weak. **weakling** *n.* feeble person or animal. **weakly** *adj.* **1.** weak or sickly. —*adv.* **2.** feebly. **weakness** *n.* **1.** being weak. **2.** failing. **3.** self-indulgent liking. **weak-kneed** *adj. Informal* lacking determination.

weal[1] *n.* raised mark left on the skin by a blow.

weal[2] *n. Obs.* prosperity or wellbeing, esp. in *the common weal.*

weald *n. Obs.* forested country.

wealth *n.* **1.** riches. **2.** abundance. **wealthy** *adj.* **wealthier, wealthiest. wealthiness** *n.*

wean *v.* **1.** accustom (a baby or young mammal) to food other than mother's milk. **2.** coax (someone) away from former habits.

weapon *n.* **1.** object used in fighting. **2.** anything used to get the better of an opponent. **weaponry** *n.* weapons collectively.

wear *v.* **wearing, wore, worn. 1.** have on the body as clothing or ornament. **2.** show as one's expression. **3.** (cause to) deteriorate by constant use or action. **4.** endure constant use. **5.** *Informal* tolerate. —*n.* **6.** wearing or being worn. **7.** things to wear, e.g. *leisure wear.* **8.** damage caused by use. **9.** ability to endure constant use. **wearable** *adj.* **wearer** *n.* **wearing** *adj.* tiring. **wear and tear** damage or loss from ordinary use. **wear off** *v.* gradually decrease in intensity. **wear on** *v.* (of time) pass slowly. **wear out** *v.* **1.** make or become useless through wear. **2.** exhaust or tire.

weary *adj.* **-rier, -riest. 1.** tired or exhausted. **2.** tiring. —*v.* **-rying, -ried. 3.** make or become weary. **wearily** *adv.* **weariness** *n.* **wearisome** *adj.* tedious.

weasel *n.* small carnivorous mammal with a long body and short legs.

weather *n.* **1.** day-to-day meteorological

conditions of a place. —v. **2.** (cause to) be affected by the weather. **3.** come safely through. **under the weather** *Informal* slightly ill. **weather-beaten** *adj.* worn, damaged, or (of skin) tanned by exposure to the weather. **weathercock, weathervane** *n.* vane revolving to show which way the wind is blowing. **weatherman** *n., pl.* **-men.** *Informal* person who forecasts the weather on television or radio.

weave *v.* **weaving, wove** or **weaved, woven** or **weaved. 1.** make (fabric) by interlacing (yarn) on a loom. **2.** compose (a story). **3.** move from side to side while going forwards. **weaver** *n.*

web *n.* **1.** net spun by a spider. **2.** skin between the toes of a duck, frog, etc. **webbed** *adj.* **webbing** *n.* strong fabric woven in strips.

weber [vay-ber] *n.* SI unit of magnetic flux.

wed *v.* **wedding, wedded** or **wed. 1.** marry. **2.** unite closely. **wedded** *adj.* **1.** of marriage. **2.** firmly in support of an idea or institution. **wedding** *n.* act or ceremony of marriage. **wedlock** *n.* marriage.

Wed. Wednesday.

wedge *n.* **1.** piece of material thick at one end and thin at the other. —v. **2.** fasten or split with a wedge. **3.** squeeze into a narrow space.

Wednesday *n.* fourth day of the week.

wee *adj.* small.

weed *n.* **1.** plant growing where undesired. **2.** *Informal* this ineffectual person. —v. **3.** clear of weeds. **weedy** *adj.* **weedier, weediest. 1.** full of or like weeds. **2.** *Informal* (of a person) thin and weak. **weed out** *v.* remove or eliminate (what is unwanted).

weeds *pl. n. Obs.* widow's mourning clothes.

week *n.* **1.** period of seven days, esp. one beginning on a Sunday. **2.** hours or days of work in a week. **weekly** *adj., adv.* **1.** happening, done, etc. once a week. —n., pl. **-lies. 2.** periodical published once a week. **weekday** *n.* any day of the week except Saturday or Sunday. **weekend** *n.* Saturday and Sunday.

weep *v.* **weeping, wept. 1.** shed tears. **2.** grieve or lament. **3.** ooze liquid. **weepy** *adj.* **weepier, weepiest.** liable to cry. **weeping willow** willow with drooping branches.

weevil *n.* small beetle which eats grain etc.

weft *n.* cross threads in weaving.

weigh *v.* **1.** measure the weight of. **2.** have a specified weight. **3.** consider carefully. **4.** be influential. **5.** be burdensome. **weigh anchor** raise a ship's anchor or (of a ship) have its anchor raised. **weighbridge** *n.* machine for weighing vehicles by means of a metal plate set into the road.

weight *n.* **1.** heaviness of an object. **2.** object of known mass used for weighing. **3.** unit of measurement of weight. **4.** heavy object. **5.** importance or influence. —v. **6.** add weight to. **7.** burden. **weightless** *adj.* **weightlessness** *n.* **weightlifting** *n.* sport of lifting heavy weights. **weightlifter** *n.* **weight training** physical exercise using weights to improve muscles.

weighting *n.* extra allowance paid in special circumstances.

weighty *adj.* **weightier, weightiest. 1.** heavy. **2.** important. **3.** causing worry. **weightily** *adv.*

weir *n.* river dam.

weird *adj.* **1.** unearthly or eerie. **2.** strange or bizarre. **weirdly** *adv.*

weirdo *n., pl.* **-dos.** *Informal* peculiar person.

welch *v.* same as WELSH.

welcome *adj.* **1.** received gladly. **2.** freely permitted. —n. **3.** kindly greeting. —v. **-coming, -comed. 4.** greet with pleasure. **5.** receive gladly.

weld *v.* **1.** join (pieces of metal or plastic) by softening with heat. **2.** unite closely. —n. **3.** welded joint. **welder** *n.*

welfare *n.* **1.** wellbeing. **2.** help given to people in need. **welfare state** system in which the government takes responsibility for the wellbeing of its citizens. **welfare work** work to improve the wellbeing of people or animals.

well[1] *adv.* **better, best. 1.** satisfactorily. **2.** skilfully. **3.** completely. **4.** prosperously. **5.** suitably. **6.** intimately. **7.** favourably. **8.** considerably. **9.** very. —adj. **10.** in good health. **11.** satisfactory. —interj. **12.** exclamation of surprise, interrogation, etc.

well[2] *n.* **1.** hole sunk into the earth to reach water, oil, or gas. **2.** deep open shaft. —v. **3.** flow upwards or outwards.

wellbeing *n.* state of being well, happy, or prosperous.

well-built *adj.* strong and muscular.

well-disposed *adj.* inclined to be friendly or sympathetic.

well-done *adj.* **1.** (of food, esp. meat) thoroughly cooked. **2.** accomplished satisfactorily.

well-heeled *adj. Informal* wealthy.

wellies *pl. n. Informal* wellingtons.

wellingtons *pl. n.* high waterproof rubber boots.

well-known *adj.* famous.

well-meaning *adj.* having good intentions.

well-nigh *adv.* almost.

well-off *adj.* fairly rich.

well-spoken *adj.* speaking in a polite or articulate way.

well-to-do *adj.* moderately wealthy.

well-worn *adj.* **1.** so much used as to be affected by wear. **2.** (of a word or phrase) stale from overuse.

welsh *v.* fail to pay a debt or fulfil an obligation.

Welsh *adj.* **1.** of Wales. —*n.* **2.** language or people of Wales. **Welsh rabbit, rarebit** dish of melted cheese on toast.

welt *n.* **1.** raised or strengthened seam. **2.** weal. —*v.* **3.** provide with a welt.

welter *n.* **1.** jumbled mass. —*v.* **2.** (of the sea) roll. **3.** lie drenched, esp. in blood.

welterweight *n.* boxer weighing up to 147lb (professional) or 67kg (amateur).

wen *n.* cyst on the scalp.

wench *n. Facetious* young woman.

wend *v.* go or travel.

wensleydale *n.* type of white cheese of flaky texture.

went *v.* past tense of GO.

wept *v.* past of WEEP.

were *v.* **1.** form of the past tense of BE used after *we, you, they,* or a plural noun. **2.** subjunctive of BE.

we're we are.

weren't were not.

werewolf *n.* in folklore, person who can turn into a wolf.

Wesleyan *adj.* **1.** of or relating to John Wesley (1703–91), who founded Methodism. —*n.* **2.** member of the Methodist Church.

west *n.* **1.** (direction towards) the point on the horizon where the sun sets. **2.** region lying in this direction. **3.** (W-) western Europe and the US. —*adj.* **4.** in, going towards, or (of the wind) blowing from the west. —*adv.* **5.** in or to the west. **westerly** *adj.* in, towards, or (of the wind) blowing from the west. **western** *adj.* **1.** of or in the west. —*n.* **2.** film or story about cowboys in the western US. **westerner** *n.* person from the west of any specific region. **westernize** *v.* adapt to the customs and culture of the West. **westward** *adj., adv.* **westwards** *adv.*

wet *adj.* **wetter, wettest. 1.** covered or soaked with water or another liquid. **2.** not yet dry, e.g. *wet paint.* **3.** *Informal* (of a person) feeble or foolish. —*n.* **4.** moisture or rain. **5.** *Informal* feeble or foolish person. **6.** *Brit.* moderate Conservative politician. —*v.* **wetting, wet** *or* **wetted. 7.** make wet. **wetly** *adv.* **wetness** *n.* **wet blanket** *Informal* person who has a depressing effect on others. **wetland** *n.* area of marshy land. **wet nurse** woman employed to breast-feed another's child. **wet suit** close-fitting rubber suit worn by divers etc.

wether *n.* castrated ram.

whack *v.* **1.** strike with a resounding blow. —*n.* **2.** such a blow. **3.** *Informal* share. **4.** *Informal* attempt. **whacked** *adj.* exhausted. **whacking** *adj. Informal* huge.

whale *n.* large fish-shaped sea mammal. **a whale of a** *Informal* very large or fine example of (something). **whaling** *n.* hunting of whales. **whaler** *n.* ship or person involved in whaling. **whalebone** *n.* horny substance hanging from the upper jaw of toothless whales.

wham *n.* **1.** sudden forceful blow or the sound produced by it. —*v.* **whamming, whammed. 2.** strike or cause to strike with great force.

wharf *n., pl.* **wharves, wharfs.** platform at a harbour for loading and unloading ships. **wharfage** *n.* accommodation at or charge for use of a wharf.

what *pron.* **1.** which thing. **2.** that which. **3.** request for a statement to be repeated. —*adv.* **4.** in which way, how much, e.g. *what do you care?* —*interj.* **5.** exclamation of surprise, anger, etc. **what for?** why? **whatever** *pron.* **1.** everything or anything that. **2.** no matter what. **whatnot** *n. Informal* similar unspecified things. **whatsoever** *adj.* at all.

wheat *n.* **1.** grain used in making flour, bread, and pasta. **2.** plant producing this.

wheaten *adj.* made of the grain or flour of wheat. **wheatear** *n.* small songbird. **wheatgerm** *n.* vitamin-rich embryo of the wheat kernel. **wheatmeal** *adj., n.* (made with) brown, but not wholemeal, flour.

wheedle *v.* coax or cajole.

wheel *n.* **1.** disc that revolves on an axle. **2.** pivoting movement. —*v.* **3.** push or pull (something with wheels). **4.** turn as if on an axis. **5.** turn round suddenly. **wheeling and dealing** use of shrewd and sometimes unscrupulous methods to achieve success. **wheeler-dealer** *n.* **wheelie** *n.* manoeuvre on a bike in which the front wheel is raised off the ground. **wheelbarrow** *n.* shallow box for carrying loads, with a wheel at the front and two handles. **wheelbase** *n.* distance between a vehicle's front and back axles. **wheelchair** *n.* chair mounted on wheels for use by people who cannot walk. **wheel clamp** immobilizing device fixed to one wheel of an illegally parked car. **wheelwright** *n.* person who makes or mends wheels as a trade.

wheeze *v.* **1.** breathe with a hoarse whistling noise. —*n.* **2.** wheezing sound. **3.** *Old-fashioned slang* trick or plan. **wheezy** *adj.* **wheezier, wheeziest**. **wheezily** *adv.*

whelk *n.* edible snail-like shellfish.

whelp *n.* **1.** pup or cub. **2.** *Offens.* youth. —*v.* **3.** produce whelps.

when *adv.* **1.** at what time. —*conj.* **2.** at the time that. **3.** although. **4.** considering the fact that. —*pron.* **5.** at which time. **whenever** *adv., conj.* at whatever time.
▷ Some people dislike the use of *when* in definitions: *famine is when food runs low,* but it is very common in informal usage. More formally, write *...a situation/condition in which.*

whence *adv., conj. Obs.* from what place or source.

where *adv.* **1.** in, at, or to what place. —*pron.* **2.** in, at, or to which place. —*conj.* **3.** in the place at which. **whereabouts** *adv.* **1.** at what place. —*n.* **2.** present position. **whereas** *conj.* **1.** but on the other hand. **2.** considering that. **whereby** *conj.* by which. **wherefore** *Obs.* —*adv.* **1.** why. —*conj.* **2.** consequently. **whereupon** *conj.* at which point. **wherever** *adv.* at whatever place. **wherewithal** *n.* necessary funds, resources, etc.
▷ *Where* includes the ideas *to* and *at* so

avoid the use of these prepositions: *where was it?* (not *where was it at?*).

wherry *n., pl.* **-ries. 1.** barge. **2.** light rowing boat.

whet *v.* **whetting, whetted. 1.** sharpen (a tool). **2.** increase (appetite or desire). **whetstone** *n.* stone for sharpening tools.

whether *conj.* used to introduce an indirect question or a clause expressing doubt or choice.

whew *interj.* exclamation expressing relief, delight etc.

whey [way] *n.* watery liquid that separates from the curd when milk is clotted.

which *adj., pron.* **1.** used to request or refer to a choice from different possibilities. —*pron.* **2.** person or thing referred to. **whichever** *adj., pron.* **1.** any out of several. **2.** no matter which.

whiff *n.* **1.** puff of air or odour. **2.** trace or hint.

Whig *n.* member of a British political party of the 18th–19th centuries that sought limited reform.

while *conj.* **1.** in the time that. **2.** despite the fact that. **3.** whereas. —*n.* **4.** period of time. **whilst** *conj.* while. **while away** *v.* pass (time) idly but pleasantly.

whim *n.* sudden fancy. **whimsy, whimsey** *n., pl.* **-sies, -seys. 1.** capricious idea. **2.** light or fanciful humour. **whimsical** *adj.* **1.** fanciful. **2.** full of whims. **whimsicality** *n.*

whimper *v.* **1.** cry in a soft whining way. —*n.* **2.** soft plaintive whine.

whin *n.* gorse.

whine *n.* **1.** high-pitched plaintive cry. **2.** peevish complaint. —*v.* **3.** make such a sound. **whining** *n., adj.*

whinge *Informal* —*v.* **1.** complain. —*n.* **2.** complaint.

whinny *v.* **-nying, -nied. 1.** neigh softly. —*n., pl.* **-nies. 2.** soft neigh.

whip *v.* **whipping, whipped. 1.** strike with a whip, strap, or cane. **2.** *Informal* pull, remove, or move quickly. **3.** rouse into a particular condition. **4.** urge by or as if by whipping. **5.** beat (esp. eggs or cream) to a froth. **6.** *Informal* steal. —*n.* **7.** cord attached to a handle, used for beating animals or people. **8.** call made on members of Parliament to attend for important divisions. **9.** politician responsible for organizing and disciplining fellow party members.

10. whipped dessert. **whip hand** advantage. **whiplash injury** neck injury caused by a sudden jerk to the unsupported head. **whipping boy** scapegoat. **whip-round** *n. Informal* collection of money.

whippet *n.* racing dog like a small greyhound.

whir, whirr *n.* **1.** prolonged soft buzz. —*v.* **whirring, whirred. 2.** (cause) to make a whir.

whirl *v.* **1.** spin or revolve. **2.** be dizzy or confused. **3.** drive or move at high speed. —*n.* **4.** whirling movement. **5.** confusion or giddiness. **6.** bustling activity. **whirlpool** *n.* strong circular current of water. **whirlwind** *n.* **1.** column of air whirling violently upwards in a spiral. —*adj.* **2.** much quicker than normal.

whisk *v.* **1.** beat (esp. eggs or cream) to a froth. **2.** move or remove quickly. —*n.* **3.** egg-beating utensil. **4.** quick movement.

whisker *n.* **1.** any of the long stiff hairs on the face of a cat or other mammal. —*pl.* **2.** hair growing on a man's cheeks. **by a whisker** *Informal* only just. **whiskered, whiskery** *adj.*

whisky *n., pl.* **-kies.** spirit distilled from fermented cereals. **whiskey** *n., pl.* **-keys.** Irish or American whisky.

whisper *v.* **1.** speak softly, without vibration of the vocal cords. **2.** rustle. —*n.* **3.** soft voice. **4.** something whispered. **5.** rustling. **6.** *Informal* rumour.

whist *n.* card game in which one pair of players tries to win more tricks than another pair. **whist drive** social event at which whist is played.

whistle *v.* **1.** produce a shrill sound by forcing the breath through pursed lips. **2.** make a similar sound. **3.** signal by a whistle. —*n.* **4.** instrument blown to make a whistling sound. **5.** whistling sound. **blow the whistle on** *Informal* inform on or put a stop to. **whistling** *n., adj.*

whit *n.* not a whit not the slightest amount.

white *adj.* **1.** of the colour of snow. **2.** pale. **3.** light in colour. **4.** (of coffee) served with milk. —*n.* **5.** colour of snow. **6.** white part. **7.** clear fluid round the yolk of an egg. **8.** (W-) member of the race of people with light-coloured skin. **whiten** *v.* make or become white or whiter. **whiteness** *n.* **whitish** *adj.* **white blood cell** same as LEUCO-CYTE. **white-collar** *adj.* denoting nonmanual

salaried workers. **white elephant** useless or unwanted possession. **white fish** any sea fish with white flesh used as food. **white flag** signal of surrender or truce. **white goods** large domestic appliances such as cookers and fridges. **white-hot** *adj.* very hot. **White House 1.** official residence of the US president. **2.** US presidency. **white lie** minor unimportant lie. **white paper** report by the government, outlining its policy on a matter. **white sauce** thick sauce made from butter, flour, and milk or stock.

whitebait *n.* small edible fish.

Whitehall *n.* **1.** street in London where the main government offices are sited. **2.** British Government.

whitewash *n.* **1.** substance for whitening walls. —*v.* **2.** cover with whitewash. **3.** *Informal* conceal or gloss over faults.

whither *adv. Obs.* to what place.

whiting [**white**-ing] *n.* edible sea fish.

whitlow *n.* inflamed sore on a finger or toe, esp. round a nail.

Whitsun *n.* week following **Whit Sunday,** the seventh Sunday after Easter.

whittle *v.* cut or carve (wood) with a knife. **whittle down, away** *v.* reduce or wear away gradually.

whizz, whiz *v.* **whizzing, whizzed. 1.** make a loud buzzing sound. **2.** *Informal* move quickly. —*n., pl.* **whizzes. 3.** loud buzzing sound. **4.** *Informal* person skilful at something.

who *pron.* **1.** which or what person. **2.** used to refer to a person or people already mentioned. **whoever** *pron.* **1.** any person who. **2.** no matter who.

WHO World Health Organization.

whoa *interj.* command used, esp. to horses, to stop or slow down.

whodunnit [hoo-**dun**-nit] *n. Informal* detective story, play, or film.

whole *adj.* **1.** containing all the elements or parts. **2.** uninjured or undamaged. **3.** healthy. **4.** (of a number) not containing a fraction. —*n.* **5.** complete thing or system. **on the whole** taking everything into consideration. **wholly** *adv.*

wholehearted *adj.* sincere or enthusiastic.

wholemeal *adj.* **1.** (of flour) made from the whole wheat grain. **2.** made from wholemeal flour.

wholesale *n.* **1.** sale of goods in large

quantities to retailers. —*adj., adv.* **2.** dealing by wholesale. **3.** extensive(ly). **wholesaler** *n.*

wholesome *adj.* physically or morally beneficial.

whom *pron.* objective case of WHO.

whoop *n., v.* shout or cry to express excitement.

whoopee *interj. Informal* cry of joy.

whooping cough *n.* infectious disease marked by convulsive coughing and noisy breathing.

whoops *interj.* exclamation of surprise or of apology.

whopper *n. Informal* **1.** anything unusually large. **2.** huge lie. **whopping** *adj.*

whore [hore] *n.* prostitute.

whorl *n.* **1.** ring of leaves or petals. **2.** one turn of a spiral. **3.** something coiled.

whortleberry *n.* bilberry (also **blaeberry**, **huckleberry**).

whose *pron.* of who or which.

why *adv.* **1.** for what reason. —*pron.* **2.** because of which.

WI 1. Wisconsin. **2.** *Brit.* Women's Institute.

wick *n.* cord through a lamp or candle which carries fuel to the flame.

wicked *adj.* **1.** morally bad. **2.** mischievous. **wickedly** *adv.* **wickedness** *n.*

wicker *adj.* made of woven cane. **wickerwork** *n.*

wicket *n.* **1.** set of three cricket stumps and two bails. **2.** ground between the two wickets on a cricket pitch. **3.** small gate. **wicketkeeper** *n.* fielder positioned directly behind the wicket.

wide *adj.* **1.** large from side to side. **2.** spacious or extensive. **3.** having a specified width. **4.** far from the target. **5.** opened fully. —*adv.* **6.** over an extensive area. **7.** to the full extent. **8.** far from the target. **widely** *adv.* **widen** *v.* make or become wider. **wide-awake** *adj.* **1.** fully awake. **2.** alert or observant. **wide-eyed** *adj.* **1.** naive or innocent. **2.** surprised or frightened. **widespread** *adj.* extending over a wide area.

widgeon *n.* same as WIGEON.

widow *n.* **1.** woman whose husband is dead and who has not remarried. —*v.* **2.** make a widow of. **widowed** *adj.* **widowhood** *n.*

widower *n.* man whose wife is dead and who has not remarried.

width *n.* **1.** distance from side to side. **2.** quality of being wide.

wield *v.* **1.** hold and use (a weapon). **2.** have and use (power).

wife *n., pl.* **wives.** man's partner in marriage. **wifely** *adj.*

wig *n.* artificial head of hair. **wigged** *adj.*

wigeon *n.* duck found in marshland.

wigging *n. Brit. slang* reprimand.

wiggle *v.* **1.** move jerkily from side to side. —*n.* **2.** wiggling movement. **wiggly** *adj.* **wigglier, wiggliest.**

wight *n. Obs.* person.

wigwam *n.* N American Indian's tent.

wilco *interj.* expression in telecommunications etc., indicating that the message just received will be complied with.

wild *adj.* **1.** (of animals) not tamed or domesticated. **2.** (of plants) not cultivated. **3.** not civilized. **4.** lacking restraint or control. **5.** violent or stormy. **6.** random. **7.** *Informal* furious. **8.** *Informal* excited. **wilds** *pl. n.* desolate or uninhabited place. **wildly** *adv.* **wildness** *n.* **wild-goose chase** futile search or undertaking. **Wild West** western US, which was lawless during settlement.

wildcat *n.* **1.** European wild animal like a large domestic cat. —*adj.* **2.** (of a strike) sudden and unofficial.

wildebeest *n.* gnu.

wilderness *n.* uninhabited uncultivated region.

wildfire *n.* **spread like wildfire** spread quickly and uncontrollably.

wildlife *n.* wild animals and plants collectively.

wile *n.* trick or ploy. **wily** *adj.* **wilier, wiliest.** crafty or sly.

wilful *adj.* **1.** headstrong or obstinate. **2.** intentional. **wilfully** *adv.* **wilfulness** *n.*

will[1] *v., past.* **would.** used as an auxiliary to form the future tense or to indicate intention, ability, or expectation.
▷ *Will* is normal for discussing the future. The use of *shall* with *I* and *we* is a matter of preference, not of rule. *Shall* is commonly used for questions in Southern England but less often in the North and Scotland.

will[2] *n.* **1.** faculty of deciding what one will do. **2.** directions written for disposal of one's property after death. **3.** desire or wish. **4.** attitude towards others, e.g. *ill will.* —*v.* **5.** use one's will in an attempt to do (something). **6.** bequeath (property) by a will. **7.** wish or desire. **willing** *adj.* **1.** ready or inclined (to do something). **2.** done or given readily. **willingly** *adv.* **willingness** *n.* **willpower** *n.* ability to control oneself and one's actions.

willies *pl. n. Slang* nervousness, jitters, or fright, esp. in *give one the willies.*

will-o'-the-wisp *n.* **1.** pale light sometimes seen over marshes at night. **2.** elusive person or thing.

willow *n.* **1.** tree with thin flexible branches. **2.** its wood. **willowy** *adj.* slender and graceful.

willy-nilly *adv.* whether desired or not.

wilt *v.* (cause to) become limp or lose strength.

wimp *n. Informal* feeble ineffectual person.

wimple *n.* garment framing the face, worn by medieval women and now by nuns.

win *v.* **winning, won. 1.** come first in (a competition, fight, etc.). **2.** gain (a prize) in a competition. **3.** get by effort. —*n.* **4.** victory, esp. in a game. **winner** *n.* **winning** *adj.* charming. **winnings** *pl. n.* sum won, esp. in gambling. **win over** *v.* gain the support or consent of (someone).

wince *v.* **1.** draw back, as from pain. —*n.* **2.** wincing.

winceyette *n.* cotton fabric with a raised nap.

winch *n.* **1.** machine for lifting or hauling using a cable wound round a drum. —*v.* **2.** lift or haul using a winch.

wind[1] *n.* **1.** current of air. **2.** hint or suggestion. **3.** idle talk. **4.** breath. **5.** flatulence. **6.** scent borne by the air. —*v.* **7.** render short of breath. **8.** get the scent of. **windy** *adj.* **windier, windiest. windward** *adj., n.* (of or in) the direction from which the wind is blowing. **windbag** *n. Slang* person who talks much but uninterestingly. **windbreak** *n.* fence or line of trees providing shelter from the wind. **windfall** *n.* **1.** unexpected good luck. **2.** fallen fruit. **wind instrument** musical instrument played by blowing. **windmill** *n.* machine for grinding or pumping driven by sails turned by the wind. **windpipe** *n.* tube linking the throat and the lungs. **windscreen** *n.* front window of a motor vehicle. **windsock** *n.* cloth cone on a mast at an airfield to indicate wind direction. **windsurfing** *n.* sport of riding on water using a surfboard propelled and steered by a sail. **windswept** *adj.* exposed to the wind.

wind[2] *v.* **winding, wound. 1.** coil or wrap around. **2.** tighten the spring of (a clock or watch). **3.** move in a twisting course. —*n.* **4.** winding. **5.** single turn or bend. **wind up** *v.* **1.** bring to or reach an end. **2.** tighten the spring of (a clock or watch). **3.** *Informal* make tense or agitated. **4.** *Slang* tease.

windlass *n.* winch worked by a crank.

window *n.* **1.** opening in a wall to let in light or air. **2.** glass pane or panes fitted in such an opening. **3.** display area behind the window of a shop. **4.** opportunity to see or understand something not usually seen, e.g. *a window on the workings of Parliament.* **window-dressing** *n.* **1.** arrangement of goods in a shop window. **2.** attempt to make something more attractive than it really is. **window-shopping** *n.* looking at goods in shop windows without intending to buy. **windowsill** *n.* ledge below a window.

wine *n.* **1.** alcoholic drink made from fermented grapes. **2.** similar drink made from other fruits. **wine and dine** entertain or be entertained with fine food and drink.

wing *n.* **1.** one of the limbs or organs of a bird, insect, or bat that are used for flying. **2.** one of the winglike supporting parts of an aircraft. **3.** projecting side part of a building. **4.** part of a car body surrounding the wheels. **5.** *Sport* (player on) either side of the pitch. **6.** faction of a political party. —*pl.* **7.** sides of a stage. —*v.* **8.** go very fast. **9.** wound slightly in the wing or arm. **winged** *adj.* **winger** *n. Sport* player positioned on a wing. **wing commander** middle-ranking commissioned air-force officer. **wingspan** *n.* distance between the wing tips of an aircraft, bird, or insect.

wink *v.* **1.** close and open (an eye) rapidly as a signal. **2.** twinkle. —*n.* **3.** winking. **4.** smallest amount of sleep.

winkle *n.* shellfish with a cone-shaped shell. **winkle out** *v. Informal* extract or prise out.

winnow *v.* **1.** separate (chaff) from (grain). **2.** examine to select desirable elements.

winsome *adj.* charming or winning.

winter *n.* **1.** coldest season. —*v.* **2.** spend the winter. **wintry** *adj.* **wintrier, wintriest. 1.** of or like winter. **2.** cold or unfriendly.

winter sports open-air sports held on snow or ice.

wipe v. **1.** clean or dry by rubbing. **2.** erase (a tape). —n. **3.** wiping. **wiper** n. (also **windscreen wiper**) device that automatically wipes rain etc. from a windscreen. **wipe out** v. **1.** destroy completely. **2.** Slang kill.

wire n. **1.** thin flexible strand of metal. **2.** length of this used to carry electric current. **3.** fencing made of wire. **4.** telegram. —v. **5.** provide with wires. **6.** send by telegraph. **wiring** n. system of wires. **wiry** adj. **wirier, wiriest. 1.** like wire. **2.** lean and tough. **wire-haired** adj. (of a dog) having a stiff wiry coat. **wire netting** net made of wire, used for fences.

wireless n. Old-fashioned same as RADIO.

wisdom n. **1.** good sense and judgment. **2.** accumulated knowledge. **wisdom tooth** any of the four large molar teeth cut usu. after the age of twenty.

wise[1] adj. **1.** having wisdom. **2.** sensible. **wisely** adv. **wiseacre** n. person who wishes to seem wise.

wise[2] n. Obs. manner.

-wise adv. suffix **1.** indicating direction or manner, as in clockwise, likewise. **2.** with reference to, as in businesswise.
▷ The ending -wise can frequently be replaced by -ways: sidewise/sideways; lengthways/lengthwise. Adding -wise to a noun to create the meaning 'in respect of', as in Defencewise, Scotland are strong, is generally unacceptable except in very informal usage.

wisecrack Informal —n. **1.** flippant or sardonic remark. —v. **2.** make a wisecrack.

wish v. **1.** want or desire. **2.** feel or express a hope about someone's wellbeing, success, etc. —n. **3.** expression of a desire. **4.** thing desired. **wishful** adj. too optimistic. **wishful thinking** interpretation of the facts as one would like them to be, rather than as they are. **wishbone** n. V-shaped bone above the breastbone of a fowl.

wishy-washy adj. Informal insipid or bland.

wisp n. **1.** light delicate streak. **2.** twisted bundle or tuft. **3.** anything slender and delicate. **wispy** adj. **wispier, wispiest.**

wisteria n. climbing shrub with blue or purple flowers.

wistful adj. sadly longing. **wistfully** adv. **wistfulness** n.

wit[1] n. **1.** ability to use words or ideas in a clever and amusing way. **2.** person with this ability. **3.** speech or writing showing wit. **4.** (sometimes pl.) practical intelligence. **witless** adj. foolish.

wit[2] v. Obs. be or become aware of (something). **to wit** that is to say; namely.

witch n. **1.** person, usu. female, who practises (black) magic. **2.** ugly wicked woman. **3.** fascinating woman. **witchcraft** n. use of magic. **witch doctor** in certain societies, a man appearing to cure or cause injury or disease by magic. **witch-hunt** n. campaign against people with unpopular views.

witch- combining form same as WYCH-.

with prep. **1.** by means of. **2.** in the company of. **3.** possessing. **4.** in relation to. **5.** in a manner characterized by. **6.** because of. **7.** understanding or agreeing with. **within** prep., adv. in or inside. **without** prep. **1.** not having, accompanied by, or using. **2.** Obs. outside.

withdraw v. **-drawing, -drew, -drawn.** take or move out or away. **withdrawal** n. **withdrawn** adj. unsociable.

withe n. strong flexible twig, esp. of willow, suitable for binding things together.

wither v. wilt or dry up. **withering** adj. (of a look or remark) scornful.

withers pl. n. ridge between a horse's shoulder blades.

withhold v. **-holding, -held.** refrain from giving.

withstand v. **-standing, -stood.** oppose or resist successfully.

withy n., pl. **withies.** same as WITHE.

witness n. **1.** person who has seen something happen. **2.** evidence or testimony. **3.** person giving evidence in court. —v. **4.** see at first hand. **5.** give evidence. **6.** sign (a document) to certify that it is genuine. **witness box** place in a court where a witness stands to give evidence.

wittingly adv. intentionally.

witty adj. **wittier, wittiest.** characterized by clever humour or wit. **wittily** adv. **witticism** n. witty remark.

wives n. plural of WIFE.

wizard n. **1.** magician. **2.** person with outstanding skill in a particular field. **wizardry** n.

wizened [wiz-zend] adj. shrivelled or wrinkled.

woad n. blue dye obtained from a plant.

wobble v. 1. move unsteadily. 2. shake. —n. 3. unsteady movement. 4. shake. **wobbly** adj. **wobblier, wobbliest.**

wodge n. Informal thick lump or chunk.

woe n. grief. **woeful** adj. 1. miserable. 2. causing woe. 3. pitiful. **woefully** adv. **woebegone** adj. looking miserable.

wok n. bowl-shaped Chinese cooking pan, used esp. for frying.

woke v. past tense of WAKE[1]. **woken** v. past participle of WAKE[1].

wold n. open downs.

wolf n., pl. **wolves.** 1. wild predatory canine mammal. —v. 2. eat ravenously. **cry wolf** raise a false alarm. **wolf whistle** whistle by a man indicating that he thinks a woman is attractive.

wolfram n. tungsten.

wolverine n. carnivorous mammal of Arctic regions.

woman n., pl. **women.** 1. adult human female. 2. women collectively. **womanhood** n. **womanish** adj. effeminate. **womanly** adj. having qualities traditionally associated with a woman. **womanize** v. (of a man) indulge in casual affairs with women. **womanizer** n. **Women's Liberation** (also **women's lib**) movement for the removal of social and economic inequalities between women and men.

womb n. hollow organ in female mammals where babies are conceived and develop.

wombat n. small heavily-built burrowing Aust. marsupial.

won v. past of WIN.

wonder n. 1. emotion caused by an amazing or unusual thing. 2. wonderful thing. —v. 3. be curious about. 4. feel wonder. —adj. 5. spectacularly successful, e.g. a wonder drug. **wonderful** adj. 1. remarkable. 2. very fine. **wonderfully** adv. **wonderment** n. **wondrous** adj. 1. Old-fashioned wonderful. 2. strange. **wonderland** n. real or imaginary place full of wonders.

wonky adj. -**kier, -kiest.** 1. Informal shaky or unsteady. 2. not working properly.

wont [rhymes with **don't**] n. 1. custom. —adj. 2. accustomed.

won't will not.

woo v. 1. seek to marry. 2. seek zealously. 3. try to persuade. **wooer** n.

wood n. 1. substance trees are made of. 2. timber. 3. firewood. 4. (also pl.) area where trees grow. **wooded** adj. covered with trees. **wooden** adj. 1. made of wood. 2. without expression. **woody** adj. **woodier, woodiest.** **woodbine** n. honeysuckle. **woodcock** n. game bird. **woodcut** n. 1. engraved block of wood. 2. print made from this. **woodland** n. forest. **woodlouse** n. small insect-like creature with many legs. **woodpecker** n. bird which searches tree trunks for insects. **wood pigeon** large Eurasian pigeon. **woodwind** adj., n. (of) a type of wind instrument made of wood. **woodwork** n. 1. parts of a room or building made of wood. 2. skill of making things in wood. **woodworm** n. insect larva that bores into wood.

woof n. cross threads in weaving.

woofer n. loudspeaker for reproducing low-frequency sounds.

wool n. 1. soft hair of sheep, goats, etc. 2. yarn spun from this. **woollen** adj. **woolly** adj. **woollier, woolliest.** 1. of or like wool. 2. vague or muddled. —n. -**lies.** 3. knitted woollen garment. **woolgathering** n. daydreaming. **Woolsack** n. Lord Chancellor's seat in the British House of Lords.

woozy adj. **woozier, wooziest.** Informal weak, dizzy, and confused.

word n. 1. smallest single meaningful unit of speech or writing. 2. chat or discussion. 3. brief remark. 4. message. 5. promise. 6. command. —v. 7. express in words. **wordless** adj. inarticulate or silent. **wordy** adj. **wordier, wordiest.** using too many words. **wording** n. choice and arrangement of words. **word-perfect** adj. (of a speaker or actor) knowing one's speech or role perfectly. **word processor** keyboard, microprocessor, and VDU for electronic organization and storage of text. **word processing** n.

wore v. past tense of WEAR.

work n. 1. physical or mental effort directed to making or doing something. 2. paid employment. 3. duty or task. 4. something made or done. 5. decoration of a specified kind, e.g. needlework. —pl. 6. factory. 7. total of a writer's or artist's achievements. 8. Informal full treatment. 9. mechanism of a machine. —v. **10.** (cause to) do work. **11.** be employed. **12.** (cause to) operate. **13.** cultivate (land). **14.** manipulate, shape, or process. **15.** (cause to) reach a specified condition. **16.** accomplish. —adj. **17.** of or for work. **work to rule** adhere strictly to all working regulations to reduce the rate of work as a protest. **work-to-rule** n. **workable** adj. **worker** n. **workaday** adj. ordinary. **workaholic** n. person addicted to work. **workforce** n. total number of workers. **workhouse** n. Hist. institution where the poor were given food and lodgings in return for work. **working class** social class consisting of wage earners, esp. manual workers. **working-class** adj. **working party** committee investigating a specific problem. **workman** n. manual worker. **workmanship** n. **1.** skill of a workman. **2.** skill exhibited in a finished product. **work out** v. **1.** accomplish by effort. **2.** solve by reasoning or calculation. **3.** devise or formulate. **workout** n. session of physical exercise for training or fitness. **workshop** n. **1.** room or building for a manufacturing process. **2.** session of group study or practice of a subject. **worktop** n. surface in a kitchen, used for food preparation.

world n. **1.** the planet earth. **2.** mankind. **3.** society. **4.** sphere of existence. —adj. **5.** of the whole world. **worldly** adj. **1.** not spiritual. **2.** concerned with material things. **3.** wise in the ways of the world. **worldwide** adj. applying or extending throughout the world.

worm n. **1.** small limbless invertebrate animal. **2.** shaft with a spiral thread forming part of a gear system. **3.** Informal wretched or spineless person. —pl. **4.** illness caused by parasitic worms in the intestines. —v. **5.** crawl. **6.** insinuate (oneself). **7.** extract (information) craftily. **8.** rid of worms. **wormy** adj. **wormier, wormiest. wormcast** n. coil of earth excreted by a burrowing worm. **worm-eaten** adj. eaten into by worms.

wormwood n. bitter plant.

worn v. past participle of WEAR.

worry v. **-rying, -ried. 1.** (cause to) be anxious or uneasy. **2.** annoy or bother. **3.** (of a dog) bite repeatedly. —n., pl. **-ries. 4.** (cause of) anxiety or concern. **worried** adj. **worrying** adj., n.

worse adj., adv. **1.** comparative of BAD or BADLY. —n. **2.** worse thing. **worst** adj., adv.

1. superlative of BAD or BADLY. —n. **2.** worst thing. **worsen** v. make or grow worse.

worship v. **-shipping, -shipped. 1.** show religious devotion to. **2.** love and admire. —n. **3.** act or instance of worshipping. **4.** (W-) title for a mayor or magistrate. **worshipper** n. **worshipful** adj. **1.** worshipping. **2.** in titles, honourable.

worsted [wooss-tid] n. **1.** type of woollen yarn or fabric. —adj. **2.** made of worsted.

wort [wurt] n. infusion of malt used to make beer.

worth adj. **1.** meriting or justifying. **2.** having a value of. —n. **3.** excellence. **4.** value or price. **5.** amount to be had for a given sum. **worthless** adj. **worthy** adj. **worthier, worthiest. 1.** deserving. **2.** having value or merit. —n., pl. **worthies. 3.** Informal notable person. **worthily** adv. **worthiness** n. **worthwhile** adj. worth the time or effort involved.

would v. used as an auxiliary to form the past tense or subjunctive mood of, express a request, or describe a habitual past action. **would-be** adj. wishing or pretending to be.

wouldn't would not.

wound[1] n. **1.** injury caused by violence. **2.** injury to the feelings. —v. **3.** inflict a wound on.

wound[2] v. past of WIND[2].

wove v. a past tense of WEAVE. **woven** v. a past participle of WEAVE.

wow interj. **1.** exclamation of astonishment. —n. **2.** Informal astonishing person or thing.

wpm words per minute.

WRAC Women's Royal Army Corps.

wrack n. seaweed.

WRAF Women's Royal Air Force.

wraith n. **1.** apparition of a person seen shortly before his or her death. **2.** ghost.

wrangle v. **1.** argue noisily. —n. **2.** noisy argument.

wrap v. **wrapping, wrapped. 1.** fold (something) round (a person or thing) so as to cover. —n. **2.** garment wrapped round the shoulders. **wrapper** n. **1.** cover. **2.** loose dressing gown. **wrapping** n. material used to wrap. **wrap up** v. **1.** fold paper round. **2.** put warm clothes on. **3.** Informal finish or settle (a matter).

wrasse n. colourful sea fish.

wrath [roth] n. intense anger. **wrathful** adj.

wreak v. **1.** inflict (vengeance). **2.** cause (chaos).

wreath n. twisted ring or band of flowers or leaves used as a memorial or tribute. **wreathe** v. **1.** form into a wreath. **2.** encircle. **3.** twist round.

wreck n. **1.** accidental destruction of a ship at sea. **2.** wrecked ship. **3.** remains of something destroyed. **4.** person in very poor condition. —v. **5.** cause the wreck of. **wrecker** n. formerly, person who lured ships onto the rocks in order to plunder them. **wreckage** n. wrecked remains.

wren n. small brown songbird.

Wren n. Informal member of the Women's Royal Naval Service.

wrench v. **1.** twist or pull forcefully. **2.** sprain. —n. **3.** forceful twist or pull. **4.** sprain. **5.** difficult or painful parting. **6.** adjustable spanner.

wrest v. **1.** take by force. **2.** twist violently.

wrestle v. **1.** fight, esp. as a sport, by grappling with and trying to throw down an opponent. **2.** struggle hard with. **wrestler** n. **wrestling** n.

wretch n. **1.** despicable person. **2.** pitiful person. **wretched** [**retch**-id] adj. **1.** miserable or unhappy. **2.** worthless. **wretchedly** adv. **wretchedness** n.

wrier adj. a comparative of WRY. **wriest** adj. a superlative of WRY.

wriggle v. **1.** move with a twisting action. **2.** manoeuvre oneself by devious means. —n. **3.** wriggling movement.

wright n. maker, e.g. playwright.

wring v. **wringing, wrung. 1.** twist, esp. to squeeze liquid out of. **2.** clasp and twist (the hands). **3.** obtain by forceful means.

wrinkle n. **1.** slight crease, esp. one in the skin due to age. —v. **2.** make or become wrinkled. **wrinkly** adj.

wrist n. joint between the hand and the arm. **wristwatch** n. watch worn on the wrist.

writ n. written legal command.

write v. **writing, wrote, written. 1.** mark paper etc. with symbols or words. **2.** set down in words. **3.** communicate by letter. **4.** be the author or composer of. **writing** n. **writer** n. **1.** author. **2.** person who has written something specified. **write-off** n. Informal something damaged beyond repair. **write-up** n. published account of something.

writhe v. **1.** twist or squirm in or as if in pain. **2.** be very embarrassed.

WRNS Women's Royal Naval Service.

wrong adj. **1.** incorrect or mistaken. **2.** immoral or bad. **3.** not intended or desirable. **4.** not working properly. —n. **5.** something immoral or unjust. —v. **6.** treat unjustly. **7.** malign. **wrongly** adv. **wrongful** adj. **wrongfully** adv. **wrongdoer** n. person who acts immorally or illegally.

wrote v. past tense of WRITE.

wrought [**rawt**] v. **1.** Lit. past of WORK. —adj. **2.** (of metals) shaped by hammering or beating. **wrought iron** pure form of iron used for decorative work.

wrung v. past of WRING.

WRVS Women's Royal Voluntary Service.

wry adj. **wrier, wriest** or **wryer, wryest. 1.** dryly humorous. **2.** (of a facial expression) contorted. **wryly** adv.

wt. weight.

WV West Virginia.

WWI World War One.

WWII World War Two.

WY Wyoming.

wych-, witch- combining form (of a tree) with pliant branches.

wych-elm n. elm with large rough leaves.

wynd n. Scot. narrow lane or alley.

X

X 1. indicating an error, a choice, or a kiss. **2**. indicating an unknown, unspecified, or variable factor, number, person, or thing. **3**. the Roman numeral for ten.

X-chromosome *n*. sex chromosome that occurs in pairs in the females of many animals, and as one of a pair with the Y-chromosome in males.

Xe *Chem*. xenon.

xenon *n*. colourless odourless gas found in very small quantities in the air.

xenophobia [zen-oh-**fobe**-ee-a] *n*. fear or hatred of people from other countries. **xenophobic** *adj*.

Xerox [**zeer**-ox] *n*. **1**. ® machine for copying printed material. **2**. ® copy made by a Xerox machine. —*v*. **3**. copy (a document) using such a machine.

Xmas [**eks**-mass] *n*. Christmas.

x-ray *n*. **1**. stream of radiation that can pass through some solid materials. **2**. picture made by sending x-rays through someone's body to examine internal organs. —*v*. **3**. photograph, treat, or examine using x-rays.

xylem [**zy**-lem] *n*. plant tissue that conducts water and minerals from the roots to all other parts.

xylophone [**zile**-oh-fone] *n*. musical instrument made of a row of wooden bars played with hammers.

Y

Y *Chem.* yttrium.

yacht [yott] *n.* **1.** large boat with sails or an engine, used for racing or pleasure cruising. —*v.* **2.** sail in a yacht. **yachting** *n.* **yachtsman, yachtswoman** *n.*

yahoo *n.* crude coarse person.

yak[1] *n.* Tibetan ox with long shaggy hair.

yak[2] *v.* **yakking, yakked.** *Slang* talk continuously about unimportant matters.

Yale lock *n.* ® cylinder lock using a flat serrated key.

yam *n.* sweet potato.

yank *v.* **1.** pull or jerk suddenly. —*n.* **2.** sudden pull or jerk.

Yankee, Yank *n. Slang* **1.** person from the United States. **2.** *US* person from the Northern United States.

yap *v.* **yapping, yapped. 1.** bark with a high-pitched sound. **2.** *Informal* talk continuously. —*n.* **3.** high-pitched bark.

yard[1] *n.* **1.** unit of length equal to 36 inches or about 91.4 centimetres. **2.** spar slung across a ship's mast to extend the sail. **yardarm** *n.* outer end of a ship's yard. **yardstick** *n.* standard against which to judge other people or things.

yard[2] *n.* **1.** enclosed area, usu. next to a building and often used for a particular purpose, e.g. *builder's yard*. **2.** *US* garden of a house.

yarmulke [yar-mull-ka] *n.* skullcap worn by Jewish men.

yarn *n.* **1.** thread used for knitting or making cloth. **2.** *Informal* long involved story. **spin a yarn** *Informal* tell a long involved story.

yashmak *n.* veil worn by a Muslim woman to cover her face in public.

yaw *v.* (of an aircraft or ship) turn to one side or from side to side while moving.

yawl *n.* two-masted sailing boat.

yawn *v.* **1.** open the mouth wide and take in air deeply, often when sleepy or bored. **2.** (of an opening) be large and wide. —*n.* **3.** act of yawning. **yawning** *adj.*

yaws *n.* infectious tropical skin disease.

Yb *Chem.* ytterbium.

Y-chromosome *n.* sex chromosome that occurs as one of a pair with the X-chromosome in the males of many animals.

yd. yard.

ye [yee] *pron. Obs.* you.

yea *interj. Old-fashioned* yes.

yeah *interj. Informal* yes.

year *n.* **1.** time taken for the earth to make one revolution around the sun, about 365 days. **2.** twelve months from January 1 to December 31. **3.** any period of twelve months. **4.** group of people who have started a course at the same time. —*pl.* **5.** a long time. **6.** age. **yearly** *adj., adv.* (happening) every year or once a year. **yearling** *n.* animal between one and two years old. **yearbook** *n.* reference book published annually containing details of the previous year's events.

yearn *v.* (foll. by *for*) **1.** want (something) very much. **2.** feel tenderness. **yearning** *n., adj.*

yeast *n.* fungus used to make bread rise and to ferment alcoholic drinks. **yeasty** *adj.*

yell *v.* **1.** shout or scream in a loud or piercing way. —*n.* **2.** loud cry of pain, anger, or fear.

yellow *n.* **1.** the colour of gold, a lemon, etc. —*adj.* **2.** of this colour. **3.** *Informal* cowardly. —*v.* **4.** make or become yellow. **yellow card** *Soccer* piece of yellow pasteboard shown by a referee to indicate that a player has been booked. **yellow fever** serious infectious tropical disease. **yellowhammer** *n.* European songbird with a yellow head and body. **Yellow Pages** *pl. n.* ® telephone directory which lists businesses under the headings of the type of business or service they provide.

yelp *v., n.* (give) a short sudden cry.

yen[1] *n., pl.* **yen.** main unit of currency in Japan.

yen[2] *n. Informal* longing or desire.

yeoman [yo-man] *n., pl.* **-men.** *Hist.* farmer owning and farming his own land. **yeomanry** *n.* **1.** yeomen. **2.** in Britain, former volunteer cavalry force. **yeoman of the**

guard member of the ceremonial bodyguard of the British monarchy.

yes *interj.* **1.** expresses consent, agreement, or approval. **2.** used to answer when one is addressed. —*n.* **3.** answer or vote of yes. **yes man** person who always agrees with his or her superior.

yesterday *adv., n.* **1.** (on) the day before today. **2.** (in) the recent past.

yet *adv.* **1.** up until then or now. **2.** still. **3.** now. **4.** eventually. —*conj.* **5.** nevertheless.

yeti *n.* same as ABOMINABLE SNOWMAN.

yew *n.* evergreen tree with needle-like leaves and red berries.

YHA *Brit.* Youth Hostels Association.

Yiddish *adj., n.* (of or in) a language of German origin spoken by many Jews in Europe and elsewhere.

yield *v.* **1.** produce or bear. **2.** give up control of, surrender. **3.** give in. **4.** agree (to). **5.** grant or allow. —*n.* **6.** amount produced. **yielding** *adj.* **1.** submissive. **2.** soft or flexible.

yippee *interj.* exclamation of joy.

YMCA Young Men's Christian Association.

yob, yobbo *n. Slang* bad-mannered aggressive youth.

yodel *v.* **-delling, -delled. 1.** sing with abrupt changes between a normal and a falsetto voice. —*n.* **2.** act or sound of yodelling.

yoga *n.* Hindu method of exercise and discipline aiming at spiritual and physical wellbeing. **yogi** *n.* person who practises yoga.

yoghurt, yogurt, yoghour *n.* slightly sour custard-like food made from milk that has had bacteria added to it, often sweetened and flavoured with fruit.

yoke *n.* **1.** wooden bar put across the necks of two animals to hold them together. **2.** frame fitting over a person's shoulders for carrying buckets. **3.** *Lit.* oppressive force, e.g. *the yoke of the tyrant.* **4.** fitted part of a garment to which a fuller part is attached. —*v.* **5.** put a yoke on. **6.** unite or link.

yokel *n. Offens.* person who lives in the country and is usu. simple and old-fashioned.

yolk *n.* yellow part of an egg that provides food for the developing embryo.

Yom Kippur *n.* annual Jewish religious holiday.

yon *adj. Old-fashioned or dialect* that or those over there.

yonder *adj., adv.* (situated) over there.

yonks *pl. n. Informal* very long time.

yoo-hoo *interj.* call to attract attention.

yore *n. Lit.* the distant past.

yorker *n. Cricket* ball that pitches just under the bat.

Yorkshire pudding *n.* baked batter made from flour, milk, and eggs and often eaten with roast beef.

you *pron.* refers to: **1.** the person or people addressed. **2.** an unspecified person or people in general.

young *adj.* **1.** in an early stage of life or growth. —*n.* **2.** offspring, esp. young animals. **3.** young people in general. **youngish** *adj.* **youngster** *n.* young person.

your *adj.* **1.** of, belonging to, or associated with you. **2.** of, belonging to, or associated with an unspecified person or people in general. **yours** *pron.* something belonging to you. **yourself** *pron.*

youth *n.* **1.** time of being young. **2.** state of being young. **3.** boy or young man. **4.** young people as a group. **youthful** *adj.* **youthfulness** *n.* **youth club** club that provides leisure activities for young people. **youth hostel** inexpensive lodging place for young prople travelling cheaply.

yowl *v., n.* (produce) a loud mournful cry.

yo-yo *n., pl.* **-yos.** toy consisting of a spool attached to a string, by which it is repeatedly spun and reeled in.

ytterbium [it-**terb**-ee-um] *n.* soft silvery element.

yttrium [**it**-ree-um] *n.* silvery metallic element used in various alloys.

yucca *n.* tropical plant with spikes of white leaves.

yucky, yukky *adj.* **yuckier, yuckiest** *or* **yukkier, yukkiest.** *Slang* disgusting, nasty.

Yugoslav *n.* **1.** person from Yugoslavia. —*adj.* **2.** of Yugoslavia.

Yule *n. Lit.* Christmas (season).

yummy *adj.* **-mier, -miest.** *Informal* delicious.

Yuppie *n.* **1.** young highly-paid professional person, esp. one who has a fashionable way of life. —*adj.* **2.** typical of or reflecting the values of Yuppies.

YWCA Young Women's Christian Association.

Z

Z *Chem.* atomic number.

zabaglione *n.* Italian dessert of egg, sugar, and wine.

zany [zane-ee] *adj.* **zanier, zaniest.** comical in an endearing way.

zap *v.* **zapping, zapped. 1.** *Slang* kill (by shooting). **2.** change television channels rapidly by remote control. **3.** move quickly.

zeal *n.* great enthusiasm or eagerness. **zealot** [zel-lot] *n.* fanatic or extreme enthusiast. **zealous** [zel-luss] *adj.* extremely eager or enthusiastic. **zealously** *adv.*

zebra *n.* black-and-white striped African animal of the horse family. **zebra crossing** pedestrian crossing marked by black and white stripes on the road.

zebu [zee-boo] *n.* Asian ox with a humped back and long horns.

Zen *n.* Japanese form of Buddhism that concentrates on learning through meditation and intuition.

zenith *n.* **1.** highest point of success or power. **2.** point in the sky directly above an observer.

zephyr [zef-fer] *n.* soft gentle breeze.

zeppelin *n.* *Hist.* large cylindrical airship.

zero *n., pl.* **-ros, -roes. 1.** (symbol representing) the number 0. **2.** point on a scale of measurement from which the graduations commence. **3.** lowest point. **4.** nothing, nil. —*adj.* **5.** having no measurable quantity or size. **zero hour** time at which something is set to happen. **zero in on** *v.* **1.** aim at. **2.** *Informal* concentrate on.

zest *n.* **1.** enjoyment or excitement. **2.** interest, flavour, or charm. **3.** peel of an orange or lemon.

zigzag *n.* **1.** line or course having sharp turns in alternating directions. —*v.* **-zagging, -zagged. 2.** move in a zigzag. —*adj.* **3.** formed in or proceeding in a zigzag. —*adv.* **4.** in a zigzag manner.

zilch *n.* *Slang* nothing.

zinc *n.* bluish-white metallic element used in alloys and to coat metal.

zing *n.* *Informal* quality in something that makes it lively or interesting.

Zionism *n.* movement to found and support a Jewish homeland in Israel. **Zionist** *n., adj.*

zip *n.* **1.** fastener with two rows of teeth that are closed or opened by a small clip pulled between them. **2.** short whizzing sound. **3.** *Informal* energy, vigour. —*v.* **zipping, zipped. 4.** fasten with a zip. **5.** move with a sharp whizzing sound. **6.** rush.

zircon *n.* mineral used as a gemstone and in industry.

zirconium *n.* greyish-white metallic element that is very resistant to corrosion.

zither *n.* musical instrument consisting of strings stretched over a flat box and plucked to produce musical notes.

zloty *n., pl.* **-tys, -ty.** monetary unit of Poland.

Zn *Chem.* zinc.

zodiac *n.* imaginary belt in the sky within which the sun, moon, and planets appear to move, divided into twelve equal areas, called signs of the zodiac, each named after a constellation.

zombie, zombi *n.* **1.** person who appears to be lifeless, apathetic, or totally lacking in independent judgment. **2.** corpse brought back to life by witchcraft.

zone *n.* **1.** area with particular features or properties. **2.** one of the divisions of the earth's surface according to temperature. —*v.* **3.** divide into zones. **zonal** *adj.*

zoo *n., pl.* **zoos.** place where live animals are kept for show.

zoology *n.* study of animals. **zoologist** *n.* **zoological** *adj.* **zoological garden** zoo.

zoom *v.* **1.** move or rise very rapidly. **2.** make or move with a buzzing or humming sound. **zoom lens** lens that can make the details of a picture larger or smaller while keeping the picture in focus.

Zr *Chem.* zirconium.

zucchini [zoo-keen-ee] *n., pl.* **-nis, -ni.** *US* courgette.

Zulu *n.* **1.** member of a tall Black people of southern Africa. **2.** language of this people.

zygote *n.* fertilized egg cell.

Collins English Dictionary

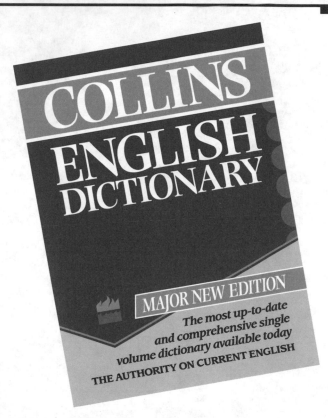

With 3.5 million words of text, the third edition of the COLLINS ENGLISH DICTIONARY is the most up-to-date and comprehensive single volume dictionary available today.

Collins French Pocket Dictionary

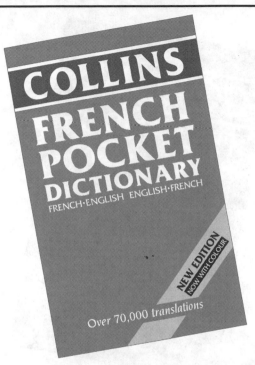

With over 40,000 key references, the **COLLINS FRENCH POCKET DICTIONARY** is the ideal portable companion to the language. Its use of a second colour for headwords and subentries makes both immediately accessible. Further titles in the series include the **COLLINS GERMAN POCKET DICTIONARY**, the **COLLINS SPANISH POCKET DICTIONARY**, the **COLLINS ITALIAN POCKET DICTIONARY**.

Collins Thesaurus in A-Z Form

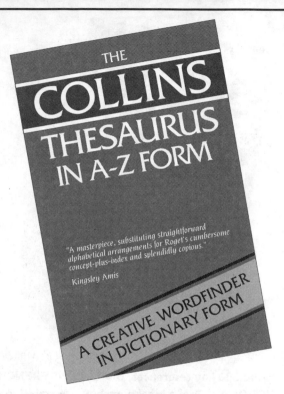

"A masterpiece, substituting straightforward
alphabetical arrangements for Roget's
cumbersome concept-plus-index and splendidly
copious."

Kingsley Amis

Collins Dictionary & Thesaurus in One Volume

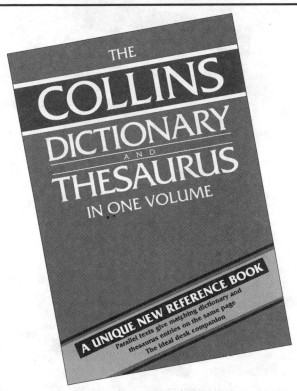

THE

COLLINS

DICTIONARY

AND

THESAURUS

IN ONE VOLUME

A UNIQUE NEW REFERENCE BOOK

Parallel texts give matching dictionary and thesaurus entries on the same page

The ideal desk companion

Hailed as indispensable, this unique new reference book combines two essential books in one, with parallel texts offering matching dictionary and thesaurus items on the same page.

Collins On-line

COLLINS ON-LINE is a bilingual dictionary that combines the power of the modern computer with the authority and scholarship of Collins Dictionaries. Business people, secretaries, journalists, translators, students and teachers - indeed everyone who requires quick accurate translation at their fingertips - will find **COLLINS ON-LINE** an invaluable aid in their work.